Nineteenth-Century Literature Criticism

Guide to Gale Literary Criticism Series

For criticism on	Consult these Gale series
Authors now living or who died after December 31, 1999	*CONTEMPORARY LITERARY CRITICISM (CLC)*
Authors who died between 1900 and 1999	*TWENTIETH-CENTURY LITERARY CRITICISM (TCLC)*
Authors who died between 1800 and 1899	*NINETEENTH-CENTURY LITERATURE CRITICISM (NCLC)*
Authors who died between 1400 and 1799	*LITERATURE CRITICISM FROM 1400 TO 1800 (LC)* *SHAKESPEAREAN CRITICISM (SC)*
Authors who died before 1400	*CLASSICAL AND MEDIEVAL LITERATURE CRITICISM (CMLC)*
Authors of books for children and young adults	*CHILDREN'S LITERATURE REVIEW (CLR)*
Dramatists	*DRAMA CRITICISM (DC)*
Poets	*POETRY CRITICISM (PC)*
Short story writers	*SHORT STORY CRITICISM (SSC)*
Black writers of the past two hundred years	*BLACK LITERATURE CRITICISM (BLC)* *BLACK LITERATURE CRITICISM SUPPLEMENT (BLCS)*
Hispanic writers of the late nineteenth and twentieth centuries	*HISPANIC LITERATURE CRITICISM (HLC)* *HISPANIC LITERATURE CRITICISM SUPPLEMENT (HLCS)*
Native North American writers and orators of the eighteenth, nineteenth, and twentieth centuries	*NATIVE NORTH AMERICAN LITERATURE (NNAL)*
Major authors from the Renaissance to the present	*WORLD LITERATURE CRITICISM, 1500 TO THE PRESENT (WLC)* *WORLD LITERATURE CRITICISM SUPPLEMENT (WLCS)*

ISSN 0732-1864

Volume 114

Nineteenth-Century Literature Criticism

Excerpts from Criticism of the
Works of Novelists, Philosophers, and Other
Creative Writers Who Died between 1800
and 1899, from the First Published Critical
Appraisals to Current Evaluations

Lynn M. Zott
Project Editor

GALE®

THOMSON

GALE

Detroit • New York • San Diego • San Francisco • Cleveland • New Haven, Conn. • Waterville, Maine • London • Munich

THOMSON
GALE

Nineteenth-Century Literature Criticism, Vol. 114

Project Editor
Lynn M. Zott

Editorial
Jenny Cromie, Kathy D. Darrow, Elisabeth Gellert, Edna M. Hedblad, Jelena O. Krstovi, Michelle Lee, Jessica Menzo, Thomas J. Schoenberg, Lawrence J. Trudeau, Maikue Vang, Russel Whitaker

Research
Nicodemus Ford, Sarah Genik, Tamara C. Nott, Tracie A. Richardson

Permissions
Margaret Chamberlain

Imaging and Multimedia
Dean Dauphinais, Robert Duncan, Leitha Etheridge-Sims, Mary K. Grimes, Lezlie Light, Michael Logusz, Dan Newell, David G. Oblender, Christine O'Bryan, Kelly A. Quin, Luke Rademacher

Composition and Electronic Capture
Carolyn Roney

Manufacturing
Stacy L. Melson

LIBRARY OF CONGRESS CATALOG CARD NUMBER 84-643008

ISBN 0-7876-5978-9
ISSN 0732-1864

Printed in the United States of America
10 9 8 7 6 5 4 3 2 1

Contents

Preface vii

Acknowledgments xi

Literary Criticism Series Advisory Board xiii

Preface

Since its inception in 1981, *Nineteeth-Century Literature Criticism* (*NCLC*) has been a valuable resource for students and librarians seeking critical commentary on writers of this transitional period in world history. Designated an "Outstanding Reference Source" by the American Library Association with the publication of is first volume, *NCLC* has since been purchased by over 6,000 school, public, and university libraries. The series has covered more than 300 authors representing 29 nationalities and over 17,000 titles. No other reference source has surveyed the critical reaction to nineteenth-century authors and literature as thoroughly as *NCLC*.

Scope of the Series

NCLC is designed to introduce students and advanced readers to the authors of the nineteenth century and to the most significant interpretations of these authors' works. The great poets, novelists, short story writers, playwrights, and philosophers of this period are frequently studied in high school and college literature courses. By organizing and reprinting commentary written on these authors, *NCLC* helps students develop valuable insight into literary history, promotes a better understanding of the texts, and sparks ideas for papers and assignments. Each entry in *NCLC* presents a comprehensive survey of an author's career or an individual work of literature and provides the user with a multiplicity of interpretations and assessments. Such variety allows students to pursue their own interests; furthermore, it fosters an awareness that literature is dynamic and responsive to many different opinions.

Every fourth volume of *NCLC* is devoted to literary topics that cannot be covered under the author approach used in the rest of the series. Such topics include literary movements, prominent themes in nineteenth-century literature, literary reaction to political and historical events, significant eras in literary history, prominent literary anniversaries, and the literatures of cultures that are often overlooked by English-speaking readers.

NCLC continues the survey of criticism of world literature begun by Gale's *Contemporary Literary Criticism* (*CLC*) and *Twentieth-Century Literary Criticism* (*TCLC*).

Organization of the Book

An *NCLC* entry consists of the following elements:

- The **Author Heading** cites the name under which the author most commonly wrote, followed by birth and death dates. Also located here are any name variations under which an author wrote, including transliterated forms for authors whose native languages use nonroman alphabets. If the author wrote consistently under a pseudonym, the pseudonym will be listed in the author heading and the author's actual name given in parenthesis on the first line of the biographical and critical information. Uncertain birth or death dates are indicated by question marks. Single-work entries are preceded by a heading that consists of the most common form of the title in English translation (if applicable) and the original date of composition.

- The **Introduction** contains background information that introduces the reader to the author, work, or topic that is the subject of the entry.

- A **Portrait of the Author** is included when available.

- The list of **Principal Works** is ordered chronologically by date of first publication and lists the most important works by the author. The genre and publication date of each work is given. In the case of foreign authors whose works have been translated into English, the list will focus primarily on twentieth-century translations, selecting those works most commonly considered the best by critics. Unless otherwise indicated, dramas are dated by first performance, not first publication. Lists of **Representative Works** by different authors appear with topic entries.

- Reprinted **Criticism** is arranged chronologically in each entry to provide a useful perspective on changes in critical evaluation over time. The critic's name and the date of composition or publication of the critical work are given at the beginning of each piece of criticism. Unsigned criticism is preceded by the title of the source in which it appeared. All titles by the author featured in the text are printed in boldface type. Footnotes are reprinted at the end of each essay or excerpt. In the case of excerpted criticism, only those footnotes that pertain to the excerpted texts are included. Criticism in topic entries is arranged chronologically under a variety of subheadings to facilitate the study of different aspects of the topic.

- A complete **Bibliographical Citation** of the original essay or book precedes each piece of criticism.

- Critical essays are prefaced by brief **Annotations** explicating each piece.

- An annotated bibliography of **Further Reading** appears at the end of each entry and suggests resources for additional study. In some cases, significant essays for which the editors could not obtain reprint rights are included here. Boxed material following the further reading list provides references to other biographical and critical sources on the author in series published by Gale.

Indexes

Each volume of *NCLC* contains a **Cumulative Author Index** listing all authors who have appeared in a wide variety of reference sources published by the Gale Group, including *NCLC*. A complete list of these sources is found facing the first page of the Author Index. The index also includes birth and death dates and cross references between pseudonyms and actual names.

A **Cumulative Nationality Index** lists all authors featured in *NCLC* by nationality, followed by the number of the *NCLC* volume in which their entry appears.

A **Cumulative Topic Index** lists the literary themes and topics treated in the series as well as in *Classical and Medieval Literature Criticism, Literature Criticism from 1400 to 1800, Twentieth-Century Literary Criticism,* and the *Contemporary Literary Criticism* Yearbook, which was discontinued in 1998.

An alphabetical **Title Index** accompanies each volume of *NCLC*, with the exception of the Topics volumes. Listings of titles by authors covered in the given volume are followed by the author's name and the corresponding page numbers where the titles are discussed. English translations of foreign titles and variations of titles are cross-referenced to the title under which a work was originally published. Titles of novels, dramas, nonfiction books, and poetry, short story, or essay collections are printed in italics, while individual poems, short stories, and essays are printed in roman type within quotation marks.

In response to numerous suggestions from librarians, Gale also produces an annual paperbound edition of the *NCLC* cumulative title index. This annual cumulation, which alphabetically lists all titles reviewed in the series, is available to all customers. Additional copies of this index are available upon request. Librarians and patrons will welcome this separate index; it saves shelf space, is easy to use, and is recyclable upon receipt of the next edition.

Citing *Nineteenth-Century Literature Criticism*

When writing papers, students who quote directly from any volume in the Literary Criticism Series may use the following general format to footnote reprinted criticism. The first example pertains to material drawn from periodicals, the second to material reprinted from books.

Kim McQuaid, "William Apes, Pequot: An Indian Reformer in the Jackson Era," *The New England Quarterly,* 50 (December 1977): 605-25; excerpted and reprinted in *Nineteenth-Century Literature Criticism,* vol. 73, ed. Janet Witalec (Farmington Hills, Mich.: The Gale Group, 1999), 3-4.

Richard Harter Fogle, *The Imagery of Keats and Shelley: A Comparative Study* (Archon Books, 1949), 211-51; excerpted and reprinted in *Nineteenth-Century Literature Criticism,* vol. 73, ed. Janet Witalec (Farmington Hills, Mich.: The Gale Group, 1999), 157-69.

Suggestions are Welcome

Readers who wish to suggest new features, topics, or authors to appear in future volumes, or who have other suggestions or comments are cordially invited to call, write, or fax the Project Editor:

Project Editor, Literary Criticism Series
The Gale Group
27500 Drake Road
Farmington Hills, MI 48331-3535
1-800-347-4253 (GALE)
Fax: 248-699-8054

Acknowledgments

The editors wish to thank the copyright holders of the excerpted criticism included in this volume and the permissions managers of many book and magazine publishing companies for assisting us in securing reproduction rights. We are also grateful to the staffs of the Detroit Public Library, the Library of Congress, the University of Detroit Mercy Library, Wayne State University Purdy/Kresge Library Complex, and the University of Michigan Libraries for making their resources available to us. Following is a list of the copyright holders who have granted us permission to reproduce material in this volume of *NCLC*. Every effort has been made to trace copyright, but if omissions have been made, please let us know.

served. Reproduced by permission of *Studies in Romanticism* and the author.—Sweezy, Paul M. and Leo Huberman. From ***The Communist Manifesto, Principles of Communism, and The Communist Manifesto after 100 Years.*** Modern Reader Paperbacks, 1968. Copyright © 1968 by Modern Reader Paperbacks. All rights reserved. Reproduced by permission.—Ty, Eleanor. From ***Women, Revolution, and the Novels of the 1790's.*** Edited by Linda Lang-Peralta. Michigan State University Press, 1999. Copyright © 1999 by Michigan State University Press. All rights reserved. Reproduced by permission.— Wright, Judith. From ***Australian Writers and Their Work: Charles Harpur.*** Lansdowne Press, 1963. Copyright © 1963 by Lansdowne Press. All right reserved. Reproduced by permission.

THE PHOTOGRAPH APPEARING IN *NCLC*, VOLUME 114, WAS RECEIVED FROM THE FOLLOWING SOURCE:

Harpur, Charles, photograph. Reproduced by permission of the National Library of Australia.

Literary Criticism Series Advisory Board

The members of the Gale Group Literary Criticism Series Advisory Board—reference librarians and subject specialists from public, academic, and school library systems—represent a cross-section of our customer base and offer a variety of informed perspectives on both the presentation and content of our literature criticism products. Advisory board members assess and define such quality issues as the relevance, currency, and usefulness of the author coverage, critical content, and literary topics included in our series; evaluate the layout, presentation, and general quality of our printed volumes; provide feedback on the criteria used for selecting authors and topics covered in our series; provide suggestions for potential enhancements to our series; identify any gaps in our coverage of authors or literary topics, recommending authors or topics for inclusion; analyze the appropriateness of our content and presentation for various user audiences, such as high school students, undergraduates, graduate students, librarians, and educators; and offer feedback on any proposed changes/enhancements to our series. We wish to thank the following advisors for their advice throughout the year.

The Communist Manifesto

Friedrich Engels and Karl Marx

The following entry presents criticism of Engels and Marx's political pamphlet, *Manifest der Kommunistischen Partei* (1848; *The Communist Manifesto*). For information on Engels's complete career, see *NCLC,* Volume 85. For information on Marx's complete career, see *NCLC,* Volume 17.

INTRODUCTION

Early in 1848, two young German intellectuals set forth their plan for proletarian revolution against the prevailing socio-economic forces in Europe, which in their eyes were corrupt. *Manifest der Kommuntischen Partei* (*The Communist Manifesto*), the slim volume outlining their plan, has been described as the most influential secular document in world history, ranked behind only such religious works as the Bible and the Koran for the impact it has had on world events. Indeed, it has been characterized as the Socialist movement's "holy" book. Calling for workers of the world to unite, *The Communist Manifesto* examines the oppression felt by the working class in Europe, analyzes the unequal distribution of wealth under the capitalist system, and provides a vision for a new way of life, wherein the proletariat fights for and wins economic and social equality with the ruling bourgeois class. With the Russian Revolution in the early part of the twentieth century, *The Communist Manifesto* was catapulted from being an important philosophical text to being the framework for a new nation. Communism and the Soviet Union, both of which have their birth in this text, went on to become globally polarizing forces. The Cold War can be considered a result, in large part, of the diametrically opposed socio-economic philosophies held by the communist East and the capitalist West. While the late twentieth century saw the Soviet Union crumble, leaving capitalism seemingly the victor, the socialist plan sparked by *The Communist Manifesto* nevertheless remains a strong influence on the world's political and philosophical thought, and *The Communist Manifesto* itself is assured an eminent place in the history of human experience, both for the revolutionary philosophy it presents and for the way it changed the face of nation-building.

TEXTUAL HISTORY

The first step to understanding the *The Communist Manifesto* is to understand its authors. Karl Marx, who is generally considered the primary author of both the text and the philosophy that has come to bear his name, was born in Germany in 1818. He received a university education, studying law and then philosophy. Shortly after he received his degree, his anti-bourgeois sentiment growing, he realized he could not participate in the German education system. He turned to journalism—a pursuit that would help support him for the rest of his life. In this capacity he began developing his revolutionary ideas, until he was forced out of Germany in 1843. For the next several years his involvement with revolutionary, anti-capitalist organizations increased and he continued to develop his theories by studying economic science and pursuing literary study. In 1844 he met Friedrich Engels. Engels grew up in the same area of Germany as Marx, and came from a similar class and educational experience. Sent by his father to England to represent the family in its textile business, Engels observed first-hand the exploitation of textile workers, and the injustice of the industrial capitalist system. Independently, both men published critical works that questioned the existing European socio-economic system, but upon their meeting in 1844, they found in each other not only a lifelong friendship, but an intellectual partnership that would take them both to new philosophical heights. Their friendship and intellectual partnership led them to discuss all of their intellectual projects together; their mutual influence was so great that it is difficult for critics to determine where in their joint works Engels' thought ends and Marx's begins. In *The Communist Manifesto* the authors put forth a theory of history, an analysis of capitalism, and an outline for socialism. Their call for proletarian revolution was met with interest from other disaffected bourgeois intellectuals, hope from the increasingly mobilized working class, and fear from the supporters of the existing system. The manifesto was quickly translated and published in most European languages. It gave birth to modern Socialism, and helped change the world order; it was espoused by revolutionaries across Europe, and saw its greatest victory in 1918 with the Russian Revolution. Marx and Engels continued to hone and develop their socialist theories, and both went on to publish prolifically on the subject. Numerous essays, lectures, and articles picked up where *The Communist Manifesto* left off. The authors revised its preface liberally as it went through multiple editions, and they saw world changes resulting from the manifesto's influence. While the specifics of their proletarian revolution were to change as the social, economic and political climates changed, Marx and Engels always maintained the accuracy of the ideas put forth in *The Communist Manifesto*. Upon its fortieth anniversary, Engels decided that the preface could no longer be revised, as the text was then an historical document and needed to be preserved as such. Theories of socialism and communism continued to evolve, but the *The Communist Manifesto* was a finalized text. It went through no further revisions at the hands of its authors, but its influence did not lessen, as the Socialist and Communist movements of the twentieth century held to its ideals and built new societies from its revolutionary plan.

MAJOR THEMES

Divided into four parts, *The Communist Manifesto* begins with a theory of world history based on class struggles, and provides an explanation of the abuse of the working class by the bourgeoisie. The evils perpetrated upon the working class—the proletariat—are enumerated, and the injustice of the capitalist economic system, whereby a few get rich off the labor of many, is outlined. In the second section of *The Communist Manifesto* the virtues of communism are portrayed. Marx and Engels anticipate and refute the objections of the bourgeoisie and demonstrate the benefits to be gained by all through communism. The third and fourth chapters deal largely with contemporary social movements, whose inadequacies are outlined. While support for these groups is given, the ultimate virtue of the plan put forth in the previous sections is maintained. Throughout the entire manifesto, the workers of the world are called to unite and throw off the oppression of bourgeois capitalist society, so that after the proletarian revolution, a new society based on equality—economic, social, and political—could be built.

CRITICAL RECEPTION

Since the time of its initial publication, *The Communist Manifesto* has sparked a wide range of reactions, from early intellectual and revolutionary enthusiasm, to vicious condemnation, to fervent adherence to its philosophy. For millions of people *The Communist Manifesto* has served as an essential text, greatly affecting their ways of life. It has influenced nation-building, affected social and economic policies, and played a very important role in world politics as nations drew alliances during the Cold War. Vast amounts of commentary have been produced by both pro-communist and anti-communist scholars and critics. Marx and Engels themselves contributed to the debates through their numerous revisions of the preface to *The Communist Manifesto*. Upon the text's seventy-fifth anniversary, Algernon Lee explored the European influences on Marx and Engels as they were formulating their ideas. With *The Communist Manifesto*'s one hundredth birthday, Paul M. Sweezy and Leo Huberman reexamined the text's history and its international significance. Some critics have explored the authors' own lives and education in an effort to elucidate *The Communist Manifesto*. Others have detected a wide and diverse range of influences on the work, including Romanticism, French materialist philosophy, millenarianism, Darwinism, and gothic melodrama. Rhetorical analyses of the text have been conducted, as have

economic, political, cultural, and philosophical readings. Since the collapse of the Soviet Union *The Communist Manifesto* has increasingly been examined as an historical document, as the product of a particular historical moment. As one of the most important secular documents in human history, however, *The Communist Manifesto* remains assured of its place in the literary canon, and the philosophy it espouses retains a certain force in contemporary social, economic, and political thought.

PRINCIPAL WORKS

Friedrich Engels

"Briefe aus dem Wuppertal" ["Letters from Wuppertal"] (essays) 1839; published in *Telegraph für Deutschland*

*Schelling und die Offenbarung: Kritik des neuesten Reaktionsversuchs gegen die freie Philosophie (essay) 1842

Die Lage der arbeitenden Klasse in England [The Condition of the Working Class in England in 1844] (essay) 1845

*Po und Rhein (essay) 1859

*Savoyen, Nizza und der Rhein (essays) 1860

Essays Addressed to Volunteers (essays) 1861

Der deutsche Bauernkrieg [The Peasant War in Germany] (essay) 1870

†Herr Eugen Dührings Umwälzung der Wissenschaft: Philosophie; Politische Oekonomie; Sozialismus [Herr Eugen Dühring's Revolution in Science; or Anti-Dühring] (essays) 1878

Die Entwicklung des Sozialismus von der Utopie zur Wissenschaft [Socialism, Utopian and Scientific] (essay) 1882

Der Ursprung der Familie, des Privateigenthums und des Staats [The Origin of the Family, Private Property, and the State] (essay) 1884

Ludwig Feuerbach und der Ausgang der klassischen deutschen Philosophie [Ludwig Feuerbach and the Outcome of Classical German Philosophy] (essay) 1888

‡Revolution and Counter-Revolution (essays) 1896

"Die deutsche Reichsverfassungskampagne" ["The Campaign for a German Constitution"] (essay) 1902

"Grundsätze des Kommunismus" ["Principles of Communism"] (essay) 1932

The Fourteenth of March 1883: Frederick Engels on the Death of Karl Marx (essay) 1933

Dialektik der Natur [Dialectics of Nature] (essay) 1935

Karl Marx

Misère de la philosophie: Résponse à la "Philosophie de la misère" de M. Proudhon [The Poverty of Philosophy] (essay) 1847

Der achtzehnte Brumaire des Louis Bonaparte [The Eighteenth Brumaire of Louis Bonaparte] (history) 1852

Zur Kritik der politischen Ökonomie [A Contribution to the Critique of Political Economy] (history) 1859

§Die Klassenkämpfe in Frankreich 1848 bis 1850 [The Class Struggles in France, 1848-1850] (essay) 1895

Ökonomisch-philosophische Manuskripte [Economic and Philosophic Manuscripts of 1844] (essays) 1932

Karl Marx: Early Writings (essays, histories, and criticism) 1963

Selected Letters: The Personal Correspondence, 1844-1877 (letters) 1981

Karl Marx and Friedrich Engels

Die heilige Familie, oder Kritik der kritischen Kritik: Gegen Bruno Bauer und Consorten [The Holy Family; or, Critique of Critical Critique] (essay) 1845

"Die deutsche Ideologie" ["The German Ideology"] (treatise) 1846

Manifest der kommunistischen Partei [The Communist Manifesto] (pamphlet) 1848

Das Kapital: Kritik der politischen Ökonomie [Capital: A Critical Analysis of Capitalist Production.] 3 vols. (essay) 1867-94

Historisch-Kritische Gesamtausgabe. Werke, Schriften, Briefe. 12 vols. (essays, histories, criticism, and letters) 1927-35

*These works were published anonymously.

†The essays in this collection were originally published as a series of articles in the Social Democratic party organ *Vorwärts* between January 1877 and June 1878.

‡The essays in this collection were originally published as a series of articles under Marx's name in the *New York Daily Tribune* in 1852.

§This work was written between 1850 and 1859.

CRITICISM

Algernon Lee (essay date 1926)

SOURCE: Lee, Algernon. "Essentials of Marx: General Introduction." In *The Essentials of Marx,* pp. 1-24. New York: Vanguard Press, 1926.

[*In the following excerpt, Lee discusses the political climate in Europe at the time Marx and Engels were solidifying their theories on economics and class, and maintains that they were influenced by French materialist philosophers, the German philosopher Hegel, and the British economists. Lee finds that the authors of the* Communist Manifesto *recognized three burgeoning movements—the struggle for political democracy, the trade union movement, and the appearance of underground revolutionary societies—all of which were filtered into their fluid conceptualization of Socialism, Communism, and Marxism.*]

In the field of social history all beginnings are relative. Back of whatever we may call the date of origin of any institution or movement lie the conditions and tendencies out of which it grew. With this qualification, 1848 may be counted as the birth-year of modern Socialism, and the issuance of the **Communist Manifesto** as the first step in the development of a new social force which, challenging all the accepted ideas, assailing all the established institutions, threatening all the vested interests of aristocratic and of capitalist society, boldly set itself the task of putting an end to the exploitation of man by man and of building from the bottom up a free and classless world. Obstructed by the ignorance and self-distrust of the very classes whose cause it champions, beaten down again and again by savage persecution, broken again and again by dissension within its ranks, it has rallied more strongly after each defeat, surer of itself after each schism. Launched by an obscure little group of hunted exiles, at the end of seventy-eight years it counts its adherents by the tens of millions, its organizations spread all over the civilized world, and in a number of the leading countries of Europe a slight further increase of strength will put the powers of government definitely into its hands. Such a movement is worth the trouble of understanding, even in a land where it is for the moment at low ebb.

The three little works reprinted in this volume have an importance out of all proportion to their size. Whoever has really mastered their contents—something which cannot be done in a single hasty reading—holds the clue which will guide him in any further study of the Socialist movement and its theories. Some account of their authors and of their historic setting may help the reader to grasp their significance.

. . . . .

Karl Marx was born at Trier or Treves, not far from the Rhine, in March, 1818. He came of a highly cultured family, Jewish by race though not by religious belief. From his youth on he showed an insatiable thirst for knowledge and an unusual capacity for thorough and critical thinking. His first interests were in literature and languages, which he learned with great ease, but history and philosophy soon won his attention. In several years of study at the universities of Bonn and Berlin he prepared himself first for the practice of law and then, changing his plans, for the life of a teacher of philosophy. Hardly had he taken his doctor's degree, however, when it became clear to him that he could never be servile enough to the ruling powers to hold a professorship in the Germany of those days. He next turned to journalism, both as a means of livelihood and as a channel for self-expression. For a short time in 1842-'43 he edited the *Rheinische Zeitung* (Rhenish Gazette) at Cologne, but resigned when its proprietors decided to soften its opposition to the reactionary policies of the Prussian government. Marx left Germany shortly before the issuance of an order for his arrest. Settling for the time in Paris, he collaborated on the *Deutsch-Französische Jahrbücher* (German-French Yearbooks), but was expelled by the French government in 1845 and found refuge at Brussels. Here in 1847 he published his **Poverty of Philosophy,** in answer to Proudhon's *Philosophy of Poverty.* In this book the whole future development of his economic thinking is broadly foreshadowed, and it is important also as beginning to draw the line between what were later to be known as the Socialist and Anarchist movements. The next year the Belgian government, subservient to that of France, drove him again into exile.

At Paris and Brussels, besides carrying on a tireless literary activity, of which the writings just mentioned represent but a portion, Marx had plunged into a profound study of economic science, had come into contact with refugees from many parts of Europe and with the underground movements of discontent which were then becoming very active, and had also been watching with keen interest the efforts of the British working class on both the industrial and the political field.

It was at Paris in 1844 that he met Frederick Engels, with whom he was for the rest of his life so closely associated, both as personal friend and as fellow thinker, that it is hard to say just how much either of them may have contributed to the other's work. Engels, who was two years younger than Marx, was a native of the industrial city of Barmen, also in the valley of the Rhine. Representing his father in the textile business, he had already spent some years in England, and in that country he resided mostly until his death in 1895. A man of keen and powerful mind, while his interests lay largely in the same field with those of Marx, he was more conversant than was his friend with natural science and anthropology on the one hand, and on the other hand with business and practical affairs. Within a few months after their first meeting he published his ***Condition of the Working Class in England,*** which was in certain aspects an epoch-making book. Of his later works the one best known to English readers is ***Socialism, Utopian and Scientific,*** published in 1880.

It is perhaps significant that both these men were born and reared in the Rhine country. There for centuries the forces of French and of German civilization had met and fought and trafficked, producing a blended culture of a rich and active type. Lying between the old republican strongholds of Switzerland and the Low Countries, and itself in the Middle Ages studded with all but independent free cities, it had preserved traditions of liberty which the rule of the Hapsburgs, the Bourbons, and the Hohenzollerns had been able to repress, but not altogether to destroy, and which had been quickened into life at the beginning of the century, when Napoleon's arms had brought into Western Germany at least some of the emancipatory results of the French Revolution. Moreover, its great navigable river was the principal thoroughfare by which British travel and trade penetrated Central Europe, and into its valley machine industry, born in England, was transplanted earlier than into almost any other part of the Continent. Altogether, it was a fit nursery for internationalist, democratic, and scientifically forward-looking revolutionists.

· · · · ·

Three powerful intellectual currents, drawn from three great and diverse nations, were assimilated, transformed, and made to produce something greater than themselves in the thought of Marx and Engels.

First there is the influence of the French materialistic philosophers of the later eighteenth century—such men as Di-

derot, Helvetius, d'Alembert, and Holbach. These had been forerunners of the Great Revolution, spirits of denial, ruthless critics of church and state and social convention, doubters and questioners, unwilling to believe anything on authority, confident of the power of human reason to solve every problem it might take up. Their great contribution was that they looked always to material facts, not to metaphysical abstractions nor to the alleged will of God, for the explanation of the nature of man and of society. Their weakness was that, on the whole, their thought-method was static, dealing with supposed eternal truths, not sufficiently recognizing the fact of continuous change.

The second of these influences was that of the German philosopher Hegel, who died in 1831. Marx and Engels always avowed themselves his disciples, though they turned his system topsy-turvy in using it. To Hegel, abstract ideas were the sole reality, material things but their fleeting shadow. In this respect, his philosophy was at odds with the whole trend of modern science, and on this point Marxism takes a diametrically opposite view. But Hegel's immense service was that he thought in terms of process or evolution. Instead of saying simply "This is and that is not," he said "In every moment of its being, everything is ceasing to be what it was and becoming what it is not yet." His working-out of this conception—his so-called dialectic thought-method—cannot be explained in further detail here. A good idea of it can be obtained from Engels' ***Socialism, Utopian and Scientific.*** In the hands of Marx, Engels, and their successors, who combined it with reliance on observed fact as the raw material for thought, it became an instrument, not only for exploring the past and explaining the present, but for predicting the general course of future development with a degree of certainty such as no other social thinkers have attained.

To these must be added a third influence—that of the British economists, foremost among whom stood and still stands David Ricardo, author of the *Principles of Political Economy,* published in 1817. Just as Hegel was the accepted philosophical champion of Prussian nationalist monarchy, and as Marx, in developing Hegel's system, made it the philosophy of democratic internationalism, so had Ricardo's work been hailed as a complete justification of industrial capitalism, and in like wise did Marx, not destroying but fulfilling it, make it demonstrate the antisocial and ultimately self-destructive nature of the capitalist system, and thus turn it to the service of the revolutionary proletariat.

Ricardo unquestioningly accepted production for sale, private ownership of the means of production, and the relations of landlord to tenant and of employer to wage-worker as things eternal for the future, if not in the past. Taking these for granted, he analyzed with marvelous acuteness the normal inner workings of a system of production and exchange founded upon them. In the light of his demonstration, the economic laws of value, of rent, of wages, and so forth seemed to have the same validity as the laws of gravitation or of chemical affinity. The processes by which, in the capitalist system, the incomes of wage-worker, landlord, investor, and enterpriser are determined appeared as "natural" and therefore as little to be resisted or found fault with as the motions of the earth and the alternation of the seasons. As for poverty—well, the physical world too had its painful aspects, such as cyclones and earthquakes, which those who suffered from them must bear as best they could.

To this system of thought, so comfortable for the new ruling class, Marx did two things. First, Marx the economist carried Ricardo's analysis a little farther, completed the statement of the law of value and of wages, and thereby exhibited the capitalist pure-and-simple as a parasite pure-and-simple. In other words, he showed that the actual capitalist is a collaborator in production only in so far as he still functions, not as owner of capital, but as director of industry; and that, in proportion as the growth of capital itself divorces these two functions, the capitalist becomes socially useless and harmful. In the second place, for Marx there were no finalities. Marx the historian saw the capitalist form of property as but the latest in a series of property systems, each of which by its own full development destroys itself and at the same time evolves its successor. To the strictly economic analysis he added the social-psychological analysis which brought to light the perfectly normal process by which capitalism "produces its own grave-diggers."

Such, in brief, are the roots of the theoretical system of Marx and Engels, which is the theoretical system of modern Socialism.

But Marx and Engels did not make modern Socialism out of nothing. They probably would not have worked out their theories, and even if they had done so the theories would have remained barren, had there not already existed the vague and unlinked elements of a movement of social discontent, which they were able to understand, to which they devoted themselves, and which their clear thinking greatly helped to unify, to guide, and to inspire. Here again three main sources are to be noted, with one or two minor ones.

. . . . .

The speculative radicalism of such men as Rousseau, Condorcet, Priestley, Godwin, and Shelley spent itself mostly in literary effort, and never constituted an actual movement. Yet it did something to break down conservative traditions and to generate moral enthusiasm.

The Utopian socialisms of Saint-Simon, Fourier, Owen, Cabet, and other ingenious picturers of society "as it ought to be" had a little more nearly the character of a movement. In so far, however, as the attempt was made to realize their dreams by founding colonies and communities, not only did these fail, but they retarded the movement of the working class as a whole in the same way as a mirage retards the desert traveler by diverting him from his right course. On the other hand, each of these four thinkers rendered a real service by his illuminating criticism of certain aspects of the existing social order.

Of the three really vital tendencies that merged to form modern Socialism, the most general was the striving for political democracy. Even in the United States, manhood suffrage did not become fairly universal till the 1840's. Nowhere in the Old World did it prevail at that time, but in the more advanced nations of Western Europe it was being vigorously demanded. In each country, when the rising capitalist class undertook to wrest power from monarchs and aristocrats, it needed the help of all the lower classes and accordingly made democracy its slogan. In France the democratic movement triumphed in 1789-94, and then the bourgeoisie promptly kicked away the ladder by which it had climbed. Under the Directory, the Consulate, the Empire, the Bourbon Restoration of 1814-30, now broader and now narrower sections of the propertied classes monopolized political power. In the revolution of 1830 the Paris workers bore the brunt of the fighting, but when the old government had been overthrown, the propertied classes united to seize upon the fruits of victory; and as a result, under the Orleans Monarchy, not only the artisans and wage-workers, but even a large part of the lower middle class, were excluded from political activity. Germany was yet far behind France on the road toward popular self-government. Only in some of its thirty or forty loosely connected states did even the richer bourgeois share power with the aristocrats. It was therefore still possible for the middle classes to hold democratic opinions, except in so far as they were deterred by fear of what the lower classes might do if once the revolution got under way.

As for Great Britain, by the later 1820's there came a powerful protest against the continued political monopoly of a small fraction of the population, composed chiefly of great landowners. The wage-working class, here larger and more self-conscious than in any other country, joined heartily in the movement. Violent revolution was near at hand; but in 1832 the reactionaries gave way—just enough to avert the crisis, not an inch more. The Reform Bill largely increased the representation of the industrial districts and lowered the property qualification for voters enough to take in the upper and most of the lower middle class. This gave the capitalists a dominant influence and left the urban and rural workers voteless and unrepresented. Paralyzed for a moment by the unforeseen treachery of their bourgeois allies, the workers soon rallied and launched an independent movement commonly known as Chartism, from their "People's Charter" or statement of demands, which included manhood suffrage, secret ballot, equal districts, annual elections, and payment of members. The life of this movement was marked by three great waves of activity, with intervals of depression. Its third high tide came in 1848, simultaneously with revolutionary crises all over Western and Central Europe. By 1852 it had ceased to exist. In form, Chartism was only a demand for political democracy; but, being almost exclusively a movement of wage-workers, it inevitably focussed attention on economic questions and was essentially a movement of social revolution. Not one of its specific aims was achieved till long afterward, yet its efforts were by no means wasted.

Through the fear which it put into the hearts of the ruling class it did much to promote labor legislation and other valuable reforms. What is more, it educated the workers, trained them in organized struggle, made them class-conscious.

. . . . .

Second among the roots of modern Socialism we must name the trade-union movement. In England some unions had existed as early as 1720. Throughout the eighteenth century, however, this kind of organization was confined to a few of the skilled hand trades. The unions were neither large nor numerous, they were locally isolated and often short-lived, and they could hardly be said to constitute a movement. But in the 1760's, 70's, and 80's the invention of the steam engine, the spinning jenny and mule, the power loom, and many other kinds of power-driven machinery brought about a great change known as the Industrial Revolution. Large factories came into existence, whose competition was ruinous to many of the old hand trades. Industrial capital was rapidly increased and concentrated. Its owners became the economically dominant class, while thousands of petty manufacturers went to the wall. Artisans and craftsmen by the tens of thousands, whether self-employers or employed in small shops, lost their custom or their jobs. In place of these old types of workingmen came a new one—the modern proletarian, necessarily a city dweller, unable to own his home, have a garden, or keep a cow, absolutely dependent on daily wages for his daily bread. Women and children could now do what had been men's work. The labor market was glutted, unemployment became chronic, wages went down, and at the very moment when wealth was being piled up as never before, the working people were plunged into unprecedented misery, from which they hardly began to emerge till the middle of the nineteenth century. Their sufferings incited them to revolt, their individual helplessness forced them to think of united action, their aggregation in mill towns and mining centers made it easier for them to organize, their increased mobility suggested general instead of merely local organization. A real trade-union movement was beginning to be born when, as a part of the general system of reaction to which the British ruling classes resorted in their fear of the effects of the French Revolution, parliament in 1799-1800 passed the Combination Acts, which made mere membership in a union a criminal offense. For twenty-five years these laws were drastically enforced, and the normal growth of trade unionism was held in check. Secret organizations of course were formed, but spies and provocators easily found their way into them, and had much to do with inciting the campaign of machine-breaking and other violence known in history as the Luddite disturbances, for which many working-men were hanged.

On the repeal of the Combination Acts in 1824-25 there was a hectic outburst of union organization and of strikes, followed by a sharp decline. Next came the attempt to organize the working class as a whole, rather than the various trades and industries, culminating in 1834 in the Grand National Consolidated Trades Union, which hoped to make a complete social revolution by means of the general strike. This was a fiasco, at once ridiculous and sublime. In the early 1840's there began a slow but steady growth of labor organization of a very conservative type, chiefly in the more skilled and better paid trades, but consciously revolutionary unionism did not revive in Great Britain for more than fifty years.

The story of unionism in Western and Central Europe down to the middle of the century need not detain us so long. In these regions the factory system arose from thirty to sixty years later than in Great Britain. The workingmen felt the competition of British machine-made goods, which caused great misery among them, and of course stirred them to discontent; but only in a few localities had any considerable proletariat of the modern type come into existence at the time of which we are speaking. In general, too, the poorer classes had even less of civil rights and political liberty than their British comrades, and were therefore less able to organize on the economic field. As early as 1791 the National Assembly of the new-born French republic enacted a penal statute which forbade "any sort of combination of citizens of the same profession or trade"—a law which was rigorously enforced against labor unions, but not against employers' associations. Legislation such as this prevailed almost without interruption on the Continent until the 1860's, and in some countries much longer. Naturally there were many attempts of workers to unite secretly for economic resistance, but they had little success. It took the genius of a Marx to see in 1848 the vast historical significance of the trade unions.

. . . . .

And so we come to the third of the main sources of modern Socialism as a movement—that is, to certain of the underground revolutionary societies which inevitably were formed under a regime which gave no open outlet to the discontent of the oppressed classes. There were of course many secret societies which pursued only political aims of a more or less democratic character, and which had no necessary connection with the movement of the working class. But, from the time when it became evident that the French Revolution had only put a new ruling class in the saddle, conspirative organizations among the lower strata of the population, aiming to translate the formula "Liberty, Equality, Fraternity," into economic fact, were always on the order of the day. The earliest and most famous was the Society of Equals led by François Noel Babeuf, which in 1795-96 planned to overthrow the French government by armed insurrection, nationalize the land, and reorganize the whole population on a communistic basis. The plot was discovered, Babeuf and one other were guillotined, a number were imprisoned or driven into exile, and the society disappeared. But for more than half a century thereafter, especially in France, but also in other parts of Europe, groups of a more or less similar sort were forever being formed, unearthed, broken up, and formed again.

This underground communism was in general of a utopian character. That is, to use Plekhanoff's expression, "starting from an abstract principle it sought to devise a perfect society." Like the Saint-Simonians or the Fourierites, each group had its ready-made scheme, which was in general based, not on a study of the actual tendencies of economic development, but on some particular conception of justice or equality or other moral abstraction. But whereas the former expected all "good" people, regardless of class, to accept their proposals as soon as they understood them, these conspirative communists were free from that illusion. They did not imagine that they could persuade the propertied classes to abdicate; they relied, perhaps not specifically on the working class, but at any rate on the "poor and oppressed" in general, who they thought, would rally to them whenever they were ready to raise the standard of revolt and impose the new system by armed force. In a sense, too, their schemes were often backward-looking, in that they aimed to revive local small-scale production by hand labor, rather than to socialize the economies of the now rapidly developing system of great machine industry. In these respects, however, some clarification of ideas went on among the underground communists in the course of the half-century. As, with the growth of modern industry, "the poor" came to be more nearly synonymous with "the wage-working class," this type of communism took on a more definite class character. In any event, it kept alive a seed-fire of social aspiration among masses whose wretchedness might otherwise have reduced them to utter degradation and impotence.

In 1836 there was organized a society which called itself the League of the Just and which had its headquarters for some time in Paris, but afterwards in London. In the beginning its membership was made up almost wholly of Germans and German-speaking Swiss. There were among them few industrial wage-workers of the modern type. The majority were skilled hand workers—tailors, shoe makers, watch makers, cabinet makers, and so forth—and with these were mingled a good many intellectuals whose ideas had set them at odds with existing institutions and who more or less understandingly sympathized with the working class. Many of them, and those the most prominent, were political refugees. At first a conspirative group of the 'Babeuvist type, the League of the Just developed rather into a propaganda society, which sought to prepare the way for a mass movement. While not able itself to throw off the veil of secrecy, it organized wherever possible workingmen's educational societies, which held open meetings for the discussion of social questions, and in which its own members naturally played the leading part. This kind of activity reacted upon the mother organization. Utopian creed gradually gave way to critical thinking. At the same time, through the adhesion of a considerable number of Scandinavian, Dutch, Hungarian, Polish, Russian, and other exiles and of some English workingmen, it acquired an international character.

Marx and Engels were in touch with this organization as early as 1844, though they did not join it till 1847. Early in this year it was becoming obvious that another revolu-

Title page of The Communist Manifesto, *1848.*

tionary crisis was near at hand, and the leaders of the League of the Just felt that it was necessary for that body to define its ideas more clearly and to determine upon a course of action to be pursued when the open struggle should begin. For this purpose two congresses of the League were held in London, one in August, the other at the end of November. Engels was a delegate to both gatherings, Marx only to the second one.

At the August meeting the society was thoroughly reorganized on a more democratic basis, the propaganda of communistic ideas and the organization of the toiling masses for self-directed action were definitely accepted as its purpose, its international character was strongly emphasized, and the passing of its former utopian, sentimental, and conspirative aspects was symbolized by the adoption of a new name—that of Communist League—and by the substitution for its old motto, "All men are brothers," of the aggressive slogan, "Proletarians of all countries, Unite!" The November congress, at which English, French, German, Belgian, and Swiss branches were represented, devoted ten full days to a thorough discussion of principles and of the manner in which they were expressed in a manifesto which it had been resolved to put forth. The proposals of Marx and Engels were accepted and by a unanimous vote these two men were commissioned to put them into final shape for publication in the name of the League.

Early in February, 1848, they fulfilled this mandate by delivering to the printer the original German text of the **Communist Manifesto,** which was almost immediately translated and published also in the French language.

. . . . .

In that same month the storm burst in Paris. The monarchy fell, and for a little while the Second Republic seemed to offer a possibility for the realization of the communist ideal of economic freedom and equality. But the upper and lower bourgeoisie joined forces and, with the support of the peasant class, made it clear that the rights of labor must count for nothing as against the interests of profit-making property. In June the proletariat met reaction with revolt, but their rising was drowned in blood. The mutual antagonisms of the propertied classes then broke loose and soon destroyed the republic. In its place, from 1852 till 1870, stood the Second Empire of Louis Napoleon, founded on the consent and promising to serve the interests of the masses of the people, but undemocratic in its very essence, and in practice increasingly dominated by financiers, militarists, priests, and police-spies.

In the year 1848 revolutionary disturbances had broken out also in Germany, Austria, Hungary, Switzerland, Italy, and elsewhere, and were participated in by the most varied elements, some striving only for national independence, some for more or less complete democratization of government, some looking beyond political to social-economic aims. The Communists fought bravely wherever they saw an opening. But within two years the forces of reaction had triumphed all along the line. On the surface, it looked as though nothing had been gained, and not until the sixties did the revolutionary elements even begin once more to raise their heads. One thing, however, had been gained—a fund of bitter but valuable experience.

Marx himself went back to Germany early in 1848, where he edited the *Neue Rheinische Zeitung* (New Rhenish Gazette) and threw all his energies into the struggle. When the fight was lost he returned to London, and here he dwelt from that time till his death in 1883. For a number of years he and his family suffered great hardship, his only regular income being the pound a week that Greeley's *New York Tribune* paid for his correspondence on European affairs. Most of his other writing was unremunerative. Engels was able to spare him a small sum from time to time. Later, when Engels became fairly wealthy, Marx's modest wants were amply cared for, and such was the relation between the two friends that this involved no sense of patronage or dependence.

Marx's activities and his writing henceforth fall into two classes—those which have to do directly with current events in the movement, and those which embody the systematic statement of his economic thought. Yet these are by no means unconnected. Marx the publicist was also Marx the theoretician; for him every question of organization or party tactics involved the application of scientific principles, while theoretical study was valuable only as it enabled the movement to understand the world and guide its own conduct.

Under the first head come three works of contemporary history—**Revolution and Counter-Revolution,** which deals with Germany in 1848; **The Class Struggle in France** and **The Eighteenth Brumaire of Louis Bonaparte,** which together cover the rise and fall of the Second Republic. To this group belong also the statutes of the International Workingmen's Association and several addresses of its General Council, in the period from 1864 to 1873, among them those called forth by the Paris Commune of 1871, generally known under the title **The Civil War in France.**

The lull in revolutionary activity which prevailed for a dozen years after 1850 and again, at least in France, for a long time after 1871, gave Marx more leisure than he had hitherto been able to devote to strictly economic research and thought. In 1859 his studies in this field bore fruit in the publication of a volume entitled **A Contribution to the Critique of Political Economy.** This, however, was but the prelude to a greater work. In 1867 appeared the first volume of his monumental work **Capital,** dealing with "The Process of Capitalist Production." Poor health, as well as preoccupation with the affairs of the contemporary movement, hampered Marx in the further prosecution of this work. At his death in 1883 he left a huge mass of manuscript, in various stages of completion, which Engels, now sixty-three years of age, undertook to edit and publish. In 1893 and '94 respectively, he brought out the second and third volumes, which deal with "The Process of the Circulation of Capital" and "The Process of Capitalist Production as a Whole." When Engels died in 1895 there remained a considerable manuscript, treating in a critical manner of the history of economic thought, which was subsequently edited by Karl Kautsky and published under the title **Theories of Surplus Value.**

While performing this vast labor, Marx found time for a very heavy correspondence—the letters exchanged between him and Engels alone fill four large volumes—and for many lectures, besides writing numerous articles for German, French, and English periodicals. Some of these minor works are of inestimable value.

. . . . .

This introduction makes no pretence either to explain, even in broad outline, the body of economic and historico-philosophical thought known as Marxism, or even hastily to sketch the development of that indomitable Socialist movement of which Marxism is the theoretical expression. All that has been attempted in the preceding pages is to point out the sources from which both the movement and the theory were derived and the circumstances under which they first took definite form, thus indicating their place in the whole social-political history of the modern world, and to tell so much of the life-story of the two great thinkers and leaders as is necessary to that end. It remains to say a few words which may help to the understanding of the three small Marxian classics contained in this volume, or to forestall certain possible misunderstandings.

The **Communist Manifesto,** whose origin has already been related, is a truly unique work. In form it is the campaign address of a special group issued in a special emergency.

But the campaign has proved to be an age-long one, and the group has grown into a world-wide class movement. Moreover, while the writers of this proclamation of course could not foresee just how remote victory might be, nor just what vicissitudes might intervene, they knew well enough that 1848 was to be but one battle in a very prolonged conflict, and that the class struggle then beginning to take definite shape involved issues far more fundamental than had any revolution of the past. They knew also that, while historical events are acts of human will, yet what men will to do is determined by the conditions under which they act, and above all by their economic status and relations. In their view, therefore, all class struggles were explainable and predictable through study of the development of the means of production and exchange and the forms of property. Accordingly, when called upon to write a campaign document, they wrote not only as party leaders and agitators, but also as historians—and again, as historians not of the past only, but of the future as well. Through whole pages of the first section they give in the present tense a vivid account of historical processes which, even in England, the first home of modern industrial capitalism, had at that time hardly more than well begun. Three-quarters of a century later we can find some error in the details of their prediction, but in its essentials it has been or is being fulfilled.

The reader will note that the *Communist Manifesto* consists of four sections. Of the first section and a large part of the second—to the exclusion, however, of the "immediate program" near its close—it may with some qualification be said that they are as live now as when they were first given to the world. The third and fourth sections deal in the main with movements and tendencies that no longer exist, at least in their old forms. If read without due recognition of this fact, they are in part unintelligible, in part misleading. To the serious student of social history, however, they have their value.

At this point we must take up the question of party names. Marx and his associates in 1848 called themselves Communists and spoke critically, in some cases scornfully, of various species of Socialism and Social-Democracy. To the casual reader this may be confusing. He may conclude that only those who now bear the name of Communists can rightly claim to be Marxians, and that the existing Socialist or Social-Democratic parties deserve all the reproaches Marx heaped upon those who were so called in 1848. This is by no means the case.

It is necessary to remember that words often change their meaning in the course of time. Especially is this true of the names of parties. Many examples might be given, but two must suffice. In the history of France and also of several Latin American republics, the advocates of a decentralized form of government have always been known as Federalists; but when we speak of Federalism in the United States, we mean the party which, during the first thirty years of our national existence, strove to exalt the powers of the central government. In France or in Mexico, Jeffer-

son would have been called a Federalist; in this country it was Hamilton who bore that name. Again, the Jeffersonian opponents of centralization and upholders of "states' rights" called themselves Republicans; but ever since 1856 we have had a Republican party proclaiming and acting upon the principle for which Hamilton stood in his time.

Just such a shifting of names has taken place in the history of the revolutionary movement of the proletariat. Within twenty-five years after the *Communist Manifesto* was written, its authors were calling themselves Socialists, while the name of Communist was becoming attached to certain elements with whom they sharply disagreed—especially to those who dreamed of dissolving modern society into innumerable little "communes" or autonomous communities. The conflict between the tendencies represented by Marx and by Michael Bakunin, which culminated in a complete splitting of the International in 1872-73, made it necessary to distinguish more sharply. As the Socialist name might be claimed by either wing, the Marxians often preferred to be designated as Social-Democrats. In the course of time the followers of Bakunin—notable among them Peter Kropotkin—took to calling themselves Communist-Anarchists; moreover, toward the end of the century their movement rapidly declined; thenceforth Socialist and Social-Democratic remained as synonymous appellations, either of which might be applied to such men as Engels, Bebel, Liebknecht, Kautsky, Bernstein, Adler, Plekhanoff, Turati, Guesde, Lafargue, Vaillant, Jaurès, Vandervelde, Hyndman, Hardie. In some countries the party bore one of these names, in some the other; and there were variant titles, such as Labor party, Independent Labor party, Socialist Labor party, Social-Democratic Labor party, while at one period the word "Collectivist" was often used to designate the same ideas and tendencies.

Finally, the problems raised by the World War and the Russian Revolution brought on another great schism in the Socialist movement. By 1919 it was everywhere so definitely split into two distinct camps that it was no longer possible for both to use the same party name. On the one side stood the Bolshevist or majority wing of the old Russian Social Democracy, with Nikolai Lenin as its foremost leader, and along with it larger or smaller groups in all other countries. These resumed the party designation which had been used by Marx and his associates in the 1848 period. They constitute the Communist parties of the various countries (that of the United States calls itself Workers' party) which are linked together in the Third or Communist International, with headquarters at Moscow. On the other hand, those who reject Bolshevist theory and tactics continue to call themselves Socialists or Social-Democrats, and their national organizations are affiliated with the Socialist and Labor International, whose headquarters are at Zurich. Each of these factions claims for itself and more or less emphatically denies to the other the right to be considered as the legitimate continuation of the movement which first took definite form with the issuance of the *Communist Manifesto.* The plan of this introduction does not permit a discussion here of these conflicting claims.

It has been said a little ways back that "with some qualification" the greater part of the *Communist Manifesto* may be considered as live today as it was in 1848.

One qualification has to do with the tone of the controversial parts. In our day many readers are scandalized at the vehemence with which the spokesmen of the Communist League hurled back the accusations of their adversaries. Let those who are shocked read what pious clergymen and learned professors in this country have written against Paine and Jefferson, against Jackson, against the Abolitionists, against the early advocates of Woman Suffrage—not to mention the utterances of many eminent "hundred-percent Americans" during and since the war—and they will get some idea of the flood of shameless slander which it was necessary for Marx and Engels to repel. Certainly they wrote with passion and sometimes exaggerated for the sake of emphasis. Rhetoric has its place, when there is honest feeling behind it. And after all, what made their most savage taunts rankle so deeply is the fact that in substance they were true.

The second and more important qualification is of a different sort. Of the *Communist Manifesto,* even more than of most books, it is to be said: "The letter killeth, but the spirit giveth life." To be valuable, Marx's writings must be read in a Marxian spirit. That which makes Marxism one of the greatest products of the human intellect is its power of growth through self-criticism. Marx himself had scant patience with those who froze his living thoughts into frigid formulas, who treated a historical analysis as if it were meant to be a sacred code. Superficial or disingenuous opponents of Socialism cannot be prevented from speaking of the *Communist Manifesto* as "the Gospel according to Saint Karl" and by their own shallow interpretation making much of it appear false and absurd. The intellectually honest student, not to say the intelligent Socialist, in reading this little book, will say to himself: "This is the way a great thinker expressed his thought under such-and-such circumstances at such-and-such a stage in the development of the capitalist system and of the working-class movement. What can I draw from it to help me, not in flooring an opponent nor in 'putting over' some pet project, but in understanding the problems of the movement at this later stage of its development?" To one who uses it thus, the study of the *Communist Manifesto* is worth all the effort it may cost.

. . . . .

The inclusion in this volume of Engels' elaborate introduction makes it superfluous to say much here about *Wage-Labor and Capital,* which, although it bears Marx's name, may be regarded as a joint work, in view of the very thorough editing it underwent at the hands of his surviving friend.

Marxian economic and social theory cannot be fully stated in the space of forty pages; but as nearly as that is possible, it is done in this remarkable work. It is more than a statement of economic theory, for it leads up to a conclu-

sion whose importance as a rule of working-class tactics can hardly be overestimated. There is no better illustration of Marx's masterly use of dialectic than in his treatment of the paradox that the interests of capitalists and wage-workers as individuals, and likewise those of the bourgeoisie and the proletariat as classes, are at the same time mutually dependent and diametrically opposed. It follows that the right policy for the working class is not one of opposition pure-and-simple, any more than it is one of collaboration pure-and-simple; that anything which hampers or distorts the normal growth of capitalism retards or perverts the progress of the working class as well; that the emancipation of labor can be achieved only when the full development of capitalism and of the class struggle within it shall have endowed the proletariat with the capacity to "grasp this sorry frame of things entire" and—not

> shatter it to bits and *then*
> Remold it nearer to the heart's desire—

not just to destroy capitalism and afterward build something else in its place, but to bring it to an end by the positive process of transforming it into that desired something-else. It is at this point that Socialism parts company with Anarchism and Anarcho-Syndicalism, as well as with agrarian and petty-bourgeois movements such as that of our Populists in the 1890's; and at this point, the Socialists hold, Neo-Communism has parted company with Marx.

To set the reader on the right track for understanding *Value, Price, and Profit,* which is much more difficult than the other two works here presented, it is necessary to impress upon him the fact that in writing it Marx was not trying to state his economic theory as a whole, but was dealing with one specific question—a very practical question, which he characteristically treated as one of theory. We have no record of the speeches of Weston, to which this is a reply. It is clear, however, that Weston upheld a thesis which is dear to the hearts of all enemies of the labor movement, but which, alas! is too often accepted in good faith by men of Weston's type—workingmen or honest friends of labor who have begun to think in the field of economics but have not thought far enough—the thesis, namely: That every increase in the workers' wages results in at least an equal increase in their cost of living, and that accordingly it is a waste of energy for them to struggle for higher wages. If this were true, trade unionism would be a tragic mistake. Marx took up the task of showing that it is not true. Such is the origin of this rather abstruse, but yet fascinating work, which lay in manuscript till some years after its author's death, and was then printed with but slight editing by his daughter Eleanor and her husband Edward Aveling.

In addition to the three works printed in full in this volume there are included at the end small portions of three other books, each of which standing by itself has a certain completeness. First comes the short passage in the preface to Marx's *Critique of Political Economy* in which the materialistic conception of history is tersely summarized. The second is a chapter on "The Historical Tendency of Capitalist Accumulation" which occurs near the end of the first volume of **Capital.** Finally, we include the first page or two of **The Eighteenth Brumaire of Louis Bonaparte,** in which Marx contrasts the proletarian revolution—"the revolution of the nineteenth century," as he too sanguinely calls it—with all the revolutions of the past. . . .

One closing word—let no one suppose that he can gain a real knowledge of Socialism as a living movement from the study of books alone. To vitalize what he gets from such study, he should observe the movement itself by following its periodicals and propaganda literature and if possible by attending Socialist mass meetings and lectures.

Howard Selsam (essay date 1948)

SOURCE: Selsam, Howard. "The Ethics of the *Communist Manifesto*." In *A Centenary of Marxism,* edited by Samuel Bernstein and the editors of *Science and Society,* pp. 22-32. New York: Science and Society, Inc., 1948.

[*In the following essay, Selsam examines the ethical basis of* The Communist Manifesto *and the moral questions it raises. He also explores how the text passes judgment on capitalism, calling for its end, while at the same time eulogizing it as a good system that once worked.*]

One hundred years is a nicely rounded period in terms of which to pass judgment on a doctrine or a document, to evaluate or re-evaluate it. How does it stand the test of time? Can it be used today or is it only of antiquarian interest? Of the **Communist Manifesto** we can also ask: Has its ethics been repudiated or confirmed? Has the world acquired a new ethic which supersedes that of the **Manifesto**? How has the century that has passed illuminated the ethical issues it raised? Can the bourgeois world today avoid, as it tries to evade, the moral judgment pronounced on it by Marx and Engels?

But the question can be raised as to whether the **Communist Manifesto** is a moral document, whether it embodies an ethic in the sense of an all-embracing system of morality. It plainly does not if one seeks an explicit system of fully developed premises from which a body of conclusions logically flows. The young Marx and Engels were not writing a textbook on ethics but were drawing up the theory and program of a revolutionary movement. They were revolutionaries, however, by principle—deeply concerned with philosophy and problems of scientific method. This fact alone required them to seek a rational foundation for their condemnation of the existing order and their demand for its overthrow. At the same time their experience with capitalism and their scientific analysis of it led them to an ever stronger and clearer moral revulsion against it.

It is often said today that Marxists repudiate all morality, that they deny the validity of ethical judgments, that they eliminate the "moral factor" from history, whether past or

in the making. As absurd and untrue as such pronouncements are, they have this much justification—Marx and Engels early became weary of the *mere* "ethical" examination of capitalist society, of *mere* moral assaults on it. The utopians had done enough of that. Besides, capitalism had neither come into being because of moral considerations nor would it pass away because of them. Scientific analysis is required to understand it and a mighty organized physical force is required to overthrow it.

Nevertheless, the reading of the **Manifesto** reveals that Marx and Engels had the "highest" moral reasons for abhorring capitalism and seeking to achieve socialism. But such moral reasons, they believed, were rooted in the historic process itself as scientific study reveals it to us; not imposed upon it by any whim or fancy of this or that individual or class. Such an approach does not take ethics out of the realm of human life and place it in some impersonal or cosmic force, for the simple reason that for the authors of the **Manifesto** the historic process is a human one; it is men making history. If this be forgotten we get not Marx but Hegel or Spencer, not a scientifically grounded morality but philosophical idealism or social Darwinism. For Marx and Engels, as materialists, of all things in the heavens or on the earth, good and evil are to be found only in human society. Ethics arises and has its nexus alone in human life. And as dialecticians, they can see "man" only in the form of real men, of men living in society in constant process of change and development in accordance with ascertainable laws.

It is our purpose, on the basis of these few introductory considerations, to elucidate the ethical principles that are employed in the **Manifesto** and that are revealed by it. As far as possible attention will be limited to this single document, to the question of its ethical premises and conclusions. For here is the heart of Marxism, and we can well ask today, amidst so much moral confusion and hypocrisy in high places, what moral principles the **Manifesto** offers the contemporary world as well as what ethical grounds it has for urging the workers of the world to unite.

Much more attention is conventionally paid to relatively incidental moral issues raised in the **Manifesto** than to the basic ethical philosophy it employs. A few of these should be noted, if only to show their essentially incidental character. The bourgeoisie, it stated for example, "has left no other nexus between man and man than naked self-interest, than callous 'cash payment.' It has drowned the most heavenly ecstasies of religious fervor, of chivalrous enthusiasm, of philistine sentimentalism, in the icy water of egoistical calculation. It has resolved personal worth into exchange value, and in place of the numberless indefeasible chartered freedoms, has set up that single, unconscionable freedom—Free Trade. In a word, for exploitation, veiled by religious and political illusions, it has substituted naked, shameless, direct, brutal exploitation."[1] In other writers of the period such a statement would constitute an absolute indictment of capitalism. Not so for Marx and Engels. Here it has a dual character, depending on the use to be made of it. On one side it points to a progressive feature of capitalism, its tearing asunder "the motley feudal ties that bound man to his 'natural superiors,'" and thus enabling the working class to see their oppression without illusions. On the other side, it presents the essential inhumanity of capitalist relations.

Similarly, in Section II of the document many ethical questions are raised in the discussion of such charges as: the communists seek to abolish private property, they threaten the destruction of culture; they seek abolition of the family, of countries and nationality. The first and obvious answer given to these questions is that the bourgeoisie has done these things far beyond the communists' power to add or to detract, and the authors sometimes with biting wit and sometimes with passionate seriousness discuss the charges. But the real answer occurs at the end of the discussion and is often missed. It points in the direction of our subsequent analysis. The answer is: "The charges against communism made from a religious, a philosophical and, generally, from an ideological standpoint, are not deserving of serious examination."[2] This is because all such arguments are from the standpoint of the bourgeoisie, for they are expressions of the ruling ideas of the age which are inevitably "the ideas of its ruling class." Marx and Engels believe, in short, that the proletarian condemnation of the bourgeois order is so profound and so devastating, its justification for revolution so overwhelming, that the bourgeoisie has lost all right to question the proletariat in this manner. Bourgeois moral principles are but the ideological expression of its class rule, and once the latter is under sentence the former cannot be invoked in its behalf.

The central feature of the *Manifesto* from an ethical viewpoint is that it passes judgment on a whole order of society and finds it wanting. It pronounces the death sentence on capitalism and demands that the sentence be carried out. But even while passing sentence, it reads a eulogy of its victim. It *was* a great system, "it has accomplished wonders"; it "has created more massive and colossal productive forces than have all preceding generations together."[3] A paean of praise is sung to the achievements of the bourgeois system. Its world, however, is not good enough, and its greatest achievement is that it makes possible and necessary the transition to socialism. Thus it is the reasoned judgment of the *Manifesto* that capitalism will be remembered in history as that system of *class* society which prepared the way for the abolition of classes.

But when we look for the grounds upon which such sweeping condemnation is passed we find none of the conventional ethical ideas of the philosophers. Neither "right" nor "justice" is anywhere invoked. There is no appeal to a "golden mean" or a "moral law." Men are neither told that they do nor that they should follow their self-interest or pursue their happiness. Sympathy, benevolence, charity are sarcastically scorned. None of the traditional moral appeals are made; no accepted standards invoked. Why? The clue is to be found in this simple statement: "The commu-

nist revolution is the most radical rupture with traditional property relations; no wonder that its development involves the most radical rupture with traditional ideas."[4] Professor E. H. Carr, in writing of Marxism correctly said: "A true revolution is never content merely to expose the abuses of the existing order, the cases in which its practice falls short of its precept, but attacks at their root the values on which the moral authority of the existing order it based."[5] Since in this case the attack is not only on the existing order, but on the very form of all previous historic society as well, its attack on their moral authority cannot be made by means of the moral ideas or precepts derived from them. If "the history of all hitherto existing society is the history of class struggles," then all previous ethics, too, is at least suspect, for it "moves within certain common forms or general ideas which cannot completely vanish except with the total disappearance of class antagonisms."[6]

The problem is highlighted by the use of two terms, throughout the *Manifesto*, which ordinarily have a moral meaning and which are frequently taken to have such in Marxist usage. Indeed, a first reading of the *Manifesto* might easily lead one to conclude that the basic ethical concept hinges on a judgment of *exploitation*. Historical society has always been divided into exploiters and exploited: the worker is exploited by the capitalist, and so on. But the careful study of the whole document reveals that these are not expressions of moral judgment but are simply descriptions of social relations. No ethical conclusion is intended, none is derived from these terms. To the objection that they are weighted terms the answer might be given that they have been used for ages to describe a feature of class-property relationships. It is clear, further, from the Marxist use of them here as elsewhere that they contain no essential moral element, inasmuch as they are used in relation to slavery and feudalism, as well as capitalism, and these systems are not condemned forthright but are recognized as having had progressive phases in the sense of having made contributions to human social development.

This brings us to the root of the problem, which is found only in the conception of the historic process itself. But this, too, can be viewed only from the standpoint of one or another class in society—in this case, obviously, that of the proletariat. The concepts of class and history are here so interwoven that neither can be taken without the other. The basis of the moral judgments of the *Manifesto* is to be found only in the historical position of the proletariat. Hegel quoted from Schiller that the "history of the world is the world's court of judgment."[7] This is equally true for Marx and Engels, except that for them such judgment is pronounced not by a world spirit but by the historical process itself, and the instrument of the historical process has been the struggle of classes. Under capitalism it is the proletariat which necessarily pushes this struggle to its logical conclusion and is therefore the leading class and the best representative, today, of history's judgment.

In this approach there is no need for an eternal moral law. Capitalism is bad because the proletariat finds it so from the standpoint of its own class needs and interests. It became bad at the point when the proletariat, having become conscious of itself as a class, could also project a plan for the reorganization of society without classes and give birth to communist theory and practice. These arose precisely because "the bourgeoisie is unfit any longer to be the ruling class in society and to impose its conditions of existence on society as an overriding law. It is unfit to rule because it is incompetent to assure an existence to its slave within his slavery, because it cannot help letting him sink into such a state, that it has to feed him, instead of being fed by him."[8] (If this seems an exaggeration or appears to the reader not to describe existing conditions, let him only think of capitalism today on a world scale and of the economic dilemma of the United States in relation to the world market; of the simple fact that no one can buy the products we must sell to maintain our economic system unless we give them the money to do so.)

There still seem to be, however, conventional moral premises in the *Manifesto.* One could even claim to find one of the chief dicta of Kant's moral law, namely, that men should be treated as ends only, never as means. Marx and Engels say: "All that we want to do away with is the miserable character of this appropriation [that is, the personal appropriation of the products of social labor] under which the laborer lives merely to increase capital, and is allowed to live only in so far as the interest of the ruling class requires it."[9] And Marx wrote years later: "The worker himself appears in the [bourgeois] conception as what he really is in capitalist production—a mere means of production; not as an end in himself and the goal of production."[10] The words may be the same as Kant's, but both the theoretical basis and the practical application are vastly different. Unlike Kant, Marx and Engels find no such rule in "the starry heavens above us" or in "the moral law within us." Nothing in heaven or earth, in short, has decreed that men *ought* to treat their fellows as ends only, never as means. Nothing, that is, except men themselves as a result of the concrete condition of their social development. It is doubtful whether Kant really meant by this any more than Adam Smith meant when he described capitalism's "obvious and simple system of natural liberty" as that system in which "Every man, as long as he does not violate the laws of justice, is left perfectly free to pursue his own interest his own way, and to bring both his industry and capital into competition with those of any other man, or order of men."[11]

For the authors of the *Manifesto* such a principle as Kant's is unquestionably moral in nature. But it originated, as all moral principles do for them (as also for Spinoza), in the strivings and desires of men. Marx and Engels are not here invoking an *a priori* moral principle to justify the attack on capitalism and the demand for a socialist world, but rather should be understood as describing the fact that the workers are becoming aware that they are being treated only as a means to production and are demanding that they be the end of production.

The whole problem of the ethical judgment of the *Manifesto* will appear in clearer light if we recognize the basic Marxist thesis that ethics or morality, like all other forms of ideology, arise out of and reflect specific modes of production and resultant class interests. Heretofore, however, every class struggling to maintain and justify its power or struggling to become the ruling class, represented its needs and desires in the form of eternal principles, commandments, and so on. Or, in the case of the radicals among the early bourgeoisie, as dicta of human nature, inviolable laws of human conduct, such as the pursuit of self-interest. Marx and Engels have, through their whole philosophy of historical materialism, forsworn any attempt to justify the claims of the modern working class in this way. This does not mean at all that the working class cannot and does not adduce ethical principles to support its demand for the overthrow of capitalism. It means that the working class cannot and does not need to derive its principles from anything other than its own interests which are eventually those of mankind as a whole. It means that the working class has discovered that it is exploited, that it doesn't like being exploited, and means to do away with exploitation. It means that the conditions of modern industry—the productive forces developed by capitalism taken together with the capitalist relations of production—are such that the workers cannot see any good reason why they who do the work of the world should not themselves reap the fruits of their labor, that is, be the end of production.

These simple assumptions of the *Manifesto,* factual in the first instance rather than moral, are pointed up by the eulogy given capitalism for its development of the productive capacities of society. It is precisely capitalism that has, through its inherent compulsion to revolutionize the instruments of production,[12] created the conditions which both enable and impel its "slaves" to demand its overthrow. It has created the conditions which first make it possible for man to be the end of production, not the means. It has created the conditions which make it possible for all exploitation to be abolished. To put it in ethical terms and somewhat fancifully, behind the demands and new ethical understanding of the proletariat stand all the slaves and the serfs of the ages. They could struggle only to change the condition of their servitude, while the modern proletariat, thanks to its creator, capitalism, can abolish servitude. Engels expressed this most clearly in his original draft for the *Manifesto.* "The slave can become free by rupturing one relation of private ownership, the relation of slavery; the proletariat can achieve emancipation only by destroying private property relations in their entirety."[13]

Our first conclusion is that the ethical principles employed in the *Manifesto* are expressions of the world-outlook, the needs and interests, the hopes and desires of the working class. At this point we stand only on the revolutionary doctrine that no ethical principles of ruling-class ideologists are sufficient for the class struggle of the proletariat. The only conclusion possible is that they must formulate the moral principles of their struggle. No higher authority is invoked, no eternal truths, no ultimate principle of righteousness. Just as it is the doctrine of the *Manifesto* that the workers must achieve their own liberation (a doctrine not to be confused with any denial of the need for allies, in the form both of individuals who come over to the workers and groupings of the petty bourgeoisie, the farmers, etc.) so must it necessarily follow that the ethics of their struggle must be theirs and can't be anyone else's.

But this is only the first major conclusion or generalization that can be drawn from the *Manifesto,* basic and indispensable as it is. It called for the abandonment of reliance on all forms of altruist approaches—approaches which for Marx and Engels can lead only to confusion and compromise, to the attempt to alleviate the class struggle, not eliminate it. This is that without which no one is a Marxist, but at best a utopian socialist, for, as the *Manifesto* observed, "Only from the point of view of being the most suffering class does the proletariat exist for them." The ethics of the utopians, like their "fantastic pictures of future society" correspond not to the position in society and the understanding of a developed proletariat but only to the "first instinctive yearnings of that class for a general reconstruction of society."[14] Communist principles, on the contrary, are not invented but discovered. They express the actual relations of capitalist society,[15] in that developed form when it has already produced its own "gravediggers." And the only moral justification its grave-diggers require is that the system is inimical to their needs and interests, stands in the way of their living the life they want to live. And, thanks to society's newly developed productivity, a life they can live under new social and economic relations.

Fundamental as is the position described above, it is not the whole picture. A second equally important ethical idea runs through the *Manifesto* as it does through all the subsequent writings of Marx and Engels. The struggle of the working class for the overthrow of capitalism is justified and right not only because it expresses their needs and interests, hence their ethics, but because their ethics is the highest or best possible at this stage of history. This is so because, in the nature of things, moral judgments reflect reality, and the judgments of the workers today reflect the contradictions in this reality. As Engels eloquently expressed it: "When the moral consciousness of the masses declares this, that, or the other economic phenomenon to be wrong, as happened at one time in the case of slavery and at another in the case of serfdom, this means that the phenomenon in question has already outlived its time, that new economic conditions have arisen, thanks to which the old ones have become intolerable, and must be swept away."[16]

There is a direction of history, Marx and Engels believe, which the struggle of the working class is carrying forward. This is expressed in many places in the *Manifesto.* They call reactionary, for example, the fight of the lower middle class against the bourgeoisie: "for they try to roll back the wheel of history."[17] They say again, "In bourgeois

society, . . . the past dominates the present; in communist society, the present dominates the past."[18] There is a "march of modern history" the feudal socialists are unable to comprehend, and they forget further "that the modern bourgeoisie is the necessary offspring of their own form of society."[19] But this conception of the direction of history from a lower to a higher form appears most clearly of all in the very analysis of the achievements of capitalism. What are some of these "achievements" which merit the praise of capitalism's foremost enemies? It has established the world market, "the universal interdependence of nations." "It has been the first to show what man's activity can bring about" by accomplishing wonders of production. It "draws all, even the most barbarian, nations into civilization." By creating great cities it "has thus rescued a considerable part of the population from the idiocy of rural life." Unlike all previous industrial classes, the bourgeoisie "cannot exist without constantly revolutionizing the instrument of production, and thereby the relations of production, and with them the whole relations of society." But the heart of it all is the fact that the bourgeoisie "during its rule of scarce one hundred years, has created more massive and more colossal productive forces than have all preceding generations together." It has developed fabulous instruments of production and communication, cleared continents, changed the course of rivers. It has in a word subjected "nature's forces to man." And they ask, "what earlier century had even a presentiment that such productive forces slumbered in the lap of social labor"?[20]

The greatness of the bourgeois world lies in its development of productive forces, in its increase of man's mastery over nature. But this was an inevitable development out of feudalism; such is the direction of social evolution. Right here is found the fatal weakness of capitalist relations. For capitalism "is like the sorcerer who is no longer able to control the powers of the nether world whom he has called up by his spells."[21] The capitalist forces of production come into conflict with capitalist relations, are fettered by them. Only the proletariat can take the next step, can free the forces of production from capitalist fetters, can create such social relations as can carry ever further mankind's ability to produce, man's mastery over nature. History is therefore on the side of the working class, or to put it better, the working class in its revolutionary struggle is on the side of history. Engels had made such an approach in his early draft. He wrote: "It is obvious that hitherto the productive forces had not been developed widely enough to provide a sufficiency for all members of society, and that private property had not yet become a chain, a hindrance, to these productive forces. . . . [These] mighty and easily multiplied productive forces have vastly outgrown the bourgeois and his private property and thus constantly involve society in colossal disturbances—the abolition of private property is not only possible but necessary."[22]

The objection can be raised at once that this proves nothing, that it is a circular argument, that there is already a moral judgment implicit in such an interpretation of history. Why is increasing productivity good? Why should it be taken as an index of progress? Why is man's increasing mastery of nature desirable? Have there not been, and are there not still noteworthy opponents of such views? Marx and Engels, neither in the **Manifesto** nor elsewhere argue this point. Perhaps, because they consider it irrelevant. They are social scientists, not "moralizers." Like Hegel they do not believe in placing personal whims and fancies up against that scientific knowledge which explores "the march of cold necessity in the subject-matter." But better still, they know, first, that history moves that way; second, that the proletariat becoming class conscious under the conditions created by capitalism will struggle to free the productive forces from private property relations. Finally, they know that the members of the classless society of the future will recognize the prevailing ideological attacks on communism for what they are: the moral cynicism or nihilism of those who would hold back the wheel of history.

There is no other way. Either ethics and morality are derived from the concrete changing conditions of human life or they are not. Materialism must insist that they have no other basis. Under the conditions of class struggle Marx and Engels are discussing, therefore, the inevitable tendency is for two positions to crystallize, that of the bourgeoisie and that of the proletariat. But when the struggle is seen in its broadest historical terms, they can say that the position of the proletariat conforms to the needs and interests of the human race as a whole.

On one side, recurrent crises, war, famine, mass misery, reversion to barbarism. On the other side, free men freely developing their relations with one another and with nature in the interests of all. On one side, each for himself, "dog eat dog," men as means to profits and as appendages to the machine; on the other side, men as the end and goal of production, guided by the principle that "the free development of each [is] the condition for the free development of all." The proletariat works for the interests of all men in furthering its own interests; that is why it has the allies without which, as Lenin said, it could never win. Marx and Engels, taking their stand only on the concrete and ever changing nature of men in society in constant development are led by all their studies to believe that the ethics of the proletariat is a higher ethics than is that of the bourgeoisie, higher in the sense that it represents a movement in a direction which mankind, in its subsequent historical development, will pronounce good. And here history's judgment means, of course, nothing but the collective opinions of men in historical development. In reference to any particular form of society at any particular time, such a judgment is relative. From the standpoint of the historical process as a whole it is absolute. But it is absolute only in the sense of direction, not as a state or stage conceived as eternally existing or as realized at any one time.

This paper has sought to bring forward only two points: (1) that the ethics employed in the **Manifesto** is simply the expression of the needs, hopes and desires of the modern working class, and (2) that this ethics alone accords with the necessary and desirable (in the sense of being desired)

direction of social evolution. To forget the first is to leave out the very soul of Marxism: its partisanship in the class struggle. To ignore the second is to deprive Marxism of both its historical perspective and its moral power. It is no "mere" class doctrine. It is not pragmatism which has no ends or goods beyond the immediate situation and thus supports or becomes opportunism at every turn. It is not an amoral taking of sides nor a loyalty for loyalty's sake. The essential unity of the two points inheres in the Marxist recognition that it is the nature of capitalism itself which compels the working class, in struggling for its emancipation, to struggle for the emancipation of all oppressed humanity. It is the nature of capitalist relations which has created a class that must struggle to abolish all classes. It is the capitalist development of productivity that makes the abolition of all classes, of all exploitation of man by man, possible for the first time in history. In short, it is the historic process itself which requires the working class to liberate all mankind, and which gives concrete meaning to the word "liberation" for the majority of the world's population.

It is no exaggeration to say that this is the first document in history to achieve any such organic unity of scientific social analysis with ethical ideals. Previous attempts at social science had either sought to eliminate values or had added on, extraneously, values derived from religious or secular traditions. In the first case no rational guide for action was possible. In the second, the values were divorced both from what in fact existed and also from any possible effective program of action.

The success of Marx and Engels was due to the fact that they derived their values from their scientific study of capitalist society itself, and they were able to make such a study because they approached the subject from the standpoint of the proletariat.

Notes

1. Karl Marx and Frederick Engels, "Manifesto of the Communist Party," in Karl Marx, *Selected Works* (New York, International Publishers, n.d.), I, p. 207 f.

2. *Ibid.,* p. 225.

3. *Ibid.,* p. 208 and 210.

4. *Ibid.,* p. 226.

5. Edward Hallett Carr, *The Soviet Impact on the Western World* (New York, 1947), p. 94.

6. Marx and Engels, *op. cit.,* p. 226.

7. *Hegel's Philosophy of Right,* transl. by T. M. Knox (Oxford, 1942), sect. 340.

8. Marx and Engels, *op. cit.,* p. 218.

9. *Ibid.,* p. 221.

10. Marx, *Theorien über den Mehrwert,* ed. by Karl Kautsky (Berlin 1923), II, p. 334.

11. Adam Smith, *The Wealth of Nations* (New York, Modern Library, 1937), p. 651.

12. Marx and Engels, *op. cit.,* p. 208 f.

13. *The Communist Manifesto,* ed. D. Ryazanoff (New York, 1930), p. 322 f.

14. Marx and Engels, *op. cit.,* p. 238.

15. *Ibid.,* p. 219.

16. Quoted by D. Ryazanoff in his edition of *The Communist Manifesto,* p. 172.

17. Marx and Engels, *op. cit.,* p. 216.

18. *Ibid.,* p. 221.

19. *Ibid.,* p. 230.

20. *Ibid.,* p. 206–10.

21. *Ibid.,* p. 211.

22. In Ryazanov, *op. cit.,* p. 329.

Paul M. Sweezy and Leo Huberman (essay date 1949)

SOURCE: Sweezy, Paul M., and Leo Huberman. "*The Communist Manifesto* after 100 Years." In *The Communist Manifesto. Principles of Communism. "The Communist Manifesto" after 100 Years,* edited by Paul M. Sweezy and Leo Huberman, pp. 87-113. New York: Modern Reader Paperbacks, 1968.

[*In the following essay, originally published in 1949, Sweezy and Huberman provide an overview of the history of socialism and discuss the* Communist Manifesto *in terms of historical materialism, class struggle, the nature of capitalism, the inevitability of socialism, and the road to socialism.*]

THE HISTORICAL IMPORTANCE OF THE *MANIFESTO*

What gives the **Manifesto** its unique importance? In order to answer this question it is necessary to see clearly its place in the history of socialism.

Despite a frequently encountered opinion to the contrary, there was no socialism in ancient or medieval times. There were movements and doctrines of social reform which were radical in the sense that they sought greater equality or even complete community of consumer goods, but none even approached the modern socialist conception of a society in which the means of production are publicly owned and managed. This is, of course, not surprising. Production actually took place on a primitive level in scattered workshops and agricultural strips—conditions under which public ownership and management were not only impossible but even unthinkable.

The first theoretical expression of a genuinely socialist position came in Thomas More's *Utopia,* written in the early years of the sixteenth century—in other words, at the very threshold of what we call the modern period. But *Utopia* was the work of an individual genius and not the reflection of a social movement. It was not until the English Civil War, in the middle of the seventeenth century, that socialism first began to assume the shape of a social movement. Gerrard Winstanley (born 1609, died sometime after 1660) was probably the greatest socialist thinker that the English-speaking countries have yet produced, and the Digger movement which he led was certainly the first practical expression of socialism. But it lasted only a very short time, and the same was true of the movement led by Babeuf during the French Revolution a century and a half later. Meanwhile, quite a number of writers had formulated views of a more or less definitely socialist character.

But it was not until the nineteenth century that socialism became an important public issue and socialists began to play a significant role in the political life of the most advanced European countries. The Utopian socialists (Owen, Fourier, St. Simon) were key figures in this period of emergence; and the Chartist movement in Britain, which flourished during the late 1830s and early 1840s, showed that the new factory working class formed a potentially powerful base for a socialist political party.

Thus we see that socialism is strictly a modern phenomenon, a child of the industrial revolution which got under way in England in the seventeenth century and decisively altered the economic and social structure of all of western Europe during the eighteenth and early nineteenth centuries. By 1840 or so, socialism had arrived in the sense that it was already widely discussed and politically promising.

But socialism was still shapeless and inchoate—a collection of brilliant insights and perceptions, of more or less fanciful projects, of passionate beliefs and hopes. There was an urgent need for systematization; for a careful review picking out what was sound, dropping what was unsound, integrating into the socialist outlook the most progressive elements of bourgeois philosophy and social science.

It was the historical mission of Karl Marx and Friedrich Engels to perform this task. They appeared on the scene at just the right time; they were admirably prepared by background and training; they seized upon their opportunity with a remarkably clear estimate of its crucial importance to the future of mankind.

Marx and Engels began their work of transforming socialism "from Utopia to science" in the early 1840s. In the next few years of profound study and intense discussion they worked out their own new socialist synthesis. The **Manifesto** for the first time broadcast this new synthesis to the world—in briefest compass and in arrestingly brilliant prose.

The **Manifesto** thus marks a decisive watershed in the history of socialism. Previous thought and experience lead up to it; subsequent developments start from it. It is this fact which stamps the *Manifesto* as the most important document in the history of socialism. And the steady growth of socialism as a world force since 1848 has raised the *Manifesto* to the status of one of the most important documents in the entire history of the human race.

HOW SHOULD WE EVALUATE THE *MANIFESTO* TODAY?

How has the *Manifesto* stood up during its first hundred years? The answer we give to this question will depend largely on the criteria by which—consciously or unconsciously—we form our judgments.

Some who consider themselves Marxists approach the *Manifesto* in the spirit of a religious fundamentalist approaching the Bible—every word and every proposition were literally true when written and remain sacrosanct and untouchable after the most eventful century in world history. It is, of course, not difficult to demonstrate to the satisfaction of any reasonable person that this is an untenable position. For this very reason, no doubt, a favorite procedure of enemies of Marxism is to assume that all Marxists take this view of the *Manifesto.* If the *Manifesto* is judged by the criterion of one-hundred-percent infallibility it can be readily disposed of by any second-rate hack who thus convinces himself that he is a greater man than the founders of scientific socialism. The American academic community, it may be noted in passing, is full of such great men today. But theirs is a hollow victory which, though repeated thousands of times every year, leaves the *Manifesto* untouched and the stature of its authors undiminished.

Much more relevant and significant are the criteria which Marx and Engels themselves, in later years, used in judging the *Manifesto.* For this reason the prefaces which they wrote to various reprints and translations are both revealing and important (especially the prefaces to the German edition of 1872, the Russian edition of 1882, the German edition of 1883, and the English edition of 1888). Let us sum up what seem to us to be the main points which emerge from a study of these prefaces:

(1) In certain respects, Marx and Engels regarded the *Manifesto* as clearly dated. This is particularly the case as regards the programmatic section and the section dealing with socialist literature (end of Part II and all of Part III).

(2) The general principles set forth in the *Manifesto* were, in their view, "on the whole as correct today as ever" (first written in 1872, repeated in 1888).

(3) The experience of the Paris Commune caused them to add a principle of great importance which was absent from the original, namely, that "the working class cannot simply lay hold of the ready-made state machinery and wield it for its own purposes." In other words, the "ready-made state machinery" had been created by and for the existing ruling classes and would have to be replaced by new state machinery after the conquest of power by the working class.

(4) Finally—and this is perhaps the most important point of all—in their last joint preface (to the Russian edition of 1882), Marx and Engels brought out clearly the fact that the *Manifesto* was based on the historical experience of western and central Europe. But by 1882 Russia, in their opinion, formed "the vanguard of revolutionary action in Europe," and this development inevitably gave rise to new questions and problems which did not and could not arise within the framework of the original *Manifesto.*

It is thus quite obvious from these later prefaces that Marx and Engels never for a moment entertained the notion that they were blueprinting the future course of history or laying down a set of dogmas which would be binding on future generations of socialists. In particular, they implicitly recognized that as capitalism spread and drew new countries and regions into the mainstream of modern history, problems and forms of development not considered in the *Manifesto* must necessarily be encountered.

On the other hand, Marx and Engels never wavered in their conviction that the *general principles* set forth in the *Manifesto* were sound and valid. Neither the events of the succeeding decades nor their own subsequent studies, profound and wide-ranging as they were, caused them to alter or question its central theoretical framework.

It seems clear to us that in judging the *Manifesto* today, a century after its publication, we should be guided by the same criteria that the authors themselves used twenty-five, thirty, and forty years after its publication. We should not concern ourselves with details but should go straight to the general principles and examine them in the light of the changed conditions of the mid-twentieth century.

THE GENERAL PRINCIPLES OF THE *MANIFESTO*

The general principles of the *Manifesto* can be grouped under the following headings: (a) historical materialism, (b) class struggle, (c) the nature of capitalism, (d) the inevitability of socialism, and (e) the road to socialism. Let us review these principles as briefly and concisely as we can.

HISTORICAL MATERIALISM.

This is the theory of history which runs through the *Manifesto* as it does through all the mature writings of Marx and Engels. It holds that the way people act and think is determined in the final analysis by the way they get their living; hence the foundation of any society is its economic system; and therefore economic change is the driving force of history. Part I of the *Manifesto* is essentially a brilliant and amazingly compact application of this theory to the rise and development of capitalism from its earliest beginnings in the Middle Ages to its full-fledged mid-nineteenth-century form. Part II contains a passage which puts the case for historical materialism as against historical idealism with unexampled clarity:

> Does it require deep intuition to comprehend that man's ideas, views, and conceptions, in one word, man's consciousness, changes with every change in the conditions of his material existence, in his social relations and in his social life?

What else does the history of ideas prove, than that intellectual production changes its character in proportion
as material production is changed? The ruling ideas of
each age have ever been the ideas of its ruling class.

When people speak of ideas that revolutionize society,
they do but express the fact, that within the old society,
the elements of a new one have been created, and that
the dissolution of the old ideas keeps even pace with
the dissolution of the old conditions of existence.

CLASS STRUGGLE.

The *Manifesto* opens with the famous sentence: "The history of all hitherto existing society is the history of class
struggles." This is in no sense a contradiction of the theory
of historical materialism but rather an essential part of it.
"Hitherto existing society" (Engels explained in a footnote
to the 1888 edition that this term should not be interpreted
to include preliterate societies) had always been based on
an economic system in which some people did the work
and others appropriated the social surplus. Fundamental
differences in the method of securing a livelihood—some
by working, some by owning—must, according to historical materialism, create groups with fundamentally different
and in many respects antagonistic interests, attitudes, aspirations. These groups are the classes of Marxian theory.
They, and not individuals, are the chief actors on the stage
of history. Their activities and strivings—above all, their
conflicts—underlie the social movements, the wars and
revolutions, which trace out the pattern of human progress.

THE NATURE OF CAPITALISM.

The *Manifesto* contains the bold outlines of the theory of
capitalism which Marx was to spend most of the remainder of his life perfecting and elaborating. (It is interesting
to note that the term "capitalism" does not occur in the
Manifesto; instead, Marx and Engels use a variety of expressions, such as "existing society," "bourgeois society,"
"the rule of the bourgeoisie," and so forth.) Capitalism is
pre-eminently a market, or commodity-producing,
economy, which "has left no other nexus between man and
man than naked self-interest, than callous 'cash payment.'"
Even the laborer is a commodity and must sell himself
piecemeal to the capitalist. The capitalist purchases labor
(later Marx would have substituted "labor power" for "labor" in this context) in order to make profits, and he makes
profits in order to expand his capital. Thus the laborers
form a class "who live only so long as they find work, and
who find work only so long as their labor increases capital."

It follows that capitalism, in contrast to all earlier forms of
society, is a restlessly expanding system which "cannot
exist without constantly revolutionizing the instruments of
production, and thereby the relations of production, and
with them the whole relations of society." Moreover, "the
need of a constantly expanding market for its products
chases the bourgeoisie over the whole surface of the globe.
It must nestle everywhere, settle everywhere, establish
connections everywhere." Thanks to these qualities, "the

bourgeoisie, during its rule of scarce one hundred years,
has created more massive and more colossal productive
forces than have all preceding generations together." But,
by a peculiar irony, its enormous productivity turns out to
be the nemesis of capitalism. In one of the great passages
of the *Manifesto,* which is worth quoting in full, Marx and
Engels lay bare the inner contradictions which are driving
capitalism to certain shipwreck:

> Modern bourgeois society with its relations of produc-
> tion, of exchange and of property, a society that has
> conjured up such gigantic means of production and of
> exchange, is like the sorcerer who is no longer able to
> control the powers of the nether world whom he has
> called up by his spells. For many a decade past the his-
> tory of industry and commerce is but the history of the
> revolt of modern productive forces against modern con-
> ditions of production, against the property relations that
> are the conditions for the existence of the bourgeoisie
> and of its rule. It is enough to mention the commercial
> crises that by their periodical return put the existence
> of the entire bourgeois society on its trial, each time
> more threateningly. In these crises a great part not only
> of the existing products, but also of the previously cre-
> ated productive forces, are periodically destroyed. In
> these crises there breaks out an epidemic that, in all
> earlier epochs, would have seemed an absurdity—the
> epidemic of overproduction. Society suddenly finds it-
> self put back into a state of momentary barbarism; it
> appears as if a famine, a universal war of devastation
> had cut off the supply of every means of subsistence;
> industry and commerce seem to be destroyed. And
> why? Because there is too much civilization, too much
> means of subsistence, too much industry, too much
> commerce. The productive forces at the disposal of so-
> ciety no longer tend to further the development of the
> conditions of bourgeois property; on the contrary, they
> have become too powerful for these conditions, by
> which they are fettered, and so soon as they overcome
> these fetters, they bring disorder into the whole of bour-
> geois society, endanger the existence of bourgeois prop-
> erty. The conditions of bourgeois society are too nar-
> row to comprise the wealth created by them. And how
> does the bourgeoisie get over these crises? On the one
> hand, by enforced destruction of a mass of productive
> forces; on the other, by the conquest of new markets,
> and by the more thorough exploitation of the old ones.
> That is to say, by paving the way for more extensive
> and more destructive crises, and by diminishing the
> means whereby crises are prevented.

THE INEVITABILITY OF SOCIALISM.

The mere fact that capitalism is doomed is not enough to
ensure the triumph of socialism. History is full of examples which show that the dissolution of a society can
lead to chaos and retrogression as well as to a new and
more progressive system. Hence it is of greatest importance that capitalism by its very nature creates and trains
the force which at a certain stage of development must
overthrow it and replace it by socialism. The reasoning is
concisely summed up in the last paragraph of Part I:

> The essential condition for the existence and for the
> sway of the bourgeois class, is the formation and aug-
> mentation of capital; the condition for capital is wage

labor. Wage labor rests exclusively on competition between the laborers. The advance of industry, whose involuntary promoter is the bourgeoisie, replaces the isolation of the laborers, due to competition, by their revolutionary combination, due to association. The development of modern industry, therefore, cuts from under its feet the very foundation on which the bourgeoisie produces and appropriates products. What the bourgeoisie therefore produces, above all, are its own grave-diggers. Its fall and the victory of the proletariat are equally inevitable.

THE ROAD TO SOCIALISM.

There are two aspects to this question as it appears in the *Manifesto*: first, the general character of the socialist revolution; and, second, the course of the revolution on an international scale.

The socialist revolution must be essentially a working-class revolution, though Marx and Engels were far from denying a role to elements of other classes. As pointed out above, the development of capitalism itself requires more and more wage workers; moreover, as industry grows and the transport network is extended and improved, the workers are increasingly unified and trained for collective action. At a certain stage this results in the "organization of the proletarians into a class, and consequently into a political party." The contradictions of capitalism will sooner or later give rise to a situation from which there is no escape except through revolution. What Marx and Engels call the "first step" in this revolution is the conquest of power, "to raise the proletariat to the position of ruling class, to win the battle of democracy." It is important to note—because it has been so often overlooked—that basic social changes come only after the working class has acquired power:

> The proletariat will use its political supremacy to wrest, by degrees, all capital from the bourgeoisie, to centralize all instruments of production in the hands of the state, i.e. of the proletariat organized as the ruling class; and to increase the total of productive powers as rapidly as possible.

This will be a transition period during which the working class "sweeps away by force the old conditions of production." (In view of present-day misrepresentations of Marxism, it may be as well to point out that "sweeping away by force" in this connection implies the orderly use of state power and not the indiscriminate use of violence.) Finally, along with these conditions, the working class will

> have swept away the conditions for the existence of class antagonisms and of classes generally, and will thereby have abolished its own supremacy as a class.

> In place of the old bourgeois society, with its classes and class antagonisms, we shall have an association, in which the free development of each is the condition for the free development of all.

So much for the general character of the socialist revolution. There remains the question of the international course of the revolution. Here it was clear to Marx and Engels that though the modern working-class movement is essentially an international movement directed against a system which knows no national boundaries, "yet in form, the struggle of the proletariat with the bourgeoisie is at first a national struggle." And from this it follows that "the proletariat of each country must, of course, first of all settle matters with its own bourgeoisie." At the same time, Marx and Engels were well aware of the international character of the counter-revolutionary forces which would certainly attempt to crush an isolated workers' revolution. Hence, "united action of the leading civilized countries at least, is one of the first conditions for the emancipation of the proletariat." Thus the various national revolutions must reinforce and protect one another and eventually merge into a new society from which international exploitation and hostility will have vanished. For, as Marx and Engels point out:

> In proportion as the exploitation of one individual by another is put an end to, the exploitation of one nation by another will also be put an end to. In proportion as the antagonism between classes within the nation vanishes, the hostility of one nation to another will come to an end.

As to the actual geography of the revolution, Marx and Engels took it for granted that it would start and spread from the most advanced capitalist countries of western and central Europe. At the time of writing the *Manifesto,* they correctly judged that Europe was on the verge of a new revolutionary upheaval, and they expected that Germany would be the cockpit:

> The Communists turn their attention chiefly to Germany, because that country is on the eve of a bourgeois revolution that is bound to be carried out under more advanced conditions of European civilization and with a much more developed proletariat than that of England was in the seventeenth, and of France in the eighteenth century, and because the bourgeois revolution in Germany will be but the prelude to an immediately following proletarian revolution.

This prediction, of course, turned out to be overoptimistic. Not the revolution but the counter-revolution won the day in Germany, and indeed in all of Europe. But at no time in their later lives did Marx and Engels revise the view of the *Manifesto* that the proletarian, or socialist, revolution would come first in one or more of the most advanced capitalist countries of western and central Europe. In the 1870s and 1880s they became increasingly interested in Russia, convinced that that country must soon be the scene of a revolution similar in scope and character to the great French Revolution of a hundred years earlier. No small part of their interest in Russia derived from a conviction that the Russian revolution, though it would be essentially a bourgeois revolution, would flash the signal for the final showdown in the West. As Gustav Mayer says in his biography of Engels, speaking of the later years, "his speculations about the future always centered on the approaching Russian revolution, the revolution which was to clear the way for the proletarian revolution in the West." (English translation, p. 278.) But "he never imagined that his ideas might triumph, in that Empire lying on the very edge of European civilization, before capitalism was overthrown in western Europe." (P. 286.)

THE GENERAL PRINCIPLES OF THE *MANIFESTO* A HUNDRED YEARS LATER

What are we to say of the theoretical framework of the *Manifesto* after a hundred years? Can we say, as Marx and Engels said, that the general principles are "on the whole as correct today as ever"? Or have the events of the last five or six decades been such as to force us to abandon or revise these principles? Let us review our list item by item.

HISTORICAL MATERIALISM.

The last half century has certainly provided no grounds whatever to question the validity of historical materialism. Rather the contrary. There has probably never been a period in which it was more obvious that the prime mover of history is economic change; and certainly the thesis has never been so widely recognized as at present. This recognition is by no means confined to Marxists or socialists; one can even say that it provides the starting point for an increasingly large proportion of all serious historical scholarship. Moreover, the point of view of historical materialism—that "man's ideas, views, and conceptions, in one word, man's consciousness, changes with every change in the conditions of his material existence, in his social relations and in his social life"—has been taken over (ordinarily without acknowledgment, and perhaps frequently without even knowledge, of its source) by nearly all social scientists worthy of the name. It is, of course, true that the world-wide crisis of the capitalist system, along with the wars and depressions and catastrophes to which it has given rise, has produced a vast outpouring of mystical, irrational theories in recent years, and that such theories are increasingly characteristic of bourgeois thought as a whole. But wherever sanity and reason prevail, both inside and outside the socialist movement, there the truth of historical materialism is ever more clearly perceived as a beacon lighting up the path to an understanding of human society and its history.

CLASS STRUGGLE.

The theory of class struggle, like the theory of historical materialism, has been strengthened rather than weakened by the events of the last half century. Not only is it increasingly clear that internal events in the leading nations of the world are dominated by class conflicts, but also the crucial role of class conflict in international affairs is much nearer the surface and hence more easily visible today than ever before. Above all, the rise and spread of fascism in the interwar period did more than anything else possibly could have done to educate millions of people all over the world to the class character of capitalism and the lengths to which the ruling class will go to preserve its privileges against any threat from below. Moreover, here,

as in the case of historical materialism, serious social scientists have been forced to pay Marx and Engels the compliment of imitation. The study of such diverse phenomena as social psychology, the development of Chinese society, the caste system in India, and racial discrimination in the United States South, is being transformed by a recognition of the central role of class and class struggle. Honest enemies of Marxism are no longer able to pooh-pooh the theory of class struggle as they once did; they now leave the pooh-poohing to the dupes and paid propagandists of the ruling class. They must admit, with H. G. Wells, that "Marx, who did not so much advocate the class war, the war of the expropriated mass against the appropriating few, as foretell it, is being more and more justified by events" (*The Outline of History,* Vol. II, p. 399); or, with Professor Talcott Parsons, Chairman of the Social Relations Department at Harvard, that "the Marxian view of the importance of class structure has in a broad way been vindicated." (*Papers and Proceedings of the 61st Annual Meeting of the American Economic Association,* May 1949, p. 26.)

THE NATURE OF CAPITALISM.

In political economy, bourgeois social science has borrowed less from, and made fewer concessions to, the Marxian position than in historiography and sociology. The reason is not far to seek. Historical materialism and class struggle are general theories which apply to many different societies and epochs. It is not difficult, with the help of circumlocutions and evasions, to make use of them in relatively "safe" ways and at the same time to obtain results incomparably more valuable than anything yielded by the traditional bourgeois idealist and individualist approaches. When it comes to political economy, however, the case is very different. Marxian political economy applies specifically to capitalism, to the system under which the bourgeois social scientist lives (and makes his living) here and now; its conclusions are clear-cut, difficult to evade, and absolutely unacceptable to the ruling class. The result is that for bourgeois economists Marxian political economy scarcely exists, and it is rare to find in their writings an admission of Marx's greatness as an economist stated so specifically as in the following: "He was the first economist of top rank to see and to teach systematically how economic theory may be turned into historical analysis and how the historical narrative may be turned into *histoire raisonnée.*" (J. A. Schumpeter, *Capitalism, Socialism, and Democracy,* 1st edition, p. 44.)

Does the neglect of Marx as an economist indicate the failure of the ideas of the *Manifesto*? On the contrary; the correlation is an inverse one. What idea has been more completely confirmed by the last century than the conception of capitalism's restless need to expand, of the capitalist's irresistible urge to "nestle everywhere, settle everywhere, establish connections everywhere"? Who can deny today that the periodical return of crises is a fact which puts the "existence of the entire bourgeois society on its trial, each time more threateningly"? Who can fail to see that "the conditions of bourgeois society are too narrow to comprise the wealth created by them"? In short, who can any longer be blind to the fact that capitalism is riddled with contradictions which make its continued existence—at least in anything like its traditional form—impossible and unthinkable?

THE INEVITABILITY OF SOCIALISM.

There are, of course, many who, recognizing the dire straits to which the capitalist world has come, believe that it is possible to patch up and reform the system in such a way as to make it serve the real interests of society. But their number is diminishing every day, and conversely the great international army of socialism is growing in strength and confidence. Its members have every reason for confidence.

When the *Manifesto* was written, socialism was composed of "little sects," as Engels told the Zurich Congress of the Second International in 1893; by that time, two years before his death, it "had developed into a powerful party before which the world of officialdom trembles."

Twenty-five years later, after World War I, one sixth of the land surface of the globe had passed through a proletarian revolution and was, as subsequent events showed, securely on the path to socialism.

Three decades later, after World War II, more than a quarter of the human race, in eastern Europe and China, had followed suit.

If capitalism could not prevent the growth of socialism when it was healthy and in sole possession of the field, what reason is there to suppose that it can now perform the feat when it is sick to death and challenged by an actually functioning socialist system which grows in strength and vigor with every year that passes? The central message of the *Manifesto* was the impending doom of capitalism and its replacement by a new, socialist order. Has anything else in the whole document been more brilliantly verified by the intervening hundred years?

THE ROAD TO SOCIALISM.

Much of what Marx and Engels said in the *Manifesto* about the general character of the socialist revolution has been amply confirmed by the experience of Russia. The working class did lead the way and play the decisive role. The first step was "to raise the proletariat to the position of ruling class." The proletariat did "use its political supremacy to wrest, by degrees, all capital from the bourgeoisie, to centralize all instruments of production in the hands of the state, . . . and to increase the total of productive powers as rapidly as possible." The conditions for the existence of class antagonisms have been "swept away." On the other hand, the relative backwardness of Russia and the aggravation of class and international conflicts on a world scale have combined to bring about the intensification rather than the dismantling of state power in the USSR. The achievement of "an association in which the

free development of each is the condition for the free development of all" remains what it was a century ago, a goal for the future.

It is also true that an important part of what is said in the *Manifesto* about the international course of the revolution has been corroborated by subsequent experience. The socialist revolution has not taken the form of a simultaneous international uprising; rather it has taken, and gives every prospect of continuing to take, the form of a series of national revolutions which differ from one another in many respects. Such differences, however, do not alter the fact that in content all these socialist revolutions, like the bourgeois revolutions of an earlier period, are international in character and are contributing to the building of a new world order. We cannot yet state as a fact that this new world order will be one from which international enmity will have vanished, and the quarrel between Yugoslavia and the other socialist countries of eastern Europe may seem to point to an opposite conclusion. The present status of international relations, however, is so dominated by the division of the world into two systems and the preparation of both sides for a possible "final" conflict, and the existence of more than one socialist country is such a recent phenomenon, that we shall do well to reserve judgment on the import of the Yugoslav case. In the meantime, the reasons for expecting the gradual disappearance of international exploitation and hostility from a *predominantly* socialist world are just as strong as they were a hundred years ago.

We now come to our last topic, the geography of the socialist revolution. Here there can be no question that Marx and Engels were mistaken, not only when they wrote the *Manifesto* but in their later writings as well. The socialist revolution did not come first in the most advanced capitalist countries of Europe; nor did it come first in America after the United States had displaced Great Britain as the world's leading capitalist country. Further, the socialist revolution is not spreading first to these regions from its country of origin; on the contrary, it is spreading first to comparatively backward countries which are relatively inaccessible to the economic and military power of the most advanced capitalist countries. The first country to pass through a successful socialist revolution was Russia, and this was not only not anticipated by Marx and Engels but would have been impossible under conditions which existed during the lifetime of their generation.

Why were Marx and Engels mistaken on this issue? We must examine this question carefully, both because it is an important issue in its own right and because it is the source of many misconceptions.

At first sight, it might appear that the mistake of Marx and Engels consisted in not providing explanatory principles adequate to account for the Russian Revolution. But we do not believe that this reaches the heart of the problem. It is, of course, true, as we pointed out above, that during the 1870s and 1880s Marx and Engels denied the possibility of a *socialist* revolution in Russia. But at that time they were perfectly right, and it is not inconsistent to record this fact and at the same time to assert that the pattern and timing of the Russian Revolution were in accord with the principles of the *Manifesto.* What is too often forgotten is that between 1880 and World War I capitalism developed extremely rapidly in the empire of the tsars. In 1917 Russia was still, *on the whole,* a relatively backward country; but she also possessed some of the largest factories in Europe and a working class which, in terms of numbers, degree of organization, and quality of leadership, was almost entirely a product of the preceding three decades. Capitalism was certainly more highly developed in Russia in 1917 than it had been in Germany in 1848. Bearing this in mind, let us substitute "Russia" for "Germany" in a passage from the *Manifesto* already quoted above:

> The Communists turn their attention chiefly to Russia, because that country is on the eve of a bourgeois revolution that is bound to be carried out under more advanced conditions of European civilization and with a more developed proletariat than that of England was in the seventeenth, and of France in the eighteenth century, and because the bourgeois revolution in Russia will be but the prelude to an immediately following proletarian revolution.

Clearly, what Marx and Engels had overoptimistically predicted for Germany in 1848 actually occurred in Russia seventy years later. What this means is that, *given the fact that the socialist revolution had failed to materialize in the West,* Russia was, even according to the theory of the *Manifesto,* a logical starting point.

Furthermore, there is no contradiction between Marxian theory and the fact that the socialist revolution, having once taken place in Russia, spread first to relatively backward countries. For Marx and Engels fully recognized what might be called the possibility of historical borrowing. One consequence of the triumph of socialism anywhere would be the opening up of new paths to socialism elsewhere. Or, to put the matter differently, not all countries need go through the same stages of development; once one country has achieved socialism, other countries will have the possibility of abbreviating or skipping certain stages which the pioneer country had to pass through. There was obviously no occasion to discuss this question in the *Manifesto,* but it arose later on in connection with the debate among Russian socialists as to whether Russia would necessarily have to pass through capitalism on the way to socialism. In 1877 Marx sharply criticized a Russian writer who

> felt obliged to metamorphose my historical sketch [in *Capital*] of the genesis of capitalism in Western Europe into an historico-philosophical theory of the *marche générale* imposed by fate upon every people, whatever the historic circumstances in which it finds itself, in order that it may ultimately arrive at the form of economy which will ensure, together with the greatest expansion of the productive powers of social labour, the most complete development of man.

(Marx and Engels, *Selected Correspondence,* p. 354)

And Engels, in 1893, dealt with the specific point at issue in the Russian debate in the following terms:

> . . . no more in Russia than anywhere else would it have been possible to develop a higher social form out of primitive agrarian communism unless—that higher form was *already in existence* in another country, so as to serve as a model. That higher form being, wherever it is historically possible, the necessary consequence of the capitalistic form of production and of the social dualistic antagonism created by it, it could not be developed directly out of the agrarian commune, unless in imitation of an example already in existence somewhere else. Had the West of Europe been ripe, 1860-70, for such a transformation, had that transformation then been taken in hand in England, France, etc., then the Russians would have been called upon to show what could have been made out of their commune, which was then more or less intact.

(*Selected Correspondence,* p. 515)

While this argument is developed in a particular context, it is clear that the general principle involved—the possibility of historical borrowing—applies to, say, China today. Unless both the theory and the actual practice of socialism had been developed elsewhere it is hardly likely that China would now be actually tackling the problem of transforming itself into a socialist society. But given the experience of western Europe (in theory) and of Russia (in both theory and practice), this is a logical and feasible course for the Chinese Revolution to take.

Thus we must conclude that while of course Marx and Engels did not expect Russia to be the scene of the first socialist revolution, and still less could they look beyond and foretell that the next countries would be relatively backward ones, nevertheless both of these developments, coming as and when they did, are consistent with Marxian theory as worked out by the founders themselves. What, then, was the nature of their mistake?

The answer, clearly, is that Marx and Engels were wrong in expecting an early socialist revolution in western Europe. What needs explaining is why the advanced capitalist countries did not go ahead, so to speak, "on schedule" but stubbornly remained capitalist until, and indeed long after, Russia, a latecomer to the family of capitalist nations, had passed through its own socialist revolution. In other words, how are we to explain the apparent paradox that, though in a broad historical sense socialism is undeniably the product of capitalism, nevertheless the most fully developed capitalist countries not only were not the first to go socialist but, as it now seems, may turn out to be the last? The *Manifesto* does not help us to answer this question; never in their own lifetime did Marx and Engels imagine that such a question might arise.

THE PROBLEM OF THE ADVANCED CAPITALIST COUNTRIES

To explain why the advanced capitalist countries have failed to go socialist in the hundred years since the publication of the *Manifesto* is certainly not easy, and we know of no satisfactory analysis which is specifically concerned with this problem. But it would be a poor compliment to the authors of the *Manifesto,* who have given us all the basic tools for an understanding of the nature of capitalism and hence for an understanding of our own epoch, to evade a problem because they themselves did not pose and solve it. Let us therefore indicate—as a stimulus to study and discussion rather than as an attempt at a definitive answer—what seem to us to be the main factors which have to be taken into account.

If we consider the chief countries of Europe, certain things seem clear. First, even under conditions prevailing in the middle of the nineteenth century, Marx and Engels underestimated the extent to which capitalism could still continue to expand in these countries. Second, and much more important, this "margin of expansibility" was vastly extended in the three or four decades preceding World War I by the development of a new pattern of imperialism which enabled the advanced countries to exploit the resources and manpower of the backward regions of the world to a previously unheard-of degree. As Lenin concisely put it in 1920: "Capitalism has grown into a world system of colonial oppression and of the financial strangulation of the overwhelming majority of the people of the world by a handful of 'advanced' countries." (*Collected Works,* Vol. XIX, p. 87.) (This development only began to take place toward the end of Marx's and Engels' lives, and it would have been little short of a miracle if they had been able to foresee all its momentous consequences.) Third, it was this new system of imperialism which brought western Europe out of the long depression of the 1870s and 1880s, gave capitalism a new lease on life, and enabled the ruling class to secure—by means of an astute policy of social reforms and concessions to the working class—widespread support from all sections of society.

The other side of the imperialist coin was the awakening of the backward peoples, the putting into their hands of the moral, psychological, and material means by which they could begin the struggle for their political independence and their economic advancement.

In all this development, it should be noted, Russia occupied a special place. The Russian bourgeoisie, or at least certain sections of it, participated in the expansion of imperialism, especially in the Middle and Far East. But on balance Russia was more an object than a beneficiary of imperialism. Hence few, if any, of the effects which imperialism produced in the West—amelioration of internal social conflicts, widespread class collaboration, and the like—appeared in Russia.

To sum up: imperialism prolonged the life of capitalism in the West and turned what was a revolutionary working-class movement (as in Germany) or what might have become one (as in England) into reformist and collaborationist channels. It intensified the contradictions of capitalism in Russia. And it laid the foundations of a revolutionary movement in the exploited colonial and semicolonial coun-

tries. Here, it seems to us, is the basic reason why the advanced capitalist countries of western Europe failed to fulfill the revolutionary expectations of the *Manifesto.* Here also is to be found an important part of the explanation of the role which Russia and the backward regions of the world have played and are playing in the world transition from capitalism to socialism.

But, it may be objected, by the beginning of the twentieth century the United States was already the most advanced capitalist country, and the United States did not really become enmeshed in the imperialist system until World War I. Why did the United States not lead the way to socialism?

Generally speaking, the answer to this question is well known. North America offered unique opportunities for the development of capitalism; the "margin of expansibility" in the late nineteenth century was much greater than that enjoyed by the European countries even when account is taken of the new system of imperialism which was only then beginning to be put into operation. There is no space to enumerate and analyze the advantages enjoyed by this continent; the following list, compiled and commented upon by William Z. Foster in a recent article ("Marxism and American Exceptionalism," *Political Affairs,* September 1947), certainly includes the most important: (1) absence of a feudal political national past, (2) tremendous natural resources, (3) a vast unified land area, (4) insatiable demand for labor power, (5) highly strategic location, and (6) freedom from the ravages of war.

American capitalism, making the most of these advantages, developed a degree of productivity and wealth far surpassing that of any other capitalist country or region; and it offered opportunities for advancement to members of the working class which—at least up until the Great Depression of the 1930s—were without parallel in the history of capitalism or, for that matter, of any class society that ever existed. (On this point, see the article on "Socialism and American Labor," by Leo Huberman, in the May 1949 issue of *Monthly Review.*) This does not mean, of course, that the United States economy was at any time free from the contradictions of capitalism; it merely means that American capitalism, *in spite of these contradictions,* has been able to reach a much higher level than the capitalist system of other countries. It also means that capitalism in this country could go—and actually has gone—further than in the European imperialist countries toward winning support for the system from all sections of the population, including the working class. It is thus not surprising that the United States, far from taking the place of western Europe as the leader of the world socialist revolution, has actually had a weaker socialist movement than any other developed capitalist country.

We see that, for reasons which could hardly have been uncovered a hundred years ago, capitalism has been able to dig in deep in the advanced countries of western Europe and America and to resist the rising tide of socialism much longer than Marx and Engels ever thought possible.

Before we leave the problem of the advanced countries, however, a word of caution seems necessary. It ought to be obvious, though it often seems to be anything but, that to say that capitalism has enjoyed an unexpectedly long life in the most advanced countries is very different from saying that it will live forever. Similarly, to say that the western European and American working classes have so far failed to fulfill the role of "grave-diggers" of capitalism is not equivalent to asserting that they never will do so. Marx and Engels were certainly wrong in their timing, but we believe that their basic theory of capitalism and of the manner of its transformation into socialism remains valid and is no less applicable to western Europe and America than to other parts of the world.

Present-day indications all point to this conclusion. Two world wars and the growth of the revolutionary movement in the backward areas have irrevocably undermined the system of imperialism which formerly pumped lifeblood into western European capitalism. The ruling class of the United States, threatened as never before by the peculiar capitalist disease of overproduction, is struggling, Atlas-like, to carry the whole capitalist world on its shoulders—and is showing more clearly every day that it has no idea how the miracle is to be accomplished. Are we to assume that the western European and American working classes are so thoroughly bemused by the past that they will never learn the lessons of the present and turn their eyes to the future? Are we to assume that, because capitalism was able to offer them concessions in its period of good fortune, they will be content to sink (or be blown up) with a doomed system?

We refuse to make any such assumptions. We believe that the time is not distant when the working man of the most advanced, as well as of the most backward, countries will be compelled, in the words of the *Manifesto,* "to face with sober senses his real conditions of life and his relations with his kind." And when he does, we have no doubt that he will choose to live under socialism rather than die under capitalism.

CONCLUSION

On the whole, the *Manifesto* has stood up amazingly well during its first hundred years. The theory of history, the analysis of capitalism, the prognosis of socialism, have all been brilliantly confirmed. Only in one respect—the view that socialism would come first in the most advanced capitalist countries—has the *Manifesto* been proved mistaken by experience. This mistake, moreover, is one which could hardly have been avoided in the conditions of a hundred years ago. It is in no sense a reflection on the authors; it only shows that Engels was right when he insisted in his celebrated critique of Dühring that "each mental image of the world system is and remains in actual fact limited, objectively through the historical stage and subjectively through the physical and mental constitution of its maker."

How fortunate it would have been for mankind if the world socialist revolution had proceeded in accordance with the expectations of the authors of the *Manifesto*! How much

more rapid and less painful the crossing would be if Britain or Germany or—best of all—the United States had been the first to set foot on the road! Only imagine what we in this country could do to lead the world into the promised land of peace and abundance if we could but control, instead of being dominated by, our vast powers of production!

But, as Engels once remarked, "history is about the most cruel of all goddesses." She has decreed that the world transition from capitalism to socialism, instead of being relatively quick and smooth, as it might have been if the most productive and civilized nations had led the way, is to be a long-drawn-out period of intense suffering and bitter conflict. There is even a danger that in the heat of the struggle some of the finest fruits of the bourgeois epoch will be temporarily lost to mankind, instead of being extended and universalized by the spread of the socialist revolution. Intellectual freedom and personal security guaranteed by law—to name only the most precious—have been virtually unknown to the peoples who are now blazing the trail to socialism; in the advanced countries, they are seriously jeopardized by the fierce onslaughts of reaction and counter-revolution. No one can say whether they will survive the period of tension and strife through which we are now passing, or whether they will have to be rediscovered and recaptured in a more rational world of the future.

The passage is dangerous and difficult, the worst may be yet to come. But there is no escape for the disillusioned, the timid, or the weary. Those who have mastered the message of the *Manifesto* and caught the spirit of its authors will understand that the clock cannot be turned back, that capitalism is surely doomed, and that the only hope of mankind lies in completing the journey to socialism with maximum speed and minimum violence.

Francis B. Randall (essay date 1963)

SOURCE: Randall, Francis B. "Introduction: Marx the Romantic." In *The Communist Manifesto,* by Karl Marx and Frederick Engels, translated by Samuel Moore, edited by Joseph Katz, pp. 8-41. New York: Washington Square Press, 1964.

[*In the following excerpt, originally written in 1963, Randall explores the Romantic influences on both Marx and* The Communist Manifesto, *with special focus on Marx's experience and a close reading of the first two chapters of the* Manifesto.]

Early in 1848 there were no communist states in the world and no revolutionary governments of any sort. There was no Communist party in our sense and no revolutionary organizations or even trade unions of any size. A few countries of northwest Europe and a few areas of the United States were industrializing rapidly, but there was no city in the world—even London—much bigger than two million people, and no state—even Great Britain—in which a majority of the people did not live in the country and farm for a living. Every country in the world—except the Americas and Switzerland—was a monarchy of some sort, and in most of them the king, emperor, tsar, or sultan ruled absolutely and without any formal check. Even in free America there were millions of slaves, and even in free Great Britain most men were too poor to qualify for the vote. No woman in the civilized world—save possibly Queen Victoria—was fully and legally free from control by father, husband, or some other man. Every country was what we would now call "backward," and way over ninety per cent of the world's population lived in what we would call horrible and unendurable poverty—1848 was very long ago.

Into this now vanished world Karl Marx was born in 1818, in the western German city of Treves (Trier), which still boasts of the finest Roman ruins in northern Europe. Treves then belonged to Prussia, the second most powerful of the many independent German states, and the most efficient reactionary police tyranny in Europe. Marx always detested the Prussian regime. He renounced his Prussian citizenship while still in his twenties, and spent most of his life in exile, wanted by the Prussian police.

The Marxes were a Jewish family; both father and mother had come from families of rabbis. But Marx's father, educated in the anti-religious atmosphere of the late eighteenth-century Enlightenment, gave up Judaism and the Jewish community, and became a lawyer and a Prussian official. Eventually, when Karl Marx was six, his father had himself and his whole family baptized as Lutherans not because he admired Luther or believed in Jesus, but to save his career in what was officially Lutheran Prussia, although Treves itself was a Catholic city.

An enormous amount of nonsense has been written about Marx because he was born into a Jewish family. He was never taught much about Judaism or Jewish life, and he was proud of his ignorance. He was often twitted and sneered at in his youth for being Jewish, but he never suffered much when he was young or later from the prevailing anti-Semitism, either in his career, or, so far as we can tell, in his psyche. He had few Jewish friends. He wrote a fair amount about the Jews of Europe, always regarding Judaism as a stupid superstition, and the Jews as a community caught in the vise of capitalism from which only the revolution could free them. He adopted from his Christian neighbors the habit of calling ideas and people he did not like "dirty-Jewish" whether they were Jewish or not, and when he really hated someone (for instance, Ferdinand Lassalle, a man of Jewish origin who became the greatest German socialist and trade union leader in the 1860's), Marx would call him a "dirty Jew of Negro blood." Marx was not really a Jew. Hitler thought that communism was one vast Jewish plot, citing as proof the "fact" that Marx was Jewish. But Hitler was crazy, and other anti-Communists would do well to avoid this mode of thought.

Other kinds of nonsense are written by people who know that Marx, in spite of his family background, was not really Jewish. One often reads that Marx was cut off from European society by being Jewish, and from Jewish society by no longer being Jewish, and that he was able to fathom the future socialist society because he was thus alienated from his own. One often reads that Marx had the moral indignation of a Hebrew prophet because of his Jewish background, that he was concerned with human happiness in this world rather than in the next because of his Jewish background, and that he was given to fierce self-righteousness, absolute dogmatism, and violent abusiveness because of his Jewish background. People who believe such things are usually at a loss to explain why most denouncers of the evils of early industrialism were of Christian origin, as were most socialists, and why most Christian intellectuals of the day also expressed themselves in strong terms. Marx was far outdone in alienation, in wrathful denunciation, and in dogmatic abusiveness by such sons of Christian noblemen as Mikhail Bakunin and Vladimir Lenin. Marx's Jewish background is not the key to Marx.

Marx's father wanted his son to become a lawyer like himself, and sent him through the best schools in Treves, and then, in 1835, to study law at the University of Bonn. The University was something of a country club, and young Marx joined the other students in drinking, brawling, scarring each other in dueling games, piling up debts, and joining "subversive" (*i.e.,* politically liberal) clubs. Old Marx in disgust transferred his son to the University of Berlin, which had a justified reputation for a more intellectual faculty and student body—much as an American father, a generation ago, might have transferred his son from Princeton or Williams to Columbia. By and large, it worked. Young Marx stayed at Berlin until 1841, studying law and philosophy, and he became as heavy an intellectual as any father could have wished. In one respect it did not work. Young Marx became increasingly and incurably subversive, but his father died in 1838 before he became fully aware of his son's political bent.

The intellectual world in which Marx formed his mind was one of the most complicated of any in the history of humanity. Marx belonged to the third generation of the great Romantic current in European thought and culture. Romanticism, like the other important abstract nouns in the history of culture, is not a term to be defined but a field to be explored. To most Americans today, the word "romantic" implies sentimental love stories and swashbuckling adventure tales of the Hollywood type. There were plenty of those in the Romantic age, but the term is used by historians in many broader senses. A grim realistic novel by Balzac was just as Romantic in its way as a romance by Sir Walter Scott. There were Romantic plays and poems as well as stories, Romantic painting and sculpture, Romantic architecture and music—all familiar enough. But there were also Romantic politics, Romantic history, Romantic religion, Romantic philosophy, and Romantic science—in fact, every human activity could be conducted Romantically.

It is difficult to find anything common to all the aspects of late eighteenth- and nineteenth-century European (and American) culture that historians call Romantic. A great deal of Romanticism involved the cultivation of human emotions, especially love, but also exalted joy and profound melancholy, youthful protest, delight in struggle, artistic sensibility, and many more. On public questions, a Romantic might pursue a liberal or radical course inspired by the French Revolution, or he might react conservatively against it. In either case, he would probably be much concerned with his people or nation, its characteristics, its history, its folklore and folk arts. In the natural sciences or the social sciences, a Romantic would usually be concerned with tracing the history, development, and progress of the stars, the earth, plants and animals, man, a nation, a social institution—in short, he would be concerned with *evolution,* one of the key Romantic ideas. Romantic philosophers often emphasized the evolution of the world and human society. Many Romantics participated in the revival of religion in the early nineteenth century, usually a private and emotional religion. In the arts and in literature, Romantics usually reacted against the many rules and restraints of the French Classical culture of the seventeenth and eighteenth centuries in favor of their own national traditions, of freer forms, and of greater emotional expression.

Most Romantics were concerned with some small individual part of the world, a poet with some of his own emotions, a scientist with a few specimens in his laboratory, but the more ambitious Romantics tried to build up vast philosophical or scientific systems to describe the evolution of the universe and the nature of man (e.g., Hegel's philosophy), or vast artistic syntheses to express the emotional life and predicament of man (e.g., Wagner's operas). Obviously no one Romantic personality could combine all the currents mentioned above in himself, least of all Marx. The mature Marx would have angrily denied that he was a Romantic, for he used the term in a narrower sense to denote and abuse a number of emotional, religious, and mushy-headed men he despised. He called himself a scientific philosopher and a scientific socialist. For all that, it is fair and useful to call Marx's science, philosophy, and socialism a Romantic science, philosophy, and socialism. Marx was the greatest of the high Romantic ideologists of the mid-nineteenth century, just as his contemporary, Wagner, was the greatest of the high Romantic composers, and just as another contemporary, Darwin, was the greatest of the high Romantic scientists. Marxists would still deny this heatedly, but a less partisan observer can perhaps see that Marx will always be misunderstood unless he is set against the background of his own Europe of the high Romantic age.

In his years at the University of Berlin, Marx became imbued with the following convictions that were not necessarily Romantic in themselves, but which, taken together, and taken in the peculiar emotional way of young men in Marx's day *were* Romantic: He came to believe that all the various sciences and philosophies were part of one over-arching system, which, when completed, would give a true and total picture of the universe and man. (The Romantics had transformed this faith, which they had inherited from their scientific predecessors.) He came to believe that the core of such a science and philosophy was the growth, development, progress, and evolution of the world, human society, and the individual, particularly the mechanism by which such evolution took place. He came to believe that nature and man evolve according to certain inexorable scientific laws, whose working out can be embodied but not opposed by even the greatest men, such as Napoleon. Marx and his fellow students found the most thorough statement of these views in the works of the then recently deceased philosopher, Georg Wilhelm Friedrich Hegel, but they were by no means all straightforward disciples of Hegel.

Unlike Hegel, Marx came to believe that there was no God. He even spent some time trying vainly to prove that Hegel had also been an atheist. He became sure that Europe was trembling on the edge of reaction and revolution, that existing societies were dark, cruel, tense, and unstable, and that most of mankind was ground down, unhappy, of divided mind, disaffected from society, and cut off from its own true nature. This was the unfortunate condition that Marx and his contemporaries called man's *alienation.* Such convictions were a variety of radical Romanticism, which in the Germanies was called Left Hegelianism.

Having become a radical, Marx was in no mood to take up the practice of law in reactionary Prussia when he left the University of Berlin. Instead, he became a radical journalist. Early in 1842 he joined the staff of a liberal newspaper in Cologne, the *Rheinische Zeitung.* By the end of the year the twenty-four-year-old Marx was made editor-in-chief. Five months later, in 1843, the radicalism and venom of Marx's editorials provoked the Prussian police into suppressing the whole paper. At this point Marx finally got around to marrying his fiancée of long standing, Jenny von Westphalen, a childhood neighbor of his in Treves, who came from a family of Lutheran officials and was four years older than himself. The couple moved from their homeland forever, first to Paris for four years, where Marx tried not very successfully to make a living at journalism and other writing.

During 1843 and 1844, Marx was acquiring, through his reading, another set of convictions that was to be crucial to his future doctrine. He was absorbing the books of Malthus, Ricardo, and other British economists of the earlier Romantic period. Marx accepted much of their economic analysis, but disagreed wholly with their Romantic pessimism and their Romantic reactionary political judgments of the workingmen. Instead, Marx was led to choose the industrial workingmen (for whom he adopted, Romantically, a term out of ancient Roman history, the "proletarians") as the key to the future development of society, as the great Romantic cause of his life.

In the last generation, scholars such as Professor Sidney Hook of New York University and Professor Leonard

Krieger of Yale have shown that Marx's ideas during 1843 and 1844 were exceedingly interesting and complex, and much more broad-minded and attractive to our ways of thinking than his later dogmatic obsession with proletarian revolution. More recently a New York psychoanalyst named Erich Fromm has written a curious and unconvincing book on Marx that has dwelt on this early period in an attempt to show that Marx was really a kind of existentialist sage like his Danish contemporary Kierkegaard, and that Marx was chiefly concerned with the sick divided souls of men, with their revulsion and alienation from their work and their lives. Marx, in this view, hit on revolution chiefly as a therapeutic means to heal the sick souls of the working class and the rest of humanity. If this is so, then the world has been long deceived.

By the end of 1844, Marx had established his lifelong friendship with Friedrich Engels. Engels was born in 1820 in Barmen, Prussia, a town just south of the then developing industrial district of the Ruhr. His father, a tyrannical Calvinist, was a manufacturer who owned cotton mills near the Ruhr and in England. Young Engels became converted to radicalism during a brief stay at the University of Berlin in 1841. His father at once dispatched him to England to learn the textile business. Engels learned it, and with it he learned of the grim life led by English workers in the early days of the industrial revolution. He also acquired an Irish factory girl, Mary Burns, as a mistress. He never married, but stayed with her over twenty years until her death. Engels' relationship to Mary Burns, during the height of the Victorian age, alienated him from society far more than communism could have. Since Marx and Engels discussed all projects together, even when they did not actually write a piece together, it is often hard to sort out their respective contributions. But everyone, starting with Engels himself, has judged that Marx had the more striking and original mind of the two.

During the middle 1840's, Marx and/or Engels produced a number of works in which they depicted the ghastly condition of the growing working class, engaged in vigorous debates with other radicals, and began to set forth their own version of what they called "communism" in the 1840's, which has usually been called "socialism" since 1850. Today one can usually tell the difference between the Socialist and Communist parties of any given country. Although attempts have been made to distinguish between socialism with a small *s* and communism with a small *c*—often by saving the term "communism" to indicate a more radical, more violent, or more evolved stage of "socialism"—the two words have usually been used overlappingly if not interchangeably. Attempts at formal definition, such as the old chestnut that "socialism is the public ownership of means of production, distribution, and exchange," break up on the rocks of divergent common usage.

No matter what the definition, it is clear that the socialist movement arose in the Romantic age, and is one of the major Romantic legacies to the twentieth century. The hundreds of millions of people who have called themselves Socialists and/or Communists have all believed that the system of private property they knew—whether it was in industrial capital, piles of money, landed estates, serfs, or slaves—was wrong, and that the consequent inequality between the rich and the poor was wrong, and that any exploitation of one human being by another was wrong. This highly Romantic sense of social wrong, and the consequent highly Romantic drive toward social justice, which Marx and Engels shared to a high degree, are the ethical and emotional bases of any socialist movement.

Virtually all socialists have subscribed to a characteristically Romantic solution to these social problems: to end all or much private property; to turn the land, the factories, and the banks, at least, over to the community. Beyond these essentials, socialists disagree among themselves. There is a clear distinction between the religious socialists and the atheist socialists, who are the majority. There is another clear distinction between socialists who want to accomplish their aims by peaceful political means, and those who are willing to engage in violent revolution. Some socialists want to turn private property over to national or international governments; others (including most Russian socialists up to 1917) want to turn private property over to small decentralized social units, co-operatives or village communes. Some socialists want to establish a libertarian democracy soon after the revolution; others insist on a long period of dictatorship for the sake of political consolidation and economic buildup.

Marx and Engels were atheist socialists who urged violent revolution to be followed by a brief "dictatorship of the proletariat" in the course of which much private property would be turned over to the government. Marx furthermore insisted that his was the only *scientific* socialism, based not on wishful thinking but on the inexorable laws of nature and history, which would drive men toward socialism no matter what anybody or everybody thought, felt, or did. These classifications are difficult because almost all socialist groups take their doctrines so seriously that they deny the name of socialism—and all honorable intention—to all rival socialist groups.

In 1847, while Marx was calling most other socialist thinkers in Europe "dirty Jews of Negro blood," he was kicked out of Paris and France by the French police, in order to please the Prussian police. He moved to Brussels, and then to London to join Engels. Throughout the 1840's they had been involved with one or another miniscule group of socialist intellectuals and/or workingmen. In 1847 they were most interested in the Communist League, an allegedly international group of workingmen, chiefly composed of exiled German intellectuals. They attended a minute congress of this League in London in November, 1847—indeed they dominated it. They had themselves commissioned to draw up a complete theoretical and practical party program. The Communist League lasted only long enough to see some of its members railroaded to prison in 1852 by the Prussian police. But the program of

Marx and Engels, which was printed in German and published February, 1848, in London, has survived as the first definitive statement of their variety of socialism. Their program—*The Communist Manifesto*—has become the most widely read and influential pamphlet in the history of the world.

The Communist Manifesto was allegedly addressed to the workingmen of the world (by which Marx and Engels meant Europe). In fact, it seems to be addressed as much if not more to educated middle-class people who rejected communism; there are whole pages of argument directed to such people. Today it is read mainly by students. In communist countries the pamphlet is read in all the schools; in America it is read in college courses on European history, economics, and Western civilization. To most American students it seems windy and rhetorical in style, and simultaneously radical and old-fashioned in substance. The argument can hardly have converted any American to socialism for decades. At this late date, it is wholly "non-subversive"!

Marx and Engels began with the famous sentence, "A specter is haunting Europe—the specter of communism." Nowadays this makes most people smile because it is true today as it never was in 1848, but with a wholly different meaning. At the beginning of 1848, the tsar of Russia and his fellow rulers feared a revolution, but it was a liberal revolution by the middle classes they feared, not a socialist revolution by the workingmen. Marx and Engels Romantically exaggerated the importance of their movement.

The Communist Manifesto is divided into four chapters of decreasing importance. The first chapter, "Bourgeois and Proletarians," is crucial. There are a number of ways of sub-dividing humanity—by sexes, by age groups, by religions, etc. The most characteristic Romantic way to sub-divide humanity was into nations. Most Romantic thinkers were nationalists to some degree; they were much concerned with their own nation, or people, a group that usually shared a common territory, language, religion, culture, and history. If the people had already been unified into a common nation-state—as the English, French, and Russians had—a nationalist was concerned with the past and present glories of the state, and with strengthening and perfecting the unity of the people. If the people had not yet been unified—as the Germans and the Italians had not—or if they were occupied by foreign powers—as the Irish and Poles were—a nationalist was concerned with the past glories of his people, and with political campaigns to expel the foreigners and unify the country. Nationalists tended to play down the class divisions within a people in the interest of national unity. These nationalist movements were very widespread and deep in Romantic Europe. Nationalist sentiment has been a major legacy of the Romantic age to the later Europe of the two World Wars, and to all the backward and colonial peoples of the world.

It is therefore amazing that Marx and Engels, who lived right in the middle of it all, not only failed to share the nationalist feelings of their fellow Germans, but failed to recognize the force of Romantic nationalism in others. "The workingmen have no country," they wrote in *The Communist Manifesto.* "National differences and antagonisms are vanishing gradually from day to day, owing to the development of the bourgeoisie, to freedom of commerce, to the world market. . . ." This was flatly false, more obviously and stupidly false than anything else in Marx's whole doctrine. On the eve of the revolutions of 1848, a titanic set of nationalist explosions, Marx judged that national feeling was on the way out. At the beginning of a hundred-year period in which workingmen were to become increasingly swept up by nationalist feelings, Marx declared that they had no country.

Marx's feelings, but not Marx's blindness, are explained by the fact that he and many other socialists divided humanity in another characteristically Romantic way, into social classes. At a time when most European countries were still ruled, or at least co-ruled, by kings and nobles, Marx had the vision to see that the bourgeoisie was taking over. "Bourgeoisie" had originally meant the inhabitants of cities, but by the Romantic age the term had come to mean the middle classes, whether they lived in cities or not. Businessmen from the greatest textile magnates to the smallest hole-in-the-wall shop-keepers, doctors, lawyers, teachers and other educated and professional people, all the groups that we now call "white collar workers" were part of the bourgeoisie. Marx often felt compelled to give a narrow economic definition of the bourgeoisie—"the owners of the means of capitalist production"—but he used the term to indicate the middle classes as a whole.

The proletarians had originally been the poverty stricken masses of ancient Rome, who had no property save their children (*proles*). The Roman poor had nothing whatsoever to do with factories, but Marx took over the term for modern factory workers because he liked its grand Romantic historical sweep. In spite of his formal economic definitions, Marx usually included all the urban poor in the proletarians, whether they worked in factories or not. He was convinced that with the evolution of industrial society, almost everybody would become proletarian. The peasants would be drawn into the cities by economic necessity, and most of the bourgeoisie would become bankrupt by capitalist competition, and would sink into the proletariat. This has never happened; it was one of Marx's most famous wrong predictions. As industry advances the working classes grow, but the middle classes grow more rapidly still. There has never been a country in which the industrial workers were a majority. In most advanced countries, such as America, Great Britain, and Germany, the middle classes form a majority.

In the first chapter of *The Communist Manifesto,* Marx pictured Europe as being in the throes of a tremendous struggle for "the upper hand" between the rising bourgeoisie and the developing proletariat. The struggle was marked by strikes, lock-outs, sabotage, wage slashes, bankruptcies, business crises, the simultaneous rise of industrial combines and trade unions, increasing proletarian "class consciousness" (realization of its nature and predicament), and violence. This vast dramatic clash between sharply contrasted antagonists was precisely the sort of thing a Romantic thinker would hope to find in society, especially a follower of Hegel, who believed that progress came about through "the fruitful struggle of opposite principles."

Following Hegel's Romantic tenets, Marx saw the contemporary struggle in Europe as only one chapter in the whole vast sweep of universal history, which they both believed to be a continuous evolutionary sequence of struggles between mutually interacting opposites, each struggle producing something higher that would in its turn struggle with its opposite. This supposed process of struggle and evolution, to which Hegel gave the celebrated name "dialectic," included absolutely everything, as Hegel presented it—God, spirit, reason, the universe, and man. Marx got rid of God, spirit, and some of the other abstractions, a process which he snidely called "standing Hegel on his head." This left him with an earthly, visible, tangible, material world as the scene of the evolutionary struggle—the subject matter of his celebrated doctrine, dialectical materialism. For Marx, the Romantic struggle of universal history was reduced to an economic struggle between social classes. "The history of all hitherto existing societies has been the history of class struggles."

In the first chapter of *The Communist Manifesto,* Marx sketched the dramatic history of the world, the struggles of ancient patricians and ancient slaves, of feudal lords and feudal serfs, and above all, the struggles of the bourgeoisie. For Marx, the bourgeoisie was the collective hero of a Romantic tragedy. Like many heroes of Romantic tragedies, the bourgeoisie rose from low estate against enormous odds, burst its chains and hurled the older masters from their seats of power. Like many heroes of Romantic tragedies—Prometheus and Faust—the bourgeoisie was possessed of an enormous and restless energy. Marx wrote, "It has accomplished wonders far surpassing Egyptian pyramids, Roman aqueducts, Gothic cathedrals; it has conducted expeditions that have put in the shade all former migrations of nations and crusades . . . it batters down all Chinese walls." Finally, in Marx's view, the bourgeoisie accomplished what so many Romantic heroes strove for, what only God was previously thought to have achieved: "In one word, it creates a world in its own image."

So far, Marx's bourgeoisie was the hero of a Romantic triumph beyond the dreams of Goethe or Byron. But this triumph was so Romantically extreme as to approach blasphemy. Nemesis, the goddess of retribution, lay in wait, as she did in so many other tragedies. In its pride of triumph the bourgeoisie became insolent, and in its insolence it forgot that in the depths from which it had risen so far, it was itself producing its fatal enemy, the proletariat. "What the bourgeoisie therefore produces, above all, are its own grave-diggers." The more the bourgeoisie produces, the stronger its subterranean antagonist grows. Marx believed that in the last act of this inevitable Romantic tragedy the

bourgeoisie, grown old and tyrannical, would be hurled from its thrones into the abyss, like the haughty kings and insolent titans of so many Romantic dramas. "Its fall and the victory of the proletariat are equally inevitable."

In the full sense of the term, the first chapter of *The Communist Manifesto* is a high Romantic drama on a vast scale, in which the bourgeoisie plays the role of the most immense of all Romantic tragic heroes. It was doubtless very satisfying for Marx to feel that he understood and approved the course of the grand drama of history. One might ask why Marx threw himself so wholeheartedly into revolutionary work if he was convinced that the revolution would inevitably come at a given moment, no matter what he or the rest of the world did to hurry or prevent it. The answer, of course, is that Marx was possessed of an activist temperament, like many other believers in universal determinist schemes (e.g., Mohammed and Calvin). He was constantly driven from within to write, to make speeches, to organize, to act, driven by what the arch-Romantic Goethe would have called a *Daemon,* which meant not a devil, but an insatiable psychic compulsion. It is intellectually silly for a determinist to be an activist; all the efforts of Marx and his followers to make logic out of such illogic are unconvincing. Yet for Marx and his followers, these two inconsistent mental traits seemed to go naturally together.

The second chapter of *The Communist Manifesto,* "Proletarians and Communists," is essentially an argument with bourgeois critics of communism about whether communism is good or not. This was necessary at some point, for many things may be inevitable without being desirable (e.g., death and taxes). Marx began, "In what relation do the Communists stand to the proletarians as a whole?" The honest answer would have been that they stood in no relation to the proletarians, for there wasn't any communist organization to speak of. Instead, Marx wrote as if there was already a well organized international network of Communists which sought to offer its services to the various national proletarian movements, and to co-ordinate their revolutionary work.

The communist program was "the abolition of private property." This was expected to bring a thrill of horror to any bourgeois reader, and Marx spent the rest of the chapter arguing with and/or taunting such bourgeois readers. In this mock debate, Marx changed his tone drastically from the first chapter. He no longer sang of the bourgeoisie as heroes of a high historic drama; he squabbled with them and sneered at them as if the bourgeoisie were thieving, bloated, stupid villains of some vulgar horse opera—a tone that has been adopted by most people who call themselves Marxists.

Why should the bourgeoisie squawk about losing their private property, Marx wanted to know, when they themselves have stolen all their property from the hard-working, upstanding proletarians and farmers who produced it? Why should the bourgeoisie cry out that the Communists want to abolish freedom and individuality, when the bourgeoisie have themselves enslaved the huge majority of the population in the factories? The bourgeoisie moan that the Communists want to annihilate the state, culture, religion, and the family but they have themselves deprived the workers of any state, any culture, any true religion, and any decent family life, and so on.

This is certainly the least convincing part of **The Communist Manifesto.** The charges against the bourgeoisie are so exaggerated that one realizes that Marx was not entirely serious. He depicted the bourgeoisie screaming in chorus that the Communists wanted to nationalize all women, and then went on to assert that the bourgeoisie spent its own time seducing proletarian girls, and each other's wives as well. This, in the depths of the Victorian age, was presumably a heavy jest. Even if the arguments were true, all Marx proposed in this section was to drag the bourgeoisie down into the depths with the workers, apparently for the sake of sheer revenge. In other writings he dealt with the problem more seriously, and asserted that the abolition of bourgeois privilege would lead to a tremendous resurgence of true freedom, true creativity, and true culture among the former proletariat, which would more than make up for the loss of bourgeois freedom and culture in the revolution.

The chapter ends with Marx's famous ten-point communist program, which often startles and amuses modern readers by its combination of proposals that we still regard as "communist" or otherwise extremely radical—such as the nationalization of factories, banks, transport and land—with calls for reforms long established in advanced capitalist societies—such as income and inheritance taxes, and free public schools. The program was not intended to be a detailed or well-thought-out blueprint for the future beyond the revolution, nor was Marx ever to provide such a detailed blueprint in his other writings.

The last two chapters of **The Communist Manifesto** are only of historical interest, and not much of that. First Marx explained why he was right, and why every other group that called itself socialist was inadequate, unscientific, wrong, and vile. Right or wrong, all those groups soon disappeared as Marx predicted. Then Marx indicated his support—usually qualified—for various revolutionary groups scattered around Europe, the more extremist the better. None of those groups were destined to amount to anything. At the very end of the pamphlet, Marx returned to his vein of ringing Romantic rhetoric. He insisted on "the forcible overthrow of all existing social conditions" with uninhibited abandon. "Let the ruling classes tremble at a communist revolution. The proletarians have nothing to lose but their chains. They have a world to win. Working men of all countries, unite!" Millions have thrilled to this most memorable of all appeals that have come down to us from the Romantic age.

Haig A. Bosmajian (essay date 1963-64)

SOURCE: Bosmajian, Haig A. "A Rhetorical Approach to the *Communist Manifesto.*" In *Karl Marx: "The Communist Manifesto,"* edited by Frederic L. Bender, pp. 189-99. New York: Peter Lang, 1988.

[*In the following excerpt, originally published in 1963-64, Bosmajian looks at some of Marx's literary influences and provides an analysis of the rhetorical style of the* Communist Manifesto.]

Late in February, 1848, an octavo pamphlet of thirty pages published by a German printer in London at 46 Liverpool Street, Bishopsgate, appeared for the first time with a title page which read, in part: "Manifest der Kommunistischen Partei. . . . Proletarier aller Länder vereinigt Euch." The ideas expressed in this *Manifest* had been presented, for the most part, previously in speeches, books, and pamphlets by predecessors and contemporaries of Karl Marx and Friedrich Engels. In fact, Marx and Engels, in their own writings, had previously presented the ideas that finally made up the **Communist Manifesto.** However, of the many "socialist-communist" tracts written during the eighteenth and nineteenth centuries, it was the **Communist Manifesto** which survived to be translated into almost one hundred different languages.

Why has it been the **Manifesto** which has survived to influence so many people in so many lands during the past one hundred years when other "socialist-communist" works stand undisturbed on dusty library shelves? Certainly a major factor is Marx's ability to present his content in such a form as to make the arguments appear forceful and valid, to arouse the emotions of his audience, and to make the author of the tract worthy of belief. If he were going to influence and move people, Marx realized that he would have to use all available means of persuasion, including what Aristotle called the "good style" in the *Rhetoric,* parts of which Marx had translated in his university days.[1]

There is no doubt that Marx was aware of and thoroughly conscious of various rhetoric devices. He was an avid reader of plays, speeches, poetry, and novels. He did various translations and wrote verse, the latter of questionable literary value. In a letter to his father, Marx wrote in November, 1837, that he had translated Tacitus's *Germania,* Ovid's *Tristium libri,* and parts of Aristotle's *Rhetoric.* Paul Lafargue, who married Marx's second daughter, Laura, wrote that Marx "had a preference for eighteenth century novels, and was especially fond of Fielding's *Tom Jones.* The modern novelists who pleased him best were Paul de Kock, Charles Lever, the elder Dumas, and Sir Walter Scott, whose *Old Mortality* he considered a masterpiece. Marx looked upon Cervantes and Balzac as "the greatest masters of romance," and *Don Quixote* was for him "the epic of the decay of chivalry."[2]

Two orators of whom Marx thought highly were John P. Curran and William Cobbett. Of Curran, Marx said in a letter to Engels: "I consider Curran the only great advocate—people's advocate—of the eighteenth century and the noblest nature. . . ."³ Lafargue tells us that Marx sought out and classified the characteristic expressions in some of the polemical writing of William Cobbett, "for whom he had great esteem."⁴ Many of the characteristics of Cobbett's pamphleteering and oratorical style, especially the lucidity, sarcasm, and invective, seemed to appear later in the *Manifesto.* Upon Cobbett's death in June, 1835, *The Times* commented on his style: "The first general characteristic of his style is perspicuity, unequalled and inimitable. A second is homely masculine vigor. A third is purity, always simple, and raciness often elegant. His argument is an example of acute, yet apparently natural, nay, involuntary logic, smoothed in its progress and cemented in its parts, by a mingled storm of torturing sarcasm, contemptuous jocularity, and slaughtering invective. . . ."⁵

Wilhelm Liebknecht, one of Marx's "pupils" who was for a time a daily visitor to Marx's home in London, writes in his reminiscences that "Marx attached extraordinary value to pure correct expression and in Goethe, Lessing, Shakespeare, Dante, and Cervantes, whom he read every day, he had chosen the greatest masters. He showed the most painstaking conscientiousness in regard to purity and correctness of speech."⁶ Marx's attitude towards words and language is displayed in his efforts to achieve clarity in his own works. Lafargue wrote that Marx "would not publish anything until he had worked over it again and again, until what he had written obtained a satisfactory form."⁷ It may well have been this thoroughness which delayed Marx's completion of the *Manifesto,* much to the displeasure of the Communist League. . . .

. . . . .

From the beginning of the *Manifesto,* Marx establishes that communism is a powerful force to be reckoned with; in so doing, he establishes at the same time a part of his *ethos* by identifying himself with a movement opposed by great powers, a movement which is itself powerful and which openly publishes its aims and views for all to see. He does this in the *exordium* by pointing out that "all the powers of old Europe have entered a holy alliance to exorcise" the spectre of communism and by asserting that "communism is already acknowledged by all European powers to be itself a power."

The *Manifesto*'s short *exordium* is followed by a *narration* which follows Aristotle's advice: ". . . if there is narration at all [in deliberative speaking], it must be of the past, and its object to remind your audience of what happened in the past, with a view to better plans for the future: It may be used in condemning people. . . ."⁸ After stating in his *exordium* that it is about time that the communists openly publish their views, aims, and tendencies "to meet this nursery tale of the spectre of communism with a manifesto of the party itself," he follows, in the *narration,* not with elaborations of these aims and views, but with a historical description of the growth of the bourgeois with all its evils: new forms of oppression, "naked,

shameless, direct, brutal exploitations," breakdown of the family relationship, enslavement and pauperization of the labourer. In this process of discrediting his opponents by identifying them with all that is evil, Marx has again added to his *ethos*; he has branded his adversaries as selfish, oppressive, unjust, intemperate, and dishonorable, and in the process of linking his opponents with that which is not virtuous he has focused attention upon the probity of his own character. From the very beginning, he attempts to establish character and good will, not by elaborating on his own cause and its virtues (this will come later), but by condemning his opponents, their cause, and their actions: it is the bourgeois that has "reduced the family relation to a mere money relation," it is the bourgeois that has forced labourers to sell themselves piecemeal, it is the bourgeois that has reduced poets, priests, and doctors to its paid wage-labourers. It is this bourgeois against which Marx and the communists stand.

Not only does Marx establish his *ethos* by calling his adversaries selfish, oppressive, and dishonorable; he also arouses, in the *narration,* the emotions of anger, hate, and fear. Aristotle, in his *Rhetoric,* has defined anger as "an impulse attended by pain, to a revenge that shall be evident, and caused by an obvious, unjustified, slight with respect to the individual or his friends." By portraying the bourgeois as contemptuous of and insolent to the proletariat, Marx arouses the worker's anger towards the bourgeois. Has not the bourgeois, after taking all that it can from the labourer, handed him over to "other portions of the bourgeois, the landlord, the shopkeeper, the pawnbroker?" Has not bourgeois industry benefited only the ruling class and sent the labourer "deeper and deeper below the conditions of existence of his own class?" Has not the bourgeois transformed the proletarian children "into simple articles of commerce and instruments of labor?" Has not the bourgeois taken for its own pleasures the wives and daughters of the workers? The bourgeois has shown only indifference and insolence to the plight of the labourer and his family, and as Aristotle explained, just as a sick man is angered by indifference to his illness, so too is the poor man angered by indifference to his poverty.

Marx not only attempts to arouse anger, which is always attended by a certain pleasure arising from the expectation of revenge against a particular person or persons, but he also attempts to arouse hatred which is directed not only against an individual, but also against a class. Marx obviously was interested in more than arousing his audience to anger which would induce them to wish the object of their anger to suffer; his goal was to arouse his listeners to that state in which they would wish the bourgeois eradicated. As Aristotle put it, "the angry man wishes the object of his anger to suffer in return; hatred wishes its object not to exist."

In his *narration,* Marx also seems to be trying to arouse fear, which is caused by whatever seems to have a great power of destroying us or of working injuries that are likely to bring us great pain. One way of arousing fear is to argue that others greater than the listener have suffered. "Have not men of science, lawyers, doctors become the paid wage-labourers of the bourgeois?" asks Marx. Another way of arousing fear is to portray injustice coupled with power. "Has not the bourgeois organized the workers like soldiers and placed them under the command of a perfect hierarchy of officers and sergeants?" asks Marx. However, at the same time, he is careful not to arouse so much fear as to create in his listeners the feeling that there is no hope of deliverance. The proletariat may be ruled, enslaved, and oppressed by the bourgeois, but still there is hope that things will change for the better; in fact, it is inevitable that things will get better. "Fear sets men deliberating," said Aristotle, ". . . but no one deliberates about things that are hopeless." And things are not hopeless, Marx tells the proletariat in his *narration,* which he ends with the logical conclusion to all the historical evidence he has compiled up to that point: the bourgeois is unfit to rule; society no longer can live under the bourgeois; the fall of the bourgeois and the victory of the proletariat are equally inevitable. It is on this note that the *narration* ends, a *narration* in which the word *communism* never once appears.

If the evils of the bourgeois predominate in Part I of the ***Manifesto,*** the virtues of communism pervade Part II. This is not to say that Marx ceases his attacks against the bourgeois; the attacks continue, but the perspective is different. The evils of the bourgeois, as they appear in Part II, are juxtaposed with the virtues of communism: In bourgeois society, living labor is but a means to increase accumulated labor. In Communist society, accumulated labor is but a means to widen, to enrich, to promote the existence of the laborers." In bourgeois society, "the past dominates the present; in communist society, the present dominates the past."

Section II takes on the characteristics of a debate in which logic and rhetoric are blended. Marx's character, the character of his adversaries, argument, and the arousing of emotion are all fused, thus making the whole more forceful and more moving. By using the refutative process to present his case for communism, Marx places side by side the evils of the bourgeois and the virtues of communism; he places side by side the weak objections of the bourgeois and the sensible answers of the communists: "You are horrified at our intending to do away with private property. But in your existing society, private property is already done away with for nine-tenths of the population. . . ." "Do you charge us with wanting to stop the exploitation of children by their parents? To this crime we plead guilty." This type of presentation is effective, for as Aristotle has explained, "The refutative process always makes the conclusion more striking, for setting opposites side by side renders their opposition more distinct." Marx seems to further take Aristotle's advice when the latter suggests: "You should . . . make room in the minds of the audience for the argument you are going to offer; and this will be done if you demolish the one that pleased them. So combat it—every point of it, or the chief, or the success-

ful, or the vulnerable points, and thus establish credit for your own arguments." Through this process Marx builds his case for the acceptance of the various measures the communists will put into effect once they gain control; the presentation of the positive measures comes late in Section II.

In answering bourgeois objections, Marx often takes the line that the communists cannot take from the masses that which they never had in the first place while living under bourgeois rule. The communists, he asserts, cannot take from the masses private property they never possessed; they cannot take from the masses a happy family relationship never possessed by the masses while living under bourgeois rule; they cannot abolish nationality, for "the workingmen have no country. We cannot take from them what they have not got." After answering bourgeois questions and objections with communist answers, Marx says, "let us have done with the bourgeois objections to communism," and it is only then that he presents, for the first time, the specific measures which the communists advocate.

Whereas Marx focused attention upon the probity of his character in Part I by linking his opponents and their cause with what is not virtuous, in Part II he establishes his *ethos* by associating his message with what is virtuous and desirable to his audience. Further, he minimizes unfavorable impressions of his cause previously presented by his opponents. It is his cause which wants to create a world in which children will be educated and women will be respected; it is his cause which wants to see the workers given their just rewards for their labour; it is his cause which wants a world where there will be no exploitation of one individual by another, no hostility of one nation to another. It is his cause which will be inevitably successful. Just as he added to his *ethos* early in the ***Manifesto*** by attributing injustice coupled with power to his adversaries, so too has he added to his *ethos* by joining justice and the inevitability of its success to his own cause.

Marx concludes Section II with a sentence which sets side by side "the old bourgeois society, with its classes and class antagonism," and the communist society which will be "an association, in which the free development of each is the condition for the free development of all." But he cannot conclude the ***Manifesto*** on this note.

During the eighteenth and nineteenth centuries, there were too many other "socialists" and "communists" who asserted that their movements and their philosophies were the ones that would bring to the labourers what they deserved. Marx could not ignore these other movements. He may have persuasively argued early in the ***Manifesto*** that the bourgeois was not fit to rule, but there were others who had said or were saying the same thing. He may have shown that the private property of the bourgeois should be abolished, but there were others preaching much the same doctrine. So Marx had to go on in his ***Manifesto*** to tell the world that these other "socialists" and "communists" were false prophets. In Section III, he proceeds to point out the absurdities and falsities of Feudal Socialism, Petty Bourgeois Socialism, "True" Socialism, Conservative Socialism, and Critical-Utopian Socialism. The representatives of these movements, said Marx, only *appeared* to have the answers; in some cases their analyses were incorrect; in others, their tactics were inappropriate. Some of these false prophets, Marx contended, want only to restore the old means of production and the old society; others reject the class struggle; still others, "the philanthropists, humanitarians, improvers of the condition of the working class, organizers of charity, members of societies for the prevention of cruelty to animals, temperance fanatics," want the proletariat to remain within the bounds of existing society and "cast away all its hateful ideas concerning the bourgeois." The representatives of these other movements, Marx attempted to demonstrate, were either deceitful, self-deceived, impractical pedants, innocent reformers, or starry-eyed experimenters.

Marx's *peroration* is as trenchant as is his *exordium*. After stating that the communists "everywhere support every revolutionary movement against the existing social and political order of things" and that they "labor everywhere for the union and agreement of the democratic parties of all countries," he reaches the climax toward which he has been building. "Let the ruling classes tremble at a Communist revolution. The proletarians have nothing to lose but their chains. They have a world to win. Workingmen of all countries, unite!"

From "A specter is haunting Europe—the specter of communism" to "Working men of all countries, unite!" Marx has clothed his message in a rhetorical style permeated with tropes and figures of speech. Through the use of numerous different rhetorical tropes and figures, the author of the *Manifesto* has emphasized, clarified, and elaborated through sheer repetition, through exaggeration and comparison. Marx's style is that of controversial speaking, not that of written prose. Aristotle has pointed out in his *Rhetoric* that "such devices as *asyndeta* and repetition of the same word, which are rightly enough censured in the literary style, have their place in the controversial style when a speaker uses them for their dramatic effect." To a very great extent Marx uses rhetorical stylistic devices which rely for their effectiveness not so much on silent reading as on oral presentation.

Marx was very conscious of style; in his evaluations of various personages whom he admired and some he did not admire, he would comment on their style. For instance, concerning Pierre Joseph Proudhon's *What is Property?*, Marx wrote: "This book of Proudhon's has also, if I may be allowed, a strong muscular style. And its style is in my opinion its chief merit. . . . The provocative defiance, laying the ordinary bourgeois mind, the withering criticism, the bitter irony, and, revealed hands on the economic 'holy of holies,' the brilliant paradox which made a mock of here and there behind these, a deep and genuine feeling of indignation at the infamy of the existing order, a revolutionary earnestness—all these electrified the readers of

What is Property? and produced a great sensation on its first appearance."[9] Again his concern for style is reflected in his criticism of Proudhon's *The Philosophy of Poverty*: "The style is often what the French call ampoulé [bombastic]. High-sounding speculative jargon, supposed to be German-philosophical, appears regularly on the scene when his Gallic acuteness of understanding fails him. A self-advertising, self-glorifying, boastful tone and especially the twaddle about 'science' and sham display of it which are always so unedifying, are constantly screaming in one's ears. Instead of the genuine warmth which glowed in his first attempt [*What is Property?*], here certain passages are systematically worked up into a momentary heat by rhetoric."[10] From these comments, and comments on the style of Cobbett and others, it appears that Marx favored the style which avoids the abstract and displays the concrete, which is lucid, ironic, and trenchant. His appreciation for this kind of style is reflected in the *Manifesto.*

Marx did not hesitate to pile trope and figure one upon another in succession. Perhaps he had read Longinus, who wrote: "Nothing so effectively moves, as a heap of figures combined together."[11] In the following four-sentence paragraph Marx has combined his rhetorical questions with metaphor, irony, personification, antithesis, and anaphora (beginning a series of clauses with the same word):

> Nothing is easier than to give Christian asceticism a socialist tinge. Has not Christianity declaimed against private property, against marriage, against the state? Has it not preached in the place of these charity and poverty, celibacy and mortification of the flesh, monastic life and Mother Church? Christian socialism is but the holy water with which the priest consecrates the heart-burnings of the aristocrat.

Into the two sentences preceding this paragraph, Marx incorporates balance, metonymy (use of the name of one thing for that of another associated with or suggested by it), metaphor, synecdoche (a trope which heightens meaning by substituting the part for the whole or the whole for the part), and antithesis: "In political practice, therefore, they join in all coercive measures against the working class; and in ordinary life, despite their high-falutin phrases, they stoop to pick up the golden apples dropped from the tree of industry, and to barter truth, love, and honor for traffic in wool, beetroot-sugar, and potato spirits. As the parson has ever gone hand in hand with the landlord, so has Clerical Socialism with Feudal Socialism." It is important to note that the foregoing translated lines do not have the same overall flavor and effect that the original German text has; the sentence beginning "In political practice, therefore, they join," for instance, has lost much of its impact in translation. An underlying irony in the entire sentence is lost. That particular sentence reads, in Marx's German, "In der politischen Praxis nehmen sie daher an allen Gewaltmassregeln gegen die Arbeiterklasse teil, und im gewöhnlichen Leben bequemen sie sich, allen ihren aufgeblähten Redensarten zum Trotz, die goldenen Äpfel aufzulesen und Treue, Liebe, Ehre mit dem Schacher in Schafswolle, Runkelreuben und Schnaps zu vertauschen." Obviously, the "golden apples" referred to in the English translation are not the same "golden apples" of the original German text. However, it is the English version of the *Manifesto* with which I am concerned here, and my purpose is not to examine the discrepancies between the German and English versions of the **Communist Manifesto**; but it must be remembered that some of Marx's impact and irony is lost in the translation.

To give his presentation force and clarity, Marx has made extensive use of various figures which rely for their effect on repetition of one type or another; hence we find him using accumulation, anaphora, epistrophe (ending a series of clauses or sentences with the same word), and anadiplosis (repetition of the word ending one clause or sentence at the beginning of the next). He precedes an anadiplosis with a rhetorical question: "What does this accusation reduce itself to? The history of all past society has consisted in the development of class antagonisms, antagonisms that assumed different forms at different epochs." Of the many figures, Marx is particularly fond of using anaphora and asyndeton (omission of conjunctions); he uses them singly, he uses them combined with other tropes and figures. In the following sentence he combines anaphora and asyndeton with personification and antithesis: "In this way arose feudal socialism: half lamentation, half lampoon; half echo of the past, half menace of the future; at times, by its bitter, witty, and incisive criticism, striking the bourgeoisie to the very heart's core, but always ludicrous in its effect through total incapacity to comprehend the march of modern history."

Another figure which adds to the speech-like quality of the *Manifesto* is Marx's use of *correctio*. In the first instance below *correctio* is used alone; in the second instance it is combined with the periodic sentence; in the third, it appears with antithesis and metaphor: (1) "Hence, they habitually appeal to society at large, without distinction of class; nay, by preference, to the ruling class." (2) "Capital is a collective product, and only by the united action of many members, nay, in the last resort, only by the united action of all members of society, can it be set in motion." (3) "They are therefore not revolutionary, but conservative. Nay more, they are reactionary, for they try to roll back the wheel of history."

As one would expect of a person who thought in terms of class conflict and thesis-antithesis-synthesis, Marx incorporated into the *Manifesto* many phrases, sentences, and paragraphs which rely heavily for their effectiveness on balance and antithesis. "This kind of style [antithesis] is pleasing," said Aristotle, "because things are best known by opposition, and are all the better known when the opposites are put side by side; and is pleasing also because of its resemblances to logic—for the method of refutation is the juxtaposition of contrary conclusions." One simply cannot escape the antithesis in the following sentence, which appears at the beginning of Section I to support Marx's contention that the "history of all hitherto existing society is the history of class struggles": "Freeman and

slave, patrician and plebeian, lord and serf, guildmaster and journeyman, in a word, oppressor and oppressed, stood in constant opposition to one another, carried on an uninterrupted, now hidden, now open fight, a fight that each time ended, either in revolutionary reconstruction of society at large, or in the common ruin of the contending classes." Then, at other times, the antitheses appear sentence after sentence, paragraph after paragraph:

> In bourgeois society, living labor is but a means to increase accumulated labor. In Communist society, accumulated labor is but a means to widen, to enrich, to promote the existence of the laborer.

> In bourgeois society, therefore, the past dominates the present; in Communist society, the present dominates the past. In bourgeois society capital is independent and has individuality, while the living person is dependent and has no individuality.

To emphasize and clarify, Marx not only uses antithesis, but he also sets similarities side by side; sometimes the balance and antithesis are combined: "Just as it has made the country dependent on the towns, so it has made barbarian and semibarbarian countries dependent on the civilized ones, nations of peasants on nations of bourgeois, the East on the West."

Marx uses the device of disputation to display the thoughts of his opponents, to anticipate objections, and to answer those objections. He uses the figure synchoresis, whereby the speaker, trusting strongly in his own cause, freely gives his questioner leave to judge him. This particular device reappears often in Section II of the **Manifesto** combined with irony. His procedure here is to present the adversary's contentions and then to answer them; for the first time he begins to refer to his opponents as "you." Edmund Wilson has pointed out that Marx's opinions seem always to have been arrived at through a close criticism of the opinions of others, as if the sharpness and force of his mind could only really exert themselves in attacks on the minds of others, as if he could only find out what he thought by making distinctions that excluded the thoughts of others."[12] By using this procedure in Section II, Marx cuts into his adversary's contentions with a savage irony, discrediting them and at the same time pointing out the positive features of communism:

> You are horrified at our intending to do away with private property. But in your existing society, private property is already done away with for nine-tenths of the population. . . . You reproach us, therefore with intending. . . .

> In a word, you reproach us with intending to do away with your property. Precisely so; that is just what we intend.

> "Undoubtedly," it will be said, "religion, moral, philosophical and judicial ideas have been modified in the course of historical development. But religion, morality, philosophy, political science, and law, constantly survived this change."

"There are, besides, eternal truths, such as Freedom, Justice, etc., that are common to all states of society. But communism abolishes eternal truths, it abolishes. . . ."

What does this accusation reduce itself to? The history of all past society has consisted in the development of class antagonisms, antagonisms that assumed different forms at different epochs.

Just as the *Manifesto* begins with "the spectre of communism" and "this nursery tale of the spectre of communism," so too does it end with the proletarians having nothing to lose but "their chains" and with "a world to win." Excellence of style, wrote the author of *On the Sublime,* comes from five sources, the third of which consists "in a skilful application of figures, which are twofold, of sentiment and language."[13] These figures, continued Longinus, "when judiciously used, conduce not a little to Greatness."[14] The proof that Marx has "judiciously used" his rhetorical tropes and figures is in his ability to disguise the means he has employed, so that he seems to be speaking "not with artifice, but naturally."

Notes

1. Karl Marx, *Selected Works* (New York, 1933), I, p. 85.

2. Ibid.

3. Karl Marx and Friedrich Engels, *Selected Correspondence,* trans. Dona Torr (New York, 1934), p. 281.

4. Marx, *Selected Works,* p. 84.

5. G. D. H. Cole, *The Life of William Cobbett* (London, 1947), p. 431.

6. Marx, *Selected Works,* p. 111.

7. Ibid., p. 91.

8. All the quotations from Aristotle are taken from Aristotle, *The Rhetoric of Aristotle,* trans. Lane Cooper (New York, 1932).

9. Marx and Engels, *Selected Correspondence,* pp. 169-70.

10. Ibid., p. 173.

11. Longinus, *On the Sublime,* trans. William Smith (London, 1752), p. 97.

12. Edmund Wilson, *To the Finland Station* (New York, 1940), pp. 152-53.

13. Longinus, op. cit., p. 24.

14. Ibid., p. 85.

Harold J. Laski (essay date 1967)

SOURCE: Laski, Harold J. Introduction to *The Communist Manifesto,* by Karl Marx and Frederick Engels, pp. 3-105. New York: Pantheon Books, 1967.

[*In the following excerpt, Laski provides brief character studies of Karl Marx and Friedrich Engels, and presents a section-by-section analysis of the* Communist Manifesto.

The critic acknowledges that the Manifesto *is an immensely important document because it pulls from an enormous body of thought and writing to lay out a concise logical whole that goes beyond thought and philosophy to offer a revolutionary plan for the workers of the world.*]

I

The ***Communist Manifesto*** was published in February, 1848. Of its two authors, Karl Marx was then in his thirtieth, and Friedrich Engels in his twenty-eighth, year. Both had already not only a wide acquaintance with the literature of socialism, but intimate relations with most sections of the socialist agitation in Western Europe. They had been close friends for four years; each of them had published books and articles that are landmarks in the history of socialist doctrine. Marx had already had a stormy career as a journalist and social philosopher; he was already sufficiently a thorn in the side of reactionary governments to have been a refugee in both Paris and Brussels. Engels, his military service over, and his conversion to socialism completed after he had accepted the view of Moses Hess that the central problem of German philosophy was the social question, and that it could only be solved in socialist terms, had already passed nearly fifteen months of his commercial training in his father's firm in Manchester by the end of 1843. He had gained a deep insight into English conditions. He had come to understand the meaning of the conflict between the major political parties, the significance of Irish nationalism, then under the leadership of Daniel O'Connell, and all the stresses and strains within the Chartist Movement; he appreciated the meaning of Chartism, and he had joined its ranks. He realised how great had been both the insight and the influence of Robert Owen. He had been an eager reader of the *Northern Star,* and had been on friendly terms, after the summer of 1843, with George Julian Harney, then, under Feargus O'Connor, the main influence on the paper, and one of the few Chartists aware of conditions and movements on the European Continent. He had written a good deal in Owen's paper, *The New Moral World,* among his contributions being a very able essay on Carlyle's *Chartism,* and a really remarkable attack on the classical political economy. In the months of his return to Barmen, from the autumn to the end of the winter of 1844-45, he had published his classic ***Condition of the Working Class in England,*** influenced, no doubt, by the earlier and interesting work of Buret,[1] but with a freshness and a power of philosophic generalisation far beyond Buret's grasp. He had already become certain that the antagonism between the middle classes and the proletariat was the essential clue to the history of the future.

No partnership in history is more famous than that of Marx and Engels, and the qualities of each were complementary to those of the other. Marx was essentially the thinker, who slowly, even with anguish, wrestled his way to the heart of a problem. At times a writer of remarkable brilliance, he was not seldom difficult and obscure because his thought went too fast or too deep for words. Erudite in an exceptional degree—his pre-eminence in scholarship was recognised by all the young Hegelians of his German years—he had something of the German gelehrte's impractical nature, a passion for systematisation, not a little of that capacity for stormy ill-temper which often comes from the nervous exhaustion of a mind which cannot cease from reflection. He had fantastic tenacity of mind, a passion for leadership, a yearning, never really satisfied, for action; born of the difficulties he encountered from the outset of his career, he had too, a brooding melancholy, a thirst for recognition, which made him too often suspicious and proud, and, despite the noble self-sacrifice of his life, in a special way a self-centred personality who, outside his family, and a very small circle of friends of whom Engels was always the most intimate, found it, normally, much easier to give others his contempt or his hate than his respect and his affection. There were deeply lovable traits in Marx's character; but they emerge much more clearly in his private life than in his capacity either as agitator or as social philosopher. All his immense power, moreover, both of diagnosis and of strategy, rarely enabled him to conceal his inner conviction of intellectual superiority, so as to remain on easy terms with the rank and file in each phase of the movement he was eager—mostly selflessly eager—to dominate.

Engels had a quick and ready mind. He was always friendly, usually optimistic, with great gifts both for practical action and for getting on with others. He knew early where he wanted to go, but he had the self-knowledge to recognise that he could neither travel alone, nor be the leader of the expedition. Widely read, with a very real talent for moving rapidly through a great mass of material, he was facile rather than profound. He was utterly devoid of jealousy or vanity. He had a happy nature which never agonised over the difficulties of thought. After a brief moment of doubt at their first meeting, he accepted the position of *fidus Achates* to Marx, and it never occurred to him, during a friendship of forty years, marked only by one brief misunderstanding, to question his duty to serve Marx in every way he could. He was a better organiser than Marx; he had a far more immediate sense of the practical necessities of a situation. He was far quicker in seeing what to do than to recognise the deep-rooted historical relations out of which the necessity for action had developed. If Marx showed him vistas of philosophy he had never realised, he explained to Marx economic realities with a first-hand insight Marx could otherwise hardly have obtained. Not least, he made Marx see the significance of Great Britain in the historical evolution of the mid-nineteenth century at a time when Marx still thought of Germany as the central factor in its development. Without him Marx would have been in any case a great social philosopher of the Left; with him it became possible for Marx to combine superb intellectual achievement with immense practical influence. Their partnership was made when the practitioners of socialism were incoherent groups of doctrine and of agitation. When it ended they had laid the foundations of a world movement which had a well-integrated philosophy of history, and a clear method of action for the future directly born of that philosophy.

When Marx and Engels, then, came to write the **Communist Manifesto** they were not only close friends, but they combined an insight built on firm philosophic foundations with a breadth and depth of historical and contemporary knowledge unequalled in their day in its relevance to the problems of social development. They had both been enchanted by the Hegelian dialectic; they had both been driven, almost from the moment of their original acquaintance with it, first to the Hegelian Left, and then beyond it to the point where, as Marx said, it was necessary to stand Hegel on his head. They both knew from intimate personal acquaintance the deep tyranny of the German princes, always dull, always petty, and always bureaucratic. They both saw that the state-power was used to maintain a special system of legal relations which were set in a given historical mode of production; and they had both realised that nothing could be expected from the aristocracy, and little from the middle classes, except what the proletariat became self-conscious enough to realise it must take. They both understood that, without this self-consciousness, nothing could prevent the exploitation of the wage-earners by their masters; and that every social agency, from the pietism of the Churches, through the pressure of the newspapers and the censorship exercised over them, to the brutal and deliberate use of the army and the police, would be employed to break any rebellion against this exploitation. They knew that every society was a class-society, that its education, its justice, its habits, were limited by their subordination to the demands of the class which owned the instruments of economic power. They had come to see, in the famous aphorism of Marx, that "the ruling ideas of an age were the ideas of its ruling class." They had come to see also that freedom is never given from above, but must be taken from below; yet it can only be taken by men who have philosophy as well as habit. They had both seen through the hollowness of the official churches, and measured the gap between their actual and official practice. Not least, as Marx was later to add to his famous addition to the **Theses on Feuerbach,** they had both come to have an intensely practical view of the mission of philosophy. "Hitherto," Marx was to write, "it was the mission of philosophers to interpret the world: now it is our business to change it." It was to secure that change that their unique partnership had been formed.

Nor was the historical basis of their approach less ample in its survey when they came to write the **Communist Manifesto.** Marx was not merely a philosopher of competence and a jurist of considerable knowledge. He had read widely in German history. He had made a special and profound study of the eighteenth century in France, and, in quite special fullness, of 1789 and its consequences; and, with his usual omnivorous appetite, he had begun those remarkable studies of English economic history and theory which were to culminate, in 1867, in the publication of the first volume of **Capital.** Engels knew the working-class movement in England from the end of the Napoleonic wars in massive detail. He knew the Chartist and trade union movements as one who had not only seen them from the inside, but with a perspective of historical knowledge and insight into contemporary European conditions that were hardly rivalled anywhere at the time. It is, in particular, important to emphasise that, apart from their specialised knowledge, both Marx and Engels, and especially Marx, had an extraordinarily wide general cultivation; each could say, with truth, that *nihil a me alienum putat* had been a choice of inner obligation. They were both polymaths; and one of the striking characteristics they shared, from an early age, was an appreciation of the significance of science in the context of each epoch in which its major developments influence human relations. Few eminent thinkers in social philosophy had, at their age, so superbly prepared themselves for the task which lay to their hand.

* * *

III

The *Communist Manifesto* has passed beyond the stage where it requires any eulogy. It is admitted by every serious student of society to be one of the outstanding political documents of all time; in the influence it has exerted it compares with the American Declaration of Independence of 1776, and the French Declaration of Rights of 1789. Its character is unique, not only because of the power with which it is written, but also because of the immense scope it covers in its intense brevity. It is a philosophy of history, a critical analysis of socialist doctrines and a passionate call to revolutionary action. In each of these phases, it is written as a deliberate and provocative challenge. Its aim is to make the working class conscious of a great historical mission, and to communicate to it the deep sense of urgency about that mission which Marx and Engels themselves possessed. Its savage invective is intended to strip the veil from those bourgeois foundations of the existing order the concealment of which is one of the ways in which capitalist civilisation hides its real purposes from the workers whom it makes its slaves. But its invective is intended also to safeguard the workers from being deceived by other doctrines, claiming to be socialist, which, in the judgment of Marx and Engels, are intended to turn the workers from their vital task of abolishing a society built on the exploitation of one class by another and so building the classless society. The *Manifesto,* it must be added, is a remarkable feat of compression; and though its ringing sentences make it, on a first reading, seem simple and straightforward, there are, in fact, behind almost every phrase of it the marks of profound intellectual conflict, without the grasp of which the reader is only too likely to miss both the decisiveness of the document and its great complexity. For one of the purposes of the *Manifesto* is the definition of a doctrine which, though rooted in the massive discussions which had taken place ever since the conspiracy of Babeuf and, in particular, since the French Revolution of 1830, was intended to supersede all competing theories, and thus to unify a chaos of ideas into a philosophy which bound the workers together and prepared the basis of action.

The originality of the *Manifesto* does not lie in any single doctrine that it enunciates. It draws upon an immense body of literature, not all of it socialist, in which a number of the doctrines which lie at the heart of classical Marxism had already been set out with clarity and with vigour. Its originality lies in the skill, first of all, with which these doctrines are woven together so as to form a logical whole; and, second, in putting in the perspective of ultimate revolutionary prophecy the outlines of an immediate programme so conceived as to be directly related to the demands of the workers in the major European countries, as these had been born out of their practical experience of capitalist domination. Two other things, moreover, must be said. It is evident from the whole content of the *Manifesto* that when it was written both Marx and Engels were convinced that the day of reckoning was close at hand, and this was why there was a certain apocalyptic note of urgency about their discussions. It is not less evident that they believed—of course quite mistakenly—that the birthplace of the social revolution they anticipated was certain to be Germany. No one can seriously doubt that they had immensely overestimated the degree to which revolutionary socialist ideas had penetrated the German working class; and brave as was the fight they put up in particular places, remarkable as was the literature they published in their cause, their enthusiasm allotted to the German movement a priority it was far from ready to assume. On any detached analysis the France of 1848 was, alike in ideas and in action, far more mature than the Germany of the same years; it is impossible not to feel that this emerges in Marx's own two classic pamphlets, *The Eighteenth Brumaire of Louis Napoleon* (1852) and the *Class Struggles in France* (1850). Anyone who compares these with his account of the German struggles of the same years, cannot fail to note what it is difficult not to call an almost Utopian element in his description of German events and their implications. They pitched their expectations of the outcome of the German Revolt unjustifiably high; they tended to exaggerate both the influence and the significance of their own supporters. It may even be doubted whether they fully realised how deep were the internal divisions in the movement they sought to lead; or how difficult was the achievement of that democratic centralism which the *Manifesto* put forward as the basis of organised proletarian action.

It is, moreover, obvious, both from their references to the Owenite movement and to Chartism, that, though Marx and Engels were aware of important trends in English thought, they tended to underestimate their significance both for doctrine and for action. Even though Engels' studies had since 1842 brought him into close contact with the English workers' movement, it is doubtful if at this stage he fully understood its possibilities; Marx who, apart from two brief visits to England in 1845 and 1847, knew only of the British movement at second hand from Engels, had hardly begun those massive studies of English political activity and theory which, in the *Critique of Political Economy* (1859) and the first volume of *Capital* (1867), were to bear such remarkable fruit. It was not until they had both settled down in England, after the failure of revolution in France and Germany, that they really began to grasp the full importance of an English tradition which not only bourgeois economists like Sir William Petty, Adam Smith, Malthus and Ricardo had their share in making, but in which that classical tradition had been challenged by Owen and his followers, by Hodgskin and Bray; only then did they understand how much more was to be gained from a full study of the English scene than from that of France or of Germany. Here, they began to see, was already the most mature expression of capitalism's habits; and they could only prophesy its outcome by the careful and detailed study of its operation. But, by that time, the *Communist Manifesto* had already taken a dogmatic position in their thinking; and their tendency, henceforward, was to judge the English movement less by the scene which unfolded itself before their eyes, than by the degree to which they could fit its postulates of action into those they had so stoutly defended in the *Manifesto.* In the early years of their exile, they assumed that the habits of the English trade union movement were due to their theoretical backwardness; they awoke with relative slowness to its significance alongside the magnificent slogans with which the French and German workers were accustomed to decorate their doctrines. It was not until both men had realised that the English movement was to be the context in which the major part of their lives was likely to be passed that they gave it the full consideration it deserved. Even then, when they could desert its analysis for the large-scale *Weltanschaung* of some German or French doctrinaire, they continued to feel far more at home in socialist exegesis. However much Engels made himself at home with English habits it is important to remember that Marx was always a German who lived, very consciously, *in partibus infidelium,* and was never able to alter the categories of his thinking from those of his native land. Engels, for him, was always a remarkable source of fertile English illustration; the core of Marx's approach was Franco-German experience. Late in life, he realised the significance of Russia; but England was an illustration of a thesis in the main largely formed when he first entered the library of the British Museum.

IV

The actual construction of the *Communist Manifesto* is brilliantly simple. Affirming, with justice, the dread of communism felt by the governments of Europe, it goes on to insist that the struggle between classes is the central clue to historical change. But whereas in previous periods the structure of society is a "complicated arrangement," in the new "epoch of the bourgeoisie" society is being ever more "simplified" by being forced towards the dual division between bourgeoisie and proletariat. The *Manifesto* emphasises the revolutionary part the bourgeoisie has played in history, its relentless drive to make the "cash nexus" the only bond between men. It has dissolved innumerable other freedoms for the one freedom which gives it command of the world market—freedom of trade. It lives by exploitation, and its unresting search for markets means an unending and profound change in every aspect of life. It gives a "cosmopolitan character to production and consumption in every country." It compels the breakdown of

national isolation; as it builds an inter-dependent material universe, so it draws, as a common fund, upon science and learning from every nation. It means the centralisation of government, the supremacy of town over country, the dependence of backward peoples upon those with more advanced methods of production in their hands.

The *Manifesto* describes with savage eloquence how the development of bourgeois society makes the workman a wage-slave exploited by the capitalist. The latter spares neither age nor sex. He makes it increasingly impossible for the small producer to compete with him; on every side economic power is increasingly concentrated and the little man, in every category of industry and agriculture, is driven into the dependent condition of the working class. So ruthless is this exploitation that in sheer self-defence the workers are compelled to combine to fight their masters. They form unions, ever more wide, which come at last to fight together as a class and as a political party representative of that class. If the battle sways backwards and forwards, with gains here and losses there, the consolidation of the workers as a class hostile to their exploiters has one special feature which distinguishes it from all previous struggles between rulers and ruled; the working class becomes increasingly the self-conscious, independent movement of the immense majority, in the interest of the immense majority. If at first it struggles within the framework of the national state, it soon becomes evident that this struggle is but one act in a vast international drama. A time comes in the history of capitalism when "its existence is no longer compatible with society." It cannot feed its slaves. It drives them to revolution in which a proletarian victory is inevitable.

The *Manifesto* then turns to the special functions of Communists in the working-class movement. It insists that the Communists do not form "a separate party opposed to other working-class parties." They have no interest apart from the workers. More than this: "They do not set up any sectarian principles of their own," says the *Manifesto,* "by which to mould and shape the proletarian movement." Their task is to insist on the international solidarity of the working class, to stand in its vanguard in each country, to aid, by their deeper theoretical grasp of the movement of history, in the workers' drive to the conquest of power. They do not aim at the abolition of individual private property, but of that bourgeois form of the ownership of the instruments of production which deprives nine-tenths of society of the capacity to acquire individual property. Communists admit freely that they desire to abolish the bourgeois corruption of the family and to replace home education by social education. They do so because the bourgeois family is a means of exploiting the labour of women and children, and because bourgeois education means its subordination to the ends of the ruling class. If Communists are charged with seeking to abolish love of country, the *Manifesto* answers that the workers can have no country until they are emancipated from bourgeois domination; with their acquisition of political power, the hostility between nations will disappear. So, also, it will change traditional ideas in religion and philosophy. Since it puts experience on a new basis, it will change the ideas which are their expression.

The *Manifesto* recognises that the emancipation of the workers will never come in exactly the same way in every country; differences in development make that inevitable. Yet it suggests a programme of measures, "generally applicable" in advanced countries, which will enable the workers to win the battle of democracy. When this victory has been won, under these conditions class distinctions will disappear and the state-power will wither away, since it is necessary only to preserve class-distinctions. In its place there will be a free association of citizens "in which the free development of each will be the condition of the free development of all."

Such a summary as this, of course, is bound to do injustice to the superb sweep of the *Manifesto* itself. But it is important to dwell upon it for the implications upon which it insists. First, perhaps, a word is useful on the title of the document itself. It was to have been the "Catechism" by way of question and answer, from the Communist League; it became the *Communist Manifesto.* What is the reason for the change? Partly, no doubt, the decision of Marx and Engels to alter what would have been an essentially temporary domestic piece of propaganda into one that would have permanent historical value. It is hard not to believe that they called it a *Manifesto* in tribute to the memory of the Babouviste *Manifesto of the Equals.* They always recognised Babeuf as a real precursor, and do honour to him in their own work. The word *Communist,* it may fairly be suggested, has a double implication. On the one hand, it emphasises the relation of their work to the Communist League, by which they were authorised to undertake it; on the other, it serves to mark their own sense of profound separation from the "true" socialists of Germany, and especially of Karl Grün, against whom their criticism was so evident in the *Manifesto* itself. They reproached "true" socialism with sentimentality, with pretentiousness, and with an abstract approach to concrete problems which deprived them of any sense of reality. One can already see the depth of their hostility to Grün in articles they had written against him in August and September, 1847.[2] It would not be surprising that they should choose a title for their pronouncements which at once looked back to a great revolutionary predecessor, and avoided the danger of any confusion with a group whose "socialism" seemed to them no more than a vapid humanitarianism.

What lends support to this view is the emphatic declaration of Marx and Engels that the Communists do not form a separate party. On the contrary, they are ready to work with all working-class organisations genuinely dedicated to the socialist task; more, they repudiate any claim to "sectarian" doctrines of their own which might result in their separation from the rest of the working-class movement. It is vital to insist upon this emphasis. However critical Marx and Engels may be of other socialist principles than their own, their regard for unity among the working-class forces is paramount. That is shown by their careers from the very outset. Engels lent his support to Chartism even before the appearance of the *Manifesto*; yet there must have been few among its leaders who had any real insight into the doctrines of which he was the exponent. He and Marx were often bitterly hostile to the German Social Democratic Movement; they attacked Lassalle, Liebknecht, Bebel, Kautsky. But they never sought to found a separate German Communist Party. The hostility of Marx to the dominant elements in French socialism is obvious from his attack on Proudhon as early as 1847; but though he and Engels always encouraged the "Marxist" elements in the French party, the *Civil War in France* (1871) of Marx himself shows their anxiety to assist it, even when they thought its policy mistaken. Indeed, Section IV of the *Manifesto* itself insists upon this view. The Communists support the Chartists in England and the Agrarian Reformers in America; they "ally themselves" with the Social Democratic Party in France; they support the radicals in Switzerland, "without forgetting that the party consists of contradictory elements"; in Poland they support "the party that has seen in an agrarian revolution the means to national freedom, that party which caused the insurrection of Cracow in 1846"; in Germany they fight with any bourgeois elements which see the need to "act in a revolutionary manner against the absolute monarchy, the feudal landlords, and the little middle class."

The *Manifesto,* without question, insists that the Communists enter into relations with other groups to give them direction, to spread their own revolutionary creed, to make the workers aware of the "hostile antagonism" between bourgeoisie and proletariat. They "openly declare that their ends can be attained only by the forcible overthrow of all existing social conditions." But this declaration follows upon the announcement of three purposes which must be kept closely in mind if it is to be fully understood. They support "every revolutionary movement against the existing social and political order of things." In every movement, moreover, whatever its stage of development, they put the question of property in the first place. "Equally," says the *Manifesto,* "they labour everywhere for the union and agreement of the democratic parties of all countries."

If all this is read in the context of Engels' famous introduction to Marx's *Class Struggles in France,*[3] which he wrote in 1895, and of the joint *Address of the Central Council of the Communist League,*[4] it is clear that the *Manifesto* is presenting a doctrine of permanent revolution. By that famous phrase they do not mean a continuous series of attempts to seize the state-power by the workers in the manner advocated by Blanqui. They had learned that revolution was an art, and that it needs certain special historical conditions if it is to be successful. They meant that when an alliance of the progressive forces in society overthrows the reactionary forces, the workers must not allow bourgeois democrats or social reformers to stop at the point where private ownership of the means of production remains unchallenged. They must always drive them on from this reformist outlook to the revolutionary stage where direct attack is made on private property. Even if the conditions do not permit of success, at least they will have done much to educate those workers who are not yet class-conscious into a realisation of their position. And, with the coming of universal suffrage, the revolutionary idea will, by force of historical circumstances, enable the Communists to

> conquer the greater part of the middle section of society, petty bourgeois and small peasants, and grow into the decisive power in the land, before which all other powers will have to bow, whether they like it or not. To keep this growth going without interruption, until of itself it gets beyond the control of the ruling governmental system, not to fritter away this daily increasing shock force in advance guard fighting, but to keep it intact until the day of the decision—that is our main task.[5]

The continuation is not less significant. "The irony of world history," wrote Engels,

> turns everything upside down. We, "the revolutionaries," the "rebels," we are thriving far better on legal methods than on illegal methods and revolt . . . The parties of order, as they call themselves, are perishing under the legal conditions created by themselves . . . and if we are not so crazy as to let ourselves be driven into street fighting in order to please them, then nothing else is finally left for them but to break through this legality so fatal to them.[6]

Nothing here written by Engels means that he assumed the likelihood that the final transition from capitalism to socialism would be peaceful. On the contrary, it is quite evident that he expected the peaceful forces of socialism so to develop that their strength became a threat to the interests of property. That threat, he prophesied, would lead the interests of property themselves to break the Constitution. Where that occurred Social Democracy would then be free to act in its own defence. That, for him, is the moment when a revolutionary struggle would begin. He did not neglect the danger that progress towards socialism might be halted by war on a global scale. "No war is any longer possible for Prussia-Germany," he wrote,[7]

> except a world war, and a world war indeed of an extension and violence hitherto undreamed of. Eight to ten millions of soldiers will mutually massacre one another and, in doing so, devour the whole of Europe until they have stripped it barer than any swarm of locusts has ever done. The devastations of the Thirty Years' War compressed into three or four years; and spread over the whole Continent; famine, pestilence, general demoralisation both of the armies and of the mass of the people produced by acute distress; hopeless confusion of our artificial machinery in trade, industry and credit, ending in general bankruptcy; collapse of the old states and their traditional state-wisdom to such an extent that crowns will roll by dozens on the pavement, and there will be no one to pick them up; absolute impossibility of foreseeing how it will end, and who will come out of the struggle as victor; only one result is absolutely certain: general exhaustion, and the

establishment of the conditions for the ultimate victory of the working class. This is the prospect when the system of mutual outbidding in armaments, driven to extremities, at last bears its inevitable fruits. This, my lords and gentlemen, is where, in your wisdom, you have brought old Europe. And when nothing more remains to you but to open the last great war dance—that will suit us all right. The war may perhaps push us temporarily into the background, may wrench from us many a position already conquered. But when you have unfettered forces which you will then no longer be able again to control, things may go as they will; at the end of the tragedy you will be ruined, and the victory of the proletariat will either be already achieved, or, at any rate, inevitable.

Nor does he fail to note, in a letter to Sorge, of 7 January 1888, that "American industry would conquer all along the line, and push us up against the alternatives: either retrogression to production for home consumption . . . or—social transformation . . . but once the first shot is fired, control ceases, the horse can take the bit between his teeth."[8]

To this should be added what Marx and Engels had to say in the edition, prepared by the latter, of Marx's famous address to the General Council of the First International on the Civil War in France which arose out of the defeat of Louis Napoleon in the Franco-Prussian War. "In reality," wrote Engels, in his preface of 18 March 1871,[9]

> the state is nothing but a machine for the oppression of one class by another, and, indeed, in the democratic republic, no less than in the monarchy; and, at best, an evil inherited by the proletariat after its victorious struggle for class supremacy, whose worst sides, the proletariat, just like the Commune, cannot avoid leaving to lop off until such time, at the earliest possible moment, as a new generation, reared in new and free social conditions, will be able to throw the entire lumber of the state on the scrap-heap. Of late, the Social Democratic philistine has once more been filled with terror at the words: dictatorship of the proletariat. Well and good, gentlemen, do you want to know what this Dictatorship looks like? Look at the Paris Commune. That was the Dictatorship of the Proletariat!

No one can examine this section of the *Manifesto* honestly without coming to two conclusions, especially when it is set in the light of the subsequent comments upon its meaning by its own authors. They did not expect that capitalist society would be transformed into socialist society without violent revolution. They were insistent that the people who shared their views must never divide the organised working-class forces, that it was their duty to avoid sectarianism, and that they must not form a separate party. Their task was to be the vanguard of their party, to proclaim, indeed, their views, to do all in their power to get them accepted as the basis of action, but still to remain within the political ranks of the organised working class. More than this: in the last edition of the *Manifesto* edited by Engels, though he remained emphatic in his belief that violence would accompany the final disappearance of capitalism, he was also emphatic that the workers would be foolish to rely upon the old methods of street-fighting at the barricades, because new methods and new weapons had altered the situation in favour of the armed forces and the police. Fighting might still be necessary, but it would be folly for the workers to abandon legal methods until a stage had been reached when the position they confronted compensated for the new strength a capitalist society possessed in the power at the disposal of the state authority.

Under what circumstances did the workers reach that position? The answer, surely, is given by the fact that Marx saw the dictatorship of the proletariat as the outcome of the Paris Commune when France was defeated by Prussia in the war of 1870. Engels saw it, as is evident from the preface of 1895 to the *Manifesto,* and from his introduction to Borkheim's book, as the outcome of the catastrophic conditions produced by global war. It is of decisive importance to consider these views in the light of the interpretation that Lenin himself put upon them. He pointed out, with perfect fairness, the immense step taken by Marx between the publication of the *Manifesto* and the *Eighteenth Brumaire,*[10] and between these pamphlets and both the *Letters to Kugelmann* and the *Civil War in France,*[11] he draws attention, too, again quite fairly, to a similar change in the outlook of Engels between the production of the *Manifesto* and the careful analysis of the *Anti-Dühring*;[12] but the vital outlook of Lenin is set out in his classic *State and Revolution* and the documents therewith connected. It is sufficient here to say that Lenin was here concerned to establish to the comrades in Leningrad the necessary conditions of successful revolution; for he, like Marx and Engels, was careful to distinguish his outlook from that of Blanqui. He thought it necessary, first, that the armed forces of the state-power should be disloyal. He thought that the machinery of the state must be in ruins; there must be widespread revolutionary disturbance among the working class, as evidenced by strikes and demonstrations and there must be a solid and coherent working-class power able to lead the working class to the conquest of power. On these conditions, working-class victory was a possibility with a real prospect of success. Here, it will be noted that Lenin is considering a condition in which the overwhelming breakdown of the machinery of government opened the prospect of new orientations.[13] The breakdown of ancient state-powers as the outcome of the war of 1939 had resulted in something akin to that which Lenin had foreseen. That was the result of defeat in war. The form of state has remained unaltered in the states which remained victorious in that struggle. Lenin was pretty clearly right in insisting that the "democratic republic," based on universal suffrage, was the last rampart of bourgeois socialism rather than the first of democratic socialism in the Marxian sense of that term; that can be seen from utterances like those of Macaulay and of Daniel Webster. But nothing in his discussion deals with the fundamental point of whether and why that extreme Left he represented was justified in dissenting from the continuous insistence of Marx and Engels that the working class opposed to the imposition of bourgeois capitalism should

Friedrich Engels, 1820-1895.

form a separate party from the old social democrats. In this regard, the famous split between Bolsheviks and Mensheviks, at the Congress in London in 1903, was an innovation unconsidered by his predecessors. Whether it was wise or unwise, together with all the immense consequences to which, since the foundation of the Third International in 1919, it has led, lies outside the scope of this introduction.

V

From this remarkable analysis, the *Manifesto* goes on a little cursorily and haphazardly, to consider the literature of socialism which had appeared up to 1848. It condemns, first of all, what it calls "reactionary" socialism as a form of capitalism the roots of which lie deep in a feudal outlook. It seems probable that the author had in mind, without naming them, two groups of thinkers. On the one hand they were attacking the attempts of men like Herman Wagener and Bismarck who were seeking an alliance between the Prussian Crown and the proletariat, primarily at the expense, immediately, of the bourgeoisie, but ultimately, of the proletariat. These were seeking, in the old technique, how first to divide in order that their royal master might govern without question. They were in all probability attacking also the *soi-disant* socialism of Louis Rousseau and Villeneuve-Bargemont in France, who sought, by putting the French unemployed into agricultural colonies, to prevent them from strengthening the army of the proletariat by leaving the supporters of the "juste milieu" face to face with their bourgeoisie. Above all, they were dismissing that "Young England" group, of which Disraeli, as in *Sybil,* with some support from George Smythe and, at a remoter distance. Thomas Carlyle, supplied the ideas, and for which Lord John Manners provided, with occasional support from Lord Ashley (the later Earl of Shaftesbury), the political leadership. They, together with the Christian Socialists, of whom F. D. Maurice and Charles Kingsley were the outstanding figures, were groups of which Engels, with his accustomed prescience, had already seen the danger in his *Condition of the Working Class in England in 1844.*

Engels, at least, had not failed to understand the importance of Carlyle's *Chartism* (1840) and of his *Past and Present* (1843); he had already written about them in the *Deutsch-französische Jahrbücher.*[14] He had fully understood the reality of their horror of the new factory system, the new poor law, the invasion of happy lives by the new and grim industrialism. But the *Manifesto* regarded this type of socialism as no more than feudalism, however much its plea might be garbed in eloquence. Marx saw that they loathed the effects of industrialism; but he realised that they wanted to go backwards to a paternalistic feudalism, not forward to a democratic socialism. They were afraid of a rebellion from the oppressed, and they hoped to buy it off by paternal concessions which would still leave Tory Democracy in power. Since this was in its essence aristocratic and would, as in the Ten Hours Bill, improve factory conditions without removing the indignity of an unemancipated class, the *Manifesto* rejects this attempt to return to "Merrie England" as an effort without serious meaning for socialists who had really grasped the problem before the proletariat.

They then turned to the analysis of petty-bourgeois socialism. The *Manifesto* admits freely the achievements of this school of doctrine, at the head of which, both for France and England, it places the distinguished name of Sismondi. But it argues that, apart from its important criticism of modern production, the petty-bourgeois school has no positive aim but to restore "the old property relations, and the old society." It is therefore dismissed as both "reactionary and utopian"; "this form of socialism," says the *Manifesto,* "ended in a miserable fit of the blues."

This is far from being a fair picture. It is true enough that Sismondi announced his hopeless sense of bankruptcy before the results of the new system of production, the outcome of which he described so well. But it is curious that there is no tribute to French writers like Buret—to whom Engels owed a special debt—and Vidal, still less to Constantin Pecquer, who had the keen insight to see that the *petit bourgeois* is part of a numerous class which forms, as it were, the rag-bag into which are thrown both bankrupt peasants and outmoded craftsmen.[15] Nor is it fair to the remarkable English school, like Hodgskin and Thompson and Bray, some knowledge of whom it is difficult to sup-

pose was absent from men as eagerly interested in Chartism as Marx and Engels. It may be that the abrupt brevity with which the "petty bourgeois school" is dismissed is partly due to their failure to depict the revolution, the coming of which is, of course, the main prophecy of the *Manifesto*; this leads naturally into the bitter attack that is made, in the next section, on "true" or German socialism.

This attack may be regarded as the final breach of Marx and Engels with that Hegelian Left to which both of them had once belonged. It is the demonstration not only that its leaders were living by concepts and not by things, but also that the result of their effort was merely to serve the ends of German reaction. It is here that Marx and Engels break with their own past. They have done with Ruge and Moses Hess, with Karl Grün and Hermann Kriege. The stride beyond Hegel which Feuerbach had taken, which was in large part the basis of "true" socialism, now is declared not only inadequate but also deceptive. The votaries of "true" socialism are using the great principles of revolutionary experience and thought in France to elucidate a situation to which they are inapplicable. They fail to see that French socialism is an attack upon a bourgeoisie already in power. In Germany this is not the case. There the bourgeoisie has only begun to fight against the feudal aristocracy. To fight for socialism under these conditions is to delay the success of the bourgeois revolution by frightening it with the threat of a proletarian attack for which the conditions are completely unripe. "True" socialism, the *Manifesto* argues, thus "served the governments (of Germany) as a weapon for fighting the German bourgeoisie." It thus delays the march of the necessary historical development by serving up as "eternal truths" concepts the value of which depends wholly upon their relevance to the concrete situation. The "true" socialists are thus guilty of an abstract philosophy which appears like a call to arms; but it is a call which can have no other result than to aid the victory of feudal reaction by seeking a revolutionary temper in a class which has not yet decisively appeared upon the historic stage.

That Marx and Engels were wholly right in their attitude to "true" socialism was shown conclusively by the events of 1848 in Germany. There is indeed an important sense in which their criticism of German socialism has remained valid right down to our own time. The "true" socialists, as they said, borrowed the formulae of French socialism. They then not merely refrained from universalising them. What was worse, they made their realisation seem a special German mission, the task to be accomplished by a German nation which was a "model" nation, by a German "petty philistine" whom they looked upon as the "typical man." It is a high tribute to the insight of Marx and Engels that they had thus perceived what, indeed, they had begun to realise as early as 1845, that "true" socialism was deeply infected with the taint of German romanticism; and that this, in its nationalist form, gave to the socialist expression of its ideals the same arrogant sense of a superior place in the fulfilment of their purpose as, upon another plane of thought, Fichte and Hegel gave to Germany as a compensation for its humiliation by Napoleon. When Hess called the German people the nation "at once the most universal and the most European," he was claiming for it the same supreme place in the hierarchy of socialist effort as was Hegel when he made the Prussian monarchy coincide with the ultimate purpose of the absolute. It was an analogous reliance upon what the *Manifesto* calls "speculative cobwebs embroidered with flowers of rhetoric" which made German socialism in 1914 so overwhelmingly take up arms in an imperialist war and in 1918-19, by manipulating concepts instead of realities, rejoice, as the Weimar Republic was built, in the success of a revolution that had not yet happened. There is no part of the *Manifesto* more rich in understanding than the bitter paragraphs in which Marx and Engels so severely attack men with whom, but recently, they had been in close alliance. Nor should we omit to note the important sense in which this criticism is as much directed against an earlier phase of their own thinking at it is against their friends. It is because Hess and Grün had failed to see that the idealist methodology of Hegel, and even of Feuerbach, could never be the basis of an effective Socialist movement, that they were handled with so determined a severity.

The section on literature continues with a discussion of "conservative or bourgeois" socialism. "The socialistic bourgeois," says the *Manifesto,* "want all the advantages of modern social conditions without the struggles and dangers necessarily resulting from them. They desire the present state of society without its revolutionary and disintegrating elements. They wish for a bourgeoisie without a proletariat." The "conservative" socialist may be an economist or a humanitarian; he is found among "hole and corner reformers of every kind." If he systematises his doctrine, he emerges with a body of ideas like those expounded by Proudhon in his *Philosophie de la Misère.* Or he may refrain from system-making, and devote his attention to attacks on revolutionary movements intended to persuade the workers of their folly. Political reform will not do. Nor is anything gained by abolishing the bourgeois relations of production. In the eyes of the "conservative" socialist the supreme need is a change in "the material conditions of existence." When we analyse what he means by this change, we find that it is no more than "administrative reforms" which, though they simplify the work and diminish the cost of government, leave the relations between capital and labour unchanged. He is in favour of free trade, or protective duties, or prison reform, for the benefit of the working class. What, nevertheless, is vital to his outlook is that the proletariat should cease to hate the bourgeoisie, and accept the capitalist system as final. By that means the "social New Jerusalem" can be built without the haunting fear that revolution is necessary to its establishment.

It is obvious enough that this attack is directed against the men whose palliatives Marx agreed with Proudhon in dismissing with contempt in his *Poverty of Philosophy*— Proudhon himself, be it noted, being added by Marx to the list of those to be so dismissed. Michel Chevalier, Adolphe Blanqui and Léon Faucher in France, with their remedies

of technical education, profit-sharing and state-compensation for workers displaced by the development of machine-technology, are typical examples of this kind; they have, as the *Manifesto* says, to mitigate the harsher consequences of capitalism without interfering with the relations of production upon which it is based. The reference to free trade is, I think, pretty obviously an arrow launched against Cobden and Bright and their supporters in the Anti-Corn Law League who believed that the social problem would be solved by the adoption of universal free trade; and this view is the more likely since both Marx and Engels, and especially Engels, had seen at first hand how the propaganda of the League had done much to break the hold of the Chartist Movement upon the workers. It is reasonable to suppose that the reference to tariffs is primarily a thrust at Friedrich List—who had died only the year before—and his system of German national economy based upon a closed customs union as the unit of prosperity. If this is so, it links the *Manifesto* to the growing economic literature from America, the famous *Report on Manufacture* (1791) of Alexander Hamilton, for example, and the works of Henry C. Carey, to which we know Marx and Engels gave careful attention, though without being convinced that the protectionists had found an answer to the central issue of productive relations. What they were rejecting was the notorious doctrine of the "harmony of interest" between capital and labour, which, though Adam Smith at the rise and John Stuart Mill at the end of the first half-century of classical political economy had already seen it to be fallacious, was still the main ground upon which the growth of trade unions was discouraged and repressed. Men of good will, the *Manifesto* says in effect, can never build a society capable of justice by philanthropy of palliatives. It is nothing less than the whole system of productive relations that must be changed.

In a sense, the final section on previous socialist literature, which deals with what the *Manifesto* calls "critico-Utopian" writers, is a little disappointing. It quite properly emphasises the fact that the literature of the first proletarian strivings produces "fantastic pictures" of future society, that it thinks of the workers as a suffering rather than a revolutionary class, that it appeals, for the most part, to ethical principles beyond and above class-antagonism, that it seeks to change society "by peaceful means" and "by small experiments." It agrees that Babeuf, Owen, Cabet and Fourier attack the existing foundation of their civilisation at its roots, that they are "full of the most valuable materials for the enlightenment of the working class." But their proposals are dismissed as "purely Utopian," and though it is admitted that they were themselves "in many respects revolutionary," it is insisted that their followers have always "formed merely reactionary sects." "They therefore endeavour," wrote Marx and Engels, "and that consistently, to deaden the class struggle, and to reconcile the class-antagonisms. . . . They sink into the category of the reactionary conservative socialists, differing from them only by more systematic pedantry." They became, we are told, the violent opponents of working-class political action. Like the followers of Owen who oppose the Chartists, and the followers of Fourier who oppose the *Reform-istes,* they have a "fanatical and superstitious belief in the miraculous effects of their social science."

The praise is grudging, and a good deal of the criticism is, in fact, unfair. It is unfair to Babeuf, to whom, through Buonarrotti, the debt of Marx and Engels themselves was great. It is unfair to a great deal of Bronterre O'Brien's work, to the remarkable trade union achievements of John Doherty, and to the profound writer in the *Poor Man's Guardian* of 1831 whom Beer, the careful historian of British socialism, has given good reasons for thinking was a self-educated working man. No doubt it is fair to conclude that Owen and Saint-Simon, Hodgskin and Fourier, with all their piercing insight into social conditions, never had faith enough in the working class to believe that it could accomplish its own emancipation, or enough interest in political action to recognise the real nature and function of the state-power. But it ought to be compared with the tribute—which Marx approved—paid to Owen, Saint-Simon and Fourier by Engels in 1874 in his preface to the reprint, as a book, of the article he had written in 1850 for the *Neue Rheinische Zeitung* on the Peasants' War in Germany of the sixteenth century. "Just as German theoretical socialism will never forget," he wrote,

> that it rests on [their] shoulders . . . three men who, in spite of all their fantastic notions and Utopianism, have their places among the most eminent thinkers of all times, and whose genius anticipated innumerable ideas the correctness of which we are now scientifically proving, so the practical workers' movement in Germany must never forget that it has developed on the shoulders of the English and French movements, that it was able directly to utilise their hardly-bought experience, and that it could now avoid the mistakes that were unavoidable at the time they made them. Without the English trade unions and the French workers' political struggles before them, without the great impulse given, in particular, by the Paris Commune, where should we be now?

And that eulogy was repeated in the quite masterly preface which Engels wrote to the English edition of 1892, of his *Socialism, Utopian and Scientific.* There, though the same point is made as in the *Manifesto* itself, it is made in a perspective far more just and profound. "Scientific socialism," as Engels again wrote in a footnote to a German reprint of the same work, "is not an exclusively German, but just as much an international, product."

What is the reason for this difference of emphasis? It lies, I suggest, in the desire to show in the *Manifesto* that "true" socialism is a species of the genus Utopian socialism and can make no claim to be regarded as scientific. Marx and Engels belittled the achievements of the Utopians in 1847 because their victory over men like Grün and Hess in Germany itself was not yet complete, and the valuation they then made of their great predecessors was part of a polemic in which they were not yet sure of victory. In 1878, their outlook held the field, still more fully in 1892; and they could afford to be more generous about the men who

laid the foundations of the edifice they themselves had brought so remarkably to completion. That is essentially the attitude of Marx himself when he sought to assess his own personal contribution to socialist philosophy.[16]

VI

The final section of the *Manifesto* is essentially an outline of the correct Communist strategy in view of the coming struggle. The Communists, it affirms, will fight for the immediate interests of the workers, without losing sight of the need to assist the emergence of the future in their aid to the present. Thus, if in France they support the social democrats—the party led by Ledru-Rollin—that will not prevent them from seeking to correct the tendencies in that party which are no more than an empty tradition handed down from the Revolution; if in Germany they support the bourgeoisie in its revolutionary struggle against absolute monarchy, the feudalism of the landlords and the reactionary outlook of the petty-bourgeois elements, that will not prevent them from awakening the workers to the realisation that, once the bourgeois revolution has been accomplished, the proletarian revolution must begin.

The Communists concentrate their efforts on Germany, Marx and Engels say, because a successful bourgeois revolution there, in the conditions of the nineteenth century, where the proletariat is so much more advanced than it could have been either at the time of the English or of the French Revolutions, is bound to be the prelude to an "immediate and subsequent" proletarian revolution. Their general position assumes three clear principles. They must support every revolutionary movement against the conditions of the time. They must make the question of property—that is, the ownership of the means of production—the central issue in every movement in which they participate. They must, finally, "labour everywhere for the union and agreement of the democratic parties of all countries." Their position is thus unmistakable. They will always support working-class parties, even when these are not communist, without forming a separate party of their own; even though such a party may have an inadequate programme, its proletarian character makes it the appropriate instrument through which to exercise communist influence. Where the party they support, like that of Ledru-Rollin, is not proletarian, they support it because it offers the workers the chance first of a greater rôle in politics, and second, of great social reforms.

The position of the *Manifesto* on Germany needs a somewhat more elaborate analysis. It says quite clearly that Germany is on the eve of a bourgeois revolution, and that its makers must be supported because their success will be the prelude to a proletarian revolution. We have to put this affirmation alongside the insistence of Marx and Engels themselves, at the Communist Congress in London, not many weeks before the writing of the *Manifesto* that the antagonism between the bourgeoisie and the workers is more developed in England—an inference clearly drawn from their judgment upon Chartism—than in any other country. We must compare it further, as Charles Andler has pointed out in his remarkable commentary on the *Manifesto,*[17] with the passage in Marx's article on the Hegelian philosophy of Law, published in 1844, where he argued that Germany could no longer make a partial revolution, since the only class in Germany capable of revolutionary action was the "class of the purely *déclassés.*" That class could not, in his submission of 1844, seek for any rights but those of all humanity, since it had been bowed down by suffering to a point where nothing less would enable it to reaffirm its manhood. It thus, in his view, became the proletariat; and when it made its revolution it would, by suppressing itself, inaugurate the classless society.

The change in the *Manifesto,* compared with the article of 1844, admits of a simple explanation. As Andler rightly points out, in the three years that intervened between them Marx himself had ceased to be a "true" socialist, like Grün and Hess, and had come to realise the full significance of historical materialism. He no longer, therefore, thought conceptually, but concretely, of the German workers; and he realised in 1847 that they could not move directly to revolutionary emancipation since German capitalism had not yet developed sufficiently to make them in a full sense a proletariat bent on freeing itself by revolution from its chains. This was later pointed out by Engels in the remarkable articles he wrote for the New York *Tribune* in 1861-2.[18] "The working-class movement itself," he wrote,

> is never independent, is never of an exclusively proletarian character, until all the different elements in the middle class and, particularly, its most progressive element, the large manufacturers, have conquered political power, and remodelled the state in terms of their needs. It is then that the inevitable conflict between the employer and the employed becomes imminent, and cannot be adjourned any longer; that the working class can no longer be put off with delusive topics, and promises never to be realised; that the great problem of the nineteenth century, the abolition of the proletariat, is at last brought forward fairly, and in its proper light.

The reason why Marx and Engels in the years immediately preceding 1848 looked to Germany for the revolution they were expecting has, I think, one personal and two historical grounds. The first is that they were, after all, Germans, with the passionate nostalgia of the exile for his native land; no one can fail to see in their correspondence that, with all the width of their interest in other countries, the interest they took in German development had an intensity which put it on a different plane. They recognised, moreover, that the revolutionary content had, at least for the time being, gone out of the English movement, as was proved in the abortive Chartist demonstration in London on 10 April 1848, and that it would provide no opportunity of vital change. But in Germany, as Engels wrote in the New York *Tribune,* in the second of his articles, "people were either constitutional monarchists or more or less clearly defined socialists or communists." So sharp an antithesis made it natural, therefore, to look to Germany for some important opportunity. "With such elements," wrote Engels,

the slightest collision must have brought about a great revolution. While the higher nobility and the older civil and military officers were the only safe supporters of the existing system; while the lower nobility, the trading middle classes, the universities, the schoolmasters of every degree, and even part of the lower ranks of the bureaucracy and military officers, were all united against the government; while behind these there stood the dissatisfied masses of the peasantry, and of the proletarians of the large towns, supporting, for the time being, the Liberal Opposition, but already muttering strange words about taking things into their own hands; while the bourgeoisie was ready to hurl down the government, and the proletarians were preparing to hurl down the bourgeoisie in its turn; this government continued obstinately in a course which must bring about a coalition. Germany was, in the beginning of 1848, on the eve of a revolution; and this revolution was sure to come, even had the French Revolution of February not hastened it.

That explains the special significance the *Manifesto* attached to German events. But Marx and Engels did not look upon those events as isolated and complete in themselves. They were a part only of a much vaster perspective in which the proletariat of one country could be seen handing on the revolutionary torch to the proletariat of another. That is why the *Manifesto* appeals to the workers of all countries to unite. The famous sentence which concludes it is not the formula of an empty ritual. It is inherent in the whole *Manifesto* as an expression of the interdependence of a class which, as capitalist society takes the whole world into its grasp, must act internationally if it is to act successfully. It is the anticipation of what Marx was to say, some sixteen years later, in his inaugural address to the First International. "To conquer political power," he told the meeting in St. Martin's Hall,[19]

> has become the great duty of the working classes . . . One element of success they have—numbers; but numbers weigh only in the balance if united by combination, and led by knowledge. Past experience has shown how disregard of that bond of brotherhood which ought to exist between the workmen of different countries, and incite them to stand firmly by each other in all their struggles for emancipation, will be chastised by the common discomfiture of their incoherent efforts . . . The emancipation of the working classes requires their fraternal concurrence.

The men who had lived through ardour to failure in 1848 were there reaffirming their conviction that the "immediate combination of the still disconnected movements" in different countries was the indispensable condition of working-class emancipation; to achieve it was not "a local nor a national, but a social, problem, embracing all countries in which modern society exists, and depending for its solution on the concurrence, practical and theoretical, of the most advanced countries." So only could the workers throw off their chains.

VII

Time has added to the lustre of the *Communist Manifesto*; and it has achieved the remarkable status not only of being a classic, but a classic also which is directly relevant to the controversies which rage a century after it was written. Inevitably, therefore, it has become the subject of rival interpretations; and it is not seldom read as though its eminent authors were still fighting for one or another of the different schools of contemporary socialist thought. It is, indeed, hardly an exaggeration to say that, under the leadership of the Communist Party of Soviet Russia, an attempt has been made to secure the prestige of the *Manifesto* for those only who accept the leadership and direction of Moscow, and to argue that it has no meaning outside the canons of orthodoxy which first Lenin, and later Stalin, have applied to its scrutiny. One may go even further and suggest that those who do not accept these canons are regarded by the adherents of the Muscovite school with the same furious indignation as Marx and Engels regarded the "true" socialists of their own day.

Of certain things there can be no doubt at all. Marx and Engels were both convinced that the victory of the proletariat, and the consequential establishment of a classless society would normally be established by violent revolution. They were convinced, also, that only by the alliance of the working classes in the most advanced countries would a proletarian revolution in any one of them be able to hope that its successful consolidation might be seriously expected. They were emphatic that Communists must not form a party which separates itself from the mass organisations of the working class; and they insisted that Communists must, while they ceaselessly bear in view the ultimate and decisive proletarian revolution, never forget the high importance of helping to realise those lesser, if more immediately realisable, gains which improve the position of the worker. They were ready to make alliances with non-working-class parties, if the result of their joint action was strategically progressive. When, jointly, they republished the *Manifesto* in 1872, they remarked that while its "general principles . . . are, on the whole, as correct to-day as ever," nevertheless "the practical application of the principles will depend, as the *Manifesto* itself states, everywhere and at all times, on the historical conditions for the time being existing." On that account, they said, the revolutionary measures they proposed in 1848 needed "no special stress." They thought, also, that the immense industrial development since the *Manifesto* first appeared, as well as "the practical experience" of the February Revolution and of the Commune made some of the measures obsolete. Above all, they argued, one thing especially was proved by the Commune, viz., that "the working class cannot simply lay hold of the ready-made state machinery, and wield it for its own purposes." This last sentence is a quotation from Marx's famous pamphlet, the *Civil War in France*; and in a letter written to Kugelmann on 12 April 1871,[20] during the existence of the Paris Commune, Marx explained what this meant by referring his German admirer to the last chapter of his *Eighteenth Brumaire* where "you will find that I say that the next attempt of the French Revolution will be no longer, as before, to transfer the bureaucratic-military machine from one hand to the other, but to *smash* it; and this is essential for every real people's

revolution on the Continent." The virtue of the Commune was that it was elected by universal suffrage, had a majority of working men "or acknowledged representatives of the working class," and was "a working, not a parliamentary body, executive and legislative at the same time," the members being elected for short terms, and subject to recall. In his preface to the reprint in 1891 of the *Civil War in France,* Engels wrote that "of late, the Social Democratic Philistine has once more been filled with wholesome terror at the words 'Dictatorship of the Proletariat.' Well and good, gentlemen, do you want to know what the Dictatorship looks like? Look at the Paris Commune. That was the Dictatorship of the Proletariat."

Almost all these phrases have been the subject of violent conflict, of which the best known, perhaps, is that between Lenin and Trotsky, in one camp, and the German social democrat Karl Kautsky in the other; Rosa Luxembourg, who was martyred in the Spartacus revolt of 1919, and the Russian Menshevik leader, Jules Martov, may fairly be described as occupying an intermediate position between the two extreme interpretations. It is impossible here to enter upon the kind of detailed and special scrutiny of texts in which not only is every word important, but in which, also, what is really a subjective valuation of their importance in their total context, plays a very considerable part. It must suffice to examine certain major themes in the dispute, and, somewhat dogmatically, to suggest the main results of research about them.

It is quite clear that both Marx and Engels expected that most proletarian revolutions would be successful only after heavy fighting, and that the only possible exceptions they saw to this rule were Great Britain, the United States and, perhaps, Holland. They thought that the critical moment would come for Great Britain when Ireland and India had secured their independence, since this would deprive Great Britain of a source of exploitation which enabled it, in a considerable degree, to give its proletariat a bourgeois character and outlook. They were confident that, in all cases, the arrival of the working class in power would mean a period of transition marked by the dictatorship of the proletariat.

No phrase has been subject to so much misinterpretation as the "dictatorship of the proletariat." Let us be clear at once that neither for Marx nor for Engels was it the antithesis of democracy; for them, its antithesis was the "dictatorship of the bourgeoisie" which, as they believed, obtained in every country, even when concealed by formally democratic political institutions, so long as the ownership of the means of production remained in middle-class hands. Marx and Engels meant by the "dictatorship of the proletariat" an organisation of society in which the state-power was in the hands of the working class, and used with all the force necessary to prevent it being seized from them by the class which formerly exercised its authority. They assume that the representatives of the working class will use the state-power to change the relations of production and to repress any attempt to interfere with this change. But it is obvious from Engels' identification of the Paris Commune with proletarian dictatorship that he regards it as based on the support of the majority, that it employs the technique of universal suffrage, and that its acceptance of the people's rights to frequent elections, and to the recall of their representatives implies full popular participation in the working of the dictatorship. It is obvious, further, from Marx's account of the Commune as a legislature and executive in one, that it denies the validity of the separation of powers, and assumes that the dictatorship is exercised through the elected body based upon popular choice and subject to public opinion, through the right of each constituency to recall any representative it may have chosen; that, surely, was what Marx meant when he wrote that "nothing could be more foreign to the spirit of the Commune than to supersede universal suffrage by hierarchic investiture." Marx even points out that the "great bulk of the Paris middle class . . . the wealthy capitalist alone excepted" admitted that "this was the first revolution in which the working class was openly acknowledged as the only class capable of social initiative"; he noted that it supplied the republic with the basis of really democratic institutions; and he compares the peace and order it secured within Paris, with the fanatically repressive atmosphere of Versailles under the domination of Thiers.

From this angle, it seems to me inescapable that Marx and Engels did not conceive the dictatorship of the proletariat to mean the dictatorship of the Communist Party over the rest of the community, that is, the centralisation of the state-power in the hands of a single party, which imposes its will by force on all citizens outside its ranks. It is conceivable that the struggle for the state-power may be so intense that the government has no alternative but to proclaim a state of siege until it has consolidated its authority. It is undeniable, also, that a workers' government in possession of the state-power may find it necessary to penalise persons or parties who threaten its safety, in the same way as the British Government found it necessary to assume drastic powers when it was threatened by invasion after Dunkirk in 1940. It was, I think, this second situation that Marx and Engels had in view. They assumed that the use of the state-power by and for the workers would mean an expansion, and not a contraction, of democratic forces; it would permit, that is, vastly greater numbers to participate in social life effectively than is possible when democratic institutions operate only within the framework of capitalist production. They could not, therefore, have envisaged the Communist Party acting as a dictatorship over the working class and excluding all other parties from the right to share in, and influence over, the exercise of power.

I think this view is borne out by other evidence. The *Manifesto* itself declares quite explicitly that Communists are the vanguard of the working class. They are not its masters; they are in the forefront of the co-operative effort to abolish capitalist society. Still more important, the Communists do not form a separate party of their own. They ally themselves with other organisations, especially of the working class, which aim at the same end as themselves,

or may objectively be regarded as assisting that end even though unconsciously. That was why, for example, the Communist League supported Ledru-Rollin in 1845, even though he hated Communism. That was why, also, they persuaded the First International to support the Paris Commune, and why those of its members, who were also members of the International, cooperated in its heroic struggle with others who did not belong to it. Unless, indeed, Marx and Engels had taken this view, they would have been arguing that the dictatorship of the proletariat means the rule of that party leadership to the guidance of which any political organisation of large size must give heavy responsibilities. They never argued for this outlook. On the contrary, their deepest concern was to make the state-power, when it passed into the workers' hands, not only the organ through which the capitalist relations of production were transformed into socialist relations of production, but the organ also through which the unreal democracy of capitalist society became the real democracy of socialist society. Repression in all its forms was for them a transitory necessity. That was why they could argue that, with the establishment of socialism, the state would "wither away."

The "withering away" of the state is another famous phrase that has been much discussed and much misunderstood. In one sense it is a purely logical inference from the definition of the *Manifesto.* The state is there defined as the "executive committee of the bourgeoisie." Obviously, therefore, as the power to govern is taken out of the hands of the bourgeoisie by the workers, the state as a bourgeois institution ceases to exist because being in the workers' hands it becomes transformed into a proletarian institution. Marx and Engels then argued that its coercive authority, the army, for example, the police, and the civil service, would have so to be adapted as to be capable of use by the workers for socialist purposes, as they had been adapted by the bourgeoisie to be used for capitalist purposes. They thought in 1872, as Marx had suggested 20 years before, that a socialist society would have to "break" the political machinery of the régime it took over in order to make the adaptation successful. What did they mean by "breaking" the machinery of the capitalist state? The answer is, I think, that it was to be deprived of that character of an "hierarchical investiture" which, as Marx had written in *Civil War in France,* prevented the defective power of numbers from being authoritative. The organs of government were to be genuinely democratised. They were to be in and of the new proletarian society, not, as in capitalist society, over and above the workers, separated from them by caste-like walls, so that they could impose upon the workers the discipline necessary to maintain in its fullness the capitalist mode of production. The defence forces, the police and the civil service were to have no special privileges, and no special place in the new régime. Their members were to be looked upon as workers performing a necessary social function in the same way as any other groups of workers. They were to be deprived of their "hierarchical" attributes.

It should be added that when Marx and Engels spoke of the "withering away of the state" there is no reason to suppose they believed that in a socialist country the hopes of the philosophical anarchists would be fulfilled and that all authority would be the outcome of express assent to its orders. No doubt both of them strongly believed that as the private ownership of the means of production passed away there would be far less need for a coercive apparatus in society. That was a natural view for them to take since they held that it was the private ownership of those means which was responsible for most of what was evil in the social process. Their insistence that the state-power was essentially used to protect that private ownership from attack was, of course, held with great emphasis by Adam Smith himself. "It is only under the shelter of the civil magistrates," Adam Smith wrote,[21] "that the owner of that valuable property, acquired by the labour of many years, or perhaps many successive generations, can sleep a single night in security." Marx and Engels agreed with the implications in Adam Smith's statement, though the inference they would have drawn was different. But there is nothing to suggest in all they wrote that with the establishment of a socialist society government itself becomes unnecessary. They rarely spoke of what a socialist society would be like; and the few references they did make to its character only justify us in saying that they looked to a fuller and freer expression of individuality when the capitalists' fetters upon the forces of production had been finally removed.

Some discussion is desirable of the materialist conception of history which is the vital thread upon which the whole of the *Communist Manifesto* hangs; the more so because it continues to be strangely misrepresented by historians and social philosophers. It is not a claim that all actions are the result of economic motives. It does not insist either that all change is economically caused. It does not mean that the ideas and behaviour of men are fatalistically predetermined and that, whether he will or no, the emergence of a socialist society is inevitable. It is the argument that, as Engels puts it,[22] "production and, with production, the exchange of its products, is the basis of every social order; that in every society which has appeared in history, the distribution of the products, and, with it, the division of society into classes or estates, is determined by what is produced, and how it is produced, and how the product is exchanged." This is the basis from which Marx and Engels were led to that philosophy of history which led them to part company with their former allies, the Left Hegelians, whose conceptions are attacked in the *Manifesto*. For it led them to see that the way in which the total social production is divided in a community is not the outcome of the purposes, either good or bad, of the members of the community, but of the legal relations which arise out of given modes of production, and that these legal relations are independent of the wills of those engaged in production. Since changes in the modes of production and exchange are ceaselessly taking place, legal relations which were, at one time, adapted to the conditions of that time, cease to be adapted to them. It is in this disproportion between legal relations in the community and the forces of production in it that the changes in men's ideas of good

and bad, justice and injustice, are to be found. That class in a community which legally owns the means of production uses the state-power to sanction that division of the product of which it approves. It therefore seeks through the coercive authority at the disposal of the state-power, to compel the general acceptance of its approved division; and systems of values, political, ethical, religious, philosophical, are ways in which, directly or indirectly, men express their agreement or disagreement with the nature of the division which the owners of the instruments of production endeavour to impose.

This does not mean that changes may be regarded as irrelevant to the ideas of men; but it does mean that men's ideas are continually evolving as their minds come to realise that changes in the methods of production and exchange render some ideas obsolete and require new ideas. As feudalism became transformed into capitalism, the legal relations it implied hindered the full use of the forces of production. The values the feudal system had been able to maintain before the advent of the capitalist method of production emerged became no longer acceptable. Then, as Engels wrote, "the bourgeoisie shattered the feudal system, and, on its ruins established the bourgeois social order, the realm of free competition, freedom of movement, equal rights for commodity owners and all the other bourgeois glories." Now, the *Manifesto* argues, changes in the forces of production have rendered the legal relations of capitalism obsolete in their turn; and socialism emerges as the claim to new relations, and, therefore, to new values which the workers, as the class which suffers most from this obsolescence, seek to put in its place.

No serious observer supposes that the materialist conception of history is free from difficulties, or that it solves all the problems involved in historical interpretation. But no serious observer either can doubt that it has done more in the last hundred years to provide a major clue to the causes of social change than any other hypothesis that has been put forward. There can really be no valid reason to deny that, over the whole space of recorded history, class struggle has been a central principle of its development. Nor can it be denied that class struggle is intimately bound up with the relations of production in some given society and the ability to develop the full possibilities of the forces of production at any given time. It is equally clear, on any close analysis, that the class which owns the instruments of production uses the state-power to safeguard that ownership, and seeks to repress the emergence of ideas and values which call that ownership into question. Anyone, moreover, who examines objectively any period in which the mode of production is rapidly changing, the age of the Reformation, for example, or the period between the two world wars, cannot fail to note that they are also periods marked by the grave instability of traditional values and of traditional institutions. There is nothing in the theory of the *Manifesto* which argues more than that the occurrence of such a period means that, if the traditional values and institutions continue to function in the new economic setting, they will deprive large numbers of their means of living, and that they will, therefore, seek to emancipate themselves from a position of which they are the victims. To do so, as Marx and Engels point out, they must possess themselves of the state-power that they may adapt the relations of production to the implications of the new order. And, on the argument of the *Manifesto,* since the passage from capitalist to social ownership marks the end of a history in which the instruments of production have been predominantly the possession of one class, the transition to public ownership means, when it is successfully effected, the emergence of the classless society.

It is this doctrine which the *Manifesto* is concerned to get accepted by socialists as against the other doctrines with which it was competing. It was not enough, Marx and Engels were saying in effect, for some men or group of men to proclaim a new principle as true and hope by the force merely of rational argument to persuade others to see also that it is true. What makes the new principle acceptable is the fact that changes in the mode of production have produced the material environment which makes it seem the natural expression of what people want. The duty to be tolerant is rarely likely to receive wide acceptance when it is advanced as an abstract metaphysical obligation. But when intolerance hinders the attainment by society of a full command over its material resources, men begin to see a validity in arguments advanced on its behalf, some religious, some ethical, some political, some economic, the strength of which had not previously been apparent to them. All the world applauded Robert Owen so long as he made the operation of that "revolution" in the mind and practice of the "human race" a philanthropic experiment confined to his own factories in New Lanark. But when he argued that his principles were so obviously rational that all social organisation should be adapted to their application, the world turned angrily upon him and showed him that, in the absence of the necessary material conditions, a principle which has justice and truth and reason on its side will still be unable to conquer the world by the inherent force of its own virtue. It is not until men see that the "anarchy of social production" caused by capitalism in decay can be replaced "by a socially planned regulation of production in accordance with the needs both of society as a whole, and of each individual," that they are prepared to get rid of capitalism.

"The forces operating in society," wrote Engels,[23]

> work exactly like the forces operating in nature: blindly, violently, destructively, so long as we do not understand them and fail to take them into account. But when we once have recognised them, and understood how they work, their direction and their efforts, the gradual subjection of them to our will, and the use of them for the attainment of our aims, depends entirely upon ourselves. And this is quite especially true of the mighty, productive forces of the present day.

That is, I think, the central principle which underlies the whole of the *Communist Manifesto*; it is the social appli-

cation of Bacon's great aphorism that "nature, to be commanded, must be obeyed." It is our attempt to show that every pattern of social institutions presupposes a stage in the development of productive forces, and that those who seek for the achievement of the pattern in which they believe will succeed only if their aim is justified by the character of those productive forces at the time when they make their effort. That was why, though Carlyle and Ruskin saw the evils of their own day, their remedy was an anachronism when they preached it; they preached a sermon to men who, as it were, had already left their church. That was why, to take a contemporary instance, the New Deal of President Roosevelt was able only to assuage temporarily the wounds he sought to heal; for those wounds were not some temporary infliction, but the symptoms of a disease far more deep and deadly than he was prepared to recognise.

One last aspect of the *Manifesto* required to be clarified. Why was it given this title? Those who sponsored it had not thought of it in that form; it was rather a catechism, more easily capable of being memorised, that they had in mind. The word "Communism" had no special sanctity for them; their organisation, in one or another of its forms, had operated under a variety of names. It is not a question we can answer with any certainty; Engels himself did not deal with it in the recollections he wrote later—themselves not always accurate—of how it came to be composed in the form in which we have it. Perhaps it was a "Manifesto" in half-conscious tribute to the memory of the Babouvian *Manifeste des Egaux,*[24] a salute to one of the supreme documents of that French Revolution which Marx and Engels recognised as one of the great climacterics of history, and from which they learned so much; perhaps it is also due to a faint recollection of the once well-known pamphlet which Victor Considerant had published shortly before.

Why "communist" and not "socialist" Manifesto? Obviously, in the first instance, because it was the official publication of the Communist League. We have little other evidence on which to base speculations. It was possibly the outcome of a recollection of the Paris Commune in the French Revolution, an institution to which all socialists did homage. It was possibly a desire to distinguish the ideas for which they stood from socialist doctrines which they were criticising so severely. The one thing that is certain, from the document itself, is that the choice of the term "Communist" was not intended to mark any organisational separation between the Communist League and other socialist or working-class bodies. On the contrary, Marx and Engels were emphatic in their insistence that the Communists do not form a separate Party and that they ally themselves with all the forces which work towards a socialist society. The idea of a separate communist party dates from the Russian Revolution; it had no place in the thought either of Marx or of Engels.

IX

Few documents in the history of mankind have stood up so remarkably to the test of verification by the future as the *Communist Manifesto.* A century after its publication no one has been able seriously to controvert any of its major positions. All over the world the crises of capitalism have grown both more frequent and more profound. The fact that America has reached its last internal frontier has brought into being there precisely the same problems, if on a vaster scale, as in Europe, and the rising nationalisms of the Far East and the Pacific, while they hasten the decay of capitalism in the older industrial societies, quite obviously prelude their rise in the new. For, unmistakably, whether in Japan or China, whether in India or Indonesia, the central problem is the sheer misery of the masses; and our experience makes it clear that, within a capitalist framework, there is little likelihood of its effective mitigation. Nor is anyone likely to look at the prospect either in Latin America or in Africa and conclude that in either continent the business of government is carried on with the consent, or for the good, of the governed. Vice in both may pay to virtue the homage of occasional hypocrisy, but, in the intervals between those tributes, the squalor and vigour with which the many are exploited by the few, have changed less their character than the rhetoric under which they seek to conceal themselves.

But it is in Europe, above all, that the principles of the *Communist Manifesto* have found their fullest vindication by far. It is not only that even after two world wars fought in the name of democracy and freedom each of them has either perished altogether, or is in grave danger; it has been shown that, whereas in Great Britain and Scandinavia, deep historical traditions give to democracy and freedom an exceptional strength, the regard of the Right for their form is greater than their regard for their substance. The British Labour Party won a notable electoral victory at the close of the second World War. It has thus embarked upon the tremendous task of beginning to build the foundations of a socialist society in Great Britain in a period when, a large part of Europe having been devastated by war and the resources of the victorious powers, like Great Britain itself, drained almost to breaking-point, its task, both as a Socialist Party, and as a Government, is to ask for the continuance of great sacrifices from a people fatigued by the immense effort of war. To keep its authority, as Mr. Attlee himself has said,[25]

the Labour programme must be carried out with the utmost vigour and resolution. To delay dealing with essentials would be fatal. To show irresolution or cowardice would be to invite defeat. A Labour Government should make it quite plain that it will suffer nothing to hinder it in carrying out the popular will. In all great enterprises it is the first steps that are difficult, and it is the way in which these are taken that makes the difference between success and failure.

It is not, I think, merely patriotic emotion that makes British socialists feel that here, as nowhere else, the truth of their principles will be tested. It was in Great Britain that capitalist society first came to full maturity in the generation subsequent to the Napoleonic Wars. It was largely from the observation and analysis of that maturity that Marxism became the outstanding philosophic expression of socialist principles and methods; and it was largely from British socialist writers, and the early British socialist movement, alike on its political and on its trade union side, that Marx and Engels moved to the understanding that men make their history by their power, through their grasp of the forces which make it move, to give a conscious direction to that movement. Mr. Attlee has never been himself a Marxist; but there is not a word in the sentences of his that I have quoted which could not have been eagerly accepted by the authors of the *Communist Manifesto*; and they would, I think, have inferred from them that in the degree to which the first Labour Government with a majority puts the spirit of those phrases into operation, it would fulfil the great objectives for which it was formed. By unbreakable loyalty to its own principles it could lead its own people, even in the hour of crisis, to cast off its chains. A British working class that had achieved its own emancipation could build that working-class unity everywhere out of which the new world will finally be won.

Notes

1. *La Misère des Classes Laboreuses en France et en Angleterre* (Paris, 1840. 2 volumes).

2. They were originally printed in the *Westphalische Dampfboot*; they were reprinted in the *Neue Zeit* for 1895-6 (vol. I, pp. 51 et seq.).

3. I use the full text as published in *Selected Works of Karl Marx* (Moscow, 1935), vol. II, p. 169. Marx's analysis originally appeared in the *Neue Rheinische Zeitung* from March to June, 1850.

4. It was written at the end of March, 1850.

5. Engels, op. cit., vol. II, p. 189.

6. Ibid.

7. Preface to Borkheim's *In Memory of the German Martyrs who died for their Fatherland 1806-1807*, quoted in *Correspondence of Marx and Engels* (London, 1934), p. 456. Cf. also ibid. p. 429, 455.

8. Preface to Borkheim's *In Memory of the German Martyrs who died for their Fatherland 1806-1807*, quoted in *Correspondence of Marx and Engels* (London, 1934), p. 456, and pp. 489-91.

9. *Selected Works,* vol. II, p. 460.

10. *The State and Revolution* in *Select Works* (London, 1937), vol. VII, p. 5.

11. Letter of 12 April, 1871, and cf. Lenin, op. cit., p. 27.

12. Ibid., p. 16.

13. As is made clear in the preface to the first edition of the *State and Revolution.* "An international proletar-

ian revolution," Lenin writes, "is clearly maturing. The question of its relation to the state is acquiring practical importance."

14. Paris, 1844, pp. 152-81.

15. C. Pecquer, *Des Intérêts du Commerce* (1844), vol. II, pp. 208-9.

16. *Letters to Kugelmann,* 12 April 1871.

17. *La Manifeste Communiste, Introduction Historique et Commentaire* (Paris, 1901), p. 204.

18. *Germany: Revolution and Counter-Revolution.* These articles, first published as a book in England in 1896, were long supposed to have been written by Marx. It is, of course, clear that Engels wrote them in the fullest consultation with him. The quotation in the text is from the first article.

19. *Selected Works,* vol. II, p. 440.

20. Cf. Lenin's comment, preface to *Letters to Kugelmann* (London, 1934), pp. 16-19.

21. *Wealth of Nations.* Bk. V, chap. 1, S. 2.

22. *Socialism, Utopian and Scientific,* S. 3.

23. *Socialism, Utopian and Scientific,* S. 3.

24. Written by Sylvan Maréchal.

25. *The Labour Party in Perspective* (London, 1937).

S. S. Prawer (essay date 1976)

SOURCE: Prawer, S. S. "World Literature and Class Conflict." In *Karl Marx and World Literature,* pp. 138-149. London: Oxford University Press, 1976.

[*In the following excerpt, Prawer details the literary devices and references present in the* Communist Manifesto, *while also examining the origins and intentions of the work.*]

> National one-sidedness and narrow-mindedness become more and more impossible, and from the numerous national and local literatures there arises a world literature.
>
> (*MEW* [*Werke*] IV, 466)

(I)

'The combination of scientific analysis with moral judgment', Bottomore and Rubel have said, 'is by no means uncommon in the field of social studies. Marx is unusual, and his work is exceptionally interesting, because, unlike any other major social thinker, he was the recognized leader, and subsequently the prophet, of an organized political movement.'[1] The document, however, which was to do more than any other to ensure such recognition, the *Manifesto of the Communist Party,*[2] went al-

most unnoticed when it first appeared in London in February 1848. Composed jointly by Marx and Engels at the invitation of the Communist League, this manifesto is pervaded from the very start by what may justifiably be called 'literary' imagery: metaphors, images, from oral and written literature, from publishing, and from theatrical performance. 'A spectre is haunting Europe', the famous opening words proclaim; and lest we mistake the fictional source of this image, Marx and Engels proceed at once to speak of the need to confront 'this nursery-tale [*Märchen*] of the spectre of Communism with a manifesto of the party itself'.[3] Many related images follow: 'spectacle' (*Schauspiel*), 'song of lamentation' (*Klagelied*), 'lampoon' (*Pasquill*), 'pocket-edition (*Duodez-Ausgabe*) of the New Jerusalem'; and, more elaborate than these, a 'palimpsest' image which Marx and Engels may well have borrowed from Heine:

> It is well-known how the monks write silly lines of Catholic saints *over* the manuscripts on which the classical works of ancient heathendom had been written. The German literati reversed this process with profane French literature. They wrote their philosophical nonsense beneath the French original. For instance, beneath the French criticism of the economic function of money, they wrote: alienation of humanity . . .[4]

German readers, in fact, will more than once feel that the **Communist Manifesto** is itself a palimpsest: that beneath the utterances of Marx and Engels they detect those of German poets. This may be just a matter of an image, or a phrase, that brings reminiscences of another context with it:

> The aristocracy, in order to rally the people to them, waved the proletarian alms-bag in front for a banner. But the people, as often as it joined them, *saw on their hindquarters the old feudal coats of arms,* and deserted with loud and irreverent laughter.
>
> [my italics][5]

. . . erblickte es auf ihrem Hintern die alten feudalen Wappen . . .—no reader of Heine will fail to hear the echo of *Germany. A Winter's Tale*:

> Das mahnt an das Mittelalter so schön
> An Edelknechte und Knappen,
> Die in dem Herzen getragen die Treu
> Und auf dem Hintern ein Wappen.
>
> This is a beautiful reminder of the Middle Ages,
> Of noble servants and squires,
> Who bore loyalty in their heart
> And a coat of arms on their behind.[6]

Another and more complex kind of palimpsest effect is produced by the following passage:

> Modern bourgeois society with its relation of production, of exchange, and of property, a society that has conjured up such gigantic means of production and of exchange, is like the sorcerer [*gleicht dem Hexenmeister*] who is no longer able to control the powers of the nether world that he has called up by his spells.[7]

In Goethe's poem 'The Sorcerer's Apprentice' (*Der Zauberlehrling*) it is the apprentice who calls up spirits he cannot, in the end, subdue, and it is the master, the *Hexenmeister,* who repairs the damage. In *The Communist Manifesto* the master-sorcerer himself has lost control: the magnitude of that disaster can be best felt if we perceive Goethe's contrasting text in and through that of the *Manifesto.*

The terms 'literature' and 'literary', *Literatur* and *literarisch,* occur frequently in *The Communist Manifesto,* and are used in three different ways. The first example is to be found only in the German version; it is absent from the familiar English translation:

> Thus arose petty-bourgeois socialism. Sismondi was the head of this school, notably in France but also in England.

> Es bildete sich so der kleinbürgerliche Sozialismus. Sismondi ist das Haupt dieser Literatur nicht nur für Frankreich sondern auch für England.[8]

Here the term *Literatur* denotes 'the body of technical books, pamphlets, etc., that treat of a given subject, and the writers who produce it'.

The sentence about Sismondi occurs in a section of *The Communist Manifesto* which is entitled *Socialist and Communist Literature* and opens as follows:

> Owing to their historical position, it became the vocation of the aristocracies of France and England to write pamphlets against modern bourgeois society. In the French Revolution of July 1830, and in the English reform agitation, these aristocracies again succumbed to the hateful upstart. Thenceforth, a serious political struggle was altogether out of the question. A literary battle alone remained possible. But even in the domain of literature the old cries of the restoration period had become impossible.

> In order to arouse sympathy the aristocracy was obliged to lose sight, apparently, of its own interests and to formulate its indictment against the bourgeoisie in the interest of the exploited working class alone. Thus the aristocracy prepared itself the vengeful satisfaction of singing scornful songs [*Schmählieder*] about their new master and whispering into his ear more or less sinister prophecies of coming catastrophe.[9]

Here 'literature', it would seem, denotes more than just the 'pamphlets' mentioned in the opening sentence. Poems, plays, and novels could qualify for inclusion if they had some sort of political slant or 'message'. We find one such novel, Étienne Cabet's *Journey to Icaria* (*Voyage en Icarie. Roman philosophique et social,* Paris, 1840 and 1842), mentioned a little later in this section.[10] This is, of course, the work to which 'communism' owes its very name; and it had already figured prominently in *The German Ideology* where it was used, through contrast and comparison, to show up the plagiarisms and misunderstandings which Marx and Engels ascribed to Karl Grün and other 'true socialists'.[11] Literature is not, for Marx, a

separate, self-enclosed region. Poems like those of Heine and the song of the Silesian weavers, novels like those of Gustave Beaumont, Étienne Cabet, and George Sand, plays like Gustav Freytag's *The Journalists* (which Marx was to see much later in life), are clearly related to other, more utilitarian forms of writing, and may profitably be discussed alongside these.

The Communist Manifesto uses the term 'literary', however, in yet another sense—one which will not surprise readers of Marx's earlier works. In the section devoted to 'German or "true" Socialism', Marx and Engels discuss, once again, the introduction of French socialist and communist writings in eighteen-and nineteenth-century Germany:

> German philosophers, would-be philosophers, and *beaux esprits* eagerly seized on this literature, only forgetting that when these writings immigrated from France into Germany, French social conditions had not immigrated along with them. In contact with German social conditions, this French literature lost all its immediate practical significance, and assumed *a purely literary aspect* [*ein rein literarisches Aussehen*] . . . Thus, to the German philosophers of the eighteenth century, the demands of the first French Revolution were nothing more than the demands of 'Practical Reason' in general, and the utterance of the will of the revolutionary French bourgeoisie signified in their eyes the laws of pure Will, of Will as it was bound to be, of true human Will generally.
>
> [my italics][12]

Here 'purely literary' implies—as so often in Marx—a world of words floating loose, words cut off from things, cut off from social and political reality. The Manifesto goes on to describe this effect, in terms which carry suggestions of the sentimental, belletristic, and rhetorical, as a 'robe of speculative cobwebs, embroidered with flowers of rhetoric, steeped in the dew of sickly sentiment . . .', and to make the important point that such literature, however ethereally interpreted, is in nineteenth-century society itself an item of commercial transaction. Its writers and translators are concerned with the sale of their commodity (*Absatz ihrer Ware*) among the German public.

As such terms show, and as is not surprising in such a context, *The Communist Manifesto* bids us look at the way writers function in modern society, and concludes that romantic illusions can no longer hide the actualities of the market-place: 'The bourgeoisie has stripped of its halo every occupation hitherto honoured and looked up to with reverent awe. It has converted the physician, the lawyer, the priest, *the poet,* the man of science, into its paid wage labourers' [my italics].[13] Even poetry, then, is a commodity in the modern world and subject to its economic laws. Nor are poets exempt from that determination of men's thoughts which the *Manifesto* proclaims in uncompromising terms: 'Your very ideas are . . . outgrowths of the conditions of your bourgeois production and bourgeois property.'[14] And if writers are in this way a *product* of their society and the social groups for whom they write, those social groupings in their turn are affected by the writings they have indirectly produced and inspired: 'With very few exceptions, all the so-called socialist and communist publications that now circulate in Germany belong to the domain of *this foul and enervating literature*' [my italics].[15] The nemesis of converting writers into paid hirelings is that their productions enervate their readers instead of enlivening and refreshing them with new ideas, new hopes, and new energies.

But if a nation's writings are the product of economic and social conditions, they will alter as those conditions alter—and *The Communist Manifesto* itself is clearly seen, by its authors, as a sign of the inevitability of change as well as a call to effect change:

> Does it require deep intuition to comprehend that man's ideas, views, and conceptions, in one word, man's consciousness, changes with every change in the conditions of his material existence, in his social relations and in his social life? What else does the history of ideas prove, than that intellectual production changes its character in proportion as material production is changed? The ruling ideas of each age have ever been the ideas of its ruling class.[16]

The Communist Manifesto, we must infer, heralds the coming change by its resolute adoption and proclamation of ideas which, its authors think, will become those of the proletariat, the ruling class of a future in which 'the free development of each' will be 'the condition for the free development of all'.

The passage about the relation of consciousness to material existence which I have just quoted has often been attacked, by non-Marxists, as bleakly deterministic. Yet as René Wellek has rightly pointed out, Marx's wording seems designed to obviate this charge. Consciousness, he avers, changes *with* the conditions of material existence. 'If', René Wellek comments, 'one interprets the word "with" freely, no complete economic determinism is yet proclaimed; the intellectual life of man changes *with* the transformation of economic order. A parallelism, an analogy is taught—not one-sided dependence.'[17]

Marx and Engels proclaim, in particular, one great change in literature; a change that Goethe had foreseen in his old age, when he looked at the way increase in international exchange of material goods was bringing related increase in intellectual and spiritual traffic and interchange. The old Goethe therefore spoke, more and more frequently, of 'world literature', *Weltliteratur.*[18] For Goethe, such 'world literature' did not imply an abandoning of national characteristics. On the contrary, each national literature would be valued by readers abroad for its distinctiveness and difference, for the special instrumental colour it added to the symphony of world literature. Through becoming conscious of the specific contributions of other nations and learning to value them, we would also learn to value our own. Our own literature, it is true, would to some extent

change its character through such contacts; but this would be an enrichment, and the resulting symbioses, like Goethe's own *West-Eastern Divan* and *Chinese-German Seasons and Times of Day,* would continue to bear the imprint of the specific national culture within which the foreign works had been received, as well as that of their authors' genius and individual bent.

Such a conception was clearly congenial to Marx and Engels, who had described in *The German Ideology* how one generation after another learnt to develop further the material wealth, capital, and forces of production it had inherited:

> In the course of this development, the circles which act upon one another expand—and the more they do this, the more the pristine isolation of individual nationalities is annihilated by perfected means of production, exchange and commerce [*Verkehr*] and a consequent division of labour between different nations, the more history becomes world history.[19]

The Communist Manifesto supplements this with speculations about the effect such developments will have on literature:

> The bourgeoisie has through its exploitation of the world market given a cosmopolitan character to production and consumption in every country. To the great chagrin of reactionaries, it has drawn from under the feet of industry the national ground on which it stood. All old-fashioned national industries have been destroyed or are daily being destroyed. They are dislodged by new industries, whose introduction becomes a life and death question for all civilized nations, by industries that no longer work up indigenous raw material, but raw material drawn from the remotest zones; industries whose products are consumed, not only at home, but in every quarter of the globe. In place of the old wants, satisfied by the production of the country, we find new wants, requiring for their satisfaction the products of distant lands and climes. In place of the old local and national seclusion and self-sufficiency, we have intercourse in every direction, universal interdependence of nations. And as in material, so also in intellectual production. The intellectual creations of individual nations become common property. National one-sidedness and narrow-mindedness become more and more impossible, and from the numerous national and local literatures there arises a world literature.[20]

What is chiefly remarkable about this passage, as about so many others in Marx's work, is the compliment it pays to the nineteenth-century bourgeoisie. Not for him the out-and-out anti-capitalism of the German Romantics, or of Thomas Carlyle—he never forgot the extent to which the order he wanted to overturn had in fact served the cause of progress. And what 'progress' meant in this context had once again been clearly spelt out in *The German Ideology,* where Marx and Engels had looked forward to a time when 'separate individuals will be liberated from the various national and local barriers, be brought into practical connection with the material and intellectual production of the whole world and be put into a position to acquire the capacity to enjoy this all-sided production of the whole earth (the creations of man)'.[21]

The Communist Manifesto goes on to consider the part a victorious working class would play in a process which affects literature along with all other spheres of life:

> National differences and antagonisms between peoples are daily more and more vanishing, owing to the development of the bourgeoisie, to freedom of commerce, to the world market, to uniformity in the mode of production and in the condition of life corresponding thereto.
>
> The supremacy of the proletariat will cause them to vanish still faster.[22]

It may well be thought that ***The Communist Manifesto*** does not, in this passage, make enough allowances for resistance to the trends it detected: national antagonisms and differences have not vanished as fast or as universally as the logic of production and commerce seemed to suggest. Marx came, in fact, to realize this and consistently distanced himself, in his later life, from would-be followers who underestimated the power of national feeling. In 1866 he ridiculed French delegates to a Council meeting of the First International for announcing 'that all nationalities and even nations were "antiquated prejudices"'. For these delegates, he added, 'negation of nationalities seemed to mean their absorption into the model French nation'. Later still he praised the Russian economist Flerovsky because he had 'a great feeling for national characteristics', and he took up the cause of the Irish as 'a national question'.[23]

The prophecy of ***The Communist Manifesto*** has not, however, gone wholly unfulfilled. We have seen, in this our twentieth century, a world-wide dissemination and mingling of 'national and local' literatures, through translations, paperbacks, theatre-tours, broadcasts, films, and television, which have transformed our cultural perspective in ways that would not have surprised Marx. 'World literature' has arrived with a vengeance—as a vast Imaginary Museum, as a great Library of Babel.

The Communist Manifesto is essentially a call to action. As such it commits itself, in the main, to what one might call a Dives and Lazarus view—or better, perhaps: a Master-Slave view—of modern society: the opposition of two classes, haves and have-nots, bourgeoisie and proletariat. But as a Polish scholar has pointed out,

> if all political or religious struggles are to be interpreted as class struggles, if we are to correlate the various literary and artistic trends with underlying class relations, if we are to look for a reflection of class interests and class prejudices in moral norms, then we must make use of a greater number of classes than the two basic ones in ***The Communist Manifesto***.[24]

This may help to explain why one can detect, in Marx's works, three-layered and other multi-layered models of class structure as well as the dichotomous one of the ***Mani-***

festo; and also, perhaps, why, when Marx at last addresses himself to a definition of 'class' in what was later to become volume III of ***Capital,*** his manuscript should so tantalizingly break off before the definition has properly begun.

What, then, of the intellectual, what of the artist, and his class-affiliations? Here we must remember what had been said about 'oppositional' writers and thinkers in ***The German Ideology.*** Such men, Marx and Engels had there suggested, can oppose dominant ideas because of the contradictions in society itself at any given moment. They can identify themselves with forces already at work in their society, or in similar societies beyond the frontiers of their own country; forces which are destined to change radically the socio-economic relations obtaining in a given society and hence, ultimately, to change intellectual and artistic life too. 'A portion of the bourgeoisie', we read, therefore, in ***The Communist Manifesto,*** 'goes over to the proletariat; in particular a portion of the bourgeois ideologists, who have raised themselves to the level of comprehending theoretically the historical movement as a whole.'[25] In this dynamic situation the bourgeois intellectual—whether as artist, as economist, or as historian—can free himself, through the exercise of his theoretical consciousness, from the shackles of the class to which he would seem to belong by birth and upbringing. ***The Communist Manifesto*** is clearly written from the point of view of men who think they have done just that; men who have constituted themselves champions of the proletariat and now address the bourgeoisie in that role:

> You are horrified at our intending to do away with private property. But in your existing society, private property is already done away with for nine-tenths of the population, its existence for the few is solely due to its non-existence in the hands of those nine-tenths. You reproach us, therefore, with intending to do away with a form of property the necessary condition for whose existence is the non-existence of any property for the immense majority of society. In one word, you reproach us with intending to do away with your property. Precisely so; that is just what we intend.

The famous last sentence of the ***Manifesto*** is the more dramatic because here, for the first time, the authors directly address *the proletariat* instead of the bourgeoisie.

The Communist Manifesto was based on a 'catechism' drafted by Engels—but its final redaction belongs entirely to Marx. A single page of the manuscript, preserved by chance, shows how much trouble he took over the filing and refining of its formulations; and an outline plan for section III demonstrates the careful attention he paid to coherent and ordered presentation of his case. To him, therefore, must go the credit for the lucid over-all structure of the ***Manifesto,*** for its clear exposition, its subtle changes of tone and perspective, its indignation and humour, its powerful imagery, its skilful deployment of revolutionary slogans,[26] and its use of a multitude of rhetorical devices not for their own sake, but for the sake of the social message that was to be conveyed. David McLellan has listed some of the devices Marx constantly used in his works, though not always with the appositeness and the success characteristic of their use in the **Manifesto**: 'climax, anaphora, parallelism, antithesis and chiasmus'. To this should be added the distinctive rhythm and word-music of the **Manifesto** in its original German. The opening lines afford as good an example as any with their tolling word-repetitions, their linking alliterations and assonances (some of which I have underlined below), and their effective pairing of less and less well-matched partners, first monosyllabic titles (*der Papst und der Zar*), then polysyllabic names with two main stresses separated by four slacks (*Metternich und Guizot*), and finally the more intricate rhythms of the last deliberately ill-matched pair (*französische Radikale und deutsche Polizisten*).

> Ein Gespenst geht um in Europa—das Gespenst des Kommunismus. Alle Mächte des alten Europa haben sich zu einer heiligen Hetzjagd gegen dieses Gespenst verbündet, der Papst und der Zar, Metternich und Guizot, französische Radikale und deutsche Polizisten.

> A spectre is haunting Europe—the spectre of Communism. All the powers of old Europe have entered into a holy alliance to track down and exorcise this spectre: Pope and Tsar, Metternich and Guizot, French radicals and German policemen.[27]

Marx did not always write with such distinction—but at his best he shows a command of didactic and polemical prose which assures his work a place in the history of German literature as well as in the history of ideas and political action. . . .

Notes

1. *BR* [*Selected Writings in Sociology and Social Philosophy*] 40.

2. From now on this work will be called by its better-known title: *The Communist Manifesto*.

3. *SW* [*Selected Works in Three Volumes*] I, 108; *MEW* [*Werke*] IV, 461.

4. *SW* I, 131; *MEW* IV, 486. Heine used the palimpsest image in *Die Harzreise* and *Französische Maler*. The image is not, however, an uncommon one.

5. *SW* I, 128; *MEW* IV, 483.

6. Even the famous phrase which concludes *The Communist Manifesto* may be an echo of Heine. In his essay on Ludwig Marcus (*Ludwig Marcus. Denkworte*) Heine had spoken 'of that fraternal union of the workers of all lands [*Verbrüderung der Arbeiter in allen Ländern*], of that wild army of the proletariat [*von dem wilden Heer des Proletariats*], which is bent on doing away with all concern about nationality in order to pursue a common purpose in Europe, to call into being a true democracy'. Cf. Dolf Sternberger, *Heinrich Heine und die Abschaffung der Sünde* (Hamburg and Düsseldorf, 1972), p. 360.

7. *SW* I, 113; *MEW* IV, 467.

8. *SW* I, 130; *MEW* IV, 484.

9. *SW* I, 127; *MEW* IV, 482-3.

10. *SW* I, 136; *MEW* IV, 491. Marx had mentioned Cabet's Utopian novel before—in the letters to Ruge published in *Deutsch-Französische Jahrbücher* (*MEW* I, 344).

11. *MEW* III, 507 ff.

12. *SW* I, 130-1; *MEW* IV, 485-6.

13. *SW* I, 111; *MEW* IV, 465.

14. *SW* I, 123; *MEW* IV, 477.

15. *SW* 132; *MEW* IV, 488.

16. *SW* I, 125; *MEW* IV, 480.

17. R. Wellek, *A History of Modern Criticism 1750-1950*, Vol. iii, p. 235.

18. Cf. F. Strich, *Goethe und die Weltliteratur* (Berne, 1946), pp. 13-103.

19. *MEW* III, 45.

20. *SW* I, 112; *MEW* IV, 466.

21. *GI* 55.

22. *SW* I, 124-5; *MEW* IV, 479.

23. Letters to Engels, 20 June 1866 and 12 Feb. 1870—*MEW* XXXI, 228-9 and XXXII, 443; to S. Meyer and A. Vogt, 9 Apr. 1870—*MEW* XXXII, 668.

24. S. Ossowski, *Class Structure in the Socialist Consciousness,* trans. S. Patterson (London, 1963), p. 88. It is not irrelevant to recall that Disraeli's *Sybil; or The Two Nations* had been published in 1845, and that a character in Heine's *William Ratcliff* had as early as 1822 divided mankind into two warring nations: the wellfed and the hungry.

25. *SW* I, 117; *MEW* IV, 471-2.

26. '*The Communist Manifesto* is almost an anthology of revolutionary rhetoric, and some of its most effective slogans are borrowed. Werner Sombart has shown that "The proletarians have nothing to lose but their chains" and "The workers have no country" are Marat's, and that "the exploitation of men by men" is from Bazard. The nexus of "cash payment" is Thomas Carlyle's, and had been quoted in Engels' *The Condition of the Working Class in England in 1844 . . .*' (S. E. Hyman, *The Tangled Bank* (1966 edn.), p. 100.)

27. *MEW* IV, 461. Cf. Pamela Hansford Johnson, 'The Literary Achievement of Marx', *The Modern Quarterly*, New Series, ii (1946-7), 240: 'This paragraph demonstrates two of his most notable stylistic traits. Firstly, the brief simple statement in the form of a metaphor, followed by a long and rolling sentence of

qualification. Secondly, the use of bathos, the sharply descending curve of glory from the Pope to the German police spy. Examples of bathetic irony abound throughout his work . . .'

List of Abbreviations

BR Karl Marx, *Selected Writings in Sociology and Social Philosophy,* ed. T. Bottomore and M. Rubel (Harmondsworth, 1963).

MEW Karl Marx, Friedrich Engels, *Werke.* Herausgegeben vom Institut für Marxismus-Leninismus beim ZK der SED (Berlin, 1956-68).

SW Karl Marx and Frederick Engels, *Selected Works in Three Volumes* (Moscow, 1969).

Rondel V. Davidson (essay date 1977)

SOURCE: Davidson, Rondel V. "Reform versus Revolution: Victor Considérant and the *Communist Manifesto.*" In *Karl Marx: "The Communist Manifesto,"* edited by Frederic L. Bender, pp. 93-104. New York: Peter Lang, 1988.

[*In the following essay, originally published in 1977, Davidson examines the influence Victor-Prosper Considérant's* Manifest de la démocratie pacifique *(1843) had on Marx and Engels' philosophy and their subsequent writing of the* Communist Manifesto. *The critic considers arguments that the* Communist Manifesto *is a mere translation of Considérant's work, and demonstrates where the two works are similar and where they are fundamentally different.*]

Despite voluminous publications relating to the development of Marxism, the specific origins of the **Communist Manifesto** remain subject to scholarly debate. One of the most important and unresolved controversies deals with the relationship between Marx and Engels' publication of 1848 and the French Fourierist, Victor-Prosper Considérant's *Manifeste de la démocratie pacifique,* originally published in 1843 as the introduction to his newspaper, *Démocratie pacifique,* and reissued in book form under the title, *Principes du socialisme, Manifeste de la démocratie au XIXe siècle,* in 1847. What little scholarship has been produced on this subject is extremely polemical, superficial and inconclusive. For a more acurate assessment of the contributions of Marx and, more particularly, of Considérant to nineteenth-century socialism, a comprehensive understanding of the connection between these two documents is imperative.[1]

Although several scholars have noted the relationship between Considérant's thought and that of Karl Marx, no one has made a thoroughgoing comparison of the two manifestoes. In an effort to discredit the communist movement, anti-Marxist writers have made much of the argument that Marx and Engels drew heavily from Con-

sidérant's manifesto. Writers such as Sorel (n.d.:32) and Cohen (1946:111) have accused Marx of plagiarizing from the *Manifeste de la démocratie pacifique,* and Brandes (1925:115) states in his biography of Ferdinand Lassalle that the **Communist Manifesto** is "almost a mere translation from Victor Considérant . . ."

The only serious attempt to analyze the two manifestoes was made by the Russian anarchist, W. Tcherkesoff. In *Pages of Socialist History* (1902:56-57), Tcherkesoff, referring to the first section of the *Manifeste de la démocratie pacifique,* declares, "In these fifty short pages the famous Fourierist, like a true master, gives us so many profound, clear and brilliant generalizations, that even an infinitesimal portion of his ideas contains in entirety all the Marxian laws and theories—including the famous concentration of capital and the whole of the *Manifesto of the Communist Party,*" and he concludes, "This 'Manifesto,' this Bible of legal revolutionary democracy, is a very mediocre paraphrase of numerous passages of the 'Manifesto' of V. Considérant." To prove this point, Tcherkesoff cites and compares numerous quotations from both documents which indeed reflect a striking similarity in both content and phraseology. Tcherkesoff, however, is guilty of utilizing a familiar technique of deceptive propaganda. He conveniently omits statements from both works which indicate substantial differences in the basic concepts of the two socialists. Partly because of its excessively polemical nature and partly because of its errors of omission, Tcherkesoff's work remains inconclusive and has received little recognition.

Pro-Marxist writers have responded to these charges of plagiarism by a rather effective ruse of their own—they have, by and large, ignored them. Most Marxian accounts of the development of the **Communist Manifesto** do not mention Victor Considérant. The only serious attempt by a pro-Marxist to counter these charges was made by Bernstein. Writing in *Science and Society,* Bernstein (1949:58-67) recognizes these allegations against Marx and simply declares that they are false. Without comparing the two documents or without indicating the contents of Considérant's manifesto, he proceeds to acclaim the originality and profundity of the Communist document. As with the anti-Marxist polemics, Bernstein's vague generalities prove of little value to the serious student of socialism.

Unfortunately, the most able scholars have passed over the opportunity to resolve this controversy. While briefly alluding to a possible connection between the two manifestoes, intellectual historians such as Barzun (1958:177), Lichtheim (1961:61-62), and Hammen (1969:171), in their otherwise brilliant and penetrating analysis of Marxism, refrain from describing the relationship. None of these writers makes any attempt to compare the two works or to indicate what Considérant's manifesto contains or how it might be considered a forerunner of the communist declaration. Their failure to clarify the problem has left a serious hiatus in the history of socialism.

It is certain that Marx and Engels were thoroughly familiar with the activities and writings of Victor Considérant.

Despite the fact that most United States' historians have inexplicably ignored Considérant's role in European history, he was one of the best known and most influential social critics of the period 1836-1849. After having obtained the rank of captain in the French army, he abandoned a secure military position for an uncertain career as a socialist writer and propagandist. As the leader of the Fourierist movement, Considérant, more than any other individual, popularized its ideas. He authored over 20 books, numerous pamphlets and essays, and edited three newspapers. His publications, particularly *Destinée sociale* (1836-1844) and the *Exposition abrégée du systéme phalanstérien de Fourier* (1845), brought Fourier's ambiguous and sometimes preposterous ideas out of obscurity, rationalized them and placed them before the public. Under Considérant's leadership, the *École societaire,* the official Fourierist society, organized branch societies in almost every major city in Europe and in the United States and disseminated propaganda throughout the world.

Considérant played a significant role in the French Revolution of 1848, serving the Second Republic in the Constitutional Assembly, the Luxemburg Commission, the Constitutional Committee, the Committee of Work and the National Assembly. As a result of his bitter opposition to the presidency of Louis Napoleon Bonaparte, Considérant was exiled from France in 1849. In 1855, he established an unsuccessful, although important, communal experiment near Dallas, Texas, known as *La Réunion.* When Napoleon III lifted the ban on him in 1869, Considérant returned to Paris where he lived the remainder of his life as a socialist sage of the Latin Quarter. He died in Paris in 1893, a citizen of the United States (Davidson, 1973:277-296; Bourgin, 1909:7-9, 121-125; Dommanget, 1929:167-214).

When Marx arrived in Paris in November 1843, Considérant and his numerous publications were as well known as those of Louis Blanc, Pierre-Joseph Proudhon, Louis-Auguste Blanqui, Etienne Cabet, and Ledru-Rollin. By mid-nineteenth century standards, Considérant's books and his newspapers were circulated widely. The *Manifeste de la démocratie pacifique* was probably a more influential document in socialist history prior to the 1870s than was the *Communist Manifesto.* In addition to its publication in newspaper form in 1843, Considérant's manifesto went through three editions in book form in Paris, two in 1847 and one in 1849, and it was published in Italy in 1894 (Bo, 1957:11-14).

Although Marx was anxious to contact Considérant on his first visit to the French capital, no relationship ever developed between the two. Arnold Ruge attempted to induce Considérant, along with several other Paris radicals and socialists, to collaborate with Marx in writing for their proposed German-French publication, *Deutsche-Französische Jahrbücher.* Considérant refused any contact with the German radicals. He apparently did not know, in 1843, who Marx was, and he was unwilling to associate himself with the revolutionary image of Ruge. There is no evidence to indicate that Marx and Considérant ever met during any of Marx's visits to Paris. Moreover, the voluminous letters and manuscripts of both men which have been preserved indicate that the two never corresponded with each other. Although Considérant ("Correspondances," 1826-1893) did join the First International in 1871, he never considered it a Marxist organization, and he had no contact with the Marxist members.

What relationship existed between Marx and Considérant was theoretical and confined specifically to the impact of Considérant's writings on the development of Marx's thinking during the formative years of 1843-49. By their own admissions, Marx and Engels were thoroughly familiar with Considérant's writings, particularly his newspaper and the *Manifeste de la démocratie pacifique.* In fact, the two communists frequently indicated their respect and preference for the Fourierist critique of contemporary society (*Rheinische Zeitung,* 1841-1842). This affinity is particularly evident in Engels' unpublished essay, **"A Fragment from Fourier on Trade."**

The **Communist Manifesto** clearly demonstrates Considérant's influence on Marx and Engels' thinking. The charge of plagiarism stems from the similarity between the two manifestoes concerning their analysis of nineteenth-century society in general and capitalism in particular. In this regard, the *Manifeste de la démocratie pacifique* definitely foreshadows the **Communist Manifesto.** Throughout Marx and Engels' declaration, the rhetoric parallels Considérant's. Such words as "class struggle," "class war," "feudal lords," "oppressed proletariat," and "exploitation" appear profusely in both documents. In a few places, whole sentences demonstrate a striking similarity. For example, in the Fourierist manifesto Considérant (1847:10-11) stated, "Society tends to split more and more distinctly into two great classes: a small number possessing all or nearly all the domain of property, of commerce and of industry; and the great numbers possessing nothing, living in absolute collective dependence on the holders of capital and the machines of work, compelled to hire out for an uncertain salary and always losing their power, their talents, and their forces to the feudal lords of modern society." In the declaration of 1848, Marx and Engels (1964:3) proclaimed, "Society as a whole is more and more splitting up into two great hostile camps, into two great classes directly facing each other—bourgeoisie and proletariat." Regarding the development of economic imperialism Considérant (1847:22-23) declared, "Industrial nations try mightily to obtain foreign markets for their manufactured goods. England, tormented by overproduction of goods, makes superhuman efforts to pour her products over all the earth. She breaks open by cannon shot the closed doors of the Chinese Empire. She incessantly crosses the globe with arms in hand demanding consumers." And in the **Communist Manifesto** (1964:7), one reads, "The need of a constantly expanding market for products chases the bourgeoisie over the whole surface of the globe. . . . The cheap prices of its commodities are the heavy artillery with which it batters down all Chinese walls, with which it forces the barbarians' intensely obstinate hatred of foreigners to capitulate." Regarding the affinity of rhetoric it is interesting to note that Considérant (1847:45-46) used the term "communism" with the exact same meaning as did Marx and Engels. Apparently, the two adopted the term as Considérant had defined it in the Fourierist declaration. In the *Manifeste de la démocratie pacifique,* Considérant attacked those he termed as "Political Communists" for attempting to dupe the proletariat into establishing "Egalitarian Communalism" and for propounding the destruction of private property through revolution and force.

In addition to phraseology, Considérant pointed to the same societal defects as did Marx and Engels. In fact, Considérant's attack on nineteenth-century capitalism is a more comprehensive analysis. According to Considérant (1847:1-2), the past was characterized by the exploitation of one class at the expense of another. In ancient society the free men oppressed the slaves, and in the feudal society, the nobility "trampled under foot" the peasants and serfs. The French Revolution of 1789 supposedly established freedom and equality by destroying the old order, by proclaiming equality before the law, and by creating a system of political democracy through various forms of representative government. But, as Considérant (1847:4-6) argued, the Revolution only destroyed the old order; it did nothing to organize and guarantee the principles of equality and democracy which it theoretically proclaimed. In reality, the Revolution of 1789 was a destructive force which replaced an old form of feudalism with a "new feudalism." The new feudalism created a different, but no less powerful and oppressive aristocracy based upon capital and not land.

Under the mask of protecting individual freedoms, the systems of laissez-faire economics and free enterprise forced the masses of working people into abject slavery. In Considérant's opinion, the term free enterprise was an insidious catch phrase which had been utilized by one class of people to subjugate another class. He argued that economic anarchy was as bad as political anarchy. Under the prevailing system of "anarchical competition" and "blind warfare," a few individuals possessed all the advantages, capital, education, talent, and powerful positions in society. The proletariat, the most numerous class, could not possibly compete on an equal basis with the upper classes because they had no capital, no education, and no opportunity to develop their skills. Thus, he concluded, "The system can lead to nothing but general bondage, the collective infeudation of the masses who are destitute of capital, of the instruments of work, of education, and of industrial arms, to the endowed and well-armed capitalist class."

According to the Fourierist, the system not only enslaved the lower class, but it progressively increased their misery. Unregulated capitalism produced a process of triple competition which resulted in the continual depreciation of workers' salaries. Competition between entrepreneurs for markets motivated them to lower prices and this, in turn,

forced them to lower salaries. Because the ranks of the proletariat were rapidly increasing, competition between workers for jobs forced them to agree to work for lower wages. Finally, scientific and technological advances forced the worker to compete with machines for employment. These three forms of rivalry placed the worker in a defenseless position (Considérant 1847:8-9).

The proletariat was not the only class which suffered from anarchical competition. Considérant (1847:9-10) was one of the first nineteenth-century writers to sound the alarm for the middle class. According to him, the large entrepreneurs "sucked up" and "progressively crushed" small and middle-sized industry, commerce, and agriculture. At the present rate of attrition, the middle class would soon be reduced to the position of proletariat and would disappear from the social and economic scene.

With the exploitation and decline of both the lower and middle classes, the system of unlimited competition led directly to the establishment of monopolies. Considérant (1847:11) declared, "Our system of free enterprise is a colossal mechanism of enormous power, which incessantly sucks up the national riches to concentrate them in the great reservoirs of the new aristocracy and which creates the starving legions of the poor and the proletarian." Moreover, this development of monopolies created serious economic and political problems. The consolidation of wealth, both in terms of capital and land, established a "vicious circle" which would stop the flow of products and result in economic chaos and instability. Because only a few controlled the money, the masses, whose salaries continually depreciated, were unable to purchase all the goods. The outcome was overproduction followed by economic depression. He (1847:23) argued, "The most civilized nations collapse under the deadly weight of overproduction, and the legion of workers, falsely stripped of purchasing power by the conditions of their salary, cannot participate in the consummation of this exorbitant production: Is it not logical that this inhuman industrial regime which threatens fatal ruin to the consumers and which so miserably remunerates the workers destroys itself by closing all markets and channels of consummation?"

In addition to economic instability, the system produced two alarming political consequences. First, the concentration of wealth in the hands of a few resulted in the "infeudation of the government to the new aristocracy." With economic power came political domination. In Considérant's mind, it did not matter what political system prevailed in what country; they all succumbed to economic domination. The "financial barons" controlled the king in France, the czar in Russia, and the Parliament in England. Even in the United States, which was so proud of its democracy, the economic giants had subjugated the Congress (Considérant 1847:12-13, 42, 70-71). Second, the free enterprise system, with its overproduction and cyclic tendencies, led directly to economic imperialism. Because of the masses' deficient purchasing power, capitalist countries sought colonial empires as an outlet for their goods. Often this frantic search resulted in the use of force and imperialistic war. Again, the political structure made no difference. England, supposedly the most liberal and democratic of the European nations, most vigorously pursued the subjugation of foreign peoples for the purpose of economic domination (Considérant 1847:23-24).

The defects and inequities in the social and economic structure above delineated, created a "social hell" characterized by the division of classes into two warring camps. Considérant's manifesto (1847:20) is profuse with statements such as, "The capitalist and the workers are in flagrant warfare. The workshop of production, of distribution, and of remuneration is nothing but an eternal battlefield." But the deplorable conditions of the majority of people in Europe could not continue indefinitely. Considérant argued that the masses would not starve while the "financial lords" amassed great wealth. If reform did not come, violent revolution would erupt between the haves and have nots. As he put it, "If the wisest minds in the governments, the intelligent and liberal bourgeoisie, science, and technology do not perceive this problem, it is certain that the movement which is dominating European societies [laissez-faire capitalism] will lead directly to social revolution, and we will march to a European Jacquerie" (Considérant 1847:13-14).

Anyone familiar with the *Communist Manifesto* can see that the above summary of the critique of laissez-faire capitalism found in the *Manifeste de la démocratie pacifique* could almost serve as a résumé of "Part I" of the communist declaration. Indeed, recent scholarship has emphasized the diverse French origins of many of the ideas expressed in the communist document. But most of these writers have concluded that Marx and Engels made an important contribution by drawing a proliferation of concepts together from numerous sources and synthesizing them in their manifesto.[2] It must be stated categorically, however, that Considérant's publication synthesized and lucidly expressed all of Marx and Engels' critical interpretations of nineteenth-century society several years before the publication of the *Communist Manifesto.* As demonstrated, the basic components of the Marxian analysis of unregulated capitalism—the growth of monopolies, the concentration of wealth, the political preponderance of big business, the exploitation of the proletarian masses, the destruction of the middle class, class antagonism, over-production, cyclical tendencies in the national economy, economic imperialism, and the historical development of classes based on economic conflicts of production, an idea Marx considered as one of his most original and important contributions—are enunciated with much detail and clarity in the *Manifeste de la démocratie pacifique*—in fact he expressed most of the concepts in various other writings as early as 1832. See, for example, Considérant (1832; 1835).

Although both manifestoes attacked the social and economic structure with an almost identical analysis and both demanded a complete reorganization of society, the similarity ends at that point. Anyone who reads the two docu-

ments in their entirety will note that following the criticism of capitalism Marx and Considérant went their separate ways. In terms of both the model social structure and the methods to be employed to establish their utopian societies, the two documents differ markedly. Regarding the means to the ends, a fundamental and significant conflict must be noted between the two declarations. Marx and Engels looked to class war and revolution to overturn the prevailing system. Moreover, they viewed the proletarian revolution as inevitable and as historically determined by economic forces.[3] Although Considérant recognized the possibility of such a conflict and even predicted civil war if reform did not come, he rejected revolution as a solution. As a pacifist, Considérant denounced all forms of violence and war. More important, he believed that revolution simply replaced one form of tyranny with another. The Revolution of 1789 provided the best example. As a result of that conflagration, the capitalistic class had replaced the old feudal nobility as the masters and oppressors of society. In Considérant's mind, future revolutions would be no better, as he (1847:21) declared, "When a class of people make a revolution for the purpose of redistributing the wealth, and when they are victorious, they do not share their spoils. They pursue the conquered and take everything."

Fundamental to this disagreement over revolution and the use of force was a difference between Considérant's and Marx's attitude toward the proletariat. Although Considérant's clearly defined the class conflict as an historical development, he did not consider class struggle as inevitable or as an instrument for social progress. He consistently rejected the Marxian appeal to only one class. Although the Fourierist program called for total amelioration of the destitute position of the working people, Considérant (1847:24, 51-53) viewed the inequities of nineteenth-century society as a threat to all classes, and in his manifesto he petitioned all elements of society to support a reform program for the lower ranks of society. As with the use of force, he argued that any program appealing to only one class would increase class antagonism and hatred and could never create a harmonious society.

Considérant's concept of democracy reflects his aversion to revolution and class dictatorship. In explaining why he chose the term "Peaceful Democracy" for the title of the manifesto and for the title of his newspaper, he warned that various revolutionary groups were perverting the concept of democracy. Because of the growing popularity of the term democracy, particularly among the lower classes, radical parties were seizing the term and using it as "a flag of revolution and war." Considérant (1847:60-62, 67) argued that true democracy could never be based on the use of force; democracy and coercion were antithetical. Democracy must be based on "intellectual combat" as opposed to force, because "martial arms" could never destroy ideas. Democracy, as he indicated, implied the organization and guarantee of political, social, and economic freedom and equality of opportunity for all classes, not just the proletariat. In his mind, any democratic structure must be based upon the voluntary and peaceful reorganization of society, and the majority must never be allowed to crush the minority.

Marx clearly understood this intrinsic conflict between his concept of revolution and Considérant's attitude of peaceful democracy. Attempting to negate the influence of those advocating class amelioration by satirizing their views, Marx and Engels (1964:58) declared, "They, the followers of Fourier, Saint Simon, and Owen, endeavor, therefore, and that consistently, to deaden the class struggle and to reconcile the class antagonisms. They still dream of experimental realization of their social Utopias, of founding isolated 'phalansteres,' of establishing 'home colonies,' of setting up a 'Little Icaria,' duodecimo editions of the New Jerusalem, and to realize all these castles in the air, they are compelled to appeal to the feelings and purses of the bourgeoisie." Although Marx and Engels were ridiculing the Fourierists, Considérant would not have objected to the basic premise of the above quotation, only to its tone.

Finally, regarding the ultimate, perfect society, the manifestoes differ on many points. It is somewhat true, as Lansac (1926), and others have noted, that there are similarities between Marx's communal structure and the Fourierist phalanstery. When Marx and Engels (1964:33-41, 62) called for an international movement based upon "the union and agreement of democratic parties of all countries" and the abolition of nationalism, the "centralization of the means of communications and transportation in the hands of the state," the "establishment of industrial armies," the "combination of agriculture and manufacturing industries," the "gradual abolition of the distinction between town and country," "free education for all children in public schools," "the combination of education with industrial production," and the political, economic and social emancipation of women, they were reiterating programs which Considérant (1836; 1840; 1842; 1844; 1847), and others, had been advocating for several years. In a more general sense, both Marx and Considérant sought to create a social and economic structure which would effect a compromise between individual needs and aspirations and the needs of society as a whole. Particularly, both hoped to create a social structure which would allow the individual to act in his own best interest and to be able to do so without adversely affecting others in society. And it is interesting that Marx and Engels (1964:41) referred to their proposed social structure as "an association in which the free development of each is the condition for the free development of all." As every social and political activist of the 1848 period understood, the term *association,* made popular earlier by the Saint-Simonians, belonged to the Fourierist domain. When Considérant and a few of his colleagues founded the Fourierist movement in 1832, they selected the name *École sociétaire* (Association School) for their official organization, and the Fourierists always referred to their phalanstery as an association in which individual activities would improve society (Considérant 1847:20-22).

Despite these specific and general parallels in their proposed social organizations, Considérant and Marx differed significantly in their concepts of an association. These fundamental contradictions are clearly demonstrated in the two manifestoes. Marx and Engels (1964:25-31, 62) in adopting the labor theory of value, proposed the establishment of a totally equalitarian society based upon the complete abolition of private property and private capital. Considérant never accepted the labor theory of value nor the concept of equalitarian communalism. In fact, Considérant, or Fourier for that matter, should not even be classified as a socialist, at least not in the pure definition of socialism. In the *Manifeste de la démocratie pacifique* and in other writings, Considérant rejected the idea of totally abolishing private capital and private property holding. He argued that the development of property holding was a civilizing and essentially historical development which was now impossible to destroy. He declared that "the sentiment of property is a formal element of human individuality," and that it would be dangerous and impossible to destroy the individual drive to collect personal wealth through property and capital. Rather than abolish private wealth, Considérant declared, "On the contrary, it is a question of finding and establishing the most perfect, the most secure, the most free, the most mobile, and, at the same time, the most social forms of property holding by harmonizing the individual interests with the general interests. It is necessary to unite property, not by promiscuous and egalitarian communalism, confused and barbaric, but by the *Hierarchical Association,* a voluntary and intelligent combination of all individual property" (Considérant 1847:45).

Considérant viewed the association as an arrangement whereby private property and capital would be united with labor. His communal structure depended on the investment of private capital and property. The phalanstery would serve simply as the tenant, and remuneration would be based upon the input of capital and labor. For the practical application of this principle, Considérant abolished salaries in the association and devised an elaborate system of dividends, the rudiments of which were first propounded by Fourier, which would be distributed to all participants in proportion to the amounts of capital, labor, and talent contributed by each. Considérant's concept of talent included not only managerial skills, as has been assumed by some students of Fourierism, but included any particular proficiency which added measurably to the wealth of the commune. Annually, the value of all production would be divided, three twelfths for skill, four twelfths for capital, and five twelfths for labor. Thus, the Fourierist association provided, not for the abolition of property and capital and the completely equal distribution of wealth, but for a combination of capital value and labor value based on a more equitable relationship than presently existed under laissez-faire capitalism. It is significant to note, however, that labor would receive a slightly higher share of the profits than capital in Considérant's system.

The preceding comparison of the ideas expressed in the **Communist Manifesto** and in the *Manifeste de la dé-*

mocratie pacifique, thus, demonstrates a similarity in some areas but a marked divergence in others. With regard to critical analysis of laissez-faire capitalism, Considérant clearly predates Marx. Whether or not Marx and Engels lifted ideas from Considérant's document, it is certain that they were familiar with the *Manifeste de la démocratie pacifique,* that it influenced their thinking both positively and negatively, and, concerning the critique of society, Marx had nothing new to add.

Concerning methods, solutions, and proposed social structures, however, the two documents are profoundly antithetical. The claim that the **Communist Manifesto** is "almost a mere translation of Victor Considérant," is a distortion of the facts. All three writers, Marx, Engels, and Considérant, would have rejected such an interpretation. History must continue to recognize Marx, for better or for worse, as the prime popularizer of the ideas of the proletarian revolution and dictatorship. Conversely, historical scholarship needs to accord Victor Considérant a more significant role for his early synthesis of unregulated capitalism and for his proposals for a more equitable social structure based upon a voluntary and democratic association of capital and labor.

Notes

1. Although Marx expressed many of the ideas found in the *Communist Manifesto* in earlier writings, particularly his and Engels' *The Holy Family* (1845), and *Poverty of Philosophy* (1847), none of these works predates the first publication of Considérant's manifesto in August, 1843. Since the *Communist Manifesto* represents a more comprehensive and a more thoroughly developed expression of Marx's concepts than these earlier writings, this essay will focus its analysis on the manifesto of 1848. Also, in frequently referring to Marx and his contributions in this article, I do not intend to neglect Engels and his important role in drafting the *Communist Manifesto*. Of particular significance is Engels' unpublished essay of 1847, "Principles of Communism," which the two used as a starting point for their manifesto of 1848. Although certainly a coincidence, it is interesting to note that Engels drafted this document while he was in Paris at almost the same time Considérant's manifesto appeared in book form under the similar title, *Principes du socialisme.*

2. In a weak moment, Marx himself admitted that he borrowed many of the ideas found in the *Communist Manifesto* in a now famous letter to Joseph Weydemeyer, March 5, 1852. It is also important to note that numerous other writers had been or were attacking laissez-faire capitalism in a similar vein, most notably Sismondi and Proudhon. But none of their expositions on society compares so closely with Marx as does Considérant's manifesto.

3. For interpretations of Marx's concept of revolution, see Tucker (1970), Schaff (1973), and Hook (1973).

Works Cited

Barzun, J. *Darwin, Marx, Wagner: Critique of a Heritage.* Garden City: Doubleday and Company, 1958.

Bernstein, S. "From Utopianism to Marx," *Science and Society* 14.1 Winter 1949-50: 58-67.

Bo, D. D. *Charles Fourier e le Scuola Societaire.* Milan: Feltrinelli Editore, 1957.

Bourgin, H. *Victor Considérant, son oeuvre.* Lyons: Imprimeries réunies, 1909.

Brandes, G. *Ferdinand Lassalle.* New York: Bernard G. Richards Co., 1925.

Cohen, M. R. *The Faith of a Liberal.* New York: Henry Holt and Co., 1946.

Considérant, V. "La Civilisation ruinant ses pauvres," *Phalanstère* (Paris, 1832) 2.25-27.

———. *Destinée sociale.* Paris: Bureau de La Phalange, 1835.

———. *Nécessité d'une dernière débâcle politique en France.* Paris: Librairie phalanstérienne, 1836.

———. *De la politique générale et du rôle de la France en Europe.* Paris: Bureau de La Phalange, 1840.

———. *Bases de la politique positive, Manifeste de l'École sociétaire.* Paris: Librairie phalanstérienne, 1842.

———. *Chemins de fer.* Paris: Librairie sociétaire, 1844.

———. *Principes du socialisme, Manifeste de la démocratie au XIXe siècle.* Paris: Librairie phalanstérienne, 1847.

———. *Le Socialisme devant le vieux monde ou le vivant devant les morts.* Paris: Librairie phalanstérienne, 1849.

Davidson, R. V. "Victor Considérant and the Failure of La Réunion." *Southwestern Historical Quarterly* 76.3 (January 1973): 277-96.

Dommanget, M. *Victor Considérant, sa vie, son oeuvre.* Paris: Éditions sociales internationales, 1929.

Hammen, O. J. *The Red '48ers: Karl Marx and Friedrich Engels.* New York: Charles Scribner's Sons, 1969.

Hook, Sidney. "Myth and Fact in the Marxist Theory of Revolution and Violence," *Journal of the History of Ideas* 34.2 (April-June, 1973): 263-80.

Lansac, M. *Les conceptions méthodologiques et sociales de Charles Fourier.* Paris: Librairie philosophique de J. Vrin, 1926.

"Les Correspondances de Victor Considérant." 1826-1893. Housed in the Archives Nationales (Paris).

Lichtheim, G. *Marxism: An Historical and Critical Study.* New York: Praeger Publishers, 1961.

Marx, K. and Engels, F. *The Communist Manifesto.* Ed. Paul M. Sweezy and Leo Huberman. New York: Monthly Review Press, 1964.

Rheinische Zeitung. 1841-1842. (Cologne).

Schaff, Adam. "Marxist Theory on Revolution and Violence," *Journal of the History of Ideas* 34.2 (April-June, 1973): 263-80.

Sorel, G. *La décomposition du Marxisme.* Paris: Alcan, n.d.

Tcherkesoff, W. *Pages of Socialist History: Teaching and Acts of Social Democracy.* New York: C. B. Cooper, 1902.

Tucker, Robert C. *The Marxian Revolutionary Idea.* New York: W. W. Norton & Co., 1970.

Donald Clark Hodges (essay date 1999)

SOURCE: Hodges, Donald Clark. "Conclusion: Assessing the *Manifesto*." In *The Literate Communist: 150 Years of "The Communist Manifesto,"* pp. 185-98. New York: Peter Lang, 1999.

[*In the following excerpt, Hodges looks at the* Communist Manifesto*'s literary and religious tradition, and its importance to Russia in the late nineteenth century. He also follows its influence into the twentieth century as it affected the Russian revolution, the rise of Soviet power, and the subsequent fall of the Communist bloc.*]

> The *Manifesto* of Marx and Engels begins with the balance sheet of historical evolution at the threshold of the crucial year 1848. A new balance sheet is called for today.
>
> Lucien Laurat, *Le Manifeste communiste de 1848 et le monde d'adjourd'hui* (1948)

How has the *Manifesto* stood the test of time? As Engels proudly observed, "the history of the *Manifesto* reflects, to a great extent, the history of the modern working class movement." Besides hope for the toiling masses—albeit a false hope—he believed that it had opened their eyes to the reality underlying the surface of modern society. *Would that it were so!*

Looking backward, one is struck by two sides to the *Manifesto*'s ledger. On one side, it appealed to workers and intellectuals alike, as the German Social Democratic and the Bolshevik parties gained adherents. On the other side, its popularity was ephemeral, as seen by the loss of interest in the *Manifesto* after these parties enjoyed their stint in power.

After 150 years of the *Manifesto,* its eclipse stares us in the face. Neither the humanist highroad nor the egalitarian low road to communism turned out to be passable. There is, however, a third communist alternative—an expanding public sector of free goods and services—a pacifier of the discontented and a sanctuary for the insecure.

For almost a century and a half, the *Manifesto* has been the centerpiece of communist ideology, the leading manual of international communism. It still ranks as one of the modern world's most consequential political documents. It helped to establish the first mass-based socialist parties in the 1860s and 1870s, and it paved the way to the 1917 Bolshevik Revolution. As one of America's leading historians notes, "the Russian Revolution . . . [was] arguably the most important event of the century," while its repercussions "would be felt in every corner of the globe."[1] If the Russian Revolution was that important, then no less consequential was the *Communist Manifesto* that fueled it.

The *Manifesto*'s invaluable service to the communist movement was to transform it from a sect into the secular equivalent of a church, a worldwide mass movement whose only rivals in greatness, numbers of adherents, and geographical expansion were Islam and Christianity. Just as St. Paul's Christology helped to sanitize the spiritualized communism of Jesus and the Apostles, so Marx's humanism helped to defang the secular communism of Babeuf, Buonarroti, Blanqui, and their disciples. And as Christianity took the heart out of the messianic doctrine of the carpenter from Nazareth, so Marxism toned down the revolutionary communism of Blanqui's German followers with the socialist humanism of the *Manifesto.*

If communist extremists were ever to join forces with trade unionists in struggles for the workers' daily bread, it was necessary for communists to moderate their demands. Wrote Kautsky in the first major updating of the *Manifesto, The Class Struggle* (1892), an exposition of the Erfurt Program of German Social Democracy: "In their [Marx and Engels'] *Communist Manifesto* . . . they laid the scientific foundation of modern socialism. They transformed the beautiful dreams of well-meaning enthusiasts into the goal of a great and earnest struggle."[2]

As a public relations coup, the *Manifesto* was a success; like the religious faiths it resembled, it came to mean all things to all men. It thus offers a prime illustration of Machiavelli's dictum that "the great majority of mankind are satisfied with appearances."[3] Bakunin's and Lenin's readings of the *Manifesto* made a brief for relentless class struggle, but its humanist and demoliberal readings justified Khrushchev's reforms and Gorbachev's perestroika, leading to the eventual breakup of the Soviet Union.

The *Manifesto* was meant to be open-ended, to be continually revised in response to economic changes and the appearance of new political forces. Yet in 1872 Marx and Engels decided it was a "historical document which we have no longer any right to alter." So their amendments to it were not incorporated into the text. It was superseded in 1891 by the Erfurt Program of German Social Democracy and again in 1919 by the program of the Communist Party of the Soviet Union. But German Social Democrats and Russian Communists could not agree on whether the Russian Revolution was a bastard or a "legitimate child of *The Communist Manifesto.*" If illegitimate, then the *Manifesto* did not represent a rupture with the liberal democratic tradition in the West; otherwise it did.[4]

Wherever Socialist and Communist parties have contended for power, the *Manifesto* has outshone all rivals on the Left. But once entrenched, those parties favored their own manuals of revolution at the *Manifesto*'s expense. Paradoxically, the *Manifesto*'s eclipse is correlated rather with the strength than with the weakness of the parties it represented.

Before the turn of the century there had been more German editions than English and French ones combined. Between the time of the first Russian translation in 1869 and half a century later in 1919, however, there were more than twice as many editions in the former Czarist Empire and its Soviet successor than in Germany during the same period. The *Manifesto* topped its original record of six German editions in 1848 on at least three occasions. In 1899 and again in 1905 and 1917, the number of new Russian editions reached two digits.[5] For the most backward and despotic regime in all of Europe was on the eve of a combined liberal-democratic revolution that would soon match the Great French Revolution of 1789.

It is hardly surprising that both 1905 and 1917 saw the publication of a record number of editions. The first Russian revolution occurred in 1905. Although it failed, it was followed by a second, this time successful, revolution in February 1917 and by the Bolshevik seizure of power eight months later.

But why was the *Manifesto* such a big hit in 1899? That was the year of the first student general strike. Despite its innocent origins, that strike came under the leadership of an "organizing committee"—militants of the new Russian Social-Democratic Labor party founded in 1898. The student strike has been aptly described as the "prelude to the Russian Revolution."[6] Thanks to the work of the "organizing committee," Russia's restive students and burgeoning intellectuals began rallying behind the *Communist Manifesto.*

The high point in the *Manifesto*'s reception was reached in 1905-1906, and that point was nearly attained again in 1917-1918. Then the *Manifesto* began facing stiff competition from N. Bukharin and E. Preobrazhensky's *The ABC of Communism*—a commentary on the Communist party's new 1919 program. A few years later, in his bid for power after Lenin's premature death in 1924, Stalin published his best-selling *Foundations of Leninism,* which soon overtook the *Manifesto* in total sales.

Stalin's book reigned supreme until 1938, when it was displaced by the *History of the Communist Party of the Soviet Union (Short Course),* drafted by a commission of the Party's Central Committee under Stalin's active supervision. As many as twelve million copies of the Russian edition and another two million in the other languages of the Soviet Union were initially published in October. A decade later, some two hundred editions had appeared in more than sixty languages, amounting to some thirty-four million copies. The distribution of the *Short Course* so

dwarfed the circulation of the *Communist Manifesto* that at the Party's Eighteenth Congress in March 1939, Stalin's presumptive heir, Andre Zhdanov, announced that "since the inception of Marxism, no Marxist book has ever had such wide circulation."[7]

The *Manifesto* would never recover from this literary coup. Two decades later it was again overshadowed, this time by the *Short Course*'s successor, *Fundamentals of Marxism-Leninism.* Under the general editorship of Otto V. Kuusinen, the new manual responded to the Bolshevik party's change of line beginning with the Twentieth Party Congress in 1956. When the first edition was followed in 1963 by a second revised edition, the *Manifesto* continued to lose ground.

The successive revisions and adaptations of the *Manifesto* point to failures as well as successes on the part of those who attempted to translate its precepts into practice. When the Communist League in 1852 and the International Working Men's Association in 1872 failed to live up to the *Manifesto*'s program and strategy, Marx scuttled both organizations. When the Socialist International during World War I refused to implement the 1912 Basel Manifesto's reaffirmation of the *Manifesto*'s opposition to national wars and imperialism, it too fell apart. Lenin founded the Communist International in 1919 with the aim of implementing the *Manifesto*'s program, but Stalin dissolved it during World War II under pressure from the Soviet Union's Western allies—when it, too, was no longer an asset to socialism but a liability.

Contrary to expectations, socialism made the *Manifesto*'s communism increasingly irrelevant. The *Manifesto* was a huge success as a socialist manifesto. But the hopes raised by Stalin's second Bolshevik Revolution were dashed when Khrushchev's communism failed to deliver the goods, when Gorbachev's humanism proved to be a mirage, and when Soviet citizens regretfully concluded that socialism had not lived up to its promises. So the *Manifesto* had outlived its usefulness, save for the boondocks and backwaters of world civilization.

During the Bolshevik struggle for power, the *Manifesto* provided the rationale for a grand alliance of workers, peasants, and petty bourgeois toward the ultimate conquest of the state. But once in power, the alliance dissolved. The same *Manifesto* that had furthered the unified and concerted action of the parties of discontent became a cause of dissension. Universal self-development was supposed to flourish with the extension of civil liberties to all, followed by the institution of universal suffrage and the replacement of private property in the means of production by collective ownership. But socialism under Bolshevik leadership began by trashing the humanist and demoliberal legacies and then reviving them. In effect, a Leninist revolution built the Soviet Union, and a Marxist counterrevolution destroyed it. The *Manifesto* cut both ways.

Lenin placed a lid on humanism and its demoliberal offspring by giving precedence to uncivil "Reds" over civil "Pinks," by loosening the reins on equalizing tendencies, and by attempting to build socialism and communism simultaneously instead of sequentially. Stalin succeeded in abolishing capitalism and fulfilling the promise of socialism in the Soviet Union, but at the same time offered nominal support to humanism, liberalism, and democracy. Khrushchev's new program gave a major impetus to humanism, liberalism, and democracy, but prepared the ground for Gorbachev's betrayal that nullified communism altogether.

Such was the logic of unintended consequences that took its toll *beginning* with Khrushchev's and *ending* with Gorbachev's phoney communism. In both instances the contradiction between personal and collective fulfillment was resolved by the path of least resistance. By then the *Manifesto* had lost most of its appeal. Although Khrushchev made one last effort to salvage it, Gorbachev looked to the Western legal tradition for inspiration.

We have seen that the *Manifesto* is not just a communist manifesto; it can be read as a humanist, demoliberal, technocratic, and socialist manifesto, and as a set of guidelines to a future anarchism. By preserving part of this ideological heritage, the *Manifesto* effectively compromised its goal of communist revolution.

In view of the foregoing, is it feasible to rewrite the *Manifesto,* to revive its ailing body? Or should one give it a decent burial? Bernstein claimed that neither the Marxist building nor its scaffolding was any longer salvageable. More recently, Lucien Laurat notes that it is time "to oppose [to Paleomarxism] a new synthesis embodying the scientific socialism of our times . . . [since a] new balance sheet is called for today." But if Laurat is correct in claiming that the managerial elites share power with the capitalists, then his updating of the *Manifesto*'s socialist program would tend to play into the hands of Bakunin's nonmanagerial elites.[8]

The Achilles heel of the *Manifesto* was its assimilation of the so-called progressive ideologies that competed with communism—the humanist credo of the supreme worth of the individual, the demoliberal legacy of civil rights and majority rule, the technocratic utopia of salvation through scientific and material progress, and the socialist class struggle against the bourgeoisie. This constellation of social preferences virtually defines modernism in political philosophy.

The *Manifesto*'s communism is obsolete because of its modernist premises. Unrestrained economic growth on behalf of universal self-cultivation leads up a blind alley. More work implies less leisure for those on the industrial treadmill. Technocracy represents a threat to communism, because the producers of the economic surplus can be made to produce more when the screws are tightened, not loosened. To push at once for optimum economic growth and for the abolition of exploitation is to push in opposing directions. Thus far, the former push has been the more forceful; for the latter requires immense outlays for welfare and education that cut into the reserves set aside for research and development. The *Manifesto,* however, suggests we can have the best of both possible worlds!

The multiplication of needs in response to increasing wealth means that the more one gets, the more one wants. That is not to say that the *Manifesto* favors consumption for its own sake. Marx's humanism makes a brief for high-quality over low-quality consumption, the enjoyment of music, art, and literature rather than the enjoyment of material possessions. But he set no limit to the educational treadmill other than the vacuous condition that the free development of each must be compatible with the free development of all. Why vacuous? Because "free development" opens the door to privileged shares in the economic surplus needed to defray the higher costs of a liberal arts education at its higher levels.

The *Manifesto*'s cult of self-development claims to be universally applicable. To become fully literate in the arts and sciences, however, their devotees must become industrially exempt and give priority to what is higher instead of lower on the scale of being. Lenin loved the theater, according to his wife Krupskaya, but he was driven to sacrifice the liberal arts for the sake of ordinary literacy. His urge for personal fulfillment did not stop him from trying to close down the pride and joy of Russia's intellectual and artistic circles—the Bolshoi Theater. As he instructed Vyasechslav Molotov: "I propose the Politburo issue the following orders . . . keep just a few dozen artistes for Moscow and Peter[sburg] to perform (as singers and dancers on a self-financing basis), that is, avoid any large expenditure on scenery. . . . Give not less than half the billions thus saved for the liquidation of illiteracy and [for] reading rooms." As one hostile critic observed, "a lowering of the nation's intellect would be the price for raising the general population's awareness."[9]

Although the *Manifesto*'s goal of free development is utopian, it can be achieved on a limited scale. For those unwilling to wait for communism prior to their own emancipation, however, humanism becomes a sanction for egoism under conditions of exploitation. It is this humanist-sanctioned selfishness that communists find intolerable. The *Manifesto*'s slogan, "The proletarians have nothing to lose but their chains," is a communist slogan, but it hardly fits the *Manifesto*'s goal of the free development of all.[10]

The vicious side of humanism has been traditionally concealed by a veil of hypocrisy. Britain's governing classes, according to Bernard Shaw, consist of "people who, though perfectly prepared to be generous, humane, cultured, philanthropic, public spirited and personally charming, are nonetheless unalterably resolved to have money enough for a handsome and delicate life." For that purpose they will "batten in the doors of their fellow-men, sweat them in fetid dens, shoot, stab, hang, imprison, sink, burn and destroy them in the name of law and order . . . for a sufficient income is indispensable to the practice of virtue."[11]

Marx's claim to fame was that he made communism credible. Instead of Babeuf's "principle of equalization" to be achieved by leveling downward, he proposed to raise ordinary workers to the status of a literate communist like himself. He believed that self-cultivation, a patrician ideal, was what every proletarian secretly wanted.

This is what theologians mean by original sin. In the Biblical account of the fall, Eve is tempted to eat of the forbidden fruit because of the serpent's prodding. Lucifer, the Light-Bearer, assures her that her eyes will be opened, that she will become wise like the gods (Gen. 3:4-6). Eve then shares the fruit with Adam. Did Lucifer lie? On the contrary, God confirms the serpent's words: "Behold, the man has become as one of us" (Gen. 3:22). But as punishment for aspiring to divine heights, they must thereafter suffer the consequences by being driven from paradise.

Man's fate, according to Milton, is to aspire to a higher form of life, to human self-fulfillment, not just to knowledge of good and evil. But "This higher degree of life . . . cannot be but to be Gods, or Angels, [i.e.] Demigods."[12] For Milton, paradise is lost because Adam and Eve want to be more than merely human, to be superman and superwoman—a godlike condition with a style of life inaccessible to the immense, underlying population. But like Icarus in the Greek myth, when they fly too close to the sun, the wax melts on their wings and they plunge to their death in the sea. For man's cardinal sin, no less than Lucifer's, is to set himself in glory above his peers.

Renaissance man claimed nothing less. Castiglione's "Courtier" not only was a perfect horseman for every saddle, but also "set all his delights and diligence to wade in everie thing a little farther than other men." To what purpose? For the sake of excellence. Socrates' lover, the great Alcibiades, "excelled . . . everie man in the thing that he had most skill in. So shall this our Courtier passe other men, and everie man in his owne profession."[13]

This Renaissance credo is thinly disguised in Marx's celebrated *Manifesto*: "In place of the old bourgeois society . . . we shall have an association in which the free development of each is the condition for the free development of all"—a condition at the opposite extremity from "universal asceticism and social leveling in its crudest form." But how in this world of irremediable scarcity is the multiplication and refinement of one person's needs to be prevented from infringing on the needs of others?

Milton was right. Humanism is the offspring of presumption and self-adulation compounded by the most insidious and unrestrained selfishness. It is but a short distance from "Man is the measure of all things" to the tempting but deceptive conclusion that, since I am a man, "I am the measure of all things." Remember Faust! There is no more a limit to the craving for knowledge—the apple of discord—than there is to the desire for money or other tangible assets needed for fulfillment. In the Marx-Engels correspondence between 1844 and 1855, one finds references to the great literary figures of both the ancient and modern worlds, but not a single line on Milton. Evidently, the father of literate communists had not studied Milton; or, if he had, he found nothing in Milton's work worth citing.

Like wealth, knowledge is a form of power. Wrote Mencius (390-305 BC): "There are those who use their minds and there are those who use their muscles. The former rule; the latter are ruled. Those who rule are supported by those who are ruled."[14] Evidently, nothing has changed in this respect some 2,300 years later! There's *progress* for you!

For Marx, man's goal is to become rich in needs rather than rich in the sense of wealthy, as if money were not a condition of both. It is clear from his early writings that a mature communism aims to sever the link between cultivation of the personality and the accumulation of material wealth. It is unrealistic, however, to believe that riches, and therefore freedom from time-consuming cares and the burdens and frustrations of everyday life, are *not* conditions of human excellence. Although one can enjoy music, art, and literature without "owning" them, ownership is a mighty boon to enjoying them.

Like precious jewels, books filled with knowledge do not come cheaply. What the ancient Cynic, Lucian of Samosata (ca. 125-180 AD), said about luxuries that have become necessities applies to books as well as to jewels: "All that costly array of means of enjoyment which you so gloat over is obtained only . . . through how many men's blood and death and ruin. To bring these things to you many seamen must perish; to find and fashion them many laborers must endure misery."[15]

No wonder that the pampered will be punished—if only in the hereafter! With 2,000 years of hindsight and another 2,000 years of foresight, Lucian spelled out what they deserved. "Whereas many lawless deeds are done in life by the rich who plunder and oppress and in every way humiliate the poor: Be it resolved by the Senate and people [of Hades] that when they [the pampered] die . . . their souls be sent back into life and enter into donkeys until they have passed two hundred and fifty thousand years in the said condition, transmigrating from donkey to donkey, bearing burdens and being driven by the poor." *There's* a communist for you—with a vengeance![16]

Louis-Ferdinand Céline, the French misanthrope and cynic, was not one to take the doctrine of original sin and divine punishment as sacred truth. But he astutely recognized its usefulness in unmasking Marx and the Marxists' humanist hoax. At least the Church says we are inherently vile and acquisitive, unlike Marxists who believe in human perfectibility and a classless society. The one good thing about Christianity, he told his Soviet hosts in 1936, is that it acknowledges human beings to be the greatest scum on earth. But Marxist humanists have the gall to dress up a turd and call it a caramel.[17]

Marx objected to communism for being crude and ascetic. But precisely those features define its perennial nature. The ideas of equality, sharing, and caring owe their existence to a memory of what used to be, "a small voice left over from our kindergarten experience, a sort of super ego or conscience . . . to a memory buried deep in the primitive brain, a memory of things past when sharing and loving were much more in vogue than in contemporary life." At the dawn of civilization, people who were barely human learned to survive through solidarity and group action, through what Kropotkin called "mutual aid." Primitive communism is a "natural phenomenon in the sense that the sharing, equality, and caring which characterized it flowed out of the extended family network on which the tribe was based."[18]

However, primitive or fraternal communism is irretrievably naïve. It demands more of both workers and their leaders than either is prepared to deliver. To expect leaders of a Marxist party to risk their necks in a struggle from which they would not emerge as beneficiaries is to expect too much. To suppose that a Marxist party in power would act on the few hints of communism in the *Manifesto* is tantamount to "expecting the Catholic Church to preach and practice the tenets of primitive communism held by the first Christian communities."[19]

Pre-Marxist communism suffers from an ascetic virus and the voluntarist foible of believing in a "new man" capable of renouncing the good things of life, in a "new era" to be ushered in by acts of heroism and the sheer discipline of will. Experience shows that it, too, is slated for defeat, not just from without but also from within. Since subtracting from human needs is as self-destructive as multiplying them, communism is the loser either way.

The vain and interminable search for individual happiness, according to Céline, is the bête noire of communism. "That's what makes life so difficult! What makes people so poisonous, disgusting, intolerable. . . . It's out of happy people that the best damned are made!" A genuine communism, he believed, would not sacrifice the spirit of fraternity to the selfish pursuit of personal well-being—especially since one cannot honestly have both. "Communism, above all, is much more the sharing of all troubles than the sharing of wealth." But it demands also that wealth be shared, really shared, instead of the socialist principle of rewarding each according to his work. "I'm all in favor, me, of sharing! I've never wanted anything else! There! My four halfpennies on the table! . . . I'll put all I have on the table. If there's a *total* share-out." But that is not what the masses want.[20]

The typical proletarian, says Céline, is infected with ambition. He emulates his social betters. The most ardent working-class militant "has about as much desire to share with his luckless brother worker as has the winner in the national lottery." One becomes a communist not only out of self-interest, but also because of deep feelings for others. Communists are born, not made. "Communism is a quality of the soul. A spiritual state which can't be acquired." As he lays down the conditions of his egalitarian and ascetic—but also eminently aesthetic—communism: "Income . . . to be based on what is necessary to provide for the basic needs of each human being, and *not* on the

kind of work performed *nor* on the degree of responsibility." In this way the absence of differences due to unequal incomes would make possible the total reform of the nation, as a "*family* whose members care for one another."[21]

By appealing to human selfishness and by relying on material instead of moral incentives to get workers to produce more, Céline concludes, Soviet communism was a monstrous imposture. But are ordinary people as yet ready for communism? On the contrary, they are too depraved to appreciate it. No matter! "What is attractive in communism, its great advantage if truth be told, is that it sets out to unmask man at last." Like the Fathers of the Church, it promises happiness not in this world, but in the New Jerusalem that never arrives. It tells us that original sin is not a myth, that man is basically a rat. As in George Orwell's *1984,* in a real pinch most people will betray their closest friends. "Do it to Julia! Not me!"[22]

Céline offers no hope for humankind. But is such an ultra-degree of cynicism warranted? We have seen that the Scylla and Charybdis of modern communism are respectively its sectarianism and its ecumenicism—the pre-Marxist legacy and Marx's revision of this legacy in the *Manifesto.* It would be stretching credibility to claim that either one is feasible. But like Odysseus, cannot communists steer a middle course between the wreckage on both shores?

Indeed, traces of a third communist project may be found in the *Manifesto.* As Marx interpreted the *Manifesto*'s "Communistic abolition of buying and selling," the cooperative economy that replaces capitalism includes—besides the exchange of goods for labor certificates that do not circulate and therefore do not function as money—a welfare sector for the common satisfaction of needs, such as schools, health care, and relief for those unable to work. In the lower stage of communism the exchange sector prevails in matters of distribution; but with the progress of industry and the overcoming of scarcity the sector of free goods and services expands until it becomes the dominant sector. Hence, "To each according to his needs"![23]

The *Manifesto*'s transitional program favors a "community of goods" to be achieved in conjunction with income redistribution. It combines upward and downward leveling through a set of halfway measures, including gradual socialization, the restriction of wage labor, the application of rents to public purposes, a progressive income tax, and the abolition of the right of inheritance. Having ridiculed the identification of communism with Babeuf's Republic of Equals and the placing of the principal stress on equality, Marx's communist alternative was to raise the welfare sector to the leading position in the cooperative economy.

The future of communism and the future of welfare *are* thus closely connected. Escalating pressures from below combined with grudging concessions from above have made welfare the least objectionable road to social peace. Since "all modern market economies are to some degree welfare economies,"[24] the *Manifesto*'s prognosis of a future communism has borne fruit without, as well as with, the direct intervention of Communist parties.

The modern Welfare State first took root in Marx's Germany. The term "Wohlfahrsstaat" was coined by journalists to describe Bismarck's comprehensive program of workers' insurance against sickness and accidents in a series of laws in 1883, 1884, and 1885; and another in 1889 insuring the aged and disabled. "Bismarck, the revolutionary against his will," wrote Engels, became the first European statesman to introduce "Staatssozialismus" (State Socialism)—later, a model for every other country in Europe.[25]

What led to this startling innovation? In order to curb the growing influence of German Socialists under the influence of the revived 1848 *Manifesto,* Bismarck relied on the age-old strategy of the carrot and the stick. The stick was the Anti-Socialist Law (1878-1890); the carrot was the Welfare State. As the Iron Chancellor declared in 1884, "assure him [the workingman] of care when he is sick and maintenance when he is old . . . *then* if the state will show a little more Christian solicitude for him, the Socialists will sing their songs in vain."[26]

Welfare communism is defined by a sector of free goods and services either completely or partially subsidized by the state. With the emergence of strong Labor and Social Democratic parties in the early twentieth century, public welfare made impressive gains in Germany, Austria, France, the United Kingdom, the British Dominions, and Scandinavia. In response to the worldwide depression of the 1930s, World War II, and the postwar economic boom, the United States and the other market economies in Europe developed similar but more modest welfare programs.

Welfare communism also had a counterpart in the former Soviet Union and in Eastern Europe, and in still larger measure in both China and Cuba during the 1960s. In both countries efforts were made to bridge the gap between Marx's lower and higher stages of communism by reducing wage differences and by gradually withdrawing goods from commercial circulation.[27]

Contrary to popular belief, communism is not just an ideal, myth, utopia, ideology, political movement, or any combination of these. Although no longer a "historical movement going on under our very eyes," communism is a fact of life common to all contemporary societies. As a spin-off of the *Manifesto*'s communism, it has become feasible in miniature—especially when the sector of subsidized goods is not acknowledged as communist.

Although whittled down and partly scuttled in the new Russia and in Eastern Europe under post-Communist rule, welfare communism is here to stay. However, welfare has an underside; it is not what it appears. It leaves intact the social status of Mister Drudge Forlyfe, Esquire. First, it is a token communism—like "Bread and Circuses" in the ancient world—marginal to and overshadowed by the private and public sectors where buying and selling are the rule. Second, it is a communism that has passed its zenith, that is currently eroding under pressure from the technocrats concerned with making their firms and national economies "competitive." Third, it is a Machiavellian device for managing social unrest, for preventing social explosions under both late capitalist and postcapitalist conditions, "a political response to political disorder." That is the *sinister* reality of communist welfare—a device for regulating the poor.[28] Thus the welfare carrot serves the interests of old and new masters, not just working stiffs.

Far from attaining the final abolition of buying and selling, the *Manifesto* has to its credit only socialism and welfare in small and easily digested doses. Socialism was no ordinary achievement. But was exploitation abolished—other than capitalist-induced misery? On the contrary, the *Manifesto* contributed to making revolutions, but the exploited and oppressed got only a token share of the benefits.

For the semiprivileged but exploited workers—those earning more than the minimum but less than the average wage—conditions have markedly improved. On this score, Céline is mistaken. But for those at the bottom of the social pit, Céline is right. For the Lazarus-layers of society there are only degrees of Hell.

When not inventing heavenly kingdoms, people fabricate earthly substitutes. The various forms of communism are witness to this extravagant levity among communist thinkers. After 150 years of trial, the *Manifesto*'s communism is in agony almost everywhere. Yet it would be hazardous to predict the long-range outcome. The communist phoenix does more than self-destruct; it has a two-thousand-year history of rising from the ashes.[29]

Notes

1. Richard Pipes, *The Russian Revolution* (New York: Vintage, 1991), xxi.

2. Karl Kautsky, *The Class Struggle (Erfurt Program),* trans. W. E. Bahn (New York: Norton, 1971; orig. pub. 1892), 199.

3. Machiavelli, *The Prince* and *The Discourses,* 182; from *The Discourses,* 1:25.

4. Marx and Engels, "Preface to the German Edition of 1872," in Bender, 44; and Harrington, "The Democratic Essence of Socialism," in Bender, 109.

5. Bert Andréas, *Le Manifeste Communiste de Marx et Engels* (Milan: Feltrinelli, 1963), Appendix: Tableaux Synchronoptique (1848-1919), 380-382.

6. Pipes, *The Russian Revolution,* 6-7.

7. Paulo Spriano, *Stalin and the European Communists,* trans. Jon Rothschild (London: Verso, 1985), 79, 80.

8. Laurat, "If One Were to Rewrite the *Communist Manifesto* Today," in Bender, 146, 147.

9. Volkogonov, *Lenin,* 356, 357.

10. See my *Socialist Humanism: The Outcome of Classical European Morality* (St. Louis: Warren H. Green, 1974), 281-315, 330-337.

11. George Bernard Shaw, "Preface" to *The Irrational Knot,* in *The Works of Bernard Shaw* (London: Constable, 1930-38). Cited by Paul A. Hunwert, *Bernard Shaw's Marxian Romance* (Lincoln: University of Nebraska Press, 1973), 10.

12. John Milton, *Paradise Lost,* ed. Merritt Y. Hughes (New York: Odyssey, 1935), 9:934-937.

13. Ibid., 1:39; and Castiglione, *The Book of the Courtier,* 41.

14. John M. and Patricia Koller, *A Sourcebook in Asian Philosophy* (New York: Macmillan, 1991), 483.

15. Lucian of Samosata, "Cynicus," as cited by Farrand Sayre, ed., *Diogenes of Sinope* (Baltimore, MD: J. H. Furst, 1938), 8.

16. Lucian of Samosata, "A Journey to Hades," as cited by John Jay Chapman, ed., *Lucian, Plato and Greek Morals* (Boston: Houghton Mifflin, 1931), 334. For a contemporary equivalent of this communist transmigration of souls, see Hodges, *Sandino's Communism,* 126-140, 182-186.

17. Cited by Florence King, *With Charity Toward None: A Fond Look at Misanthropy* (New York: St. Martin's Press, 1992), 131.

18. James R. Ozinga, *The Recurring Dream of Equality: Communal Sharing and Communism Throughout History* (Lanham/New York/London: University Press of America, 1996), 1-2. See Piotr Kropotkin, *Mutual Aid, A Factor of Evolution* (London: William Heinemann, 1915), 11-62.

19. Nomad, *Rebels and Renegades,* 119.

20. Merlin Thomas, *Louis Ferdinand Céline* (London/Boston: Faber & Faber, 1979), 126, 127, 140. Cited from Céline's pamphlet, *Mea Culpa* (1936), and *Bagatelles pour un massacre* (1937).

21. Ibid., 157 and 169. From Céline's *L'Ecole des cadavres* (1938).

22. Ibid., 125-126. From Céline's pamphlet *Mea Culpa*; and George Orwell, *1984* (New York: Signet, 1950), 197, 215, 218.

23. Marx, "Critique of the Gotha Programme," *Selected Works,* 2:22-24.

24. George N. Halm, *Economic Systems: A Comparative Analysis,* rev. ed. (New York: Holt, Rinehart and Winston, 1961), 270-271.

25. See Engels' letters of 23 April and 13 November 1885 in Marx and Engels, *Selected Correspondence,* 460, 464.

26. Cited by Walter Phelps Hall and William Stearns Davis, *The Course of European History Since Waterloo,* 4th ed. (New York: Appleton-Century-Crofts, 1957), 310.

27. On the guiding principles and prospects of these Communist "heresies," see Donald C. Hodges, *The Bureaucratization of Socialism* (Amherst: University of Massachusetts Press, 1981), 155-160, 163-168, 168-173.

28. Frances Fox Piven and Richard A. Cloward, *Regulating the Poor: The Functions of Public Welfare* (New York: Pantheon, 1971), 3-8, 104-111, 196-198; and Hodges, *America's New Economic Order,* 154-163.

29. A revival of interest in the Manifesto occurred in anticipation of its 150th anniversary. See Karl Marx, *The Communist Manifesto,* Introd. by Mick Hume (Chicago: Pluto Press, 1996); K. Marx and F. Engels, *The Communist Manifesto,* Introd. by A. J. P. Taylor (Harmondsworth: Penguin, 1997); Karl Marx, *The Communist Manifesto,* Introd. by Eric Hobsbawm (London: Verso, 1998); and Mark Cowling, ed., *The Communist Manifesto: New Interpretations,* trans. Terrell Carver (New York: New York University Press, 1998).

Aijaz Ahmad (essay date 1999)

SOURCE: Ahmad, Aijaz. "The *Communist Manifesto* in Its Own Time, And in Ours." In *A World to Win: Essays on the "The Communist Manifesto,"* edited by Prakash Karat, pp. 14-47. New Delhi: LeftWord Books, 1999.

[*In the following essay, Ahmad looks at the* Communist Manifesto *as both Marx's first mature work and a transitional text in the development of his philosophy. The critic also examines the* Manifesto's *conception of the bourgeoisie and the Marxist perspective on the laws of history.*]

It is said that the Bible and the Quran are the only two books that have been printed in more editions and disseminated more widely than **The Communist Manifesto.** This brief and terse text thus has a pre-eminent position in the entire history of secular literature. Some sense of the breadth of its influence can be gauged from the fact that some 544 editions are known to have been published in 35 languages—all of them European languages, one might add—even prior to the Bolshevik Revolution; there must have been during that same period other editions which are not known, and infinitely greater number of editions were to be published, in very many more languages, European and non-European, *after* the Revolution of 1917. It is worth emphasizing, furthermore, that, unlike the two religious books that are said to have had a wider circulation, the **Manifesto** is barely one hundred and fifty years old: rather a young text, all things considered. It is much too early to fully assess the influence this young little pamphlet has had in the past and is likely to have in the future.

One can also say without fear of refutation that the ***Manifesto*** has been more consequential in the actual making of the modern world than any other piece of political writing, be it Rousseau's *Social Contract,* the American Constitution and the Bill of Rights, or the French 'Declaration of the Rights of Man and the Citizen'. The first reason is of course the power of its political message which has reverberated throughout the world and determined the destinies of a large cross-section of humanity over the past one hundred and fifty years. Then there is the style itself: no call to arms has ever been phrased in a language of such zest, beauty and purity. Third, there is the stunning combination of diagnosis and prediction. Marx describes the capitalism of his own times and predicts its trajectories into the indefinite future with such force and accuracy that every subsequent generation, in various parts of the world, has seen in the ***Manifesto*** the image of its own times and premonition of the horrors yet to come. And, fourth, concealed in the direct simplicity of its prose, like the labour of the tailor that disappears into the coat,[1] is the *distillation* of a multifaceted philosophical understanding that had arisen out of a series of confrontations with the thinkers most influential in the Germany of his times: Hegel, Feuerbach, Proudhon, Stirner, Bruno Bauer, Sismondi, the 'True Socialists' and the all the rest whom the authors of the ***Manifesto*** broadly describe as 'would-be universal reformers'.[2]

Much of the richness of the ***Manifesto*** is owed to the fact that it is the text of an intellectual and political transition. Marx alone—and then, increasingly, Marx and Engels together—had written so very much before coming to draft the ***Manifesto*** that one now quite forgets how very young (not quite thirty years old) he really was. This is the first *mature* text of a very young man. So, it *concludes* certain lines of argument Marx had been developing previously—in his first significant text, ***Critique of Hegel's Doctrine of the State*** and **"A Contribution to the Critique of Hegel's Philosophy of Right: An Introduction"**; and then in **"The Jewish Question"**, the *Economic and Philosophical Manuscripts* (also knows as **"Paris Manuscripts"**), the famous **"Theses on Feuerbach"**, and *The German Ideology.* Of these, Marx published only the *Critique* and 'The Jewish Question' in his own lifetime; the rest were drafted mainly for self-clarification and were then 'abandoned'—in the famous self-ironical phrase about *The German Ideology*—'to the gnawing criticism of mice'. These texts, together with *The Holy Family, The Poverty of Philosophy,* and a number of minor essays of that time serve both as a prelude to the formulations that are so familiar to us now from the ***Manifesto,*** but also as a series of confrontations with the most influential tendencies in the Philosophy, Economics and Political Thought that were central to the intellectual universe within which Marx had first learned to think. They are, in short, oppositional texts, texts in which Marx stutters and stammers, refuses other people's thoughts, tries to think his own thoughts and define his own premises, tries to come out from under the whole weight of that immensely powerful body of thought that has come down to us under the labels

of the Enlightenment, post-Enlightenment, Romanticism, Anarchism, utopian socialism, not to speak of the discourse of Rights and the fetishization of the market and the State.

Those earlier texts include passages and entire sections of great originality. However, virtually all of them are written in opposition to some particular writers or tendencies, i.e., Hegel and the others we have mentioned above. This kind of focussed criticism is continued in the latter section of the ***Manifesto*** as well, but the memorable first part can be viewed as perhaps the first of Marx's texts that is written entirely in the declarative, in opposition to not this or that thinker, this or that tendency in thought, but in opposition to bourgeois society as a whole. It is a text written at the end of a difficult apprenticeship, so as to scatter the spectres that had haunted European thought until that time and to define a new kind of relationship between political economy, history and philosophy, with the ambition of *realizing* the aims of philosophy through a double movement. This double movement consisted, on the one hand, of a theory of history which makes concrete the intellectual project of philosophy by explaining the fundamental motion of the material world in its generality—what postmodernism these days dismisses as a 'modes of production narrative'. But, on the other hand, it also demanded from philosophy that its ethical project be materialized as the *praxis* of a revolutionary transformation of an ethically intolerable world—what postmodernism now dismisses as 'the myth of Progress'.

Marx's mature studies of the world economy in general, and of the principles of capitalist economy in particular, belong of course to the period after the composition of the ***Manifesto.*** The engagement had begun much earlier, however, as we see in the systematic and constantly improving expositions of the subject in *The Economic and Philosophical Manuscripts* and *The German Ideology* which he did not publish in his own lifetime, as well as *The Poverty of Philosophy* which he did. A principle that had struck him quite early was that the rate and quantum of historical change in the forces and relations of production was much quicker under capitalism, and tended to get even quicker in each successive phase, as compared to antecedent modes of production where changes in the relations of production remained relatively limited and the pace of technological change relatively very slow; not 'unchanging' as he sometimes hastily said, but on the whole glacially slow. As a fundamental methodological principle, then, Marx adopted the view that it is impossible to grasp the essence of capitalism if we were to study it as a static reality, or mainly as it quite evidently is at a given time. Rather, the pace of change within this mode of production required that it be studied as a *process,* whose past had to be understood historically and whose future trajectory could be deduced from its past and present with reasonable degree of accuracy, not in all details but in its overall structure. This explains why the pic-

Karl Marx, 1818-1883.

ture that the **Manifesto** presents of capitalism tells us so little about how capitalism was in his own time, and tells much more of how it had been and how it was likely to unfold.

Even so, within the larger corpus of Marx's work the **Manifesto** cannot be regarded as a text of some final illumination. As was said above, it is a *transitional* text, the *first* mature text of a very young man. It not only transits from earlier texts but also gropes toward those more comprehensive studies that were to follow over the next many years. The range of that corpus is breathtaking. Three preoccupations were paramount in that whole range of work, however. There was, first, the effort to offer the most incisive, most detailed account of the capitalist mode of production as such: the first principles and the first premises for an account of the modern world as a whole, from the standpoint of labour, production and the struggle of classes. The massive **Grundrisse,** which too Marx drafted only for self-clarification, in 1857-58, and of course the three volumes of **Capital** and **Theories of Surplus Value** are the key texts of that historic project. Second, there was extensive engagement with the history and politics of his own time as these unfolded all around him; among numerous such texts, **"The Class Struggle in France",** first published as a series of articles in 1850, and **"The Eighteenth Brumaire of Louis Bonaparte",** composed two years

later as yet another series of articles, are the most magisterial. Rarely, if ever, has journalism risen to such heights of analytic and theoretical grandeur. Finally, there are equally numerous writings of Marx as a militant of the labour movement, most famously the **"Critique of the Gotha Program"** which he drafted almost thirty years after the **Manifesto,** in the wake of the experience of the Paris Commune and, thanks to that experience, directly concerned, in whatever preliminary fashion, with what a Communist society of the future may in broad outline strive to be. All three preoccupations of later life—the history and political economy of capitalism as a whole; contemporary politics of the ruling classes; the premises of the labour movement—are foreshadowed in the **Manifesto** itself. If it refines the general statement of the materialist conception of history as it had been defined up to **The German Ideology,** its thrust toward a theory of the political economy of capitalism would be immeasurably improved by the time Marx came to write **Capital.** It is on the basis of this whole edifice, with the **Manifesto** serving as a beam in the middle, that later masters of Marxism, such as Lenin and Rosa Luxemburg, were to make seminal contribution to the Marxist theory in general as well as to a fuller understanding of their own time, notably on the issue of imperialism and the actual strategy and tactics of the labour movement.

APPROACHES TO THE *MANIFESTO*

There are many ways of looking at the **Manifesto.** Each one of its significant proposition had received detailed, though sometimes less rigorous, treatment in the earlier texts and was to surface again, often in very much more precise and enriched forms, in later writings. The pithy characterization of the state executive as 'the managing committee of the whole bourgeoisie', for example, would be understood in a much more nuanced and dialectical fashion if we were to read it in the perspective of the far more detailed treatment of the subject in the earlier **Critique of Hegel's Doctrine of the State** and **"The Jewish Question"** and the later, maturer **"The Eighteenth Brumaire".** Similarly, the cryptic comment on the nature of consciousness in Section Two—'Does it require deep intuition to comprehend that man's ideas, views and conceptions, in one word, man's consciousness, changes with every change in the conditions of his material existence, in his social relations and in his social life'—can be usefully compared with the sharper formulation of twelve years later, in the 'Preface' to **The Critique of Political Economy**: 'It is not the consciousness of men that determines their existence, but, on the contrary, it is their social existence that determines their consciousness'. Indeed, this had been a constant theme in Marx's writing after he had developed his own critique of Hegel's idealism soon after finishing his university education. But our understanding of these very condensed formulations can be vastly enriched through a reading of **The German Ideology** where Marx makes the fundamental point that *all* consciousness is intrinsically class consciousness in the sense that all consciousness is *formed* within class society, from the moment of birth onward, so that one may have the consciousness of the class into which one is born or one may adopt the consciousness of some other class (e.g., a proletarian internalizing a consciousness propagated by the capitalist system) but there is no such thing as a *class-less consciousness.* Antonio Gramsci was to make much of this insight, for example, arguing that since one imbibes one's consciousness from different and conflicting segments of society, individual consciousness is necessarily a contradictory and incoherent consciousness which can be made coherent only through great effort of education, reflection and practical interaction with others who are comrades in the same struggle. A reading of this kind, where elements of the thought expressed in the *Manifesto* are systematically related to the more detailed exposition of those same elements in other, earlier and later texts of Marx, as well as to the thought of later Marxists, is perhaps the most fruitful way of approaching the *Manifesto.* In itself, individual sentences in the text can mislead as to what Marx thought on the subject.

Or, one can read the *Manifesto* as a text of its own time. For all its timeless grasp of the fundamental premises of capitalist society, it is also a text very much of its time, i.e. of the working class movement living with a great sense of urgency because all could see that a great revolutionary upheaval was fast approaching in which the proletariat would be necessarily involved, so that the correct political standpoint was a matter not only of the long future but of the very palpable present. And, indeed, the first edition of the *Manifesto* was published in London weeks before the revolution of 1848 broke out in Paris and spread like wildfire through what today would be known as thirteen different countries in Europe. It was expected, as undoubtedly happened, that the urban proletariat would provide the bulk of the revolutionary mass, and the *Manifesto* was very much a call for the international class *unity* and political self-organization and *autonomy* of the proletariat, across the diverse countries, in a way that the proletariat had not been united in independent action in the previous revolutionary upheavals. Programmatic statements like 'The Communists do not form a separate party opposed to other working class parties' would be opaque to today's reader without grasping that (a) the Communist League was so small an organization that an attempt to convert it into a political party in today's sense would have been futile and sectarian at best; (b) that the various segments of the working class were deeply fragmented along the ideological lines that are dealt with in Section III so that ideological struggle against those other tendencies was perceived as being a precondition for the subsequent formation of the 'party of the whole'; (c) that most European countries at the time had nothing resembling a constitutional, representative government, so that the unity not only of different sections of the politically active proletariat but also of what in Section IV are described as 'democratic parties' was seen as a precondition for a successful revolutionary offensive;[3] and (d) that the formulation is directly connected with the central emphasis on the unity of the class as a whole, which was then reflected with the call to arms with which the text concludes: 'Workers of the World, Unite!'[4]

One could also read the *Manifesto,* especially Section I, purely from the philosophical point of view. It is well to recall that Marx's original training, and a very rigorous training at that, was in philosophy. He was deeply steeped in the thought of Spinoza, Kant, and Hegel, not to speak of scores of lesser philosophers such as Feurbach who had been at the time very influential among German youth, especially in contestation with the thought of Hegel. At every step in his philosophy of history Marx is engaged with various aspect of Hegel's thought. His conception of the proletarian consciousness as the 'true' consciousness, for example, is directly in line with the Master-Slave dialectic in Hegel's *Phenomenology* where Hegel argues that the slave always knows more about himself *as well as the Master,* hence about society as a whole, because he needs to know not only about himself but also the whole condition of his enslavement, including specially the character and conduct of the master, whereas the master need know nothing about the slave more than that the latter labours for him.

By contrast, Marx's theory of the state as inevitably the instrument of the ruling class is counterposed directly against Hegel's view of the state as a superior, disinterested mechanism for reconciling antagonisms in civil society—indeed, Marx's theory of the State, which is stated so economically in the *Manifesto,* arose initially out of his close, critical, passage-by-passage reading of Hegel when he was still a student. One could go even further and argue that it was his rejection of the Hegelian concept of the state as the highest form of social synthesis, and his theoretical discovery that the state exists not as a resolution of social conflicts but as a precise *expression* of those conflicts, which eventually led him to posit the theory of class struggle itself, i.e., the idea that class conflict is the most fundamental conflict in any society and that no state authority can be neutral in, or suspended above, this conflict. This Marx had first argued philosophically, while settling his accounts with Hegel, well before he set out to prove the thesis empirically, through a careful study of the laws of political economy.

In another direction, his sweeping denunciation of commerce as being a mechanism of conquest and exploitation of the dominated peoples and regions is counterposed directly against Kant's view of commerce as an instrument of peaceful exchange and friendship among nations. One could offer many more such examples of his engagements with philosophical masters of the past, in a wide range of philosophical discourses from political theory to ontology. The main point here, however, is that just as Marx was to later become a master of political economy essentially by formulating an unassailable critique of political economy, he was already launched, well before drafting the *Manifesto,* on a critique of philosophy so fundamental and extensive that Balibar, the contemporary French philosopher, has called it an 'anti-philosophy'.[5] Marx was determined, in other words, never to become a philosopher in the sense in which German Idealists, for example, were philosophers, even though so much of the language of *German Ideology* itself is imbued with the language of that idealism. One would want to add that this 'anti-philosophy' was possible precisely because of the extent to which he had mastered the philosophical discourse as such. Marx is in fact so deeply conversant with philosophical concepts—theory of consciousness, dialectics, the universal and the particular, and so on—and he uses them so casually that one does not quite feel the weight of philosophical thought that undergirds the lightness and clarity of his prose. I have myself published an essay on his radically new way of employing and re-defining the concept of 'universality' in the *Manifesto* which simply overturns, on this particular subject, the whole legacy of eighteenth and nineteenth century European philosophy.[6]

There are so many approaches to the *Manifesto* that if one were to adopt them all one could go on writing virtually indefinitely. My main concern throughout the present reflection on the text is to demonstrate, mainly by giving examples, how rich and complex and elusive a text this brief pamphlet really is. I have by and large refrained from commenting on the latter sections of the *Manifesto,* although those too are replete with surprises. A reflection on the varieties of 'reactionary socialism', and on 'utopian socialism', may at the end in fact bring us closer to some strands in the dominant Indian political discourse, including that of Gandhi who was himself deeply influenced by the utopian movement (though not by the specific utopians Marx discusses) and by conservative, right-wing critiques of capitalism, as in Carlyle or Tolstoy or Ruskin. All that I have set aside, for lack of space. In the rest of this essay, I want to comment only on a few more issue at some length, which too shall bring up some related concerns: In what sense, and to what extent, is the bourgeoisie perceived to be revolutionary? And, what is the Marxist conception of the 'laws' of history? In his portrait of globalization as it was to unfold over time, does Marx give us an equally accurate picture of the capitalist economy as well as the attendant political and aesthetic forms? And, what do we learn about the proletariat, then and now?

'REVOLUTIONARY' BOURGEOISIE?

Numerous commentators have noted that whereas the *Manifesto* declares the proletariat to be the revolutionary class of the future ('grave-diggers' of the bourgeois order), the great exploits that it narrates are those of the bourgeoisie as it overturns the older order and establishes its dominion over the surface of the entire globe.[7] Some have even made out that Marx suffers from the progressivist ideology of nineteenth century positivism in which the bourgeoisie is the real hero of modernity and history is the history of constant improvement. While the former point has considerable merit, the latter is simply absurd.

The main principle of narration in the *Manifesto* is not that of a teleological unfolding of Progress (a unilinear development that always goes in the direction of greater improvement) but that of a contradictory process of both construction and destruction that proceed simultaneously until the point where the process becomes incapable of resolving or even containing the contradictions it has produced: *that* is the moment of revolutionary rupture, if the proletariat succeeds in making a revolution, or a moment of 'mutual destruction of contending classes', as the *Manifesto* puts it, if no revolutionary resolution is found.[8] If history was always moving in the direction of progress, there would be no need for revolution as such. We shall come momentarily to how Marx, and then later Marxists have conceived of the progressive role of the bourgeoisie in relation to the antecedent modes of production and their correlative political structures. Suffice it to say here that the authors who associated the capitalist mode of production with what the *Manifesto* calls 'a universal war of devastation' or who wrote the following lines, could hardly be thinking of the role of bourgeoisie as simply and mainly a revolutionary role in the positive sense of that word:

> It [capitalism] has resolved personal worth into exchange value, and in place of the numberless, indefeasible chartered freedoms, has set up the single, unconscionable freedom—Free Trade. In one word, for exploitation, veiled by religious and political illusions, it has substituted naked, shameless, direct, brutal exploitation. . . . It has converted the physician, the lawyer, the priest, the poet, the man of science, into its own paid wage-labourers. . . . It compels all bourgeois nations, on pain of extinction, to adopt the bourgeois mode of production; it compels them to introduce what it calls civilization in their midst, i.e., to become bourgeois themselves. In one word, it creates a world in its own image.

That ironic phrase, 'what it calls civilization', reminds one of a superbly contemptuous phrase that Engels was to use later for the colonizing European bourgeoisie: 'civilization-mongers'. This is the language of outrage and denunciation, not of unalloyed enthusiasm.

The other point—that the *Manifesto* treats the proletariat as only an ascendant revolutionary class and tells mainly of the exploits of the bourgeoisie—is certainly correct. This has to do with Marx's punctual method of describing the existing conditions and deducing from them the future directions. It is worth recalling here that even limited trade union rights in the most advanced capitalist country, Britain, were at the time less than a quarter century old; that the first political party which could be viewed as a working class party, namely that of the Chartists, was itself less than a decade old and could hardly be described as 'revolutionary'; even the successful struggle for an 8-hour day was to come very much in the future, and mass working class parties in Europe itself were not to arise until the 1880s, some forty years after the publication of the *Manifesto.* The Communist League, whose manifesto Marx was writing, was a small organization of German emigres in London with even smaller branches in some cities of the Continent. The revolutionary role of the proletariat that Marx was visualizing and theorizing for the future was so very much greater than anything that could be associated with that Communist League that even the name of the organization does not appear in the text of what was its own manifesto. The *Manifesto* does not tell of the revolutionary achievement of the working class for the good reason that in all the revolutions up to that time the proletariat had played a large but a subaltern role, under the flag of the bourgeoisie, and Marx was drafting a call to arms that would put an end to that subaltern position and would for the first time bring the proletariat on to the stage of history as a revolutionary class in its own right. What is important here is not that Marx has no revolutionary exploits of the proletariat to celebrate. What is much more important is the quality of the prediction. If his description of capitalism itself gives us an image of a capitalism not the way it was in 1848 but what it was to become much later, his conception of the revolutionary agent also has that same extraordinary orientation toward the future.

As for the bourgeoisie, it is conceived as a class that has undoubtedly played a revolutionary role in relation to the older regimes of exploitation but, in the same sweep, it is also conceived as class that can no longer extricate itself from the cycle of crises (e.g., 'the epidemic of overproduction') and a 'universal war of devastation'. What, then, has been the revolutionary role?

The *Manifesto* conceives of the bourgeoisie as a *revolutionary* class in two radically different senses, drawing alternately on the very different historical experiences of Britain and France. There is, on the one hand, the *objectively revolutionary* role that has to do mainly with the economic sphere and the social relations necessary for the expanded reproduction of this sphere. Here, Marx draws mainly on the experience of the British capitalist class and focuses on this bourgeoisie's need to constantly revolutionize the forces and relations of production, optimize the pool of the propertyless, maximize the rate of surplus value, generalize the wage relation and 'the cash nexus', and carry market relations to the farthest corner of the earth. This is the logic of industrial capitalism *per se,* and even though only in Britain had such an industrial bourgeoisie fully emerged as the dominant class, Marx had the acumen to see that such was going to be the fate of every other national bourgeoisie which hoped to compete with the more advanced one. Britain was of course to remain in the lead during the rest of his lifetime but other such centres were to soon develop, notably in Germany and the United States even more than France, giving rise to a kind of imperialist rivalry that was qualitatively different from colonial competitions of the mercantilist era.

On the other hand, however, there was also what one might call the *subjectively* revolutionary role of the bourgeoisie which had to do largely with the political sphere and which had been most marked in the French Revolution and the subsequent revolutionary upheavals in many parts of the Continent, including later upheavals within France itself, right up to 1848. Whereas the modern British state had evolved on the basis of a class compromise between the new bourgeoisie and the old aristocracy, with the latter

also transforming itself into a bourgeoisie of the ground-rent, as Engels in particular was to emphasize in his writings on Britain, it was the French Revolution, with its Jacobin and even communistic elements, that had sought to fully destroy the *ancien regime* as well as the whole social edifice upon which it had rested. The Restoration there had only led to successive revolutionary upheavals, with the aim of erecting a modern, secular, representative state. If the revolutionary role of the British capitalist class in the economic sphere had led to polarization of classes and universalization of 'the cash nexus', the political revolutions of the French bourgeoisie had sought to create civic and juridic equality of citizens, the class cleavages notwithstanding. If the British bourgeoisie had done all it could to keep the proletariat out of the political process, not even granting a minimum of trade union rights until the third decade of the nineteenth century, the French bourgeoisie had, in each of its revolutionary surges, sought to organize the unprivileged and the proletarianized masses for active participation in the struggle for civic equality, though it too stringently suppressed aspirations of the working classes to organize themselves in autonomous 'combinations' (as these were called at the time). If British political economy had perfected the theory of the free market, the philosophical representatives of the French bourgeoisie had formulated the most extensive thought on social, political, and religious freedoms. And, if British factory production was to set the pattern for later industrializations in the rest of the world, especially in the imperialist core, it was the French theories of 'Liberty, Equality, Fraternity' which have marked the nature of oppositional political agitations right down to our own day. It is in this specific sense that Marxism appropriates the Enlightenment project but also tries to supersede it by concentrating on removing the class virus, and it is precisely on the issue of the class character of the Republican notion of 'freedom' that Marx had criticized the French revolutionary thought the most stringently.

As Germans settlers in Britain, with intimate knowledge of such places as Paris and Brussels, Marx and Engels well understood this whole range of bourgeois experience in Europe. Nor did they romanticize the 'revolutionary' role of either the British or the French bourgeoisie. If the chapters on primitive accumulation in *Capital* tell the story of the many swindles out of which the British bourgeoisie was born, and if Engels' *Conditions of the Working Class in England* details the moral and material degradation of the great majority that was inherent in the 'revolutionary' phase of the British capitalist class, Marx's mature work was conceived as a *critique* of primarily British political economy as an illusory science that merely reflects the phenomenal form of the capitalist mode of production; *inter alia,* he shows how unfree the so-called 'free market' really is, and how freedom of the market itself leads to monopoly. Similarly, in analyses of the British state, they had shown how much the aristocracy had been absorbed in its key institutions, especially the Armed Forces and the colonial governments. As for the French Revolution, Marx had contemptuously written of 'the self-conceit of the political sphere' precisely in relation to the French representative state and its juridic equalities, and as early as **"The Jewish Question"** (1843), well before the *Manifesto,* he had also shown, through careful analyses of the 'Declaration of the Rights of Man' and of key clauses of the French Constitution, how juridic equality was based on much more fundamental inequalities and how the right to private property is the most fundamental right guaranteed therein. In their numerous writings, Marx and Engels make quite explicit the distinction between the British and French experiences, showing how neither is capable of completing the revolutions they have set in motion; as the *Manifesto* puts it, 'The conditions of bourgeois society are too narrow to encompass the wealth created by them'.

In the condensed, epic prose of the *Manifesto,* however, they present these two tales of the respective bourgeoisies as a single story of the structural imperative inherent in the generalization of the capitalist mode of production as such, as if the bourgeoisie that had revolutionized the forces of production was the same that was revolutionizing the political structures. Some writers, including many admirers of this text, have viewed this condensing of the respective experiences into one as a weakness, an overgeneralization and an inaccurate characterization of the French bourgeoisie. That is to a certain extent true. The weakness would surely be more significant if we were dealing with a descriptive text that would require distinctions of that kind. Instead, the very method of the *Manifesto* assumes that each national bourgeoisie shall grow in historical conditions specific to it and that in the process of its own maturation each national bourgeoisie is beset with its own set of anachronisms and its own realties of uneven development. What is of central importance, however, is that no mature system of capitalist production can arise without generalized 'free' labour which must then be translated, sooner or later, into juridic equality, all the more so because this formal equality of otherwise unequal citizens is itself a reflection of the capitalist market that organizes commodity exchange in the language of equivalences. Thus, it did not matter, from the historical standpoint of the long-term trend, that production in the Southern United States of Marx's own time was based on unfree, slave labour, despite the Bill of Rights that had bravely, and with no small degree of duplicity, proclaimed that 'All men are created equal'. What mattered, rather, was that the United States could not emerge as a uniform labour market and an industrialized society without, sooner or later, abolishing slavery and establishing some kind of juridic equality among its citizens. That process spanned over a hundred years or so, from the abolition of slavery during the 1860s to the Civil Rights legislations and movements of the 1950s and 1960s. But the process did occur, even though that newly-won juridic equality rests on top of a whole heap of social and economic inequalities, along lines of race as well as class.

But this question of the revolutionary role of the bourgeoisie we could approach from another angle as well. Since the *Manifesto,* many Marxists have addressed a particular question: when does the bourgeoisie *cease* to be a revolutionary class? At the most general level, Lenin argued that the decisive turn in Europe came with (a) the completion of the process of forming nation-states in the latter half of the nineteenth century; (b) the emergence of the revolutionary movements of the working class during roughly the same time; and (c) the onset of imperialism which established the supremacy of 'coupon-clippers' within Europe and prevented the consolidation of the classes of modern capitalism in the colonies—an onset that Lenin dates also from about the 1880s. Within the colonies, however, the emergent national bourgeoisies could play a constructive role in anti-colonial struggles but the attempt had to be made to organize a leading role for worker-peasant coalitions within the liberation struggles. For Russia itself, Lenin argued that capitalism had produced sufficient concentrations of the proletariat in key areas of class conflict for the struggle for a socialist revolution to begin, and that contradictions of Russian capitalism were such that neither the economic task of further, full-fledged, independent industrialization nor the political task of creating a modern state could be left to the bourgeoisie.

Generally, Marxists have tended to argue that the shift in the role of the bourgeoisie as a 'revolutionary' class comes between the aborted revolutions of 1848, immediately after the publication of the *Manifesto,* and the short-lived Paris Commune of 1871. In other words, the bourgeoisie's fear of the proletarianized masses which was already palpable during the revolutions of 1848 turned, after the Commune, into a full-fledged nightmare of a possible proletarian revolution. Antonio Gramsci, however, makes an arresting point. He argues that the bourgeoisie's fear of the proletariat goes back to the French Revolution itself. It had fully mobilized the proletarianized masses in the course of its own struggle against the *ancien regime,* but then counterrevolutionary terror came as soon as it became clear that the masses were gathering on a platform of radical equality, with increasing talk of the abolition of property and full democratization of state administration, that threatened the supremacy of the bourgeoisie itself. The masses were of course suppressed. Gramsci argues that the European bourgeoisie learned from that experience so well that in every subsequent revolutionary upheaval the bourgeoisie always compromised with the landowning classes in defence of the rule of property as such. He traces the reactionary character of the bourgeois regimes in nineteenth century Europe, especially in Germany and Italy, to this enduring class compromise on the part of the bourgeoisie. In the case of Italy, with which he was mainly concerned, he argues that the weakness of parliamentary democracy and the rise of fascism were both related to the crisis created by the rise of the most modern capitalist relations arising in one sector of the economy, mostly in Northern Italy, and the most backward and anachronistic structures persisting in the rest of the country, especially in the South. This extreme form of uneven development he traces to the fact that the bourgeoisie never really confronted the landowning classes, even though it played a relatively progressive role in obtaining independence and unity of the Italian nation-state. According to this argument, then, the revolutionary role of the bourgeoisie came and went rather quickly.

This sheds interesting light on the role of the bourgeoisie in India. Some sections of it certainly played a progressive role during the struggle for Independence. However, five countervailing factors should also be noted. First, key sectors of the Indian bourgeoisie, such as the house of Tata, remained closer to the colonial authority than to the national movement. Second, even those who drew closer to the national movement, mainly through Gandhi's mediation, such as the Birlas, adopted an attitude of collaborative competition with regard to the colonial authority, while fully anti-colonial positions were more common among sections of the smaller bourgeoisie. Third, the bourgeoisie was always suspicious of mass movements and, during the crucial two years between the end of the Second World War and the moment of Independence, as the revolutionary wave began to rise, the bourgeois leadership was no less keen on a quick settlement than the British themselves, even if it meant partition of the country; better partition than revolution, it effectively said. Fourth, after Independence the bourgeoisie made a far-reaching alliance with the landed classes, old and new, making impossible land reforms that would radically alter the conditions of life for the poor peasants, the rural proletariat, the bonded labourers, the *adivasis* and the like. It thus preempted the chance of extensive social reforms in the antiquated, traditional society which are simply not possible without radical re-distribution of land and other agricultural resources in the first place. The most advanced forms of capitalist development in some areas has been combined with the most extensive backwardness of social and property relations in much of the country. Much of the social pathology we witness today, giving rise to all manner of fascistoid violences, is ultimately rooted in this fact. Finally, the fear of the proletariat and the peasantry has meant that this bourgeoisie has found it easier to compromise with imperialism than to undertake radical transformation of Indian society, even for its own purposes; they would rather have an extremely restricted home market and an unhealthy, socially backward, illiterate or semi-literate work-force than undertake a social transformation that may slip out of their control. Instead of a 'revolutionary' bourgeoisie, we have something of a permanent, pre-emptive counterrevolution, which only goes to show that in a society such as the one we have, even the tasks of a bourgeois revolution cannot be fully carried out except within a socialist transition.

ARE THERE 'LAWS' OF CAPITALISM?

Schematically speaking, we could say that the *Manifesto,* and the science of Marxism of which this is a document of very great importance, is built around two kinds of principles or 'laws'. One set consists of 'laws' pertaining to the very motion of the capitalist mode of production which are fundamental and immutable throughout the whole history of this mode, without which capitalism would cease to be capitalism as such. Three such laws can be summa-

rized here, simply to illustrate a part of this theoretical core, or what Marx might have called the 'rational kernel' of this theory.

There is, first, the proposition that throughout its history, capitalism drives toward greater and greater polarization between the fundamental classes. This does not mean that no intermediate classes or strata are present at any given time; indeed, with the increasing complexity of administration, management and technical expertise required for expanded reproduction of capital, such intermediate strata arise all along the axis of this class polarization. What the law means, rather, is that the means of production for the expanded reproduction of capital tend to get concentrated at one end of the class polarization, while the increasingly more numerous majority gets proletarianized (i.e., loses control over these means of production) and is forced to sell its labour-power, whether in the 'organized' or the 'unorganized' sector, and whether on the full-time, permanent basis or as casual and temporary labourers. 'Repression' or 'poverty' are punctual features of this class relation, but what defines it as specifically 'capitalist' is the category of 'exploitation', i.e., expanded reproduction and accumulation of capital by one class that appropriates the labour-power of the other class. It is in relation to this polarization of classes that the concept of class struggle is derived, and the main point is that all classes, especially the two polar classes, the bourgeoisie and the proletariat, participate in this struggle. We tend to think of class struggle only in relation to the proletariat, as revolutionary struggle. Marx's point is that the possessing class itself wages a brutal and permanent struggle in defence of its own class interests, through violence and threats of violence, through exploitations both extensive and intensive, by maintaining a permanent army of the unemployed, and through thousand other means in the social, political, economic, ideological and cultural arenas. Class struggle has, in other words, not one side but two.

Second, there is the iron 'law' of increasing globalization of the capitalist mode of production, first extensively by bringing more and more territories and populations under its dominion, and then intensively by constantly imposing newer and newer labour regimes and processes of production, which are first invented at the core of the system and then get enforced in its peripheries as and when the need arises. This globalizing tendency was there well before the Industrial Revolution came about and is an ongoing process today, in myriad forms. No pre-capitalist mode had this constant expansion as an inherent law of its own reproduction; capitalism does. The feudal lords of Britain had neither the design nor the capacity to extend their feudal mode into the rest of the world; the British bourgeoisie was increasingly embroiled in perfecting precisely such designs and capacities. Today, when some celebrated theorists in the advanced capitalist countries are talking of 'late capitalism', 'post-imperialist capitalism', even a 'postmodern' and 'cybernetic' capitalism in which production is said to have been replaced by information technologies, the basic fact is that, according to the calculations of the World Bank, the number of workers in the 'modern' (i.e. fully capitalist) sector has doubled during the thirty years between 1965 and 1995, the very years when capitalism is said to have abolished historic forms of labour (a book was recently published in the United States, by eminent labour theorists in the postmodern Left, simply called *Post-Work*).

The third such law that we can cite as a permanent feature of capitalism is the class nature of the state, i.e., that no capitalist society can exist and reproduce itself without a state that is the state of the bourgeoisie as a whole. Now, on the Left at least, we take this for granted. On Marx's part, this was a revolutionary discovery. For the political theory that he had inherited, from the Enlightenment and the French Revolution and right up to Hegel, the normal and desirable state was one that stood above all classes and fractions of civil society, mediating their disputes and itself embodying the General Will. It is in this sense that Hegel had described the bureaucracy as 'a universal class'; in other words, a class that represented not the interest of a particular class but a universal interest, of the whole society. It is directly in response to Hegel's description of the bureaucracy as the universal class that Marx was to say so emphatically that only the proletariat is *potentially* a universal class, since as an object of universal exploitation it has no particular interests to defend, and that the proletariat can actually *become* such a 'universal class' through a revolutionary re-structuring of society into one where 'the free development of each is the precondition for the free development of all'—free, above all, from exploitation. This definition of 'freedom'—as a freedom, first of all, from exploitation—was also a new one. Through a dense and brilliant analysis of some founding texts of the French Revolution—'Declaration of the Rights of Man' as well as some key clauses of the Republican Constitution—Marx had shown in **"The Jewish Question"** that the fundamental freedom granted by the Declaration is the right to private property, that the fundamental right granted was the right to defend one's property against encroachment by others, and that the core of legal government were laws pertaining to right and freedom of property. This, he argued, was certainly an advance over the arbitrary powers of the monarchical state, but, in a dialectical move, freedom from exploitation was now posited as the *true* freedom that could only be guaranteed through abolition of capitalism as such, as against the *illusory* and class-based freedom of private property as guaranteed by documents of the bourgeois revolution. The main point, in any case, was that a state that guaranteed the right to private property, hence the system of exploitation, could not possibly represent, either in theory or in practice, the General Will. Such a state had to be a class state, and that class society could not be abolished without simultaneously abolishing the class state.

Such are some of the fundamental 'laws' of motion under capitalism, and without some strict conception of such laws Marxism ceases to be a coherent theory. This does not mean that such laws function in exactly the same way in all places and all times. It does mean, though, that capitalism cannot exist without the operation of such laws. However, most of what passes for 'laws of history' or 'laws of nature' and even 'laws of political economy' are in fact what we might call *laws of tendency,* i.e., the view that since capitalism is on the whole an intelligible structure a correct understanding of the existing structure can reasonably predict that, all else being equal, certain phenomena would tend to take particular directions and particular forms. For example, Marx speaks in the **Manifesto** of the inherent tendency of capitalism toward periodic crises, and he speaks specifically of 'the epidemic of overproduction'. In later, more mature studies of political economy, he was to closely demonstrate that the inherent tendency in the average rate of capitalist profit was toward decline, thanks to competitions of various sorts, crises of overproduction, etc. These are obviously laws of tendency that gives to capitalism a peculiarly unstable character. However, the rate of profit does not *always* fall, not in every period, not in every branch of production, not in all phases of the class struggle, not in every national space of investment. The bourgeoisie is always trying to maintain at least a constant, if not rising, rate of profit. Much of the drive behind imperialist expansion and exploitation of more and more regions and peoples of the world is precisely to stabilize and push up these rates in the core countries; and the bourgeoisie wages an unremitting class struggle against workers everywhere to simultaneously raise the productivity of labour, depress the wage rate and yet expand the market for its products—by raising, for example, the level of consumer debt, by extending to them a purchasing power beyond their earned incomes, so that the capitalists can sell their products while also collecting interest on the generalized debt. We have, in other words, not a teleological unfolding of an iron law but the contradictory structure of tendencies and counter-tendencies.

Broadly speaking, the guiding principle here is that, as Engels was to put it, 'men make their own history but they make it in circumstances given to them'. History is, in other words, a dynamic and ever changing mix of intentions and constraints. The choices people make and the outcomes they produce are deeply constrained by the 'circumstances given to them'. However, they could not make 'their own history' if intentions did not matter and if tendencies inherent in the system could not be reversed. Indeed, revolution is a moment where intentions—the subjective factor; the collective human agency—would confront the constraints and transform them in radically new directions.

GLOBALIZATION, ECONOMY, AND CULTURE

This distinction between laws that are fundamental to the structure as a whole and laws that are only laws of tendency can be grasped if we look at the way the **Manifesto** speaks of (a) the process of globalization strictly in terms of the expansion of capital on the one hand, and (b) on the other, the probable consequences it attempts to foresee in diverse other areas, such as on the issue of 'national specificity' or on the issue of a 'world literature' arising in the distant future out of the dissolution of national literatures.

It is really quite extraordinary how frequently words like 'global' and 'universal' appear in the brief first part of the *Manifesto.* A very considerable conquest of the globe had been happening since at least the early part of the sixteenth century, driven largely by very powerful merchants' capital. The colonization of the Americas, the extermination of the bulk of their populations, the mass enslavement of Africans (thirty million slaves shipped out of Africa, with half of them dying before reaching the American and Caribbean shores), the network of trading and military posts all along the coasts of Africa and Asia, the virtually complete colonization of India itself—all this, and much more, had happened by the time the *Manifesto* was drafted. Indeed, the process had been much accelerated after the Industrial Revolution (it was actually Engels who was to call it that). Between 1770 and 1848, the British alone acquired Australia, New Zealand, South Africa, in addition to most of India, while France took chunks of North Africa.

How different was Marx's view of all that can be gauged from the fact that Hegel, the philosopher whom Marx admired as well as fought against the most, had seen in this wave of colonization a necessary and welcome solution, one almost ordained by nature itself, for the surplus population of Europe. Marx's great achievement was that he saw this process as part of what the *Manifesto* calls a 'universal war of devastation', connected it all with the inherent nature of capitalism, and then tried to make this perception a key element in the consciousness of the European working class itself. It needs to be said, however, that the colonialism of his day was nothing like the imperialism about which Lenin was to write some seventy years later and the beginning of which Lenin himself was to date around the 1880s, i.e., not in the days of Marx's youth but in the very last years of his life. And, during the seventy years since Lenin wrote his famous pamphlet, *Imperialism, the Highest Stage of Capitalism,* some of the basic features of imperialism have again changed more radically than they did during the previous seventy years.

The astonishing fact is that when Marx writes specifically of the economic and technological expansion of capitalism on a global scale, and of the deep penetration of capitalist logic into regions very remote from Europe, today's reader tends to think not of the capitalism and colonialism of Marx's time but the capitalism and imperialism of our own time—despite all the historic shifts that have taken place and that have transformed the processes of globalization in very fundamental ways. He asserts that 'modern industry has established the world market', that 'the bourgeoisie . . . must nestle everywhere, settle everywhere, establish connections everywhere', and that 'in place of the old local and national seclusion and self-sufficiency, we have intercourse in every direction, universal interdependence of nations everywhere'—at a time when most

of Europe itself, let alone the rest of the world, did not have industrial economies. Even France was then an overwhelmingly rural society and Germany, which was to emerge by the end of the nineteenth century as one of three most industrialized societies alongside Britain and France, was at that time not even a unified nation-state. Similarly, Marx speaks here of capitalism's drive to unify the globe through a 'revolution' in transport—at a time when steamboats and railways were a bare novelty. The first steamboat had sailed from the Americas to Europe in 1819, and as late as 1840 railways in England itself covered merely 843 miles of track. Yet the vivid metaphors of speed and compression that Marx employs in speaking of the world having been transformed into a single entity through industry, technology, the global chase of commodities and the 'cash nexus', conjures up in the reader's mind today's world of jet travel, international TV channels, globalized patterns of fashions and fast foods, and the computerized network of stock exchanges across the globe where billions of dollars can be moved around in seconds. In rapid, sharp strokes necessary for so brief a text, Marx condenses description and prediction in a single sweep. He sees what is there already, and he grasps the long-range dynamics at work behind and beyond what he actually sees, so that if one sentence of the *Manifesto* gives us the capitalism of 1848 the very next one gives us an image of what was yet to be, in the indefinite future, right up to our own and beyond. What is of key importance here is the firmness and accuracy with which Marx was able to perceive the future development of capitalism by grasping its inexorable operative laws.

But there is also a structure of secondary formulations—also regarding 'globalization'—essentially deductive and speculative in nature, about the likely consequences of this capitalist logic as it was expected to unfold in diverse areas of national formations, the arts, etc. Several of those formulations had to do with the kind of world European expansion into the rest of the world was to make. Here, in areas that are at some distance from economy as such, and which are areas essentially of political and cultural forms, two kinds of problems arise. The first, and in the long run less significant historically and theoretically, is the uncritical use of some inherited categories which was at best unpleasant, e.g., the description of capitalist Europe and precapitalist China as 'civilized and 'barbarian' respectively. The second kind of problem pertains to the kind of expectation which subsequent history has proved to be wrong, especially in relation to the colonized countries. As colonialism fully matured and at length gave us what Lenin was to designate as 'imperialism', which is still very much with us, national differences, far from disappearing, in fact became more recalcitrant and more hierarchically structured. Nationalism itself was to have a history very different from what we can deduce from the *Manifesto.* Some of the correctives came in the later writings of Marx and Engels themselves, other and even more substantive ones came from a later generation of Marxists, Lenin and Rosa Luxemburg in particular.

When Marx drafted the **Manifesto** he had studied great many things, but there is very little evidence that he had really studied the whole complexity of the colonial enterprise. It was only later, after the revolutions of 1848 had been defeated and he settled down to a life-long exile in London the next year, that he undertook any systematic study of colonialism, especially after Engels persuaded him to undertake the writing of some journalistic pieces for the *New York Herald Tribune* regularly, mainly in order to make a little money. This study then meant that both Marx and Engels started paying much greater attention to the actual events of colonial history as it unfolded over the next three or four decades, and this they did to the extent that it was possible to grasp those events from accounts in the British press. As I have argued at some length elsewhere, it was in those later years that Marx became much more thoroughly disillusioned with the 'progressive' results that he had expected of colonialism earlier, in his youth, and that both he and Engels began affirming the right of resistance on the part of the colonized peoples.[9]

With all the benefits of hindsight one hundred and fifty years later, one can make four points with some degree of certainty. One is that Marx and Engels themselves were to understand the phenomenon of colonialism much better in later years than they did at the time of writing the **Manifesto**; in 1847-48, they fully understood the key role of colonialism in the global expansion of the capitalist mode but not that, far from unifying the globe politically, colonialism would divide and sub-divide the world into numerous entities large and small, so that 'national specificity' would on the whole rather increase than decline.[10] Second, even though they understood colonialism much better in later years, the structure itself was to alter very drastically and a wholly more complex and in some ways quite different theoretical apparatus would then be required, which was to be the focus of attention for a later generation of Marxists, Lenin most particularly, but also Bukharin, Luxemburg, Hilferding, and some of the Austro-Marxists such as Otto Bauer, who were to make very seminal contribution to theories of colonialism as well as nationalism. Third, if the political consequences could not be gauged with precision, less still was it possible to do so with respect to the cultural consequences; far from there arising a 'world literature' in any meaningful sense, as the **Manifesto** had envisioned, the cultural consequences of colonialism were such that the literatures of the colonized people were to remain regional and/or national, while in the global marketplace of capitalism they were always subordinated to the literatures of the advanced metropoles. Finally, Marx's own discovery that the rate and quantum of change under capitalism is greater than under any previous mode, and that this rate of change increases in every succeeding phase, also means that the world has by now changed so very much since the time not only of Marx but also of Lenin or even Gramsci that an immense new theoretical labour is required to understand the world as we now have it.

This discrepancy between the stunning prescience of Marx's summation of the fundamental structure in the strictly economic sphere, and the much less assured a touch in foreseeing the coming changes in some of the political and cultural spheres, can perhaps be looked at from another angle as well. Several years after drafting the **Manifesto,** in a famous formulation in his 'Preface' to **A Critique of Political Economy** of 1859, Marx was to write:

> . . . a distinction should always be made between the material transformation of the economic conditions of production, which can be determined with the precision of natural science, and the legal, political, religious, aesthetic, or philosophic—in short, ideological forms in which men become conscious of their conflict and fight it out.

What is striking about this distinction is that only 'the transformation of the economic conditions of production' are said to be available for being 'determined with precision', in a scientific manner. The 'consciousness' of that fundamental conflict is said to belong elsewhere—in 'the legal, political, religious, aesthetic, or philosophic' forms—which evidently cannot be 'determined' with equal 'precision' even though—or, more likely, *because*—that is where people actually 'fight it out', so that, presumably, those forms are less the outcome of objective structural laws and much more 'determined' by the very way human subjects 'fight it out' in collective struggles that take not only 'legal, political' forms but also 'religious, aesthetic, or philosophic' forms. According to this principle, then, it is only logical that Marx could foresee with far greater precision much of the course that the globalization of the capitalist mode of *economic* production was to take but could not predict with anything like that degree of precision what 'political' or 'aesthetic' forms were to ensue.

Proletariat, the 'Universal Class'

Marx conceptualized the proletariat as a 'universal class' at a time when no country in Asia or Africa could be considered as having something resembling a modern proletariat. In the larger American countries, like the U.S. and Brazil, there were many more slaves than proletarians. Russia was steeped in serfdom; certainly the whole of Eastern and Southern Europe, and much of the rest as well, was predominantly agrarian. The term 'universal class' was used, I believe, in two senses. The first was in part a philosophical proposition: since what all proletarians have in common is an experience of exploitation and a location in processes of production that were collective as well as impersonal, they had an inherent (within the class, a universal) interest in a revolution against the system of exploitation as such; and since the system of exploitation could not be abolished piecemeal, nor could it be abolished without abolishing *both* capital and 'wage-slavery' at the same time, along with all the political, social and ideological superstructures that arose on the premise of that exploitation, the proletariat could not emancipate itself without abolishing the system as a whole, emancipating society as a whole; it was the class *par excellance* of universal emancipation.

That was the first sense and, as pointed out earlier, it was initially a philosophical proposition posited in opposition to Hegel's description of the *bureaucracy* as a 'universal class'. But there was also the other sense that since capital had an inherent drive toward globalization, i.e., toward establishing its dominion in all corners of the earth, it was destined to constantly increase the number of proletarians around the globe so that, eventually, the proletariat would come to be comprised of the great majority of humanity, spread universally in all parts of the world: a world proletariat, in other words, over and above all national bounds. Universal in *scale* as well! This was also projected as a process of greater class polarization ('simplification of the class structure', as the ***Manifesto*** calls it) as well as absolute immiseration of the majority.

This is what has now come to pass, for the first time in history: not in Marx's time, not in Lenin's time, but in ours.

I have mentioned earlier that according to World Bank calculations the number of proletarians doubled in the course of the thirty years between 1965 and 1995. This number in now said to stand at roughly two and a half billion (i.e., two thousand five hundred million) of whom 120 million are said to be currently unemployed, roughly one billion are said to subsist on less than a dollar a day, and many unknown millions are said to have stopped looking for work. Needless to add that the overwhelming majority of this immiserated bulk lives in the poorer continents of Asia, Africa, and Latin America. For China alone, the World Bank calculates that there is, besides the employed and semi-employed proletariat, already a 'floating population' of 80 million who have ceased to be peasants and are not yet part of the 'modern' sector and that over a hundred more million peasants will leave the Chinese countryside over the next decade or so to look for work in the cities. Similar processes are at work in other countries of Asia, Africa and Latin America as well. The same statistics also suggest that no more than 12 to 15 per cent of labouring activity is now left on the surface of this earth which is not in one way or another, directly or remotely, connected with the world market; well over 80 per cent now produces for this integrated market—a novel 'universalization' in its own terms. As regards increasing immiseration, the May 1998 issue of *Monthly Review* published the following statistical table about shifts of wealth from the poor and the middling to the rich over a short span between 1965 and 1990:

SHARES OF WORLD INCOME, PER CENT

	1965	1990
Poorest 20 per cent	2.3	1.4
Second 20 per cent	2.9	1.8
Third 20 per cent	4.2	2.1
Fourth 20 per cent	21.2	11.3
Richest 20 per cent	69.5	83.4

The long and short of it is that for 80 per cent of the people around the globe share of wealth was cut by half in the course of barely 25 years, or over roughly a single generation, while the share of the lower 40% at the later point dropped to just over 3 per cent of the total. What is also significant is that the share of the second highest 20 per cent—presumably, the so-called 'middle class' or even perhaps 'upper middle class'—also saw its share in total wealth cut by almost half. So much for the expansion or the financial security of this 'middle class'! For the average share to be cut so drastically, at least a good number must have fallen into the category of 'low income' or even 'poor' and great many more must have seen their standards of living decline sharply and perhaps their levels of indebtedness rising proportionately. What is striking in any case is the absolute polarization: roughly 3 per cent of the income for 40 per cent of the people and 83 per cent of the wealth for the top 20 per cent.

Thus, increasing polarization, immiseration, proletarianization and primitive accumulation are ongoing processes in our own time. In the imperialist centres of the world which have experienced the highest concentration of accumulated capital, and where the processes of proletarianization and primitive accumulation were completed earlier, the emphasis has shifted more toward intensive exploitation and accumulation of relative surplus value, based on more advanced technologies. In formations of backward capital, the intensity of labour rather than of capital is still very substantially at the heart of 'globalization'; for China, which has had spectacular though now declining success in expanding its exports, something like three-fourths of all exports are now labour-intensive whereas less than forty percent were labour-intensive a decade ago when the volume of exports was much more limited. The great increase in exports is owed, in other words, not so much to any technological 'modernization' of the process of production but to the more methodical, more intensified exploitation of labour.

Simply in terms of the global spread, the proletariat is now infinitely more 'universal' than ever before, which then means that, in objective terms, the imperative for workers of the world to unite is greater than ever before. This universal proletarianization does not come without its own problems, however. As David Harvey puts it:

> The workforce is now far more geographically dispersed, culturally heterogeneous, ethnically and religiously diverse, racially stratified, and linguistically fragmented. . . . Differentials (both geographical and social) in wages and social provision within the global working class are likewise greater than they have ever been.[11]

Problems of this kind, as regards stratification within the working class, which compound the difficulty of obtaining working class unity, are then further compounded by several other factors such as increasing proportion of casual and temporary work as against more secure full-time employment; increasing weight of the 'unorganized' sector relative to the 'organized' one; great mobility and transience of the labour force, as well as the greater mobility of capital itself, and so on.

In sum, then, capital has more than completed what was once conceived as its historic mission: it has created a single world market and it has taken the process of proletarianization deep into the farthest nook and corner of this earth. Obtaining working class unity, starting at the point of habitation and production and spiralling up to national levels and across the nation-states, shall be the more exacting task for militants of a socialism yet to come. When the *Manifesto* reminds us that 'every class struggle is in essence a political struggle' it calls upon us to recognize that same distinction which I tried to clarify a bit earlier with the help of Marx's formulation in his 'Preface' to *A Critique of Political Economy* of 1859. Let me repeat that formulation for greater emphasis:

> . . . a distinction should always be made between the material transformation of the economic conditions of production, which can be determined with the precision of natural science, and the legal, political, religious, aesthetic, or philosophic—in short, ideological forms in which men become conscious of their conflict and fight it out.

In order to transform the class struggle that is forever going on in 'material transformation of the economic conditions of production' into a properly 'political struggle', all the 'ideological forms in which men become conscious of their conflict and fight it out'—legal, political, religious, aesthetic, or philosophic forms—need to be addressed together. Otherwise, those issue of subjective consciousness and objective stratification which divide the working classes of the world cannot be addressed. The more diverse the populations that get proletarianized, the more diverse will have to be the forms that are designed to bring about that unity. For, as the scope of proletarianization has escalated rapidly, every 'political struggle' has become accordingly more complex, encompassing a greater variety of 'forms' ('religious, aesthetic' etc.). For, one bitter lesson we have learned in the course of this process is that the fact of immiseration itself does not produce a consciousness of class unity. For that, the domain of consciousness has to be addressed in the very forms in which it experiences the world, and those forms are social and ideological in nature.

Notes

1. The vivid phrase, 'labour of the tailor that disappears into the coat', is from Louis Althusser who coined it in an entirely different context.

2. *The Communist Manifesto* has always been published as the joint product of Marx and Engels. That is not entirely inaccurate. In the present essay, however, I refer punctually to Marx as the author of this text. This calls for some explanation. The simplest reason is a matter of stylistic convenience; it is easier to refer to one author than constantly refer to both of them. There is also the question of historical accuracy in the strict sense, on two counts. First, we *know* that the final draft was prepared by Marx alone, at a time when Engels was not available for consultation

and the Communist League was threatening punitive action against 'Citizen Marx' for the delay; the responsibility was his and was perceived to be as such. Second, any comparison between the text of the *Manifesto* with the two earlier texts, 'Draft of a Communist Confession of Faith' and 'Principles of Communism', which Engels had produced only a few months earlier, would show how very sweeping were Marx's departures from those preparatory materials. Quite aside from the radical revision of substance, virtually every sentence in the key first Part, 'Bourgeois and Proletarians', bears the inimitable signature of Marx's style, demonstrating, as was usual in his writing, that Marx was one of the great stylists in the history of nineteenth century prose. Engels' contribution to this text was substantive but more indirect, in the sense that the materialist conception of history which the text so pithily summarizes was developed by both of them together, notably in *The German Ideology*. Earlier versions of this conception are also to be found in such texts as *The Economic and Philosophical Manuscripts* which belong to Marx alone, and in *The Holy Family* which began as a 15-page pamphlet by Engels and which Marx then expanded into a whole book. As Engels himself always recognized, Marx was the senior partner in what they humourously called their 'joint firm'.

3. It is in this perspective that 'to win the battle of democracy' is seen as 'the first step in the revolution' for establishing 'the political supremacy of the working class'. Elsewhere, 'dictatorship of the proletariat' would itself be described as 'democracy carried to its fullest' and as the right of the majority to act in the interest of the majority. Since the majority is necessarily proletarianized under capitalism, and since democracy is conceived of as rule of the majority, Marx sometimes uses words 'proletarian' and 'democratic' to mean the same thing, and the phrase 'dictatorship of the proletariat' was initially designed to convey the same nuance. All of that is at least very confusing for today's reader but makes perfect sense when the standpoint is understood.

4. As indicated partially in the previous note, the terminology of the *Manifesto* can pose many problems for the unwitting reader. In his famous commentary on the *Manifesto*, Ryazanoff points out that in the foreword to the original German edition of *The Condition of the Working Class in England*, Engels tells us that he makes use of words like worker, proletarian, working class, non-possessing class, and proletariat to refer to the one and the same phenomenon. Some of that generalized sense of the word 'proletariat' is there in the *Manifesto* as well; much of what got called the 'Paris proletariat' then was comprised of the more pauperized craftsmen, struggling shopkeepers, and a variety of proletarianized urban clusters living as often by wit as by wage but overwhelmingly outside modern factory production. A further

example refers to the much maligned formulation regarding 'the idiocy of rural life'. Hobsbawm points out that the original German word 'idiotismus' is much closer to the Greek 'idiotes' which has the meaning not of 'stupidity' or 'soft-headedness' but of 'narrow horizon' or 'isolation from wider society' and, more interestingly, 'a person concerned only with his own private affairs and not with those of the wider community'. The import of Marx's use of the word 'idiot' is thus closer to 'isolated' in one sense and 'individualist' in another. This, then, is connected with the crucial Marxist distinction between the individual character of peasant production and the collective character of the production of the industrial proletariat. There are numerous other misunderstandings of this kind, pertaining to our text, which are unfortunately much too common.

5. Etienne Balibar, *The Philosophy of Marx,* London 1995; French original, 1993.

6. Aijaz Ahmad, '*The Communist Manifesto* and the Problem of Universality', *Monthly Review,* June 1998.

7. The most stimulating statement of this problem can be found in Ellen Meiksins Wood, '*The Communist Manifesto* After 150 Years', in *Monthly Review,* May 1998; reprinted in the new edition of the *Manifesto* issued from the Monthly Review Press, 1998. In the following couple of paragraphs I have drawn upon but also partly departed from that very fine-grained analysis.

8. Rosa Luxemburg was to summarize these *alternative* possibilities in a pithy phrase when she said that capitalism does not *necessarily* lead to socialism, so that the choice facing humankind was 'socialism *or* barbarism'. Looked at from the vantage-point of today, Marx's own phrase 'mutual destruction of contending classes' is more apt than might appear to those who are unduly impressed by the achieving side of capitalist domination today. Examples are myriad, but we shall confine ourselves to only one. A fundamental contradiction that is inherent in the profit-driven capitalist mode is the destruction—first rather slow, and then increasingly more massive destruction—of a kind of environment that is necessary for sustaining human life, so that we now have an ecologically unsafe planet to the extent that survival of the human species into the coming some centuries cannot be confidently predicted, affecting all the 'contending classes' equally.

9. Aijaz Ahmad, *In Theory: Classes, Nations, Literatures,* London 1992; Delhi 1994; pp. 228-29. Two passages, from Marx and Engels respectively, should clarify this point. The first, from Marx, occurs in a letter written rather late in life (to Danielson, in 1881):

> In India serious complications, if not a general outbreak, are in store for the British government.

What the British take from them annually in the form of rent, dividends for railways useless for the Hindoos, pensions for the military and civil servicemen, for Afghanistan and other wars, etc., etc.,—what they take from them *without any equivalent* and *quite apart* from what they appropriate to themselves annually *within* India,— speaking only of *the value of the commodities* that Indians have to gratuitously and annually *send over* to England—it amounts to *more than the total sum of the income of the 60 million of agricultural and industrial laborers of India.* This is a bleeding process with a vengeance.

> [Italics in the original]

And, well before Marx referred to colonialism as a 'bleeding process with a vengeance', Engels had this to say about what we today call 'national liberation':

> There is evidently a different spirit among the Chinese now. . . . The mass of people take an active, nay, a fanatical part in the struggle against the foreigners. They poison the bread of the European community at Hongkong by wholesale, and with the coolest meditation. . . . The very coolies emigrating to foreign countries rise in mutiny, and as if by concert, on board every emigrant ship, fight for its possession. . . . Civilization mongers who throw hot shell on a defenseless city and add rape to murder, may call the system cowardly, barbarous, atrocious; but what matter it to the Chinese if it be but successful? . . . We had better recognize that this is a war *pro aris et focis,* a popular war for the maintenance of Chinese nationality.

> ('Persia and China', 1857)

10. In the imperialist core this 'national specificity' is of course declining at the current, far more mature stage, as indicated for example in the ongoing European integration. Such was not to be the case in the rest of the globe, however, and even in Europe this is a very recent and still very, very uneven process.

11. David Harvey, 'The Geography of Class Power', *The Socialist Register 1998,* Merlin Press (in UK) and Monthly Press (in USA), 1998.

Irfan Habib (essay date 1999)

SOURCE: Habib, Irfan. "The Reading of History in the *Communist Manifesto.*" In *A World to Win: Essays on the "The Communist Manifesto,"* edited by Prakash Karat, pp. 48-67. New Delhi: LeftWord Books, 1999.

[In the following essay, Habib considers the primary goal of the Communist Manifesto *to have been the formulation of a concise text that contextualized history and took thought in a new direction by solidifying and then disseminating the ideas that would lead to revolution. However,*

the critic explains, the text and its theories evolved with time, and this evolution should be kept in mind by subsequent students of Socialism and The Communist Manifesto.]

Set to draft **The Communist Manifesto** for publication early in 1848, Marx and Engels were called upon to give a popular form to their understanding of philosophy, history, economics and politics, and to frame a practical programme on this basis. The effort was at once both summation and creation: summation of principles that they had come to grasp both independently and together in the preceding five years, and creation to deal with lacunae that to be filled up. The task was brilliantly performed making the **Manifesto** undoubtedly the most important single document in the annals of the Communist movement. There is no need of special justification, therefore, to analyse its contents with exceptional care.

I

The Communist Manifesto is a product of that basic departure from the materialism of the Young Hegelians which led to the initial formulation of Marx's own conception of history. In 1845 when he wrote his Theses on Feuerbach, the very first thesis was as follows:

> The chief defect of all previous materialism—that of Feuerbach included—is that things, reality, sensuousness are conceived only in the form of the *object, or of contemplation,* but not as *sensuous human activity, practice,* not subjectively. . . . Feuerbach wants sensuous objects, really distinct from conceptual objects, but he does not conceive human activity itself as *objective* activity.

The matter is further elaborated in the third thesis:

> The [Feuerbachian] materialist doctrine concerning the changing of circumstances and upbringing forgets that circumstances are changed by men and that the educator must himself be educated.

The theses lead up to the following celebrated finale:

> The philosophers have only *interpreted* the world in various ways; the point is to *change* it.[1]

The crucial importance of these Theses has often been ignored by critics of Marxism (and, unluckily, some of its followers as well), who attribute to it a very determinist aspect, as if 'material' factors simply determine consciousness, which then merely serves as a medium for bringing about changes that those material circumstances have made 'inevitable'. Such interpretations have often relied upon Marx's Preface to **A Contribution to the Critique of Political Economy** (1859), in which he speaks of how 'the mode of production of material life conditions the general process of social, political and intellectual life,' and goes on to assert that 'it is not the consciousness of men that determines their existence but, on the contrary their social existence that determines their consciousness'.[2]

But if we look at these words closely, we musk ask, what, after all, 'production of material life' consists in. Surely, human labour (and, therefore, human consciousness) is the driving element behind all processes of production, and man's social being itself is the result in a large part of his own practice. The 'consciousness' that man's social being 'determines' or sets limits to is, then, only what stands outside the realm of material production, the seemingly pure realm of intellect. The position is clarified in Marx's conclusion that mankind always 'sets itself only such tasks as it is able to solve; since closer examination will always show that the problem itself arises only when the material conditions for its solution are already present or at least in the course of formation'.[3] It, however, still remains of decisive moment for human intellects to correctly discover the soluble question and define its solution: 'the educator must himself be educated'. And once individuals have grasped the questions to be taken up, the ideas attained have to be propagated in order to have practical consequence. This surely constitutes 'the significance of "revolutionary", of "practical-critical", activity' of which Marx speaks in his Theses on Feuerbach.[4] Gramsci, the Italian Communist thinker in his *Prison Notebooks* argued insightfully that 'fatalism' (i.e. determinism, the belief in the inevitability of a certain process) is at best 'the clothing worn by real and active will when in a weak position'. He urged that 'it is essential to demonstrate the futility of mechanical determinism'; for otherwise it would become 'a cause of passivity, of idiotic self-sufficiency'—a fatal position for any revolutionary movement.[5]

While Marx and Engels paid full attention to limits on immediate 'practice', set by the historically inherited circumstances, they did not subscribe to any belief in any automatic or blind force of history. The action to change the world could come only by the diffusion of ideas leading to revolutionary practice. It was, therefore, inherent in the philosophical conclusions they had reached in 1845-46, that they should now come forward with a clear clarion call for revolution—which was the main object of **The Communist Manifesto**. The **Manifesto** is thus a splendid monument to the confident belief of Marxism's founding fathers that it was for thinking men, not blind 'matter', to rise and overthrow the existing order.

II

Complementing Marx's and Engels's belief that theory must lead to revolutionary practice, was their application of the dialectical method to history, which implies that changes are to be seen as the results of the interplay of contradictions. Dialectics came to Marx from Hegel, but, as he put it in his Preface to the second German edition of **Capital,** I (1873), the 'mystified form' which had been given to dialectics by Hegel needed to be transformed into a 'rational form'. In this form,

> it [dialectics] includes in its comprehension and affirmative recognition of the existing state of things, at the same time also the recognition of the negation of that state, of its inevitable breaking up, because it regards

every historically developed social form as in fluid movement, and therefore takes into account its transient nature not less than its momentary existence, because it lets nothing impose upon it and is in its essence critical and revolutionary.

And he then goes on to speak of the 'contradictions inherent in the movement of capitalist society'.[6]

Whether what Marx did with Hegel's dialectics was merely an inversion ('turned right side up again', as Marx said in the Preface above quoted), or a fundamental 'break' with Hegel (as Althusser has urged)[7] is an important question; but whatever the answer, Marx's use of dialectics to fashion his vision of history is hardly to be disputed. Marx's application of dialectics to society and history first appeared appropriately enough in his **'Introduction to the Critique of Hegel's Philosophy of Law',** an article written in March-August 1843. It was here that the concept of a major contradiction in society, the contradiction of classes, was identified. The struggle it gave rise to must result in 'part of civil society emancipating itself and attaining universal supremacy'.[8] In Marx's and Engels's joint work *The Holy Family,* written the following year, and published in 1845, the relationship between 'the proletariat and [men of] wealth' is presented as one of 'antitheses',[9] and Engels in a speech in 1845 spoke of this as a 'contradiction which will develop more and more sharply'.[10]

In *The German Ideology* (1845-46), the next step was taken of sketching a succession of major classes based on different 'property relations', the development from one social formation to another taking place as a result of class struggle. Here it is assumed that human society from the very beginning had a form of 'division of labour', giving rise to a corresponding form of 'property'. As the division of labour become more and more complex, the forms of property changed, giving rise to corresponding classes, with mutually antagonistic interests. Thus, first, there was 'tribal property' with patriarchal relations growing into slavery; then 'ancient communal and state property' where 'the class relations between citizens and slaves are now completely developed'. The third form was 'feudal or estate property', which had 'landowners' on one side and 'the enserfed small peasantry' on the other.[11] From out of these relationships developed the system of manufactures; and then, with large scale industry, came the modern 'bourgeois society', with possessors of 'industrial capital' being confronted by 'the proletarians'.[12]

It was clearly this understanding of the past attained within some five or six years by Marx and Engels that found its ultimate generalization in the sentence with which the main text of the *Manifesto* begins: 'The history of all hitherto existing society is the history of class struggles. 'Despite such modification of the words 'all hitherto existing society' that Marx and Engels were to make later, this sentence undoubtedly represents the core of the materialist conception of history, and the basic premise on which any Marxist historiography can be constructed.

III

The reason why Marx and Engels came later to restrict the application of classes and class struggles to only the later (or historical) periods of 'all hitherto existing society' was because zoological science and social anthropology, which had seemingly lagged behind the progress of philosophy and political economy, made up the lag in the period following the *Manifesto.* In *The German Ideology* it had been assumed by Marx and Engels that the appearance of mankind, the formation of society and the division of labour were all inseparable and simultaneous events. Natural scientists had not as yet seen any evolutionary sequence in the origins of the various species, including *homo sapiens;* and there was yet no answer to the assertion that man, with his specific anatomical structure, was created all at once. In his Paris Manuscripts of 1844, Marx had found it easier to refute the conception of the creation of the world, by bringing up the results of geological observation, which pointed to spontaneous evolution. But for human evolution at the anatomical plane, there was nothing that Marx could urge, except to assert vehemently the fact of man's 'self-creation, his own formation process';[13] but this, on the basis of knowledge then available, could be valid only for the social, not anatomical, history of man. The current scientific belief still relied on the dictum of the immutability of each species that had been so authoritatively pronounced by Linnaeus (d. 1778).

The scientific breakthrough came with the publication of Charles Darwin's *Origin of Species* in 1859. Evolution (and, therefore, dialectics) was at work even in the anatomical formation of man; and, no wonder, Marx was extremely excited by Darwin's great discovery.[14] This immediately opened the question of the transition from ape to man (on which Engels was to write a pamphlet in 1876),[15] and the nature of the evolution of society. In his 1844 Paris Manuscripts Marx had distinguished man from animals by his ability to produce more than what he immediately needed;[16] but now this capacity could also be seen as an acquired one after man had anatomically evolved.

The solution, for Marx and Engels, came to hand, when in 1877 the American anthropologist Lewis H. Morgan published his *Ancient Society, or Researches in the Lines of Human Progress from Savagery through Barbarism to Civilization.* Marx took copious notes from the book, though death (1883) prevented him from critically evaluating the results of Morgan's researches. But Engels carried out the required undertaking and published his *Origin of the Family, Private Property and the State* in 1884. In the Morganian state of 'savagery', human society existed, with production 'essentially collective'; the producers being also the consumers. The 'division of labour' came late, and, as it evolved, generated classes, until 'with slavery, which reached its fullest development in civilization, came the first great development of society into an exploiting and an exploited class'.[17] Classes and class struggles thus originated at a late stage in the time-span of human existence, when man could produce, and, therefore, be forced to produce, a surplus—and this the exploiting class could seize.

Once this decisive elucidation of the origin of class divisions in human society had been made, it became necessary for Engels to introduce a note in the 1888 English edition of the *Manifesto* to the effect that the phrase 'all hitherto existing society' should be modified to cover only the period of 'written history'. Since writing in all societies originated long after the ages of 'savagery' and 'barbarism' were past, this was a good counsel of caution. But Engels's note made it clear that what he wished to exclude was not the entire period previous to written history (now generally called prehistory), but the period of 'the primitive communistic society' when owing to the low level of production and collective organization, classes did not exist. Only when the primitive society decayed, did 'separate and finally antagonistic classes' appear on the scene.

IV

In its short description of the pre-modern classes, based mainly on European history, the *Manifesto* follows the longer description attempted in *The German Ideology,* already mentioned.[18] It particularly underlines two important points, both relating to the nature of class struggle in pre-modern epochs.

First, the class struggle though 'uninterrupted', was 'now hidden, now open'. In other words, since class interests were always in contradiction, class conflict was always present. But the extent to which the struggle was grasped as a class struggle in the contestants' consciousness varied: this seems the best way of how the words 'now hidden, now open' are to be understood. Here a passage in *The German Ideology* may again be taken to have presaged more explicitly what the *Manifesto* here touches on, with rather tantalizing brevity:

> . . . all struggles within the state, the struggle between democracy, aristocracy, and monarchy, the struggle for the franchise, etc., etc., are mere illusory forms—altogether the general interest is the illusory form of common interests—in which the real struggles of the different classes are fought out among one another.[19]

In other words, written records of the past cannot, of themselves, always be expected to give a direct explicit exposition of the class struggles as were then taking place. Marx was to note in his Preface to *A Contribution to the Critique of Political Economy* that a period of social transformation cannot be judged 'by its own consciousness' in the same way as 'one does not judge an individual by what he says about himself'.[20] One major change from earlier times brought about by the rise of capitalism is that the oppressed class, the proletariat, is becoming more and more conscious of its own existence as a class and of the fundamental antagonism between itself and the owners of capital.

The second feature of pre-capitalist formations that the *Manifesto* mentions, explains why the class struggle could so often remain dormant in the consciousness of the oppressed classes. This was because of the complexity of those earlier class structures:

> In the earlier epochs of history, we find almost everywhere a complicated arrangement of society into various orders, a manifold gradations of social rank. In ancient Rome we have patricians, knights, plebeians, slaves; in the Middle Ages, feudal lords, vassals, guild masters, journeymen, apprentices, serfs; in almost all of these classes, again, subordinate gradations.

In *The German Ideology* Marx and Engels had already explained how such complexities in medieval Europe hindered the development of class struggle.[21] In that text a further important point was made, that such complexity was to be expected in all societies where human relations were based not purely on exchange, but on custom and other social institutions ('personal relations'). But things change, when, as in modern bourgeois society, individuals are 'independent of one another and are only held together by exchange'. Here as labour (or, as Marx would say later, labour power) itself becomes a commodity, in conditions of 'large-scale industry', the class contradictions become overwhelmingly dominant and sharper.[22]

This conclusion is repeated in more vibrant language in the *Manifesto*:

> Our epoch, the epoch of the bourgeoisie, possesses, however, this distinctive feature: it has simplified the class antagonisms. Society as a whole is more and more splitting into two great classes directly facing each other: Bourgeoisie and Proletariat.

These ideas about the nature of class structures and class struggles were offered in the *Manifesto* in respect of Europe, to which till then the knowledge of Marx and Engels had been largely restricted. But in the 1850s Marx began to read extensively about India, and it clearly seemed to him that the caste system was another form of those complex gradations which had marked pre-bourgeois societies in Europe. Writing in 1853 he saw that the foundations of the caste system lay in 'hereditary divisions of labour', divisions that, as he noted later, were carried to the extreme of 'conversion of fractional work into the life-calling of one man'. By their divisiveness, the castes constituted 'decisive impediments to Indian progress and Indian power'. Yet these divisions, like the pre-modern gradations in Europe touched upon in the *Manifesto,* could not withstand the introduction of bourgeois conditions: 'Modern industry, resulting from the railway system will dissolve the hereditary divisions of labour, upon which rest the Indian castes . . . '.[23]

Marx might have been optimistic here, and did not allow for the continuing ideological backwardness which would sustain the caste system, even after its main economic basis in the form of division of labour had been removed or curtailed. But what is important for us is that within almost five years of composing the *Manifesto,* he was essentially recognizing a prospective historical process in India similar to the one that had taken place in Europe—a complex of class gradations being immensely simplified by the onset of capitalist relations. Here, therefore, there was no desire in Marx to seek any exceptionalism for areas outside Europe.

V

It will be noticed that in the *Manifesto* there is not yet any use of the term 'mode of production'. The term with its sense definitely established occurs in the *Grundrisse,* Marx's extensive manuscript notes, composed in 1857-58;[24] but the *locus classicus* for the term is the Preface to *A Contribution to the Critique of Political Economy,* which Marx published early in 1859 immediately after *Grundrisse.* In the Preface the 'mode of production' appears as the sum total of 'the relations of production'—the base—and the 'legal and political institutions' and 'forms of social consciousness' which correspond to it. A 'mode of production' having passed its prime begins to decay from its own contradictions, whereafter 'an era of social revolution' ensues, leading to the rise of new 'superior relations of production'. And so 'in broad outline' Marx could distinguish 'the Asiatic, ancient, feudal and bourgeois modes of production' as successive social formations.[25]

It could be said that the succession of ancient, feudal, and bourgeois modes, with slave, serf and wage-labour as the respective defining basic forms of relations of production, is implied in the text of the *Manifesto* (and in the earlier *German Ideology*), as we have seen. Essentially, what the Preface to the *Critique* does, is to put that description into a more theoretically refined mould, through a clearer application of the dialectical method to social history.

The reference to the Asiatic mode is, however, one singular addition, since there is no trace of it in the *Manifesto* or earlier writings. Marx and Engels appear to have become interested in the economic formations outside Europe for the first time in 1853; and there is much reflection in the *Grundrisse* (1857-58) on the Indian ('Asiatic') community and the despotic states that arose to exploit these communities.[26] When Marx listed the 'Asiatic' as the earliest mode, preceding the ancient and feudal, he probably had in mind not a territorial mode but the earliest form of 'tribal property' which he thought lasted in Asia much longer than in Europe. This becomes clear from his statement in the *Grundrisse* that

> Slavery and serfdom are thus only further developments of the form of property resting on the clan system. They necessarily modified all of the latter's forms. They can do this least of all in the Asiatic form.[27]

The intrusion of the 'Asiatic' in a succession of 'modes' was not without its problems, especially since its persistence would imply, as Marx rather incautiously stated in 1853, that

Indian society has no history at all, at least no known history. What we call its history is the history of successive intruders who founded their empires on the basis of that unresisting and unchanging society.[28]

Clearly, the emergence of individual petty production within the community, the production of a marketable surplus and so the emergence of a commodity sector along with the presumed 'natural' economy of the village, the appearance of a 'despotic' power, taking 'rent' as 'tax', processes recognized by Marx himself as taking shape within the 'Asiatic' system, meant that the Asian continent, or India (to Marx, the main ground for his 'Asiatic' evidence), could not be devoid of historical change.[29] One should moreover remember that the denial of history to India, expressed in 1853, was never repeated by Marx and Engels; and that, while in 1888 Engels did suggest a modification to the 'history of class struggles' formulation in the *Manifesto* in order to accommodate the stage of primitive communism, he proposed no further modification in order to provide for the history-less 'Asiatic Mode'. There is, therefore, no doubt the universality of the *Manifesto*'s principal historical dictum about class struggle continued to be upheld by its authors, as applying to all societies blessed by the exploitation of one class by another (as the 'Asiatic' mode in its 'despotic' form certainly was). There could be no exceptions to this rule.[30]

VI

The *Manifesto* provides us with a sketch of the emergence and development of the bourgeoisie, tracing its origins to 'the serfs of the Middle Ages', from amongst whom 'sprang the chartered burghers', from whom, in turn, came 'the first elements of the bourgeoisie'. In Marx's usage the terms 'bourgeoisie' and 'capitalists' are not always synonymous. 'Bourgeoisie' is generally the broader term, representing not only the owners of capital, who employ wage-labour in modern industry—and to whom he restricts the term 'capitalist' in *Capital*—but is a much larger class with much earlier origins, and includes merchants, and pre-industrial manufacturers, from whose fold 'the modern bourgeois', the industrial capitalists proper, have arisen.

The *Manifesto* identifies two important factors for the rise of the bourgeoisie and the emergence of capitalism. The first was the growth of the market, initiated by the discovery of America and the rounding of the Cape of Good Hope, which resulted in Europe's access to the 'East-Indian and Chinese markets, the colonization of America, [and] trade with the colonies . . .'. These markets required production on a scale for which the feudal craft-guild system was unsuitable; large workshops had, therefore, to be established, with 'division of labour' not, as previously, between guilds but within 'each single workshop': this was the basis of 'the manufacturing system', which was ultimately dissolved or transformed by machinery into the modern factory system.

This account was based on Marx's and Engels's economic and historical studies, carried on till that date. The relationship of market to production was at the heart of the great controversy between the Mercantilists and their opponents, out of which controversy the science of Political Economy originated. The increase in productivity caused by the division of labour within the workshop had been classically emphasized by Adam Smith in 1776.[31] And the transformation wrought by machinery was especially studied by Ricardo in a new chapter added to his text in 1821.[32] Marx had already discussed in his ***Poverty of Philosophy*** (1847) the matter of the markets ('the increase of commodities put into circulation from the moment trade penetrated to the East Indies, by way of the Cape of Good Hope; the colonial system; the development of maritime trade'), of the 'workshop' of the 'manufacturing industry', and of the transformation in the division of labour brought about by machinery,[33] what the ***Manifesto*** does is to reproduce the essential points made there.

But, if the ***Manifesto*** sums up what classical Political Economy had already expounded with regard to the growth of bourgeois relations of production, it necessarily lacked what came to be Marx's own crucial contribution to the history of capitalism, viz. the theory of the primitive or primary accumulation of capital. In 1857-58 in the ***Grundrisse*** Marx made some important observations about 'the original accumulation of capital', but this was done mainly in order to show that not money, but social changes, helped to bring such accumulation about.[34] These remarks can hardly be considered to anticipate the main theory that was presented in all its fullness in the last portion of ***Capital,*** Volume I, Part VIII: 'The So-called Primitive Accumulation'.[35]

Marx here begins by pointing out that the initial circuit of capitalist production can take place only when possessors of capital and free labourers can come together 'face to face'. This is made possible only if the former have accumulated wealth (convertible into capital) outside of, or previous to, capitalist production, and the latter have been 'freed' of their means of production as petty producers. There must therefore be a process of 'expropriation' of the one class by the other before capitalist production can begin. It is this process that constitutes 'Primitive Accumulation'.[36]

Marx describes two such major processes or forms of primitive accumulation: one, internal; the other, external. Taking England as the classical case he describes at length how the English peasant was deprived of his land, from the period of the Tudor enclosures to the private and parliamentary enclosures of the eighteenth century.[37] Primitive accumulation here was achieved by brute force, its principal moments those when

> great masses of men are suddenly and forcibly torn from their means of subsistence, and hurled as free and 'unattached' proletarians on the labour market. The expropriation of the agricultural producer, from the soil, is the basis of the whole process.[38]

The second process, the external, consisted of the forcible plunder and expropriation of colonial peoples:

> The discovery of gold and silver in America, the extirpation, enslavement and entombment in mines of the aboriginal [Amerindian] population, the beginning of the conquest and looting of the East Indies, the turning of Africa into a warren for the commercial hunting of black skins, signalized the rosy dawn of the era of capitalist production. These idyllic proceedings are the chief momenta of primitive accumulation.[39]

Of these proceedings Marx then offers a trenchant account, touching on the colonial regimes of terror, the loot of India, the slaughter of the Amerindian people and, not the least, the African slave trade.[40]

This picture of the rise of capitalism is profoundly different from that given in the ***Manifesto,*** where we see burgesses growing into modern bourgeois by simple expansion of trade and gains from production. But Marx now dismisses this simple mode of growth (transformation of guild-masters and artisans into 'full-blown capitalists' through 'gradually extending exploitation of wage-labour and corresponding accumulation') as a process that would have given only 'snail's pace' to the development of capitalist production.[41] Primitive accumulation, forcible expropriation, internal and external, could alone give the necessary pace and scale to capital accumulation. Force was central to this process—the whole process of primitive accumulation illustrated how 'force is the midwife of every old society, pregnant with a new one. It is in itself an economic power.'[42]

One must, therefore, realise that the description of the rise of capitalism in the ***Manifesto*** is seriously incomplete. The forcible expropriation of the peasants and colonial peoples (as against simple conquests of rural and colonial markets) do not appear in the ***Manifesto***: even the infamous trans-Atlantic slave trade is not mentioned. This was because, as we have seen, the ***Manifesto*** had basically accepted what classical Political Economy had till then taught about the growth of production through an expansion of the market and forms of division of labour. Marx subsequently made his own historical discoveries, leading to another decisive break (comparable to the one in the realm of surplus value) from the legacy of Adam Smith and Ricardo.

VII

At the time of the drafting of the ***Manifesto,*** Marx was well aware of the effect of England's industrial development on crafts and employment in non-capitalist countries. In 1845-46, he and Engels noted in ***The German Ideology*** how 'if in England a machine is invented [it] deprives countless workers of bread in India and China'.[43] A year later in the ***Poverty of Philosophy,*** while speaking of economists' optimism with regard to 'improvement', Marx asked sarcastically whether they 'were thinking of the millions of workers who had to perish in the East Indies so as to procure for the million and half workers employed in the same [textile] industry in England three years' prosperity out of ten'.[44]

These statements are not repeated in the *Manifesto,* though it does say that 'all old established national industries have been destroyed or are being destroyed', where the authors might have had in mind colonial craft industries as well. Then follows a passage which touches upon the new condition of dependence that capitalism was imposing on the rest of the world:

> Just as it [the bourgeoisie] has made the country dependent on the towns, so it has made barbarian and semi-barbarian countries dependent on the civilized ones, nations of peasants on nations of bourgeois, the East on the West.

It should be recognized that this dependence is visualized in the *Manifesto* in economic terms, not political. 'The prices of its commodities', it says a few lines earlier, 'are the heavy artillery with which it [the bourgeoisie] batters down all Chinese walls, with which it forces the barbarians' intensely obstinate hatred of foreigners to capitulate'. Yet as Marx was himself later to note, it had been not cheap prices, but canon with which Britain forced China to open its markets to opium and other goods through the infamous First Opium War, 1840-42.[45]

In a very important (but rather neglected) article of 1859 Marx noted that Chinese goods could not be undersold by British exports because Britain did not yet have the necessary political power in China to undermine the position of Chinese rural producers, in the way it had done in India.[46] And with respect to India, Marx had seen as early as 1853 that the Free Traders needed first to conquer it ('to get it') 'in order to subject it to their sharp philanthropy'.[47] In 1859, again, he remarked on the financial burdens England had to accept 'for the "glorious" reconquest of India' after the 1857 Revolt, for the purpose of 'securing the monopoly of the Indian market to the Manchester free traders'.[48] It nearly seems as if Marx was anticipating the notion of imperialism of free trade, which Gallagher and Robinson introduced in a seminal article published almost a hundred years later, in 1953.[49] In general, Marx's attitude towards colonialism hardened perceptibly as he read more about it. One can see from his articles in the *New York Daily Tribune* in the 1850s what harsh and uncompromising indictment of the colonial system he was capable of.[50]

Since the *Manifesto* precedes its authors' attainment of the recognition of colonialism as a necessary adjunct of free trade, it naturally does not put forward any explicit objective of colonial emancipation. But within very few years of its publication, Marx himself was savouring the prospect of a free China and free India. In 1850 he closed a report on China with the words:

> When in their imminent flight across Asia our European reactionaries will ultimately arrive at the Wall of China, . . . who knows if they will not find there the inscription: 'The Chinese Republic—Liberty, Equality, Fraternity.'[51]

And three years later, he was looking forward to 'the Hindus [Indians] [having] grown strong enough to throw off the English yoke altogether'.[52]

VIII

The Communist Manifesto was written to meet an important need—the need to put in a short text the main principles of Communism, a task that was brilliantly performed—the stirring language conveying the main ideas without loss of precision. If the *Manifesto* was written in time to offer to the proletariat a guide before it entered the revolutionary upsurge of Europe in 1848, its value has only grown further in that today, after the grave retreat of socialism on the world scale in the last decade and more, the working class of all countries needs to be rallied to the cause of socialism still more urgently and more resolutely. But these very circumstances also require that Marxian theory should be closely and critically grasped. One needs, therefore, to look at the *Manifesto*'s contents carefully in the light of the stage in the evolution of Marxism at which it was written. The perception of historical development, especially of the development of capitalism, was considerably enriched by Marx and Engels in the years after the publication of the *Manifesto.* The present paper is an attempt to indicate in what areas we must supplement the theoretical framework of the *Manifesto* by drawing upon the later discoveries and insights of its authors. A reading of the *Manifesto,* with these kept in mind, can surely help us to serve its cause only still better.

Notes

1. 'Theses on Feuerbach', the original version, as published in English translation in Karl Marx and Frederick Engels, *Collected Works,* V, Moscow 1976, pp. 3-5. Emphasis as in the original. The final thesis reappears in *The German Ideology,* composed by Marx and Engels in 1845-46, in the following words: '. . . in reality and for the *practical* materialist, i.e. the *communist,* it is a question of revolutionizing the existing world, of practically coming to grips with and changing the things found in existence'. Ibid., pp. 38-39. The portion containing this passage seems to be omitted in S. Ryazanskaya's translation of *The German Ideology,* Moscow 1964; it should have come on p. 39.

2. *A Contribution to the Critique of Political Economy,* translated by S. Ryazanskaya, edited by M. Dobb, Moscow 1978, pp. 20-21.

3. Ibid., p. 21.

4. Marx and Engels, *Collected Works,* V, p. 1.

5. *Selections from the Prison Notebooks of Antonio Gramsci,* edited and translated by Quintin Hoare and Geoffrey Nowell Smith, New York 1971, pp. 336-37. Also see Louis Althusser, *For Marx,* translated by Ben Brewster, Harmondsworth 1969, pp. 105-06, n. 23.

6. *Capital,* I, translated by S. Moore and E. Aveling, edited by F. Engels, London 1889, photographic reprint, edited by Dona Torr, London, 1938, pp. xxx-xxxi. All references to *Capital* are from this edition unless otherwise specified.

7. Althusser, *For Marx,* pp. 89-116, 203-04, etc.

8. For a summary and analysis of this article, of signal importance in the development of Marx's thought, see David McLellan, *Marx Before Marxism,* London 1980, pp. 142-57. The quoted words are given on p. 152.

9. *Collected Works,* V, pp. 35-36.

10. Ibid., p. 224.

11. *Collected Works,* V, pp. 32-36.

12. *Collected Works,* V, pp. 66-89; *The German Ideology,* translated by Ryazanskaya, pp. 66-85.

13. See McLellan, *Marx Before Marxism,* pp. 190-91.

14. Marx wrote to Lassalle (16 January 1861): 'Darwin's book is very important and serves me as a natural scientific basis for the class struggle in history. . . . Despite all deficiencies, not only is the death-blow dealt here for the first time to 'teleology' in the natural sciences, but its rational meaning is empirically explained'. Marx and Engels, *Selected Correspondence,* Moscow 1956, p. 151.

15. *The Part Played by Labour in the Transition from Ape to Man,* Moscow 1949.

16. McLellan, *Marx Before Marxism,* pp. 171-72.

17. Engels, *The Origin of the Family, Private Property and the State,* Moscow 1948, pp. 247-50, to be read with the Preface to the first edition (pp. 13-14).

18. One can compare the passages in the *Manifesto* with the detailed description of forms of property and corresponding classes in *The German Ideology, Collected Works,* V, pp. 32-35; *The German Ideology,* translated by Ryazanskaya, pp. 32-36.

19. *Collected Works,* V, pp. 46-47; *The German Ideology,* translated by Ryazanskaya, p. 45.

20. *A Contribution to the Critique of Political Economy,* p. 21.

21. *Collected Works,* V, pp. 64-66; *The German Ideology,* translated by Ryazanskaya, pp. 64-66.

22. *Collected Works,* V, pp. 63-64; passage not traceable in Ryazanskaya's translation.

23. 'The Future Results of British Rule in India' (*New York Daily Tribune,* 8 August 1853), in Marx and Engels, *On Colonialism,* Moscow 1976, p. 85. The reference to division carried to fractional work is from *Capital,* I, p. 331.

24. See *Grundrisse,* translated by Martin Nicolaus, Harmondsworth 1973, p. 495 (Marx, *Pre-capitalist Economic Formations,* translated by Jack Cohen, edited by E.J. Hobsbawm, pp. 94-95), for possibly the first occurrence of the term, with a clear indication of sense.

25. *A Contribution to the Critique of Political Economy,* pp. 20-22.

26. *Grundrisse,* pp. 473-86; *Pre-capitalist Economic Formations,* pp. 70-82.

27. *Grundrisse,* p. 493; *Pre-capitalist Economic Formations,* p. 91.

28. 'Future Results of British Rule', *On Colonialism,* p. 81.

29. I venture to refer to my own detailed discussion of problems in Marx's changing perceptions of the Asiatic Mode in 'Marx's Perception of India', *Essays in Indian History: Towards a Marxist Perception,* New Delhi 1995, pp. 16-35.

30. But see Hobsbawm, who attributes the view to Marx that 'the Asiatic society' is 'not yet a class society, or if it is a class society, then it is the [its?] most primitive form'. Introduction to *Pre-Capitalist Economic Formations,* p. 34. There are no statements in Marx and Engels to support this extreme inference.

31. *An Inquiry into the Nature and Cause of the Wealth of Nations,* I, London 1910, pp. 4-11.

32. David Ricardo, *The Principles of Political Economy and Taxation;* London 1911, pp. 263-71 (Chapter XXXI, 'On Machinery').

33. *Collected Works,* VI, pp. 184-87; *The Poverty of Philosophy,* Moscow n.d., pp. 151-57.

34. *Grundrisse,* pp. 259, 506-10.

35. *Capital,* I, pp. 736-800. It is, perhaps possible that 'primary' may be a better rendering than 'primitive' as in Eden and Cedar Paul's translation of *Capital,* I, London 1951, II, p. 790. But since 'primitive' is authorized by Engels, who supervised the Moore-Aveling translation, and has been in general use, it seems better to stick to it here.

36. *Capital,* I, pp. 736-39.

37. Ibid., pp. 740-57.

38. Ibid., p. 739.

39. Ibid., p. 775.

40. Ibid., pp. 775-78, 784-85.

41. Ibid., p. 774.

42. Ibid., p. 776.

43. *Collected Works,* V, p. 51; *The German Ideology,* translated by Ryazanskaya, p. 60.

44. *Collected Works,* VI, p. 160; *The Poverty of Philosophy,* p. 113.

45. In 1853 Marx spoke of 'British canon forcing [opium] on China', *New York Daily Tribune* (*NYDT*), 14 June 1853, *On Colonialism,* p. 19.

46. *NYDT,* 3 December 1859; *Collected Works,* XVI, p. 539. For some reason this article is not included in *On Colonialism.*

47. *NYDT,* 11 July 1853; *On Colonialism,* p. 49.

48. *NYDT,* 30 April 1859; *Collected Works,* XVI, p. 286; omitted in *On Colonialism.*

49. John Gallagher and Ronald Robinson, 'The Imperialism of Free Trade', *Economic History Review,* second series, VI, 1953, pp. 1-15.

50. The two major collections of these articles are *On Colonialism,* used in this paper, and Shlomo Avineri (ed.), *Karl Marx on Colonialism and Modernization,* New York 1969; the latter is the more extensive collection. The volumes of the *Collected Works* are not only the most comprehensive in their coverage, but have the most accurate texts as well.

51. *Neue Rheinische Zeitung,* No. 2 (1850); *On Colonialism,* p. 18.

52. *NYDT,* 8 August 1853; *On Colonialism,* p. 85.

FURTHER READING

Criticism

Bender, Frederic L. "Historical and Theoretical Backgrounds of the *Communist Manifesto.*" In *Karl Marx: "The Communist Manifesto,"* edited by Frederic L. Bender, pp. 1-39. New York: W. W. Norton & Company, 1988.

> Analyzes the historical and theoretical influences on *The Communist Manifesto.*

Hobsbawm, Eric. Introduction to *The Communist Manifesto* by Karl Marx and Frederick Engels, pp. 1-29. London: Verso, 1998.

> Provides an overview of *The Communist Manifesto,* the events surrounding its creation, and the social and political movements it inspired.

Hodges, Donald Clark. "Introduction: Understanding the Manifesto." In his *The Literate Communist: 150 Years of the "Communist Manifesto,"* pp. 1-14. New York: Peter Lang, 1999.

Examines *The Communist Manifesto*'s history and its influence on Russian and Soviet Communism, and considers whether Soviet Marxism self-destructed as a result of its "communist legacy" or as a result of its Marxist component.

Karat, Prakash. Introduction to *A World to Win: Essays on "The Communist Manifesto,"* edited by Prakash Karat, pp. 1-13. New Delhi: LeftWord Press, 1999.

> Provides an overview of the history of *The Communist Manifesto* upon its one hundred fiftieth anniversary.

Lansbury, Coral. "Melodrama, Pantomime and *The Communist Manifesto.*" *Browning Institute Studies* 14 (1986): 1-10.

> Analyzes the *Communist Manifesto* as a gothic melodrama, using Monk Lewis' *The Last Spectre* (1797) to illustrate the communist text's use of social reversal.

Taylor, J. A. P. Introduction to *The Communist Manifesto,* by Karl Marx and Frederick Engels, pp. 7-47. London: Penguin Books, 1967.

> A survey of events surrounding the writing of *The Communist Manifesto,* and an examination of its purpose and content.

Toews, John E. "Introduction: Historical Contexts of the *Communist Manifesto.*" In *The Communist Manifesto,* by Karl Marx and Frederick Engels, edited by John E. Towes, pp. 1-59. Boston: Bedford/St. Martin's, 1999.

> A comprehensive examination of the historical context of *The Communist Manifesto* from its own time up through the late twentieth century, with attention to how the fall of the Soviet Empire has informed contemporary understanding of the text.

Tuveson, Ernest L. "The Millenarian Structure of *The Communist Manifesto.*" In *The Apocalypse in English Renaissance Thought and Literature: Patterns, Antecedents, and Repercussions,* edited by C. A. Patrides and Joseph Wittreich, pp. 324-41. Manchester, England: Manchester University Press, 1984.

> Explores the call to revolution set forth in *The Communist Manifesto* as it resembles the millenarian dream.

Charles Harpur
1813-1868

Australian poet, essayist, and short story writer.

INTRODUCTION

Described as an original and distinctive poet of ideas, Harpur is considered one of the best and most prolific of Australia's colonial writers. His poetry, which includes "The Creek of the Four Graves" and "A Storm in the Mountains," displays Harpur's astute observational skills, knowledge of local history and evolving culture, and sense of moral responsibility. Although criticized at times for his awkward, even clumsy poetic structures, particularly in his landscape narratives, Harpur is recognized by Judith Wright as "the first to assert the independence, the specialness, of the Australian . . . ."

BIOGRAPHICAL INFORMATION

Harpur was born on January 23, 1813, in Windsor, New South Wales. His parents, Joseph and Sarah (Chidley), had been sent to Australia as convicts from Ireland and England. Harpur's father took on positions as chief constable, town clerk, farmer, and schoolmaster to care for his growing family. Young Charles attended his father's school, but little else is known about his education. Harpur's biographer, J. Normington-Rawling, records that Harpur read extensively, probably borrowing books from the private collection of Samuel Marsden, his father's patron. Harpur began to write at the age of eleven or twelve and many scholars believe that by 1826 he was publishing verses in a local newspaper, the *Sydney Gazette*. Harpur's life changed dramatically in 1829 when his family and friends faced a harsh depression, leaving his father without funds and unable to care for his children. Harpur, out of necessity, left his family to work on the Hunter River as a woodcutter and hunter. Harpur's determination to be content with a limited income while studying, meditating, and writing is implied in his poem, "To the Spirit of Poesy." By the age of twenty, Harpur was writing steadily and publishing poems, political essays, and letters in colonial newspapers. While living in Sydney, he unsuccessfully drafted a play and attempted acting, with both endeavors garnering ridicule in the *Sydney Monitor*. Harpur also mixed with political radicals and reformers in Sydney and held a number of jobs, including teaching, farming, and clerical work. Harpur considered this the loneliest episode of his life, although he also believed it made him a better poet. In 1843 Harpur met Mary Doyle, whose parents were initially opposed to their daughter's relationship with a man of such little means, the son of convict parents. After seven years of courtship and much effort to persuade

her father, however, Harpur and Doyle were married in 1850. Meanwhile, Harpur was busily writing his "Rosa Sonnets," and in 1845 his first volume of poems, *Thoughts: A Series of Sonnets,* was published. Later, Harpur acquired the position of Gold Commissioner on the southern goldfields, allowing him to provide comfortably for his family of five children. In 1866 Harpur faced a two-fold blow: he lost this government position and severe floods destroyed his farm. But the worst was yet to come. His second son, Charles, was killed in a hunting accident. Harpur's poems during this period reflect his deep sadness and sense of loss, his disappointment at the criticism leveled at his works—which, critics claim, was due in part to his social background—and his struggle with tuberculosis. Harpur died on June 9, 1868.

MAJOR WORKS

Critics have outlined four major periods in Harpur's life which distinctly affected his writing: his early years, known as the Windsor or Hawkesbury period, 1813-30;

the Sydney period, 1830-39, in which Harpur experienced some measure of success as well as the first real criticism of his work; the Hunter River period, 1839-59, a time in which his first collection of poems was published; and the Euroma period, 1859-68, which left the poet disillusioned, disappointed, and struggling to support his family. In his early poetry and prose, Harpur emerged as a landscape poet, a painter in words with a style that was both original and distinctly Australian. Harpur's best-known poem, "Midsummer Noon in the Australian Forest," reflects the influence of Wordsworth, but also the independent, inventive spirit that would characterize most of his works. Harpur struggled throughout his career to define a singularly Australian style, and he took considerable pride in his self-appointed role as "Australia's First Poet." The subject of his nature poetry—mountains, trees, clouds, an endless sky, and bright starlight—carry a sense of the enormity and depth of Australia itself, as seen in *Songs of Australia—First Series,* published in 1850. Harpur's time in Sydney also left deep impressions, as he felt overlooked and unappreciated by those in established literary circles. His feelings are expressed in such poems as "The Sorrows of Chatterton" and "Genius Lost." Harpur's best poetic work, *The Bushrangers; A Play in Five Acts, and Other Poems,* was published in 1853 and included a longer version of "The Creek of the Four Graves." This narrative poem displays Harpur's ability to treat historical events movingly, as he describes a clash between colonial settlers and Australian Aborigines. Some of Harpur's poetry, like "The Creek," contains religious elements, contrasting God's benevolence and forgiveness with man's sinful inclinations. Critics note Harpur's technique of moving from general to specific—as in "The Coastal View" and "A Storm in the Mountains"—and point out that it mirrors the methods of scientific discovery during the latter part of the eighteenth century. Harpur's Euroma period saw the publication of *A Poet's Home* in 1862, *The Tower of the Dream* in 1865, and the writing of "The Witch of Hebron," considered by many to be Harpur's best blank verse work. "The Witch of Hebron" recounts the transmigration of a soul through five different lives as punishment for prideful sin and is indicative of Harpur's belief in the persistence of the soul beyond death. Written during a time in which he felt an extreme sense of neglect and abandonment, the poem encompasses the themes of love, hate, good and evil, space and time, and poverty and luxury.

CRITICAL RECEPTION

Judith Wright asserts that a fair and accurate assessment of Harpur's works cannot be based solely upon *Poems,* the collection of his works published in 1883 after his death. This collection, edited by H. M. Martin with a forward by Harpur's wife Mary, contains serious omissions and excisions that, according to Wright, are essential to the understanding of many of Harpur's poems. Wright compares *Poems* with early manuscripts now housed at the Mitchell Library in Sydney to shed light on the purpose and import of Harpur's works. She notes competent narrative, excellent landscape descriptions, and originality in Harpur's

published verse, but emphasizes that a true characterization of the depth of his subject matter can only be discerned when passages from these manuscripts are restored. This evaluation echoes Harpur's initial reception by his colonial contemporaries, who, while noting semantic errors, hailed Harpur's *The Bushrangers; a Play in Five Acts, and Other Poems* as poetry of the very highest order. Later critics would not be so kind, however, describing Harpur's writing as awkward, clumsy at times, and even of "earnest ineptitude." Elizabeth Perkins discusses Harpur's emphasis on self-consciousness and the need to instruct, with too much effort in conveying his new Australia within established poetic terms and diction rather than truly and freely expressing himself. Adrian Mitchell and others have focused on Harpur's propensity to revise his poetry, with sometimes unsuccessful or confusing results. Critics also lament the lack of a common foundation for analysis, with many of Harpur's poems existing in several different revisions and no clear means of determining dates of completion. However, most scholars agree with Leonie Kramer's statement that, despite his technical imperfections, Harpur "knew what poetry is, and how poets learn their craft; he appointed himself good masters, and taught himself what to accept and adopt and how to present his individual perceptions, while drawing on the tradition he made his own."

PRINCIPAL WORKS

"Rhymed Criticisms with Prose Notes" (poetry) n.d.
"The Importance of a Rhyme or A Story of the Old Dock-Yard" (short story) 1845
Thoughts: A Series of Sonnets (poetry) 1845
Songs of Australia—First Series (poetry) c. 1850
The Bushrangers; A Play in Five Acts, and Other Poems (poetry) 1853
A Poet's Home (poetry) 1862
The Tower of the Dream (poetry) 1865
Poems (poetry) 1883
Selected Poems of Charles Harpur (poetry) 1944
Rosa: Love Sonnets to Mary Doyle (poetry) 1948
Charles Harpur (poetry) 1973
The Poetical Works of Charles Harpur (poetry) 1984
Charles Harpur: Selected Poetry and Prose (poetry, prose) 1986

CRITICISM

Judith Wright (essay date 1963)

SOURCE: Wright, Judith. In *Australian Writers and Their Work: Charles Harpur*, pp. 5-32. Melbourne: Lansdowne Press, 1963.

[*In the following excerpt, Wright addresses Harpur's family background, early employment, and the unprofessional editing of a posthumous edition of his works. The essay concludes with an attempt to summarize the importance of Harpur's work in Australia's literary canon.*]

I

Many poets have been born in unfortunate circumstances; some have lived and died unfortunate; but poets can usually trust to a posthumous future for justice. Few are as unlucky as Charles Harpur, Australia's first and least-regarded poet.

Harpur was born under precisely that cloud which in early-Victorian Australia was least forgivable—he was the son of convicts. His father, Joseph Harpur, an Irishman, was indicted in London for highway robbery, with others, and was sentenced to death. Reprieved and transported, he arrived in Sydney in November 1800, at the age of 24, and was later assigned to the service of John Macarthur, "the Perturbator" of the young colony.

Sarah Chidley, Charles's mother, seems to have been about thirteen or fourteen when she was tried at Taunton in 1805 for what we would now think a very minor offence, and sentenced to seven years' transportation. She reached Sydney in 1806, and was apparently also assigned to the Macarthurs, where she met Joseph Harpur. Charles was their second son and third child (the eldest son, also named Joseph, was himself a remarkable man, something of a versifier, and later a politician).

Charles was born in 1813. His father, who had evidently earned the goodwill of John Macarthur, had now been made Government schoolmaster at Windsor, on the Hawkesbury River. His qualifications for the post we do not know—he was described officially at the time of his trial as "a labourer", but it seems he may have been an attorney's clerk, and clearly he was literate enough to encourage his sons' ambitions. So Charles and his brother received at least some education, and Charles seems to have had access to a private library, or libraries, where he read all he could. The Windsor schoolmaster may quite well have been on amicable terms with the local clergymen, who included in their number Rowland Hassall at Parramatta, and the Rev. Henry Fulton at Castlereagh on the Nepean, an Irish clergyman who, like Joseph Harpur himself, had been transported. The excitable and controversial Samuel Marsden, the "flogging parson", may also have allowed the use of his library to the studious young man, in spite of his prejudices.

At any rate, Joseph Harpur and his young family seem to have spent a few comparatively peaceful and happy years in Windsor, until Charles' sixteenth year. In the little town with its central square, its Greenway church and the bridge across the river, Charles discovered his love for poetry and determined on his vocation. Later, in **"The Dream By the Fountain"**, he wrote of those days, making the Australian Muse address him:

> For I felt thee—ev'n then, wildly, wondrously musing
> Of glory and grace by old Hawkesbury's side,

> Scenes that then spread recordless around thee suffusing
> With the purple of love—I beheld thee, and sighed.
> Sighed—for the fire-robe of thought had enwound thee,
> Betokening so much that the happy must dread,
> And whence there should follow, howe'er it renowned thee,
> What sorrows of heart, and what labours of head . . .

What kind of boy was this, who dreamed of glory by a river in a convict colony, and suffused its landscape with love? In a manuscript book[1] dated 1851, he gives us a self-portrait:

> "I was earnestly imaginative, simple of mind, and single of heart. I could greatly venerate whatever I could believe in, as being righteous and true. I was affectionate to all-forgivingness—perhaps to weakness. I was proud to my sorrow. I was impolitic to my loss— that is, in worldly matters: for in things spiritual there is nothing, in the end, to be gained by policy. I was naturally social, though solitary in my habits from wounded goodwill, and from a shyness superinduced by the everlasting evilness of my circumstances: for I know, of my own hard experience, that men in general can only value the fortunate. I was (as I am still) an enthusiast in the cause of human liberty and progress: liberty in all directions and progress infinite . . . To complete the portrait with its most perilous details—I was wilfully good or wilfully wicked; fiery as a furnace; daring as a devil; and lastly, sensual, but in the best sense of the word . . ."

Self-portraits are automatically suspect; few of us can look ourselves, even our younger selves, steadily in the eye and put down what we see without faltering. But the man who speaks to us through Harpur's poetry—even the least interesting and least successful of his verses—the man who with an impetuous heat protested to the end of his days against injustice in man or fate, and dreamed to the end of his days of the recognition that was always denied him, must have been much of the fiery yet gentle temper that he shows us here.

Charles Harpur began to write verse, and to publish it, very early. That he loved the country round Windsor, and the great river that runs through that fertile plain, we know from his poetry. But the recurrent image that haunts him is of the Blue Mountains, whose foothills lead up and away from the Hawkesbury plain; the mysterious mountains that must have obsessed his mind in his youth as they did the minds of many of the settlers on the coast. He gives us many splendid pictures of them; the best known comes from his narrative poem, **"The Creek of the Four Graves"**:

> . . . O what words, what hues
> Might paint the wild magnificence of view
> That opened westward! Out extending, lo!
> The heights rose crowding with their summits all
> Dissolving as it seemed, and partly lost
> In the exceeding radiancy aloft;

And thus transfigured for awhile they stood
Like a great company of archaeons, crowned
With burning diadems, and tented o'er
With canopies of purple and of gold.

So Harpur began his life with a certain advantage, for a poet who had to lay the foundation for a transition from the English to the Australian atmosphere in poetry. The fertile cultivated countryside of the Hawkesbury Valley, the almost English grace of the little town, planned by Governor Macquarie, stone-built—even though built in bitterness by convict labour—made as it were a natural stepping-stone between the old and the forbidding new.

Today we cannot realise how forbidding that untouched, unknown, unlimited wilderness must have seemed. Australia—what was it? It was scarcely even the germ of a country, scarcely even a vision, except to the most prescient, among whom the boy by the Hawkesbury was certainly one. It was a dubious and strife-torn convict settlement at the forgotten end of the world, a dump for the unwanted. And the free settlers, the respectable of the community, felt this most bitterly of all. England was not merely the home to which they all hoped, sooner or later, to return; it was a cult, it was an image of worship, it was Respectability. They clung the more to their cult, that the unrespectable, the convicts, the Irishmen, the ticket-of-leave men with old scars on backs and ankles, were so far from sharing it. To the respectable, the very existence of these shoddy and rebellious men sharpened their nostalgia and negated any image of Australia that might begin, somewhere, to take shape.

So a literature could hardly be respectable that had its source in, and tried to affirm, this tatterdemalion country. What was not English and had not been praised by the English magazines, could not be allowed to be poetry. To write of Australia as she looked and was—the dark wild land, with its savage and miserable outcasts and its life of monotony relieved by rum and quarrels; with its few influential men, its constant political intrigues and squabbles, and beyond them the ancient silence—would have been to win no friends and find no publishers.

The picture was dark; Harpur in his young idealism gilded it, but with the gold of a Utopia that the material-minded settlers cared little for. And Harpur, son of a convict and an Irishman, was by his birth precluded from being the poet of respectability that the influential men might have recognised—if they had wanted a poet at all.

So an Australian poet was doomed, since an Australian poetry was not yet possible. In fact, how could such a poetry begin to be written? The English tradition was built in an island of safety and pride, of rain and greenery, of power and confidence. Here, it sometimes seemed, none of these things existed. Moreover, Christmas came in the summer heat and Easter in autumn; the old rituals became a kind of nonsense, the English customs stood on their heads. The stars were in the wrong places, the trees shed bark instead of leaves, the animals were comic nightmares, the

very plants and birds were strange. The natives were obstinately unamenable; they would not work, nor would they fight, except in a ragged guerrilla warfare that ate away at the outskirts of settlement. It was no time and no climate for poetry.

Harpur understood this, but he went on obstinately with his determination to be a poet for all that—to be the first Australian poet, no hanger-on of the other side of the world.

> Lyre of my country, first falls it to me
> From the charm-muttering Savage's rude-beating hand
> To snatch thee . . .[2]

he wrote; but he knew that on that strange lyre he might not yet have the art to play.

Yet, though the English tradition was oddly out of place, was even perhaps irrelevant, in this country, it must somehow be adapted. Harpur set himself earnestly to learn all he could. He read whatever he could get hold of; he made copious notes, and many of them were astute. A young man with as little teaching and encouragement as Harpur might laboriously find out much for himself; but he could not, without a sensitive and independent taste, have written, for instance, of Chaucer's rhymed couplet:

> It is the true English heroic couplet, not composed, like Pope's, of two lines having each a caesural balance, but flowing freely forth, and yet at the same time open to every variety of modulation. And notwithstanding all that has been said to the contrary, I cannot help thinking the true English heroic verse the best of all kinds of verse—entire, compact, continuous, and yet admitting of all the heroic pauses being located anywhere in it, from the first syllable to the last.[3]

He wrote, also, a number of critical verses on various of the English poets, each in the particular style of the poet—no mean feat for any versifier, and carried out well enough to make those critics who have denigrated his technical powers look foolish, if they could read them. Unluckily, they cannot read them, for like so much of Harpur's work they are buried in manuscript form in the Mitchell Library in Sydney.

All this was training. But for what Harpur was himself to write, experience was also necessary. What kind of experience did Harpur's life afford, to a young poet all faith and ardour and determination?

In 1829, when Charles was sixteen, his family life came to an end. His father had been given a small grant of land, and the family had been relatively well off. But in 1829 depression came. Many small settlers were ruined, and Joseph Harpur among them. The Harpur family had to break up, and Charles went away to work on the Hunter River, inland from Newcastle, probably as a farm-labourer.

When he was twenty years old, Charles's verses began to appear in various of the Colony's newspapers, and thereafter he wrote, and was published, fairly continuously. He was at this time in Sydney, where he found occasional employment. He also produced the first draft of a play, on an Australian bushranging theme, which began by being called **"The Tragedy of Donohoe,"** but in its later form was re-titled **"The Bushrangers."** It is interesting as his first attempt at a serious handling of an Australian theme; but Harpur's gifts were not dramatic, and the play was never acted. Most of it was, however, published later, in successive issues of the Sydney *Monitor.*

The latter part of this time in Sydney seems to have been the unhappiest period of Harpur's life. He was a target for criticism, and his temperament did not allow him to take this quietly. He made some friends—including perhaps, W. A. Duncan, later editor of the *Weekly Register*—but he probably made many more enemies; he seems to have been unhappily in love, and he began to realize the difficulties of his chosen career of writing. For a time he worked as a clerk in the Post Office, but a crisis came in his life; he began, according to his own account, to drink, and in 1839 he left Sydney in despair of making his way there, and returned to the Hunter Valley and his old life of hard work and few pence.

It is not often easy to date his poems accurately, but perhaps it was at this time that he wrote two of his most characteristic poems, **"The Dream by the Fountain"** quoted earlier, and **"To the Spirit of Poesy"**. A few verses must be quoted from the second poem:

> Yet do not thou forsake me now,
> Poesy—with Hope together.
> Ere this last severest blow
> Did lay my struggling fortunes low,
> In love unworn have we not borne
> Much wintry weather?
>
> . . . Ah misery, what were then my lot
> Among a race of unbelievers,
> Worldly men who all declare
> That Gain alone is good and fair
> And they who pore on Beauty's lore
> Deceived deceivers?
>
> Half at rest upon thy breast
> How often have I laid me, musing
> That in the golden eventide
> All the dead to Thought allied
> Around me dwelt, unseen yet felt,
> Great hopes infusing . . .
>
> But if there lives, as love believes,
> All underneath this silent heaven,
> In yon shades, and by yon streams,
> As we have seen them in our dreams,
> A deathless race—still let thy grace
> My being leaven!
>
> Thy mystic grace, that face to face
> Full converse I may hold with nature,
> Seeing published everywhere
> In forms, the soul that makes her fair;
> And grow the while to her large style
> In mental stature.

So he seems to have resolved that he would live as simply as possible, working for a bare existence, and meanwhile practise his vocation.

His brother Joseph was acting as postmaster at the small settlement of Jerry's Plains, on the Hunter. Charles accordingly went to Jerry's Plains, and here he seems for a time to have subordinated his life to writing, remaining content with the barest of livings from labouring work, or from acting as proxy postmaster for his brother, with perhaps occasionally a few shillings from such newspapers as paid their contributors.

Harpur's life in Sydney had led him into the company of reformers and radicals, and had left him with an abiding desire to take part in the political issues which then affected all Australians. He now wrote articles, letters to newspapers, political lampoons and squibs in verse and prose, as a supporter of Wentworth's campaign for responsible government and an advocate for the cessation of transportation, in opposition to the "squattocracy". He was now, in fact, a red-hot democrat, and, unlike his contemporary William Wentworth, he was always to remain so.

His political writing was of course ephemeral, and is now little more than a curiosity; but it was often amusing and satirical, and usually much above the political writing current at the time, most of which was scurrilous and unrelieved by wit.

He remained on the Hunter for the most part of ten years until 1849. It was a time of isolation and loneliness, with few people he could talk to with any freedom. But, though his almost outcast state preyed on his mind and his pride, and his lack of companions threw him back too much upon himself, he nevertheless felt that this hard life, with its loneliness, had a reality about it that was useful to him as a poet. So, in a quaint note on Tennyson, he writes:

> [He is] an old-world Towney, a dresser of parterres and a peeper into Parks. I am a man of the woods and mountains—a wielder of the axe, and mainly conversant with aboriginal nature: a man made stern and self-reliant, and thence plain and even fierce, by nearness (if I may so speak) to the *incunabula mundi.* Hence poetry, with him, should be nice and dainty, rather than wise and hearty: while to affect my admiration, it must be free, bold and open, even at the risk of being rude.[4]

Four years after leaving Sydney, he met at Jerry's Plains the "Rosa" of his sonnets, Mary Doyle. She was the daughter of a settler and landowner, who, naturally enough, neither trusted nor approved of this poverty-stricken young man, a democrat and firebrand, and the son of convict parents. The Doyles were much opposed to the match, but Mary continued to cling to her thoughts of marrying this impossible young poet.

It was seven years before the Doyles finally gave way; and the sonnets give a hint that they had almost succeeded in forcing Mary into another match meanwhile. However,

Harpur and Mary were at last married, when Harpur was thirty-seven years old. During the time since their meeting, he had written the **Sonnets to Rosa,** which now form the only volume of his poetry that readers can obtain, since they were edited and published in 1948 by C. W. Salier.

However, not long after his first meeting with Mary, in 1844, Charles had returned to Sydney for some time, in an attempt to mend his fortunes and become a more "suitable match" for her. This visit was a fruitful one, since now he met the young Henry Parkes, who had come to Sydney and set up as an ivory-turner, and who later paid tribute to his friendship with Harpur and with W. A. Duncan, "his chief advisers in matters of intellectual resource".

During this time in Sydney Harpur may have had regular employment on a newspaper. Certainly Duncan published his first small book of verse, **Thoughts,** a volume of sonnets. Duncan himself had strong enemies; about this time he ran into trouble, as the owner and editor of the *Weekly Register,* which had antagonised the squatting interests by supporting Gipps's land policy.

Parkes reviewed Harpur's book for the *Register* and gave it exaggerated praise. The critics moved in to the attack immediately; the mark was too good to let the opportunity pass, and Duncan's unpopularity with the moneyed interests sharpened the hostility to his protégé. Sore and angry, Harpur retaliated with a satire on the refusal of Australian critics to see good in anything Australian—a satire which probably did no good to his cause, but Harpur could never submit quietly to unjust criticism.

The *Register* was forced to cease publication in 1845, and journalism failed to provide Harpur with a living, but when, in 1850, he married, a living had become important. He took up teaching, his father's profession, for a time; but he was untrained, and, when the school at which he was teaching came under the control of the National Board, he had to come to Sydney again to obtain his qualification.

But now the Doyles stepped in, and his father-in-law assisted him to obtain a sheep-farm, whereupon he gave up teaching (which he may not have been sorry to do). He had once written a verse to Parkes, his faithful correspondent for a time, in which he regretted his inability to make a living at his chosen work:

I sometimes wish my Muse a monthly nurse,
Or something else—or even something worse;
For here I'm still "poor Jack", without the shiners,
And hence unwelcome to all sorts of Tiners.
While others dip their fleecy flocks, and store
Bright gold, I've only so much *verse* the more—
. . . A vagrant, and the cause still, all along,
This damn'd unconquerable love of Song.[5]

However, now that he was in fact "dipping his fleecy flocks" like other men, he could not help fretting at his isolation and the hard work which kept him from his beloved writing. He was distant from his Sydney friends—

Deniehy the ill-fated poet who had helped and encouraged him, Stenhouse, Parkes, and Robertson, later Sir John Robertson, with whose cause of land reform Harpur was passionately involved. Happy as he seems to have been with Mary, he suffered from the lack of their intellectual companionship, and probably he felt that, while much was going on in Sydney, he was cut off from sharing in the new ferment.

Nevertheless, he still wrote a great deal. Wentworth, whom he had supported in earlier years in his battle for constitutional government, was now himself a member of the "squattocracy", and advocating an Australian peerage. Harpur's reaction to this, when it was first proposed, had been characteristic:

> In Sheepshanks we behold a destined peer
> And Oxtail's stockmen shall "my-lord" his son![6]

he wrote, and added a tart note on the future of Australia should it become "a bad copy of the national perditions of Europe. Wherever there are palaces, there are hovels: and this should determine us in Australia to have as few of either as possible."

Now he continued to attack the various attempts to establish an aristocracy of property. In fact, the radical papers of the 'fifties contain a great deal of Harpur's best political writing. It has been said that he was one of John Robertson's most valued advisers, in his programme of land reform. He was that rare bird, a poet with practical foresight and ability. He seems to have been quite a successful farmer during these years, in spite of his numerous other interests; yet none fought more eagerly than he did against the encroachments of the privileged squatters, and few saw more clearly what was likely to happen to Australian land-settlement policy if that encroachment was not curbed.

How much, if anything, he had to do with the formulation of the free selection legislation is not known; but Robertson seems to have considered him worth helping. In 1859, when Robertson was Minister for Lands, he appointed Harpur assistant gold commissioner on the southern goldfields, at Araluen.

It was a good post, and for the first time in his life Harpur enjoyed a steady salary. He bought a farm at Eurobodalla, near Nerrigundah, where Mary and his five children were to live, and divided his time between his commissionership and the farm, while yet continuing to write whenever he could.

Harpur must at this time have been working at high pressure. The numerous interests which divided his attention seem to have become too much for him; he was too frequently absent from the farm to be able to manage it properly, and gradually it ate up his savings. His health began to suffer, and when, after seven years, Government retrenchment deprived him of his commissionership, he had few resources left. He applied for compensation for the loss of his position, but there were delays and excuses, and while he was fretting and waiting, disastrous floods ruined his farm.

He was already a sick man, and the long wet season, and his losses and disappointments aggravated his illness. The final blow came early in the autumn of 1867, when his beloved second son Charley, a boy of remarkable promise, was accidentally shot when out hunting.

Harpur was by now far gone in tuberculosis, and the terrible depression of the disease, added to his misfortunes, make his last few poems painful to read. He could not have helped feeling himself neglected and forgotten, a failure, when his friends Parkes and Robertson were now men of note and high in public affairs, and his own life-long dedication to poetry and politics had left him with nothing to show.

His hopes had once been high—after his first retreat from Sydney he had written in a notebook:

> At this moment I am a wanderer and a vagabond upon the face of my Native Land—after having written upon its evergreen beauty strains of feeling and imagination which, I believe, "men will not willingly let die." But my countrymen, and the world, will yet know me better! I doubt not, indeed, but that I shall yet be held in honour both by them and by it.[7]

But he had grown old in the service of his Muse, and his poems, as he sadly wrote, had "gone a-begging as it were—and in vain—about the land of their inspiration, for publication in the form of a presentable Book."[8]

So all his circumstances combined, now, with his disease, to kill him, not quite two years after his loss of his position, in his fifty-sixth year.

II

To assess Harpur as a poet, it is first of all necessary to look carefully at the only collection of his work that purports to represent him. It is a book published in 1883, put together after Harpur's death and from manuscripts left by him, with a brief foreword by Mary Harpur. This foreword, which has apparently been taken as a guarantee that Mary approved of the contents of the book, has perhaps, sadly enough, prevented until recently any critical examination of the book in relation to Harpur's surviving manuscripts.

But it is clear now, from recent research[9], that the poems were, in fact, edited by a man (one, H. M. Martin), whose qualifications for the work were, to say the least, uncertain, and who took an oddly high-handed attitude, not only to Harpur's work, but to his widow's own preferences. The result has been disastrous to Harpur's reputation—since most, if not all, of these poems exist otherwise only in manuscript form or in forgotten files of newspapers, and no questions, apparently, were ever asked as to how authentic the versions published in the volume actually were.

There are, in fact, many serious excisions from the more important poems; other important poems have been omitted altogether, or have had lines or whole sections transposed by the editor without indication of the fact. Worse still, while the important poems have been cut and emasculated, the slighter and more sentimental or technically unsatisfactory poems (some of which, in all likelihood, Harpur himself would not have included) have all gone in. The result has been a book which not only does not represent Harpur's poetic work, but actually, in vital respects, misrepresents it.

For instance, among the important poems from which Martin removed sections or verses is that by which Harpur has long been best known—**"The Creek of the Four Graves"**. As this poem stands in the collected volume, it is a very competent narrative, with some good incidental description of landscape, and with some striking images and verses. What it lacks is what may be called "deepening"—the kind of comment that gives the reader a clue to why the poem is being written, why it seems to the poet that the subject is important.

We can still read **"The Creek of the Four Graves"** as an interesting, but rather dated, set-piece about a massacre by aborigines in early Australian history. If we read it perceptively, we may be momentarily interested by the emphasis on the setting—on the beauty and calm of the night in which the party of men are murdered, on the vastness of the scene in which the drama takes place. But not until a missing verse has been restored does this contrast between violence and calm make its proper balance within the poem:

> For see, the bright beholding Moon, and all
> The radiant Host of Heaven, evince no touch
> Of sympathy with man's wild violence—
> Only evince in their calm course, their part
> In that original unity of Love
> Which, like the soul that dwelleth in a harp,
> Under God's hand, in the beginning chimed
> The Sabbath concord of the Universe.[10]

This verse has its links and echoes throughout the poem—it is, in fact, a pivotal verse, important to our understanding of the *meaning*. Without it, the poem is devitalised.

This is not an isolated instance of ignorant and biased editing. There are plenty of others. In another descriptive poem, **"A Storm in the Mountains"**, there is an even more flagrant omission. As this poem stands in the 1883 volume, it is a descriptive essay, so to speak, following the storm from its inception to its end. No human figure appears, no comment is made. The description is good—at times even excellent—but the poem lacks life, for it is never referred to a human level—it, too, is apparently a set-piece, with no purpose beyond the external observation. But a key passage has again been omitted:

> Strange darings seize me, witnessing this strife
> Of Nature's powers, and heedless of my life

I stand exposed. And does some fatal charm
Hold me secure from elemental harm
That in the mighty riot I may find
How wide the externality of Mind? . . .
Soul wildly drawn abroad—a Protean force
Clothing with higher life the Tempest in its course![11]

Quite apart from the fact that this, too, is obviously an important passage in the poem, it has remarkable interest in itself, as an extension of early Romantic thought. It goes beyond the Wordsworthian doctrines of the relationship of man and nature, and implies the whole question of the relationship, beyond this, of thoughts to things, that relationship which, in England, Coleridge had first pointed out when he undermined the whole Wordsworthian attitude to nature in his two lines:

O Lady, we receive but what we give,
And in our life alone doth Nature live . . .

It is a verse that repays study; and in the poem in which it occurs, it is climactic.

There are other omissions, not less serious; but these two instances give us a clue to what has been the motive behind the excisions. The clue is reinforced by a letter from Martin to Mary Harpur, quoted by C. W. Salier in an article[12], regarding **"The Creek of the Four Graves"**.

Martin writes: "We had intended to publish extracts . . . but not to print it in its entirety . . . It is very undesirable to have any lines printed which may serve as a handle for carping criticism . . . The *descriptive* parts of the Poem have always excited our warm admiration."

The effect Harpur's editor aimed at, in fact, was to present him as a tame nature-poet, and to prune away all that could make him a centre of controversy—all, in fact, that makes Harpur important and interesting as a poet. No wonder he has been so tragically neglected by criticism and ignored by the poets and writers who followed him.

I think that I have said enough to make it clear that all estimates of Harpur which have been based on the 1883 volume alone, without reference to the manuscripts, are unsoundly based and ought, in fairness to the critics as well as to Harpur, to be blotted from the record. The poet we have to deal with is an unknown, because a censored, figure.

Why was this censorship imposed? And why has it never been lifted? The answer, I think, reflects no credit on Australia. It seems that the original dismissal of his work—that which began in his own lifetime—had its source in two facts: his convict origin and his radical opinions. It was, of course, reinforced by the fact that during the period when Harpur was writing actively, there was little, if any, national feeling for, or encouragement of, Australian writing. This only began to emerge when Kendall was fighting for recognition, and it came too late to save Kendall himself from his fate.

But it is stranger—and more deplorable—that our ignorant dismissal of Harpur should have continued up to the present day, and that Harpur's lone and difficult fight for poetry and for his radical opinions should have been so far forgotten that he has even been referred to recently[13] as "a middle-class" writer! This is the kind of irony that would have made even Harpur incredulous at the blows of fate.

Having said all this, it is time to look at Harpur as he really was. To begin with, he was, above all, a poet conscious of his responsibilities. He not only read all that he could get hold of in English poetry; he attempted to train his critical faculties with notes and brief essays on the poets he read, and to train his sense of language and rhythm with various poetic exercises. He wrote, as I have said, a number of **"Rhymed Criticisms"**, in which he used the particular style and versification of a poet to express his own verdict on the poet's work.

On Dryden, for instance:

Not much I love him, yet perforce admire
The vigorous rage of his material fire!
Though prodigal of verse, and coarse of phrase,
Built durably are all his better Lays.
His lines, like pleasant brooks, now warbling go,
And now, like mountain floods, they thunder as they
        flow . . .[14]

And throughout his life he seems to have revised and reworked his earlier poems, though not always with good effect. His manuscript books, therefore, often contain several versions of a single poem, apparently written at different dates, and it is not easy to decide which version is definitive, until more work is done on the dating and collating of the manuscripts.

Not only did Harpur feel his responsibilities as an artist; he expressly declared his own dedication to poetry, notably in the poem **"The Dream by the Fountain"**, which he may well have written during his first retreat from Sydney to the Hunter Valley between 1839 and 1844. In **"The Dream"**, he makes his Muse address him—not the Muse of the old world, nor even the Muse of Wordsworth, his mentor, who was Nature herself—but "the Muse of the Evergreen Forest", of the Australian bush.

The term "evergreen forest" is significant. No one would refer to the Bush nowadays in such a fashion; it is almost English in its implications, just as the paintings, say, of Martens and Buvelot, those early Australian artists, are almost English in their vision of the landscape. But the difference is there—this new element, this strangeness of the forest that does not lose its leaves. The transition has begun.

Just so it began in those early paintings, where the detail of the strange trees is blurred and lost in a kind of generalisation, so that they are almost—but not quite—English trees. Yet it is not the likeness that seems important, when we study such paintings; it is the difference, which, momentous yet gradual, deepens and widens with the years until the vision of Australia emerges through the memories of England.

It is the same process that is at work in Harpur—the movement out of the past and into an unknown future. Harpur was conscious of this movement, and of its necessity; it makes him everywhere emphasise the future, not the past:

> Listen, rejoined one, [*says his Muse*], I promise thee
>   glory
> Such as shall rise like the daystar apart,
> To brighten the source of Australia's broad story,
> But for this thou must give to the Future thy heart.
>
> Be then the Bard of thy Country! O rather
> Should such be thy choice than a monarchy wide!
> Lo, 'tis the land of the grave of thy father;
> 'Tis the cradle of Liberty! Think, and decide.[15]

There is a new note here; and for its sake we can disregard the language which may sound to our ears (though we must not forget that it did not so sound in Harpur's time) stale and rhetorical. Listening without prejudice, we can hear the noble naivety of a large nature, behind the language of a now-tarnished political vision. What remains important is not the vision (which was to be betrayed), but the dedication and the hope.

If we begin by taking Harpur purely at the value set on him by the editor of the 1883 volume—as a descriptive poet—we will not get a fair view of his poetry, but we will at least be able to judge the accuracy of his eye and the truth of his transcription. Using only passages from the 1883 volume, it is easy enough to discover what most moved him in nature; significantly, it is to mountains, clouds and the play of light that he most often recurs. This emphasis on the features of his landscape that were most generalised, and therefore easiest to translate from the terms of English vision into his new country, also allowed him to bring into his landscape poetry something new, and especially Australian—the sense of enormous space, space which seems to dwarf even the mountains, and light which floods and changes everything below it.

One passage has already been quoted from **"The Creek of the Four Graves"** which illustrates this. Here is another from the same poem; where the mountains are seen

> Against the twilight heaven—a cloudless depth
> Yet luminous with sunset's fading glow;
> And thus awhile in the lit dusk they seemed
> To hang like mighty pictures of themselves
> In the still chambers of some vaster world.

In **"A Storm in the Mountains"**, the hills are seen at noon:

> . . . in the breeze that o'er
> Their rough enormous backs deep-fleeced with wood
> Came whispering down, the wide upslanting sea

> Of fanning leaves in the descending rays
> Danced interdazzlingly, as if the trees
> That bore them were all thrilling—tingling all
> Down to the roots, for very happiness:
> So prompted from within, so sentient seemed
> The bright quick motion.

And it is worth pointing out that this passage contains remarkable instances of Harpur's powers of observation and description. Anyone who has seen the movement of the leaves of a forest of gum-trees in wind and sunlight will agree on the aptness of the adverb, "interdazzlingly"—the leaves being set in a vertical, not a horizontal plane, reflect light sideways from one leaf to another, not upwards as in a forest where the leaves are held horizontally—and this sight Harpur saw and perhaps described for the first time, with care and love.

In **"A Storm in the Mountains"** he describes, too, the movement of moonlight over the hills:

> . . . And now the moon arose
> Above the hill, when lo! the giant cone
> Erewhile so dark, seemed inwardly aglow
> With her instilled irradiance . . .
> Then her full light in silvery sequence still
> Cascading forth from ridgy slope to slope,
> Chased mass by mass the broken darkness down
> Into the dense-brushed valleys . . .

This last passage is one which Martin mutilated. I quote it as it appears in the published volume, for convenience in checking; but the passage is even more impressive in manuscript.

These are the enduring images of Harpur's poetry—light, mountains, great forests, and a vision of space that seems unlimited. The descriptions may seem to us impersonal and lacking in detail—Harpur wrote no poems to "lesser celandines" or their equivalent in the terms of Australian wildflowers; but perhaps the picture he leaves with us is the truer for that. A wide, almost undifferentiated landscape—a flood of light—a height of sky; that must have been the first and most lasting vision of Australia to her first settlers.

And that Harpur was, in fact, a close and delighted observer of the events and inhabitants of his world of forests, he gives plenty of proof. Take the account of the changes in the sky as the storm rises:

> . . . Now with a slow gradual pace
> A solemn trance creams northward o'er its face [the
>   sky's]
> Yon clouds that late were labouring past the sun,
> Reached by its sure arrest, one after one,
> Come to a heavy halt, the airs that played
> About the rugged mountains all are laid;
> While drawing nearer far-off heights appear,
> As in a dream's wild prospect, strangely near.

or of the advance of a bushfire:

> . . . down the flickering glades
> Ghastfully glaring, huge dry-mouldered gums

Stood 'mid their living kin as banked throughout
With eating fire expelling arrowy jets
Of blue-tipped, intermitting, gaseous flame,
Boles, branches, all! like vivid ghosts of trees.

("The Bushfire")

And he has a brief but precise description of the flight of the squirrel-glider:

Startlingly near and phantom-like to see
The sharp-voiced bidawong streams from the tree.

("Lost in the Bush"—manuscript)[16]

and of the dingo's voice:

. . . the lank dingo's long and weary cry
Comes wildly wailing from some covert nigh.

("Lost in the Bush"—ms.)

In **"The Kangaroo-Hunt"**, too, though it is youthfully ambitious and introduces too many worn poetic tricks, peopling the Bush with eighteenth-century abstractions such as Love, Hope and the rest, the glimpses of that now vanished forest that Harpur knew remain enchanting.

In **"The Kangaroo Hunt"**, which occupies a complete manuscript book, Harpur tried a method of versification that shows how conscious he was of the necessity for a new approach to technique, in this new country. He explains in his preface to the poem: "When composing it, I conceived that such an unconfined, many-metred structure of verse as might be varied and paragraphically moulded (after the manner of a musical movement) to the peculiar demands of every occasion, and appear therefore to result spontaneously from the very nature of the things depicted, would be most conducive to . . . effective treatment."

The attempt was, on the whole, unsuccessful. It was too difficult a task, at that stage of the Colony's history, to write epic narrative verse about an event like a kangaroo-hunt—which might have seemed merely curious and ludicrous to an overseas reader, but would certainly seem no more than foolish inflation of a common event to Harpur's fellow-countrymen. But Harpur's notion of "a paragraphically moulded verse (after the manner of a musical movement)" interestingly anticipates a good deal of experiment which we think of as purely twentieth-century; and though the poem is unsuccessful, it is evidence of his originality that he made the attempt at all.

Purely as narrative verse, **"The Kangaroo-Hunt"** is also unsatisfactory; the story is tenuous and forms only a peg on which to hang descriptions and dissertations, in the manner of an inferior poem by Wordsworth. But Harpur's narrative poetry was to improve. **"The Creek of the Four Graves"** has much more tension and a strong underlying structure; description is better balanced with narration; and at times the telling of the story reaches a climax where the verse is excitingly counterpointed with the events, in a

strenuously dramatic shape. For instance, where the leader of the exploring party hears the stealthy approach of the natives to attack the camp:

. . . With a strange horror gathering to his heart
As if his blood were charged with insect-life
And writhed along in clots, he stilled himself
And listened heedfully, till his held breath
Became a pang. Nought heard he; silence there
Had recomposed her ruffled wings . . .

The gasping of the h-sounds and the hissing sibilants in the first sentence, and the placing of the caesuras, show that Harpur was a much better technician than his early critics thought him.

The long poem, **"The Tower of the Dream"**, which his editor has placed at the beginning of the 1883 volume, was separately published during Harpur's lifetime, in 1865. We have no date for its composition, nor do I know whether Harpur had read Browning's "Childe Roland" before it was written. It would be thought a tiresomely symbolic invention nowadays, with its lake and tower, and the maiden and monster that inhabit the tower; its inner well and Gothically alarming gates and staircases; and the poem is a great deal too long to sustain the atmosphere which Harpur evokes so well in the opening passages.

The subject, however, is one that any twentieth-century poet might dare to use, if we forget the Freudian overtones that the cast and scenery have acquired since Harpur's day. The poem is about the division of conscious life from the unconscious powers that can so vividly image and enact in our dreams scenes of extraordinary and compelling grandeur; and about the attempt of the poet to overcome that division and free his soul to cross the boundaries of sleep, and conquer its mystery. The maiden is a kind of Psyche, a messenger of light to the poet; together they are to defy the law that holds mortal men back from discovering the mysteries of Sleep. But when the winged horse is already saddled for the journey, the nameless monster of the tower snatches away the lady, and an airy chorus sings that the attempt is doomed:

The gulf we are crossing may never be crossed
By a mortal, ah, never!
The doom holds forever . . .

The poem is, in fact, about the division within the life of the poet, and of man, between conscious knowledge and unconscious forces—a theme which is strangely modern, though treated in a nineteenth-century style, and one which shows once more that Harpur was preoccupied with problems that are still significant for us—that he was, in fact, a thinking, rather than a lyrical, poet.

His two longest and most remarkable poems are both printed in mangled and foreshortened forms, in the 1883 volume. **"The Witch of Hebron"**, which contains much of Harpur's best blank verse, has lost well over 400 lines, and many passages essential to an understanding of the poem's meaning have gone. **"Genius Lost"**, a poem-series on the death of Chatterton, is treated even more summarily—of its 2,300 lines only a few chosen lyrics and choruses are included, and the verses with which the editor chose to end the poem are in fact not part of the original poem at all, but imported from another poem-series, **"Autumnal Leaves"**. Moreover, there is no indication that the poem's subject is Chatterton, so that a good deal of the point even of what has been included is lost.

In the manuscripts, the poem is a series of monologues, and Harpur explains that the plan was to make the book (for it is in fact a book, though never published) "a psychological step-by-step development of the lonely conceptions and peculiar sufferings that are . . . leading (the poet) to a disastrous self-inflicted end: while the Choruses annexed to them are spiritual cognitions of these peculiar moods and sufferings."[17]

"Genius Lost" is one of the most ambitious and largely-conceived poems of Australian literature. Though built of separate lyrics and choruses, it is structurally sound and the links between the separate passages are subtle and firm. In it, though it was written in his youth, Harpur solved problems of construction which are far beyond Kendall's powers, and triumphantly showed that the task he undertook was not beyond him.

His strength as a poet probably lay rather in construction than in the lyric forms which, even in his own day, were more popular than long poems and narratives. This is a measure of the particular kind of mental power that he possessed; he could be banal and awkward, and there are long passages of fustian in his worse poems, but his thought had depth and enterprise, and he attacked his special poetic problems (of which he had many) with fore-thought and intelligence. The pity is that not one long poem has survived intact in the 1883 volume (except **"The Tower of the Dream"**—and this no doubt only because Martin was not quite sure what Harpur was talking about) so that it is not possible for the student to discover for himself where Harpur succeeds and where he fails.

Harpur is, in fact, a far more interesting, because a more thoughtful and controversial, poet than that volume implies. Consider the ambition of an obscure colonial poet who could embark on a long blank-verse dissertation on **"The World and the Soul"**, from a point of view which combines Darwinian theory with an unorthodox—almost an Oriental—religious view of the universe and its purpose. The subject itself was forbidding, and Harpur's treatment of it was unconventional enough to have alarmed even a more enterprising nineteenth-century editor than Martin, who, in fact, omits it from his edition altogether.

The poem is in blank verse; it begins before the appearance of man on earth, and traces the events which lead up to the first appearance of the Soul, or consciousness (the two seem, in Harpur's treatment, interchangeable), the spirit for which the earth's evolution was preparing.

Yea, thus for countless centuries, beneath
The sun and moon and stars, did all the bare
And shapeless hills show ghastly in their light,
And the dull waters gleam, although as yet
Through all those patient periods immature,
No soul intelligent, save God alone,
Might know them, as their maker . . .[18]

But man is only earth's present king; he is destined to yield before "new successions in the scheme of life", "progressive changes in the sum / And increment of that divine Idea / Whereof the Earth's so solid-seeming bulk / Is, with its fleshly populations whole / The vesture."

So far, Harpur's picture of the universe seems a strange anticipation of the Nietzschean notion of the superman. But the difference is soon apparent; to Harpur the "intelligent soul" is not, as for Nietzsche, a law to itself, but is subject to and forms part of a larger whole, and bears the responsibility of its own immortality, in God. The soul, Harpur says:

. . . complete
In her sole being, evermore aspires,
An ultimate of all that went before,
A spirit of Thought, and thence a child of that
In which the world began and hath its end . . .
. . . Thus, ancestrally a spark
From God's internal brightness, goes she forth
To die not, but to clothe for evermore
Her mighty life and wondrous faculties
In robes of beauty and of use . . .

And further, Harpur visualised the soul as travelling on by transmigration through

. . . those
Innumerable other worlds, that strew
The neighbouring heavens with seats of being, such
As host on host, yet farther forth, enrich
Infinite spaces, populous alike
With kindred glories, that exist in Him;
As being but the million-featured modes
Of his star-seeing Thoughts—each several thought
A shining link in one eternal chain
Of progress—to Perfection. Here we rest.

This notion of the soul as part of the all-consciousness of the universe, as it were a mode of the thought of God, allows Harpur to set the emphasis on the progression of consciousness, "the increment of that divine Idea", rather than on the advancement of man as a species. It is an attempt to respiritualise the world which, after Darwin, could be seen less and less as creative in itself, and in fact was seen more and more as a machine for physical evolution.

Moreover, it is a step beyond the thought of Wordsworth, for whom Nature is herself a spiritual manifestation of the force that "rolls through all things", a teacher, guide and nurse to man. Harpur sets the emphasis on the intelligence of the soul—on its capacity for conscious use of nature, as material for the enrichment of the soul—as "robes of beauty and of use".

It is just at this point that Harpur can make the transition between poetry and politics. As a poet, his notion of man is not of a political animal, but of the vehicle of an immortal soul, which is both the expression of "a divine Idea" and itself part of that idea, and whose task is the divinization, as it were, of the external world. Only after this is understood can we see Harpur's occupation with politics for what it was—not a mere antagonism of "have-not" versus "have", but a reasoned, passionate and even religious conviction based on a world-view that allowed equality to all men, not as a material right, but as a spiritual duty.

This poem, with a few others, gives us an illuminating elevation from which to see Harpur's life and work. While he is seen only as the author of the poems in the 1883 volume, it is not possible to understand either his enlightened radicalism, or his total dedication to poetry. If we realise that both these aspects of his nature stem from a spiritual, not an economic, conviction of the importance of human thought and action, he steps into place as one of our most interesting and most misjudged poets. We can understand, and begin at last to believe in, his own assertion of his importance to Australia's future generations; and we can see his deliberate choice of "the future" as against his own immediate advantage as the great gesture it really was. It is his vision of the soul as "a spark from God" that gives his radicalism its obstinate passion, and his devotion to poetry its enthusiasm.

But many men have been devoted to poetry, without leaving any permanent memorial in the form of good poems behind them; and also, though perhaps less often, good poems have been written by men who cared little for the future of the human race. What we need to know about a poet is not what he thought, but what he wrote. What kind of poetry can we best remember Harpur by?

The two or three poems by which he is, in fact, usually represented—**"A Midsummer Noon in the Australian Forest"**, **"A Basket of Sun-Fruit"**, **"The Creek of the Four Graves"** (in its emasculated and edited form)—are chosen for their descriptive qualities. But Harpur was a more interesting, because a more thoughtful, poet than this choice implies. His longer poems, even if they were available to the reader, would be too long to quote; but reading Harpur in even the 1883 volume, his qualities are seen to be sterner and more durable than his editors would have us believe. The besetting fault of sobriety and earnestness is pedestrianism (Wordsworth's own fault), and Harpur does not always avoid it; but certainly his most characteristic poetry is that of his middle period, and we miss his special idiosyncratic flavour if we represent him only by the few poems we know.

One of the few complete poems in the 1883 volume which does illustrate him at his strongest is the threnody for his father. It is too long to quote in full; but the extracts given at least indicate the general shape and strength of the poem:

> I stand in thought beside my father's grave,
> The grave of one who, in his old age, died
> Too late perhaps, since he endured so much
> Of corporal anguish, sweating bloody sweat,
> But not an hour too soon—no, not an hour!
> . . . For his bruised heart
> And wounded goodwill, wounded through its once
> Samsonian vigour and too credulous trust
> In that great Delilah, the harlot world,
> Had done with fortune . . .
> Nor was there, in the lives of those he loved,
> Even had he been susceptible of cheer,
> Enough of fortune to warm into peace
> A little longer ere he passed away,
> The remnant of his chilled humanity.
> . . . Not less must death the great inductor be
> To much that far transcends time's highest lore,
> Must be at worst a grimly grateful thing,
> If only through deliverance from doubt,
> The clinging curse of mortals.
> . . . But the dead
> Have this immunity at least; a lot
> Final and fixed, as evermore within
> The gates of the Eternal. For the past
> Is wholly God's, and therefore, like himself,
> Knows no reverse, no change—but lies forever
> Stretched in the sabbath of its vast repose.

This poem—as stern and solid as a granite monument—contains much of the essential Charles Harpur. Unlike most of his contemporaries, in England as in Australia, he does not allow himself sentimentalism or self-pity, unless in the form of protest; he looks on facts clear-eyed and his verse is as plain and firm as his feeling. To have written this poem, and a few more, is enough to prove his quality as a poet and as a man.

What of Harpur's place in Australian literature? To all appearance, he was robbed of his proper due and influence by almost total neglect, in his lifetime and after it; and it would not be unexpected if he seemed quite outside the general current of later writing. In fact, it is surprising to find in Harpur's work the fountainhead from which first issue the two opposing and mingling themes and preoccupations of most of our later writers—the twin themes of exile, of the European consciousness faced with the distasteful necessity of change and readaptation; and of hope, the Utopian but recurrent hope of human brotherhood at last become possible at the far end of the world from Europe. Australia Deserta, Voss's land of self-discovery, was sung first of all by Harpur in his fashion:

> My country, though rude yet and wild be thy nature,
> This alone our proud love should beget and command.
> There's room in thy broad breast for Manhood's full
>   stature . . .
>
> **("Never Mind")**[19]

As for the theme of exile from European culture, even though from his circumstances Harpur had little enough respect for traditions and laws that had driven his parents from their own country, he felt bitterly enough the lack of appreciation and intelligent friendship in the harsh materially-minded community of early Australia. His ponderously named **"Sonnet on the Fate of Poetic Genius in a Sordid Community"**[20] is a lament for his isolation:

> Hapless is he who meditates the Nine
> Where Greed is rampant, with intent to build
> Enduring verse; for there none deem divine
> His eloquent art, however he be skilled . . .
> To Misery wedded then, as to a wife,
> And bearing that worst load, a loving heart
> Unloved, adown the narrow ways of life,
> What hath he gained by his harmonious art? . . .

But he did not fall into the trap of cultivating either theme to the exclusion of the other; he balances his sense of isolation as a poet, of exile from a tradition, against his hope for Australia as the land of the future, where men may learn to live as fully developed human beings in harmony with each other. There is a note in his unpublished **"Discourse on Poetry"** which is relevant:

> Yet it is terribly true that Poetry is not bread . . . I know all this as well as the prosiest mortal alive. But since a very man—a man spherical and so far godlike in the build of his mind . . . cannot live by bread alone . . . all sordid objections to the value of Poetry are forever invalid.[21]

"Spherical and so far godlike in the build of his mind"—it is a sweeping idea, and it implies in the man who could voice it a personal aim far beyond that of the politician, even beyond that of the poet. It stems from Harpur's faith that the soul of man is "a divine spark", "a child of that in which the world began and hath its end". It was this notion that he struggled to realize in himself; and when he contemns the "clod-like" minds of those he lived among, and longs for Pope's satirical mastery to denounce the stupidities and injustices of his society, it is not only a personal disappointment that drives him, but a more disinterested emotion on behalf of the visioned enlargement of man's capacities that he never ceased to hope for.

So Harpur is not so much a landscape poet as a poet of humanity. Kendall saw this, when in his obituary poem he says of Harpur,

> No soul was he to sit on heights
> And live with rocks apart and scornful.
> Delights of men were his delights
> And common troubles made him mournful.[22]

The human figure is always present in his landscapes to act as a point of final reference; his semi-humorous **"Lost in the Bush"** and **"Ned Connor"** are lively pictures of the life and people he knew, and the fiery sincerity of much of his political satire and lampooning still carries across the years.

How important is Harpur's part in our literary inheritance? In spite of our blank ignorance of what he was and did, he remains the most significant, because the most many-sided and thoughtful, of our nineteenth-century poets, until Brennan began writing at the end of the century. Our ignorance of him is our loss. Poetry is not just a matter of what is being written here and now; it is a living and interconnected body that draws its nourishment from the past as much as the present. We cannot ignore our poetic roots, if we are to write poetry that is fully aware of its surrounding influences.

I have spoken of Harpur's understanding of the necessity to adapt the English tradition in poetry, to toughen its delicacies and subtleties, to make it "free, bold and open, even at the risk of being rude", in order to express the new kind of life being lived by the generation who had, like himself, been born far from the gentilities of English civilization. It was the first step towards an expression of the meaning of the new continent, and perhaps the most important. It was obviously not possible for Harpur to reject that tradition; we did not, after all, come here with wholly empty pockets, and what we brought was precious and relevant to our own existence and our future.

But Harpur was more than a mere translator of English poetic techniques and attitudes into new terms. He was the first to assert the independence, the special-ness, of the Australian—the new man, the first white generation in an unknown country. Not only in his radical political verse, or in his attempts to describe the country and its life, but in the man himself, those qualities are asserted. No poet has been more independent in thought and feeling (it was just this quality of independence and lack of convention which his editor so deplored in him that it scarcely appears at all in the 1883 volume). In the best of his poetry one finds, not only an adaptation of what was best and most durable in the English tradition, but a freshness and strength of thought and feeling, and an ardency of vision, that perhaps could only be found in a generation suddenly presented with a new country and the possibility of making a new life within it.

Harpur's tragedy was that the narrow-mindedness and neglect that darkened his life spread their shadow also over his work, and so effectively that even today we know very little of what he really thought and wrote. He himself almost lost faith, in the end, that future generations would in fact accept him as a poet; but at the end of his life the young Kendall generously acknowledged and praised his work, hailing him as a master.

Yet if he could have guessed what would in fact happen to his life-work after his death, the epitaph he once wrote for himself would have had a wry sound for him:

> But fame he sought not through a gainful hand
> (This of my being let the future tell)
> Nor through the arts of popular command;
> But in retirement, where the Muses dwell,
> That his life's legacy might be a well
> Pierian, in a wide and thirsty land.[23]

Notes

1. Manuscript book in Mitchell Library numbered C383.

2. "To the Lyre of Australia", Ms. book numbered A87.

3. *Rhymed Criticisms with Prose Notes,* Ms. book No. C376.

4. Ms. book A90.

5. "To Henry Parkes", Ms. book A87.

6. "The New Land Orders", Ms. book, 1847-48.

7. Ms. book, 1847-48.

8. Ms. book A89. (This book is dated at Euroma, 1863.)

9. *Southerly* No. 1, 1951. Article by C. W. Salier.

10. Ms. book A87.

11. Ms. book A89.

12. See Note ([9]).

13. *The Australian Legend,* Russel Ward, p. 57. (O.U.P., 1958.)

14. See Note ([3]).

15. *Poems,* by Charles Harpur. Published by George Robertson, Melbourne Street, Adelaide, 1883.

16. Ms. book A89.

17. Do.

18. Do.

19. Ms. book A90.

20. Do.

21. Ms. book A87.

22. Kendall's poem "Charles Harpur", published in *Leaves from Australian Forests.*

23. "To James Norton, Esq.", Ms. book A90.

Bibliography

The manuscript books referred to are in the Mitchell Library, Sydney, and I am indebted to the Librarian for permission to examine them.

For information on the facts and dates of Harpur's life, I warmly thank his biographer, Mr. Normington-Rawling, whose book on Harpur's life has recently been published by Angus & Robertson Ltd.

Other authorities: P. B. Cox, whose address to the Royal Australian Historical Society was published in the society's journal, 1939; H. M. Green, *Fourteen Minutes* (Angus & Robertson), pp. 6-11; C. W. Salier, article in *Southerly* No. 1, 1951, and ensuing correspondence.

Brian Elliott (essay date 1967)

SOURCE: Elliott, Brian. "The Eye of the Beholder." In *The Landscape of Australian Poetry,* pp. 57-74. Melbourne: F. W. Cheshire, 1967.

[*In the following excerpt, Elliott establishes Harpur as an original, impressionist landscape poet whose works, although flawed, are perceptive and poignant.*]

. . . The first poet who may be considered to belong firmly to the Australian repertory is Charles Harpur.[1] That he was an original poet is fairly to be claimed, in spite of much in his work that appears acquiescent or imitative. An admirer of Wordsworth and of Shelley, he still adhered in many ways to the notions (and particularly the prosody) of an earlier generation. Like his friend—until they quarrelled—Parkes, he found himself torn between twin impulses to elevate and to moralise his song. But his instrument was always in either case, the intimate landscape image.

It is not easy to become excited about all that Harpur wrote; it was of its period, often pedestrian; but what redeems a great deal of it is the fact that poetry was a completely spontaneous idiom with him. His verses are never showy because his mind was not showy. It was steady, perceptive, and at its best creative; but it was not the mind of an extraordinary genius, merely of a man sensitively and responsively adapted to the landscape in which he grew up. It was natural to him to feel the desire to express himself in terms of it. But he had no urge to explain or justify it; he did not see it as merely picturesque. Hence he did not address himself primarily to an audience abroad; his purpose was to observe, recognise and absorb it for himself and others like him. Though Wordsworth taught him much, it was not Wordsworth's landscape he was concerned with, nor Wordsworth's emotions that were to be realised. When he did find successful expression, the manner was romantic but the substance was closer to a late eighteenth century formal, reflective delight in physical nature, than to the giddy joys and aching raptures of a nineteenth century style. Harpur's pleasures were more of sedate recognition than of exhilaration and self-projection. The landscape that pleased him did so, usually, because he accepted it not merely as formally beautiful, but also as typical and representative. Each glimpse was an epitome of the whole.

The pleasures of recognition are compatible with the techniques of impressionism. Harpur, prompted by native inspiration alone, set up impressionism in Australia much about the same time as it was evolving abroad. Impressionism seems the natural approach to the Australian landscape problem: to discover its physical and its spiritual identities at one and the same stroke.

The effect is well seen in Harpur's best-known lyric, **'Midsummer Noon in the Australian Forest.'** The point of the poem rests in impressions shared between poet and reader. These are as valid now as when the words were written,[2] no doubt because the poet selects for emphasis not only details that every reader recognises as generally true or typical, but also experiences associated with his own happy childhood spent in the bush. No poet nurtured on simple buttercups and daisies could have sung this dry song of the cicada in the glare of an Australian summer day:

> Not a sound disturbs the air,
> There is quiet everywhere;

Over plains and over woods
What a mighty stillness broods.

All the birds and insects keep
Where the coolest shadows sleep . . .

. . . the ever-wakeful rill,
Whose cool murmur only throws
Cooler comfort round repose.

        . . . . lazily,
Tired summer, in her bower
Turning with the noontide hour,
Heaves a slumbrous breath ere she
Once more slumbers peacefully.

The happiness of this dwelt entirely in recollection. The poignancy of the sentiment is enhanced by the suggestion that these reflections indicate an end and a beginning: the mood is of childhood at its exquisite terminus, expectant upon the brink of adult sorrow:

Oh! 'tis easeful here to lie
Hidden from noon's scorching eye,
In this glassy cool recess
Musing thus of quietness.

The poem is imperfect. It gains—it even coheres better—if we cull it over and dwell on fragmentary echoes. It is not that the details are better poetry than the whole; they are in a few cases even defective (at least, to a carping judgement; for example, 'dragon-hornet' for the harmless dragon-fly; 'locust' for cicada). Unquestionably the best value is in the general effect. But the disposition of the detail was new and valid. In every presentation of landscape during the colonial period, 'total effect' (whether or not wholly visual, as Harpur's was not) might be successfully intuitive, but analysis in detail was usually more difficult because it called for clear, specific identifications.

A more considerable poem than **'Midsummer Noon'** was **'The Creek of the Four Graves,'** a heroic fragment. The story concerned a clash by night between settlers pushing out into new country and the Aborigines whose territory they were violating. Harpur was, for his time, liberal in his views about Aborigines, although his knowledge of them hardly extended to an informed appreciation of their tribal life. (Nor, really, did anybody else's.) He portrayed the blacks here as ruthless, yet justified by their lights.[3] One man lives to tell the tale, finding shelter in a wild creek whose ruggedly eroded bank supplies a precarious hiding place:

So went the chase. Now at a sudden turn
Before him lay the steep-banked mountain creek;
Still on he kept perforce, and from the rock
That beaked the bank, a promontory bare,
Plunging right forth and shooting feet-first down,
Sunk to his middle in the flashing stream,
In which the imaged stars seem'd all at once
To burst like rockets into one wild blaze.
Then wading through the ruffled waters, forth
He sprang, and seized a snake-like root that from

The opponent bank protruded, clenching there
His cold hand like a clamp of steel, and thence
He swung his dripping form aloft, the blind
And breathless haste of one who flies for life
Urging him on; up the dark ledge he climbed . . .
There on its face a cavity he felt,
The upper earth of which in one rude mass
Was held fast bound by the enwoven roots
Of two old trees, and which, beneath the mound,
Over the dark and clammy cave below,
Twisted like rotting snakes. 'Neath these he crept,
Just as the dark forms of his hunters thronged
The steep bold rock whence he before had plunged.

So extraordinary a disappearance puzzles the blacks; their superstitions are aroused:

        Keen was their search but vain;
There grouped in dark knots standing in the stream
That glimmered past them moaning as it went,
They marvelled; passing strange to them it seemed;
Some old mysterious fable of their race,
That brooded o'er the valley and the creek,
Returned upon their minds, and fear-struck all
And silent, they withdrew.

The poem concludes:

Four grassy mounds are there beside the creek,
Bestrewn with sprays and leaves from the old trees
Which moan the ancient dirges that have caught
The heed of dying ages, and for long
The traveller passing then in safety there,
Would call the place—The Creek of the Four Graves.

Upon these passages a few remarks may be offered. Prosodically the verse is competent, or better than competent; and there is no echo in it of any other poet.[4] Descriptively, the detail is remarkably clear: the incident of the escape (by hiding in a cavity under the roots of a tree) called for great precision, and the presentation is adequate. The sentence structure may be a little uneven, and here and there faulty. In diction, there is a wide gulf between 'that from the opponent bank protruded' and 'twisted like rotten snakes'; a contrast between stilted convention and lively observation. But an Australian style, outlook and aptitude are emerging. The lines about the stars reflected in the disturbed water might grace poetry anywhere, yet this imagery of bright starlight is also very 'typically' Australian. The presence of a still, reflecting pool in a creek which elsewhere 'moaned as it went' might well be a shade more intelligible to readers familiar with Australian streams than to most others—though this point obviously cannot be urged too far. The allusions to the fear felt by the blacks, and to the existence of 'some old mysterious fable' suggests that Harpur's understanding of the black people would have been open to a better knowledge of their life, had any systematic clarification been available.[5]

The closing lines indicate another interesting and very widespread characteristic of colonial landscape-poetry: a persistent pre-occupation with minor local tradition and the naming of places.[6] The names of persons and places became increasingly a vehicle of romantic assertion. Gordon was more attached to names than Harpur, while with A. B. Paterson and other balladists they provided an outlet for much resourceful virtuosity.

The worst that may be said about Harpur's writings is that they have a dull, flat evenness of tone. The quoted poems are exceptional. They show that, given strong feelings and a subject matter well fortified with local interest, the colonial limitations were not too inhibiting. **'The Creek of the Four Graves'** has a freshness and authenticity not to be seen in the work of other poets: the effect of a combination of observed detail, well selected, and a vivid sense of pioneering history dramatically in action. It is very vividly local poetry. Not so distinguished, yet still interesting, are a number of other pieces, the best-known of which are **'A Coast View'** and **'A Storm on the Mountains.'** But both these poems, though they embody essentially truthful landscape (or seascape) impressions, are marred with literariness; a danger Harpur was aware of, but not clearly enough to avoid it. The first (and shorter) poem describes a vista of calm sea, then dwells on the possibilities of storm. It is a good short piece of formal impressionism in blank verse. But literary decoration of an outmoded kind spoils it:

> High 'mid the shelves of a grey cliff, that yet
> Riseth in Babylonian mass above . . .
>   I sit alone,
> And gaze with a keen wondering happiness
> Out o'er the sea.

This 'keen wondering happiness' is free and true to the poet's feeling; but 'Babylonian mass' is a dead weight. The **'Storm'** describes in simple plan the approach, violence, and after-impression of a mountain squall.

The point of view is the poet's as a young boy—evidently the most deeply receptive period of his imaginative life—and the substance of the poem is excellent, the vision true. But it is cast in couplets, and although it begins with an easy relaxed measure like the boy's own motion:

> A lonely boy, far venturing from home
> Out on the half-wild herd's faint tracks I roam; . . .

—before long the literary strait-jacket is on him, and this excellent Australian landscape-material has begun to move in startled jerks, simply because the couplet form does not suit it—or Harpur. The description of the eagle's death might have been considered striking in a contemporary of Pope's:

> See in the storm's front, sailing dark and dread,
> A wide-winged eagle like a black flag spread!
> The clouds aloft flash doom! short stops his flight!
> He seems to shrivel in the blasting light!
> The air is shattered with a crashing sound,
> And he falls, stonelike, lifeless, to the ground.

It is so well done, it is a pity it should be so out of place.[7] Evidently proud of his eagle, the poet introduced a second one and again achieved a startling but wasted couplet:

> A swift bolt hurtles through the lurid air,
> Another thundering crash! the peak is bare!

Probably only one eagle was intended, but in the end Harpur could not decide between the treatments. Literature had run away with him.

It is unnecessary here to do more than mention Harpur's ambitious literary poetry which stood outside the range of landscape. It is now forgotten and it is doubtful if there can ever be any very valid reason for recalling it. There could be few demonstrations so convincing, of the contention that colonial poetry in Australia was (for whatever reason) inseparably bound to the landscape image. Poems like the ambitious **'Genius Lost'** (an autobiographical, allusive poem ostensibly about Chatterton),[8] **'The Tower of the Dream'** and **'The Witch of Hebron'** achieve nothing original or new in themselves, and only expose the fallibility of colonial literature when its writers desert what is nearest, and most vital to their imaginative existence, in order to pursue literary illusions. Colonial poetry *almost*[9] collapses unless it is supported by the vital image.

Harpur gave himself and his contemporaries good advice in 'The **"Nevers" of Poetry'**:

> Never say aught in verse, or grave or gay,
> Which you in prose might hesitate to say.

Of course there was more to it than that, and he did not always keep this counsel anyway. When he wrote at his best, the flatness in his style, which has been complained of, was capable of resolving itself into a valuable simplicity or plainness. But in order to attain that level, he had to find the proper stimulus. It only came when his heart was full of intimate communings with the bush, mostly remembered from childhood. Then, and then only, he came inspired to poetry—not with literature, nor rational enlightenment nor noble morals (though he remained all his life a moral poet)—but with the warm image of all that he had experienced of visible, audible, and tangible nature, the true landscape.

     . . . . .

G. B. Barton[10] said of Harpur, 'Suffering in the first instance from a narrow culture, he never seems, unfortunately, to have found the limits of his power, nor the direction in which it lay. He has written a mass of verse that will never compensate for the labour it cost him.' But it was inevitable that a poet to whom the activity of making verses was sheer second nature, should accumulate 'a mass of verse', and almost inevitable that only a small proportion should be of high quality. What is strange, perhaps, is that contemporary judgement should for once be so sure. **'The Creek of the Four Graves'** was approved by a discerning few. Yet Harpur persevered with his cabinet-pieces, which all fell flat.[11] It was the same with all other colonials; their landscape poetry alone was much regarded. Yet they one and all would have liked to scintillate in verse that would bring a flattering approval in the London reviews. No colonial poet did so shine. Nothing that R. H.

Horne wrote in Australia had the success of his *Orion,* written before he left England. Perhaps Alfred Domett's Maori epics should be considered an exception, but he lies outside our range; and it is doubtful if these poems are still read.

Notes

1. Charles Harpur (1813-1868) was born at Windsor, New South Wales, of convict parentage. Studious by disposition, he became a relatively learned man although his entire life was spent in Australia and a great part of it in remote country places. See the biographical study, *Charles Harpur, An Australian* (J. Normington-Rawling, Sydney 1962). His posthumously issued collected *Poems* (1883) is badly in need of revision and supplementation.

2. For some interesting remarks on the poem's composition and revision, see the article 'Charles Harpur', by C. W. Salier, *Australian Quarterly,* XV, Dec. 1943, p. 85.

3. There is an interesting comparison to be drawn between Harpur's poem and the work of the Canadian poets Joseph Howe and Charles Mair, approximately his contemporaries. Howe's *Acadia* describes a clash between Indians and white settlers, with a half-committed sympathy for the barbarians, and Mair's *Tecumseh* portrays the barbarian as hero. The finest modern verse account of such a clash is E. J. Pratt's *Brébeuf and his Brethren*; but that is a historical reconstruction, while Harpur's poem was closer to a contemporary narrative.

4. This cannot be said of all Harpur's poetry. But imitativeness, the besetting sin of colonial poetasters, was the last of his. His poem *The Cloud,* for example, which recalls Shelley's, manages to remain distinct from its model in mood and diction. That he *could* imitate appears from his parody of Wentworth:
   And, O Britannia, shouldst thou cease to have
   One born Obstructionist, one titled Knave . . .

   (See Normington-Rawling, *op. cit.,* p. 190).

5. Did the fugitive happen to take shelter in a tabu place? If so, Harpur does not see it in that light. Presumably the story has some historical foundation.

6. Already foreshadowed in the sentiments expressed by Lang (p. 61).

7. It is also a pity the passage should so naively recall the death of the partridge in *Windsor Forest.* This is to equate thunderbolts with a shot from a muzzle-loader.

8. Only fragmentarily preserved in the published collection, *Poems* (1883).

9. There must of course be a limit to dogmatism. Harpur had some success with non-landscape themes.

10. An interesting, and early, critic of Australian literature. He published two volumes in 1866: *Literature in New South Wales* and *Poets and Prose Writers of New South Wales.* Harpur is discussed in both.

11. Kendall's professed admiration of *The Tower of the Dream* (see pp. 107, 109) hardly contradicts this. No doubt it was sincere, but it was also consolatory.

Vijay C. Mishra (essay date 1977)

SOURCE: Mishra, Vijay C. "Early Literary Responses to Charles Harpur." *Westerly* no. 4 (December 1977): 88-93.

[*In the following essay, Mishra surveys the early responses to Harpur's poetry, concluding that the lavish praise Harpur received comments more upon the reviewers than on the poet himself.*]

> There's a path to redemption—but *that* shall we miss,
> Till we seek it no more in the old warring manner
>
> —Charles Harpur

'. . . Australia has now produced a poet all her own, to atone for the indiscretions of poetasters among her adopted sons.' So wrote Henry Parkes in his review of Charles Harpur's first published volume, *Thoughts, A Series of Sonnets,*[1] which appeared in the *Register* of 22 November 1845.[2] The enthusiasm with which Parkes greeted the publication of verses by a 'native' poet who had already made his presence felt through contributions to various magazines and newspapers in the colony,[3] echoed the sentiments expressed in an earlier review of Harpur's short volume in the *Australian Chronicle*.[4] The *Chronicle* detected in it verse of some creative merit and eagerly pronounced that at long last Australia had found grace in the eyes of the Muses. Thus the *Chronicle* contended that Charles Harpur was one of those whose literary pursuits 'were fitted to crown his country with a diadem of poetry worthy of herself, and of her children'. Yet these reviews were not restricted to prophetic prognostications alone, they also pointed out the more concrete aspects of Harpur's verse. Parkes, for instance, felt that 'Mr. Harpur was . . . not unworthy to be named with these august sons of genius (i.e. Shakespeare, Milton and Wordsworth)' and the *Chronicle* critic complimented Harpur on his 'great flow of words . . . rich stores of imagination'. This young 'sonnet-writer', as Parkes called him, was however not without 'affected piety and pure patriotism'.[5] Unwittingly perhaps—though a more deliberate action is certainly discernible—Harpur was raised to the heights of the first genuine 'bard of the country', a position which agreed closely with Harpur's own self-proclaimed position as stated in **'The Dream of the Fountain'** which appeared in the *Chronicle* of 14 March 1843. In that poem the Muse of Poetry urged the poet to:

> Be then the Bard of thy Country! O rather
>   Should such be thy choice than a monarchy wide!
> Lo! 'tis the Land of the grave of thy father!
>   'Tis the cradle of Liberty!—Think and decide.[6]

In some ways, much of the literary reputation and the critical positions surrounding Charles Harpur arises from the inevitable conflict between cultural and historical significance on the one hand—Harpur was, after all, the first major poet of the country—and the aesthetic foundations of these assumptions on the other. As Henry Parkes' own evocation demonstrates, too often 'criticism' aligned Harpur with the poetic 'greats' without attempting to distinguish Harpur's personal strengths.[7] Analogies of this sort are quite often nothing more than subconscious projections of an underlying sense of social and cultural uncertainty, the need to assert indigenous culture without denying its links with the overall European civilisation. In the absence of a strong 'popular opinion'—the type of 'opinion' which was partly responsible for Gordon's elevation—assertions of this sort became all the more important. Yet popular 'literary opinion' is another matter and many people did write in praise of Harpur (though, it is equally true that a large number did not always concur). However, even literary opinion found Harpur slightly evasive at times, refusing to fit into the preconceived patterns of the writers concerned. A study of this sort cannot ignore the difficulties Harpur presented the critics of the time, difficulties, which, in part, can be explained by the collision of the literary expectations of the times against a very individualistic expression of poetry on the part of Harpur. It remains one of the great mysteries of Australian literary history that Australia's first major poet was a 'difficult' poet who, even consciously, remained slightly aloof from the prevailing tastes of the period, tastes which, as Dr Webby has so aptly demonstrated, were still circumscribed by Shakespeare, Milton, Scott and Burns.[8]

Moreover, it cannot be denied that part of the uncertainty also arose from Harpur's strong mystical bent which infused his somewhat 'traditional' romanticism with an element of the unknown which inevitably made readers uncomfortable. Thus the *Hawkesbury Courier* of 30 July 1846 wrote about Harpur's **'The Poet Boy's Love Wishes'**:

> The above lines are very pretty, but the genius of the Bard, we think, soars too high for our comprehension. If it was somewhat more confined to terrestrial objects we should have read the verses with somewhat greater satisfaction.

Similarly, some eight years earlier (1838), James Martin in an article entitled 'The Pseudo-poets' (later included in 'The Australian Sketchbook') had, on slightly different grounds, repudiated Harpur for producing 'nothing colonial'. It is thus not surprising that Harpur's contemporary reputation became awkwardly inconclusive and even ragged: occasional outbursts followed by long periods of almost total silence.

Some months before the publication of *Thoughts,* the *Colonial Literary Journal*[9] published a letter by A SON OF THE SOIL in which lavish praise was endowed upon the poet. In the letter the author praised Harpur's work for the 'cause of Australian literature' and continued with the compliment, 'the name of Charles Harpur is a magic-word for those of his countrymen who have aught of communion with the graceful and the beautiful in intellect'. 'The native bard of the southern isle', the author added, '(should) come forward and occupy that place which his exalted abilities entitled him—as the guiding altar of his countrymen in the glorious and soul-elevating paths of literature,—of a literature NATIONAL and "Australian".' Something of an evangelical role is early thrust upon Harpur by this rather 'effulgent' enthusiast who himself writes in a lush, romantic style complete with a liberal garnishing of loaded romantic terminology. Yet the fact that the writer signs himself (and so boldly) 'A SON OF THE SOIL' surely explains a lot of the nature of the inherent in Harpur. With this also comes the pre-ordained role of Harpur within the cultural history of Australia. Whether Harpur agreed with the exact meaning of that role remains, as we have seen, an 'undefined' phenomenon. No doubt, Harpur, the author of **'The Dream of the Fountain'**, had a strong sense of his poetic vocation but, he did not, one gathers from contemporary reports, want to be a simple poet voicing the virgin melodies of the Australian bush. When later editors such as Martin detected this, they were quick to excise the non-descriptive elements from his poetry. Few poets, it is true, have suffered because what they were was precisely what they were denied.

Newspaper articles and notes appended to poems of Charles Harpur continued to put across the view that Australian writing had come of age with Harpur. This sense of euphoria, broken occasionally by James Martin's criticism, continued until the more volatile 1850's when for the first time Harpur's contributions to colonial culture began to be seriously questioned. In the 1840's, however, the applause was always there. The note preceding the republication of Harpur's **'To an Echo on the Banks of the Hunter'**[10] in the *People's Advocate* of 20 January 1849 is typical of the period:

> We venture to assert that the following is the most beautiful poem belonging to the infant literature of this country. A still, deep, shining power pervades it . . . (Mr. Harpur's) is a wayward and erratic genius; but we consider this production alone would stamp him as a true poet.[11]

The poem is quite self-consciously Wordsworthian with the usual pantheistic delight in 'swift murmurs', 'the whisperings' and the 'spirit of the past'. It is, however, a much better poem than many others written by Harpur. Here is the first stanza as it appeared in 1849:

> I hear thee, Echo, and I start to hear thee,
>   With a strange tremour; as among the hills
> Thy voice reverbs, and in swift murmurs near me
>   Dies down the stream, or with its gurgle low
> Blends whisperingly—until my bosom thrills
> With gentle tribulations, that endear thee,
>   But smack not of the present. 'Twas as though
> Some spirit of the past did then insphere Thee
>   Even with the taste of life's regretted spring—
> Waking wild recollections, to evince

My being's transfused connexion with each thing
Loved though long since.[12]

The precise reason why readers found this poem attractive is much more difficult to establish. If one uses 'Australian impressions' as a criterion then surely no other contemporary poem could have been further removed. If, however, even in the absence of local colouring people accepted this as indigenous verse, then it would not be totally incorrect to say that no one was too clear in his mind about the direction poetry should take in the young country. That Harpur is indeed being praised for sincerely capturing English ideals seems to me to be the only incontrovertible verdict one can give.

Yet it would be wrong to assume that part of if not the only real problem in the 1840's was an almost total absence of critical stance. Criticism—and creativity for that matter—did not exist in a vacuum in the colony. If major yardsticks by way of established men of letters and literary journals did not exist, there was still no dearth of speakers willing to elaborate on poetic ideas—especially Coleridgean and Romantic—to responsive audiences in Sydney. A slightly different perspective on national literature was given in a reprint of an article by the American Unitarian and sometime teacher of Ralph Waldo Emerson, Dr William Channing. The article entitled 'The Importance and Means of a National Literature' appeared on Saturday 14 April 1838 in *The Colonist*. Echoing the American experience, Channing related literature to culture, society and the overall progress of human life. 'We maintain', he wrote, 'that a people, which has any serious purpose of taking a place among the improved communities, should studiously promote within itself every variety of intellectual exertion . . . Mind is the creative power . . . It should train within itself, men able to understand, and to use, whatever is thought and discovered over the whole earth . . . the whole mass of human knowledge must exist . . . in its higher minds.'[13] Dr Channing's article was also a strong plea against provincialism and it emphasised that the creation of local literature should not mean that overseas trends ought not be completely ignored or that the works of the past should be by-passed. 'The more we receive from the other countries', he added, 'the greater the need of an original literature.' Four years later, Hastings Elwin's translation of Metatasio's *Observations on the Poetics of Aristotle* was published by Kemp and Fairfax, the owners of the *Sydney (Morning) Herald*.[14] The level of intellectual activity in the colony suggests that Harpur was quite possibly aware of a good many currents and crosscurrents in the literary thought of the time. We know for certain that Harpur knew Emerson's ideas very well.[15] Thus Harpur is not, as has been suggested by a number of twentieth-century apologists,[16] a man who needs sympathy because of his essential isolation from 'culture'. That handicap was no doubt there: Harpur could not have had the exposure of a Gordon, for instance. But this is no feasible criterion on which to make judgments about Harpur because first it is not totally accurate and second it takes us to areas of conjecture verging on the sentimental.

Channing's American notes were used by R. K. Ewing who delivered a number of lectures on poetry at the Sydney School of Arts during 1844-46. The series ended in late June 1846 with a lecture which was partly devoted to "Colonial Poetry".[17] In it Ewing referred to about twenty colonial poets including H. Halloran, W. C. Wentworth, Henry Parkes and Charles Harpur. In the *Spectator* report, however, it was felt that Mr Ewing 'might have devoted more time to analyze the beauties and less to the defects of Australian poetry'. At the same time the *Spectator* did note that 'there was much justice in his examination of the extravagantly high claims set up for Mr C. Harpur by some injudicious friends'. In spite of this concession, the *Spectator*, like much contemporary criticism, wished to have it both ways: 'Yet, that gentleman has produced compositions of much merit' and 'Whatever be his faults we will forgive them, if it be only that some lines of his **"To an Echo on the Banks of the Hunter"** formed the inspiring theme for the following beautiful stanzas by Mr Henry Halloran'.[18] S. P. Hill's interpolation is typical of the 'damning with faint praise' which often occurs in the period. But no real definition of the special peculiarities or flavour of Australian poetry is actually given in defence. Without mentioning Harpur by name, the *Spectator* continued, 'their art (the Art of Australian poets) is no more trick of versification, but is a genuine growth of nature, having their root deep in their hearts—hearts accustomed to meditate with earnestness and feel with truth, upon the great duties and interests of mankind'.

In his June 1846 lecture, Ewing had referred to the claims made by Parkes about Harpur in his November 1845 review of Harpur's *Thoughts*. Parkes had suggested that Harpur was not unworthy of the genius of poets such as Shakespeare, Milton and Wordsworth. It is true, as Parkes pointed out in a letter to the *Spectator* of 4 July 1846, that Mr Duncan, the editor of the *Register*, had in fact cautioned him that 'it was a piece of extravagance to compare Harpur with Wordsworth'. As we have already seen, the comparison was in fact made by Parkes, though in his defence Parkes quickly pointed out that he did not feel that Harpur would ever 'attain to their (Shakespeare, Milton and Wordsworth's) universal fame'.[19] Parkes left Harpur 'to take care of his own reputation' which, he felt, Harpur 'is well able to defend'.

And, indeed, Harpur wasted no time in getting himself involved in this mini Ewing-Parker-Harpur-Milton controversy, a controversy which, with some changes in cast, was to emerge again later in his career. Charging the editor of the *Spectator* of collusion with Mr Ewing ('that he and yourself had laid heads together upon the matter'), Harpur fumed with the wrath of a weather-beaten journalist and quipped at the 'intolerable nonsense' and the 'subterfuge' which was 'gross as the nature of a bog, and vile as the odour of the fox'.[20] In tone and sentiment at least, Harpur's violent outburst had already been equalled by his earlier letters to newspapers, especially those written in protest against editorial emendations of his poems.[21]

Thus by the time **The Bushrangers: A Play in Five Acts and Other Poems** appeared in 1853,[22] Harpur had been the centre of lively and vigorous discussions in the Australian literary scene. But the exact nature of that enthusiasm, the responses to Harpur primarily as a poet, demonstrates a certain amount of discomfort in critical stance. What the critics and the newspapers of the period in fact sought was an 'epic' voice in Australian literature to strengthen cultural claims about the colony's 'maturity'. In this way wild comparisons to Homer, Milton and Shakespeare were made to assert one's own search for permanence in art and aesthetics. Hence the early literary responses to Harpur reflect a critical stance which has been pervasive since—an uneasiness arising out of a conflict between an uncertainty as to the literary worth of a writer against the feeling that indigenous culture should be encouraged and asserted at all times. Not surprisingly, then, to this day Harpur's reputation, while saved of the excesses of the early period, still continues to survive inconclusively.

Notes

1. Sydney, W. A. Duncan, 1845, 8 vo. 16pp. Mitchell Library copy (C378) inscribed by the author to Mrs Parkes, 1 November 1845, with holograph notes by Sir Henry Parkes, 1895.

2. Duncan's newspaper to which Harpur had contributed poems pseudonymously under 'A Spirit of the Past' etc. Parkes also reviewed a work by G. F. Poole which was peremptorily dismissed.

3. For instance, the *Currency Lad* published a poem by Harpur as early as 4 May 1833. Another poem by 'Stebii' (Charles Harpur) appeared in Tegg's *Literary News,* 2 December 1837.

4. *Australian Chronicle,* 5 November 1845.

5. *Australian Chronicle, op. cit.*

6. Martin's 1883 edition of *Harpur Poems* has 1.1 'bard of the country', 1.3 'land' and 1.4 'Liberty! think'. This is followed by J. McAuley, *The Personal Element in Australian Poetry,* Angus & Robertson, 1970.

7. Harpur himself was very conscious of the larger 'tradition'. See Harpur holograph 'Discourse on Poetry', 32 mo. n.d., Mitchell Library, C386. Also *Sydney Morning Herald,* 30/9/1859 for a report of a lecture given by Harpur.

8. Webby, E. A. "Literature and the Reading Public 1800-1850: A Study of the Growth and Differentiation of a Colonial Literary Culture during the Earlier Nineteenth Century", PhD thesis, Sydney University, August 1971. 4 Vols.

9. *Colonial Literary Journal,* 8 February 1845.

10. First appeared in the *Chronicle,* 7 March 1843. In the same year the *Chronicle* also published Harpur's 'Loneliness of Heart', 'The Dream of the Fountain', 'Sonnet to My Friend, Mr. J. J. Walsh', 'Sonnet, De- scription of the Prospect from Mount View, South of Jerry Plains' etc.

11. Note by Edward John Hawkesley, Editor of the *People's Advocate,* founded in December 1848 and sympathetic towards colonial poetry.

12. The text is the same as the one which appeared in 1843. In the final copy made by Harpur in 1865 (Mitchell A87, MS No. 6), however, the following changes were made: 1.2 . . . strange shock, as from among . . . , 1.3 . . . voice, reverbing, in swift . . . , 1.5 . . . whisperingly, until . . . , 1.7 . . . Present . . . , 1.8 . . . Spirit . . . thee, 1.9 . . . Spring.

    Martin made further changes in the 1883 edition of *Harpur Poems* and completely altered the final stanza.

13. It is worth remembering that like many other advocates of 'literary tradition' Channing also used the example of the Greeks as his overall paradigm.

14. So J. Normington-Rawling, *Charles Harpur, An Australian,* Sydney, Angus & Robertson, 1962, p. 102. However, *Webby, op. cit.,* Vol. III, p. 345, observes '. . . an anonymous translation of Observations . . . rendered into English with biographical notice of the author (Sydney, 1842)'.

15. The Mitchell Library copy of Emerson's *Eight Essays* (1852) is in fact the copy which was actually owned by Harpur and has 1855 inscribed in it.

16. Notably H. M. Green and E. Morris Miller.

17. *Spectator,* 1 July 1846. The lectures on poetry were generally of a high quality. The basic assumptions of his criticism were Platonic and Coleridgean: the 'ideal beauty' is the 'sublimer emanation' than the 'soul of poetry, which is energy' said Ewing in connection with Byron whose poetry, he felt, belonged to the latter category. The review was written by S. P. Hill.

18. Poem beginning 'And I in early youth had hopes as deep' quoted in full by the *Spectator.*

19. *Spectator,* 4 July 1846.

20. *Spectator,* 18 July 1846.

21. *Chronicle,* May 1844, for instance.

22. *The Bushrangers: A Play in Five Acts and Other Poems,* Sydney, W. R. Piddington, 1853.

Noel Macainsh (essay date 1978)

SOURCE: Macainsh, Noel. "Charles Harpur's 'Midsummer Noon'—A Structuralist Approach." *Australian Literary Studies* 8, no. 4 (October 1978): 439-45.

[*In the following essay, Macainsh analyzes repetition, rhyme schemes, and allegory in Harpur's "Midsummer Noon" to emphasize its value as structurally sound poetry.*]

Charles Harpur's poem **"A Midsummer Noon in the Australian Forest"** is widely anthologised. The editor of *The Penguin Book of Australian Verse,* Professor Harry Heseltine, says of the poem that it arguably makes a 'definitive contribution to the direction and pattern of our poetic history'.[1] Nevertheless, and despite the considerable critical notice of the poem, it seems to the present writer that adequate attention has yet to be given to the structure of the text itself, as well as to its unique place in Australian literature, if not to its place among the relatively few examples of its genre in literature generally. Rather, the critics have pronounced brief, varying summary judgements on the 'total effect' of the poem while giving as much attention or more to its alleged defects, chief of which are outmoded diction and breaches of a presumed contract to supply the reader with accurate natural description.

For example, the late James McAuley, in what is perhaps the most recent discussion of Harpur's poem, states that the poem 'in a modest way, transcends mere description. It creates a sentiment, and celebrates the value of quiet "musing" or contemplation'.[2] However, this is McAuley's only recognition of the poem's transcendence of 'mere description' in a close examination largely taken up with tracking down putative faults in Harpur's knowledge of dragon-flies.

Brian Elliott, in his *The Landscape of Australian Poetry,* calls the poem 'this dry song of the cicada' and states that its mood 'is of childhood at its exquisite terminus'.[3] Although Elliott implies that the poem's 'total effect' is 'successfully intuitive',[4] he nevertheless pronounces the poem to be imperfect, and instances Harpur's presumed misnaming of both the dragon-fly and the cicada. Other, and similar examples could be cited from the critics.

In view of this state of criticism on Harpur's poem, it is thought worthwhile to attempt here a so-called text-immanent approach, a structuralist analysis, in the belief that it will bring hitherto unnoticed features of Harpur's poem to light and will show that his presumed misnaming of insects and use of outmoded diction may have more justification than the critics so far have conceded him. This procedure of course does not obviate the complementary consideration of personal, social, cultural factors in the production and reception of Harpur's poem. But, as a preliminary operation, criticism must start out from 'structure', that is from comprehension of the system of relations internal to the text itself, and this is what appears to be relatively lacking in the case of Harpur's **'Midsummer Noon'**.

A pre-condition of structural analysis of literary texts is a knowledge of the results of structural linguistics, the basic principles of which were formulated by Ferdinand de Saussure in the years 1906 to 1911. The transfer of the structural method from linguistics to literary analysis is based primarily on the thesis that literary language is a deviation from normal language and should be analysed accordingly.

De Saussure has explained the function of language on the basis of selection of elements from paradigms and their combination into syntagms. A paradigm is explained here as a class of units which, from a certain aspect, are equivalent to each other, while differing when seen from another aspect. The paradigm is equal to a store of similar but differing signs, from which a sign is selected for use in discourse. It unites absent signs into a virtual memory sequence, that is, signs that are not actually present in the discourse are virtually present; or as de Saussure has it, paradigmatic relationships are 'associative'. According to this view of language, each sign is selected from a specific store of other signs, which themselves do not occur in actual discourse but are virtually present by unconscious association. Each of the other signs is like the one selected, but they also oppose it in at least one respect. Furthermore, each sign is determined by its relationship to the signs that precede or follow it on the syntagmatic axis of the discourse as a whole. These paradigmatic and syntagmatic relationships characterise the sign at the levels of both expression and content.

These considerations, together with the work of Roman Jakobson, Claude Levi-Strauss and others, have led to the paradigmatic structural analysis of literature practised initially by the French critic Roland Barthes. Barthes' method does not purport to provide answers to all questions concerning the rules governing a text, but it is thought to be sufficiently productive as a heuristic device to apply here.

Whereas a traditional interpretative approach would firstly ask of Harpur's poem what is the significance of the 'birds and insects', 'hills' and 'plains', and so on, so as to set up more or less essential relationships between these things and the assumed meaning of the poem, Barthes' method requires that the corresponding things or signs be released from their syntagmatic conjunction and be comprehended as members of a paradigm. This involves the detection of 'repetitions', as structural phenomena, at whatever level they occur, whether phonetic, phonological, morphematic or syntactic, as these always prove themselves ultimately to be phenomena of meaning.

Harpur's poem is as follows (the version given is from *The Penguin Book of Australian Verse*):

"A Midsummer Noon in the Australian Forest"

Not a sound disturbs the air,
There is quiet everywhere;
Over plains and over woods
What a mighty stillness broods!

All the birds and insects keep
Where the coolest shadows sleep;
Even the busy ants are found
Resting in their pebbled mound;
Even the locust clingeth now
Silent to the barky bough:
Over hills and over plains
Quiet, vast and slumbrous, reigns.

Only there's a drowsy humming
From yon warm lagoon slow coming:

'Tis the dragon-hornet—see!
All bedaubed resplendently,
Yellow on a tawny ground—
Each rich spot nor square nor round,
Rudely heart-shaped, as it were
The blurred and hasty impress there

Of a vermeil-crusted seal
Dusted o'er with golden meal.
Only there's a droning where
Yon bright beetle shines in air,
Tracks it in its gleaming flight
With a slanting beam of light,
Rising in the sunshine higher,
Till its shards flame out like fire.

Every other thing is still,
Save the ever-wakeful rill,
Whose cool murmur only throws
Cooler comfort round repose;
Or some ripple in the sea
Of leafy boughs, where, lazily,
Tired summer, in her bower
Turning with the noontide hour,
Heaves a slumbrous breath ere she
Once more slumbers peacefully.

O 'tis easeful here to lie
Hidden from noon's scorching eye,
In this grassy cool recess
Musing thus of quietness.

Firstly, certain "repetitions" occur in the very title of Harpur's poem. By syntagmatic conjunction and important position as title, these repetitions signal a fundamental compositional ordering in the poem, namely that of space.

The first repetition involves the words **'A Midsummer Noon'**. The repetitive element here is that of the zenith, common as height of year and height of day. We also notice here the internal syntagm of heat and height; the heat element is intensified by association with a specific point in time, that of mid-day of mid-summer. The second repetition involves the phrase 'in the Australian Forest'. The word 'forest' on its own may induce in some readers a sense of the vertical, but the qualifier 'Australian' has a broad, geographical association, such that the concept 'in the Australian Forest' acquires a predominantly broad, horizontal character. The syntagmatic element of space formed by the title is essentially that of a vertical dimension penetrating a horizontal. If one considers the given totality of objects in Harpur's poem as defining a space, then in so doing one abstracts all properties of these objects except those that are defined by space-like relations. Already at the level of merely ideological modelling, the language of spatial relations is one of the basic means to comprehend reality. The directions of "heaven" and "hell", "right" and "left", "ahead", "behind", and so on, have long been modelling aids for social, religious, political and moral comprehension of the world. In the world of Harpur's poem, space is essentially the shape of an inverted cone. That is, there is a vertical dimension, and a horizontal dimension having maximum range above and restricted

extent below, tending to a point-focus. The slanting sides of the cone find physical definition in 'a slanting beam of light', ripples and wave-like expressions, which will be returned to shortly. The elements distributed on this vertical axis are, at the upper end: a vastness, 'a mighty stillness', a reigning slumbrous quietness, a 'scorching eye', a brooding over plains and woods. At the lower end are: all the birds and insects, the poet, coolness, shadows, hiding, sleep, the pebbled mound, a grassy recess, the woman 'summer'.

After the opening stanza has quickly indicated the top of the vertical scale, the second stanza describes the elements at the bottom, and then returns the reader's gaze upwards. The 'pebbled mound' (line 8) is the lowest point here. The image of the locust clinging silently to the bough reverses the direction to upward, preparing for the formal repetition of lines 1 and 2, as the conclusion of stanza 2.

Here, there would be a breaking-off of the poem, if it were not that the opening line, 'Not a sound disturbs', together with the antithetical discordant rhyme of lines 3 and 4, generates an on-reaching tension. A consideration of stanza 1 will make this clearer.

The first two lines of stanza 1 exhibit semantic parallelism, such that for non-poetic reading, the information given by the second line is redundant. However, read as poetry, the parallelism becomes 'stylistic symmetry', for which there is ample precedent in literary history; the Bible, for example, having many such repetitions.

Lines 3 and 4, which constitute the second half of the opening sentence of the poem show anaphoric repetition of 'over' in line 3 and, less overtly, phonemic repetition of "d" and "t" elements. Also, the "e"-vowel of 'mighty' in line 4 repeats that of 'quiet' in line 2. As with lines 1 and 2, we note that lines 3 and 4 taken together show semantic parallelism with the preceding lines, such that we could again speak of redundancy at the informational level but of stylistic symmetry as poetry. The structural effect of all these devices is to intensify the poem's opening statement.

We now consider Harpur's rhyme. At the lowest poetical level, we can distinguish in general between equivalences of position and those of sound. The point of intersection of these two classes of equivalence is defined as rhyme. All types of equivalence, including such secondary equivalences, generate the formation of additional semantic units. We can also define rhyme further as the congruence in sound of words or their parts in a position marked by reference to the rhythmical unit with accompanying semantic incongruence.

In Harpur's poem, lines 1 and 2 exhibit exact end-rhyme, 'air' and 'everywhere'. However, the effect on the reader here is hardly a rich one because the semantic incongruence is weak; along with the congruence of sound we find that the meanings of 'air' and 'everywhere', in the present context, are virtually the same. In place of similarity of sound and contrast of meaning, we are confronted with two kinds of similarity. We are thus conditioned by the initial rhyme-pair to an uneventful congruence.

The second rhyme-pair, lines 3 and 4, however, contrasts strongly with the first by offering incongruence at both levels. 'Woods' and 'broods' offers eye-rhyme as well as final consonantal rhyme, but is an off-rhyme with regard to vowel sound. The sound of 'broods' at the end of the fourth line is as disturbing as it is unexpected, being intensified also by the following exclamation mark. As such, it returns the reader involuntarily to the opening statement of the poem, 'Not a sound disturbs the air', creating an antithetical response, a disquiet requiring subsequent resolution. The tension thus created is met by the opening of stanza 3, 'Only there's a' (line 13), introducing the dragon-hornet. This opening is anaphorically repeated as the opening of the next sentence (line 23), which introduces the second insect, 'yon bright beetle'.

With the dragon-hornet, stanza 3 also introduces the horizontal direction, at a level well down on the vertical axis. The dragon-hornet is 'slow coming' from 'yon warm lagoon'. The direction of motion is from a near periphery, into the centre. The hornet which is defined as a 'large, strong, social wasp having an exceptionally severe sting'[5] is conjoined here with a fiery, monstrous and mythical animal. It is the only active creature mentioned so far in the poem. The other, less fearsome creatures, already mentioned, are inert. The dragon-hornet itself emits only a 'drowsy humming', here exhibiting alliteration and metrical parallelism, and is 'slow'. The paradox of fearsome name and mild behaviour is paralleled by that of its description, 'bedaubed resplendently', where the element of bedaubing, that is, to soil, smear, defile, paint coarsely, to lay or put on without taste,[6] is conjoined with the element of magnificence, brilliant lustre or handsome accoutrement. The first specification of this bedaubing (line 17) is 'yellow on a tawny ground', which repeats the implicit imagery of the noon-day sun, the 'scorching eye' shining down over the tawny "ground" of woods and plains. The 'resplendence' is incongruent with 'tawny', must therefore associate with 'yellow'; hence the dragon-hornet's markings are an image in miniature of a bird's-eye view (or 'scorching' sun's-eye view) of the world at large. Next, lines 18-19 convey the information that each 'rich spot' is 'rudely heart-shaped'. The spots are resplendent yellow daubs, heart-shaped but lacking the proper perfection of that shape, and are as though due to the blurred and hasty impress of a 'vermeil', that is bright-red, crusted seal. These red 'hearts' are as if 'dusted' over with 'golden meal'. There is a repetition of imagery here, with the incongruence that 'yellow on a tawny ground' now becomes gold on a bright-red ground.

Immediately, at the end of the description of the first active creature, the dragon-hornet, we are paratactically introduced to the second, 'yon bright beetle'. The relativising opening of the previous sentence, 'Only there's a', (line 13) is repeated here for the sentence introducing the second creature (line 23).

The paradigm of the active insect reveals here certain incongruencies. Whereas the first insect was a 'dragon-hornet', this second one is a relatively milder 'beetle'. The sound it emits is not a 'drowsy humming' but merely a 'droning'. The yellow spots of the first insect are here the single spot of the 'bright beetle' shining in the sunlight. Its motion is not horizontal, 'slow coming' in, but is a 'rising' in 'a slanting beam of light', repeating in its direction the upward-pointing 'locust' image at the end of stanza 2. But whereas stanza 2 concluded with a return to the upper end of the vertical axis, the upward motion here does not reach as far. The beetle rises till its 'shards flame out like fire' or, as a later version has it, 'Its shards flame out like gems on fire'. We note that the word 'shards' has meanings both of a shell-like wing-cover of a beetle and of a fragment, especially of broken earthenware. The movement upwards, against the 'slanting beam of light', leads to an apparent flaming out. There are repeated associations here, in both insect-descriptions, of cultural heritage, of the "Golden Age of Time" that Harpur is known to have been drawn to. The incongruence of the dragon-hornet's fierce name, and the resplendent hearts on its wings, with its mild behaviour, is paratactically matched here by the incongruence of the beetle's transfiguring rise into the light while droning. That both of these insects suggest further associations, for instance, with the sacred scarab of the Egyptians, a symbol of re-birth, or with Icarus, with the incongruence of earth-bound creatures who bear the spotted glory of age-old aspirations to conquest and transcendence, goes without saying, but cannot be pursued further here.

Suffice it to say that this second insect-motif is a repetition in diminuendo of the first. The insect rises, but the counter-direction of the 'slanting beam of light' remains to direct the reader still further downward to subsequent elements, initially to the 'rill', the third and only other thing that is 'not still'. The poem thus includes the four "elements", fire, air, earth and water. Though the activity of the rill is congruent with that of the two insects, it represents a still further step to insentience. The parallel here is that of wakefulness and water, of water that coolly 'murmurs'. As the spatial focus of the poem narrows in, the manifestation of life decreases. High above, there is a vast, mighty, brooding consciousness while far below there is only the mindless murmur of the rill. The form of the rill associates with the 'slanting' beam of light, with the 'ripple in the sea' of leaves, with the 'breath' heaved by 'summer' and with "summer's" turning with the 'noontide hour'. This slanting, wave-like motion in each case peters out downward, towards the unconscious and inert. Summer is depicted as a woman, lazy, tired, who turns over with the 'noontide' and then sinks once more into slumber. She is allusive of 'yon warm lagoon' from which the dragon-hornet comes. She is at the bottom of the inverted cone of space, where the poet also lies, 'easeful', 'hidden from noon's scorching eye', with the woman, 'summer'. He is 'musing thus of quietness'. Above, there is the 'scorching eye' and the vast stillness that broods, that is meditates with morbid persistence, or rests fixedly, over plains and woods.

Harpur's poem, like all artistically structured texts, models both a universal and a particular object, in this case a universal experience of midsummer noon and its particular occasion in the Australian forest. The blemishes that Harpur's critics point to are not blemishes of this structure as such, but are blemishes only when seen from the standpoint of an 'imitation' theory of art, requiring detailed naturalistic fealty to the specifically Australian setting of Harpur's experience. Harpur himself was clearly not so much interested in entomology or promoting Australianness in landscape as in drawing on his reader's associations so as to best structure for himself and them a unique experience transcending 'mere description'.

Harpur's poem deals with a particular time of the day and year. An important example of the moods associated with the rhythmic progression of the times of the day and year is the sequence of moods of the seasons as it declares itself in progression from early morning, through the rising life of later morning, over the height of day, into the evening sun, or into the gathering dusk and finally comes to rest in the growing stillness of night. What the sympathetic witness feels here is not only a sequence of psychic states or a change of light in which the world and life appear, but that these states when seen more deeply are also various forms of access to hidden depths of reality only accessible in this way. In this sense, one can speak of a metaphysic of the times of day.

However, in seeking for poetical examples of the experience of midday, such as may have influenced Harpur, one makes the perhaps surprising discovery that whereas there are numerous examples of morning, evening and night poems, there is strikingly little poetry about the height of day as such. In the older, North European literature, this may be due to climate; the noon not being as striking as in hot climates. However, even in hot climates, the mid-day theme, as such, is not often dealt with.

It is noted here in passing that while Australian critics have sought for various possibilities of influence on Harpur's poem, including Andrew Marvell's 'The Garden',[7] no one so far has mentioned John Clare's poem 'Noon', which seems to the present writer a much more likely influence:

> All how silent and how still;
> Nothing heard but yonder mill: . . .

However, though various poems could be cited as possible influences on Harpur's work, none of these poems exhibits the same clarity of structure of the mid-summer noon-day experience as does Harpur's poem itself.

What is more striking, however, is that if one extends one's purview to literary examples of the heightened noonday experience in the wider world of European literature, then one finds certain quite unique experiences expressed, such as might appear to be merely the marks of a particular perhaps idiosyncratic author, were it not that the same features are to be found with some regularity, repeated in the works of other authors, often in similar words and images.

For example, Judith Wright, in her *Preoccupations in Australian Poetry*,[8] has spoken of Nietzschean elements in Harpur's poetry. There can of course have been no direct influence, since Nietzsche's works would not have been available here until after Harpur's death. However, it is of interest that the experience of midday probably signified for Nietzsche his deepest experience and was of basic significance for his entire philosophy. As can be seen from 'Zarathustra' and 'The Wanderer', the experience of 'The Great Midday', as Nietzsche termed it, was one of stillness in heat, in which no sound or leaf stirred, in which the great god Pan slept, having an expression of eternity on his face. All living creatures were still, it was only the ever-springing fountain that played. Here, man experiences release from the passage of time, is lifted above individuation, is only a perceiving and knowing being, is empowered with an hitherto unknown fineness of perception— 'one sees much that he never saw'. This release from time is a contentment but a heavy, ambivalent one, having a menacing overpowering quality from its proximity to death.

Other poems that come to mind, on the midday theme, and which were certainly unknown to Harpur, are those of Paul Valery ('Cimetière marin'), Stéphane Mallarmé ('Tristesse d'Eté', 'L'Après Midi d'un Faune', which certainly influenced Christopher Brennan's 'Noon' poem[9]), Leconte de Lisle ('Midi'), and Gabriele d'Annunzio ('Meriggio').

From these various witnesses, including Nietzsche, one can discern some general features of the midday experience: The experience of midday is that of a stillness in which all life has come to rest and no sound is to be heard. The silence of midday is a quiescence both of human life and of surrounding nature, related to sleep and death. Borne by this stillness, in and around him, the poet feels himself to be at ease and harmony with surrounding nature. It is properly a returning of a pantheistic, even basically Pan-like and pagan experience that finds its full intensity only in hot zones (here Southern Europe). Merged with the surrounding stillness of life and borne by it, the poet feels himself freed from the fetters of individual existence. He merges into the nameless ground of eternity. The experience thus shows itself as a lifting above the flow of historical time into the higher plane of eternity. As a typically recurring symbol of this, there appears the closed circle. In brief, the experience of midday is a revelation of the world in its completeness, reached just at the height of the day. The midday, and the height of summer as midday of the year, and maturity as the midday of life, thus fuse to an inseparable unity.

The midday experience is of a rare, rather sombre happiness. The lifting above the limits of individual existence has a releasing and joyful effect but since the completed maturity of this existence simultaneously signifies the end of individuation, the illuminating experience of eternity is also accompanied by the shadowy premonition of death. This gives the easeful experience of midday an associated character of anxiety and foreboding. The experience is properly ambivalent.

From the foregoing, it can be seen that Harpur's poem too shares these general features. Naturally, there are departures of detail. Nature, for Harpur, is represented by the woman, 'summer', not the great god Pan. His diction,[10] as of the locust that 'clingeth' to the 'barky bough', suggests, like Nietzsche's, the Old Testament, as might also the 'scorching eye' above; though these elements when taken together with other elements of the poem might just as well suggest Egyptian, pagan times. In any case, great antiquity is implied. Also, the tension of Harpur's poem, related to the polarity of joyful release and the foreboding of death, is less marked than in the poetry of Nietzsche and d'Annunzio or even in that of Brennan. However, there is no doubt that the Australian poet, as the structure of his poem reveals and despite his possible inaccuracies of natural description, has shared a unique and valuable experience with his fellow poets.

Notes

1. Harry Heseltine, ed., *The Penguin Book of Australian Verse* (Ringwood, Vic: Penguin Books, 1972), p.32.

2. James McAuley, The Rhetoric of Australian Poetry, *Southerly,* No. 1, (1976), 5.

3. Brian Elliott, *The Landscape of Australian Poetry* (Melbourne: Cheshire, 1967), p.67.

4. p.68.

5. *Webster's International Dictionary.*

6. Ibid.

7. Leon Cantrell, 'Marvell and Charles Harpur', *Australian Literary Studies,* 6 (1973), 88-90.

8. Judith Wright, *Preoccupations in Australian Poetry* (Melbourne: O.U.P. [Oxford University Press], 1965), p.15.

9. cf. Elliott, pp.266-7.

10. Elizabeth Perkins, in an unpublished M.A. thesis on Harpur, University of Queensland, has suggested that 'not one word in the poem would have seemed alien to a colonist' (p.126).

Vijay Mishra (essay date 1978)

SOURCE: Mishra, Vijay. "Charles Harpur's Reputation 1853-1858: The Years of Controversy." *Australian Literary Studies* 8, no. 4 (October 1978): 446-56.

[In the following essay, Mishra analyzes the changes in Harpur's literary reputation during a period of intense self-examination by the Australian literary community of the mid-nineteenth century.]

Between 1853 and 1858 there was a dramatic change in the literary reputation of Charles Harpur. Prior to 1853 Harpur had produced a volume of verse, *Thoughts, A Series of Sonnets,* and had been a regular contributor to various newspapers since 1833. There were, no doubt, minor disagreements as in the Ewing-Parkes-Milton controversy which occurred soon after Parkes' very warm appraisal of Harpur's slim volume,[1] but these were not major criticisms of the poet. 1853, however, began with the publication of Harpur's second volume and by 1858 Harpur had become the centre of one of the major literary controversies of the period. Moreover, much more fundamental questions relating not only to the intrinsic worth of Harpur as a poet but also to the overall direction of Australian literature began to be raised and discussed in earnest. This change in literary responses as it relates to Charles Harpur is one of the more interesting episodes of mid-nineteenth century Australian literary history and deserves a closer look.

Charles Harpur's second volume, *The Bushrangers: A Play in Five Acts and Other Poems,* appeared in 1853.[2] It was dedicated to N. D. Stenhouse 'by one who, though unacquainted with him, has learned to appreciate his character and talents'.[3] The play, **'The Bushrangers'**, was itself a reworking, though ever so slightly, of **'The Tragedy of Donohoe'** which Harpur had sent to the *Sydney Monitor* when he was barely twenty one.[4]

Daniel Deniehy,[5] a close friend of Harpur and a fluent man of letters in his own right, reviewed the volume for the *Empire* of 22 April 1853. Invoking Channing's claim[6] that the 'men of a nation are not alone its noblest but its only genuine products', Deniehy recapitulated, though with greater gusto and erudition, Parkes' earlier (1845) judgment on 'native genius':

> This little volume contains the most satisfactory proof of the existence of native genius of a high order, that has been yet offered to the public . . . . In the book before us, the reader will not only find exquisite poetry, a rare and delicate imaginative loveliness; but above all an impress of character noble and masculine . . . .

That 'self-moulded intellect' of Harpur was, to Deniehy, a microcosmic expression of the larger destiny of Australia, the expression, indeed, of a free, poetic spirit growing independently of alien influences. After admitting Harpur's defects ('petty defects of execution lying here and there on the surface of his compositions . . .'), Deniehy's main argument returned to the fact that like himself, the poet was 'native born': he belonged 'to the soil, and grew . . . .' Implicit in this adulation is thus an attempt at edification not unlike those which had been already showered upon Harpur. Still, Deniehy was a remarkably good critic and in fact pre-dates those critics whom Brian Kiernan felt 'drew the same organicist analogies as did social scientists like Comte, Taine or Herbert Spencer'.[7] Indeed, part of the problem with Deniehy's review is that it ends up as an aesthetic exercise in itself. However, Deniehy made poetic as well as purely cultural observations. He agreed that 'the miscellaneous poems' (some of the best that Harpur ever wrote) are 'far superior to *The Bushrangers*':

There is evidence in them of profounder and maturer thought, of a clearer perception of the aims and ends of poetry, perhaps, also, of a completer mastery of expression. The materials of which the drama is composed seem scarcely to have arrived at the requisite state of fusion in the poet's mind, when he commenced his labour; at all events it is quite obvious in the play itself that they have not been sufficiently wrought up.

Sonnets such as **'His mind alone is kingly . . .'**, **'There's a rare Soul of Poetry which may be'**, **'The manifold Hills forsaken by the sun'** are singled out for particular attention. But it is **'The Creek of the Four Graves'** which captures Deniehy's imagination and which, he feels, would best support 'Mr. Harpur's claims to a laurel'. The great strength of the poem is its unified sensibility: 'In Harpur nature is related to the soul of the spectator, gazing, looking and thoughtfully awake . . . .' It is indeed remarkable that this aspect of Harpur was seen so early by Deniehy. That Harpur is not simply a literal realist but one who transforms the world into his own inner consciousness and expresses it in terms of an image, is precisely what Judith Wright discovers about Harpur a century later.[8] For Deniehy, however, the exercise was more an extension of his very real interest in Coleridgean criticism. Thus when he writes that **'The Creek of the Four Graves'** 'has the perfect inward organisation and harmony of a Poem in the severe philosophical sense, and is everywhere alive with the creative imagination—the true "faculty divine"' he is not really talking about the poem itself; rather he is speaking about the poetic process in Coleridgean-Romantic terms.

Nor does Deniehy lose sight of Milton. According to him the following lines have 'a contour . . . of Miltonic grandeur':

Yea, thence surveyed, the Universe might have seemed
Coiled in vast rest,—only that one dim cloud,
Diffused and shapen like a mighty spider,
Crept as with scrawling legs along the sky;
And that the stars, in their bright orders, still
Cluster by cluster glowingly revealed
As this slow cloud moved on,—high over all,—
Looked wakeful—yea, looked thoughtful in their
  peace.

Yes, 'Miltonic grandeur' indeed! But only if attempt at cosmic considerations and echoes of epic tone (however dismal) are themselves taken to be Miltonic. Surely, on a purely poetic level, there is something amiss in the metaphorical dissonance created by the image of a scrawling spider! But the criticism may well express Deniehy's own rather conservative position about 'native genius': for that genius to be poetically great, it must stand the test of the epic poets, especially Milton and Homer. The epic has, ironically, remained a great Australian dream in literature.

Perhaps the final few lines of Deniehy's article say more than anything else about the distance Harpur criticism—in terms of his reputation and not in terms of the quality of the criticism itself—had reached by 1853: **'"To an Echo on the Banks of the Hunter"** . . . alone would have ob-

tained for Harpur a seat among the serene creators of Immortal things.' The poem referred to appeared some ten years before and was praised by people as diverse as 'A SON OF THE SOIL' and Edward John Hawkesley for very much the same reasons as suggested by Deniehy.[9]

The *Freeman's Journal* also welcomed **The Bushrangers** with much enthusiasm.[10] 'Seldom has a more grateful and pleasing duty fallen our lot', wrote the reviewer with a sense of excitement verging on the hyperbolic. The poet 'is possessed of poetic talents of a very high order . . . he is no "mere jangling rhymester", but one endowed with all those rare and tender sympathies of "mind" that constitute a *true poet*'. Such adulation, however, did not lose sight of the important cultural role which Harpur must actually perform: 'Australia is yet destined to occupy no mean position in the Temple of the Muses'. Like Deniehy, the reviewer did not consider **'The Bushrangers'**, the play, worthy of much critical attention. Echoing in some ways the advice given to young Harpur by Smith Hall of the *Sydney Monitor* in May 1834,[11] he felt that the subject of the play was scarcely appropriate. **'The Creek of the Four Graves'** is again mentioned but it is **'The Bush Fire'** and **'Morning'** which fill the *Freeman's Journal* critic with agonising romantic raptures. Of **'The Bush Fire'** he wrote: 'This is truly poetry of the very highest order, redolent of the most exquisite harmony and breathing a tenderness of sentiment perfectly enchanting'. Having expressed the 'nation's' indebtedness to Harpur for 'the rich intellectual banquet', the reviewer concluded with a strong plea that 'Australia should stretch forth no niggard hand to welcome her only "Son of Song"'. Two points raised here, however, need some emphasis. Harpur is considered Australia's *only* poet and his real strength is in the field of 'Song': Harpur the sonneteer rather than Harpur the descriptive poet and the satirist. Deniehy—and Henry Parkes before him—had tried to show Harpur's more traditional strengths and without stating it categorically, they were more inclined to see him in terms of something akin to the epic poet: hence the analogies to Milton and a subsequent one, by Deniehy, even to Homer. Unfortunately, such criticism was never allowed to develop along purely aesthetic lines; the need, almost compulsive, for eulogy and the development of poetry strictly Australian was such that when tempers did flare up, as we shall see later, judgments on Harpur very quickly became enmeshed in larger issues about art, culture and literature in the colony.

The reviewer of the *Maitland Mercury*[12] placed Harpur among 'English poets' but, like the reviewers of the *Empire* and the *Freeman's Journal,* he also felt that Harpur had written a 'poor play, poor in reading, and we should judge, poor on the stage'. The poems, however, could stand scrutiny from the standpoint of perhaps the 'finest poets'. Raising canons of criticism similar to Deniehy's, the *Maitland Mercury* praised the very considerable descriptive powers of the poet and felt that **'The Creek of the Four Graves'** 'would alone entitle the author to be held a true poet'. Among others entitled to some praise were: **'The Bush Fire'**, **'Morning'**, **'A Poet's Home'**,

'The Manifold Hills', **'The Leaf Glancing Boughs'**, **'The Voice of the Native Oak'**, **'Emblem'** and **'The Dream by the Fountain'**. The reviewer, moreover, did not lose track of what Deniehy had raised some three weeks before. Harpur's great strength as a poet was his 'fine appreciation of the harmonies existing between the mind of man and the sights and sounds of nature'. A new aspect of the *Mercury* review was that the 'amatory verse' and 'the misanthropic bits of poetry' were also considered. Of the former the reviewer felt that they 'want heart' and the 'females depicted are creatures of the poet's imagination rather than true women'.[13] The misanthropic element arose because 'Mr. Harpur gave way to a temporary à la Byron feeling once so common with English poetasters . . .'. It is important to note that this Byronic tendency is noticed by a contemporary reviewer, and evaluated for what it is worth, a mild lapse and no more. It would be unwise to make much more of the Byronic in Harpur's verse or, for that matter, the verse and prose of Harpur's contemporaries.[14] The review ends with a statement in which is implicit a faint dream of the great Australian work of art: 'The man who could write **"The Creek of the Four Graves"** could surely write a larger work of the same high merit.' The 'epic dream' was to remain unfulfilled, for Harpur wrote little after 1853 to equal or excel the poems published in the 1853 volume.

Praise was also forthcoming from slightly different quarters. A 'Currency Lass' (Adelaide Ironside) sang Harpur's praise in a poem published in the *Advocate* which extolled Harpur in terms of the usual virtues of Patriotism, Liberty and Truth. Henry Halloran, whom some considered superior to Harpur much to Harpur's chagrin, wrote a moving, albeit slightly pompous sonnet:

> A new Achilles by the old walls stands
>   Of this grey Troy, the World—and calls aloud—
>   Burning for battle with the False and the Proud,
> He lifts his fierce immitigable hands,
> Or as another Orpheus, he commands
>   The stoutest hearts to tears—all inly-bowed—
>   While from his own throngs forth a various crowd
> Of Hopes and Fears with their illusive bands.
> Sweet thoughts are gathering in my own moved
>   mind—
>   Remembered tones are in my ravished ear,
>   Angelic forms, unutterably dear,
> Come round me, like rich odours in the wind,
> And I am gazing on thy pages, blind,
>   With a loud-beating heart—and many a hurrying
>   tear.[15]

Except for James Martin's strong objections[16] to Harpur's pretensions to colonial poetry, there was little, if any, real reaction against Harpur from men of letters in the colony. There were a few minor instances of disagreement but these really involved semantic niceties. Ewing (1846), it is true, had some reservations and the *Spectator* had easily concurred with Ewing's judgment. Harpur himself was, however, more than certain of his position and had quickly pointed out that Ewing's criticism was in fact a conspiracy by the establishment against local talent, a theme which he

was to hammer with greater vehemence later in life. In spite of these minor fluctuations in reputation, accidental asides rather than closely argued points of view, Harpur remained the self-proclaimed bard of Australia and most men of letters agreed, or silently assented though with a slight quirk.

In terms of literary history, if we wish to look for a watershed in Harpur's reputation that watershed was Daniel Deniehy's lecture on Charles Harpur delivered in the hall of the Mechanics' Institute in late November, 1857.[17] It is ironic that, as in the case of the Ewing-Parkes-*Spectator* controversy of the mid-forties, once again it was a reference to Harpur's poetic 'antecedents' which resulted in violent disagreements. The *Sydney Morning Herald* of 27 November 1857 referred to the lecture with the rubric *Harpur-Homer-Milton* and opened with the remark: 'Such is the order of excellence in which, according to Mr. Deniehy, the names of the greatest poets the world has yet produced should stand.' In a letter to the editor the following day Deniehy pointed out that he did not have such a literal meaning in mind when he delivered the lecture. However, there is little doubt that he had actually said this in an attempt to restore Harpur's reputation which had been on the wane despite glowing newspaper reports some four years ago. But the exaggeration obviously misfired; Harpur never regained the quiet literary deference he enjoyed in the mid-fifties.

Tempers didn't quite flare up when the *Morning Herald* bemoaned the passing of rigid literary standards: 'We can imagine no worse indication of the progress and mental status of a community than that its standards of excellence should be the writers of trashy poetry.' The 'Correspondent' who wrote the report declared that there was 'irreverence, if not impiety' in the idea that writers of 'namby-pamby, wishy-washy, milk-and-water verses' should be made equal to Homer and Milton. With mock condescension, the report went on to suggest that Harpur was not as bad as most of the other colonial poets, indeed he was the 'best of them'. In an equally mocking tone and with quite deliberate undercutting, the 'Correspondent' referred to Deniehy's praise of **'The Creek of the Four Graves'** in the following terms:

> Mr. Harpur it seems has written some verse entitled **'The Creek of the Four Graves'** . . . [Mr. Deniehy thought] . . . there was nothing superior to it in the whole range of poetry. There was in Pope's Homer some descriptions of a similar order, but this poem was not surpassed even by the productions of the great bard of Greece.

In the absence of Deniehy's own notes it is reasonable to conjecture that in his praise of colonial poetry—echoing the contents of his 1853 review in part—Deniehy had perhaps over-stepped the mark. Nevertheless the *Freeman's Journal* which reported the lecture the following day was not quite so scathingly bitter. From this report it becomes clear that Deniehy had also referred to the influence of Wordsworth on Harpur but felt that Harpur 'chiefly formed his [own] style'. During the lecture, it seems, Deniehy was actually reciting verses from Harpur, especially **'The Creek of the Four Graves'** and **'To an Echo on the Banks of the Hunter'** and within the context it is not odd that Deniehy made the remark that **'The Creek . . .'** was among the best in the whole range of verse. Deniehy had also referred to the American experience and had felt that the Australian search for a national literature may well follow a similar path. According to the *Freeman's Journal,* the only comparison to the 'greats' was apparently made in the remark: '[Harpur had] . . . earned laurels which would bear comparison with those which adorned the brows of the greatest of these poets who had sung the gentle passion from Petrarch downwards.'

In a letter to the editor of the *Sydney Morning Herald*[18] Deniehy strongly refuted that paper's report of the day before. Charging that the contents of the article were 'grossly untrue', he added that 'no opinion was expressed in the lecture that Homer and Milton *have* equals'. Nor had he compared Harpur to Homer and Milton. He conceded that Harpur had chosen Milton and Wordsworth as his models but added that he never mentioned Homer's poetry and did not say that Harpur's translations of Homer were superior to Pope's.[19] Yet Deniehy is unable to completely answer the reports of both the *Morning Herald* and the *Freeman's Journal* which, we have seen, wrote quite similar reviews. Deniehy's protestations make it even more clear that his final defence (i.e. that the acoustics of the hall and his own voice are partly responsible for the misrepresentation of his argument) is simply meant to camouflage the issue while keeping his own estimate of Harpur intact. One doubts if Deniehy actually believed in that estimate. My own contention, that he felt an evangelical enthusiasm was needed to resurrect Harpur's fledgling reputation, is perhaps closer the mark. Naturally, the *Sydney Morning Herald* in its "Notes of the Week"[20] made no retraction and simply reiterated a view which has always been responsible for much of the misunderstanding which has developed around Harpur:

> It is clear, however, that he [Deniehy] lauded the Australian poet as deserving a very conspicuous niche in the temple of fame. Without saying or insinuating one word depreciatory of Mr. Harpur's talent, we may be permitted to express a doubt as to the prudence of claiming such preeminence for "persons and things Australian" as will assuredly be laughed at, and that most heartily, in Europe.

Harpur did not get directly involved in this controversy, quite possibly because it was all over within a week. No mention is made of the Deniehy lecture again in either the *Morning Herald* or the *Freeman's Journal.* Harpur's personal commitment to his family and the rather austere life he was leading in Jerry Plains could also account for this uncharacteristic aloofness on the part of the poet to events in Sydney. But more simply, he may not have heard of Deniehy's lecture and its aftermath till well after the hatchets had been buried. When we hear from Harpur again it is not, however, in an entirely new context. In an article

called 'The **"Nevers" of Poetry'** published in Henry Parkes' *Empire,*[21] he is once again the Currency Lad asking for a fair go from the colonials. This time it is Mr Fowler of the *Month* who must bear the brunt of his charges. The poem, 'The **"Nevers" of Poetry'** is Harpur's contribution to 'the canonical foundation' of Australian literature on behalf of 'all who have hitherto vainly endeavoured to lay down a few of the foundation stones of an Australian literature'.[22] It is Fowler's attitude to local talent which must be repudiated: '. . . Mr. Fowler has come hither, all the way from Fatherland, for the express purpose of founding for us *natives a national literature,* on a critical basis . . . .' Accusing Fowler of applying double standards, Harpur claimed that anything by himself or by Halloran, for example, is always considered 'defective' or 'imitative' whereas there is no limit of praise given to new English verse.[23] It seems more likely, however, that a more personal reason explains this outburst. The *Month* had refused to publish poems by Harpur in spite of the fact that earlier on in a letter to the *Month* Harpur had spoken very highly of Fowler's endeavours.

The same day, Mr. Fowler replied to Harpur's article in the 'Postscript' to the *Month.*[24] Interpreting Harpur's 'The **"Nevers" of Poetry'** as a fight by proxy employed by the editor of the *Empire* (Henry Parkes), Fowler accused the paper of harbouring 'jackals' and sycophants who could be used to pass complimentary judgments on its own editor. Yet, the *Month* scornfully retorted: '. . . the highest honor to which we, in our literary capacity, aspire is to be execrated in the same production in which Mr. Parkes, in *his* literary capacity, is exalted'. While the rest of the article is really a contribution to a perennial journalistic vendetta, some significant comments are made about Harpur's verse which merit attention. Maintaining that a 'critical basis' is essential for any national literature, Fowler showed that Harpur's own poem, 'The **"Nevers" of Poetry'** fell into the very errors it aimed at condemning; the poem breaks down on its own postulates by falling for 'Fowler's Shelley-mocking strain'.[25] But Fowler also demonstrates some of Harpur's strengths and weaknesses:

> We have read lines of great beauty from his pen; but grace and precision—and, what is more, musical concord—he has, of a certainty, never displayed. True poetic feeling, true poetic fervour, he possesses in an eminent degree, but he is as destitute of poetic culture just to the same extent, we should say, as he is conceited over his imaginary possession of it.

This is the first time that a reference to 'poetic culture' is made with reference to Harpur. Interpretations may vary as to its exact meaning but its importance no doubt lies in the larger cultural issues which are implicit in the statement. True, the concept of culture referred to is not Arnoldian; nevertheless the fact remains that a poet must be defined within a larger tradition of poetic continuity. Harpur had always made claims to 'culture' in his writings though that 'culture' had been consciously cultivated by the poet. His translations from Homer were perhaps another expression of it, and his natural intellectual bent simply reinforced this interest. What exactly that 'culture' meant to colonial poetry we shall never know. Was it simply an awareness of the past as Deniehy and Parkes had shown, was it a question of some form of an aristocratic expression of values or, finally, was it something which the colony couldn't possibly possess simply by virtue of its historical background? Even if answers were forthcoming, in literature at any rate, the answers themselves become enmeshed into larger issues concerning aesthetics, art and morality. The legacy of the controversy itself, however, remained, and continues to remain, a distinct feature of Australian literary history.

Notes

1. See Henry Parkes' review in the *Register* of 22 November 1845. See also *Spectator,* 1 July 1846 for a summary of Ewing's lectures and the *Spectator* of 4 July 1846 for Parkes' reply.

2. *The Bushrangers: A Play in Five Acts and Other Poems* (Sydney: W.R. Piddington, 1853).

3. See A. M. Williams, 'N. D. Stenhouse: A Study of a Literary Patron in a Colonial Milieu', M. A. thesis, Sydney University, 1963, pp.75-78 for details of relationship between Stenhouse and Harpur.

4. *Sydney Monitor,* 10 May 1834. A number of suggestions were addressed to Harpur who was variously called 'the ingenious youth', 'a native of Windsor' and 'a currency lad'.

5. See Frances Devlin Glass, 'Daniel Henry Deniehy (1828-65): A Study of an Australian Man of Letters', PhD Thesis, A.N.U., 1974. My thanks to Dr Glass for answering a number of queries.

6. Dr William Channing, the American Unitarian and teacher of Ralph Waldo Emerson, whose article, 'The Importance and Means of a National Literature', was reprinted in *The Colonist* of Saturday 14 April 1838. His strong plea against provincialism was taken up by a number of local critics.

7. Brian Kiernan, *Criticism* (Melbourne: O.U.P. [Oxford University Press], 1974), p.10.

8. Especially, Judith Wright, *Preoccupations in Australian Poetry* (Melbourne: O.U.P., 1965), pp.1-18. 'If Nature is accepted as Harpur accepted it, as part of man and of his consciousness, the strange and the unusual lose their repugnance . . . .' (p.18).

9. See the *Colonial Literary Journal,* 8 February 1845 and the *People's Advocate,* 20 January 1849.

10. *Freeman's Journal,* 18 May 1853. It is of some importance to literary history to note that in spite of this review, no further mention of Harpur is made in the *Freeman's Journal* that year. There is also a singular absence of 'popular judgment' (letters, etc.) on Harpur.

11. A change of the hero's name (to Walmesley or Webber) and a reworking of the mainly Shakespearian plagiarisms were some of his suggestions. See also note 4.

12. *Maitland Mercury,* 14 May 1853.

13. The observation was, of course, not true so far as the sonnets' inspiration is concerned. The 'woman' in the sonnets was Mary Doyle whom Harpur married in 1850 after a lengthy courtship.

14. See Barry Argyle's *An Introduction to the Australian Novel 1830-1930* (Oxford: Clarendon Press, 1972). Argyle looks at a number of characters in Australian fiction in terms of the Byronic hero e.g. pp.107ff: Henry Kingsley's George Hawker is considered in Byronic terms.

15. I owe this reference to J. Normington-Rawling, *Charles Harpur, An Australian* (Sydney: Angus & Robertson, 1962), p.184. Normington-Rawling does not give his source and so far I have not been able to locate it.

16. James Martin 'The Pseudo-Poets' (1838) in *The Australian Sketchbook.*

17. *Freeman's Journal* had a report on the lecture a day after the *Morning Herald* comment and mentioned that the lecture had been delivered on Monday evening. It would be reasonable to conjecture from this (without referring to old almanacs) that Deniehy delivered his lecture on 25 November 1857.

18. *Sydney Morning Herald,* 28 November 1857.

19. During the 50s Harpur translated a number of pieces from Homer, in particular the famous night scene in the VIIIth book of the *Iliad* and the battle piece from the XVIIIth book of the *Iliad.* Deniehy, according to the newspaper reports, spoke very highly of these translations. In a letter to Stenhouse, Richard Rowe, author of *Peter Possum's Portfolio,* also commented favourably on these translations. For details of publication and reference to Tennyson's translations of the same passages see G. W. Salier, 'Charles Harpur's Translations from the *Iliad*', *Southerly,* 7 (1946), 218-222.

20. *Sydney Morning Herald,* 30 November 1857.

21. *Empire,* 9 March 1858.

22. Apart from himself, Harpur also mentioned the names of the following local poets: Wentworth, Dr. Lang, Martin, Norton, Parkes, Halloran, Deniehy and Dalley.

23. Harpur also referred to Fowler's own poetry and dismissed it as verse 'so indeterminate a (in) quality, as to depend wholly for its value . . . upon the mood in which we regard it'.

24. *Month,* 1 (9 March 1858), 159-162.

25. Fowler does pick up a fundamental contradiction in Harpur's alleged poetics and his practice. Never 'turn a rich *sunset* into a red *rain*' cautions Harpur; yet he uses this very image in ll.6-8 of 'The "Nevers" of Poetry':

True feeling rains them in unfeigned distress
Or save when doubts that over Love may lour,
Like summer clouds, break in a sunny shower.

Leonie Kramer (essay date 1983)

SOURCE: Kramer, Leonie. "Imitation and Originality in Australian Colonial Poetry: The Case of Charles Harpur." *Yearbook of English Studies* 13 (1983): 116-32.

[*In the following essay, Kramer highlights word choice and construction in Harpur's poetry to address early influences on his work. Kramer also analyzes the poet's later attempts to merge the form of his Continental "mentors" with an original Australian style.*]

'Australian poetry', writes Vivian Smith, 'starts with the indelible stamp of the cultivated amateur'.[1] It also starts with a mixed inheritance, with established modes of poetic address (particularly odes and elegies) and their accompanying eighteenth-century linguistic fashions; and with an expectation of imaginative freedoms and renovated forms and language promised by the experiments of Romanticism and supported by the hope of adventure in a new land.

Although the very earliest attempts at verse (such as Michael Massey Robinson's celebratory and occasional odes) were, like the clothes of the first arrivals, rather indicative of their origins than appropriate to their new life, they were not without some fortuitous relevance to the colonial situation. The neo-Classical rhetoric of the rise and fall of civilizations and the taming of the wilderness might not have found an echo in every bosom, but it was adaptable to the frequently expressed hopes for the colony. When he wanted to describe the failure of an attempt to educate the aborigines in farming and other skills, and the abandonment of the village built for the purpose, Charles Tompson turned naturally to Goldsmith's *The Deserted Village* for a model. More ambitious, William Charles Wentworth wrote a long ode in couplets (*Australasia*, 1823), celebrating the new British colony and describing some of the highlights of its short history. Barron Field, who published the first little book of verse (1819), found it extremely difficult to accommodate strange animals and plants within the poetic conventions available to him and was derided for his efforts. Yet these early attempts, however clumsy, to versify observations upon the new land initiated change in the forms of expression. But it was not until Charles Harpur began to write in the 1830s that real progress was made towards capturing the realities of Australian experience in poetry. It is ironical that a man who tried so hard to establish himself as a poet, and poetry as an indigenous growth, should have been unpopular in his life and still largely neglected 120 years after his death.

Among the many subjects of literary debate in the nineteenth century, imitation was one of the most sensitive. Originality (interpreted in a narrow though ill-defined sense) seemed to many critics to be a necessary condition of a distinctive literature. An anonymous reviewer of Charles Tompson's *Wild Notes from the Lyre of a Native Minstrel* (1826), writing in the *Sydney Gazette,* suggests to Tompson 'the propriety of letting his similes and metaphors be purely Australian. He will soon find his account in doing so, as they will infallibly possess all the freshness of originality. In this respect he has a decided advantage over all the European poets, because here nature has an entirely different aspect'.[2] The reviewer's complaint that Tompson 'imitates too closely the style of others' has some force when one compares his 'Black Town' with Goldsmith's *The Deserted Village.* But it is not easy to determine the substance of some later critics' objections to Kendall's debt to Tennyson and Swinburne, or to evaluate the accusations of plagiarism against Adam Lindsay Gordon. When one considers the skill with which Wyatt and Surrey anglicized the Petrarchan sonnet, or the adaptation of Juvenalian and Horatian satire to English subjects, it is not at all clear why colonial poets should have attracted adverse criticism for trying to accommodate their sentiments and their experiences of Australian life within the English lyrical, satirical, and discursive modes. There was the obvious difficulty of finding new words for new objects; a poet of nature was more often dealing with the novel than with the familiar, and sometimes had to attempt an approximate description by means of an English analogy or conventional epithet. Uncertainty about the audience could tempt the writer into relying on recognized ways of describing the unfamiliar; so the mountain barrier west of Sydney becomes the Appenines, with the odd result of taming the wilderness by means of a misnomer.

There are some explanations of the sensitivity to imitation which must remain speculative. One is that in their desire to promote a distinctive literature, representative of the realities of colonial experience, commentators were simply not interested (and possibly not able) to argue the niceties of the relationship between imitation and originality. Another, even more speculative, is a growing desire to reject the formalities of traditional modes, and to hope that fresh ones, better suited to the interests of the colonists, would develop from popular forms such as the ballad, the narrative, the adventure story, the traveller's tale, the yarn, and simple lyric. In other words, one might be observing rebellion against the supremacy of the English tradition, a kind of literary republicanism, with a bias towards popular rather than learned expression.

In any enquiry into the relationship between imitation and originality in nineteenth-century Australian poetry, Charles Harpur is a test case. Judith Wright credits Harpur with making a virtue of necessity 'by combining the English poetic tradition with the best that its lonely colony had to offer, to speak in the voice of a new country without rejecting what English tradition could give'. But even her sympathetic and perceptive account of his poetry does not resolve the problem of his poetic voice. For example, she writes that 'he was prudent and honest enough to recognize that an Englishman in process of becoming an Australian must speak with an English voice before finding his true accent'. Yet it is difficult to see how one can describe Harpur as 'an Englishman in process of becoming an Australian', since he was born of convict parents in 1813 at Windsor, New South Wales. Even more surprising is the statement that 'it would, of course, have been impossible for him at this time to have had the kind of appreciation of the Australian landscape that is possible nowadays'.[3] For the Hawkesbury River and the ruggedly beautiful Blue Mountains along the foothills of which the Hawkesbury flows were his terrain. He knew no other environment. It was to him what the Lake District was to Wordsworth, and it is not surprising that he should have turned to Wordsworth for guidance in defining his perceptions of the natural world.

There is still no complete edition of Harpur's work, and there are considerable problems in dating even some of his major poems. Harpur worked over his poems many times and published in newspapers and journals as he revised. He published only two collections in his lifetime: *Thoughts: A Series of Sonnets* (1845) and *The Bushrangers and other Poems* (1853). An earlier collection, *Wild Bee of Australia: A Series of Poems with Prose Notes* (c. 1851), was prepared for publication but did not appear. In 1863 he prepared a manuscript for local publication; and in 1867-68 he made a selection of his poems for Thomas Mort to take to London. When Mort did not go Harpur continued his revisions, and this manuscript collection is the final version of his work. Until these manuscripts were used by Adrian Mitchell as the copy-text for a selection of Harpur's work published in 1973,[4] the only available text was a corrupt one edited by Henry Martin in 1883.[5] Martin ignored Harpur's own selection in the 1867-68 manuscripts, and made substantial 'corrections', thus changing significantly the direction and style of Harpur's work.[6]

Harpur had a strong sense of vocation. In designating himself 'Charles Harpur, An Australian'[7] he might seem to be declaring a rather crude nationalism; but his efforts were in fact directed not towards a mere assertion of nationalistic sentiment, or a rough application of local colour, but towards a considered analysis of political and social life (in his satires), and of the qualities of the landscape and the moral reflections it gave rise to (in some of the lyrics and the longer poems). It is in the longer poems that one most clearly sees evidence of Harpur's attempts to express, partly through the mediating influence of English poetry and partly through forging his own style, his developing perception of the land, past and present. These poems bear witness to the interplay of imitation and originality in a manner which disallows any simple account of the one or the other.

Although Harpur worked over his poems so carefully in the 1860s, writing them out in his meticulous hand many times, it is now clear that the major revisions, and in particular the additions to the longer poems, were made in the 1850s. In about 1841, after a period in Sydney, Harpur had returned to the Hunter Valley (where he had worked

as a labourer much earlier in his life); and for some ten years or more he was only occasionally employed. This situation continued (except for an attempt at sheep farming after his marriage in 1850) until 1859, when he was offered a position as an assistant gold commissioner. The years of insecurity and restlessness from 1840 into the 1850s were also those in which he read extensively, and rethought much of his poetry.

'A Storm in the Mountains' (published in 1856)[8] is one of the few of his longer works which appears to have been written for the first time in this decade and for which, to date, no earlier version has been found. The poem is in two parts, the first describing gathering storm clouds, the instinctive reactions of the birds and animals to the approaching storm, the first flash of lightning and the first thunder clap; the second describing the height of the storm, the 'strife of Nature', its dying away, and its aftermath, 'the freshened scene', silent and at peace. The poem is set in Harpur's territory, the escarpments and 'vast-backed ridges' of the Blue Mountains, seen on a hot summer day. Its inhabitants are native birds and insects (Harpur includes a lengthy note on the Australian grasshopper) and dingoes, and there is a reference to the 'half-wild herd's dim tracks' as a faint reminder that there is settlement even in this 'rude peculiar world'. Most interesting of all, the whole event is seen through the eyes of a boy 'far venturing from his home', 'A lonely Truant, numbering years eleven'.

A link between **'A Storm in the Mountains'** and Wordsworth's *The Prelude* seems more than probable. Into the mind of Wordsworth's Winander boy, who died at the age of eleven, the 'visible scene' with 'all its solemn imagery' enters 'unawares'.[9] Harpur's boyhood self wanders among the crags and comes upon a pool scooped out, like the 'rocky basin' in Wordsworth's 'An Evening Walk', 'by the shocks of rain-floods plunging from the upper rocks', and here he drinks and muses.[10] He is sufficiently observant to detect a change in the scene transmitted by the instinctive reactions of living things. He notices, for example, that the 'locusts' cease flying and climb to the top of the tallest grasses, as they in fact do, he explains in a footnote, to escape sudden floods. Harpur's boy is just as finely attuned to his natural world as is the Winander boy, or the young Wordsworth of *The Prelude,* but he is not in communion with it. The storm is merely a part of nature; it does not speak directly to him nor he to it. The perceptions are those of a solitary observer, not unlike the young Wordsworth, with 'a listless, yet enquiring eye'; but the sentiments have more in common with those of Thomson's *The Seasons* or Cowper's 'A Thunder Storm' than with the intensity of Wordsworth's passionate hauntings.

Within **'A Storm in the Mountains'** the perspective shifts from the child's view to the adult's, as he passes from musing to curiosity, to wonder, and finally to the sense of standing exposed before the possibility of finding 'How through all being works the light of Mind'. The inwardness of the early part of the poem (where Wordsworth's influence seems strongest) gives way to a cheerful description of the calm evening scene, then to a rather bland statement about the purging of 'pestilence' and the return of peace. So does Harpur, in his own phrase, 'moralise the agony', though not without recovering at the last moment a glimpse of the earlier awareness when he notes 'even 'mid the sylvan carnage spread . . . some pleasantness unmarked till now' (Mitchell, pp. 55-62).

In **'A Storm in the Mountains'** Harpur has profited by Wordsworth's example in his attempt to describe both the changing moods of nature and his changing perceptions of landscape. He is also indebted, probably to Cowper, for a reasonably flexible and expressive rhymed couplet. His language draws on eighteenth-century poetic diction in the use of words and phrases such as 'prospect', 'sable bosom', and 'the elements of social life', or in lines like

> O'er all the freshened scene no sound is heard,
> Save the short twitter of some busied bird.
>
> (l. 188)

But there are other literary ingredients too, such as a modest Miltonic simile which begins

> as Travellers see
> In the wide wilderness of Araby
> Some pilgrim horde at even, band by band
> Halting amid the grey interminable sand.[11]
>
> (l. 43)

There are echoes of the Romantic poets in 'some else-viewless veil' and 'Why congregate the swallows in the air', and in the admiration of wildness and turbulent nature. Yet Harpur speaks in his own voice, even though with traces of the accent of the literary past. There is awkwardness and lack of polish in his phrasing, as in

> Here huge-piled ledges, ribbing outward, stare
> Down into haggard chasms; onward there,
> The vast backed ridges are all rent in jags,
> Or hunched with cones, or pinnacled with crags.
>
> (l. 5)

The roughness comes not from any attempt to declaim, or to apply local colour to the canvas, but from a determination to fix his perceptions accurately. His effort has some curious results, as when his local terms bump into imported ones. In the line 'Or list the tinkling of the dingle-bird', 'tinkling' is the right word, and 'dingle-bird' is a local name for the 'bell-bird'; but 'list' is not assimilated into the native context. Having acknowledged this, however, one must also acknowledge that **'A Storm in the Mountains'** is a well-constructed poem, and that Harpur shows a real ability to dispose its elements. It is certainly not a mechanical performance or a bland imitation, but an energetic exposition, through contrasting sets of images, of an outbreak of natural violence within what Adrian Mitchell calls 'a transcendent stability, a serene world of larger vision' (p. xxvii). **'A Storm in the Mountains'** is evi-

dence of Harpur's understanding of the ways in which the English poets could help him, of his determination to shape his perceptions in his own way, and of his struggle for a poetic style.

The textual history of his long poem **'The Creek of the Four Graves'** is in essence an account of his poetic development, and through it can be plotted his changing sense of the possibilities of what began as an unadorned narrative poem and ended as a quite ambitious blending of narrative action, local history, landscape art, and moral reflection. Behind **'The Creek of the Four Graves'** might well be a real incident, as there is in his very early poem (possibly a rehearsal for this one?) **'The Glen of the Whiteman's Grave'** (it is interesting that the word 'Whiteman' is used in the earliest text of **'The Creek of the Four Graves'**). One might also posit a literary source for the poem in Wordsworth's *The Brothers*:

> In our churchyard
> Is neither epitaph nor monument
> Tombstone nor name—only the turf we tread
> And a few national graves.
>
> (l. 12)

Thus speaks the 'homely Priest of Ennerdale' in a poem in which Leonard Ewbank is welcomed back from a journey which has taken him from one of the highest peaks in the Cumberland mountains as 'far as Egremont'.

In all, four different versions of **'The Creek of the Four Graves'** have been located (five if one counts the corrupt Martin text), and two fragments. The first version of 202 lines was published in *The Weekly Register* over three issues in August 1845. It is a compact tale of four men who, under the leadership of Egremont (the source of the story), go off into 'the wilderness' beyond the limits of settlement in search of new pastures. They camp in the bush on a radiant moonlit night, are attacked by aborigines, and savagely slaughtered, only Egremont escaping by hiding in a hollow in the river bank. Description of the setting is concise and exact, and slightly elaborated only in order to draw a contrast between the serenity and beauty of the natural world and the brutality of man. There is no explicit censuring of aborigines, but there is a brief moral about unity and love. One of the four murdered men is singled out for special attention. He resists the violence of the attack because having 'lived with misery nearly all his days' he still hopes for 'the taste of good' and cannot bear to die, desolate, having lived so. Egremont, as he keeps watch, is filled with thoughts of home, because of some

> subtile interfusion that connects
> The cherished ever with the beautiful
> And lasting Things of Nature.
>
> (l. 66)

Egremont's 'musing' is more a matter of sentiment than perception, in keeping with the sobriety of the tale and the measured tone of its narration, as they are introduced by the first line, 'I *tell* a settler's tale of the old times'.

In the telling Harpur allows himself only as much detail as is strictly necessary to the simple embroidery of the tale. The landscape references are brief. As the journey begins the sun sets beyond a mountain range and the travellers pass a 'nameless creek'; and when darkness falls there is an effective but brief description of the dark ranges beyond the watch-fire's circle. The blank verse is sturdy, and the language (for the most part) echoes the regular certainties of the eighteenth-century discursive mode. The meal is 'dispatched | By the keen edge of healthful appetite'. Horses are called 'cattle', and the unexplored mountains are 'new eminences'. But though the dominant manner of the poem is plain, and its rhythms those of the eighteenth century, it catches up other echoes. From Milton Harpur surely takes 'the empyreal things of God', from Wordsworth the 'subtile interfusion', and probably from Shakespeare 'multitudinous', which he uses elsewhere. It is Harpur, though, who observes that the creek is 'fringed with oaks and the wild willow', as he feels for words for new trees; and who has the wallaroo looking forth from the mountains; and who, much more inventively, refers to a cloud that 'Crept, as with scrawling legs, across the sky'.

The second version of the poem was published in 1853 in **The Bushrangers** (the first 130 lines of this version, in Harpur's hand, are in the manuscript of the unpublished **Wild Bee of Australia,** 1851; Mitchell Library MS C376). It is 257 lines long. In the first line Harpur announces what seems to mark a change of direction away from the plain narrative, 'I *verse* a Settler's Tale of the old times', and as though to insist on this point he changes the 1845 version's 'encreasing flocks and herds' to 'augmenting'. Horses are still 'cattle', but instead of being too precious for the 'trackless depths' of the wilderness (1845) they are now too precious for the 'mountain routes' and 'brush lands perilously pathless' (of 1853).

The additions in this first paragraph of the poem establish a pattern that persists throughout. The additional lines are chiefly descriptive, and indicate an attempt to be much more detailed and specific as well as more decorative. The mountains that in 1845 were 'ne'er visited' are now 'barrier mountains' (there is a particular reference here to the time of the events of the poem, which must be before 1813, the date of Harpur's birth, when the Blue Mountains were first crossed). Harpur, then, has now added an exact temporal perspective of forty years to the poem's action. He has also added a perspective which, perhaps, is possible only to the man born in the colony at the time when the mountains were conquered. This detail, like his references to the mountains as the Appenines and the aborigines as Indians, suggests that he is consciously addressing foreign readers, not just to inform them but to give them a link between the unknown and the known.

Through the additional passages of description he begins to develop an analysis of the awareness of the observer (his narrator Egremont) which was missing from the 1845 text. It is not just that the sunset over the Blue Mountains is described at length, but that it is described from within the intensely appreciative understanding of the narrator. So he does not simply add to the *poetic* effects by, for example, comparing the mountains to 'rampires' (which in one manuscript is changed, not in Harpur's hand, to 'ramparts'). The wilderness is now seen to be beautiful as well as wild; and Harpur describes the breeze that stirs the forest leaves as 'prompted from within', not in the Wordsworthian sense of reciprocity between the lover of nature and the spirit of nature but as a property of a universal order. A further descriptive detail reinforces this idea. The account of the travellers' supper in the 1845 text ends somewhat abruptly with their seeing 'the Wallaroo look forth'; in the fragment of *c.*1851 this prominent local feature retreats into a larger background. In the luminous sky as the sunset fades the woods on the ridges look even more distinct:

> Even like a mighty picture of themselves
> Hung in some vaster world.

> (l. 54)

It is not elegantly phrased; but it is an original image of distance, perspective, and space, appropriate both to the actual scene, to the sentiment of the occasion, and especially to the percipience of the narrator.

The 'one long cloud' of the 1845 text ('with scrawling legs') is now, in addition, 'diffused and shapen like a mighty spider'. The metaphor is elaborated, at some cost to the language, but not for merely decorative effects. It introduces a sense of strangeness, even menace, which is one of the devices Harpur uses in this version to heighten the dramatic effects. Some Miltonic echoes have been noted in the 1845 text; in this version he draws more extensively on Milton as he begins to develop the moral of the tale, and an early sign of this is an extended description of the moon rising. In the 1845 text Harpur in a slightly laboured manner describes the way in which the moon outlines the mountain ridges so that the 'shrubs' fringing its summit look as though they are growing out of the moon itself. It is a sharp observation which Harpur struggles valiantly to put into words. In the *c.*1851 fragment the word 'shrubs' (which is quite inappropriate to the forest scene) becomes 'trees', but in order to preserve the observation Harpur expands it to read

>   whilst the trees
> That fringed its outline, their huge statures dwarfed
> By distance into brambles . . .

> (l.99)

The other significant change is of a quite different order. Where in 1845 the moon 'was seen | Ascending slow', in the 1853 text it is 'seen | Conglobing', a word which he takes from Milton. One would like to think it is not an accident that Harpur also adds to this text the notion that the attacking aborigines 'in their enmity . . . come | In vengeance', thus humanizing and making more specific the notion of 'diabolic rage' present in the 1845 text. He omits, on the other hand, the brief moral about 'Unity and Love' of the 1845 text.

The next complete text of the poem, with the title **'The Creek of the Graves'** is at present known only in a printed cutting pasted in one of Harpur's small notebooks (Mitchell Library MS C384). It was printed either in or by the *Braidwood Dispatch* and could have been issued as a pamphlet, and I shall refer to it as the 'Braidwood' text. There is no date, but it is certainly later than the 1853 text. Harpur moved to Braidwood in October 1859 and left in December of the same year. The most likely date seems to be the early 1860s. What looks like a version of the text (a fragment 100 lines long) appears in the manuscript **'Poems and Prose Pieces 1855-58'** (Mitchell Library MS B78). The 'Braidwood' text is 346 lines long, and is in detail very close to the final manuscript version of 1867-68.

A marked feature of this text is its changed sense of audience. In both the earlier versions Harpur addresses himself to his narrative and descriptive task without making any concessions to readers unfamiliar with the landscape of the poems. The first indication that he is thinking differently (possibly with the hope of an English audience in mind) comes in the *c*.1855-58 fragment referred to above. In the 1845 text the 'oaks and the wild willow' would have misled an English reader interested in Australian vegetation. Now Harpur, while preserving the 'wild willow', goes to considerable pains to identify the 'oak' as the casuarina, or, as it is popularly called, the she-oak. In doing so, he both invents an interesting and original image and offers an explanatory comment for a foreign reader about the creek

> duskily befringed
> With the tall feathery upward tapering oak
> The sylvan eyelash ever, as it were,
> Of the Australian waters.
>
> (l. 22)

He refines this image further in the 'Braidwood' text to read:

> The sylvan eyelash always of the yet
> Remote Australian waters
>
> (l. 25)

remembering that he is looking back to the early days of settlement.

Approximately one third of the additional eighty-eight lines of this 'Braidwood' text are small revisions, like the one already quoted, which elaborate descriptive detail and in particular attempt to define more clearly the reactions of Egremont to the attack and to plot his escape more closely. But there are two passages, one of eight lines and one of twenty-five, which introduce quite new material and show that Harpur has moved a long way from the simple narrative structure of the 1845 text. Again, as in the use of the word 'conglobing' in the 1853 text, the new emphasis is prepared for by a quite simple change. In the earlier versions the four weary travellers fall asleep under 'the wide gaze of Heaven' secure in the knowledge that they are be-

ing watched over by their master, Egremont. In the 'Braidwood' text Harpur capitalizes 'Master'. It would be unwise to attach much importance to this, were it not for the character of the passage which Harpur adds to the description of the rising moon:

> Thus o'er that dark height her great orb conglobed,
> Till her full light, in silvery sequence still
> Cascading forth from ridgy slope to slope,
> Like the dropped foldings of a lucent veil
> Chased mass by mass the broken darkness down
> Into the wooded valleys, where it crouched
> And shrunk and struggled, like a dragon doubt
> Glooming some lonely spirit lost to Truth
> Though shining out of heaven.
>
> (l. 121)

In *Paradise Lost,* Book VII, Milton, describing the creation of the earth, writes:

> Darkness profound
> Cover'd th' Abyss: but on the watrie calme
> His brooding wings the Spirit of God outspred,
> And vital vertue infus'd, and vital warmth
> Throughout the fluid Mass, but downward purg'd
> The black tartareous cold infernal dregs
> Adverse to life; then founded, then conglob'd
> Like things to like, the rest to several place
> Disparted, and between spun out the Air,
> And Earth self-ballanc't on her Center hung.[12]
>
> (l. 233)

Harpur has taken over the general sense of this passage, and his use of the word 'conglobed' gives access to the implied analogy between the banishing of darkness and doubt, and God's creation of light, and of earth out of chaos.

The longer passage, which is the penultimate paragraph of the poem, builds on this reference. It draws the conclusion that the world has been cursed by the deeds of Man, who has made 'This glorious residence, the Earth, a Hell'. The passage about 'Unity and Love', dropped from the 1853 text, is reintroduced in this fuller statement; and Harpur even manages references to the moon and stars looking down both on Sidonian (in the final version changed to Arcadian) dancers on the village green, a hermit at his vigils, and a 'monster battlefield', just as they looked, on the night of the poem, on the 'doomful forest'. There is no suggestion here that Harpur is unable to view his world for himself; on the contrary, he widens his gaze to take in those scenes of life removed in time and place from his own, and shows considerable confidence in doing so. He has also, of course, adjusted the structure of the poem so that it is no longer a simple action with a simple moral, but an action exemplifying by imagery and reference the fallen state of the world.

It is now clear that by the time Harpur came to revise the poem for the final manuscript version of 1867-68 (which is 410 lines long) he had only to attend to relatively minor but significant details.[13] Most of the additions are to descriptive passages, and they show that Harpur is even more conscious than in the 'Braidwood' text of a possible foreign audience (some of these changes are marked in Harpur's hand on the 'Braidwood' text). The image of the 'sylvan eyelash' is enlarged to read:

> The sylvan eyelash always of remote
> Australian waters, whether gleaming still
> In lake or pool, or bickering along
> Between the marges of some eager stream.
>
> (l. 25)

It is interesting to note what seems to be a concession on Harpur's part to an English audience in those last two lines, and especially in the phrase 'eager stream'. It seems not unreasonable to suggest that Harpur was quite capable of using English poetic diction purposefully, and not simply for want of a suitable local idiom. It should be noted in passing that not all the additions to the original 1845 text are for the best. For example, what was then a simple camp fire, becomes, from *c.* 1851 onwards 'A wilder creature than 'twas elsewhere wont'. Sometimes, too, he actually suppresses the local detail, as when he changes 'tea-trees' to 'trees' in the 'Braidwood' text. Other concessions, such as the use of the term 'Indians' and 'Appenines', are preserved in the final revision.

In the final text Harpur adds one new passage, interesting for its attempt to draw areas of reference into the poem and for what it might reveal of his reading and use of allusion. It is a paragraph in which he searches for words and 'hues' with which to paint the scene, when the sun has set behind the mountains but has left in its wake 'exceeding radiancy aloft'. The mountains are

> Like a great company of Archeons, crowned
> With burning diadems, and tented o'er
> With canopie of purple and of gold.
>
> (l. 49)

Here Harpur offers a Miltonic flourish, a classical reference, and a glance at Byron. At the time this passage was added to the poem, Harpur was revising his own translations of ten similes from Homer.[14] There is little doubt that he intends the simile to refer to the Archons, the chief magistrates of ancient Athens. But his spelling of 'Archons' in the manuscripts fluctuates, and the form 'Archeons' is not to be found in the dictionary. It may be that Harpur's interest in geological history led him to conflate the word 'Archon' with 'Archaean', thus bringing together his observation of the actual landscape and his literary experience.[15] This passage demonstrates Harpur's ability to use his sources to define an individual view of the subject. It also clearly indicates that the descriptive and narrative elements are used emblematically. There is a real point of comparison between the spectacle and colour of the mountains at sunset and the brilliance of an imagined legendary host; but he is also preparing early in the poem for the notion of heavenly splendour from which

man's inhumanity to man marks such a miserable fall. The landscape images are integrated with the ideas projected in the poem.

From this examination of the textual history of **'The Creek of the Four Graves'** one can see that Harpur depends, in the final version, much more on ideas than on action as a principle of organization. Further evidence of this shift in emphasis is his strengthening of Egremont's role as narrator. Harpur probes Egremont's feelings and reactions more deeply than in the early version, and also tries to recreate a sense of the experience he undergoes. He thus brings to the poem a double perspective, by creating awareness of the poet's perception of the past, as well as of the narrator's.

In working out his purposes Harpur, as has been seen, develops a language in which there are recognizable borrowings. Harpur advised Kendall to 'study Milton & Wordsworth for a blank verse style, and combine the master-movements of the two'.[16] From Milton he learnt how to express his sense of the beauty of the world (as exemplified by his own natural environment) and his sense of its betrayal and violation by the cruelty and violence of man. He adopts words and patterns of imagery which support his perceptions. From Wordsworth he learnt how to express his sense of the interpenetration of things in the natural world, and to report on what is revealed to the 'inward eye'.

In registering these influences, Harpur is also acknowledging the clear line of descent from Shakespeare to Milton and the Romantic poets. From the beginning of his poetic career he was in search of a vocabulary appropriate to his view of poetry as 'the vehicle of earnest purpose'.[17] A particular group of words, much favoured by him, will illustrate more precisely the nature of his debt to the past, and the way he uses the riches he mined. The group includes *intergrowth, interdazzlingly, instilled, insphere, ingathered, interfusion, interwrithing,* and *intermingled,* most of which are to be found in Shakespeare and/or Milton, and which are used, in different combinations and with very different connotations, by Harpur (two of these, *interdazzlingly* and *interwrithing* seem to be his own invention, and both are most apt to their contexts). His adaptation of such words to his own purposes is inventive, and gives his poetic speech those qualities which, he felt, made him so unsympathetic to Tennyson: 'Poetry, with him, should be nice and dainty, rather than wise and hearty; while to affect my admiration, it must be free, bold, and open, even at the risk of being rude.'[18] Certainly this group of words reflects Harpur's earnest striving for an accurate verbal representation of certain natural scenes and events.

A textual history comparable to that of **'The Creek of the Four Graves'** lies behind a much more ambitious poem, **'The World and the Soul'**, which was also put into its final form in 1867-68. The first printed version of this poem appears in *The Atlas* on 4 September 1847 under the title **'Geologia'** (48 lines). It presents a very brief geological history of the earth up to the appearance of man, and then goes on to speculate that 'novel Orders' might still spring from 'our mother Earth's prolific womb', concluding that, whatever changes might come about, man's soul is immortal. It has been suggested that Harpur was probably influenced by Lyell's *Principles of Geology* (1830), and more specifically by Robert Chambers's *Vestiges of the Natural History of Creation* (1844).[19] Two manuscript versions of the poem, accompanied by a long prose note, belong probably to the early 1850s; the second of these runs to eighty-nine lines. Harpur almost doubles the length again in the 1863 manuscript (154 lines); and adds a further sixty lines in about 1866. The final version is 211 lines long.

The additions, of two main kinds, correspond to the developments observed in **'The Creek of the Four Graves'**. First, Harpur greatly elaborates his original spare description of the history of the earth gathered from 'the crude records' of geological remains; secondly, he adds to his speculations about the future, and to his reasons for confidence in the Soul's immortality and in the 'divine necessity' which guarantees the emergence of a 'state yet more exalted'. From the very modest beginning of 1847 Harpur developed over twenty years a poem which, though clotted and laboured at times, nevertheless contains passages of real imaginative strength. Harpur's 'Old billowy Hawkesbury' seems to be recognized in the Creation

> Of rivers in their broad abundant flow
> Through boundless depths of bloomy boughs, all
>   tossed
> And billowing in the breeze.
>
> (l. 82)

And there is a kind of ingenuous imaginative realism in his description of the herd of mammoths

> As into the dim spaces of the dense
> And bordering woods it passed, and onward then
> Crashed, munching as it went.
>
> (l. 55)

Harpur has a metrical sense; and he presses towards his conclusion with vigour, making use of a range of acquired vocabulary appropriate to his subject (though not to be described as merely 'poetic') while struggling to clarify his own thoughts. The additions to the original **'Geologia'**, like those to **'The Creek of the Four Graves'**, are not mere verbal embroidery but an extension of the meaning of the poem beyond description or narration.

Harpur travels further long the road of conceptualization in his longest poem, **'Genius Lost'**, of which there appear to be six versions dating from 1837 to 1867. It is evidently inspired by Wordsworth's lines on Chatterton from 'Resolution and Independence'. He suggests some affinity between his struggles and Chatterton's, but he fails to convey that sense of immediacy which marks his best poems. The ideas are attenuated, and the verse is ponderous and prosaic. What he said of Coleridge's early poems is applicable to this one. It is 'too mouthy to be rightly musical'.[20]

At the other extreme, Harpur attempted a substantially descriptive long poem. In 1860 he published, over seven issues of the *Australian Home Companion,* a poem of nearly 1200 lines, **'The Kangaroo Hunt'**. There is reason to believe that all or most of it was written nearly twenty years earlier, since an extract from Part III (under the title **'Australian Scenery'**, described as being 'From **'The Kangaroo Hunt'**, an unpublished poem') was published in *The Weekly Register* on 1 November 1843. In the poem itself, and in the long prose notes which accompany it, Harpur displays his intimate knowledge of native trees and birds and shows considerable skill in describing them. He uses a flexible rhyming tetrameter verse form, with occasional varying line lengths, and his diction is an odd mixture of local terms and awkward poetic constructions. In his preface Harpur describes his versification as 'designedly irregular', remarks that since writing the poem he has come to know Coleridge's *Christabel,* and affirms that in writing **'The Kangaroo Hunt'** he had read nothing 'that was professedly imitative of it [that is, of *Christabel*] . . . My design, therefore, was so far original'. In one of the notes, which is really a gloss on lines which extol the character and physique of native-born Australians, he argues for a national educational system on the ground that 'our career as a race should be full of boldness and invention, and as little imitative as possible'. The poem strives for this objective, and it is ironical that Harpur's attempt at originality should not have met with the success which elsewhere attends his sensible use of models. Here, one feels the lack of a basic structure of ideas; and the metrical form is an awkward one for so long a poem.

By contrast, in another purely descriptive poem, the short lyric **'A Midsummer Noon in the Australian Forest'**, where Marvell is clearly his mentor, Harpur's fresh perception overcomes the occasional clumsiness of his language:

> Even the grasshoppers keep
> Where the coolest shadows sleep;
> Even the busy ants are found
> Resting in their pebbled mound
>
> (l. 5)

and he acknowledges his debt to Marvell in the last lines;

> O 'tis easeful here to lie
> Hidden from Noon's scorching eye,
> In this grassy cool recess
> Musing thus of Quietness.
>
> (l. 39)

In the lyrical mode, as in the satires and lampoons, where he draws on various models from the seventeenth century onwards, he manages to bring about an accommodation between the inherited mould and the new substance it receives.

Harpur's choice of subjects for poems such as **'A Storm in the Mountains'**, **'The Creek of the Four Graves'**, **'A Flight of Wild Ducks'**, **'The Bush Fire'**, and many others allowed him scope for his detailed observation; but he is judicious in his use of local detail and is rarely content merely to describe or record. In poems such as **'A Coast View'** or **'The Bush Fire'** (where Egremont again appears) Harpur's originality consists in his thoughtful choice of poetic form (**'The Bush Fire'**, like **'The Creek of the Four Graves'** develops an action, but reaches beyond it) and in the way he organizes his poetic language so that it can range from a relatively unadorned narrative style to the heightened diction which always accompanies, though not always with equal force or conviction, his approach to the subject of transcendence or to the wonders and terrors of nature.

In his decorous use of the resources of English poetry Harpur draws on his many years of close study and reflection on the work of a number of English poets, from Chaucer to the Romantics. This studious approach to his poetic task is recorded in a series of **'Rhymed Criticisms'**, which he began publishing in the 1840s. Each poet is analysed in verse paragraphs in a style 'something betwixt the heroic rhyme of Dryden and that of Cowper', followed by prose notes. These, which are later than the verse paragraphs, combine detailed comment on stylistic characteristics with general reflection on the qualities of the verse. They reveal an attentive, sensitive, and perceptive reader, and also, interestingly, changing views. His admiration for Dryden increases, his liking for Pope diminishes; he comes to regret his early severity about Byron, while defending its justness; he cannot now read Moore 'with any continuous relish', finding him lacking in 'repose'; Wordsworth, 'a great poet', is nevertheless 'too persistently didactic' and 'not infrequently . . . lean in thoughts or feeling, and verbose in expression'; and while he has admired Coleridge 'more than any of his contemporaries', he finds his poetry inferior to Wordsworth's 'in imaginative sanity'; he continues to admire Shelley, but not to recommend his poems 'as an early study' because they are 'too morbid in their beauty'.

His analysis of Milton has a special interest, given the debt Harpur owes him. He sees as Milton's most characteristic quality 'a certain picturesque and ideal suggestiveness'. He stoutly defends Milton against the 'critical prate', as he calls it, that there is a 'falling off' in the later books of *Paradise Lost*. He pays special attention to Books VII-XI. Milton's account of the Creation in Book VII clearly influenced him deeply, as has been seen; and he asks that close attention be given, in Book XI, to the passage describing Adam and Eve awaiting the arrival of Raphael and to the later 'vision pictures' in the same book. There are reflections of both the substance and tone of these sections in Harpur's works, and his admiration of them is a clue to his search for an enriched narrative and discursive style.

These compact prose and verse criticisms are the product of repeated reading, close study, and revision, and confirm the evidence of the textual history of Harpur's poems. He understood that a close acquaintance with poetry in all its forms is the first step towards the forging of a distinctive style; and only a concept of originality which excludes all access to traditional resources could deny it to him. He was neither a great thinker nor a great poet. But he knew what poetry is, and how poets learn their craft; he appointed himself good masters, and taught himself what to accept and adopt and how to present his individual perceptions, while drawing on the tradition he made his own. He could have done none of these things had he not been able to see for himself and test the accomplishment of others against his capacities and needs.

Notes

1. 'Poetry', in *The Oxford History of Australian Literature,* edited by Leonie Kramer (Melbourne, 1981), p. 275.

2. *Sydney Gazette,* 1 November 1826, p. 3.

3. *Preoccupations in Australian Poetry* (Melbourne, 1965), pp. 8-9.

4. *Charles Harpur,* edited by Adrian Mitchell, Three Colonial Poets, Book 1 (Melbourne, 1973).

5. This text was also reproduced in *Selected Poems of Charles Harpur,* edited by Kenneth H. Gifford and Donald F. Hall (Melbourne, 1944), and in *Charles Harpur,* selected by Donovan Clarke, Australian Poets Series (Sydney, 1963).

6. For a fuller account of Martin's editing, see C. W. Salier, 'Harpur and his Editor', *Southerly,* 12 (1951), 47-54.

7. See J. Normington-Rawling, *Charles Harpur, An Australian* (Sydney, 1962), p. 23.

8. *The Empire,* 15 July 1856, p. 2. This version has 159 lines. There are 209 lines in Mitchell Library MS A89 (1863). This is Adrian Mitchell's copy text.

9. See Wordsworth's poem 'There was a Boy' (1800) which reappears in *The Prelude,* v. 364-97.

10. The 1856 text is subtitled 'My First Poetical Conception'. In a later footnote Harpur wrote that 'from the very coming-on of the storm he became possessed with the intention of eventually describing it', thus emphasizing that he, like Wordsworth, early felt the urge to poetry. This note is in Mitchell Library MS A97, No. 2.

11. Note Wordsworth's reference to 'Araby' in *The Prelude,* v. 497.

12. *The Poetical Works of John Milton,* edited by H. C. Beeching (London, 1944).

13. For this text see Mitchell's edition, pp. 3-15.

14. There are three MS versions of these passages 'one undated, the second dated 1867, and the third 1868' (C. W. Salier, 'Charles Harpur's Translations from the *Iliad*', *Southerly,* 7 (1946), 218-23.

15. This could be a reference to J. D. Dana's *Manual of Geology* (Philadelphia and London, 1863), where Dana refers to man as 'the Archon of mammals' (p. 573). Dana is recorded as having proposed the word Archaean for the oldest geological period (pre-Cambrian era). See *Webster's New Twentieth Century Dictionary of the English Language* (Cleveland, Ohio and New York, 1945), p. 93. Dana visited the Hunter Valley in 1840.

16. Letter to Kendall, 7 July 1866. See Mitchell, p. 193.

17. 'My Own Poetry', Mitchell, p. 125.

18. From 'The Nevers of Poetry, footnote 15', Mitchell, p. 126.

19. There was much discussion of the subject in Sydney in the 1840s. See Normington-Rawling, p. 155.

20. *Rhymed Criticisms,* Mitchell Library MS A89 (1863).

Michael Ackland (essay date 1984)

SOURCE: Ackland, Michael. "God's Sublime Order in Harpur's 'The Creek of the Four Graves.'" *Australian Literary Studies* 11, no. 3 (May 1984): 355-70.

[*In the following essay, Ackland compares Harpur's treatment of the union of man, nature, and God in "The Creek of the Four Graves" with that of poet John Milton.*]

'The Creek of the Four Graves' has long been a rallying-point for the defence of Charles Harpur's poetic standing. Published separately in 1845 and reissued in the 1853 collection entitled **The Bushrangers: A Play in Five Acts and Other Poems,** it was singled out for special praise by the *Maitland Mercury,* while Daniel Deniehy writing in the *Empire* felt that it would 'best support' Harpur's 'claims to a laurel'.[1] Even severe critics of the self-appointed bard of Australia have acknowledged its power. G. B. Barton, for instance, in his pioneering survey of *Literature in New South Wales* (1866) praised the poem for its 'dramatic power' and its 'landscape painting', although in general he judged the poet to be self-conceited, and lacking the basic skills of his craft.[2] Similarly, G. A. Wilkes offers qualified recognition of Harpur's ability to capture large, natural 'effects' in this poem; but finds the overall impression left by his verse to be one of 'earnest ineptitude'.[3] Harpur then, and this his best known work, have met with only limited acclaim. Although its individual felicities are applauded, on the whole it is adjudged 'a heroic fragment', chiefly notable for its 'lively observation'.[4] But, as I hope to demonstrate, this 'settler's tale' transcends purely descriptive categories to take its place within the tradition of prophetic, blank verse narrative, which Harpur had encountered in the works of his two great English mentors, Milton and Wordsworth.[5]

Harpur, no less than Milton or Wordsworth, saw himself as a visionary or bard, whose mission was to lay bare the well-springs of natural and human life, and ultimately 'to justify the ways of God to men'. **'The Creek of the Four Graves'** represents arguably his most complete attempt to work within this tradition. As in Book I of *The Prelude,* so here Harpur's poetic precursors are evoked through the choice of their common verse form, and through veiled references to their characteristic settings and concerns. The conceptual framework of the poem is evidently Miltonic in origin. Man is envisaged as a violent, fallen creature; nature as a battle-ground of opposing principles:

> Some dread Intelligence opposed to Good
> Did, of a surety, over all the earth
> Spread out from Eden—or it were not so![6]

Moreover, Milton's epic offers us allusive 'keys' to scenes in the poem, which are crucial to an understanding of Harpur's vision of loss and redemption. As we shall see, the camp-site of Egremont's party evokes the nuptial bower of Adam and Eve; Harpur's splendid description of the rising moon recalls Raphael's account of the first day of creation; and the poem's frequent references to violent, untimely death gain wider resonances when seen in the context of *Paradise Lost.* These mythic parallels, however, are subsumed in a pervasive awareness of the natural sublime. Here landscape, as in Wordsworth's verse, is suffused with spiritual and inner reality.[7] It is at once a promise of and a setting for redemption. Against this backdrop Harpur portrays the continual struggle between reason and instinct and, as I shall argue, the re-enactment of man's fall. For in **'The Creek of the Four Graves'** early colonial experience is placed within a larger teleological framework inherited from the old world; and the reader is asked to recognize the possibility of human regeneration even in this vast, wild and unknown continent.

In **'The Creek of the Four Graves'**, Charles Harpur establishes a powerful sense of Divine immanence through his portrayal of sublime phenomena. Part I emphasizes the presence of rampire-like mountains which, in the descriptive verse tradition of the eighteenth century, had established themselves as the supreme example of the natural sublime. They dominate the entire action, and are presented as 'dissolving' in the 'exceeding radiancy' advocated by Edmund Burke, or as obscured by that darkness which is even more productive of sublimity. In Part II the rising moon provides the occasion for an awed celebration of creative Divinity, and one which reveals a sacramental conception of nature: that is, a concern with outer reality as a type or emblem of the moral, the intellectual and the religious. These wider concerns, in turn, are underlined through the adaptation of Miltonic scenes, so that Harpur is able to develop Egremont's tale into a dramatic account of the place of error and salvation in God's universal order.

Like so much of Harpur's verse, Part I of **'The Creek of the Four Graves'** is conceived of primarily in pictorial terms. The second stanza, which describes the countryside through which the explorers pass, is picturesque in a dual sense. Its visual details are ordered in accordance with the

principles of composition to be found in landscape painting, with mountains, forest, and 'the windings of a nameless creek' occupying respectively the back-, middle-, and
fore-ground of the verbal canvas; while the overall depiction is characterized by that roughness and complexity in a
wild, natural scene so sought after by devotees of the picturesque, as defined by William Gilpin.[8] This informing
habit of vision becomes increasingly evident in the speaker's stress on the 'wildly beautiful', and in his emphasis
on the scenic and pictorial qualities of the landscape:

> Before them, thus extended, wilder grew
> The scene each moment—beautifully wilder!
>
> . . . . .
> . . . O what words, what hues
> Might paint the wild magnificence of view.

(pp. 3-4)

The description, grounded as it is on the Horatian concept
of *ut pictura poesis,* is thoroughly eighteenth century.[9]
Like the English descriptive poets, Harpur's verse fulfils
Simonides' famous dictum that 'Painting is mute poetry,
and poetry a speaking picture'. Moreover, there seems no
reason to doubt that Harpur was aware of these concepts,
because in a later poem, **'The World and the Soul'**, he
refers explicitly to the Sister Arts tradition, which is based
on these notions. There poetry is seen to be engendered by
the Soul, as are painting and sculpture, which operate
through their own cognate 'languages'.

> And thence descending in her [Soul's] influence, grew
> More intimate and plastic,—till at last
> Semblance idealised in hues, or wrought
> From the rude rock into a life which spake
> The language of immutable loveliness,
> Adorned the abodes of Learning, and the shrines
> Of Worship, and of Virtue;—Sister Arts,
> Three Sister Arts in fellowship divine—
> A triune glory of exalted *Soul.*

(p. 42)

But significantly, for Harpur these arts, far from representing a pure aesthetic, are imbued by spiritual presence, and
take their place with other manifestations of 'the evoking
word of God!' (p. 43).

Dominating Harpur's verbal picture are 'unknown
mountains', and through their depiction the picturesque elements of the scene are absorbed into a profound experience of the natural sublime. As M. H. Nicolson has demonstrated, mountains play a vital role in man's shifting
view of the relationship between Divinity and nature.[10]
Once regarded as blots and warts on the landscape, and
hence as apparent signs of God's displeasure with erring
man, they came in the course of the seventeenth and eighteenth centuries to form the focal point of a new psychology or 'aesthetics of the infinite'. Man, marvelling at the
magnitude of interstellar space, transferred emotional responses once reserved for the Divinity to the heavens and
then, by a natural progression, to the vastest objects on
earth—mountains. These phenomena characterized by vast

dimension and wild inaccessibility led observers to experience an expansion of spirit and mingled feelings of joy
and awe, as they achieved a greater sense of God's presence. In the words of Edward Young's popular eighteenth
century meditative poem, *Night Thoughts*:

> . . . great objects make
> Great minds, enlarging as their views enlarge;
> Those still more godlike, as these more divine.[11]

The distinctive transitions associated with the aesthetics of
the infinite emerge in Harpur's presentation of the mountain range:

> Before them, thus extended, wilder grew
> The scene each moment—beautifully wilder!
> For when the sun was all but sunk below
> Those barrier mountains,—in the breeze that o'er
> Their rough enormous backs deep fleeced with wood
> Came whispering down, the wide upslanting sea
> Of fanning leaves in the descending rays
> Danced interdazzlingly, as if the trees
> That bore them, were all thrilling,—tingling all
> Even to the roots for very happiness:
> So prompted from within, so sentient, seemed
> The bright quick motion—wildly beautiful.
> But when the sun had wholly disappeared
> Behind those mountains—O what words, what hues
> Might paint the wild magnificence of view
> That opened westward! Out extending, lo,
> The heights rose crowding, with their summits all
> Dissolving, as it seemed, and partly lost
> In the exceeding radiancy aloft;
> And thus transfigured, for awhile they stood
> Like a great company of Archeons, crowned
> With burning diadems, and tented o'er
> With canopies of purple and of gold!

(pp. 3-4)

The portrayal moves down, and then upwards, from the
sun to the tingling trees and back to the celestial image of
transfiguration, with the mountains mediating each transition. While the depiction conveys the rugged indomitabil-
ity and magnitude of natural forms, it also stresses the
presence of ubiquitous, incessant movement throughout
this enduring landscape. The breeze 'whispers down', 'descending rays' cause 'fanning leaves' to dance and thrill.
Ethereal currents are met by an answering terrestrial response, and the union is signalled by the prefix in
'interdazzlingly' and by the potentially cosmic image of
the dance. Implicitly, the passage leads us to ask what
causes this 'thrilling', this 'very happiness', which is
prompted from within and without; to ponder what is the
essence of the 'wildly beautiful'. The scene of 'barrier
mountains' has been transformed imperceptibly into one of
'bright quick motion', as the so-solid-seeming-mass
'dissolves' to admit the presence of irradiating Divinity.
Well may the speaker wonder how he is to paint the ineffable. The cause is truly 'lost / In the exceeding radiancy
aloft'. It is not just the mountains, but our awareness of
the poem's setting which is thus 'transfigured'; and the
closing image of Archeons clad in the purple and gold of

kings unmistakably evokes the archetype of all presiding authority. The picturesque has been ennobled with the sublime. What began primarily as an aesthetic depiction has been infused with a moral and religious significance, felt again in Harpur's final allusion to the scene's picturesque qualities:

> And thus awhile, in the lit dusk, they [the mountains]
> seemed
> To hang like mighty pictures of themselves
> In the still chambers of some vaster world.
>
> (p. 5)

The concluding line lends a metaphysical dimension to the concept of *ut pictura poesis* by referring the whole tradition back to a Divine archetype. It should also alert us to view the action depicted in terms of a vaster order, presided over by an Unmoved Mover.

This notion of immanent Godhead is expressed most clearly at the beginning of Part II in the sublime evocation of the rising moon. Again the depiction is conveyed in picturable terms and yet is redolent with spiritual implications, for the greatest objects of nature are transformed by the presence of God's surrogate, the moon, elsewhere termed by Harpur 'Infinitude's dark Spouse' (p. 33):

> Meanwhile the cloudless eastern heaven had grown
> More and more luminous—and now the Moon
> Up from behind a giant hill was seen
> Conglobing, till—a mighty mass—she brought
> Her under border level with its cone,
> As thereon it were resting: when, behold
> A wonder! Instantly that cone's whole bulk
> Erewhile so dark, seemed inwardly a-glow
> With her instilled irradiance; while the trees
> That fringed its outline,—their huge statures dwarfed
> By distance into brambles, and yet all
> Clearly defined against her ample orb,—
> Out of its very disc appeared to swell
> In shadowy relief, as they had been
> All sculptured from its substance as she rose.
>
> (p. 7)

Here terrestrial and celestial, mountain and moon, are fused to create an emblem of life as Divine vesture. By implication, the natural world is always 'inwardly aglow / With . . . instilled irradiance': an idea rephrased in the concluding lines, where the image of external reality emanating from the source of light suggests both God's indwelling presence and His unmoved transcendence. Nature is at once, in Harpur's words, 'nourished into being / Upon the bosom of Almighty Power / Illimitably active' and formed 'in strict / Coincidence with Eternal Verity' (p. 33).[12] Again the scene hangs like a painting whose full significance depends on a Divine archetype, just as the relief-sculpture stands out from the underlying and supporting substance.

Traditionally, however, the natural sublime is not evoked for merely aesthetic ends, but as a stimulus to moral and religious speculation of the kind which Harpur introduces through his adaptation of Miltonic set-pieces, as in Egremont's first-night camp-site. Given the capacity of the 'wildly beautiful' countryside to assume aspects of a last Eden or a blemished paradise, the primary context almost inevitably evoked by the camp-site is the paradisial bower from *Paradise Lost*:

> Thus talking, hand in hand alone they passed
> On to their blissful bower; it was a place
> Chos'n by the sovran Planter, when he framed
> All things to man's delightful use; the roof
> Of thickest covert was inwoven shade,
> Laurel and myrtle, and what higher grew
> Of firm and fragrant leaf; on either side
> Acanthus, and each odorous bushy shrub
> Fenced up the verdant wall; . . .
> . . . Here, in close recess
> With flowers, garlands, and sweet-smelling herbs
> Espousèd Eve decked her first nuptial bed.
>
> (IV. 689-97, 708-10)[13]

Harpur, however, is portraying life as it is experienced in a fallen world. As a result of man's original disobedience, Divinity is now only a sensed stellar presence, glimpsed through the interlacing growths of the explorers' 'bower':

> The simple subject to their minds at length
> Fully discussed, their couches they prepared
> Of rushes, and the long green tresses pulled
> Down from the boughs of the wild willows near.
> Then four, as pre-arranged, stretched out their limbs
> Under the dark arms of the forest trees
> That mixed aloft, high in the starry air,
> In arcs and leafy domes whose crossing curves
> And roof-like features,—blurring as they ran
> Into some denser intergrowth of sprays,—
> Were seen in mass traced out against the clear
> Wide gaze of heaven . . .
>
> (p. 6)

Although the Edenic bower of Milton's depiction is richer and more intricately constructed, it shares the major characteristics of the natural shelter under which Egremont's party sleeps. Both consist of shady roof and walls formed by the 'intergrowth' of local vegetation; the whole furbished by a Divinely-inspired nature. And the putative parallel is strengthened by Harpur's final depiction of the camp-site, where it becomes, by ironic inference, the first-night 'nuptial bed' of mutilated corpses. God is absent from the immediate scene, but his surrogate, the moon, is described gazing

> As peacefully down as on a bridal there
> Of the warm Living—not, alas! on them
> Who kept in ghastly silence through the night
> Untimely spousals with a desert death.
>
> (p. 14)

Nature's original order is here subverted. Man is at once the culprit and the victim of his primal pact with violent death.

Adaptation of Miltonic teleology is also evident at the commencement of Part II. There the ascent of the radiant moon is developed into a portrayal of the conflict between reason or truth and chaos-wreaking error:

> Thus o'er that dark height her great orb conglobed,
> Till her full light, in silvery sequence still
> Cascading forth from ridgy slope to slope,
> Like the dropt foldings of a lucent veil,
> Chased mass by mass the broken darkness down
> Into the dense-brushed valleys, where it crouched,
> And shrank, and struggled, like a dragon doubt
> Glooming some lonely spirit that doth still
> Resist the Truth with obstinate shifts and shows,
> Though shining out of heaven, and from defect
> Winning a triumph that might else not be.
>
> (pp. 7-8)

The assimilation of traditional material is complete. But the use of 'conglobed' and subsequent references to a brooding, wingèd spirit (to be quoted later) direct attention to what, for Harpur, would have been the familiar context of these images: Messiah's creation of the earth, as described in Book VII of *Paradise Lost*.

>   . . . Darkness profound
> Covered th' abyss; but on the wat'ry calm
> His brooding wings the Spirit of God outspread,
> And vital virtue infused, and vital warmth
> Throughout the fluid mass, but downward purged
> The black tartareous cold infernal dregs
> Adverse to life; then founded, then conglobed,
> Like things to like, the rest to several place
> Disparted, and between spun out the air,
> And earth self-balanced on her center hung.
>
> (VII. 233-42)

While recognition of the Miltonic original is not indispensable, it does underscore the burden of Harpur's portrayal, which invites us to see each rising of God's resplendence as a re-enactment of the miracle of creation; as a taming of chaos and all those forces 'adverse to life'. 'Dragon doubt' may not be entirely routed, but its continued existence serves as a pretext for God to display His untiring benevolence and care for this world. Earth, however, is fallen; and from its defective condition the force of darkness may extort some sense of victory. Yet the very description of his actions as 'shifts and shows' suggests the insubstantiality of his gains, while his portrayal as a 'lonely spirit' implies a beleaguered rather than triumphant state. God's supremacy, then, is unassailable, but He does not exercise absolute control over every aspect of existence. The stars are watchful yet detached; and 'Silence', described with the attributes of Milton's 'Spirit', seems unconcerned by the impending triumph of error in the temporalized abyss:

>   . . . Silence there
> Had recomposed her ruffled wings, and now
> Brooded it seemed even stiller than before,
> Deep nested in the darkness . . .
>
> (p. 8)

Here as elsewhere, recognition of Miltonic parallels highlights the broader significance of Egremont's tale. For Harpur, no less than Milton, is concerned with the grand issues of human community and universal order. In the initial camp-site scene he creates an image of domesticity, supportive fellowship, and reciprocal delight, surrounded by the threatening unknown of the wild. The fire is 'well-built', and conductive to a calming, 'steadier mood': positive values reinforced by the 'fuming pipes', described as 'full charged', and as giving off 'tiny clouds over their several heads / Quietly curling upward' (p. 6). These attributes will be played off against Egremont's 'death-charged tube', and a cloud of a more sinister sort:

> Yea, thence surveyed, the Universe might have seemed
> Coiled in vast rest,—only that one dim cloud,
> Diffused and shapen like a mighty spider,
> Crept as with scrawling legs along the sky;
> And that the stars, in their bright orders, still
> Cluster by cluster glowingly revealed
> As this slow cloud moved,—high over all,—
> Looked wakeful—yea, looked thoughtful in their
>   peace.
>
> (p. 7)[14]

Contrasts are thereby established between peaceful and threatening, or between constructive and destructive action, as epitomized by the shift from pipe to firearm; and a habit of mind revealed which can draw a metaphysical truth from both the upward path of pipe-smoke and the obscuring drift of a dark, ponderous cloud. The 'tiny clouds' are specifically designated 'types' of 'comfort' drawn from social activity, and this 'comfort' rests finally on the belief in a presiding universal order, imaged in the stars which 'high over all— / . . . looked thoughtful in their peace'. Yet all around between man and the object of his faith lurks a world of uncontrolled instinct, whose type is the spider-cloud. For man, the problem posed is how to tame the forces within and without, so as to attain a permanent vision of, or access to, the 'bright orders' that lie beyond the wilderness.

With the sublime setting established, Harpur attempts to come to terms with the presence of evil and violence in the creation. Part II opens with an image of ongoing terrestrial struggle, subsumed within an all-embracing Divine order, and then portrays the reverberations of these hostilities within the human sphere. Specifically man, in the person of Egremont, moves from peace and fellowship to the position of blood-stained outcast, through the slaughter of his own kind. In Part III the sequence is reversed. The individual instance expands into the cosmic, as Egremont is saved and bloodshed averted through Divine intervention. Furthermore, both sections contain important references to loving domesticity and to sacred charity. These concepts are invoked to contrast with man's violent deeds, and to give the main action a redemptive outcome. The pessimism engendered by man's brutality is thus qualified by showing the survival of saving bonds between microcosm and macrocosm: bonds which enable Egremont to move from the condition of erring man in the wilderness of instinct to that of enlightened participation in supportive, human community.

As **'The Creek of the Four Graves'** was revised and expanded, its depiction of violence assumed a thoroughly Miltonic cast. In the 1853 version of the poem, Egremont is only an observer, not a participant in the murderous deeds. The original text reads:

> Egremont, transfixt
> With horror—struck as into stone, saw this,
> Then turned and fled! Fast fled he, but as fast
> His deadly foes went thronging on his track![15]

In the final version he returns blood for blood, and the description of his gun as a 'death-charged tube' underscores the wider ramifications of his passionate deed. Moreover, this emphasis on unnatural, man-produced violence is elevated to a focal-point of terrestrial evil in a passage from Part III, which was also a later addition to the 1853 text:

> O God! and thus this lovely world hath been
> Accursed for ever by the bloody deeds
> Of its prime Creature—Man. Erring or wise,
> Savage or civilised, still hath he made
> This glorious residence, the Earth, a Hell
> Of wrong and robbery and untimely death!
> Some dread Intelligence opposed to Good
> Did, of a surety, over all the earth
> Spread out from Eden—or it were not so!
>
> (p. 14)

Similarly, in *Paradise Lost* man's act of disobedience, the very partaking of the apple, is presented in terms of a mortal blow to creation.

> Earth trembled from her entrails, as again
> In pangs, and Nature gave a second groan;
> Sky loured and, muttering thunder, some sad drops
> Wept at completing of the mortal sin
> Original . . .
>
> (IX. 1000-1004)

This dire vision haunts successive scenes of the epic, until it culminates in Michael's historical panorama. As the archangel tells Adam, 'from that sin derive / Corruption to bring forth more violent deeds' (XI. 427-28), the first of which is the brutal slaying of Abel by Cain who

> Smote him into the midriff with a stone
> That beat out life; he fell, and deadly pale
> Groaned out his soul with gushing blood effused.
>
> (XI. 445-47)

Harpur, in an unpublished note entitled **'Poetic Descriptions of Violent Death'**, quoted and underlined the above passage, stating 'I know of nothing so terrible in this kind, as Milton's account in Paradise Lost of the death of Abel'.[16] And **'The Creek of the Four Graves'** reinforces this assertion. There, as in *Paradise Lost,* the archetypal transgression and its consequences are characterized by violent acts, which are antithetical to the love and unity, or community, informing God's original order.

The association of fallen existence with death and violence is dramatized through the encounter with the blacks. The description of the attacking aborigines is purposefully generalized, and teleological references are inwoven with colonial experience to drive home parallels between temporal and sacred history. This is both a local conflict and an acting-out of man's original errors:

> But there again—crack upon crack! And hark!
> O Heaven! have Hell's worst fiends burst howling up
> Into the death-doom'd world? Or whence, if not
> From diabolic rage, could surge a yell
> So horrible as that which now affrights
> The shuddering dark! Ah! Beings as fell are near!
> Yea, Beings, in their dread inherited hate
> And deadly enmity, as vengeful, come
> In vengeance!
>
> (p. 9)

Harpur, in revising the earlier version of this passage, added 'death' to 'doomed world', and expanded the line 'Beings in their enmity as vengeful, come' to include the concept of 'dread inherited hate'. He thereby linked the assault with that hellish enmity which caused the loss of paradise; and created a complex structure of comparisons which expressly associates Satan's fiends and their black counterparts in terms of fellness and vengeance. Harpur's prime concern throughout, however, is not to denigrate the aborigines, but to make them representative. The blacks are called 'Savages', Egremont is termed 'our sage friend'. These designations link them respectively with two broad human types, who are alike in their proclivity to violence: 'Erring or wise, / Savage or civilised, still hath he [man] made / This glorious residence, the Earth, a Hell'. Yet Harpur's categories, despite his well-known sympathy for the mistreated aborigines, do reveal the bias of his age. To a man who affirmed contemporary beliefs in Western progress and Christianity, heathens, like hellish reprobates, are necessarily erring. Inherited cultural models are also discernible in the closing depiction of the marauders. Their conception of events is only 'crude', just as their benighted condition leaves them in a state of primitive fear when confronted with the apparently inexplicable:

> His vanishment, so passing strange it seemed,
> They coupled with the mystery of some crude
> Old fable of their race; and fear-struck all,
> And silent, then withdrew . . .
>
> (p. 14)

Civilized and rational man, however, should know better. Consequently, attention is focused on Egremont's response to wild, untamed instinct; and on the Christian ideal of charity or mercy.

Through the reactions of Egremont, Harpur explores the conflict in man between rational and instinctive forces. These two sides of human nature first emerge in the description of Egremont on guard-duty, immediately before the fatal attack. The scene opens with his response to positive, loving values, centred on the image of home:

> There standing in his lone watch, Egremont
> On all this solemn beauty of the world,

Looked out, yet wakeful; for sweet thoughts of home
And all the sacred charities it held,
Ingathered to his heart, as by some nice
And subtle interfusion that connects
The loved and cherished (then the most, perhaps,
When absent, or when passed, or even when *lost*)
With all serene and beautiful and bright
And lasting things of Nature . . .

(p. 8)

A 'subtle interfusion' of 'sacred charities' is shown to link upper and lower, inner and outer realms. Far-reaching and invisible bonds are hinted at, which interlink man, God and nature; redeeming bonds which are always present, even though individuals may succumb to 'dragon doubt'. Moreover, the 'fall' and eventual regeneration of 'our sage friend' are implicitly prefigured by the stressed passage in parentheses. As a prelude to this process, we then see Egremont shocked by a sudden noise into 'wild surmise', so that he seeks cover

Against the shade-side of a bending gum,
With a strange horror gathering to his heart,
As if his blood were charged with insect life
And writhed along in clots, he stilled himself,
Listening long and heedfully, with head
Bent forward sideways, till his held breath grew
A pang, and his ears rung . . .

(p. 8)

Here as so often in the poem, realistic psychological depiction has wider implications. The phrase 'gathering to his heart' clearly echoes the preceding 'ingathered to his heart', and so invites a comparison of his two mental states. Thought and sacred charities have been swept away by horror; the reference to his blood 'charged with insect life' perhaps suggests the ascendancy of the wild or instinctual; while the image of writhing clots is contrasted with the calm he is able to enforce on this occasion. This momentary usurpation of thought by instinct, moreover, foreshadows the temporary triumph of chaotic passion when 'his blood again rushed tingling', and he explicitly kills.

For Harpur, man remains the arbiter of his own destiny. All depends on his right and continued use of reason. Egremont is termed 'their thoughtful Master', and it is specifically this attribute which links mankind with the 'thoughtful' interstellar order. Yet defects do exist. The savage attack, for instance, erupts from beyond the bright circle of communal firelight, hinting at dire complicity between man and untamed nature.[17] Egremont also feels this pull, and becomes morally one with the vengeful 'murderous crew', when he instinctively fires his 'death-charged tube' from within the shadows of the forest. Man is thus the battle-ground of rival forces. He may confirm the violent, unreasoning acts which transformed paradise into 'the death-doom'd world' or, by aligning himself with the 'sacred charities' of loving community, confirm the remaining bonds of the original covenant between man, God, and nature. The murderous encounter represents then, in the widest sense, a struggle between black and white for control of the fallen 'garden'. While separate cultures clash for possession of the land, larger forces struggle for possession of man.

Counterbalancing the vision of man in the grasp of infernal instinct is Harpur's frequently neglected picture of humanity's indomitable striving after spiritual fulfilment. The onslaught of the blacks is swift and brutal. Three explorers are instantly clubbed to death; the fourth resists his fate in vain. It is not that he fears natural death, but he is unwilling to forego the 'human good' he has promised himself, and the legitimate hope of unselfish utility: 'the consciousness of having shaped / Some personal good in being;—strong myself / And strengthening others' (p. 10). At one level, of course, this poor child of misery, and the terse contrast drawn between his heroic response and that of 'Fortune's pampered child', reflect Harpur's democratic predilections, while there seems to be more than a little of the poet's own bitter experience in his description of the man's unappeased soul-hunger in an unappreciative world. Yet his final struggles against harsh reality have much in common with the ennobling Romantic ethic of eternal striving, and with Harpur's ideal of ever pushing 'onward' after related personal and spiritual fulfilment:

. . . against them still
Upstruggled, nor would cease: until one last
Tremendous blow, dealt down upon his head
As if in mercy, gave him to the dust
With all his many woes and frustrate hope.

(p. 11)[18]

The apparent despair of the concluding words is qualified arguably by the emphasis laid on mercy in the ensuing lines. In the 1853 text, the concept of mercy is evoked in this scene primarily as condemnation of the blacks, described as 'merciless foes' and 'the merciless'. But as revisions gradually transformed a local into a universal conflict, these comments were deleted; and the onus of judgment placed on the reader through the added lines: 'Fast! for in full pursuit, behind him yelled / Wild men whose wild speech hath no word for *mercy*!' Implicitly a distinction is drawn between Egremont who, we are pointedly told, acts 'from instinct more than conscious thought' and the detached observer. To 'wild men', like the unenlightened blacks or the momentarily overthrown Egremont, whose deeds indicate no notion of mercy, the death-blow to the poor man must seem to 'frustrate hope'. Harpur's text, however, is tantalizingly ambiguous concerning the man's spiritual state: 'So should I [be] . . . / . . . more than now prepared / To house me in its [the grave's] gloom . . .' (p. 10). Preparation is not entirely denied—only fulfilment and completion remain unachieved. This positive intimation is also supported by the man's devotion to selfless good and by his intuitive projection of the grave in homely and life-giving terms. Furthermore we, the readers, are explicitly reminded of the Christian concept of mercy, and thereby of the Pauline faith built upon the knowledge that man is dust and to dust will return. What appears only profound physical abasement may in fact be a precondition for the man's being raised a spiritual body. Nor should we forget the inference that salvation is perhaps most possible when it is apparently 'absent, . . . passed, or even . . . *lost*'.

Themes of mercy and regeneration dominate the closing scenes between black and white. The opening of Part III presents the successive stages of Egremont's immersion in nature, as he is re-admitted into that 'subtle interfusion' which links all spheres of life. First he plunges 'to his middle in the flashing stream', then he is submerged below the very ground. This progression, moreover, is marked by constant references, implicit or explicit, to God's presence. In the description of the stream there is again an interlinking of earth and sky, and an echo of the earlier image of brooding spirit or 'Silence' in the qualifier 'ruffled':

> Plunging right forth and shooting feet-first down,
> Sunk to his middle in the flashing stream—
> In which the imaged stars seemed all at once
> To burst like rockets into one wide blaze
> Of interwrithing light. Then wading through
> The ruffled waters, forth he sprang . . .
>
> (p. 12)

Throughout Egremont's helplessness is emphasized. He has 'no time . . . for thought'; he is 'blind' in the profoundest sense. Only mercy can redeem the erring soul, and Harpur is at pains to stress that Egremont owes his salvation not to good fortune, but to Divine charity working through himself and the natural world, in response to an appeal from a far-distant, loving heart.

> When in its face—O verily our God
> Hath those in his peculiar care for whom
> The daily prayers of spotless Womanhood
> And helpless Infancy, are offered up!—
> When in its face a cavity he felt,
> The upper earth of which in one rude mass
> Was held fast bound by the enwoven roots
> Of two old trees,—and which, beneath the mould,
> Just o'er the clammy vacancy below,
> Twisted and lapped like knotted snakes, and made
> A natural loft-work. Under this he crept,
> Just as the dark forms of his hunters thronged
> The bulging rock whence he before had plunged.
>
> (p. 12)

Thus Egremont returns, to borrow Milton's phrase, to 'earth's hallowed mold' (V. 321)—except that this is nature in a postlapsarian world. The creation itself, like its prime creature, is ambivalently constituted: a point driven home by the passage added to the 1853 text which likens the overlapping roots to 'knotted snakes'. Nonetheless, the place of refuge proves a second fertile 'bower', though subterranean, for Egremont will be reborn from this 'cavity' or 'clammy vacancy', like man from the womb or original clay, or like Earth itself from the abyss. Here in the microcosm God re-enacts the founding miracle re-peated every day with the arising of His celestial effulgence. Egremont emerges 'renewed', and will take a further step towards redeeming his blood-deed by reintegrating himself with the 'sacred charities' centred on 'Home'.

Egremont's dramatic escape leads to a final and traditional attempt to 'justify the ways of God to men'. At the centre of the section lies Harpur's explicit statement of his Miltonic teleology. The primal pattern of fall and redemption is acknowledged, as is its recurrence in man's continual propensity to sin. Preceding events are recalled through references to 'Erring or wise, / Savage or civilised' (p. 14), and imaged in the contrasting choices open to mankind. Unenlightened 'spousals' with inherited violence produce a desert of death; the alternative 'bridal' between earth and heaven leads to Egremont's emergence from the rival bower of humid life. These dual images are then refracted and integrated into an all-embracing vision, which reaches from the highest ethereal beings to fallen souls in their most repulsive states:

> For see the bright beholding Moon, and all
> The radiant Host of Heaven, evince no touch
> Of sympathy with Man's wild violence;—
> Only evince in their calm course, their part
> In that original unity of Love,
> Which, like the soul that dwelleth in a harp,
> Under God's hand, in the beginning, chimed
> The sabbath concord of the Universe;
> And look on a gay clique of maidens, met
> In village tryst, and interwhirling all
> In glad Arcadian dances on the green—
> Or on a hermit, in his vigils long,
> Seen kneeling at the doorway of his cell—
> Or on a monster battle-field where lie
> In sweltering heaps, the dead and dying both,
> On the cold gory ground,—as they that night
> Looked in bright peace, down on the doomful Forest.
>
> (p. 15)

Here the concept of a surviving 'unity of Love' serves not only as a stark contrast with, but as a promise of possible redemption from, 'Man's wild violence'. Various paths are open to mankind; and three alternatives are envisaged which find correlatives in Egremont's tale. Most obviously, the 'monster battle-field' recalls this 'terrible hour / Of human agony and loss extreme'. This devastation is played off against two images of achieved spiritual harmony. The way of the hermit is one of self-denying asceticism. Fate may be seen to force on the fourth poor adventurer an analogous course: transfiguration bought at the cost of rigorous mortification of the flesh. The maidens' more joyous dance is a terrestrial manifestation of the original 'sabbath concord'; and women, both here and elsewhere in the poem, are closely associated with sacred and life-affirming actions. Egremont's return 'Home' aligns him with the regenerative values centred on 'the gay clique of maidens . . . interwhirling', though the gap that separates him from their innocent pleasure is felt in the comparable whirling of wintry leaves that marks the graves of his companions:

. . . four long grassy mounds
Bestrewn with leaves, and withered spraylets, stript
By the loud wintry wingèd gales that roamed
Those solitudes, from the old trees which there
Moaned the same leafy dirges that had caught
The heed of dying Ages: these were all;
And thence the place was long by travellers called
The Creek of the Four Graves . . .

(p. 15)

God may be high above the creation; but Egremont's survival and the burial of the mutilated corpses testify to the existence of an enduring covenant. Following the lead of man, the seasons now deck the graves as a pledge of the remaining bond between man, God and nature, and as a sign of the ultimate powerlessness of that 'dread Intelligence opposed to Good'. In a postlapsarian world of 'dying Ages', simple Arcadian delights may rarely be attainable; but Harpur affirms that violence and sin can be redeemed through the ever-present possibility of spiritual spring. The heavens maintain 'their part', the rest is up to individual man.

Like the sculptured relief standing out from the stone, the 'freshness and authenticity' of Harpur's vision in **'The Creek of the Four Graves'** rests on his profound sense of tradition.[19] Archetypes inform not only his view of nature, but also his response to Australia. Unlike many of his later compatriots, Harpur sought to understand colonial experience in terms of great inherited concepts. These enabled him to acknowledge boldly the strangeness of events, and yet to find assurance and that larger prophetic vision which he felt to be so necessary to his native land. In this poem, adaptation and assimilation characterize his borrowings. *Paradise Lost* is used allusively to demonstrate the continual reenactment of the primal myth, while the familiar Romantic compact between man, God and nature becomes a means of drawing instructive patterns from pioneer-experience. Moreover, we chance observers have been involved, no less than the aborigines portrayed, in what Adrian Mitchell refers to as the 'imaginative assimilation' of events.[20] But unlike them, our concept of mercy provides a path beyond the 'fear-struck' condition of unreclaimed wilderness, as the savage reverence of terror is subsumed in an enlarged awareness of God's sublime benevolence. To receive this vision, Harpur leads his reader to an imaginative height similar to that enjoyed by Milton's Michael and Adam in paradise, except that now the prospects of Eden are in Australia; their fulfilment in the hands of each of us.

Notes

1. Quoted in J. Normington-Rawling, *Charles Harpur, An Australian* (Sydney: Angus and Robertson, 1962), pp. 181-83.

2. Quoted in J. Normington-Rawling, 'A Currency Lad Poet: The Significance of Charles Harpur', *Quadrant*, 7 (1963), 18.

3. G. A. Wilkes, 'Introduction' to *The Colonial Poets* (Sydney: Angus and Robertson, 1974); and *The*

Stockyard and the Croquet Lawn: Literary Evidence for Australia's Cultural Development (Melbourne: Arnold, 1981), p. 60.

4. Brian Elliott, *The Landscape of Australian Poetry* (Melbourne: Cheshire, 1967), pp. 68 and 70. Even Judith Wright, Harpur's most sympathetic commentator, claims that such verse 'is, and is intended to be, descriptive and narrative only' (*Preoccupations in Australian Poetry* [Melbourne: Oxford Univ. Press, 1965], p. 15).

5. Commentators have, of course, noted links between 'The Creek of the Four Graves' and the works of these poets. Judith Wright, for instance, in *Charles Harpur* (Melbourne: Oxford Univ. Press, 1977) describes its landscape as a 'Wordsworthian treatment' (p. 26); Adrian Mitchell in his introduction to *Charles Harpur* (Melbourne: Sun Books, 1973) refers to 'Miltonic aborigines' (p. xxv); and Harry Heseltine, in his introduction to *The Penguin Book of Australian Verse* (Middlesex: Harmondsworth, 1972), suggests that the poem should be more carefully considered in terms of 'Harpur's Miltonism' (p. 31) and its use of 'archetypal narrative' (p. 32): issues to which this paper addresses itself directly.

6. Adrian Mitchell, ed., *Charles Harpur* (Melbourne: Sun Books, 1973), p. 14. Future page references to this edition will be cited parenthetically in the text. After its reprinting in 1853, Harpur extensively revised 'The Creek of the Four Graves' until it reached the expanded form preserved in Mitchell Library ms. A87. Mitchell's text is based on this handwritten copy, which is dated Euroma 1867, and designated 'final copy'. At a still later date Harpur made minor alterations to the text; but Mitchell has apparently concluded that these brief emendations lack the authority of the full copperplate text, which Harpur had transcribed as part of a definitive collection of his poems. Throughout I have attempted to ensure that my case retains its validity irrespective of the ms. variant accepted. Thus, for instance, although Harpur later substituted 'arose' for 'conglobed' in II. 16, the Miltonic resonance is still present owing to the earlier use of 'conglobing' (II. 4) to describe the same scene. Readers interested in the revised Euroma 1867 text will find it reproduced in *The Colonial Poets*, pp. 16-27.

7. My concern in this paper is with their shared, general preoccupations, not with putative parallels between their works. Harpur's portrayal of the natural sublime was no doubt influenced by Wordsworth's, but then both their productions were also informed by a host of other eighteenth century works which dealt with sublime phenomena.

8. On the vogue of the picturesque see Christopher Hussey, *The Picturesque: Studies in a Point of View* (1927; rpt. London: Cass, 1967); Elizabeth Wheeler Manwaring, *Italian Landscape in Eighteenth Century*

England (1925; rpt. London: Cass, 1965); and J. R. Watson, *Picturesque Landscape and English Romantic Poetry* (London: Hutchinson, 1970).

9. Jean Hagstrum provides a thorough survey of this tradition in *The Sister Arts: The Tradition of Literary Pictorialism and English Poetry from Dryden to Gray* (Chicago: Univ. of Chicago Press, 1958).

10. Marjorie Hope Nicolson, *Mountain Gloom and Mountain Glory: The Development of the Aesthetics of the Infinite* (Ithaca, N.Y.: Cornell Univ. Press, 1959).

11. Charles Cowden Clark, ed., *Young's Night Thoughts* (Edinburgh: Nichol, 1865), IX. 1064-66.

12. The lines are from 'The Spouse of Infinitude', while in 'The World and the Soul' the infinite heavens are described as being 'bosomed all in Him!' (p. 44).

13. All quotations from *Paradise Lost* are from Douglas Bush, ed., *Milton: Poetical Works* (Oxford: Oxford Univ. Press, 1969).

14. The contrasting clouds are also linked verbally. For the participle 'coiled', although qualifying 'universe', is contextually associated with the spider-cloud, and recalls the 'curling' action of the smaller pipe-clouds. These contrasts, however, were not available to a reader of the early 1853 text of the poem. They were produced by revisions which introduced the references to both the 'tiny clouds' and the 'death-charged tube'. Similarly, textual expansions were also responsible for the related contrast in Part II between Egremont's thoughts of 'sacred charities' and his horrified, instinctive reactions to an unexpected alarm.

15. Charles Harpur, *The Bushrangers, A Play in Five Acts and Other Poems* (Sydney: Piddington, 1853), p. 68.

16. Mitchell Library ms. C376, pp. 541-42.

17. This association is implied strongly in Part III, where the outlined trees are described in almost human terms, as 'All standing now in the keen radiance there / So ghostly still, as in a solemn trance' (p. 13); and the searching blacks are metaphorically linked with the surrounding forest in the phrase 'till the fretted current boiled / Amongst their crowding trunks from bank to bank' (p. 13).

18. See the poem 'Onward' in Charles Harpur, *Poems* (Sydney: Robertson, 1883), pp. 75-77.

19. The comment quoted is from Elliott, *The Landscape of Australian Poetry*, p. 71.

20. Mitchell, *Charles Harpur*, xxvi. Mitchell, however, seems to limit unduly the coherence and ambitious expansiveness of Harpur's thought when he concludes: 'The attempt at acclimatization is both the subject and the process of the poem; the experiment is fascinating and not wholly a failure' (xxvi).

Elizabeth Perkins (essay date 1984)

SOURCE: Perkins, Elizabeth. Introduction to *The Poetical Works of Charles Harpur*, pp. xi-xliii. London: Angus & Robertson Publishers, 1984.

[*In the following excerpt, Perkins details Harpur's education, family circumstances, and controversial episodes in the poet's youth. Perkins then balances an explanation of Harpur's weaknesses as a lyricist with his originality, spirit, and narrative skill.*]

I

Sir Henry Parkes's autobiographical *Fifty Years in the Making of Australian History*, published in 1892 when Parkes was seventy-seven, begins with an account of the political movement of the forties and fifties which eventually brought self-government to the eastern Australian colonies. "It is impossible," he wrote, "in view of the marvellous progress of New South Wales during the last forty years, to overvalue the importance of that first popular movement in Australia. It formed truly a new epoch in Australian life. A people, emerging from the indistinct mists of scattered settlement in a wild country, claiming to be ripe for freedom and representative institutions. A public spirit was awakened never more to be lulled to rest."[1]

When Parkes reached the colony from England in 1839, his first acquaintances, he says, were Charles Harpur, William Augustine Duncan and Henry Halloran. Halloran, more conservative in every way than Harpur, was Harpur's chief rival as poet in New South Wales for some thirty years. Duncan was founding editor of the *Australasian Chronicle* and the owner-publisher of the *Weekly Register*, a leading organ of political comment and literature between 1843 and 1845. Parkes, the liberal English craftsman, inspired by Daniel O'Connell and William Cobbett; Halloran, born in Cape Town, the son of a clergyman, a staunch Anglican and successful civil servant; Duncan, Scottish-born Catholic convert, newspaper owner, political reformer, littérateur, and civil servant; and Harpur, son of emancipist parents, transcendentalist, republican in theory, poet and aesthetician, consciously transmitting the English literary heritage and interpreting the new physical and spiritual landscape, epitomise some of the distinctive forces that contributed to Australian social history. The influence they represent lies between the purely political and the purely intellectual, and there were, of course, strong forces at work in the colony that were quite outside their interests and capacities. It is therefore difficult to define precisely what their influence achieved—although Parkes's rôle as owner of the *Empire*, member of the Legislature, Premier and promulgator of Federation, may be roughly estimated—but they were thinkers as well as participants, men to whom abstract principles were of greater concern than material interests. It is as easy to underestimate the contribution of such citizens to history as it is to exaggerate the tangible effects of their influence.

At a time when the clergyman and the journal editor ruled the middle-class intellectual roost, when there were scores of small papers and periodicals of all shades of political and religious persuasion for each monopolist daily and weekly circulating now, and when printed articles and public lectures filled the place taken today by radio and television, men like Parkes, Duncan, Harpur, and Halloran had considerable effect in determining the character and quality of colonial life. The imperial policies of Britain had more obvious repercussions, and the growth of pastoral, agricultural, mining and trading enterprise reacted more dramatically and immediately on economic life. But the fabric of colonial society, which sustained the operations of overseas interests and commercial speculation, and which was the basis for higher intellectual achievement and the refinements of cultured wealth, was the life of that part of the middle-class which was independent in spirit, curious in mind, and aspiring in its emotional reach.

To call this life bourgeois or liberal, whenever and wherever it appears, is to misrepresent its complexity and constrain its boundaries. It is a social force that lives by tradition and grows by revolution; it nourishes itself through reverence and iconoclasm. It is best defined by what it is not. It is not primitive, not slavish, not aristocratic, not cowardly, not self-sacrificing, not destructive, not well-disciplined, not mercenary, not loyal to its own interests, and not materialistic. In Australia, Harpur's poetry was the clearest and most comprehensive literary expression of this social force before the eighteen nineties.

The reader of Harpur's work sees at once that Harpur was not a great poet, but finds the poetry almost inexhaustibly interesting. Undeniably, Harpur had a great natural gift for poetry, and he was, if the phrase still has meaning, great in soul. He had several defects of personality, but his irascibility and sense of moral aspiration never fell into meanness or hypocrisy. He came to feel that society had treated him badly, and to some extent it did.

Harpur's biographer, James Normington-Rawling, could only speculate about the details of a considerable part of the poet's life, and little has been added since then to our knowledge of his activities.[2] It is usual to divide his life into four periods, determined by his chief place of residence: the Windsor or Hawkesbury period 1813-1830; the Sydney period 1830-1839; the Hunter River period 1839-1859; and the Euroma period 1859-1868.

He was born at Windsor on the Hawkesbury River on 23 January 1813, the third child of Sarah and Joseph Harpur, both emancipists under the enlightened governorship of Macquarie. His father was an Irishman transported for complicity in an armed robbery, but he must have been a man of some education, for at the time of Charles's birth he was schoolmaster of the Windsor Government School, and he enjoyed the patronage of the severe but energetic Samuel Marsden. In Harpur's writing, his first seventeen years are described in Wordsworthian terms as a time of happiness, hope, and inspiration, saddened only by the death of a three-year-old brother in 1825. Lack of educational opportunity was apparently not one of his early difficulties, although precisely by whom he was taught, apart

from his father, is not known. None of the four Harpur sons who survived infancy had the chance of attending the Sydney College inaugurated by R. D. Lang in 1829, or the rival Australian College, also patronised by Lang and opened in 1832, and this probably weighed against Harpur socially when he entered literary circles in Sydney in the thirties. But Harpur received a thorough grounding in grammar and composition, and had read a great deal of English literature before he came to Sydney. Possibly he obtained books from a private library. Marsden collected a large library for the use of Australian convicts while he was in England, and there is evidence that books were readily lent to those genuinely interested in them by churchmen and other benefactors. No juvenile writing by Charles remains from this time. By 1830 the family's prosperity, prestige and security were in jeopardy, and they moved to Parramatta. The sons had now to make their own way in the world, and Harpur's Sydney period began.

Normington-Rawling's research indicates some of the ways in which Charles supported himself between 1830 and 1842, and he appears to have lived most of the time in Sydney. He was employed in various capacities, for four years, as a clerk in the Post Office. This employment ended abruptly in 1839 when Harpur fell out with the Postmaster-General. Many of Harpur's later problems may have been avoided had he settled for a clerical position in the Public Service, as Halloran and later Duncan did. But although clerical work could keep him in reach of the congenial new intellectual liberal circle, and provide him with a modest living and time for writing, it is as easy to imagine the colonial-born Reuben Kable, the hero of Alexander Harris's *The Emigrant Family* (1849), sitting on Bob Cratchit's stool in Scrooge's office, as Harpur permanently tied to a clerical post in Sydney. Moreover, clerical positions were not as readily available to Harpur as they were to some, partly because of a change in the social climate of the colony. The thirties were a period of poetic activity for him, but it was also then that he acquired some bitter experience which coloured his immediate social contact and some of his later poetry.

As the son of a respected schoolmaster and parish clerk, with the friendship of churchmen like Marsden and Thomas Hassall, with brothers and sisters and other friends who treated him as an equal and even as a leader, and under the emancipist-oriented governorship of Macquarie, the young Harpur grew into a first-generation Australian, a Currency Lad, willing to doff his cap to no one simply because rank demanded it. The heavily satiric portrait of the magistrate Tunbelly's treatment of the Doorkeeper in Harpur's drama, **"Stalwart the Bushranger"**, indicates his opinion of the respect the élite demanded from native-born employees. After the governorship of Darling, the free settlers held the power in Sydney as never before, and whatever occurred politically, the Exclusionists dominated socially. Mrs Charles Meredith, a shrewd observer, described the position of the emancipist in Sydney in 1839, and remarked on the stringency with which class distinctions were maintained by free settlers.

Of course a large proportion of the population are emancipists (convicts who have served their allotted years of transportation), and their families or descendants; and a strong line of demarcation is in most instances observed between them and the free emigrants and settlers. Wealth, all-powerful though it be,—and many of these emancipists are the richest men in the colony,—cannot wholly overcome the prejudice against them, though policy, in some instances, greatly modifies it. Their want of education is an effectual barrier to many, and these so wrap themselves in the love of wealth, and the palpable, though misplaced importance it gives, that their descendants will probably improve but little on the parental model.[3]

Mrs Meredith's observation throws light on several aspects of Harpur's life and work. Although he never overtly refers to his emancipist parentage in his verse or prose, it did determine some of the limitations and possibilities of his early years in Sydney. Circumstances were better for the lawyer, politician and critic Daniel Deniehy, born in Sydney in 1828, the son of wealthy emancipist parents, educated at the Sydney College and under a private tutor in England, and widely travelled in Europe. Yet even Deniehy, who was loved and respected by many, including Harpur, died of alcoholism in 1865. The thirties were particularly inimical to the recognition of emancipists, and Harpur was a poor man who scorned to compensate for social inferiority by acquiring mercenary importance, as many others did. Harpur was not a nineteenth-century democrat, and he believed in an aristocracy of the intellect to which he felt he belonged. He scorned money and rank, but it hurt him severely that the intellectual leaders of the community, busying themselves with the affairs of the Australian Library and the Mechanics' Institute and School of Arts, could not recognise him as a member of their aristocracy. It is clear from his work that he was deeply marked by his years in Sydney. Some of this emerges from the long poem called **"The Sorrows of Chatterton"** or **"Genius Lost"**, which is ostensibly about the boy-poet Thomas Chatterton who took his own life in 1770 at the age of seventeen. Harpur supplied notes to the last version of this poem, and from these, and from the verses themselves, we have one picture of Harpur as he saw himself in his twenties.

There is enough evidence in the social history of the time to explain why an ingenuous Currency Lad with emancipist parentage would be likely to meet social embarrassment as he grew older. Yet Harpur was so determined to cast himself in the rôle of the poet that it was almost necessary for him to endure the full cycle of poetic agony. The happy, fruitful childhood fashioned in freedom and harmony with nature, and giving rise to dreams of high patriotism in the service of the Muse of Australia, was a reality. And although disillusionment during the transition from childhood to manhood is a commonplace theme of poets, the loss of economic and social security at the age of seventeen was a harsh reality for Harpur.

Harpur always gave his year of birth as 1817, although his family recorded it correctly. As his parents were not formally married until Samuel Marsden performed the ceremony in 1814, Harpur may have wanted to avoid social embarrassment. On the other hand, the ideal of the boy-genius Chatterton may have prompted Harpur to present his first work as that of a very young poet indeed. It is not easy to decide that Harpur did not to a degree, wittingly and unwittingly, give his life some elements of the legendary bardic fate. If he did, it is clear enough that life co-operated.

Harpur's personality did not make life in Sydney any easier for him. He appeared first in the public eye as a somewhat ridiculous and aggressive figure in a report published by the *Sydney Monitor* on 18 December 1833. It concerned the dismissal of a case brought by the plaintiff Harpur against the actor-manager of the Theatre Royal.

COURT OF REQUESTS THEATRICALS—

Harpur vs. *Levey*—The plaintiff sought to recover the sum of 3£. from the defendant, the Proprietor of the Theatre Royal, for services performed. The plaintiff, a soft-bearded native youth, stated, that he had engaged with Mr Levey in the mainfold characters of *Captain Arlington,* in the MUTINY OF THE NORE; *Count Friburg,* in the MILLER AND HIS MEN, & c. & c.; besides which, he was *open* to play ROMEO to any lady's JULIET; *Rigdum Funnidos,* in that very entertaining farce of CRONONHOTONTHOLOGOS; *Mr Gadabout,* in the LYING VALET; or, to transform his person into the veri similitude of any Hero that might be nominated by the Stage Manager; and all for the sum of 3£. per week, and *find his own, & c.* Mr Levey cut the thread of this harangue, by stating, that the plaintiff understood as much of theatricals as the candle snuffer's apprentice, and he had discharged him. Plaintiff insisted, that notwithstanding that he had not *taken out his degrees* at home, yet he could "tear a passion to rags" with any gentleman of the *corps.* Mr Levey was obstinate as to the plaintiff's ignorance, and added, that he blushed to own, that a disciple of Thespis should be so totally unacquainted with the etymology of his *vernicular* tongue. Plaintiff challenged Mr Levey to a trial of their prosodaical talents, which Mr Levey declined, but by way of composition, made the following proposition;—that if the plaintiff would ascend the table and recite a portion of any play, so that it should be applauded by His Honour the Commissioner and the audience, he (Mr L.) would pay the demand. Plaintiff accordingly threw himself into "attitude," amidst roars of laughter, and shouted, "Do you take me for an ass?" Mr Levey politely told him that the opera of *Midas* was in rehearsal, which would afford him an opportunity of shewing off. The Commissioner interfered, and with much difficulty brought the parties to moderation. The plaintiff produced a written agreement, and Mr Levey, in return, produced a document to show, that the plaintiff had consented to withdraw from the Theatre for one month, at the end of which time, Mr Levey was to re-engage him, provided the funds of the Establishment would admit of it.—*Case dismissed.*

There is little doubt that this is Charles Harpur at twenty years of age, so one of his first efforts to support himself in Sydney was to get a short-lived job as an actor; it is known that Levey, unfortunately, was not over-scrupulous in his treatment of his employees.

Some six months later Edward Smith Hall, the editor of the *Sydney Monitor,* published a more generous picture of Harpur as a young playwright. Under the heading "Australian Literature" Smith Hall described the appearance in his office of a "youth of an open and ingenuous countenance" who came to ask advice about publishing a tragedy in blank verse.

> Feeling quite confident that we should have to condemn the work, so far as our inferior judgment might guide us, we considered it only *charitable* to prepare the ingenuous and modest youth for the endurance of those *pangs and throes,* which a condemnation of his *maiden production* would, as of course, bring upon him; and accordingly we began in our tenderness, to inculcate the necessity for his preparing himself for disappointment, and to discourse to him with freezing kindness, on the policy of his bending in future his attention and talents (for talents we felt confident from his physiognomy he possessed) to something more substantial and profitable, than writing *blank-verse tragedies*; informing him for his comfort, that it had so happened he had, of all the paths to literary fame, chosen *the most rugged, steep, and devious.*
>
> The ingenuous youth bore our icy but parental counsel, with that modest but firm steadiness of feature, for which the young men of this extraordinary country are remarkable; so that we were vastly encouraged to pour in our cold water in *still more copious drafts*; but we at length finished our benumbing polar lecture, with a promise, that we would certainly read his play, and tell him candidly what we thought of it; and finally we invited him to call again in a few days.

The publication of extracts from **"The Tragedy of Donohoe"** in the *Sydney Monitor* in February 1835, and a small but steady flow of poems accepted by other journals, may have aggravated Harpur's natural pride beyond ordinary human bearing. Normington-Rawling suggests that Harpur clashed with the young James Martin, later Premier and Chief-Justice of New South Wales, at the inaugural meeting of the Literary and Debating Society which was held in April 1838. In July of that year, the eighteen-year-old Martin published the *Australian Sketch-Book* which castigated Harpur in a chapter on "The Pseudo-Poets" of New South Wales. The god Apollo is heard judging the efforts of four Sydney poets, including Halloran, for whom he predicts the eminent position in Australian literature that Harpur seems already to have envisaged for himself. The god's treatment of Harpur is coloured by Martin's dislike of the young poet's manner. Harpur's poor discrimination in verse-making is apparently in keeping with his churlish appearance and conduct, and he is described as a "tall, bleary-eyed, pert-looking, cocks-combish person" who "strutted boldly forth" and "walked consequentially" to the judgment seat.[4] He is allowed some possible innate genius, which is at present rough and uncouth because his mind is rude and uncultivated and his soul is destitute of the cheering rays of literature and science. He is advised to study the works of the ancients to learn the intricacies of the human heart and elevate his conception of mankind. "The vanity of this man was beyond all conception," says the narrator; and Apollo is almost offended by the arrogance with which he presents his blank-verse tragedy, "The Thieves of Attica, or the Depredation of a Robber". Apollo pronounces this drama worthy of the most unqualified contempt, a coarse and ridiculous production which he cannot contemplate without abhorrence and disgust. Martin must have had some words of Harpur in his mind when he represented him as saying, "Homer . . . had genius and fire, and Hesiod, had harmony and ease, but all these qualities, are blended in me—I have the majesty of the one, combined with the beauty of the other." Infuriating as Harpur possibly was, he received a cruel dismissal: "It has not yet been clearly ascertained, whether he followed the suggestions that were given him by Apollo, or relinquished all claims to fame, and committed suicide, to escape the jeers and mockeries of an unfeeling, a fastidious and criticizing world."

Harpur survived of course. But by the end of 1839 he had left Sydney and begun the Hunter River period of his life, undertaking a variety of jobs in the Jerry's Plains and Singleton district. It is known that he worked on his brother's property, farmed with mixed success, undertook some local government duties, and taught as a schoolmaster at Farnborough. He lost this position because he could not or would not attend the Model School in Sydney for training when the voluntarily-supported school came under the National Board. He took a prominent part in local affairs, and for a time worked industriously to change the Singleton Temperance Society into a Total Abstinence Society. This conscientious extremism is typical of Harpur's life, for he had several bouts of intemperance, although he mastered the problem in a way that his brother Joseph, Henry Kendall, Daniel Deniehy and other eminent men of the time could not. In 1843 he met Mary Doyle, the twenty-three-year-old daughter of a respected settler, and when Harpur eventually satisfied her father that he could keep her adequately, they were permitted to marry in 1850. Many poems record the vicissitudes of this long courtship, including the **"Rosa"** sonnet sequence, which is published in this edition in the final, slightly more sophisticated version called **"Nora or Records of a Poet's Love"**.

During the Hunter River period, Harpur made extended visits to Sydney, and in 1845 Duncan published Harpur's first volume of poems, ***Thoughts, A Series of Sonnets.*** Although Parkes names Harpur as one of his first acquaintances in New South Wales, they did not meet until 1844, but as the poems which passed between them before their meeting indicate, each man found much in the other to admire and each encouraged the other in his involvement in public affairs. These affairs included land reform, the struggle of Gipps with the squatters, the abolition of transportation, the composition of the Legislative Council of 1842, the treatment of Aborigines, and above all, the terms under which the Australian colonies should receive self-government by the Act of 1850, and the nature of the Constitution that would finally emerge. Harpur's work was in advising Parkes and in writing prose and verse to the many papers and journals, some of which sprang up specifically to conduct a campaign for one or another group or faction. There is little evidence that Harpur was more directly engaged in organising political opinion, and his residence in the Hunter Valley made continuous involvement impossible. Parkes remembered him and Duncan as "my chief advisers in matters of intellectual resource and enquiry."[5]

No historical account can supply the kind of record of the political struggles of the forties and fifties that is found in Harpur's verse. Without necessarily sympathising with Harpur's point of view, the reader finds that a poem, or even a mere "squib", or one of the "Bits", elaborates or neatly sums up the principles which underlay opposition to or support of a government proposal or public practice in the colony. There is, of course, additional interest in the plentiful prose notes, and the ingenious use to which Harpur could put an apparently disinterested poem like **"A Basket of Summer Fruit"** which, dedicated to "the Mammon-trapped clerks of Sydney", and printed in the *People's Advocate* for 18 March 1854, justified a lengthy comment on the fixing of land prices beyond the range of workingmen in order to keep a good supply of labour in Sydney. Yet the poems seen in isolation, as they are in this edition, show more clearly how a poet's work can create a picture of a real place and time. Much of Harpur's poetry from the Hunter River period does not have specific social origin, and these were his most productive years. Verse in general was flourishing in New South Wales, and writers other than Harpur took up the same issues and subjects. Allowing that Harpur published poems two or even three times in different journals, and the one poem in different versions, he nevertheless remains the most prolific writer of the time. Without prejudice, he may also be considered to write consistently the best verse that appeared, and his longer poems that were either not published or published only in part, are the most distinguished colonial achievements in poetry during his lifetime and for many years after.

During the fifties Harpur attempted to settle himself permanently as a grazier and farmer, and in 1855 wrote to Parkes for a loan of "£100 or £150 for two years at a reasonable rate of interest, with security" to assist him in buying up a station on the Namoi River. Parkes's refusal prompted the poem **"A Friend in Need"**, and the following letter, which is as disinterested a piece of evidence as may be cited on some aspects of Harpur's personality:

Granbelang, near Singleton. 15 March 1855

Dear Sir,

I received your letter in reply to the one in which I requested you to lend me £100 or £150; and I confess it disappointed me a good deal on several accounts—on some, indeed, quite beyond my own present need and interests. But why did I apply to you? I had lately seen your contributions in no less than sums of £50 *flung down,* as it were, at the call of objects afar off and dubious; and I naturally thought that a man to whom such sums seemed but as the loose cash and out turnings of his pockets, on the occasion of his changing his coat or

trowsers, was at least in a position to benefit an old friend with the loan of £100 or so, at a *reasonable interest and a good security*—an old friend, too, that he had assured on several occasions that he "loved him like a brother"—and who, moreover, was at that precise juncture at the very turning point of victory or disaster in a long and cruel battle with the world! But I was not thoroughly aware, it would seem, even up to the time of making that request, how little such an expression as that I have above quoted from one of your own letters,—how *little,* I say, it may mean even in the mouths of the best. You must permit one to say also, that I think it would have been in quite as good taste for you to have gone directly to your refusal, as to have beaten round about it through such an ostentatious display of your own marvellous prosperity. Yet you must not think from this expression of feeling, that I envy your worldly well doing. On the contrary I rejoice at it.

No doubt, I could raise £100 or more, by the sale of some of my property—but to have to raise it in this way just now would be almost ruinous to me. All my horses, except those I shall need for travel and daily use, are unbroken, and to sell them in this condition would be to sell them for next to nothing. Or to sell any of my sheep, they being a mixed flock and not butchers' meat, would be absolutely to give them away; while my cattle are 400 miles away, running on terms at John Doyle's station on the Barwin, and it will take a year or more before I can have them collected upon the station (200 miles distant) upon which I am endeavouring to establish myself permanently.

As to the matter of my book, the following extract from Mr Pennington, dated 25 Jan(uary) 1853, will explain to you the position in which I have conceived myself as hitherto standing with regard to the printing and publicity expenses.

"There is no news of the subscription list, but I can recollect all the parties whom I solicited, and Deniehy will be able to do the like. There is little fear of our fulfilment of our guarantee in this respect; at all events to you let not this be any farther a matter of concern. Mr Parkes has with his wonted consideration done all that was needful to ensure the publication. The rest is a matter between him and your friends and well wishers."

The letter from which I transcribe this was in reply to one of mine in which I had stated that I wished the first proceeds of the sale of the book to be applied to the covering of whatever amount the subscriptions on the whole might run short of the expense, for which I knew you would otherwise be answerable.

In the same letter Mr Pennington requested me to inform him how I wished the books to be distributed amongst the booksellers and so forth; and I immediately wrote to him detailing my wishes on that head: namely, I wished to present each of the subscribers with a copy, to send me 100 copies and to have the rest of the edition distributed amongst the Sydney Booksellers. A copy, I think, was also to be sent to the editor of each of the colonial journals.

The 100 copies to be sent to myself I got—but what was done with the rest of the edition I do not know, nor have I been able to learn up to the present time although I have written no less than three letters to Mr Pennington on the subject, to neither of which has he ever thought it worth his precious while to make any reply. But the whole matter must now be enquired into; and it will be incumbent upon all concerned in it, I think, to furnish me forthwith with a clear and straight-forward statement.

I do not know whether you will be able to read this easily; for my sight is so much impaired at a short range that I can hardly see either to read or write.

You might still do me a good office, if you will in this way. I think if you were to show my letter to Mr James Norton Sen'r (as at my request) stating your own in-ability to serve me, that he would either himself lend me the amount or procure me the loan of it, upon the terms there offered.

> I remain, dear Sir
> Your very obed't Servant
> Chas Harpur

P.S. On the other side there is a lyric at your service, if you care to accept of it for the Empire. The name upon which it is written should lift it out of the range of all of our petty and private differences.

> C. H.

The lyric accompanying this letter was the poem **"George Washington"**.

In August 1859 Harpur was made a Gold Commissioner on the fields around the Tuross River south of Sydney. His various commissions entailed moving about the Goulburn and Araluen districts, but he settled his family on a farm, which he called "Euroma", at Eurobodalla. The Euroma period began well for Harpur, who now belonged in some measure to the literary circle of Sydney centred on Nicol Drysdale Stenhouse, "Australia's first and probably only important nineteenth-century literary patron."[6] Parkes, De-niehy, Henry Kendall and W. H. Pennington were among the open admirers of Harpur's work. Harpur benefited from the use of Stenhouse's library, and Stenhouse intro-duced the poet-lecturer when he spoke on "The Nature and Offices of Poetry" at the Sydney School of Arts in September 1859. To have the respect of a cultured, kindly and influential man like Stenhouse meant much to Harpur. Yet Harpur's personal and immediate contact with the Stenhouse circle was limited by distance and lack of funds for travel. In 1862 Kendall began the correspondence which was to help the older poet with encouragement and criticism and the placing of his poems in colonial newspa-pers.

Although there is evidence that Harpur did not always please his superiors, his work on the goldfields was his most successful venture into public office and he seems to have discharged a difficult job with considerable ability. In 1866 the position was abolished, but Harpur did not let the retrenchment pass without protest, and wrote to Parkes setting out what seem cogent reasons why the post should be retained:

Euroma, via Bodalla. 3 February 1866

My dear Parkes,

I congratulate you on your having at length mounted to the "top of the tree", though, I opine, you will find that that same top of the political tree is just now no bed of roses whereupon to "repose your wearied virtue." Still you have, no doubt, right manfully "served up" to the position—and it is greatly better I suppose that a man should at any time be worn out with work (of which you will have no stint), than that he should be eaten away by the rust of any sort of idleness. Perhaps even to *die in harness,* if on a right road, would be a wise man's choice: and wisdom I think you have.

As for myself, poor-unprovided-for devil that I happen always to be, I am in no small terror just now of that diabolical Spectre to all officialdom, yclept *Reduction* albeit I believe that my particular berth is one as little deserving of abolition as any in the country—due re-gard being had to the efficiency of the Government ser-vice. It is so, in fact, on the six several grounds follow-ing: 1st. There is no other magistrate resident within a distance on all hands of 35 miles. 2nd. The nearest other Gold Field—viz Araluen—is 70 miles distant by the only practicable road. 3rd. Moruya, the head quar-ters of the Police Magistrate (as proposed in the reduc-tion scheme of the late ministry) is 35 miles distant from even Nerrijundah the trading township of the Gulph Diggings. 4th. These same Gulph Diggings, with Nerrijundah for Centre, are a congeries of separate Fields, lying some of them 15 miles apart, and extend-ing upward and laterally over 40 miles of country. 5th. All mining disputes require to be settled at once or as they arise, much more than any other kind of legal dis-putes do—all work having to be suspended pending their settlement; and they require also to be *dealt with upon the spot.* 6th. The right settlement of them re-quires also that the adjudicating magistrate should have considerable experience in the deciding and adjusting of such disputes, which are often, not only greatly, but *peculiarly* complicated.

From what is above said, it will be obvious, I think, that no Police Magistrate, stationed at Moruya, could be the Commissioner of such a scattered Gold Field as well except in *name* only—and to the wholesale ne-glect of its mining interests.

Moreover, my dear Parkes, having now the power and the opportunity, you will, I doubt not, be duly influ-enced by the spirit of the wise man's saying: "How can he get wisdom who holdeth the plough and whose talk is of bullocks? But they—the men of mind and study—"will maintain the state of the world"—will keep it from becoming a dungheap. While in proof of my be-ing the right man in the right place, need I say more than this: I have now had sole charge of the Gulph Gold Fields for a period of four years, during which time I have had to decide *some hundreds* of mining disputes—perhaps a thousand altogether;—and yet not one of these judgments of mine has ever been appealed from? What other Commissioner in the service can point to his official work as being thus characterised? Not one other of them all.

Remember Mrs Harpur and myself to Mrs Parkes and all the young folk, and believe me yours

> very truly
> Chas Harpur

Parkes, who had become Colonial-Secretary under James Martin in January 1866, apparently could not help Harpur in saving his position, and judging by Harpur's next letter, he mildly rebuked him for breaching official etiquette in making the private submission. Harpur took this well, at first, contenting himself with the subtle reproach of enclosing the "perfected" version of an earlier sonnet beginning "Dear Henry, though thy face I have not seen", in his next letter to Parkes.

Parkes was also obliged to deny Harpur's claim upon the Civil Service Superannuation Fund, and received from Harpur the following reply which, if it is a true statement of the matters it deals with, must arouse sympathy for the unhappy poet:

> Euroma, via Bodalla. 28 June 1866

My dear Sir,

I am in receipt of your favor of the 21st instant and at another time, I intend to write to you an answer to it in full—in which, I doubt not, I shall be well able to show you that the ex parte statement of volunteer informers and self-constituted spies are in no wise to be depended upon, but rather that the reports of such characters—always base to detestible—are to be ever taken with much salt: that the "freaks" you speak of as being all known in Sydney were either sheer lies, or mere minor matters of morals and manners that have been most egregiously distorted into enormities, or invidiously magnified out of all life-likeness: and with which in fact the Government had properly nothing to do.

But in the present note I intend to touch upon nothing but the superannuation Fund. You sue that I have no claim upon that Fund. Why, when a common constable is turned adrift, he is allowed a month's pay for every year of service. And such was the rule, I believe, throughout the whole civil service previous to the passing of the Superannuation Act, which was to make all officialdom more easy in mind as to the future, and which to that end has exacted from me monthly ever since it came into operation the sum of £1-3/4. For what, as it turns out? To provide a comfortable retiring allowance for a few favored old fogies some twenty years hence—and who, all of them, will, until then, have been comfortably lapped—not in superannuation lavender, but in what is nearly as good—big and constant pay: not a mere pittance which at a dear outpost was barely a living! This surely is not just. And I think Mr Martin (being a logical lawyer) will at once see that it is not.

> I remain, dear Sir,
> Yours very truly
> Chas Harpur

P.S. As this is the last letter but *one* which it is likely I shall ever write to you, perhaps you will do me the favor of answering it.

> C. H.

On 1 July 1866 Harpur shrugged off the business as far as he could, and scribbled the date and the following lines:

> This day I've lost my office, and again am a free man,
> With the wide world for my oister, which I'll open if I can.

But in a letter to Kendall a few days later, he again repudiated the importance of his "freaks" of conduct with which no manly government would condescend to become acquainted, and berated Parkes for having perpetrated dishonesties that would have hanged a less subtle man—perhaps a reference to the shifts to which Parkes resorted in the late fifties when the *Empire* was declared insolvent. Harpur received some monetary compensation for his loss of office, but he lived barely two years in retirement, harassed by bad seasons, ill health and much bitterness and uneasiness about the reception of his life's work. Finally, the shock of the death of his second son Charles, aged thirteen, who died in a shooting accident in March 1867, and the effect of a hard winter, hastened his death by consumption on 9 June 1868.

The few letters cited here, and the following volume of poetry, show the worst and best of Harpur as man and poet. It is as a poet that he matters now, and since little clear evidence was brought forward in his lifetime or later as to how morally serious his misconduct was, it was probably more uncomfortable for those who knew him than harmful to his family or the community. In summary, Harpur's life is not a prepossessing tale, but in spite of everything, there was a certain quality about the way he lived.

How he actually lived is more obvious in his minor verse than in his best work. Whether he was describing "the grinning self-contempt" of the "votary of the bowl", as in **"The Drunkard"**, or recounting in ballad form a tale of barbarity against an Australian native, as in **"The Spectre of the Cattle Flat"**, or writing in praise of the Maori leader Hone Heke, or complimenting his friend W. A. Duncan in verse, or abusing the same friend for his attitude towards the Constitution of 1855, or dedicating a volume of poems to Wordsworth, there is always present an unmistakable dignity. It is the dignity of a basically puritan soul, of a free man, the dignity of a man like Thoreau. It is, in fact, a colonial dignity. Yet it is also the dignity of a man consciously dedicated to a high and solemn office. When Harpur's work is considered against the background of his place and time, one recognises in it that "high seriousness" of the nineteenth century, which, though it may sometimes be ridiculed, cannot be derided.

II

Many of Harpur's poems are already known to the public, and have been discussed in various contexts by critics and historians. A selected Bibliography of comments and reviews of his work appearing since his death is supplied, and a list of some nineteenth-century journals relevant to a study of his life and writing.

The greater number of poems and verses will be new to most readers, and of these very few will not be disappointing, simply because they achieve so much yet fail to give absolute poetic pleasure. The greatest general defect of Harpur's poetry is its self-consciousness which too often turns seriousness to solemnity, inspiration to exhortation, pain to melodrama, and delight to didacticism. A too conscious and conscientious concern with transmitting an inherited poetic and interpreting a new life and land in the terms of that poetic, is responsible for the formal diction and pedanticism that affect almost all his work. The damage is greatest to those poems describing the poet's response to nature, because such poems take their life from the freshness and immediacy with which the response is conveyed. Harpur's nature poems live chiefly by the intensity of his feelings, which even his self-conscious formality does not conceal.

Harpur believed he was innovative and original to the limits of poetic freedom, but his passionate respect for the tradition of the best English poetry circumscribed his creativity in form and technique. He would have shown a more truly creative genius had he produced poetry in which form and tone were more closely related to the milieu in which it was written, or to the ruggedness of his own mind.

Ratiocinative and philosophical poems are also affected by the Miltonic and neoclassical decorum of diction and sentence structures. His ideas were contemporary and often in advance of his time. He was not only taught by English and American liberal thinkers but had the chance independently to develop ideas similar to theirs, and his pleasure, even exultation, in recognising that there were others who thought as he did, is often apparent. Yet although the poetic styles of Whitman, or Clough, appear to keep pace with the new cast of their ideas, Harpur's style is as anachronistic to his nineteenth-century political and religious liberalism as it is to the physical landscape of his Australian environment.

The new expression we seem to ask of Harpur need not have been as radical a departure from earlier modes as that made by Whitman in the 1855 edition of *Leaves of Grass,* but a comparison between poems by Harpur and by Whitman shows up another reason for our dissatisfaction with Harpur's work. Harpur was determined to teach. When his poem **"A Coast View"**, first written in the late fifties, is set beside Whitman's "On the Beach at Night Alone" (1856) and "The World Below the Brine" (1860), the comparison shows how Harpur's didactic intentions affect what is technically a competent poem.

The blank verse of the poem is not at fault—it is structurally accurate and conveys meaning with enough clarity—and it adds dignity to the description and intensifies the significance of the poet's statement. The tone of the poem is distinctly Harpurian. That is to say, the expression is rhetorical, employing compound and sometimes unusual epithets and qualifying and modifying phrases, the mood is serious, and the purpose clearly instructive.

The seascape comes into focus with surprising clarity, considering that Harpur gives as much generalised description as particular detail. The poem then goes beyond evocative description to indicate that such a scene has a wider relevance for the spirit of man. The landscape and its inhabitants are placed in the context of homage to the creator of this beauty. The exclamation

> yet, O God!
> What a blind fate-like mightiness lies coiled
> In slumber, under that wide-shining face!

occurring early in the poem, counters what would otherwise be a general pantheism with a definite concept of a creative deity. This doctrine is well assimilated within the poem and establishes its philosophical basis. If this is achieved deftly and poetically, what makes the poem fail as a whole?

The overt didacticism of the poet is the chief single weakness of the poem. A preoccupation with instruction has become the overriding concern of Harpur's intellect and emotional energies, and his imagination and instinct no longer have free play. Scrupulous observation, precise and delicate narration, and the most careful relating of physical detail to the forces of the spiritual world, cannot overcome the deadening effect of his need to teach. The poem does not exist in its own right, but as a means of instruction. Neither the scene nor the poet's response is allowed to speak for itself. The poet as teacher is fighting the poet as poet, and the latter loses.

The lesson set out in the close of the poem is derived from Wordsworth, but is also a genuine part of Harpur's experience of nature:

> How nourishing is Nature to the soul
> That loves her well!

In a didactic poem the lesson is not out of place, since a didactic poem purports to be nothing more than a well-penned piece of sermonising in verse. But Harpur intended **"A Coast View"** to be more than sermonising in competent blank verse, and its rhetoric and emotional energy show that it aimed at the sublime.

A poem such as this indicates how the weaknesses of any school or style are magnified in the work of a minor follower, and the weaknesses of romanticism are apparent in Harpur's search for similes to link the natural to the spiritual world. It is seen by comparison how skilfully and how narrowly Wordsworth and Coleridge avoided falling into the stance of an uninspiring lecturer on the appreciation of nature. Harpur does not always avoid this danger. The guiding finger directs the reader to look where Harpur is looking. The reader's imaginative eye dares not wander at all, and finally lapses into sullen blankness. The looser rhetoric of Byron's address to the deep and dark blue ocean encourages an imaginative response which all Harpur's precision fails to arouse.

In the first stanza, the simile of "a lover's dream" sits uncomfortably with the careful mapping of the contours and limits of sky and horizon, but the movement of cloud, in Harpur's recurrent image of expansion and massing, is pleasingly carried from the first into the second stanza. The reader is about to move with the poem when Harpur commands him to withdraw his eye from heaven to behold the wonders of the coast. The injunction, "Withdrawing now the eye from heaven, behold . . ." betrays the poet's relentless control of the reader, whereas it is the poem that should hold, not the poet.

In the description of the cliff formations, the idea of an exotic architecture is extended with similes of Assyrian arches and Babylonian buttresses. This is an inventive use of the Gothic tradition and the passage evokes both the wild, eroded coastline and the crumbling ruins of Gothic landscapes. The weird and rugged Australian coast is thus tamed and assimilated by an acceptable aesthetic convention.

The poet next shows that this rude prospect lies under the cherishing care of creative forces: "Yet even mid these rugged forms the warm / And gentle ministry of Spring . . ." Nevertheless, the minuteness of Harpur's observation is negated by a stultified phrase applied to the seabirds. Some odd sense of decorum, or perhaps a tendency to generalise a concept, or more possibly an echo from Milton, prompts Harpur to juxtapose a lyric phrase like "silver pinioned wanderer in the winds" with the ponderous euphemism of "conjugal convention" to describe the birds' mating.

The sentiment of the final lines is not Wordsworth's, but is taken from an essay by Emerson:[7]

> Nay, even a scanty vine,
> Trailing along some backyard wall, shall speak
> Love's first green language; and (so cheap is truth)
> A bucket of clear water from the well
> Be in its homely brightness beautiful.

Harpur seems to be indicating an Emersonian cyclic pattern in nature, and in art as represented by his own poem, because here he draws a unifying comparison between the measureless expanse of ocean with which the poem begins, and the bucket of well-water with which it ends.

In theory, it is easy to sympathise with Harpur's self-conscious colonial pride in his attempt to show that Australian scenery offers as many lessons as any region in Europe. But the poem, with its promise and half-achievement, could not survive his self-consciousness.

Whitman was also a teacher, but he had almost two centuries of American poetry behind him to Harpur's bare half-century of Australian verse, and Whitman was not self-consciously singing a traditional aesthetic in a new land. "On the Beach at Night Alone" and "The World Below the Brine" use chiefly Whitman recitative, and cataloguing or lists, derived from Emerson's prose technique and the He-braic psalms and poetic books of the Old Testament. As the medieval poems of St Francis of Assisi, and those of the eighteenth-century Christopher Smart, for example, take the same form, it cannot be said that Whitman is writing a completely new kind of verse:

> Sluggish existences grazing there suspended, or slowly
>   crawling close to the bottom,
> The sperm-whale at the surface blowing air and spray,
>   or disporting with his flukes,
> The leaden-eyed shark, the walrus, the turtle, the hairy
>   sea-leopard, and the sting-ray,
> Passions there, wars, pursuits, tribes, sight in those
>   ocean-depths, breathing that thick-breathing air, as
>   so many do,
> The change thence to the sight here, and to the subtle
>   air breathed by beings like us who walk this sphere,
> The change onward from ours to that of beings who
>   walk other spheres.

(from "The World Below the Brine")

Both poems are didactic, in that description leads to a statement of Whitman's Emersonian belief in the mystical unity of all life. The myriad forms, from the inhabitants of the sea floor, through ocean, air and other spheres, to angelic or spiritual ways of being, are set out as progressive, evolutionary manifestations of the one all-embracing soul. The poems celebrate the enormous variety of the forms and the awesome concept of their unity. The ideas and the mood of Whitman's poems are similar to those of Harpur's **"A Coast View"**, but Whitman stands outside his poems and lets them create their own wonder and instruction:

> As I watch the bright stars shining, I think a thought
>   of the clef of the universes and of the future.
> A vast similitude interlocks all,
> All spheres, grown, ungrown, small, large, suns,
>   moons, planets,
> All distances of place however wide,
> All distances of time, all inanimate forms,
> All souls, all living bodies though they be ever so dif-
>   ferent, or in different worlds,
> All gaseous, watery, vegetable, mineral processes, the
>   fishes, the brutes, . . .
> This vast similitude spans them, and always has
>   spann'd,
> And shall forever span them and compactly hold and
>   enclose them.

(from "On the Beach at Night Alone")

Although recitative is not necessarily more spontaneous than blank verse, Whitman's verse is more vital than Harpur's, and not only because the poems are shorter. "On the Beach at Night Alone" is in sonnet form, but its force is in its compact unity, not in its brevity. This lyric, which is one of the "clef" poems with which Whitman hoped to unlock the mystery of the universe, was originally a much longer poem. Whitman compressed the poem, whereas Harpur invariably lengthened any poem he revised, and his additions are usually explanations and elaborations. Whitman's two poems simply describe and state. The economy of his means and intention achieves a new, fresh poetry that is found only rarely in Harpur's work.

A number of poems of varying reach and depth transcend Harpur's didacticism and life beyond the attack of the criticism directed at **"A Coast View"**. The reader will find sonnets that are almost perfect in their kind, and **"A Mid-Summer Noon in the Australian Forest"**, **"A Rural Picture"**, **"A Musical Reminiscence"**, **"The Bower by Moonlight"**, **"Monodies II"**, **"To a Comet"**, **"The Silence of Faith"**, **"The Babylonian Captivity"** (a paraphrase of Psalm 137), and **"To an Echo on the Banks of the Hunter"**, are among the shorter pieces which move the reader by their achievement, not only within a particular genre, but as poetry, pure and simple.

The best known longer poems, like **"The Creek of the Four Graves"**, **"The Glen of the Whiteman's Grave"**, **"A Storm in the Mountains"** and **"The Kangaroo Hunt"** have already prompted many responses from direct literary criticism to Judith Wright's poem "Extinct Birds" and Robert Dixon's analysis of the scientific accuracy of the prose notes to **"The Kangaroo Hunt"**. The references to flora and fauna within the poem, and the prose notes, included in this edition, led Dixon to the conclusion:

> Although there appears to be no direct evidence that Harpur had read Gould's books, it is not unlikely that during the twenty years he spent revising **"The Kangaroo Hunt"** his interests would have led him to seek out the latest publications of the celebrated ornithologist. His reading was probably more casual than systematic, yet the ornithological and zoological embellishments of the poem reveal a mind surprisingly well attuned to the spirit of the new scientific approach to the study of ornithology. Like other literary figures of the nineteenth century whose interests also embraced natural history, Harpur's accomplishments as a scientific observer were by no means inconsiderable, even when measured against the work of a professional like John Gould.[8]

"The Kangaroo Hunt", like several other longer poems, is *interesting* poetically for what it attempts, but it does not provide much aesthetic satisfaction. It is a pastoral poem, with an epigraph from the work of the puritan poet satirist George Wither, whose five partly allegorical pastorals were written under the title of *The Shepherd's Hunting* (1614). If Harpur had studied Wither closely, the seventeenth-century poet's sardonic self-sufficiency and resolute independence probably pleased him. Wither was imprisoned on several occasions under James I, and found much consolation in poetry, and the lines from his fourth eclogue are an apt epigraph for a poem by Harpur. Harpur explains the aesthetic conventions of the poem in his preface, and it may be argued that it is irrelevant for a literary critic to approach the work on any grounds other than those Harpur has given.

Other longer poems printed here for the first time since Harpur's death, and some which have not been printed before, also must be met on their own terms. If the pleasure the reader finds in exploring poems like **"The Slave's Story"**, **"Genius Lost"**, **"The Olden Warrior"**, **"The Tower of the Dream"** and **"The Witch of Hebron"** is not purely the pleasure derived from poetry, it is nevertheless a lively one. The longer satires like **"The Scamper of Life"**, **"The Temple of Infamy"** and **"Castle Carnal"** show how well Harpur understood the techniques of Dryden, Pope, Byron, and the Shelley of "The Triumph of Life". Deprived of the prose notes, the poems must stand by themselves as satire on human folly, and their interest may therefore be diminished as is the interest of "Absalom and Achitophel" under the same conditions. Harpur's criticism in verse, **"The 'Nevers' of Poetry"** and **"Poetical Studies"**, here printed without the accompanying prose, show Harpur to be a shrewd and acute evaluator and a sensitive admirer of poetry. The reader will only wish Harpur had followed more closely his own prescriptions and admonitions, and yet it will be admitted that in all Harpur's satiric work the dexterity of his verse is remarkable.

This edition includes a sampling of Harpur's translations and paraphrases, omitting only some of the renditions of Homer and some paraphrases of the psalms. References will be found in the Bibliography to articles speculating on Harpur's little Latin and less Greek, and it is reasonably certain now that he probably knew Latin and Greek "roots" well enough to use English words with subtlety, but that his translations from the "Iliad" were actually adaptations of Cowper's translation, which Stenhouse had in his library. It is also unlikely that Harpur read German, and his **"Imitations from the German"** are paraphrases of poems he had read in translation. **"The Dream by the Fountain"** borrows, without acknowledgement, a fair amount from Goethe's "Zueignung", but Harpur normally acknowledges his adaptations somewhere in the different versions of the manuscripts. A review of Sir Edward Bulwer Lytton's translation of *The Poems and Ballads of Schiller* (Edinburgh 1844) in the *Atlas* of 21 December 1844 quoted "Thekla" from *Wallenstein* in both Bulwer Lytton's and Coleridge's versions; and also a translation of Schiller's "Ideals", made by "C. N.", an Australian Colonist. The review probably suggested Harpur's **"Thekla's Song"**, which he included later in *Poems in Early Life,* and the passionate outburst called **"To the Spirit of Poesie"**, which borrows from Schiller's "Ideals".

Harpur wrote quite a handful of trivia, sometimes rewriting very slight, tediously skittish or romantic verses with more care than the subject or treatment warrants. An editor sees some point in James Martin's criticism in the *Australian Sketch-Book* of the rubbishy lovers' complaints that appeared in Sydney newspapers in the thirties. Yet not very many of Harpur's pieces are utterly worthless, and many slight poems which were intended as words for music seem quite suitable for the purpose. His first published poem, printed here under the title **"Australia Huzza"**, and a nostalgic lyric, **"Old Billowy Hawksb'ry"**, appear in one manuscript as **"Two National Songs to the Same Measure"**. They may be sung to the tune of "The Ash-Grove", as may several other of his songs and lyrics. A number of exhortatory songs for various causes are found in this collection, and Harpur was upset that Isaac Nathan, who had written settings for Byron's Hebrew Melodies before he came to Sydney, did not see fit to put any of Harpur's pieces to music.

The compendium of small verses that Harpur published under various headings, and rewrote in different sequences in the manuscripts, are collected together here in the form of one hundred and forty-five Bits, an extension of Harpur's original collection under that title. Some are morally tendentious, but the majority are often politically apt, neatly epigrammatic, and even witty, and a few are even mildly scurrilous, reminding the reader of Juvenal or Petronius.

Two of the little known longer poems are of special interest—**"Genius Lost"** because it is as much about Harpur as about Thomas Chatterton, and because its form is as operatic as that of Shelley's "Prometheus Unbound"; and **"The Witch of Hebron"**, because it is the last poem Harpur began, and its strange and powerful narrative is written with great fluency. Harpur was writing his dramatic monologue, **"Genius Lost"** or **"The Sorrows of Chatterton"** at the same time as Alfred de Vigny in Paris was presenting his melodrama, *Chatterton*. Harpur says he began **"The Sorrows"** in 1836, and de Vigny's play was first presented at La Comédie Francaise in 1835, but whether or not Harpur had read about the French play is not known. To treat creatively the story of Chatterton seems to have had cathartic value for both the aristocratically minded Frenchman and the republican Australian, and Maurice Shroder's comment about de Vigny's *Chatterton* applies equally well to Harpur's figures of the boy-poet.

> . . . for Chatterton subsumes more than the character of the lamentable dying poet. He contains as well the qualities of the martyred genius, the poet who seems to be expiating in suffering the superior nature he has received from God. When the Quaker reproaches him for being too good, too pure, Chatterton replies, '. . . I have made up my mind not to disguise myself, and to be myself to the very end, always to listen to my heart, whether it speaks in compassion or in indignation, to resign myself to fulfilling the law of my being'. He is a man of feeling, unable to staunch the flow of his emotions; he is a man of imagination as well, and he can no more deny his dreams than he can the voice of his heart: '. . . I have never been able to curb the tumultuous overflowing of my soul in straight and narrow canals. It has always flooded its banks, in spite of me.' And, in line with the Romantic ethic, Chatterton knows that his gifts are a curse. The Quaker need not point out that 'imagination and introversion are two diseases that no one pities'; Chatterton himself calls his poetic genius 'the fatal enemy born with me, the bad fairy which was surely with me in the cradle'. He feels, as did all the fatal heroes from René to Manfred, the weight of impending doom: he cannot rid himself of his superior nature, he must accept the destiny of martyrdom that is necessarily his.[9]

Whoever reads sympathetically and critically through Harpur's collected poems will realise how closely he himself fits the portrait drawn by Shroder, and yet his aesthetic is also neoclassical, and his ethical principles loftily puritan. Strangely as this second-generation romanticism consorts with the Miltonic concept of the divine poet, with the Augustan satirist, or with Gray's meditative scholar or frenzied bard, they are all found in Harpur's concept of the poet—the poet as Chatterton and the poet as Charles Harpur.

"Genius Lost" relies to some extent on Wordsworth's descriptions of his boyhood and on Shelley's "Queen Mab" and "Prometheus Unbound", and the hero has a Promethean passion for reforming the world through the influence of the exquisite beauty of his thought and poetry. The poem was apparently intended to contain ten monologues, but the eighth monologue and the opening lines of the tenth section are missing in the final manuscript. Without making any alterations, this edition prints the work as a connected piece. Each section presents a fairly compact narration, description and argument, and is followed by a Chorus of the Hours and sometimes a Semi-Chorus. It is clear from this and other longer poems, that Harpur had considerable architectonic skill.

The argument of **"Genius Lost"** is not tightly structured, however, and tends to be very repetitive of the brilliant hopes of youth, the cruelty of the present, the loss of Love, Faith and Hope, and despite all these, the eventual coming of a new age. It is difficult to see precisely what has brought about Chatterton's death, although certainly society is largely responsible, and perhaps the effects of a Beatrice and Dante experience of love.

The forging of the Rowley manuscripts is briefly alluded to, but Harpur's poem does not suggest (as de Vigny's play does) that the disgrace attendant upon the exposure of the "forgeries" has anything to do with the poet's death. Rather Harpur goes to the heart of the matter and seems to suggest that loneliness and despair are the causes of Chatterton's suicide. Nevertheless it is the coldness and bad faith of the world that give rise to loneliness and despair. Tedious as much of the introspective complaints of Chatterton are, they carry enough realism to justify Harpur's claim that he has written "a Psychological Poem". In the postscript he says:

> In the design of the Poem, the monologues are a psychological, step by step development of the lonely conceptions and peculiar sufferings that are but too surely leading such a wild and unfriended, though noble nature, to a disastrous, self-inflicted end; while the Chorusses annexed to them, are spiritual cognitions of these peculiar moods and sufferings—but raised and illumined throughout by prophecies of a general good in predestined reservation, and thence, by inference, of a better era for the lowly born children of Genius: and moreover, they are pointed and *practicalised,* as it were, by frequent suggestions of such intellectual efforts and means as might be conducive to the speedier advent of such a desirable era.

Finally he adds "a few words having a self-reference":

> It is for the reader to determine how far, and in what way, he may be affected by this Poem; but to me its author, I can most truly affirm, it has been an exceed-

ing benefit. It proved the occasion—undesigned indeed—of the purging away of much 'perilous stuff' that weighed upon my heart and life up to, and during, the period of its composition . . . And moreover, its composition became to me the means (especially the Chorusses) of balancing the account of suffering—whether *real,* as affecting myself, or *imaginary,* as attributed to Chatterton—with instinctive prophecies of that sure, though distant reversion, which is for ever taking a wider hold upon the distance of the human race, through the self devotion and recorded thoughts and experience of its more gifted individuals.

The figure of the poet that emerges from **"Genius Lost"** is humanly frail, but possessed of a spirit that transcends its human frailties and acts as a catalyst for all that is divine, beautiful, ennobling and enriching within the universe. Something of this radiant vision surrounded Harpur throughout his awkward colonial existence and his own all too human encounter with life.

"The Witch of Hebron" shows in every way that it was written much later than **"Genius Lost"**: a short version is dated 1863 and the longer poem bears the inscription, "Composed 1868". Harpur may have read a good deal of Southey and Byron, and even William Beckford's "Vathek", as well as De Quincey's "The Daughter of Lebanon" before he began **"The Witch of Hebron"**, because his poem is thoroughly saturated with the mood and trappings of the oriental Gothic. There is also something distinctly Harpurian about the tone and texture of the poem, and his social and moral preoccupations are assimilated with some success into the exotic tale. What is unexpected is a tone of detached irony in Part VI of the poem, and it is this section that reminds the reader of some of the incidents and settings in "Vathek".

"The Witch of Hebron" tells the story of the transmigration of a soul through five different lives, transmigration being a concept that illustrates perfectly an idea Harpur was fond of, the notion that "soul is form". The resemblance to De Quincey's prose tale is not great, but there is sufficient similarity to make it likely that Harpur had let his own creative talent re-work the story of the beautiful daughter of Lebanon who, lying in fever and near to death, tells her story and her repentance to a rabbi, and is granted at death her wish to be reunited with her twin sister in the house of her father. De Quincey's story is studiously Christianised. Harpur's story is Hebraic, and concludes with an open metaphysical speculation:

> Only a pool
> Gleamed flat before him, where it seemed erewhile
> The splendid Structure had adorned the view!
> Perplexed in mind, the Rabbi turned again
> And hurried homeward, muttering as he went:
> 'Was it a Vision? Can these marvels be?
> But what indeed are all things, even those
> That seem most solid—Dust and Air at last!'

The mysticism involved in this poem is interesting, for it is seen that the *one* soul retains its identity through all five transmigrations. This indeed is the horror of its punishment. Nevertheless the *quality* of this soul alters, so that in another sense there are five souls represented in the story—the soul of the stricken lady with whom the poem begins and ends; the soul of the Machiavellian, evil Egyptian of the court of the Ptolemies of five hundred years before; the bestial soul of the lion into which he is transformed at death; the soul of the eagle which is raised one degree higher, and indeed shows something of nobility, a fact which hardly surprises Harpur's readers; and the soul of the Circassian maiden sold to the Persian court. And yet these five transmigrations represent not change of soul, perhaps, but changes of *personality* through which each personality remembers its state in former existences. If this poem seriously represents Harpur's metaphysical belief about the soul it could explain to some extent the reason for his insistence on the individuality of the soul which does not evolve, and yet may change and remain in motion. The theory is not clear in detail, but as a concept it compels interest.

As in Harpur's other pieces about human evil and retribution, the psychological interest is convincing. The cruel and ambitious Egyptian who speaks through the lady's person in Part II of the poem is another typical Gothic hero, proud, revengeful, embittered, and utterly unscrupulous. He has no history of social mistreatment, however, to explain his evil conduct, and when confronted by the fiend Sammael in the desert, he willingly sells his soul for one hundred years of power. Part III begins with his return to the scene of his earlier power and downfall: "Out of the Desert—I returned to Egypt", he continues, and perhaps Harpur was aware of the literary irony behind the reversal of the tradition that holds that the desert experience is symbolic of spiritual chastening and repentance. In Egypt the young man, restored to extraordinary beauty, beats down his enemies and mounts almost to the throne of Ptolemy himself. Harpur paints a vivid picture of the viciousness and decadence of the Egyptian court, against which the crimes of the damned man at least assume a *magnificence* of evil. The implication here is that such evil as his is only possible where society itself is weak and corrupt.

> And yet, behold,
> The more I trampled on mankind, the more
> Did fawning flatterers throng me as I swept
> On set days of processional display,
> Like a malignant meteor through the Land!
> The more I hurled the mighty from their seats,
> And triumphed o'er them, prostrate in the dust,
> The human hounds that licked my master hand
> But multiplied the more!

Harpur's poetry is a constant search for examples of human greatness and nobility, and the force with which he draws pictures of evil, corruption and meanness shows that his preoccupation with good and evil was no mere literary or social convention. **"The Witch of Hebron"** fittingly culminates his work. It is perhaps the most detached of all his poems, yet its vigour and conviction are sometimes overwhelming. It deals with love, hate, beauty, space, time, good, evil, luxury and deprivation—all those things which fascinated the eager, reflective, ascetic and sensuous soul of the poet. And yet in the reader's memory, the narrator's voice holds a trace of Chaucerian irony, as though Harpur, whose spiritual vision was accustomed to eternity, had at last begun to see the affairs of men in the same perspective.

It may be left to living poets to deny that Harpur has had any influence on Australian poetry. He certainly had imitators in his own generation, but since his poetry has been almost inaccessible for more than a century his later influence could not possibly be great. It is his spirit, rather than his practice, that may inspire other writers. Historians of Australia's social development have found him representative rather than influential. The distinction is a fine one, and it was suggested earlier that even if his lasting social and political influence is intangible, his poetry is the unique expression of certain cultural forces that have contributed to Australian society. Parkes called him "one of the most genuine of Australian poets", and when one turns the pages of the collected poems, the phrase is seen to confer a certain distinction both on Harpur and on colonial Australia.

Notes

1. Henry Parkes, *Fifty Years in the Making of Australian History* (London: Longmans, Green, 1892), p. 16.

2. J. Normington-Rawling, *Charles Harpur, An Australian* (Sydney: Angus and Robertson, 1962).

3. Mrs Charles Meredith, *Notes and Sketches in New South Wales, during a residence in that colony from 1839 to 1844* (London: Murray, 1844), pp. 50-51.

4. James Martin, *Australian Sketch-Book* (Sydney: James Tegg, 1838), p. 169.

5. Parkes, p. 8.

6. Anne-Mari Jordens, *The Stenhouse Circle. Literary Life in Mid-Nineteenth Century Sydney* (Melbourne: Melbourne University Press, 1979), p. 1.

7. See, for example, Emerson's essay "Nature" in *Essays* (Second Series), 1844.

. . . Cities give not the human sense room enough. We go out daily and nightly to feed the eyes on the horizon, and require so much scope, just as we need water for our bath. There are all degrees of natural influence, from those quarantine powers of nature up to her dearest and gravest ministrations to the imagination and the soul. There is the bucket of cold water from the spring, the wood-fire to which the chilled traveller rushes for safety—and there is the sublime moral of autumn and of noon.

Harpur's copy of Emerson's *Eight Essays* in a London edition of 1852, which includes the essay quoted from, is held in the Mitchell Library.

8. Robert Dixon, "Charles Harpur and John Gould", *Southerly,* No. 3 (1980), p. 328.

9. Maurice Z. Shroder, *Icarus, The Image of the Artist in French Romanticism* (Massachusetts: Harvard University Press, 1961), p. 136.

M. Ackland (essay date 1988)

SOURCE: Ackland, M. "Innocence at Risk: Charles Harpur's Adaptation of a Romantic Archetype to the Australian Landscape." *Journal of the Australasian Universities Language and Literature Association* 70 (November 1988): 239-59.

[*In the following essay, Ackland demonstrates Harpur's linking of the possibility of redemption for man with the relatively untouched Australian landscape.*]

Charles Harpur, it is now agreed, is a poet of ideas, but the precise nature of his thought remains largely unexplored. Repeatedly his works express faith in a suffusing Divinity, and the related recognition that trust in a Providential presence demands a corresponding advocacy of 'the capacity of human nature for good' (**'Have Faith'**, A92).[1] Yet these major tenets of his thought, taken in isolation, provide no clear understanding of why an avowed 'Settler's tale', such as **'The Creek of the Four Graves'**, should contain scenes of violent death and a plaint on man's primal disobedience:

> O God! and thus this lovely world hath been
> Accursed for ever by the bloody deeds
> Of its prime Creature—Man. Erring or wise,
> Savage or civilised, still hath he made
> This glorious residence, the Earth, a Hell
> Of wrong and robbery and untimely death!
> Some dread Intelligence opposed to Good
> Did, or a surety, over all the earth
> Spread out from Eden—or it were not so!
>
> (pp. 171-72)

In what follows, I wish to demonstrate the centrality of these inherited ideas to Harpur's self-professed mission as 'the bard of thy country'. For this vision of existence as a struggle between death-affiliated forces and God's benevolent influence is related to the poet's preoccupation with how man would shape the largely untouched landscape of *terra australis*. Was he irredeemably fallen, or could a terrestrial paradise, free from the Old World's failings, be restored through the generous, loving acts of mankind? What forces would oppose this Edenic rebirth, and to what extent would we need to revise our socially-sanctioned notions of rights and duties, or material success and spiritual failure? Harpur sought to offer answers to these pressing issues; and his poetry reveals many instances of the familiar Romantic motif of innocence betrayed or at risk, adapted to meet the demands and conditions of the newly-founded colony.

In Harpur's works, God's beneficent intention is never at issue, though man is portrayed as having the ability to 'mar its just design' (**'Providential Design'**, p. 565). To the poet's eye creation offers constant indices of an 'ultimately perfect Plan'. It is evident each day in the arising sun's radiant majesty, when God re-enacts His founding creation of order from chaos, and confirms His promise that regenerative light will triumph over the forces of darkness. Similarly, it appears in each new human being who represents a birth of unspoilt Edenic innocence, a spring-time potential which, as in the beginning, may make or unmake his natural and human surroundings. Nevertheless, man's propensity to sin is not underplayed. Harpur's measured and characteristic view is summarised in 'Eden Lost', where he asserts that stars, sun, moon, birds and beasts

> Are loyal to their mould as on
>   Creation's earliest day.
> 'Tis Man alone—dishonest Man,
>   Who schemes a plan
> Excluding brotherhood!
> He only, with disnatured mind,
> Becomes the Tyrant of his kind:
>   He! in his lordly mood.
>
>   (p. 406)

To explain man's fall away from nature into sin thus becomes a major concern, as well as to lead his audience beyond the labyrinth of recurrent erring towards paradisiacal possibilities under the southern cross. To this end his works focus on a diverse range of violent deeds which repeat primal error, and each of which has a specific bearing on Australian experience. In **'The Slave's Story'** and **'The Spectre of the Cattle Flat'**, for example, encounters between blacks and whites serve to direct the reader towards values which transcend the accepted dichotomies of 'Erring or wise, / Savage or civilised'; while in other poems, such as **'The Murder of the Lamb'** and **'The Glen of the Whiteman's Grave'**, Harpur examines the growth of error and the potential for its eclipse in God's 'prime Creature—Man'. In all these works, as we shall see, the dictates of mercy gradually supplant those of retribution.[2] The uncomprehending Cain-like actions of an ostensibly Christian world are exposed, the source of man's 'bloody deeds' is explored, and a way pointed back to the garden landscape through Christ-like acts based on charity, forgiveness, and selfless love triumphant.

The poet's preoccupation with man as the battleground of opposing instincts, and his related advocacy of inner reform, are well illustrated by **'The Slave's Story'** and **'The Spectre of the Cattle Flat'**. Here, too, characteristic attempts are made to involve the reader in moral and spiritual judgments; while the interaction of blacks and whites is used to undermine the presumed superiority conferred on Europeans by their enlightened religion and advanced civilization. Harpur's blacks, at worst, are no more savage than their white foes and, at best, exhibit a natural gentility and charitable disposition long abrogated in the whites by the gross material dictates of their society. **'The Slave's Story'**, for instance, tells how a happy 'Indian' family extends generous hospitality to a forlorn whiteman. Their guest, however, proves to be the pitiless captain of a slave-ship, who is fated not only to act inhumanely towards blacks, but also to slaughter his fellows and himself on a subsequent voyage. A parable constructed around absolute contrasts, the poem counterbalances a vision of European man *in extremis* with the incorruptible good instilled in nature's child. The captain is raised among pirates and knows no spiritualizing influence. Steeped in evil, his life becomes increasingly violent until it is terminated by hunger in the midst of tropical plenty. The black, in contrast, is nurtured solely on the bosom of unspoilt nature; and is still capable of disinterested acts of charity even after the dehumanizing experience of slavery. As a free man, the measure of his bounty was his final thought before going to bed of how he would furnish his guest with provisions next day to spare him the ordeals of thirst and hunger in the 'desert track'. This same generosity of spirit remains unbroken, as is seen in his concluding benediction to the passing traveller. A tale which inverts inherited cultural categories, and compels us to 'read black' where narrow sectarian interest usually perceives white, **'The Slave's Story'** demonstrates the repeated moral of Harpur's treatment of the innocence at risk theme: that brotherhood can and must be recognized, or man will ultimately sink to the self-destructive level of a maddened beast. Man's savage deeds are the poet's abhorrence, irrespective of whether their perpetrator be black or white; although the European, in acting against what should be his better knowledge, is arguably more reprehensible than the supposed 'savage'.

'The Spectre of the Cattle Flat' expands this stark contrast of native humanity with 'Christian' ingratitude into a general portrayal of man's Cain-like impulses. The setting is a camp-fire, where stockmen vie for status through accounts of bloody atrocities which they have wreaked on the blacks. The first speaker's boast provides an unconscious subversion of the parable of the Good Samaritan:

> One tells how, after a fierce fray,
>   A wounded Chief he found
> Dark-lying, log-like, on his way,
>   Sore gashed with many a wound,
> And how, as there alive he lay,
>   He staked him to the ground.
>
>   (p. 188)

The second recalls an act of racial genocide, when 'a tribe entire . . . was pent, and held at bay, / Till there, like sheep, in one close heap, / Their slaughtered bodies lay.' Ned Connor, however, claims superiority for his murderous deed because it was not motivated by a counterthreat: 'What is there in an open stroke / To boast of? Ye but slew / Those who'd have done, each hell-black one, / The same or worse to you.' He coolly shoots a black who, in return for a promised knife, has led him home. Short-sighted cunning overcomes his physical plight as a lost stockman, but confirms his condition of moral and spiritual error: 'I raised my gun, as if in fun— / I fired! and he was *dead*!' Furthermore, the precedence claimed for and accorded his crime is virtually meaningless. Fratricide emerges from the accounts of these whitemen as the distinctive and accepted condition of humanity, while religious associations like 'hell-black' are evoked only to sanction unchristian acts. Natural innocence, in the stockmen and slavers alike, has been overlaid by the experience of Western civilization. Through it they have gained such developed instruments of death as knife and gun, and thoroughly debased attitudes which discern in native trust only exploitable gullibility. Thus, as Harpur grimly concludes of man in Part I of **'The Slave's Story'**,

> Oh learn how like a Upas Tree
> (Not fabled) *his* dread cruelty
> Can make a scene that else might tell
> Of Paradise, a type of Hell!
>
> (p. 438)

Opposed to this awareness of man's intransigent heart is a vision of nature redolent with benevolent and supernatural influence. Part I of **'The Slave's Story'** creates an image of nature ever-renewed, which will provide the reader with grounds for hope even in the wake of the slaver's disruptive actions. Successive images drawn from pagan and Christian mythology are used to portray the setting in terms of the world's 'earliest style'. First the tropical isle is likened to 'a vast shield of fretted gold / Dropt by some worsted Elder God'; and then, following this legend of Olympian strife, to '*one* Altar graven / From the rude mass of things terrene / By Time inspired with Eden lore.' The island affords a paradisiacal vision of what might be; the allusions pinpoint the source of its eclipse in our over-reaching pride and subsequent violence. Within this unspoilt tropical setting man's generosity is the overflow of creation's plenitude, and this perfect harmony finds its emblem in the native's home:

> That hut my dwelling had been;
> 'Twas joisted in four living trees
> That met aloft high o'er the roof
> In domes of solid shade sun-proof;
> And from its wicker door the sheen
> Of a clear brook might just be seen.
>
> (p. 440)

Ideally man and nature are mutually supportive; and life, not death, informs their relationship. Cultivation and local vegetation are interblent, heightening each other's bounty and affording a landscape where the meeting of aspiring finite and answering infinitude is continual: 'Far as might range the wandering eye, / The vast uprising main was seen / To meet the bending Sky.' Even in the sullied realm portrayed in **'The Spectre of the Cattle Flat'** something of the primal bond remains, as witnessed in the supernatural occurrences. The contest for status among the stockmen in a blood-peerage terminates only with the discovery that the water-container is mysteriously empty. The synonymous phrases 'heart of sin' and 'heart of stone', used to describe Ned Connor, are translated into a dry waterpail in the midst of nature's plenty. Fittingly, the very essence of life is denied to those who boast of its violent

disjunction. In the subsequent quest for water Connor, and through him his companions, will be brought face to face with an indigenous manifestation of those moral and spiritual values which they have repeatedly contravened.

Here as elsewhere in Harpur, man emerges first as the agent and finally as the victim of oppressive acts. A spiritually divided sinner, he can be a cold enactor of blasphemy and yet a prey to indwelling remorse. This constellation of ideas, of course, is a familiar one in Romantic literature, and there is much in the plot and narrative mode of the poems to recall works such as 'The Rhyme of the Ancient Mariner'.[3] Like Coleridge's protagonist, Harpur's villains return death for a potentially life-saving act, and are punished by an absence of sustenance in the midst of teeming creation. But whereas the reasons for the mariner's deeds and the death of his shipmates remain unspecified except as givens of a larger existential design, which moves us from innocence through experience to restored unity, Harpur locates the source of all fatal action in man alone.[4] Specifically, suffering has external and internal causes, attributable to the wilful denial of that basic brotherhood manifested in others and in the heart's spiritual promptings. These innate bonds can be consciously suppressed but not annulled, as seen in both Harpur poems. There the eclipse of daylight and rational strategies brings man into open confrontation with the conflicting sides of his character. The slaver asleep assumes the aspect of another Cain. His fair face reveals 'the shadow as of crime or care, / Or secret hate', while his apparent youth is belied by 'lines of grey'. Later in the tale, he rises 'ghastly as a ghost / . . . raging, murder mad', butchers half his crew, and brings about his own death. Driven by mysterious impulses, he becomes the manifestation simultaneously of his crime and its avenger, affording the final enactment of his fratricidal life and its spiritual consequence: self-slaughter. Similarly in **'The Spectre of the Cattle Flat'**, the murderer becomes the object of a supernatural counter-force which, though 'dreadful to the eye', was 'more so to the thought'. Whatever the phenomenological status of the apparition, its buffeting torment of Connor accurately reflects a retributive dread arising from a guilty conscience. His mortal shot is now answered by a series of blows and by an overwhelming stench 'decayedly of the earth', which will eventually mortify his proud heart. Simulated death, the reawakening of consciousness, and the terminal pangs of remorse follow in quick succession; and his violent fate links him with the 'base Enslaver', of whom it is said:

> Fit end, though terrible and sad,
> For one so violently bad
> Even in his evils,—if ever sane
> We may account the sons of Cain.
>
> (p. 446)

Ironically, each man becomes the ghost of his former self, or even assumes what, to conventional eyes, may seem temporary insanity, before he can bring to a close the physical acts which have all but consumed his spiritual existence.

In these works, however, vengeful retributive deeds are integrated into a larger pattern concerned with the possibility of moral growth, enlarged sympathy, and the recognition of fraternity. Harpur's preoccupation with the need for man to meliorate his worst impulses or, preferably, to maintain his best is clearly illustrated by revisions to **'The Spectre of the Cattle Flat'**. Originally entitled **'Ned Connor'**, the story was expanded to ensure that the fate of the main protagonist would assume a truly representative cast. The first major change was the addition of stanzas three and four, which afford accounts of the butchery done by Connor's associates. As a result they are fully implicated in the crime of fratricide, and participate in the supernatural ordeals. Next Harpur altered the description of Connor's temporary unconsciousness from 'A moment— and then all was tame / Forgotten, painless, past' to the straightforward simulation of death.[5] The earlier suggestions of peace, cessation and forgetfulness scarcely accord with the notion of an unrelenting process of spiritual arousal, which climaxes in his physical prostration and constant supplication for mercy. Finally, the morally inclusive perspective introduced by the opening expansion is assured by adding a last stanza. The initial version of the poem concludes with the stockmen still largely detached from the main drama. They simply acknowledge Connor's error and bury him by the stream. The added lines, however, explore their motivation, and suggest that they have been involved in an analogous process of spiritual growth:

> There did they bury him, to ease,
>   A crudely pious dread,
> That sought, so choosing, to appease
>   Some Influence from the *dead,*
> Which there had brought for his crime, they thought
>   God's doom on a Murderer's head.

(p. 197)

For the first time in the poem dread and death are placed in an overtly religious context; and man chooses openly to act on the interrelated dictates of Divinity and common humanity. Enlightenment is by no means complete, but all Connor's auditors, both within and without the poem, have been brought to awareness of a supernatural mystery informing creation. Theirs is a propitiatory act of atonement, an acknowledgement of brotherhood and of that original compact which still links all inhabitants of nature's primal realm.

The crucial function of the audience's response in Harpur's dramatic narratives is even more evident in **'The Slave's Story'**, where a surrogate reader-audience, in the person of a 'pitying Traveller', becomes imaginatively involved in the reaffirmation of charity in a humanly brutalized environment. Unlike Coleridge's wedding-guest, who seems repeatedly disturbed by and desirous of escape from the mariner's tale, Harpur's chance auditor displays untiring patience and the solace of pity throughout. Moreover, given his liberty of movement in a setting dominated by slavery, we may assume him to be white. He thus affords an implicit alternative to the slaver's crew, and demonstrates that Western civilization, while providing the lucra-

tive incentive to inhuman acts, need not always annul the well-springs of charity. His freely-given sympathy elicits a corresponding spiritual blessing from the slave, couched in terms of a Divine design which guarantees the ultimate survival of merciful benevolence: 'never—never mayest thou need / Ere God shall shield thee in thy grave, / Such pity as thou has shown indeed / So freely to a Slave' (p. 447). The threatened bond of faith and brotherhood is thereby restored; and even civilized man proves himself worthy of a place in nature's order. A benediction, intended originally for the fair betrayer, finds its meet object in one willing to assume the burden of humanity. Here the process of denaturalization lamented in 'Eden Lost' is arrested. A simple act within the reach of everyman marks a giant step towards rooting up the cruel, Upas-like growths of man's mind, which poison and constrict the otherwise 'bounteous . . . fair, / And genial' aspects of natural existence. The Edenic setting of section I, Harpur implies, is always present, though we are spiritually deadened to its regenerative potential by our violence and unthinking deeds.

Harpur's espousal of the role of imaginative sympathy and active deeds of charity in restoring or, perhaps more accurately, maintaining 'this glorious residence, the Earth' emerges clearly in the last works for discussion, **'The Murder of the Lamb'** and **'The Glen of the Whiteman's Grave'**. In the first of these genuine contrition, such as Connor experiences, is translated into saving acts; and the cycle of fatal retribution is also symbolically transcended through the typological assimilation of the Cain motif to the dictates of the new dispensation.[6] This **'Legend of the Sheep Fold'**, as it is subtitled, tells how the unrequited passion of a young shepherd for a dazzlingly white lamb turns to cruelty, when the boy leaves it tied up in rushes to be slain by a marauding beast of the night. Yet light will eventually conquer evil. For the boy, tormented by his conscience, confesses his deed and begins a restorative process based on extending charity to God's creatures. Present here are the major elements of previously discussed works: natural innocence destroyed; the mysterious progress of the soul which transforms acts of love into those of hate; evocation of the supernatural, not merely as a dramatic device by which to effect retribution, but as evidence of a suffusing and ever-operative spiritual dimension; and bloody, fratricidal acts, presented as a recurrent dilemma which affects all existence but emanates solely from man. Here, however, the dialectic of evil is converted into one of ultimate good through an elaborate Cain-Abel typology, created by Harpur's substitution of a lamb for the human victim, and by making the Cain-like culprit 'a keeper of sheep', and not the biblical 'tiller of the soil'. Most obviously, the first change facilitates the conventional linking of prototypal violence with the crucifixion, when the 'Spectre' of the murdered creature appears 'so white— / And lo, from its side ran blood!' This visionary ordeal, in turn, makes the shepherd lad a victim of the same spite and cruelty which slew his 'brother'; and so completes his earlier identification by occupation with the Abel figure. Alternatively a Cain or an Abel, the boy becomes the focal-point of man's apparently conflicting responses, and the means of their resolution.

Central to Harpur's depiction of these events is his belief in the interconnectedness of existence. Here as in other poems, nature appears as an ever-renewed but ever-endangered primal garden:

> And now the golden Eventide
>   Is glowing in the west—
> Glowing like a Summer bride
>   Upon old Winter's breast!
> O how can Hate in all the wide
> And beautiful world thus beautified
>   Dare harbor unconfest—
> Nor casting off his hellish scroff,
>   Transform to a Spirit blest?
>
> (p. 210)

The creation is envisioned in terms of an ongoing spiritual wedding, and the controlling seasonal metaphor suggests a mistaken tardiness, or plain contrariety, in man's response to its regenerative impulse. This withheld or 'unconfest' union, it will be suggested, arises from fundamental incomprehension on the part of individuals. Like Egremont in **'The Creek of the Four Graves'** and the poet's other blood-sinners, the boy is 'wild-willed' and, most importantly, subject to ambivalent motivation. He is, according to the shepherd's definitive prescription, 'brave at heart and good, / Though given at times to hate.' He responds instinctively with love to the innate bond of life he feels with a lamb, only to be greeted with an inversion of his best impulses: 'But only *fear* was living there— / Not what he yearned to trace.' The result is a baffling and ultimately tragic lack of communication, arising from the inappropriateness of the boy's naive expectations:

> O had it been a thing with speech
>   Tow'rd which his love did glow,
> Some sympathy within their reach
>   Fond words had taught to flow;
> And through the might of his strange delight
>   To have wakened a kindred mood,
> Had kept its fountain pure and bright,
>   And welling forth for good.
>
> (p. 208)

The protagonist is mankind in its spiritual infancy and maturing self-awareness. His innate purity and intuitive quest for sympathy or extended fellowship are demonstrated, but so too is his limited view of what nature offers. Individual failure to grasp comprehensively the inherent pattern of existence causes it to assume a negative aspect, so that in his once clear 'eye there lurks some sad / Life-urking mystery.' Man's subjective perception begins to eclipse God's; and the benevolent influence of the solar eye on events is temporarily replaced by the circumscribed, subverting awareness of the boy. In place of mild and radiant love, cruelty 'glares outward from his mind'. Appropriately, the sense of thwarted love turns his thoughts to Cain, and the archetypal blood-deed arising from incomprehension. For as in the case of the primal murderer, his apparently rejected gifts lead to vengeance against his nearest kinsman and to Divine intervention.

Regeneration in Part III of the poem is dependent on interrelated external and internal impulses. This redemptive process comprises three phases: remorse, contrition and eventual salvation, when repeated prayers and deeds of atonement will have purged 'his young life . . . of a crime'. The first phase is introduced by the ewe's plaint, described as 'that mournful Mother's wail', and ends with memories of his own mother, who instilled in him the merciful precepts which cause 'his wilful heart . . . [to] quail.' The kinship between all nature's creatures is thus reasserted through the evocation of a common source of nurturing love, which finds its spiritual type in the climactic vision of the murdered lamb. Similarly the states of victim and victimizer are subtly interlinked. The boy, rising 'from his thorny bed', standing 'ghostly stiff' and pierced with remorse, becomes the counterpart of his victim; just as he answers the 'low wild moan' of a solitary, suffering spirit aloft with his own 'fearful groan'. The second stage of his regeneration depends on this recognition of, and identification with, the crime. Like the Ancient Mariner, he openly confesses his sin and bursts involuntarily into inward supplication:

> Thus lay he—till his heart did break
>   Into a wondrous prayer,
> That God, the Father of All, would take
> Sweet pity upon him for sorrow's sake,
>   Thus lowly lying there!
> Nor let the wrong that he had done,
> Being tempted of the Evil One,
>   Some deadlier fruitage bear!
>
> (p. 215)

The crisis of the soul's disease is now passed. The individual heart is restored as God's temple;[7] and the fruits of primal error become the means to that 'inner paradise, happier far' which results from the positive application of increased knowledge. In ensuing stanzas emphasis falls on 'mystic Influence', 'healing' and spiritual enlightenment which teach man that the supernatural and physical consequences of his blood-deed require 'sorrow true and penance due', as well as a voluntary pledge to care for 'the firstlings of his flock' (Genesis, 4:4). For as the sage shepherd argues, 'of all ways, the best / For righting the wrong thou hast done to *one,* / Is justice to the rest.' Justice is tempered with mercy, and their claims reconciled through expanded understanding of the appropriate terms in which to respond to the ordained unity of creation. Red blood, which spelt vengeance in the old dispensation, assumes here its Christian identification with the redemptive operation of grace, which we may witness in the salvation of a single murderer or in one of God's natural epiphanies. Hence in the final lines guilt and crime, likened only to 'a thin white mist', are dispelled by the transfiguring 'golden ray' of presiding Divinity to reveal 'the first / Red flash of the perfect day'. The shadowy doubts which haunted the prospect are 'shrunken' or 'burst' in response to the broken and restored heart of this spiritual everyman.

The fullest expression of violence eclipsed and guilt transformed into expansive sympathy occurs in **'The Glen of the Whiteman's Grave'**, a work which affords a triumphant close to the poet's treatment of the innocence at risk motif by emphasizing the good inherent in man and creation. As Harpur's biographer Normington-Rawling notes, the poem was inspired by the murder of a 'settler named Clementson';[8] though Harpur's description of funeral mounds in both **'The Glen of the Whiteman's Grave'** and **'The Creek of the Four Graves'**, which is based on Clementson's resting-place, is intentionally generalized through suppression of the victim's name. In **'The Glen of the Whiteman's Grave'** we are told pointedly that the name is 'Deep carved in the bark of a grand old Tree'; but its wider significance resides in its being *'The name of a murdered man'*: a phrase which Harpur underscores. The particular is thereby elevated into the universal, as the poet prepares to take up the drama of individual atonement for the actions of humankind where **'The Slave's Story'** left off, through concentrating on the response of a chance auditor to a tale of Cain-like betrayal. The speaker tells first of his solitary pilgrimage, motivated by a camp-side story, to the forest grave of a young man murdered by whites; while Part II offers a meditation there on how others, whether relatives or strangers, blacks or whites, are affected by the event. Throughout the emphasis is not so much on the act of betrayal and fratricide, as on its spiritually regenerative consequences. For the poet-speaker will provide confirmation of each man's Christ-like potential to redeem the errors of his fellows, when he descends to the grave and arises enlightened and imaginatively strengthened through his sympathetic sharing in the experience of untimely death.[9]

Part I of the poem focuses on the actual state or potential of creation through a series of elaborate vignettes that image either harmony or discord perceived in nature, depending on which influences predominate in the speaker's mind. As a lone traveller on the heights of sun-drenched mountains, he perceives the scene as an ennobling vista of vast, wild ranges merging with the heavens, 'like a dusky main / Of monster breakers flowing high / And wide along the shoreless sky' (p. 218). The prospect is one of primal concord. Mountains are likened to 'old-world Kings', or appear in 'tribe-like groups'; and the aspiring acts of peaks and perceiving mind find their type in a kindred image: 'High as soar the eagle's wings'. Upon his descent into the gloomy 'melancholy Glen' which houses the grave, the speaker looks back on the same objects from a lower vantage-point, and discerns the awesome ruins of a broken, fallen world. Though still 'mingled', all is 'unblent', 'rudely wild' and fragmented, with the very peaks seeming to rend the sky. The movement into a realm that knows sin and violent death is everywhere apparent; but so too is the sensed potential of individual intellect to discern here causes for hope. To the speaker's eye, the glen from afar can seem 'a huge gap between / Two craggy walls', and 'a time-hewn path / For the giant Pan of so wild a place'. It provides at once a magnified projection of the scar-like grave at its heart and a suggestion that the spirit behind

creation can turn acts of despoliation to life-giving ends. Similar antitheses are mediated by the same setting at sunset:

> A few grey cloud-shreds only were
> Seen in the vault of heaven to stir,
> As cobwebs, dim and torn, might wave
> From the marble dome of a mighty cave.
>
> (p. 219)

A chilling sense of death is present, transforming clouds to cobwebs and the world to a tomb. Yet there is also a promise of afterlife in the imaged oneness of a creation whose upper part consists of heaven. Moreover, with earth itself assuming the aspect of a tomb, we are invited to realize that the pilgrim's quest after the dead individual in fact embraces the fate of all. Imperceptibly topography and metaphysical implications have been interwoven by the light of mind; much as the described journey becomes the physical correlative of the previous imaginative response to the tale of murder. This too carried him from a setting of unity or community by the camp-fire, through images of wilderness, to 'some grey / Abysm in the Far Away'. But then as now, the stated physical and emotional predominance of 'grey' mediates, not suggestions of termination and vacuity, but of the grave as a threshold to broader prospects and vastly enlarged consciousness.

This play of antitheses, together with the possibility of hope emerging from the lap of despair, finds its most detailed projection in the description of the burial mound at the close of Part I. In this third tableau the speaker's contrition, his impelling 'sympathetic load', enables him to discern a regenerative kinship between natural and human life. The process of identification begins when the gloom-dispelling rays of the sun withdraw from the grave 'As Hope's last flickering gleam might fade / From the face of a doomed Man' (p. 220). Moreover, the use of 'might' should alert us that hope is no more unconditionally banished from the following setting than it was in a comparable scene in **'The Creek of the Four Graves'**, when Egremont witnessed the death of the poor man:[10]

> Only one tuft of grass did wave
> Above that sterile desert Grave
> Bestrewn with leaves and withered sprays,
> And only one blue flower did gaze
> Timidly up, as near I trod,
> From 'twixt the dry lips of a broken clod.
> O 'twas a desolate, dreary thing,
> That Grave in the else-green lap of Spring—
> In the else-unbroached primeval sod!
>
> (pp. 220-21)

As always, responsibility for despoliation rests with mankind, just as nature continually extends relief and evidence of a covenant maintained. From the midst of man-created indices of death and drought flowers a solitary emblem of regeneration. Evoking hope and the virgin through the colour blue, it appears like an anticipatory response to the speaker's ensuing prayer that 'not one human child / Of the Earth should be laid in the lonely cold / Of a Grave so wild!' Compassion not dread is awakened by this 'desolate dreary thing'. Certainly the grave will next recall to the viewer's mind the primal past of murdered Abel; but with this spiritual enlargement of the scene also comes the knowledge that 'Spring's healing hand, after many a year' does 'flower . . . [the tomb] with purple and gold!' Creation rewards the speaker's journey of selfless atonement with a vision of Edenic bounty encompassing a single scar-like plot 'bestrewn with leaves and withered sprays', as if in sign of gracious mourning and affirmative charity towards man's repeated Cain-like acts. Nature's face, although bearing the traces of human sin, provides everywhere evidence that temporal does merge with eternal: that even parched lips may yield up saving words of forgiveness and renewal.

The topographical transitions of Part I, signalling shifts from primal unity through untimely devastation to hope restored, find their imaginative and human analogues in the meditations of Part II. The speaker, kneeling at the grave-side in response to 'a spirit of dread', invokes the past of the murdered man in terms of the geographically contrasted but spiritually linked realms of England and Australia. In this visionary sequence, England serves as the first garden, the state of loving accord characterized by the cherishing bonds of village and familial care. By contrast, in the New World 'felons bent to slay' and 'savage mountains' suggest not harmonious community but postlapsarian desolation and solitude. Further, the English new-chum affords an image both of innocent everyman sallying forth into the forbidding landscape of experience; as well as of the poet-elect in man, faced with the task of reconciling ideality and actuality:

> A visionary Youth, methought,
> On he came, all wonder-wrought
> With the dreary grandeur massed
> Aloft in shapes so wild and vast,
> And which his memory oft compared
> For contrast, with the rural joy
> Of scenes in England . . .

(p. 221)

In his death, then, we mark an eclipse of creative potential—but only to recognize its continued existence in the narrator, who passes beyond physical and temporal bounds in his imaginative perusal of the consequences of violent death. Hence even cumulative images of bereavement can provide grounds for faith. Significantly his account focuses on human response. First the parents 'mourning hopelessly' for their lost promise of life's continuation are evoked; then we are invited to see the instinctive but Christianly unreclaimed reactions of a passing black. He avoids the place, 'nor dares to halt', and hushes the play of 'his Boys' in pointing admonishingly at 'the Whiteman's Grave'. Finally, the very glen is 'that primeval waste' to the lone speaker's enlarged perception; though as in Part I the imaged nadir of despair provides cause for joy. For whereas the parents failed imaginatively ('they *saw* not' the grave), and the black, like his counterparts in **'The**

Creek'**, was unable to overcome superstitious dread; to the poet-speaker alone is given the capacity to approach and daringly reassert the bonds between men, nature and God.

The reaffirmation of this constantly threatened covenant is achieved in the final section through a complex series of identifications. Like the shepherd boy, the speaker's troubled spirit will be restored through an intuitive revelation of suffusing order and individual responsibility. He identifies with 'a Brother's sorrow' and unconsciously acts to cover or redeem this 'bleak scar in the Earth's . . . mould' (p. 221). The corporeal and spiritual blow rendered creation in the murder of young, spring-time life is mollified by the physically prostrate and mentally abased figure of the speaker, weeping and lying by the grave. From this strongly felt experience of blood-crime and its consequences for all existence springs a 'deepened' understanding of how death can provide a site for rebirth, or woe the starting-point for 'wisely sympathetic strength' (p. 223).[11] The key-note of this evolution is 'stretched'. It marks his first sighting of the burial place, 'And now the sought for Grave I found— / Against me stretched in lonely mound / Was darkly seen.' It recurs with the allusion to Cain, 'O God! / That first bleak scar in the Earth's new mould / Which stretched over Abel in Eden of old', and is enacted by the speaker at the grave. The iterated concept links past to present, marks stages in an ongoing process, and evokes a sense of that universal kinship from which will emerge the mysterious well-spring of regeneration. In each instance, living creation is measured by its response to death. The physical as well as poetic deeds of the speaker arguably complement and complete the shrouding, healing action of 'Earth's new mould'; just as they answer the implied injunction of the opening scene for affirmative, individual acts. Scars may point to injuries, but they also indicate an overall wholeness sustained. In this scheme, the speaker's arisal from the grave confirms a direct continuation of the visionary potential endangered with the eclipse of the new-chum. It also affords an act that transcends the physical termination of death, as well as evidence of the capacity of humanity in the New World to redeem its accumulated burden of guilt. Again we witness a dramatisation of Harpur's major theme: that 'this lovely world', in the words of **'The Creek of the Four Graves'**, may still prove a 'glorious residence', if 'its prime Creature—Man' can overcome savage passion through awareness of Divinely sanctioned ties which interlink all aspects of creation. The poem concludes with images of life's apparently antagonistic impulses resolved. There the generosity of man and nature are shown to conspire in soothing 'a dying child' with 'wreaths of flowers', and the 'moon's beams' are imaged as 'smoothing / O'er some benighted wild'—figures which suggest that even untimely death and unillumined wildness are parts of an ultimately just design.

Here as in the other poems surveyed, Harpur's use of the innocence at risk theme is informed by the belief that dread primal recurrence can only be countered by the charitable extension of love and forgiveness. This the speaker enacts physically through his pilgrimage and mentally through his narrative which, by means of studied transitions, attempts to engage its audience imaginatively in an unfolding spiritual progress. The text slips effortlessly from 'I' to 'we', from the presumably physical givens of the opening scenes to the frankly fictional constructs of Part II, as the poem becomes an overt act of inclusion, a call for responsible participation, and an instrument for the enlargement of sympathy which it preaches. Characteristically the process of genuine atonement is presented as one of identification by potentially alienated man with his slaughtered brother; and with this union comes a transformed perception of nature, seen no longer as an inhospitable, Cain-tormenting waste, but as a kindly ministering presence:

> Yea, wept as we are fain to weep
> When some great load is on the brain,
> As given by Nature so to keep
> The saddest thinking sane;
> And sweet for future use, I trow,
> When we shall understand at length
> What beauty of soul, and grace to know,
> And wisely sympathetic strength
> Was born to us of Woe.
>
> (p. 223)

The passage provides a bare summation of Harpur's beliefs. As this and previous works have shown, murder is antithetical to all that distinguishes existence. It is hateful, ugly, grace-denying and marks an uncomprehending denial of fraternity. Together, these implied attributes constitute a receipt for the insanity which motivates all the poet's blood-sinners from Egremont to the shepherd boy, those lineal 'Sons of Cain'. Opposed to this vision of evil rampant is the spiritualizing gift of nature to 'the brain'—that seat and source of primal strife. Sanity, in this context, means faith in an unshaken celestial presence ever able and willing to turn evil to higher good, and to maintain in man those redeeming Christian virtues of charity and love. Unobtrusively the poem attains the status of prophecy, distilling from present problems a spiritual knowledge which is synonymous with grace; and ensuring, through our involvement in the pilgrim-poet's response, the unbroken operation of creative potential in humankind as well as in nature.

According to Harpur man, though fallen, is redeemable. Certainly 'some dread Intelligence opposed to Good' has spread 'over all the earth', but error may emerge as a station in a necessary process of maturation. Life under the condition of full consciousness may be viewed as a blessing and not as a punishment or curse, while the young or intellectually benighted may progress through emulation of bardic precepts. Ours remains the primal choice, and with it the fate of a young nation. True children of the earth, we feel the pull of savage, destructive impulse, and yet we remain subject to the same regenerative pulse which energizes all creation. Against recurrent error, Harpur offers examples of selfless charity which, through healing wounds and forging sympathetic bonds, provides the groundwork for a God-ordained democracy. Thus charity becomes, in the poet's words, 'all mankind's concern', and 'the core / Of Wisdom's social aim' (**'Charity'**, A87). Transcending economic and religious demarcations, it elevates the individual to his original status as 'man-god' and becomes, in Harpur's verse and theoretical pronouncements, synonymous with the annulment of violence and the restoration of paradisiacal existence through Christ-like acts of faith in mankind. Moreover charity, in his dramatic narratives, provides the touchstone for judging the torch-bearers of Western civilization in the New World. In the culturally superior whites, acquisitive rights are often shown to have eclipsed natural humanitarian duties, and material success to have annulled Christian concerns. As a corrective Harpur preaches the thinly veiled republican doctrine of righting individual wrong through 'justice to the rest', and the accompanying vision of an all-encompassing natural kinship. In the spring superabundance of creation, or in the innate reverence which distinguishes the actions of his narrators, the passing blacks and the very seasons, he offers us evidence of a Providential presence maintained. Its influence guarantees the renewal of 'a nameless flower' or the spontaneous act of disinterested charity in 'a nameless scene', and with them a new Adamic chance for mankind in the preserved spiritual garden of this world.

Notes

1. Quotations from Harpur's writings are accompanied either by a reference to their Mitchell Library manuscript source, or by a page reference to Elizabeth Perkins, ed., *The Poetical Works of Charles Harpur* (Sydney: Angus and Robertson, 1984).

2. The same is true for Harpur's other major works, stretching from his early youthful drama, 'The Bushrangers', through to his last ambitious poem of epic scope, 'The Witch of Hebron'. For further detailed treatment of these concerns see my essay 'God's Sublime Order in Harpur's "The Creek of the Four Graves"', *Australian Literary Studies,* 11 (1984), 355-70.

3. J. J. Healy in *Literature and the Aborigine in Australia: 1770-1975* (Brisbane: Queensland Univ. Press, 1978), noting this possible source, posits that the poem 'was an effort to construct, in narrative terms, a fundamental breach of the moral order'; but limits and even distorts the work's implications by concluding: 'The European in Australia, for Harpur, was part of a disturbed moral order; his killing of the Aborigine initiated and manifested this fundamental disturbance' (p. 95). As the poet's works repeatedly indicate, he maintained that Australia represented a new chance for mankind. The coming of the white was not reprehensible *per se*; but only in so far as he brought with him the errors of a fallen, botched Old World, and attempted to re-establish them in the new colony, as Harpur explains, for instance, in the opening lines of his sonnet on 'The New Land Orders' (pp. 635-36).

4. The Australian is also careful not to suggest that the humans' evil-doings are in any way part of a presiding spiritual design. Heaven is thereby absolved of blame, but remains free to intervene supernaturally in order to awaken a sense of contrition and genuine repentance.

5. The text of the earlier version appears in *The Bushrangers, a Play in Five Acts, and Other Poems* (Sydney: Piddington, 1853), p. 86.

6. On the Romantic and mid-nineteenth century use of these motifs see George K. Anderson, *The Legend of the Wandering Jew* (Providence, R.I.: Brown Univ. Press, 1965), pp. 174-275; and Leslie Tannenbaum, 'Lord Byron in the Wilderness: Biblical Tradition in Byron's *Cain* and Blake's *The Ghost of Abel*', *Modern Philology,* 72 (1975), 350-64; and 'Blake and the Iconography of Cain', in *Blake in his Time,* ed. Robert N. Essick and Donald Pearce (Bloomington: Indiana Univ. Press, 1978), pp. 23-34. In the latter, Tannenbaum draws attention to the Romantic use of the Cain motif to stress the possibilities of forgiveness, reconciliation and sympathy, as well as the bond between man and Divinity (pp. 29-32): points also emphasized in Harpur's treatment of the Cain-centred typology.

7. Interesting confirmation of this reading is supplied by the A92 version of the poem, where Harpur substitutes 'templed' for the qualifier 'tempted', used in the A89 and A95 texts.

8. Normington-Rawling, *Charles Harpur, An Australian* (Sydney: Angus and Robertson, 1963), p. 32.

9. The motifs are familiar Romantic ones; and Hartman traces them authoritatively in *Wordsworth's Poetry: 1788-1814* (New Haven: Yale Univ. Press, 1964). Harpur, of course, was well read in Romantic poetry, particularly that of Wordsworth, to whom he owes much in theme and technique, as Judith Wright describes in *Preoccupations in Australian Poetry* (Melbourne: Oxford Univ. Press, 1965), pp. 7-10.

10. The scene is discussed in some detail in Michael Ackland, 'God's Sublime Order in Harpur's "The Creek of the Four Graves"', *Australian Literary Studies,* 11 (1984), 367-68.

11. Here as so often in Romantic poetry Nature, or an indwelling presence both within and without the speaker, seems to motivate his unpremeditated acts. His tears spring from thought and are 'as given by Nature'—a telling simile which suggestively pinpoints the source of his atoning deeds in a force mediated through but not necessarily synonymous with the natural creation. For further examination of these concerns in Harpur's verse, see my 'Cognitive Man and Divinity in the Short Descriptive Verse of Charles Harpur', *Southern Review,* 16 (1983), 389-403; and 'Charles Harpur's "The Bush Fire" and "A Storm in the Mountains"': Sublimity, Cognition and Faith', *Southerly,* 43 (1983), 459-74.

Adrian Mitchell (essay date 1992)

SOURCE: Mitchell, Adrian. "Writing up a Storm: Natural Strife and Charles Harpur." *Southerly* 53, no. 2 (1993): 90-113.

[*In the following essay, originally delivered as a lecture in 1992, Mitchell considers the reasons and methods for reading Australian colonial poetry and focuses on Harpur's efforts to combine new experiences and expressions of thought with a sense of the familiar.*]

Australian colonial poetry is considered, if it is considered at all, more with sorrow than delight. The colonial writer lived with the inevitability of failure, one recent commentator tells us, leaning over the counter of the post-colonial theory store.[1] Others concede that the poetry is not all that great, though acknowledging obliquely that some of the poets, and Charles Harpur not least, did have a hankering after greatness. Somewhere behind that is a principle of diminishing returns: the more the hankering, the more unlikely the greatness. For one reason or another, the Colonial poets no longer have the power to capture the imagination; perhaps, it is admitted, they never did, or rarely.

Yet they do have something to offer, as we occasionally find. Here and there a remarkable image, a set of wonderful lines, even whole poems that lift themselves above the disappointing mire. Those lines get read attentively, and inspected carefully by at least a few of the literary historians, and suggestions are made about why those bits and pieces are impressive. But there is less and less of this as the years and anthologies wheel by; the colonial poets receive less and less space in the total representation of Australian writing. Perhaps that is inevitable: if the anthologies aren't going to get any bigger then necessarily the apportionment of early material will shrink.

It occurs to me that something less mechanical is at work, however: that the colonial poets are disappearing not because we have forgotten about them, but because we have forgotten how to read them. This is not just a matter of taste and judgement, of objections that the poetry is too prone to eighteenth-century English poetic diction for example, and therefore has nothing to contribute to a post-Romantic and insistently, exclusively Australian literary tradition. Yes, it is true that much of the verse is lame, or ingenuous, or bathetic, or "artificial". But that is largely beside the point, for I have no doubt that it would be possible to demonstrate the same sort of objections in modern Australian poetry. The question of distinctive Australianness is likewise unreasonably distorted in discussions about our literary origins and literary connections. Indeed, although it is often enough proposed that there is a rather interesting correspondence between development in Australian poetry and in Australian painting, I find an extraordinary disagreement in just this particular—that whereas art historians can quite comfortably indicate the obligations that experimental young avant-garde painters of the modernist movement—Nolan, Tucker, Boyd, Drysdale—

had to Europe, to suggest that Australian poets actually imitated anything European is enough to turn the nationalist literary historian apoplectic. No one suggests that Nolan and Boyd and co. are less than Australian, and we have all delighted in their success in directing world attention to Australian painting. But for *poets* to learn anything from anywhere else is a cultural scandal, it seems. The extraordinary thing is that this objection in relation to literature is no new thing. It was at large in the middle of the colonial era, in the nationalist nineties, and in various manifestoes through the first part of this century; it was very much an issue in the sixties, and it is back again, if it ever went away, in the current passion for critical theorising, with its ideological inner-spring mattress.

The question that needs to be put is not, I suggest, why read colonial poetry, but *how* do we read colonial poetry? The "why" really presumes the other, and notions of taste and judgement have to be held in abeyance until we can recognize what it is that we are reading. To read colonial poetry we need to retrieve a forgotten language; and we need to retrieve a context, a context of ideas, as well as a literary context. And when that is learned, we are in a position to understand something else about colonial poetry, that it isn't absolutely independent, and has no aspiration to be absolutely original, just as contemporary writing also benefits from imitating developments and experiments from elsewhere. It is the process of *adaptation* that is interesting and results in a distinctive Australian statement. This question of originality and imitation was addressed by Professor Kramer in an article that I have been keeping my eye on, "Imitation and Originality in Australian Colonial Poetry: The Case of Charles Harpur"; and in these remarks this evening I am attempting no more than a footnote to her exemplary discussion; taking up a case from her case, like a matching set of travelware perhaps.

The general problems I am raising here, about the inability to read, about a forgotten language and a forgotten context, are not confined to Australian circumstances. Much as we know we are meant to admire Shelley, for example, we find it difficult to focus on concepts like ideality—however important that may have been for him, however much a key to his poetic thought, we are impatient with it. The word is a furry soapbubble at best; it doesn't know whether it is froth or bubble, whether to rise or fall, and its function is just to blow away. Similarly we make no attempt to see what is intended by the language of eighteenth-century poetry:

> O vale of bliss! O softly-swelling hills!
> On which the Power of Cultivation lies,
> And joys to see the wonders of his toil.

wrote James Thomson in *Summer* (ll. 1435-7). O for goodness' sake, modern readers think, if we get that far. It means nothing to us, it is too vague and generalized. It comes as something of a surprise then, to read (probably) Oliver Goldsmith in *The British Magazine*:

> We cannot conceive a more beautiful image than that of the Genius of Agriculture, distinguished by the implements of his art, imbrowned with labour, glowing with health, crowned with a garland of foliage, flowers, and fruit, lying stretched at his ease on the brow of a gently swelling hill, and contemplating with pleasure the happy effects of his own industry.

On this comment Donald Davie has rightly remarked that the writer "probably contributes nothing that was not in Thomson's intention. For Thomson could count on finding in his readers a ready allegorical imagination, such as seems lost to us today. The loss is certainly ours".[2] And it is true—we don't read with Goldsmith's appreciation. Yet it ought not to be quite foreign to us.

Something of that allegorical imagination is required for Keats' "Ode to Autumn", for example, likewise for Charles Harpur's **"A Midsummer Noon in the Australian Forest"**: "Over hills and over plains / Quiet, vast and slumbrous, reigns," he writes; or

> Tired Summer, in her forest bower,
> Turning with the noontide hour,
> Heaves a slumbrous breath, ere she
> Once more slumbers peacefully.

Language, idiom, habits of mind, these are just a little of what we need to retrieve if we are to revive interest in and acquaintance with colonial poetry; just as we need to identify other signals, such as reference and allusions, a much more vexed question. Henry Kendall felt the need to address this particular issue in his "Prefatory Sonnets" to *Leaves from Australian Forests* (1869); it was clearly something that needed to be said in advance of his own poetic practice, that on the one hand his ambition was to write directly to, and from, the experience itself of Australian forests; and on the other that what he wrote was inevitably coloured by his reading of other poetry.

I

> I purposed once to take my pen and write
>   Not songs like some tormented and awry
>   With Passion, but a cunning harmony
> Of words and music caught from glen and height,
>   And lucid colours born of woodland light,
> And shining places where the sea-streams lie;
> But this was when the heat of youth glowed white,
>   And since I've put the faded purpose by.
> I have no faultless fruits to offer you
>   Who read this book; but certain syllables
>   Herein are borrowed from unfooted dells,
> And secret hollows dear to noontide dew;
> And these at least, though far between and few,
>   May catch the sense like subtle forest spells.

II

> So take these kindly, even though there be
>   Some notes that unto other lyres belong:
>   Stray echoes from the elder sons of Song;
> And think how from its neighbouring, native sea
> The pensive shell doth borrow melody.
>   I would not do the lordly masters wrong,
>   By filching fair words from the shining throng
> Whose music haunts me, as the wind a tree!

Lo, when a stranger, in soft glooms
Shot through with sunset, treads the cedar dells,
And hears the breezy ring of elfin bells
    Far down by where the white-haired cataract
    booms,
He, faint with sweetness caught from forest smells,
    Bears thence, unwitting, plunder of perfumes.

In that heady, swirling mix, one of the tinkling notes is surely Keatsian; but who can be sure? The point is not so much where it comes from as what Kendall makes of it, and from it. Something has come from somewhere: the poetry is a combination of imitation and originality, and imitation does not imply imaginative inadequacy, and colonial dependence. Rather it indicates how art always is. You could argue that were any poem, any painting absolutely original, we possibly could not understand it.

While Kendall is the occasion of the Herbert Blaiklock lecture series, he is not the subject of this particular lecture. It is Charles Harpur we attend to this evening; Harpur, Kendall's elected mentor and esteemed correspondent. And when Harpur died, it was Kendall who defended his literary reputation. Here is a passage from Kendall that not only argues for Harpur as a poet, but also presents Kendall's credentials as a perceptive and responsive critic. It comes from an article Kendall published in the *Freeman's Journal,* 9 December 1871, the second in a series of "Notes Upon Men and Books"; and in it we see again Kendall asserting on the one hand local responsiveness, and on the other negotiating a complaint about imitativeness, in the sense of derivativeness:

> Charles Harpur was a son of the forests—a man of the backwoods—a dweller in wild and uncouth country; and his songs are accordingly saturated with the strange fitful music of waste and broken-up places. This was a singer whose genius was ripened, so to speak, by the sun and winds of outside wildernesses; mountains were his sponsors; and from them he received his lyrical education. As Tennyson's elder songs are filled with the mournful, monotonous melody of the North-easter sweeping over there across the Lincolnshire fens, so Harpur's most characteristic and most maligned lyrics have, incorporated with them, the full, strong, *lawless* music of the Australian hills. And this music, native to rugged places where cliff, and gorge, and tree conspire to break it into fragments, has a rhythm of its own altogether unlike that which pulsates through the sustained winds of the open lowlands—a rhythm restless and broken, but, for all that, melodious. That the Australian poet was influenced to a considerable degree by the healthy, masculine genius of the great Lake Bard is a fact beyond all question; still, it is equally clear to us that Harpur stands as much apart from Wordsworth as the latter does from the author of the *Seasons.* The grand, austere toiler who thought out that marvellous poem *The Excursion,* and who left behind him the most remarkable ode in the English language, was—like the two other singers we have named—on his strongest ground when set face to face with external Nature; but, then, there is a broad subjective element in the verse he has left us, that is nowhere to be met with in the writings of Thomson and Harpur. The most characteristic

poems of Harpur and the author of the *Seasons* are purely descriptive—being that and nothing more; and it is from this point of view that the critic must judge, in order to be fair to the Australian poet without underrating his indebtedness to Wordsworth.

The two propositions are quite clear. Harpur's poetry expresses in its cadences and rhythms, its music, the strange fitfulness of waste and broken-up places; and his Wordsworthianism is Wordsworth with a difference, in which the subjective self is, as with Thomson, separate from the nature description.

But closer reading suggest this is a most peculiar defence. First, Kendall has not so much characterized Harpur, or his poetry, as matched him to a particular context. It hardly seems worth elaboration, so Kendall has presumed, that the place Harpur comes from, the natural landscape he expresses, *is* a waste and broken-up place. This is *not* the same order of nature as Wordsworth's Cumberland hills; this is the wilderness.

Second, the determination to represent Harpur as a lyric poet, a musical poet, a singer, is a projection of Kendall's own image of the poet, and more particularly of himself as poet. You might have noticed his reference to Tennyson's "elder songs", and remembered the phrase about "echoes from the elder sons of Song"—this passage relates closely to his own situation. For Kendall, the poet is almost automatically a "singer". For Adam Lindsay Gordon, the poet constructs a necklace of rhyme; for Harpur, however, the poet is more like a prophet—especially, he almost seems bitterly to remember, in being without honour in his own land. These are different orientations in one of the ongoing debates in the nineteenth century about the poet's relation to society. The poet might be a man speaking to men, or the unacknowledged legislator of mankind; or he might be nearly anonymous. It is a strange argument, to defend Harpur against his obligations to Wordsworth by asserting that he is actually closer to Thomson. Especially it is strange when Harpur himself had written to Kendall, urging him to abandon his decadent Tennysonian tendencies and to concentrate on Wordsworth and Milton:

> Study Milton and Wordsworth for a blank verse style, and combine the master-movements of the two. Wordsworth will teach you how to loosen and modernise Milton's, so as to make it eloquent; and Milton will show you how to put thunder into Wordsworth's.

> (letter to Kendall, 7 July 1866)

Harpur knew what he wanted from other poets and he knew what he wanted and wouldn't get. It would seem then a much more vigorous defence to notice his desire for thunder in the poetic line, and his blunt assertion that Wordsworth doesn't have it. Whatever Harpur's indebtedness to Wordsworth, he was not merely imitative, he was not merely Wordsworth and water—not even Wordsworth and stormwater. The originality of Harpur is in that he knew his own mind, exercized his own judgement, and learned what he needed from whichever poet—Wordsworth or Milton, or Homer or Shakespeare. Of course, Wordsworth was in fact most often the model for him.

Nowhere is this more apparent than with the poem **"A Storm in the Mountains"**, the poem about a boyhood experience which established for him that he would be a poet. Professor Kramer has summarized the case:

> A link between **"A Storm in the Mountains"** and Wordsworth's *The Prelude* seems more than probable. Into the mind of Wordsworth's Winander boy, who died at the age of eleven, [i.e. the same age as the youthful Harpur], the "visible scene" with "all its solemn imagery" enters "unawares". Harpur's boyhood self wanders among the crags and comes upon a pool scooped out, like the "rocky basin" in Wordsworth's "An Evening Walk", "by the shocks of rain-floods plunging from the upper rocks", and here he drinks and muses. He is sufficiently observant to detect a change in the scene transmitted by the instinctive reactions of living things. He notices, for example, that the "locusts" cease flying and climb to the top of the tallest grasses, as they in fact do, he explains in a footnote, to escape sudden floods. Harpur's boy is just as finely attuned to his natural world as is the Winander boy, or the young Wordsworth of *The Prelude,* but he is not in communion with it. The storm is merely a part of nature; it does not speak directly to him nor he to it. The perceptions are those of a solitary observer, not unlike the young Wordsworth, with "a listless, yet enquiring eye"; but the sentiments have more in common with those of Thomson's *The Seasons* or Cowper's "A Thunder Storm" than with the intensity of Wordsworth's passionate hauntings.[3]

The influence of Wordsworth, she notes, is strongest in the earliest part of the poem, which concentrates on the inwardness of the experience. As the storm rumbles off, so does the poem into a kind of artificial coda, a bland statement about the purging of pestilence and the return of peace.

The Wordsworthian markings here are prominent; Professor Kramer's point is well-taken. But notice that like Henry Kendall she has inserted another name into the discussion, not Cowper for his "Thunder Storm", but James Thomson of *The Seasons.* That is a hint that I shall follow up later. For in Kendall's double argument there is that other proposition, about the nature of Nature in Australia; a point raised incidentally by Professor Wilkes in the introduction to his anthology *The Colonial Poets.* The bush as Harpur described it has for the most part vanished, he remarks;

> it no longer seems to us quite so vast, so unknown, so overwhelming. Harpur also saw it in a particular way. The bush in his poetry is not simply a huge presence dwarfing man; it is also a source of elemental violence, as savage as it is unaccountable.[4]

And Vivian Smith, in *The Oxford History of Australian Literature,* extends the perception in an interesting direction:

If later writers have concentrated on the arid monotonies of the Australian landscape, merging their sense of its social and cultural limitations with the sense of the repetitive sameness of the land, Harpur emphasised its picturesque, dramatic and more violent qualities, again rather in the manner of the early colonial landscape painters. Harpur had behind him the late eighteenth century and early Romantic tradition of descriptive and landscape poems, but it is worth noting how frequently his titles and subjects, **"The Bush Fire"**, **"The Creek of the Four Graves"**, **"Dawn and Sunrise in the Snowy Mountains"**, **"A Coast View"**, **"A Storm in the Mountains"**, **"The Kangaroo Hunt"**, are also found as the titles and subjects of some of the most important colonial paintings—from Glover, Roper, Martens and Buvelot, to von Guérard and Chevalier. There is in the poetry, as in the painting, the same sense of vastness, with the emphasis on vision and views, a sense of the sublime. A detailed study of landscape in Australian poetry would, I believe, show a gradual development away from the dramatic panoramas and the large view of the first colonial artists to a microscopic focus on things in the landscape, to the tiniest insects, plants and animal life—so that now a mere boulder or pebble or a bird can be invested with the sense of the sublime and mysterious once found only in an enormous coastal view or mountain sweep.[5]

And he is right about that, of course; there is just such a pattern. But notice something further. The titles of early colonial poetry, and painting, tend to form into another pattern too, not only from vastness to minuteness, but from general to particular. The titles of Harpur's poems are often of a general or representative kind: **"A Coastal View"**, **"A Midsummer Noon in the Australian Forest"**, **"A Storm in the Mountains"**; though yes, we also find **"The Creek of the Four Graves"**, **"The Bush Fire"**, which is on the way to specifying particularity, as Kendall does with his proper titles and exact place names, or Adam Lindsay Gordon with his predication of the individual, the singular, the discrete. Harpur, that is, represents the point of transfer between an initial affirmation of the general, to the recognition of the particular; and in this he also imitates the process of rational or scientific enquiry which had become prominent in the latter half of the eighteenth century, and which reinforced the practice of periphrasis in poetry, replicating as that does the system of botanical or zoological classification—the singular identified as an example of a class or species. In perception and discrimination Harpur's poetic eye works in a recognizable manner. But it is not exclusively that of the lingering eighteenth century, for he also makes the bridge to the colonial Romantic determination to see exactly and closely—he establishes at least a colonial beach-head, if that bridging is not a sufficiently autonomous and dramatic moment for Phillip Mead, amongst others.

Harpur does in fact represent an important cultural moment. Though there are, as we learned from C. P. Snow and others who shall not be mentioned here, two cultures. In that other culture, Harpur again has a point. He was writing towards a perception of what is normative here in Australia, which is not, it seems, normative over there: the normative is relativized. By which I mean that the world to which the Europeans came, kept on being different, kept on resisting expectations from the very beginning. The case for this can be traced out in terms of myth, by showing how Australia as both place and experience kept on actualizing, if in subtly transformed ways, the legendary Antipodes. Everything turned out to be a cunning reversal, an inversion, an anomaly.

. . . . .

Or one can turn to the phenomenal events which met European arrival, and observe what kind of conceptual determination emerges from that.

For example, I understand that when Ken Stewart gave the Blaiklock Lecture several years ago, he began by referring to Captain Cook's journal. "Winds southerly, a hard gale with heavy squalls attended with showers of rain and a great sea", Cook wrote of 18 April 1770: typically, as we have come to learn from our familiarity with this part of the world, the weather cleared and then worsened again, to "a large hollow sea . . . rowling in upon the land". Cook was not much impressed by rough seas—Joseph Banks, with a livelier imagination and a livelier vocabulary, expressed anxiety to a much greater degree. The simple point is that Cook's journal is almost necessarily a discontinuous narrative. Every detail is a discrete fact; there is no pattern of experience to inform the writing other than retrospectively, and whether storms were frequent or not in this part of the world could not be guessed at.

When the First Fleet arrived in Botany Bay, with Cook's journal as a kind of carefully read instruction manual, Phillip and his officers found that, with all due respect to the Great Navigator, it was an eminently unsuitable place for settlement; and not just because Cook's fine meadows turned out to be a "rotten spongy bog", in Major Ross's irritated phrase, but because the Bay was, and is, exposed to storms, open to the heavy seas which (by the time of his published report) Phillip had learned to expect would roll in from the East. As a naval man he evidently had his weather eye out.

With the relocation of the fleet to Port Jackson, almost the first thing that happened was, you may remember, a violent storm, a Hawthornian or Melvillean thunderstorm. Ships dragged at their anchor, endangering life and limb; a bolt of lightning smashed a large gumtree under which the officers had penned their personal livestock—and both tree and livestock were destroyed. The early journals describe all this, but none as far as I know interprets these events in any symbolic or intentional way, none relates it to any of the anarchy attendant on the unloading of the convicts, or to the perverse civilization now being established at the end of the world. That kind of commentary is left for the gothic imagination of novelists like Hal Porter and Thomas Keneally.

What did happen was that Captain Hunter was very soon observing that these coastal storms were frequent, that it was a characteristic of this part of the world, and that those sailing to Sydney should be careful to avoid getting caught on a lee shore.

> Our passage, since we came round Van Diemen's Land, had been attended with much bad weather, very violent squalls, and a thick haze; particularly with the wind from the eastward: I had before observed, that in the winter-time, upon this coast, we were subject to much bad weather . . . During the Summer months we were sometimes subject to thunder, lightning, and strong squalls; but in general the weather is fine. If in the fairest weather you observe it to lighten in the lee part of the horizon, you should prepare for a squall from that quarter, which is in general pretty severe.[6]

And second, since lightning had struck that gumtree, and all around Sydney there were burnt gumtrees, maybe gumtrees attracted lightning. Slowly this hypothesis was revised, as the colonizers observed how Aborigines hunted for possums, or set fire to large tracts of bush; and the storm theory at least in *that* particular, quietly lapsed.

Hunter knew what he was talking about when he warned of the dangers of being driven into shore with no leeway to tack out to sea again. He had had the narrowest of escapes in Storm Bay, Tasmania, an escape he acknowledged as providential. At the very last minute the wind had shifted the merest two points of the compass, and with the *Sirius* heeled right over he had just managed to escape being wrecked on a group of rocks. In low visibility, with prodigious seas breaking, "the gale not in the least likely to abate and the sea running mountain high, with very thick weather, a long dark night just coming on, and an unknown coast", the *Sirius* was in more than just a spot of bother. With the narrowest shift in the wind, they managed to clear the danger:

> . . . I do not recollect to have heard of a more wonderful escape. Every thing which depended upon us, I believe, was done; but it would be the highest presumption and ingratitude to Divine Providence, were we to attribute our preservation wholly to our best endeavours: his interference in our favour was so very conspicuously manifested in various instances, in the course of that night, as I believe not to leave a shadow of doubt, even in the minds of the most profligate on board, of his immediate assistance![7]

And he gives that one of his rare exclamation marks.

Providence does not often rate a mention in early Australian encounters, of either a testing or a priorising kind. Luck or irony is more the measure of experience; there is an appreciation that events do have a discernible pattern, and that they bear upon an individual outcome. But gratitude of Hunter's kind is noticeable for its rarity; more frequent is a celebration of amazement, possibly on occasion the sort of astonishment that Burke proposed as supporting the sublime.

Here for example is an account by Mary Ann Parker, wife of the captain of the *Gorgon,* bringing Lt. Governor Philip Gidley King and his wife out to Sydney. In fact Mrs Parker appears to be relying on her husband's log, for it is a more objective passage of writing than is normal with her. The purpose of her book was to present an interesting narrative, to be *amusing* in the period sense of that word, rather than to impose her own perceptions and reflections:

> The ensuing day, being Sunday, was pleasant and serene, as if to afford us an opportunity of imploring a continuance of the Divine Protection, which we had hitherto experienced in a singular degree.
>
> On Monday the 19th [September], at noon, . . . a point of land appeared in sight, called by Captain Cook *Long Nose,* on account of its pointed shape. At sun-set the hovering clouds seemed to forebode the event of the evening; at eight came on a tremendous thunder-squall, attended with most dreadful lightning and constant heavy rains, which continued upwards of an hour and a half. About *half* past *eight* the lightning struck the pole of the main-top-gallant-mast, shivered it and the head of the mast entirely to pieces; thence it communicated to the main-top-mast, under the hounds, and split it exactly in the middle, above *one third* down the mast; it next took the main-mast by the main-yard, on the larboard side, and in a spherical direction struck it in six different places; the shock electrified every person on the quarter-deck; those who were unfortunately near the main-mast were knocked down, but recovered in a few minutes: this continued until about *half* past *ten,* when a most awful spectacle presented itself to the view of those on deck; whilst we who were below felt a sudden shock, which gave us every reason to fear that the ship had struck against a rock; from which dreadful apprehension we were however relieved upon being informed that it was occasioned by a ball of fire which fell at that moment. The lightning also broke over the ship in every direction: it was allowed to be a dismal resemblance of a besieged garrison; and, if I might hazard an opinion, I should think it was the effect of an earthquake. The sea ran high, and seemed to foam with anger at the feeble resistance which our lone bark occasioned. At midnight the wind shifted to the westward, which brought on fine clear weather, and I found myself at leisure to anticipate the satisfaction which our arrival would diffuse throughout the colony . . .[8]

The long sentence full of connecting, disconnective semicolons, and the curiously flat trajectory of this as recreated experience, are to my mind reminiscent of Defoe. It presents itself as authentic in just his way; and it does not reflect on itself as extraordinary. It is an episode that invites a Melville. But that, of course, is not what we get. Rather, the episode is inserted between the rather cosy remembrance of Sunday (the point being that in the stormy passage from Cape Town there had not been too many sunny Sundays) and their imminent arrival in Sydney Harbour, and the relief they will bring to the anxious settlement. Which is to say that the passage, like the experience it recreates, is an extraordinary irruption of the disorderly into an otherwise fairly serene, sufficiently amusing voyage; and it occurs along the NSW coast. Mrs Parker evidently did not feel as strongly as Dr Johnson: "I would not for my amusement wish for a storm" he wrote early in his journey into Scotland.[9]

As a pattern in her writing, Mrs Parker clearly fancied this procedure of occasional interruption, for it is repeated on the way home, when the ship is caught amongst icebergs and the combination of beauty and terror are consciously identified and acknowledged. The icebergs are obviously dangerous; they are very big, very numerous, and much too close. Spray from the waves freezing on to them, makes the most fantastic forms: the combination is here exactly that exquisite mixture of pleasure and apprehension Edmund Burke had identified as underlying the sublime. In other words, Mrs Parker had a way of recognizing and articulating this experience, and indeed of contextualizing it, as evidenced by her references to the common distress felt at the death of Sir Hugh Willoughby and his crew, frozen to death in Elizabethan times in quest of the north-east passage, and remembered much as Sir John Franklin was to be in the mid-nineteenth century. The tragedy of Sir Hugh was part of the common culture; it is also, one notes in passing, identified in Thomson's own note to *Winter,* his first poem. Violent storms off the NSW coast did not, however, have an available context at this early moment in colonial history (1795).

By the time Charles Sturt was presenting his account of Australia in 1833, it was already well established—at least to his satisfaction—that unruliness in climatic behaviour was only to be expected:

> In the course of the day we crossed the line of a hurricane that had just swept with resistless force over the country, preserving a due north course, and which we had heard from a distance, fortunately too great to admit of its injuring us. It had opened a fearful gap in the forest through which it had passed, of about a quarter of a mile in breadth. Within that space, no tree had been able to withstand its fury, for it had wrenched every bough from such as it had failed to prostrate, and they stood naked in the midst of the surrounding wreck. I am inclined to think that the rudeness of nature itself in these wild and uninhabited regions gives birth to these terrific phenomena. They have never occurred, so far as I know, in the located districts.[10]

"The rudeness of nature in these wild and uninhabited regions": that is what sponsors such terrific phenomena. That is what is consequent upon "waste and broken-up places". Sturt is not a slovenly writer; on the contrary, he is very careful and thoughtful. So his evidence of the nature of Nature in Australia, its comparative disorderliness, is intriguing. Elsewhere he draws attention to a kind of moral ennervation, a feebleness in the unconvincing rivers, which have not enough flow to wash their sandbars out to sea. Nature in Australia is not as it is in Europe—and that is a scientific observation as well as something like a poetic fact. Furthermore, this barbaric, unreformed Nature is in the wilderness, not in the located, that is, civilized districts. For Sturt, the poetic proposition about Art improving Nature is inseparable from observable fact, evidence from what is these days called the real world.

The poets had of course been alert to Sturt's perception all along. I give as just one brief example Michael Massey

Robinson, who in his "Ode for the King's Birth Day 1811" (*Sydney Gazette,* 8 June 1811) resumes for us some of the themes I have been identifying:

Time was, when o'er THIS dread expanse of land
No TRAIT appear'd of Culture's fost'ring hand:
And, as the wild Woods yielded to the Blast,
Nature scarce own'd the unproductive Waste.
O'er rugged Cliffs fantastic Branches hung,
Round whose hoar Trunks the slender Scions clung,
　Impervious Mountains met the ling'ring Eye,
　Whose cloud-cap't Summits brav'd the Sky.
　Rocks, whose repulsive Frown access defied,
　And Bays, where idly ebb'd the slumb'ring Tide—
　Unless some Straggler of the NATIVE RACE,
　In crude Canoe expos'd his sooty Face;
　With lazy Motion paddled o'er the Flood,
Snatch'd at the spear-struck Fish—and hugged his Food.

But when BRITANNIA'S Sons came forth, to brave
The dreary Perils of the length'ning Wave;
When her bold Barks, with swelling Sails unfurled,
Trac'd these rude Coasts, and hail'd a new-found World.
Soon as their Footsteps press'd the yielding sand,
A sun more genial brighten'd on the Land:
Commerce and Arts enrich'd the social Soil,
Burst through the gloom and bade all Nature smile.

You see by that Robinson is no great threat as an original poet. But notice the trope and the terms that are caught up in it. Robinson didn't work all this out for himself. He *was* a derivative poet, about as derivative and imitative as you can get. What he demonstrates is the intersection of a literary, a poetic convention (and conventionality) and empirical (well, maybe empirical) actuality. There are storms in poetry and storms in local fact, and for once lack of invention is protected by circumstantial reality. The terms and the experience are both to hand. This is not a big storm, it is a brief storm, with the sun coming out one might think too suddenly, too sudden for good form—but that, by experience, is what actually happens here. These are coastal storms, expressing instability rather than say profound Wagnerian themes. Or to analyse more closely, here is initially a wilderness, a wasteland that Nature would scarce own; this is how it is before cultural contact, before Civilization comes, Nature unimproved by Art. And when Britannia's sons arrive from over the sea, the sun bursts through the gloomy clouds. Creation, in a sense, recurs; smiling Nature is a Providential Nature, the sun figures that God who is also light, genial in the sense of generating, creating, engendering. It is a standard topos. One further detail though, a line that will come in useful later— "Impervious Mountains met the ling'ring Eye". This sense of the listless undirected look, this passive regard, in relation to storms, mountains and waste and broken places, will be discovered again. But chiefly remember Sturt's premise of a rude nature, a condition wherein things are "wilder than 'twas elsewhere wont" as Harpur proposes in **"The Creek of the Four Graves"**. That and not just sheer distaste informs say Barron Field's complaint that this is a place where

　　　　Nature is prosaic,
Unpicturesque, unmusical, and where
Nature reflecting Art is not yet born.

When Sturt first entered Sydney Harbour he "speculated on the probable character of the landscape": the hills, which must have been covered with the same undifferentiated "dense and gloomy wood which abounded everywhere else" had in fact been over-run by skill and industry, and "a flourishing town stands on the ruins of the forest". This is the eighteenth-century triumph of Art over Nature. A fundamental proposition about the nature of Nature is encoded in all these descriptions, and the storms that occur in the early writing, whether imaginative or factual, all confirm that particular concept.

These storms are in the early literature. In this country we haven't had many really big storms, that is, storms in our writing. We have mainly floods and droughts and bushfires: occasionally in the north-west we have cockeyed bobs. Once we had our national act together and entered the halcyon days of pastoral dreaming, all our worries were occasional plagues of rabbits and locusts, said Hanrahan. There is, I suggest, a patterning of dominant tropes in our literature, and the early writing is much taken up with storms. A simple, extra-literary explanation is that people coming to this country came by sea, and the storms were encountered at sea, or along the coast.[11] Once settlement pushed into the interior, you got beyond the storm zone; and the context of experience, especially hazardous experience, changed. It's obvious enough, no doubt.

But there are some prominent instances in our colonial writing. The storm at the end of Marcus Clarke's *His Natural Life* is a case in point—a storm that performs the same restorative cleansing function that we have begun to discern, but which also completes the waste and destruction of life, almost in revulsion against the very anarchy and violence which it in itself represents—a storm of moral disaffection. That kind of image in turn is replaced or displaced by a different kind of trope, the relentless abrading wind at the end of Henry Handel Richardson's *Fortunes of Richard Mahony* for example. Increasingly that becomes the dominant version of Australia—the eroding forces, not the confrontational ones; and stoicism replaces fatalism, the wilderness surrenders to the desert. We have no *Lear*-like storms. Patrick White's *Eye of The Storm* doesn't make that translation adequately.

Charles Harpur's **"A Storm in the Mountains"** partakes of the early configuration of course. His is a vivid response to a direct experience:

the author, young as he was, and from the very coming on of the storm, became possessed with the feeling that it was for him eventually to make a poem of it, and was thereby led to observe its startling and dangerous manifestations throughout, with a singularly daring attention. And in this way, the conception, which is here elaborated, was crudely stirring within him, I say, even then.

(Mitchell Library MS A93)

There is a difference immediately. This storm is seen as a process, a movement, a dramatic narrative; not as a "site", nor as artificial contrivance, nor as symbolic. It is an event, with a beginning, a middle and an end. Yet it is to be made into a poem; more than that, the experience confirms not what the experience is to become, but what the boy is to become; so that in another sense it is after all symbolic.

But one thing more, for my guess is that Harpur not only recognized the innate poem, or the nascent poetic impulse there, but recognized also that here was a direct, or direct enough, correlation between the world of real experience and the world of poetry: he saw, and saw vividly, how poetry was about reality. For there is a poetic model for what he saw, and what he writes.

And what is that? From Kendall to Kramer the answer has already been given, and my modest addition is to ascertain in just what way Harpur is obliged to James Thomson's *The Seasons*—and specifically (just to contain the discussion to a manageable limit), to the poem "Summer".

Thomson was an enormously popular poet. The Appendix to Ralph Cohen's *The Art of Discrimination: Thomson's The Seasons and the Language of Criticism* (1964) lists the hundreds of editions of *The Seasons* following its publication in 1730. It supplied the occasion for numerous illustrations, it prompted musical compositions (e.g. by Haydn); and it was frequently and variously imitated. It was a major cultural force, for it not only influenced how people thought about poetry, but also how they thought about nature. Harpur may not have been much impressed by Dr Johnson's estimation of Thomson's mind as one that "at once comprehends the vast, and attends to the minute" (*Life of Thomson*), but Wordsworth had esteemed Thomson as the next poet to Milton (thereby discounting Marvell, Dryden, Pope). There is not between the two of them, he claimed, "a single new image of external nature; and scarcely . . . a familiar one from which it can be inferred that the eye of the Poet had been steadily fixed upon his object" (*Essay Supplementary to the Preface*, 1815). That proposition of the "strikingly external" sits right at the centre of the most important, most conceptually ambitious stanza of Harpur's **"Storm"**, held there in direct relation to the working out of another perception of immanent force.

Thomson's poem is organized around the sequence of events of an ideal day. Harpur's poem, which recounts the events of the storm—its onset, the storm itself, its aftermath—is likewise set against the course of a day. To some extent Harpur takes up the model that Thomson much more clearly adapts, the georgic—not in any exact imitation of Virgil but in the general generic sense of a poem

dealing with "matters of fact, descriptions of material objects and accounts of physical processes (with or without their supernatural causes), dressed out with a stylistic artifice which emphasized their dignity and importance."[12] Harpur was never much impressed by stylistic artifice, though he has his momentary lapses; and he structured his poems more tightly than the georgic required. But certainly he was intent on representing matters of fact—and, given some of his notes to his poems, vain about the accuracy of his descriptions of material objects, physical processes. And like Thomson—speculatively, in imitation of Thomson—he modified the georgic in the direction of what has become identified as the "excursion" poem, with its emphasis on meditation as well as precise description, and its persistent attraction to images of vastness and ruin. "Magnificence, vastness, ruin—no three words could better sum up the effects for which the 'excursion' poets were striving. In most of them a theory of the 'natural Sublime' was implied."[13]

One important difference between Harpur and Thomson however is in Harpur's determination to wrestle with intimations of the ineffable, with the something far more deeply interfused. Thomson does not enquire so energetically into the mysteries. Yet it would be a misrepresentation to suggest he was content with some bland sense of Providence; for the one particular passage which most demands our attention, Thomson's account of a summer storm, arrives just as Harpur's does, at a reflection of

> That sense of powers exceeding far his own,
> Ere yet his feeble heart has lost its fears . . .
>
> (ll. 1242-3)

while the poem "Summer" as a whole ends with a meditation on the workings of reason and imagination.

In other words, Thomson's poem provides Harpur with both a specific model, and with a general conceptual model: and one might also add in passing, Harpur adopted Thomson's practice of revising and amending and enlarging his poems. Let me give some examples of specific correlation.

First, as to material. One of the most sensational episodes in "Summer" is the destruction, by a bolt of lightning, of the young maiden Amelia while she is being embraced by her lover Celadon. This is, I hasten to add, an entirely innocent and virtuous love:

> From his void embrace,
> Mysterious Heaven! that moment to the ground,
> A blackened corse, was struck the beauteous maid.
> But who can paint the lover, as he stood
> Pierced by severe amazement, hating life,
> Speechless, and fixed in all the death of woe?
>
> (ll. 1214-1219)

It is difficult to take this seriously, just as difficult as taking seriously the desperate attempts of illustrators to capture Celadon's astonishment (not to mention Amelia's . . .); and just as difficult, in Harpur's case, to read with suitable concern and distress of the eagle zapped by the lightning:

> Short stops his flight!
> His dark form shrivels in the blasting light!
> And then as follows a sharp thunderous sound,
> Falls whizzing, stone-like, lifeless to the ground!
>
> (ll. 98-101)

Yet readers were much affected by Thomson's story. It was based on a real event, and Pope wrote an epitaph upon the lovers. In Harpur's case, there is genuine awe created in the lines just preceding, as the storm-front bulges over the eagle, bloats, grows frightfully luminous.[14] That is, Harpur is more successful at expressing the immediacy of the storm; he is bathetic in narrating the bare facts of what happened, and to some extent that can be true of Thomson too.

Thomson's summer storm begins

> A boding silence reigns
> Dread though the dun expanse—save the dull sound
> That from the mountain, previous to the storm,
> Rolls o'er the muttering earth . . .
>
> (ll. 1116-1119)

Harpur has, though a little later in his poem,

> Portentous silence! Time keeps breathing past—
> Yet it continues! May this marvel last?
> This wild weird silence in the midst of gloom
> So manifestly big with latent doom?
> Tingles the boding ear . . .
>
> (ll. 110-114)

and he had used "dun" just previously in reference to the legions of the storm. Thomson turns to the reaction of animals to the coming storm—birds flying low, the tempest-loving raven intimidated, the cattle all listening in "fear and dumb amazement". Harpur likewise begins by observing that the creatures and insects of the bush give the first intimations of the approaching storm. With the sudden crashing explosion of thunder comes wind, comes lightning, come sheets of rain. Storms will be storms, no doubt, and that is likely enough what happens; what interests me is the poetic vocabulary which Harpur has taken over. Thus Thomson:

> overhead a sheet
> Of livid flame discloses wide, then shuts
> And opens wider, shuts and opens still
> Expansive, wrapping ether in a blaze.
> Follows the loosened aggravated roar,
> Enlarging, deepening, mingling, peal on peal
> Crushed horrible, convulsing heaven and earth
>
> (ll. 1137-1143)

and so on. That "discloses" is Harpur too, and so is "convulsing". And the sheets of lightning opening and shutting are, I think, where Harpur gets his restless heat flares,

"like the dazzling hem / Of some else viewless veil held trembling . . ." (ll. 21-22). Thomson has a smouldering pine shattered and blackened; Harpur blasts an ancient gumtree.

Harpur emphasises, by underlining, the *red* hills; and that directs us to the lines in Thomson

> various-tinctured trains of latent flame,
> Pollute the sky, and in yon baleful cloud,
> A reddening gloom . . .
>
> (ll. 1110-1112)

Harpur uses the adjective "latent" several times: it appeals to him. The Thomson passage also suggests where the otherwise rather surprising adjective "polluted" comes from in Harpur—surprising that it should be there at all, but he does not take up Thomson's image, which is of explosive natural gases.

These and other verbal correlations suggest very strongly the presence of Thomson somewhere in the organizing of Harpur's recollections; that is, his storm is both a real storm and a poetical storm.

There is more; there is always more. The lonely Boy, the perhaps Wordsworthian boy, roams "out on the half-wild herd's dim tracks". The point has been made that if this is the wilderness, the waste and broken place ("vast-backed ridges . . . all rent in jags"), so too, in Thomson's tropic vision, under the "bright effulgent Sun" (and isn't that exactly Harpur!), on the vast savannas where great Nature dwells, "naught is seen / But the wild herds . . ." (ll. 703/4); though these are not quite the herds Harpur has in mind.

Harpur's storm occurs in "A rude peculiar world"—that is, the kind of rudeness and peculiarity that Charles Sturt had registered. It is *sui generis*—"the productions of this singular region seem peculiar to it, and unlike those of any other part of the world"[15], which corresponds to the kind of extreme nature that Thomson identified in the Welsh mountains, with their loud "repercussive roar", their heaped rude rocks, and smitten cliffs. This is an unruly nature; this is where the thunder gets to in Thomson, the climax just before the episode of Celadon and Amelia. The point is not just the poetic echoing, or verbal reverberation (what other kind could there be?). It is more importantly what Harpur discovers through his resumption of Thomson—not just the unruliness of the heavens in the unruly mountains, but the spill-over of that into the realm of human affairs. The potential for disaster that Harpur explores is requisite as a donnée against which his conviction of being unharmed in the midst of all this elemental strife is asserted.

One last example: the young boy looking about him on the mountainside turns "a listless, yet enquiring eye". That is not too distant from Thomson's "unfixed, wandering eye" (1.692); nor from Michael Massey Robinson's "lingering eye". For the philosophical question is what can be seen in the undifferentiated wilderness? How, in an as yet uninformed realm of Nature, can the eye see, how can the mind determine what the eye is to see? This is the question which comes back at the high point of Harpur's poem—how, he asks (and it seems it is a question asked well after the event), how may he find

> How through all being works the light of Mind?
> Yea, through the strikingly external see
> My novel Soul's divulging energy!
> Spirit transmuting into forms of thought
> What but for its cognition were *as nought!*

(ll. 166-170)

This is ambitious verse. Harpur has moved well past what he could learn from Thomson to get to this point. Indeed, the density of the Thomson allusions is in the first part of his poem; he goes past that. Besides, though his eye had been listless, it was nevertheless *enquiring*; just as in **"Midsummer Noon"** the meditating mind had not turned over to slumber in the noontide hour, but was awake and alert to the stillness and quietness. In his own way Harpur seems to have stumbled on Wordsworth's recognition of the appropriate condition of the mind for the creative process to begin; though in the case of **"A Storm in the Mountains"** the distinction has to be made between the mind or eye as passive and perceiving, and the mind as actively engaging with experience—here, of the storm.

What Harpur shows is, I think, particularly his own: he has positioned himself in the midst of the storm, and yet he is virtually detached from it, daring, heedless, secured by some destined charm, some deep intimation that all this is to be patterned, is to be created or recreated, by the novel, innovating soul. And in this I see Harpur as formulating a response to experience, taking up an attitude to experience, that seems on the evidence characteristic of Australian writing—a narrative relationship of half-commitment, partly involved in and partly removed from what is being said, passive and active agent simultaneously—just as we find in novels and short stories and autobiographies participants who tell their own story by telling someone else's story, or fail to notice that they're in fact telling their own. Like David Malouf's Frank Harland, they stand side on to their own art. Harpur does not write as the Thomsonian philosopher poet in Stoic contemplation of the greater harmonies of the universe; nor does he really grapple with the Wordsworthian "something far more deeply interfused", though both those are of interest to him. He recognized the difficult moral and spiritual progress we have made, and he recognized the precariousness of that attainment: he did not have Wordsworth's confidence about that. Yet it is both the difficulty and the precariousness of the attainment that makes it meaningful, valuable, to Harpur. In the mundane world he railed against the fragile social order, and in his personal life likewise he had only the most tenuous control—witness his distress at the death of his favourite son, his anger at the death of his father. On the mountain, in the

midst of the storm, Harpur met something grander and greater, something which took him out of himself while it enclosed and included him completely; which happened, but which also he encountered in some equivalent form in Thomson's poem. What we find in **"A Storm in the Mountains"** is Harpur being both imitative and original, continuing a tradition and evolving his own response. He went past Thomson, but Thomson gave him his start. It is that combination of conventionality and independence that defines the colonial moment.

But poetry is not defined in terms of moments, colonial, post-colonial or any other; at least not in Harpur's estimation of it. In an incompletely revised **"Discourse on Poetry"** which Harpur had intended to be introductory to the whole of his poems, he wrote of it as "a high and even sacred thing".

> And it is the peculiar office of the Poet, to bring these vital, but subtle influences into the mental neighbourhood of all men;—to make them intimately felt by all. But he does not create them. Everywhere existing in the constitution of the universe in its relation to Man, and thence by reflection in whatever is truly reproduced from it by human invention or art, they are but ingathered, as to a magnetic centre, by his sovereign imagination; not so much for self-enjoyment, as to be again given forth in immortal Poetry—that is condensed or sublimated in spirit, and chastened or harmonized formally.

(Mitchell Library MS A87)

He is like Coleridge perhaps—"The further I ascend from animated Nature (i.e. the embracements of rocks and hills), from men and cattle, and the common birds of the woods and fields, the greater becomes in me the intensity of the feeling of life. Life seems to me then a universal spirit that neither has nor can have an opposite."[16] If the colonial wilderness was undifferentiated experience, invoking the storm, it is no small thing for Charles Harpur to have discovered a means of ingathering sensation, and affirming life as an unopposed universal spirit.

Notes

1. See Phillip Mead, "Charles Harpur's Disfiguring Origins: Allegory in Colonial Poetry", *Australian Literary Studies,* XIV.3 (May 1990), pp. 279-296.

2. Davie and the Goldsmith passage are quoted in the Introduction to *The Seasons and the Castle of Indolence by James Thomson,* ed. James Sambrook (Clarendon Press, 1972; 1984), p.xv.

3. Leonie Kramer, "Imitation and Originality in Australian Colonial Poetry: The Case of Charles Harpur", *The Yearbook of English Studies,* XII.1983, pp.119-120.

4. G. A. Wilkes, ed., *The Colonial Poets* (Angus & Robertson, 1974), p.[viii].

5. Vivian Smith, "Poetry", *The Oxford History of Australian Literature,* ed. Leonie Kramer (Oxford University Press, 1981), pp.279-280.

6. John Hunter, *An Historical Journal of the Transactions at Port Jackson and Norfolk Island . . .* (fascimile, Library Board of South Australia, 1968), p.86.

7. *Ibid.,* p.84.

8. Mary Ann Parker, *A Voyage Round the World . . .* (1975; reissued Hordern House Rare Books, 1991), pp. 65-68.

9. Samuel Johnston, *A Journey to the Western Islands of Scotland* (1775; Penguin, 1984), p.45.

10. Charles Sturt, *Two Expeditions into the Interior of Southern Australia* (Smith, Elder and Co., 1833), vol II, pp.18-19.

11. See Ralph Abercromby, *Three Essays on Australian Weather* (White, 1896). He draws attention particularly to "the so called 'Southerly Burster', which is perhaps the most remarkable of the 'squall' winds which are found in various parts of the earth" (p.iii).

12. Sambrook, pp.x-xi.

13. Marjorie Hope Nicolson, *Mountain Gloom and Mountain Glory: The Development of the Aesthetics of the Infinite* (Cornell University Press, 1959), p.333.

14. John Arthos, in *The Language of Natural Description in Eighteenth-Century Poetry* (University of Michigan Press, 1949), notes that it is as old as Democritus that the eagle announces thunder (p.35).

15. Sturt, vol. I, p.xiv.

16. Quoted W. H. Auden, *The Enchafed Flood* (Faber & Faber, 1951), p.75.

Uli Krahn (essay date 2000)

SOURCE: Krahn, Uli. "'How Nourishing Is Nature': Imaginary Possession of Landscape in Harpur and Skrzynecki." *Southerly* 60, no. 3 (Winter 2000): 29-38.

[In the following essay, Krahn explores the techniques that Harpur and Peter Skrzynecki employ to express ownership of the culture and landscape of Australia.]

Notions of place have been central in the cultural self-definition of settler colonies like Australia, since difference in place is the most visible marker distinguishing the colony from the imperial motherland.[1] In Australian literary discourses, place is very much tied up with landscape, presumably as difference in landscape foregrounds the distinguishing difference of place.[2] Landscape is thus used to emphasise the distinctiveness of Australia, from earliest colonial writings to the present day discourses of nationalism, literature and tourism. As landscape is supposed to define Australia, it is by extension used to define true Australianness. One of the most poignant metaphors of this long-standing belief is A. G. Stephens's "English spectacles", spectacles that do not allow a true perception of the Australian landscape, and thus need to be replaced by "clear Australian eyes", which can perceive, and afterwards represent, the land "as it really is".[3] The assumption of an artistic realism which can provide such transparent and unmediated access to reality has long been debunked in literary criticism. Yet the notion that writers immersed in any culture not "native Australian" are hindered from proper perception of the Australian landscape by their cultural baggage is still relatively pervasive in cultural discourses and popular belief. I will make an oblique critique of such assumptions by studying the processes of coming to terms with landscape and place in two writers who are commonly associated with this "alien", non-Australian cultural baggage, Charles Harpur as a colonial writer, and Peter Skrzynecki as a "migrant" or "multicultural" writer. With this choice I intend to bring together two discourses of Australian literary criticism which have long been kept strictly separate, as if they represented totally different modes of writing and experience.

Paul Carter suggests that both the colonial and the migrant environment share a sense of improvisation, hybridity and tolerance of cultural ambiguities.[4] This notion provides a theoretical nexus where the works of migrant and colonial writer can be linked. Both Harpur and Skrzynecki are writers of transition and mediation where "alien" and "Australian" experience meet and, according to some critics, "true Australianness" of perception and representation is achieved.[5] From a biographical point of view, both occupy unexpectedly similar positions vis a vis Australia. Harpur was a currency lad raised to the cultural contradictions of Australian self-definitions springing up amidst an official culture which Judith Wright describes as obsessed with the "cult" of all things English.[6] Skrzynecki, on the other hand, was the child of Polish migrants who grew up in Australia, Europe being little but a culturally transmitted cherished memory.[7] I want to focus on the way both writers take imaginary possession of place, making the Australian landscape home. For Harpur, writing the Australian landscape involves confronting an environment which may be familiar from personal experience, yet largely lacks an indigenous cultural mindset in which to approach it, so that the processes of imaginary possession move into the foreground of his endeavour to write consciously Australian poetry. In Skrzynecki's writing, a mental framework for the land is largely already in place, yet needs to be adapted for his specific cultural background. Thus, although both write from rather different positions, there is a shared need to develop a mode of imaginary possession while bearing the ambiguities and uncertainties involved with transforming cultural conceptions of landscape into new and hybrid shapes.

Harpur's mode of imaginary possession of Australia is based on his sense of mission, which blends Wordsworthian notions of the poet as the bard of his people with politically radical Christian progressivism. This combination constitutes a multifaceted and flexible ideology for writing the land. Politically, Harpur embraces contemporary radicalism and republicanism from a Christian point of view, in the venerable tradition of English radicalism which interprets Christianity so as to demand equality and government by popular consent.[8] It seems to me that this radical political dimension allowed Harpur to create a speaking position for himself, both as a socially somewhat disdained currency lad of convict stock, and for his project of writing Australian poetry in a culture where Australia itself was largely deemed an unfit subject for poetry. Instead of accepting dominant values, Harpur puts himself in an aggressive opposition to the colonial establishment he defines as English, thus creating an Australian speaker as defined by his opposition to England and Englishness. With this stance, Harpur somewhat prefigures the radical nationalism of the 1890s, which relied on a very similar blend of radical politics with an anti-English attitude to create a distinctive Australian identity. Harpur strongly emphasises this Australian distinctiveness, claiming in "A Note on the Australian-born Whites from **'The Kangaroo Hunt'**" that "we are neither English, nor Irish, nor Scotch; but Australians; and our career as a race should be full of boldness and invention, and as little imitative as possible".[9] He is equally firm in his belief that Australia should not only be distinct from Britain, but should utilise political opportunities which could never be realised in England. In **"The Tree of Liberty"** (**"A Song for the Future"**) Harpur describes Australia as a place of utopian hope, where the "tree of liberty" which was wrecked by greed in the Old World can finally offer its bounties to everybody.[10] Harpur's democratic republican stance thus transfers special significance on Australia while it rejects the order of the Old World; he creates a view of Australia as a New Eden, where the hopes of humanity can finally be fulfilled.

This politically informed re-interpretation of Australia allows a perception and representation of the land itself which focuses on its beauty and promise as well as its distinctiveness. As indicated above, Harpur's vision of Australia is ideologically underpinned by a brand of Christianity which understands humanity as a march towards perfection (neatly blending theology with pre-Darwinian philosophy of progress). This position is set out in detail in **"The World and the Soul"**, which describes the formation of the earth and creatures on it and their evolution towards the ascension of man.[11] Yet as the text itself makes clear, man himself is also bound eternally to struggle with his low and primal instincts in order to better himself.[12] This underlying religious dimension suffuses Harpur's perception of Australia with a metaphysical dimension, as Australia becomes a place of immense spiritual promise and hope. Michael Ackland suggests that Harpur manages to turn around previous colonial notions of Australia as a primal, undifferentiated and potentially threatening wilderness in need of civilisation, and instead makes the land itself the repository of the good;[13] Harpur's religious ideology therefore allows for a redefinition of Australia as a place where God is present in nature. Of course, finding God in nature is nothing new in the context of European thinking, but a venerable theological tradition revived in

this particular shape by Wordsworth and other Romantic poets of nature. Harpur's feat lies in daring to apply this way of seeing to the Australian landscape, which was previously overwhelmingly not defined in such a manner.

Harpur's relatively new view of Australian nature as "a repository of sacred love"[14] dominates the writing of landscape in poems such as **"A Coastal View"**. This text presents the poetic self alone amidst a savage coastal scenery, watching and contemplating in the manner recently popularised by overseas Romantic nature poetry: "I sit alone / And gaze with a keen wondering happiness / Out o'er the sea". The speaker feels happy in his isolation in the Australian wilderness—even more, he rejoices in the presumed absence of civilisation which most pre-Romantic writing, English as well as Australian, found rather disconcerting. The speaker describes at length and in extensive detail the landscape around him, and finds delight in its untamed oddity:

> The coast how wonderful. Proportions strange
> And unimaginable forms, more quaint,
> More wild and wayward than were ever dreamt
> By a mad architect . . .

The text continues to compare this coast with all that signifies the archaic, the mysterious and the exotic in contemporary writing such as "pyramidic structures", "old Assyrian trowels", "minarets" and "Babylonian vastness". The speaker seems to consciously employ stereotypes of antipodean monstrosity in the metaphor of the "mad architect", yet at the same time negates their Otherness as he emphasises his love for and delight in the landscape, and the presence of God in it. The list of Orientalist comparisons suggests the sources of Harpur's fascination with this coast in darker Romantic fantasies by Coleridge and Shelley. Yet whereas English Romantics revelled in such imagery with a self-conscious mixture of attraction and repulsion, Harpur appropriates the antipodean Otherness in its force and curious attraction. In a classic move of postcolonial writing, Harpur turns the exotic into the familiar, as the speaker is shown to be connected to this strange landscape by the force of love:

> How nourishing is Nature to the soul
> That loves her well! . . .
> [. . .]
> And hence, when thus beloved, not only here
> By the great Sea, or amid forests wild,
> Or pastures luminous with lakes, is she
> A genial Ministress—but everywhere!
> Whatever testifies of her is good . . .

The text's imaginary possession of the land thus rests on what Ackland describes as Harpur's transformation of nature into the "focal point of a sacramental relationship" between God and man.[15] This notion of nature as a place where man communicates with God and with his inner self is itself a highly Wordsworthian approach to nature, which Harpur appropriates for his purpose of writing distinctly Australian poetry. Such a positive and hopeful approach to nature allows Harpur to incorporate even aspects of the Australian experience which previous writers would have thought of as extremely terrifying and inhospitable, such as bush fires and storms. Some critics regard Harpur's perception of something more than wilderness in need of civilisation in the Australian landscape as his greatest achievement in establishing an Australian poetry.[16] Yet this consciously Australian view of the landscape largely relies on notions of nature, religion and poetry Harpur adapted from English Romanticism, thus creating Australian distinctiveness by appropriating and fusing elements from diverse cultural sources.

The processes of imaginary possession in Harpur's poetry are not always purely ideal, but can also suggest a very concrete claim of possession. **"The Creek of Four Graves"** describes settlers' search for new land, and shows the settlers both mentally and physically in personal harmony and communion with nature. In contrast, Aborigines disrupt this harmony like "Hell's worst fiends", and brutally slay some of the settlers. Yet one settler manages to escape, and nature itself seems to be on his side, offering him shelter in an overhang of rather feminine metaphorical dimensions. Nature with all her spiritual force here becomes a direct supporter of white colonisation and Aboriginal dispossession. The text also describes a very tangible form of taking possession, the process of naming, as the setting of the narrated events is thereafter known as the Creek of the Four Graves.[17] Furthermore, the graves themselves constitute yet another aspect of claiming possession by burying settlers in the land.[18] J. J. Healy suggests the text ought to be read not simply as a colonialist tale vilifying Aborigines while celebrating settlement, but rather as a reflection of man's eternal strife against man.[19] While this seems to me a reasonable interpretation of the poem's metaphysical concern, the poem exemplifies the profound ethical problem of all imaginary possession of the land. Imaginary possession of Australia can never be entirely innocent, as it is part of the colonial enterprise of actually claiming the land in a physical way, and by these means dispossessing its original owners. **"The Creek of the Four Graves"** shows the complex entanglement of Harpur's writing with colonial discourses of the time; Ackland suggests that Harpur's writings hover between writing against earlier discourses by re-evaluating Australian nature, and actively supporting discourses of colonial possession.[20]

I want now to suggest a reading of Peter Skrzynecki's approach to landscape in an attempt to show some of the potential links between colonial and migrant intellectual environments. Not only does Harpur's culturally hybrid way of creating a distinctly Australian poetry survive in "migrant" writing in general, but Harpur's particular mode of approaching nature as a signifier for a metaphysical beyond is a strategy which more than a hundred years later can still be used successfully in Australian nature poetry. Like Harpur, Skrzynecki excels in precise and personal descriptions of Australian nature which ultimately derive their force and justification from viewing nature as a place

of spiritual meaning.[21] Poems like "Anvil Rock"[22] and "A Walk at 'Edge'"[23] approach nature as a place of special significance for the self, a place which ultimately points even beyond the self into some metaphysical realm. The speaker of the poems is situated in the Australian landscape which he searches, with varying success, for insights of a personal and general nature, in "Anvil Rock" literally trying to read hidden meanings from the rockface. "Anvil Rock", similar in theme to Harpur's **"A Coastal View"**, focuses on the rock "shaped by centuries of wind and sea-spray / it stands on a platform ledge / below the headland like an ancient signpost". Unlike Harpur's poem, the text describes nothing strange or wild in the scenery, maybe since today various cultural frameworks are available which allow appreciation of Australian nature without emphasis on its antipodean unruliness. Yet like Harpur, Skrzynecki approaches nature as a signifier for something else, describing the rocks as literally pointing beyond the world of sensory perception: "fixed in the earth like a compass / that points to a direction / somewhere between the sea and sky".[24] This vaguely Romantic idea of nature as a repository of personal and supernatural truth persists in much of Skrzynecki's poetry. Although many of the more exuberant claims and hopes of Romanticism have fallen away, nature can still thus be appropriated by defining it Romantically, as a place where personal and metaphysical insights can be gleaned by the solitary and reflective poetic self.[25]

As in some of Harpur's texts, the processes of imaginary possession for Skrzynecki also encompass the writing of history. Glenda Sluga points out that Skrzynecki writes the "suppressed" history of migration which has not yet made its way into the annals of official Australian history, thus creating place and identity for the migrant experience in poems like "Old Hostel Site".[26] Yet "Old Hostel Site" also suggests a profound ambiguity towards writing such a history. While the text creates and asserts identity in the way suggested by Sluga, it also subverts the distinctness of the migrants' identity by the direct intervention of nature itself, as nature seems to take over both place and the speaker's mind:

> Where a wagtail breaks into song—
> Barking dogs
> Rip
> At Air
> And the illusions
> Of rediscovery I brought along.

Nature's intervention in history becomes even clearer in "Shortcut through Rookwood Cemetery."[27] At the significant site of the grave of previous migrants, who made the land their own by the ultimate act of being buried in it, the speaker declares:

> Nearly every month, I've stopped
> To read the names,
> Some like mine, others more harsh,
> Grouped together
> Like an electoral roll

That's never to be changed:
The Z and Y of a foreign heritage
That finally surrenders
To a landscape's claim.

Nature itself erases the differences of culture here, such as the difference of "new" and "old" Australian signified by names on the gravestones. It also appears to turn the process of imaginary possession around, as nature herself claims the people instead of people claiming the land. The Romantic notion of the landscape as a spiritual force allows the speaker to present nature as finally overriding cultural differences, uniting Australians of all cultural backgrounds as one; the migrant problem of making the alien land home can be neatly overcome by such a philosophy which assigns nature an active role in the process of making the new land one's own.

Nevertheless, Skrzynecki's use of Romantic approaches to nature is not naively anachronistic, but reflects the different circumstances of contemporary life. Instead of Harpur's hopeful and utopian look into the future, Skrzynecki's view is more resigned and directed towards the past, for instance in the emphasis in "Anvil Rock"[28] on nature's antiquity. In "A Walk at 'Edge'", the speaker recounts an excursion into landscape where the search for meaning in nature is frustrated—the land remains silent:

[. . .]
each braved the assault of winds
in a silence that was as withdrawn
as the earth that our fingers traced over—
that found lines of stone as rusty as sediments
in a river that human hands
had never disturbed and only petals
had stained the colour of a swallow's throat.
There was no answer to what
we searched for, no handful of knowledge
to bring back through an assembly
of awkwardly gesturing branches,
no souvenir to retrieve on a later occasion.[29]

Yet in a truly postmodern manner, nature's silence does not stop the speaker from repeating the gesture of expecting nature to provide entrance to some beyond, as "another heath beckoned / from the northern green horizon". As in "Anvil Rock", the Romantic attraction of nature is not so much the actual access to the deeper truths Harpur enjoyed, but the simple promise of a beyond—the speaker's inability to attain what is promised des not keep him from seeking it further. Although contemporary modes of thought seem to have reduced humanity's access to deeper truths in nature, the very act of seeking these truths still seems worthwhile repeating, even if there is little hope of fulfilment—while the search itself enables the speaker to make the land home.

Overall, I would suggest that both Harpur and Skrzynecki rely on a somewhat similar strategy of imaginary possession which is essentially derived from English Romanticism. Faced with landscapes for which both need to create a new cultural framework, they succeed in this task by interpreting the land both as an extension of the self and as a signifier of supernatural meaning. This particular poetic strategy allows both to create very detailed and often very loving poetic representations of Australian landscapes. Both writers also paradoxically emphasise the writing of a distinctly Australian landscape and poetry by adapting foreign literary modes. There is nothing surprising about this, as despite their many differences, both colonial and migrant writers' creativity is almost inevitably based on utilising and exploiting cultural ambiguity. Far from blurring the perception of Australia, I would argue that such "English" or generally "foreign" spectacles may not be a liability but an asset, providing cultural opportunities and insights as uniquely Australian in their particular hybridity as the "clear Australian eyes" of the native born.

Notes

1. Elleke Boehmer, Colonial and Postcolonial Literature (Oxford: Oxford University Press, 1995), p. 213.

2. Kevin Magarey, "Place, Landscape, Saussure, Region and Two Australian Colonial Poets", in P. R. Eaden and F. H. Mares (eds.) Mapped but not Known: The Australian Landscape of the Imagination (Adelaide: Wakefield Press, 1986), p. 106.

3. John Barnes, "'Through Clear Australian Eyes': Landscape and Identity in Australian Writing", in P. R. Eaden and F. H. Mares (eds.), p. 86.

4. Paul Carter, "Lines of Communication: Meaning in the Migrant Environment", in Sneja Gunew and Kateryna O. Longley (eds.) Striking Chords: Multicultural Literary Interpretations (Sydney: Allen and Unwin, 1992), p. 9.

5. Judith Wright, Charles Harpur (Melbourne: Lansdowne Press, 1963), p. 30; Michael Griffith, "Peter Skrzynecki: 'the revelation of a Landfall beyond any known map,'" Southerly, 54, 1994, pp. 119-128.

6. Judith Wright, p. 7.

7. Peter Skrzynecki, "Paradox of the empty socks (or Slowing down to hurry up)", in Sneja Gunew and Kateryna O. Longley (eds.), pp. 52-54.

8. Michael Ackland, That Shining Band: A Study of Australian Colonial Verse Tradition (St. Lucia: University of Queensland Press, 1994), p. 42.

9. Michael Ackland (ed.), Charles Harpur: Selected Poetry and Prose, (Ringwood: Penguin, 1986), p. 21.

10. Ibid., p. 21.

11. Ibid., p. 103.

12. As I am not entirely sure whether Harpur means "men" or "men and women" in his writings about "mankind", I deem it cautious to accept his gender specific form without changing it to the more inclusive forms popular today.

13. Michael Ackland, That Shining Band, pp. 43.

14. Ibid., p. 47.

15. Ibid., p. 77.

16. Judith Wright, p. 30; see also Adrian Mitchell, "Writing up a Storm: Natural Strife and Charles Harpur", Southerly, 53, 1993, pp. 90-113.

17. For the significance of naming see Paul Carter, The Road to Botany Bay: An Essay in Spatial History (London: Faber and Faber, 1987).

18. Elizabeth Webby, "The Grave in the Bush", in Dennis Haskell (ed.) Tilting at Matilda: Literature, Aborigines, Women and the Church in Contemporary Australia (Fremantle: Fremantle Arts Centre Press, 1994), pp. 30-38.

19. J. J. Healy, Literature and the Aborigine in Australia (St. Lucia: University of Queensland Press, 1978), p. 96.

20. Michael Ackland, That Shining Band, p. 20.

21. Michael Ackland (ed.), Charles Harpur: Selected Poetry and Prose, p. 44.

22. Michael Griffith, p. 19.

23. Peter Skrzynecki, Easter Sunday (Sydney: Angus and Robertson, 1993), p. 33.

24. Ibid., p. 118.

25. Ibid., p. 33.

26. For such a reading of Skrzynecki's poetry, see Michael Griffith, p. 125.

27. Glenda Sluga, "Dis/Placed", Meanjin, 48, 1989, pp. 153-60; Peter Skrzynecki, The Aviary (Sydney: Edwards and Shaw, 1978), p. 10.

28. The Aviary, p. 48.

29. Easter Sunday, p. 118.

FURTHER READING

Biographies

Jordens, Ann-Mari. "Harpur and Kendall." In *The Stenhouse Circle: Literary Life in Mid-Nineteenth Century Sydney,* pp. 83-106. Melbourne: Melbourne University Press, 1979.

Tracks the literary careers of Henry Kendall and Harpur, acknowledging the support of patron Nicol Drysdale Stenhouse.

Normington-Rawling, J. *Charles Harpur, an Australian.* Sydney: Angus and Robertson Ltd., 1962, 334p.

In-depth narrative of Harpur's childhood, early influences, marriage, work, and ambitions.

Criticism

Ackland, Michael. "Charles Harpur's Republicanism." *Westerly* 29, no. 3 (October 1984): 75-88.

Defines Harpur's political views based upon moral, social, and religious ideas in his writing.

———. "'Though Urged by Doubt . . .': Charles Harpur and the Nineteenth-Century Crisis of Faith." *Journal of the Australasian Universities Language and Literature Association* 64 (November 1985): 154-74.

Comments on death, religious doubt, and the matter of faith as manifested in Harpur's poems.

———. "Poetic Ideal versus 'the hard Real' in Charles Harpur's 'The Tower of the Dream.'" *Southerly* 47, no. 4 (December 1987): 380-94.

Explication of Harpur's dream-poem, with the consideration of dreams as poetry.

———. "Inspiration Versus Moonshine in Harpur's 'The Importance of a Rhyme.'" *Southerly* 49, no. 4 (December, 1989): 636-42.

Discusses Harpur's view of inspiration and the poet's role in society through a consideration of Harpur's short prose.

Cantrell, Leon. "Marvel and Charles Harpur." *Australian Literary Studies* 6, no. 1 (May 1973): 88-90.

Discusses Marvel's influence on Harpur's style, word choice, and subject matter.

Hope, A. D. "Three Early Australian Poets." In *Native Companions: Essays and Comments on Australian Literature, 1936-1966,* pp. 103-26. Sydney: Angus and Robertson Ltd., 1974.

Discusses neglect and distorted criticism of the works of Harpur, William Charles Wentworth, and Kendall.

Kane, Paul. "Charles Harpur and the Myth of Origins." *Australian Literary Studies* 13, no. 2 (October 1987): 146-60.

Develops Harpur's quest for recognition as Australia's first poet of note.

Mead, Philip. "Charles Harpur's Disfiguring Origins: Allegory in Colonial Poetry." *Australian Literary Studies* 14, no. 3 (May 1990): 279-96.

Discusses the use of allegory in Harpur's "The Dream by the Fountain" and "The Witch of Hebron," among others.

Miller, E. Morris. "Poets and Poetry: New South Wales." In *Australian Literature from Its Beginnings to 1935,* Vol. 1, pp. 18-102. Melbourne: Melbourne University Press, 1940.

Provides historical background for Harpur's literary development and briefly compares Harpur's works with those of Henry Kendall and Adam Lindsay Gordon.

Perkins, Elizabeth. "Harpur's Notes and Kendall's Bell Birds." *Australian Literary Studies* 5, no. 3 (May 1972): 277-84.

Presents evidence of Kendall's study and appropriation of Harpur's poetry and notes in the writing of his "Wild Kangaroo."

——. "Emerson and Charles Harpur." *Australian Literary Studies* 6, no. 1 (May 1973): 82-88.

Brief comparison of Harpur's works with the philosophy of Ralph Waldo Emerson. Also presents marginal notes by Harpur from the book *Eight Essays,* by Emerson, with commentary from Perkins.

——. "An Early Australian Short Story by Harpur." *Australian Literary Studies* 7, no. 3 (May 1976): 327-33.

Discusses Harpur's short story "The Importance of a Rhyme," noting how it reveals aspects of his personality and style.

——. "The Religious Faith of Charles Harpur." *Quadrant* 6 (June, 1979): 29-35.

Contemplates religious themes expressed in Harpur's poetry.

——. "Towards Seeing Minor Poets Steadily and Whole." In *Bards, Bohemians, and Bookmen,* edited by Leon Cantrell, pp. 39-55. Queensland: University of Queensland Press, 1976.

Highlights literary significance of the works of Harpur, Kendall, and Adam Lindsay Gordon, with particular attention given to the personality and style of Harpur.

Wright, Judith. "Charles Harpur." In *Preoccupations in Australian Poetry,* pp. 1-18. Melbourne: Oxford University Press, 1965.

Discusses Harpur's early years, influences, and the treatment of landscape in his poetry.

Mary Hays
1760-1843

English novelist, essayist, and biographer.

INTRODUCTION

An important writer on women's rights in the late eighteenth and early nineteenth centuries, Hays is best known for her two novels and her feminist polemic, *Appeal to the Men of Great Britain in Behalf of Women* (1798). Among her contemporaries she is ranked second only to her friend Mary Wollstonecraft in advancing such feminist causes as sexual autonomy, intellectual freedom, and political power.

BIOGRAPHICAL INFORMATION

Hays was born in 1760 in Southwark, near London, to a large family of religious Dissenters. She became engaged at a young age to John Eccles, also a Dissenter, who served as her mentor and friend, as well as her intended husband. Although neither family approved of the match initially, both eventually consented; however, Eccles became ill and died before the couple married. Grief-stricken, Hays buried herself in intellectual pursuits. The preacher Robert Robinson, with whom her family was acquainted, introduced her to a radical circle of intellectuals led by London publisher Joseph Johnson; the group included John Disney, George Dyer, and William Frend. Hays began writing and reviewing books for various publications, among them the *Critical Review,* the *Analytical Review,* and particularly, the *Monthly Magazine.* She was able to earn a meager living from her work, which at first consisted of poems and a prose fable. With the encouragement of her friends, she soon turned to weightier and more controversial subjects such as theology and women's rights. After reading Mary Wollstonecraft's 1792 attack on conventions, titled *A Vindication of the Rights of Woman,* Hays, along with her sister Elizabeth, produced *Letters and Essays, Moral and Miscellaneous* (1793), a collection of pieces on various feminist issues; she later published anonymously another feminist polemic, *Appeal to the Men of Great Britain in Behalf of Women.* Meanwhile, she became friendly with Wollstonecraft, whose work she admired and whose advice she often sought.

Inspired by English philosopher William Godwin's *Enquiry Concerning Political Justice,* Hays wrote to the author and began an intellectual correspondence that would last many years. In January of 1796, Hays served as matchmaker for Godwin and Wollstonecraft, who married the next year. At about the same time, Hays was pursuing William Frend, whose rejection of her advances formed the basis of her autobiographical first novel, *Memoirs of Emma Courtney* (1796). She continued to produce feminist pieces for the *Monthly Magazine,* and completed a second novel, *The Victim of Prejudice* (1799).

By the end of the eighteenth century, the Reign of Terror in France had made all revolutionary and reform causes, including feminism, extremely unpopular in England, and Hays moderated her position somewhat. Although she was leading a much more secluded life after the turn of the century, she continued to write, producing a six-volume series of biographies on famous women, several didactic novels, and in 1821, her last publication, *Memoirs of Queens, Illustrious and Celebrated.* Hays continued to live in and around London for more than twenty years after she stopped publishing, but she eventually lost contact with the members of the literary circles she had earlier enjoyed. She died in 1843 at the age of 83.

MAJOR WORKS

Hays's first important work was her 1793 collection *Letters and Essays, Moral and Miscellaneous,* written with her sister Elizabeth, although the former's name appeared alone on the title page. The collection includes pieces on topics generally considered acceptable for female writers as well as those on issues more conventionally reserved for males, including works on politics and philosophy. Hays's first novel, *Memoirs of Emma Courtney,* combines the features of two popular genres of the time: the first-person narrative associated with the English Jacobins was interspersed with elements of the epistolary form associated with the Novel of Sensibility. As narrator, Emma espouses many of the same reformist opinions on social and cultural issues held by Hays, and also like Hays, she openly declares her affections to a man—considered unseemly behavior for a woman both in fiction and in life.

Two years later Hays anonymously published her feminist tract *Appeal to the Men of Great Britain in Behalf of Women,* a work often compared to Wollstonecraft's *A Vindication of the Rights of Woman.* Although considered less strident than Wollstonecraft's text, *Appeal* offers evidence of women's oppression taken from the experiences of everyday life, rather than from a purely theoretical standpoint. This emphasis on the concrete also informs Hays's second novel, *The Victim of Prejudice,* a work that deals with seduction, imprisonment, suicide, rape, and prostitution. Like Hays's earlier work, the novel is concerned with the economic and social oppression of women, but adds issues of social class to those of gender. The heroine, Mary, is thus doubly victimized not only as a woman, but also as a poor woman, dependent on the generosity of her benefactor.

After the turn of the century, amid an antifeminist backlash, Hays's writing became more temperate. *Female Biography* consists of six volumes of some 290 biographies of varying lengths on famous women from Anne Boleyn to Catherine the Great. Curiously, Hays did not include a biography of Wollstonecraft, although she had earlier written two obituaries of her friend—one for the *Monthly Magazine* and another for *The Annual Necrology, for 1797 to 1798.* Some critics believe Hays was avoiding further controversy by omitting Wollstonecraft from the compilation.

CRITICAL RECEPTION

Hays was severely criticized by her contemporaries not only for the unconventional ideas on social reform manifested in her writings, but also for her unconventional approach to courtship in her personal life. Her unsuccessful pursuit of William Frend, and later of Charles Lloyd, made her the object of ridicule among the literary circles of London. Some modern critical evaluations of Hays repeat the personal gossip that hounded her during her lifetime. M. Ray Adams, for example, focuses less on Hays's writings than on her perceived "unfeminine" qualities, on her lack of physical attractiveness, and on her pursuit of men. According to Adams, "in her relations with men she carried out the doctrines of reason, sincerity, and the emancipation of woman with a thoroughness that shocked her own sex, as well as the men for whose favor she bid. With her, woman was the hunter, man the game." But later critics dismiss the personal scandal and concentrate on her serious work as a social reformer and champion of feminist causes. Katharine M. Rogers compares Hays's arguments on behalf of women's rights with those of her friend, Mary Wollstonecraft, pointing out that while Wollstonecraft grounded her arguments in rational theory, Hays used experience to shore up her position. According to Rogers, Hays's approach is "disarmingly common-sensical," and as such it complements, rather than competes with, the work of Wollstonecraft. "Together, the two authors make the points that need to be made on the theoretical and the domestic level," according to Rogers.

Terence Allan Hoagwood extends the comparison between Hays and Wollstonecraft to their novels, examining Wollstonecraft's unfinished novel *The Wrongs of Woman, or Maria,* together with Hays's *The Victim of Prejudice,* claiming that although the former begins to take on similar issues, the latter "is a finished work, sophisticated alike in its social theory, its narrative design, its historical hermeneutic, and its pervasive feminism." Hoagwood also condemns earlier criticism that concentrated on Hays's personal life as "malicious gossip," claiming that "Hays's

vigorously intellectual social criticism was belittled by propagandistic focus on her supposed flirtations. Even in the twentieth century, *Emma Courtney* has sometimes been trivialized, as if it were primarily about nothing more important than the author's private feelings for a particular man. In 1800 Charles Lloyd tried to start a rumor that Hays had flirted with him; and this humiliating triviality has sometimes seemed to eclipse the important contributions that Hays made in feminism, social theory, and fiction."

PRINCIPAL WORKS

Cursory Remarks on an Enquiry into the Expediency and Propriety of Public or Social Worship: Inscribed to Gilbert Wakefield [as Eusebia] (pamphlet) 1791

Letters and Essays, Moral and Miscellaneous [with Elizabeth Hays] (letters and essays) 1793

Memoirs of Emma Courtney 2 vols. (novel) 1796

Appeal to the Men of Great Britain in Behalf of Women (essay) 1798

The Victim of Prejudice 2 vols. (novel) 1799

Female Biography; or Memoirs of Illustrious and Celebrated Women of All Ages and Countries 6 vols. (biographies) 1803

Family Annals; or The Sisters (novel) 1817

Memoirs of Queens, Illustrious and Celebrated (essays) 1821

CRITICISM

The Anti-Jacobin Review and Magazine

SOURCE: "The Reviewers Reviewed." *The Anti-Jacobin Review and Magazine* 3, no. 11 (May 1799): 54-58.

[*The following review compares the author's own conservative assessment of Hays's* Memoirs of Emma Courtney *and* The Victim of Prejudice *to past critiques of these works.*]

Emma Courtney, . . . appeared about three years ago. The Monthly Review of April, 1797, thus speaks of it:—

> "These memoirs rise beyond the class of vulgar novels, which aspire only to divert the unoccupied mind by occasional illusion from an irksome attention to the daily occurrences and trivial incidents of real life."

Meaning, as we suppose, to praise this attempt of the "fair writer" to find other employment for the female mind, than that which nature, situation, and sex, have designed it.

> "This author," they proceed "attempts the solution of a moral problem which is eminently important, viz. Whether it be prudent in minds of a *superior mould,* whether it will bring to them a greater balance of happiness, in the whole account, to exempt themselves from the common *delicacies and hypocrisies* of life, and, on all occasions, to give vent to their *wildest feelings* with *conscientious sincerity,* or patiently to submit to the *incumbent mountains* of circumstances, without one *volcanic effort* to *shatter the oppressive load* into ruin."

Setting aside this slang of modern philosophy, the plain question is—Whether it is most for the advantage of society that women should be so brought up as to make them dutiful daughters, affectionate wives, tender mothers, and good Christians, or, by a corrupt and vicious system of education, fit them for revolutionary agents, for heroines, for Staels, for Talliens, for Stones, setting aside all the decencies, the softness, the gentleness, of the female character, and enjoying indiscriminately every envied privilege of man?

The aim of this novel is to claim for the female sex the rights of the latter character. The heroine for such she is literally meant to be, is, even in early years, described—

> "—as active, blythsome, bounding, sporting, romping, light, gay, alert, and full of glee; as offending all the pious ladies at church by her gamesome tricks."

She is next pourtrayed in still stronger terms:—

> "My desires were impetuous, and brooked no delay; my affections were warm, and my temper irascible; opposition would always make me vehement, and coercion irritated me to violence. . . . never but once do I recollect having received a blow, but the boiling rage, the cruel tempest, the deadly vengeance it excited in my mind, I now remember with shuddering."

An excellent beginning this, and fully calculated to produce the fruit intended. The next advance of her mind is effected by the perusal of Plutarch:—

> "I went down into the dining-room, my mind pervaded with *republican ardour,* my sentiments elevated by a *high-toned philosophy,* and my bosom glowing with the *virtues* of patriotism."

Does not this out-Helen even the wife or mistress of Stone? Not less alive does she appear to have been to the softer affections—let her speak for herself:—

> "In the course of my researches the Heloise of Rousseau fell into my hands—ah! with what transport, with what enthusiasm, did I peruse this dangerous, enchanting work! How shall I paint the sensations that were

excited in my mind? The pleasure I experienced approached the limits of pain—it was *tumult*—all the *ardour* of my character was excited."

That the mind here displayed should run into errors of no inferior enormity, was naturally to be expected, and, of course, we all along find her disdaining all those holy restraints which the wisdom and virtue of ages have esteemed necessary for the controul of human passions. But, lest we should be supposed *prejudiced* against her, we will quote her own sentiments on some important points:—

> "The wildest speculations are less mischievous than the torpid state of error. He who tamely resigns his understanding to the guidance of another, sinks, at once, from the dignity of a rational being, to a mechanical puppet, moved, at pleasure, on the wires of the artful operator. Imposition is the principle and support of every varied description of tyranny, whether civil or ecclesiastical, moral or mental; its baneful consequence is to degrade both him who is imposed on, and him who imposes—*obedience* is a word which ought *never to have had existence,*" &c. &c.

What stuff is here!—but a little more, and we have done with the filthy labour:—

> "To the profession my objections are still more serious; the study of the law is the study of chicanery—the church is the school of hypocrisy and usurpation!—you could only enter the Universities by a moral degradation, that must check the freedom and contaminate the purity of the mind, and, entangling it in an inexplicable maze of error and contradiction, *poisoning virtue at its source,*" &c. &c.

On the subject of female chastity she is consistent with herself, in her defence for offering her honour to a man who avoided her. "*Individuality of affection,*" she says, "*constitutes chastity;*" or, in other words, the mistress is, in all respects, as honourable as the wife, provided she hath but one lover. If such a sentiment does not strike at the root of every thing that is virtuous, that is praiseworthy, that is valuable, in the female character, we are at a loss to discover by what wickedness they are to fall.

The tale of this novel is not at variance with the opinions we have extracted. That it is in all points reprehensible, in the highest degree, would be doubted by none, but the Monthly Reviewers, and their liberal fellow-labourers. Their concluding remark upon it is worthy of them:—

> "Many remarkable and several *excellent* reflections [precious guardians of a nation's literature] are interspersed, and the whole displays great intellectual powers. There are also sentiments which are open to attack, [indeed!] and opinions which require serious discussion; but we leave every reader to form his or her own judgement."

Had the tendency of this novel been favourable to virtue, honour, religion, morality, the liberality of these critics would have been less conspicuous. But we have already bestowed, perhaps, too much notice on this performance. We must now speak to this lady's second production, namely, *The Victim of Prejudice*—of what prejudice?— the old story: A young lady, of at least equal ardour in the cause of liberty and of love as even Emma herself, is restrained by some few limits which the world has thought proper to fix to certain unruly passions. The heroine of the tale, "Mary," [we are sick of Mary,] is educated according to the plan of Rousseau: no check, no controul; freedom of enquiry, and extravagance of hope, however dangerous, and however fallacious, are the prevailing features of this performance; the same indiscriminating and mischievous censure of every thing society has hitherto deemed sacred, and necessary to its existence, is here most lavishly displayed.—In the *dishonour,* as we old fashioned moralists should call it, of "*Mary,*" there is something like an imitation of Clarissa; but how unlike to the original!—In conformity to the general spirit of this authoress, and her party, (for that she is of *the party* her quotations from Godwin, Holcroft, Mary Wollstonecraft, Helvetius, Rousseau, &c. most clearly evince,) religion is utterly, and with zealous care, excluded from her writings. The pious addresses of Clarissa to her Creator, affect the heart of the reader with the most delightful and grateful sensations; while the furious declamation of "*Mary*" to the God of nature, and the God of reason, excite no sentiment but disgust.

The event of this story is such as might be expected from its title: Mary, after a sturdy opposition to the best opinions and practices of the world, sinks in the unequal contest; and, while suffering under the effects of her extravagant desires, thus laments her fate:—

> "Almighty *nature,* [is this like Clarissa?] mysterious are thy decrees—the vigorous promise of my youth has failed: the victim of a barbarous prejudice, [namely, that she was not allowed to marry the son of a man of high rank,] society has cast me out from its bosom."

Again, in conclusion:—

> "Ignorance and despotism, combating frailty with cruelty, may go on to propose *partial* reform in one invariable melancholy round; reason derides the weak effort; while the fabric of superstition and crime, extending its broad basis, mocks the toil of the visionary projector."

To the very last she is true to her principles.—Our opinion of these two novels is now clearly known, and we have said more of them than their intrinsic merit could possibly entitle them to expect. We have noticed them merely to guard the female world against the mischievousness of their tendency, "lest the venom of the shaft should be mistaken for the vigour of the bow."—As *usefulness* seems to be the watchword of this author and her friends, we will tell her how she may be much more useful than she can possibly make herself by devoting her time to literary labours—*to your distaff, Mary, to your distaff.*—On the *style*

of her writings it is needless to remark; who stays to admire the workmanship of a dagger wrenched from the hand of an assassin?

Monthly Review (essay date 1800)

SOURCE: *Monthly Review* 31 (January 1800): 82.

[*In the following review of Hays's* The Victim of Prejudice, *the protagonist Mary Raymond is depicted as a character worthy of both love and pity owing to the disreputable circumstances surrounding her birth and history.*]

Mary, the heroine of this little tale, is, to the credit of the author's pencil, a spirited and affecting sketch, but somewhat out of nature; and the principle which it is designed to inculcate by no means follows from the premises. By the novels which issue from this school, love, which is a transient passion, is to be complimented, in all cases, at the expence of the regulations and institutions of society; and a respect for virtue and decorum is to be classed in the list of vulgar prejudices. Love, which is generally our happiness, may and will sometimes be our misery. The wisest and the best are often the slaves and victims of circumstances:—Mary is one of those victims,—though amiable, noble, and virtuous, the circumstances of her birth prevented her from being the most eligible match for a man of virtue having virtuous connections, and wishing to have a virtuous offspring. Descended from a mother who was both a prostitute and a murderer, and who expiated her crimes on the gallows, shall we term the objection of the Hon. Mr. Pelham's father to the marriage of his son with her a mere prejudice? Must not William Pelham himself, had he been permitted to marry the lovely and amiable Mary, have had cause to blush when the children who might have been the fruit of their union came to inquire into the history of their mother? According to the fixed laws of nature, we suffer from the vices of our parents; and this, with every wise man, will be a very strong motive to virtue; since the evil resulting from a deviation from her paths will not terminate in ourselves. We must love and pity such a character as Mary Raymond: but her misery results rather from a general sentiment of detestation of atrocious crimes, than from any act which is entitled to the appellation of tyranny.

J. M. S. Tompkins (essay date 1938)

SOURCE: Tompkins, J. M. S. *The Polite Marriage,* pp. 150-90. London: Cambridge University Press, 1938.

[*In the following excerpt, Tompkins analyzes how Hays's notably brash, Godwinian character and philosophical beliefs are reflected in her novels, particularly* The Memoirs of Emma Courtney.]

Of all the small writers whom [we] commemorate, Mary Hays is the least likely to be quite forgotten. This is not because of the quality of her literary work, which is, with the exception of **The Scotch Parents,** the worst we have handled, since she rejected the discipline of eighteenth-century taste and acquired no other; but because she passed many years of her life on the edge of a circle that is still intrinsically interesting to us. She was the occasion of characteristic utterances by Lamb, Southey and Coleridge, and is to be found modestly posted in explanatory footnotes to their correspondence. She knew Mary Wollstonecraft, and was counted by the *Anti-Jacobin* among those "philosophesses" who blasphemously controverted the real nature of woman in their vindication of her political and economic rights; and she deposited a great deal of confidence in the cool bosom of William Godwin. Her novels, **The Memoirs of Emma Courtney** and **The Victim of Prejudice,** are occasionally cited as documents in the history of feminism; and recently a collateral descendant, Miss A. F. Wedd, has published a selection from the love-letters of her girlhood, followed by the letters addressed to her in middle life by Mrs Eliza Fenwick, with an introduction based on family papers.[1] What follows is little more than a leisurely reconsideration of all this material, paying less attention to her not very important contacts with the romantic poets than to her self-portrait in **Emma Courtney,** that astonishing blend of complacence and a white sheet.

[Mary Hays and Elizabeth Griffith] were born within about thirty years of each other, but the cleft between their two generations was more than usually deep, and the difference in temperament between them is reinforced by differences in modes of thought and expression. Mrs Griffith had asserted that the only philosophy a woman ought to have was resignation. Miss Hays was strenuously philosophical and not at all resigned. She was a Godwinite, measuring right and wrong by the scale of social utility. She accepted the mechanical theory of the Universe and managed to harmonize it with Christianity. Her mouth was full of catchwords and quotations, and she did, with painful labour and some sophistication, seek to understand what happened to her in the light of these beliefs; but in the contortions with which she accepted her fate resignation was the last posture she tried. Hers is the clamour of constant outrage. A distempered civilization has wronged her; she has a case to bring against the prejudices of society; and the brawling, repetitive egoism with which she brings it contrasts strongly with Mrs Griffith's plaintive delicacy. Confession was at once a need of her nature and her strongest weapon of offence. Her scientific interest in her own case quelled shamefastness as it must have quenched her sense of humour and her fear of ridicule; moreover the consequences of injustice must be exhibited in order that justice may be done. In her lifetime her friends bore the brunt of her vehement and undesired candour; and now she has found another ear.

"You never wrote . . . an all-of-the-wrong-side sloping hand, like Miss Hayes" (*sic*), says Lamb in a letter to

George Dyer. The tiny fact, thrown out in a soothing, mirthful expostulation with the ruffled Dyer, who had been pricked by an allusion to his hieroglyphics, rejoices the heart as that of Edmund Gosse was rejoiced when he found it recorded that Joseph Warton read the Communion Service in a remarkably awful manner. Its appropriateness is perfect. Her reaction from the ethics of womanhood as the eighteenth century had understood them, from reserve, complaisance and submission, had indeed sent Miss Hays sloping all of the wrong side. Her chance of establishing herself in an upright position, never very good in one of her temperament, was destroyed when the death of her first lover and her repeated failures to attract another left her deepest needs unsatisfied; and in her quest for fulfilment she was led into acts of aggression that are a comic parody on the sexual honesty which her friends, the philosophers, declared to be more modest than concealment. None the less, she remained courageous, generous and determined to profit by her experiences. She looked forward to the emancipation of womanhood and the regeneration of society, and she looked steadily forward, unlike many of her friends, to a life beyond the grave. She was a grotesque, but, in the eighteenth-century meaning of the word, a respectable one.

Mary Hays was one of a family of sisters, and when she met John Eccles she was living with her widowed mother in Gainsford Street, Southwark. John Eccles lodged so near that, as their romance developed, they could communicate by signs from window to window; a book laid against hers meant that she was alone and could be visited, while his drawn curtain in the early morning, when she is already up and penning her daily letter, brings down on him an arch rebuke. They had met at chapel; both were liberal dissenters with a taste for a good sermon, but Eccles soon makes it clear that those provided at their place of worship would not ensure his attendance if it were not for the presence of Mary. She was then about nineteen, small—her short legs were to provide material for caricature—with few personal charms, as she sadly admitted in hope of contradiction, impulsive, enthusiastic, intermittently prudish, and very much occupied with her own sensibility. To Eccles she appeared "a little girl with dark hair and features soft as the peaceful messengers of heaven", and he was very soon assuring her—assuring and reassuring became his daily portion—that compared with her not even Petrarch's Laura would attract a moment's attention from him. Their letters begin early in 1779, when she was about nineteen, and are soon charged with all the emotions of interrupted affection. John Eccles was without immediate prospects; his home was at Fordingbridge in Hampshire, where he had worked in his father's business, but his endeavours to enlarge and improve it had been checked by paternal disapproval, and he was now in London, lending some kind of unpaid or slightly paid assistance in a friend's office, with a good deal of time on his hands. Mr Eccles senior, when his son made known to him the state of his affections, refused to take the matter seriously, and Mrs Hays had to intervene to separate the lovers. There were at least two parting scenes, rich in emotion. Mary abstained from food for twenty-four hours and relinquished her night's rest in order to be in a fit state to bid John Eccles farewell; her apologetic lover found the flesh too weak to fulfil his part of the vigil; but he made amends by a description of his face in the morning. "I am now looking in the glass," he wrote to the exigent and unhappy girl over the way, "and really I pity myself. I am observing the force of passion; in what strong colours it lives in every feature; how visible the marks of love and disappointment sit there." They met and parted, but not for long. Mary was tenacious and Eccles was unemployed, and both were certainly in love. A clandestine daily correspondence began, of enormous bulk and inevitably monotonous quality, and presently there were clandestine excursions too, to Vauxhall and further afield to Greenwich. Sister Betsy aided and abetted, and the indulgent Mrs Hays, we must believe, turned a blind eye. No doubt even then Mary was ill to cross.

There is little intellectual substance in the letters and no literary grace. Yet the lovers plainly feel themselves to be cultivated people; they enjoyed mediocre sentimental poetry; Eccles called himself Mary's "literary beau" and was prepared to argue on behalf of the immortality of the soul from the evidence of dreams, while Mary already shows a taste for disputation. She meant to be a good girl and had to discuss the why and how. Their letters, then, show none of the reflective range of Henry and Frances, but they convey character, of an immature kind, with equal vigour though less pleasurably. Mary was, as Miss Wedd has observed, at once daring and prim; she committed herself to Eccles's keeping on country excursions, but at the least lover-like demonstration complained that he treated her with "extreme freedom" and anxiously probed his opinion of her delicacy. She was very much agitated over her delicacy and discussed it a good deal. She accepted it, as all educated girls of her generation did, as one of her most important obligations, for without delicacy what becomes of the civilizing function of women? But she was also sure of the importance of candour and sincerity. Delicacy probably meant restraint, but it could not mean concealment. Her inability to conceal, or to consider the sensibilities of others when her own were in full play, was a permanent trait of her character, and in later years transformed her conception of delicacy into a highly aggressive virtue; but she never ceased to use the word. At present, however, she had many scruples about the exact balance of the two qualities, and Eccles had often to compose them. He told her, in heartfelt compliment, that she had invariably been honest; she had never played the artful with him; he would "venture to oppose *decent* freedom against an *affected* reserve: the former is one of the loveliest parts of your character, 'tis where I see you with the most affectionate sensations." Decent freedom, however, might not perhaps include embraces. "I cannot help thinking I was too passive last night (you know what I mean)," writes Mary with misgiving; "I cannot reconcile my conduct to those strict rules of delicacy which I had determined ever to adhere to." Delicacy and a certain kittenish playfulness defeated candour when it came to putting a name to the sensations

which absorbed her. She availed herself of asterisks or a simple cipher and reminds him in melting quotation that "May is the month of L 452!"

Eccles did not have an altogether easy time. He had to write every day, and he had to assure his Maria (sometimes Polly, but more often the statelier syllables) not only that he wanted to write, but that he had plenty to write about and would have plenty, however long the correspondence lasted. He had to digest, in a single missive from his lady, the most irritating suspicions and the most plaintive appeals for pity on behalf of "your poor little girl", who "has been early initiated to sufferings", and he was goaded into writing indignant letters which he sometimes tore up next day, and sometimes sent as a warning, accompanied by a remorseful postscript. She feared his displeasure with an excessive timidity and provoked it by her restless qualms. "Am I not a little monopolizing girl to confine you in this manner?" she writes, seeking to disarm censure by the implied flattery. "But you must forgive me, for as Mrs Digby says: 'I cannot bear a rival in love or friendship.'" John forgave her. "All things considered, I think I am a good kind of young man," he writes with meek humour. Once he was driven beyond his patience, and for some days tried to affect indifference to his little girl; but it was a vain expedient and most uncomfortable, for: "Whilst I looked at her with a countenance dégagée, the warmest perplexities reigned within." Once or twice, too, he wrote her a manly and reasonable protest against their "petty tumults", and presently he feels able to congratulate her on having overcome them. Their prospects also had brightened. Mary's tenacity had at last forced the family into action. One of her brothers-in-law had been pressed into service; acceptable proposals, including some sort of partnership for the young man, had been made to Mr Eccles senior, and by July 1780 Mary Hays and John Eccles were publicly engaged. What followed is quickly told. Eccles, whose health had given Mary cause for anxiety for some weeks, grew rapidly worse. It was thought that his native air might check the decline, and he prepared to leave London. Before he left, Mary went to his lodgings and sat by his bed. She never saw him again, nor did he even reach Fordingbridge. He died at Salisbury, in the house of a relation, in his last wanderings often calling on the name of "his dear Miss Polly Hays", and attempting to sing or repeat a line or two of the hymns they had sung together in Chapel.

Mary received the news with the full violence of her nature.

> Wild, distracted, and outrageous, I accused Providence, and my Creator! I stamped on the earth in an agony of despair, and made the house echo with my cries; at last my spirits were exhausted, and I sunk into insensibility and stupidity: for three days refused all refreshment—I shed no tears—my senses were confused—my head seemed disordered—I talked calmly but very incoherently—my eyes were fixed, and I scarcely changed my position.

Her friends were very naturally alarmed. Her mother permitted her to put on mourning for her lover, and she vowed never to quit it. The Eccleses invited her to Fordingbridge, and, while considering whether the visit would make her feel better or worse, and whether she wanted to feel better or worse, she began an impassioned correspondence with the eldest Miss Eccles. She was always fiercely competitive in her griefs, and was now concerned to prove that her loss was far greater than a sister's could be. "He was all I saw in the creation," she wrote. ". . . May this heart cease to beat should it ever be capable of feeling emotions of tenderness for any other than its first, and only love." She went to Fordingbridge in the autumn and vowed eternal fidelity to Eccles, kneeling on his grave. She was then twenty, and before a month is over, with that saving honesty that always struggles out from beneath her emotionalism, she is admitting that she has experienced some soothing moments, blended perceptions of scenery, conscious innocence and pride in the quality of her own tenderness. The Eccles family worked hard to entertain her. We hear of an excursion to the New Forest, to drink tea in a keeper's lodge and return by moonlight, and of discussions with Mr Eccles, in which the relative merits of Charles I and Cromwell were debated, and his Arminian principles wrestled politely with his young guest's Unitarianism. Mary liked Hampshire.

> "The country abounds with murmuring brooks and purling streams, which you know are objects I am partial to," she wrote to her mother, adding: "I am become quite a drinker of their ale, which I think very fine. In mentioning my amusements I forgot to tell you, that I have bought a little rabbit, which I have rendered quite tame; it eats out of my hands and sleeps in my chamber, in a basket of tow—he is now sitting by my side, munching some bran.—But how trifling is all this! how foreign to my heart! a heart labouring under mixed pain, and the deepest regrets! struggling with sorrow that dissolves it in tenderness and anguish."

Her youthful vitality was reasserting itself, but the blow had been heavy. On the anniversary of her loss she is still wearing mourning and hoping for death. Devotion seemed her only refuge; she had loved John Eccles idolatrously, and he had been taken from her.

At this point we lose sight of the girl Mary Hays. When she reappears some eleven years later, it is as Eusebia, friend of philosophers, authoress of a pamphlet on public worship, "a disciple of truth", according to her own description, "and a contemner of the artificial forms which have served but to corrupt and enslave society". Eccles was not forgotten, but she no longer wore sables for him; indeed, if we may trust the caricature of her in Miss Elizabeth Hamilton's *Memoirs of Modern Philosophers,* her dress was eccentric and gaudy. The wig, which too precariously crowned Miss Bridgetina Botherim, cannot with certainty be brought home to Mary Hays, but when the ungentlemanly *English Review* called her "the baldest disciple of Mrs Wollstonecraft", there was perhaps more than literary criticism to barb the taunt. She was aware that she was out of the ordinary, and felt that her eccentricities were the natural and not unsympathetic result of her experiences. In her *Letters and Essays, Moral and Miscellaneous* (1793), she tells with altered circumstances the story of her own frustrated love. The heroine, like Mary, abandons herself to grief, till, shocked to perceive herself on the brink of hypochondria, she rallies her forces for a deliberate recovery. The impressions of her tragedy "became at length the remembrance of remembrances, and if they betrayed her into some little whimsicality of character, the deviations were such as to the humane and philosophic eye, tracing back effects to causes, rendered her more dear and interesting". Her pen played a part in her convalescence, dimly seen in the scarcity of record. The love-letters, preserved, as Miss Wedd describes them, in a careful and beautiful transcription by Mary's friend, Mrs Collier, were edited by Mary herself with an introduction and notes. She embarked upon but failed to finish a tale, *Edwin,* which was to enshrine Eccles as its hero. We hear also of a criticism of the moral tendency of *Werther,* which was sent by a friend to the *Universal Magazine* and afterwards reprinted in the second edition of the English translation. But it was by way of her religious interests that Miss Hays climbed on to a wider stage. At some point the devotionalism that assuaged her grief for John Eccles must have stiffened into a course of solid reading. She belonged to a reasoning, intellectual sect and liked the forms of argument. When therefore the scholar and controversialist Gilbert Wakefield, whose religious views harmonized in general with her own, proposed his opinion that public devotions are in some sort a corruption of the act of worship, which should be solitary, inward and contemplative, Mary, though with some showy trepidation in her preface and conclusion, was able to write him a sensible rejoinder. Her little pamphlet, *Cursory Remarks on an Enquiry into the Expediency and Propriety of Public or Social Worship* (1792), was well received by her dissenting friends and by the press. The *English Review* amiably referred to it as an "elegant and polite little performance". Ministers and prominent laymen wrote to her, and the indulgent circle of friends and relations, which all records invite us to presume, was widened to include men of some public importance. The dissenting background—in particular the Unitarian background—is constant throughout her life. She knew the family of the Reverend Robert Robinson, and George Dyer, that absent-minded scholar, who had been tutor there, arranged a tea party for her to meet Dr Priestley. The Reverend Hugh Worthington of Salter's Hall encouraged her to write her *Letters and Essays,* and Dr Disney of Essex Street Chapel obligingly preached some sermons that she wrote. A long and polite letter came from Cambridge from a recent convert to Unitarianism, the mathematician and Hebrew scholar, William Frend, whose propagation of his new opinions had already cost him his tutorship at Jesus College, and was in a year's time to bring on him a prosecution in the Vice-Chancellor's Court and a sentence of banishment from the University. They had not then met, but, complimenting her on her "sentiments unsophisticated by scholastick learning", he expressed the wish that they might one day discuss their common faith together. Meanwhile George Dyer had brought her Mary Wollstonecraft's *Vindication of the*

Rights of Women, and, strongly stimulated by a manifesto which endeavoured, in her own words, to "restore degraded woman to the glory of rationality, and to a fitness for immortality", she wrote to the author and presently made her acquaintance at the house of Johnson the publisher. A cool and friendly criticism of the **Cursory Remarks,** touching with a firm finger its passages of egoism, remains to prove the shrewdness and kindliness of the greater Mary. Both these last names are of great importance in the life of Miss Hays; from Mary Wollstonecraft she learnt that feminism which, in her own crude version, became her constant creed, and in William Frend she thought she saw a successor to John Eccles.

The painful affair with William Frend—if that may be called an affair where all the activity is on one side while the other remains distressed and repellent—took place before Mary Hays begins to move across the pages of Lamb and Southey. She had already, however, enrolled herself among the philosophers, the circle of literary thinkers in close sympathy with the French Revolution, whose social theories were given their most challenging and unmitigated expression in Godwin's *Political Justice.* This small circle overlapped the larger one of the liberal dissenters and entry into it must have been easy enough, especially as she could rely on the good offices of George Dyer. She was by now ripe for their society. Her busy, imitative mind had worked itself into many of their positions—had indeed, we suspect, occupied them with a joyous leap. **Letters and Essays,** a book whose title-page is adorned by Socrates and Burns, while Epicurus, Lavater, Rousseau, Hartley and "the excellent Dr Priestley" enrich its pages, contains some emphatic avowals of her new beliefs. "Our nature is progressive", writes this "convert to the doctrines of materialism and necessity"; and again: "The doctrine of mechanism inspires also charity and forbearance. A Necessarian may pity, but he cannot hate." It is plain, too, that she has accepted from Mary Wollstonecraft the idea that the passions in their action unfold reason; it was a useful notion to her.

Another axiom of the *Vindication,* that independence is the soil of every virtue, probably accounts for her action in leaving home and living in lodgings in Hatton Gardens. The literal interpretation is characteristic of her. Whatever small patrimony or allowance she had was eked out by literary earnings. The circle she now moved in included many writing women, Mrs Inchbald, Mrs Barbauld, Miss Alderson and others, and, helped by Dyer, she got work on the *Critical Review* and elsewhere. It was early in 1795 that she met William Godwin. She had approached him in the preceding October by writing to ask for the loan of his book, *Political Justice,* which she was anxious to read, but could not get from the libraries nor afford to buy. The philosopher, to whom the request appeared rational, lent her his book and, according to Mary, invited her to "a free disclosure of [her] opinions in the epistolary mode". One doubts whether the impulse really came from him, but he accepted the situation with kindness and discretion. She might write to him as much as she liked, but he was not to

be expected to answer. He was a busy man, and a brief note or a call now and then was all he could spare. She took advantage of this concession to pour out to him the whole story of her pursuit of an unwilling man. There has been some doubt as to the identity of her quarry. Miss Wedd says that Mary withheld his name even from Godwin, but it seems unlikely that he did not know it, and Crabb Robinson is sure that it was Frend, who was by now settled in London, writing and teaching. "She confided to me on our first acquaintance that she was wretched," he writes, "the consequence of an attachment where a union was impossible. . . . The man whom she accused of deserting her was William Frend." And again: "Frend could not meet the love of Mary Hays with equal love. . . . Hence desertion." Godwin himself has been proposed as the object of her affections; this Miss Wedd denies, and his appearance as Mr Francis in **Emma Courtney** does little to support the suggestion. He is there the astringent friend and monitor who opposes Emma, bewilders her and convicts her of error; and the picture reflects the slight chill that seems to have gone out from Godwin; he exercises her sensations without gratifying them, Emma says, and his manners repress even while they invite confidence. It is also to be considered that, when Godwin married Mary Wollstonecraft, Miss Hays was not one of the friends who were offended by that queer but happy union, but remained on friendly terms with them both. It is certainly possible that at some time in her headlong emotional career Godwin attracted her, but this can have been no more than a secondary affliction; the storms, the anguish, the pathetic, ridiculous obstinacy, were for another.

For the purposes of our impression of Mary Hays, however, it does not much matter who the beloved was. There was no interaction of personalities; he is seen dimly, an averted figure, through the shower of her protestations, the mists of her tears. The hero of **Emma Courtney** does not help us much. There is very little of him and what there is reminds us rather of Werther than of a Unitarian mathematician. There is no sign in either of her novels that she ever studied or understood a man. This man was the Object of her Sensibilities, but she was far more aware of them than of him. He remains then an undifferentiated Object, of whom it is difficult to predicate anything but embarrassment and a kindly temper. His humanity is evident in the final astonishing incident of this distressing affair. It had dragged on for years, but Mary had at last accepted his negative; he would not enable her to fulfil her capacities for devotion by attaching herself to him; he was deaf to the argument from social utility, and she must remain a frustrated being. She was crushed but not immobilized. Something yet remained for a philosophess to do and with considerable gallantry she undertook it. A letter to Godwin of 9 March 1796 recounts how, accompanied by a female friend, she went to call on him.

> I made my friend announce and precede me to his apartment, and notwithstanding this precaution, which I conceived delicacy required, my entrance most completely disconcerted him (I had never, from motives easy to be conceived, visited him before)—"I am come

(said I smiling) to call upon you for the exercise of less than a christian duty, the forgiveness, not of an enemy, but of a friend—I have no doubt been guilty of errors, who is free?"—I held out my hand—He took it, and replied to me, with a degree of cordiality. The past was no further alluded to.—I ask'd him, if he would, with our friend present, come and drink tea with me, to this he assented without hesitation. A few days since, they fulfilled their engagement, two other friends were also of the party. Whether he will ever think proper to call on me again, I know not, but as I conceived, *I had not been faultless,* and as it is particularly painful to me to cherish severe feelings, where I have before felt affection, I do not repent of what I have done, but feel myself relieved by it.

Mary could regard her behaviour with some complacence. It was rational and courageous; it was also extremely tenacious. William Frend would not marry her; he perhaps refused—if gossip and ***Emma Courtney*** are to be believed—to make her his mistress; he must then be firmly transplanted to the ground of friendship, or at worst acquaintance; somehow, at some angle, he must still be built into the fabric of her life.

Godwin's friendship and counsel were a great stay to her in this crisis. She covered vast sheets of paper to him, reporting her progress as a convalescent. Within a month of her acceptance of defeat she admits that she is better than she has been, "though certainly *very far from happy*". Her self-esteem, never a very substantial structure, had been rudely shaken. She builds it up by insisting on her superior sensitiveness, on the ardour and importance of her affections. She dreads lest Godwin should lose patience with her, and wearies him still further with insistent explanations. She explains and explains, and some of the explanations are good. "I will confess, then," she writes, "that I am not sufficiently disinterested to expect to be happy. I want a certain number of agreeable sensations for which nature has constituted me." Some of them, on the other hand, are both trivial and elaborate. She perceives fine shades of disapproval or irritation in the behaviour of her friends and hastens with anxious humility to put things right. A pointer to one of her fusses is seen in a postscript to one of Godwin's notes: "I have not the slightest suspicion of you having disgusted Mr Holcroft by interrupting the discussion on Sunday by your departure." A more notable occasion was the cold morning of 10 March 1796, the day after she had sent Godwin the letter describing her visit to Frend. She was lazily dressing by her sitting-room fire—not her usual custom as she eagerly explains—when Godwin entered the house to make an early call, and caught some glimpse of her in *négligé* as she fled across the passage—a misadventure to be laboriously accounted for in the epistolary mode the moment her toilet was complete. To Godwin she sent the first pages of ***Emma Courtney,*** and as she saw her novel take shape under her hands and read his guarded approval, she began to count her blessings. She was, at least, no longer convulsed by uncertainty. She could admit the balmy consolations still offered her by many gentle, benevolent spirits. She had been for a walk and enjoyed it.

I have the luxuries of cleanliness, of temperate plenty, I have moral and intellectual powers, I am free from the sting of remorse, I foster no corrosive nor malevolent passions—if there are any who have injur'd me, I wou'd return it only with kindness—And there are still some who look with an eye of tenderness on my faults, and who love my virtues—A gentle and kindly emotion swells my bosom—*I am not miserable this evening!*—How I prate to you of myself and my feelings!

The walk was perhaps in obedience to the counsels of George Dyer, given from a plane of intellectual acceptance to which she never climbed. "Pray take care of your health," he wrote to her, apparently at about this time. "Do not be a martyr to philosophy, which you will be if you do not take more exercise, be a little more foolish, and look at the world with all its awkward things, its clumsy, lumpish forms, its fools, its cockscombs, and its scoundrels, with more endurance."

The Memoirs of Emma Courtney was autobiographical to the point of including letters sent by the authoress to the "inflexible being"—a fact that was well-known to all her friends and all her enemies. She must have begun to write it immediately after she had received the final repulse, for it was published in the same year (1796). Its emotion therefore is not recollected in tranquillity. Crabb Robinson says that the book attracted attention as a novel of passion, but, though the description has a meaning in its historical context, it calls up to the modern reader comparisons that ***Emma Courtney*** is quite unfitted to sustain. Aphra Behn wrote novels of passion, and so did Charlotte Brontë, but Miss Hays's work has neither the social poise of the one nor the lyrical intensity of the other. She was not a real novelist. She had no invention; characters and scenes do not live in her imagination, except as incentives to discussion, and her dialogue speedily becomes a harangue. When she has to devise action, it is melodramatic and uninteresting, and, whereas it is certainly true that the subject of the book is a woman who passionately desires the love of a man, the exposition of that craving and of the starvation that underlay it was by way of pedantic analysis; an analysis, moreover, predominantly in the terms of mind, though we need not for that reason assume that Mary Hays was unaware of what was happening to her. The philosophers she knew insisted on the supremacy of mind over matter, and to one who had failed so notably to charm there must have been some consolation in shifting her appeal on to the grounds of intellect. Nevertheless, Crabb Robinson was doubtless right, and it was as a novel of passion by a woman that ***Emma Courtney*** was noticed. When in the second half of the eighteenth century women had taken publicly to their pens, indulgent critics had expressed the hope that now the world would be treated to a picture of love from the woman's point of view. Hitherto, however, women novelists had been too much occupied with domestic ethics and romantic reverie, too closely bound by a conception of delicacy that regarded the avowal of passion as the mark of a bad, or at least an undisciplined, woman, to carry their analysis very far. Mary Hays was one of the first to break the taboo.

Emma Courtney was written for the "feeling and thinking few" and was offered to them as an essay in philosophic fiction, a contribution, through its study of the progress of one strong, indulged passion, to the science of human nature. It would be easy to go through the book picking out the sophistries, the betraying compensations, yet the impression that is strongest as one re-reads it is that of the blundering courage and the occasional shrewdness of the author. It was by no means wholly a self-justification; the heroine's hazardous experiment in taking upon herself the initiative in love-making was meant "to operate as a *warning,* rather than as an example", and whilst there is some comfort in the thought that "it is the vigorous mind that often makes fatal mistakes", there is nothing but naked self-knowledge in Emma's cry: "Alas! my own boasted reason has been, but too often, the dupe of my imagination." It is true that Emma, marching into her confessional, carries with her something more of beauty, a greater cogency and composure of rhetoric, than belonged to her creator, even as she carries the knowledge that her love had wakened a response, a knowledge that Mary, once her girlhood was over, never enjoyed; but one cannot grudge the devotee of "utility" these few decorations.

The book has little plot, no more than is necessary to get the characters into position for the harangues, and to veil, with some slight show of decency, the conditions under which the letters were originally written. The incidents may be considered, as the author suggested, as illustrative of the workings of a distempered civilization, but this is probably not the aspect under which they will present themselves to the unprejudiced mind. The heroine, Emma Courtney, is the only daughter of a clever, dissipated man, and is brought up, happily enough, in the household of her aunt. There are touches here which pretty certainly reflect the author's girlhood. We are told of an impulsive, candid, vain, affectionate child, whose "tastes were all passions", growing up in an indulgent household, surviving with some spirit the painful shock of the transition to school life and the more painful experience of shortened means and loss of friends. In the "melancholy and oeconomical retirement" to which the family are now relegated, her solace is the circulating library, where her rate of consumption is ten to fourteen novels a week. Fiction now bestirs itself, and Emma's father, conscious that he can make no provision for her, resolves at least to strengthen her mind for her conflict with society, by introducing her to solid reading and to society where she will hear free speculative discussion. Her reading, which begins with Plutarch's *Lives,* extends to Descartes, polemic divinity and Rousseau's *Héloïse,* which charms her by "the wild career of energetic feeling". At her father's dinner table, where ladies do not have to retire before the talk becomes interesting—"a barbarous and odious custom"—she meets company that corresponds to the Godwin-Wollstonecraft circle, and collects material for reflection. Her father's death terminates this phase of her history, and the break-up of her aunt's household makes her dependent upon a hitherto unknown uncle with a harsh overbearing wife, in whose house she improves her acquaintance with the philosopher,

Francis, and is sought in marriage by a young physician, Montague, whose offer she rejects. Her innocent but unorthodox conduct with Francis exposes her to the censure of her relatives, and she leaves them to go and live with Mrs Harley, a widow, in whose son Augustus she is already deeply interested. Augustus is a lawyer who has given up his profession and lives upon a legacy of £400 a year which he will lose if he marries. He lectures Emma on astronomy and philosophy from his sick-bed, but does not show himself otherwise aware of her gathering emotions, and after he has returned to London she is constrained to explain them to him in a letter beginning: "Suffer me, for a few moments, to solicit your candour and attention." The rest of the book consists largely of the letters in which she requests his affections, demonstrates why she ought to have them and systematically lays down the arguments that justify "the deviation of a solitary individual from *rules* sanctioned by usage, by prejudice, by expediency". It is a situation, she feels, that involves all her future usefulness and welfare. It is necessary for her to be esteemed and cherished. She cannot satisfy herself by venerating abstract virtue.

> "Is it possible", she writes, with her emphatic punctuation, "that a mind like yours, neither hardened by prosperity nor debased by fashionable levity—which vice has not corrupted, nor ignorance brutalized—can be wholly insensible to the balmy sweetness, which natural unsophisticated affections, shed through the human heart? . . . I make no apologies for, because I feel no consciousness of, weakness. An attachment sanctioned by nature, reason, and virtue, ennobles the mind capable of conceiving and cherishing it: of such an attachment a corrupt heart is utterly incapable."

She meets his probable rejoinders at each point, with the adroitness of a desperate jack-in-the-box. She may be idealizing him, she admits, but her sentiments are not the less genuine, and without some degree of illusion and enthusiasm life languishes. She concludes this summons to surrender with one prudent afterthought; will he inform her if his heart is free?

In the distress of spirit that follows his polite but to her mind inconclusive reply, she pours herself out to Francis, arguing down her recurrent misgiving about an action that she would by no means recommend to general imitation. "If the affections are, indeed, generated by sympathy, where the principles, pursuits and habits are congenial—where the *end,* sought to be attained, is—

> 'Something than beauty dearer'

you may, perhaps, agree with me, that it is almost indifferent on which side the sentiment originates." Nevertheless: "Those who deviate from the beaten track must expect to be entangled in thickets and wounded by many a thorn." Through these thickets she plunges, courting, one feels, the longest thorns. "In company I start and shudder from accidental allusions, in which no one but myself could trace any application." Her former frustration sharpens the edge of her anxiety. To what future, unconceived periods will the inscrutable Being who made her for an end, of which she believes herself capable, defer the satisfaction of a capacity which "like a tormenting *ignis fatuus,* has hitherto served only to torture and betray?"

From the melancholy into which she falls, in spite of Francis's philosophical ministrations, she is raised by the need of earning her living. She goes to London and begins work as a governess, and the "conscious pride of independence" does her good. Thus stimulated she writes to Harley again, admitting his right to be master of his own affections, but entreating him for an hour's frank conversation to put an end to all her doubts. "I would compose myself, listen to you, and yield to the sovereignty of reason. . . . I am exhausted by perturbation. I ask only certainty and rest." This letter extracts from him a vague reference to obligations that constrain him, which she still refuses to consider final, and three months later she returns to the attack, begging him this time for his friendship and assuring him that she is capable of a disinterested attachment. "Why am I to deprive you of a faithful friend", she asks unexpectedly, "and myself of all the benefits I may yet derive from your conversation and kind offices? I ask, why?" For a time they meet for reading and discussion of impersonal questions, but this attempt to rise above "the prejudices that weaken human character" is defeated by Emma's unsleeping determination to extract Harley's secret from him as the only means to her peace. Under her remonstrances he becomes "captious, disputatious, gloomy and imperious", and is at last driven to admit a prior attachment. Emma, who hitherto under every repulse and coldness has resumed her pen, resumes it once more, to enforce the importance of unequivocal sincerity and to point out the harm his reserve has done her. "You have contemned a heart of no common value, you have sported with its exquisite sensibilities—but it will, still, know how to separate your virtues from your crimes." After this Parthian shot of ungenerous generosity, she ceases to see him. In her wretchedness Francis comes to her aid once more, and she survives a low fever, and sets her face to the undelightful future. But the book does not end here. Fiction allowed of a more striking conclusion than life, and Emma meets Augustus Harley twice more. The first time is at his mother's death-bed, where they have a most exhausting scene during a thunderstorm, and Emma learns that he is married and the father of two children, but cannot avow his position publicly without forfeiting his income. Years pass before she sees him again, and then, when she has long been the calm and useful wife of the physician, Montague, and the mother of a daughter, a stranger is flung from his horse passing through the town. It is, of course, Augustus. In her husband's absence she takes him in, tends him with devotion exclusive of all her other duties and receives his dying confession. He had loved her all the time. The end of the book is rather startling; Montague's jealousy, when he hears of his wife's behaviour, leads him precipitately to seduction, child-murder and suicide. Mrs Wollstonecraft felt her sympathy stop at this place, and Mrs Robinson, also a novelist, declared that the husband should have been suffered to die a natural death. Mary Hays, however, meant to trace the chain of evil effects that depends from a "confused system of morals" and a tragic personal frustration. Even at this point she does not cease to afflict her heroine. Emma devotes herself to the education of her daughter and of Augustus Harley's surviving child. At fourteen the younger Emma dies, and then the prematurely old and sad woman learns that her adopted son is involved in an unhappy love affair. For his sake, she says with almost Brontesque intensity, she has "consented to hold down, with struggling, suffocating reluctance, the loathed and bitter portion [potion?] of existence"; for his sake, to sustain him in his struggles, to impress on him the paramount importance of candour, she unseals her lips and tells him her story. By this device Mary Hays endeavoured to give an air of considered judgment and desolate calm to a book which was, in effect, an interim explosion of a permanently troublous temperament.

The parts of the narrative which diverge from the facts of autobiography need no comment; they are of a kind to explain themselves, and they are not the parts that attracted contemporary attention. Nor was it much directed to the "series of errors and mortification" which formed for Mary Hays the justification of her book, since they were intended to commend self-control; for Emma's misfortunes were quite overlooked in the glare of her deplorable enterprise. She, a female, pursued a male; not comically—at least in the author's intention—and not viciously—for even during the thunderstorm Emma calls on Augustus to acknowledge that her "wildest excesses had in them a dignified mixture of virtue"—but honourably and necessarily as an indispensable prerequisite to her social usefulness. The impressive letter, in which she "methodizes" under five heads all the objections that Augustus can possibly have to her and patiently refutes them one by one, was calculated to remain longer in the memory than her sad and humbled confession to Francis: "I am sensible, that by my extravagance, I have given a great deal of vexation (possibly some degradation) to a being, whom I had no right to persecute, or to compel to choose happiness through a medium of my creation." A clumsy forerunner of the Shavian huntress woman, humourless, charmless, and too raw and unhappy to be really formidable, she made her attack not in the name of a mystical Life-Force but of General Utility. The mainspring of her activity, however, was not philosophic. What we see in Emma—what Mary Hays intermittently saw in herself—is the passionate temperament that seizes on the precepts of philosophy and forces them to subserve its own desires. "Philosophy, it is said, should regulate the feelings," remarks Emma, "but it has added fervor to mine." The notes of mournfulness and pride are mixed as she considers the tumult of her soul. All her life she has been a victim to the enthusiasm of her feelings, "incapable of approving or disapproving with moderation", but in this vehemence she sees a great stimulus to mental growth. "What are passions, but another name for powers? The mind capable of receiving the most forcible impressions is the sublimely improveable mind." It is with this sense of the enormous potential richness of her character that she reproaches Harley for rejecting "a mind like mine", and points out that in arresting her natural affections he is guilty of the same crime as the ascetics of monastic institutions. When she turned to philosophy, she selected instinctively those precepts that would sanction the spontaneous habits of her temperament; the candour that Mary Wollstonecraft declared to be more truly delicate than concealment, to cover the boundless communicativeness of a heart that "panted to expand its sensations"; Godwin's pronouncement that social utility is the only criterion of morals, to justify the demands of her affections for satisfaction; and his insistence on "the irresistible power of circumstances, modifying and controuling our character", to lighten her sense of responsibility. She also acknowledged with her whole heart the duty of self-examination, which can be a strict discipline but is easily deflected into an indulgence by the self-absorbed. It is to her credit as a striving human soul, "a human being loving virtue" as she pathetically insists, that she is able at times to apply these precepts, however maladroitly, to their proper end; the mists of delusion dissolve, her dreams collapse, she is self-convicted of some part of her inordinate egoism, and in floods of tears—those sudden inconvenient outbursts of weeping that are so uncomfortably lifelike in *Emma Courtney*—but with considerable courage, she retrieves her integrity and sets to work to build up her life again. Miss Hamilton was right and amusing when she set forth—she hardly needed to parody—her Bridgetina's convenient invocations of the principle of social utility. It is a phrase continually on Emma's lips. It enhances her dissatisfaction, her rebellious sense that the vigour of life in her is running to waste, her melancholy craving to "feel the value of existence" once more, by presenting to her the notion that not only she herself but society loses by her frustration. Utility is brandished as a threat in the anguished pedantry of her letters to Harley. "I have said, on this subject, you have a right to be free," she begins, with more superfluous points than usual; "but I am, now, doubtful of this right: the health of my mind being involved in the question, has rendered it a question of *utility*—and on what other basis can morals rest?" But there are times when the principle is applied without sophistication, as it is near the end of the book, where Emma clings to her denuded life in order that she may be of service to Harley's son, and writes with some fineness: "It is not to atone for past error, by cutting off the prospect of future usefulness."

The character of Emma Courtney, then, which is also the character of Mary Hays, provides in its not ignoble pretensions and its self-deluding folly the right material for comedy; and, though it is a comedy with an infusion of the grotesque—it raises loud laughter as well as soft smiling—Miss Hamilton's farcical Bridgetina, relieved against a monitory background of calamities, by no means represents it. Miss Hays did not, naturally, regard herself in a comic light; indeed, early in her life she avowed that she had "no great relish for what is termed humour". It was not by humour that she was saved from regarding her destiny as purely tragic but, once more, by philosophy. What she had to recount was a history of error and its consequences; and, since error could *ex hypothesi* be eradicated, not only would there come a time when no such history could take place, but her own individual fate was in some measure retrievable. "Let us reap from the past all the good we can," she writes in her last letter to Harley, "a close and searching knowledge of the secret springs and foldings of our own hearts." The science of morals, she believed, was not incapable of demonstration, but it required patient and laborious experiment. As such a laborious and fruitful experiment she considered her own struggles.

Miss Hays's career as a novelist may be dispatched before we pursue the career of her affections. She made one more effort, *The Victim of Prejudice,* published in 1799. In this book she aimed at a purely fictitious embodiment of the thoughts that exercised her, and the result is a crowded, melodramatic, extravagant story in which the injustice of society in punishing an involuntary lapse from chastity in the heroine is exemplified by the quite exceptional villainy of a lascivious baronet. Mary, beautiful, candid, courageous, a student of mathematics and astronomy, is a more enlightened and worse-fated Emma. Like Emma she argues her way through the book in pedantic, impassioned tirades; like Emma she is violently upset by her emotions and suffers cold shudders and burning heats. Nevertheless she is represented as a completed character, resolute and schooled in self-control. She is destroyed by the social conventions which her reason has rejected, because, as the authoress sadly remarks, while the conduct of the world is in opposition to the principles of philosophers, education will be a vain attempt. There must, in fact, be martyrs. There were moments when Miss Hays regarded herself as a martyr; but neither she nor Emma—if one can distinguish between them—were blameless in their defiance of society; their histories were avowedly examples of intellectual error. In Mary Miss Hays conceived the preparation and martyrdom of a spotless victim. It will be noted that she is never content to write of the ordinary. Beauty, malice, stupidity, wisdom and passion are always in extremes with her, and this takes all validity from her parable of the world as it is. After this book her essential literary barrenness overcame her. A letter from Southey of May 1803 shows that she had asked him to suggest subjects for a novel. He directs her attention to the use she could make of travel books for the background of an exotic story and to the studies in unusual temperaments that remain to be made; but nothing came of his advice. Her creative impulse, slight as it was, began and ended in autobiography. She sketched the face in her mirror and then, redoubling the beautifying touches of the first draft, made it the basis of an ideal portrait. After that she devoted her clumsy pen to industrious compilations, edification and a livelihood.

It is possible to find a number of reasons why she did not make her relations with Charles Lloyd the basis of a novel, of which the most obvious are the sameness of the material to that of *Emma Courtney,* a dawning sense of ridicule and the experience of savage criticism. Her abstention leaves us dependent upon the comments of the friends of both parties, but since these included Coleridge, Southey, Manning and Lamb, we may well feel more confidence in the chorus than we should have done in the monologue. The chorus is not heard, however, until the catastrophe; it does not accompany the earlier parts of the action. It was an explosion of irritation on the part of Lloyd early in 1800 that set the discussion going between his friends; but he had already been for some years the target of Mary Hays's regard. Traces of their acquaintance are plain to be seen in his novel, *Edmund Oliver,* which came out in the summer of 1798, and it may be that it is he to whom a note of Godwin's of December 1797 refers, a man whose confidence Mary Hays enjoys and by whom Godwin is instinctively repelled. As we follow these clues backwards we come very near the termination of her hopes in Frend, and perceive, as we might have expected, that her affections could not remain unfocused long.

Charles Lloyd, the son of a Quaker family of bankers in Birmingham, was fifteen years younger than Mary Hays. At twenty-two he was a delicate, nervous, self-conscious young man, and when he came to London in the late autumn of 1797 he had already several major crises behind him, and was deeply shaken in health and spirits by them. He had exchanged banking in Birmingham for the practice of poetry and philosophy with Coleridge at Nether Stowey. He had forsaken the faith of his fathers and been retrieved by Coleridge from scepticism to Christianity. In London he shared rooms with Lamb's cheerful friend, Jem White, and wrote *Edmund Oliver,* in which by an impertinent use of Coleridge's personality and life in the name-part he testified to the waning of the friendship between them. The book also testifies by the allusions to Mary Hays in the character of the anti-heroine, Lady Gertrude Sinclair, to the interest she felt in the romantic, suffering but rather unreliable young man.

Miss Hays's share in Lady Gertrude has not, I think, been hitherto noticed, and contemporary reviewers, who pounced upon the identity of her other simulacrum, Miss Bridgetina Botherim, omitted to mention this one. The allusions seem to me deliberate and unmistakable, but they do not contribute the whole outline of the figure, for Lady Gertrude, like Bridgetina, has to represent a more completely subversive mode of thought than Miss Hays ever acknowledged. She has to be an atheist, as Bridgetina was but Mary Hays never became. She has to be extremely beautiful, to add the seductions of passionate feminine charm to those of false philosophy. Moreover, since the purpose of the book is to express abhorrence at the dangerous "generalizing spirit" of Godwinite philosophy, the overleaping of specific individual duties in the name of general liberty or benevolence, she has to be brought through betrayal, despair and delirium to suicide, for which if we seek a prototype we must look beyond Mary Hays to hostile conceptions of the career of Mary Wollstonecraft. Nevertheless, in spite of these differences, Lady Gertrude's love-letter to Edward D'Oyley is in many ways so clear a

pointer to the author of *Emma Courtney* that there must have been malice in the intention. Edward D'Oyley, in spite of his Quaker parents and the blurred echo in his surname, does not stand for Charles Lloyd in character, though as recipient of Lady Gertrude's letter he seems to stand temporarily in his shoes. He is the villain of the piece, the corrupter and destroyer of Lady Gertrude, the figment of a shocked but not a strong imagination. Lloyd's own appearance is in the shape of Charles Maurice, the staid, benign, home-and-country-loving mentor of the unstable hero—a tell-tale reversal of the original relations between himself and Coleridge.

The love-letter, in which Lady Gertrude adjures D'Oyley to spurn his Quaker parents' grovelling minds and tell them he is resolved on a connection with her, contains two acknowledged quotations from *Emma Courtney* and several parallels to the sentiments and arguments of that book. It is a letter in which the woman takes the initiative, claiming a return of affection on the strength of the sympathy of minds; it is vehement in tone, propping emotional appeals upon Godwinite assumptions. "Promises, what are they?" asks Lady Gertrude. "Snares! fetters for the mind! . . . We should be decided only by the principles of the present hour." By rejecting such bonds the mind will acquire "an incredible elasticity, fitting it to the occasion". All prejudices must be destroyed and the search for truth must proceed by means of the boldest speculations and even by the collision of opposing principles, since "he who would walk erect in the difficult path of life, must often have fearlessly plunged amid the intellectual chaos; from thence he will derive stores hitherto undiscovered, and by repeating his efforts will bring new combinations from the unassimilated and unarranged elements of moral science". This is so close to Emma Courtney's letters to her adopted son, where she bids him "think freely, investigate every opinion, disdain the rust of antiquity, raise systems, invent hypotheses, and, by the absurdities they involve, seize on the clues of truth" that it can hardly be called a parody. At one point Lloyd deserts Emma Courtney to touch distinctly on the life of her creator. Lady Gertrude, like Mary Hays, deems it her duty to be perfectly sincere, and, while proposing a liaison with D'Oyley, is constrained to tell him that she "was once beloved by a youth of most interesting manners, and returned his love". This oddly pathetic and characteristically misplaced summoning of the shade of John Eccles must, one supposes, have occurred in some letter to Lloyd himself; it fits easily enough into Lady Gertrude's career, but not at all into her character; its curious air of awkward elderly maidenliness recalls Crabb Robinson's insistence that, whatever Mary Hays's principles may have been, her conduct was perfectly correct, and makes Lloyd's easy indiscretions difficult to excuse.

Outside this letter there are no demonstrable allusions, and the story soon diverges from any relation to that of Miss Hays. But the whole picture of Lady Gertrude before she is plunged into tragedy looks like the revenge of a quiet man who has been made uncomfortable, and the cause of the discomfort is spitefully underlined at the end of the book, where Edith Alwynne, the girl who is to draw Edmund Oliver out of the chaos of his sentiments and opinions into the happy discipline of domestic life, refuses to have her love for him brought, however indirectly, to his notice, since she doubts in any case of the "*propriety of a female being the first agent in these affairs*". The italics are Lloyd's; and one feels that as he wrote his gathering irritation drove him beyond his original plan. He set out to draw in Lady Gertrude, as his first pages inform us, "a woman of warm affections, strong passions, and energetic intellect, yielding herself to these loose and declamatory principles, yet at the same time uncorrupted in her intentions". Such a woman Mary Hays was; by this time, too, she has recognized, like Katisha, that she was an acquired taste, only to be appreciated by an educated palate; but when she advanced upon Charles Lloyd, prepared to take years to train him to love her, he failed to hear music in the purring of that bewildered tiger, and in feline anger scratched back. The sketch he gives of Lady Gertrude's manner, however, at the beginning of the book, seems uncoloured by spleen and entirely fulfils our expectations of what would be appropriate to Mary Hays. "Gertrude's temper was ardent—her manners earnest and impressive—she never spoke or moved but the soul beamed in her full eye.—She was impatient of control yet enthusiastic in her desires to diffuse happiness; impetuous and quick in her resentments, yet ever soliciting an admission into the stranger's breast." The last phrase is particularly revealing, and if we correct this romanticized impression by Miss Hamilton's amusing account of Bridgetina at a party, sitting "screwed up for a metaphysical argument", and seizing the first chance to launch into a premeditated harangue of second-hand materials, we get a possible picture of Mary Hays as she approached forty. Something of both versions is suggested by Southey's casual outline of her in 1797. He has met Mary Hays, he writes, "an agreeable woman and a Godwinite", who writes in the *Monthly Magazine* under the signature of M. H., "and sometimes writes nonsense there about *Helvetius*". He uses the word "nonsense" twice, but with a not unkindly inflection. Godwin talks "nonsense" about the collision of minds and Mary Hays echoes him, but he liked her well enough to dispute with her upon the moral effects of towns and maintained a friendly correspondence with her.

Whatever "nonsense" Godwin talked about the collision of minds—no doubt as a means of reaching truth—the collision of Mary's and Lloyd's was productive chiefly of perplexity and distaste in the minds of their friends. She wrote to him and, unlike Godwin, he answered, but, again unlike Godwin, with his tongue in his cheek. Coleridge calls it a "ranting, sentimental correspondence", and adds, on Lamb's authority, that Lloyd "frequently read her letters in company as a subject for *laughter,* and then sate down and answered them quite *à la Rousseau*". This was probably before he went up to Cambridge in Autumn 1798, as Manning, who became his tutor in mathematics and his friend, declares that he did not babble out her follies; but one may assume that her letters pursued him thither, and that in some fashion he continued to answer them. He had not

the gentleness of Frend to a woman who was a pest; moreover, his irritation must have increased when he himself fell in love. There are contradictory statements as to the date of his marriage to Sophia Pemberton; Samuel Lloyd, in his book *The Lloyds of Birmingham,* gives it as 12 February 1799, but Lamb, writing in September to Lloyd's brother, Robert, speaks as if it were still in the future, and Mr E. V. Lucas would place it soon after the date of his letter. One suspects some connection between this marriage and the angry breach of Lloyd's relations with Mary Hays, and for this the later date would be more suitable as it was during January and February 1800 that their friends were discussing the affair; but Lloyd stayed up at Cambridge for some time after his wedding, and it is possible that it was not made public at once. At all events, whether nettled by some remonstrance of hers—she had once more cause to bewail a lack of "unequivocal sincerity"—or uneasily jesting away some touch of conscience, he first slighted her character in public and then sent her an apology, so odd and slyly barbarous that, if Lamb's version is a fair epitome of it, we must assume it to have been wrung out of Lloyd by some extreme exasperation. He had heard everywhere, he said, that she had been in love with Frend and with Godwin, and that her first novel was a transcript of her letters to Frend. Further, he had said himself that he thought she was in love with him. "In the confounding medley of ordinary conversation, I have interwoven my abhorrence of your principles with a glanced contempt for your personal character." In this fashion Sophia Pemberton's husband, soon to shake the dust of cities off his feet and retire to a pastoral solitude among the Lakes, made his apology. "My whole moral sense is up in arms against the Letter," writes Lamb. It was an added touch of ugliness in his sight that Lloyd had given it to his young sister Olivia to copy.

Mary displayed her grief and her correspondence to all her friends, to the disgust of Manning who inclined to be of Lloyd's faction. A loftily disapproving note, embracing both parties to the embroilment, is heard in a letter from Coleridge to Southey. Poor Lloyd, he remarks, is an unstable man. "Every hour new-creates him; he is his own posterity in a perpetually flowing series, and his body unfortunately retaining an external identity, *their* mutual contradictions and disagreeings are united under one name, and of course are called lies, treachery and rascality." So much for Lloyd. Of Miss Hays's intellect, he explains carefully, he thinks not *contemptuously* but certainly *despectively,* setting it lower than Southey does. "Yet I think you likely in this case to have judged better than I; for to hear a thing, ugly and petticoated, ex-syllogize a God with cold-blooded precision, and attempt to run religion through the body with an icicle, an icicle from a Scotch Hogtrough!—*I* do not endure it." The reference, I think, is to her Unitarianism—a position that Coleridge had deserted. The last word on what, so far as we know, was Mary Hays's last disappointment in love comes from a cooler Lamb, who does not go back on his judgment, but does not intend to break with Lloyd because he has faults. It comes in the shape of a proposal to Manning that one day they shall discuss "In what cases and how far sincerity is a virtue?" Not truth, he explains, "who, meaning no offence, is always ready to give an answer when she is asked why she did so and so; but a certain forward-talking half-brother of hers, Sincerity, that amphibious gentleman, who is so ready to perk up his obnoxious sentiments unasked into your notice, as Midas would his ears into your face un-called for." On this definition, there does not seem much room for discussion.

During the last years of the century many things must have combined to hurt Mary Hays. The intellectual climate changed with the French war and grew hostile to liberalism and to the hopes and speculations of her friends the philosophers. Mary Wollstonecraft died and Godwin, with a family to keep, drew in his horns and walked warily. The *Anti-Jacobin* was founded and she fell under its appalling scourge. She had known something of adverse criticisms before, the hectoring jollity of those blows that send the victim reeling. The *English Review,* which had been polite to the **Cursory Remarks,** settled the **Letters and Essays** with the observation: "Female philosophers, while pretending to superior powers, carry with them (such is the goodness of providence) a mental imbecility which damns them to fame." **Emma Courtney** received some kind words from the liberal reviews, but it was not long before they were muzzled, and among the authors tainted with revolutionism, whom the clerical reviewers of the *Anti-Jacobin* haled out for public penance, Mary Hays was not overlooked. She figured with her dear friend, Mary Wollstonecraft, and with Ann Yearsley in the Reverend Richard Polwhele's vicious attack, *The Unsex'd Females* (1798). In this poem the "Arch-priestess of female Libertinism" calls upon her sex to lay aside their winning weakness, to despise Nature's law and aspire to blend "mental energy with Passion's fire", and one by one, as they respond, their brows are scored with a savage slash of the pen. Mary Hays gets off as lightly as any one. No doubt the ineptness of the one line which dispatches her—"And flippant Hays assum'd the cynic leer"—in which every important word is wrong, is accounted for by the footnote: "Mary Hays, I believe, is little known"; but this was not comforting. By May 1799 the *Anti-Jacobin* had looked her up, had found her assertion that "individuality of affection constitutes chastity", and proceeded to slaughter both her novels in a grand retrospective review, culminating in the growl: "*To your distaff, Mary.*" "As to the style of her writings," concluded the reviewer on a milder note, "it is needless to remark; who stays to admire the workmanship of a dagger wrenched from the hand of an assassin?" This was good measure, but they had not yet done with her; her private life, which indeed she had not kept private enough, remained to be exploited. Three months later they saw their chance. A harmless-looking book, John Walker's *Elements of Geography, and of Natural and Civil History,* already four years old, turned out to have been dedicated to the fair sex, whose well-wisher, the author, had rather foolishly and quite irrelevantly taken up the right of a woman to make a proposal to a man. The reviewer came down on Walker like a load of bricks. Let him ask Mary

Hays. She would tell him that the "privilege of addressing" led a woman nowhere but to the loss of the "fascinating charms of female reservedness". And so forth, without any decency.

On top of these assaults came Miss Hamilton's *Memoirs of Modern Philosophers* (1800). This is an amusing and sensible book, and not unkindly. Miss Hamilton can see much to praise in Mary Wollstonecraft and in Godwin, but she mistrusts the effect of their theories on uncontrolled and undiscriminating minds, and in Mary Hays she has an example ready to her hand. To be sure, she denies that her characters are drawn from life, but this is no more than the satirist's safe-guarding of his right to exaggerate, caricature and sharpen the follies of the type by the addition of the eccentricities of an individual. Reviewers, at least, had no difficulty in recognizing Mary Hays in Miss Bridgetina Botherim; all the marks were there—the short, unlovely figure, the phonographic reproduction of Godwin's philosophy, the pedantically amorous pursuit of a reluctant man. It was certainly Miss Hays, but a Miss Hays stripped of even such dignity as the *Anti-Jacobin* had left her, no more a dagger-bearing assassin, but the ridiculous aberration of a small provincial society, the comrade and dupe of shoddy "philosophic" tradesmen and rascally adventurers, as negligible as a spluttering squib against the massive good sense of the English people. The incidents that Miss Hamilton contrives, to make nonsense of her theories and sensibilities, are woundingly funny, and as Miss Hays had no capacity for fun ("I do not care for wit and humour", remarks Bridgetina, well in character) there can have been nothing to soften the impact of Miss Botherim on her mind. Apart from gratuitous humiliations, when Miss Hamilton in sheer high spirits rolls the blue and yellow finery, the stiff turban with its ribbon and the frizzled wig in the mud, she had to endure the comic perversion of her watchwords and the burlesque of her sentiment. Bridgetina quotes screeds from *Political Justice* in a small shrill voice and congratulates a friend, who has broken his arm, on the glorious opportunity he now enjoys of proving the omnipotence of mind over matter; she steeps herself in Rousseau, abandons her imagination to "the solemn sorrows of suffocating sensibility" and calls it renovating her energies. Feeling in herself "the capacity for increasing the happiness of an individual", she searches anxiously for a suitable recipient of her devotion, fixes on the local dentist, with unfortunate results, and replaces him by the young doctor, Henry Sydney, whom she addresses in inflexible love-letters that are terribly close to the original. The degree of parody is often slight; Miss Hamilton's cool hand has only to arrange side by side expressions that in **Emma Courtney** are separated, to bring out with comic force the interested and specious arguments of that heroine.

> "How shall I describe my sufferings?" says Bridgetina, analysing her "importunate sensibility" to an unwilling confidante. "How shall I recount the salt, the bitter tears I shed? I yearn to be useful (cried I) but the inexpressible yearning of a soul which pants for general utility is, by the *odious institutions of a distempered*

civilization, rendered abortive. O divine Philosophy! by thy light I am taught to perceive that happiness is the only true end of existence. To be happy it is necessary for me to love! Universal benevolence is an empty sound. It is individuality that sanctifies affection. But chained by the cruel fetters which unjust and detested custom has forged for my miserable and much-injured sex, I am not at liberty to go about in search of the individual whose mind would sweetly mingle with mine. Barbarous fetters! cruel chains! odious state of society! Oh, that the age of reason were but come, when no soft-souled maiden shall sigh in vain."

This is fair play enough for a satirist, though painful for the victim. Miss Hamilton, enjoying laughter, was not angry with its victim; she confined her sense of the dangers of liberal and especially non-Christian thought to another part of the book, and used Bridgetina for her sport. There is no venom in her, but her ringing cuffs must have made Miss Hays's head ache. They come most thick and fast in Bridgetina's ratiocinations over Henry Sydney's affections.

> "Why should he not love me?" she demands. "What reason can he give? Do you think I have not investigated the subject? Do you think I have not examined every reason, moral and physical, that he could have against returning my passion? Do not think I have learned to philosophize for nothing."

Not for nothing, certainly, since she can put down the superior attractiveness of Julia's youthful beauty to the "unjust prejudices of an unnatural state of civilization", and see in her own surrender to her emotions "a link in the glorious chain of causation, generated in eternity". In her last letter to Sydney Miss Hamilton allows herself to enhance the colouring, while sticking close to the line of argument in *Emma Courtney.*

> "You do not at present see my preferableness," admits Bridgetina, "but you may not always be blind to a truth so obvious. How can I believe it compatible with the nature of mind, that so many strong reiterated efforts should be productive of no effect? Know, therefore, Doctor Sydney, it is my fixed purpose to persevere. I shall talk, I shall write, I shall argue, I shall pursue you; and if I have the glory of becoming a moral martyr, I shall rejoice that it is in the cause of general utility."

As a final insult, Miss Hamilton closed her spirited performance by convincing her Bridgetina of error; there is no martyrdom, but a recantation.

It is with pleasure that we contemplate the appeasing process of the years. Mary Hays had little innate faculty for peacefulness, but as time passed and wounds healed into scars, that ached only when the weather was bad, she did manage to settle down. She clung to her feminism. "I have at heart the happiness of my sex, and their advancement in the scale of national and social existence," she declares in the preface to *Female Biography* (1803), and advises her young readers to "substitute, as they fade, for the evanes-

cent graces of youth, the more durable attractions of a cultivated mind". But she is careful to describe herself as "unconnected with any party and disdaining every species of bigotry", and she does not include Mary Wollstonecraft in her compilation. Matilda Betham, another of Lamb's acquaintances, whose *Biographical Dictionary of Celebrated Women* appeared the year after, does include her; but Miss Betham, a miniature painter, could perhaps better afford whatever risk attached to the mention of that courageous and reprobated woman than could Miss Hays, who was writing primarily for young people, and now or a little later tried her hand at teaching for a living. Still, it is an unexpected timidity, the shrinking, perhaps, of a battered fighter from another bruise.

There are very few facts to give substance to the last forty years of her long life. Miss Wedd tells us that there was at one time a suggestion, which never matured, that she should join the Southey household at Keswick; that she lived for some time with a married brother at Wandsworth and helped with his children—a solid family backing was to be presumed behind her experiment in solitary housekeeping—and that she taught for a year in a school at Oundle. The letters of Eliza Fenwick show that by about 1811 or 1812 she was living with her mother again, so the wanderings may have been due rather to restlessness than necessity. She knew narrow means, but had not to fear distress. She continued to wield her pen. *Female Biography; or, Memoirs of Illustrious and Celebrated Women of all ages and countries. Alphabetically arranged,* came out in 1803; it consists of six volumes of tabloid lives. At this time she was meditating a history of manners in England from the accession of the Stuarts, a grandiose project from which Southey gently dissuaded her. Instead, she turned her attention to the youthful mind and produced in *Harry Clinton; a Tale of Youth* (1804) a reworking of Brooke's *Fool of Quality.* I have not seen this book, nor the three volumes of *Historical Dialogues for Young Persons* which followed in 1808. They seem to have been the fruit of her experience as schoolmistress and aunt. From 1814 to 1824 she lived at Hot Wells, Clifton, boarding with a Mrs Pennington, who was acquainted with Mrs Siddons, Mrs Piozzi and Hannah More (a William Pennington, Esq., was inducted as Master of the Ceremonies at Hot Wells in 1785 and this may well have been his widow), and here the fringe of Hannah More's mantle seems to have touched her, for she became interested in one of the many benevolent enterprises of Bristol, the Prudent Man's Friend Society, and wrote two short tracts, *The Brothers; or Consequences. A Story of what happens every day* (1815), and *Family Annals; or the Sisters* (1817), to recommend it to "that most useful Part of the Community, the Labouring Poor". The Society existed "for the purpose of promoting provident habits and a spirit of independence among the poor"; it acted as a bank for their savings and made small loans to deserving cases without charging interest. The tracts were written in simple language and in the form of dialogues, with the scenes laid in humble life. The *Gentleman's Magazine* approved them as well-timed and sensible publications and wished that they could be introduced into the family of every labourer in the Kingdom. It is not given to many writers to be attacked by the *Anti-Jacobin* as a subversive and dangerous force and to be praised by the *Gentleman's Magazine* as a wholesome influence, to pass from discipleship to Mary Wollstonecraft to harmony with Hannah More. However, the old leaven worked in her still. Once more in her *Memoirs of Queens Illustrious and Celebrated* (1821) she lifts her voice on behalf of the moral rights and intellectual advancement of woman, and expresses her concern that the general training of her sex is rather for "the delights of the harem" than to render them the companions and counsellors of men. What, one wonders, did Miss Hays know of the delights of the harem?

This was her last book. She was then about sixty years old and speaks of herself as "declining in physical strength and mental activity", though actually she lived till 1843. Hot Wells was not her final resting-place, as it was Mrs Piozzi's and Miss More's; she came back to the Kentish edge of London, living first at Maze Hill and afterwards at Camberwell, near her girlhood's home; and since her papers were preserved with care in a sister's family, we may assume that there was domestic kindness round her in her old age.

These are scanty facts to spread over half a lifetime, not uncharacteristic but not very informative. But there is something to add that shows Mary Hays in a new and pleasing character, as a steady, wise and generous friend. These are the letters of Eliza Fenwick, written to her between 1798 and 1828, and printed by Miss Wedd in her *Fate of the Fenwicks*. It is probable that her confused and ill-disciplined but by no means poorly endowed nature had always displayed this capacity, and that her relations with her own sex had formed a background of sobriety to her extravagant designs on the other. She met Mrs Fenwick in Mary Wollstonecraft's circle, and the two women sat together by her childbed and deathbed and remained fast friends. Mrs Fenwick, burdened with children and impeded by a shiftless husband, writes from various places in England and Ireland, and, at widening intervals, from Barbadoes and the United States. She makes Mary Hays the confidant of all her enterprises, her literary undertakings, her positions as governess, the education of her son, the launching of her daughter as an actress, the establishment of her schools in Barbadoes and on the mainland and of the lodging-house in New York. For most of her English schemes Miss Hays helped to find the money. Travelling expenses, books, and the younger Eliza's stage dresses came somehow out of her narrow income. There was always a margin for "active kindness" and a "generous loan". In 1811 Mary and Mrs Hays are taking care of the boy Lanno (Orlando) while his mother and sister are in Ireland. He was a prepossessing child, according to Mrs Fenwick, "in whom a sort of Gentlemanly temper was visible from infancy; so that it was said of him at four years old that he was born to be a plenipotentiary." Lanno—who never became a plenipotentiary, but died of fever in Barbadoes in 1816—was then in his early teens, and Mary is

asked to fortify him with undeviating integrity. "Do not say that you regret that he is not your son," writes the grateful mother, "for he is yours. You are performing all the most useful, the highest, the *moral* duties of a mother." It was wise comfort, and doubtless the activity had been more comforting still; but one divines the tone of the letter that drew such an answer from busy and preoccupied Mrs Fenwick. She comments once, with an air of wonder, on the differences in their natures and fates. Eliza Fenwick, after a full and painful life, felt herself "stealing towards the grave [it was still far off and across the Atlantic] without any of those blank, lonely desolate feelings that you, dear Mary, gifted with extraordinary resources, and connected with a numerous and in a great degree kind and amiable family, too often participate". She notes with straightforward sympathy the "faithful pourtrayings of unmerited wrongs and consequent sufferings" which her friend's letters often contain. Mrs Fenwick, teaching, dress-making, accommodating herself to incessantly changing and arduous conditions, wondered, pitied and admired; asked help and returned thanks with a simple frankness that speaks well of both parties in the process; poured forth her grief at the loss of her son, revealed at long last the unhappiness of her daughter's marriage, and in old age sent rare but warm letters of news and enquiry, breathing a hardy and not uncheerful acceptance of toil and sorrow, across a severing ocean to her "dear, prudent, considerate Friend".

To give this help and receive this acknowledgment is perhaps a small but an unassailable achievement. It is not the work of Bridgetina Botherim, nor do we find, at least in Mrs Fenwick's letters, any reference to social utility. On this ground Mary Hays was a success, and needed no philosophical terminology to make her defeat palatable; she was an effective benefactor, giving with stable benevolence to one who needed and therefore took without embarrassment. She was summoned and replied. The voice was not the voice she had hoped to hear, but it certainly enabled her to contribute to, though never to perfect, the happiness of an individual. There was no apathy in her and no silence round her; and though melancholy and restlessness may at intervals have clouded her mind, she can hardly have become sour.

Note

1. *The Love-Letters of Mary Hays* and *The Fate of the Fenwicks* (Methuen). For permission to quote from these books I am indebted to the author and the publishers.

M. Ray Adams (essay date 1947)

SOURCE: Adams, M. Ray. "Mary Hays, Disciple of William Godwin." In *Studies in the Literary Backgrounds of English Radicalism,* pp. 83-103. Lancaster, PA: Franklin and Marshall College, 1947.

[*In the following essay, Adams provides an overview of Hays's major writings and discusses Hays's relationship with William Godwin and Mary Wollstonecraft.*]

Mary Hays was one of that remarkable coterie of women, including Mary Wollstonecraft, Amelia Alderson, Mrs. Reveley, Mrs. Fenwick, and Mrs. Inchbald, who afforded William Godwin a sort of philosophic seraglio. Little is known of her life: no biographical sketch of her exists. As the information left by others is sparse, we must depend much upon her supposedly autobiographical novel, *Memoirs of Emma Courtney.* She lived to be eighty-three, but the last forty years of her life are without a record. Soon after the decade of the French Revolution she became enveloped in an obscurity which has never lifted. Once the immediate revolutionary impulse had spent itself, she seems to have written nothing more. But in the revival of the fame of Godwin and Mary Wollstonecraft, to both of whom she was as faithful as their shadows, she perhaps deserves more attention than she has received. In her blind discipleship she innocently reduced many of Godwin's philosophical maxims to absurdities. She thus made herself the laughing-stock of those conservatives whose sympathies were narrowed by mere respectability as well as of certain liberals whose convictions did not give them such reckless courage.

Particularly in her relations with men she carried out the doctrines of reason, sincerity, and the emancipation of woman with a thoroughness that shocked her own sex as well as the men for whose favor she bid. With her, woman was the hunter, man the game. Since nature was very unkind to her in both face and figure, she had to resort wholly to philosophy, and Cupid's wings were promptly clipped. Rousseau's dictum that "energy of sentiment is the characteristic of a noble soul" she accepted with a vengeance. Though she adopted Godwin's belief in the power of reason to direct feeling, she did not exemplify it in practice.

If we are to accept the *Memoirs of Emma Courtney* as an adumbration of her early life, she received her first draught of republican ideas from her childhood reading of Plutarch, the perusal of whom she finished with "her mind pervaded with republican ardour, her sentiments elevated by a high-toned philosophy, and her bosom glowing with the virtues of patriotism."[1] As a child, too, she wept over the sorrows of St. Preux.

In 1792, at the age of twenty-two, she made her literary debut with a reply to Gilbert Wakefield's *On the Propriety of Public Worship,* published as No. I of *Letters and Essays* (1793). The influence of Price and Priestley, at this time very strong, kept her from openly breaking away from the Christian religion. She was more attracted to Unitarianism than to any of the forms of popular dissent because it "divested Christianity [as she put it] of the corruptions of scholastic jargon on the one side and of fanatic mysticism on the other."[2] But to her the ennobling of feeling was as true a part of religion as the satisfaction of the reason. She could not abide the emotional aridity of high church Anglicanism. In fact, her rationalism never became as soulless as Coleridge, who could not abide the image of Reason set up for God, later made it appear:

> To hear a thing, ugly and petticoated, ex-syllogize a God with cold-blooded precision, and attempt to run

religion through the body with an icicle, an icicle from a Scotch Hog-trough! *I* do not endure it; my eye beholds phantoms and "nothing is but what is not."[3]

She condemned the idea that "salvation should be the reward of sound opinions." Certainly she was the disciple of no arid deism in 1796 when she wrote:

> After having bewildered ourselves amid systems and theories, religion returns to the susceptible mind as a *sentiment* rather than as a principle.[4]

Just when she came to know Godwin personally is not clear. That she was certainly one of the earliest converts to *Political Justice* is evident in her *Letters and Essays,* published within the same year as Godwin's book. Since she undoubtedly was drawn about this time into the circle of the liberal bookseller Joseph Johnson, her own publisher and the friend of Godwin, it is very probable that she and Godwin met in 1793. At any rate "in 1795 or early 1796 he appears to have received a proposal of marriage from Mary Hays,"[5] she having already courted William Frend with no success.[6] The story of her courtship of Godwin is supposed by Godwin's latest biographer to be told in *Emma Courtney* under the guise of the heroine's attachment to Augustus Harley.

The friendship with Mary Wollstonecraft began in some frank criticism[7] which she, as Johnson's reader, had made in Paris of the preface of Miss Hays's *Letters and Essays.* She probably sought the first opportunity of a personal acquaintanceship during Miss Wollstonecraft's short stay in England in the spring of 1795 or at least soon after her final return in October. During the long agony of Mary's separation from Imlay, which was finally confirmed in March, 1796, Mary Hays, as we may safely conjecture from their later intimacy, did what she could to help her. Now that she saw her own suit with Godwin fruitless, she decided, it seems, to bestow him upon her friend. At any rate, it was at her home and by her invitation that Godwin in January, 1796, renewed his originally not very auspicious acquaintanceship[8] with Mary Wollstonecraft. It was not long thereafter that their enmity melted into friendship and their friendship into love. Mary Hays was generous enough—and wise enough—to urge upon the couple their formal union. She was among the few friends to whom the secret of the marriage was first imparted. Twelve days after the ceremony on May 29, 1797, Godwin wrote to her:

> My fair neighbour desires me to announce to you a piece of news which it is consonant to the regard that she and I entertain for you, you should rather learn from us than from any other quarter. She bids me remind you of the earnest way in which you pressed me to prevail upon her to change her name, and she directs me to add, that it has happened to me, like many other disputants, to be entrapped in my own toils; in short, that we found that there was no way so obvious for her to drop the name of Imlay, as to assume the name of Godwin. Mrs. Godwin—who the devil is that?—will be glad to see you at No. 29, Polygon, Somers Town, whenever you are inclined to favour her with a call.[9]

Her constancy toward the Godwins was scrupulously kept. On August 31, Godwin called at her house to deliver the news of the birth the day before of Mary Godwin, who was to become the wife of Shelley. Mary Hays was Mrs. Godwin's faithful attendant during the last four tragic days that ended in death on the morning of September 10, and she wrote for the grief-distracted husband some letters[10] which he could not bring himself to compose.

In the literary circle at Johnson's after the publication of **Emma Courtney** in 1796 she enjoyed for a while a certain celebrity. She was among the "London lions or literati" whom Lamb's George Dyer took Southey to see in March, 1797. "Mary Hays is an agreeable woman and a Godwinite," Southey wrote to Cottle.[11] She introduced the young Crabb Robinson to her circle, and in 1799 he accompanied her on a visit to Johnson, then confined in King's Bench Prison for selling Gilbert Wakefield's *Reply to the Bishop of Llandaff,* an intemperate revolutionary attack upon Pitt's government.

After this what little we hear of her takes the form of ridicule or downright defamation, occasioned either by her eccentricities or by her disturbing ideas. As late as 1816, when she was forty-six, Lamb saw her "prim up her chin" for George Dyer. An unreciprocated passion for Coleridge's friend Charles Lloyd led her into an imbroglio from which Lloyd himself did not escape with credit. Having vehemently attacked Godwin's ideas on marriage, Lloyd was very ill chosen by Miss Hays as a subject upon which to try out those ideas about "Sincerity" (Lamb calls it "a certain forward-looking half-brother of Truth") which Godwin had taught her. He wrote her a letter in answer to her advances in which, as he put it, was "interwoven his abhorrence of her principles with a glanced contempt of her personal character."[12] He disagreed with her on the question when and how far sincerity is a virtue. Nevertheless, he seems for a time to have taken her cue for the sake of amusement merely. For this both Southey and Coleridge condemned him. Coleridge wrote January 25, 1800 to Southey:

> Charles Lloyd's conduct has been atrocious beyond what you stated. Lamb himself confessed to me that during the time in which he [Lloyd] kept up his ranting, sentimental correspondence with Miss Hays, he frequently read her letters in company, as a subject for *Laughter,* and then sate down and answered them quite *à la Rousseau!*[13]

Her writings were not so "strange and wild" as her detractors made them appear. In principle she went no further than her radical contemporaries. In her **Letters and Essays** she attacks the monarchial idea with the downrightness of Paine, and she echoes Priestly on materialism and Godwin on necessity. Her materialism, she urges, is not inconsistent with the belief in a future life, the evidence of which she takes from the New Testament and not from philosophical theory. The materiality of the soul, which involves its dissolving with the body, does not affect the attributes of the Deity, for he can restore to the spirit its identity just as easily as he might keep it from becoming extinct. To her, necessity does not involve "a blind fatality within us," since action is determined by the bent of nature and the force of motive. To allow philosophical free-will is "indeed binding the Deity by a kind of necessity." There is nothing distressing about the moral implications of necessity:

> A necessarian may pity, but he cannot hate. He will likewise be active, as he knows the end strictly to depend on the means. His ideas by no means open the door to licentiousness; for, should he have an enlightened understanding, he sees happiness to be the result of order and that vice and folly are synonymous terms.[14]

Though she has the metaphysical and theological urge, her intellectual faculties do not appear deep or original.

With the boldness of Mary Wollstonecraft she declares for the intellectual independence and dignity of her sex. The mental slavery of women which "chains them down to frivolity and trifles" and deprives them of "the glory of rationality" is condemned with Wollstonecraftian vigor. She stands for the legitimate demands of human nature which are ignored by strict religious codes. And she appeals on behalf of those women who have the rudiments of taste, but who, for lack of training must display them only in "drawing the pattern, shading the colours for a carpet or a fire-screen, and . . . fancying the ornaments to decorate their persons." She is not above an appeal to men's self-interest and vanity:

> Lovers of truth! be not partial in your researches. Men of sense and science! remember, by degrading our understandings, you incapacitate us for knowing your value, and make coxcombs take the place of you in our esteem . . . How impolitic to threw a veil over our eyes, that we may not distinguish the radiance that surrounds you![15]

Her controversy on Helvetius with several correspondents in the *Monthly Magazine*[16] reveals a doughty champion of ideas who is deep in the radical ferment. She will have nothing to do with "the obsolete notion of innate ideas"; insists that "a particular train of circumstances rather than an inborn peculiar attitude leads to a preference of one study over another" and that differences of national character are directly traceable to differences in government; restates and reaffirms the principles of the sensational psychology; appeals to "universal experience" against "the notion of natural powers"; and declares that virtue no more than knowledge is born with us.

Miss Hays was the author of two novels, **Memoirs of Emma Courtney** (1796) and **The Victim of Prejudice** (1799). **Emma Courtney** is certainly one of the most readable novels of the time. It is, as the *Monthly Review* observed, "above the class of vulgar novels,"[17] comprising in fact the investigation of a moral problem—whether the expression of sincere feeling should be fettered by an established system of conduct which may be merely a fosterer of false delicacy and hypocrisy.

Emma Courtney, a beautiful and accomplished but poor woman, voluntarily submits herself to the tutorship of a celibatarian philosopher, Mr. Francis, who encourages her to use her reason. But she allows reason to become "the auxiliary of her passion," or rather she makes passion the "generative principle" of reason. She falls in love with a young man, Augustus Harley, without means, who loves her as a brother and esteems her as a friend, but who, in order to inherit a small fortune, is bound not to marry. With the conviction that it is a pernicious system of morals "which teaches us that hypocrisy can be virtue" and that "the Being who gave to the mind its reason gave also to the heart its sensibility," she reveals to him her passion and urges him to be as "ingenuous" as she. Into Emma's correspondence with Harley the author was said by Charles Lloyd to have inserted her own love-letters to Frend and Godwin.

The heroine finally writes Harley a letter[18] in which her passion for him is given full expression and in which she musters all the powers of reason against every possible species of objections to their union except the "invincible obstacle of his marriage to another." Since she is the enemy of all obscurity and mystery in personal relations, she has the "magnanimity" to declare her love directly. She proposes to break what appears to be his emotional resistance by a grand frontal attack with the artillery of reason. She is esteemed and respected.

> How, then, can I believe it compatible with the nature of mind that so many strong efforts and reiterated impressions can have produced no effect upon yours? . . . My own sensibility and my imperfect knowledge of your character may have combined to mislead me. The first, by its suffocating and depressing powers, clouding my vivacity, incapacitating me from appearing to you with my natural advantages—these effects would diminish as assurance took place of doubt. The last every day would contribute to correct. Permit me, then, to hope for as well as to seek your affections, and if I do not at length gain and secure them, it will be a phenomenon in the history of mind.

To meet the financial obstacles and make it possible for him to retain his legacy, she is willing to enter into a union without legal or ecclesiastical sanction and thus make it "wholly the triumph of affection." In this way principle would rise above prudence, "for the individuality of an affection constitutes its chastity."

The one "invincible obstacle" she later discovers: Augustus is married to another woman, whom he dislikes. Emma in despair marries a former lover. Augustus' wife dies. He, accidentally wounded, is brought to Emma's house, where he dies in her arms. Her husband becomes jealous, and his progressive degeneration sets in apace. Infidelity, infanticide, and finally suicide bear him to an ignominious end. Emma is left to devote herself to her own children and Augustus's child, to whom the book is addressed.

The violent abuse visited upon Mary Hays for this book was based upon the misunderstanding that she intended unreservedly to commend her heroine. Unfortunately her own conduct toward Godwin may have led to this interpretation, and her later infatuation for Lloyd may have confirmed it with many people. But, in the light of her experience with Godwin, one must conclude that the book was written more as an apology to him than as a challenge to others. It was really written to teach the danger of indulging an extreme sensibility. "The errors of my heroine," she plainly writes in the preface, "were the offspring of sensibility, and . . . the result of her hazardous experiment is calculated to operate as a *warning* rather than as an example."[19] What is this warning? That passion should submit to the control of reason rather than that reason should be guided by passion. The young son of Augustus Harley has loved a girl who has married another. Emma tells the story of her own life to this son in order to warn him of the consequences of enslavement to passion and of the continual use of reason to justify its dictates, of which error he seems already guilty. The power of a strong affection, she shows, may enslave reason just as it may put a host of syllogisms to flight.

Emma Courtney had come to grief because she had not acted upon Mr. Francis's, or Godwin's advice. In their philosophic correspondence Mr. Francis warns her, in answer to a letter full of romantic aspirations, against "fostering an excessive sensibility instead of cultivating her reason."[20] He, indeed, has no sympathy for her romantic madness. "Had you worshipped," he writes her, "at the altar of reason half as assiduously as you have sacrificed at the shrine of illusion, your present happiness might have been enviable."[21] The person of truly independent mind will not have his happiness thus in another's keeping. In fact, the teaching of the novel had been plainly put in *Letters and Essays* three years before:

> Unrestrained sensibility is ever selfish; properly regulated, it will give energy and interest to virtue; but, flattered and fostered, it is a mere specious name for imbecility.[22]

Emma's feelings towards her husband had nothing of the morbid excess which the Godwinian reason condemns. There is nothing here of the mere emotional distemper often called love. She tells him:

> I feel for you all the affection that a reasonable and virtuous mind ought to feel—that affection which is compatible with the fulfilling of other duties. We are guilty of vice and selfishness when we yield ourselves up to unbounded desires and suffer our hearts to be wholly absorbed by one object, however meritorious that object may be.[23]

Emma's career, then, illustrated the dangers of the effervescent Rousseauistic philosophy untempered by the sedative doctrines of Helvetius and Godwin. These are conveyed to her in the letters of Mr. Francis.

Mr. Francis is Godwin, too, in his teaching that "vice originates in mistakes of the understanding," that women are degraded by the customs of society, that inequalities of society are "the source of every misery and of every vice," that the soldier's trade is murder, and that utility is the basis of morals. But Emma's mind could not rise with Mr. Francis's into the rarefied atmosphere of abstractions and dwell there:

> My mind has not sufficient strength to form an abstract idea of perfection. I have ever found it stimulated, improved, advanced by its affections.[24]

Augustus Harley, whom Brown[25] mistakenly equates with Godwin, is a political liberal only to the extent that he has foregone the privileges of the eldest male in the division of the family estate and has relinquished the law because of its chicanery; but we are told nothing about his philosophical ideas.

For the doctrine of sincerity she draws upon Holcroft; for those of feminine emancipation, upon Miss Wollstonecraft. The checking of the natural man by suppressing our affections instead of expressing them with unequivocal sincerity "injures the mind, converts the mild current of gentle and genial sympathies into a destructive torrent and . . . has been one of the most miserable mistakes in morals."[26] In a letter[27] to Mr. Francis she puts the case of woman denied what should be the inheritance of her nature:

> While men pursue interest, honour, pleasure, as accords with their several dispositions, women who have too much delicacy, sense, and spirit to degrade themselves by the vilest of all interchanges, remain insulated beings, and must be content tamely to look on without taking any part in the great, though often absurd and tragical, drama of life.

She will "not recommend to general imitation" that the woman shall take the initiative in love. But she asks in her letter:

> When mind has given dignity to natural affections; when reason, culture, taste, and delicacy have combined to chasten, to refine, to exalt, to sanctify them—is there then no cause to complain of rigour and severity, that such minds must either passively submit to a vile traffic or be content to relinquish all the enduring sympathies of life.

The observance of artificial precepts under such circumstances is consistent neither with the voice of nature nor with the dignity of mind. Of the privileges of thinking, too, she saw woman so long deprived that she was careless of claiming and hardly capable of exercising them. The puerilities of feminine conversation made Emma Courtney seek the society of men. It was in a rebellious mood that at a party she noted "the adjournment of the ladies into the drawing room, whither I was compelled, by a barbarous and odious custom, reluctantly to follow, and to submit to be entertained with a torrent of folly and impertinence."[28]

The Victim of Prejudice is the undistinguished story of a beautiful and virtuous girl whose mother is both a prostitute and a murderess. The daughter is educated according to the plan of Rousseau, and prays to the God of nature and of reason. She becomes the victim of prejudice when the circumstances of her birth make impossible her marriage with a man of worth and breeding. The book is a protest against the injustice of society's visiting the sins of the parents upon the children. It won short shrift from that journalistic baiter of radicalism, the *Anti-Jacobin Review*:

> To your distaff, Mary, to your distaff! On the style of her writing it is needless to remark; who stays to admire the workmanship of a dagger wrenched from the hands of an assassin?"[29]

But her next publication received the disapprobation even of such tolerant organs as the *Monthly* and *Annual Reviews*. This was her ***Female Biography,*** issued in six volumes in 1803. It was a project which Mary Wollstonecraft would have highly approved, though it is of very uneven literary excellence. By presenting the accomplishments of women who reflect the greatest credit upon their sex, the author hoped to excite a rivalry nobler than that of beauty and equipage, and to "substitute, . . . for the evanescent graces of youth, the more durable attractions of a cultivated mind."[30] One instance of her liberal prepossessions will have to suffice. The account of the martyrdom, under Henry VIII, of Anne Askew, the fearless advocate of the exercise of the private conscience in religion, is thus concluded:

> All who have attached important consequences to speculative theology, have . . . employed it for the extirpation or the annoyance of those who, doubting the propriety of a *standard mind,* have presumed to exercise their own judgments.[31]

Both of the above reviews object to the biographer's indifference to the moral implications in the lives of women more noted for their talents than for their virtues, accounts of whom, thinks the *Annual Review,* "might have been sacrificed with advantage to the *sacred ignorance . . .* of female youth."[32]

But what most stirred up the watch-dogs of the public conscience was the ideas about marriage in ***Emma Courtney,*** especially the opinion that "the purity of an attachment consists in its individuality." The *Anti-Jacobin Review,* with incredible lack of charity, buried her, along with Helen Maria Williams, Godwin, and Mary Wollstonecraft, under an avalanche of abuse. It thought that the book "outhelens even the wife or the mistress of Stone," and declared that it "cannot but think the forbearance of the philosopher Godwin and his worthy disciples to act up to the principles which they professed when so glorious an opportunity occurred for reducing them to practice, was an instance of unphilosophical pusillanimity."[33]

Lloyd attacks her by indirection in his novel *Edmund Oliver* (1798). Gertrude Sinclair, a devotee of "general principles," breaks her troth with her childhood lover, Edmund Oliver, using Godwin's philosophy concerning promises as her defense. She then takes the initiative in love and practices Miss Hays's "Sincerity" with her paramour, Edward D'Oyley, a "dashing modern democrat" whom she has met at a "reading party" conducted by a circle of Godwinians at Bristol and whose impulses are vitiated by his philosophy. She and D'Oyley enter into intimate relations without benefit of marriage; but she is soon thereafter afflicted by her conscience though having sincerely acted from the beginning in conformity with what she regarded as "sublime and elevated notions." D'Oyley, who turns out to be a married man, finally abandons her. She bears his illegitimate child, is disowned by her family, and ends miserably, the victim of Godwin's philosophy. The author quotes from *Emma Courtney* as the inspiration for Gertrude's decision to go to any absurd length in the exercise of the understanding and as the source of such ideas as the following:

> Love is not as some suppose a blind and unreasoning instinct—it is a passion that may be heightened, and perhaps owes its origin to physical sympathies, but its growth, like that of any other of our qualities, depends on the permission of the will, on the perception of fitness in the object.[34]

The *Memoirs of Emma Courtney* was the chief begetter of Mrs. Elizabeth Hamilton's *Memoirs of Modern Philosophers* (1800), an anti-revolutionary novel in which "some of the opinions conveyed to the young and unthinking through the medium of philosophical novels, is exhibited in the character of Brigetina,"[35] who, the author further tells us, "seems indebted to Emma Courtney for some of her finest thoughts."[36] To Miss Hays's Brigetina Botherim, Holcroft plays Mr. Glib and Godwin plays Mr. Myope. As a character Brigetina is burlesqued far too much to be convincing, and the real problem of Mary Hays's book is blandly ignored. Reputedly learned and exceedingly homely, Bridgetina has stuffed her head so full of metaphysics under the influence of Glib and Myope that she is unfitted for the common duties of life and quite unconscious of her lack of looks and manners. She seizes every occasion to parrot Godwinian precepts about gratitude, necessity, duty, the system of rewards and punishments, the domestic affections, perfectibility, general benevolence, marriage, general utility, ecclesiastical tyranny, and the omnipotence of mind over matter—sometimes even to the exasperation of Mr. Myope himself. She besieges the heart of Henry Sidney, but neither her effusions of sensibility nor the bombardment of the artillery of reason avails. She considers her contempt of chastity "as an exalted proof of female heroism and virtue."[37] But, like Emma, little as she in her philosophy seems to value her chastity, she never surrenders it. She, Glib, and Myope become enamoured of the idea of emigrating to the land of the Hottentots, where they expect to find the Age of Reason exemplified.[38] Vallaton, a philosophic rake and disciple of Myope, seduces Julia, Bridgetina's sister in philosophy, and sets off for France, with all the money collected for the Hottentot enterprise, in the company of Emmeline, a time-worn French wanton who goes under the name of "the Goddess of Reason." Bridgetina is finally brought to her senses by the deathbed plea of the ruined Julia that she "in the sober du-

ties of life forget the idle vagaries which our distempered brains dignified with the name of philosophy."[39]

Whether Mary Hays's militant and romantic radicalism ever became subdued to this extent or whether she was content all her life to suffer, like Emma Courtney, "the moral martyrdom of those who have courage to act upon advanced principles," we do not know. But against the opprobrium which her unconventional ideas won her, we can set the testimony of Henry Crabb Robinson, who knew her until her death, who had very little tolerance for moral derelictions, and whose opinion will be conclusive enough to most modern readers:

> She confessed Mary Wollstonecraft's opinions with more zeal than discretion. This brought her into disrepute among the rigid, and her character suffered—but most undeservedly. Whatever her principles may have been, her conduct was perfectly correct.[40]

There is no evidence, however, that she ever brought her own reason into submission to the established system of conduct which a prudential world lays upon every freeborn spirit.[41]

Notes

1. *Memoirs of Emma Courtney* [2 vols., 1796], I, 23.

2. *Letters and Essays* [1793], p. 48.

3. Letter of January 25, 1800, to Southey; see *Letters of Samuel Taylor Coleridge,* edited by E. H. Coleridge (Boston, 1895), I, 323.

4. *Memoirs of Emma Courtney,* I, 53.

5. Ford K. Brown, *The Life of William Godwin* (New York, 1926), p. 109. Of this proposal Godwin discreetly makes no mention.

6. Associate of Coleridge at Cambridge, whence he had been expelled for freethinking in 1793.

7. Mary Wollstonecraft reproved for her "vain humility" in pleading the disadvantages of her education as an excuse for defects, and for her foolish thirst for that praise usually bestowed as a matter of form by men upon the work of women but denied by them in private. Her critic was simply attempting to stiffen the feminine spine. For Mary Wollstonecraft's letter, see W. Clark Durant's supplement to his edition of Godwin's *Memoirs of Mary Wollstonecraft* (1927).

8. See Godwin's letter to Miss Hays, Ford K. Brown, *op. cit.,* p. 114.

9. *Ibid.,* pp. 118-119.

10. The letter to Mr. Hugh Skeys is very expressive of her attachment to Mary Wollstonecraft. See C. Kegan Paul, *William Godwin: His Friends and Contemporaries* (London, 1876), I, 282.

11. Joseph Cottle, *Reminiscences of Samuel Taylor Coleridge and Robert Southey* (London, 1847), p. 152.

12. *Works of Charles Lamb,* edited by E. V. Lucas (London, 1912), V, 157.

13. *Letters of Samuel Taylor Coleridge,* I, 322.

14. *Letters and Essays,* p. 180.

15. *Ibid.,* pp. 20, 80, 26. These references are grouped in the order of the quotations above.

16. See numbers for February, June, and September of 1796 and January of 1797.

17. XXIII, 443.

18. II, 44-48.—All the quotations in this paragraph are from this letter.

19. I, 4.

20. I, 63.

21. II, 71. In answer to this, she points out to him an essential paradox of Godwin's philosophy. All her calamities in love, she declares, have flowed "from chastity having been considered a sexual virtue"; and, since, as he has shown, we are the creatures of impression and bound by the inexorable chain of necessity, the philosopher is shrinking from his own principles. Mr. Francis dodges the problem and begins to turn the course of her ideas in order to relieve her emotional tension.

22. P. 85.

23. II, 116.

24. II, 18. The emotional dryness of Godwin's philosophy has undoubtedly been overdrawn by his critics. In this connection, see B. Sprague Allen, "William Godwin as a Sentimentalist," *PMLA* [*Publications of the Modern Language Association*], XXXIII (1918), 1-29. Mr. Allen concludes: "Whether he would have admitted it is a question, but the fact is that the inmost shrine of his philosophy might be entered by way of either the reason or the feelings. The preference seems to have been for the latter way, if we can judge by the character and writings of his most ardent disciples." Among these disciples this was particularly true of Mary Hays. Perhaps Mr. Francis is too austere a portrait for the Godwin whom she knew.

25. See *op. cit.,* p. 110. There seems to be nothing as a basis for such identification but the mere report that Miss Hays introduced some of her letters to Godwin into the correspondence between Emma and Harley. Godwin, as Mr. Francis, is given the dignified rôle of philosophical mentor, a part which we know he played in real life. Emma's love for Mr. Francis is purely platonic. Brown also confuses Augustus Harley with his son.

26. II, 55.

27. I, 118-124.

28. II, 31.

29. III, 58.

30. P. iv.

31. I, 111. It is strange that the life of Mary Wollstonecraft was not included in this work, though Miss Hays had written her obituary for the *Monthly Magazine* (IV, 232-233).

32. I, 612.

33. I, 55; V, 39-40.

34. I, 40-41.

35. P. xv.

36. II, 85n.

37. III, 106.

38. This burlesque of the Pantisocratic scheme is unfair to Godwin and his followers, who did not preach reversion to the state of noble savagery and in whose picture of the perfect society there was nothing of the primitive.

39. III, 349-350.

40. *Diary, Reminiscences, and Correspondence,* edited by Thomas Sadler (Boston, 1869), I, 37. See also *Henry Crabb Robinson on Books and their Writers,* edited by Edith J. Morley (London, 1938), I, 130-131, 234-235; III, 843.

41. In fact, Robinson in a note on her death remarks that she had "stuck fast" in her liberal opinions (*Ibid.,* II, 629).

Some of the obscurity which has enveloped Miss Hays's youth and later maturity has been dispelled by J. M. S. Tompkins in "Mary Hays, Philosophess," *The Polite Marriage* (Cambridge, 1938). She has had access to family letters not available to me and has thus been able to present more fully than here the emotional nexuses that make up so large a part of any biography of Mary Hays. The few facts unearthed about her later life show her feminism unimpaired, though her radicalism otherwise was subdued to an active benevolence among "the labouring poor."

Burton R. Pollin (essay date 1971)

SOURCE: Pollin, Burton R. "Mary Hays on Women's Rights in the *Monthly Magazine*." *Etudes Anglaises* 24, no. 3 (July-September 1971): 271-82.

[*In the following essay, Pollin examines Hays's contributions to the late eighteenth-century reform movement in the form of letters and essays she produced for the* Monthly Magazine.]

While sifting the earliest issues of the *Monthly Magazine* for references to William Godwin, I was struck by the frequent mention of his name in the letters to the editor, from

February 1796 through September 1797, chiefly on the subject of women's rights and education[1]. The series included several signed "M. H." and terminated with one signed by Godwin's friend, Mary Hays. Two of the very few studies of this ardent and curious suffragette, I discovered, mentioned her contributing to a "controversy on Helvétius" under these initials, but failed to examine or even identify the printed articles[2]. They obviously relied for their information upon Southey's statement in a letter to Joseph Cottle, of March 13, 1797, soon after he met Mary Hays. Southey says, "She writes in the 'Monthly Magazine' under the signature of M. H., and sometimes writes nonsense there about *Helvetius*." He adds that she is "an agreeable woman, and a Godwinite," the author of "an uncommon book," which has been "much praised and much abused."[3] Southey, who continued his friendship with Mary Hays for the rest of her long life (1760-1843), never felt inclined to revise that generally favorable opinion.

Mary Hays had enlisted herself among the liberal intellectuals of London and vehemently espoused the cause of women's rights in 1792 when Mary Wollstonecraft's *Vindication of the Rights of Woman* was published. Since her life has been at least sketchily treated by A. F. Wedd, M. Ray Adams, and J. M. S. Tompkins, there is need to mention only her literary activities concerning the subject of women's rights through the 1790's[4]. Her first work, significantly a controversial pamphlet, by "Eusebia", comprised ***Cursory Remarks on Gilbert Wakefield's Enquiry into the Expediency and Propriety of Public Worship*** (1792). Among those who admired her work was the prominent, scholarly William Frend, one of the three or four men whom Mary rather daringly and unsuccessfully courted[5]. When George Dyer brought to her Mary Wollstonecraft's newly published *Vindication of the Rights of Woman,* she sought out the author and became an ardent disciple. Her miscellany, ***Letters and Essays, Moral and Miscellaneous*** (1793), betrays this new adherence in its expressions of admiration. In view of her later comments on William Enfield's *Monthly Magazine* article, there is interest also in her citing his *History of Philosophy*[6]. Mary Hays's fledgling book, with its inserted poems, tale, and essays—several reprinted from the *Universal Magazine*—led to her further association with the literati of London, including Godwin, and to her reviewing in such monthlies as the *Critical Review* and the *Analytical Review.* An important figure on the *Analytical* was Mary Wollstonecraft. After Mary Wollstonecraft's return from France, dejected by the desertion of the American Gilbert Imlay, Miss Hays became her close friend in 1795. She deeply regretted an unfortunate coolness which had resulted from the Wollstonecraft-Godwin meeting in 1791 and managed to reintroduce them in January 1796. Although unaware of the steady ripening of their relationship into intimacy, she appears to have approved of their marriage on March 29, 1797.[7] Some critics have carelessly alleged that Mary Hays had been in love with Godwin, who had allowed her to send him long "philosophical" and sentimental letters, several of which were inserted into her novel, ***Memoirs of Emma Courtney*** (1796)[8]. In reality, a careful reading of the book and of the evidence shows Godwin as cast in the role of a "trusted friend", i.e., the philosopher, Mr. Francis, who warned "Emma-Maria" about the danger of mentally indulging her unreciprocated amour. The real object of her passion this time was apparently William Frend, just as Charles Lloyd would become the object in 1799. (The latter was to mock her rather callously in his novel *Edmund Oliver,* which represented a break with Jacobinical ideas as well as liberal friends, such as Godwin[9].) In 1796, Mary, still single, was apparently eager for a discussion of the prejudicial position of women in society.

A good point of departure was the anonymous "Enquirer" series beginning in the first issue of the new liberal journal, the *Monthly Magazine,* published by the well-known Richard Phillips, February 1796[10]. Phillips had engaged Dr. William Enfield, former tutor at Warrington Academy, adviser to Ralph Griffith of the *Monthly Review,* to which he contributed, and author of the very popular schoolbook, *The Speaker,* and *Institutes of Natural Philosophy,* as I have indicated above[11]. According to Godwin's manuscript journal, he had met him in 1794[12]; Godwin was sure to note Enfield's use of the *Enquiry concerning Political Justice* in "Enquirer" Nos. 1 and 4 (February and May 1796). In turn, Godwin probably used the title of his series for his own book of essays, *The Enquirer,* being written during 1796[13]. Godwin could have had no doubt about Enfield's authorship, which must have been an open secret to the liberal literati of London, including Mary Hays (she is mentioned in his journal for visits received or paid at least twice in 1795, thirty-seven times in 1796, and twenty-three times in 1797). In fact, in Enfield's obituary notice in the *Monthly Magazine* of November 1797, the editor John Aikin wrote: "His cast of thoughts was free, enlarged and manly, as was proved in *The Enquirer,* which so much gratified the liberal readers of the *Monthly Magazine*[14]."

At this time Mary Hays was seeking an important forum for presenting her candid and fervent views on the invidious position accorded women by an unjust society. Enfield's first topic was provocative: "Ought the Freedom of Enquiry to be restricted?" He gave the standard answer of the Rational Dissenters. Every man has a natural right to enquire after truth. It is a birthright, manifested by man's curiosity, enriched by experience. Diminish a person's ideas and you reduce his humanity and bring him closer to the animals. As knowledge and truth advance, so does the happiness of society. It is the evil policy of government to conceal the truth and to discourage enquiry. Here Enfield, obviously drawing his argument from Godwin, cites the *Enquiry concerning Political Justice* on the consequences of the removal of "all restriction and discouragement from enquiry" (I, 4). He concludes with a firm hope that man's progress will not be "retarded by coercive restrictions". Thus far Enfield says nothing on the subject of the special restrictions placed upon the education of women. But the editor either deliberately or coincidentally printed a letter from "J. T." in the same issue (I, 26-29), consisting largely of quotations from two opposing sides of a related question—whether all men's capacities at present are indefinitely or unreservedly susceptible to that educational development which will improve his physical and moral condition and achieve a foreseeable "perfection". Helvetius's *Treatise on Man* would naturally serve to present complete environmentalism and the denial of inborn inequalities. Long quotations from the translation by Hooper are given, to the effect that man's personality is only "the product of his education", interpreted as the total of impressions impinging upon sensibility[15]. In this view a Newton or a Shakespeare is merely the effect of numerous, unfathomable but none the less external causes which, if exactly duplicated, might produce a like product. To support his own belief in inborn differences of memory, judgment, and imagination, "J. T." counterposes a paragraph from Juan Huarte de San Juan, whose work on the growth of intelligence had had much publicity and popularity throughout Europe, including England, where Richard Carew in 1594 and later (1698) Edward Bellamy had issued translations of this "educational classic[16]". It is the Bellamy translation (1734 ed.) that is cited to prove that inborn predispositions of mind or personality make the young students fit for certain subjects, such as languages, or logic, or astronomy; to force them into the wrong discipline is to doom them to misery and failure. Huarte's psychology is rooted in the medieval theory of the four humors and the notion of the disciplinary value of different subjects; nonetheless Huarte may be given credit for a good statement of "professional orientation[17]". It is not surprising that his work was still being cited when we consider that the very popular Lavater gives four pages to eighteen "aperçus" drawn from his pages, several with critical comments, in the fifth volume of *Physionomie*[18]. Among the London literati Lavater was well known, for the standard translation was that of Thomas Holcroft (1789), and Mary Wollstonecraft herself had prepared an abridgment for Joseph Johnson, though it had not been published[19].

In April 1796, "Enquirer III" raises a different aspect of the great issue, whether all mankind can be ameliorated: "Are Literary and Scientific Pursuits suited to the Female Character?" (I, 181-184). Enfield presents his balanced and, on the whole, pro-female viewpoint through a charming dialogue between the frivolous coquette Sophia, ironically named after the mate that Rousseau gave to Emile, and the sober female philosopher Eliza, who admirably presents her case for producing enlightened mothers and wives. The arbiter is Aunt Margaretta, who favors a cultivated understanding, providing "the imagination and affections" are not neglected. Plain Mary Hays, as we shall see, must have identified herself with Eliza[20]. The May 1796 issue included a letter from "Christiana" discussing Mary Wollstonecraft's *Letters Written . . . in Sweden, Norway and Denmark* of January 1796 (I, 278-296). This criticizes two phrases which, in their carelessness, vitiate the effectiveness of the work of a "writer of considerable eminence". The letter shows the importance attached to Mary Wollstonecraft's name, as well as the editorial balance in presenting varied viewpoints.

The opponents begin to join forces in the issue of May 1796, with the printing of a letter from "A. B.", animadverting on "Enquirer III" (I, 289-290). Briefly he notes that "women ought to be better educated than they are" but denies that they equal men in mental power. Often their education has equaled Shakespeare's but never has there been his female equivalent. This item was bound to feed the flames of the debate, and Mary Hays had already prepared for the June 1796 issue a long letter, signed "M. H.", attacking Mr. "J. T." (I, 385-387). She defends the ability of everyone to learn anything through "use and exercise", speaking of "natural fitness" as an "occult phrase" and of the "notion of innate ideas" as "obsolete". Yet, at that very time, her mentor Godwin, whose *Political Justice* of 1793 she was echoing here, was in the process of revising his basic ideas about innate aptitudes[21]. Although environments may differ for all individuals, she admits, yet the major influences come from the climate of opinion induced by the prevailing government, as Helvétius has maintained[22]. Briefly and not very skillfully she summarizes Godwin's sketch of the development of perception through the external stimulation of the senses. As a novelist, she characteristically emphasizes the need for tracing the development of motives and the "progress" of one's opinion. The notion of inborn powers is "monstrous and hypothetical". "Virtues as well as talents are the product of education." Hence why seek for virtuous qualities in statesmen, brokers, or lawyers, she asks, as though she has read Godwin's startling essay, "Of Trades and Professions", in *The Enquirer* (pp. 212-239), even now aborning. The melodramatic Mary Hays then wrenches out of context from Godwin a concept basic to her own stormy and manhunting career: "The true methods of generating talents are to rouse attention by a lively interest, by a forcible address to the passions, the springs of human actions."

Two magazine numbers later, in July 1796, Mary is apparently attacking "A. B.'s Strictures on the Talents of Women", signing herself simply "A Woman". The sentiments, style, and allusions to *Political Justice* are characteristic of her work. A passage from Godwin's work on the development of mind from "absolute ignorance" through impinging impressions is first given. She grants the preponderance of male geniuses in the history of intellectual attainments, but then tacitly raises the argument of Mary Wollstonecraft, that women have both a neglected and a "perverted" education. The same attack upon Rousseau's "eccentric and erroneous opinions" is made[23] in language which is more impassioned than eloquent: "Endeavours were still made to sophisticate and entangle the truths which could no longer be suppressed" (II, 470). Perhaps self-consciously the very plain Mary Hays ends with a sarcastic denial for womankind of any wish to be at once "the most lovely and the wisest part of the human species".

The August 1796 issue contains an attack upon the letter of "A Woman" from "C. D.", initials which suggest a staff writer's contribution, since there would not have been time for a reader to have sent in his reply for the issue of the following month. Moreover, we now have anti-feminist replies, first from "A. B." and then from "C. D.". This also provides evidence that the magazine sought a balance of views, for the writer calls the quotation from Godwin "turgid inanity". He seizes upon "A Woman's" admission of inborn inequality of strength between man and woman to expound upon a probable native difference in intellect, which is associated with decreased opportunities, he says, for "cultivating the intellect enjoined by the needs and cares of pregnancy and motherhood" (II, 526-527). Such arguments, of course, goad feminists beyond the bounds of cool, logical refutation. Immediately following this letter is another from "T. S. N." on the allied subject of Hume's denial that "physical causes" of air and climate "influence the genius and nature of Man" (II, 527-530). The writer regards Hume's arguments as "plausible rather than valid", but finally concludes that physical causes may, indeed, be counteracted by others which are more powerful, at least in civilized society. Soon this phase of the topic will be absorbed into the feminist conflict.

The September issue brings a contribution from a new polemicist, ironically named "Philogynes". In a good piece of satire he contends that we too often regard talents as manifested best by works of literature or eloquent speeches, whereas the persuasion wrought by "a smile, a glance of the eye, or a very few words" clearly shows women to be the superior sex. Men can rebel against that superior power only as celibates or "worn-out batchelors", proof of women's supremacy of talents (II, 611-612). A more serious rejoinder, specifically to the previous defense of Helvétius by Mary Hays, is made by "S. R." in the same issue (p. 629). He contends that "all arguments deduced from experience and analogy" are directly "opposed to the fashionable philosophy of Helvétius". Since the organs of different individuals vary, why cannot the brains differ in size and consistency, thereby altering the capacity to reason. Moreover, the Jesuits, cited by "M. H.", certainly study the dispositions of their pupils from the beginning of their training. In the next issue, "A. B." joins the fray again (II, 696-697), specifically answering the May, 1796 letter of "A Woman". With deft sarcasm he raises the old argument of the need to attend to the home and the children rather than to intellectual pursuits; asks why Queen Elizabeth, so educationally privileged, could not surpass Shakespeare and Bacon; and finally generously opens up the field for intellectual development to the women with leisure and finances, while yet maintaining women to be, on the average, mentally inferior to men.

This letter, whether "planted" or actually received, was clearly intended to stimulate further discussion. This came in the November 1796 issue, again from "A Woman", whose long letter (II, 784-787) is chiefly a lively refutation of "C. D.'s" note in the August issue; this scarcely proves male "superiority", she sarcastically asserts. She uses the Helvetian concept of human beings as "similarly and commonly well organised" to deny that marked inferiority of structure may, indeed, produce an "ideot" (sic). More important is the social tendency to imitate and follow power-

ful examples—a fact which may justify Hume's depreciating physical causes in favor of the social or the moral causes. (Clearly, she has paid attention to the intervening letters on allied topics.) Women have been deprived of rational education and of the incentives fostering a Shakespeare or a Newton. Using Godwin's phrases she declaims against the "odious and pernicious . . . monopoly of mind" by men, upon whom she calls to open the field of enquiry for both sexes. Her postscript objects to the narrow definition of "education" applied by "A. B." in citing Shakespeare versus Queen Elizabeth. A little coda appears in the December issue in "A Woman's" correction of misplaced quotation marks in her excerpt from Hume (II, 850).

At the beginning of 1797 there was no decrease in the controversy among these epistolists, for "C. D." returns with a blunt denial of woman's equality and a complaint that "A Woman" has somehow brought the equality of all mankind into an argument which rested upon the differences of the two sexes. He also declares a sentence about considering non-appearing causes as "not existing" to be both meaningless and undiscoverable in Hume's "Essay on National Character", this last being "C. D.'s" manifest error (III, 4). The *Monthly Magazine*'s editor himself, in February, indicates the provenance of the sentence in Hume's revised edition of the "Essay"; this is certainly a kindly solicitude for the reputation of his female correspondent[24].

The last two installments in the controversy are those of Mary Hays, or "M. H.", indicating either a suppression of opposing letters or growing loss of interest in the theme. In March 1797, the opening suggests a contrived debate: "I am encouraged by your insertion of my defence of the talents of women, in reply to the strictures of A. B. and C. [she omitted the suitable 'D.'] to address you, etc." (III, 193-195). Citing "an eloquent advocate for the rights of her sex" (probably Mary Wollstonecraft), she pleads against the artifice and despotism of female education and augurs later ideas of Godwin, advocate of candor, in the view that such an education is "enough to destroy" the "whole character" and "to poison the whole community". Women's financial dependence upon men, leads to marriage for "mercenary and venal motives (the worst kind of prostitution)". Within the confines of one paragraph, she traces the decline and fall from virtue of a wife subject to a capricious despot, epitomizing the plight of Jemima in Mary Wollstonecraft's *The Wrongs of Woman* and her own *Emma Courtney* (1796). While the ensuing depravity is deeply entangled with the system of property (Godwin's contention in *Political Justice,* Book VIII, although not footnoted by Miss Hays here) yet "its deplorable consequences" can be lessened by an improved "female Education". She proposes a training for the "trades and professions" which are suitable for women, to enable marriage to be less mercenary in motive; family support may then be shared by both partners. She ends on a note drawn from the first edition of *Political Justice,* that government must ensure that "one moral and mental standard is established for every rational agent". Mary seems unaware that Godwin has dropped this expectation of a fundamentally vicious establishment, from his second edition[25]).

Her next letter, of May, 1797, on the subject of talents shows a new humility and consciousness of weakness of argument, which is probably the result of the shift in opinion in Godwin's latest work, *The Enquirer* (III, 359-360). Here he had begun to retract his view of the absolute equality and "tabula rasa" purity of all minds or "organs of perception" at birth[26]. Mary herself speaks of the preface to the work of this "eloquent philosophic writer". The resultant article by her is a potpourri of borrowed statements about the connection of knowledge and virtue, of mental powers and lively sensations, of sense and reason, of talents and power, and finally of hampering government and the need for free enquiry. Her interest in motives causes her in conclusion to allude to Godwin's tracing "the principles" of mind. Her admiration of *The Enquirer,* incidentally, is echoed in August, 1797 (III, 119), in the *Monthly Magazine*'s "half-yearly retrospect of the state of Domestic Literature" asserting that Godwin correctly "wishes to make all men, children of reason" through reform in education and in manners in general.

Following this psychological interest, "M. H." made her penultimate contribution in September 1797 (IV, 180-181). It is an interesting defense of novel-writing in the interregnum between her own two novels, **Emma Courtney** and **Victim of Prejudice** (1799). The first had been widely criticized for the indecorous, overly-susceptible Emma, who steadfastly pursues the diffident Augustus Hartley for years, to her own catastrophic end[27]. The letter cites Johnson's view, in the *Rambler,* that "the most perfect models of virtue ought only to be exhibited", for the impressionable readers. On the other hand, Johnson's view that "Vice should always disgust wherever it appears", says Mary, ignores the gradations and mixtures of human character. In a passage that might have been the kernel of Godwin's later famous explanation of how he wrote *Caleb Williams* (in his new preface to *Fleetwood,* as reprinted in 1832), Mary shows her intention as a novelist: "To describe life and manners in real or probable situations, to delineate the human mind in endless varieties, to develop the heart, to paint the passions, to trace the springs of action, to interest the imagination, exercise the affections, and awaken the powers of the mind." It is not through contemplation of perfect beings that we learn but rather through "tracing the pernicious consequences of an erroneous judgment, a wrong step, an imprudent action, an indulged and intemperate affection . . . How deep is our regret, how touching our sympathy, how generous our sorrow, while we contemplate the noble mind blasted by the ravages of passion, or withered by the canker of prejudice!" Every contemporary reader would be prepared for her summarizing allusion to the character of Ferdinando Falkland in *Caleb Williams.* She concludes: "Fictitious histories, in the hands of persons of talents and observation . . . would become a powerful and effective engine of truth and reform." Here we can see the social and literary credo of Mary Hays, novelist.

It is interesting to note the way in which the *Monthly Magazine* treated Mary Hays's two novels, one of which fell within the period of her letters on the female cause. In the "Half-yearly Retrospect" of January 1797 (III, 47) we find a single sentence on the first: "Miss Hays's **Emma Courtney,** written to show the danger of indulging extreme sensibility, is an interesting and instructive performance abounding with just and liberal sentiments, and evidently the production of a well-cultivated and enlightened mind." Surely Mary was satisfied with this judgment. Her second novel was heralded by the magazine in December 1798 (VI, 456) as follows: "Miss Hays will speedily publish her long expected **Victim of Prejudice** which has only been delayed by the printer. The lady is at present engaged upon a biographical work of great and lasting interest to the female world, to contain the lives of illustrious women of all ages and nations . . ." When the novel finally came out, the *Monthly*'s "Retrospect" in July 1799 (VII, 542) called it a "pathetic and instructive story, displaying its author's strong natural powers, and an unrestricted freedom of thinking, which to some timid spirits may give displeasure. We confess that with us Miss Hays is a favourite author, although, in the present volumes, if we had time and room, we could point out several parts which are objectionable". The growth of anti-Jacobin abuse against liberal works was making the staff more cautious, as its occasionally sharp criticism of Godwin's new publications at the turn of the century shows.

It is fitting that the name of Mary Hays should be signed for the first time in the *Monthly Magazine* in connection with the death of Mary Wollstonecraft, her chief inspirer in the cause of women's rights. Godwin's wife died on the 10th of September 1797, ten days after the birth of little Mary. Indeed, Mary Hays had been called in by the distraught husband to help nurse his wife at the end[28]. In the September issue of the *Monthly* (pp. 232-233) appears an anonymous obituary notice, by Mary Hays, which quite naturally emphasizes her "exertions to awaken in the minds of her oppressed sex a sense of their degradation" One assumes that she is not straying from her Helvetian convictions in speaking of Mrs. Godwin's "admirable talents and . . . masculine tone of understanding". We recognize many of the threads in her previous articles, as when she notes Mary's perception of "those partial evils, destructive to virtue and happiness, which poison social intercourse and deform domestic life". The only demerit—and it is only tangentially mentioned—is Mary's attempted suicide. No one reading her eulogy could fail to perceive the distress of a loyal friend and disciple. Obviously she was proud of the notice, for in the issue of October 1797 (p. 245), she speaks of her "desire and intention" to affix her name in respect and affection for her "late admirable friend". She apologizes for not giving further particulars, which will be furnished to the public soon "by a far abler hand", namely, Godwin's in *Memoirs* of Mary Wollstonecraft. Perhaps one should also note that the *Monthly* provided a second obituary notice, of one paragraph, in July 1798, alluding to the *Memoirs* and *Posthumous Works,* which had been published in the interim (V, 493-494). This one is colder in style than that of Mary Hays, who obviously did not write: "She had faults and transcendant virtues, but let us not examine her frailties now[29].

After the death of Mary Godwin, the friendship of Mary Hays and Godwin waned and visits became rather infrequent[30]. The Godwin journal records the following references to Mary Hays: 1798, four; 1799, five; 1800, two. Mary was no less devoted, however, to the great causes which had engaged her attention in the *Monthly Magazine* series: women's rights and the enlightenment of mankind. We find her, for example, visiting Joseph Johnson in prison, to which he had been sent for publishing the "seditious" pamphlet of Gilbert Wakefield—her former contestant of 1792. The last of her letters to the editor of the *Monthly Magazine* was published in July 1800 (IX, 523-524), in affirmation of two enlightened articles on the nature of mania, by her friend Dr. John Reid, with her name signed. The final sentence is characteristic: "Any mental emotion indulged to excess may . . . induce maniacal derangement[31]". She returns to her major theme in *Female Biography* (1803), announcing in the Preface: "My pen has been taken up in the cause, and for the benefit, of my own sex, and their advancement in the grand scale of rational and social existence . . . A woman who, to the graces and gentleness of her own sex, adds the knowledge and fortitude of the other, exhibits the most perfect combination of human excellence[32]." Clearly, to Miss Hays, because of their sensibility, women are not merely men's equals but actually the superior half of humankind. Since the female biographies were of the illustrious dead of the distant past, Mary should not be contemned for omitting her friend Mary Wollstonecraft. Nor should she be blamed for writing two short tracts in 1815 and 1817 in the style of Hannah More; since the start of her career in 1792 with the pamphlet on public worship, she had never adopted the blatantly anti-religious opinions of Godwin and Holcroft.

The proof of this moderation despite the savage attacks upon her is, perhaps, her continued friendship with Henry Crabb Robinson, who offers the best sketches of Mary Hays in the nineteenth century: her failure in 1813 to reside at Southey's home as her "*too* sentimental letter" had tried to arrange and her "over-strained sensibility joined to precise manners" which will make her offensive and ridiculous to many intrinsically "below herself"; his seeing more of her, in 1819, in Pentonville, and finding her "correct in her conduct", of a "kind disposition", now become "more cheerful and agreeable in company, being less sentimental"; her death, in 1843, she being "a very worthy woman", very "liberal in her opinions" in which she "had stuck fast[33]". Robinson's allusion to Mary's friendship with Southey offers an opportunity to indicate the opinion of the Poet Laureate in May 1799, not long after the period of the *Monthly Magazine* articles. Southey thought Charles Lloyd much at fault for reading to friends with jests his correspondence with Mary Hays, who was being deliberately deceived about his feelings. Later in the year Southey wrote to Coleridge: "She is worth seeing. For, with all her mistaken notions, she has genius, more than

most of the lady writers." Soon afterwards, he wrote again: "She is a woman perhaps erroneous in all points of first importantce, but a woman of talents and I believe of a good and warm heart. I like and esteem her . . . one of those persons whom twenty years hence it will be pleasant and gratifying to have seen[34]". Perhaps the additional "sight" of Mary Hays afforded to us through her uncollected articles in the *Monthly Magazine* will confirm Southey's opinion and give us a sense of the sincerity and fervor of her feelings on one of the great issues of her day.

Notes

1. My gratitude should be expressed to the ACLS and the New York State University Research Foundation for grants which enabled me to consult materials in the British Museum, April, 1968.

2. M. Ray Adams, *Studies in the Literary Backgrounds of English Radicalism* (Lancaster, Penn., 1947), Ch. III, "Mary Hays, Disciple of William Godwin", pp. 83-103, mentions: "Her controversy on Helvetius with several correspondents in the *Monthly Magazine* . . . see numbers for February, June, and September of 1796 and January of 1797 (p. 90)"; these months are inaccurate. See J. M. S. Tompkins, *The Polite Marriage* (Cambridge, 1938), "Mary Hays Philosophess", pp. 150-187; for her reiteration of Southey's information about her writing in the *Monthly Magazine,* see, p. 179.

3. Charles Cuthbert, Southey, ed., *The Life and Correspondence of Robert Southey* (New York, 1851), p. 96.

4. A. F. Weed, *The Love Letters of Mary Hays (1779-1780)* (London, 1935), summarizes her life, pp. 1-13, and also gives letters exchanged by Mary Hays, William Frend, and William Godwin, pp. 220-248.

5. *Henry Crabb Robinson on Books and Their Writers* (London, 1938), I, 5 and 235 lays the pursuit and rejection entirely to Frend's account.

6. *Letters and Essays,* pp. v-vi, 11, 26, 28, 106, 183-184, and 14.

7. Ralph M. Wardle, *Mary Wollstonecraft* (Lincoln, Nebraska, 1966; reprint of 1951), pp. 259-260. See also his *Godwin and Mary* (Lawrence, Kansas, 1966), for many references to Mary Wollstonecraft's letters.

8. E.g., C. B. A. Proper, *Social Elements in English Prose Fiction* between 1700 and 1832 (Amsterdam, 1929), p. 196.

9. Kenneth Curry, ed., *New Letters of Robert Southey* (London, 1965), I, 187-188. For Lloyd's "apostacy" see *Edmund Oliver* (Bristol, 1798), I, 7-10, 114, 128-129, 151-152; II, 102-104 and also Lloyd's *Letter to the Anti-Jacobin Reviewers* (Birmingham, 1799), pp. 19-20.

10. The best study of the orientation and importance of the *Monthly Magazine* is by Geoffrey Carnall, *Re-*

view of English Studies, N.S. V (April 1954), 158-164. For Phillips the inadequate *DNB* article is still the best source.

11. Walter Graham, *English Literary Periodicals* (London, 1930), pp. 210-211 and *Cambridge History of English Literature,* X, 385 and XIV, 399.

12. The journal was consulted in the Pforzheimer Library, in microfilm, through the courtesy of Lord Abinger and Mr. Carl H. Pforzheimer, Jr.

13. The ascription of the period, of one year, February 1796 to February 1797 is made in *Shelley and His Circle* (Cambridge, Mass., 1961), I, 152 and confirmed by the daily journal entries.

14. *Monthly Magazine,* IV, 400-402. Lewis Patton also refers to this notice, in his reply, in the *Review of English Studies,* XVI (1940), 188-189, to Dorothy Coldicutt's effort to attribute the "Enquirer" series to Coleridge, in the same periodical, XV (1939), 45-60.

15. W. Hooper, trans., *Treatise on Man* (London, 1810 reprint of 1777 ed.), pp. 3, 13-14, and 27-28.

16. Juan Huarte, *Examen de ingenios para las ciencias* . . . 1575, 1578, 1593; Leyden, 1593; Antwerp, 1603; Alcala, 1640; Leyden, 1652; Amsterdam, 1662; Madrid, 1668, London, 1590 (?), 1594, 1596, 1604, 1616; translated by Bellamy, 1698, 1734; Lyon, 1597; Paris, 1619, 1645, 1661; Lyon, 1668; Paris, 1675; Wittenberg, 1785; Venise, 1582, 1586, 1590, 1600.

17. See Elias F. Haiek, "Juan Huarte: iniciador del estudio de la individualidad", pp. 3-12 in *Museo Social Argentino* (Buenos Aires, 1933), especially, p. 6.

18. Johann Kaspar Lavater, *L'art de Connaître les hommes par la Physionomie* (Paris, 1807), V, 49; VI, 105-112. The original version, of 1775-1778 in German, was dedicated to H. Fuseli, then Lavater's close friend and fellow reformer in Zurich and, as London artist, the object of Mary Wollstonecraft's ardent attention in 1792.

19. Wardle, *Mary Wollstonecraft,* p. 107.

20. Frequently cited is Coleridge's letter of January 25, 1800, to Southey, calling Mary Hays "A Thing, ugly & petticoated . . .", q.v. in Earl Leslie Griggs, *Collected Letters of . . . Coleridge* (Oxford, 1956), I, 563.

21. *Political Justice,* Book I, Ch. IV, given in F. E. L. Priestley's edition (Toronto, 1946), III, 141-142; for discussion see III, 95-96, and my *Education and Enlightenment in the Works of . . . Godwin* (New York, 1962), pp. 26-27.

22. She cites the Hooper translation of *De l'Homme*: II, Ch. V, 102-106; X, 171-179: XI, 179-181.

23. See Mary Wollstonecraft, *A Vindication of the Rights of Woman* (London, 1929), Ch. II, p. 23 and V. p. 88.

24. For the full text see *The Works of David Hume* (Boston, 1854), III, p. 224.

25. *Political Justice* (1793), I, IV, section 3, deleted in 1796; given in Priestley's edition, III, 245-247, and discussed at length in *Education and Enlightenment,* Chapters I and II.

26. See Priestley, Introduction to *Political Justice,* III, 95-96, and David Fleisher, *William Godwin* (New York, 1951), pp. 119-124.

27. She received a full share of anti-Jacobinical abuse, directed chiefly against Godwin. See B. Sprague Allen, *Modern Philology,* XVI (August 1918), 57-75, "The Reaction Against William Godwin", specifically, p. 60. Miss Hays was the particular target of Elizabeth Hamilton's *Memoirs of Modern Philosophers,* in the character of Bridgetina, as is stated in the 1802 French translation's preface. For a full discussion of the pointed parallels with and borrowings from Godwin see Jean de Palacio, "La Fortune de Godwin en France: Le Cas d'Elizabeth Hamilton", *Revue de Littérature Comparée,* XLI (1967), 321-341.

28. Wardle, *Mary Wollstonecraft,* p. 305.

29. However, the notice of Mary Godwin by Mary Hays in the *Annual Necrology, 1797-98* (London, 1800), pp. 411-420, was much "more restrained and apologetic" than this earlier one, as Wardle, *ibid.,* p. 322, notes.

30. It ceased in 1800 according to A. F. Wedd, *op. cit.,* p. 10. See *Shelley and His Circle,* I, 141, for a letter from Godwin to Mary Hays, of October 22, 1797, concerning a quarrel which will preclude "intimacy" but not friendship.

31. Dr. Reid's contributions to the journal were VIII (December 1799), 876-877; IX (November, 1800) 342-345; and IX (June, 1800), 427-429. Her approval of his views may reflect her friendship for one who had bitterly reviewed Lloyd's attack in *Edmund Oliver* for the *Analytical Review,* as H. C. Robinson, *op. cit.,* I, 5, reports.

32. *Female Biography* (1st American edition, Philadelphia, 1807; from London ed., 1803), Preface, pp. iii and iv. Richard Phillips, publisher of the *Monthly Magazine,* published this work.

33. H. C. Robinson, *op. cit.,* I, 124-125, 131, 234-235; and II, 629.

34. Kenneth Curry, ed., *New Letters of Robert Southey* (New York, 1965), I, 210 and 215.

Katharine M. Rogers (essay date 1987)

SOURCE: Rogers, Katharine M. "The Contribution of Mary Hays." *Prose Studies* 10, no. 2 (September 1987): 131-42.

[*In the following essay, Rogers describes Hays's writings on women's rights, comparing them to those of her friend*

Mary Wollstonecraft, whose approach was more theoretical than Hays's.]

Over a lifetime of writing, from her **Letters and Essays, Moral and Miscellaneous** (1793) to her **Memoirs of Queens** (1821), Mary Hays argued for women's rights and celebrated their achievements. Like her friend Mary Wollstonecraft, she was an ardent feminist whose assertion of the rights of women was reinforced by the ideals of the French Revolution. Mary Astell and other predecessors had argued that women have immortal souls to develop independent of their obligations to the family and that traditional marriage, requiring cheerful submission to a husband regardless of his character and behaviour, is oppression. But the political theorists of the French Revolutionary era legitimized a more radical interpretation of woman's role. Their assertion of human equality undermined the hierarchy of the family, and their belief that goodness is achieved by freedom rather than restraint undermined the restrictive morality imposed on women and even suggested that they had a right to express sexual passion.

Both Wollstonecraft and Hays wrote book-length tracts arguing for women's rights—*A Vindication of the Rights of Woman* (1792) and **Appeal to the Men of Great Britain in Behalf of Women** (1798)—and flawed polemical feminist novels—Wollstonecraft's *The Wrongs of Woman* (1798) and Hays's **Memoirs of Emma Courtney** (1796) and **The Victim of Prejudice** (1799). Both had a weakness, shared with most late eighteenth-century writers of English, for stilted rhetoric and overblown sentimentality and melodrama. On the other hand, both, at their best, used a forceful downright style, animated by personal experience and passionate commitment to their cause. What Wollstonecraft said of her style in the *Vindication* applies equally well to Hays: moved by "energetic emotions" and "wishing rather to persuade by the force of my arguments than dazzle by the elegance of my language, I shall not waste my time in rounding periods, or in fabricating the turgid bombast of artificial feelings, which, coming from the head, never reach the heart."[1] We see this plain style consistently in Hays's non-fiction, especially where she is inspired by indignation at oppression of women, for example in her life of the Protestant martyr Anne Askew, a victim of religious intolerance and patriarchal tyranny (**Female Biography**, 1802).

Hays might perhaps be dismissed as a lesser Wollstonecraft. But actually her work complements that of the more brilliant and charismatic feminist. It is true that Wollstonecraft was stronger as a theorist. She was the first to recognize that all forms of the moral double standard would have to go if women were to achieve equal rights; she grounded her whole argument in the *Vindication* on her refutation of the idea that virtue should be differently defined for men and women (Chapters 2 and 3, demolishing "The Prevailing Opinion of a Sexual Character"). Hays, like most feminists before her, opposed the abuses and extremes of the double standard; for example, she

noted that the drive to distinguish oneself, natural and proper in both sexes, is called vanity in women, while in men it is dignified as ambition, a term which "is too sublime for woman; and is reserved to varnish over the passions, and crimes of man."[2] But she did not see that the principle itself had to be refuted.

Conceding (or rather boasting) that there is a natural "extreme delicacy" in the female character (32-3) or that overbearing is even more unbecoming in women than in men (121), Hays left the way open for restricting women's development and stripping them of the means to assert their rights.[3] Insisting that a decent woman would gladly give up mental development if it interfered with her duties "as daughter, sister, wife, or mother" (202-3), she implied that women are more obligated to sacrifice themselves than are men. Moreover, she ignored Wollstonecraft's insight that independence is fundamental to self-respect (85), burbling that any woman who has "ever experienced the nature of a true and virtuous attachment . . . would . . . rather a thousand times owe her happiness to the indulgence of an amiable man whom she loves, than to any other circumstance that imagination can suggest" (275-6). But if Hays yielded to sentimental fantasy in theory, she had sufficient practical sense to recognize its irrelevance to the actual world: she went on to note that, since most marriages do not meet her ideal, we must rely on law and the concept of rights to avoid sacrificing "the multitude . . . to a *possibility.*" Hays's more positive view of female dependence may result from sentimental naiveté, since she never tried marriage, or perhaps from her happier experiences with men, for her father was exemplary and her courtship happy until cut short by the death of her fiancé.[4]

The contrasting structures of the *Vindication* and the **Appeal** suggest Wollstonecraft's more theoretical approach. She starts by outlining what institutions are pernicious or beneficial to human society, proceeds to argue that virtue is the same in man and woman, goes on to attack on intellectual and ethical grounds the theories of Rousseau and other eighteenth-century writers on women. Hays's basic strategy, on the other hand, is to confront conventional formulas with daily experience, so as to demonstrate by common sense their internal inconsistencies and their deviations from what actually happens and what is obviously desirable. Where Wollstonecraft discusses "The Prevailing Opinion of a Sexual Character" or "the Pernicious Effects . . . [of] the Unnatural Distinctions Established in Society," Hays exposes the self-contradictions in "What Men Would Have Women To Be." Women are expected to love and depend on their husbands, and at the same time to accept their unfaithfulness with equanimity; they are encouraged to develop emotionality, small-mindedness, and weakness as endearing feminine characteristics, and at the same time expected to bear insult and misfortune with perfect fortitude. Though they must not presume to lay claim to the masculine quality of wisdom, "strange to tell! there it must be in full force, and come forth on all convenient occasions" (48). To suppose that "all that firmness of character, and greatness of mind commonly esteemed masculine" can be united with "that universal weakness, which men first endeavour to affix upon women for their own convenience, and then for their own defence affect to admire," "really . . . requires more than female imbecility and credulity" (56-7).

Wollstonecraft is more interested in general situations than specific relationships; she thinks more in terms of social structure, Hays in terms of what happens within the home. Wollstonecraft's rhetoric is strongest when she is analysing concepts, as when she acutely distinguishes between the gentle forbearance required of all Christians and the weak subservience enjoined on wives (117). But she does not concern herself with working out these concepts in terms of everyday living. Hays demonstrates the practical consequences. She notes that the virtues allotted to women, however undervalued, put an extra moral burden on them; for these are the virtues which are hardest to attain "and which occur most commonly in life" (60-1). She suggests that men try teaching women virtue by example rather than by precept, "for really the one has a wonderful effect upon people, and the other very little" (63).

She shows how oppressively the double standard actually operates in married life. It promotes discord by encouraging men to expect inordinate devotion from women while not demanding anything much from themselves, and to attach inordinate importance to their own will. No reasonable woman expects her husband to continue a romantic lover, but men "do seriously suppose that their wives are to turn out, the angels, their imaginations had painted. Or if they do not seriously suppose it . . . they act precisely as if they did." While they do not think about fulfilling their own share of the contract, they eagerly insist on women's matrimonial duties. Further, "they place their happiness, and what they seem to value more,—their consequence,—in being indulged and humored beyond all reasonable bounds, in whatever mode their fancy or passions suggest" (85-7). Here Hays acutely notes the pernicious effects of the male habit of valuing self-importance over happiness and defining that self-importance in terms of domination over women.

Hays describes what happens in a family when female virtue is defined to include uncritical submission.

> There are no vices to which a man addicts himself, no follies he can take it into his head to commit, but his wife and his nearest female relations are expected to connive at, are expected to look upon, if not with admiration, at least with respectful silence, and at awful distance.

A wife who tries in any way to restrain her husband from excessive drinking is "accused at all hands of driving him to pursue in worse places, that which he cannot enjoy in peace at home" (51-2). If women protest against injustice, men use the resulting unpleasantness as a pretext to deprive them of the few rights they have.

Hays characteristically illustrates her point with a homely fable of a brother and sister carrying their eggs to market. When Peggy asks John to give her an equal share of the eggs, he responds by asking for even more, "which you know will be quite the same as if you had them yourself, or indeed better; as I shall save you the trouble of carrying them, shall protect you and the rest of your property, and shall besides give you many fine things when we get to the fair." When she does not cheerfully acquiesce, he exclaims, "How horribly ugly you look whenever you contradict me! I wish poor Ralph the miller saw you just now, I'm sure he'd never look at you again." Finally, on the grounds that she has provoked him beyond all bearing, he seizes her eggs against her will and spends all the proceeds himself. "Such," Hays comments, "are the weighty arguments used to deprive women of rights." Moreover, she points out, if women practise the forbearance that is demanded of them, they are no better off. Men just use it to comfort their own consciences and to maintain the status quo: "Silence and submission are looked upon as proofs of acquiescence and content; and men will hardly of themselves, seek to improve a situation, with which many are apparently satisfied" (72-5).

Both authors demolish the consoling theory that women do not need power because they can govern by sweet submission, but again Hays is more concerned with practical results. Wollstonecraft summarily dismisses the recommendation that women cultivate a "winning softness . . . that governs by obeying" on the grounds that such an argument is an insult to rational creatures (101). Hays takes pains to show why it is useful to men and why it is proved false by daily experience. Since men "are ashamed in this enlightened age" actually to preach "passive obedience . . . even to women," they govern by redefining it as female amiability. To claim rights, they say, is masculine and insufferable in women and can only antagonize men; but women have everything to hope for when they entreat indulgences as favours. "Then it is," Hays goes on,

> that we hear of the heavenly softness of the sex, that with a glance can disarm authority and dispel rage. Then it is that we hear them tell, with as much earnestness and gravity as if it were true . . . that in woman's weakness consists her strength, and in her dependence her power. That . . . men are vested with authority over women . . . for their mutual good. . . . That it is indeed rather a nominal authority taken up for conveniency's sake; for that upon the whole, what women lose of power in an acknowledged way, and in name, they make up for in the private scenes of life, &c. &c. &c.

> (113-17)

The simple repetitive rhetoric—"Then it is . . . that . . . that" helps to build a cumulative derisive effect, culminating in that final "&c. &c. &c." In recognizing the persuasive power of earnestness and gravity, Hays acutely exposes the grounds on which our supposedly logical minds accept many conventional absurdities: bland assurance is no argument, but nevertheless it is hard to refute.

Hays's approach here is particularly useful for answering the conduct book writers of her period, who supported self-serving patriarchal morality by making outrageous assertions with an utter confidence that disarms doubt. Thomas Gisborne, for example, a respected and popular writer, assured women that Providence had thoughtfully "implanted in them a remarkable tendency to conform to the wishes and example" of whomever they happened to live with.[5] Such absurdities can be better confuted by a common sense dismissal than by the most sophisticated theoretical argument. In the same spirit, Hays does not labour to argue against Pope's outrageous line "Most women have no characters at all" ("Of the Characters of Women," line 2). She merely calls it "very silly," adding that this great wit wrote many silly lines on women (31).

Wollstonecraft argues that women should disdain to exert influence through charm and softness (103); Hays, more cogently, shows that it does not work. If a woman is ugly, or old, or even too familiar to be interesting because she is a man's own wife, she enjoys no dominion through male chivalry; indeed, without law to support her, she cannot even obtain common justice (119-20). "This is a way indeed," Hays briskly concludes, "of cutting short every proposal for bettering the situation of women, and of quashing every hope or desire of a general improvement" (114), but it can hardly stand up to rational examination.

As she was more interested than Wollstonecraft in looking at problems and inequities as they occur in daily life, Hays was also more concerned with practical solutions. She suggests, for example, that marriages, like other relationships, would work out better if the parties defined beforehand the obligations on each side. The best way to avoid perpetual quarrels in marriage, with one party complaining of oppression and the other of disobedience, is to set out rules: this will minimize confusion, set due bounds to authority on the one hand, and on the other increase the likelihood that just commands will be obeyed (287-8). Thus Hays anticipates marriage contracts such as are being formulated by feminists today.

Wollstonecraft tends to develop abstractly even her case-histories. She analyses the qualities of a type, but makes no effort to sketch a particular example.[6] Her account of the fate of an unmarried woman trained in dependence is logically convincing but devoid of human interest. Indeed, after telling how the narrow-minded wife drove her husband's dependent sister into cheerless exile, Wollstonecraft points out that the two women "may be much upon a par with respect to reason and humanity, and, changing situations, might have acted just the same selfish part" (157-8). Thus she effectively demonstrates the baneful effects of failing to develop women's minds and hearts, but does not engage the interest that attaches to particularized characters. Hays, on the other hand, does just that in an early feminist essay in her *Letters and Essays, Moral and Miscellaneous.* Her story of Sempronia and her daughters may have been inspired by Wollstonecraft's bare reference to "a very good woman—as good as such a narrow mind would allow her to be," who carefully kept her daughters from novels, but left their minds so empty that they had nothing to think of but sex and marriage (307). Hays

fleshed out this example by giving each of her narrowly educated women a realistically individualized character and career.

Sempronia, who valued herself on knowing no book but the Bible, trained her four daughters "with unrelenting rigour to the duties of non-resistance and passive obedience."

> The sole accomplishments which this notable lady deemed necessary to constitute a good wife and mother, were to scold and half starve her servants, to oblige her children to say their prayers, and go sedately to church, and to make clothes and household furniture from morning to night.

This regimen so undermined the girls' health and spirits that their mother, because she did love them, took them to Brighton. There Serena's "languid charms" attracted Melville, a romantic and cultured young businessman. Her bashful meekness "awakened his tenderness, and flattered his vanity"; he construed the silence produced by her mother's repression as "delicate timidity" and anticipated the pleasure of instructing her "lovely ignorance." But he learned, soon after their marriage, that ignorance is not lovely. Serena would interrupt his reading of the most passionate scene in *Hamlet* to remark on a passing carriage or pet her lap dog. Though she "would smile when he smiled, and weep when he frowned," he realized that this was not sweet feminine compliance but insipid passivity, since the little will she had from nature had been quenched by her mother. Wearied by such meaningless acquiescence, her husband, in desperation, "vainly exhorted her sometimes to have a taste of her own; for he would even have preferred opposition to the dead calm in which their days languished."[7]

Martha, the second daughter, illustrates the disaster which results when a woman of naturally strong will is provided with no rational principles to control it. Her mother's arbitrary tyranny had done no more than temporarily restrain her violent passions and increase her eagerness to escape into marriage, which she saw merely as an opportunity to indulge in the free spending and fun her mother had forbidden. Her liveliness and housewifely upbringing attracted a tradesman who did not mind her ignorance because he had no interest in culture; all he required was a cheerful companion and an economical housekeeper. But he too was disappointed, as she unthinkingly pursued extravagance and dissipation, resisting his attempts to control her with temper tantrums. Her education had given her neither reasonable morality nor worthy values, and affection for her husband had no restraining power, since she had married him only to escape from her mother's discipline. They lapsed into constant quarrelling, in desperation he isolated her in the country, and she took to drink and died (67-72).

The younger daughters, lacking their sisters' good looks and sharing their want of mental attractions, remained unmarried. Ann was instantaneously converted by a fiery

Methodist sermon that she happened to hear, for "Her religious ideas (if ideas they could be called) had been taken upon trust" and "she had no notion that belief must be founded upon evidence." Lacking understanding of religion, she thought she was zealous when in fact she was merely gratifying her pride and her spleen by belonging to a narrow circle of true believers. She "grew every day more narrow and morose" and finally sank into religious melancholia (72-3, 78-9). Charlotte, the youngest daughter, had more intellect than the others, though not enough to rise above her narrow upbringing. In youth she exercised her mind "by forming many little plans" for her wardrobe and the furnishings of her house after she married. When this hope failed, she gave way to chronic envy and disappointment. With nothing to offer in society once she had lost the charms of youthful liveliness, yet forced to seek company because she lacked inner resources, she spent her days in visiting from house to house, spying on her neighbours, collecting and circulating anecdotes, though she did this "without malice, merely to enliven the insipidity of a commerce, where neither the heart, nor the understanding had any share" (80-83).

Through concrete examples, carrying the authenticity of familiar experience, Hays has made her case for encouraging women to form ideas and think out rational moral principles. Though her characters are exempla rather than fully developed individuals, she has provided enough detail to make them plausible and to engage our interest. She makes us sympathize with Melville and Charlotte because she shows us how both are victims of society. Melville made his fatuous and selfish marriage choice because he accepted the conventional limited view of women; Charlotte was small-minded and mischievous because her mind had been systematically cramped. Most of Hays's contemporaries would have stereotyped her as an old maid motivated by the spite supposedly inherent in that character.

Hays and Wollstonecraft, both of whom were religious, had to deal with the orthodox Judaeo-Christian rationale for oppressing women. But where Wollstonecraft summarily dismisses Moses' "poetical story" of Eve's creation from Adam's rib and seduction of him (109), Hays less radically applies common sense to examine its relevance to the subjection of women. Why should Eve's punishment of subjection to her husband extend to all succeeding women, since no one suggests that Adam's punishment of a lifetime of physical labour extends to his upper-class male successors? (3-4). Hays's tone, as well as her argument, is disarmingly common-sensical.

Her subject is the humorous incongruities in laws which should be derived from moral principles but are in fact determined by what is convenient in shifting circumstances—between what is preached at one time and what at another, between what is required and what is reasonable to expect. She makes her case in a plain, colloquial style appropriate to showing that it is perfectly evident to common sense. Her simple repetitive structures are those of a popular preacher. (She enthusiastically attended Dissenting sermons and argued the advantage of public worship in *Letters and Essays* [6-8].) She often speaks familiarly to her readers. Having demonstrated from Biblical texts that God did not mean woman to be inferior to man, she goes on: "I shall endeavour next to convince my readers, as much as I am myself convinced, that reason goes hand in hand with religion in opposing the claims of the one sex, to a right of subjecting the other" (25). It is as if she were sitting down with men to show them how things are, confident that they will agree with her once they look at the issues: if men would consider her subject with attention, "they would of themselves be inclined to do justice" (68-9). Her choice of title, an *Appeal to the Men* rather than a *Vindication* of woman's rights, implies not so much a desire to conciliate as a hope that men, once appealed to, will see the inconsistencies of their present demands on women and form more just and rational expectations. Accordingly, her tone is less adversarial than Wollstonecraft's, more good-natured and easy-going. Where Wollstonecraft seems to see chivalry as a male plot to hoodwink women, Hays sees it as sincere self-delusion. Thinking about beautiful young women works men "up to a temporary sentiment of love and tenderness for the whole sex," which naturally causes them to suppose that women in general "have no need of law or right on their side, and have only to be seen to be obeyed" (118).

In the same way, Hays is more tolerant of women's failings: since women cannot conform to men's ideal and yet as the weaker party must appear to do so, "is it wonderful" if they are trifling and hypocritical? "I believe I may readily answer the question. It is not wonderful. It is perfectly in the course of nature. It is an effect, resulting of necessity from a cause" (75-6). If "women do avail themselves of the only weapons they are permitted to wield"—"petty treacheries—mean subterfuge—whining and flattery—feigned submission"—they cannot be blamed, "since they are compelled to it by the injustice and impolicy of men. . . . Necessity acknowledges no law, but her own!" (91). Hays's homely, concrete approach, her constant awareness of actual women in actual situations, makes her more tolerant than the more idealistic and doctrinaire Wollstonecraft.

While Hays sees men as potentially well-disposed, she also recognizes their natural human selfishness; she appeals to their sense and good nature, but at the same time is shrewdly aware of their motives for resisting change. There is a wistfulness in her hope that men would examine their treatment of women "with the same impartiality, which they would expect and demand, in any case where their own interest were concerned" (105). That power relationships work most smoothly when authority and obligations are clearly defined is a simple and obvious truth and "now very readily acknowledged, in all matters except where women are concerned. It is astonishing . . . that principles of private and domestic justice, do not at least keep pace in the minds of men, with those of a public and political nature." Actually, though, it is not so astonishing. "With respect to each other [men] enforce justice, because

they have power so to do;—where the weaker sex is concerned . . . what cannot be *enforced,* remains *undone*"
(288).

Where Wollstonecraft tends to generalize about men, Hays
talks to them directly. She exhorts them to "come forth
and look Reason boldly in the face," although

> most of you would rather face a cannon, or see a spec-
> tre; but take courage, for though she will speak some
> dreadful truths to your consciences, yet you must agree
> at last, if you bring not the fiend Prejudice in your
> train. If you do bring her, it is as if a man brought his
> mistress along when he was going to be reconciled to
> his wife.
>
> (29-30)

Hays often uses homely similes to prove her point. If
women seem to conform to the contradictory and oppressive demands men lay upon them, it is only because "by
preparatory tortures any mode of conduct, however unnatural, may be forced upon individuals"—turkeys and
bears can be taught to dance, provided the turkeys are
blinded and the bears set on hot iron (57-8). By visualizing in concrete detail a cherished conservative analogy between a political constitution and a building, she neatly reverses its implications. Conservatives liked to compare
attempts to modify the British Constitution to assaults on
the foundation of a noble building, and warned that it was
wiser to put up with inconveniences than to risk bringing
the building down on one's head.[8] Hays examines that
figurative building more closely and exposes the actual
motives for preserving it:

> they look upon it as probably the wisest, and as cer-
> tainly the easiest method for themselves, to let remain
> as long as it can, a fabric; which though from the be-
> ginning not built of the best materials, and certainly
> upon the very worst possible foundation; and which
> though propped up . . . by trash, and rubbish of every
> sort, that best suited the conveniency of successive un-
> dertakers; yet accommodates one way or other all par-
> ties;—but particularly well, those who only have it in
> their power to make a change.
>
> (101)

Hays seems to be conceding a point to the opposition
when she admits that there are some saintly women who
will accept any treatment whatsoever without protest. She
goes on, however, to suggest her opinion of them by an
artful turn of metaphor: "When a man falls in with such a
woman, he should cherish her as the apple of his eye when
alive; and afterwards pickle or preserve her, or stuff her
like some new species in the cabinet of a virtuoso," since
such paragons are not only rare, but a vanishing species
(272-3).

Hays's feminist works, then, complement the *Vindication.*
She fleshes out Wollstonecraft's analysis with examples
from daily life and lowers her rhetoric to a familiar no-
nonsense tone. Together, the two authors make the points

that need to be made on the theoretical and the domestic
level. Actually, Hays was closer than Wollstonecraft to the
feminist mainstream. Mary Astell, writing a century earlier, used the same downright, practical style when she detailed a wife's duties as those of a devoted upper servant.[9]

Unfortunately, Hays's plain directness did not carry over
into her novels. There, she felt the need to work up passion and pathos, and accordingly lost touch with realistic
observation as she developed her characters into vehicles
for high-flying emotions. The story of Sempronia's daughters succeeds because it aims to be no more than a moral
fable, which does not require deep psychological insight
or emotional involvement; and its prose is as effectively
plain as its content. On the other hand, Emma Courtney,
the idealized and partially autobiographical heroine of
Hays's first novel, speaks with consistent pomposity, soft-
ening into lachrymose sentimentality. Here, for instance, is
Emma reproaching her Augustus for failing to answer an
importunate letter:

> If . . . from having observed the social and sympa-
> thetic nature of our feelings and affections, I suffered
> myself to yield, involuntarily, to the soothing idea, that
> the ingenuous avowal of an attachment so tender, so
> sincere, so artless as mine, could not have been unaf-
> fecting to a mind with which my own proudly claimed
> kindred:—if I fondly believed, that simplicity, modesty,
> truth—the eye beaming with sensibility, the cheek man-
> tling with the glow of affection, the features softened,
> the accents modulated, by ineffable tenderness, might,
> in the eyes of a virtuous man, have supplied the place
> of more dazzling accomplishments, and more seductive
> charms . . . surely my mistakes were sufficiently hu-
> miliating![10]

Hays's autobiographical involvement with Emma, together
with her aim of raising her to a dignity proper to the refined heroine of a sentimental novel, led to inflation of her
emotions and her language. Hays did the same thing in her
love letters to her fiancé, where she posed as a heroine of
sensibility.[11] But in works where she did not let herself get
sentimentally involved, she was able to express her mind
and feelings without pretentious flourishes.

We see the same dual style in other late eighteenth-century
women writers, such as Hannah More. More, perhaps the
most admired intellectual woman of her period, poured
forth volumes of edifying discourses and an equally edifying novel, all in a stupefyingly stilted style. Yet even she
could become lively and direct when dealing with everyday experience, when expressing common sense instead of
conventional generalizations. Her most interesting writing
is in the *Cheap Repository Tracts* (1795-8), where she addressed an uneducated lower-class audience on subjects
which concerned them, and which also, because of wom-
en's particular involvement in domestic life, concerned
women. Moreover, as she spoke more naturally and presented what she knew by experience, she occasionally
slipped from her usual role as spokeswoman for the establishment. Personal feminine insight appears when she de-

flates the idealism of the radical philosopher Fantom by noting that Mrs. Fantom hardly dared to speak; for, "in his zeal to make the whole world free and happy, [Mr. Fantom] was too prudent to include his wife among the objects on whom he wished to confer freedom and happiness."[12] Feminist indignation occasionally breaks through even in the more formal *Strictures on the Modern System of Female Education* (1799), and when it does, it expresses itself in plain terms. Men chat frivolously while everyone is at the dinner table, More complains, conserving their intellects until the ladies have withdrawn. If strong truths should ever happen to be addressed to women, they "are either diluted with flattery, or kept back in part, or softened to their taste." With similar tartness, More punctures the complacency of mediocre conventional women who take pleasure in ridiculing intelligent ones, exclaiming

> with much affected humility, and much real envy, that "they are thankful *they* are not geniuses." Now, though one is glad to hear gratitude expressed on any occasion, yet the want of sense is really no such great mercy to be thankful for; and it would indicate a better spirit, were they to pray to be enabled to make a right use of the moderate understanding they possess.[13]

More is more consistently pompous than the radicals Hays and Wollstonecraft, partly because her contemporaries' exaggerated admiration for her intellect made her feel she should maintain an edifyingly formal style, and partly because most of the time she was repeating conventional opinions on women rather than personally observed experience. When Hays indulges in artificial, inflated rhetoric, it is because she feels compelled to rise to a proper level of romantic sensibility. Women may have been particularly liable to succumb to contemporary vices of style because, less secure than men, they would have felt more pressure to conform to what was considered appropriate. The sentimentality and evasive circumlocution we occasionally find in Hays and Wollstonecraft were expected from feminine tenderness and delicacy.[14]

But all three of these very different women wrote effectively when they plainly expressed their feelings of derision or resentment or when they plainly reported on occurrences of everyday life. Even Wollstonecraft, the best theoretical intellect of the three, was at her best in voicing heartfelt indignation at the hypocrisy, the falsehood, the injustice and oppression which she could daily observe in men's treatment of women. Hays wrote forcefully only when she was responding to domestic experience—that is, the experience which all women, however exceptional, were immersed in as men were not. When she was, her downright, common-sense exhortations to men to be fair to women make a distinctive contribution to the feminist tradition.

Notes

1. Mary Wollstonecraft, *A Vindication of the Rights of Woman,* ed. Miriam Brody Kramnick (Harmondsworth: Penguin Books, 1982), p. 82. All subsequent citations from Wollstonecraft will refer to this text.

2. Mary Hays, *Appeal to the Men of Great Britain in Behalf of Women,* intro. Gina Luria (New York: Garland, 1974), p. 77. All subsequent citations from Hays will refer to this text unless otherwise indicated.

3. Even more egregiously, Hays severely restricted the occupations suited to woman's nature and to "delicacy and propriety" (193-9). Where Wollstonecraft argued that women could "be physicians as well as nurses" (261), Hays prated that the practice of medicine by a woman was so indelicate as to induce nausea.

4. It is these initial relationships which would have set her basic attitude. In later life, Hays had less happy experiences with men—notably her unrequited love for William Frend (dramatized in *Emma Courtney*) and the friendship with Charles Lloyd which ended in his publicly slandering her.

5. Thomas Gisborne, *An Enquiry into the Duties of the Female Sex* (1797) (New York: Garland, 1974), p. 116.

6. The only exception is Jemima in *The Wrongs of Woman,* who, though not a rounded novelistic character, is a moving illustration of the oppression of lower-class women.

7. Mary Hays, *Letters and Essays, Moral and Miscellaneous,* intro. Gina Luria (New York: Garland, 1974), pp. 34-40.

8. See John Dryden, *Absalom and Architophel,* lines 801-6; Edmund Burke, *Reflections on the Revolution in France* (New York: Rinehart, 1959), pp. 40, 207, 306-7; and Bernard N. Schilling, *Dryden and the Conservative Myth: A Reading of "Absalom and Architophel"* (New Haven: Yale U.P., 1961), pp. 73, 220, 252. Two of Hays's contemporaries, Charlotte Smith in *Desmond* and Mary Wollstonecraft in *A Vindication of the Rights of Men,* also turned this architectural metaphor to radical ends, but not in a context of women's rights. See *Before Their Time: Six Women Writers of the Eighteenth Century,* ed. Katharine M. Rogers (New York: Ungar, 1979), p. 86, and *A Mary Wollstonecraft Reader,* ed. Barbara H. Solomon and Paula S. Berggren (New York: New American Library, 1983), p. 254.

9. Mary Astell, *Reflections upon Marriage, Occasioned by the Duchess of Mazarine's Case,* in *Before Their Time,* pp. 41-2. Hays included Astell in *Female Biography.*

10. Mary Hays, *Memoirs of Emma Courtney,* intro. Gina Luria (New York: Garland, 1974), 2:3-4.

11. See *The Love-Letters of Mary Hays (1779-1780),* ed. A. F. Wedd (London: Methuen, 1925), e.g. p. 35.

12. Hannah More, *The Complete Works* (New York: Harper, 1835), 1:8-9.

13. Hannah More, *Strictures on the Modern System of Female Education* (New York: Garland, 1974), 2:45, 71.

14. Mary Poovey has discussed this tendency in Wollstonecraft; see her *The Proper Lady and the Woman Writer: Ideology as Style in the Works of Mary Wollstonecraft, Mary Shelley, and Jane Austen* (Chicago: U. of Chicago Press, 1984).

Terence Allan Hoagwood (essay date 1990)

SOURCE: Hoagwood, Terence Allan. Introduction to *The Victim of Prejudice,* by Mary Hays, pp. 3-12. Delmar, NY: Scholars' Facsimiles & Reprints, 1990.

[*In the following essay, Hoagwood discusses the connections between Hays's polemical writings and her novel* The Victim of Prejudice.]

Mary Hays's ***The Victim of Prejudice*** (1799) is an important feminist novel, intellectually and aesthetically. Its author was a prominent figure among British writers who, during the period of the French Revolution and afterward, advocated feminist and politically radical forms of thought. A friend of William Godwin, Mary Wollstonecraft, Joseph Priestley, and many others in the radical circles working in London in the 1790s, Hays wrote polemical literature as well as fiction, contributing to the periodical press and writing novels, biographies, and works of political and philosophical argument. ***The Victim of Prejudice,*** her second novel, is the most advanced and intellectually important fiction that she ever wrote. This novel has, unfortunately, long been thought—even by some of the foremost contemporary specialists in women's literature of the eighteenth century—to be nonexistent except in French translation;[1] the present edition is the first publication of the novel since its first edition of nearly two hundred years ago.

Treating directly such social topics as rape, child molestation, madness, imprisonment, economic hardship, prostitution, and suicide, ***The Victim of Prejudice*** shares concerns with Mary Hays's other works—including her ***Appeal to the Men of Great Britain in Behalf of Women*** (1798)—and with works by her friends, Mary Wollstonecraft and William Godwin. These concerns include a theory of social determinism and class conflict founded in a critique of "custom" and "prejudice"; in twentieth-century terms such a critique amounts to a theory of ideology. Her novel is a valuable document in the history of English radicalism, no less than the history of the novel and the history of literature by and about women.

As Jane Rendall has usefully observed, feminist argument was in the eighteenth century associated with political polemics and activities in the American and French Revolutions.[2] Much feminist literature by women tends to explore conjunctions among *kinds* of social conflict (e.g., economic and sexual), and more broadly Hays treats the relationships between what is apparently personal and what is profoundly political. For example, ***The Victim of Preju-*** *dice* shares some concerns with Agnes Maria Bennett's *The Beggar Girl and Her Benefactors* (1797), including the conjunction of narrowly economic facts with emotional and attitudinal structures ("They despise me for my poverty," says Bennett's eponymous beggar girl). An important principle is the recognition that emotions and attitudes are broadly social in origin and in effect, rather than merely personal or individualistic phenomena. These ideas came to reappear with some frequency in fiction by women: Fanny Burney, for example, a far more conservative thinker and writer than Hays, produces in 1814 (in *The Wanderer*) a fictional presentation of problems special to women without wealth or family connections. More ideologically akin to Hays, Susanna Pearson had also written of conjunctions of social and political issues, as in her *Poems* of 1790, where she writes of the African slave trade and the French Revolution.[3]

Mary Hays was born to a family of dissenters, like so many of the intellectual radicals in England during the period of the French Revolution. In a community whose center was the home and publishing house of Joseph Johnson (No. 72 St. Paul's Churchyard), Hays came to know many of the most influential among these radical thinkers—Joseph Priestley (whose awesome productivity included volumes of radical political philosophy, including a reply to Burke's *Reflections on the Revolution in France*), Theophilus Lindsey (the founder of Unitarianism), William Frend (who was discharged from Cambridge for his dissenting publications on religious and political issues), William Godwin (who had been a dissenting minister for five years and whose *Enquiry Concerning Political Justice* [1793] was perhaps the most influential work of political philosophy published in England in the revolutionary decade), and Mary Wollstonecraft (who, like Paine and like Priestley, also wrote an important reply to Burke's *Reflections on the Revolution in France,* and whose subsequent *Vindication of the Rights of Woman* is one of the earliest and most influential volumes of feminist argument in England).

In fact, Hays read Wollstonecraft's *Vindication of the Rights of Woman* promptly on its first publication in 1792, and there ensued an important intellectual relationship between the two women. Hays sent to Wollstonecraft the manuscript of a collection of her short pieces for Wollstonecraft's responses and advice prior to their publication as a volume. The volume appeared in 1793 as ***Letters and Essays, Moral and Miscellaneous,*** a book that includes an essay singularly important in the conceptual background of ***The Victim of Prejudice.*** In an essay entitled **"On the Influence of Authority and Custom on the Female Mind and Manners,"** Hays writes, "of all bondage, mental bondage is surely the most fatal," and a patriarchal "despotism . . . has hitherto . . . enslaved the female mind."[4]

In 1791 Hays met Godwin at a dinner at the house of Joseph Johnson. In 1794 she wrote to Godwin, asking him to lend her a copy of his *Enquiry Concerning Political Justice,* of which she had heard but which she had been unable to see.[5] Her friendship with Godwin deepened intellectually, and he began to encourage her to embody in fiction her social vision, including her feminist perspective. In 1796 Hays arranged a meeting of Wollstonecraft with Godwin and with Thomas Holcroft, another radical thinker and writer in the circle of Joseph Johnson. Wollstonecraft had not seen Godwin since 1791, and Hays's reintroduction of the two writers to each other nurtured an important intellectual flowering. Hays's friendship with both writers flourished: they read each other's works and exchanged advice; Wollstonecraft asked Hays to write reviews of fiction for *The Analytical Review,* including Hays's 1796 review of *The Gossip's Story* by Mrs. Jane West; and Hays published two separate tributes to Wollstonecraft after her death in 1797.

In 1796 and 1797 Hays published a series of articles in *The Monthly Magazine* presenting arguments of a kind that reappear in her later work, including **The Victim of Prejudice**; these are arguments on feminism and environmentalism, contending that social forces shape and determine human minds and lives. **Memoirs of Emma Courtney** (1796), her first novel, presents a critique of social conventions in the fictional context of frustrated love. Here, Hays integrates material from her relationships with Godwin and with Frend—adapting, in fact, some documents from her intellectual correspondence with Godwin. Thus Hays engages her fiction with real-life issues, including social problems involving "prejudices the most venerated." Frend had, of course, been removed from his office at Cambridge for blasphemy and sedition. As Kenneth L. Moler has said, the novel takes a largely social theme: "in a more enlightened social order, [the heroine of **Emma Courtney**] would not have been condemned to a life of frustration and disappointment by archaic prejudices and institutions."[6] Jane Spencer, author of the only extended discussion of **The Victim of Prejudice,** has observed that **Memoirs of Emma Courtney** and **The Victim of Prejudice** together constitute a feminist analysis of social institutions, though it is the second novel that deals more rigorously with difficult issues including "the whole range of social institutions."[7]

The passages in **Emma Courtney** which criticize conventional marriage, institutionalized religion, and the oppression of women are coherently related to works that Hays had been writing and publishing in the polemical press for some years, including **Letters and Essays, Moral and Miscellaneous**; subsequently, in 1798, Hays published anonymously a sustained work of surprisingly comprehensive feminist argument, **Appeal to the Men of Great Britain in Behalf of Women.** As Gina Luria has noticed, it is significant that this work was reviewed in only two contemporary periodicals.[8] Counter-revolutionary war abroad was accompanied by repressive developments at home. Already in 1794 Pitt had arranged for the suspension of habeas corpus. In 1797-98, Thomas Paine was tried and convicted of treason (for the publication of *Rights of Man*); Paine's lawyer, Thomas Erskine, was tried for sedition, having published in 1797 his own *View of the Causes and*

Consequences of the War with France (which nonetheless went through forty-eight editions).[9] Coleridge, among others, testified at the trial of Frend for sedition; and Wordsworth and Coleridge learned of a spy who had been sent to watch them as they looked, in ways that made the government suspicious, over the English Channel. Joseph Johnson, publisher for Hays, Wollstonecraft, and other radicals, was prosecuted and imprisoned in 1798 for publications that seemed, to frightened governmental authorities, seditious. Under these conditions radical political opinion was driven underground or abroad. A violent riot in Birmingham, which was probably instigated by government agents, chased Priestley first to London and then to America; Paine was already in France when he was convicted of treason in England. For writers who remained in England the discourse of radical opposition was displaced into the safer forms of figurative language, where covert and symbolic presentation of ideological issues became a norm for British Romantic writing.[10]

The repressive and even dangerous conditions in England in 1798 drove Hays's feminist argument into anonymity, but that argument was not wholly suppressed: in the **Appeal** Hays argues forcibly that "the world has ever been, and still is, more guided by custom and prejudice, than by principle" (p. 128), and these customs and prejudices are singularly injurious for women. Custom, prejudice, and opinion are not *merely* mental things, because they arise in material conditions: "all opinions degrading to women, are grounded on the rude ideas of savage nations, where strength of body is the only distinguishing feature" (p. 131). Further, systems of ideas produce material effects: "the cultivation of the minds and morals of women, is considered as the one thing needful—the first object in their education—the foundation, upon which any solid hopes of future improvement may be placed;—or any thing really beautiful can be raised" (p. 204).

This dialectical linkage of ideological and material formations is, in a general way, common to the circle of radical thinkers to which Hays belonged. Wollstonecraft had argued that the imperfection of all modern governments arises from the fact that their constitutions had been formed in times of ignorance, prejudice, and superstition.[11] The most generalized philosophical exposition of that dialectical linkage is by Godwin, who argues that mind and nature and society, or human intellect and the material and social worlds, are connected in reciprocally determining ways, and the results are profoundly political: "the opinions of men [are], for the most part, under the absolute control of political institution," while reciprocally "the happiness men are able to attain, is proportioned to the justness of the opinions they take as guides in the pursuit."[12] The development of this mode of thought in connection with gender relations, however, is accomplished rather by Wollstonecraft (in the *Vindication of the Rights of Woman*) and by Hays (in the **Appeal**). The exploration of the theory in artistic forms appears then in Wollstonecraft's *Wrongs of Woman* (incipiently) and in Hays's **The Victim of Prejudice,** fully elaborated and finely wrought.

The aesthetic design of *The Victim of Prejudice* is also striking: the novel embeds hermeneutic models, fictionalizing writing itself and displaying acts and models of interpretation within its plot. Often in the novel important issues are disclosed in letters between characters, and even in letters discovered by third parties; some features of reality and history are available to the characters only in written form, and interpretation always mediates reality in these cases. In one centrally important instance, a letter from Mr. Raymond to the heroine, Mary, reports the contents of another letter, written by her mother in the distant past (Mary had never known her own mother). One of the novel's themes is the continuity of women's experience, and this theme works itself out through the troubled medium of hermeneutic and historical distance.

The reality of Mary's mother as a determining influence in Mary's life, even though Mary did not know her, is a salient issue in the novel's intellectual structure. The analogy between her mother's history and Mary's own amounts to a theme, which the novel socializes: relations of class and gender, and the relatively rigid machinery of social institutions, account for much of the parity between the women's stories. All of the relevant history, however, comes to Mary thrice mediated: the history is interpreted by Mary's mother, who encodes her story in the letter; it is again interpreted by Mr. Raymond, who re-encodes it for Mary a generation later; and it is interpreted by Mary in *her* narrative, which constitutes the novel.

. . . . .

Epistolary fiction had long been mediating its histories in character's writings, of course. Perhaps the most monumental epistolary achievement of the eighteenth century is Richardson's *Clarissa,* which, like *The Victim of Prejudice,* narrates a rape;[13] in women's fiction the narrative form had also been used fairly extensively, of course—as in Agnes Maria Bennett's *Agnes-de-Courci, A Domestic Tale* (1789). *The Victim of Prejudice* makes an intellectual use of this design which is new and important: Hays writes a novel which is *not* a domestic tale, but rather social criticism of a much larger scale. The author's theories of history, society, and knowledge are repeatedly articulated, in her polemics as well as her fiction; these theories entail a conjunction between material history and intellectual forms, and especially the conjunction between social relations (including the oppression of women) and "education" in the broad, cultural, eighteenth-century sense of mental formation. The novel persistently and effectively engages its social themes with this theory of mental formations. Those social themes include preeminently the oppression of women and the determining power of economic and social-class structures. The theory with which Hays analyzes those issues is—like Godwin's, like Wollstonecraft's—a dialectical one, arguing for the reciprocal determinism of material and intellectual structures at the level of culture and ideology. *All* of the major events in the heroine's life—including her childhood molestation and finally her impending death—arise as effects of societal structure, and not as unique personal accidents.

The plot of the novel is, in one sense, a progressively deepening understanding that Mary herself gains, an understanding of the large-scale social relationships which have in many ways determined the lives of her mother, herself, and virtually all women in the society she knows. Mary Wollstonecraft's closely related but never completed novel, *The Wrongs of Woman, or Maria,* begins to thematize exactly these issues, simultaneously historical and hermeneutic in its concerns.[14] In contrast, *The Victim of Prejudice* is a finished work, sophisticated alike in its social theory, its narrative design, its historical hermeneutic, and its pervasive feminism.

After the publication of *The Victim of Prejudice* in 1799, an increasingly conservative environment in England tended to inhibit recognition and appreciation of Hays's work. The French invasion of the peaceful Swiss in 1798 had inflamed opposition at home to Jacobin arguments. There had been reason to fear a French invasion of Britain since 1796, when peace negotiations had been unsuccessful, and the expansion of war in 1798 created an environment hostile to writers who had been active in the defense of the French Revolution, including writers like Hays, and like Wordsworth and Coleridge and Southey, three men who seemed to turn conservative at about this time. Hays, however, continued to write and to publish treatments of women's issues and educational issues, and works of fiction. In 1803 she published *Female Biography; or Memoirs of Illustrious and Celebrated Women of All Ages and Countries*; she published tales and also instructive or doctrinal volumes for years, including *Family Annals, or The Sisters* in which, as late as 1817, Hays returns to the environmentalism of Helvetius, a set of arguments that she had treated in 1796 and 1797 in the *Monthly Magazine* during her more openly Jacobin period.

The governmental and public pressures that drove so many writers into apparent compliance and conservatism in the early nineteenth century brought two perhaps predictable sets of problems for Hays's reputation. One problem concerns malicious gossip: Hays's vigorously intellectual social criticism was belittled by propagandistic focus on her supposed flirtations. Even in the twentieth century, *Emma Courtney* has sometimes been trivialized, as if it were primarily about nothing more important than the author's private feelings for a particular man. In 1800 Charles Lloyd tried to start a rumor that Hays had flirted with him; and this humiliating triviality has sometimes seemed to eclipse the important contributions that Hays made in feminism, in social theory, and in fiction.

A second issue has been entirely practical in its consequences: her most important novel and perhaps her best book was for political reasons immediately greeted with hostile reviews. It has remained out of print ever since. The publication of the present volume resolves both sorts of problems: not only is the novel again available, but it is in itself proof against the belittling criticisms of contemporaries. The novel engages itself with social issues so explicitly, profoundly, and totally, and in such a finished novelistic form, that the quality, depth, and range of Hays's thought is apparent again, as it was when—191 years ago—this novel was last available.

Notes

1. Janet M. Todd, "Mary Hays," in *Biographical Dictionary of Modern British Radicals,* vol. 1: 1770-1830, ed. Joseph O. Baylen and Norbert J. Gossman (Sussex: Harvester Press, 1979): "In 1799, Hays published her second novel, *The Victim of Prejudice* (Paris, 1799), which exists now in only a French edition" (p. 217). Fortunately the novel's first English edition *does* exist, though only a very few copies have been traced. The present volume is a reproduction of the copy in the Van Pelt Library of the University of Pennsylvania.

2. Jane Rendall, *The Origins of Modern Feminism: Women in Britain, France and the United States, 1780-1860* (New York: Schocken Books, 1984), especially pp. 33-72.

3. Valuable sources of information on women writers of the period include *A Dictionary of British and American Women Writers 1660-1800,* ed. Janet Todd (Totowa, N.J.: Rowman and Littlefield, 1985); Moira Ferguson, *First Feminists: British Women Writers 1578-1799* (Bloomington: Indiana University Press, 1985), p. 413; and *British Women Writers: A Critical Reference Guide,* ed. Janet Todd (New York: Continuum [Frederick Ungar], 1989).

4. Mary Hays, *Letters and Essays, Moral and Miscellaneous* (London, 1793; rpt. New York: Garland, 1974), pp. 19-20.

5. See Hays's letter to Godwin, in *Shelley and His Circle,* ed. Kenneth Neill Cameron (Cambridge: Harvard University Press, 1961), 1:139.

6. Kenneth L. Moler, *Jane Austen's Art of Illusion* (Lincoln: University of Nebraska Press, 1968), p. 198.

7. Jane Spencer, *The Rise of the Woman Novelist: From Aphra Behn to Jane Austen* (Oxford: Basil Blackwell, 1986), pp. 130-131. On *The Victim of Prejudice,* Spencer points out that "Hays is explicit in tracing the heroine's wrongs to social causes, and makes an open attack on male dominance and the oppressive ideology of natural female chastity" (p. 132).

For brief mentions of *The Victim of Prejudice* (which is the only sort of mention ever made of the novel in the twentieth century, apart from Spencer's good discussion), see Moler, *Jane Austen's Art of Illusion,* p. 200n.; Gina Luria, introduction to *Appeal to the Men of Great Britain in Behalf of Women* (New York: Garland, 1974); Moira Ferguson, *First Feminists,* p. 413; Janet Todd, "Mary Hays," in *A Dictionary of British and American Women Writers 1660-1800,* p. 157; Alice Browne, *The Eighteenth-Century Femi-*

nist Mind (Brighton: Harvester Press, 1987), p. 169; and (most helpful among these brief accounts) Jane Spencer, "Mary Hays," in *British Women Writers: A Critical Reference Guide.* Earlier general accounts of Hays include A. F. Wedd, *The Love Letters of Mary Hays* (London: Methuen, 1925), pp. 1-13; J. M. S. Tompkins, *The Polite Marriage* (Cambridge: Cambridge University Press, 1938), pp. 150-87; and M. Ray Adams, *Studies in the Literary Backgrounds of English Radicalism* (1947; rpt. New York: Greenwood, 1968), pp. 83-103. Especially useful in connection with Hays's political (and specifically feminist) arguments is Burton R. Pollin, "Mary Hays on Women's Rights in the *Monthly Magazine,*" *Etudes Anglaises* 24, 3 (1971): 271-82.

8. Gina Luria, introduction to *Appeal,* p. 14.

9. See Bruce Gronbeck, "Thomas Erskine," in *Biographical Dictionary of Modern British Radicals,* 1:162.

10. I discuss symbolic ideological discourse in the period in my essay, "Fictions and Freedom: Wordsworth and the Ideology of Romanticism," in *Power's Presents: Reproducing Texts, Representing History,* ed. Jeffrey Cox and Larry Reynolds, a collection of essays not yet in print.

11. Mary Wollstonecraft, *A Vindication of the Rights of Men* (London, 1790; rpt. Gainesville, Fla.: Scholars' Facsimiles & Reprints, 1960), p. 19.

12. William Godwin, *Enquiry Concerning Political Justice and Its Influence on Morals and Happiness,* ed. F. E. L. Priestley (Toronto: University of Toronto Press, 1946), 1:26.

13. On the rape in *Clarissa* and issues in social criticism, see Terry Eagleton, *The Rape of Clarissa: Writing, Sexuality and Class Struggle in Samuel Richardson* (Oxford: Basil Blackwell, 1982), especially pp. 56-69, 72-73, and 82-83: Eagleton effectively argues against "the offensive suggestion that Clarissa desires her own violation," and observes that "if virtue is necessary it is also an encumbrance, since to behave well in a predatory society is the surest way to unleash its violence."

14. An excellent account of Wollstonecraft's novel in this connection is Tilottama Rajan, "Wollstonecraft and Godwin: Reading the Secrets of the Political Novel," *Studies in Romanticism* 27 (1988): 221-51.

Eleanor Ty (essay date 1993)

SOURCE: Ty, Eleanor. "Breaking the 'Magic Circle': From Repression to Effusion in *Memoirs of Emma Courtney,*" and "The Mother and Daughter: The Dangers of Replication in *The Victim of Prejudice.*" In *Unsex'd Revolutionaries: Five Women Novelists of the 1790s,* pp. 46-72. Toronto: University of Toronto Press, 1993.

[*In the following excerpt, Ty discusses* Memoirs of Emma Courtney, *suggesting that the novel's true thesis, despite Hays's stated intentions to the contrary, is to demonstrate the fatal consequences of female repression. Ty further examines Hays's* The Victim of Prejudice *and claims that it is far more pessimistic than* Emma Courtney, *and that it may represent the author's rewriting of Richardson's* Clarissa *from a female perspective.*]

In the preface to her first novel Mary Hays contends that 'the most interesting, and the most useful fictions' are those that delineate 'the progress' and trace 'the consequences of one strong, indulged passion or prejudice.'[1] That *Emma Courtney* was to be about the perils of a woman's excessive passion is evident from Hays's defensive attitude towards her heroine:

> I meant to represent her, as a human being, loving virtue while enslaved by passion, liable to the mistakes and weaknesses of our fragile nature . . . the errors of my heroine were the offspring of sensibility; and . . . The result of her hazardous experiment is calculated to operate as a *warning,* rather than as an example.
>
> (xviii)

While Hays's avowed intent was to teach through a negative model, what actually happens is that the lesson is often lost or sublimated as the reader gets enticed into the novel. The moral, which has to do with the consequences of indulged passion, becomes increasingly contradictory and ambiguous. In fact, the unstated but undoubtedly calculated thesis of the work seems to be the fatal repercussions of repression on the eighteenth-century middle-class woman.

Female repression or limitation occurs on three levels in *Emma Courtney*: firstly, restraint in speech and language; secondly, professional restrictions; and lastly, sexual repression. Emma's excessive response to her specific situation shows the dangerous effects of these forms of limitation on an intelligent woman of the 1790s. As Wollstonecraft was to do in *Wrongs of Woman,* in her two novels of the decade Hays makes use of the sentimental novel with its standard conventions—acute sensibility, the distressed heroine, exhibitions of pathos, a plot of sudden reversal[2]—as a medium for her feminist dialectics. In contrast to conservative writers such as Jane West and Hannah More, who advocated compliance and restraint in women, Hays like Wollstonecraft argues that these artificially instilled qualities only serve to create havoc in a female subject. Forced into a culturally produced rather than natural subject-position, a woman, such as Emma Courtney in fiction or Mary Hays herself in real life, became a potentially catastrophic site of ideological struggle. Caught between her need to conform to the feminine ideals of submission and silence, and her desire to participate in the traditionally designated 'masculine' modes of activity and expression, an eighteenth-century woman often became an emotional and mental outcast, fitting into neither sphere. Thus, while the novel seems to be about one woman's struggle with her passion—a fairly common subject of sentimental fiction—it is actually a public statement about sexual politics.

In her two prose tracts written in the revolutionary decade Hays similarly verbalizes her disapproval of the passivity, docility, and submission required of a middle-class woman. Disagreeing with the conservative thinkers who believed that these were desirable qualities in women, Hays maintains that subordination and lack of proper education kept women in 'a state of PERPETUAL BABYISM.'[3] In her *Appeal to the Men of Great Britain in Behalf of Women* (1798) she writes: 'Women . . . ought to be considered as the companions and equals, not as the inferiors—much less as they virtually are,—as the slaves of men' (127). Like Wollstonecraft and Smith, Hays took advantage of the currency of the revolutionary language to speak of woman's plight.[4] In *Letters and Essays* (1793), for example, Hays protests against what she calls 'mental bondage,' contending that the 'female mind' is 'enslaved,' and the 'understandings of women . . . chained down to frivolity and trifles.'[5] Using post-revolution are rhetoric, she argues that 'the modes of education, and the customs of society are degrading to the female character, and the tyranny of custom is sometimes worse than the tyranny of government' (*Letters and Essays,* 11). Published just shortly after the fall of the Bastille, *Letters and Essays* deliberately uses such politically suggestive words as *bondage, chains, tyranny,* and *slavery.*

For Hays, women are not naturally inferior, but they, like 'any race of people' or 'any class of rational beings' who are 'held in a state of subjection and dependence from generation to generation by another party,' are liable to 'degenerate both in body and mind' (*Appeal,* 69). This belief is a version of the Godwinian notion that people are products of their external circumstances rather than of their birth.[6] Again comparing gender relations to political activity, Hays says that men maintain their authority 'by the same law by which the strong oppresses the weak, and the rich the poor' (*Appeal,* 28). She asks 'man' to examine his conscience and to judge whether he holds his 'empire by force alone; or if it is founded on the eternal and immutable laws of nature, and supported by justice and reason' (*Appeal,* 28). Assuming that the 'men' to whom the *Appeal* is addressed are enlightened, Hays frequently implores them to use their judgment and sense of justice to reassess their treatment of women.[7]

While in her prose tracts Hays relies on 'reason' to convince the audience of her arguments, in her novels she counts on sentiments and sensibility to arouse sympathy in her readers for her cause. Both *Emma Courtney* and *Victim of Prejudice* are deliberately dramatic and emotional, full of sensational events, plots, and characters. These elements intensify Hays's rational arguments, illustrating and thematizing graphically the reasonable and logical contentions found in her essays. The pathos and extreme emotion that are characteristic of the genre become harnessed for a dialectical purpose. As in Wollstonecraft's fiction metaphors are frequently 'literalized,' as Hays translates a linguistic construct or a figure of speech and makes it real.

One of the androcentric practices *Emma Courtney* seems to be questioning, for example, is the objectification and the silencing of women. In the *Appeal* Hays similarly questions:

> Since . . . the beneficent Creator of all, has dealt out to his children of this world his portions of intelligence, and all his benefits, with so impartial an hand, that we are not only entitled, but irresistibly impelled to claim equality in his paternal inheritance; why should women be excluded from having, and giving their opinions, upon matters of importance to themselves?
>
> (154)

In her novel she demonstrates one possible tragic effect of women's exclusion from linguistic practice, from the symbolic order of the Father. Speech and silence become crucial themes that run through the text. In Emma's youth, for instance, authority and defiance of that authority are shown through a manipulation of language. While as a child Emma had grown up 'in joy and innocence,' running 'like the hind,' frisking 'like the kid,' and singing 'like the lark,' in her adolescent years at boarding-school, this freedom is curtailed: 'I was obliged to sit poring over needle work, and forbidden to prate;—my body was tortured into forms, my mind coerced, and talks imposed upon me, grammar and French, mere words, that conveyed to me no ideas' (14). As punishment for bad behaviour Emma 'was constrained to learn, by way of penance, chapters in the Proverbs of Solomon, or verses from the French testament' (15).

While Hays does not relate Emma's problems to gender here, the needlework and the torturing of her body 'into forms' suggest that these restrictions were specifically designed for females. Language is paradoxically forbidden and imposed on women as a means of conformity and discipline. Emma cannot 'prate,' but she has to learn verses written by authoritarian patriarchs. However, here as in her later years, Emma soon learns to 'turn everything upside down,' as Irigaray says.[8] Writing from a mode of 'forbidden speech' or hysteria,[9] she revenges herself by satirizing her 'tyrants in doggrel rhymes' (15). While this scenario may seem childish and insignificant, it is an early indication of the rebellious way in which Emma deals with social and linguistic restraints. In her adult years Emma similarly seeks to escape power and cultural constraints through writing in an unorthodox manner.

Emma's relationship to the two most important male figures in her life—to her father and to her beloved Augustus—is similarly signalled by the absence and thereafter effusion of speech. Both seem to be negative illustrations of the Burkean ideal of the benevolent patriarch as they provide Emma with neither protection nor support. Mr Courtney, for example, refuses 'the title of father' because 'his conduct gave him no claim to the endearing appellation' (28). As an only parent, he does not supervise Emma's education, but is content merely with 'occasional remarks and reflections' to her (19). On his deathbed, where 'a gloomy silence' reigned, he delivers a long lecture to Emma in preparation for her life of poverty and dependence. Emma is not allowed to answer and 'make[s] no comment on the closing scene of his life' (30). Her dealings with her parent illustrate in a very literal manner woman's exclusion from the symbolic world of the Father. Even when matters relate directly to her upbringing or her future, Emma is never consulted or permitted to speak for herself.

At the Morton household wherein Emma is consigned by her father, she is also besieged by problems of speech and communication. Here she cannot seem to make herself understood. The women of Morton Park are full of superficial language: Mrs Morton's voice is 'loud and discordant'; Sarah Morton is 'loquacious' and sarcastic; while Ann is described as a 'prattler' (33, 53). Emma's intentions are misread twice by the family. When Emma offers to assist Mrs Morton in the education of her children, she is accused of possessing 'vanity' (35). When she shows her appreciation for Mr Francis's conversation and friendship, she is charged with exhibiting indecorous 'partial sentiments' for him (42). The only person whom Emma finds a kindred spirit is the neighbour, Mrs Harley, whose address is 'engaging,' and with whom Emma reads, walks, and talks (54). Because Mrs Harley is the only one whom Emma can speak and converse properly with, it is not surprising that her affection for this woman of 'cultivated understanding' is soon transferred to her son, Augustus Harley.

Even before meeting him, Emma calls Augustus 'the St. Preux, the Emilius of [her] sleeping and waking reveries' (59). Because Emma has been largely excluded from meaningful speech and communication up to now, she seems to expend all her repressed energies in her letters to Augustus. Augustus becomes the dubious recipient of numerous letters from Emma informing him of her 'pure' affection (80) for him. Just as Emma had 'revenged' herself as an adolescent by writing forbidden and disruptive 'doggrel rhymes,' she now rebels against her restrictive environment by pouring out her innermost wishes in her epistles. In a rather unprecedented manner for an eighteenth-century middle-class woman, Emma ventures to confide her sentiments to Augustus, disregarding '*rules* sanctioned by usage, by prejudice, by expediency' (80). She tells him: 'Remember, *that you have once been beloved, for yourself alone,* by one, who, in contributing to the comfort of your life, would have found the happiness of her own' (81). Emma's radical declaration may be somewhat limited since, as Janet Todd points out, 'what the heroine wants is the conventional romantic ending albeit brought about by unromantic means: marriage to Harley proposed by herself.'[10] However, while her goal may be conventional, I believe that the importance of Emma's proposal lies elsewhere.

In expressing her ardour, Emma is not only asserting the existence of female desire, but also challenging the objectification and silencing of women. By professing her feelings, she ceases to be merely the 'object of transaction' in a cultural exchange, as Irigaray puts it (*This Sex,* 85), but becomes a subject initiating desire. Historically, her choice of Augustus is significant because it supports the Godwinian and Jacobin emphasis on individual merit rather than on birth, fortune, and heredity. Emma stresses that she loves Augustus for himself alone, and not for his ancestral name or family. In fact, she is aware of the 'tenure,' or the peculiar terms specifying that he remain single, upon which he retains his fortune (81). Willing to sacrifice economic considerations and social position, Emma argues that her love is one that results from the 'laws of nature' (89). It occurs 'when mind has given dignity to natural affections; when reason, culture, taste, delicacy, have combined to chasten, to refine, to exalt . . . to sanctify them' (89). Quoting Rousseau, she contends that 'moral, mental, and personal qualifications' can make even a 'union between a prince and the daughter of an executioner' suitable (103). Like Holcroft in *Anna St. Ives* Hays is implicitly suggesting an opposition to rank based on class and promoting instead distinctions based on individual merit, a revolutionary notion which would have horrified a conservative thinker such as Burke.

Ironically the effect on Augustus of Emma's announcement of her love is to render him silent. In fact, there is a perverse kind of gender or role reversal in the novel upon which Hays does not comment. As Emma acquires more powers of speech, the men around her seem to become more inarticulate or ineffective. Augustus repeatedly evades Emma's queries on the state of his heart and postpones replying to her letters. Her plea for 'one hour's frank conversation' with him is ignored (99), and Emma, like the reader, is left uncertain of his response to her passion until almost the end of the novel. Like Wollstonecraft, Hays was hesitant or perhaps unwilling to allow herself and her readers the possibility of escape through sheer romantic fantasy. Instead she resorts to the sentimental, possibly because of her own thwarted romances in real life, or perhaps because she felt the tragic ending would serve the purposes of her dialectical novel better. Emma's experiment does not bring her connubial felicity but illustrates how the silencing and the repression of females lead to tragedy and misplaced affections. It may be, as Irigaray suggests, that writing as a 'hysteric,' that is, forced to mime and reproduce a language that is not her own but 'masculine language,' Hays could not yet write adequately about herself and her needs (*This Sex,* 136, 137). Irigaray argues that by 'virtue of the *subordination* of feminine desire to phallocratism,' the full power of woman is still 'kept in reserve' and 'paralysed' (*This Sex,* 138).

Aside from verbal and linguistic repression, Hays shows how an eighteenth-century woman suffers from limitations in her choice of profession. Self-educated, intelligent, and energetic, Emma finds that a single woman with no fortune had virtually no means of subsisting independently in the 1790s in England. 'Dependence' is what Emma wishes to avoid, and it becomes a key word that runs through the novel. The career alternatives opened to Emma were either marriage or forms of servitude,[11] against which she exclaims:

> Cruel prejudices! . . . hapless woman! Why was I not educated for commerce, for a profession, for labour? Why have I been rendered feeble and delicate by bodily constraints, and fastidious by artificial refinement? Why are we bound, by the habits of society . . . Why do we suffer ourselves to be confined within a magic circle, without daring . . . to dissolve the barbarous spell?
>
> (31)

This plea for a means of self-support is a direct transcription of Hays's arguments in her *Appeal to the Men of Great Britain,* where she complains that men have been 'monopolizing trades' such as tailoring, hairdressing, millinery, mantua- and stay-making which women could easily do (200-1). In the *Appeal* she also uses the same metaphor of the 'magic circle,'[12] this 'prison of the soul' out of which women 'cannot move, but to contempt or destruction' (111). In *Emma Courtney* Hays illustrates the convictions she had articulated in her prose: while Emma was 'active, industrious, willing to employ [her] faculties in any way,' she 'beheld no path open . . . but . . . the degradation of servitude' (164). This tangible example of the 'iron hand of barbarous despotism' (164) thematizes graphically in fiction the implications of the 'magic' circle or social limitation on women's lives.

That this 'magic circle' is a result of social and cultural conditioning rather than of nature is demonstrated in the novel. Hays begins by having the heroine 'trace' the events of her life, as Emma is convinced 'of the irresistible power of circumstances, modifying and controuling our characters, and introducing, mechanically, those associations and habits which make us what we are' (6). Echoing Godwinian philosophy, Hays then shows how economic and social circumstances, education, and background mould Emma into the 'victim of . . . a distempered imagination' that she becomes (77). In her childhood and adolescent years Emma is 'interpellated' by the literature that she happens to read.[13] 'Attached' to books, she says, '. . . stories were . . . my passion, and I sighed for a romance that would never end' (12). Unaware of gender distinction, she acted the part of both the male and female protagonists of the stories: the 'valiant knight—the gentle damsel—the adventurous mariner—the daring robber' (12), even identifying with the 'grecian heroes' in the *Lives* of Plutarch (21). As she gets older however, she falls prey to sentimental fiction: 'I subscribed to a circulating library, and frequently read, or rather devoured—little careful in the selection—from ten to fourteen novels a week' (17). These novels, and the '*Héloïse* of Rousseau,' the 'dangerous, enchanting work' which Emma peruses with 'transport' (25), make her believe that she is a heroine of sensibility. Full of self-pity,[14] she often describes herself in clichéd sentimental terms, calling herself, for example, 'a poor, a friendless, an unprotected being,' and a 'deserted outcast from society—a desolate orphan' (35, 74). Paradoxically, while her reading has made her yearn for heroism and romance in her youth, it also makes her eager to adopt the subject-position of the suffering female victim depicted in the novels.

Most significantly, however, Emma's education and her reading make her aware of women's economic and mental imprisonment, their confinement within the 'magic circle.' Hays's heroine proves to be antithetical to the conservative ideal of the docile, submissive woman content with her domestic sphere, an ideal proposed by writers such as More and West. Emma realizes that she suffers from intellectual and spiritual deprivation: '. . . my mind panted for freedom, for social intercourse, for scenes in motion, where the active curiosity of my temper might find a scope wherein to range and speculate' (31). For her, the kinds of things women were supposed to be interested in were not rewarding. She complains of the 'insipid routine of heartless, mindless intercourse . . . domestic employment, or the childish vanity of varying external ornaments' (85) which are 'insufficient to engross, to satisfy, the active, aspiring mind' (86).

Insightfully, Hays contends that this limitation of woman's sphere can cause psychological damage and eventually destroy intelligent women. In ***Appeal to the Men of Great Britain,*** she says that women as well as men possess a 'passion to distinguish themselves,—this rage to excel' but 'when applied to woman it commonly receives the denomination of vanity' or 'pride' (77). Because of the denial of this impulse women are driven to do foolish things:

> Driven and excluded from what are commonly esteemed the consequential offices of life; denied . . . any political existence; and literary talents and acquirements, nay genius itself . . . nothing in short being left for them, but domestic duties, and superficial accomplishments and vanities—Is it surprising, that instead of doing as men bid them . . . that spoiled by prosperity and goaded on by temptation and the allurements of pleasure, they give a loose rein to their passions, and plunge headlong into folly and dissipation . . . to the utter extinction of thought, moderation, or strict morality?

> (*Appeal*, 81-2)

In Emma Courtney this argument is repeated by the heroine:

> While men pursue interest, honor, pleasure, as accords with their several dispositions, women . . . remain insulated beings, and must be content tamely to look on, without taking any part in the great, though often absurd and tragical drama of life. Hence the eccentricities of conduct, with which women of superior minds have been accused . . . the despairing . . . struggles of an ardent spirit, denied a scope for its exertions! The strong feelings, and . . . energies . . . forced back, and pent up, ravage and destroy the mind which gave them birth!

> (86)

What happens to Emma is a literal transcription of this contention: instead of being able to direct her strong energies to a useful channel, Emma becomes strongly infatuated and obsessed with an admirable man with a doubtful past.

While Augustus Harley is not a villain, he is rather like Wollstonecraft's Darnford in *Wrongs of Woman* in that he is a hero largely created by the heroine's imagination. Part of his attraction stems from the fact that he is the son of Emma's friend, but part of it arises from his willingness to assist Emma 'in the pursuit of learning and science . . . astronomy and philosophy . . . languages . . . criticism and grammar, and . . . composition' (71). In other words, he widens Emma's mental horizons and encourages her development in a way that no one else had before. Subsequently, at a dinner party, Emma listens with admiration to a discussion on the slave trade in which 'Mr. Harley pleaded the cause of freedom and humanity with a bold and manly eloquence, expatiating warmly on the iniquity as well as impolicy of so accursed a traffic' (115). Like Emma, Augustus, too, is an advocate of 'freedom and humanity.' She feels a sympathy between them, a 'union between mind and mind,' but also knows that her emotions are aided by her 'imagination, ever lively,' which 'traced the glowing picture, and dipped the pencil in rainbow tints!' (103).

The fact that Augustus, who seems to shun Emma throughout the novel, actually reciprocates her feelings and admits that he has loved her adds a touch of irony to the lesson of restraint that Hays seems to be inculcating in her readers. All along, Hays cautions that Emma's conduct '*is not what I would recommend to general imitation*' (89). Emma seems to be exposing and humiliating herself by her constant harassment of Augustus with detailed proofs of her affection and with her queries: 'Had he, or had he not, a *present, existing engagement*?' (109). At the height of her passion she even offers herself to him without the sanctity of marriage: 'I breathe with difficulty—*My friend*—I would *give myself to you*—the gift is not worthless' (126). This sensational declaration of the heroine's willingness to give herself physically to a man is made even more shocking by Emma's admittance of the existence of sexual desires. Emma's reading has not only enriched her mind, but has also made her aware of her sexuality, as she explains: 'I am neither a philosopher, nor a heroine—but a *woman, to whom education has given a sexual character*' (120). As one critic remarks, Emma longs for the 'twin sources of masculine power; knowledge and sex.'[15] To eighteenth-century readers women who wished to meddle in 'masculine' spheres of learning were already considered freaks or 'unsex'd,' but women who desired both erudition and passion were virtual monsters.[16]

It is not coincidental that Foucault credits the eighteenth century with the beginning of the production of sexuality, when 'specific mechanisms of knowledge and power centering on sex' were formed.[17] Foucault argues that among a number of developments at this time were the 'hysterization of women's bodies' and the 'socialization of procreative behavior' (104). Both the character Emma Courtney and the author Hays are affected by the period's fear of woman's sexuality and the overt way in which Hays attempted to discuss it. Because it was widely known that ***Emma Courtney*** was based on her unrequited love for

William Frend, the Cambridge mathematician and rebel, who had advocated many of Godwin's beliefs, Hays became the target of a number of censures. Frequently the attacks on Hays's ideas were accompanied by unjust invectives against her person. In a letter to Robert Southey dated Saturday, 25 January 1800, an irascible Samuel Taylor Coleridge wrote:

> Of Miss Hays' intellect I do not think so highly as you, or rather, to speak sincerely, I think, not contemptuously, but certainly very despectively thereof [*sic*].— Yet I think you likely in this case to have judged better than I—for to hear a Thing, ugly & petticoated, ex-syllogize a God with cold-blooded Precision, & attempt to run Religion thro' the body with an Icicle . . . If do not endure it![18]

Another assault came from Charles Lloyd, who satirized Coleridge and the excessive, uncontrolled sensibility of the English Jacobins in his novel *Edmund Oliver* (1798). In the work Hays appears as Lady Gertrude Sinclair, a passionate girl of very advanced principles who is throwing herself at a revolutionary who turns out to be a hypocrite.[19] As in Hamilton's *Memoirs Modern Philosophers*, *Edmund Oliver* replicates passages from **Emma Courtney** verbatim, which, though meant to satirize, also created more publicity and certainly reinforced Hays's notoriety. That Hays's novel and her person should inspire a number of writers to depict her in their works, albeit negatively, is an indication of the disruptive power of her revolutionary ideas. In addition, in **Emma Courtney** itself, the heroine's declaration of her passion causes some to believe that she is hysterical. Harley refuses to acknowledge her sexual desires, while Mr Francis believes that her conduct is a sign of 'moon-struck madness' (142).

Hays's novel created an outrage and became a target for satires because she used her fiction to transgress the boundaries allocated to women by the male-dominated culture. Her heroine's declaration openly challenged the notions of female propriety and modesty as prescribed by the conservatives. What Irigaray says of women's sexuality applies to Hays's Emma Courtney: '. . . what they desire is precisely nothing, and at the same time everything . . . Their desire is often interpreted, and feared, as a sort of insatiable hunger, a voracity that will swallow you whole' (*This Sex*, 29). Indeed, fear is undoubtedly one of the reasons why **Emma Courtney** inspired the number of parodies and caricatures that it did. Hays's insistence on the moral aspects of her tale does not, in fact, lessen its revolutionary implications. While Emma complains that she is 'hemmed in on every side by the constitutions of society' and that she perceives 'the magic circle, without knowing how to dissolve the powerful spell' (86), she does succeed in breaking this 'magic circle' in many ways. Emma reverses eighteenth-century courtship conventions by infringing on the masculine right to selection, openly acknowledges her sexual longing, breaks out of silence, and becomes a subject rather than an 'specularized' object of male desire. Her repentant covering letters to Augustus, Jr, at the beginning and end of the memoirs do not, ultimately, negate her achievement or the power of her tale. The virtues that she tries to instil in the young Augustus—'vigor' of the mind, 'self controul,' the 'dignity of active, intrepid virtue'—are very worthy, but the didactic lessons seem pale and lifeless in comparison to the narration of the potency and frenzy of forbidden and 'contemned love' (198-9).

Another way in which the sense of women's limitations and imprisonment within the 'magic circle' is reinforced is through the circular and repetitive structure of the narrative. Emma's sexual and intellectual frustrations, her feelings of being a 'miserable, oppressed, and impotent woman' excluded from expanding her 'sensations' (146), are reflected in the novel's textual confinement of the reader. As Emma writes and rewrites the same argument, as she repeatedly confronts Augustus with identical proofs of her sincerity and affection based on reason, it is difficult not to be exasperated by her seemingly futile efforts. Emma's narrative, with its tedious, but very real and urgent, supplications, encircles and confines the reader just as she is in fact 'hemmed in' by her lack of alternatives or choices. I suggest that rather than lose patience with the heroine, Hays wishes that her readers would cease to tolerate the social and cultural institutions or structures that are responsible for her plight. As in Wollstonecraft's *Wrongs of Woman* repetition, inactivity, and confinement are designed to instigate revolt and reaction in the reader.

Finally, the ambiguous and rather hasty resolution of **Emma Courtney** betrays Hays's ambivalent feelings about the power of emotions and passion. According to Lacanian myth, Hays, like Wollstonecraft, is writing from the position of the daughter. Her text therefore reveals both a strong penchant for what Kristeva calls the semiotic realm, and a desire to conform to the symbolic world, with its emphasis on language and reason. In 'From One Identity to an Other' Kristeva says that 'semiotic processes prepare the future speaker for entrance into meaning and signification,' but points out that 'language as symbolic function constitutes itself at the cost of repressing instinctual drive and continuous relation to the mother.' Poetic language is useful because it signifies 'what is untenable in the symbolic, nominal, paternal function.'[20] Critic Patricia Elliot suggests that 'as such, poetic language reveals the process through which subjects are constituted, a process repressed by a rationality that assumes the conscious ego to be master in its own house.' She notes that 'from Kristeva's perspective this rationality marks another instance of sacrifice . . . in the process of establishing coherent social and symbolic identities.'[21] Through Emma, Hays reveals the cost of this sacrifice, and by implication, the need for change in the construction of women's identity. As Catherine Belsey puts it, 'It is this contradiction in the subject—between the conscious self, which is conscious in so far as it is able to feature in discourse, and the self which is only partially represented there—which constitutes the source of possible change.'[22]

Near the end of the novel Emma believes herself cured of 'the morbid excess of a distempered imagination' and marries a second-rate suitor, Montague, because she owed him 'life, and its comforts, rational enjoyments, and the opportunity of usefulness' (172). However, this peaceful relationship based on 'a rational esteem, and a grateful affection' (171) is quickly destroyed when Emma accidentally encounters Augustus before his expiration. After Augustus's deathbed confession that Emma's 'tenderness early penetrated [his] heart' and that he has loved her all along (180), Emma becomes ill and in her delirium 'incessantly call[s] upon the name of Augustus Harley' (182), thereby negating her assertions that she is now completely ruled by reason rather than passion.

Indeed, even as she terminates her memoirs with the entreaty to young Augustus to learn from 'the errors of [her] past life' (198), and to escape 'from the tyranny of the passions' (199), she also says in a rather contradictory manner: 'The social affections were necessary to my existence, but they have been only inlets to sorrow—*yet still, I bind them to my heart!*' (198). Her half-hearted repentance and her romantic narrative do not actually condemn pure passion as much as the conventions of society which do not tolerate its expression. Though she claims that her 'affections' have only brought her 'sorrow,' she is nevertheless unwilling to let them go. Clinging to her feelings, she fails in her attempts to follow the advice of her philosopher friend, Mr Francis. In fact, the weak and rather impotent authority of Francis's admonition is another indication of Hays's distrust of the Law of the Father. Francis, the paternal figure, points out to Emma that her conduct has been 'moon-struck madness, hunting after torture' and that 'disappointed love' cannot be catalogued as one of the 'real evils of human life' (142), but his sagacious counsel is wasted on the ardent Emma. Emma refuses his abstract rationalism and insists that her sorrow is real: 'That which embitters all my life, that which stops the genial current of health and peace is whatever be its nature, a real calamity to me' (144). For Emma, reasoning powers cannot take the place of or compete with emotional strength. She maintains that 'my reason was the auxiliary of my passion, or rather my passion the generative principle of my reason' (145). As with Wollstonecraft, Hays was attracted to both of these forces and tried to work out in her fiction the place of each in a woman's life.

Similar to a Gothic novel such as Radcliffe's *Mysteries of Udolpho, Emma Courtney* ends with a sense of order, sanity, and normality after having taken the reader through what seems to be a world of uncertainty, doubts, heightened emotions, and tensions. Both Emily St Aubert and Emma Courtney appear to be 'cured' of excessive sensibility after their experience in the dark maze of agitation, passion, and imagination. However, despite the moralistic beginning and ending of Hays's novel, the tendency of the whole work is still towards feeling, sensation, and the free expression of one's sentiments. As in *Udolpho* the most exciting and innovative parts of the novel are those that deal with the excesses, the effusions of passions, the mystery of the unknown. The strong middle part of the work, where the heroine gives 'loose rein' to her passion, to her

emotional and bodily drives, her 'semiotic' self, subverts and undermines the lesson of good sense that the narrator tries to teach. It is as if Hays felt compromised by the demands of the critics and the conservative writers into tacking a moral onto her powerful tale depicting female desire.

In addition to the tension between the moral and the effect of the work, another revolutionary aspect of Hays's novel is in its unusual conclusion. In the final scene of *Emma Courtney* we do not see the conventional heterosexual couple ending the novel but a tableau of a mother and child dyad. Like Wollstonecraft's in *Mary, a Fiction,* Hays's resistance to the Burkean notion of paternal authority is shown in her refusal to let her heroine submit to the name of the Father. Instead Hays resorts to the maternal and places her hopes on the youth of the next generation. While Emma had identified herself with the sentimental heroine in her younger years, in her middle age she is very much a female survivor, outliving both the prevaricating Augustus and her weak-willed husband. Though she is still affected by her memories, the 'long forgotten emotions' (198), she looks forward to a new and better society in which 'men begin to think and reason; reformation dawns, though the advance is tardy' (199). This belief in the Godwinian notion of the perfectibility of humankind, though laudable, was difficult to sustain; and, by her next novel, Hays became more pessimistic about the ability of society to reform.

. . . . .

Despite its contradictory message towards freedom of expression and excessive feeling *Emma Courtney* maintained the hope shared by the radical intellectuals of the 1790s that the example of the French Revolution would bring about change in England. By the time Mary Hays wrote her second novel, *The Victim of Prejudice* (1799), however, this glimmer of hope was fast disappearing. Hays was much more pessimistic in her attitude at the close of the revolutionary decade, and this outlook resulted in a novel less idealistic and more sombre in tone than her first one. In spirit and intent *Victim of Prejudice* is closer to Wollstonecraft's *Wrongs of Woman* in that it presents a catalogue of possible 'wrongs' or acts of social injustice perpetrated on the eighteenth-century middle-class female.

Using elements of the sentimental and the Gothic novel, Hays sets out to disprove and dispel the Burkean myth of the benevolent country squire as an adequate miniature head or 'monarch' of the residents of his estates. Sir Peter Osborne, the representative patriarch, is the complete opposite of the Burkean ideal and is devoid of any sense of kindness or generosity towards his tenants. In fact, he deliberately takes advantage of his authority to gratify his selfish desires for seduction and revenge. Other issues Hays attempts to deal with in her second novel are the objectification of women in a male-dominated society, and their lack of social and economic power. As in *Emma Courtney* the theme of dependence becomes important and is fictionalized in the work. Indeed much of *Victim of Prejudice* is a transcription of the feminist contentions found in her prose writings, *Letters and Essays* and, especially, *An Appeal to the Men of Great Britain.* Literalization occurs at various levels in the novel: the metaphor of the confinement of women in the 'magic circle' becomes a physical reality; horrors and nightmares discovered in ancient papers are enacted and become 'real'; and finally, a woman's sense of helplessness, most often imagined in the form of sexual violation and its consequences, materializes and becomes literal.

Similar in tone and ideology to Godwin's *Things As They Are; or, The Adventures of Caleb Williams,* by which Wollstonecraft's *Wrongs* was also influenced, Hays's *Victim* attempts to expose the corruption of such man-made institutions as the court and legislative systems which favour persons of wealth and rank. Jane Spencer says that '*The Victim of Prejudice* is a study of the obstacles in the way of female independence, the ideal that animated Wollstonecraft in *The Rights of Woman.*'[23] But the novel also deals with the complexities of mother-daughter relations, and with more general concerns such as social prejudices which tend to distinguish worth according to birth, reputation, and fortune and blind people to an individual's personal merit.[24] Like Caleb Williams the heroine sees herself as a victim of society, describing herself rather sentimentally but nevertheless appropriately as a 'child of misfortune, a wretched outcast from [her] fellow beings.'[25] Using language borrowed from the revolutionary decade of the 1790s, she addresses her memoirs to the 'victim of despotism, oppression, or error, tenant of a dungeon,' her successor in her prison cell, whom she calls 'fellow sufferer' (1:ii, iii). While Emma Courtney is metaphorically confined in her 'magic circle,' Mary Raymond, the 'victim' of a 'barbarous prejudice' (2:230), is incarcerated in a literal prison as she writes her autobiography.

According to Mary's reconstruction of her life, her history has been like a fall from paradise to a dungeon or hell. Treated like a beloved daughter by her benevolent guardian, Mr Raymond, Mary grows up with a 'robust constitution, a cultivated understanding, and a vigorous intellect' (1:6). Like Emma she has had a liberal education, learning the rudiments not only of 'French, Italian, and Latin,' but also 'geometry, algebra, and arithmetic' (1:8). She has been taught to 'triumph over the imperious demands of passion, to yield only to the dictates of right reason and truth' (1:65-6). However, as in *Emma Courtney,* theory and knowledge of how to act do not necessarily lead to success in practice. These lessons fail to save her from the cruelty and persecutions of the Gothic-like villain, Sir Peter Osborne, who happens to catch Mary stealing a cluster of grapes from his greenhouse one day. Admiring her innocence and beauty, Osborne tauntingly calls her 'a true daughter of Eve' (1:28) because of her transgression. This appellation becomes ironically appropriate because shortly after her theft of the forbidden fruit, Mary is expelled from her Edenic idyll, loses her 'innocence' in both the physical and mental senses, and becomes subjected to the continual harassment of the powerful Sir Peter. Instead of extricating her from her difficulties, Mary's learning has

only made her aware of the peculiar social conditions which contribute to her plight.

Another irony of this appellation is that it links the then virginal Mary with the temptress figure of Eve. It is perhaps not coincidental that two of the most prominent women of the Bible are seen to be fused in the character of Mary. In Osborne's limited understanding all women are stereotyped as both the mother and the whore. Mary unwittingly becomes the object of Osborne's desire and never gets a chance to articulate her wishes or speak as a subject. He only sees her as his specularized 'other,' projecting his desire onto her, and refuses to treat her as the individual she is. His stereotypical and automatic categorization of her is a form of victimization which becomes a literalization when, through his manipulations, she is later reduced to a 'daughter of Eve,' or a figure of temptation in the eyes of men.

Aside from being the object of desire, Mary also represents the oppressed and the defenceless. In her next encounter with Osborne she receives lashes from his whip while trying to shelter a hare from him. Mary is linked to the little animal lexically: she describes it here as a 'panting victim' while she later depicts herself as a 'helpless, devoted victim,' 'panting, half-breathless with emotion' (1:46; 2:128). Implicitly Hays suggests that the aristocratic Osborne desires to sport with her much in the same way he does with the hare, chasing it and eventually killing it in the guise of adventure. According to the Burkean ideal of the benevolent patriarch, as lord of the manor and of the surrounding estates, Osborne should be the benefactor and protector of his tenants. However, Hays shows the inadequacy of this ideal as Sir Peter abuses his privileges of power and peerage, giving in to his lascivious needs, to his 'sport,' rather than considering the good of the community, of which Mary is part.

Earlier, in her *Appeal to the Men of Great Britain,* Hays had expressed her reservations about giving power to men merely on the basis of their gender: 'As matters now stand, it is very difficult to decide, where authority should in prudence begin, or where it ought in justice to end.'[26] Protesting against 'things as they are,' she asks: '. . . in forming the laws by which women are governed . . . have not men . . . consulted more their own conveniency, comfort, and dignity, as far as their judgement and foresight served them than that of women?' (158-9). In *Victim of Prejudice* she demonstrates how 'having no hand in forming [the laws],' women become the 'sufferers' (*Appeal,* 159). Mary is not the only 'victim' in the novel: she seems destined to repeat or replicate the sensational and melodramatic life of her mother. At one time admired and beloved by Mr Raymond, the Mary of the first generation was also a 'victim of the injustice, of the prejudices of society' (1:162). Seduced and abandoned by a man whom she had trusted, she became a prostitute out of desperation. Then, after giving birth to her illegitimate daughter, she murdered her lover in a tavern brawl and later died on the scaffold for her crime. Like her daughter, the mother blames society for her destruction: '*Law* completes the triumph of injustice. The despotism of man rendered me weak, his vices betrayed me into shame, a barbarous policy stifled returning dignity, prejudice robbed me of the means of independence . . .' (1:168). In the eyes of the world the degrading circumstances surrounding Mary's birth are enough to exclude her from respectable society. Her education and accomplishments, her dignity and character, signify nothing. Mary laments: 'While the practice of the world opposes the principles of the sage, education is a fallacious effort, morals an empty theory, and sentiment a delusive dream' (1:78).

Despite her determination not to fall prey to seduction like her mother, the second Mary ends up with an equally tragic fate. The younger Mary's worst nightmares are literalized in the novel, which is thereby given an unreal, Gothic-like quality. As she peruses the memoirs of her mother, Mary becomes the intradiegetic reader, or the reader within the narrative, whose reactions to the tale gauge our own. She is unable to transcend the imprisoning web of the narrative, and becomes enmeshed by the words. She feels 'a sense of oppression, almost to suffocation,' after reading her mother's story and goes out into the 'dark and stormy' night in order to relieve herself of her anguish (1:175). Literally trying to wash away her pain, she stays out in the howling wind and rain, but finds herself unable to escape the narrative:

> I recalled to my remembrance the image of my wretched mother: I beheld her, in idea, abandoned to infamy, cast out of society, stained with blood, expiring on a scaffold, unpitied and unwept. I clasped my hands in agony; terrors assailed me till then unknown; the blood froze in my veins; a shuddering horror crept through my heart . . .
>
> (1:176)

Because Mary was abandoned as an infant, the image that she sees here of her mother is an imagined rather than a recollected one. The terror that she experiences is not only for her mother's experiences in the past, but also for herself, as she feels the danger of replicating her mother's life in the future.

Replication and literalization are made more explicit in yet another instance. After her rape Mary sees her 'wretched mother' in 'visionary form':

> One moment, methought I beheld her in the arms of her seducer, revelling in licentious pleasure; the next, saw her haggard, intoxicated, self-abandoned, joining in the midnight riot; and, in an instant . . . covered with blood, accused of murder, shrieking in horrible despair . . . Then, all pallid and ghastly, with clasped hands . . . and agonizing earnestness, she seemed to urge me to take example from her fate!
>
> (2:95-6)

The ghostly, Gothic-like nightmare of her mother ends with Mary clasping her parent 'in a last embrace' (2:96). It is as if Mary subconsciously desired to be linked with her mother and her disgrace. This realization of something that happened a generation ago seems to be a physical and mental manifestation of the desire to return to the marginalized and outcast maternal.[27] Like Wollstonecraft, Hays demonstrates the ambivalence a woman feels, for the world dominated by the Father. For these female writers the emphasis of maternal figures, dreams, and nightmares, of the disruptive, suggests a move in the direction of the pre-Oedipal mother-child relation, even if this move frequently entails danger, death, or exclusion from the symbolic order.

This mother-daughter link and the subsequent literal re-enactment[28] of the first Mary's written memoirs create much of the tension and sense of foreboding in the novel. As Mary imagines her mother 'abandoned to infamy, cast out of society, stained with blood . . . unpitied and unwept' (1:176), she is also ironically prescribing and envisioning her own future in many ways. Except for the murder of her seducer Mary's life follows that of her mother's, as she is systematically seduced, abandoned, and cast out of society. That Hays understood the consequences that arise from a return to the maternal is revealed when she associates it with betrayal and exclusion from the male symbolic order. Attractive as the mother-daughter connection may seem to be, its cost is undeniably high. Through a replication of the mother's life in the daughter's, Hays shows how challenging the patriarchal system can lead to some form of female punishment in contemporary eighteenth-century culture. The attempts of both the first- and the second-generation Mary to rebel, oppose, and curtail masculine will and desire only create further constraints in their lives. Yearning for more space and freedom, they become physically and spiritually more constricted and circumscribed. In her depiction of the failure of the maternal Hays recognized that the refusal to yield to the Father's law brings about marginalization and isolation under the specific historical and social circumstances in which she and her heroines lived.

Furthermore, the seduction and abandonment of Mary Raymond is not only a transcription of events that have already transpired within the text, but also a replication, or what Margaret Homans would call a 'literalization,' of a more figurative earlier text. The device of the kidnapped heroine was common enough by the 1790s;[29] however, the details of Mary's ravishment and violation closely parallel that of a mid-century novel, *Clarissa*. There is evidence to suggest that Hays was rewriting Samuel Richardson's *Clarissa* from a feminist perspective. Earlier, in an essay entitled **"On Novel Writing"** published in the *Monthly Magazine* of September 1797, Hays expressed her disagreement with Samuel Johnson, who believed that fictional narratives should exhibit 'perfect models of virtue.'[30] She cites and criticizes Richardson's Clarissa as an example of a character who is depicted too perfectly: '. . . the character of Clarissa, a beautiful superstructure upon a false and airy foundation, can never be regarded as a model for imitation. It is the portrait of an ideal being, placed in circumstances equally ideal, far removed from common life and human feelings' ("**On Novel Writing,**" 180). According to Hays, Richardson's novel violates principles of 'truth and nature' and abounds with 'absurd superstitions and ludicrous prejudices' ("**On Novel Writing,**" 180). Preferring the 'real' to the ideal, Hays questions: '. . . why should we seek to deceive . . . by illusive representations of life? Why should we not rather paint [life] as it really exists, mingled with imperfection, and discoloured by passion?' ("**On Novel Writing,**" 180).

Hays's rejection of 'illusive' or figurative representations can be explained with the help of Chodorow, Kristeva, Irigaray, and others as a manifestation of a woman writer's lingering attachment to pre-Oedipal, literal language, as opposed to a son's wholehearted embrace of the symbolic, figurative language associated with the father. In the depiction of women in literature figurative or ideal representations often entail the death or destruction of the real.[31] That Hays was aware of, and uncomfortable with, this notion is revealed in her opposition to iconic representations of good and evil. Arguing that such delineations are not 'consistent with truth and fact,' she writes: 'Human nature seems to be at an equal distance from the humiliating descriptions of certain ascetic moralists, and the exaggerated eulogiums of enthusiasts. Gradations, almost imperceptible, of light and shade, must mingle in every true portrait of the human mind' ("**On Novel Writing,**" 180). Hence, in ***Victim of Prejudice*** the heroine is neither the virgin Mary, despite her name, nor the temptress Eve, as Sir Osborne believes. She is not 'wholly or disinterestedly virtuous or vicious' ("**On Novel Writing,**" 180), but a complex and probable human being.

That Hays intended her readers to think of *Clarissa* as an intertext to her own novel is confirmed by the many similarities between the two works. Like Clarissa, Mary is from an untitled middle-class family and is courted by an aristocrat. Both heroines are transported from their homes by deceit to the London residences of the villain/rakes. Both are raped and dishonoured by their abductors and live long enough to exclaim against their fate in writing, Clarissa in her numerous epistles and Mary in her memoirs. However, even more significant are the differences between the two texts. Hays reworks the Richardsonian material according to her beliefs: her heroine is not a paragon, nor is she placed in ideal circumstances. Radically changing the denouement, Hays does not end her novel with the triumphant death of the heroine, but instead uses the tragic events to illustrate powerfully the injustice of later-eighteenth-century social customs and laws, and the abuse of patriarchal authority. Unlike Richardson, Hays does not shift the focus away from the realistic, brutal consequences of the rape to a more ethereal, spiritual realm; rather, she dwells on the sordid details of the miserable existence of her heroine after her sexual defilement. Hays's Mary, unlike Richardson's Clarissa, does not transcend the physical and the corporeal to become a symbolic representation of Christian fortitude or female virtue, but remains rooted in the social and the real.

Using Gothic elements enabled Hays to increase her heroine's sense of terror and helplessness. Some of these techniques include Osborne's elaborate machinations to get her to his London mansion, confinement in a chamber with the door locked on the outside, and Mary's midnight wandering, in an effort to escape, in the dark halls and corridors of the house on the night of the grand dinner. While these circumstances may remind one of Radcliffe's *Udolpho,* the end result is quite different. For Mary's terrors, unlike most of Emily St Aubert's, are not imagined ones, and her fears of rape become literalized that night. And while Osborne apologizes for his behaviour the next day, maintaining that his action 'had not been premeditated, but was the mere result of accident and a temporary effervescence of spirits' (2:80), he increasingly becomes the obsessive and cruel tyrant who inhabits the imaginations of Gothic maidens like Emily. However, unlike Emily, Mary does not need to resort to fantasy or to the symbolic: her horrors are all too real and literal.

Following the rape Hays uses a stock character of sentimental fiction, that of the suffering heroine, or virtue in distress, to illustrate her beliefs of gender and class inequality. Mary's plight reveals how the existing justice system fails to protect and, in fact, aids in oppressing the wronged in society. Because of her mother's reputation as a whore and murderer, her insufficient knowledge of the city, and her lack of social connections, Mary finds it difficult to convince anyone that she was brutally violated. She threatens Osborne with legal proceedings, but he jeers at her: 'Who will credit the tale you mean to tell? . . . Who would support you against my wealth and influence? How would your delicacy shrink from the idea of becoming, in open court, the sport of ribaldry, the theme of obscene jesters?' (2:85-6). As Hays suggests in her advertisement, because of the 'too-great stress laid on the reputation for chastity in woman,' Mary has difficulty in retaining her dignity and self-respect. Paraphrasing Godwin's philosophy, she demands 'liberty,' and proclaims: 'when the mind is determined,' one cannot 'fetter the body' by 'feeble restraints' (1:82, 81). However, her worthy resolutions soon fail: she cannot battle hunger, cold, and poverty with her philosophic ideals. In her struggle to be independent Mary is unable to overcome eighteenth-century gender and class prejudices, and the value system of materialistic and morally corrupt society. Eventually she succumbs to despair, unable to conceive of herself as something other than a victim, or the tragic heroine of sentimental fiction.

While we may be bothered by Mary's stubbornness and her insistence on her freedom at all cost, we cannot help but sympathize with her lack of choice as she desperately clings to the only thing left intact: her self-esteem. Preferring 'disgrace, indigence, contempt' to 'the censure of [her] own heart' (2:110-11), Mary tries to find work as a companion, attempts to teach drawing, aspires to learn engraving, embroidery, even copying, but is rejected in all trades because she is a woman with a tarnished reputation. All the men she encounters view her as only a sexual being, not a serious worker. She complains:

I sought only the base means of subsistence amidst the luxuriant and the opulent . . . I put in no claims either for happiness or gratification . . . yet, surely, I had a right to exist—For what crime was I driven from society? I seemed to myself like an animal entangled in the toils of the hunter.

(2:143)

The metaphor of the hunter and prey is a version of the imagery of imprisonment which radical writers often used.[32] But with Hays, and often with other women writers, this metaphor ceases to be merely figurative and instead becomes literalized in the novel. Mary literally becomes a 'prey' with whom Osborne sports.

As Osborne 'entangles' her in his 'toils,' Mary's freedom increasingly becomes curtailed. The theme of dependence found in **Emma Courtney** is reiterated in Hays's second novel. Mary, like Emma Courtney and Wollstonecraft's Jemima, objects to the fact that she has very limited or virtually no means of existing independently of men. As Hays had pointed out earlier in **Letters and Essays,** 'young women without fortunes, if they do not chance to marry . . . have scarce any other resources than in servitude, or prostitution.'[33] Hays continues: 'I never see, without indignation, those trades, which ought to be appropriated to women, almost entirely engrossed by men, haberdashery, millinery, & even mantua-making' (**Letters and Essays,** 84-5). In the **Appeal** she objected to the way girls were brought up: 'Indeed there is something so very degrading in the idea of breeding up women, if allowed to be rational beings at all, merely with the view of catching at a husband' (227). While Emma, out of desperation, eventually succumbs to the enticement of marriage with Montague, Hays's second heroine resists absolutely the traditional solution of marriage. Mary refuses her childhood companion William Pelham's sincere offers of marriage because of her notions of duty and honesty. Later she turns down Mr Raymond's proposal that she wed an honest local farmer and become the 'prettiest dairy-maid in the country' (2:30) because her heart is with William. If Emma Courtney's fault is an over-indulgence of sensibility, Mary Raymond's is an exalted sense of honour and self-righteousness. In many instances Mary seems to glory in anticipation of her suffering. After the rape, for example, she refuses William's affection and financial assistance saying: '. . . let my ruin be complete! . . . Dishonour, death itself, is a calamity less insupportable than *self-reproach*' (2:110-11). While it is undoubtedly true that Osborne's will and the implicit condonation of society are responsible for most of her miseries, her exaggerated sense of heroism and desire for independence also contribute to her agony.

That Hays was influenced by Richardson's *Clarissa* and by Godwin's *Caleb Williams* is evident in her depiction of Sir Peter Osborne. He is as villainous, cruel, and full of stratagems as the wealthy and powerful Lovelace or Ferdinando Falkland. But Hays's anti-hero also shares some affinities with Radcliffe's Montoni from the *Mysteries of*

Udolpho. Radcliffe and Hays each recognized and made explicit the link between economic and sexual dependence. Both Montoni's and Osborne's abuses of power involve a deprivation of the heroine's material possessions, a parallel which reveals both female authors' awareness of the close connection between money, property, and power.[34] In **Victim of Prejudice** Osborne places Mary at his mercy by systematically stripping away her every means of self-support. First he forces the Nevilles, with whom Mary is staying, to quit the country, thereby using up the little amount of money Mr Raymond intended for Mary. Subsequently he gives her a choice of a debtor's prison, 'famine and destitution,' or the enjoyment of a 'lavish fortune' and pleasure as his mistress (2:167). As his prey Mary chooses 'desolation, infamy, a prison, the rack, death itself' rather than life with Osborne (2:169). At this point the 'magic circle' that Hays wrote about metaphorically in her first novel and in her prose essays becomes literalized into a real enclosure. Mary is no longer merely figuratively or spiritually confined, but physically imprisoned.

To emphasize the falsity of Burke's ideal of the benevolent patriarch Hays deliberately creates an anti-paternal lord in Osborne. Osborne's relentless pursuit of Mary culminates in his emotional and physical abuse of her while she resides with an elderly servant who is trying to cultivate a farm leased on Osborne's property. As squire of estates Osborne offers no protection or aid to his tenants, but instead takes advantage of his power as 'monarch' of the countryside to pursue his prey further. This time he is humbled, implores Mary's forgiveness, and offers her a '*legal*' title to his hand and fortune' (2:204). However, Mary, in her most Clarissa-like heroic manner, refuses his proposal. Without prospects or fortune, she still dares to exclaim: 'Think not that I would ally my soul to your's; my haughty spirit, wounded, but not crushed, utterly contemns you' (2:205). In the spirit of the Richardsonian heroine she claims that she wishes but 'to die decently and alone' (2:206).

The conclusion to **Victim of Prejudice** is melodramatic and sentimental. While Clarissa, true to her tragic form, can will herself to die gracefully within a relatively short time after her violation, Mary lives on for two to three years after her resolution to depart from her 'joyless existence' (2:216). Hays does not even allow Mary to expire with the proper dramatic stage effect of a tragic heroine. Writing from the position of a hysteric, Hays is, to use Irigaray's term, 'miming,' and at the same time questioning, a patriarchal means of resolving the loss of female subjectivity. While she is unable to break out of the literary convention of 'killing off' the fallen woman, the prolonged survival of Mary after her sexual violation reveals a hesitancy in following the prescribed formula. The fact that Mary continues to live and fight for her dignity and self-sufficiency long after her loss of virginity is an indication of Hays's defiance of the popular belief in the male ability to manipulate the female through controlling her body. Mary is not merely a 'specularized' object or mirror which reflects a man's desire or his condition: she does not immediately wither to death after being assaulted and then left by a man.

As a contrast to Mary, Hays presents Mrs Neville as an example of a woman who is nothing but a mirror reflection of a man. The whole episode of Mary's reunion with the Nevilles seems rather odd and out of place located as it is in the concluding chapter of the novel. The Nevilles return to England in time to rescue Mary from her 'deadly torpor' (2:214) and nurse her back to health. However, shortly after, Mr Neville perishes from a fatal illness, followed by his wife, who dies from grief. On her deathbed Mrs Neville confesses to Mary that she has been a 'feeble victim to an excessive, and therefore blameable tenderness' (2:225). The use of the word *victim* here links Mrs Neville to Mary and to her mother, who have also described themselves as victims. However, in contrast to the two Marys, Mrs Neville's victimization has been one in which she willingly participated. She explains:

> My husband was worthy of my affection; but I adored him with a fondness too lavish, an idolatrous devotion, in which every other duty has been at length absorbed . . . I modelled to his my temper, my character, my words, my actions, even the expression of my feelings. I had no individual existence; my very being was absorbed in that of my husband . . . I was the slave, and am at length become the victim, of my tenderness.
>
> (2:226, 228)

Rather belatedly Mrs Neville recognizes the loss of herself as an autonomous subject in her lifelong devotion to her husband. She is nothing but a negative of her husband, a victim of what Irigaray calls the 'feminine,' which 'has never been defined except as the inverse, indeed the underside, of the masculine.'[35]

The differences stand out between Mrs Neville, who has, in Irigaray's words, maintained a 'lack of qualities,' remained 'in unrealized potentiality,' in order to 'ensure . . . that the male can achieve his qualifications,'[36] and Mary, who has, conversely, always acted as a subject and has refused the position of Other. But what is more significant is their similarity: both Mrs Neville and Mary in their extreme positions remain in 'unrealized potentiality' and are both 'victims' of society. In introducing the Neville case rather obtrusively in the last chapter, Hays reveals her mistrust of the submissive, dependent, and docile ideal female described by conservatives such as Jane West and Hannah More. In other words, though she is portraying the failure and ultimate demise of the independent woman, she is not endorsing her opposite. In fulfilling the duties of a wife, Mrs Neville, too, has suffered because of social and cultural expectations of that role. For Hays, it is still better to have rebelled and lost, than never to have rebelled at all. While Mary may be bodily confined at the end, her spirit of freedom and desire for self-reliance make her life more memorable than those of a dozen Mrs Nevilles.

In fact, in *Letters and Essays* Hays had maintained with assurance that 'bolts and bars may confine for a time the feeble body, but can never enchain the noble, the free-born

mind; the only true grounds of power are reason and affection' (23). However, this bold confidence of the earlier work is curtailed by the time we come to the end of *Victim of Prejudice.* The strong-willed heroine is reduced to a despairing and distressed sentimental sufferer, whose only desire is that 'the story of [her] sorrows should kindle in the heart of man, in behalf of [her] oppressed sex, the sacred claims of humanity and justice' (2:231). Since hope of restitution seems lost to her, she bequeaths it rather wistfully to the reader of her memoirs. This pathetic end of the once energetic heroine seems rather disappointing in the light of Hays's earlier vigorous and spirited attacks on men and the customs of eighteenth-century society. It may be a result of the change in climate by the end of the 1790s. No longer were the revolutionaries as optimistic in their belief in reason and the perfectibility of man as at the beginning of the decade. With Robespierre's Reign of Terror and the Napoleonic invasions, the example of France and the revolution proved to be a negative one. In addition, the death of Wollstonecraft in 1797 and the publication of the *Memoirs* of her life certainly did not aid the feminist cause. Like many other Jacobins, Hays was viewed with hostility and retired from the public sphere shortly after the publication of her second novel.

However negative and sentimental the ending of *Victim of Prejudice* seems to be, the work still stands as a powerful reminder of the difficulties faced by a middle-class woman desiring independence in the late eighteenth century. While Hays did not provide her readers with pat solutions to the problems she has raised, her contribution to social change may lie in her vivid depiction, articulation, and literalization of female constraints and victimization. Her observations about tyrannical governments can be applied to gender subjugation: 'It appears to men that all monarchical, and aristocratical governments, carry within themselves the seeds of their dissolution; for when they become corrupt, and oppressive to a certain degree, the effects must necessarily be murmurs, remonstrances, and revolt' (*Letters and Essays,* 17). Hays believed that 'a benevolent mind cannot view with indifference its fellow-creatures sinking into depravation and consequent misery' (*Letters and Essays,* 16). Perhaps Hays felt that the mere portrayal of women as 'victims' in her novel was a step in the direction of social awakening, if not revolt.

Notes

1. Mary Hays, *Memoirs of Emma Courtney* (1796), introd. Sally Cline (London: Pandora 1987), xvii. Subsequent page references are to this edition.

2. See Janet Todd, *Sensibility: An Introduction* (London: Methuen 1986), 1-6 for a description of sentimental literature and the cult of sensibility.

3. Mary Hays, *An Appeal to the Men of Great Britain in Behalf of Women,* introd. Gina Luria (New York: Garland 1974), 97

4. Katharine M. Rogers, in 'The Contribution of Mary Hays,' *Prose Studies* 10, no. 2 (Sept. 1987) 131-42,

compares Wollstonecraft's prose style and arguments to those of Hays and notes that Wollstonecraft's approach was more theoretical.

5. Mary Hays, *Letters and Essays, Moral and Miscellaneous,* ed. Gina Luria (New York: Garland 1974), 19-20

6. See William Godwin, *Enquiry Concerning Political Justice,* ed. and abridged K. Codell Carter (Oxford: Clarendon 1971), 28.

7. Katharine Rogers points out that Hays's tone reflects the choice of the title of the *Appeal.* Hays's attitude is 'less adversarial than Wollstonecraft's, more good-natured and easy going' ('The Contribution of Mary Hays,' 138).

8. Luce Irigaray, *Speculum of the Other Woman,* trans. Gillian C. Gill (Ithaca, NY: Cornell University Press 1985), 142

9. Luce Irigaray, *This Sex Which Is Not One,* trans. Catherine Porter (Ithaca, NY: Cornell University Press 1985), 136

10. Janet Todd, *The Sign of Angellica: Women, Writing and Fiction, 1660-1800* (London: Virago 1989), 245

11. In *Women, Power, and Subversion: Social Strategies in British Fiction 1778-1860* (Athens: University of Georgia Press 1981), 14-22, Judith Lowder Newton discusses the effects of industrialization on middle-class women and its manifestations in literature. While industrialization meant rising economic and social power for middle-class men, women were increasingly being allocated to the domestic sphere.

12. Janet Todd points out that this 'magic circle' is probably from a 'Wollstonecraftian feminist context' and echoes the 'enchanted circle' of Mary Astell (*The Sign of Angellica,* 246).

13. In 'Ideology and Ideological State Apparatuses' Louis Althusser includes literature among the 'ideological apparatuses which contribute to the process of *reproducing* the *relations of production,* the social relationships which are the necessary condition for the existence and perpetuation of the capitalist mode of production.' See Catherine Belsey's summary of his, Roland Barthes's, and Jacques Lacan's theories of subjectivity in *Critical Practice* (London: Methuen 1980), 56-84.

14. In *The Sign of Angellica* Janet Todd emphasizes the self-pitying aspects of Emma Courtney and Wollstonecraft's Mary (237, 245). While Emma does tend to ask her readers to sympathize with her at the beginning, the ending shows a strengthening of her fortitude and a sense of her resignation, if not acceptance of her lot.

15. Gina Luria, 'Mary Hays: A Critical Biography' (Ph.D. diss., New York University, 1972), 297

16. In *The Unsex'd Females,* introd. by Gina Luria (New York: Garland 1974) Richard Polwhele included

Hays in Wollstonecraft's band of 'Gallic freaks' who mixed 'corporeal struggles' with 'mental strife' (7, 21). See also Felicity A. Nussbaum, *The Brink of All We Hate: English Satires on Women 1660-1750* (Lexington: University Press of Kentucky 1984), 4ff. for a discussion of the learned lady as a frequent target of satire.

17. Michel Foucault, *The History of Sexuality: An Introduction,* vol. 1, trans. Robert Hurley (New York: Vintage 1990), 103

18. Samuel Taylor Coleridge, *Collected Letters,* 4 vols, ed. Earl Leslie Griggs (Oxford: Clarendon 1956-66), 1:563

19. In *Jane Austen and the War of Ideas* (Oxford: Clarendon 1976), 109, Marilyn Butler says that this relationship bears more resemblance to Mary Wollstonecraft's affair with Gilbert Imaly. However, Lady Gertrude Sinclair's many passages verbatim from *Emma Courtney,* documented with footnotes, suggest that the target was more likely Hays. See Charles Lloyd, *Edmund Oliver,* 2 vols (Bristol: J. Cottle 1798).

20. Julia Kristeva, 'From One Identity to an Other,' in her *Desire in Language: A Semiotic Approach to Literature and Art,* ed. Leon S. Roudiez, trans. Thomas Gora, Alice Jardine, and Leon Roudiez (New York: Columbia University Press 1980), 136, 138

21. Patricia Elliot, *From Mastery to Analysis: Theories of Gender in Psychoanalytic Feminism* (Ithaca, NY: Cornell University Press 1991), 213

22. Belsey, *Critical Practice,* 85

23. Jane Spencer, *The Rise of the Woman Novelist: From Aphra Behn to Jane Austen* (Oxford: Basil Blackwell 1986), 132

24. In *Jane Austen and the War of Ideas* (Oxford: Clarendon Press 1975), Marilyn Butler says that 'it is still possible to draw a critical divide where [Richard] Whately puts it: between the advocates of a Christian conservatism on the one hand, with their pessimistic view of man's nature, and their belief in external authority; on the other hand, progressives, sentimentalists, revolutionaries, with their optimism about man, and their preference for spontaneous personal impulse against rules imposed from without' (164-5). Hays is clearly of the latter camp, as she believes in individual worth, rather than the judgment of external authority.

25. Mary Hays, *The Victim of Prejudice,* 2 vols (London: J. Johnson 1799), 1:i. Subsequent page references are to this edition.

26. Mary Hays, *An Appeal to the Men of Great Britain in Behalf of Women,* introd. Gina Luria (New York: Garland 1974), 287

27. Extrapolating from the theories of Klein, Horney, and Deutsch, Marianne Hirsch, in *The Mother/*

Daughter Plot: Narrative, Psychoanalysis, Feminism (Bloomington: Indiana University Press 1989), suggests that narratives of female development 'would not be linear or teleological but would reflect the oscillations between maternal and paternal attachments as well as the multiple repressions of the female developmental course.' (102).

28. One instance of 'bearing the word' that Margaret Homans discusses occurs when the text 'performs linguistic operations—translation, transmission, copying' of the language of other authors (*Bearing the Word* [Chicago: University of Chicago Press 1986], 31). Here Hays does not actually 'bear the word' of another, but she does replicate her own story or fears.

29. For example, Charlotte Smith's *Emmeline; or, The Orphan of the Castle* (1788), Ann Radcliffe's *The Mysteries of Udolpho* (1794), and Elizabeth Inchbald's *A Simple Story* (1791) featured abducted maidens. However, in these novels the heroines escape before they are actually violated.

30. M. H. "On Novel Writing," *Monthly Magazine* (Sept. 1797), 180

31. See Homans, *Bearing the Word*, 4ff.

32. See, for example, William Godwin, *Things As They Are; or, The Adventures of Caleb Williams,* ed. David McCrachen (London: Oxford University Press 1970), vol. 3, chapters 8-10; and Mary Wollstonecraft, *Mary and the Wrongs of Woman*, ed. Gary Kelly (Oxford: World's Classics 1976), 178.

33. Mary Hays, *Letters and Essays, Moral and Miscellaneous,* ed. Gina Luria (New York: Garland 1974), 84

34. In Radcliffe's *Mysteries of Udolpho* Signore Montoni attempts to coerce both his wife and Emily to sign over their properties to him. Emily's lawful possession of the estates and her refusal to give them up are her means of asserting the little power she has at Udolpho (see vol. 3, chap. 5).

35. Luce Irigaray, *This Sex Which Is Not One,* trans. Catherine Porter (Ithaca, NY: Cornell University Press 1985), 159

36. Luce Irigaray, *Speculum of the Other Woman,* trans. Gillian C. Gill (Ithaca, NY: Cornell University Press 1985), 165

Terence Allan Hoagwood (essay date 1996)

SOURCE: Hoagwood, Terence Allan. "Literary Art and Political Justice: Shelley, Godwin, and Mary Hays." In *Shelley: Poet and Legislator of the World,* edited by Betty T. Bennett and Stuart Curran, pp. 30-38. Baltimore: The Johns Hopkins University Press, 1996.

[*In the following essay, Hoagwood suggests that Hays, Shelley, Godwin, and Wollstonecraft all drew from the ideology of the* philosophes *and incorporated their political philosophies within their novels and poems.*]

Shelley's major poems represent a dialectical theory that, like works by William Godwin and Mary Hays, is developed from arguments expressed by the *philosophes* and the *ideologistes.* Thinking about ideology combines with political pressures in the 1790s and again in the post-Waterloo years to move social and political philosophy into symbolic forms. Poetry is politicized in a hermeneutic way: The interpretive operation that is induced by the figural mode of symbolic fiction is taken into the fiction as its subject and theme. The theory of representation that is a political theory in Godwin's *Political Justice* becomes both an aesthetic form and a political contention in the symbolic figurations of novels, including Hays's ***The Victim of Prejudice,*** and also in Shelley's major poems.

Epipsychidion, Adonais, and *Hellas* take as their subject, and deliver as their contention, historical understanding and not historical events. The disjunctions in tone and narrative within individual poems, like the disparate points of view within the lyrical drama, represent multiplicity and change among mental frames. Understood as collective rather than individual varieties, and placed within a frame of historical time, these multiplicities of mental frames relativize the authority of beliefs and thus exhibit critically the fictionality of political forms of authority.

In France and England alike, the conjunctural pressure of political events submerges social and political philosophy in safely figural forms. Condorcet died in prison; Joseph Johnson, who published Hays's ***The Victim of Prejudice*** in 1799 and who was imprisoned in the same year (for publishing a supposedly seditious work by Gilbert Wakefield), also published a translation of Condorcet's great last work, written in prison, in 1795. Holbach wrote highly subversive treatises under the ancien régime; he smuggled his manuscripts to Holland, where they were printed as books, which were then smuggled back into France. He maintained anonymity and confusion about the authorship of his works: One edition of his *Système de la nature* is ascribed on the title page to Mirabaud; his *Christianity Unveiled* is sometimes attributed to Boulanger.[1]

In 1793, as *Political Justice* was being published, Thomas Muir and Thomas Palmer were sentenced to deportation on charges of sedition. In the same year, the Seditious Publications Act was passed. In 1794 twelve persons, including Thomas Holcroft and John Thelwall, were indicted on charges of treason; Godwin knew most of the indicted people personally. In 1795, the Treasonable and Seditious Practices Act and the Unlawful Assemblies Act were passed. Godwin wrote in protest of all these proceedings.[2] Godwin was also concerned for his political and personal safety: He wrote to Thelwall, who was imprisoned in the Tower, saying that he feared "to expose myself to the caprice of persons who . . . have . . . seized a despotical power into their hands."[3] In the same month in which these trials took place, he also published his novel *Caleb Williams.* The sequence is recurrent and important: Political suppression and persecution grow severe, and radical polemics attacking the suppression are moved into figural form.

An excellent but unjustly neglected writer whose work illustrates this pattern as tellingly as Godwin's or Shelley's is Mary Hays, who had met Godwin at the house of Joseph Johnson in 1791. Hays had read Mary Wollstonecraft's *A Vindication of the Rights of Woman* when it was first published in 1792, and an important intellectual friendship ensued among the three writers. In 1796 and 1797, Hays published a series of articles in the *Monthly Magazine* on the philosophy of Helvetius and more largely on the power of social forces to determine human lives and minds. Her epistolary novel ***Memoirs of Emma Courtney*** (1796) is a critique of social conventions, including especially sentimental fictions of romantic love and the power of such fictions to enslave and destroy women. In 1798, she published (anonymously) ***An Appeal to the Men of Great Britain in Behalf of Women,*** which presents arguments about the power of ideology in sustaining sexual inequality. In 1799, she published (under her own name) ***The Victim of Prejudice,*** in which the trope of writing models the inscription of social codes and the economic oppression of women is figured in a narrative of imprisonment. There is no evidence that Shelley knew Hays, or that he was self-consciously indebted to her work. Similarities in their artistic and polemical works reveal something much more important than personal influence: With Wollstonecraft and Godwin, Hays and Shelley participate in the elaboration of a theory of ideology from the *philosophes,* and they participate too in the submergence of that social and historical theory in aesthetic forms.[4]

In an essay of 1793, Hays writes that "of all bondage, mental bondage is surely the most fatal"; patriarchal "despotism . . . has enslaved the female mind."[5] In 1794, Godwin advised Hays to put her arguments about the condition of women and the power of custom and prejudice in the form of fiction; *Memoirs of Emma Courtney* does exactly that, and more effectively still *The Victim of Prejudice* represents the impoverishment of women, rape, imprisonment, violence, and the ideological structures that are correlative with these forms of suppression.

A more complex issue arises when these works, outwardly coerced into the form of submergence, take in that submergence as a theme. Hays's novels induce a hermeneutic operation, narrate acts of interpretation and the consequences of those acts, and also require a transcoding of themselves, as fictive signs of the actual times; the fictional signifiers are signs of "things as they are" (to quote the title of Godwin's novel known conventionally as *Caleb Williams*). That submergence becomes a theme of the fictions. This hermeneutic theme is a repetition in the contentions of verbal art of the material condition of suppression under which the art is produced.

The dialectical linkage of mental and material structures is a common theme among the circle of radical thinkers to which Hays belonged: Wollstonecraft writes that the imperfect governments in Europe "have arisen from this simple circumstance, that the constitution was settled in the dark days of ignorance when the minds of men were shackled by the grossest prejudices."[6] Holbach had argued that whole classes of society had first become enslaved precisely when ruling classes learned to exploit "ignorance" and "prejudice."[7] Godwin argues that "the opinions of men [are,] for the most part, under the absolute control of political institution."[8]

In the ***Appeal,*** Hays argues forcibly that "the world ever has been, and still is, more guided by custom and prejudice, than by principle" (128). Custom, prejudice, and opinion are not merely mental things, because they arise in material conditions: "all opinions degrading to women, are grounded on the rude ideas of savage nations" (131). Furthermore, systems of ideas produce material effects: "the cultivation of the minds and morals of women, is considered as the one thing needful . . . the foundation, upon which any solid hopes of future improvement may be placed;—or any thing really beautiful can be raised" (204). In a letter of 1820, Shelley repeats Hays's point: "The system of society as it exists at present must be overthrown from the foundations with all its superstructure of maxims & of forms before we shall find anything but dissappointment [sic] in our intercourse with any but a few select spirits" (*PBSL* [*The Letters of Percy Bysshe Shelley*] 2:191).

In Hays's ***The Victim of Prejudice,*** characters singly and collectively act in ways that exhibit the social production of ideas and (in dialectical corollary) the power that those ideas then represent. There is no dualism of circumstances and sentiment, of real and ideal; the structures of sentiment and of mentality are themselves social formations. Shelley's poems—for example *Prometheus Unbound* and *Hellas*—share this theme with Hays's novel: the thematizing of the hermeneutic operation as a political act within the outwardly safe and symbolic figurations of the literary art. The works come to be about the interpretive operations that they embody and require. Their political meanings include the contention that the institutions of social life and power also rest upon fictions that require such acts of interpretation.

From Newton (in terms of physical science) and Locke (in terms of philosophy of mind), Condillac developed a philosophy of the *sensibilité physique*: all knowledge derives from physical sensation. For the *philosophes,* the importance of this contention was not metaphysical but political. The "legislator-philosopher" (a phrase from Helvétius that Shelley uses in *A Philosophical View of Reform* 1819-1820 [7:20]) can achieve a reformation of society by way of a total system of reeducation founded in a total environmental determinism.

Godwin writes that he has "slight estimation" for any ethics "which confines itself to . . . the offices of private life"; he is, he says, concerned rather with "communities and nations."[9] For Godwin and Hays, as previously for Helvétius, the argument for environmental determinism is not an abstractly philosophical contention. Differing in this way from Condillac, who was interested chiefly in epistemology, Helvétius sought from the doctrine of the *sensibilité physique* a social and political program. The *power* of intellectual operations, therefore, is emphasized by the same philosophy that insists that intellectual operations are socially and materially *determined*. The relationship between thought forms and material and social determiners is dialectical.

"Perhaps government," Godwin writes, "insinuates itself into our personal dispositions, and insensibly communicates its own spirit to our private transactions." Godwin states what Shelley was to repeat in the *Defence of Poetry*: "Were not the inhabitants of ancient Greece and Rome indebted in some degree to their political liberties for their excellence in art, and . . . in the moral history of mankind? Are not the governments of modern Europe accountable for the slowness and inconstancy of its literary efforts?"[10] Political and artistic forms are identified in the ground of their being and in the reciprocity of their mutual determinations.

Godwin's notoriously misunderstood concept of perfectibility is also a repetition and transformation of French arguments: Cabanis argues tenaciously through twelve treatises (all of them gathered in his *Rapports du physique et du moral de l'homme*) that environmental determinism, dialectically understood, implies a human capacity to progress indefinitely. Cabanis was interested in evolutionary models of biological explanation, and he was also interested in a political theory of progress founded in the open-ended developmentalism that the theory of evolution implies.

In *Outlines of an Historical View of the Progress of the Human Mind*, Condorcet argues also from the materialism of the *sensibilité physique*, and he argues that the development of a society is subject to the same laws as the individual development of faculties. From historical determinism proceed "perpetual variations." Condorcet says that "no bounds have been fixed to the improvement of the human faculties . . . the perfectibility of man is absolutely indefinite."[11]

In the *Appeal*, Hays joins Wollstonecraft in the contention that to raise women from mental degradation is to release them from political and economic bondage as well. From this context of political philosophy, a historicist conception of humankind and human institutions emerges, and so does a hermeneutical philosophy whereby interpretation is seen as a vital political act. Like Shelley in the first chapter of *A Philosophical View of Reform*, Condorcet says that the historical form of conception is necessary for a philosophical understanding of political history.

Condorcet's *Outlines of an Historical View* divides human history into ten epochs—a period of hordes, a pastoral epoch, a period in which writing is developed, a period in which the human mind progresses in ancient Greece, a fifth in which the sciences progress until their decline in the Christian dark ages, an epoch that culminates in the

restoration of learning after the Crusades, a revival of learning that includes the invention of the printing press, an epoch "to the Period when the Sciences and Philosophy threw off the Yoke of Authority" (178), a "Ninth Epoch: From the Time of Descartes, to the Formation of the French Republic" (224), and the tenth epoch, "Future Progress of Mankind" (316).

Condorcet explains how it is that historicism produces not advocacy but rather understanding of intellectual formations in a context of historical change: "from the general laws of the development of our faculties, certain prejudices must necessarily spring up in each stage of our progress, and extend their seductive influence beyond that stage." He explains the reactionary operations of ideology in this way: "men retain the errors of their infancy, their country, and the age in which they live, long after the truths necessary to the removal of those errors are acknowledged" (16). Referring in his *Essay on Christianity* to "national and religious predilections which render the multitude both deaf and blind" (7:243), Shelley follows Condorcet on this point. Major poems, including *Hellas*, which juxtaposes religions and thematizes their historical vanishing, are about that historicizing conception.

Here is one example of Godwin's pursuing the same point: "There is a degree of improvement real and visible in the world. This is particularly manifest, in the history of the civilized part of mankind, during the last three centuries. The taking of Constantinople by the Turks (1453) dispersed among European nations, the small fragment of learning, which was, at that time, shut up within the walls of this metropolis. The discovery of printing was nearly contemporary with that event. These two circumstances greatly favored the reformation of religion, which gave an irrecoverable shock to the empire of superstition and implicit obedience."[12] In *A Philosophical View of Reform*, Shelley almost precisely reproduces this historical account from Godwin (2:5ff.), an account also mirrored in Condorcet's historical explanations.

The issues involve political justice and also literary art. In the *Essay on Christianity*, Shelley explains some implications of this historicist theory regarding the rhetorical forms that contingency mandates for writers who would overthrow those reigning prejudices. He writes that "the established religion of the country in which I write renders it dangerous to subject oneself to the imputation of . . . abolishing old [gods] . . . the metaphysician and the moralist . . . may . . . receive something analogous to the bowl of hemlock for the reward of his labors" (6:241). In consequence Shelley prescribes for politically insurrectionary discourse a cloaked form: A revolutionary writer adjusts his language and his forms to their social and historical context and "secures the prejudices of his auditors"; Shelley notes that "all reformers have been compelled to practice this misrepresentation" (6:243).

The issues involve literary art, but also political justice. Not only rhetorical form, but also the content of understanding is determined by the historical idea. Shelley writes that, during the French Revolution, "the oppressed, having been rendered brutal, ignorant, servile and bloody by long slavery . . . arose and took a dreadful revenge on their oppressors." He explains the reciprocal determination of morality and material conditions: this pernicious desire for revenge "arose from the same source as their other miseries and errors and affords an additional proof of the necessity of that long-delayed change" (7:13), which is of course the democratic revolution. As Shelley says in a letter of the same year, both the foundations of society and the superstructure of ideational forms need to be overthrown (Shelley to Leigh Hunt, May 1, 1820, *PBSL* 2:191).

Among the *ideologistes,* the act of interpretation is positively advocated and equally positively politicized. The condition of being that historical materialism describes for human experience entails an exigency of interpretation: because mental, moral, political, and material things are produced by forces operating historically, they require exegesis. The meanings of mental and material things are the determining forces that produced them. To understand anything, therefore, is to perceive the determinants of its production. As Plotinus once said, "finding everything to be made up of materials and a shaping form, . . . one naturally asks whence comes the shaping form"; "produced is to producing principle as matter is to form."[13] In the philosophy of the *ideologistes* and later in Shelley's *A Philosophical View of Reform* and *Hellas,* the producing principle is history.

I suggest, therefore, that Marx makes a mistake in the *Theses on Feuerbach* when he characterizes the French materialists and after them Feuerbach as mechanistic in their explanatory model, in contrast to his own dialectical explanations. The *sensibilité physique* in the arguments of the *philosophes* did entail a dialectical activity of thought and thing, the conformations of mentality configuring and in that sense determining material formations. The *philosophes* did construct a model of activity, action, force, and production, in place of a model of static and passive machinery. This fact about the explanatory model of the *philosophes* is something that Marx is concerned to conceal or deny, but it is something that it will be valuable to recover, as it is centrally important for interpretation of the ideological argumentation of the French writers and the English—Godwin, Hays, Shelley—who carry on their line of argument.

Shelley quotes Holbach to illustrate the contention wherein historicity mandates a hermeneutic response to the social world: "Man's earliest theology made him at first fear and adore the very elements and material and gross objects. . . . their anxious imagination labors continuously to create for itself chimeras which plague them until their knowledge of nature disabuses them of the fantoms which they have always so vainly adored." The "educated person ceases to be superstitious."[14] Likewise in *Hellas,* Ahasuerus and Shelley alike disavow any belief in supernatural agency, and Shelley's own disavowal of Christianity, in his notes to that play, opens a critical distance on passages including the famous chorus "The world's great age begins anew" (lines 1060-1101). This chorus voices a reactionary desire that Shelley's historicism discredits; his play historicizes and therefore relativizes such illusions, assimilating Christianity with pagan and Mahometan myths. *Hellas* does not endorse any of these religions or their codes of superstitious abstraction. The operation of the Greek chorus's ideological framework, like the operation of Mahmud's interpretive scheme, is shown to be constructed of socially and temporally relative thought-forms. The play is about the succession of belief systems, and not the credibility of any of them; the succession disallows the credibility. As Doris Lessing has said, "the merest glance at history would have told them . . . that their certitudes were temporary."[15]

The conceptual content of that passage in *Hellas* is an argument for the political act of interpretation; cognition does not stop at the ingestion of a signifying form but proceeds by way of historical dialectic to a construction of the "producing principle" that is its meaning. In Shelley's quotation from Holbach, the example is the myth of deity; in *Hellas,* examples include the Greek Christian's ideologically determined desire for the stability of eternity in the face of historical change. The desire to evade and to deny historical change, under the form of superstition and idealist delusion, is treated critically in the play, as a product of historical forces.

For Shelley and for the *ideologistes,* interpretations arrive at both skepticism and a theory of evolution: in *Hellas,* as in Volney's *The Ruins,* "Worlds on worlds are rolling ever / From creation to decay" (lines 197-98). For these two contentions—skepticism and evolutionary theory—the form of the interpretive operation is a higher order meaning. The largest contention of this school of political philosophy—which is the school of Holbach, Helvétius, Godwin, Hays, and Shelley—is the contention that cultural forms are products of cultural forces and that political progress depends upon the hermeneutic operation that discloses those cultural forces and their temporality.

Whatever the particular reference, therefore, that a Shelley poem or a Hays novel might make, whatever its contentions (about George III, or the Peterloo massacre, or property law, or rape), a higher-order level of meaning is advocacy of interpretation. Shelley's poems, like the poetry and drama and fiction of many of his contemporaries and predecessors in the radical movement in England, are designed to induce hermeneutic acts. They are in that way *about* the interpretive operations that they produce, and this sequence (I repeat) is a political act because of the dialectical theory of ideological forms in which it is grounded and toward whose goals it aims its interventions.

Notes

1. [Paul Henri Thiry, Baron d'Holbach], *The System of Nature; or The Laws of the Moral and Physical World. Translated from the French of M. Mirabaud* (London: G. Kearsley, 1797); *Christianity Unveiled;*

Being an Examination of the Principles and Effects of the Christian Religion. Translated from the French of Boulanger, by W. M. Johnson (London: Richard Carlile, 1819).

2. William Godwin, *Cursory Strictures on the Charge Delivered by Lord Chief Justice Eyre* (London: Daniel Isaac Eaton, 1794) (first published in the *Morning Chronicle,* October 21, 1794); *Considerations on Lord Grenville's and Mr. Pitt's Bills* (London: Joseph Johnson, 1795).

3. Godwin to Thelwall, September 18, 1794, quoted by William St Clair, *The Godwins and the Shelleys: A Biography of a Family* (1989; Baltimore: The Johns Hopkins Univ. Press, 1991), 127.

4. For accounts of Mary Hays, see Gina Luria's introduction to Hays's *Appeal* (New York: Garland, 1974); Jane Spencer, "Mary Hays," in *British Women Writers: A Critical Reference Guide,* ed. Janet Todd (New York: Continuum [Frederick Ungar], 1989); and Terence Allan Hoagwood's introduction to Hays's *The Victim of Prejudice* (Delmar, N.Y.: Scholars' Facsimiles, 1990). Gary Kelly, *Woman, Writing, and Revolution* 1790-1827 (Oxford: Clarendon Press, 1993) appeared after the present essay was written, and discusses Hays in Chapter 3.

5. Mary Hays, *Letters and Essays, Moral and Miscellaneous* (1793; rpt. New York: Garland, 1974), 19-20.

6. Mary Wollstonecraft, *A Vindication of the Rights of Men* (London: Joseph Johnson, 1790), 19.

7. Paul Henri Thiry, Baron d'Holbach, *The System of Nature; or, Laws of the Moral and Physical World,* trans. H. D. Robinson (Boston: J. P. Mendum, 1853), 13-14.

8. William Godwin, *Enquiry Concerning Political Justice and Its Influence on Morals and Happiness,* ed. F. E. L. Priestley (Toronto: Univ. of Toronto Press, 1946), 1:26.

9. *Political Justice.* I:vi-vii.

10. Ibid. 14-5, 5-6.

11. Marie Jean Antoine Nicolas Caritat. Marquis de Condorcet, *Outlines of an Historical View of the Progress of the Human Mind,* translator anonymous (London: Joseph Johnson, 1795), 3-4.

12. *Political Justice.* 1:450-51.

13. Plotinus in *The Essential Plotinus,* trans. Elmer O'Brien (Indianapolis, Ind.: Hackett 1961), 18-19.

14. I quote Holbach's *System of Nature,* as quoted in Shelley's note to *Queen Mab,* from the translation by E. F. Bennett that is reproduced in *Shelley's Prose; or, The Trumpet of a Prophecy.* ed. David Lee Clark (Albuquerque: Univ. of New Mexico Press, 1954), 354.

15. Doris Lessing, *Prisons We Choose to Live Inside* (Montreal: CBC Enterprises, 1986), 23.

Abbreviations

We have adopted *Shelley's Poetry and Prose,* ed. Donald H. Reiman and Sharon B. Powers, 3rd ed. rev. (New York: W. W. Norton, 1981) as a standard for references to works by Shelley quoted in this volume. Occasionally, authors will refer to other Shelley texts not included in that edition. For other poetry, we have referred to the Oxford Standard Authors edition of *The Complete Poetical Works of Shelley,* ed. Thomas Hutchinson (1905); rev. G. B. Martthews (1970); cited as *OSA.* Citations for other prose works are keyed to the Julian Edition of *The Complete Works of Percy Bysshe Shelley,* ed. Roger Ingpen and Walter E. Peck, 10 volumes (London: Ernest Benn, 1926-30). For correspondence, references are to *The Letters of Percy Bysshe Shelley,* ed. Frederick L. Jones (Oxford: Clarendon Press, 1956)—cited as *PBSL*—and *The Letters of Mary Wollstonecraft Shelley,* ed. Betty T. Bennett (Baltimore: The Johns Hopkins University Press, 1980-88), cited as *MWSL.* Byron's poetry is quoted from *The Complete Poetical Works of Lord Byron,* ed. Jerome J. McGann (Oxford: Clarendon Press, 1980-93), and his familiar prose from *Byron's Letters and Journals,* ed. Leslie Marchand (Cambridge: Harvard University Press, 1972-94), cited as *BLJ.*

Sandra Sherman (essay date 1997)

SOURCE: Sherman, Sandra. "The Feminization of 'Reason' in Hays's *The Victim of Prejudice.*" *The Centennial Review* 41, no. 1 (winter 1997): 143-72.

[*In the following essay, Sherman discusses* The Victim of Prejudice *as a departure from Hays's belief that reason was instrumental for achieving the independence of women.*]

Mary Hays's novel, **The Victim of Prejudice** (1799), is read alongside a cadre of "revolutionary" texts inspired by events in France, rebutting the *Reflections* of Edmund Burke (1790) which idealized patriarchalism.[1] Yet its address to texts which challenged Burke, and aligned themselves with Mary Wollstonecraft's *Vindication of the Rights of Woman* (1792), is pessimistic, complicated by what Eleanor Ty terms a "change in climate by the end of the 1790s." After the Reign of Terror and Napoleonic invasions, "no longer were the revolutionaries as optimistic in their belief in reason and the perfectibility of man as at the beginning of the decade."[2] Hays's rendering of "reason" as fractured into unmanageable, incommensurate counters that shift and collide, distinguishes **The Victim of Prejudice** even from contemporary, less optimistic texts. She focuses on cognitive breakdown, evincing a universe resistant to woman's mental appropriation, inclined towards excruciating ironies of entrapment. As Ty notes, the heroine's "learning has only made her aware of the peculiar social conditions which contribute to her plight," rather than releasing her from it.³

In Hays's postrevolutionary epistemology, women's mental exertion is subject to distortion by affective imperatives that reinscribe patriarchal limits, subverting strategies—represented in hopeful, revolutionary terms of "reason"—through which women might become autonomous subjects. The heroine, Mary, cites the vulnerability of reason when confronted by conflicting claims of guardian and lover, both of whom invoke it:

> . . . my reason became weakened by contradictory principles. Thus, the moment the dictates of virtue, direct and simple, are perplexed by false scruples and artificial distinctions, the mind becomes entangled in an inextricable labyrinth, to which there is no clue, and whence there is no escape.⁴

In this article, I trace cumulative warpings of reason in *The Victim of Prejudice* that render it "perplexed," and cast "the mind" as "an inextricable labyrinth" troped by patriarchal suggestion. I examine Hays's departure from texts promoting reason as instrumental to woman's moral/financial "independence," and her use of imaginative prose to "[dis]entangle" tensions created by her own revolutionary exhortations.

In Wollstonecraft's *Vindication,* as in Hays's version of the same argument, reason and independence are co-ordinate, linked through a program of education focused on autonomy.⁵ *The Victim of Prejudice* refuses this position, depicting women's reason as constituted by ideology premised on female subjection. "Reason" is a mirage, reproducing male-engendered norms that seem "natural."⁶ The displacement is crucial to Hays's postrevolutionary rejoinder.⁷ Deploying fiction as a heuristic, *The Victim of Prejudice* tests the theoretical bases of "revolution" in emotionally-fraught encounters with dominant norms. It weighs women's ability to pursue "reason" when historically validated, seemingly evident imperatives alter the contours of reason.⁸

Thus while the text challenges Burke, it also takes issue (on a practical level) with texts (including the author's own) whose politics of "reason" it would ideally adopt. By casting as problematic the notion of female subjectivity premised on rational pursuit of virtuous autonomy, *The Victim of Prejudice* resonates with Wollstonecraft's posthumous novel, *Maria, Or the Wrongs of Woman* (1799), which bemoans the deadening (but not dead) hand of ideology that the *Vindication* still sought to defeat. *Maria*'s most vivid minor character, the former prostitute Jemima, recalls "independence, which only consisted in choosing the street in which I should wander, or the roof, when I had money, in which I should hide my head."⁹ Both novels show women as "entangled," compromised subjects. *The Victim of Prejudice,* however, educes the irony that compromise inheres in the touted instrument of female subjectivity, "reason," a radically unstable formation as likely to entail "entangl[ing]" imperatives as to stand against them.¹⁰

From Hays's ironic perspective, women's approach to autonomy is circular. Seeking shelter from patriarchal institutions, women are drawn to "enlightened" men—expositors of "reason"—whose power to provide shelter *depends on* their position relative to patriarchal institutions. "Rational" autonomy falls into affectivity, entailing a train of dependence that warps the ideological revolution required to escape it. Even when women regard themselves as rational, "rationality" short-circuits. Female autonomy cannot therefore be realized, as in the *Vindication,* merely by women's accession to reason since "reason" is always already contingent.

When Mary's guardian, Mr. Raymond, claims to "shelter her from [the] world," Mary calibrates his claim against his dim view of her own capacity. Automatically, she acquiesces in Raymond's assertion, accepting patriarchal benevolence—compromising her independence, though she does not see it that way—instead of challenging patriarchal formations that make "shelter" necessary:

> "No sir," replied [Mr. Raymond], "I have not the happiness of calling this lovely girl mine, except by adoption. She is an unfortunate orphan, whom it is equally my duty and my delight to shelter from a world that will hardly be inclined to do her justice, and upon which she has few claims."
>
> There was something in the tone of Mr. Raymond's voice . . . that thrilled through my heart with a new and indescribable sensation. . . . a powerful and irresistible emotion; throwing my arms around the neck of my benefactor, I burst into tears, and sobbed upon his bosom.
>
> (8)

Grateful to be saved from "[in]justice," Mary accepts that "she has few claims," that the "world" negates her autonomy, making "shelter" her best hope. The excluded middle in Raymond's argument—that rational women *make* claims—eludes Mary, stirred to acquiesce by a spirit of deference. This spirit, a "powerful and irresistible emotion," inhibits Mary's capacity to calculate undeferentially, outside affective relationships and outside (what amounts to the same thing) patriarchal ideology. Her response, reproducing ideological convention, concedes emotional dependence, a concession fostered by Raymond. Moreover, out of love, Mary is predisposed to crediting Raymond, the conduit of a disempowering ideology and the source of Mary's fear—two sides of the same coin.¹¹ Fearing injustice, encouraged to do so, she falls back onto patriarchal "shelter," literally onto its "bosom."

In evoking the rational/emotional matrix through which Mary defines existence, Hays configures a paradox. In the 1790s, "reason," "independence," had altered the lexicon of female subjectivity, as it had regarding subjectivity in general. Yet a world "hardly inclined to do . . . justice" without reference to gender and class, precipitates emotional strategies in women (rationalizations, not reason) that constrain their potential to reason independently. The grey area between ideologies—"revolution" and accommodation—constitutes the text's mental terrain, presented as Mary's own autobiographical struggle.[12] Reason and independence subsist as *discourse,* discussed, valorized, evoked; but they are warped by persistent necessity. In the end, reason and affectivity reduce to a false dichotomy, absorbed by patriarchal norms.

Raymond becomes the pivotal figure in Mary's address to revolutionary discourse, encouraging her to apply reason and be true to her own best principles ("amidst the vicissitudes and the calamities of life, a firm and an independent mind is an invaluable treasure" [38]), even as he warns her away from independence as potentially ruinous ("the imperious usages of society, with a stern voice, now command us to pause" [31]). As rendered by Hays, Raymond personifies the dilemma of postrevolutionary patriarchy: compelled by the new logic of female subjectivity, it cannot yet imagine (due in part to its own passivity) that such logic might prevail. Women are caught in the cross-current, their education liberalized while they are effectively constrained. When Raymond tells Mary that "certain prejudices" forbid her marrying despite a mutual love, Mary cites the ironies of Raymond's position, which extend to that of enlightened patriarchy generally:

> Unhappy parent! unhappy tutor! forced into contradictions that distort and belie thy wisest precepts, that undermine and defeat thy most sagacious purposes!—While the practice of the world opposes the principles of the sage, education is a fallacious effort, morals an empty theory, and sentiment a delusive dream.
>
> (33)

Raymond's recoil from the "wisest precepts," debasing his education of Mary into a "fallacious effort," demands that Mary negotiate the "contradictions."[13] That is, Raymond manifests patriarchy's persistent power to shape discourse (even that [en]gendered by women, e.g. Wollstonecraft) and women's response to it. Even after he lays down (and follows) social "prejudices," Raymond continues to invoke women's rational independence ("a firm and independent mind"), tailoring its meaning, however, to serve his prescription for Mary. Mary is placed in, and accepts, a reactive status, continually acknowledging Raymond's "claims" on her capacity to discern (his "just and irresistible claims" [40], "just claims upon my fortitude" [45]), even when she fails to understand (and struggles to accept) his sociology.[14]

No study of *The Victim of Prejudice* examines Raymond's relation to postrevolutionary epistemology and to "claims" made on women's touted capacity to reason independently.[15] I shall do that, setting Hays's text against Wollstonecraft's prescriptions for women's autonomy, and Hays's struggle with the issue up to *The Victim of Prejudice.*

. . . . .

The *Vindication* defines subjectivity as epistemological agency. "Every being may become virtuous by the exercise of its own reason." "The most perfect education. . . .

enable[s] the individual to attain such habits of virtue as will render it independent" [103]. Subjectivity is a rational, autonomous address to the world. Wollstonecraft bridles when women concede autonomy, eschewing reason for "sentiments" of patriarchal ideology: "Indignantly have I heard women argue in the same track as men, and adopt the sentiments that brutalize them, with all the pertinacity of ignorance" (206). If ignorance were dispelled, women could snap "the adamantine chain of destiny" by which they "are never to exercise their own reason, never to be independent, never to rise above opinion" (121). The discursive "track" on which ideology runs—"opinion"—ratifies women's irrational turn: "by the prevailing opinion, [women assume] that they were created rather to feel than to reason" (155). "Feeling" is consequent upon entrapment in discourse. Reason overcomes discourse, entailing autonomous self-reflexivity.

Such logic pivots on "rational will," a perfected agency that "only bows to God" (121). Women should, therefore, "acquire virtues which they may call their own, for how can a rational being be ennobled by anything that is not obtained by its *own* exertions?" (141, orig. emph). Reason personalizes the "discerning [of] truth. Every individual is in this respect a world in itself" (143). If a rational self is a "world," woman's subordination is contingent, persistent only because "man is ever placed between her and reason" (143).

Male mediation casts women as "dependent . . . on man [for] . . . advice . . . neglecting the duties that reason points out" (155). By opposing male "advice" to neutered "reason," Wollstonecraft assumes that female reason can be independent of "prevailing opinion," i.e. ideology. Hence she exhorts women to act *on themselves,* as if from a standpoint outside ideology:

> It is time to effect a revolution in female manners—time to restore to them their lost dignity—and make them, as a part of the human species, labour by *reforming themselves* to reform the world.[16]
>
> (135, italics added)

She assumes the possibility of and endeavors to construct conditions for unmediated female subjectivity. Her project (unlike Hays's) elides the notion that such conditions may irretrievably be "prejudiced" against autonomy.

The invocation to "labour," as a type of extension into the "world," concatenates the pursuit of autonomy with material production. In Wollstonecraft's logic, independence is both moral ("virtuous") and economic (i.e. "virtuous and useful" [264]):

> [T]o render her really virtuous and useful . . . she must not be dependent on her husband's bounty for her subsistence during his life, or support after his death; for how can a being be generous who has nothing of its own? or virtuous who is not free?
>
> (264)

The co-ordinate relationship between moral and economic agency, in which both are required to constitute the autonomous female subject, requires that women be educated for "useful" work. Reason has an instrumental concomitant, enabling a woman to survive even in adversity: "a proper education, or, to speak with more precision, a well-stored mind, would enable a single woman to support a life with dignity" (117). For Wollstonecraft, exhortation transmogrifies into outcome: a woman *can* work, can "support a life," provided her mind is "well-stored." "Education" becomes an overdeterminant, obscuring systemic impediments to women's initiative such as the gendered division of labor.[17]

Wollstonecraft castigates a government that "does not provide for honest, independent women, by encouraging them to fill respectable stations" (267). What "stations"? She ignores evidence that women's employability was collapsing in the industrial revolution. As Clara Reeve noted, "there are very few trades for women; the men have usurped two-thirds of those that used to belong to them; the remainder are overstocked."[18] The *Vindication* constructs a Robinson Crusoe myth for women, suggesting they can achieve autonomy merely by learning it.[19]

Contingencies elided in Wollstonecraft's analysis erupt into *The Victim of Prejudice,* evincing a persistent *ancien regime* and an economy administered by men. The novel's disillusion stands against Hays's early texts, which comport with the *Vindication,* invoking (sometimes skittishly) reason's liberatory potential and eschewing the cognitive dissonance broached in *The Victim of Prejudice.* Hays's *Letters and Essays* (1793) assumes that "reason" is uninflected by "feelings" and able to dominate them: "Is there any cause to apprehend that we may subject our feelings too much to the guidance of reason?"[20] From the hindsight of Mary's ordeal in *The Victim of Prejudice, Letters and Essays* sounds idealizing, too attentive to revolutionary formulae: "Let those who love influence seek it by surer methods; bolts and bars may confine for a time the feeble body, but can never enchain the noble, the free-born mind" (23). "Mind" is the constitutive site of autonomy, isolating "reason" from needs that conventionally entail women's dependence. Reason becomes the avatar of revolution ("it is time for degraded woman to assert her right to reason, in this general diffusion of light and knowledge" [84]); it constitutes freedom from dependence, assuring its own purity.

In her first novel, *The Memoirs of Emma Courtney* (1796), Hays still accepts the possibility of mental purity. Emma's "philosopher" friend, Mr. Francis, tells her:

> He, who tamely resigns his understanding to the guidance of another, sinks at once, from the dignity of a rational being, to a mechanical puppet, moved at pleasure on the wires of a mechanical operator.
>
> (49)

Echoing the *Vindication,* Mr. Francis insists that "*Obedience,* is a word, which ought never to have had existence" (49).

Yet *Emma Courtney* is less convinced than *Letters and Essays* that "reason" subserves independence. While Emma invokes "reason," she enacts its inevitable defusion by patriarchy. Her text wavers, evincing frustration with reason. While experiencing throes of unrequited love for Augustus Harley, Emma insists that "reason and self-respect sustain me" (127), but the claim seems rote, self-flattery to quell uncertainty. She is in fact becoming unhinged, and admits that "I am, at least, a reasoning maniac: perhaps the most dangerous species of insanity" (142). The notion of a "reasoning maniac," evinced in the brief that Emma compiles for Harley touting her perfection as a lover, constitutes an ironic retort to Hays's question in *Letters and Essays*: "whether . . . we may subject our feelings too much to the guidance of reason." Clearly, the answer is yes. Reason *can* be implicated in "feelings"; it can exacerbate obsession into "insanity." In so doing, it assumes an ironic relation to emotion: rather than "subject[ing] our feelings," it makes them grotesque.

Upon admitting an "insanity" linked to reason, Emma affiliates with a loss of autonomy generic to women, admonishing Mr. Francis:

> Why call woman, miserable woman, oppressed, and impotent, woman—*crushed, and then insulted*—why call her to *independence*—which not nature, but the barbarous accursed laws of society, have denied her? *This is mockery!*
>
> (143)

The link between reason and "emancipation" invoked by Emma even *in extremis,* snaps when Emma subjects it to "laws of society." Intransigent social formations—"laws"—overwhelm theory. Her outburst against independence issues to the "philosopher" Mr. Francis, who is cast as insensitive for advice that fails to distinguish between prerogatives of men and women. "Laws" keep women in subjection, whether or not they adopt "reason." The view from women's experience, rather than from untested "reason," establishes enlightened discourse as gendered, its heroism ill-suited to women.

Like *The Victim of Prejudice, Emma Courtney* depicts reason's frustration in a male-dominated regime of solicitous, ultimately disempowering concern. Harley dismisses Emma's desire to stanch her dependency; it is deferred to another day with her silent complicity, motivated by her respect for and emotional attachment to Harley:

> I struggled for more fortitude—hinted at the narrowness of my fortune—at my wish to exert my talents in some way, that should procure me a less dependent situation—spoke of my active spirit—of my abhorrence of a life of indolence and vacuity.
>
> He insisted on my waving [sic] these subjects for the present. "There would be time enough, in future, for their consideration. In the mean while, I might go on improving myself, and whether present; or absent, might depend upon him, for every assistance in his power."
>
> (74-75)

The encounter, parallel to Mary's conversation with Raymond, initiates a pattern in Hays's fiction in which male "shelter" blunts female contemplation of independence. In both cases, a woman's gratefulness and affectivity consume energies that would otherwise, necessarily, be channeled towards the world:

> [Harley's] soothing kindness, aided by the affectionate attentions of my friend, gradually, lulled my mind into tranquility. My bosom was agitated, only, by a slight and sweet emotion—like the gentle undulations of the ocean, when the winds, that swept over its ruffled surface, are hushed into repose.
>
> (75)

Both Mary and Emma experience emotional repletion in the male's sheltering gesture, assimilating themselves into stillness suggestive of sexual consummation. Indeed, Emma's reference to "gentle undulations . . . hushed into repose" bespeaks a desire for Harley, sublimated into a lapsed "struggle" for independence. The "vacuity" of which Emma complains—mental and economic—is valenced to emotional vacuity; when it is provisionally filled, insistent "revolutionary" concern abates. As Emma directs her mental capacities towards a passion for Harley, she rationalizes that she cannot be the person of revolutionary myth:

> The mind must have an object:—should I desist from my present pursuit [of Harley], after all it has cost me, for what can I change it? I feel, that I am neither a philosopher, nor a heroine—but a *woman, to whom education has given a sexual character.* . . . Ambition cannot stimulate me.
>
> (117)

Like Mary, Emma excludes the middle term: neither abject nor heroic, she could still pursue an "ambition" encompassing autonomy. But she accepts affectivity as her limit, ironically pursuing Harley instead of enterprise.

Hays's last important text prior to *The Victim of Prejudice* was the *Appeal to the Men of Great Britain in Behalf of Women* (1798). While the text acknowledges obstacles to autonomy, it reasserts the confident spirit of *Letters and Essays*:

> [A] development of mind would undoubtedly enable [women] to see and reason upon what principles, all the other regulations of society were formed,—which however they may deviate in execution, are evidently founded on justice and humanity—and would consequently enable them to bring home and apply those principles to the situation of their sex in general.
>
> (97)

In the *Appeal,* "justice" is female, dispelling female despair:

> But shall the time never come—Ah! surely it must—when the mysterious veil formed by law, by prejudice, and by precedent, shall be rent asunder,—when justice herself shall appear in all the beauty of simplicity. . . .
>
> (100)

The logic constructs a Whiggish ascent towards equality, a knowledge shared with men of civil, cultural mysteries. That is, where men and women are educated towards the same (rational) end, their social capacities will be the same.

Together, the three texts preceding *The Victim of Prejudice* constitute a troubled matrix, in which Hays valiantly asserted the imminence of revolution, even as she articulated its dissipation within the affective/economic limitations of women. Thus *The Victim of Prejudice* is a key text, resolving Hays's discursively unstable relation to revolutionary ideals. It inverts the premises of Hays's nonfiction, exposing them to psychological imperatives of real human beings, intensifying the reproach to revolutionary discourse in *Emma Courtney.*[21]

. . . . .

Chapter 1 of *The Victim of Prejudice* begins with Mary's education. Raymond, who has "contempt for vulgar prejudices," encourages in her "a cultivated understanding, and a vigorous intellect" (5). Yet lingering over such enlightenment are signs that Raymond's "contempt" for prejudice is tinctured with acquiescence, a weakness that could perplex Mary's "understanding." When Mr. Pelham presents his sons, Edmund and William, for tutoring by Raymond, he requires they be kept from "improper acquaintance, or humiliating connections" (8). He enquires into Mary's status. Raymond identifies her as adopted, "an unfortunate orphan" whom it is his "duty and delight to shelter" (8). Mary, however, bursts into tears, and perceives her sudden incongruity when Raymond recoils from the passion "he had unwarily excited" (9). Raymond, it seems, wishes not to display before Pelham the attachment between himself and Mary. Withdrawing his embrace, he "propose[s] that [Mary] should accompany the young gentlemen into the garden." In the text's first ironic reversal, the "garden" becomes an anti-paradise, a place of expulsion from fatherly shelter:

> For the first time in my life, I had been sensible to an embarrassment, and a temporary feeling of depression and apprehension; a prelude, as it should seem, to those anxieties and sorrows which have since pursued me with unmitigated severity. . . .
>
> (9)

Implicit in Raymond's action and the "depression" it causes is Mary's sense that paternal "shelter" is unstable, that at a fundamental level fathers may reverse premises (and promises). Raymond's bivalent shelter/expulsion instantiates the logic of his relationship with Mary. As the text proceeds, his preceptorship subverts counsel that it also promotes, leaving Mary (as she is with William) "weakened by contradictory principles."

William, with whom Mary shares an intense affection, compounds Mary's early exposure to epistemological uncertainty. Tempted by grapes in Sir Peter Osborne's greenhouse, he urges Mary to filch them, appealing to a mutual affection. Mary capitulates: "To a young casuist these reasonings bore a specious appearance: assuming the respectable forms of generosity and tenderness, they dazzled and finally prevailed" (13-14). The passage evokes the chameleon quality of "reasonings," the capacity of "specious" arguments to "assum[e] . . . respectable forms." Its movement depends on Mary's fascination with "reasonings" (they "dazzled"), and its ironic consequence: her response to a man's "reason" through emotion, whereby his urgings seem to rise from her own.[22]

Yet if Mary is a "casuist," it is to vindicate "right" and "wrong"—in practical terms, "justice." Returning home, wounded by Sir Peter who discovered the theft, she lauds "blows acquired in the cause of humanity and friendship" (22) and asks: "Have you not taught me, dear father, that, in the cause of *right* we should contemn bodily pain?" (23). Mary idealizes absolutes, the correlative of "cause[s]." Well into her narrative, she reflects the *Appeal*'s conviction that "justice herself shall appear." Only later does she acknowledge that reason's revolutionary coordinate, justice, is also implicated in gender and class. Such early optimism explains why only "temporary . . . apprehension" grips her on expulsion to a garden—a "world"—of "anxieties and sorrows."

Writing her memoirs from a perspective of a subject in collapse ("Despair nerves my hand; Despair justifies the deed" [168]), Mary reconstructs the mental processes of agents whose minds affected hers. In the chapter preceding the dreadful encounter where Raymond observes *You can never be the wife of William Pelham*" (32), Mary imagines his thoughts:

> Painful suspicions assailed him: he began to doubt whether, in cultivating my mind, in fostering a virtuous sensibility, in imbuing my heart with principles of justice and rectitude, he had not been betraying my happiness.
>
> (25)

The passage imaginatively recreates the enlightened male's dilemma: having "cultivat[ed]" a woman's mind and imparted notions of justice, Raymond suspects such notions may backfire. He responds to revolutionary discourse, aware of a disjunction between the life of the "mind" and life. The virtuous man is in a bind. Unable to ignore texts such as the **Vindication** and **Appeal,** neither can he accommodate their logic to his own experience.[23] Where "prejudice" is normative (Mary is an orphan, William is wealthy) such men reinscribe injustice. In Raymond's custody, Mary's education becomes an instrument of ironic inversion, implicating revolution (and its male supporters) in women's emotional, epistemological breakdown.

Yet whatever misgivings Mary projects onto Raymond of "betraying my happiness," he initially adopts the revolutionary line, arguing that Mary was educated towards "happiness":

> The first and most earnest purpose of my cares and precepts has been, by forming you to virtue, to secure your *happiness*: for this *end,* I have laboured to awaken,

excite, and strengthen, your mind. An enlightened intellect . . . affords us an inexhaustible source of power, dignity, and enjoyment.

> (28)

The problem with Raymond's formulation, which he links to "habits of self-government and independence of mind" (28), is that he equates "independence" with rational submission to prejudice, a compromise of "independence" that acknowledges the undertow of class and gender. In effect, Mary must reason her way out of reason's prerogatives, deny passion for a man above her station, find "happiness" with less "power, dignity, and enjoyment." While Raymond tells her to "triumph over . . . passion . . . yield only to the dictates of right reason and truth" (29), he deploys revolutionary language to reinforce the *status quo,* endorsing *non*-revolutionary ends that jibe with Burkean apologetics.

Mary's response betrays the depth of Raymond's ambivalence towards female autonomy. Having raised her to be "independent," he clearly imparted as well an allegiance to himself entailing patriarchal conventions of deference. Mary exclaims:

> Name the sacrifice you require; distrust not the mind you have formed; your dictates and those of *reason* are the same, they have ever been uniform and invariable. Behold me, my father, resigned to your will!
>
> (30)

In this jarring passage, Mary makes no distinction between mentor and patriarch, deploying language of abject submission as she cleaves to Raymond's "reason." She is guided by emotion. Ironically, though Raymond warned her away from "passion," he welcomes (is "visibly affected" [30] by) her zealous embrace of his "dictates." In this embrace, Mary recapitulates Raymond's inversion of revolutionary language, using it to recuperate patriarchal norms. The continuity of Mary's mental processes with Raymond's is stunning. Mary abdicates rational autonomy to "the mind you have formed," to "dictates" that "are the same" as "reason." While this cannot seem "reasonable" to Raymond, Hays does not mean it to; his reaction evinces the enlightened male's complicity in female dependence.

Irony compounds as Raymond admits that if "right reason and truth" must "triumph over . . . passion," it is *unreason* that dictates such "triumph." Alluding to his pledge to Pelham to preserve William from "any improper acquaintance, or humiliating connections," Raymond states:

> Were it not for certain prejudices, which the world has agreed to respect and to observe, I should perceive your growing tenderness with delight . . . but I am responsible to another tribunal than that of *reason* and my own heart for the sentiments and conduct of this young man, and I dare not betray my trust. . . . [T]he imperious usages of society, with a stern voice, now command us to pause. Her mandates, often irrational, are, nevertheless despotic: contemn them,—the hazard is certain, and the penalty may be tremendous.[24]
>
> (31)

Raymond accepts William as a pupil because he needs income;[25] he enforces Pelham's prejudices ("the imperious usages of society") not out of conviction, but in deference to money and power—to Burkean class structure—as to law, "another tribunal." Yet why does Raymond accommodate this "tribunal" of injustice? He *could* refuse Pelham, whose exactions are repugnant to enlightened aims.[26] However, Raymond is willing to compromise ideology, to teach reason but accept the "often irrational." He asks Mary to do likewise, instantiating the predicament of the enlightened man: mediating between classes and genders, he may "betray" his own and others' autonomy (and hence revolution) under financial pressure. It is Pelham's "trust" Raymond "dare not betray."

Mary is bewildered by Raymond's advice, which he mystifies into "a subject too subtle for reasoning" (36). What could be *more* subtle than reason? In fact, subtlety is not the issue, but reeducation, an unlearning of what Mary was taught: "time and experience can only evince the propriety of my conduct" (36). Raymond shifts from inculcating "reason" to advocating its opposite, a gross empiricism subservient to ideological reality. This departs from his prior recommendation that reason be the basis of Mary's stifling her passion for William. He seems uncertain, though his compromise with Pelham suggests he was never firmly committed to reason. In any case, by opposing "reason" and "experience," Raymond evinces Hays's own tense relation to revolution, already evident in *Emma Courtney*. It is Mary, the absolutist—the Hays of the *Appeal*—who seeks to reconcile justice with her situation:

> What tyranny is this? When reason, virtue nature, sanctify its emotions, why should the heart be controlled? who dare control it? . . . For the first time in my life, I was ready to accuse my guardian of injustice and caprice. It was many hours ere I reasoned myself into more composure.
>
> (35)

But Mary's "reasoned" composure is an affective response, the consequence of love for Raymond: "I confide, without shrinking, in your judgment and affection" (37). He accepts her "shrinking" from her own "judgment," or rather, he allows her to identify with his.

In light of Raymond's recasting of "reason" as compliance with prejudice; denial of "reason" in justification of his conduct; and delight in Mary's deferral of rational autonomy, his parting words (prior to Mary's leaving his household) seem strained: "[A] firm and an independent mind is an invaluable treasure and a never-failing support" (38). What can he mean, having so disorganized and dismissed the rational life? For Raymond, the "independent mind" still yields to governing norms ("contemn them,— the hazard is certain").[27] It dwells (if uneasily) in ideological compromise, a split consciousness that allows Raymond to obey a "tribunal" he hates, eschewing "reason and my own heart." It allows him to assuage guilt—"I impose no fetters. I will trust to the rectitude of your feel-

ings" (45)—knowing that Mary, who responds through "feelings," will affiliate her mind to his: "my patron read in my eyes the law I imposed on myself" (45). Raymond wants Mary to internalize norms he cannot (without guilt) "impose," making them seem a natural consequence of Mary's moral/intellectual deference.

Away from Raymond at the Nevilles, Mary's conviction wavers. She struggles with "senseless prejudices to which I have tamely submitted, whose nature I am utterly unable to comprehend" (48). But as on the previous occasion, she "reason[s]" herself into "composure" when William (who learns of her retreat) challenges her integrity: "[Y]ou are a victim of control, you have tamely submitted to a tyranny that your heart disavows" (52). Mary responds with the fractured "reason" she has "reasoned" herself into as a result of her affection for Raymond:

> Mr. Raymond, in the sacrifice which he requires of us, is guided by considerations the most disinterested: he imposes nothing, he appeals to my reason and affections, and his claims are resistless.
>
> (53)

Mary's assertion that Raymond is "disinterested," elides his admission that he "dare not betray" Pelham's "trust." Even more basic are Mary's contradictions. If Raymond "requires" sacrifice, how is it that he "imposes nothing"? If he casts his action as "too subtle for reasoning," how is it that he "appeals to reason?" Is "reason" compatible with "resistless" "claims"? The key to Mary's denial/confusion is her pernicious coupling (at Raymond's behest) of "reason and affections," driving her to defer to Raymond, to abandon rational autonomy. In this formulation, Mary's state makes "sense": Raymond is caught in a force field of contradiction (revolution and Mr. Pelham) which he negotiates by making Mary seem to herself the initiator of "sacrifice." She struggles to naturalize the counterintuitive, to "impose" "tyranny" on herself.

The narrative of Mary's mother inscribes Mary into, indeed virtually enforces Mary's perplexed relation to Raymond. Her mother (also named Mary) regrets eloping with a cad "raised by fashion and fortune to a rank seducing to my imagination," for whom she rejected young Raymond "whose reason would have enlightened me" (63). Failure to appreciate Raymond, she believes, led to forsaken paternal shelter and a life of blasted virtue:

> Unaccustomed to reason, too weak for principle, credulous from inexperience, a stranger to the corrupt habits of society, I yielded to the mingled intoxication of my vanity and senses, quitted the paternal roof, and resigned myself to my triumphant seducer.
>
> (63)

From her prison cell, she consigns the fruit of her dissipation—Mary—to Raymond, pleading that he "cultivate her reason," "rouse her to independence," "teach her to contemn the tyranny that would impose the fetters of sex upon her mind" (69). Yet the missive's subtext complicates this plea, endorsing a "paternal roof" whose virtue devolves onto Raymond, valencing female "independence" with "enlightened" male shelter. *This is why Raymond shows Mary the letter.* If it adopts rhetoric of the *Vindication* and *Appeal,* it also speaks from the position of Raymond's compromising ideology, offering compromise as balm to "inexperience." The letter serves Raymond's ends, admonishing Mary against men "raised by fashion and fortune" (read: William), and establishing Raymond personally and generically ("the paternal roof") as proper arbiter of Mary's "independence."

Raymond uses the letter to constrain Mary's "independence"—her class-jumping attachment to William—since a consummation would challenge his sexuality, repressed since he lost Mary's mother to another wealthy, fashionable young man. Though Raymond imposes a discipline of "reason" on *Mary,* it operates through her to deny *William* sexual opportunity missed by Raymond with Mary's mother.[28] In the battle to possess Mary (Raymond her mind, William her mind and thereby her body), Mary is her mother's surrogate; "reason" masks irrational forces at work in Raymond, sublimated into paternal concern.[29] The mother's admonitions are refracted through Raymond's will to an effect she may never have intended. Hays's insight is in exposing the contingency of "reason," its potential absorption into male sexual contention. Raymond's gloss on the mother's letter is deeply ironic as he tells Mary: "In the eye of the world, the misfortunes of your birth stain your unsullied youth: it is in the dignity of your own mind that you must seek resource" (71). Not Mary's "birth," but Raymond's failure to have caused it, produces "misfortune." It precipitates his assault on her "dignity," his arrogating her "own mind" into service of *his* sexual conflicts.

Since William's contention with Raymond turns on the proper application of "reason," he turns Raymond's logic on its head, claiming that "reason indignantly revolts" at the "senseless chimera" he urges (75). Astonishingly, Mary seems to do the same:

> I do not deny that I am sensible of its injustice; an injustice that my reason and my affections equally contemn.
>
> (76)

Logically, in yet another troping of "reason," Mary is allied with William. But Raymond has so warped the rational autonomy he seems to recommend, that in her ultimate response Mary falls back on Burkean apologetics: "who am I, that I should resist . . . the customs which use has sanctioned . . . ?" (76)[30] Her posture is a stunning abdication of Wollstonecraft's "rational will," collapsing into its opposite. As if directly countering Wollstonecraft, she tells William: "it is virtue to submit to a destiny, however painful, not wilfully incurred" (77). With its reinscription of Burke and denial of his most vociferous female opponent, Mary instantiates an almost brain-dead acquiescence in the status quo. Hays depicts the power of patriarchy, operant through a single, well-meaning (but tortured) father, to disrupt forces promoting reason and justice for women.[31]

Volume 2 concerns Mary's quest for economic "justice," the chance to pursue financial independence outside marriage. She is initially optimistic: "I am young, active, healthy, and able to labour" (93). Her grit tests by way of experience prescriptions in the *Vindication* and the *Appeal.* They are sorely tried. Upon arrival in London she is kidnapped to the house of her nemesis, Osborne, who rapes and tries to confine her. But Mary rebels, claiming she will take him to law: "Think not, by feeble restraints, to fetter the body when the mind is determined and free" (117-18). Confronting this most unregenerate representative of the old order, Mary throws down the gauntlet. Responding to his taunt that residence with him has "irretrievably injured [her] reputation" (118), and to his question, "Who would support you [at law] against my wealth and influence?" (119),[32] Mary claims that her "spirit . . . rises above the sense of its wrongs," that she "will seek, by honest labour, the bread of independence" (119).

Back on the streets of London, "friendless and unknown" (121), she encounters William, who nurses her through delirium. During this time of "wandering reason" (123), her "wandering"—not "reason"—disinters history, embodied in her fallen mother: her "visionary form . . . seemed to flit before me. . . . [A]ll pallid and ghastly, with clasped hands, streaming eyes, and agonizing earnestness, she seemed to urge me to take example from her fate" (123). Mary's mother is History, the gendered, alternative trajectory to a theorized "reason" that (as Mary loses her "mind") seems almost irresistible.[33] Yet Mary interprets history as the plea of "reason" against the overdetermination of events. She "sought to recall . . . reason" (123), to reinstate "rational will." Thus William's ministrations fail. Now married to an heiress of his father's choice, he pleads with Mary to let him serve her. But Mary, intent on avoiding a "fate" as William's mistress, invokes the same rhetoric that previously turned him away: "With a mind, a resolution, yet unimpaired, I do not, *indeed I do not,* yield to despair" (128).

This is more than a refusal of William. It is a refusal to concede that her "mind" is already captured by patriarchal formations, that history *inscribed* Mary's fate when she "sacrificed" William to Raymond. *In* history, Mary succeeded her mother in Raymond's "family romance," a narrative belonging to a male. But Mary does not project from her mother's experience—does not imagine history as proleptic, the seed of emplotted narrative—and so she imagines a future "independent" of history, "determined" by her own "resolution, yet unimpaired." *The Victim of Prejudice,* not the "victim of prejudice," connects history to a woman's fate. In Mary's "determined" search for economic justice, Hays reflects on women's revolutionary "mind," bound to a gendered destiny but convinced it can break free. William challenges Mary's idealism, claiming that "the consolations of a spotless fame were for ever denied [her]; that the prejudices of the world, unrelenting to [her] sex, would oppose to all [her] efforts insuperable barriers" (128). But idealism dies hard. Invoking the moral self-reflexiveness of early revolutionary discourse, Mary vows to accept "ruin . . . but not the censure of my own heart" (128-29). From a position of such radical theoretical detachment, *The Victim of Prejudice* redacts Hays's own conflicts, ranging discourse against history as to the "fate" of women's "mind."

For Mary, history remains in "visionary form," foreboding but refused. A domestic position falls through when the elder Pelham, claiming "motives of justice," recounts Mary's "residence at the house of a libertine baronet," her *seductions* of his son," and "infamous" birth (135). When a messenger transmits these "cruel calumnies," Mary passes into reverie:

> O God! how terrible were the first indignant feelings that rent my heart on the perusal of this barbarous recital! New to world, to its injustice, the wrongs I had suffered appeared to me as a dream, the reality of which was wholly inconceivable.
>
> (135)

How can such treachery seem dreamlike? Pelham twists history, claiming as "justice" "injustice." His rendition emerges *as* history, strained through patriarchal *imprimatur.* Such authority allows him to hijack epistemology: Mary's potential employer (a woman!) finds it "not possible . . . to doubt . . . the principal facts alleged" (137).[34] Not only is Mary caught in history, but in a version that bespeaks patriarchal dominance in history, enforced by female complicity. Yet Mary associates Pelham's calumny, and the rebuff that follows, with "dream," ontologically "inconceivable." Just as the "visionary form" of her mother fades, leaving the trajectory of history but a faint streak in Mary's "mind," so this latest indignity is assimilated to a diaphane. Though Mary recalls her mother—"'O wretched and ill-fated mother! . . . what calamities has thy frailty entailed upon thy miserable offspring!'" (136)—once again, *as* history her reality is disallowed. Reacting to the rejection of her attempt to explain, Mary shakes off a wish to have been "strangled . . . at birth," turning history on its head:

> This new instance of injustice operated to mitigate than to increase my distress . . . my spirit, conscious of its purity, rose with dignity superior to its woes.
>
> (137)

Mary's "dream"-world, without a history inscribed by men, without her mother as avatar of such history, seems perverse, obsessed with spiritual "purity" which no one notices or values. In Mary, "rational will"—which should snap the link between history and "destiny"—is its ironic opposite: narcissism, debased autonomy, the last refuge of "revolution" when it has nowhere to go.

Mary's sojourn through London takes her to a series of deceptive employments. When she takes up "the art of drawing and colouring plants and flowers" (138), a profession recommended to women, her employer tries to seduce her, taunting, "Sir Peter Osborne and Mr. Pelham found less difficulty" (140). Yet again, with agonizing predict-

ability, Mary faces history: "I perceived that the fatal tale of my disgrace pursued and blasted all my efforts" (140). Her response seems overtly narcissist:

> "I am guiltless," I repeated to myself; "why then should I then affect disguise, or have recourse to falsehood? In every honest and consistent means of safety I will not desert myself . . ."
>
> (140)

Mary insists on herself ("myself . . . myself"), as if she were historically transcendent, her own construction. Yet in a context where economic autonomy is repeatedly filched, such insistence is out of place, a parody of revolutionary exhortation.[35] The language of female autonomy comes full circle: self-assertion does not issue in success, it is incapable of effecting change.

Mary continues to look for work as an engraver, an embroiderer. She almost succeeds in becoming a companion, until Osborne gossips to the family about "former incidents" in Mary's life, claiming that her "present distress" is "wilful" (145). She is then arrested for debt. Osborne turns up offering her release, a "legal settlement . . . independence" (150) in exchange for Mary's favor. But she reviles him. His usage of her, his smug derogation of language ("independence"?) evinces the decadent potential of a prerogative asserted (arrogantly) by the elder Pelham and (defensively) by Raymond. When Osborne leaves, he invokes Mary's frailty relative to his will, her subjection by a legal machine that he controls: "Let the law, then, *for the present* . . . take its course" (151).

Miraculously, Raymond's old servant, James, finds Mary and pays her debt. With money left him by Raymond, he has, moreover, rented a farm from Osborne, and together they set off to work it. Still believing she may "triumph over [her] malignant fortune" (155), Mary defines "triumph" as *a*political economy, a state of "mind":

> Let us rather look forward; my mind, unviolated, exults in its purity; my spirit, uncorrupted, experiences, in conscious rectitude, a sweet compensation for its unmerited sufferings. The noble mind, superior to accident, is serene amidst the wreck of fortune and of fame.
>
> (156)

The mind's "unviolated . . . purity" recuperates Mary's violated chastity. Her history is erased. She claims agency for herself independent of prior personal narrative, subverting "ideology" by *dis*entangling self from discourse. But in this rarefied arena of "spirit," "superior to accident," Mary's economy is a zero-sum: "uncorrupted" "mind" is "sweet compensation" for "sufferings," while fortune's "wreck" remains unrecovered. For her, economy is coterminus with mind.

But as she begins to farm, "tast[ing] the sweets of independence" (159), weather ruins her crops, she is harassed for debt, and Osborne haunts the area spreading gossip. Mary is helpless against "the influence of wealth and power, the bigotry of prejudice, the virulence of envy" (163). No one intervenes. James dies. Osborne seizes the day, finally offering "*legal* title to his hand and fortune" (164). But Mary shuns him, demanding he restore "my fame, my honour, my *friend,* my unbroken mind" (165). "Mind" and the accoutrements of virtue—"fame . . . honor"—are still Mary's obsessive concern. However, her rhetoric consigns them to the past. She acknowledges that "toils that entangle," debauch "unviolated . . . purity."

After Osborne departs, Mary's situation becomes desperate. Her creditor sues out a writ against her. She molders in jail, recalling her mother, history, which she can no longer dismiss:

> Involved, as by a fatal mechanism, in the infamy of my wretched mother, thrown into similar circumstances, and looking to a catastrophe little less fearful, I have still the consolation of remembering that I suffered not despair to plunge my soul in crime . . . and struggled in the trammels of prejudice with dauntless intrepidity. *But it avails me not!* . . . [E]njoyment, activity, usefulness hope, *are lost forever.*
>
> (168)

Mary acknowledges defeat, the failure of "mind" to overcome material conditions, to procure revolution over "prejudice." After two years, "reason faultered and nature yielded" (169). In Mary's *experience,* mind becomes as vulnerable as physical "nature"; it is not disembodied "rational will," persevering "superior to personal injury" (119).

Mary is rescued by the Nevilles, but too late. Mrs. Neville remarks: "over your stronger mind, *injustice* has triumphed, and consigned you to an early grave" (172). Mary's potency, her reality as a counter to "prejudice," is diminished to that of Mrs. Neville, who admits "I had no individual existence; my very being was absorbed in that of my husband" (173). Heroic womanhood and that of the utmost banality share a common inconsequence. In such an equation, Hays's indictment of revolutionary discourse is extreme: it is as if it never were.[36] Mary answers such discourse in terms of total negation: "the powers of my mind wasted, my projects rendered abortive . . . *I have lived in vain!*" (174). Her only qualification of such negativity is itself submissive to history—male-engendered history: she hopes to become history, "kindl[ing] in the heart of man, in behalf of my oppressed sex, the sacred claims of humanity and justice" (174).[37] Her words evoke "reason" as a bare, ruined category, reproaching Mrs. Neville but routing revolutionary vision:

> Reason derides the weak effort; while the fabric of superstition and crime, extending its broad base, mock the toil of the visionary projector.
>
> (175)

It might be the epitaph of revolution, except that its sentiments became common coin. That same year, in *A Letter to the Women of England,* Anne Frances Randall wrote of generic despair that projects Mary's life into universals:

> Supposing that a WOMAN has experienced every insult, every injury, that her vain-boasting, high-bearing associate, man, can inflict: imagine her, driven from society; deserted by her kindred; scoffed at by the world; exposed to poverty; assailed by malice; and consigned to scorn: with no companion but sorrow, no prospect but disgrace; she has no remedy. She appeals to the feeling and reflecting part of mankind; they pity, but they do not seek to redress her: she flies to her own sex, they not only condemn, but they avoid her. She talks of punishing the villain who has destroyed her: he smiles at the menace, and tells her, *she is,* a WOMAN.
>
> (7-8)

Hays's chillingly modern perception is that "the feeling and reflecting part of mankind" menaces revolution by seeming to support it.

Notes

1. On Hays's literary context, and the sorority of writers whose ideas she shared, see Eleanor Ty, *Unsex'd Revolutionaries: Five Women Novelists of the 1790s* (Toronto: U of Toronto P, 1993), as well as Ty's introductions to *The Victim of Prejudice* (Peterborough: Broadview P, 1994), and Hays's *Memoirs of Emma Courtney* (Oxford: Oxford UP, 1996). See also Gary Kelly, *Women, Writing, and Revolution 1790-1827* (Oxford: Clarendon P, 1993), and *Revolutionary Feminism: The Mind and Career of Mary Wollstonecraft* (New York: Saint Martin's P, 1992); Marilyn Butler, *Jane Austen and the War of Ideas* (Oxford: Oxford UP, 1975); Mary Poovey, *The Proper Lady and the Woman Writer: Ideology as Style in the Works of Mary Wollstonecraft, Mary Shelley, and Jane Austen* (Chicago: U of Chicago P, 1984). In *Jane Austen: Women, Politics, and the Novel* (Chicago: U of Chicago P, 1988), Claudia Johnson describes Burke's patriarchalism: "in self-proclaimed contrast to crazed French ideologues who would break with time-honored traditions in order to create a new society based on rational principles, Burke apotheosizes . . . the retired life of the country gentleman, the orderly transmission of property, the stabilizing principle of generational continuity, the grateful deference of youth to venerable age, and of course the chastity of wives and daughters which can guarantee the social identity of men and heirs" (5).

2. *Unsex'd Revolutionaries* 71.

3. *Unsex'd Revolutionaries* 62. The irony of female "reason" was that it failed to liberate, producing only a disappointed self-awareness. In *A Letter to the Women of England on the Injustice of Mental Subordination* (London, 1799), Anne Frances Randall remarks: "woman is taught to discriminate just sufficiently to know her own unhappiness" (84).

4. *Victim of Prejudice* 54.

5. Wollstonecraft argues that if women are "really capable of acting like rational creatures, let them . . .

cultivate their minds, give them the salutary sublime curb of principle, and let them attain conscious dignity by feeling themselves only dependent on God." The goal is agency: "I do not wish [women] to have power over men; but over themselves." Miriam Brody, ed., *A Vindication of the Rights of Woman* (New York: Penguin, 1992) 121, 156. Mary Poovey notes that Wollstonecraft never escaped "the myth of personal autonomy," failing to see that an "individual's opportunities" are in "important respects, delimited by one's position within culture." *The Proper Lady* 109. In *Letters and Essays, Moral and Miscellaneous* (London, 1793), Hays argues that "the vulgar of every rank," "terrified at the very idea of our feeling and asserting our rights to rationality, raise innumerable cavils and objections, all originating from the same source, a pertinacious and jealous adherence to a narrow and mistaken self-interest, and the petty word AUTHORITY" (22).

6. In a stunningly modern intuition, Hays suggests that (even revolutionary) "reason" does not transcend ideology, but reproduces it. For theorizations of ideology elaborating this position, see James Kavanagh, "Ideology," in Frank Lentricchia and Thomas McLaughlin, eds., *Critical Terms for Literary Study*, 2nd. ed. (Chicago: U of Chicago P, 1995) 306-20, and Julian Henriques, *et al.*, *Changing the Subject: Psychology, Social Regulation and Subjectivity* (London: Methuen, 1984).

7. David Simpson notes that "in the writings of the late eighteenth century there is an unusually widespread preoccupation with the problem of knowledge. . . . All specifications of what 'is' come to be accompanied by concerns about 'who's asking,' and why. . . . Not a little of the long- and short-term failure of the rationalist project of the 1790s, as argued by Paine, Godwin, and others, must be explained in reference to the sheer anachronism, then and since, of proposing to defend a model of objectivity so much at odds with other besetting contemporary convictions." See "Romanticism, Criticism, and Theory," in Stuart Curran, ed., *The Cambridge Companion to British Romanticism* (Cambridge: Cambridge UP, 1993) 1-24, 21, 22. Hays suggests that when it is a woman "who's asking," the "problem of knowledge" is acute. She reflects "besetting . . . convictions" concerning the pathology of patriarchy.

8. On the capacity of imaginative literature to tease out contingent meanings of abstract concepts, see Wai Chee Dimock, *Residues of Justice: Literature, Law, Philosophy* (Berkeley: U of California P, 1996). Speaking of "justice" (one might substitute abstract "reason") Dimock observes: "We might think of literature, then, as the textualization of justice, the transposition of its clean abstractions into the messiness of representation. We might think of it as well as the historicization of justice, the transposition of a universal language into a historical semantics: a language given meaning by many particular contexts, saturated with the nuances and inflections of its many usages" (10).

9. Janet Todd, ed., *Mary; Maria / Mary Wollstonecraft. Matilda / Mary Shelley* (New York: New York UP, 1992) 85.

10. Anca Vlasopolos expresses the common view that after the *Vindication* was published, Wollstonecraft's oeuvre (including her private, unpublished writing) "increasingly recognizes the role of emotions, of grand passions in shaping a human being's mind and experience." See "Mary Wollstonecraft's Mask of Reason in *A Vindication of the Rights of Woman*," *Dalhousie Review* 60 (1980): 462-71, 469. The *Vindication* was, of course, Wollstonecraft's manifesto for extending the Rights of Man to women—for masculinizing female epistemology by separating "reason" and "feeling"—and so I treat it as the benchmark for Hays's own idealizing aspirations. Hays's ultimate view that reason is ideologically freighted, and hence aligned with the disruptive potential of emotion, distinguishes her epistemology from Wollstonecraft's. While the war *between* reason and emotion is the common coin of late eighteenth-century women's texts, Hays complicates this dichotomy.

11. Raymond's proleptic knowledge of the "world"—it "*will* hardly be inclined" to favor Mary—comports with and reinforces his power as patriarch, taken for granted by Mary. On the mutual engagement of power and knowledge, see Michel Foucault, *Power/ Knowledge: Selected Interviews and Other Writings*, ed. Colin Gordon (New York: Pantheon, 1980), and Henriques 115-18. Mary's commitment to Raymond (her incapacity to attenuate the relationship by questioning his acumen) reflects a definition of self as tied to the relationship. In *Toward A New Psychology of Women* (Boston: Beacon P, 1976), Jean Baker Miller notes that "women's sense of self becomes very much organized around being able to make and then to maintain affiliation and relationship" (83).

12. The "Female Novel of Education and the Confessional Heroine," *Dalhousie Review* 60 (1980) 472-86, Virginia Tiger observes that Hays "creates a confessional heroine whose defining characteristic is the capacity to think. Traditionally, when confessional novels center on the *thinking* heroine, the critical action is not outward, but rather the inward progress to judgment . . ." (472).

13. Raymond—the "father"—is a riposte to Burkean family romance: operating at the level of epistemology, he disorganizes the "daughter's" apprehension of language within the social convention of "shelter." As such, he adumbrates modernist themes. In "The Paradox of the Individual Triumph: Instrumentality and the Family in *What Maisie Knew*," *South Atlantic Review* 53.4 (1988): 77-85, Lee Heller notes that in Henry James's novella, "the family, that place

where first meanings are assigned, is the source of this instability ["where identity and meaning are contingent"], not a safe haven from it (as it is in so many nineteenth-century novels). . . . What Maisie must learn is that 'language is contextually, not absolutely significant—meaning arises out of what language does, not what it is'" (79-80).

14. Mary's grateful imputation to Raymond of "claims," typifies late eighteenth-century disciplinary regimes. By that time, fathers no longer controlled daughters by intimidation, educating them instead to become "self-regulating, self-policing" agents of the paternal will. See Caroline Gonda, *Reading Daughters' Fictions 1709-1834: Novels and Society from Manley to Edgeworth* (Cambridge: Cambridge UP, 1996) 32. In *Their Fathers' Daughters: Hannah More, Maria Edgeworth, and Patriarchal Complicity* (Oxford: Oxford UP, 1991), Elizabeth Kowaleski-Wallace argues that such "new-style patriarchy" dispensed with overt paternal prerogative, appealing instead to "reason . . . and noncoercive exercise of authority." Instead of threatening punishment, it operated "according to the more compelling themes of guilt and obligation" (110). The girl "internalized the voice of paternal authority as her own" (21); she "must say [yes] sincerely and as though she has posed the question herself" (Lynda Zwinger, *Daughters, Fathers, and the Novel: The Sentimental Romance of Heterosexuality* [Madison: U of Wisconsin P, 1991] 8); her "desire for paternal approval becomes an effective method of control" (Gonda, *Reading* 179). Training daughters to be dependent on paternal love and esteem, made them "least likely to view [fathers] critically" (Kowaleski-Wallace, *Fathers' Daughters* 97). Paternal discipline and patriarchal "ideology" constituted reciprocal, internalized brakes on female autonomy.

15. Even Ty's exemplary study sees Hays's attack on patriarchy as seeking "to disprove and dispel the Burkean myth of the benevolent country squire as an adequate miniature head or 'monarch.'" In the context of Burkean myth, she characterizes Raymond as Mary's "benevolent guardian." *Unsex'd Revolutionaries* 60, 61.

16. I disagree with Poovey's judgment that "Wollstonecraft is generally *not* challenging women to *act*. When she calls for a 'revolution in female manners,' for example, she is not advocating a feminist uprising to overthrow manners but rather a general acquiescence in the gradual turning that the word 'revolution' was commonly taken to mean in the eighteenth century." See *The Proper Lady* 79 (orig. emph.). Without debating "feminist," I suggest that "revolution" resonates with the cataclysm in France, and as such implies that women should "act" to obtain the means of production of autonomous subjectivity. Wollstonecraft's concatenation of reason and agency resonates with a "humanist position [that] tends to see the individual as the agent of all social phenomena and productions, including knowledge.

The specific notion of the individual contained in this outlook is one of a unitary, essentially noncontradictory and above all rational entity." Her account differs, therefore, from those presenting the individual "not as a pregiven entity but as a constituted 'always-already social' being, a being locked in ideological practices." Henriques 93, 95.

17. On this point, see Mary Poovey, above at n. 5, and Moira Gatens, "'The Oppressed State of My Sex': Wollstonecraft on Reason, Feeling, and Equality," in Mary Shanley and Carole Pateman, eds., *Feminist Interpretations and Political Theory* (University Park: Pennsylvania State UP, 1991) 112-28.

18. Reeve, *Plans of Education* (London, 1792) 119-20. The notion that appropriate, remunerative work could be had by most women conflicts with economic reality and contemporary literary representations. In *Women Writing About Money: Women's Fiction in England, 1790-1820* (Cambridge: Cambridge UP, 1995), Edward Copeland notes that "the spectre of lessened expectations haunts women's fiction" of the period" (37). In *Women, Power, and Subversion: Social Strategies in British Fiction, 1778-1860* (Athens: U of Georgia P, 1981), Judith Newton observes that what lay behind an "incursion [by her father and "Daddy Crisp"] upon [Frances] Burney's status and autonomy was to a large degree the declining economic stature of genteel young women in the eighteenth century, for women of all stations had lost and were continuing to lose their previously recognized economic value" (26). In *The Age of Manufactures 1700-1820: Industry, Innovation and Work in Britain* (London: Routledge, 1994), Maxine Berg states that as the century progressed, "the introduction of new technology further increased unemployment for women" (150). "Women were left to perform the manual tasks while men used the efficient equipment," which effectively "'enhanc[ed] the prestige of men'" (155). In *London in the Age of Industrialization: Entrepreneurs, Labour Force and Living Conditions, 1700-1850* (Cambridge: Cambridge UP, 1992), L. D. Schwarz notes that "when they were no longer employed in service, eighteenth-century women were reputed to crowd into the few available jobs that paid any money worth earning, and to compete with each other for work and for pay" (17). "The restrictions on female employment were one of the major causes of the poverty and exploitation suffered by women" (46). On men's organized efforts to keep women out of the labor market and to depress their wages, see Anna Clark, *The Struggle for the Breeches: Gender and the Making of the British Working Class* (Berkeley: U of California P, 1995) 119-40. Mary Ann Radcliffe's *The Female Advocate: Or, An Attempt to Recover the Rights of Women from Male Usurpation* (London, 1798), castigated "the vile practice of men filling such situations as seem

calculated, not only to give bread to poor females, but thereby to enable them to tread the paths of virtue" (409).

19. For the classic reading of *Crusoe* as "self-made" man, typifying emergent capitalism, see James Watt, "*Robinson Crusoe* as Myth," in Norton Critical Edition of *Robinson Crusoe* (New York: Norton, 1975) 311-31. See also Isaac Kramnick, *Bolingbroke and His Circle: The Politics of Nostalgia in the Age of Walpole* (Cambridge: Harvard UP, 1968) 188-204. Kramnick argues that Crusoe typifies a type of "projecting man . . . shaping his own world and his own destiny" (194).

20. Hays, *Letters and Essays, Moral and Miscellaneous* (London, 1793) 21.

21. Hays's use of "experience" to test theory was becoming a feature of women's novels. As Tiger points out, "the novel offered a place for women writers to respond creatively—beyond protest at privation—to their generic concerns, their shared experience of being female. Eighteenth-century radical and conservative women seized upon the novel, transforming an atraditional literary *genre* into a medium for female, sometimes feminist education." "The Female Novel of Education" 476. Hays's attempt to calibrate theory and experience anticipates modern feminist advocacy. In *Breaking Out: Feminist Ontology and Epistemology* (London: Routledge, 1993), Liz Stanley and Sue Wise argue that while feminists tend to "*go beyond* the personal, into structural and more abstract work which develops [its] themes in more conventionally theoretical forms," they should attend to work "deeply rooted in variations in, and kinds of, *experience*" that can "help us to understand, in a way that abstract theory can't, the complexities and contradictions of our own, and other women's, experience" (77). See also Joan W. Scott, "Experience," in Judith Butler and Joan W. Scott, eds., *Feminists Theorize the Political* (London: Routledge, 1992) 22-40.

22. With William as tempter, Mary becomes a type of Eve, losing her innocence before men as she did once already when Raymond expelled her. Troped as Mary/Eve (virgin/whore), hence as a staple of patriarchal discourse, Mary cannot avoid compromise *by* such discourse. On the ideology of the virgin/whore, see Marina Warner, *Alone of All Her Sex: The Myth and the Cult of the Virgin Mary* (New York: Vintage Books, 1983).

23. Both the *Vindication* and *Appeal* exhort men. Neither explores the confusion, even guilt, such exhortation provokes. In Raymond, power to affect a woman's life, combined with impotence to dispel "prejudice," triggers moral/emotional contradiction. For another approach to this dilemma, see John P. Farrell, *Revolution as Tragedy: the Dilemma of the Moderate from Scott to Arnold* (Ithaca: Cornell UP, 1980), citing the gulf between "revolution as a thought and revolution as an action" (30).

24. Raymond admits that Mary's "childish association [with William] has been a reciprocal source of moral and mental improvement" (31). His sudden effort to separate them therefore wrenches Mary, recapitulating Raymond's dismissal of her to the garden (traceable as well to the elder Pelham's dictates). In both cases, Raymond acts to disrupt patterns he seemed to reinforce, disorganizing Mary's sense of security, continuity, and the "natural" order of things. In this respect, Raymond's actions distort what Veronica Machtlinger refers to as the "development of a positive Oedipus complex and its attendant wishes directed toward the father." See "The Father in Psychological Theory," in Michael E. Lamb, ed., *The Role of the Father in Child Development,* 2nd ed. (New York: Wiley and Sons, 1981) 113-53, 139. Machtlinger argues that "this would be ideally a relationship in which the girl would 'discover' and experience the first extensions of her femininity in a 'safe' relationship with an admiring and responsive father. . . . It is difficult to conceive of a girl developing a healthy and secure gender identity without such a gradually developing awareness of what her femininity is and means to her" (139). Raymond instead suppresses Mary's emerging sexuality, negating her healthy and innocent feelings towards William. Machtlinger departs from Sigmund Freud, who abandoned the parallel Oedipus complex for girls. See "A Child is Being Beaten: A Contribution to the Study of the Origins of Sexual Perversions," in *Standard Edition,* vol. 17 (London: Hogarth, 1955).

25. Mary's notes that "some embarrassments of a pecuniary nature assisted in determining my patron . . . to acceed the more readily to the proposal of his friend" (7).

26. As the *Vindication* observes: "From the respect paid to property flow, as from a poisoned fountain, most of the evils and vices which render this world such a dreary scene to the contemplative mind" (257).

27. Hays dramatizes what was perceived as intellectual misfeasance, where knowledge is imparted to women but its use prohibited. In *A Letter to the Women of England on the Injustice of Mental Subordination* (1799), Anne Frances Randall states: "The parent . . . who enlightened [a woman's] understanding, like the dark lantern, to spread its rays internally only, puts into her grasp a weapon of defence against the perils of existence; and at the same moment commands her not to use it. Man says you *may* read, and you *will* think, but you shall not . . . employ your thoughts beyond the boundaries which we have set up around you. . . . Why expand the female heart, merely to render it more conscious that it is, by the tyranny of custom, rendered vulnerable?" (83-84).

28. Raymond's attempt to deny sexual opportunity to William is a species of the "cognitive mastery" one

male asserts over another by seducing a female. See Eve Kosofsky Sedgwick, *Between Men: English Literature and Male Homosocial Desire* (New York: Columbia UP, 1985), 56. His suggestion that Mary marry a local farmer would "consummate" such "mastery," constituting as well a typical, patriarchal marriage of convenience.

29. Elizabeth Fishel observes that "the Patriarch's posture as a moral arbiter is often used to camouflage the irrepressible sexuality he makes every effort to repress. So before she can be a free agent, the daughter of the Patriarch must come to terms with both her father's repressed sexuality and her own burgeoning sexuality." *The Men in Our Lives: Fathers, Lovers, Husbands, Mentors* (New York: William Morrow, 1985) 67. It is possible, moreover, that an eighteenth-century reader would have seen Mary's dismissal to the Nevilles as instantiating Raymond's fear of his own attraction to her—is she her mother's surrogate in still another sense? On father/guardian attraction to the daughter/ward in eighteenth-century novels, see Gonda, *Reading,* ch. 1.

30. In *Reflections on the Revolution in France* (London, 1790), Burke opined: "Thanks to our sullen resistance to innovation, thanks to the cold sluggishness of our natural character, we still bear the stamp of our forefathers." See Geoffrey Tillotson, *et al.,* eds. *Eighteenth-Century English Literature* (Fort Worth: Harcourt, Brace, Jovanovich, 1969) 1282.

31. Raymond yields to the extent of telling Mary that William should "try the world, and prove his boasted strength." If he remains uncorrupted, he may claim Mary's "invaluable heart" (81). However, Raymond knows that Mary has internalized his "wishes" ("I see in you all that my most sanguine wishes presaged" [57]), and that appearing not to "impose" will only strengthen his moral authority. When William in fact proposes to Mary prior to departing for two years at his father's behest, Mary speaks as if her father's mouthpiece: "What! shall I first bind my fate to your's, and then suffer you . . . to expose your yet-uncertain virtue to the contagion of the world?" (84). Unlike the young man who seduced Mary's mother, William *does* seek to marry Mary; but she rejects him, anticipating that class-based norms (which bewilder her) will nonetheless wreck the marriage. This is Raymond's logic.

32. Osborne's question reflects the assumptions of Squire Falkland in Godwin's *Caleb Williams* (London, 1794), which attacks class bias in the legal system. On the substantial impediments to convictions for rape in the eighteenth century, see Anna Clark, *Women's Silence, Men's Violence: Sexual Assault in England 1770-1845* (London: Pandora, 1987).

33. Hays perceives history as a heuristic, "not exclusively as the record of changes in the social organization of the sexes but also crucially as a participant in the production of knowledge about sexual difference." See Joan W. Scott, *Gender and the Politics of History* (New York: Columbia, 1988) 2.

34. James Turner notes that "as consumers and as traders, women whose sexual 'credit' was broken could not obtain financial credit or employment." "Court records show that sexual defamation did have serious economic consequences." "Male discourse and gesture actually did control reputation, and that reputation translated directly into financial life or death." See "'News from the New Exchange': Commodity, Erotic Fantasy, and the Female Entrepreneur," in Ann Bermingham and John Brewer, eds., *The Consumption of Culture 1600-1800: Image, Object, Text* (London: Routledge, 1995) 419-39, 427.

35. In A *Theory of Parody: The Teachings of Twentieth-Century Art Forms* (New York: Methuen, 1985), Linda Hutcheon proposes that parody inheres in "trans-contextualization," radical displacement into an inappropriate context.

36. In *The Mother/Daughter Plot: Narrative, Psychoanalysis, Feminism* (Bloomington: Indiana UP, 1989), Marianne Hirsch argues that women's novels of the nineteenth century indulge a fantasy of "the heroine's singularity based on a disidentification from the fate of other women, especially mothers" (10). Hays refuses, indeed repudiates, such fantasy. Hirsch also observes that "female plots . . . attempt to subvert the constraints of dominant patterns [i.e. of patriarchal discourse] by means of various 'emancipatory strategies'—the revision of endings, beginnings, patterns of progression," and that such a process of "resistance, revision, and emancipation" is "a *feminist* act defining a *feminist* poetics" (8). Hays eschews such "strategies," denying Mary any "heroic" singularity.

37. Gary Kelly argues that English "revolutionary" novelists frequently show "how self-reflection and its resultant political consciousness can break the cycle of institutional reproduction of evil and error"; this new consciousness is "expressed socially, as a confessional self-vindication or warning to others—the text of the novel itself or an inset narrative within it." See "Romantic Fiction," in Curran, ed., *Cambridge Companion* 196-215, 204. Hays, however, short-circuits the monitory aspirations of both Marys' texts, compounding the irony of trying to "break the cycle" of patriarchy by producing monitory texts.

Tilottama Rajan (essay date 1998)

SOURCE: Rajan, Tilottama. "Autonarration and genotext in Mary Hays' *Memoirs of Emma Courtney.*" In *Romanticism, History, and the Possibilities of Genre: Re-forming Literature 1789-1837,* edited by Tilottama Rajan and Julia M. Wright, pp. 213-39. Cambridge: Cambridge University Press, 1998.

[*In the following essay, Rajan refutes critics who consider* Memoirs of Emma Courtney *scandalously autobiographical, suggesting instead that the novel is a self-conscious attempt to explore the relationship between experience and textuality.*]

I

Mary Wollstonecraft's The *Wrongs of Woman,* long written out of the canon by being used as a source-book for her life, has recently become an object of serious attention. Mary Hays' **Memoirs of Emma Courtney** (1796),[1] however, remains the victim of a reduction of text to biography that fails to recognize its complex interimplication of textuality and reality. Hays' novel is based on the story of her unreturned passion for the Cambridge radical William Frend. Its autobiographical nature led contemporaries to see it as a scandalous disrobing in public, and the novel is still dismissed as a monologic transfer of "life" into "text." **Memoirs,** however, self-consciously draws upon personal experience as part of its rhetoric, so as to position experience within textuality and relate textuality to experience. From the distinctions by Schiller and the Schlegels onwards, between classicism as impersonal and Romanticism as the revelation of personality, the inscription of the author in the text has been a characteristically Romantic move: expressive not of the egotistical sublime, but of the text as the unfinished transcription of a subject still in process. Hays' text can be seen as part of a larger (post)-Romantic *intergenre* that I shall call autonarration, which is also used (though differently) by male writers such as Rousseau and Wordsworth. Far from collapsing the boundary between life and text, autonarration effects a series of "trans-positions" (to borrow Kristeva's term)[2] among ideology, life, and fiction. The transposition of personal experience into fiction recognizes "experience" as discursively constructed. That Hays draws on her own experience is a way of authorizing what she does, and of reciprocally implicating the reader in the text. But it is also a way of putting the finality of the text under erasure, by suggesting that what it "does" or where it ends is limited by its genesis in the life of a conflicted historical subject.

This paper argues for the importance of Hays' novel to both the feminist and Romantic traditions, and in the process works out a phenomenology of autonarration. But because the novel is relatively unknown, it is necessary to begin by describing it and by saying something about Hays herself. Mary Hays was born in 1760 into a middle-class family of Rational Dissenters near London.[3] Her early engagement to a fellow Dissenter John Eccles ended in tragedy when he died shortly before their marriage. Through the preacher Robert Robinson she met some of the leading intellectuals of the day, and eventually became a member of Joseph Johnson's radical circle. Thereafter Hays made a tenuous living by writing and reviewing, and produced essays, other novels, her own vindication of women's rights entitled **An Appeal to the Men of Great Britain in Behalf of Women** (1798), as well as a six-volume attempt to construct a gynocentric tradition under the title **Female Biography** (1805). Although her relationship with Robinson and William Godwin was purely intellectual, Hays became notorious among her contemporaries for throwing herself at men who apparently did not return her affections. Through Frend she met Godwin, whom she introduced to his future wife Wollstonecraft, and with

whom she carried on a long correspondence. Her letters were not only about her (non)relationship with Frend but also about its ramifications: a sexual economy that constructed women only for marriage, and the resulting predicament of single women untrained for a profession. It was Godwin who encouraged her to write a fictionalized version of her experiences. She wrote the novel, she implied to him, for reasons that were neither purely literary nor kathartic but political: "My Manuscript was not written *merely* for the public eye—another latent, and perhaps stronger, motive lurked beneath—. . . my story is *too real.*"[4]

Hays is best remembered as the author of Wollstonecraft's obituary and the person who was at her bedside when she died. But though she has consequently been identified with or dismissed as a more outrageous version of Wollstonecraft,[5] there are significant differences between the two. Hays' attitude to passion and to the tradition of romance and sentiment was more positive than Wollstonecraft's.[6] Moreover, **Memoirs** is the work of a woman who could not or did not enter the marriage circuit. For although Wollstonecraft felt it would have been more appropriate for the novel to end with the death of the male protagonist and thus the unavoidable termination of Emma's love,[7] Hays has her heroine outlive the conventional ending of novels about women in death or marriage. Curiously enough, while *The Wrongs of Woman* is about much more than its love interest, Wollstonecraft seems unable to see her way beyond Darnford's possible treachery. But although **Memoirs** seems to be about nothing *but* romantic love, the terms of Emma's life are not really defined by that love. In fact the novel is concerned less with Emma reenacting or even remembering her love than with her writing and potentially reading it, so as to understand women's representation in the symbolic order.[8]

Drawing on Hays' own letters to Frend and Godwin (who appears in the novel as Francis), the novel focuses on the one-sided correspondence between its title character and the man she chooses to love, Augustus Harley. Emma, like so many nineteenth-century characters for whom the family is an imposed structure, has lost her mother and her aunt early in life, has been brought up by an absent father, and has been transferred after his death to the care of an uncle. It is in her uncle's house that she meets the destructively passionate Montague, as well as the highly rational Francis, with whom she exchanges ideas and to whose not entirely sympathetic eyes she later confides the story of her love. Augustus enters Emma's story by way of a violent coach accident to which I shall return, and in which he saves her and Montague from death but is badly injured. Seeming to encourage her friendship at first, he later becomes evasive and refuses to answer her letters. His ostensible reason is his uncle's will, which stipulates that he will forfeit his legacy if he marries. Emma is never entirely convinced by the purely pecuniary motive but her declarations of love and pleas for frankness are met by injunctions to be less selfish and more restrained. Eventually it emerges that Augustus is actually married, to a foreign woman he no longer loves, and whose existence he has concealed for fear of losing the legacy.

This disclosure ends their (non)relationship and Emma, now under financial pressure, marries Montague. She is a faithful wife and mother until a second coach accident outside her home brings Augustus back into her life. She learns that Augustus, having been reduced to poverty, has lost his wife and two of his children to illness. Emma nurses him until he dies, and inherits the guardianship of his remaining son, Augustus Jr. From then on her marriage deteriorates, culminating in Montague's murder of his child by a servant girl and his subsequent suicide. Emma tells her story partly through a series of letters: passionately rational letters to Augustus, and rationally passionate ones to Francis, to whom she writes about the economic predicament of single women and the relationship between reason and passion. The letters are interspersed with narrative to make up the memoirs of the title. But the memoirs are also framed by two letters to the now adult son of Augustus, who is himself involved in a passionate relationship. Ostensibly Emma conveys her (hi)story as a cautionary exemplum to her adopted son. But the epistolary form is potentially transgressive, crossing the bounds of private space so as to say what cannot be said in public, and claiming a certain immediacy and presence. In putting her letters within her memoirs, Emma had allowed their radicalism to be contained within the mode of pastness. But the framing of the memoirs themselves within a return to the epistolary form suspends this cautionary closure, by once again transposing the question of passion from the past to the unresolved present.

Crucial to Hays' novel is the concept of Desire. Desire is part of the text's functioning in ways to which I shall return. But it is also thematically central to a novel that questions the opposition between reason and passion, so as to reposition female subjectivity within the psychosocial economy. Felicity Nussbaum has described how women's sexuality posed a threat to this economy in specifically material ways having to do with the inheritance of property and thus the maintenance of the class system.[9] Emma's aspirations are also subversive because of the social implications of a woman taking the initiative in love. But her desire has to do with more than sexuality. Thus I use the word partly as it is used by Lacan, for whom desire is always in excess of its object, the object being only a partial representation of something beyond it, and thus implicated in a chain of deferrals and transferences. *Memoirs* is not about Emma's desire for Augustus but about something else that is signified by that desire. Moreover, because it suggests the substitutive and still "symbolic" character of the object(s) of desire, the Lacanian term avoids the positivism sometimes associated with political reading. For marriage to Augustus remains a signifier within the symbolic order, while the further transference of Emma's desire to his son is still what Fredric Jameson calls a symbolic resolution: one that allows her to be Augustus' mother, the mother who teaches but also the mother of his desire, and yet as mother in a paradoxical position of

origination and subordination. Hays herself recognizes the nature of her project when she points in *An Appeal* to the difficulty of positing women's identity, given that men have so constructed them that "they have lost even the idea of what they might have been, or what they still might be":

> We must therefore endeavour, to describe them [women] by negatives. As, perhaps, the only thing that can be advanced with certainty on the subject, is,— what they are *not*. For it is very clear, that they are not what they ought to be, that they are not what men would have them to be, and to finish the portrait, that they are not what they appear to be.[10]

But if the currently Lacanian connotations of "desire" allow us to approach *Memoirs* in terms of the "negativity" of the signifier, there are limitations in his version of the concept. In tracing the history of desire from Jean Hyppolite's influential rereading of Hegel, through Sartre, to Lacan, Judith Butler comments on the attenuation that occurs as desire is transposed from a dialectical to a psychoanalytic and structural framework.[11] Not only does Lacan dissociate desire from any sense of subjective agency, he also denies that desire can be "materialised or concretised through language," whether directly or negatively.[12] Moreover, because he sees desire as endlessly metonymic and unsatisfiable, he dispossesses the means by which it signifies itself of historical specificity or facilitating value, making the signifier no more than a position in an empty series.

In using the word desire, then, I continue to have in mind Hyppolite's rereading of Hegel as part of a negative dialectic that is particularly (post)Romantic. Desire is the "very existence of man, 'who never is what he is,' who always exceeds himself," and who in that sense "has a future."[13] As such, it is the power of the negative in experience, as well as the reflexivity of a consciousness that must know itself partly as an other and as existing for another.[14] Put differently, Emma's love is an articulation of the imaginary within the symbolic, or in Hegelian terms of the subjective within the objective. Beginning as the idealism of a highly romantic subject who resists being confined by things as they are, Emma's desire can express itself only in the socially prescribed form of heterosexual love. Her desire is doubly negative, in the sense that it resists the symbolic order through an identification with the masculine that sets it at odds with itself. Yet this negativity is dialectical and not deconstructive, because desire makes the negative into "something to be labored upon and worked through."[15] For Emma this working through occurs through the epistolary format of the novel, which makes of self-consciousness an intersubjective process. For Hays herself it occurs through the act of writing, in which she must become other than herself in the text in order to know herself.

That Emma articulates herself through romantic love has to do with the way women have been constructed in the social text. She herself makes this point when she refuses to abandon her love of Augustus, referring to it as the mind's necessary "object" and "pursuit," and arguing, "I feel that I am neither a philosopher, nor a heroine,—but a *woman, to whom education has given a sexual character*" (*M* [*Memoirs of Emma Courtney*], 120). Thus although Hays' critics found Emma's epistolary pursuit of Augustus unseemly and her concern with her feelings narcissistic, to see the novel as fetishising desire is to miss its pathos. *Memoirs* is strategically rather than essentially about female sexuality. From the beginning Emma's desire is excessive: it exceeds the objective correlative it tries to find in Augustus Harley, and even at the end it survives the dismantling of its object. At first Augustus encourages Emma "in the pursuit of learning and science" (*M,* 71), so that her need for a relationship with him is also a desire for access to knowledge (*M,* 79). Given women's exclusion from all but the domestic sphere, this love is also a desire for the enunciative position within the social order that a woman could have only in relation to a man. But as the convenient vagueness of the word "desire" suggests, it would be wrong to give it a precise referent. For when Emma does acquire the status afforded by marriage to Montague, domesticity becomes an empty signifier that does not satisfy her.

Emma's desire is all the more difficult to characterize because it is not even initially sexual: as she says, it involves a transference of her affection for his mother (*M,* 59), in which she loves in *him* what he must inherit from *her.* What begins as a desire for everything effaced from her own patriarchal upbringing is thus androgynously transcoded onto the masculine as the only sanctioned object of adult female love. Thus it is significant that Emma's specifically sexual desire is set in motion before she actually meets him by Augustus' portrait (*M,* 59). This mobilizing of desire by an image that precedes its representation in a real person anticipates texts such as Shelley's *Alastor,* where the protagonist unites in an image "all of wonderful, or wise, or beautiful, which the poet, the philosopher, or the lover could depicture," before he actually goes in search of his epipsyche.[16] Figuring the precedence of the signifier over the signified, the portrait marks the fundamentally Romantic structure of desire, not simply as lack, but also as a form of Imagination subversively knotted into the symbolic structures of representation and the family.[17]

If the word desire suggests a non-coincidence of the subject with its object, we also need to set it beside Hays' own more positive term "passion," and to read them as intertextual glosses on each other. The frequent discussions of "passion" in *Memoirs* involve Emma's struggle to rethink the position of women by examining the identification of emotion as the site of feminine weakness. Hays' views on this subject are highly conflicted. On the one hand, in representing her memoirs as a warning against error, Emma accepts the dominant devaluation of passion and related terms such as "romanticism" and "imagination." On the other hand, Hays differs from Wollstonecraft in arguing for passion as a form of strength. Writing to

Francis, Emma asks, "What are passions, but another name for powers?" (*M,* 86).

The questioning of the hierarchy between reason and passion links Hays to a re-examination of this opposition in Romantic thinking from Blake to Schopenhauer. But whereas Schopenhauer will argue that the representations produced by reason are no more than disguised expressions of the will, Hays' protagonist suggests that passion can be deeply rational. Writing to Francis, she argues that reason and passion are not necessarily opposed, and indeed that reason begins in passion: "do you not perceive, that my reason was the auxiliary of my passion, or rather my passion the generative principle of my reason?" (*M,* 145). This statement significantly revises her earlier condemnation of herself on the grounds that "my reason was but an auxiliary to my passion" (*M,* 61). If reason is originally the elaboration of passion in a series of general principles, the outward circumference of energy as Blake would say, then passion remains vitally necessary to the reconsideration of what would otherwise congeal into law. For Emma's passion causes her to rethink the social structures that condemn that passion as outrageous, and thus her desire also becomes the site of her emergence as a political subject. Or as she tells Francis, "Had not these contradictions, these oppositions, roused the energy of my mind, I might have domesticated, tamely, in the lap of indolence and apathy" (*M,* 145).

Hays' use of the term passion remains highly conflicted, for the active thrust of the word is continually negated by Emma's acceptance of its patriarchal encoding as something that one suffers and by which one is infected. However, a reading of the term purely in terms of lack does not convey the force of Hays' project. If desire does more than eroticize female powerlessness, that is because the *discourse* of desire in the tradition to which Hays' text belongs is allied with the modes of autonarration and epistolarity. These forms, which will be the concern of the remaining two sections, implicate author and reader respectively in the process of desire. Linda Kauffman has provided a valuable account of how amorous discourse is elaborated through epistolarity, so that the text becomes a letter to the reader,[18] thus putting desire in circulation. But a further untheorized element in her discussion is the "auto-graphing" of many of the texts she describes, either by the author or by the reader. *Jane Eyre* is curiously subtitled an autobiography, and Kauffman's discussion focuses on its correspondence with Brontë's letters to Constantin Heger, the Belgian schoolmaster with whom she fell in love as a young woman. As interesting is the reception history of *The Letters of a Portuguese Nun,* which testifies to a compelling desire to make the nun into a historical person.[19] As Ruth Perry points out, eighteenth-century readers liked to see fictional characters as "real,"[20] in striking contrast to readers nursed on contemporary theory. The blurring of the line between fiction and reality potentially allowed readers to write themselves, or to pursue the trace of their desire, through the text. This conflation of the fictional and the real becomes in the Romantic period a powerfully dialectical use of the subjective as a sub-version of the objective world.

II

Memoirs of Emma Courtney can be seen as an example of autonarration, an intergenre characterized by its mixing of private and public spaces. Autonarration is part of a larger discursive formation characteristic of Romanticism, in which writers bring details from their personal lives into their texts, speaking in a voice that is recognizably their own or through a persona whose relation to the biographical author is obvious. Thus Coleridge's conversation poems are situated within his life through specific references to the time and place of their composition, to friends such as Wordsworth and Charles Lamb, and to incidents from his domestic life. Somewhat differently Shelley in *The Triumph of Life* and Keats in *The Fall of Hyperion* inscribe in their texts what are best described as subversions of themselves referred to by the pronoun "I." Subjectivity, however, is not always indicated by the use of the first person or of local and topographical markers. Thus the Byronic hero is a third person character, but is nevertheless a figure for a public persona that is recognizably a projection of the author himself.

Criticism from Eliot to the present has taught us to exile the author from a supposedly ironic or decentered text, and insofar as the Romantics deviate from this standard of impersonality, the author's presence in the text has been seen as a form of egotistical sublimity. But the author's self-representation through a textual figure is quite different from her presence. On the one hand, subjectivity offers the writer an enunciative position within the social syntax that she is precluded from occupying by the aesthetic grammar of (neo)classicism and (post)modernism. As a subject who is not quite inside the space of the public, she can articulate desires that are different from (or that defer) the received genres of experience. On the other hand, these desires are textualized rather than literalized, so that the writer, in leaving life for text, ceases to be a transcendental ego and confesses her situatedness as a historical subject. Nor is it simply the case that "life" is made into a text. For the historical (as distinct from the fictitious) first-person position also inscribes the textual within the Real, by marking its genesis in and its continued importance for a historical subject.

As a specific form of this larger discourse, autonarration involves not simply the author's entry into the text through the first-person pronoun, but a sustained rewriting in fictional form of events from the author's life. Autonarrations are not fictions but they are also not autobiographies. Thus Hays' text is a highly fictionalized version of her life in which the main character is nevertheless writing her memoirs, thus inscribing the text itself as a sub-version of the autobiographical project. I use the term autonarration rather than autobiography or self-writing quite deliberately. As a subset of biography, autobiography assumes a straightforward relationship between representation and experience

that allows the subject to tell her life-story either in the form of constative or of performative utterance: either as it was, or as it becomes through the act of rewriting. By contrast the term self-writing refers to a textual articulation of the self that is already not the real self, but the self as it is produced within existing discourses. Self-writing, however, includes diaries, journals, and letters as well as narratives. Autonarration is thus a form of self-writing in which the author writes her life as a fictional narrative, and thus *consciously* raises the question of the relationship between experience and its narrativization. It is not exclusively a women's genre, because some of Kierkegaard's writings fall within this category. Its use, however, tends to put the writer in a female subject-position.

In this sense, Wollstonecraft's first novel *Mary* is not a fully fledged autonarration, because it does no more than evoke the interimplication of life and texts through the titular reference to the author's name. *The Wrongs of Woman,* by contrast, contains sustained parallels between Maria's life and Wollstonecraft's relationship with Gilbert Imlay. These parallels, moreover, are deliberately imperfect in that Maria's lover Darnford occupies the positions of both Imlay and Godwin. He resembles Imlay in being Maria's first real lover, but in the fragmentary endings he also resembles Godwin in being the father of her second child.

The fact that the author is and is not represented by her textual surrogate has significant consequences for the reading process. For instead of generating a series of identifications in which the author recognizes her alter ego in the mirror of the text, and thus enables the reader to find and identify with the autobiographical subject within the text, the reading process involves a series of (mis)recognitions in which we cannot be quite sure of the relationship between textuality and reality. These misrecognitions generate a series of complex intertextual relationships between what is and what could be. For instance, one of the pivotal events in Wollstonecraft's life was Imlay's betrayal of the desires that she symbolically invested in him: desires that were social and political as well as romantic. That Darnford is both Imlay and Godwin narrates the possibility of a repetition that did not happen in quite that way in Wollstonecraft's life. At the same time the transposition of this betrayal into the text is effected through its displacement into an ending that she did not integrate into her novel. This displacement suspends the inevitability of betrayal, both in the text and in life: it removes the betrayal from a climactic position in the text, and by repeating it within a text, it also exposes betrayal as part of a discourse into which women are written and therefore write themselves.

As these preliminary comments indicate, autonarration puts under erasure the assumption made in autobiography that the subject can tell her own story. It is not autobiography because it is still fiction, but it is not just fiction because of its genesis in the life of a real individual. Crucial to the genre is the movement that occurs between the zones of life and fiction. We should not, however, think of the relationship between these zones as being similar to that between story and discourse. "Story" is a foundationalist concept which implies that certain events really happened in a certain order. By transposing her life into fiction, Hays recognizes that her life itself takes shape within a social text. Autonarration therefore involves a double textualization of both the narrative and the life on which it is based. At the same time its genesis in experience is crucial in complicating this textualization by inscribing the Real as what Jameson would call the absent cause of the narrative process.[21] In gesturing beyond the text to the author's "experience," it points us to something that cannot quite be represented in either the text or the public life of the author. This something is what impels her to articulate herself in the two different media of life and text, as if each requires the supplement of the other. Indeed both Hays and Wollstonecraft use a third medium, that of the political tract, although it is the mixed genre of autonarration that sensitizes us to the intertextual and supplementary position of seemingly simpler signifying materials such as "life" and political prose.

But the term life itself needs to be further broken down: into Hays' public history, and the autobiographical pre-text that precedes her interpellation into a social script. The pre-text is a provisional articulation of drives at the level of what Kristeva calls the "semiotic" (*R* [*Revolution in Poetic Language*], 25). As such it finds no adequate objective correlative in the history of Mary Hays or her fictional counterpart, but can only be sensed through a symptomatic reading of the differences between Hays' history and its further narrativization in Emma's memoirs. Insofar as we can describe it this provisional articulation involves desire: a desire that is at once metaphysical, political and sexual. However, any expression of this desire is already a narrativization of the pre-text produced within the psychosocial structures of the family. In this narrative desire attaches itself to an *animus* or more properly a masculine equivalent to what Shelley calls the epipsyche. We can note Hays' tendency to idealize men with radical political commitments: whether as mentors like Godwin, or as potential lovers like Frend. Although Johnson eventually published her *Appeal,* Emma Courtney recapitulates the position of a younger Mary Hays in having to express her views on the construction of gender in late eighteenth-century society in a series of private letters to a male correspondent. Hays sought relationships with men because they were her means of access to knowledge, and because the discourse of emotional relationships gave her a way of locating for herself an admittedly ambiguous enunciative position within the social text. Where her relationships with male mentors preserved the gender hierarchy that Emma struggles against in her correspondence with Francis, her more passionate relationships promised (at least ideally) a union with the male that would lead to a transcendence of hierarchy and difference.[22]

If Hays' public history already writes her desire in certain pre-set social forms, *Memoirs of Emma Courtney* tries to displace and defamiliarize this anterior social text. Crucial

to this process are the differences between the novel and the "events" that it symbolically transforms. These *differences,* rather than the events themselves or their fictional counterparts, are what allow us to sense the autobiographical pre-text misrepresented in Hays' public life. For it is not that Hays rewrites things as they are in her life into things as they should be in her novel: indeed Emma's life is not resolved with any more outward success than Hays' affair with Frend. Rather, by enacting her relationship with Frend in two different signifying materials, Hays dislodges the mimetic authority of either version and allows the reading process to operate in primarily negative ways that impede its premature closure. That the text does not exactly repeat Mary Hays' history opens up the possibility of a history that could have been different. On the other hand the novel, as a deflected repetition of the life, is both a deferral of that hi(story) which continues to haunt it and to reinscribe its utopian project in the structures of eighteenth-century society, and it is also a difference from its own ending, which could be written differently if transposed into an alternative set of circumstances.

We shall focus only on the most significant of the divergences between life and text: Hays' representation of Augustus. Unlike Frend, he is apolitical. Indeed his concealed passion for his foreign wife marks him as much closer to Emma than he admits, but utterly different from her in his hypocritical attitude to the feelings. Most significant of all is his secret marriage, given that Frend himself married only much later. This change is important not simply because it makes him unworthy of Emma's love, and not because it hints that she could have had Augustus if the plot of her life had been different, but because that possibility destigmatizes her desire and frees the reader from having to judge it in terms of the failure which may well be our only reason for condemning it. At the same time it is crucial that we not rewrite the plot as it is worked out in the symbolic order of Hays' history or that of Emma Courtney, by substituting for it an imaginary ending which discloses the marriage of Emma and Augustus as the text's hermeneutic secret. For this repositing of the subject within the existing social order is negated both by the displacement of the secret marriage onto a wife who is effaced from the text, and by the (dis)appearance of Emma's namesake daughter, whose early death prevents the marriage of Emma and Augustus from being consummated in the second generation. The possibility of a marriage exists as no more than a trace, which defers the outcome of Hays' life so as to make us think about it differently. But it is important that Emma's desire should not succeed, because the nature of that desire is that it exceeds its articulation as sexual desire. Augustus' unavailability renders Emma's desire pure excess, a desire that cannot have an object. It also renders this desire innocent, both of the failure that leads us to dismiss it and of the sexuality that cuts off the political radicalism of women's desire in the scandalous memoirs of writers like Charlotte Charke and Laetitia Pilkington alluded to in Hays' title.[23]

Insofar as the pre-text is accessible only through the zone of possibilities generated by the differences between Hays' and Emma's histories, we have been tacitly assuming two further areas of signification in the interaction between text and life, namely the phenotext and the genotext of the novel itself. I borrow these terms from Kristeva, who defines the phenotext as that which communicates "univocal information between two full-fledged subjects." The genotext, by contrast, is a "process" or "*path*" that articulates ephemeral structures and that can be "seen in language" but "is not linguistic" (*R,* 86-87). The phenotext, though quite different from Hays' public history, is its intratextual equivalent because both are produced within the symbolic order. It includes the mimetic and pragmatic (as opposed to expressive) dimensions of the novel: its plot, and its use of the letter as a way of forwarding the memoirs to their addressee as a cautionary tale. The genotext, according to Kristeva, is the unformulated part of the text, evident for instance in rhythm as that which exceeds statement.

Kristeva elaborates the notion of a genotext through writers such as Mallarmé and thus with reference to lyric. Moreover, her association of the semiotic with lyric and of narrative with the symbolic (*R,* 90)[24] constitutes a privatizing of the semiotic that can sometimes come across as a failure to retrieve its political potential. Yet in spite of the connection between plot and the symbolic order, writers such as Hays and Wollstonecraft choose subjective narrative rather than lyric because it provides them with a way of entering history. Where lyric allows for the expression of subjectivity, narrative positions this subjectivity in relation to the other, so as to open the genotext to political reading and so as to put it into history. One of my concerns here is therefore to explore what constitutes the genotext of *narrative,* and more specifically of autonarration. As we have seen, the genotext exists partly as an intertext or connective zone between the biographical and diegetic worlds, which is to say that it consists of the possibilities released by the negation of the various scripts into which the subject has been or could be written. But in addition the genotext is also *intra*textual. If the phenotext includes the plot and its characters as positive terms in a narrative syntax, the genotext is something the reader senses in the *form* taken by content: in the rhythms or processes of emplotment and the spaces between characters and generic components. It is also important to remember that the drives produced in the semiotic *chora* and reproduced in the genotext already bear the imprint of cultural structures. The genotext, as something which is not linguistic but is seen in language, is the overdetermined site of an entanglement between residual, dominant, and emergent discourses. Insofar as it generates the gaps in which desire can emerge, this desire is produced *within the symbolic order* as a transgression of this order.

Where the phenotext is positive in the sense of communicating information or positing identity, the genotext can be conceived only as a negativity. As negativity (which is a process) rather than negation (which is thetic) (*R,* 109-13), the genotext can be located first of all in the diacritical relations between generic components and characters. An obvious example would be the way the affirmative element in Emma's passion emerges not from what she does, but as something not quite stated and thus never confirmed in the difference between her behavior and the self-destructive passion of Montague.

A far more complex version of the functioning of *differance* and the trace as part of a genotext involves the conspicuous doubling of the first generation protagonists of Hays' novel in the second generation, combined with a simultaneous maintenance *and* reversal of the symmetry that contains the doubling within the boundaries of gender. Emma is repeated as her daughter Emma and Augustus as his son Augustus, with a symmetry that seems at first to perpetuate the gender positions of the first generation. But then Augustus' death becomes little Emma's death, while Augustus Jr. occupies the position in the plot occupied by Emma Sr., in that his own involvement in a passionate love affair provides the pretext for her to send him her memoirs. Or to put it differently, the plot in the second generation does away with the woman and allows the man to survive, but only after the man has come to resemble Emma more than his father. In a metaphoric sense the surviving Emma dies as the woman her child might have been, while her desire survives in the younger man who, by occupying a female subject-position within the social syntax, allows Emma at last to occupy the same subject-position as a man.

This complex rearrangement of the first generation in the second is genotextual, in the sense that we must read it as a psychosocial text (dis)organized by certain rhythms. As important to this text as its characters are the processes by which gender and plot functions are mapped and remapped onto each other. Implicit in my use of the word "processes" is the assumption that narrative (or at least subjective narrative of the sort written by the Romantics) is not simply the plot with its characters. Rather it is an autogenerative mechanism which produces and disposes of events and characters, in such a way that its movements are themselves a symptomatic part of the text's content. In this case the narrative begins by doubling its main characters along familial lines that preserve the separateness of male and female, by giving Emma a daughter and Augustus a son. But then it crosses these lines by partially reversing the roles played by the younger Emma and Augustus in the political economy of the text. The reversal is incomplete, because little Emma resembles Augustus Sr. only in one respect: they both die. It is, however, this incomplete turn, from the maintenance to the rearrangement of gender lines that forms a part of the genotext. The movements of the narrative are traces of something whose provisional articulation in the genotext is itself imprinted by the sexual structures of the symbolic order. In other words, Hays' vicarious self-doubling of Emma as Augustus Jr. narrates her desire for a social order in which the division between reason and passion, male and female, will no longer obtain. This desire, however, is haunted by the possibility that Emma may after all be her daughter, that her desire may die, like so many Romantic projects, before it has lived. It is also haunted by the possibility that Augustus may still be his father's son, that his future may not vindicate the rights of the woman who is no more than his adoptive and metaphoric mother in a family that is an ideal rearrangement of his actual family. Finally this desire is itself produced within the gendered economy that it resists. For the symbolic resolution it projects, provisionally and genotextually, has Emma survive through her masculine counterpart at the cost of killing off the very female self she has sought to vindicate.

At the same time this ambiguous transgression of the social order is connected to a (mis)identification with the role of mother that allows the death of little Emma to function in more than one symbolic register. Emma Sr. survives as (the younger) Augustus' symbolic mother, and can transmit her memoirs to a future reader only by assuming this role, which affords her a position in the social syntax. It seems, moreover, that she can enter the symbolic role only after transiting the literal function of motherhood. At the same time she is not really Augustus' mother, and occupies the role of literal mother only briefly. Even as it marks the loss of what she wants to preserve, little Emma's death is what enables motherhood to be no more than a rite of passage for Emma. It marks her reinscription into the structures of genre and family as the uneasy assumption of a position rather than of an identity, as symbolic rather than imaginary in Lacan's sense.[25] Implicated as it is in more than one signifying path, little Emma's death exemplifies the functioning of the genotext as process rather than thesis, as a conflictual flux that is simplified by any attempt at paraphrase.

If the genotext emerges in the spaces between characters and between characters and their roles, it can also be seen in the structuring of the plot. As distinct from "structure," a concept that codifies a mimetic reading of the plot in terms of what happens in it, what I call "structuring" or "emplotment" are concepts that call for a symptomatic reading of plot in terms of the pathology of its de(form)ation. The most crucial example here is the novel's emplotment through what is itself a highly charged signifier: the mechanism of repetition. Emma and Augustus first meet through an accident in which the coach in which she is travelling with Montague overturns and they are rescued by Augustus, with both men being badly injured. The plot ends with an uncanny recurrence of this accident, in which Augustus is fatally injured, with equally fatal ramifications for Emma's marriage to Montague.

The framing of Emma's passion in terms of violent accidents is a conspicuous departure from Hays' life, for both she and Frend lived on into their eighties. The accident inscribes the end of the affair in highly conflicted ways. In phenotextual terms, the association of passion with violence and ultimately death signifies its destructiveness. But such a conclusion in no way sums up the complexity of the relationships between characters. Throughout the novel Emma's passion has been distinguished from the ultimately murderous passion of Montague. Although she seems destined to meet Augustus, that meeting could just as easily

have occurred at his mother's house. That her love for him is associated with scenes of destructiveness is thus accidental. Or to put it differently, at the level of the genotext the accident is itself a figure for the way passion and death are associated in the symbolism of the social text. It comments on the inscription of "passion" within the symbolic order, by marking this association as *accidental,* the result of a metonymic proximity. We can locate the disturbance of the phenotext in the symmetrical neatness of the plot, which deflects our attention from the text as mimesis to the processes that produce figures mimetically as truths whose rigidity is symptomatically registered in this symmetry.

This second reading of the accident is genotextual in focusing on the text as body rather than as mimesis: in focusing not on what the text says, but on what it does not say through its resistance to the rigid skeleton of the plot. As important is the simultaneously structural and psychic mechanism by which the ending is inscribed. For the recurrence of the accident should be read not simply as another stage in the plot but also in terms of what Jameson calls the form of content,[26] or in terms of a de-formation of content that shifts attention from the event itself in the phenotext to its *structuring* as a return or repetition. The event itself, Augustus' death, is not particularly surprising. Indeed if we think of an ending as a text's self-conscious recognition of its unconscious, of what has already happened emotionally, Augustus' death is simply the plot's delayed reaction to his departure from Emma's life some years before. What is shocking is the way the story ends, with an uncanny repetition that foregrounds structure in such a way as to make form take the place of content. In marking its structural mechanisms in this way, the narrative knots the signified within the signfier, so that one must attend not only to what the text says but also to the form in which the abortion of Emma's passion is communicated. This mechanism is all the more conspicuous because it involves a symptomatic rewriting of the novel's pre-text, in which the circumstances of Hays' meeting with Frend and the eventual dissolution of their relationship are much less remarkable.

As a signifier, the mechanism of repetition is highly overdetermined, and can be read in several ways on which we can only touch. On one level, Augustus' departure from Emma's life in the same way he entered it brings the plot full circle. This circularity has the function of purgation as well as closure: the end returns to the beginning to correct it, by disposing of Augustus and thus correcting Emma's initial error. But on another level this confusion of beginnings and endings within the motif of the return undoes the entire project of ending. It is not simply that the second accident reawakens Emma's passion for Augustus, contaminating the present with the past. It also reopens the whole issue of passion as the material site of women's struggles.

At this level the repetition of the accident is connected to other forms of repetition: to the novel itself as memoir or return, and to autonarration as the author's return to her past. Repetition is most obviously a form of obsession: a return to something that cannot be disposed of because it has not yet been worked through. But it is also an occasion for revision, and in this sense it is linked to another instance of repetition in the novel: the repetition of the first generation in the second. This figure, which was to become increasingly common in nineteenth-century narrative, often signifies the taming and attenuation of the past in the present, as in Frankenstein's repetition as Walton or the return of Heathcliff and Cathy as their Victorian children.[27] The repetition of Emma's letters as her memoirs purports on one level to be just such an act of self-taming. But given the curious reversal by which it is the present that functions as a shadowy type of the past in these texts and not vice versa, the typological drive that mobilizes repetition remains curiously unfulfilled, making the figure the site of a lack. As a moment of irresolution and unfulfillment, repetition figures the survival of desire within the asceticism imposed by the symbolic order, infecting or affecting the reader with this desire, by making reading into another form of repetition. The link between repetition as a motif in the plot and the functioning of the figure on a hermeneutic as well as a diegetic level is explicitly made through Emma's forwarding of her memoirs to Augustus Jr., who as inscribed reader embodies the potential for repetition as re-vision, and as Emma's male surrogate embodies repetition as the possibility of progress.

III

Crucial to autonarration is its implication of the reader in the continuation of its project. The genre thus participates in what I have elsewhere described as the major transgeneric form of Romanticism: a transactional text whose significance must be conceived historically, and must be developed and renegotiated through its reading.[28] The question of reading is foregrounded in Hays' novel by its semi-epistolary format. Emma conveys the story of her life through her letters, and she thus displaces attention from plot to reflection, from the outside to the inside but also the other side. For unlike the Portuguese Nun, Emma does not simply write about her love to her lover: she also writes to Francis and Augustus Jr. Thus the novel is not simply about desire, but also about the communication and continuation of desire within an economy in which there is more than one reader, and thus potentially more than one law.

Much of the recent work on epistolary fiction has approached it through a vocabulary of presence and absence that emphasizes the textuality and supplementary status of the letter.[29] Alternatively, the letter has been seen socioculturally as a site of the alienation that results from the commodification of language.[30] Either way, epistolarity has been associated with a split between language and experience, and a consequent loss of power. There is no question that Emma writes her love because she cannot act it, and that both her love and her ideas are confined within the space of representation. On the other hand, the very limitations of letters are also enabling conditions. Because of

their marginality in relation to speech and print, letters were often associated with pietist or dissenting communities and thus with oppositional culture.[31] Emma herself draws attention to the advantages of the letter when she comments that she can express herself "with more freedom on paper" (*M,* 39). For her meetings with Francis are generally in the company of others, and even her occasional private walks with him are constrained by an uncertainty about his own relationship to the existing social order. Writing to him without these constraints, she can write to a subject dialectically split between the real and the ideal, between what he is and what he could be.

As the site of a crossing between actual and possible worlds, the intimate letter also blurs the boundary between public and personal space. It says what one is not supposed to say and thus renegotiates the terms of the social contract. Letters were not necessarily read only by the person to whom they were addressed, and for women they occupied a space midway between the private and the public in the information network.[32] Hays herself wrote about her relationship with Frend in letters to William Godwin. Godwin was not only a friend, he was also the author of *Political Justice.* As such he occupied a position whose ambiguity blurred the boundary between the personal and the public, and thus allowed his correspondent a strategic enunciative position on that boundary. Moreover Hays' letters may also have been read by Mary Wollstonecraft, who certainly read her novel, and who in turn wrote to Godwin and criticized him for his masculine response to Hays.[33] In publishing the novel, Hays formalized what had already happened in her writing of the letters: she placed her situation and her responses to it within a communicative circuit that was not confined to the addressee of the letters or the designated reader(s) of the novel.[34]

A discussion of *Memoirs* as a letter to the reader must begin with a curious anomaly. The novel in so many ways seems to call for a "female" reader. But whereas Wollstonecraft's Maria addresses her memoirs to her daughter, redirects them to Darnford and Jemima, and then uncertainly brings back her daughter, Emma Courtney's readers are exclusively male. However, the turn to Augustus Jr. should not be read phenotextually as the positing of an actual addressee. In writing to her daughter, Wollstonecraft's protagonist turns towards the future, but also *re*turns to someone whose fate may repeat her own. Hays turns against such doubts by allowing Emma's daughter to die. Yet in so doing she turns not to the male reader addressed in *An Appeal,* but to the wounded masculine[35] in herself: to that part of herself which cannot survive except by figuring itself as male. The recourse to a male reader must be taken in conjunction with the fact that the novel's male protagonists all die, except for Francis who simply drops out of the narration. These various deaths register the bankruptcy of the patriarchal order, and displace Emma's investment in it to the level of a signifier she is constrained to use. Moreover, the disappearance of Francis, once he has served his purpose as an intersubjective stimulus for

Emma's ideas, marks the fact that the male reader is less the designated reader of the text than a facilitating position within a communicative grammar that is still historically situated. In gendering her addressee as male, Emma allows *herself* a position from which she can be heard. Both positions (that of the writer and that of the addressee) shift even within the space of the novel, with the replacement of Francis by Augustus Jr. For Francis is characterized in sufficient detail to limit what Emma can say to him. Although she transgresses those limits by pleading her passion as well as discussing it rationally, Francis, as a representative of the liberal male public of the time, cannot really hear her. Augustus, by contrast, takes no significant part in the novel's action, and we have no way of guessing his responses. His extradiegetic status thus allows him to figure the possibility of a reading not constrained within the present order.

Through the young Augustus, in short, Emma inscribes within the text a space for (re)reading, and associates the reader with a future dialectically connected to her own past. As a figure for the reader, however, the young Augustus is ambiguously within and beyond the novel's diegesis, between the symbolic and imaginary orders. Although the relatively little we know about him leaves us free to imagine his responses to Emma's memoirs, the one thing we do know is the name of his father. Thus what the turn to Augustus allows Emma to do is painfully knotted in to what it disables her from doing. For it requires her to survive in a space that remains symbolic because, in Kristeva's words, it connects "two separated positions" (*R*, 43): that of desire and the means of its signification through an inscribed reader, through a signifier which is still part of the economy of gender.

It is therefore important to remember that Augustus is only the temporary addressee of the memoirs. Through the shift from Francis to the younger Augustus, Hays formalizes what may have been instinctive in the correspondence. She disengages us from identifying with the novel's intratextual readers, using them to create a space within the text which can and will be occupied differently by different readers. This space can be described as the "reading-function," and must be distinguished from concepts such as the "designated reader," the "implied reader," or the "superreader," in that it is a structural position within the text, rather than an ideological position identified with a certain category of person and thus given a specific content. In the writing of the novel the text's communicative grammar is necessarily given such a content in ways that are historically determined. But it is here that the embedding of the novel in the writer's biography becomes important. For by situating her text in the life of a historical subject, Hays asks us to read beyond the ways in which she herself is constrained to write its ending and to inscribe its reading.

The reading-function is implicit in the "temporal polyvalence" which Janet Altman notes as one of the features of epistolarity, but which once again has been associated with the letter as failed communication. Epistolary communication does not occur in a shared space and time like conversation, but instead involves several times: the time of the act, its writing, and its reading.[36] Introducing the notion of time as perspective, epistolarity also introduces the possibility of understanding as historical, and of history as re-reading. One of the earlier examples of amorous epistolary discourse is *The Letters of a Portuguese Nun* (1669).[37] In the movement from the nun, who writes only to her uncaring lover and writes only about her passion, to Emma Courtney who writes about social as well as amorous issues, we witness an expansion from the erotics to the politics of desire, effected through a deliberate exploitation of temporal polyvalence. In a sense, however, this expansion had already occurred in the reception history of the **Letters** and analogous texts, and had thus modified the hermeneutics of epistolarity in ways that were crucial to writers such as Hays. For although the nun writes only to her lover, real people write back to the fictional character, culminating in the multiple-authored *Three Marias: New Portuguese Letters* (1972). This process of revision had already begun in the eighteenth century, with an imaginary sequel that supplied the lover's missing responses to the nun, thus rewriting life through fiction.[38]

Crucial to the way the text reaches beyond its inscribed readers to an extratextual reader is the hermeneutics of the autonarrative genre itself. We have demarcated four zones of signification in autonarration: the autobiographical pre-text, which is entirely nondiscursive and which constitutes something like what Jameson calls the Real; the public life of the author; the phenotext of the novel; and the genotext, an area of affect and signification that is not so much in the diegesis as it is in a symptomatic *reading* of its psychotropology. Where a purely fictional text could be approached simply in terms of the last two areas, the four zones are part of the more complex dynamic of creation and reception specific to the genre under consideration. By writing their lives as texts that are themselves about women writing their lives, novelists such as Hays and Wollstonecraft register an awareness of their lives as textually constructed. On the other hand, this taking of life into the text is itself taken back into life, because the **Memoirs** have their origins in the experience of a real woman whose life will be affected by their reading. The constant crossings between life and text are represented in the novel by the way characters and functions cross over between the extradiegetic and intradiegetic worlds. As author of the memoirs, Emma is an extradiegetic narrator who is also a character in her own story, and who functions as an intradiegetic narrator in this story when she writes her memoirs for Francis. In the text itself the position of subject is thus shown as moving between the extra- and intradiegetic worlds. Similarly the function of reading is transferred between intradiegetic readers such as Augustus and Francis, who receive Emma's letters, and Augustus Jr., who does not participate in the action of the novel.

These transfers between extra- and intradiegetic worlds analogically interimplicate life and text so as to draw the extratextual reader into the text. But it is the specifically auto(bio)graphic nature of a text such as the **Memoirs** that stops this process from becoming aestheticized as the play of mirrors it becomes in many self-reflexive texts. For in making her personal life public Hays takes certain risks all too evident in the ridicule to which she was subjected, and this "signing" of her text (to borrow a word from Bakhtin)[39] asks us to reciprocate by transposing the text into our own lives. We return here to the importance of desire in this novel. Because autonarration mixes text and life, it also mixes the signifier into the signified in ways for which a purely deconstructive theory of the sign cannot account. The desire which is the subject of the novel transmits itself metonymically to its mode of functioning, so that desire is not simply what the text is about, but is also the means by which its subject is signified. Transposing her desire into the symbolic world of the novel, Hays implicates her text within the desire of a reader for whom reading too is an autonarrative process. It is through this reader that the novel's genotext enters history.

Notes

1. Mary Hays, *Memoirs of Emma Courtney* (London: Pandora Press, 1987). All references to this text (*M*) will hereafter be in parentheses in the text.

2. Julia Kristeva, *Revolution in Poetic Language,* trans. Margaret Waller (New York: Columbia University Press, 1984), 59-60. References to this work (*R*) will hereafter be in parentheses in the text.

3. My biographical information is drawn from Gina Luria, "Mary Hays' Letters and Manuscripts," *Signs* 3 (1977): 524-30; and from Luria's introduction to her reprint of Hays' *Appeal to the Men of Great Britain in Behalf of Women* (New York: Garland Press, 1974).

4. Hays continues in the same letter by insisting that her aim is to show "the possible effects of the present system of things, & the contradictory principles which have bewilder'd mankind, upon private character, & private happiness" (quoted in Luria, "Mary Hays' Letters," 529-30).

5. See for instance Claire Tomalin, *The Life and Death of Mary Wollstonecraft* (London: Weidenfeld and Nicholson, 1964), 241, 245; James Foster, *History of the Pre-Romantic Novel in England* (New York: Modern Language Association, 1949), 259-60. Another example of the automatic dismissal of Hays is provided by Allene Gregory's *The French Revolution and the English Novel* (London: G. P. Putnam, 1915). Gregory also "deals" with Hays by absorbing her into Godwin, despite her concession that the novel by Godwin to which *Memoirs* bears a "striking resemblance" was published much later (223), and despite the fact that Emma corresponds with Francis on the assumption that opposition is true friendship.

6. While sharing Wollstonecraft's sense that the Rousseauian model of romance wrote women into a male script, Hays may also have found in Rousseau a com-

pelling version of the discourse of desire. Emma Courtney is in the middle of reading *La Nouvelle Héloïse* when her father disapprovingly takes the book away, so that she reads about Julie's passion but not its correction. The resulting misprision shapes her life in ways that are both disastrous and constitutive of her subjectivity. Emma's early interest in romance is sharpened by her father's insistence that she read history, with the result that romance offers her the only available position from which she can express female desire. As such, it is a version of what Lacan calls the imaginary, which attaches the subversiveness of this desire to imagos that are part of the symbolic order.

7. *Collected Letters of Mary Wollstonecraft,* ed. Ralph M. Wardle (Ithaca: Cornell University Press, 1979), 376.

8. I use this term in the sense used by Lacan and Kristeva, to indicate the order in which we are constructed as speaking subjects: the order of syntax, which is also the order of the law and the family. This order is "symbolic" in the sense that the individual's identity within it is always other: a representation of her as something else, for and by someone else.

9. Felicity Nussbaum, *The Autobiographical Subject: Gender and Ideology in Eighteenth-Century England* (Baltimore: Johns Hopkins University Press, 1989), 179-80.

10. Hays, *Appeal,* 70, 67.

11. Judith Butler, *Subjects of Desire: Hegelian Reflections in Twentieth-Century France* (New York: Columbia University Press, 1987), 186.

12. Butler, *Subjects of Desire,* 186-87, 192-98.

13. Jean Hyppolite, *Genesis and Structure of Hegel's Phenomenology of Spirit,* trans. Samuel Cherniak and John Heckman (Evanston: Northwestern University Press, 1974), 166.

14. Hyppolite, *Genesis and Structure,* 162-68.

15. Butler, *Subjects of Desire,* 9.

16. Percy Bysshe Shelley, "Preface" to *Alastor,* in *Shelley's Poetry and Prose,* ed. Donald Reiman and Sharon Powers (New York: Norton, 1977), 69.

17. We might note in passing the frequent use of certain proto-Romantic words and concepts: "image," "imagination," and "portrait" (*M*, 53, 82, 89, 93, 122); "ideal" or "romantic" (*M* 20, 60, 80, 84, 103, 171); and "visionary" (*M*, 46, 84).

18. Linda Kauffman, *Discourses of Desire: Gender, Genre, and Epistolary Fiction* (Ithaca: Cornell University Press, 1986).

19. See Kauffman, *Discourses of Desire,* 160-78 and 92-97. Kauffman seems to endorse the feeling of the au-

thors of the *New Portuguese Letters* that "it is immaterial whether the experience and emotions described in the nun's letters is fictive or real" (283). My argument, that it is rhetorically if not factually material, is slightly different.

20. Ruth Perry, *Women, Letters, and the Novel* (New York: AMS Press, 1980), 74-80.

21. Fredric Jameson, *The Political Unconscious: Narrative as a Socially Symbolic Act* (Ithaca: Cornell University Press, 1981), 35, 81-82.

22. Augustus refers to Emma as his sister (*M,* 71), the role which Mrs. Harley ultimately assigns her (*M,* 156), and which marks the incestuous and forbidden nature of this union within the terms of the symbolic order. Similarly, Emma Jr. and Augustus Jr. are brought up as brother and sister.

23. The scandalous memoirs are discussed by Felicity Nussbaum, who describes them as the first significant form of women's self-writing other than spiritual autobiography (*Autobiographical Subject,* 180). Nussbaum sees the scandalous memoirists as both confirming and contesting the dominant ideology, and further notes the conflicted position of these writers given the relegation of "unlicensed sexuality to the lower classes" (179). I would further argue that the memoirists' identification of desire with sexuality aborts the emergent radicalism of their texts, and that Hays' representation of a love that is and is not sexual is a way of retaining her right to address a middle-class liberal audience.

24. An exception to this statement is Kristeva's recent article "The Adolescent Novel," in *Abjection, Melancholia and Love: The Work of Julia Kristeva,* ed. John Fletcher and Andrew Benjamin (London: Routledge, 1990), 8-23. Here too she focuses on a series of symbolic positions assumed by the subject of narrative. But inasmuch as these positions are experimental, her concern is (at least potentially) the *engendering* of narrative, the desire that results in the subject assuming different positions in the symbolic order.

25. The imaginary and the symbolic can be seen as different ways of relating to an identity that is always already specular. In the imaginary the subject identifies with the image (or imago) in the mirror. In the symbolic she is uneasily aware of it as a representation.

26. Jameson, *Political Unconscious,* 242.

27. A less well-known example of this motif is Arnold's "Tristan and Iseult," in which the dark passionate Iseult is repeated as Tristan's paler, fairer, and more domestic second love. Arnold's text parallels Victorian novels such as *David Copperfield* in its linking of repetition to the domestication of the Romantic, the conversion of revolutionary energy into evolutionary caution.

28. See Tilottama Rajan, *The Supplement of Reading: Figures of Understanding in Romantic Theory and Practice* (Ithaca: Cornell University Press, 1990); and "The Other Reading: Transactional Epic in Milton, Blake, and Wordsworth," in *Milton, The Metaphysicals and the Romantics,* ed. Lisa Low and Anthony John Harding (Cambridge: Cambridge University Press, 1994), 20-46.

29. Ruth Perry treats the epistolary form thematically, as an expression of separation and isolation (*Women, Letters, and the Novel,* 93-118). Roy Roussel approaches it in terms of presence and absence in "Reflections on the Letter: The Reconception of Presence and Distance in *Pamela,*" *ELH* 41 (1974): 375-99. Although her argument becomes increasingly political as the book proceeds, Linda Kauffman's early chapters associate epistolarity with a Lacanian form of desire. Thus she describes desire as "infinitely transcribable, yet ultimately elusive, and . . . therefore reiterated ceaselessly," and she refers to the "metonymic displacement of desire" (*Discourses of Desire,* 24-25).

30. Thus W. Austin Flanders in *Structures of Experience* (Columbus: University of South Carolina Press, 1984), links the letter to "the production of language as a commodity through the use of paper and writing utensils as tools and its consequent distance from primary experience" (79).

31. Katharine Goodman, *Dis/Closures: Women's Autobiography in Germany Between 1790 and 1914* (New York: Peter Lang, 1986), 77.

32. Goodman, *Dis/Closures,* 79.

33. "I think you *wrong* . . . You judge not in your own case as in that of another. You give a softer name to folly and immorality when it flatters—yes, I must say it—your vanity, than to mistaken passion when it was extended to another—you termed Miss Hays' conduct insanity when only her own happiness was involved" (*Collected Letters,* 404).

34. It is further worth noting that epistolary fictions such as the *Letters to a Portuguese Nun* often resulted in revisionary sequels. Not only were fictional letters treated as though they were about real life persons, writers/readers also responded to these novels-as-letters, by creating further fictions in order to rewrite 'life' through fiction (see Perry, *Women, Letters, and the Novel,* 72-84, 111).

35. I owe this term to Ross Woodman.

36. Janet Gerkin Altman, *Epistolarity: Approaches to a Form* (Columbus: Ohio State University Press, 1982), 129-35. Ruth Perry sees "the time lag of long-distance communication" primarily as a cause of misunderstanding (*Women, Letters, and the Novel,* 108).

37. See the account by Kauffman, *Discourses of Desire,* 91-118, 271-312. Kauffman points out that the letters

were enormously popular in the eighteenth century, provoking numerous English translations, imitations and sequels (95). It is therefore quite likely that Hays would have read them.

38. See Perry, *Women, Letters, and the Novel,* 111.

39. While recognizing that texts and actions are intersubjectively produced and do not have their origin in a transcendental ego, Bakhtin nevertheless sees the subject as implicated in his or her text. "Signature," according to Morson and Emerson, means "making an act one's own, taking responsibility for it" ("Introduction," in *Rethinking Bakhtin,* ed. Gary Saul Morson and Caryl Emerson [Evanston: Northwestern University Press, 1989], 16).

Eleanor Ty (essay date 1999)

SOURCE: Ty, Eleanor. "The Imprisoned Female Body in Mary Hays's *The Victim of Prejudice*." In *Women, Revolution, and the Novels of the 1790s,* edited by Linda Lang-Peralta, pp. 133-53. East Lansing: Michigan State University Press, 1999.

[*In the following essay, Ty discusses* The Victim of Prejudice, *claiming that Hays's concern in this novel was the construction of female subjectivity according to the hierarchies associated with class and gender.*]

In her Advertisement to the Reader, Mary Hays states that what she wants to question in ***The Victim of Prejudice*** (1799) is the "too-great stress laid on the *reputation* for chastity in *woman*" and the "*means . . .* which are used to ensure it."[1] This aim echoes that of Mary Wollstonecraft, who in *The Vindication of the Rights of Woman* (1792), had also argued that "regard for reputation" was "the grand source of female depravity" because it causes women to adopt an "artificial mode of behaviour."[2] What both writers deplored was the way the customs and society of late eighteenth-century England put more emphasis on the external sign of chastity, or reputation, than on chastity or purity itself. In their works, both Wollstonecraft and Hays sought to differentiate between outward representations of female virtue and the morality that sprang from women's understanding and strength of character. This insistence on the separation between reputation and the actual possession of virtue ultimately made Wollstonecraft, Hays, and other radical women of the 1790s the subject of much criticism and censure by the conservative thinkers of the time.[3] Their claims for moral, economic, and intellectual liberty were viewed simply as a justification for sexual freedom and licentiousness.

By the time Hays wrote ***The Victim of Prejudice,*** she had already suffered what she called "the cry of slander" due to her first novel, ***Memoirs of Emma Courtney,*** which depicted a woman's passion and pursuit of her desire.[4] Nevertheless, she continued to resist the dominant culture's

beliefs in the "proper lady" and persisted in demonstrating how the bodily experience of women differed from that of the fabular or linguistic construction of woman.[5]

In her second novel, she is concerned with the way the female subject is shaped and constructed by ideologies defined by class and gender-hierarchies. Using Edward Moore's *Fables for the Female Sex* (1744) as an intertext, she rewrites the story of the seduced woman highlighting the emotional and psychic pain, the bodily sufferings of her heroine. In Foucault's terms, one could say that ***The Victim of Prejudice*** demonstrates the way the "female body is transformed into a feminine one" by being disciplined and punished.[6] In his study of prisons, twentieth-century historian Michel Foucault argues that it was in the late eighteenth century that there was a shift in penal justice from one of corporeal punishment to a more subtle form which intends to "correct, reclaim, cure."[7] He notes that "the body now serves as an instrument or intermediary: if one intervenes upon it to imprison it, or to make it work, it is in order to deprive the individual of a liberty that is regarded both as a right and as property. The body, according to this penality, is caught up in a system of constraints and privations, obligations and prohibitions."[8]

It is such a system of constraints and deprivations that Hays illustrates in her novel. Her narrative reveals how systems of power and authority manipulate and operate to create a docile body out of one originally of "robust constitution, a cultivated understanding, and a vigorous intellect" (5). In her words, the "means" used to ensure that women paid attention to their "reputation" lead to "hypocrisy, not virtue" (1, 174).

My paper explores the roles that language and the cultural representations of women play in the construction of the heroine's subjectivity in ***Victim of Prejudice.*** It shows how the confinement of the heroine in the penitentiary is linked to eighteenth-century society's need for control and surveillance, especially of female sexuality. The heroine's lament that she has become "the victim of a barbarous prejudice" (174) is not just the story of one woman's loss, but becomes indicative of the way the culture circumscribed what it perceived to be unruly and uncontrollable in women. Through her polemical novel, Hays reveals that the violation of women's bodies and women's lives is not inevitable or natural, but is enabled by "narratives, complexes and institutions which derive their strength not from outright, immutable, unbeatable force but rather from their power to structure [women's] lives as imposing cultural scripts."[9]

From the short introduction which begins the novel, it is clear that Hays was attempting to recast one script, which Susan Staves calls the "seduced-maiden tales" in different terms.[10] Her heroine, Mary Raymond, repeatedly asserts her "innocence" in spite of her lost chastity (3). She represents herself as "a child of misfortune, a wretched outcast" from her society, someone "driven with ignomy from social intercourse" (3), rather than a sweetly pathetic fallen woman. The language, which reverberates with Jacobin polemics, is much more reminiscent of William Godwin's *Caleb Williams* or Mary Wollstonecraft's *Maria; or the Wrongs of Woman* than that of a distressed maiden. Typically, as Staves notes, the seduced-maiden tales "rely heavily on a romantic idealization of maidenly devotion to chastity, a devotion rewarded not in this life but in the purer world toward which the dying maiden so frequently turns her final glance."[11] In these literary seductions, the girl's father plays a prominent role; he is seen "both in law and in fiction" as the "chief victim."[12] While Hays's narrative follows the plots of these seduction tales to a certain extent, there are a number of important deviations worth noting. One of the crucial differences between *The Victim of Prejudice* and works such as Elizabeth Inchbald's *Nature and Art* or Amelia Opie's *The Father and Daughter,* both of which are cited by Staves, is the use of the first-person narrative. By letting her heroine tell her own tale, Hays empowers Mary Raymond's subjectivity and validates her experience rather than romanticizing her. Gary Kelly has argued that the use of the first-person or confessional mode was characteristic of Jacobin novels of the 1790s, as it was a genre that could have "political and revolutionary implications." It had the "function of showing how an individual developed from personal experience a critical consciousness about his or her own 'rights' in the face of social oppression."[13] Using this mode, Mary Raymond is able to distinguish her mental or emotional state from physical and social circumstances over which she, as a woman, has little control. Even in her last days, she judges herself by personal rather than social standards. She claims to derive "firmness from innocence, courage from despair," and, even in prison, asserts that she possesses an "unconquerable spirit, bowed but not broken" (3).

Another cultural script or narrative that Hays was revising is "The Female Seducers" by Edward Moore and Henry Brooke. This fable is part of a collection of sixteen fables published as *Fables for the Female Sex* initially in 1744 and reprinted frequently throughout the eighteenth and early nineteenth centuries. This extremely popular work from which Hays quotes in the epigraph and towards the end of the novel teaches young women about vanity, modesty, coquetry, cleanliness, and other lessons. "The Female Seducers" is one of the longer fables which does not use animals as characters and which teaches women that "honour is a woman's life."[14] In the fable, a young girl at the "crisis of fifteen" leaves her parents' care to go on a journey. Her aged parents warn her that as a woman she is "frail as fair," and that if once her foot strays from heaven's "appointed way," then "reproach, scorn, infamy, and hate" shall await her.[15] She is seduced by Sirens and by Pleasure and returns disgraced and in despair. At the end, only angels in heaven welcome the "lovely penitent" who finds no asylum elsewhere.

This fable, which is longer and contains a more developed narrative than the others in the collection, has much in common with the seduced-maiden tales. In these narra-

tives, a woman's whole subjectivity is predicated upon her sexual chastity. Once a young girl has lost her virginity, she is no longer fit for earthly society and becomes an outcast and spends the rest of her life as a penitent. What Hays does in *The Victim of Prejudice* is to call upon these narratives and to show how they are not reflections of woman's experience, but rather are ideological representations or cultural scripts which transmit a set of assumptions or values of patriarchal society. The intention of the fables is similar to those of conduct-manuals and of some domestic or sentimental novels, notably those by writers such as Samuel Richardson or Jane West. They are designed to teach young women of marriageable age that they are to be modest, chaste, and dutiful. Although critics such as Nancy Armstrong have argued persuasively that domestic fiction helped produce the modern female individual who "understood herself in psychological terms,"[16] this subject, who could represent her desire, took over a hundred fifty years to develop and she did not emerge without conflict. For the most part, domestic novels, like conduct-books, helped, in Vivien Jones's words, to "regulate social and sexual behaviour, teaching women to discipline themselves into acceptable forms of femininity in order to achieve and maintain respectability."[17] Hays, like Mary Wollstonecraft, struggled with these socially and culturally established notions of what a woman ought to be and for what qualities she should be most valued. Unlike the author of "The Female Seducers," she did not believe that "honour" in a woman's life was necessarily equated with virginity. Though her heroine, like the young girl in the fable, eventually has nothing but death to look forward to, she is unwilling to follow the script of the fable or to be defined in terms of virginity, frail beauty, seduction, or penitence. The fact that she is nevertheless forcibly cast into these roles by others demonstrates the pervasiveness of these ideologies about women, and the violence used on her to enforce them reveals the arbitrariness and unnaturalness of these positions for women.

Although the plot of *The Victim of Prejudice* substantially follows that of the fable, one of the ways in which Hays renders her text polemical is by accentuating the bodily experience of the woman. In Moore's fable, the body of the young girl is curiously absent from the narrative. For the most part, the fable describes the unnamed maiden in idealized and ethereal terms which fit with the universalizing and moralizing tendency of the fabulist. She is the daughter "too divinely fair," the "brightest beauty," who is betrayed (273, 280). When she is seduced, she is the "nymph" with "her treasure flown" (285). She becomes the "lonely Trembler" and the "lovely penitent" after her transgression (286, 288). Such epithets distance readers from identifying too closely with the actual emotional or physical state of the girl. She remains an unreal example of lost virtue and innocence. In contrast to this deliberate effect of remoteness in the fable, Hays's novel, which uses techniques we associate with realistic fiction, focuses on details and the woman's life experiences. Hays shows how various texts, language, and the ways in which women were represented in the late eighteenth century have a detrimental effect on the lives of actual women of the time.

The Victim of Prejudice is a novel whose author and heroine react to texts and textuality. Aside from Moore's *Fables,* Hays was also rewriting Richardson's *Clarissa,* as I have argued elsewhere.[18] In fact, the *Anti-Jacobin Review* condemned the novel because it was so unlike the tone and moral nature of *Clarissa*:

> In the *dishonour* . . . of 'Mary,' there is something like an imitation of Clarissa; but how unlike to the original!—In conformity to the general spirit of this authoress, and her party . . . religion is utterly, and with zealous care, excluded from her writings. The pious addresses of Clarissa to her Creator, affect the heart of the reader with the most delightful and grateful sensations; while the furious declamation of 'Mary' to the God of nature, and the God of reason, excite no sentiment but disgust.[19]

The *Anti-Jacobin* reviewers saw the comparison Hays intended, but what they found so objectionable was the "furious declamation of Mary." This declamation was Hays's repetitive critique of social practices, institutions, the legal system, and the power of the aristocracy. Unlike Clarissa who after her seduction accepts her fate with resignation and equanimity, the heroine Mary Raymond rages against her oppressors, those who defeat what she calls her "right to exist" (141). She is unwilling to accept the notion that a woman who has lost her virginity must necessarily be socially banished and must look towards heaven for redemption. Mary's attitude to life is contrary to that shown by the maiden in the fable or Richardson's heroine:

> My bosom swelled with honest indignant pride: I determined to live; I determined that the devices of my persecutors should not overwhelm me: my spirit roused itself to defeat their malice and baffle their barbarous schemes.
>
> (141)

This spirited stance is not in keeping with the passive and submissive demeanor required of the feminine subject in traditional conduct-books. It is not surprising that Hays aroused the ire of conservative thinkers of the time.

Another text which affects the heroine adversely is her mother's memoirs which Mr. Raymond presents to her. This intradiegetic text occupies a central position in Mary's life and is symbolically situated in the middle of the two-volume novel. It is the last narrative of a woman, but framed by the discourse of a man, albeit a progressive and liberal one. Mary does not have direct access to her dead mother, or to her maternal body, and her access to the body of text left by her mother is problematic. The packet containing the pages written by Mary's mother is enclosed within letters to Mary written by Mr. Raymond. He, in effect, has the task not only of introducing and ending the story, but also of directing the response of the reader. While as a former suitor of Mary's mother, he is sympathetic to her plight, his language reveals that he is very much a product of patriarchal culture and of his age. When he describes her mother to Mary, it is in romantic and idealized terms, much like the language in Moore's fable. He remembers her as "a young woman, amiable and accomplished," as "lovely Mary, whom Nature had formed in her most perfect mould" (58). The mother is presented as an object of male desire at first, and then, after her seduction, she becomes a madwoman and whore. When Mr. Raymond sees her five years later she is "a woman, with a wan and haggard countenance, her clothes rent and her hair dishevelled" (59). He perceives "the remains of uncommon beauty," but she is "stained with blood, disordered by recent inebriation, disfigured by vice, and worn by disease" (60). His representations of Mary's mother are polar opposites, showing that he can conceive of his former lover only in terms of the angel or the whore.

Mary's introduction to her mother, and to the text left by her mother then, is influenced by these representations of woman as either lovely angel or contaminated whore. Her reading of her mother's legacy is mediated by these textual depictions. As well as gathering information, Mary and we, as readers, have to learn to decipher and read the text written by the mother. The mother's narrative is that of the seduced maiden, and though in prose, has reverberations reminiscent of the paternalistic and judgmental tone of Moore's fable. The memoirs reveal that, following the codes of society, the mother's standards of right and wrong behaviour are based, not surprisingly, on sexual purity. Once she has lost her "innocence," she feels that she has also lost all dignity, self-respect, and self-worth. This disintegration affects her physically, emotionally, socially, and economically. Significantly, she increasingly speaks of herself as a victim, as someone without control over her destiny, and someone lacking in agency and subjectivity. The language she uses reflects her sense of powerlessness. She changes from active to passive voice as she writes of her fall from grace. For example, she says that at eighteen, she "rejected" an honorable man, and instead, "yielded" to a man of fortune and rank (63). After months of "varied pleasure" however, she writes: "I found myself suddenly deserted . . . thrown friendless and destitute upon the world, branded from infamy, and a wretched outcast from social life" (63). Here, she describes herself as a being to whom things are done rather than one who does things. The danger of this kind of thinking and representation is that it reinforces the notion that a seduced woman is necessarily passive and helpless, and can no longer fend for herself.

What the narrative teaches young Mary is that there is no social space open to seduced women. The seduced woman simply becomes a site of abuse or a site of pleasure for men. When she asks for her parents' help, she "was treated as an abandoned wretch, whom it would be criminal to relieve and hopeless to attempt to reclaim" (64). Other men see her as an easy target for their sexual pleasure, partly because of her low self-esteem, partly because of her poverty. Her helplessness becomes a reason and a justification for further sexual liaisons:

Unable to labour, ashamed to solicit charity, helpless, pennyless, feeble, delicate, thrown out with reproach from society, borne down with a consciousness of irretrievable error, exposed to insult, to want, to contumely, to every species of aggravated distress, in a situation requiring sympathy, tenderness, assistance,—From whence was I to draw fortitude to combat these accumulated evils?

(64-65)

This account of the mother's life inevitably scripts the woman as victim, as passive and helpless being, and prey. When she describes her life with the libertines, it is still either in the passive voice or narrated as if she had no control over her actions: "I found myself betrayed," "I was compelled," and "The injuries and insults to which my odious profession exposed me eradicated from my heart every remaining human feeling" (66-67). In addition, she has internalized the image of the sexual woman as a monstrous sickness: "I became a monster, cruel, relentless, ferocious; and contaminated alike, with a deadly poison, the health and the principles of those unfortunate victims whom, with practised allurements, I entangled in my snares" (67). These representations of women, as victim, as prey, as monster, are part of the damaging images with which the heroine has to contend when she is later placed in a similar situation. She has to learn to read herself and her body differently from her mother.

Besides texts—real, fabular, or fictional ones—another way in which the ideology of the "proper lady" is transmitted is through the disciplining, controlling, and shaping of female habits and their desire. Early on in the novel, Hays reveals how education and the prejudices of society can create and channel a woman's aspirations. As a young girl who is brought up in idyllic Wales, Mary is brought up to exercise and develop her mind and body. This system of education follows the recommendation of Mary Wollstonecraft, who encouraged women to "endeavour to acquire strength . . . of mind and body" rather than to become soft and weak creatures.[20] Mary says that she was "early inured to habits of hardiness; . . . to endure fatigue and occasional labour; to exercise [her] ingenuity and exert [her] faculties, arrange [her] thoughts and discipline [her] imagination" (5). Hays demonstrates how girls can be as physically active and dexterous as boys when given the opportunity. Her heroine narrates:

At ten years of age, I could ride the forest horses without bridle or saddle; could leap a fence or surmount a gate with admirable dexterity; could climb the highest trees, wrestle with the children of the village, or mingle in the dance with grace and activity.

(5)

While these claims may sound like idle boasting, Hays was making an important point here about the relation between women's abilities and their education. Given a liberal education where she is taught languages, geometry, algebra, arithmetic, astronomy, and other branches of natural knowledge, Mary excels and becomes a model student. In

diligence, "in courage, in spirit, in dexterity, and resource," she is equal to or perhaps slightly ahead of William, whom Mr. Raymond tutors (9).

In her *Appeal to the Men of Great Britain in Behalf of Women* which was cowritten with her sister, Hays remarked that the "abilities and capacities of sexes are so alike, that with equal advantages it were difficult to determine to whom the palms were due."[21] In this treatise, she complained that women have been "bound by chains" and "subjected as a race."[22] Similarly, in a letter published in July 1796 in *The Monthly Magazine,* Hays, writing as "A Woman," complained about the way women were excluded from certain activities:

That one half of the human species, on a self-erected throne, should prescribe bounds to, and impose intellectual fetters on, the other half; and dictate to them to what purposes they are to apply, and how far they are to be allowed to exercise, their common faculties, is not more intolerable than vain.[23]

She pointed out that "because the education of women has been uniformly *perverted,* as well as neglected, than that of men, their general inferiority then follows as a consequence."[24] In *The Victim of Prejudice,* what she tries to demonstrate is the loss of possibilities for intelligent women such as her heroine. The fact that Mary Raymond had the mental and physical potential, but fails to transcend the customary social prejudices and limitations makes her narrative all the more tragic. Her initial aspirations and desires to live a life of liberty and independence are thwarted by many "prejudices" of society.

Although she has been unfettered by gender in her childhood and early adolescence, Mary soon encounters what Hays has called the "tyranny of custom."[25] During her seventeenth year, when she is "tall, healthful, glowing," and beginning to "display all the graces and the bloom of womanhood," her guardian reluctantly acquaints her with "the manners and maxims of the world" (25). He informs her that because of her lack of a good family, she can "never be the wife of William Pelham" who had been her childhood playmate and companion (32). William's father wishes him to be "preserved from humiliating connections," and Mary's "poverty, obscure birth, and the want of splendid connections" overshadow her "beauty," "virtue," and "talents" (32). She is obliged to separate from William at the request of her guardian. This injunction has the paradoxical effect of awakening previously unarticulated desires and feelings in Mary. After their conversation, she thinks:

Many of the sentiments and reflections of my patron struck me as at once new, extraordinary, and inconsistent. My ideas were confused, my reasoning powers suspended: undefined apprehensions and suspicions arose in my mind; my principles were unhinged and my passions thrown into disorder.

(33)

What Hays demonstrates is the contradiction between social practices and reason which suggested that she and William were compatible. For the first time in her life, her heroine's "reasoning powers" were "suspended," and her "principles . . . unhinged" (33). Sandra Sherman points out that throughout the novel, Hays depicts "women's reason as constituted by ideology premised on women's subjection."[26] Sherman argues that "in Hays's postrevolutionary epistemology, women's mental exertion is subject to distortion by affective imperatives that reinscribe patriarchal limits, subverting strategies—represented in hopeful, revolutionary terms of 'reason'—through which women might become autonomous subjects."[27] Here the prohibition has a disruptive effect on her emotions as well as her body:

> Mr. Raymond's discourse had awakened in my heart new desires and new terrors, to which, till that moment, it had been a stranger. The novelty of my sensations at once surprised and alarmed me. . . . If nature had yet spoken in my heart, so soft and gentle were her whispers, that her voice had hitherto been unheeded. The caution of my patron appeared to have given a sudden and premature existence to the sentiment against which he sought to arm me.
>
> (34)

Here Hays is doing what Michel Foucault would call a genealogical analysis of female sexuality and desire. Hays reveals that it is not "nature" that speaks to Mary's heart, but the "caution" of her guardian. In other words, language, in the form of the prohibition of Mr. Raymond, creates sexual desires in Mary: "his discourse awakened . . . new desires" and gave a "sudden and premature existence" to the very sentiment which she is forbidden to experience (34).

In *The History of Sexuality,* Foucault argued that it was in the eighteenth century that there was a "hysterization of women's bodies, where the feminine body was analyzed . . . as being thoroughly saturated with sexuality."[28] As Hays shows, previous to Mr. Raymond's injunction, Mary did not view her body as a sexualized one. She had not ever thought of William as anything more than a companion and friend. However, the day after the prohibition, Mary begins to lament that she can "never be the wife of William Pelham," a wish she had not articulated before (35). She begins to see herself as a sexual being, and the energies she previously devoted to intellectual and physical pursuits are henceforth channeled into feminine ones that conform to social expectations of what a woman should be. Mary admits to William: "I knew not, that the regard I felt for you differed, in any respect, from our mutual and infantine fondness, till Mr. Raymond awakened my fears, and alarmed my tenderness, by telling me that I must separate myself from you, that 'I must never be the wife of William Pelham'" (53). In representing Mary as a dangerous threat because of her sexuality or reproductive capacity, Mr. Raymond then succeeds in colonizing and shaping Mary's body. Through language, her body is invested with ideological meanings previously unknown to her. Well-intentioned as he is, Raymond nevertheless instills in Mary the notion that her desire and her body are perverse and unacceptable to respectable society.

This scene also illustrates the relationship between power and desire. Foucault notes that "the law is what constitutes both desire and the lack on which it is predicated. Where there is desire, the power relation is already present."[29] He points out that "power's hold on sex is maintained through language, or rather through the act of discourse that creates, from the very fact that it is articulated, a rule of law."[30] In *The Victim of Prejudice,* Hays makes us aware that Mary's body becomes a highly-charged *topos* and becomes inseparable from her social identity, from her intellectual and psychic self. It is not only Mr. Pelham and Mr. Raymond, the father-figures of the novel, who construct her as sexualized being. Other men, such as her friend William, and the Gothic villain, Sir Peter Osborne, also construct Mary's identity and objectify her. Though they have very different intentions—one wishes initially to be her husband, and the other wishes to seduce her—the end result is the same for Mary. Whereas in her youth, with her "active mind," "ardent curiosity," and "an enthusiastic love of science and literature," she had been a serious student, she is increasingly unable to see herself apart from the feminized and sexualized position of wife and mistress (24-25).

William plays a much smaller role in the construction of Mary into a feminine subject than Sir Peter Osborne. Early on, he naively proposes to "purchase a cottage, and hide . . . from the world" with Mary. In a reckless moment, Mary compares their youthful passion to the sublime love between Emilius and Sophia who she thinks experienced the "most exquisite rapture" and the most "bewitching delirium" that the human mind is capable of enjoying (55-56). This is an interesting and suggestive reference because both Wollstonecraft and Hays disagreed with Rousseau's principles of education which maintained that a soft, gentle, and feminine Sophie was perfectly formed to be Emile's companion. Rousseau believed that "woman is framed particularly for the delight and pleasure of man."[31] That Mary alludes to this problematic text at a moment when she contemplates an implausible act is significant. She sees the impossibility of her relationship with William, and calls their future an "undefinable contradiction" (55). The allusion to *Emile* acts as a forewarning of what comes subsequently. For much later in the novel, William meets Mary again and proposes to restore to her all his "affections" despite the fact that he is married to another. While he claims to be following the "dictates of nature and virtue" rather than the "factitious relations of society," Mary can only interpret his proposal as an attempt to "seduce" her "judgement" (127). She refuses to become his mistress, his object of "delight and pleasure," and would rather brave "dishonour, death," than "self-reproach" (129). Though he is certainly not as villainous as Sir Peter Osborne, what he offers Mary is similarly sinister. Both William and Osborne view the seduced woman as a vulnerable and easily penetrable body.

Of all the characters in the novel however, it is Sir Peter Osborne, representative of aristocratic decadence, who wields the most power over Mary and her body. Through physical, linguistic, psychic, and economic violence, he single-handedly transforms Mary into a socially acceptable docile body. His relentless pursuit of Mary takes many forms. At their first meeting, he catches Mary trying to steal grapes from his garden and immediately calls her "a true daughter of Eve," as well as pronouncing her to be "a little beauty," "a Hebe," and "a wood-nymph" (14). These names and mythical allusions are representations of woman which are culturally constructed and instilled. They are meant to reflect man's ideals or fears of sexuality or mortality which have historically been projected unto women. Twentieth-century feminist Luce Irigaray has pointed out that feminine roles like these are difficult for women to play:

> The value of a woman would accrue to her from her maternal role, and, in addition, from her 'femininity.' But in fact that 'femininity' is a role, an image, a value, imposed upon women by male systems of representation. In this masquerade of femininity, the woman loses herself, and loses herself by playing on her femininity. The fact remains that this masquerade requires an *effort* on her part for which she is not compensated. Unless her pleasure comes simply from being chosen as an object of consumption or of desire by masculine 'subject.'[32]

From his first meeting with her, Sir Peter sees Mary as "an object of consumption or of desire." He demands a kiss from her at this and their next encounter and assaults her with violence both times. Though Mary is unharmed by these escapades, their effect is to create terror in her where there previously was none. These incidents force Mary to view her body as a vulnerable and weak one even though earlier on in her youth she had boasted that she was equal to William in "boldness and agility" and even "daring" (9). Though Mary resists these roles and refuses to play the "masquerade" of femininity for a long time, these scenes, isolated as they seem, are part of the ways in which a woman is disciplined and punished into conforming to what society expects of her.

The most overt way in which Sir Peter Osborne forces his will upon Mary is to rape her. That Hays was thinking of *Clarissa* as she wrote her novel is evident from the somewhat similar circumstances of the characters and of the rape.[33] The *Anti-Jacobin Review* had observed that in the "dishonour" of Mary there was an imitation of Clarissa, but that the heroines were quite different in the way they handled their loss of chastity. More than once in her letters, both in private and published ones, Hays has discussed the over-valuation of chastity by society. In a letter to William Godwin dated 6 February 1796, Hays wrote: "It is from chastity having been render'd a *sexual virtue,* that all these calamities have flow'd—Men are by this means render'd sordid and dissolute in their pleasures; their affections blunted and their feelings petrified; they are incapable of satisfying the *heart of a woman* of sensibility and virtue."[34] Similarly, in an essay entitled **"Improvements Suggested in Female Education,"** Hays wrote: "Sexual distinctions respecting chastity, an impor-

tant branch of temperance, have served but to increase the tide of profligacy, and have been the fruitful source of the greater part of the infelicity and corruption of society."[35] Hays was not advocating that women be lascivious, but did not approve of the way a woman's whole life and reputation were dependent upon her virginity. In her view, chastity had become a highly sought prize for men who then were unable to view women through other terms. In *The Victim of Prejudice,* Mary attempts, albeit unsuccessfully, to convince the people around her that her honour and virtue are intact despite the fact that she has lost her virginity.

Hays's concept of virtue is unlike Richardson's in *Pamela,* where virtue is equated with the guarding of the heroine's chastity. In addition, contrary to the hagiographic tendencies in *Clarissa,* what Hays highlights in her novel are physical and economic effects of the violation. She uses the narrative to make observations about women's liberty, by linking the restraints on Mary's liberty and rights after her rape to those of powerless creatures such as the hare. The hare, like her, is hunted and trapped by Osborne. In both cases, Osborne, the pursuer, uses his position and power—as a man and a member of the aristocracy to sport with the weaker. Even before the actual rape, Osborne torments Mary in the village where she resided, and even invades the privacy of the home where she stayed: "he beset my paths, haunted me daily, and overwhelmed me with adulation and offensive gallantry" (51). I point out these earlier instances of harassment because they show that the rape was not a single act of violence but the culmination of systemic abuses and injustices that men in positions of power were culturally encouraged to act out against women. In her post-structuralist analysis of rape, Sharon Marcus points out that "rape is structured like a language, a language which shapes both the verbal *and* physical interactions of a woman and her would-be assailant. . . . The language of rape solicits women to position ourselves as endangered, violable, and fearful and invites men to position themselves as legitimately violent and entitled to women's sexual services."[36] In the eighteenth century, more so than today, this attitude of weakness and vulnerability in women versus physical violence in men would have been even more pronounced.[37] In *The Victim of Prejudice,* Osborne taunts Mary not only by his body, but also through language and his economic power. After the rape, he is confident that the authorities, the law, and the members of the community would support him rather than Mary, because she is a woman with no family and because she admits to having lost her chastity. He tells her, "No one . . . will now receive you . . . even were it more worthy of you; such are the stupid prejudices of the world. What is called, in your sex, honour and character, can, I fear, never be restored to you" (119). Though Mary at first believes that she can transcend these social prejudices, she learns that the loss of reputation in woman in eighteenth-century society is destructive. Despite her best efforts, she is unable to find employment suitable to her condition.

What the last part of the novel stresses is not so much the defeat of the heroine, though such a reading is certainly possible, but the difficulty for a woman to ignore her sexed body. In *Volatile Bodies,* feminist Elizabeth Grosz points out that in Western philosophy from Plato to Descartes there has been a tradition of separating the mind from the body. This dualism is often gendered and hierarchized so that women are associated with the body, while men are linked to the mind or reason. Grosz sees an urgent need to break down the dichotomy and to "refigure" bodies. She argues, "Only when the relation between mind and body is adequately retheorized can we understand the contributions of the body to the production of knowledge systems, regimes of representation, cultural production, and socioeconomic exchange."[38] In *The Victim of Prejudice,* Hays demonstrates the way discursive constructions of woman affect the heroine physically and psychically. In other words, she highlights the near impossibility for a woman to separate her mind or spirit from her body, to live outside codes of propriety, femininity, and chastity expected of her gender.

There are a number of incidents in the novel which show the link between language, representation, and a woman's corporeal existence. Three examples here should suffice. In one of her attempts to find employment, Mary applies to a lady in London recommended by her deceased guardian. Upon checking Mary's references, the woman finds out scandalous information about her past from William's father: that Mary had attempted to seduce William; that her birth was infamous; that she was brought up by charity (135). Mary's reaction to this biased version of her past is passionate. She recounts: "O God! how terrible were the first indignant feelings that rent my heart on the perusal of this barbarous recital!" (135). Here it is the recital or narrative that creates much emotion and anguish in her. In addition, because of these representations of Mary, the woman adamantly refuses to have any further contact with her. Upon hearing this, Mary has a strong physical reaction: "Unable to say more, my tottering limbs failed me; a mist overspread my eyes; while, overpowered by the passions that crowded tumultuously upon my heart, I sunk into a swoon, and should have fallen to the bottom of the stairs but for the support of the servant" (136). In this example, we see how words can modify a woman's sense of her self. Despite her youthful claims of physical and mental agility, Mary is slowly beginning to be overcome by her sense of powerlessness and vulnerability. This negative representation also adversely influences her prospects of employment. Without giving Mary a chance to tell her story, the woman makes a decision based on Mary's loss of "reputation," rather than on her capabilities or intrinsic moral worth. Unlike Clarissa and the young maiden in Moore's fable, Mary is unable to simply ignore the world's opinion of her and turn to heaven. For Hays who also had problems with her own reputation, the realities of day-to-day living had much to do with the way people perceived a woman's sexual self. In the novel she reveals the way Mary's economic situation became dependent upon the way others chose to read her body.

In two other incidents, Mary is again defeated by malicious representations of her. In one instance, at the print shop, the master makes sexual advances towards Mary because he has heard rumors about her involvement with Sir Peter Osborne and William Pelham. When Mary resists him, he only insults her: "My dear little angel, why this distress? why these pretty romantic airs?" (140). As she escapes from his arms, she hears the "ribaldry and cruel comments of the young men employed in the business" (140). Mary makes the connection between the representation of her and her desire for liberty: "I perceived that the fatal tale of my disgrace pursued and blasted all my efforts" (140). Despite her efforts to exist as an independent woman, she is forced to acknowledge her sexuality, her femininity, and her powerlessness in combating what people expect of a woman in her circumstance. This experience is repeated when she later finds a comfortable home with James on a farm. After six months of peaceful living, Osborne discovers their rural retreat and misrepresents her past to the villagers:

> Suddenly I found myself shunned by my acquaintance, as one infected by a pestilence: every eye scowled on me, every neck was scornfully averted on my approach. The young peasants, who had been accustomed to pay me homage, leered and tittered as I passed; and the village-maidens, bridling, shunned every familiar courtesy or advance.
>
> (162)

As in the previous example, Mary's body and her sexuality are overcharged with significance. All her actions are read from her sexualized position, and her body is no longer private, but becomes a site for public viewing, for comparison, for abjection and horror. Her female body imprisons her; she becomes simply body and no mind in others' eyes. This example may be fairly extreme, but it illustrates the way women's bodies have traditionally been viewed in patriarchy. Women's bodies are inscribed with reproductive and sexual functions, and often used as a means of socioeconomic exchange.

It is not surprising that Hays ends her novel with the female body in the penitentiary. It is an appropriate metaphor for the social and cultural restrictions placed on women in the eighteenth century. What John Bender says of Defoe's contribution to the rise of the penitentiary could equally apply to Hays's work: "he showed how, in confinement, the internal forces of psychological motivation fuse dynamically with the physical details of perceptual experience. Here is the penitentiary imagined as the meeting point of the individual mind and material causes."[39] In prison, Mary writes in a fatalistic tone which echoes the language of her mother:

> Almighty Nature, mysterious are thy decrees!—The vigorous promise of my youth has failed. The victim of a barbarous prejudice, society has cast me out from its bosom. The sensibilities of my heart have been turned to bitterness, the powers of my mind wasted, my projects rendered abortive, my virtues and my sufferings alike unrewarded, *I have lived in vain*! unless the story of my sorrows should kindle in the heart of man,

in behalf of my oppressed sex, the sacred claims of humanity and justice.

(174)

Though this conclusion may sound extremely pessimistic, what Hays has delineated in her novel is the way material causes affect the mind or the psyche of a woman. Although Mary's story seems similar to that of her mother's and to the narratives of other seduced women, the difference is that we are made aware of the way society's "barbarous prejudice" works to construct and delimit the female subject through the details of Mary's memoirs. It is this hope of awakening the consciousness of humanity that motivates the author and her heroine into writing this compelling account.

Notes

1. Mary Hays, *The Victim of Prejudice,* ed. Eleanor Ty (Peterborough, Ontario: Broadview Press, 1994), 1.

2. Mary Wollstonecraft, *A Vindication of the Rights of Woman,* 2nd ed., ed. Carol H. Poston (New York: Norton Critical Edition, 1988), 131, 133.

3. See my introduction to *Unsex'd Revolutionaries: Five Women Writers of the 1790s* (Toronto: University of Toronto Press, 1993), 3-30.

4. Hays, *Victim of Prejudice,* 1. For a discussion of desire, see my introduction to Mary Hays, *Memoirs of Emma Courtney,* ed. Eleanor Ty (Oxford: Oxford World's Classics, 1996), vii-xxxvii.

5. I am using the term "proper lady" to designate the tractable, obedient woman and wife as described in conduct books of the 17th and 18th centuries. See Chapter 1 of Mary Poovey, *The Proper Lady and the Woman Writer: Ideology as Style in the Works of Mary Wollstonecraft, Mary Shelley, and Jane Austen* (Chicago: University of Chicago Press, 1984).

6. Lois McNay, *Foucault and Feminism: Power, Gender and the Self* (Boston: Northeastern University Press, 1992), 23.

7. Michel Foucault, *Discipline and Punish: The Birth of the Prison,* trans. Alan Sheridan (New York: Vintage, 1979), 10.

8. Foucault, *Discipline and Punish,* 11.

9. Sharon Marcus, "Fighting Bodies, Fighting Words: A Theory and Politics of Rape Prevention," in *Feminists Theorize the Political,* ed. Judith Butler and Joan W. Scott (New York: Routledge, 1992), 389.

10. Susan Staves, "British Seduced Maidens," *Eighteenth-Century Studies* 14, no. 2 (1980-81): 110.

11. Staves, "British Seduced Maidens," 110.

12. Ibid.

13. Gary Kelly, "Jane Austen and the English Novel of the 1790s," in *Fetter'd or Free? British Women Novelists, 1670-1815,* ed. Mary Anne Schofield and Cecilia Macheski (Athens, Ohio: Ohio University Press, 1986), 287, 286. Kelly notes that Anti-Jacobin novels tended to employ an omniscient narrator, and used wit and satire to expose the follies of youth and the New Philosophy, 289.

14. Edward Moore, *Fables for the Female Sex, in The Young Lady's Pocket Library, or Parental Monitor* (London: 1790; facsimile rprt. Bristol: Thoemmes Press, 1995), 268.

15. Moore, "The Female Seducers," 273, 277.

16. Nancy Armstrong, *Desire and Domestic Fiction: A Political History of the Novel* (New York: Oxford University Press, 1987), 23.

17. Vivien Jones, *Introduction to The Young Lady's Pocket Library, or Parental Monitor* (1790, facsimile rprnt. Briston: Thoemmes Press, 1995), vi.

18. See the introduction to *The Victim of Prejudice,* xxii-xxiv.

19. *The Anti-Jacobin Review and Magazine* 3 (April-Aug. 1799): 57.

20. Mary Wollstonecraft, *A Vindication of the Rights of Woman,* ed. Carol Poston (New York: Norton Critical Edition, 1988), 9.

21. Mary Hays, *Appeal to the Men of Great Britain in Behalf of Women* (London: J. Johnson, 1798; facsimile rprt. New York: Garland, 1974), 45.

22. Hays, *Appeal to the Men of Great Britain,* 70.

23. A Woman, "Remarks on A. B. Strictures on the Talents of Women," *The Monthly Magazine* (July 1796): 469. Burton Pollin, in "Mary Hays on Women's Rights in *The Monthly Magazine,*" *Etudes Anglaises* 24, no. 3 (1971): 271-82, first noted that these articles and those signed M. H. were probably written by Mary Hays.

24. A Woman, "Remarks on A. B.," 469.

25. Mary Hays, *Letters and Essays, Moral and Miscellaneous* (London: 1793; facsimile rprnt. New York: Garland, 1974) I:9. Hays comments, "The truth is, the modes of education, and the customs of society are degrading to the female character and the tyranny of custom is sometimes worse than the tyranny of government."

26. Sandra Sherman, "The Feminization of 'Reason' in Hays's *The Victim of Prejudice,*" *The Centennial Review* XLI, no. 1 (1997): 144.

27. Sherman, "Feminization of 'Reason,'" 143.

28. Michel Foucault, *The History of Sexuality: An Introduction, vol. I,* trans. Robert Hurley (New York: Vintage, 1990), 104.

29. Foucault, *History of Sexuality,* 81.

30. Foucault, *History of Sexuality,* 83.

31. Jean-Jacques Rousseau, *Emilius; or, A Treatise of Education, 3 vols.* (Edinburgh: J. Dickson, 1773), III, v, 7.

32. Luce Irigaray, *This Sex Which Is Not One,* trans. Catherine Porter (Ithaca, N.Y.: Cornell University Press, 1985), 84.

33. In my introduction to *The Victim of Prejudice,* I noted that, "like Clarissa, Mary is from an untitled middle-class family and is courted by an aristocrat. Both heroines are transported from their homes by deceit to the London residences of the villain and rakes. Both are raped and dishonoured by their abductors, and live long enough to exclaim against their fate in writing," xxiii.

34. Mary Hays, letter #12 to William Godwin, 6 February 1796, New York Public Library, New York.

35. M. H., "Improvements Suggested in Female Education," *The Monthly Magazine* (March 1797): 194.

36. Sharon Marcus, "Fighting Bodies, Fighting Words: A Theory and Politics of Rape Prevention," *Feminists Theorize the Political,* ed. Judith Butler and Joan W. Scott (New York: Routledge, 1992), 390.

37. Margaret Hunt, in "'The Great Danger She Had Reason to Believe She Was in:' Wife-Beating in the Eighteenth Century," *Women & History: Voices of Early Modern England,* ed. Valerie Frith (Toronto: Coach House Press, 1995), 86, notes that "Eighteenth-century English society was profoundly hierarchical, explicitly committed to male supremacy and accustomed to the belief that the use of violence was essential for the maintenance of order among subordinate groups."

38. Elizabeth Grosz, *Volatile Bodies: Toward A Corporeal Feminism* (Bloomington: Indiana University Press, 1994), 19.

39. John Bender, *Imagining the Penitentiary: Fiction and the Architecture of Mind in Eighteenth-Century England* (Chicago: University of Chicago Press, 1987), 43.

FURTHER READING

Criticism

Grove, Allen W. "To Make a Long Story Short: Gothic Fragments and the Gender Politics of Incompleteness." *Studies in Short Fiction* 34, no. 1 (winter 1997): 1-10.

> Discusses several fragments of Gothic fiction, among them Hays's "A Fragment," which appears in her 1793 *Letters and Essays, Moral and Miscellaneous.*

Jacobus, Mary. "Traces of an Accusing Spirit: Mary Hays and the Vehicular State." In *Psychoanalysis and the Scene of Reading,* pp. 202-34. Oxford: Oxford University Press, 1999.

> Uses Freud's theories to examine *Emma Courtney,* focusing on the epistolary portions of the novel.

Jones, Vivien. "Placing Jemima: Women Writers of the 1790s and the Eighteenth-Century Prostitution Narrative." *Women's Writing* 4, no. 2 (1997): 201-20.

> Examines the prostitution narrative, employed by Hays, Wollstonecraft, and others in the 1790s, as a rebellious genre.

José Asunción Silva
1865-1896

Colombian poet and novelist.

INTRODUCTION

An important writer associated with the Spanish-language movement *modernismo,* Silva committed suicide at the age of thirty, thus cutting short a promising literary career. His work, which includes a number of poems and a novel, is characterized by the same pessimism and sense of futility that haunted his life. Silva shared his writings with only a few intimate friends, and most of his work remained unpublished until the early part of the twentieth century.

BIOGRAPHICAL INFORMATION

A member of a rich aristocratic family and the eldest of six children, Silva was born November 27, 1865, in Bogotá to doña Vicenta Gómez and don Ricardo, a prosperous importer and minor writer. Silva, an eager student, was tutored at home initially and then enrolled in various private schools where his devotion to his studies and his reserved nature alienated him from his schoolmates. Although his formal education ended when he joined his father's business at the age of sixteen, he continued learning on his own in a variety of fields—languages, philosophy, science, and history. In 1885, Silva traveled with his great uncle to Paris where he lived for the next two years. During this period he was exposed to the works of such poets as Stéphane Mallarmé and Charles Baudelaire as well as the philosophical writings of Auguste Comte and Arthur Schopenhauer. While he was in Europe, civil war broke out in Columbia and Silva's father suffered severe financial losses. When his father died in 1887, the 22-year-old Silva became head of both the family and its failing import business, although he was clearly unsuited for a commercial career. He spent the next seven years trying to salvage the business and repay his father's many creditors, but his efforts were unsuccessful. In 1891, his sister Elvira died suddenly, causing the poet to withdraw into a melancholy solitude. In 1894, Silva served briefly as the secretary of the Colombian Legation in Caracas, Venezuela, where he took up with the editors of a modernist periodical and wrote what many consider his finest poetry. On his return to Bogotá in 1895, however, he suffered yet another blow through the loss of a number of his most precious manuscripts in a shipwreck. An unsuccessful attempt to secure a diplomatic post and another failed business venture plunged him into a state of disenchantment and depression. Visiting a doctor about his insomnia, Silva ex-pressed curiosity about the exact position of the heart and asked the doctor to mark the location on his chest. The next day, May 25, 1896, he died of a self-inflicted bullet wound to the heart.

MAJOR WORKS

Silva began composing poetry at the age of ten, and the poetry of his early years was based on happy childhood memories. Soon after, though, his writing became infused with melancholy and eventually gave way to pessimism and a preoccupation with death. "Muertos," "Un poema," and his best-known poem, "Nocturno III," all involve the loss of loved ones, the latter inspired by his personal grief over the death of his sister. The manuscript of Silva's only novel, *De Sobremesa,* was lost in the shipwreck of *L'Amerique* off the coast of Columbia and was rewritten from memory by Silva at the urging of a friend. Silva completed the work before he died, but it was not published until 1925, possibly because of concerns from Silva's family that the work would damage his reputation. The novel is constructed as a series of diary entries by a South American poet traveling in Europe and is, like most of Silva's work, considered highly autobiographical. Like the protagonist of *De Sobremesa,* Silva shared most of his compositions in readings with an intimate group of friends rather than publishing them. The majority of his work was, like his novel, published posthumously, including *Poesías* (1908), and *El Libro de Versos* (1928), a collection of approximately thirty poems based on his childhood and his anticipation of death and the afterlife.

CRITICAL RECEPTION

It is as a representative of *modernismo* that Silva has gained the most critical attention. Mark I. Smith (1982) reports that Silva was, like many others of his generation, attempting to break away from the older literary conventions and to create a new tradition of his own. According to Smith, Silva "possessed the eclecticism, or elasticity of mind, characteristic of the truly original artist." Smith has also studied possible sources of Silva's poetic inspiration and notes the similarities between his work and that of Victor Hugo, suggesting the influence of French Romanticism on the *modernismo* movement. "It is particularly in the handling of vague and melancholic effects (achieved through an impressionistic use of carefully chosen detail) that Silva often resembles the great French master," according to Smith.

Many critics, including Lily Litvak (1989) and Julia Palmer (1991), consider the novel *De Sobremesa* to be a characteristic modernist text that was misunderstood by Silva's contemporaries and neglected by critics until recently. Litvak calls the work "a lyric novel that subordinates action to the intensity of an instant's emotion," and claims that the work features "the disintegration of the realistic protagonist." Palmer reports that the novel is being reevaluated by scholars today, and insists that an analysis of the novel's narrative structure reveals a work that is more complex than assumed by earlier critics, who dismissed it as disorganized and lacking in unity.

Many literary scholars have traced the autobiographical elements of Silva's work, noting that the qualities that defined Silva's life and early death also characterize his poetry and his novel. One such critic, Jack Roberts (1972), believes that "there is within his work a deep melancholy, a sense of helplessness, a lack of purpose, a feeling of anxiety and desperation unequalled in modernist poetry." Litvak, too, has studied the pessimism of Silva's writing and claims that his most prominent themes are the unhappy condition of present reality, the escape to the fantastic and mysterious, and the attractiveness of death, which Litvak describes as "the primary character in his poetic universe, the decomposing factor of all that might be perfect." Silva is, according to Litvak, "a poet whose vision is directed toward the past, yet who is condemned to a coarse, rough, mediocre present, an existence that leaves him with a pessimistic, negative view of the future." Alfredo Villanueva-Collado (1997), discussing conventional notions of masculinity in the Spanish-American critical tradition, suggests that speculation on Silva's possible homosexuality may have distorted assessments of his life and work and resulted in criticism that concentrates on lengthy descriptions of the poet's physical beauty and his "dandyism" rather than on the merits of his poetry and prose.

PRINCIPAL WORKS

Poesías (poetry) 1908
De Sobremesa, 1887-1896 (novel) 1925
El Libro de Versos, 1883-1896 (poetry) 1928
Obras Completas (poetry and prose) 1965
Intimidades (poetry) 1977

CRITICISM

G. Dundas Craig (essay date 1934)

SOURCE: Craig, G. Dundas. "José Asunción Silva." In *The Modernist Trend in Spanish-American Poetry,* pp. 251-54. Berkeley: University of California Press, 1934.

[*In the following essay, Craig discusses Silva as a member of the group of Spanish-American writers associated with the early Modernist movement.*]

José Asunción Silva was born in Bogotá, Colombia, in 1865, and died there in 1896. He is properly regarded as one of the precursors of the Modernist movement, and is so grouped along with Julián del Casal, Manuel Gutiérrez Nájera, and José Martí by Arturo Torres-Ríoseco in his volume, *Precursores del modernismo* (Madrid, 1925). Blanco Fombona has asserted that Rubén Darío drew some of his inspiration from Asunción Silva;[1] but this is unlikely. The poems of Silva did not appear in book form till 1908, twelve years after the author's death. During his lifetime they circulated among his friends or appeared in local periodicals, but the likelihood that any of these local Colombian papers reached Buenos Aires, where Darío was then living, is remote. Moreover, there is no trace of the influence of Silva in Darío's *Prosas profanas* (1896), where, if anywhere, we might expect to find it. The further fact that Darío denied that Silva's work had influenced him in any way, should be conclusive. It is equally unlikely that Silva was influenced by Darío, for, although Darío's first important work, *Azul,* was published in 1888, it was little known till Juan Valera's appreciation (published by *La Nación,* Buenos Aires) gave it a wide publicity. By this time, however, all that part of Silva's work which is now extant had already been written. **"Nocturno III"** probably belongs to the year 1892 or 1893. Of Silva's last works nothing is known, the manuscript having been lost in the wreck of the "America" (1895).

The important fact is that the enthusiastic study of the more recent French writers was going on over the whole Spanish-speaking area from Chile and the Argentine Republic to Colombia and Mexico; and Darío came to be recognized as the leader of the movement because he arrived at the opportune moment to concentrate and condense, and to express with power and precision, the thoughts and feelings of a whole generation.

The complete edition of the *Poesías* of José Asunción Silva (Barcelona, 1908) is a comparatively small volume. The earlier poems, dealing with memories of childhood, are simple, natural, and sympathetic; but even in these there is an occasional touch of melancholy:

> La abuela se sonríe con maternal cariño,
> mas cruza por su espíritu como un temor extraño
> por lo que en lo futuro de angustia y desengaño
> los días ignorados del nieto guardarán.

This same way of looking at things is noticeable in his patriotic poem, *Al pie de la estatua.* His admiration and love for Bolívar are deep and sincere, yet it is not of Bolívar's great deeds as Liberator that the poet sings, but of the pettiness, selfishness, and ingratitude of his own generation. Even the children playing innocently in the garden around the statue give him a feeling of foreboding which he is unable to dispel with Gray's reflection in a similar situation:

> Yet, ah! why should they know their fate
> Since sorrow never comes too late,
> And happiness too swiftly flies?
> Thought would destroy their paradise.

No more;—where ignorance is bliss,
   'Tis folly to be wise.

This note of bitterness is seldom absent from Silva's work. In his *Día de difuntos* (in which we catch echoes of *The Bells* of Edgar Allan Poe) it is not the mournful notes of the great bells that move the poet with their

   acentos dejativos
   y tristísimos y inciertos . . .
   que les hablan a los vivos
      de los muertos,

but the ironic clang of the bell that tells the hours, and notes how easily the weeping widower finds another mate.

   Ella [the bell] ha marcado la hora en que el viudo
   habló del suicidio y pidió el arsénico,
   cuando aún en la alcoba recién perfumada
   flotaba el aroma del ácido fénico;
      y ha marcado luego la hora en que mudo
   por las emociones con que el gozo agobia,
      para que lo uniera con el sagrado nudo
   a la misma iglesia fué con otra novia.

The somber coloring of these poems is the reflection of the tragedy of the poet's life, and this may be best understood in the light of his aspirations as he reveals them in his prose work, *De sobremesa*:

   You know very well what it is: just as poetry attracts me, so everything draws and fascinates me irresistibly: all the arts, all the sciences, politics, speculation, luxury, pleasure, mysticism, love, war, all forms of human activity, all forms of life . . . all those sensations which through the urgency of my senses I require to have from day to day more intense and more delicate.[2]

And again:

   Ah! to live one's life! that is what I desire; to feel all that can be felt; to know all that can be known, to be able to accomplish all that can be accomplished!

This hunger of the spirit is one of the preëminent marks of the Modernist. For Silva, all hopes and efforts ended in frustration. The death of his father left him burdened with debt. Being a poet and a dreamer, he was never able to raise his head above business worries. His sensibility was wounded by the sordidness of his surroundings and the lack of sympathy with his ideals. His reading of pessimistic philosophy left him without faith of any kind; while the death of his beloved sister, Elvira, together with the loss of the manuscript of his last and presumably best work, and the fear of insanity, brought him to despair and finally to suicide.

His third **"Nocturno,"** in which he gives expression to his grief over the loss of his sister, is one of the most deeply moving poems in Spanish-American literature. Its gloom and utter desolation are unrelieved by any ray of hope; yet there is a haunting beauty in the lines to which translation can hardly do justice. The feeling of strangeness and mystery is heightened by the musical reiteration of certain vowel sounds,

   una noche toda llena de murmullos, de perfumes y de
      música de alas,

by an occasional assonance, and by the frequent repetition of phrases—all characteristic of the newer school of poetry. These repeated phrases provoked laughter among the critics; and, read casually, they may seem pointless; but recited by a master reader they might be made very telling. On this point Solar has an interesting note:

   Bertha Singerman has recited the **"Nocturno,"** interpreting it admirably. Her rich, warm voice, on reaching these lines,

      ¡Y eran una sola sombra larga!
        ¡Y eran una sola sombra larga!
          ¡Y eran una sola sombra larga!

   sank softly, becoming each time thinner and more tremulous—as a phantom might grow, waver, and vanish away;—the syllables lengthened out with light inflections, and the accent became less and less marked until it expired in an imperceptible whisper. No one smiled. The hearers, less schooled but more intuitive than certain critics, had understood that each line, though identical in words with the preceding, had a different signification, evoked a new aspect of the quivering, changing shade, and all remained absorbed, as if the black wings of mystery had touched their spirits.[3]

Metrically, this poem was regarded as a daring innovation, for not only are the lines of irregular length, but also the meter is built up on a foot of four syllables with the accent on the third syllable (adopted later by José Gabriel y Galán, José Santos Chocano, and Ricardo Jaimes Freyre). The regular recurrence of the accent—more regular than is usual in the best Spanish poetry—serves only to enhance the feeling of melancholy and depression that pervades the whole poem.

In Silva's later poems the bitterness of his spirit finds vent in satire against the religious life, in *Don Juan de Covadonga*; against the love of women, in *Luz de luna*; against the futility of all human endeavor, in *Filosofías*; for

   cuando llegues en postrera hora
   a la última morada
   sentirás una angustia matadora
   de no haber hecho nada;

against the grossness of the materialistic philosophy of the time, in *Futura,* in which he sees the race gathered, in the twenty-fourth century, around the statue of its patron saint,

   Sancho Panza,
   ventripotente y bonachón;

and against the Philistine density of the critics, in *Un poema.* For into one great work of art the poet had poured all the power and beauty of his soul;

   Complacido en mis versos, con orgullo de artista,
   les dí olor de heliotropos y color de amatista . . .

Le mostré mi poema a un crítico estupendo . . .
Lo leyó cuatro veces, y me dijo . . . ¡No entiendo!

It is in this satirical sense that we must interpret the last poem in the volume, *Egalité.* In his book of table-talk, *De sobremesa,* Silva resents the imputation that he is a mere *asqueroso pornógrafo,* a charge which this poem might be held to justify; but the intention is obviously ironic. Silva was a man of rare culture and sensitive spirit. For him, the mandarin represents the flower of an age-old culture. But take that away and what remains? Nothing but the mere animal; and then

> Juan Lanas, el mozo de esquina,
> es absolutamente igual
> al Emperador de la China:
> los dos son un mismo animal.

Notes

1. Blanco Fombona maintains this opinion; see *El modernismo y los poetas modernistas* (Madrid, 1929), p. 172.

2. José Asunción Silva, *De sobremesa* (Bogotá, 1926), pp. 15-16.

3. Eduardo Solar Correa, *Poetas de Hispano-América* (Santiago de Chile, 1926), p. 261.

Donald McGrady (essay date 1966)

McGrady, Donald. "Two Unknown Poems by José Asunción Silva." *MLN* 81, no. 2 (March 1966): 233-37.

[*In the following essay, McGrady reviews two previously undiscovered poems by Silva, first printed in the Bogotá newspaper* Gil Blas *upon the sixteenth anniversary of Silva's death.*]

The works of José Asunción Silva are only partially and imperfectly known. Silva published a small portion of his total production during his lifetime, and most of his extant poems were published posthumously by friends or descendants. These friends and relatives did not always respect the poet's work, but frequently retouched those passages that they considered unsuitable. Sometimes the changes reflect the prudery of the self-appointed censor;[1] in other cases the editor merely seems to have preferred a different word, occasionally introducing another grammatical form.[2] Furthermore, according to one critic,[3] some poems were reconstructed by those who had been present at the readings Silva held for his intimate friends. The result is that there are variants in even Silva's best-known poems, and his work consequently has the air of traditional poetry.[4]

An undetermined part of Silva's work is still buried in periodicals and private archives. An indication of this is my recent discovery of two unknown poems by Silva, entitled **"Resurrexit"** and **"Necedad yanqui."** These poems are found in a Bogotá newspaper: *Gil Blas,* Año III, No. 247

(May 24, 1912). Unlike its French namesake, this *Gil Blas* did not usually devote much space to literary matters. However, the issue of May 24, 1912 was dedicated in its entirety to the commemoration of the sixteenth anniversary of Silva's death. Ten poems by Silva, eight of them unpublished, were given the place of honor. The issue also contained articles on Silva by several of his closest admirers: Pedro Emilio Coll, Emilio Cuervo Márquez, Clímaco Soto Borda, Daniel Arias Argáez and Tomás Palacio Uribe.

The poems published in *Gil Blas* are: **"Paseo," "El recluta," "Avant-propos," "Egalité," "Resurrexit," "Idilio," "Madrigal," "Necedad yanqui," "Psicoterapéutica,"** and **"Zoospermos."** Of these poems, only **"El recluta"** and **"Avant-propos"** had been previously published. Today, all except **"Paseo," "Resurrexit"** and **"Necedad yanqui"** are well known. **"Paseo,"** which is easily the most mediocre poem of Silva that has been printed, was recently republished by Daniel Arias Argáez[5] and will not be considered here.

With the exceptions of **"Paseo"** and **"El recluta,"** all the poems published in *Gil Blas* belong to the vitriolic *Gotas amargas,* the collection in which Silva gave expression to his skepticism and misanthropy. During his lifetime, Silva refused to publish the collection.[6] This made it possible for his censors to suppress offensive *Gotas amargas,* or so they thought. However, when the first edition of Silva's poems was published,[7] there were many protests against the mutilation of the poet's work. Guillermo Valencia's reaction was typical: "(. . . El mismo sentimiento zalamero e hipócrita que así fue osado a poner mano sacrílega en los escritos del poeta, ha suprimido la mayor parte de *Gotas amargas.* De éstas echamos menos: *Liberté, Egalité, Fraternité*; *El conocido sabio Cornelius*; *Al través de los libros amó siempre*; *Omne animal*; *Cápsulas*; *Es en el siglo XXIV*)."[8] The editor of *Gil Blas,* B. Palacio Uribe, may have had Valencia's protest in mind, for the memorial number is primarily an attempt to make known suppressed *Gotas amargas.*

Let us now turn our attention to the unknown poems. The text of **"Resurrexit"** is as follows:

"Resurrexit"

> Para qué arrepentirnos, si es bastante
> a purgar nuestro mísero pecado
> el doliente recuerdo de un pasado
> cada vez más cercano y más distante;
>   Si no hemos de encontrar más adelante
> todo lo que nos hubo conturbado,
> ni las bocas que ya nos han besado
> ni el loco amor ni la caricia amante,
>   Ríe y no te arrepientas, que mañana
> nuestras dos almas solas irán juntas
> a explorar los misterios del Nirvana. . . .
>   Mientras que Magdalena, la divina,
> entre el coro de vírgenes difuntas
> hace un triste papel de celestina.

> (*Gil Blas,* No. 247; no pagination)

"Resurrexit" is the most sacrilegious poem by Silva that has been preserved. Its title seems to be a contumelious reference to Christ's resurrection, as contained in the Scriptures and the Creed. The theme is "Let us love today, for tomorrow we die and everything ends." This hedonistic philosophy is the result of Silva's morbid preoccupation with death and the afterlife.[9] Several of the *Gotas amargas* reflect the pessimistic conclusions at which Silva arrived concerning the hereafter. However, no other poem is so bitter as **"Resurrexit,"** which lashes out spitefully at the beliefs held by Christians. The call for non-repentance and the ill-humored scoffing at Christian doctrine are reminiscent of Nietzsche, who exercised a decisive influence on Silva.[10] The basic themes of **"Resurrexit"**—preoccupation with death, disbelief in a hereafter, refuge in riotous love—are all found in **"Filosofías,"** another *Gota amarga*. **"Filosofías"** also shares with **"Resurrexit"** a reference to the Buddhist nirvana, a word that does not appear elsewhere in Silva's poetry. The similarity of themes and the new interest in nirvana probably indicate that **"Resurrexit"** and **"Filosofías"** were written within a short time of each other.[11]

"Necedad yanqui" appears in *Gil Blas* as follows:

"Necedad Yanqui"[12]

En Nueva York. Cenando con William W. Breakhart,
comisionista yanqui de fortuna notoria,
y que, según los cálculos de gente respetable,
no baja de 350,000 dollars,
le oí decir las frases siguientes, que atribuyo
a embriaguez producida por quince o veinte copas:
  "¿Amigos suyos? Perfectly. Yo nunca tiene amigos.
¿Usted cree en esto? Ensáya. Está usted en Europa,
préstales por servicio your francs if you are in Paris
your pounds if you are in London if in Spain your onzas
well. . . . il amigo suyo es muy agradecido;
usted es very plased. . . . Entonces il es desagradado
I d'ont pay a usted nada. . . . y no es su amigo ahora
o bien el paga todo. . . . and that's is very silly
yo no es su buen amigo y dice usted le roba . . ."
  Yo he atribuído siempre aquel discurso estúpido
a embriaguez producida por quince o veinte copas

(*Gil Blas*, No. 247).

"Necedad yanqui" is a protest against materialism. It seems reasonable to assume that Silva wrote this poem during the period in which he was struggling desperately to re-establish the family fortune. After his bankruptcy of 1894, Silva was ever looking for a scheme to get rich quick. His repeated failures no doubt made him envious of successful entrepreneurs. Therefore **"Necedad yanqui"** is probably not a reflection of antipathy toward the United States, but a sour-grapes attitude toward the symbol of commercial success, the enterprising and well-heeled Yankee.[13] Silva ridicules the antisocial Mr. "Breakhart" by making him speak fractured Spanish, and by his intemperance.[14] Presumably, the mistakes in Mr. Breakhart's English are not intentional; it is impossible to say whether

they are to be attributed to Silva or to the typesetter. The rhyme and the uneven number of lines indicate that a verse is missing after line eleven.

"Resurrexit" and **"Necedad yanqui"** give us additional insight into the poetic work of José Asunción Silva. Further investigation in Colombian periodicals and archives will undoubtedly yield other poems. Silva's genius cannot be definitely evaluated until all his extant work is brought to light.

Notes

1. The most famous example is that of the "Nocturno I" (also called "Ronda" or "Poeta, di paso"). Roberto Suárez, a friend of Silva who had the manuscript, introduced several prudish changes in the version he published in *Repertorio Colombiano*, XVII (1898), p. 358: "severo retrete" for "señorial alcoba" (or "nupical alcoba," according to other versions), and "rendida tú a mis súplicas" for "desnuda tú en mis brazos." Many subsequent editions reproduced these versions.

2. Numerous examples can be found by comparing almost any two editions of Silva's poetry. An example of a different grammatical form is the substitution of "zapatitos" for the typically Colombian "zapaticos" in "Crepúsculo."

3. Baldomero Sanín Cano, note 5 in his edition of Silva's poetry (Paris, Buenos Aires: L.-Michaud, 1923?), reproduced in the Aguilar edition (Madrid, 1952), pp. 196-197.

4. On occasion, poems have been mistakenly attributed to Silva. See Daniel Arias Argáez, *Bolívar*, No. 5 (November-December, 1951), pp. 943 and 962.

5. *Ibid.*, pp. 942-943. Arias Argáez publishes other unknown poems by Silva on pp. 942, 946, 949 and 950. These poems have not been included in later editions of Silva's verse.

6. Roberto Liévano, *En torno a Silva* (Bogotá, 1946), pp. 30-31.

7. *Poesías* (Barcelona: Imprenta de Pedro Ortega, 1908).

8. *Bolívar*, No. 4 (October, 1951), p. 620. Most of these omitted *Gotas amargas* appeared in subsequent editions, but under different titles than the ones Valencia gives, which are usually the first lines; only "Cápsulas" remains the same. "Omne animal" is still lost, as is another *Gota* mentioned by Sanín Cano (Aguilar ed., pp. 196-197). Valencia's punctuation, if it is faithfully reproduced here, indicates that "Liberté, Egalité, Fraternité" is one title; but according to Liévano (p. 25), "Liberté" and "Fraternité" are different poems that have been lost. The fact that there is a known *Gota amarga* called "Egalité" supports Liévano's statement. Other poems by Silva have appeared under different titles: those called "Juntos los

dos," "Poeta, di paso" and "Nocturno" in the Aguilar ed. are "Risa y llanto," "Ronda" and "¡Oh dulce niña pálida!" (or "Dime") in earlier editions. This confusion would seem to indicate that Silva, like his admired Baudelaire, left many poems without titles, and that these were later supplied by editors.

9. Silva's obsession with death and the hereafter is evident even in his earliest poems—for example, in "Crisálidas," written when he was only fifteen.

10. See Rafael Maya, introduction to Silva's *Obra completa,* 2nd ed., Biblioteca de Autores Colombianos, No. 99 (Bogotá, 1956), p. 16. Looking in the other direction—not of Silva's sources, but of his possible influences—we find an affinity of "Resurrexit" with the novel *María Magdalena* (Barcelona, 1917), by José María Vargas Vila, the *enfant terrible* of Colombian literature. Silva's Magdalene follows his advice of "no te arrepientas" and reverts to her former immoral life, now acting as go-between among dead virgins; Vargas Vila's Magdalene goes a step farther and revels with a depraved Christ.

11. The word "nirvana" occurs twice in Silva's autobiographical novel *De sobremesa* [Bogotá, 1925], pp. 243 and 356 of the cited *Obra completa* ed. Since the themes of death, disbelief and refuge in mercenary love are also present in *De sobremesa,* it would seem reasonable to conjecture that Silva wrote the poems at more or less the same time as the novel. Silva reconstructed *De sobremesa* shortly before his death, after the original manuscript was lost in the shipwreck of the *Amérique* (1895).

12. I reproduce this poem exactly as it appears in *Gil Blas,* without correcting spelling or supplying missing punctuation.

13. I have found no evidence of anti-American feeling in Silva's other works. On the contrary, José Fernández—Silva's *alter ego,* the hero of *De sobremesa*—expresses admiration for American enterprise: ". . . mientras me consagro en alma y cuerpo a recorrer los Estados Unidos, a estudiar el engranaje de la civilización norteamericana, a indagar los *porqués* del desarrollo fabuloso de aquella tierra de la energía y a ver qué puede aprovecharse, como lección, para ensayarlo luego, en mi experiencia" (p. 244). Also see pp. 200 and 229.

14. There are also a couple of hard-drinking Yankees in *De sobremesa,* p. 271.

Jack Roberts (essay date 1972)

SOURCE: Roberts, Jack. "Life and Death in the Poetry of José Asunción Silva." *The Southern Quarterly* 10, no. 2 (January 1972): 137-65.

[*In the following essay, Roberts examines the pessimism and sense of futility that characterized Silva's life and work, pointing to the influence of Comte and Schopenhauer on his poetry.*]

When any man takes his life, it is a tragic event, but if that man happens to be a promising literary figure, the public seems particularly shocked, and, doubtless, many wonder what could have compelled him to such a choice. José Asunción Silva is usually considered the most pessimistic of the modernists. There is within his work a deep melancholy, a sense of helplessness, a lack of purpose, a feeling of anxiety and desperation unequalled in modernist poetry. A suicide at the age of thirty, Silva apparently either could not cope with his particular circumstances in life or he did not think life worthy of being prolonged.

Possessor of an extreme sensitivity from earliest childhood, Silva exhibited a search for knowledge, faith, and purpose that evaded him constantly during his short life. Added to this inherent sensitivity and quest for purpose were disastrous personal blows such as his failure in the business world, the death of several members of his family, and the loss of some manuscripts which Silva felt certain would bring him the recognition he so ardently pursued.

In the reactionary clime of Bogotá, José Asunción could not feel free to discuss new philosophies or to satisfy his voracious appetite for knowledge. Groping for a certainty to which to cling, he became entangled in various philosophical systems, especially those of positivism and of Arthur Schopenhauer. Silva could see no hope wherever he turned, and this desperation is expressed in his poetry. He could never reconcile intellect with religion. In complete agreement with Schopenhauer concerning the vanity of existence, he took his life May 25, 1896.

The poet's mind, personality, and education were such that, compounded with other circumstances, they instilled in him a sense of futility that ultimately terminated in suicide. José Asunción Silva was surely not the only man to be faced with such devastating obstacles to happiness, but he chose to commit suicide rather than combat a life filled with disappointments. What, then, in more specific terms, were those forces that determined his destiny? His poems, though few in number, give us reflections of his anguished soul, and it is there we shall turn ultimately to analyze the course and depth of his despair. The answer to why he chose as he did and why his poems manifest an increasing obsession with death is complex and must be examined in several stages. I have divided these into: (1) background and temperament; (2) positivism; (3) Schopenhauer; (4) early poems; (5) the forgotten dead; and (6) "El mal del siglo."

Since there can be no adequate comprehension of Silva's spiritual life as mirrored in his poetry without a previous knowledge of the external circumstances, let us consider the first stage.

I BACKGROUND AND TEMPERAMENT

José Asunción Silva was born the twenty-seventh of November, 1865, in Bogotá, Colombia, the oldest of six brothers and sisters. His father, don Ricardo, was an importer, a model of community life, and a *costumbrista* essayist of some repute, at least in Bogotá. Don Ricardo has been described as "un tipo de caballero perfecto," and seems to have had a charm in conversation and an acute power of observation which he passed on to José Asunción. From his mother, doña Vicenta Gómez, Silva inherited his physical attractiveness. Silva's parents were patrons of the arts and their home was a gathering place for prominent literary figures of the day. Jorge Isaacs and Rafael Pombo were frequent guests and doubtless influenced young José to demonstrate a penchant for literature, and especially for poetry, at a precocious age.

Besides being patrons of the arts, Silva's parents were at least moderately wealthy. This is one of the primary factors of Silva's youth that we must keep in mind. He did not want for anything. He grew in a carefree atmosphere, not burdened by the rigors of poverty; and more important, he became accustomed to wealth as the earliest way of life he could remember. The significance of this would be apparent later after the family lost its fortune; it would leave a bitterness in Silva that accompanies the major portion of his poetry.

Silva was reserved and taciturn by nature and some of his schoolmates, noting his fine clothes and delicate handsomeness, misinterpreted his aloofness as haughtiness and snobbery. While other children participated in the customary juvenile games, Silva sat amidst the luxury of his perfumed room and read or meditated. Arias Argáez, an intimate friend of the poet, relates how Silva stimulated the jealousy of his comrades even at the tender age of twelve by wearing his imported European suits:

> . . . sus zapatillas de charol, sus flotantes corbatas de raso, su reloj pendiente de bellísima leontina de oro y, sobre todo (detalle único entre los niños de esos tiempos) su cartera de marfil, en la cual guardaba tarjetas de visita litografiadas, que, bajo cubiertas de fino papel timbrado, enviaba en los días de cumpleaños a los amigos de su casa.[1]

It is true that Silva did not mix with the common people, but after all he was of the aristocracy by birth, and Bogotá at that time maintained a strict division of social strata: the refined class of transplanted Spaniards, and "la gran masa ignara," composed of mestizos and Indians. Since Silva was reflective and literarily inclined, it was most probably the natural bent of his personality that prevented his mingling freely rather than a deliberate attempt to be antisocial. Throughout his entire life Silva had only a very few intimate friends in whom he confided and to whom he made known his poetry. Thus he early manifested a tendency toward isolation and introspection that would characterize his most pessimistic poems.

The atmosphere of Bogotá itself cannot be left unmentioned, for in a general way it too influenced Silva. Carlos García-Prada describes Bogotá in this period as a "ciudad en busca de sí misma y de su americanidad;"[2] as a place where the ancestral mansions contained perfumed parlors that bubbled with scintillating ladies and dashing gentlemen engaged in lively conversation or dance:

> Eran los cachacos santafereños, jóvenes y viejos distinguidos que vestían de negro siempre y según las últimas modas de Londres y de París; que charlaban por lucir el implacable estilete de su *gracia,* y montaban a caballo, iban a pelear en las guerras civiles, sembraban café en sus haciendas de tierra caliente, componían endechas y epigramas, cultivaban la delicadeza—forma suprema del honor—y llevaban una flor en el ojal y en el bolsillo una pistola de dos tiros cuando iban a ver a las damas de su preferencia, mujercitas adorables que en los bailes guardaban el compás de la música con abanicos de plumas de avestruz y se acariciaban los bucles rizados del cabello con sus dedos perfumados, y que todos los domingos sin falta concurrían a misa mayor envueltas en sus mantillas negras de moaré o de crespón, y sonreían al salir ante la lluvia de flores y piropos que a su paso derramaban sus galanes.[3]

From such an account it is evident that everything in Silva's life was directed toward refinement, tactfulness, and subtlety of thought and expression. But it should also be remembered that the elite were in the minority and among such a diminished number almost everyone would have more than a superficial knowledge of what all the rest were doing. This created many tensions and volatile situations and made José acutely conscious of what was expected of him. Silva himself best explained the society of Bogotá in an interview he granted in Paris to a Czech ethnographer:

> . . . Todo el mundo conoce a todo el mundo. Las preocupaciones principales son la religión, las flaquezas del prójimo y la llegada del correo de Europa . . . Los nervios en ese aire seco, rarificado, de una misma temperatura durante el año, están en tensión constante. Para hacerse usted agradable en una sociedad en que todo el mundo conoce a todo el mundo, es necesario que se documente sobre las menudas preocupaciones del prójimo . . . Cada uno de nosotros cree estar en posesión de la verdad. Hablamos en voz alta, con cierta precipitación, golpeando los adjectivos y gesticulando copiosamente. La contradicción nos mortifica. Hemos querido hacer el mundo a nuestra imagen y semejanza, y cuando sorprendemos entre él y nosotros pequeñas diferencias, reaccionamos violentamente.[4]

Such was the tension under which Silva daily lived.

The education of this poet is of primary importance, for he could never satisfy his desire to learn. His earliest lessons were administered in the home. Later he was enrolled in the school directed by don Luis M. Cuervo, and then in another managed by Ricardo Carrasquilla. His earnestness in study sometimes provoked the anger of his classmates, who generally considered him a prideful boy. At the age of sixteen Silva left school to aid his father in the business. Though the store took up most of his time during the day, he reserved the nights for reading, an avocation of which he never tired. José had an amazing capacity for assimilation; he taught himself languages, read philosophy, science, history, and psychology. He seemed to be trying to absorb the whole of all fields of knowledge. This avid search for knowledge and especially for truth would be a recurrent theme in his poetry.

In 1885 the youth received what in his opinion was the opportunity of a lifetime—to visit Paris. His great uncle, Antonio María Silva, had invited him; José was elated at the prospect of meeting some of the authors whose works he knew. In his two short years in Paris the writings of Verlaine, Mallarmé, and particularly Baudelaire had a profound effect on his literary taste. This period in Europe was also the era of advances in the sciences, of conflict between science and religion. The positivistic doctrine of Comte was widely propagated, as were the philosophies of Kant, Nietzsche, and Schopenhauer. In varying degrees all these influences came to bear upon Silva; the pessimism of Schopenhauer would be noticeably evident in the Colombian's writing.

While José gloried in the literary clime of Paris, civil war erupted in Colombia. Bogotá was practically incommunicado for some time. The government eventually triumphed, but the badly depleted gold supply necessitated the issuance of paper money which did not have the people's confidence. Don Ricardo's trade was ruined. José cut short his happy sojourn and returned to try to keep the bill collectors from forcing his father into bankruptcy.

In 1887 José suffered a serious jolt with the world of reality—he was never to recover from it. His father died and he was left head of the household. This twenty-two year old, extremely sensitive young man was now the head of a business to which he was suited neither by inclination nor talent. But he was head of the family now, and he tried to preserve its good name and to pacify the creditors.

For seven years Silva tried to pay off his father's debts, but they were too many and he lacked business sense. He filled the store with imported rugs and exotic items which doubtless appealed to him but were quite expensive and difficult to sell. In an effort to raise more money he accepted the position of secretary of the Colombian Legation in Caracas. During the years of his failures in commerce and his brief stay in Caracas, Silva wrote his most bitter and introspective work.

Before discussing events subsequent to his departure from Caracas, one other chief point should be emphasized regarding his family. Of his five brothers and sisters, three died in infancy. His favorite sister, Elvira, died in the bloom of youth in January of 1892. Her death more than that of the others affected Silva and was responsible for the beautiful **"Nocturno III,"** for which he is best known.

With the hope of being named minister plenipotentiary to Caracas, José returned to Bogotá on the *Amérique* in 1895. Not far off the Colombian coast the ship was caught in a tempest that lasted three days. Most of the survivors considered themselves lucky to be alive. But Silva could think only of the manuscripts he had lost—***Cuentos negros, Las almas muertas, Los poemas de la carne, De sobremesa***—work which he had believed would bring him the recognition he so fervently desired. It seemed that each goal for which he strove existed only to augment his suffering.

There was yet a glimmer of hope, a spark of light. In Caracas he had made plans for a cement and tile factory. Through his persuasiveness he borrowed the capital and built the factory. He was sure this would be the plan that would make millions. But this too failed; no fewer than fifty-two suits were brought against him. Silva now began to fear for his health. He suffered from insomnia, almost certainly aggravated by thoughts of his unrealized ideals.

Though outwardly unchanged, the poet had become completely disenchanted with life. He paid a visit to Doctor Juan Evangelista Manrique on the twenty-fourth of May, 1896. Manrique relates that Silva was curious about the exact location of the heart and had him trace it on José's shirt. That night there was a gathering of ten close friends at the Silva home. They chatted amiably; no one observed any difference in Silva's behavior. The next morning they found him dead in his bed, with a bullet in his heart.

So ended the life of this man whose share of adversity seems almost incredible. We have already seen how frequent and great his disappointments were—these give us clues to many themes in his poems. But before we consider the poems themselves, there remain to be discussed two major influences on Silva's life, for without them we cannot truly appreciate the inspiration for much of his writing: positivism and Arthur Schopenhauer.

II POSITIVISM

In the last two-thirds of the nineteenth century the world witnessed grave conflicts between science and religion. Numerous philosophers were advocating systems that dispensed with God as an explanation of the universe. Men such as Comte, Spencer, Nietzsche, Schopenhauer, and Darwin stated that God was no longer essential, and, in some cases, that He was a ridiculous explanation for life. Doubtlessly, *Origin of the Species* in 1859 created more dissension and bewilderment among the followers of Christianity than any other book in the last half of the century. The story of the creation had been repudiated. Science and philosophy were exterminating God. In what would men place their faith? Many would cling tenaciously to their Christianity; some would seek other answers. One of those answers was positivism.

The term positivism in a broad sense may be applied to any philosophical system that confines itself to empirical, observable data, and excludes a priori and metaphysical speculations. In this respect the philosophers Locke and Hume belong, in varying degrees, to this classification.

In a narrow sense, the one with which we are primarily concerned, positivism refers to that philosophy devised and systematized by the Frenchman Auguste Comte in the first half of the nineteenth century. The purpose of Comte's philosophy was to explain both the existing social organizations and to guide social planning for a better future. Comte's basic theory was the "Law of the Three States." This was the law of the evolutionary progress of man's reasoning power. Human thought, said Comte, had passed through two stages, theological and metaphysical, and was now entering the positive or scientific stage. During the theological or supernatural stage, man had explained phenomena as being the acts of the gods. In the metaphysical period, these super-human agents were depersonalized and regarded as abstract forces or powers. In the positive or scientific era, the belief in powers and agents was to be discarded and pure description of observable data would represent true knowledge. As an example of this we might consider possible explanations for gravitation: (1) In the theological state men would say that divine beings moved the planets. (2) The metaphysical state would attribute gravitation to an abstract force or power of attraction and repulsion. (3) In the positive state the solution would be a simple mathematical formula on the basis of which predictions could be made, the terms of which mass and distance, are calculable from direct observation.

Comte further held that each science passed through the three evolutionary states. Sociology, which he named, arose because of practical politics. The Frenchman believed that the origin of all sciences was man's attempt to manipulate the world about him to his practical ends. Francis Bacon, Nicholas de Malebranche, and Jacques Turgot had all exhibited positivistic tendencies, but no one until Comte had systematized the thought and applied it to the history of each science. From the abbé of Saint-Pierre, Montesquieu, and Saint Simon he appropriated the concept of a need for a basic and unifying social science to explain existing social structures and devise improved ones.

Comte recognized that the religious impulse would survive the decay of revealed religion and should have an object of worship. He proposed humanity as this object. He could see the desirability of a religious framework, but he wanted the worship to be of a secular nature—reason and humanity instead of God. The Frenchman believed that the organization of the Catholic Church, divorced from its supernaturalism, might be a good model for the positivistic society. He went so far as to create a calendar, a hierarchy, and a catechism for the worship of the "Great Being," humanity.

These are the basic tenets of the positivist philosophy. The key factor to be born in mind is that this system rejected theological and metaphysical speculations. It considered essences and causes as inaccessible and dealt with effects and relationships. Upon these grounds, the positivistic philosophy failed to satisfy Silva; for, as we shall see, in his bitterest poetry he was concerned with questions that could not be answered by empirical and observable data.

III Arthur Schopenhauer

In one of his poems Silva has a character say that he suffers from ". . . el mal del siglo . . . el mismo mal de Werther, de Rolla, de Manfredo, y de Leopardi. Un cansancio de todo, un absoluto desprecio por lo humano . . .

un incasante renegar de lo vil de la existencia . . ."[5] This was the illness that weighed upon the poet's mind. Life had become unbearable, detestable. The poem quoted is one of a bitter series through which runs a philosophy of pessimism and a desire for death. Although the Colombian mentions several philosophers, Schopenhauer is the only one whom he calls "mi maestro." For this reason and because the German philosopher's special brand of pessimism is particularly akin to Silva's thinking, he is singled out here as worthy of individual study.

Besides Schopenhauer's innate pessimism, the levity with which his work was greeted when it first appeared guided him toward an even darker outlook on life. As a young professor in Berlin, he had to struggle against the cult of Hegel so steadfastly imbedded in German thinking in the first half of the nineteenth century. Schopenhauer was, to a degree, an admirer of Kant and of the English empiricists Hume and Locke. He adhered to the principle that metaphysical theories that professed to describe the nature of the world a priori and without reference to observed data were paths in the woods leading to nowhere.

The basis of Schopenhauer's philosophy is the will. Will is the concept in terms of which all that exists and manifests itself in the world can finally be made known. This will attains consciousness only in the existence of the individual, and man's overt behavior expresses his will. In Schopenhauer's opinion man possessed an unchangeable will or nature which did not permit him to make free choices. A man knew what he was from the expression of his will in overt acts. He could not choose to be this or that—he simply was. The metaphysical will was blind, without conscious purpose or direction; therefore, people merely deceived themselves into believing that they acted upon the dictates of reason. The intellect's only function was to aid the will in achieving its goals.

Schopenhauer pictured life as one long uphill battle that contains only temporary satisfactions. If existence had any intrinsic, positive value, he reasoned, we should be content simply to exist. But we are happy only while we are chasing something our will desires. If we obtain it, we fall into a state of boredom until the will stimulates us to some new hunt:

> Human life must be some kind of mistake. The truth of this will be sufficiently obvious if we only remember that man is a compound of needs and necessities hard to satisfy; and that even when they are satisfied all he obtains is a state of painlessness, where nothing remains to him but abandonment to boredom. This is direct proof that existence has no real value in itself; for what is boredom but the feeling of the emptiness of life? If life—the craving for which is the very essence of our being—were possessed of any positive intrinsic value, there would be no such thing as boredom at all; mere existence would satisfy us in itself, and we should want for nothing. But as it is, we take no delight in existence except when we are struggling for something; and then distance and difficulties to be overcome make our goal look as though it would satisfy us—an illusion which vanishes when we reach it; . . .[6]

The German philosopher felt that unless suffering was the direct and immediate object of life, that our existence fell entirely short of its aim. It was absurd, he said, to look upon the enormous amount of pain in the world and think that it existed solely by chance and with no purpose. He concluded that work, worry, and trouble form the lot of most men their entire lives. The only consolation he could find was that if there were no obstacles to overcome, man, in his leisure time, would inflict more misery upon his neighbor than they both already endured at the hands of nature. He describes life as an ". . . unprofitable episode, disturbing the blessed calm of non-existence."[7] Bitterly he states that ". . . the longer you live the more clearly you will feel that, on the whole, life is *a disappointment, nay, a cheat.*"[8]

What, for Schopenhauer, was the value of the Christian religion? Was this the best of all possible worlds? Had a God purposefully created this world?:

> There are two things which make it impossible to believe that this world is the successful work of an all-wise, all-good, and, at the same time, all-powerful Being; firstly, the misery which abounds in it everywhere; and secondly, the obvious imperfection of its highest product, man, who is a burlesque of what he should be. These things cannot be reconciled with any such belief. On the contrary, they are just the facts which support what I have been saying; they are our authority for viewing the world as the outcome of our own misdeeds, and therefore, as something that had better not have been. Whilst, under the former hypothesis, they amount to a bitter accusation against the Creator, and supply material for sarcasm; under the latter they form an indictment against our own nature, our own will, and teach us a lesson of humility. They lead us to see that, like the children of a libertine, we come into the world with the burden of sin upon us; and that it is only through having continually to atone for this sin that our existence is so miserable, and that its end is death.[9]

With such views it is interesting to note that Schopenhauer did not advocate suicide as the solution to boring, painful life. However, he did not condemn suicide on moral grounds. Lashing out against the Christian religion, he states that nowhere in either the Old or New Testaments is there any prohibition or positive disapproval of suicide. Religious teachers, in his opinion, simply fabricated a condemnation of this act and declared it morally wrong. Schopenhauer believed that monotheistic religions denounced suicide to escape being denounced by it, because a person's voluntarily surrendering his life would be a bad compliment for Him who said that "all things were very good."[10] He then points out the fact that the ancients entertained quite a different view toward suicide. To support his point, he quotes Pliny, Seneca, and several other Stoics. Convinced that there was no greater right that a man should have than to his own life and person, he concludes that suicide is not wrong morally.

But Schopenhauer considered suicide as a substitute escape from life. True moral freedom—the highest ethical goal—was to be achieved by the denial of the will to live,

the fleeing from pleasures of this life. Now if a man committed suicide, he was, according to Schopenhauer, asserting the will to live if he could do so with satisfaction. When he destroys his existence, he is escaping the painful circumstances of his life, rather than denying his will to live. The German philosopher believed that few men would not end their lives at an early age if the act constituted a purely negative character, a stoppage of existence. But there is a positive aspect involved. It is the destruction of the body, and since the body is the manifestation of the will to live, men shrink from this act.

Thus, in Schopenhauer's eyes, suicide, though not a crime, was a "clumsy experiment."[11] In killing himself, a man was asking what change death would produce in his existence, but at the same time he was destroying the body, which was the manifestation of the consciousness that asked the question and awaited the reply.

I have tried to present the fundamental parts of Schopenhauer's philosophy which I believe exercised the strongest influence upon Silva. We shall see that the poet came to agree almost wholeheartedly with the philosopher. The main discrepancy, obviously, is the choice Silva made concerning suicide.

Now that we have the proper tools and insight with which to penetrate and appreciate Silva's work, we may make a more rewarding study of his poetry and observe in it the fatal trajectory traced by his mind and soul in his hopeless struggle with life—and his obsession with death.

IV EARLY POEMS

Memories of childhood were always a chief theme for the poet, for those were his happiest days. He had not yet encountered the harsh reality that was to buffet him mercilessly. In *Los maderos de San Juan* the chief themes are the cycle of life and the *ubi sunt* motif:

> Mañana, cuando duerma la anciana, yerta y muda,
> Lejos del mundo vivo, bajo la oscura tierra,
> Donde otros, en la sombra, desde hace tiempo están
> Del nieto a la memoria, con grave son que encierra
> Todo el poema triste de la remota infancia
> Cruzando por las sombras del tiempo y la distancia
> De aquella voz querida las notas vibrarán! . . .[12]

Balancing her grandchild on her knee in the midst of joyful play, the grandmother has a premonition or fear of what pain and sorrow the future may hold for the infant. From the description she herself is well acquainted with grief; her eyes are tarnished mirrors that once reflected things and beings never to return. Tomorrow, when his grandmother is dead, the child will recall with great melancholy these times. This poem could well be taken as a parallel to Silva's life. There was nothing to mar his youth, but later events made him look back to those years with an often repeated *ubi sunt* upon his lips. Deep melancholy is present but true pessimism has not yet appeared.

A further development of the *ubi sunt* motif, plus a new element, is evident in *Los muertos*:

Y en las almas amantes cuando piensen
En perdidos afectos y ternuras
Que de la soledad de ignotos días
No vendrán a endulzar horas futuras
Hay el hondo cansancio que en la lucha,
Acaba de matar a los heridos,
Vago como el color del bosque mustio
Como el color de los perfumes idos,
    Y el cansancio aquel es triste
    Como el recuerdo borroso
    De lo que fué y ya no existe . . .[13]

The new element is his changing view of death; the fatalistic mentality is now beginning to germinate. Death is pictured here as that which terminates. Silva seems to have a greater awareness of death in this poem. In *Los maderos de San Juan* the child remembers his grandmother and joyful youth; he can still hear her voice recounting tales to him. There is not the finality, the break with the past expressed in the refrain "De lo que fué y ya no existe." The view of death in *Muertos* does not contain the consolation present in *Los maderos.* In *Muertos* the memory of things past is not a comfort but a profound weariness that finishes killing the wounded. There was much in Silva's life that had been and ceased to be: his wealth, some of his loved ones, his dreams of fame. The poet's constant reflection upon this theme eventually proved fatal.

Even when he turned his thoughts to artistic endeavors, Silva could not rid himself of this enchantment with death. In *Un poema* he tells us that he dreamed of forging a poem. What would be the mood of this poem? "Un asunto grotesco y otro trágico." And the subject matter:

    Era la historia triste, desprestigiada y cierta
    De una mujer hermosa, idolatrada y muerta, . . .

    Le mostré mi poema a un crítico estupendo . . .
    Y los leyó seis veces y me dijo . . . ¡No entiendo![14]

He chose the history of a dead woman. That his readers might feel the bitterness of her life he joined sweet syllables and created vague suggestions of mystic sentiments and human temptations. Certain that his readers would enjoy this work, he presented it to a critic, who, after reading it six times, replied that he did not understand it. The critic's statement may be applied to the poet's life. Faced with overwhelming adversities and the inability to reconcile science and philosophy with religion, Silva reached the point where this thought dominated his mind: "No entiendo." Just as the critic could not comprehend the story of the dead woman, few if any of Silva's friends understood him or the depth of his despair.

Silva would much rather have spent his time in pursuit of the ideal in art. But his father died, leaving him to assume responsibility for the business. An excellent parallel to the changes forced upon Silva by his father's death is the fate of the soldier in *El recluta.* This poem centers about a young man whose life was uncomplicated until war broke out:

sólo conoció dos órdenes
de detención y de cepo,
un planazo en las espaldas
y el modo de gritar: "¡Juego!"
hasta la tarde en que, herido
en el combate siniestro,
cayó, gritando: "¡Adios, mamá!",
el pobre recluta muerto.[15]

This unfortunate recruit led a tranquil life until war came and forced its senselessness upon him. He did not know why he had to fight; he knew only how to take orders. Though not involved in a war, Silva had to adjust to a way of life not of his choosing. Instead of devoting himself wholeheartedly to reading and composing, he had to try to sell rugs and tapestries, a task for which he had no inclination. Both the soldier and the poet, in circumstances painfully incongruous with their true natures, were fighting battles from which neither could hope to emerge victorious. The recruit struggled along until a bullet ended his plight; Silva encountered one hardship after another until he voluntarily ended his life.

A new facet of this preoccupation with death is evidenced in Silva's thoughts on the deaths of certain friends and, in particular, of his sister, Elvira. As he watched those around him die, he became aware of a new emotion that death might evoke: *angustia y frío.* Death now assumes a more active role—the thief of something precious. The anguish caused by the loss of a loved one is no better expressed in Silva's poetry than in **"Nocturno III,"** inspired by the death of his sister Elvira, whom he loved intensely. She was undoubtedly a source of comfort to him in his economic difficulties and her loss left him quite bitter:

    Esta noche
    Solo, el alma
Llena de las infinitas amarguras y agonías de tu muerte

Separado de tí misma, por la sombra, por el tiempo y
  la
             distancia,
    Por el infinito negro,
    Donde nuestra voz no alcanza,
    Solo y mudo
    Por la senda caminaba, . . .

      Sentí frío, era el frío que tenían en la alcoba
      Tus mejillas y tus sienes y tus manos adoradas,
        Entre las blancuras níveas
        De las mortuorias sábanas!
      Era el frío del sepulcro, era el frío de la muerte,
        Era el frío de la nada . . .

¡Oh las sombras que se buscan y se juntan en las
  noches de
        negruras y de lágrimas! . . .[16]

The vocabulary he employs here gives us a profound insight into Silva's state of mind: *infinitas, amarguras, agonías, frío, negruras, muerte, nada.* The length of the lines here is particularly effective. As he introduces himself, alone, the verse is short (four or five syllables), perhaps indicative of his feeling of isolation and insignificance. When he begins to speak of Elvira and the barriers that separate them, the lines become almost disproportionately long—as if in telescoping the lines he tries to express both visually and poetically the great distance between them. The sense of separation, loneliness, and frustration is overwhelming. The contemplation of death, the infinite, and nothingness has indeed taken root; it will feed upon the poet's mind to bring forth a fatal blossom.

V THE FORGOTTEN DEAD

There are several moving poems in which Silva is concerned with how quickly the dead are forgotten by the living, whether they be merely friends or lovers. In these works he skillfully intertwines the themes of death, oblivion, the Nietzschean idea of Eternal Return, and a type of posthumous infidelity—as if the now deceased beloved could be hurt by his surviving mate's treachery. There are variations within the poems, but they all share one element in common: death.

With rare poetic insight he uses a window through which to view the passage of life in *La ventana.* This particular window was constructed in colonial times. Who, he asks, would not expect to see at this window some severe-looking old patriarch or a fair-complexioned, red-lipped lady from Andalucía? Does it retain visions of its past occupants?:

> Inútil, allí, a solas
> ella miró pasar generaciones
> como pasan, con raudo movimiento,
> sobre la playa las marinas olas, . . .
> ly ora mira la turba de los niños
> de risueñas mejillas sonrosadas,
> que al asomar tras de la fuerte reja
> sonriente semeja
> un ramo de camelias encarnadas!
>
> ¡Ay todo pasará: niñez risueña,
> juventud sonriente,
> edad viril que en el futuro suena,
> vejez llena de afán . . .
>
>   Tal vez mañana
> cuando de aquellos queden sólo
> las ignotas y viejas sepulturas,
> aún tenga el mismo sitio la ventana.[17]

Even in children at play Silva can see only their ceasing to exist. In one glance his mind spans their days of childhood, maturity, old age, and death. They will occupy unknown graves; yet the window, "Inútil, allí, a solas," will keep its same place to watch other generations pass and record no trace of them. By personifying the window through a type of stream-of-conscious process, Silva effectively employs Nietzsche's theme of Eternal Return. The joys and sorrows of countless generations appear different only to the casual observer—they represent a monotonous circle of constancy to the window. Notice also the complete lack of emotion, of even compassion, on the part of the window; it merely observes, never comments, never consoles. Perhaps the poet is suggesting that there is no appropriate comment—that life makes no sense. As he looks at the children's rosy cheeks, he is obsessed with the idea of the oblivion awaiting them. This line of thinking will lead to the question dominant in his most pessimistic poetry: What is the meaning of life?

Silva sought happiness in life in many forms: art, science, philosophy, love. A man of such upbringing and refinement as his was bound to be attractive to the ladies. Many of his earliest poems he wrote in diaries and albums of the girls he courted. Once when there was a small fire in the family store, José lamented the fact that his butterfly collection had been destroyed; the butterflies had been pinned to curtains—and each one was named for a girl he had wooed. Why did Silva not marry? It is quite plausible that he believed that outside the sexual facet of love there was no lasting bond between the partners. We know from his poetry that he saw examples of this around him, of both men and women who mourned briefly for their dead mates and then resumed the social circuit as though nothing had happened. To the mind of one as sensitive as he, the facility with which dead lovers were forgotten was a shock. Santiago Argüello has commented on the place love occupied in the poet's thinking:

> El engañado de la vida, fué asimismo un equivocado del amor. Creyó que éste se bebe únicamente en la copa sexual; y como el fondo de esa copa se llama agotamiento; y como su licor se evapora como todo licor, y es finito y cambiante como todas las cosas que se hallan bajo el sexo, el poeta concluye en la negación total de ese divino dios del mundo y de los mundos.[18]

An ironic study of the fickleness of love is found in *Luz de luna.* Silva first presents us with the scene of two young lovers in a moonlit garden. The palpitating kisses upon their lips, the movements of their hands, the supreme joy each brings the other—surely they can never be happy separated from each other. Some months later the man dies. For about a year the girl mourns him, or at least she does not reveal the fact that she can ever love another. Then there is a party:

> ¡Oh girarde desnudas espaldas!
> ¡Oh cadencias del valse que mueve
> Torbellino de tules y gasas!
> Alli estuvo, más linda que nunca,
> Por el baile tal vez agitada . . .[19]

More beautiful than ever she appears. In her backless gown she is as gay as anyone amidst the waltzes, odor of perfume, and bubbling champagne. She leans slightly on Silva's arm; they leave the dance and go to the spot where only a year before the moon had watched her and her lover embrace. Will not deep sadness sweep over her? Can she help but remember his hands, his words, his kisses? But not even a sigh comes to her breast, no tear in her eyes. She says only: "Que valses tan lindos!!Que noche tan clara!" With these trifling remarks Silva provides the ironic ending of the poem. He is at a loss to understand how the girl can fail to remember one with whom she shared such intimate moments. Was this love? Had her lover meant so little to her that she is incapable of being moved? So easily are the dead forgotten!

Without a doubt the most poignant and bitter of the poems dealing with the forgotten dead is *Día de difuntos.* In my opinion there is no more vivid, suggestive, or emotionally moving composition among Silva's works. With exquisite taste he chooses his words and creates an atmosphere to rival the best lines of Edgar Allan Poe. The day is opaque, the light vague. A steady rain wets the cold, deserted city. An unseen hand seems to hurl a veil of lethal melancholy that arouses unrest in the depths of each soul. Then through the gray mists of the shadowy atmosphere the bells are heard. They ring with sad, uncertain, languid accents that speak to the living of the dead. Suddenly there is an inharmonious note present. One bell is laughing, not crying:

> Mas la campana que da la hora,
> Ríe, no llora.
> Tiene en su timbra seco sutiles ironías,
> Su voz parece que habla de goces, de alegrías,
> De placeres, de citas, de fiestas, y de bailes
> Es una voz del siglo entre un coro de frailes,
> Y con sus notas se ríe,
> Escéptica y burladora,
> De la campana que ruega,
> De la campana que implora
> Y de cuanto aquel coro conmemora,
> Y es porque con su retintín
> Ella midió el dolor humano
> Y marcó del dolor el fin . . .[20]

The bell that marks time has no pity upon the dead. It has marked the end of their joy and of their grief. This bell speaks only to the living; it entices them away from morbid thoughts. It tells of dances and pleasures to be had, and it mocks the dead. Silva asks the commemorative bells not to listen to the skeptical one:

> ¡No la oigáis, campanas!
> Contra lo imposible que puede el deseo?
> La campana del reló
> Suena, suena, suena ahora.
> Y dice que ella marcó . . .
> De los olvidos la hora . . .
> En que con la languidez
> Del luto huyó el pensamiento
> Del muerto, y el sentimiento . . .
> Seis meses tarde o diez . . .[21]

In six months all thought of and sentiment for the dead will have vanished. Amidst the chorus of bells the poet inserts a personal note: "Contra lo imposible que puede el deseo?" It seemed just as impossible for him to achieve what he desired as for that bell to cease measuring the end of life. Toward the end of the poem we find the recurrence of the forgotten lover:

> Ella que ha marcado la hora en que el viudo
> Habló de suicidio y pidió el arsénico, . . .

> Y ha marcado luego la hora en que, mudo . . .
> A la misma iglesia fué con otra novia . . .
> Y sigue marcando con el mismo modo
> La huída del tiempo que lo borra todo.
> Y eso es lo angustioso y lo incierto,
> Que flota en el sonido,
> Esa es la nota irónica que vibra en el concierto
> Que alzan los bronces al tocar a muerto
> Por todos los que han sido . . .[22]

In this poem we see firmly established the eradication of existence and memory caused by death. Making excellent use of personification and contrast, Silva almost convinces us that the two groups of bells are people who look upon life from very different points of view: one urging the living to remember the dead; the other shouting its *carpe diem* philosophy, mindful only of the living. In a broader sense this is the *ubi sunt* motif again, but it has been expanded and treated from a most pessimistic approach: neither bell really has any meaning because the dead can hear none and the living will soon join them—after having experienced the same bitterness and disillusion as those who preceded them.

Already we have seen the poet's melancholy turn to pessimism and now it becomes bitterness. There remain to be discussed only the most agonizing problems and *mal del siglo* philosophy that will finally lead Silva to seek the oblivion of death.

VI *EL MAL DEL SIGLO*

Previously I have singled out tendencies and traits inherent in Silva which later were intensified by his study of positivism and Schopenhauer. We come now to that group of poems that best illustrates the influence of positivism and Schopenhauer. I have arranged them in ascending order, in my opinion, of pessimism and despair. In the first three we shall examine, the philosophical and metaphysical problems that hounded Silva are clearly evident—"el mal del siglo"; the theme of suicide dominates the second; and the third is an intriguing, if fabricated, version of what might have happened to Lazarus (according to Silva) after his resurrection. Schopenhauer is named in two of the three selections.

The patient in *El mal del siglo* epitomizes the internal monster that fed upon Silva's mind:

EL PACIENTE:

> Doctor, un desaliento de la vida
> que en lo íntimo de mí se arraiga y nace,
> el mal del siglo . . . el mismo mal de Werther . . .
> . . . renegar de lo vil de la existencia
> digno de mi maestro Schopenhauer;

EL MÉDICO:

> —Eso es cuestión de régimen: camine
> de mañanita; duerma largo; báñese;
> beba bien; coma bien; cuídese mucho:
> ¡Lo que usted tiene es hambre! . . .[23]

Here Silva first mentions his philosopher mentor and describes the demon that takes root and grows in his most intimate being: a lassitude of everything; an absolute scorn for humanity; a detestation for the vileness of existence. These are traits certainly worthy of Schopenhauer. Analysis does nothing but augment the pain. What shall be the prescription? The doctor ironically replies that it is simply a question of regimen. Proper sleep, drink, and food will dissolve these problems. How exasperated the patient must have been when told, "You are hungry!" He was indeed hungry—hungry for the ideal, the infinite, the purpose of life. A diet would hardly suffice. Cognizant of the poet's solution to life's problems, we may venture, with relative certainty, that the young man in this poem will find only one permanent respite from his tortures—death.

Juan de Dios in *Cápsulas* reaches the same conclusion about life. Disappointed twice in love, he suffers, as a result of each affair, an attack of some disease (psychosomatic?). He is cured in both cases and the prognosis appears favorable. But then he begins to fathom the depths of life:

> Luego, desencantado de la vida,
>   filósofo sutil,
> A Leopardi leyó, y a Schopenhauer
>   y en un rato de *spleen,*
> Se curó para siempre con las cápsulas
>   de plomo de un fusil.[24]

Some inexplicable disenchantment with life has taken possession of him. He must find the cure for this last pernicious disease. After reading Schopenhauer and Leopardi, the answer is clear: what he needs is more capsules—of lead. In this last strophe Silva has given us a foreshadowing of what his solution to life's sorrows will be. Note that the name of Schopenhauer reappears, although Juan de Dios failed to follow his advice to the letter. As we have seen, the pessimistic German would have urged a withdrawal from participation in life and a cultivation of the denial of the will to live. In Schopenhauer's eyes, Juan de Dios was affirming his will to live if he could do so under more pleasant conditions.

The gloom that filled the poet's soul is poignantly expressed in *Lázaro.* How different is the poet's version of the revived man from that given in the New Testament! The Savior's voice awakens Lazarus; with trembling steps he attempts to walk. Slowly he regains his senses. He smells, palpitates, recovers his sense of touch. He is alive! His first reaction is to cry out in joy and weep from contentment. Life has been restored. Is it not a miracle, the gift of a gracious God?

Yet when we visit the graveyard again, four moons later, there is a figure weeping disconsolately:

> Cuatro lunas más tarde, entre las sombras
> Del crepúsculo oscuro, en el silencio
> Del lugar y la hora, entre las tumbas
> De antiguo cementerio,

> Lázaro estaba, sollozando a solas
> Y envidiando a los muertos.[25]

It is Lazarus, alone and sobbing in the obscure twilight. Far from rejoicing in life, he now envies the dead. It would seem that Lazarus had forgotten the misery of existence in the temporary ecstasy of regaining consciousness. It is difficult to imagine how much Silva must have hated living. The choice and treatment of his subject in this poem evidence the depth to which his soul had sunk.

One of the most interesting of Silva's poems, although not in the same vein as the majority, is *Zoospermos,* the portrait of a distinguished scientist who goes insane. Doctor Cornelius Van Kerrinken has become almost blind from looking through his microscope for extensive lengths of time. In his last years he has developed a mania for observing spermatozoides and delights in conjecturing about the future that each one might have. As the cells scurry back and forth seeking to combine and form a life, Van Kerrinken can see a definite personality in every one. One would have been a Werther, another a poet, another a loan shark. But instead of being awed by the astronomical possibilities of life in its inchoate stages, he reacts thus:

> Afortunadamente
> perdidos para siempre
> os agitáis ahora
> ¡oh puntos que sois hombres!
> entre los vidrios gruesos
> translúcidos y diáfanos
> del microscopio enorme;
> afortunadamente,
> zoospermos, en la tierra
> no creceréis poblándola
> de dichas y de horrores;
> dentro de diez minutos
> todos estaréis muertos.
> ¡Hola! espermatozoides."
> Así el ilustre sabio
> Cornelius Van Kerrinken,
> que disfrutó en Hamburgo
> de una clientela enorme
> y que dejó un in-folio
> de setecientas páginas
> sobre hígado y riñones,
> murió en Leipzig maniático
> desprestigiado y pobre,
> debido a sus estudios
> de los últimos años
> sobre espermatozoides.[26]

The question arises of why the scientist uses the term "afortunadamente" in addressing the cells. These are embryonic lives. Why will they be fortunate to die shortly rather than to realize their ultimate destination and form a human being? Judging from the rest of Silva's poetry, I think that Van Kerrinken believed that the lives the cells would engender would not be worth living; apparently he held life in general in low esteem. Some philosophers in vogue during this period maintained that the greatest good the human race could accomplish would be to let itself become extinct, thereby sparing unborn generations the recurrence of suffering and life's innate worthlessness. When man denies God, as was the intellectual fashion of the times, he must replace Him with something—positivism, humanism, psychoanalysis—or lose his mind. And let us note the scientist's fate: he went mad.

The two poems which best demonstrate the illness from which Silva suffered are *Psicopatía* and *La respuesta de la tierra.* Both have tremendous philosophical significance and excellent insight into the final stages of frustration that brought about his suicide.

A park on a beautiful spring morning is the setting of *Psicopatía.* Flowers are in bloom, the birds sing—spring seems to say, "live." There is an effervescence that should dispel the deepest gloom. But through this exuberance walks a young philosopher dressed in black:

> . . . E impertérrito sigue en su tarea
> De pensar en la muerte, en la conciencia
> Y en las causas finales! . . .
> Y él sigue su camino, triste, serio,
> Pensando en Fichte, en Kant, en Vogt, en Hegel,
> Y del *yo* complicado en el misterio![27]

A doctor and his small daughter happen to observe the young man so completely lost in thought. The doctor's daughter asks how it is possible that a man can go around with a gloomy countenance on such a lovely day. Is he sick perhaps?:

> —Ese señor padece un mal muy raro,
> Que ataca rara vez a las mujeres
> Y pocas a los hombres . . . , hija mía!
> Sufre este mal: . . . pensar . . . , esa es la causa
> De su grave y sutil melancolía . . .
> El mal, gracias a Dios, no es contagioso
> Y lo adquieren muy pocos . . .
> . . . Pero joven aquél es caso grave,
> Como conozco pocos,
> Más que cuantos nacieron piensa y sabe,
> Irá a pasar diez años con los locos,
> Y no se curará sino hasta el día
> En que duerma a sus anchas
> En una angosta sepultura fría,
> Lejos del mundo y de la vida loca,
> Entre un negro ataúd de cuatro planchas,
> Con un montón de tierra entre la boca![28]

Webster's New World Dictionary defines a psychopathic personality: "A person characterized by emotional instability, lack of sound judgment, perverse and impulsive (often criminal) behavior, inability to learn from experience, amoral and asocial feelings, and other serious personality defects: he may or may not have psychotic attacks or symptoms."[29] Sadly the young man ponders various philosophers, trying to discover a concrete basis that will tell him definitely which one is right. Not mindful of his cheerful surroundings, he contemplates death, conscience, and final causes. To this young man, representative of another side of Silva's multi-faceted personality portrayed in his poetry, the doctor could offer only this simplistic prescrip-

tion: "Do not think." The contrasting attitudes of the doctor and the young sceptic—Silva—provide us with yet another parallel to the manner in which intellectual curiosity was greeted in Bogotá. Silva asks, "Why?" Dogma says, "Believe." Such a response was small consolation to one so afflicted as he.

In my opinion *La respuesta de la tierra* is the apex in Silva's futile attempt to fulfill his need for knowledge and purpose. He enumerates every question that has exasperated him and for the last time poignantly requests an answer:

> Era un poeta lírico, grandioso y sibilino
> que le hablaba a la tierra una tarde de invierno,
> frente a una posada y al volver de un camino:
> —¡Oh madre, oh Tierra!—díjole,—en tu girar eterno
> nuestra existencia efímera tal parece que ignoras.
> Nośotros esperamos un cielo o un infierno,
> sufrimos o gozamos, en nuestras breves horas,
> e indiferente y muda, tú, madre, sin entrañas,
> de acuerdo con los hombres no sufres y no lloras.
> ¿No sabes el secréto misterioso que entrañas?
> ¿Por qué las noches negras, las diáfanas auroras?
> Las sombras vagorosas y tenues de unas cañas
> que se reflejan lívidas en los estanques yertos,
> ¿no son como conciencias fantásticas y extrañas
> que les copian sus vidas en espejos inciertos?
> ¿Qué somos? A do vamos? Por qué hasta aquí vinimos?
> ¿Conocen los secretos del más allá los muertos?
> ¿Por qué la vida inútil y triste recibimos?
> ¿Hay un oasis húmedo después de estos desiertos?
> ¿Por qué nacemos, madre, dime, por qué morimos?
> ¿Por qué?—Mi angustia sacia y a mi ansiedad contesta.
> Yo, sacerdote tuyo, arrodillado y trémulo,
> En estas soledades, aguardo la respuesta.
>
> La Tierra, como siempre, displicente y callada,
> al gran poeta lírico no le contestó nada.[30]

The poem leaves little to say about José Asunción; it is a succinct autobiography of his soul. The earth seems not to take note of man's plight. Silva unravels the thread of human emotions and aspirations and wonders about the reasons for them. Why are we born? Why do we suffer? Why do we die? What are we? Then he thinks perhaps the dead know the secret of this sad and useless life. Is there an oasis after the desert of existence? Trembling, upon his knees, the poet awaits the reply that will slake his thirst. But the earth ". . . al gran poeta lírico no le contestó nada."

Silva always sought an elusive ideal, a reality, but he pursued it only with the intellect and could not accept an intuitive truth not logically explicable. The questions he asked are metaphysical and theological, but he tried to answer them in the manner of a positivist and found it impossible. Santiago Argüello has commented in detail on the influence of positivism upon the poet:

> . . . Y al llegar Silva, con su ansiedad ideal, con su diamante presentido, busca el agua que su sed le demanda; pero la busca con la única linterna que se

vendía entonces, la del positivismo . . . y, pensando con el intelecto como único instrumento y con el beneficio ególatra como única finalidad, habría de topar con el negro desencanto del pensar, como había antes topado con el otro desencanto, negro también y frío, del amar . . . Quebró su microscopio porque no le descubrió las estrellas.[31]

We have seen the maze of philosophies in which Silva became entangled. Positivism with its demand for empirical facts and Schopenhauer's writings on the vanity of existence profoundly affected the poet. This intellectual cultivation led him to an abandonment of religion and a scorn for humanity. Reality and practicality constituted, in Silva's opinion, mediocrity, and he held only contempt for those who believed in them: ". . . La realidad? . . . Llaman *la realidad* todo lo trivial, todo lo insignificante, todo lo despreciable . . ."[32] He was a man who had to have the final answers. Life as he saw it was intolerable; he strove constantly to bring order out of the chaos.

Shortly after Guy de Maupassant went insane, Silva expressed a fear of suffering the same fate:

> ¿Loco? . . . ¿y por que no? Así murió Baudelaire, el más grande, para los verdaderos letrados, de los poetas de los últimos cincuenta años; así murió Maupassant, sintiendo crecer alrededor de su espíritu la noche y reclamando sus ideas . . . ¿Por qué no has de morir así, pobre degenerado, que abusaste de todo, que sonaste con dominar el arte, con poseer la ciencia, toda la ciencia, y con agotar todas las copas en que brinda la vida las embriagueces supremas?[33]

It was his pretension to master knowledge and art; his failure to do so never let him rest.

Finally, José Asunción Silva was a man who, paradoxically, desired faith but could not accept it intellectually. Miguel de Unamuno, another philosopher famous for his interminable struggle with life, best describes the poet's tragic life: "¿Qué hizo en su vida? Sufrir, soñar, cantar. ¿Os parece poco? Sufrir, soñar, cantar y meditar el misterio."[34]

Notes

1. Luis Alberto Sánchez, *Escritores representativos de América* (Madrid, 1957), 144.

2. José Asunción Silva, *Prosas y versos* (México, 1942), xv.

3. *Ibid.,* xv-xvi.

4. José Asunción Silva, *Poesías completas* (Madrid, 1952), 199.

5. Silva, *Prosas y versos,* 118.

6. Arthur Schopenhauer, *Studies in Pessimism* (Edinburgh, 1937), 38.

7. *Ibid.,* 32.

8. *Ibid.,* 34.

9. *Ibid.,* 24.

10. *Ibid.,* 21.

11. *Ibid.,* 22.

12. Silva, *Poesías completas,* 43.

13. *Ibid.,* 97-98.

14. *Ibid.,* 86.

15. *Ibid.,* 152.

16. *Ibid.,* 68-70.

17. *Ibid.,* 158-60.

18. Santiago Argüello, *Modernismo y modernistas* (Guatemala, 1935), 150.

19. Silva, *Poesías completas,* 94.

20. *Ibid.,* 109-10.

21. *Ibid.,* 111-12.

22. *Ibid.,* 113.

23. *Ibid.,* 118.

24. *Ibid.,* 123.

25. *Ibid.,* 93.

26. *Ibid.,* 132.

27. *Ibid.,* 101.

28. *Ibid.,* 102-04.

29. *Webster's New Word Dictionary,* College Edition (New York, 1962), 1176.

30. Silva, *Poesías completas,* 119-20.

31. Argüello, *Modernismo,* 152-54.

32. Silva, *Prosas y versos,* 35.

33. *Ibid.,* 34.

34. Silva, *Poesías completas,* 22.

Betty Tyree Osiek (essay date 1978)

SOURCE: Osiek, Betty Tyree. "*De Sobremesa*: Silva's Modernist Novel." In *José Asunción Silva,* pp. 94-139. Boston: Twayne, 1978.

[*In the following essay, Osiek provides a complete plot summary and textual history of Silva's only novel and discusses its autobiographical elements and prominent themes.*]

I THE EDITIONS

The single novel written by José Asunción Silva . . . was lost in the sinking of the ship *L'Amerique,* on his return from Caracas. But when his friend Hernando Villa, who feared Silva was going to commit suicide, asked him to rewrite one of the lost manuscripts, Silva allowed his friend to choose the one he preferred. Villa chose the novel, *De Sobremesa* (*After-Dinner Chat*), which Silva duly rewrote in his distinctive handwriting, before his suicide.[1] However, the manuscript was not published until 1925, when the first edition was produced by Cromos of Bogotá.[2] It was a small edition, and a second edition came out in 1928[3] by the same publishing house. After that, it has been included in several editions of the complete works of Silva, such as the one by the Bank of Colombia.[4]

Even after the publication of the first edition of the complete novel in 1925, several of the interpolated essays or digressions were published separately many times in anthologies, obviously out of context. The titles of the essays were often selected by the editors. Citations from these essays were used to prove different ideas that the author could not possibly have meant.

The date of Silva's death, 1896, together with the subsequent date of publication of the first edition of *De Sobremesa* in 1925, twenty-nine years later, surely reflects the attitude of his family, which delayed the publication of the manuscript in its entirety. It was not a book which in his time would have been favorite reading. The same shock value is there which often appeared in his **"Gotas Amargas" ("Bitter Potions")**. The family did not wish the complete manuscript to be published, fearing it would hurt his reputation or his family name. It was published when the times had changed enough, or Silva's worth as a poet had consecrated his name.

Even after its publication the work was mainly ignored, even though the newness of the prose style in Spanish and the subjects treated were related to those used in earlier Modernist renovation in prose. (It was similar to such novels as *A Rebours* by Joris-Karl Huysmans, published in Paris in 1884; *Il Piacere,* by Gabriele D'Annunzio, published in Milan in 1889; and *The Picture of Dorian Gray,* by Oscar Wilde, published in London in 1891.) But in Spanish America, Modernistic prose was being written in the 1870s by José Martí and Manuel Guriérrez Nájera and others, as well as by Silva, as we can see in some of his earlier essays. The first writing of *De Sobremesa*[5] probably dates from one decade later than the Modernist revolution in prose. The same currents are visible in his search for new and more aesthetic ways of writing, clothing his ideas in an original, more flexible form.

II THE PLOT

To facilitate further reference to the novel *De Sobremesa,* a detailed summary of the novel follows. Although portraying Silva's lack of organization, the résumé seemed best in a chronological arrangement, with his interpolations summarized as they appeared.

The novel begins with a Modernist description of a luxurious interior in semidarkness: "Concentrated by the gauze and lace lampshade, the tepid light of the lamp fell in a circle upon the scarlet velvet of the carpet and illuminating entirely three china cups, glazed in the depths by a trace of strong coffee, and a cut crystal glass filled with a transparent liquor glimmering with golden particles, left hidden in the dark purple shadow produced by the tone of the carpet, the hangings and tapestries, the rest of the silent chamber."[6]

Then as the candelabra is lit, we see the poet-protagonist, José Fernández, and his friends Juan Rovira and Oscar Sáenz, who are conversing after finishing a sumptuous dinner. Sáenz explains why he is silent, awed by the luxurious contrast in his friend's house to the life to which he is accustomed, that of a poor medical doctor. He enumerates the many elements which surround him in the Fernández house, which only a rich man can have. He then points out that all his friends envy Fernández because of these things, as well as his amorous adventures.

Sáenz urges him to write more poetry and not to rest on his laurels after having published only two books of poems. He reproaches Fernández for not having written a line for two years, and for dissipating his life in many different directions at the same time. Fernández replies that he is not a poet when compared with the great poets of past ages. He also attests that one cannot write poems by force of will, that they are formed within the poet by his inspiration and come out already formed. Fernández also tells his friends that many of his poems are inspired by his reading of the great poets of the past. He discloses that he dreamed and still dreams of writing great poetry by suggesting the many obscure things he feels within. But he informs them that he cannot consecrate himself to that when he has so much curiosity and enthusiasm for living and for many other things than poetry.

Sáenz says that his isolation in a luxurious house where he has social contacts with only some ten of his friends, most of whom are also somewhat eccentric, is not the most propitious way for living real life. Fernández replies, giving a long meditation on "real life," and begins by asking. "What is real life, tell me, the bourgeois life without emotions and without curiosity?"[7]

The protagonist affirms that most of the people who are alive have not really lived, and that he is doing his best to really live in every possible way. His medical friend discloses that all the refinements should be taken away from him so that he would write poetry. Fernández tells him that the skull he keeps on his desk to remind him of death shows him that his only duty is to live life to the fullest.

Yet he explains that he is still tempted to write the verses which often seem to be formed, struggling to emerge. However, he is convinced the readers would fail to understand his poems, as did the critic who called him a pornographic poet.[8] Again he reiterates the Symbolist tenet that he does not wish to express his ideas openly, but only to suggest them in his poems. This requires readers who are artists, and unfortunately, according to Silva, the public lacks artistic understanding.

Rovira interrupts this conversation between Fernández and Dr. Sáenz and urges him to read from a book which has some connection with: 1) the name of the house Fernández is building, Villa Helena; 2) with a design of three leaves and a butterfly hovering above them; and 3) with a pre-Raphaelite painting he owns. At this moment two other friends arrive, Luis Cordovez and Máximo Pérez. Luis Cordovez begins to ask also that Fernández read to him and the others from the notes he took during a trip to Switzerland. Pérez, who is ill, chimes in and asks that he read about an illness Fernández had in Europe.

Fernández begins to meditate on Helena and attributes to her supernatural power the vision he has seen that very day of a butterfly, and then, that same evening, the four requests by his friends that he read about her. He considers that perhaps these happenings are a message from Helena on the anniversary of his discovery that she had died, a time of the year when he is always emotionally ill.

Fernández commences reading from the diary covered luxuriously with an encrustation of the emblem of a butterfly fluttering over three leaves. He wrote this subjective diary during a brief stay in Europe. The first entry is dated Paris, June 3, in the 1890s. From the first line its introspective quality is obvious. It deals with José Fernández's most intimate personality. The work has a great many interpolated essays which reflect his reactions to certain happenings, books he read, and things he heard during the European trip. The essay included later in the first part concerns the reading of two books, works which were popular in the 1890s: one is a book by Max Nordau. *Dégénéréscence,* cited by Silva from the first French edition, translated from the German and published in 1894.[9] The other is the *Journal* of Marie Bashkirtseff, published for the first time in Paris in 1887.[10] Nordau, a psychologist, judges the artists of his time according to his specialization, coming to the conclusion that they are neurotic or psychological cases. Fernández is especially incensed with Nordau's treatment of Marie Bashkirtseff, a Russian artist who died of tuberculosis in Paris on October 31, 1884.[11] In her diary we see the same desires of Fernández, carried to extremes, of living life abundantly; being, seeing, and doing everything.

Silva discusses Marie Bashkirtseff's diary, in which she recorded her experiences from the age of twelve until eleven days before her death. She describes her life of luxury and her enjoyment of it, but also her rebellion against its meaninglessness. She recounts her struggles to educate herself to a higher level, her arrogance, her romantic fancies and daydreams, as well as her ambition to live to the fullest extent, and especially to gain fame as a painter. Until her death she worked at the Académie Julian, a well-known painters' academy. She also describes her struggles with her increasing pain and suffering in the final days of her fatal illness.[12]

In his work Nordau analyzed with an implacable harshness the pre-Raphaelite painters, the work of the great composer Wagner, Verlaine, and many other writers of high literary acclaim, as well as Marie Bashkirtseff. He called them "the degenerates" but admitted in his preface that they were not all criminals. He believed that many were artists who had gained numerous admirers and were the creators of a new kind of art. But all were rebels against society.[13] His book was very popular during the 1890s, and he probably made Bashkirtseff famous by including her with the other outstanding artists.

Silva was often said to have known Marie Bashkirtseff, but he did not arrive in Paris until the same month she died. Although he speaks of the Passy Cemetery, where she is interred,[14] he knew her only literarily, and perhaps not until the year before his death, when he was writing anew *De Sobremesa.* He was familiar with the article "La Légende d'une cosmopolite" by Maurice Barrés, which was included in the long section, "Trois stations de Psychotérapie" (one of the works found beside Silva's bed when he committed suicide), in which Barrés characterizes Marie as "Our Lady of Perpetual Desire."[15]

The inserted critical essay by Silva-Fernández of the books by Bashkirtseff and by Nordau, the latter work especially, shows that Silva was familiar with the literary currents of the period in France and was also aware of the great furor caused among the so-called decadent writers by the German psychologist's work. Silva was familiar with these artists, who were often considered to be decadent, because of an attitude which Silva shared, a predominantly aesthetic attitude toward art.

After this critical digression in which the author displays his literary knowledge, the protagonist, Fernández, talks about his own life. He tells of years of constant action and of passion for the luxuries of life, as well as a desire for social prominence in his native country. He describes the growth of his infinite curiosity concerning evil and complains of having tired of operating in his country, which he considers limited, with its vulgar women and its business with little challenge. These factors inspire him to leave the country and to act the part of the rich South American snob in Europe, hunting with the noblemen, dancing cotillions, and spending time in tailors' establishments. But, on the other hand, Fernández describes his opposite side. He is the collector of eighty oil paintings, four hundred watercolors and etchings, medals, bronze, marble, and porcelain pieces, tapestries, outstanding editions of his favorite authors, on special paper, bound luxuriously to his order. He is a student of science who frequents the Sorbonne to hear lectures, a speculator in the stock market, a gourmet, horseback rider, lover of magnificent women, of fine furniture, of wines thirty years old, and, above all, an analyst of himself who believes he sees clearly all the multiple impulses of his psyche.

Yet in spite of all these activities, Fernández discloses that the intense life he is living does not satisfy him, that perhaps of more worth is the laborer, or the anarchist executed for throwing a bomb, since at least he had a plan and a purpose to which he dedicated his life. But such a plan according to the protagonist is very different from the useless plans he elaborates, for example a house of commerce established in New York, a trip around the world, or a pearl-fishing trip.

An entry of June 23, in Bâle, Switzerland, gives a hint of what happened the previous day. There was a violent scene and he had to flee. He implies that by now the woman must have died, and the police probably are looking for him, although he has registered under a false name and identity. He communicates to his readers that he is to go to Whyl, Switzerland, to wait for a telegram from Marinoni, his financial adviser.

The entry dated June 29, in Whyl, discloses the contents of the telegram from Marinoni. It informs him that the girl involved, Lelia Orloff, has been seen in public and that apparently nothing serious had happened to her. Fernández does not understand how there was not a sign of a wound since he knows there was blood on his shirtsleeve.

The following day's entry explains the violence, but is lugubriously coupled with the news of the death of Fernández's grandmother, the last relative he had in the world. The letter telling of her agony describes her prayers for Fernández and repeats her last words of thanks that Fernández has been saved, by the "sign of the cross by the hand of a virgin, the bouquet of roses which falls in his night like a sign of salvation."[16]

The impression caused by his proximity to committing murder and the death of his grandmother shocks him. Then the details are given of the cause of his murderous attack with a knife on Lelia Orloff, his beautiful mistress of the past several months. From the beginning she showed a natural taste for the most luxurious in refined furnishings and possessions, and like him she needed the most profound and exquisite sensations. Her natural aristocratic bearing and tastes caused her to be very attractive to Fernández, and when he first notices that Angela de Roberto was her occasional visitor, he protested. Later, on arriving unexpectedly and learning that the two women are in the bedroom together, he reacts violently, and after breaking down the door he describes the scene, saying "I threw the infamous group to the floor on the black bearskin which is at the foot of the bed, and began striking them furiously with all my strength, stimulating screams and blasphemies, with violent hands, with my boot heels, as someone who smashes a snake. I do not know how I took out of its leather sheath the little Damasquined Toledan knife, engraved like a jewel, which I always carry with me, and I plunged it into her soft flesh twice; I felt my hand soaked with warm blood. . . ."[17]

After feeling the blood, Fernández flees, leaving her screaming. He hurries to the office of Miranda, another of his financial advisers. After getting some money and his correspondence, he goes to his hotel, where his old servant Francisco packs his luggage so that Fernández can take the first train out of the city, to Bâle, Switzerland. As al-

ways, the hero analyzes his reactions, and in this case cannot understand his violence since he is never intellectually shocked by the abnormal. In fact, he points out that the abnormal has always fascinated him as a proof of the rebellion of man against instinct. He feels it was a stupid incident, comparing it to a senseless duel he provoked for no good reason with a German diplomat.

Affected emotionally by all these events, Fernández decides to stay out in the country in a small house of an old couple to be able to think. He has sent to Paris for the books and other articles he needs, and meanwhile is going to study prehistoric America and botany. He is living quite primitively since he was unable to eat the food they prepared for him and is drinking only milk. He is surrounded by simplicity in their house and is following a regimen of mountain climbing, study, and meditation. He views nature as a kind of nirvana in which he enters. He compares the sensation with one he felt in the crossing of the ocean, when the exterior spectacle seemed to enter into his being, and he felt a pantheistic ecstasy and union with nature. He only lacks the ecstasy in the Swiss mountains. These two instances are the only times the protagonist considers nature.

Fernández feels a supreme peace in the mountains after his previous months of dissipation. He has meditated until he has come upon a plan to double or triple his fortune by selling the gold mines inherited from his father. Then he will transfer the funds to New York and found the business he had thought of starting with Carillo, who is backed by the Astors. Fernández will try to learn all he can about the fabulous development of the United States, and from New York will go occasionally to Panama to direct the pearl-fishing in person. Then, with all the capital earned, he will proceed to put into effect his political plan.

The plan which Silva puts into the mouth of his protagonist is an ultraconservative, dictatorial theory of government to enable the young, rich South American to improve his underdeveloped country. But the vision is not so implausible, since it mirrors the actual mode of government for many South American countries. The plan centers on the protagonist himself, who is to ascertain first the needs of the people through a tour of the provinces, accompanied by selected engineers and scholars. After entering into a minor political post where he engages in two years of investigation and study of governmental administration, Fernández develops a financial plan which will solve all the problems of the country. He obtains a ministry office, and using his influence gained in that office, he directs the formation of a new political party of "civilized men" who believe in science and education, and are far from religious or political fanaticism. Fernández becomes the president, through an effective publicity campaign, and in that office continues to work for improvements in public education, agriculture, mining, commerce, and industry, while promoting immigration to form a new and powerful race. Finally, after long, peaceful evolution of the established government, Fernández retires, leaving the power in the hands of "competent persons."

The protagonist discusses an alternative in case the utopian plan does not succeed through peaceful means. The people must be incited to a conservative reaction against false liberalism. The clergy must instigate the masses to arise. And a tyranny, later becoming a dictatorship, must be established through military power. A new constitution is promulgated, and revolts are kept down by the muzzling of the press, the exile of powerful opposition figures, and through confiscation of the property of the enemies of the government. With proper economic measures taken by the dictatorship with Fernández at its head, in a few years the country will be rich and peaceful. While it is impossible to be sure that Silva was considering these plans as a serious solution, even as fictional plans for his hero they show a naiveté concerning the simplicity of a government's operation, and one cannot fail to notice his lack of political ideological depth.

Fernández dreams of the success of these measures in bringing progress to his country. He visualizes the transformation of the capital to a delightful place as the Paris of Baron Haussmann. He hopes that the progress will not only be reflected in a material way, but in art, in the sciences, in a national novel, in poetry which celebrates the indigenous legends, the glorious wars of emancipation, the natural beauty, and the splendid future of the regenerated land.

He points out the incongruity of establishing a conservative dictatorship like that of Gabriel García Moreno in Ecuador or of Manuel Estrada Cabrera in Guatemala in order to bring about the sweeping changes he encompasses in his plan. But he attests that the country is tired of demagogues and of false liberties in constitutions which do not function. He feels that the people prefer the cry of a dictator who follows through on his threats, rather than that of a more platonic promise of respect for law, which is never carried out.[18]

Fernández sees himself in that faraway future retiring finally from his position as dictator to write poetry containing the supreme elixir of his many experiences—poetry of mystic tone, and apocalyptic, very different from that written when he was twenty, full of lust and fire. His last years seem peaceful and replete with philosophical pursuits, but he prognosticates that "Over my still-tepid corpse, a legend will begin to form which will make me appear as a monstrous problem of psychological complication to the generations of the future."[19]

Here he is talking about having been a dictator, and the mixed emotions that the people would undoubtedly have felt toward him. These lines are often cited as Silva's feeling about himself, yet it can be observed clearly that they are concerned solely with his fictional protagonist in his planned role as dictator.

At a break in the reading of the diary, Fernández says to his guests that he must have been mad while writing that plan. Sáenz says that it was the only time he had been lucid. Rovira tells him that being president of the republic would be degrading for Fernández. Asked if the financial part of his plan had been successful, Fernández replies that the earnings were more than expected. But when asked why he did not carry through with his plans, the doctor answers for him, saying it was because of the pleasures of life. Juan Rovira leaves, disclosing that while he loves to hear Fernández read his prose production, he does not understand anything of what he has heard. When Cordovez insists that Fernández return to his reading of the diary, Fernández begins with an entry from Interlaken, July 25. Again Fernández praises the effects of nature on man as a calmative agent and as a purification of those who retire to meditate, taking away all sensuous desires which abound in the city. With these ideas in mind Fernández thinks of the seductiveness of Lelia Orloff and laughs aloud as he savors his freedom from desire for her and for the sensual life.

The following day, July 26, Fernández continues in the same vein with a long tirade against life in the city and against the common people with their atrocious tastes unlike those of refined aristocrats such as he.

On August 5, Fernández's fifty days of abstinence are broken by Nini Rousset, a vulgar actress who had previously disdained him in Paris. She arrives at his hotel in Interlaken and seeing his name on the register comes to visit him and remains with him for the night for an orgy. Fernández detests her, but cannot resist her, even though for him she is the incarnation of all the Parisian vices.

On August 9, in Geneva, Fernández awakens after forty-eight hours under the influence of opium. He took the opium in revulsion after the night spent with Nini Rousset in his room, in order to escape from his memory of trying to choke Nini, probably because she had undone his rational and chaste plan of abstinence. She fled crying, half-dressed, from his room, and Fernández took a huge dose of opium to escape. The combination of the orgy, drinking, and the opium leaves him in a miserable physical condition when he comes to himself.

In Geneva, August 11, Fernández is having dinner in a small dining room when a young girl and her father enter. The young girl looks to Fernández like a painting of a picture by Van Dyck; her hands are like those of Anne of Austria in the painting of Rubens, and Fernández is unable to take his eyes from her. He feels that the attraction is mutual, but he is ashamed of his past life as he faces her in her innocence. He feels in her glance a compassionate tenderness resulting in peace of mind for him. He is over-excited and his imagination creates an intense understanding without ever speaking a word to the blue-eyed beauty. He hears them speaking Italian and they mention St. Moritz, among other places. Then they leave the dining room to have their after-dinner coffee served in their room. As they depart, Fernández meets her eyes again, and she seems like a supernatural being with an earthly beauty. Fernández finds on the floor a cameo which has a branch with three leaves and a butterfly fluttering above it with its wings open. He keeps the cameo to return it to her the next day and is pleased, since he thinks that it will enable him to make her acquaintance. Helena's appearance is never clarified, although isolated features are mentioned; her blue eyes, graceful carriage, and dignified poise. She shares with the Romantic and Modernist heroines such characteristics as her extreme youth, sixteen or seventeen years, her status as an orphan who had lost her mother at the age of four, her apparent physical frailty and seeming inclination to be consumptive, as was her mother.

Fernández learns that they had arrived a few hours earlier from Nice, and the Count Robert de Scilly had said that he and his daughter Helena de Scilly Dancourt, would remain two days. They did not give the name of a place where they were going. Fernández is glad that he has never had a love affair with a girl whose name was Helena.

An old friend, Enrique Lorenzana, comes to visit him and is surprised to see that Fernández looks so horribly disfigured and pale. He convinces Fernández to accompany him to a lecture on history. On walking back to the hotel in the moonlight, with the stars shining above, Fernández thinks of Helena and enters the garden of the hotel to continue his solitary walk. He looks up and sees one of the balconies on the second floor with the window open. A tall slender shadow of a woman can be seen against the gauze curtains. Fernández picks some flowers, puts his card with them, and throws them up through the window curtains into the room. Helena comes out, reminding him of a painting by Fra Angelico, and raising her hand she makes the sign of the cross as she throws him a bunch of white flowers. Fernández seems to hear the words of his dying grandmother and he nearly faints. When he recovers, all he has are the flowers, and the lights have gone out in her room.

Fernández cannot sleep without the aid of two grams of chloral hydrate, and he dreams of all the day's images, awakening at ten in the morning. He bathes, and when he is served breakfast he asks the waiter to find out if Count Scilly and his daughter have gone out. Fernández learns that they left very early in a private coach and the concierge did not hear to which station they directed the driver to take them.

Now the desperate search for the ideal, the chaste Helena, begins. Fernández has fallen in love with her, and he begins an anguished search for her as his last chance for salvation. He has only seen her twice and has dreamed of her more than actually seeing her clearly. She represents a creature of light, and he feels that she alone is capable of saving and redeeming him. The reader knows from the beginning of the novel that Fernández will never find her, but her person never dies in his soul, and in homage to his pure love for her he is constructing a villa in Colombia which is named for her. He has difficulty in beginning his search since he has no idea where she was going. He preserves the bunch of white roses in a crystal box to take with him. He has received a letter saying that the buyer of

the gold mines has agreed on the price and he must be in London on the fifteenth of the month to sign the papers. He plans to go to all the places he heard Helena and her father mention in the dining room, as soon as he finishes his business with his English bankers.

Painting is one of the main themes in *De Sobremesa*, since it creates imaginatively the dreams of the protagonist. Helena, who belonged to the family of Rossetti, a painter of the pre-Raphaelite school, is a shadow which the protagonist forms into a painting from the first time he sees her. Later, when he owns the painting of Helena's mother, the wife of the count, Helena becomes even more of an icon for him. Fernández searches for her and for her father all through Europe, finding her only in the grave, leaving him with his ideal intact but without solutions for his emotional future. From the beginning her beauty causes him to remember museum pieces, and in his first encounter with her we see the Modernist techniques of the fusion of painting and fiction.

In the entry of October 11, in London, Fernández mentions that during the two months spent in London finishing up his business deal he has taken the time to send telegrams to all the major European hotels asking about the count and his daughter, and has written letters to travel agencies trying to find them. At night he evokes her figure as he reads the poetry of Shelley and Rossetti and sometimes he calls her name and seems to see her come toward him without touching the floor. He thinks of her in terms of purity and innocence, and the phrases he uses are the verses of Dante concerning Beatrice. He meditates upon the seventy days spent chastely in London, without mixing with the society he knows would have welcomed him. His friend Enrique Lorenzana, who came to see him in Geneva after his bout with opium, sees him in London and tells him that he looks like another person. Fernández has the sensation that this is true, but wishes that he did not have the incurable nostalgia for the blue eyes of the love he has lost.

In the London entry for September 10, Fernández is preparing himself in the daytime, for development of his country, studying armaments and military maneuvers for when they will be necessary. He is still buying works of art, such as watercolors and paintings, but is experiencing no strong emotions. Nevertheless he has horrible nightmares when he again sees the three leaves on the branch and the butterfly fluttering above them. He feels that his love for Helena is like an obsession. When she appears to him he always thinks of the Latin phrase "Manibus date lilia plenis" (Give handfuls of lilies).

Fernández knows that although all this is wonderfully sentimental and ideal, he needs physiological fulfillment with some of his old mistresses. But none of them is in London. And he is revolted by the idea of buying caresses, feeling such a practice to be nearly impossible for him.

The entry for November 13 describes how an assignation is arranged by his friend Roberto Blundel with a beautiful woman, Constanza Landseer. But Fernández is unable to consummate the union because of a vision of his grandmother and of Helena, and because of a bunch of white tea roses (which Constanza has received from Nice) from which a butterfly escapes, fluttering above the flowers. Another coincidence is that the flowers are tied with the same cross-shaped ribbon as the ones which Helena tossed him. Fernández flees superstitiously from the union, hoping desperately that he can find Helena soon.

Still in London, on November 17, Fernández has talked with his Greek professor about his friend Dr. John Rivington, who has studied the pessimistic attitudes of humans and other works of experimental psychology and psychophysics. Fernández has already read the books of Rivington, and finally goes to consult with him, carrying two letters of introduction. Fernández says that he is an atheist but he is coming to the scientist with faith in his properties as a corporal and spiritual director. Rivington asks Fernández to tell him his life history, about the antecedents of his family, his life in his own country, the city in which he was raised, the present organization of his life, his plans for the future, and his present occupations. He tells the doctor of his monastic existence since his meeting with Helena, the plans he is elaborating concerning his country, and the incident of his sexual failure in the bedroom of Constanza Landseer. Asked by the doctor if he intends to marry Helena if he finds her, Fernández becomes confused, showing his shock at the idea. Dr. Rivington urges Fernández to make all his body functions a regular habit, and not to go to extremes with anything, to regularize his sexual necessities so as not to confuse them with his feelings toward Helena.

Rivington tells him to search for the girl and marry her and not to make her into a supernatural being because of the coincidence of some words said by his dying grandmother which seemed to foretell the meeting with Helena. Then Rivington begins to question Fernández about the description of Helena and finally asks him if he wishes to see his vision in a painting. Rivington takes him to see a pre-Raphaelite painting he owns which is so like Helena that Fernández feels sure it is a likeness of Helena. The doctor tells him it is a likeness of Helena's mother. He questions him about his visit to London ten years earlier and whether or not he has ever viewed paintings like this one in museums. Rivington feels that Fernández might have imagined a good part of his feelings toward Helena after seeing such a painting in his youth. Rivington advises Fernández to live a more normal life, to concentrate on less ambitious undertakings, and to search for Helena, the girl he wishes to marry. He diagnoses in Fernández a double inheritance from his ancestors; on the one hand ascetic tendencies, and on the other a desire for a wild and active life of sexual and other kinds of excitement. He advises him to leave all drug usage such as morphine, opium, or ether, because he has a predisposition for drugs and thus could easily become an addict.

Fernández blames part of the duality of his personality on his intellectual cultivation without an orderly method which, according to him, destroyed his faith and gave him an ardent curiosity to experience all the possible activities in life, both good and evil. He analyzes the feelings of terror which come to those who have intellectually denied God, and yet he fears that some of the teachings of his childhood might be true. He considers the terror of madness, sometimes induced by taking drugs, and even considers moments of deep depression, when he has felt that death by his own hand would be the only solution, but is lacking the energy to perform the act. Returning to the theme of madness he points out that he, just as many others, has felt its nearness. And he questions why it should be so disgraceful to go mad if such great artists as Baudelaire and others of equal stature have gone mad. But then he thinks of Helena, who is going to save him from all of these things he has mentioned and give him absolution.

Once again there is a break from the reading of the diary when Sáenz breaks in and tells Fernández that he has not lived the life advised by Rivington for the last eight years. Fernández says that his life is different now because he has distributed his energies equally amongst pleasure, study, and action. Also he has left off having violent, emotional affairs with women because he scorns all women, and for that reason has two affairs at once so that they counterbalance each other. Once again Fernández continues when Máximo Pérez asks his friend to resume his reading.

In the entry from London, November 20, Fernández analyzes himself and the contradictory inheritance from the side of his family which was ascetic and the side of his family which was violently active, both of which make him so changeable in his impulses. He relates the death of his mother when he was ten and his internship in a Jesuit school, from which he was then sent to the ranch of the Monteverdes, his cousins, where he lived the brutal life of the rich "patrón" (ranch-owner). The Monteverdes alternated between all types of violent activities and sexual orgies in which Fernández also took part. He feels that all these factors are the causes of his alternating between epochs of savage action, and of meditation, when he enters into a state of ascetic continence.

In the entry dated December 5, London, Fernández begins to investigate the pre-Raphaelite painters, which he admits is an example of his impracticality. But, in a long disquisition, Fernández elaborates on the idea that practical persons are inferior to the impractical ones like himself. He decides to make a return visit to Rivington and goes to his office. There in the waiting room Fernández becomes upset by the psychologically ill persons waiting to see the doctor. When he enters the office he begins to cry, and asks the doctor to assure him that he is not crazy like the people in the waiting room. He also asks the doctor to have a copy made of the painting of Helena's mother. The doctor urges Fernández to search for the girl and dream no longer. Fernández decides to go to Paris to seek her. He thinks of all the things he has done in London, studying Greek and Russian, the arts of war, agronomy, and also his studies and viewings of art, especially the pre-Raphaelite.

He also enumerates all the various things of value that he has collected during his stay.

Rivington only has partial success and admits it to Fernández. Finally, Fernández recurs to Charvet, actually a pseudonym invented by Silva for Charcot, precursor of Freud. His malady is diagnosed as neurasthenic ailments. The protagonist is ironical concerning the fancy medical terms which the psychiatric practitioners use, but nevertheless, he is cured twice from the nervous collapses he falls into.[20]

Psychotherapy is discussed at great length in Rivington's office concerning the problems of Fernández. His diagnosis seems to be a neurosis attributed in part to his contradictory inheritance, with one side of the family fanatically religious, inhibited persons, and with wild, orgiastic, antireligious persons on the other. Also, Rivington suggests that some of the protagonist's problems have resulted because he was an orphan, losing his mother when he was ten years of age, and other family members at a relatively early age, leaving him without relatives at the death of his grandmother.

With such fluctuation in his emotional states, where drugs, mysticism, and sexual orgies alternate with periods of sexual abstinence, Fernández apparently has mental aberrations. These problems cause numerous allusions to psychotherapy in the novel. It is a theme used as subject for some of the essayistic digressions, such as those on madness.[21]

On December 26 the entry explains that, once again emotionally ill, Fernández consults with Charvet. When Charvet hears of his five months of sexual abstinence, he says that Fernández should not follow such capricious behavior. But on learning that the protagonist is stubbornly bent on such behavior, he prescribes violent exercises, long hot baths, and large doses of bromides. But the suggestions give no results, and the protagonist continues to feel a violent depression. On December 27, Fernández is somewhat better, but then he becomes worse again and stays in bed for a few days. His servant, Francisco, goes to see Fernández's friends the Mirandas, who bring two doctors to diagnose his illness. The friends gossip while the doctors consider his case. Silva is very ironical in this passage, making a long enumeration of all the neuroses and psychological terms for illness which the two doctors use. They finally prescribe a purgative for Fernández, which he does not intend to take. Then his friend Marinoni says that he will go for Dr. Charvet, who comes that evening. Fernández asks for drugs to allow him to escape the horrible, anguished feeling he has. Dr. Charvet finally prescribes a medicine which has a positive effect, and within a few days Fernández is able to get out of bed. But the doctor warns him that he can have a relapse which might prostrate him at any time.

On New Year's Eve, Fernández goes out but soon begins to feel ill again. In front of a shop window, which has a great marble clock, he begins to experience all the terrors he felt before and finally loses consciousness in front of the window. He becomes conscious again in his own bed with Marinoni and Francisco his servant, accompanying him. Fernández says that he is saved, even though he has a horrible headache, since the anguished feeling which has tormented him has disappeared. In bed that night in a feverish condition, nevertheless, he is improving, and in succeeding days he finally regains his health. Charvet tells him again to enjoy life, but not excessively, and to marry and be happy.

On March 10, Rivington sends Fernández a copy of the painting of the mother of Helena, and the protagonist makes a kind of chapel, with the painting of Helena's mother on one wall and the picture of his grandmother painted for him by James McNeill Whistler on the other wall. Below the painting of Helena's mother is a bronze table he keeps filled with several different varieties of flowers ordered by telegram from Cannes. He has a chair there on which to meditate and read, a box where he keeps the jewels he has bought for her and the cameo Helena dropped in the restaurant. He also has a crystal box in which is preserved the bunch of flowers she tossed to him.

On March 10 Charvet, in one of his consultations with Fernández, sees the picture and mentions that Scilly Dancourt is an acquaintance of his. Charvet tells Fernández that Helena's mother died of tuberculosis while he was attending her, and the husband, who had a daughter four years of age, was deeply affected by his wife's death. Charvet tells Fernández the name of the only other person he knows who corresponds with Scilly, General des Zardes.

On March 20, Fernández goes to see the general. He does not know anything about Scilly at that moment, but tells Fernández that a Professor Mortha has contact with him. On seeing Mortha, Fernández is told that the only connection he has with Scilly is by mail through his bankers, Lazard, Casseres and Company. They are also financially connected with Fernández, and he goes there to investigate. He learns that they know little, but that the last check of Count Scilly was cashed in Alexandria.

Fernández meditates on April 12 on what little he has learned from his investigations except about the life of the father, previously a military man who on the death of his wife has turned to a study of religions, traveling through the world with his daughter. Fernández discloses that he has sentimentally rented for ten years the room where Helena slept in that Swiss inn, and he maintains it closed, as well as the room in the house back in his native land where his grandmother died.

On April 13 there is a long digression about what he would like to do for Helena if he were to find her. He would build her a castle and he sentimentally describes what he feels would be the reaction of the country people to her beauty: "There will be sunny mornings in which they will see us pass riding on horseback on a pair of Arabian horses over the roads which extend through the plain, and the rough country people will kneel upon seeing you, thinking you are an angel, when you look at their bodies deformed by their rustic chores with your shining blue eyes. . . ."[22]

Dated April 14 is one of the long essays in which Fernández treats of various themes such as: Ibsen, the Russians, Nietzsche, neo-Mysticism, and the theosophical centers of Paris. Sometimes one does not really understand whether Fernández is being serious about what he discusses or whether he is speaking ironically; for example, the long analysis of the trends of the epoch, where it is difficult to see whether Fernández is on the side of the anarchists or not. At times one seems to see an obvious irony, and at other times one could interpret his thoughts and ideas as his serious opinions; for example, in the following lines: "Thus with explosions of dynamite in the foundations of the palaces and striking down the most profound moral foundations, which were the older beliefs, humanity marches toward the ideal reign of justice. . . ."[23]

Another passage in which Fernández is talking about the religions of the present and especially about the Buddhists gives the reader the same doubtful feeling as to whether or not the author believed in what he was saying: "Do you still doubt concerning the Renaissance of Idealism and neo-Mysticism, you, spirit which questions the future and sees the old religions collapsing? . . . Look: from the obscure land of the Orient, the home of the gods, Buddhism and magic are returning to conquer the Western world. Paris, the Metropolis, opens to them its doors as Rome opened its doors to the cults of Mitra and Isis: there are fifty theosophical centers, hundreds of societies which investigate the mysterious psychological phenomena; Tolstoy abandons his art to publicize in a practical way charity and altruism; mankind is redeemed; the new faith lights her torches to shed light on her shadowy way."[24]

Although it is not possible to cite all the passages which would give a clearer view of Fernández's often quite perceptive ideas about the spirit of the present, this section reflects deep thought and meditation.

On April 15, the entry contains more of his evocations of the profound love he feels for Helena. The section of the diary dated April 19, however, is very different in tone from the previous evocation. Fernández enters a jewelry store, which provokes a favorite technique of the Modernists, a word picture of all the gems he sees, as well as all those which he can imagine. The following citation is only a small part of the world's gems which he paints: "Oh, sparkling stones, splendid and invulnerable, you vivid gems which slept for entire centuries in the depths of the earth, delight to the eye, symbol and summary of human riches. The diamonds shine with iridescence like drops of light. . . ."[25]

While Fernández is in the jewelry store, a girl with a Yankee accent comes in, and when she asks about a diamond necklace, she indicates that it is too expensive. Fernández offers it to her but she refuses; however, they make a date for nine that evening. After she leaves, Fernández buys the necklace to take to her as a gift. When he gives her the necklace that evening, she offers to pay for it since it is the one that she has asked her millionaire husband to buy for her without convincing him. Only after she learns he is the famous poet José Fernández does she soften and permit him to give her the necklace, thus opening the door to her seduction, not in her hotel but in his. She told him she was leaving the next day for New York, and Fernández knew that this would be his only night with Nelly, the wife of a Yankee millionaire.

Five months later, on the first of September, Fernández remembers the night with Nelly as having been only a droplet incapable of satisfying his horrible thirst. He gives a party and seduces three different girls, but none of them is really what he wants. He is searching for his lost love, Helena, and the caresses of these girls leave him with a feeling of bitterness and scorn for everything. He comments on the empty heavens because of his lack of faith. He is sure his thirst for the supreme, the absolute, is part of what causes his dissatisfaction.

His friend Rivas asks Fernández to stay with his wife, Consuelo, while he and three other friends spend the evening with four females whom he calls "horizontals." Fernández brings Consuelo flowers from his greenhouse, orchids the same as grown in Colombia and which in their youth they had looked at together. In those long-ago times, Consuelo and Fernández had felt fondness for each other before her marriage to Rivas. Fernández tells her that he has always loved her and asks her pardon. She, in turn, tells him he is her only love. Fernández asks her to meet him the next day, which she does, and their love affair begins.

Another conquest, the blonde German baroness, is seduced by the use of other wiles; Fernández playing hard to get and cool toward her. He challenges her to kiss him, and to meet with him the next afternoon. She tells him that what fascinates her in him is his scorn for the current morality. Julia Musellaro, an Italian girl, also seduced by Fernández, has libertinous conversations in her house, where she receives her guests every Tuesday evening. Fernández invites her to come to see him on Thursday morning, when they can be as pagan as they like. Fernández considers that he is perhaps behaving as a Don Juan, except in the case of Consuelo, his childhood sweetheart. He feels that he does not seduce anyone, that the seduction is mutual because of a common desire for pleasure and adventure. He meets the Italian girl later, and she has what he feels is a false story to tell him about a piece of jewelry that a "friend" needs to sell. He tells her to have it sent to him and he will send her a check.

Rivas continues sending his wife to Fernández, urging Consuelo to go sightseeing in Paris with their friend, and seems not to feel the least bit worried about his wife. Consuelo tells Fernández that everyone, including her husband, calls him "el casto José" (the chaste José).[26] Although Consuelo had been ill, she begins to improve with the affection of José and making love to him every day. For three months their idyll continues, then Rivas and his wife leave for San Sebastian, and although they invite José to accompany them, he declines. Rivas thanks Fernández for the time spent with his wife, which has resulted in her great improvement in health. In his short observations dated September 18, Fernández indicates that he does not wish to accompany them and that if they return he intends to tell Rivas that his wife should not be trusted to spend her evenings with him.

His personal record of October 1 recounts a conversation with Camilo Monteverde, first cousin of Fernández, who is considered by the protagonist to be ignorant in the subject of art, and for that reason they hardly ever talk of such themes together. His cousin's philosophy of life is to praise others' possessions highly in order that they be given to him as gifts. He lives as easily as he can without studying or working very much and says that although both are from the Andrade tree, Fernández is like Don Quixote while he on the contrary is like Sancho. In this section, as was pointed out by Bernardo Gicovate, for the first time in Spanish, Silva writes a burlesque of Ramón de Campoamor, using him as an example of intellectual mediocrity. Fernández is convinced that Monteverde has absolutely no taste in poetry because his favorite poet is Campoamor.[27] It should be remembered that Silva has often been compared to Campoamor in some of his **"Gotas Amargas."** It is obvious that the poet-protagonist of *De Sobremesa* was not seriously impressed with Campoamor's poetic talents, and that whatever respect Silva had felt for him probably no longer existed.

In his observations dated October 15, Fernández remembers Helena strongly again and returns to his meditation in the room of the paintings after an absence of several days. The flowers that had been placed there last were dead, and the room smelled of death. Fernández decided to move the things to other parts of his living quarters, and to put the paintings in his bedroom.

The diary for October 25 describes another period of searching for Helena, sending telegrams and spending ten days in investigation, with no success.

The diary now jumps to January 16, where it is revealed that Fernández has been unconscious for ten days, and again Charvet has had to be consulted. Between life and death for a few days, Fernández finally recovers and decides to leave for America to try to forget his failure to find Helena through immersing himself in mercantile operations. He returns to a cemetery where he has spent several afternoons, and there sees the emblem he has come to connect with Helena, the three leaves and the butterfly. He nearly faints, and catches himself by a column. His friend Marinoni comes to his aid, and as Fernández starts to lose consciousness in the arms of Marinoni, he sees the inscription of Helena's name and the date of her death. He

mourns her death and says that perhaps she never truly existed, but that she was his dream and was more real than what men call reality. Her early death prevents the consummation of the love Fernández feels for her, and she can then enter completely the realm of the ideal, without loss of chastity, in word or deed, becoming the perfect object for the protagonist's adoration. Fernández ends the reading of the diary and closes the book. His friends remain silent and Silva gives a last artistic description of the luxurious interior as though it were a painting.

III GENERAL CRITICAL COMMENTARY ON THE PLOT, SCENES, AND CHARACTERS

De Sobremesa lacks a well-designed and constructed plot, as most critics who have studied the novel have noted. For example, Arias Argáez cites Sanín Cano as having said that *De Sobremesa* was a work of defective construction, of arbitrary analysis and of purely subjective truth.[28] Yet there are paragraphs in which Silva shows some talent as a storyteller and also reveals his stylistic command of the Spanish language. *De Sobremesa* is a series of short narrations dated as entries in a diary. It includes incidents and episodes as well as digressions which in reality are essays. This interpolation of essays makes the novel seem rather unorganized and hard to summarize and to follow except for the unification of the plot provided by the hero of the work, José Fernández.

As the plot summary indicates, the diary relates the European trip of a rich South American, José Fernández, poet and art collector, who is beleaguered with psychological problems. He glimpses fleetingly a mysterious child-woman with whom he falls in love at first sight. He tells of the search, a kind of pilgrimage all across Europe in search of this ideal love whom he finds only in the grave.

The hero appears at times to be a stylized reflection of Silva. The character, however, is Silva and is not Silva, as in all autobiographical novels, where usually the author uses much of his own knowledge about many men, and not solely about himself. Sometimes the reader does not know whether or not Silva is referring to his own feelings or fictional ones. Nevertheless, this has not deterred many critics from quoting the majority of the words Silva puts into the mouth of his protagonist as his own thoughts and aspirations. Yet at times the character is a very different one from Silva, who at the moment of rewriting the novel was undoubtedly already decided concerning his suicide.

There can be no doubt about the reasons an author chooses to write a novel using an autobiographical approach. In this way it is possible to objectify his own contradictory psychology, and the novel is an exploration of the psychology of an artist. Since Fernández is a prose writer and poet, we are able to observe his ideas about writing poetry, ideas elaborated on by the author and put into the mouth of the hero. The narrative mode, the autobiographical novel, is one which reveals more fully the character of the hero, yet it gives a unilateral approach to the consciousness of a person, and such is the intimate diary read in a long after-dinner session with friends. Since the actual after-dinner chat is cut to such a minimum, perhaps it would have been better to entitle it *The Reading of My Diary.* The novel is so long that it does not seem plausible that it could be read at one sitting, but such acceptance of the illogical has been one of the concomitants of most types of art.

Silva wanted to write a psychological novel which would reveal the complicated psyche and soul of the artist, in this case a particular artist who showed a duality in his alternation between sexual orgies and periods of abstinence, when he would search for the ideal. When reading the summary of this unusually frank book for Silva's epoch in Colombia, it is easy to understand why his novel was not published until twenty-nine years after his death. As Juan Loveluck has said, the novel presents a kind of nonsystematic analysis of the man of the end of the nineteenth century and his basic conflicts in the world.[29] But the presentation was of a man as artist and aesthete, whose problems were often different from those of the majority of men of those years. The narration does reflect the consuming intellectual interests of the time when the pre-Freudians were beginning to elaborate their theories. The protagonist's interests are made manifest in psychology, psychopathology, and parapsychology, as well as the mental explorations which the author probably knew about personally, in Paris, when Charcot and other pre-Freudian psychological investigators were extremely popular.

In the case of Silva-Fernández, the artist (or other man), who is unable to find the sensitive spirit he craves in a woman, comes to feel completely frustrated, as if there were no being in existence who might meet him on his own footing. Then he creates an ideal of femininity, even though he must occasionally break loose and try to gain release by union with female flesh. Nevertheless, he has such revulsion for himself after these orgies that he destroys what little physiological relief he might have gained. Yet he must prove he is a man every day.

Fernández's ideal of perfect womanhood was Helena, an adolescent whom he sees only at a distance and does not know well enough to do anything but idealize her. The whole novel is in part a search for Helena, with the characteristics of a detective story in the investigation of clues to her whereabouts. But the search is fruitless and she becomes for Fernández the mystery woman, later his impossible love, and finally his muse. This idealization of Helena does not help the protagonist to have a more normal attitude toward women, nor does it prevent the sexual affairs which cause his self-revulsion. And, even though he does not leave off drugs or his encounters with other women, his self-hatred afterwards indicates that these were only substitutes for the ideal who lives solely in his memory. A less blunt and truthful writer would have left these amorous adventures out of the work, but Silva is illustrating the teaching of his day, the double standard which was ingrained in the young men from the beginning.

Often this novel has had very adverse criticism and a close study of it over many years does not cause it to gain in stature in the mind of this student of Silva's works. Yet it can be compared favorably with Modernist novels such as *Idolos Rotos* (*Broken Idols*) of Manuel Díaz Rodríquez, and others of the time. Perhaps it is not as good as the author would have liked it to be since it was reconstructed in the most terrible years which Silva suffered. He rewrote it after he had lost all the import business along with his capital and a great part of his personal property, after he had tried without success to make a career in diplomacy, after a shipwreck in which he lost much of his unpublished work, and after he had failed once again in starting the tile factory in Bogotá. He was, at the time, a complete failure, unable to find a way to maintain his mother and sister. Unemployed, he did rewrite this novel requested by his friend Fernando Villa before taking the suicide route out of all his problems. The mere fact of rewriting a long novel from memory without any notes means that it could not have the same consistency and organization of the manuscript lost in the ship *L'Amerique.* For that reason it is probably more equitable to characterize his prose writings in some of his short essays written at a much earlier time, as will be done in the next chapter.

The scenes where the novel takes place give us a cosmopolitan view of the world. It begins with the luxurious salon, where the reading of the intimate diary of a world traveler, a rich South American, takes place. The interior of the room where the protagonist reads his journal aloud, and chats with his friends, is in a South American city which is not identified, but it is probably Bogotá or perhaps Caracas. It is a novel, however, of taking a trip, an idea so dear to the mind of the young people of most epochs, especially today—taking a trip in every sense of the word. Most of the other scenes are in bedrooms where Fernández's conquests take place or in the interiors of luxurious houses, with the one exception of the few days when Fernández stays in the house of the Swiss couple. And only there, during his stay in the mountains, does the hero describe any scenes of nature. This indicates that nature did not enter into Silva's prose as an important element.

The setting is usually urban as in most of the Modernist novels. The characters also are urban. They are mostly rich, artistically knowledgeable, international, usually bilingual or trilingual, reflecting a universal culture. They are often expatriates from several different countries. Some of the characters are mature psychologists or psychiatric physicians. They are all adults or young adults. The youngest character is Helena, who is a teenager when the hero glimpses her. The protagonist is twenty-seven years old. The only child even mentioned in the novel is Helena, as a child of four when she lost her mother. This indicates that Silva was not concerned with a realistic portrayal of life, but with a psychological portrayal of the psyche of an artist. And he succeeds admirably, in spite of the disorganization apparent in the work.

IV AUTOBIOGRAPHICAL ELEMENTS

The element of fiction which is always present should not be confused, as some critics have done, apparently believing that the character created by the writer and the writer himself in his historical person are one and the same. However, Silva did use the fictional character to reflect some of the same tortures he suffered. He depicts the suffering of a young man who could not adapt to the conservative and rigid society into which he was born and whose problems were exacerbated because he was an artist who could not adapt to the society in which he found himself.

It can be said that Silva drew upon his personal experiences, and those things also that he dreamed of doing but could never afford. Some of those elements which are autobiographical are the fact that both were poets, and that Fernández expresses many of the same ideas concerning poetic theory and other subjects which Silva made clear in essays and poems. But there are differences: no ideal love is known to have played a part of any importance in Silva's life. He was never anywhere near being a millionaire, nor did he have enough money to live the luxurious life the hero lives, as for example buying a magnificent diamond necklace for Nelly to enable him to seduce her and remain with her one night.

The work is in a way a complement of the biography of Silva in that it analyzes the crisis of a poet much like himself, and the intellectual surroundings he found in Europe in those days. It is a work which also demonstrates the wide knowledge of the author in art and in literature, as well as other fields such as neuropsychology. It also shows some of his mistaken ideas, as for example the idea that thirty-year-old wines would of necessity be good ones,[30] or that the aristocracy of Europe could trace their ancestry back to Roman times.[31] There is no doubt that Silva did identify himself often with his protagonist, but it is a mistake to exaggerate out of proportion the autobiographical descriptions in the work, attributing them all to Silva, and not to the protagonist he has created out of his imagination.

One of the many ways in which Fernández is a reflection of Silva is in his dissatisfaction with his surroundings, with the bourgeois atmosphere which both the author and the protagonist reject as being mediocre, vile, and philistinian. Fernández is critical of the public, with its lack of understanding.[32] He expresses his hatred of the bourgeois life without emotions and without curiosity.[33] He is scornful of Latin American politics, manifested by the plan he elaborates to make sweeping changes.[34] He is scornful of the admirers of mediocrity,[35] of vulgar mercantile work and all the institutions of a life which is empty without the sanctuary of art.[36] Some of the other themes toward which the protagonist shows a critical attitude, probably similar to that of Silva, were: religion,[37] reality,[38] socialists,[39] the Jews,[40] the United States,[41] and even the visual pollution of Niagara Falls.[42]

Silva himself had many psychological problems, often resulting from real tragedies in his life, which were a contributing factor in his suicide. But his protagonist in the novel had many that were different from Silva's, mostly as a result of his alternating abstinence and sexual excesses, as well as his search for the ideal which was never fulfilled. Silva had to concentrate on earning a living and had little time to search for the ideal.

One suspects that the friends who listen to the reading of the diary, and those whom he meets in Paris and London and the other places Fernández visits, are taken from real-life models. However, all the women, with the exception of Consuelo, who is delineated as a live person from his native country, seem to have come from the author's wide reading, or his imagination. They lack reality, since there is little difference to be observed among them, or among his feelings for them.

More than simply mirroring Silva, the protagonist delineates the spiritual disorientation of those years, reflected by most of the Modernist writers. Fernández is a walking compendium of all the weaknesses and vacillations the Modernist artists had in resolving their lives in those days.

Like Des Esseintes in *A Rebours,* by Joris-Karl Huysmans, Fernández in many ways was the double of the author, and both writers were braving the stigma attached to the autobiographical novel, uniting the mystery of creation and autobiography. But not only in being both the creator and in part the created one does Silva show us his duality; his chosen protagonist is partly an aesthete and partly an unsatisfied man, tormented by his financial and personal difficulties. Silva therefore is behind Fernández and often comes forth with more force than the protagonist. *De Sobremesa* is a book halfway between pure autobiography and pure fiction, sometimes both at the same time, other times one or the other. *De Sobremesa* is, on the most profound level, pure autobiography; that is, on the basis of the aspirations of the soul and of the thirst for the absolute of the hero, Fernández. It does not matter that the autobiographical details of Fernández are not completely those of Silva, since the literary and artistic traits seem to blend.

Like Silva, Fernández is the author of books of poetry, two in the case of the protagonist, one in the case of the author, but Silva lost some manuscripts of poems in the wreck of the ship *L'Amerique.* The early poems of Fernández are said to be erotic, and are denigrated by him compared with the great creations found in the poetry of the past.

Fernández gives his theory of poetry, and it is a clear idea of Symbolist poetry, and perhaps it is the theory of Silva as well, since he has stated several times in poems essentially the same thing: "It is that I do not want to state, but to suggest, and in order for the suggestion to be produced, it is necessary that the reader be an artist. In imaginations deprived of faculties of this type, what effect can a work of art produce? None. Half of it is in the verse, statue, or painting, the other half in the head of the one who hears, sees, or dreams."[43]

According to a friend of Silva, Juan Evangelista Manrique,[44] the words of the protagonist of *De Sobremesa* concerning his education could be applied to Silva to describe his intellectual development: "An intellectual education undertaken without method and with crazy pretensions to universality, an intellectual cultivation which has ended up in the loss of all faith, in the burlesque of all human barriers, in an ardent curiosity for evil, in the desire to carry out all life's experiences, completed the work of other influences. . . ."[45]

Silva always desired the luxuries which surrounded him in his childhood, and after entering into the world of business, burdened with the debts inherited from his father, he was unable to obtain them in the quantity he might have wished. He reflected his lack of fulfillment of these desires by having his protagonist enjoy all of them.

The hero is profoundly interested in his own health, in his physical and mental hygiene, and this reflects the preoccupation of Silva himself during his last days when he had hypochondriac moments. But in Silva's life the sexual excesses were not possible. These preoccupations were undoubtedly wishful thinking on the part of Silva or aggrandizement of the normal pattern of Latin American youths of visiting brothels in those days. By giving so much sexual prowess to his protagonist, Silva is able to counteract in a once-removed way the reputation he himself (as well as Fernández) had gained as being the chaste, virginal young man, without experience in sexual encounters.

Some of the doctors who attend Fernández are based on real-life characters, as Charvet, and perhaps others. Charvet, as mentioned, was the veiled identity of Charcot, a pre-Freudian psychologist. The detailed description of Fernández's illness seems to be imaginary; however, Silva was always interested in reading any kind of manual, especially in psychology or psychiatry. It is true that Silva himself visited in Europe and was at many of the places where his entries are dated, but his life could not have been that of the millionaire protagonist. He must have moved in entirely different circles, if he was lucky enough to move in any circles at all in European society, except for that of the expatriates.

The European setting reflects Silva's trip to Europe, but actually little is known about what he did there except to visit Juan Evangelista Manrique, who was a medical student in Paris. Manrique testifies that Silva tried to learn all he could from him and from the persons he talked to by going to all the lectures he could attend, and by reading all the latest books. Nevertheless, it is dangerous, in the author's opinion, to equate unequivocally Silva and José Fernández since undoubtedly Silva alternates real happenings with fictional elements and modifies many of the factual elements.

V ROMANTIC ELEMENTS

One of the most constantly used characteristics of the Romantic novel is vagueness, and concerning Helena the protagonist assigns an unknown or exotic origin to the heroine, revealing the truth only gradually. Fernández is vague about names and identities, and often one has to search for the name or the identity of the characters who are his friends, or girls to whom he is making love.

In some Romantic novels, symbols and mythology are used frequently. In *De Sobremesa* they are used somewhat differently than in Romantic works in that there is an element of foreboding and terror associated with the ideal attachment which will inevitably be frustrated, as is known from the beginning of *De Sobremesa.* The supernatural symbols in the novel are connected with the words of the grandmother on her death, the throwing of a bunch of flowers by Helena to Fernández from her window, the finding of her brooch with three leaves and a hovering butterfly, and the appearance of butterflies at crucial moments. Silva uses other techniques related to the Romantics such as premonition, and open anticipation of the tragic ending.

The Romantic elements in *De Sobremesa* are mainly in tone, an exacerbated consciousness of his scorn for life. And the Modernists added to the uncovering of the sentimental life a profound literary self-consciousness concerning style and form which modify profoundly the Romantic sentimentality.

The subtle use of augury in the work gives the reader the idea of impending tragedy of the death of Helena. But it is also Modernist in the use of the emblem of the butterfly as a supernatural indication of Helena's presence, and as an indication of Fernández's belief in the supernatural. It is evident that this use of augury is to increase in the reader the anguished hope that Fernández will find Helena, but in a way, for some more observant readers, it is known from early on in the book what the outcome will be, and the interest of the reader shifts to how the actions will be accomplished.

Considering that one of the characteristics most commonly connected with Romanticism was that of an uncurbed revelation of the most intimate self, the protagonist fits that characteristic as much as any of the heroes of the Romantic novels. The "yo" (I) of the hero is the most important thing in the work and is the main theme of the novel.

The emphasis on religion, which was one of the Romantic tendencies, is present in *De Sobremesa* but in a negative way, in the lack of religion of the protagonist. Yet he is obsessed by doubts concerning his agnostic or atheistic beliefs, and thinks always of his grandmother's prayer for him when she was dying.

Probably one of the main characteristics which seems Romantic and goes against the sensibilities of the twentieth-century reader of *De Sobremesa* is the sentimental dwelling on his sorrows. Fernández even says he prefers to suffer. He has a tendency to dwell on his own grief in an overly emotional way.

In general, Romantic literature represents a reality which destroys love; and a life without love, for the protagonist, has little meaning. Such is the case with Fernández and

Helena, even though Fernández is not able to remain faithful to her physiologically. For Fernández, as for the Romantic hero, the noblest type of love is that which remains unfulfilled. The impossible love was one of the most common themes preferred in Romanticism. It became popular probably because of the belief that marriage brings out the imperfect in love, and for that reason Fernández is so shocked when he is told by Dr. Rivington that, of course, he will marry the girl. His love for her was more pleasing to him when posited from an idealizing distance. This attitude has resulted from the medieval traditions of courtly love, when marriage was not the desired state for a lover to feel an ideal passion for the beloved.

From the medieval courtly love tradition also comes the belief that the lovers who suffer the most are the most fulfilled. The suffering of Fernández is in a more modern manner with his various sexual affairs with other women. He certainly is not trying to immortalize Helena by his faithfulness, but perhaps this is a reflection of his modernity, where man no longer has the idea that he can only be happy with one woman.

Also, the preservation of the flowers thrown to him by Helena is somehow overly Romantic for the sensibilities of the present, and dates the work; but just because it reflects a taste not the same as is presently common does not mean that only in his time were such sentiments commonly felt and expressed.

Although Fernández does not compare his Helena or other lovers with blossoms or other aspects of nature as did the Romantics, there is a strong presence of flowers in the novel. The emblematic use of the three leaves and the butterfly has already been noted: Helena is identified with the bouquet of white roses she threw to Fernández, which he tries to preserve for as long as possible in a crystal box. The connection between Fernández and Consuelo is also related to flowers, orchids.

One of the most typical Romantic elements in *De Sobremesa* is the concept of love as entertained by the protagonist. The attachment is intense and spiritualized since their encounters have always been in shadows and without real communication except in symbolic gestures which, it is insinuated, might have been misinterpreted by the hero. The intensity and longevity of his attachment for Helena is reflected in his guarding zealously the bouquet of white tea roses, and also Fernández's desire to obtain a copy of the painting of Helena's mother, who was so like the daughter. His chapel, where he placed her painting and other emblems and relics, indicates these same ideas.

Although Silva rarely describes nature, in the few descriptions he does poeticize what he observes. Unlike the Romanticists, Silva does not use nature as a vehicle of his emotions. The observer does not reflect or parallel nature in his state of mind. Yet the scene in which Silva describes the ocean is a favorite scene of the Romantics, in which the hero sits alone contemplating the light of the moon. In Silva's novel it is not with melancholy feelings but in harmony with the Modernist idea that nature was the only place where the artist could expand and become part of the universe. Silva thus uses nature in two ways. One, by showing a pantheistic union with it, and the other by the Rousseauian idea of the return to pure and peaceful nature, contrasted with the vices of city life.

Also Romantic was the use of the theme of death. From the beginning it is known that the death of Helena is to terminate Fernández's search for her. This was a common Romantic approach: the story of the love of a beautiful, idealized girl ended by her death.

One of the characteristics which was Romantic as well as Modernist was Silva's preoccupation with the search for the source of the artistic inspiration, a theme returned to again and again.

VI MODERNIST TENDENCIES

In the work *De Sobremesa* there is a deep and constant reflection of a preoccupation with the new art of portraiture being painted in Europe during those years: pre-Raphaelite art. The ideal Helena of Fernández's dreams is the image of one of the paintings, and Silva adds to this emphasis by having the character descend from the family of the wife of Rossetti, one of the pre-Raphaelite painters. Fernández finally finds a portrait in the pre-Raphaelite style, not of Helena, but of her mother, who resembles her, painted shortly before her early death from tuberculosis. There is a spiritualization of Helena similar to the kind utilized in the art of the pre-Raphaelites. She is so spiritualized that she is often unreal, even in the mind of the protagonist.

In Modernist novels like *De Sobremesa,* the heroes were non-conformists and did not adapt to their society. They fought the practical businessman (even when they were as successful in business as José Fernández), and the battle was not ignored by the enemy, since they knew that the members of society looked for practical success and did not care in the least for the successes of art. Silva, however, was forced to live in both camps, at least until the liquidation of the bankruptcy, and even then had to search, without much success, for a Maecenas, a political sinecure that would allow him to live in his artistic world.

In Modernist fiction the heroes were generally "Los Raros" (the strange ones), as Rubén Darío called them, and the "neurotics," as they were called by Max Nordau. However, these heroes were idealized by the other artists in their own intellectualized atmosphere and often were obsessed by art as the only world where they could exist. The Modernists had inherited much of the Romantic tradition in these elements; for example, the cult of the sacred artist, and protest at the lack of comprehension in a vulgar and practical society which tended to frustrate the artist completely. They were often considered economic outcasts unless they could find a friend with influence who would either obtain for them a diplomatic post or give them a stipend on which to live.

The Modernist novel might seem to be a very different novel from what is normally considered to be Spanish-American. However, the novel of Modernism many times had as subject the psychological analysis of the victims of bitterness, the rebels in society, the neuropathic artists, made neuropathic by society, the persons usually of an intense refinement and hyperaesthetic sensibility. Because of this interest in such themes, the novel of Joris-Karl Huysmans, *A Rebours,* and his protagonist Des Esseintes were popular and well known among the Modernist fiction writers.

Rebellious individualism was a characteristic of Modernism, and the fact that Silva chose to rewrite this particular novel for publication after he had lost most of his manuscripts in the sinking of the ship *L'Amérique,* shows his rebellion. It was a work that would have been too disagreeable to the sensibilities of the Colombians to publish right after his death. Also, considering that when he rewrote it, he was probably already contemplating suicide, only a rebel would have chosen to redo such a shocking book, as it must have been for his times.

De Sobremesa's construction and organization were certainly not the optimum, as many critics have pointed out, and it is somewhat difficult to read in its entirety, but it is original in the analysis of the protagonist, José Fernández. The novel shows Silva's striving for a unique way of expressing his ideas in a unique style.

God is not mentioned except in a rather insolent fashion or in a deeply doubtful concern referring to His existence. However, in the consciousness of Fernández there are bits and pieces of dead religions, and a concern with religious art, and perhaps religion thus serves as one of the main themes in the novel. Fernández makes the effort to establish a new mysticism and a new mythology with his Helena, reflecting a belief in a reality which common man did not understand and perhaps the artist was doomed never to find in this life. But art might serve as a way, a kind of religion, or perhaps an aesthetic philosophy by which the poet or artist could guide his life. Silva's disquisitions on the metaphysical implications he sees around him show only an intuitive understanding without his being able to form a system or come to any order in his beliefs.

Silva shows a basically aesthetical attitude due to his concept of artistic activity as being its own end, worthy in itself and with no need for justifying it. Therefore, his prose shows that it is a literature of the senses; it vibrates with sensual elements, and it is dazzling in its display of color. It often reads like poetry in prose, and Silva always seems to be searching for sonorous turns of phrases. Also, the history of art is almost always present, and serves as one of the inspirations, perhaps equal to Silva's own intimate experiences and thoughts. Thus he used established art works for source material in his new creation, adding more artistic qualities.

Silva's protagonist showed the typically Modernist bitterness toward mediocrity. Concerning intelligence, his attitude is that it is an aristocracy to which few, like himself, belong. For him art is noble, so noble that he feels unworthy to be named in the same breath with Shakespeare and other great artists.

The author takes refuge in distance in space, in Europe rather than South America, through his protagonist, freeing himself from his own tragic life. He then chooses from among the elements around him those which represent the most aristocratic and aesthetic world; none of the conquests of his hero is less than a famous beauty. Fernández is constantly acquiring some art object, and he tries to maintain an exquisite fictional ambience around him.

The Modernist characteristic of cosmopolitanism in *De Sobremesa* is visible in several ways. In the first place, the novel has as its scene various cosmopolitan places in Europe and, although the author describes all of them, no single one seems to attract him more than any other. He speaks very few times about the beauties of nature around him, and when he does it is solely comparing them to the unfortunate aspects of the life in a large city. But these attitudes are only displayed when he is tired of the life of dissipation he leads in the city. He projects in his protagonist the desire to assimilate the ways and values of the various European societies, to become a cosmopolitan citizen of all countries. He is always engaged in the study of different and unusual subjects both in Europe and in his homeland. This reflects an interest in subjects from many different countries. The novel itself, as Silva was rewriting it, manifests his desire to participate in the community of the elite, the aesthetically initiated. In this demonstration of the aristocratic nature of Silva's tastes and ambitions, he is the same as his protagonist. He reflects a world of books and of art, which is one of the most constantly recurring themes of the work. The protagonist cultivated collections of precious objects, whole museums of art, impressionistic refinements, antibourgeois philosophies, moral crises, and miniatures of poetic prose.

One of the impulses which aimed toward personal expression of extreme individualism was an extension and modification of a Romantic tenet, but it can be distinguished in its Modernistic modality by the peculiarly literary orientation and the artistic intensity. The Modernists were often said to be uninvolved with society, but this attitude has been discounted in the present since these writers, with their intense individuality and search for the self, contributed a great deal to the understanding of man himself and of his psyche.

Silva is trying to understand one single "I," that of his protagonist, José Fernández, and exhibits a deep philosophical pessimism, considering that man's beliefs until that moment had been only illusion. According to Silva, unchangeable principles and fundamental ideals were no longer considered a standard part of man's life. The only reality, the only truth, the only irreducible core of reality was the "I." Sensibility is one of the main elements in the philosophical ideas expressed by Silva's protagonist in *De Sobremesa,* and he negates the rational worth of the ideas that unite human beings. He denies many times the social worth of literature, making it a sublime and holy sport of the select and not understood by others, even the critics.

Modernist and Romantic tendencies and elements are combined with compatible characteristics. There are only a few lingering elements of Romanticism. One of the stylistic traits which marks Silva as a Modernist most clearly is a concern for a more subtle language and a use of vocabulary which is dissimilar to that of the Romantics. Silva's diction is ornamental, often sumptuous, and he uses the techniques of word pictures or portraits. He attempts to borrow pictorial equivalents, from watercolor, oil, pastel, or etching, and emphasizes stylistic experimentation. Concerning content, Silva forms a hero of art, showing us that the heroic concept of life is not dead, but that social and political circumstances in America have changed so much, the writers could no longer be heroes of action.

VII DECADENT CHARACTERISTICS

Bernardo Gicovate has studied *De Sobremesa* as a testimony or portrait of the European decadence which was in style during the years when Silva rewrote his novel.[46] The work *De Sobremesa* can be considered to be similar to decadent novels such as *A Rebours*[47] (*Against the Grain*), by Joris-Karl Huysmans, in style as well as, to a certain extent, in the plot.

In style, Silva's work is like *A Rebours,* following the definition of the novel in which the whole is subordinated to the parts, rather than a classic style, where the opposite would be the case. Silva was predominantly interested in detail, and for that reason, perhaps, his novel seems more disorganized than it really is, because of the often overwhelming mass of minutiae given to us.

But Huysmans was a master of irony in *A Rebours* and always got his point across without leaving his reader confused as to whether he was being ironic or serious, as is sometimes the case in Silva's novel. However, if it is considered that the aesthetic attitude toward art is a decadent point of view, such a tendency can be observed many times in *De Sobremesa* just as in *A Rebours*. The use of words to give the effect of painting, and also the mention of many different paintings used as a part of the work, are utilized in Silva's novel as well as Huysmans's.

Yet the decadent spirit did not arise solely with the novel by Huysmans since it was visible in the Romantic period as well in different ways. For one thing, the Romantic as well as the decadent view of Christian religion was through an artistic, aesthetic prism which watered down its message to that of a mystic beauty and used its imagery in nonreligious or antireligious modes. In *De Sobremesa* this is visible, as is another trait, the feeling of loss and of desperation which became more pronounced the further the protagonist got from believing that God existed. And the neurosis of the hero added to the loss of an unaccustomed psychological dimension.

The idea of evasion to another period in time is observed in *De Sobremesa.* Even more pronounced in the decadent novels such as *A Rebours* is the flight to another epoch.

The correspondence established between literature and the other plastic arts is present in *De Sobremesa* and is also clearly obvious in novels like *A Rebours*. This is mainly used as a means of choice of words which are colorful and which reflect the contours and outlines of the things described.

The words in *De Sobremesa* seem to be chosen, as in *A Rebours,* less because of their meaning than for their power of evocation, their musical and plastic qualities. Silva wished to suggest rather than name specifically in his poetry. But in his prose the same desire is also visible.

Similar to the Duke des Esseintes is José Fernández in his neuroses. Yet in other ways Silva's protagonist was more Romantic in character and less sophisticated. Des Esseintes was a more refined and more anguished character than Fernández.

Silva, like Huysmans, reflects a striving for the virtues of individualism in any possible way, as observed in the prose poem on all the different kinds of precious stones, inserted in the episode when Fernández visits a jewelry store. Silva did not follow frequently the practice of inventing neologisms, but he did arrange the syntax of the Spanish language, already more flexible than the French, in original ways.

VIII LOVE AND WOMEN

Although searching for Helena almost from the beginning of the novel and worshiping her image, Fernández relapses several times from his self-imposed state of chastity and has various love affairs with women. These adventures might reflect the physiological problems of a young man with normal sexual urges who decides *contra natura* to be chaste while searching for his ideal love. They might also represent Silva's erotic fantasies, since Fernández has relations with seven women in the novel: Lelia Orloff, a Lesbian; Nini Rousset; Constanza Landseer, an Englishwoman with whom Fernández fails to consummate the union because of a reminder of Helena in a crucial moment; Nelly, the wife of a millionaire from Chicago; Consuelo, his compatriot; a German baroness; and a passionate Italian, Julia Musellaro. The friends of Fernández envy these conquests, as his friend Rovira says: ". . . Your amorous adventures . . . we all envy them in secret."[48]

These conquests live in his memory only because they are names to add to his list, like that of Don Juan. Because of the envy of his friends and acquaintances, he is especially proud that one night when he gives a party he is able to add three to his list, although he does not pretend to try to understand them. He does them favors in turn for the physiological release he can obtain from sexual relations with them. The dichotomy is clear in the case of Fernández: on the one hand the misogyny, the hatred of those women who give him the release he needs, and on the other the idealization of the one who could never disappoint him in sexual relations because of her chastity and her death before having experienced such relations.

Silva reflects a lack of knowledge about sexual relations, and indeed about human relations between the sexes. He discloses to us that the aristocratic Lelia Orloff is of plebeian origins, and wonders how a common background could have produced such an exquisite creature. He portrays her with little intellectual capacity but an immense desire to enjoy life. Then when the protagonist encounters Angela de Roberto visiting Lelia, he is angry, does not like her, and when he inquires why she is there is told bluntly that she is a friend. Then when he discovers them in a Lesbian union, his reaction is scorn, hatred, hitting out at Lelia and her friend with his hands and booted feet, and trying to stab her. His actions indicate that he felt possessive about her and did not want to share her with anyone. But aside from his possessiveness, and in spite of what he calls his fascination for the abnormal, he shows a deep-seated aversion to that relationship between them. Lelia as a character in a novel is a closed personality; she is not understood by Fernández or by the reader, and this reflects that basically Fernández felt scorn for the women he seduced, implying the same attitude on the part of the author toward a woman he might use as a sexual object.

All the seven conquests made by Fernández are either professional prostitutes or adulteresses who acquiesce easily to Fernández's charms, thus providing him with little challenge. The accounts of his nights with these women seem strangely the same and are not always very convincing: "Of that night I only remember her smiling beauty below the full, velvet curtains of my bed, in the bedroom scarcely lit by the Byzantine lamp of dark red crystal; the impression of the strong freshness and the perfume of her adolescent body and the murmur of her voice begging me to go to the United States."[49]

One of the reasons might have been that during his time it was not customary to describe sexual relations explicitly, but in other descriptions, such as the use of drugs, he was more clear. The usual dimly lit interiors indicate shame concerning the most natural of human actions, sexual union.

The oversimplicity of treatment of women by his protagonist shows that Silva was not truly acquainted with many women in his life, except for his mother and his sisters. The other women he came into contact with were stereotyped as either beings of sheer sexuality or idealized women of purity on a pedestal. He had not had the opportunity to react to an authentic, loving woman who could combine tenderness and ideal love with sensuality, and would have had difficulty adjusting to such a woman due to the dichotomy between these two in his personality.

Perhaps the heightened sensibilities aroused by the more common acceptance at the present time of woman, as well as man, as a human being with similar rights and privileges, makes the novel *De Sobremesa* seem so anachronistic. That men should scorn the personality of a particular woman who does not happen to be a virgin, making her into less of a person, into an object of scorn, is not so common in some cultures today. His double standard is not easily accepted now, although it is still in force in Colombia to a certain extent. It takes two to engage in sexual relations, and the masculine partner is no longer considered as coming out of the relationship with his virtue intact, leaving the stain solely on the female. Even in the case of the countrywoman of Fernández, Consuelo, in spite of the fact that long ago he did feel a chaste love for her, finally he scorns her. He says that if he sees her again he will close the door in her face, and will remind her husband that it is dangerous to leave his wife with a single man, even though he be called "el casto José."

Looking from another point of view at the idea of women, there is the Romantic conception that the virtuous and chaste woman can save a man and make him into a more noble character. But then as in the present, the changing of a person is not always successful, nor does the effort always provide a happy and contented relationship.

In Silva's time men often took the position that it was sinful to feel any physical desire toward the women they intended to marry, and for that reason, on Fernández's being asked if he intended to marry Helena, he is shocked because his passion contains mainly ideal sentiments and only a minimum of sensual elements. This medieval conception, which still exists in Colombia and in other countries of Latin America, is that carnal love is considered to be divorced from spiritual love. This leads to the conduct of the hero in the novel where he seduces the women who offer him little resistance, in order to ease his physiological urges. Fernández shows a basic scorn toward these women, just as though they were prostitutes, and in fact Silva may have satisfied his physiological urges in brothels, making it impossible for him to think of finding a combination of physical and spiritual love in the same person.

Fernández was a misogynist, to use a term which is milder than some which might be used today. He felt scorn toward a woman of flesh and blood, of passions and faults. He wanted an ideal woman he could put upon a pedestal to worship. This halo of faultlessness around Helena makes her lack vitality and appear to be only the painting, which is the image, not of her, but of her mother. While he physiologically needs the seven women who are his paramours, he does not even feel humanly grateful that they are giving him at least this release. The women appear as types, types reflecting the author's and protagonist's conditioning, that of the "macho" (he-man) who must prove his sexual prowess daily. Yet while proving his sexual capabilities, when they acquiesce and accept his sexual advances, he hates them for giving in to his urgings. These are the author's fantasies of rich and beautiful women, but they are still probably based on the brothel women with whom he had the most experience. Both Silva and his protagonist, Fernández, believed in absolute male superiority with both ideal and brothel women inferior to the male.

IX LANGUAGE AND STYLE

The problem of Silva and the other Modernist novelists is how to arrive at a happy medium between the plot and action of a novel and the desire of the aesthete to write an artistically elaborated prose. Several times in the novel ***De Sobremesa*** germs of some of the poems Silva wrote earlier or later with the same turns of phrase are visible. But these lyrical sections which are like brilliant poems in prose do not assure the creation of a good, solidly constructed novel. However, Silva is a fine prose writer with a musical style and fills his prose with cultural experiences. Paintings form the most constant motif in the novel, for there are the scenes the author paints, then there are the persons who are similar to paintings of the past. He incorporates painting in his novel in several ways: art within art, but also he shows an obvious tendency to have his novel move from painting to painting, from scene to scene, filled with chromatic refinements. Fernández lives in galleries of paintings, and reflects the eternal mania of turning everything, even the plastic arts, into literature. At the beginning of the novel there is a long pictorical description of the typical Modernist salon. Other techniques he uses are the mentioning of different schools of paintings, and of different paintings, such as those by Rembrandt, Fra Angelico, Sodoma, and painters of the pre-Raphaelite school. This technique ennobles and gives prestige, revealing a vast knowledge of museums. This method is used in the description of persons and creates an aristocratic beauty. Silva also uses movement to create a ritualistic atmosphere, as when Helena appears, combining the descriptions of slow and deliberate movements with her likeness to paintings.

The descriptions of the luxurious and sumptuous rooms which abound in the novel are chosen to give the sensation of the exquisite tastes of the artistically educated poet-protagonist. In addition to stylistic considerations, this reflects the compensation of the author, who was escaping his own bitter reality of failure, and was living vicariously in his protagonist some of his own best dreams. But his hero is rich and is able to enjoy the perversions and decadence of those who have all the money necessary to buy what they want. The novel presents the characters and the typical mansions of European decadence. One of the fundamental stylistic tenets of the Modernist novel was to create an original prose, and incorporate at the same time into the narrative literature a new hero, inherited from the Romantics, with an aura of the gods: the artist, set in the proper intellectual atmosphere. They adored another divinity as well, that of the aristocracy of the intelligence.

Silva's writing was uneven in ***De Sobremesa*** perhaps because it was rewritten from memory. Some of his terms are unusually colorful, but are what might be called "rubendariacos," using the terms he coined.[50] His irony at the expense of some of the characters is not comical but rather bitter, and some readers resent the author's parodies of his friends. Some of his long enumerations are boring, as for example when two medical doctors who are consulting concerning his case talk of some thirty ailments and cannot come to a common diagnosis except to give him a prescription for a purgative. Silva is inclined to give such voluminous pluralities chosen by his intuition, often felicitously, to create and give more depth to his ambience. Silva was not a bad writer of dialogue, except that speeches are sometimes longer than plausible when friends are conversing.

One other technique which adds to the poetic feeling of his prose was the use of apostrophe to give more stress to emotions. Also, he uses refrains in some poetic passages, at times repeating the same passage and at other times changing the wording slightly.

Silva reflects in the content what the writers of that period felt the novel to be, a work that does not give the reader a pleasant time, but causes him to have to think in order to penetrate into another human being, and thus perhaps to understand the universe better. Alfonso Reyes has spoken of the complex of the jungle in the Spanish-American novel, but the only jungle in ***De Sobremesa*** is the jungle of the complicated psyche of the protagonist, the jungle of the experiences of a man and of an artist.

Some of the most obvious elements in the Modernist style of Silva are the greater degree of intellectualism, the profound revelations of the consciousness of the ego, the sentimental projection of the principal characters as in the Romantic period but with Modernist differences. Above all, Silva reflects the profound desire to write in a new, artistic, more poetic, flexible prose, a more idealistic than realistic novel, leaving behind the nature settings which were favorites of the Romantics, and choosing cosmopolitan settings.

Notes

1. Miramón, [Alberto. *José Asunción Silva: Ensayo Biográfico con Documentos Inéditos.* Bogotá: Imprenta Nacional, 1937,] p. 161.

2. *De Sobremesa, 1887-1896,* 1st ed. (Bogotá, 1925).

3. *De Sobremesa, 1887-1896,* 2nd ed. (Bogotá, [1928]).

4. *Obras Completas* (Bogotá, 1965), pp. 123-310.

5. The author of this work is using the 1928 edition of *De Sobremesa,* listed in note 3. Any citations following this note will be referring to that edition. Notes will not usually be given while summarizing the plot since the elements will be chronological, giving the reader little difficulty in finding the pages.

6. *De Sobremesa,* p. 7.

7. Ibid., p. 15.

8. Ibid., p. 21.

9. The first German edition, *Antertung,* was published in 1893. The two-volume *Dégénéréscence* was translated from the German by Auguste Dietrich (Paris, 1894). Only in 1902 was the work translated into Spanish, by Nicolás Salmerón, *Degeneración* (Madrid, 1902).

10. The first edition, according to *La Grande Encyclopédie,* was published in Paris by her family, *Journal de Marie Bashkirtseff avec Portrait,* 2 vol., 1887.

11. Marie Bashkirtseff, *Journal,* Vol. 2 (Paris, 1914), p. 591.

12. Ibid., Vols. 1 and 2.

13. Max Nordau, *Dégénéréscence,* 2 Vol., translated from the German by Auguste Dietrich (Paris, 1894).

14. *De Sobremesa,* p. 28.

15. "La Legende d'une Cosmopolite," in "Trois Stations de Psychotérapie," *L'Oeuvre de Maurice Barrès,* Vol. 2 (Paris, 1965), pp. 357-68.

16. *De Sobremesa,* p. 50.

17. Ibid., p. 57.

18. Ibid., p. 63 ff.

19. Ibid., p. 74.

20. Ibid., p. 159.

21. Ibid., p. 129.

22. Ibid., p. 177. Daniel Arias Argáez in "Cincuentenario de la Muerte de José Asunción Silva," *Registro Municipal,* Bogotá, June 30, 1946, pp. 254-55, cites the long digression and testifies that it belonged to another novel by Silva which was lost in the sinking of the ship *L'Amerique,* and that probably Silva added these lines because of their beauty.

23. Ibid., p. 178.

24. Ibid., p. 183.

25. Ibid., p. 186

26. Ibid., p. 220.

27. Bernardo Gicovate, *Conceptos Fundamentales de Literatura Comparada: Iniciación a la Poesía Modernista* (San Juan, Puerto Rico, 1962), p. 124.

28. Daniel Arias Argáez, "Cincuentenario de la Muerte de José Asunción Silva," *Registro Municipal,* Bogotá, June 30, 1946, pp. 242-65.

29. Juan Loveluck, "*De Sobremesa,* Novela Desconocida del Modernismo," *Revista Iberoamericana,* Vol. 31, No. 59, January-June 1965, p. 25.

30. *De Sobremesa,* p. 46.

31. Ibid., p. 205.

32. Ibid., pp. 21, 183.

33. Ibid., p. 15.

34. Ibid., pp. 64-71.

35. Ibid., p. 133.

36. Ibid., p. 182.

37. Ibid., p. 183.

38. Ibid., pp. 133-34.

39. Ibid., p. 134.

40. Ibid., pp. 104, 172.

41. Ibid., p. 17.

42. Ibid., p. 176.

43. Ibid., p. 21.

44. Juan Evangelista Manrique, "José Asunción Silva: Recuerdos Intimos," *La Revista de América,* Paris, Vol. 6, January 1914, p. 32.

45. *De Sobremesa,* p. 127.

46. Bernardo Gicovate, op. cit. (see above, note 27), p. 124 ff.

47. *Oeuvres Complètes de Joris-Karl Huysmans,* Vol. 7, *A Rebours* (Paris, 1929).

48. *De Sobremesa,* p. 10.

49. Ibid., p. 202.

50. Silva uses this term: "rubendariacos" ("in the manner of Rubén Darío") in a letter to Baldomero Sanín Cano reproduced in José Asunción Silva, *Obras Completas* (Bogotá, 1965), p. 378.

Mark I. Smith (essay date 1982)

SOURCE: Smith, Mark I. "José Asunción Silva: The Literary Landscape." *Romance Quarterly* 29, no. 3 (1982): 283-92.

[*In the following essay, Smith examines the influence of Victor Hugo and other contemporary French and American writers on Silva's poetry.*]

The work of José Asunción Silva represents such a fine synthesis of the influences he suffered and his own original perception that there are no seams discernible. As Bernardo Gicovate has observed, "La asimilación de ideas y procedimientos heterogéneos y la absorción completa de sus lecturas en una obra variada a pesar de su exigüedad, no permite fácilmente el encuentro de reminiscencias que guíen en el estudio de las influencias extranjeras."[1] Despite this real difficulty, however, generations of critics have devoted time to determining the precise extent and nature of such influences on the Colombian modernist's work. The reason for this continued search goes beyond the simple pleasure of influence hunting, and touches on the nature of *modernismo* itself. Silva, like many of his contemporaries in Latin America, felt himself to have been born into a kind of cultural vacuum, and set about the paradoxical task of creating a tradition for himself. It was no accident that Silva, in the words of Rafael Maya, "resumió todas las características del escritor 'fin de siglo.'"[2] On the contrary, it was by an act of will that he separated himself from what he considered old and banal in art, and selected carefully the setting in which he wished his work to shine. In short, Silva, whose brilliant **"Nocturno"** was ridiculed as eccentric by the more ignorant of his contemporaries, possessed the eclecticism, or elasticity of mind, characteristic of the truly original artist. For this reason, it is better said of him than of most authors, that we cannot clearly understand his work without seeing it in the literary context to which it belongs.

As is well known, Silva's visit to France in 1884 and his exposure to the literary ambience of the time were experiences vital to his development as an artist. What is not so often mentioned is that his desire to visit that country did not arise spontaneously, but rather grew from his previous knowledge and appreciation of the great figures of French Romanticism. Victor Hugo particularly (as Héctor H. Orjuela has shown[3]) helped mold the young poet's sensibilities, and to such a degree that his presence is discernible even in Silva's most mature work.

Hugo's reputation had suffered so much in the wake of Parnassianism and Symbolism, that it is somewhat surprising to find Fernández, the decadent hero of Silva's novel *De sobremesa,* proclaiming him "padre de la lírica moderna,"[4] a distinction one might have expected him to reserve for Charles Baudelaire. In this light, it is interesting to note that when Silva, in his poem **"Triste,"** uses the phrase "lenguaje difuso" and "diálogo confuso,"[5] he need not be remembering the (to us) exhausted "confuses paroles" of "Correspondences," but rather be harking back to Hugo's various similar expression in *Les Chants du Crépuscule* (a book from which, in August of 1882, he translated a fragment[6]):

Je cherche, ô nature,
La parole obscure
Que le vent murmure. . . .[7]

On entendait des bruits glisser sur les parois,
Comme si, se parlant d'une confuse voix. . . .

(*Poésie,* I, 355)

Quand, parfois, sans te voir, ta jeune voix m'arrive,
Disant des mots confus qui m'échappent souvent. . . .

(*Poésie,* I, 354)

Several other points of resemblance exist between Hugo and Silva, and they are worth noting if only as testimony to the powerful influence of French Romanticism on the development of *modernismo.* It is particularly in the handling of vague and melancholic effects (achieved through an impressionistic use of carefully chosen detail) that Silva often resembles the great French master. The disembodied hand of **"Día de difuntos,"** for example: "Por el aire tenebroso ignorado mano arroja / Un oscuro velo opaco de letal melancolía . . ." (*Poesías,* p. 253) recalls a similar allusion to the Unknown Power that rules the universe in Hugo's "Les funérailles de Louis XVIII":

Quel bras jette les tours sous l'herbe . . .
Et quelle est la main invisible
Qui garde les clefs du tombeau?

(*Poésie,* I, 125)

And when Silva delicately invokes the nostalgia of childhood mythologies in **"Crepúsculo"**:

En estos momentos, en todos los cuartos,
Se van despertando los duendes dormidos.
La sombra que sube por los cortinajes . . .
Se puebla y se llena con los personajes
De los tenebrosos cuentos infantiles.

(*Poesías,* p. 170)

he writes much as Hugo does in his similar "A des oiseaux envolés":

Oh! certes, les esprits, les sylphes et les fées . . .
Les gnomes accroupis là-haut, près du plafond,
Dans les angles obscurs que mes vieux livres font. . . .

(*Poésie,* I, 399)

Rather than narrating the experience in a distancing past tense, both poets choose to vivify the magical moment by letting it breathe in the immediate present.

Admirers of Silva's power to evoke a twilight or a nighttime scene by use of a few telling details are aware of his fondness for the firefly, a burning point of light which serves to deepen the darkness and shadows. Beside the famous "luciérnagas fantásticas" of the **"Nocturno,"** we have also in **"Ronda"**: "Una errante luciérnaga alumbró nuestro beso . . ." (*Poesías,* p. 195). This delicate expression recalls some lines from Victor Hugo's "Crépuscule" which could almost be seen as the seed for the most famous of Silva's melancholy poems:

Vous qui passez dans l'ombre, êtes-vous des
    amants? . . .
Les mortes d'aujourd'hui furent jadis les belles.
Le ver luisant dans l'ombre erre avec son flambeau.

(*Poésie,* I, 669)

Not only is the resemblance between "errante luciérnaga" and "Le ver luisant . . . erre" intriguing, but also both **"Ronda"** and **"Nocturno"** are built around the theme Hugo sketches here, the tragic separation of lovers by the death of the beautiful beloved.

Upon occasion, one comes upon a phrase in reading Silva that bears a startling resemblance to some line by Hugo. For example, in **"Un poema,"** whose elegant alexandrines already represent an homage to French poetry, Silva exclaims that he wants to create "Ritmos sonoros, ritmos potentes, ritmos graves, / Unos cual choques de armas, otros cual cantos de aves." (*Poesías,* p. 226). Surely it goes beyond simple coincidence that long before Hugo had evoked sounds (in *Les Feuilles D'Automne*)

> Pleins d'accords éclatants, de suaves murmures,
> Doux comme un chant du soir, fort comme un
> 　　　choc d'armures. . . .
>
> 　　　　　　　　　　　　　　(*Poésie,* I, 281)

The onomatopoeic effect that both poets are reaching for, the literal translation by Silva of "choc d'armures," and his logical analogue for "chant du soir" ("cantos de aves"), can leave little doubt that he had been impressed by Hugo's couplet.

The affinity between Silva and Hugo is nowhere clearer than in some lines of the famous **"Nocturno."** Many critics have been satisfied to explain the setting and the theme of this poem from a purely biographical point of view. Baldomero Sanín Cano, for example, traced the inception of the poem to his friend's penchant for taking long evening walks: "Cuando la luna llena salía por los cerros en las primeras horas de la noche, proyectaba como espectros sobre la llanura solitaria las sombras de los que pasaban por el camino. . . ."[8] Taking a similar tack, Carlos García Prada has declared that the details that Silva uses to evoke the landscape of the **"Nocturno"** are peculiarly Colombian.[9] Although it is impossible to dismiss out of hand the opinions of such eminent critics, there is evidence enough to suggest that the landscape of Silva's poem owed as much to literature as to nature itself. For example, when the Colombian writes, "Una noche toda llena de perfumes, de murmullos / y de músicas de älas" (*Poesías,* p. 201) he is using a vocabulary and a grammatical construction strongly reminiscent of Hugo's ". . . la nuit et toi, si belles et si pures, Si pleines de rayons, de parfumes, de murmures . . ." (*Poésie,* I, 349). Even without the proof we have of Silva's having read *Les chants du crépuscule,* the development of the lines upon the *si pleine / toda llena* base, together with the parallel use of perfume and murmurs to evoke the vague sensorial impact of a nocturnal scene, would point once more to Hugo's presence in his creative memory. Two very similar lines from *Les feuilles d'automne* should not go unmentioned: "Elle court aux forêts, où dans l'ombre indécise / Flottent tant de rayons, de murmures, de voix . . ." (*Poésie,* I, 292).

A particularly noteworthy example of how Silva benefitted from his reading of French poetry is his use of the felicitous adjective "nupcial" in the fourth line of the **"Nocturno"**: "Una noche / En que ardían en la sombra nupcial y húmeda / las luciérnagas fantásticas . . ." (*Poesías,* p. 201). Although there can be no question of Silva's genius in choosing to use the word for its subtle implications of amorous innocence as well as for its euphonious n, u, and l sounds, it should be noted that it occurs in a similar

context in one of Victor Hugo's most famous poems, "Booz endormi": "L'ombre était nuptiale, auguste et solennelle . . ." (*Poésie,* II, 27). Hugo uses the adjective "nuptiale" to suggest the imminence of Ruth's marriage to Boaz, the latter being as yet unaware of his fate. Silva's use of the word suggests an atmosphere of love and intimacy in verse which evidences his ability to benefit from influences which in a lesser poet would have proved overwhelming. As has often been remarked, minor poets borrow lines, where major poets steal them outright.

Another poet who must have liked Hugo's phrasing enough to steal it was his countryman Paul Verlaine, who writes in *La bonne chanson* of "La fatigue charmante et l'attente adorée / De l'ombre nuptiale et de la douce nuit . . ."[10]. Whether it was from Verlaine or from Hugo that Silva picked up the expression "la sombra nupcial" is as impossible to determine as it would be unprofitable, although the presence of the older poet seems more pervasive in the *modernista*'s work. Verlaine, affecting a sophisticated irony, will often mock emotional modulations which Silva treats seriously. Viewed in this light, Verlaine's **"Lettre"** presents an interesting counterpart to Silva's **"Nocturno"**:

> Eloigné de vos yeux, Madame, par des soins
> Impérieux (j'en prends tous les dieux à témoins),
> Je languis et je meurs, comme c'est ma coutume
> En pareil cas, et vais, le coeur plein d'amertume,
> A travers des soucis où votre ombre me suit. . . .
> Si bien qu'enfin, mon corps faisant place à mon âme,
> Je deviendrai fantôme à mon tour aussi, moi,
> Et qu'alors, et parmi le lamentable émoi
> Des enlacements vains et des désirs sans nombre,
> Mon ombre se fondra à jamais en votre ombre. . . .
>
> 　　　　　　　　　　　　(*Oeuvre,* I, 187-188)

To admirers of the **"Nocturno"** these lines must present both suggestive similarities of expression as well as significant disparities in tone. If Silva, attracted by the idea of a union of shadows as representing the union of souls, had set out to write a somber version of Verlaine's poem, he could scarcely have done it better than with the **"Nocturno."** Not only are the basic elements of physical separation and spiritual union common to both poems, but even the phrase "Separado de ti misma" seems an echo of Verlaine's "eloigné de vos yeux." In "Lettre," however, one feels the author's irony undercutting the emotion expressed ("comme c'est ma coutume / En pareil cas"), and rather than winding up with the (perhaps, for him, overly romantic) union of shadows, Verlaine purposely engineers a drastic change in mood: "En attendant, je suis, très chère, ton valet . . ." (*Oeuvres,* I, 188).

One might speculate whether or not Silva retained for future reference the basic imagery of this poem, rejecting the debunking irony in favor of the emotional expression that was its object. He would have had all the more reason to do so considering that the first poem of *La bonne chanson* shows Verlaine treating a similar theme in a more serious manner:

Le souvenir charmant de cette jeune fille,
Blanche apparition qui chante et qui scintille . . .
    La Compagne qu'enfin il a trouvée, et l'âme
    Que son âme depuis toujours pleure et réclame.

(Oeuvres, I, 197)

Despite such general similarities, it is probable that Verlaine influenced more Silva's opinion about poetry ("De la musique avant toute chose") than his poetry itself. In fact, as far as the Colombian poet was concerned, the most important influence Verlaine exercised was probably through the work of his disciples the *verslibristes,* whose metrical experiments with the musicality of verse led to the development of the haunting rhythms of the **"Nocturno."**[11] Beyond the noted possible exception of the adjective "nupcial," there are no direct echoes from Verlaine's poetry in Silva's work.

Quite the contrary is true in the case of their Parnassian contemporary René-François Sully Prudhomme, of whom Silva's would-be connoisseur in **"Crítica ligera"** writes: "Y la elegancia aristocrática de Sully Prudhomme (el Cellini del soneto), la hechura maravillosa de sus estrofas griegas por la nitidez y la firmeza? . . . Sully es frío, y luego en sus versos se nota la preocupación de la ciencia, incompatible con la verdadera inspiración. . . ."[12] That only the first part of this judgment is shared by Silva is suggested by the following words of his hero José Fernández in *De sobremesa*: "Sentía que sus miradas se habían posado en él, que ya sabía que era un libro de poesías, de aquellas poesías de Sully Prudhomme dulces y penetrantes como femeniles quejidos" (***O.C.*** [***Obras Completas***], p. 188). In fact, the volume that Fernández is reading when his Helena looks his way is *Les solitudes* (***O.C.,*** p. 186) which appeared in 1869—and looking through this book, one finds evidence that it may well have exercised direct influence on Silva's poetry. In "La voie lactée," for example, Sully addresses the stars in the following words: "Vos leures, dans l'infini noir, / Ont des tendresses douloureuses . . ."[13]. Using an identical expression, the grieved lover of the **"Nocturno"** sees himself separated from his loved one "Por el infinito negro / Donde nuestra voz no alcanza . . ." (***Poesías,*** p. 202). It is possible that the word for word repetition might be mere accident, that "the black infity" was a cliché of the time (although I have not found it elsewhere), shared by the two poets. Still, it is suggestive that Silva's "**. . .? . . .**" (**"Estrellas que entre lo sombrío,"** *Poesías,* pp. 62-63) should resemble "La voie lactée" both in its direct address to the stars as in its juxtaposition of traditional perceptions of heavenly bodies with the new sensibility created by the scientific discoveries of the day. In this poem, Silva's lines "Nebulosas que ardéis tan lejos / En el infinito que aterra" (*Poesías,* p. 219) further corroborate Sully's fruitful influence on Silva, as they suggest a train of thought leading to the felicitous appearance of "el infinito negro" in the **"Nocturno."** A final bit of evidence indicative of the influence of *Les solitudes* on Silva's work is a line from the sonnet "Les amours terrestres": "Dans le double infini du temps et de l'espace . . ."[14]. In his essay **"El Doctor Rafael**

Núñez," Silva wrote of "la dulcísima anciana, cuyo retrato guarda como una reliquia el salón blanco de la quinta del Cabrero, y que, *separada de él por el doble infinito del tiempo y de la muerte,* le sonreía en imagen . . ." (***O.C.,*** pp. 332-33). The phrase I have underlined, which bears the thematic and rhythmic stamp of the **"Nocturno"** ("Separado de ti misma por la sombra, por el tiempo y la distancia / por el infinito negro . . ."), and which may indeed have been an echo of the poem in progress, is surely indebted to Sully Prudhomme's expression in "Les amours terrestres."

The above noted examples of direct influence from French poetry in Silva's work (in the **"Nocturno"** particularly) can gather meaningfulness when seen in a more general context, in a perspective which goes beyond the level of merely verbal correspondences. From this wider point of view, it soon becomes clear, for example, that many if not all of the atmospheric elements of the **"Nocturno"**—what one might call its special effects—existed to a significant extent in the literary *Zeitgeist.* Already in Leopardi's evocation of a nocturnal atmosphere in "Ricordanze" we find the frogs and fireflies of the **"Nocturno"**:

Delle sere io sollea pasar gran parte
Mirando il cielo, ed ascoltando il canto
Della rana rimota alla campagna!
E la lucciola errava appo le siepi. . . .[15]

Similarly, in D'Annunzio's "Nox" (*Primo Vere,* 1880):

brillano
giù per le siepi le solinghe lucciole,
la rauca rana gracida,

e li usignoli tra le fronde cantano
un bel notturno in *fa minore.* . . .[16]

Much like Silva, D'Annunzio will employ the sound of dogs barking to achieve a melancholy effect, as in "Pellegrinaggio":

Da l'aie solitarie si chiamano i cani latrando,
ed il suono propagasi triste per l'afa via lungi
rotto come a singulti. . . .

(p. 92)

And again, in "Ex imo corde":

dove ho provate voluttà sì strane

i murmuri ascoltando
de vecchi pini, a cui da lunge un cane
rispondeva latrando. . . .

(p. 8)

Closer to home, the North American Henry Wadsworth Longfellow, in *Evangeline* (another poem about the tragic separation of lovers) takes advantage of the evocative powers to be found in fireflies as well as other elements reminiscent of the **"Nocturno"**: the prairie, the moon, the young woman deeply and strangely moved:

The calm and the magical moonlight
Seemed to inundate her soul with undefinable long-
  ings
As, through the garden gate, beneath the brown
    shade of the oak trees,
Passed she along the path to the edge of the
    measureless prairie,
Silent it lay, with a silver haze upon it, and
    fireflies
Gleaming and floating away in mingled and infinite
  numbers. . . .[17]

The mood of this passage, its imagery, the variation of line lengths which are informed by a pulsing sinuous rhythm, all are clearly analogous to those of Silva's poem.

A final pictorial and thematic element that plays an important part in the **"Nocturno"** is the union of shadows which symbolizes the spiritual union of the poet and his beloved: "¡Oh las sombras que se buscan y se juntan en las noches de negruras y de lágrimas . . . (*Poesías,* p. 203). As we have seen, Verlaine utilized an analogous conceit when he wrote: "Mon ombre se fondra pour jamais en votre ombre." Beside this very similar example, others of an analogous nature abound in the work of poets who must have figured prominently among Silva's readings. His own countryman, the renowned Rafael Pombo, delicately invokes the confluence of shadows as a kind of transcendence of physical separateness:

Si a la mágica lumbre
  Del sol de ocaso
Ves que una larga sombra
  Sigue tu paso,
Mi ángel, no es esa
Tu sombra; esa es la mía
Que tus pies besa.[18]

What is absent from Pombo's poem, of course, is that shiver of the fantastic—of "ultratumba"—that Silva achieves in the **"Nocturno."** In this context, Edgar Allan Poe's "The Raven" comes to mind:

And the lamp-light o'er him streaming throws his
    shadow on the floor;
And my soul from out that shadow that lies floating
    on the floor
Shall be lifted—nevermore![19]

In Silva's vision, however, the bereaved lover is not condemned as in Poe's to be forever separated from his "lost Lenore." On the contrary, the enamoured souls that join as shadows defy all laws of time and space. A final example of this kind of almost mystic vision is to be found, once more, in the work of Victor Hugo, who in "Fantômes" exclaims:

Hélas! que j'en ai vu mourir de jeunes filles! . . .
Mon âme est une soeur pour ces ombres si belles.
La vie et le tombeau pour nous n'ont plus de loi . . .
Vision ineffable où je suis mort comme elles,
    Elles, vivantes comme moi! . . .
Je les vois! Je les vois! Elles me disent: viens!
Puis autour d'un tombeau dansent entrelacées. . . .

(*Poésie,* I, 248-249)

"¡Oh las sombras enlazadas!" is the ecstatic cry at the culmination of Silva's own exploration of the strange sympathy that can unite the souls of the living with the souls of the dead. In this last example, as in the others above, there has been no question of setting out to prove that Silva was knowingly or directly influenced by these poets (though no one would deny that he knew them), but rather to point to the fact that Silva's perceptions of nature and the general imagery of the **"Nocturno"** were clearly representative of a prevailing literary vision, a literary landscape he shared more truly with his fellow poets than with his fellow countrymen.

With respect to the discovery of certain literary influences in Silva's work, it is well to have in mind Ezra Pound's cautionary words: "'Originality,' when it is most actual, is often sheer lineage, is often a closeness of grain. The innovator most damned for eccentricity, is often most centrally in the track or orbit of tradition, and his detractors are merely ignorant. The artist is in sane equilibrium, indifferent utterly to oldness or newness, so the thing be apposite to his wants."[20] Belonging as he did to a generation of writers who—in Blanco Fombona's words—were book addicts who had printer's ink coursing through their veins,[21] Silva absorbed from the work of his masters and contemporaries precious materials he transformed and adapted to his own artistic ends.

Notes

1. Gicovate, "José Asunción Silva y la decadencia europea," *Conceptos de literatura comparada* (San Juan, P.R.: Ediciones Asomante, 1962), p. 117.

2. Maya, *Alabanzas del hombre y de la tierra* (Bogotá: Casa Editorial Santafé, 1934), p. 19.

3. Orjuela, "Estudio preliminar" to José Asunción Silva, *Intimidades* (Bogotá: Instituto Caro y Cuervo, 1977), p. 23.

4. Silva, *Obras Completas* (Bogotá: Banco de la República, 1965), p. 263. In what follows, I will refer to this edition as *O.C.*

5. Silva, *Poesías,* H. H. Orjuela ed. (Bogotá: Instituto Caro y Cuervo, 1979), p. 243. Page numbers in the text will refer to this edition of Silva's poetry.

6. Silva, *Intimidades,* p. 54. Other works by Hugo which figure in this collection include *Les chansons de rues et de bois, Les quatre vents de l'esprit,* and *Feuilles d'automne.*

7. Hugo, *Poésie* (Paris: Éditions de Seuil, 1972), I, 348. Volume and page numbers in the text will refer to this edition.

8. Sanín Cano, "Notas en la edición de la Casa Louis Michaud de París," as reproduced in *O.C.,* p. 116.

9. García Prada, "Introducción," in his ed. of Silva, *Prosas y versos* (México: Editorial Cultura, 1942), pp. xxx-xxxi.

10. Verlaine, *Oeuvres complètes* (Paris: Le Club de Meilleur Livre, 1959), I, 208. Page numbers in the text will refer to this edition.

11. Rufino Blanco Fombona pointed out Silva's obvious debt to the *verslibristes* more than fifty years ago, but it is still not generally acknowledged. See both *El modernismo y los poetas modernistas* (Madrid: Editorial Mundo Latino, 1929), p. 305, and "José Asunción Silva," *La Revista de América,* Paris, Vol. I (February, 1913), pp. 191-209 as reproduced in Betty Tyree Osiek, *José Asunción Silva: estudio estilístico de su obra* (México: Ediciones de Andrea, 1968), pp. 152-153.

12. As found in Donald McGrady, "*Crítica ligera*: una prosa olvidada de José Asunción Silva," *Thesaurus,* 24, (1969), p. 31.

13. Sully Prudhomme, *Oeuvres* (Paris: Alphonse Lemerre, 1888), II, 128.

14. *Ibid.,* III, 85.

15. Leopardi, *Canti* (Rome: Angelo Signorelli, 1967), p. 147.

16. D'Annunzio, *Tutte le Opere,* ed. Egidio Bianchetti, *Versi D'Amore e di Gloria,* I (Milan: Arnoldo Mondadori, 1959), p. 39. Page numbers in the text refer to this edition.

17. Longfellow, *Poetical Works* (London: George Rutledge and Sons, 1883), p. 96.

18. Pombo, *Poesías,* Vol. II (Bogotá: Imprenta Nacional, 1917), p. 41.

19. Poe, *Complete Stories and Poems* (New York: Doubleday and Co., 1966), p. 756.

20. Pound, *Literary Essays* (New York: New Directions, 1968), p. 280.

21. Blanco-Fombona, *El modernismo y los poetas modernistas,* p. 29. Quoted by Luis Monguió, "De la problemática del modernismo: La crítica y el 'cosmopolitismo,'" *Revista Iberoamericana,* 28, 53 (1962), p. 80.

Lily Litvak (essay date 1989)

SOURCE: Litvak, Lily. "José Asunción Silva (1865-1896)." In *Latin American Writers,* Vol. 1, edited by Carlos A. Solé and Maria Isabel Abreu, pp. 377-85. New York: Charles Scribner's Sons, 1989.

[*In the following essay, Litvak praises Silva's accomplishments as a Modernist poet, claiming that his skill in evoking the subtleties of the Spanish language was superb.*]

The author Miguel de Unamuno, in his prologue to the 1908 edition of **Poesías** by José Asunción Silva, commented,

How is it possible to reduce to ideas a pure poetry, one in which the words taper, thin, and fade to the point of becoming cloudlike, whirled about by the wind of sentiment and forced to kneel before the sun, which at its height whitens them and in its setting covers them in its golden aura? . . . To comment on Silva is like explaining the movements of Beethoven's symphonies to an audience while the notes fall upon their ears. Each individual will find in them his own sorrows, desires, and feelings.

The words of Unamuno aptly characterize the writer Silva, one of the most accomplished modernist poets and one who, more than any other poet before him, sought the most quintessential form of poetry. Silva was one of the greatest craftsmen of the Spanish language, providing it with a previously unknown scale of subtle suggestion. He was, at the same time, as his friend Baldomero Sanín Cano expressed, "analytical and coldly scrutinizing." Because of those qualities, Silva was able to reveal his entire self within his works.

According to his birth certificate, José Asunción Silva was born in Bogotá, Colombia, on 26 November 1865. The oldest of five brothers, he came from a rich and aristocratic family. His parents were Ricardo Silva and Vicenta Gómez. Among his forefathers, descendants of noble Spanish lineage, were adventurers, soldiers, scholars, nuns, and preachers.

The boy was intellectually precocious, affected by an innate sadness and a special love for all that was beautiful. A withdrawn child, he spent long hours reading in the silent, lonely house in Bogotá. He studied in various private schools, first in the institute headed by Luis M. Cuervo and later in the one directed by the celebrated costumbristic writer Ricardo Carrasquilla. At age sixteen, he left his academic work and joined his father in the administration of the family store.

Bogotá was at that time a fairly self-contained city of some seventy thousand inhabitants. It was a pure-blooded town, gray, and far from the sea and the commercial shipping lanes. Silva himself described it in the following manner: "In Bogotá, everyone knows everyone else. The primary preoccupations are religion, the vices of a neighbor, and the arrival of mail from Europe" (Alberto Miramón, *José Asunción Silva,* 2nd ed., p. 42). The city, patriarchal and isolated, might also have been considered prudish and hypocritical. Between 1880 and 1900 the echoes of Nietzscheanism, positivism, and symbolism began to be felt in the poet's environment, both in his father's store and in the Silvas' home, a gathering place for discussions about literature, politics, and news from abroad.

The house of Don Ricardo provided the city of those years with a singular element of elegance and refinement. It was, as Alberto Miramón, Silva's biographer, tells us, "noteworthy not only for its social status and the unquestionable culture and beauty of the people who frequented it, but also for its almost exaggerated luxury and refinement, or, more aptly put, for its excessive pomp. There, the furniture, the tableware, everything was unusual and unique" (p. 45).

Silva was a cultured youth. He was self-taught and possessed startling powers of assimilation, which he dedicated almost fanatically to reading. Between the ages of ten and eighteen, the boy composed his first poems. He wrote some in the albums of the girls he courted and read others to his parents and colleagues.

These adolescent verses can be placed under the sign of the Spanish poet Gustavo Adolfo Bécquer, whose influence was always to be felt in the work of Silva. From Bécquer, Silva adopted vagueness, subtlety, and musical words, pregnant with suggestion, although Silva was never as sentimental or colorist as Bécquer.

Yet even in those early years, Silva wrote poems that display his originality. In **"Crisálidas"** (**"Cocoons"**) and **"La voz de las cosas"** (**"The Voice of Things"**), the future author of **"Vejeces"** (**"Old Things"**), **"Los maderos de San Juan"** (**"The Ships of San Juan"**), and the poem that he named simply **"Nocturno"** (**"Nocturne"**) is already apparent. The latter poem, which begins "Una noche . . ." ("One night . . ."), is considered by some to be the poet's finest achievement. Silva's early material reveals the infinite yearning, the love for the past, and the obsession with death that clearly haunt his later writings.

At the age of eighteen, nourished with romantic literature from France and Spain, Silva realized one of his great dreams: to visit Europe and, above all, Paris. He visited the City of Light with his heart deeply longing for beauty and perfection. He remained in Europe for two years, a Europe that was filled with uncertainties and doubts, with political and religious rumblings. During his stay Silva became even more familiar with literature, developing his taste for Charles Baudelaire, Edgar Allan Poe, Alfred de Musset, Johann Gottfried von Herder, and the brothers Grimm. He began studies in the positivist theories of Hippolyte Taine, Auguste Comte, and Herbert Spencer. Friedrich Nietzsche and Gabriele D'Annunzio gave him a longing for the heroic, Paul Verlaine the love of soft music, and Pierre Loti the taste for the exotic and the bizarre. Arthur Schopenhauer intensified his sadness and dejection, and Marie Bashkirstev his yearning for the world beyond.

Silva returned to Colombia submerged in a deep melancholy. He had become a dandy, refined and delicate, with an extraordinary sensibility. The perfect aristocratic creole, alienated and unadapted to his world, he felt repelled by its sordid and vulgar materialism and nauseated by the growing bourgeoisie. Using a word from his contemporary society, he was a decadent. Silva possessed great physical beauty: an oval face, black hair, a sharp nose, thin lips, and long hands that were nervous and expressive. He dressed with extreme elegance, his fashion characterizing him as timid and distinguished. There are some who suppose that Silva suffered from psychological or sexual problems. It was said at times, in Bogotá, that he was crazy.

Upon Silva's return from Europe, the literary gatherings were resumed. Guests gathered in the Silvas' comfortable and luxuriously decorated library, drinking and talking while smoking Turkish cigarettes and discussing popular authors, all in an atmosphere of great refinement. Silva's dandyism continued throughout his life. Later, when he lived in Caracas, even in the midst of economic difficulty he would write, "You know that I am repulsed by cheap pleasures. So, not being able to live in *grand seigneur,* I live without pleasures" (Eduardo Camacho Guizado, *La poesía de José Asunción Silva,* pp. 16-17). In his last days he placed this order: "I ask you to buy the following and send it to me—in postal packages and wooden boxes or metal containers—twelve pounds of black tea, of the finest quality sold by the *United Kingdom Tea Co.*" (pp. 16-17).

His aestheticism is evident in his poetry and in his novel ***De sobremesa*** (***Dinner Conversation,*** 1925), which display both extravagance and luxury. His works present domestic interiors covered with fine rugs (**"Crepúsculo"** [**"Twilight"**]), walls covered with tapestries (**"Nocturno"** that begins "Poeta, di paso . . ." ["Poet, in flight . . ."]), a candle placed in a crafted goblet (**"El alma de la rosa"** [**"The Soul of the Rose"**]). His poems, such as **"Taller moderno"** (**"A Modern Workshop"**), contain an abundance of artistic and exotic objects: "un busto del Dante . . . Del arabesco azul de un jarrón chino . . . una armadura . . . un viejo retablo" ("a bust of Dante . . . a blue arabesque on a Chinese jar . . . a suit of armor . . . an old altar piece"). Silva did not employ an abundance of metaphors and comparisons, but of those that he did use, the great majority derive from luxury, wealth, refinement, gold, opal, satin, silk, lace, and the like.

His contemptuous attitude concerning the bourgeoisie can be seen in a series of satiric poems in which he attacks with cynicism the middle-class ethic and, in some compositions, religion. He rejects materialism, which, according to him, opposes idealism. In some poems he expresses social protest. With contempt for things "vulgar," he shows the contrast between the world of the "dreamer" or poet, which is delicate, sensible, elegant, and beautiful, and the world of the bourgeoisie, which is vulgar and senseless.

Another important aspect of Silva's personality was his rejection of religion. Many critics believe that his lack of religious beliefs was a decisive factor in his premature demise. His lack of faith did not, however, preclude a preoccupation with the other world. In his eagerness to obtain absolutes, Silva tried to resolve his inner conflicts through studies in the occult and esoteric beliefs, clearly manifested in his poetry, above all in the **"Nocturno"** that begins "Una noche . . ."

In 1887, after his father died, Silva made an effort to manage the family business. It was useless, as he was not temperamentally suited to such work and as his father had left overwhelming debts; soon the situation became unbearable. In 1891 his sister Elvira died suddenly from angina pectoris. Her death was the heaviest blow the poet had ever experienced, and he became even more melancholy and withdrawn from life. In the painful solitude to which he banished himself, Silva found the genesis for his poem **"Nocturno"** which immortalized him and his sister.

In 1894 Silva was named secretary of the Colombian legation to Caracas. In the Venezuelan capital, he became an important and influential figure for the young editors of *Cosmópolis* magazine, the initiator of modernism. Between 1885 and 1894 he wrote his finest poetry. Juan Ramón Jiménez, when referring to the poem **"Nocturno,"** affirms that "this nocturne, the seed of so many others, is without a doubt the most representative of the latest romanticism, and of the first modernism that was written, that lived, and that died in Spanish America" (*Sur* [*Revista Sur*] 10/79:14 [1941]). Silva was not, as so many claim, a precursor of modernism, but a real, conscious modernist, not only in his art but also in his life.

Silva returned to his homeland in 1895 on a French vessel, *L'Amérique,* which was shipwrecked on the Caribbean coast of Colombia, losing with it the best part of the poet's work. Back in Bogotá, he tried unsuccessfully to obtain a high-ranking diplomatic post. Suffering from an incurable melancholy, Silva attempted to establish a business in polychromatic cement tiles. The venture was a failure, and the poet sank into a decline. Bothered by insomnia, he consulted a doctor on 23 May 1896, and on some pretext requested that he indicate the exact location of the human heart. The doctor obliged, mapping out the pectoral region on Silva's chest and marking the location of the heart with a cross. That same day Silva's friends met in his house and spent the usual three or four hours in discussions. Rueda Vargas, one of those in attendance, relates: "It was close to midnight when, one by one, the ten who had gathered began to leave, while José lighted the path with a lamp in his hand" (Betty T. Osiek, *José Asunción Silva,* Twayne ed., pp. 46-47). The following day the poet was discovered dead in his room. He had put a bullet straight through his heart. No one heard the revolver discharge, since he had carefully closed the doors and windows. He left not even a note to explain the reasons for his suicide. The laws of Colombia did not allow the burial of Silva's body in the Catholic cemetery.

Silva's literary opus is of a reduced size since, like the protagonist of his novel *De sobremesa,* he preferred to read his compositions to friends rather than publish them, and only a small portion of his work was published. **"Los cuentos negros"** (**"Black Stories"**) was lost in the shipwreck of *L'Amérique.* **"Los poemas de la carne"** (**"Poems of Flesh"**) and the sonnets that he considered naming **"Las almas muertas"** (**"Dead Souls"**) suffered the same fate. Of those works that have been published, only a fraction appeared in newspapers and magazines during the author's lifetime. The majority of his work was published posthumously. His work consists of a book organized by the author, another containing poems that were partially

reconstructed by his friends, a series of loose poems, a novel, and some prose essays that deal primarily with literary issues. There are several poems whose authorship is doubtful.

The first book, *El libro de versos* (*The Book of Verses,* 1928), according to the author was written between 1891 and 1896, although it did contain some poetry written as early as 1883. The book consists of some thirty compositions and constitutes a biographical unity, from the evocation of Silva's childhood to the anticipated confrontation with the funereal world beyond. Silva never intended to publish the second group of poems, entitled **"Gotas amargas"** (**"Bitter Drops"**). Some of the compositions appeared in newspapers and magazines in reconstructed form, published by the poet's friends several years after his death. The third group consists of poems published, usually singly in magazines and newspapers, during the author's lifetime; in collections of Silva's work, they carry the title **"Versos varios"** (**"Various Verses"**). *De sobremesa,* Silva's last work, is a novel written over a span of years, some portions dating from 1892 and others from 1895. A group of nonpoetic items published in newspapers and magazines is entitled **"Prosas breves"** (**"Short Prose"**).

In his first stage of writing, Silva adopted the rounded, sonorous verses of the Spanish romantic style and toiled to clarify the ideas, to make them transparent. Later he developed a liking for French poetry with light, flexible, suggestive verses and musically orchestrated words.

The fundamental theme of Silva's work is the turmoil caused by his present reality. Life and the place where he lives it are repugnant; conversely, the past and the world beyond this life are mysterious and attractive. The desire to transcend this existence carries him to the gates of a world beyond the immediate and the real. He is a poet whose vision is directed toward the past, yet who is condemned to a coarse, rough, mediocre present, an existence that leaves him with a pessimistic, negative view of the future. He sees a past that is historic, sentimental, and, above all, aesthetic, a past that permits childhood mentalities and fantasies. The novel *De sobremesa,* which documents that flight from contemporary reality, is permeated with strangeness; the protagonist lives in an aesthetic world completely divorced from the American reality that surrounds him.

Another essential theme in Silva's work is death, the primary character in his poetic universe, the decomposing factor of all that might be perfect. The **"Nocturno"** that begins "Poet, in flight . . . ," one of the most beautiful poems, consists of three strophes, each based on the memory of the woman loved; the poem ends with her death in the final strophe. In the work of Silva, death becomes an obsession, sometimes revealed in its most fleshless and naked form (**"El recluta"** [**"The Recruit"**], and **"Psicopatía"** [**"Mental Disorder"**]). At other times it is adorned with morose beauty (**"Notas perdidas"** [**"Lost

Notes"]). Death prevents the enjoyment of life and love, and its wounding proximity causes anguish (**"Sonetos negros"** [**"Black Sonnets"**]). A corollary of this theme is a contempt for life. In the poem **"Lázaro"** (**"Lazarus"**), the resurrected begins to curse his new life after only a short while. At times, the weariness that Silva feels for life precipitates his willing approach to the gates of death (**"Día de difuntos"** [**"All Souls' Day"**]).

Like other modernists, Silva decorates reality with luxury. This decoration occurs on one level through the metaphors derived from precious and magnificent materials, such as gold, silver, jewels, and fine cloths: "El contacto furtivo de tus labios de seda" ("The furtive touch of your silken lips") in the **"Nocturno"** that begins "Poet, in flight . . ."; "mis sueños color de armiño" ("my ermine-colored dreams") in **"A tí"** (**"To You"**). The author also achieves these effects through the exaltation of sensory refinement:

> *Vemos tras de la neblina,*
> *Como al través de un encaje*
>
> 　　　　　　　　(**"Poesía viva"**)

> We gaze beyond the mist
> as if through lace
>
> 　　　　　　　　(**"Live Poetry"**)

> *Sobre las teclas vuela tu mano blanca,*
> *Como una mariposa sobre una lila*
>
> 　　(**"Nocturno"** that begins "A veces cuando en alta
> 　　　　　　　　　　　　noche . . .")

> over the keys your white hand flies
> like the butterfly over the lilac
>
> (**"Nocturno"** that begins "At times when at the height of
> 　　　　　　　　　　　　night . . .")

> *. . . rara historia*
> *que tiene oscuridad de telerañas*
> *Són de laúd y suavidad de raso.*
>
> 　　　　　　　　(**"Vejeces"**)

> . . . a strange history
> with the opacity of a spider web,
> a tune of lute and silk.

Silva's poetic style can be characterized by his unrealistic attitude. In his world, reality appears illuminated by a dim light through which only a faint, distant glimpse may be obtained. It is shadowy poetry, as Unamuno aptly stated. "Silva sings like a bird, but a sad bird, one that feels death approaching with the setting of the sun." In **"La voz de las cosas"** he presents the elements of his poetic world—"frágiles cosas" ("frail things"), "pálido lirio que te deshojas" ("you, a pallid lily shedding its petals"), "rayo de luna" ("a moon-ray"), "pálidas cosas" ("pallid things"),

"fantasmas grises" ("gray ghosts"), "sueños confusos" ("confusing dreams"), "ósculo triste" ("sad kiss")—that is, things that are fragile, evanescent, thin, vague, subtle, and opposed to the immutable, permanent, solid, and strong.

With this heightened poetic sensibility, Silva strives to apprehend an exterior, physical world characterized by vagueness and imprecision. The passages are delineated in dim shadows, in the twilight, beneath the moon's rays (the **"Nocturno"** that begins "At times when at the height of night . . . ," **"Paisaje tropical"** [**"Tropical Landscape"**], **"Al pie de la estatua"** [**"At the Foot of the Statue"**], **"Muertos"** [**"The Dead"**], and **"Poesía viva"**). One poem in particular, **"Día de difuntos,"** reveals this obsession with darkness and shadows. The shadow that invades the physical world has symbolic connotations, alluding to the past and to death (**"Los maderos de San Juan," "Vejeces"**) and establishing a clear relationship between the physical, exterior world, and the interior world of the poet.

Silva's poetic vision is also rendered through the other senses. Whispers occupy a position of primary importance: statements are made in hushed voices and sighs, through vague sobs; the poetic universe is "llenos de murmullos" ("full of whispers"), mysterious and vague. The sense of smell is perceived with delicacy and imprecision, associated in the poem **"Vejeces"** with a revival of the past. A similar imprecision is used to express feelings: love and nostalgia are softly and vaguely felt (**"Crepúsculo," "Luz de la luna"** [**"Moonlight"**]).

In order to create the sensation of imprecision and vagueness, Silva employs several lexical and syntactic methods. One is the use of the adjective *medio* ("half") with an adjective or another verb.

> *Del arabesco azul de un jarrón chino,*
> *Medio oculta el dibujo complicado.*
>
> 　　　　　　　　(**"Taller moderno"**)

> A blue arabesque on a Chinese jar
> half-hides the intricate drawing

> *mirar allí, sombría,*
> *medio perdida en la rizada gola*
>
> 　　　　　　　　(**"La ventana"**)

> to see there, somber
> half-lost in the wavy molding
>
> 　　　　　　　　(**"The Window"**)

> *La divisa latina, presuntuosa,*
> *Medio borrada por el líquen verde*
>
> 　　　　　　　　(**"Vejeces"**)

The presumptuous Latin emblem
half-erased by the green lichen.

Another technique is the use of adverbial phrases, in which objects, events, and sensations are compared and related by means of the word *como* ("as" or "like").

> *Mi oído fatigado por vigilias y excesos*
> *Sintió* como *a distancia los monótonos rezos!*
>
> > (**"Nocturno"** that begins "Poeta, dipaso . . .")

excess and vigilant, my fatigued hearing
sensed, *as* at a distance, monotonous prayers.

He makes comparisons, but without precision, and with the intention of being more precise, leaves one of the terms in vagueness in order to make a more attenuated comparison: ". . . cruza por su espíritu *como* un temor extraño" (". . . crossing through his spirit *like* a strange fear"), for example, in **"Los maderos de San Juan."**

Another theme in Silva's poetry is that of unreality, of fantasy and mystery. Not only is reality unraveled; it becomes totally denied. The poet abandons mundane life to enter a fantastic world. At times, a single word proves sufficient to transfer the verse from normality to unreality:

> *Por el aire tenebroso ignorada mano arroja*
> *Un oscuro velo opaco de letal melancolía.*
>
> > (**"Día de difuntos"**)

Through the gloomy air, an unknown hand throws
an obscure, opaque veil of lethal melancholy.

It is the word *ignotas* ("unknown") that places the verse in the realm of unusual suggestion.

> *En unas distancias enormes e ignotas*
> *Que por los rincones oscuros suscita . . .*
>
> > (**"Crepúsculo"**)

In unknown, enormous distances
Which rise up in dark corners . . .

Extraños ("unusual"), *ignotas* ("unknown"), *oscuros* ("dark")—such words force us to depart from our daily sphere of reality.

In order to achieve this transposition, a necessary secret communication is established between the poet and things, through which the poet is able to discover the world that lies beyond appearances. Things speak to the poet with strange voices (**"Vejeces"**). The new, unreal world opens great panoramas normally only permitted in the realm of fantasy and the unconscious.

In his excellent essay on Silva, Andrés Holguín offers the following explanation:

Perhaps the feeling of mystery in Silva is the result of some frustrated, transcendent desire. It is the sensation of the skeptic who, unable to resolve his religious feelings, falls into the abyss of nothingness. I said before that anguish is the final result of logical failure. This is especially evident in Silva. Silva is profoundly learned, intellectually curious in terms of philosophy, religion, science, and art. But nothing offers him an explanation of the world. In that is his agony born. And there, where his speculative search ends, where his reason is broken, there the night is opened into the unknown and mysterious.

> (*Revista de las Indias* 28/90:354 [1946])

Of the seventy-five poems that Silva wrote, not counting those of questionable origin, twenty-nine are based on a single metrical form: six in verses of eleven syllables, six in verses of eight syllables, five in *alejandrinos* (alexandrines), five in verses of nine syllables, four in verses of twelve syllables, two in verses of eight syllables, and one in verses of ten syllables. In other words, he used the traditional Spanish metrical forms. Thirty-two poems are composed using two or three metrical forms, based entirely on verses of eight and nine syllables.

In only three poems—**"Luz de luna," "Dia de difuntos"** and the **"Nocturno"** that begins "Una noche"—does the poet experiment with metrical novelties. In each one there is an internal rhythm that provides a constant base, yet each is composed using different meters of verse. In these works the author employs changes in meter and accent that break with the traditional rigid metrical forms, using combinations of eight, sixteen, fourteen, eleven, nine, twelve, six, and seven syllables. In these compositions Silva's stylistic restlessness may be detected; at times, the poet seems to be approaching free verse. The use of a single metrical form proved much too rigid in Silva's search for something more vague and undetermined.

Silva's vocabulary contains an abundance of verbs, most often used in the present tense to express palpitant emotion and action in progress. He also uses gerunds and participles to denote action in progress:

> *Va* tornando *en pavesas*
> *Tronos, imperios, pueblos y ciudades*
>
> > (**"Al pie de la estatua"**)

Burning into cinders
Thrones, empires, towns and cities

Likewise: "*Dándole* al aire aromado aliento" ("*Giving* to the air aromatic breath") in the poem **"Psicopatía,"** and "Y *mirando* dos rayos de la luna" ("And *looking* at the moonlight") in **"Luz de la luna."** He frequently employs the preterit to denote a completed action.

The poet often uses adjectives in groups of two, one before and one after the noun: "la divisa latina presuntuosa" ("the presumptuous Latin inscription"), "viejas cartas de amor, ya desteñidas" ("old love letters faded"), "un oscuro velo opaco" ("a dark opaque veil"). The three words are read as an isolated unit, without a respiratory pause, forming an intense image.

Multiple adjectives are sometimes linked by the conjunction *y* ("and"): "sugestiones místicas *y* raras" ("mystical *and* strange suggestions") in **"Vejeces,"** "ramilletes negros *y* marchitos" ("black *and* withered bouquets") in **"Muertos,"** and "fragua negra *y* encendida" ("black *and* red forge") in **"Psicopatía."** These condensed images eliminate the need for lengthy descriptions. Silva's adjectives often serve to displace the natural, syntactic progression of an idea, as in "y la *luz* de la luna limpia *brilla*" ("and the *light* of the moon *shines* pure") and "de *barrotes* de hierro *colosales*" ("of *colossal* iron *bars*") from **"La ventana"** or "*colores* de anticuada *miniatura*" ("*colors* of antiquated *miniature*") from **"Vejeces."** In this way the author creates an original and surprising expression of his idea.

Silva's poetry is also characterized by the repetition of sounds, words, verses, and even strophes, reinforcing through this technique the impressions that he wishes to provoke. In **"Los maderos de San Juan,"** for example, repetition is used in two ways: at the beginning of the poem in the children's poetry, with its play of repeated sounds, and later in the verses distributed among the three strophes. The accumulation of repetitions and alliterations of sounds causes the poem to move slowly, to unfold with a sad, melancholy moroseness.

Silva frequently overlaps verses. The pauses that normally would fall at the end of a verse are eliminated by the syntax of the phrase. As a result, the syntactic pause is not enforced by the rhythm, as in ". . . adivina / El porvenir de luchas y horrores" (". . . guess / the future of fights and horrors") in **"Al pie de la estatua"** or ". . . iluminaba / El paso de la audaz locomotora" (". . . illuminating / the passage of the daring locomotive") in **"Obra humana"** (**"Human Work"**).

Possibly Silva's most significant work is his poem **"Nocturno."** The crowning jewel of this opus, it is a poem constructed as a concert in vowels, with accents that enhance the words and sounds they touch, as in the line "Por los cielos azulosos, infinitos y profundos esparcía su luz blanca" ("Through the infinite, and profound azure skies, its white light spreading"). The line begins with the predominance of the *o* sound, followed by a section in *i* that alternates with *u,* and finishes with the final double *a.*

Alliterations abound: "Una noche toda llena de perfumes de murmullos y de músicas de alas" ("A night wholly filled with sounds, perfumes, and music of wings"). Most important is the placement of accents, which often produces special effects, as in the following verse, in which three grouped words are accented on the antepenult: "en que ardían en la sombra nupcial y húmeda, las luciérnagas fantásticas" ("in which fantastic fireflies burn in the nuptial and humid shadow"). The effect of the accents is a seeming desire to be identified with the flashing of the insects.

A particular effect is achieved by those verses that are linked by a peculiar rhythmic phenomenon. At the end of each verse, points of suspense are placed to maintain a vagueness that prevents rapid reading. One critic has called it an ideal overlapping reached through diverse techniques. Some of these are syntactic; the verses are full of parenthesis, making them appear static. The words of the first verse, "una noche . . ." ("one night . . .") are repeated at the beginning of the second and the third. In the second a verse is begun that does not continue; its progress is halted by means of parenthetical phrases and appositions.

The punctuation of the poem consists entirely of commas; there are no periods. At the end of each verse, one expects the continuation of the idea. The effect is that no single verse ends in itself but continues on into the next. Also contributing to this effect is the tetrasyllabic accentual base of the poem, in spite of the fact that the meter is arbitrary. The accenting produces for the ear an ideal regularity, one that foreshadows rhythmic development. The arbitrary variation of the verse's length clashes with this ideal rhythm, creating tension. Phonetic elements contribute to the development of sensations. The assonance of *a* sounds echoes in the even verses, as the sound is repeated.

Exceptional poetic possibilities are achieved through images of mysterious sounds, perfumes, and the music of wings, illuminated by intermittent fireflies and the moon's pallid light. In this unreal situation, the central action of the poem takes place: two shadows projected by the moon unite in a nuptial embrace. It is not a closeness of actual bodies, but rather of shadows, thin and evanescent, that in their embrace open this world to the world beyond.

The novel *De sobremesa* has been, until now, unjustly ignored by the critics. A characteristic modernist novel, it almost completely lacks a plot and centers exclusively on the thoughts of the protagonist, an anguished aesthete and a model of the modernist hero. José Fernández is neurotic, languid, superrefined, the classic decadent of the turn of the century.

The subject of the novel is simple. A wealthy Latin American writer gathers together in his luxurious and exotic home a group of his friends, requesting that they review the manuscript of his new work, one in which he has solved the mysteries of life. There exist in *De sobremesa* several incidents: the death of the writer's grandmother, a scene in which he stabs his lover, and his encounter with a mysterious young woman with a pre-Raphaelite face, with whom he falls passionately in love. The desperate search for this ideal lover completes the thematic development.

What stands out in the novel is the intensity of emotion provoked by the external events. One sees in these pages the typical modernist use of unusual adjectives, the association of discontinuous sensations, and the perception of what is hidden and how the hidden is linked with the visible. In this novel there are images, scenes, pictures, indicators of stationary and temporal suspense. To these impressions, the protagonist operates as actor, introspective and excessively sensitive.

De sobremesa is a lyric novel that subordinates action to the intensity of an instant's emotion. There is evident in this work the disintegration of the realistic protagonist. The protagonist of these pages loses his corporal nature, but not his humanity. Silva explores the intimate reactions of the hero in minute detail, paying greater attention to the effected impression than to the affecting action. The style is analytical in its observation of various states of being and in its description of objects, placing things observed on the same level as the contemplator.

Silva is essentially a poet of modern times. Principally with the **"Nocturno"** he delves into irrationalism and the mystery of the world beyond. He restored the use of the eleven-syllable verse favored by later modernist poets and gave it new cadences. He introduced a flexibility in the alexandrine line and created combinations of meters and verses of different measurements. He liberated traditional verse, redefining it as a musical totality with its own laws of rhythm and its own images. Silva, more than any other modernist poet, forged the Spanish language into a tool of powerful suggestiveness and delicate sounds, without falling, as even Rubén Darío did, into excessive adornment and color, never exploiting what would later become the tinsel of modernism.

Selected Bibliography

EDITIONS

INDIVIDUAL WORKS

De sobremesa. Bogotá, 1925.

Intimidades. With an introduction by Germán Arciniegas. Edited and with a preliminary study and notes by Hector H. Orjuela. Bogotá, 1977.

El libro de versos, 1883-1896. Bogotá, 1928.

El libro de versos. Fascimile edition. Bogotá, 1945.

―――. Bogotá, 1946.

COLLECTED WORKS

Los mejores poemas de José Asunción Silva. With a commentary by Manuel Toussaint. Mexico City, 1917.

Obra completa. Bogotá, 1955.

―――. With a prologue by Eduardo Camacho Guizado. Edited and with notes and chronology by Eduardo Camacho Guizado and Gustavo Mejia. Sucre, Venezuela, 1977.

Obras completas. With a prologue by Héctor H. Orjuela. 2 vols. Buenos Aires, 1968.

Poesías. With a prologue by Miguel de Unamuno. Barcelona, 1908.

Poesías. Edicion definitiva. With a prologue by Miguel de Unamuno and notes by Baldomero Sanín Cano. Paris, 1923.

―――. With a study by Baldomero Sanín Cano. Santiago, Chile, 1923.

Poesías. Edited by Franco Meregalli. Milan, 1950.

―――. Edited and with notes and an introduction by Héctor H. Orjuela. Bogotá, 1973.

―――. Critical edition by Héctor H. Orjuela. Bogotá, 1979.

Poesías completas. Buenos Aires, 1941.

Poesías completas, seguidas de prosas selectas. Madrid, 1951.

Prosas y versos. With an introduction, selection, and notes by Carlos García Prada. Mexico City, 1942.

Sus mejores poesías. Edited by Fermín Gutiérrez. Barcelona, 1955.

BIOGRAPHICAL AND CRITICAL STUDIES

Argüello, Santiago. "El anunciador José Asunción Silva." In *Modernismo y modernistas* 1. Guatemala City, 1934. Pp. 137-183.

Botero, Ebel. *Cinco poetas colombianos.* Manizales, Colombia, 1964. Pp. 15-40.

Camacho Guizado, Eduardo. *La poesía de José Asunción Silva.* Bogotá, 1968.

Capdevila, Arturo. "José Asunción Silva, el arístocrata." Prologue in *Poesias completas y sus mejores páginas en prosa,* by José Asunción Silva. Buenos Aires, 1944. Pp. 9-22.

Carrier, Warren. "Baudelaire y Silva." *Revista iberoamericana* 7/13:39-48 (1943).

Cuervo Márquez, Emilio. *José Asunción Silva: Su vida y su obra.* Amsterdam, 1935.

Fogelquist, Donald F. "José Asunción Silva y Heinrich Heine." *Revista hispanica moderna* 20/4:282-294 (1954).

Gicovate, Bernardo. "Estructura y significado en la poesía de José Asunción Silva." *Revista iberoamericana* 24/48:327-331 (1959).

Holguín, Andrés. "El sentido del misterio en Silva." *Revista de las Indias* 28/90:351-365 (1946).

Ingwersen, Sonya A. *Light and Longing: Silva and Darío. Modernism and Religious Heterody.* New York, 1986.

Jiménez, Juan Ramón. "José Asunción Silva" in "Españoles de tres mundos." *Sur* 10/79:12-14 (1941).

Lievano, Roberto. *En torno a Silva: Selección de estudios e investigaciones sobre la obra y la vida íntima del poeta.* Bogotá, 1946.

Loveluck, Juan. "*De sobremesa*: Novela desconocida del modernismo." *Revista iberoamericana* 31/59:17-32 (1965).

Miramón, Alberto. *José Asunción Silva: Ensayo biográfico con documentos inéditos.* Bogotá, 1937. 2nd ed. 1957.

Osiek, Betty T. *José Asunción Silva: Estudio estilístico de su poesia.* Mexico City, 1968.

———. *José Asunción Silva.* Twayne's World Authors Series no. 505. Boston, 1978.

Rico, Edmundo. *La depresión melancólica en la vida, en la obra y en la muerte de José Asunción Silva.* Tunja, Colombia, 1964.

Julia Palmer (essay date 1991)

SOURCE: Palmer, Julia. "Some Aspects of Narrative Structure in José Asunción Silva's *De Sobremesa*." *Revista Interamericana de Bibliografia* 41, no. 3 (1991): 470-77.

[In the following essay, Palmer identifies and describes the organizing patterns of Silva's novel.]

It has only been within the last few years that critics have begun to re-examine the previously somewhat maligned *modernista* novel ***De sobremesa.*** Initially, José Asunción Silva's story of a young poet and his anguished search for something to bring meaning to his life was not particularly well received. A close friend of Silva, Baldomiro Sanín Cano, stated, "es inferior a su obra poética y está por debajo de sus trabajos en prosa" (341).

More recently Juan Loveluck has described the work as "esta imperfecta novela reveladora" (30). In the 1970s Héctor H. Orjuela commented on several aspects of the novel's structure. He argued that, while there was a consistent thematic pattern evident in Fernández's search for Helena, overall the narrative was chaotic in form (37). Similarly, in her analysis of the work, Betty T. Osiek states that "the interpolation of essays makes the novel seem rather unorganized and hard to follow" (117), and Sonja Ingwersen has emphasized the "structural defects" of the work, noting "the relative absence of artistic control" (29).

Nonetheless, opinions regarding the value and artistry of the work are changing. Evelyn Picón Garfield states that "su considerada importancia en el ámbito de la prosa modernista es inegable" (262). Alfredo Villanuevo-Collado writes that the novel "está muy lejos de ser una obra fallida" (1987, 20). In his latest treatment of the novel Villanuevo-Collado proposes that "***De sobremesa*** está a la altura de novelas como *Rayuela* o *Cien años de soledad*" and argues that it is no longer possible to speak of the novel's lack of structure or to call Silva an inexperienced novelist (1989, 279).

Up to this point the main trend in criticism of ***De sobremesa*** has been thematic. Ferdinand V. Contino's analysis emphasized recurring aesthetic traits of *modernismo* such as chromatism and eroticism evident in the novel. Lydia D. Hazera's exploration of the artistic personality also focuses on recurring themes, duality and fear of death (1978). Ingwersen has analyzed the occultist themes of the work,

such as precious stone imagery, androgyny, and the protagonist's obsession with light (1986). Villanuevo-Collado has postulated an internal structure to the work perceiving it in terms of Silva's unifying use of alchemic and esoteric symbols (1987).

Such general discussions of the work's structure in terms of unifying themes is clearly valid, but the mere recurrence of similar ideas does not produce a satisfying analysis. A closer study of the narrative structure, however, does suggest the existence of other elements of conscious form and style. Although not complex, their very presence may serve to reinforce Villanuevo-Collado's enthusiastic defense of a work that has often been undervalued as a literary artifact because of its apparently unorganized narrative.

In this article it will be suggested that at least three separate aspects of the novel's structural organization merit attention: first, the function of the novel's frame, particularly at the two points in the text where there is an interruption of the diary; secondly, the pattern of prolepsis evident in the relating of the protagonist's love experiences; finally, the existence of a pivotal episode appearing in the center of the text which suggests a parabolic evolution of the plot.

The novel begins with the protagonist, José Fernández, agreeing to read aloud from an old diary to a circle of intimate friends. He promises that this reading will not only explain the name of his luxurious villa "Helena", and the mysterious painting of a beautiful woman, but will also enable his friends to understand why he simultaneously pursues ten different interests in his life.

Within this frame, which functions to portray his present life, Fernández reads his diary. This narration of past events provides a sharp contrast with the "here and now" of the frame which encloses the reading. Not only does the novel begin and end in José's living room, but there are also two points within the text where Fernández either stops reading or is interrupted by his friends. Why would Silva incorporate these two reappearances of the frame into the text? The answer seems to be that the returns to the present, characterized by an emphasis on his friends' emotional reactions, are designed to underline Fernández's failure to find any type of lasting fulfillment in activities that initially seemed promising.

According to his account in the diary, after brutally ending a sensually erotic affair, Fernández flees to the countryside. Refreshed by simple, clean living, one of his first ideas is to engineer a daring plan of social, political and economic rejuvenation for his homeland. As the victorious new leader, he will bring his nation out of its present darkness by creating powerful industries, reshaping the antiquated educational system, and forming a new political party that will draw support from citizens at all levels of society. Energized, Fernández carefully details his plans to reform his country, devoting many pages of his diary to the different steps he must take to prepare himself to be accepted as his countrymen's social architect.

Fernández feels that this plan will bring purpose to his life, and the triumphantly optimistic tone of these pages conveys his enthusiasm. But at this point the on-going narrative suddenly halts as he stops reading to comment, "Yo estaba loco cuando escribí esto . . ." (74).[1] His friends' reactions which now intervene are mixed. Indignant with José for his presumed superiority in aspiring to lead his country forward, Rovira states that he does not understand the connection between the diary and Fernández's present state of affairs. Mumbling, "Decididamente no entiendo nada de eso," (76) he walks out. Cordovez wonders aloud what prevented José from carrying out his carefully engineered plan. Saenz coldly criticizes Fernández for having such a detailed plan but being always unable or unwilling to invest the time necessary to make it a reality. It is clear that the reappearance of the frame-situation at this point in the text is intended to emphasize, both through the remarks of the narrator and those of his listeners, the failure of Fernández's political aspirations to provide any lasting fulfillment.

This return to the frame also underscores the situational irony created by the discrepancy between Fernández's grandiose aspirations and his sudden abandonment of them. The plan did not fail because it was impossibly large, but simply because Fernández gave up.

The constant battle for control between two distinct parts of his personality is a matter of grave concern for Fernández. The passionate, fiery side of his nature often suffocates the scholarly, knowledge-oriented side of himself. Often, the result of this duality, accompanied by the failure of either side to bring lasting satisfaction, is *abulia*. Hazera notes that *abulia* "the inability of the will to act or create" often afflicts the "intellectual and artistic protagonists of the modernist novel" (74). She argues that Fernández is a failed artist, and his lack of will to either define objectives in life or to realize his creative urge, directs him inwards "devoting creative energy to narcissistic self-analysis which is often displaced in forms of self-gratification—sexual orgies, opium intoxication, contemplation and collection of art objects" (75).

While this description of *abulia* is correct as far as it goes, it neglects to take into account that failure of the will is inseparable from lack of life-directing ideas or ideals. From this point in the novel on, Fernández's evolution is governed by his conscious or unconscious search for such sources of support.

Reading again from the diary, Fernández now turns to his emotional and sexual life and relates his affairs with Niní Rousset. A question which immediately presents itself is why Fernández's affairs with Lelia and Niní not only collapse, but end in physical violence. A possible answer might be that it is Fernández's recognition that the two women do not offer him the love ideal he is unconsciously seeking which provokes his attacks on them. His next attempted solution is that of the "paradis artificiel" of opium. But this, far from helping to dynamize his existence, only increases his lethargy.

The proof that what he is questing for is a life-orientating love ideal is supplied by his crucial encounter with the ethereally beautiful Helena. Convinced that she holds the key to permanent happiness in life, Fernández believes his salvation is imminent. She disappears, however, leaving him anxious and depressed. Unable to find solace in religion or philosophy, he looks to a "priest of science," Dr. Rivington, for an alternative intellectual ideal.

Recognizing, however, that it is an emotional ideal that Fernández needs, the doctor orders him to find Helena and marry her, suggesting that this will make his life normal once again. Rivington also severely warns his patient against his excessive swings from abstinence to over-indulgence in physical exercise, drugs, and sex. The second re-evocation of the frame occurs at this point. Saenz interrupts the reading, noting critically that Fernández has avoided that advice for eight years, always laughing at his friend's attempts to encourage moderation.

Assuming a superior attitude, Fernández calmly informs the group that the situation is different now,

> . . . he distribuido mis fuerzas entre el placer, el estudio y la acción, los planes políticos de entonces los he convertido en un *sport* que me divierte, y no tengo violentas impresiones sentimentales porque desprecio a fondo a las mujeres y nunca tengo al tiempo menos de dos aventuras amorosas para que las impresiones de una y otra se contrarresten. . . .

We can see that Fernández's reaction at this point in the text is designed to underscore the failure of two more support mechanisms that had initially seemed to promise to bring meaning to his life. Scientific rationalism, represented by Rivington himself and his logical advice to practice moderation and marry Helena, has failed to provide any way out in practice for Fernández. At the same time his inability to track down Helena leads to further debauchery which merely exacerbates the situation. The reappearance of the frame-situation at this point serves as a reminder of this and of the fact that the fleeting pleasures of the flesh have not brought lasting satisfaction.

A novel about a man's growing self-awareness, ***De sobremesa*** charts the evolution of the central character, Fernández. His changing perception of life is especially evident in his relationships with members of the opposite sex. Looking over the novel as a whole, apart from Helena with whom he never has direct contact, there are five incidents of Fernández and femininity. These five experiences represent three stages in the protagonist's growing disillusionment with life and except for the fourth affair, the narration follows an unswerving proleptic pattern.

The first two encounters are characterized by Fernández's frustration at his inability to find a life-directing goal, and his proleptic narration of these two affairs heightens the sense of drama. In his diary entry of June 23, Fernández refers, with no prior information to a blood-soaked shirt, police, and hiding.

De la tarde de ayer sólo me quedan dos sensaciones, el puño de la camisa empapado en sangre y la orla negra de la carta. . . . A estas horas debe haber muerto y la policía estará buscándome. Me hice inscribir en el registro del hotel con el nombre de Juan Simónides, griego, agente viajero, para despistarla . . . Marinoni debe telegrafiarme hoy mismo y del hotel mandarán el telegrama a Whyl . . . donde voy a esconderme en una hostería a dos kilómetros del pueblecito.

(48)

It is not until two journal entries later that Fernández provides a full explanation. He writes how he first meets Lelia Orloff at the opera and feels an immediate attraction to her. Theirs is a purely physical relationship that appeals to all of Fernández's senses. He abandons his intellectual pursuits, caught up in Lelia's attitude towards life. "La vida no es para saber, es para gozar" (55). Living only for pleasure, Fernández is able to forget his darker side. One day, however, he arrives unannounced at her apartment and finds her with another woman. Blind with rage, he beats her mercilessly and then stabs her twice with a small dagger. After this he runs away.

Unable to explain the blinding rage that motivated him to attack his lover, Fernández is shocked by his brutal reaction, but does not feel particularly remorseful, and his next affair ends with violence as well. In his entry of August 5, he relates his sado-masochistic affair with Niní Rousset, "la divetta de un teatro bufo" (81). In the next journal entry he mentions "una escena horrible" which drove him to a forty-eight hour period of opium intoxication. A few paragraphs later he explains that the night before, on a mad impulse, he attempted to choke Niní to death, but she managed to escape.

The drama created by the reordered narration of these two affairs helps to underline the passion which guides Fernández. This passion which expresses itself in violent attacks on women illustrates the uncontrollable anger that best describes the protagonist's frame of mind at this point in his life.

The next affair occurs between two events in Fernández's life that involve Helena, upon which this third encounter is hinged. When Fernández arranges a one-night stand with a prostitute, he has already met and lost Helena. Physically very attracted to Constanza, he is ready to forget his anxiety when he looks up to see Helena's profile floating above the room. Overwhelmed by fear, he runs out of the room. The guilt at his unfaithful behavior is accompanied by deepening anguish as he realizes that precisely because Helena represents ideal love and potential salvation, being without her is driving him mad. This third affair which began so passionately ends unfinished in an aborted anti-climax. Until Dr. Rivington shows him the portrait, startlingly like Helena, Fernández is unable to allow other women into his life.

The anxiety and guilt evident in the third experience with Constanza harden into an attitude of callous indifference and represent the third and final stage in Fernández's grow-ing self-awareness. In his journal entry of April 19, he chronologically relates his affair with Nelly, a young, married, American girl. When she leaves to go home, he promises to visit her, but forgets her almost immediately. He describes her as "una gota de licor para el que agoniza de sed, *sed non satiata*" (203) and realizes that he is now driven by pure carnal desire, devoid of affection or warmth.

The diary entry of September 1 follows the previously established pattern of prolepsis as he writes that, "(yo) ya había besado las tres bocas codiciadas y obtenido de ellas la promesa de las tres citas" (204). Not until a few pages later does he explain how he met, kissed, and pursued simultaneous affairs with Consuela, Olga, and Julia, all married women. He even makes a point of meeting each husband and remarks deprecatorily that they are unaware of the affairs taking place in front of them. Adultery is a sport for Fernández, now that he has given up hoping for ideal love.

Y qué me importan esas ideas sobre el amor, ni qué me importa nada, si lo que siento dentro de mí es el cansancio y el desprecio por todo, el mortal dejo, el *spleen* horrible, como un monstruo interior cuya hambre no alcanzará a saciarse con el universo, comienza a devorarme el alma? . . .

(206)

The fourth and fifth experiences chart the downward spiral in Fernández's quest to find meaning in life. He must now pursue simultaneous affairs in an attempt to quiet the inner turmoil and anguish which continue deep inside him. The first two affairs which were highlighted by Fernández's violent individual attacks on women as he sought for a life-directing goal, have turned into cold, quiet, society-oriented attacks on the institution of marriage.

His search for a meaningful ideal is characterized by violent anger. Once he meets Helena, he realizes that it is ideal love which will bring him lasting fulfillment. However, he is never able to grasp this thread of hope always just beyond his reach, which leaves him with a deepening sense of anguish. The third stage in the evolution of his character ends in the loss of his ideal, and Fernández hides his inner despair behind a mask of stony unfeeling. This evolution of self-awareness which culminates in his deliberate attacks on marriage, something he has been denied with the death of Helena, suggests a metaphor of man's fight against a life destined for despair and implies that the way to survive the existential dilemma is by losing oneself in pleasures that temporarily allow one to forget reality.

Four of the five affairs stand out because of the narrator's reordering of events in his relation of the encounters. This structural technique is significant in part because of the sense of drama of the first two affairs. The third and fifth affairs are proleptic in narration which offers a sharp contrast to their anti-climactic conclusions. Why is this technique used? It reinforces the sense of failure by letting the reader know in anticipation what the consequences of each affair will be. What evolves here is Fernández's disenchantment with life and his inability to find anything to make his life meaningful.

The reordered narrations of his exploits are also small scale duplications of the basic form of the novel, which is an explication of the consequences we see at the beginning: i.e. the villa "Helena", the mysterious painting, and Fernández's strange separation from and disenchantment with life.

The beginning of the novel acts as a prolepsis of the rest of the novel and the narrative reorderings of Fernández's exploits are all mini-reproductions of the basic underlying structure of the text.

Fernández's diary keeps a record of his growing self-awareness and the constant battle between the two disparate parts of his nature. However, the central thread of the plot concerns the protagonist's search for something to bring meaning to his life. Halfway through the text when Fernández sees Helena, he realizes he has finally come into contact with his only hope for lasting fulfillment. His encounter with Helena marks a pivotal point in the text, representing the peak of its line of evolution. The various routes he had tried in an attempt to find fulfillment in life, philosophy, poetry, politics and mere physical sexuality, have all been dead ends. His meeting with Helena marks a turning point in the text. His life changes after seeing her.

The episode's central location in the text may be related both forwards and backwards. The encounter with Helena itself is foreshadowed by the letter from Emilia relating his grandmother's death. On her deathbed, the old woman's last words are: "Benditos sean la señal de la cruz hecha por la mano de la virgen, y el ramo de rosas que caen en su noche como signo de salvación" (50). This reference to Fernández's salvation is significant because it heightens the sense of expectancy that something does exist that will save him from a meaningless life.

The night he meets Helena, Fernández watches as she genuflects and then throws him a bouquet of roses. He truly believes that she will save him, and as Hazera has noted, Helena then becomes his obsession (71). In contrast to the short-lived effects of his previous pursuits, the influence that she wields is to remain with Fernández for the rest of his life. As he begins his search for Helena, her potential as the one thing that may bring meaning to his life is reiterated by Dr. Rivington: "Ese amor puede ser su salvación" (121).

As the central episode of the text, Fernández's encounter with Helena creates a sense of anticipation that is offset by his discovery of her tomb at the end of the diary. The cold, disheartening knowledge of her death parallels the death of hope in his own life. Silva's creation of an optimistic pivotal episode that leads to anticlimax serves as further evidence of a conscious, internal design. Even more significantly it also suggests the existence of a basic,

underlying metaphor of life. The construction of an episode that marked a positive turning point in the text illustrates Silva's recognition that man experiences a sense of optimistic possibilities at some time in his life. These promising turning points, however, are only an illusion, and the hope born of them is later destroyed as man discovers the death of his "salvation" and must resign himself not only to the cruel disillusion but to an existence devoid of any lasting happiness or meaning.

The appearance of the frame-situation within the text, the proleptic pattern peculiar to the narration of the protagonist's exploits, and the existence of a pivotal episode followed by an anticlimax reveal a conscious will to order in Silva's work. These three aspects of narrative structure support Picón-Garfield and Villanuevo-Collado's assertions that *De sobremesa* should no longer be considered a rambling collection of unsophisticated and chaotic prose.

It is hoped that the identification of more elements of textual organization in *De sobremesa* than have hitherto been fully recognized will contribute to the current re-evaluation of the novel. However, it may be affirmed that the techniques which Silva employs are less significant in themselves than they are as metaphors which reinforce the underlying themes of the text: the futility of believing in a traditional "loving" God, man's search for a non-religious salvation from a meaningless life, the existence of a type of salvation, followed by the almost inevitable destruction of that salvation, committing mankind to an existence devoid of any real meaning. Silva's utilization of structuring devices to underpin the basic themes of his novel is only one aspect of a work that deserves further study since it appears to be far more complex than originally supposed.

Notes

1. All quotations from the text are from the 1920 edition of *De sobremesa* printed in Bogotá by Editorial de Cromos.

Works Cited

Contino, Ferdinand V. "Preciosismo y decadentismo en *De sobremesa* de José Asunción Silva." *Estudios críticos sobre la prosa modernista hispanoamericana.* Ed. José Olivio Jiménez. New York: Eliseo Torres, 1975, 135-55.

Garfield, Evelyn Picón. "*De sobremesa*: José Asunción Silva, El diario íntimo y la mujer prerrafaelita," in *Nuevos asedios al modernismo,* edited by Ivan A. Schulman. Madrid: Taurus, 1987.

Hazera, Lydia D. "The Spanish American Modernist Novel and the Psychology of the Artistic Personality." *Hispanic Journal,* 8 (1986), 69-83.

Ingwersen, Sonja. *Light and Longing: Silva and Dario. Modernism and Religious Heterodoxy.* New York: Peter Lang, 1986.

Loveluck, Juan. "*De sobremesa,* novela desconocida del Modernismo." *Revista Iberoamericana,* 31 (1965), 17-32.

O'Hara, Edgar. "*De sobremesa,* una divagación narrativa." *Revista Chilena de Literatura,* 27 (1986), 221-227.

Orjuela, Héctor H. *De sobremesa y otros estudios sobre José Asunción Silva.* Bogotá: Instituto Caro y Cuervo, 1976.

Osiek, Betty T. *José Asunción Silva.* Boston: Twayne, 1978.

Sanín Cano, Baldomero. *El oficio de lector.* Caracas: Biblioteca Ayacucho, 1978 or 1979.

Silva, José Asunción. *De sobremesa.* Bogotá: Editorial de Cromos, 1920.

Villanuevo-Collado, Alfredo. "*De sobremesa* de José Asunción Silva y las doctrinas esotéricas en la Francia de fin de siglo." *Revista de Estudios Hispánicos,* 21 (1987), 9-21.

———. "José Asunción Silva y Karl-Joris Huysmans: Estudio de una lectura." *Revista Iberoamericana,* 55 (1989), 273-86.

Aileen Dever (essay date 2000)

SOURCE: Dever, Aileen. "The Experience of Radical Insufficiency." In *The Radical Insufficiency of Human Life: The Poetry of R. de Castro and J. A. Silva,* pp. 7-38. Jefferson, N.C.: McFarland, 2000.

[*In the following essay, Dever compares the work of two nineteenth-century Spanish American poets, noting that the work of both was characterized by disillusionment and an awareness of human limitations.*]

Rosalía de Castro and José Asunción Silva express eternal concerns about the meaning of life and death, anticipating many themes of the existentialists. Both are writers in transition who lived in a century characterized by political chaos and ideological strife. In Spain conflict resulted as conservatives defended traditional values against the secular, progressive, and democratic trends arising in France, England, and elsewhere in the West (Kulp-Hill 15). Likewise, in Colombia the second half of the nineteenth century displayed social and religious upheaval. Tradition underwent challenge in a climate of increasing liberalism following the newly established federalist government of 1863. The influence of French and English philosophical and political ideas also contributed to the general turmoil in Colombia (Camacho Guizado, 1968: 13-14). Castro and Silva absorbed quite naturally these uncertainties and doubts, the political and religious rumblings of the times. They arrived at the disquieting realization that there is no absolute blueprint for life. Their works are permeated by anguish that relates to their feelings of abandonment in an uncertain world and their deep desire for guiding principles. Deploring the lack of enduring values and norms that would give life meaning, they consistently present the essential orphanhood of the human being. However, they do not offer solutions to the problem of existence because they believe that human beings can never discern the ultimate purpose for living. Neither philosophy, science, art, love, nor religion explain the world to them; their agony is born of the failure of human reason. Nevertheless, despite their anguish, they do not hide from their realization. Instead, they show that for human beings to comprehend reality, they must strip away the false, albeit comforting, preconceptions about life cherished for centuries. This chapter reveals how Castro and Silva, who once approached life from a conventional perspective, came to perceive being human as the experience of radical insufficiency.

THE RESTLESSNESS OF THE HUMAN BEING

THE DELUDED INNOCENCE OF CHILDHOOD

Lacking a fixed nature, humans are dynamic beings that change continuously throughout their lives. Their mutability forms part of the restlessness of being human. For both Castro and Silva, this process of change seems inevitably to lead the human being from a state of seeming innocence and faith during childhood to one of disillusionment and uncertainty during adulthood.[1] Although Castro occasionally depicts the physical and mental suffering of children (*Follas novas* 368, 399 [*New Leaves*]; *Sar* 502-503; *La hija del mar* 130 [*Daughter of the Sea*]; *El primer loco* 729 [*The First Madman*]), both she and Silva generally perceive childhood as a deluded though contented state, that is, as a time when they believed in God and in the goodness of their fellow human beings, trusted in the attainability of hopes and dreams, and thought that life was meaningful. With maturity they come to see being human as radical insufficiency because human beings can never attain a state of pure innocence. In their writings Castro (*El caballero de las botas azules* 49 [*The Gentleman of the Blue Boots*]; *Flavio* 226) and Silva (**Libro de versos** 9, 12) emphasize the fleeting nature of youthful trustfulness. Castro affirms that unmitigated, unexplained suffering is what separates the world of the child from that of the adult: "La nieve de los años, de la tristeza el hielo / constante, al alma niegan toda ilusión amada, / todo dulce consuelo" (*Sar* 460-461, "The snow of years, the ice of sadness / ever present, deny the soul cherished illusions, / every sweet consolation"). In a thematically similar poem Castro's poetic voice describes the pain of knowing that she will witness her beloved childrens' inevitable transformation from innocence (though deluded) to disillusionment as they continue living. She uses much entrapment imagery to underscore the fact that a mother cannot protect her children from the disappointment that experience brings:

Yo, en tanto, bañados mis ojos, les miro
y guardo silencio, pensando:—En la tierra
¿adónde llevaros, mis pobres cautivos,
que no hayan de ataros las mismas cadenas?
Del hombre, enemigo del hombre, no puede
libraros, mis ángeles, la égida materna.

(*Sar* 488)

I, meanwhile, with tears in my eyes, look upon them
and keep silent, thinking:—On earth
where to take you, my poor captives,
where the same chains will not imprison you?
From man, enemy of man, cannot
protect you, my angels, the maternal aegis.

Through her novelistic character Flavio, Castro powerfully illustrates how childhood ingenuousness is soon lost in the adult world. The over-all theme of the novel is the corruption of innocence as a result of experience and contact with others. Soon after his parents die, twenty-year-old Flavio leaves his ancestral home, symbol of the womb and its protection. He sets forth on a journey of initiation. Significantly, Castro often refers to Flavio not by name but simply as "the traveler" (275). Coming on a nocturnal party, he is immediately mesmerized by its impressionistic beauty (234). The scene he witnesses foreshadows the changes that will take place in him. Society corrupts Flavio just as the party unnaturally taints the unspoiled landscape. The crash of Flavio's carriage after he leaves the party to continue his journey of discovery represents his fall from innocence into the world of disillusionment (275). Subsequently, at a masquerade party symbolizing the deceptive nature of reality, women deceive Flavio into thinking that his beloved Mara has been unfaithful. Freely partaking in the experiences of life, Flavio is then seduced by carnal love and materialism. For Mara, already distrustful and cynical at fifteen, Flavio's actions confirm her pessimism about human inconstancy. Flavio also disillusions Rosa, a young girl whom he seduces and then abandons with their child (463). Fully embracing a dissolute lifestyle, Flavio disparagingly equates his former innocence with a simpleminded conception of the world (463).

Silva similarly reveals how experience transforms childhood perceptions into undeceit. The grandmother of **"Los maderos de San Juan" ("The Wood of Saint John")** is agonizingly aware that with maturity her grandchild will exchange innocence for disillusionment, just as she has:

Y en tanto en las rodillas cansadas de la Abuela
Con movimiento rítmico se balancea el niño
Y ambos conmovidos y trémulos están,
La Abuela se sonríe con maternal cariño
Mas cruza por su espíritu como un temor extraño
Por lo que en lo futuro, de angustia y desengaño
Los días ignorados del nieto guardarán.

(*Libro de versos* 12)

And while on the tired knees of the grandmother,
With rhythmical movement the child rocks
And both moved and tremulous are,
The grandmother smiles with maternal love
But her soul is shaken as if by a strange fear
Of what in the future, of anguish and disillusionment
The unforeseeable days of the grandchild will bring.

Usually, the child symbolizes the future, whereas the old represent the past. In Silva's poem, however, the grandmother is just as much a symbol of the future as of the past. As Silva interprets the grandmother's thoughts, he emphatically uses the future tense. Through her own accumulated suffering and subsequent pessimism she vividly portrays what her grandson's life and worldview will be like. Silva constantly returns to the alexandrines accented in -án, the knell of fatality. This -án is a derivative of the nursery rhyme, **"Los maderos de San Juan" ("The Wood of Saint John")**. Used as a refrain that fuses past, present, and future, the nursery rhyme acquires substantial depth to become, as the poem progresses, an almost sinister reminder of innocence and simplicity lost as the child matures. The nursery rhyme represents, then, through contrast, the lack of lighthearted exuberance and gaiety in adulthood. Another device Silva employs to emphasize his theme of disillusionment is repetition. The stanza quoted above, the penultimate, is exactly the same as the second stanza except for a slight variation in the first line. Not only does Silva deepen the pathos and contribute to the heavy and melancholic mood of the poem through this repetition, but he also eloquently creates the sensation of foreshadowing as to the child's ominous future. The child will only be able to recapture the happy past through memory as a disillusioned adult.

Nevertheless, both Castro and Silva view the deluded innocence of childhood more favorably than the disillusionment of adulthood. In "Padrón y las inundaciones" ("Padrón and the Floods") Castro recalls the golden days of childhood and adolescence spent in the manor house when "la esperanza, ahora huida, andaba agitando entonces sus luminosas alas" (635, "hope, now gone, would flutter then its luminous wings"). With deep feelings of *saudade* Silva and Castro look back to childhood: "Feliz edad de plácidos engaños" (**Intimidades** 184, "Happy age of blissful delusions" [**Private Thoughts**]).[2] Sensitively they portray human yearning for the lost paradise of childhood "por saberse constitutivamente, como hombre, *desterrado* de esta seguridad, en la que no se moría. Es por tanto, la saudade, una expresión biológico-afectiva de este ser-arrojado-en-el-mundo" (Rof Carballo 128, "knowing themselves to be constitutively, as human beings, exiled from this security, in which one never dies. Therefore, *saudade* is a biological-affective expression of this being hurled into the world").

Silva in particular writes about the blend of fantasy and reality that makes childhood such a special state, as opposed to disillusioned adulthood (**Libro de versos** 8-9,14-16). Implicitly, he conceives childhood innocence as the candid acceptance of, and belief in, ultimate authority, both human and divine, as well as a lack of motivation to attempt a rational understanding of existence (**Libro de versos** 8-9). In this stage of life practical considerations are nonexistent, and the child organizes "horrísona batalla / En donde hacen las piedras de metralla / Y el ajado pañuelo de bandera" (**Libro de versos** 9, "horrendous battle / In which stones serve as ammunition / And the crumpled handkerchief as a flag"). Unwittingly the child imitates one of the horrible realities of adult life. In another poem Silva contrasts Bolívar's somber statue with the children who play at the foot of its pedestal: "Un idilio de vida sonrïente / Y de alegría fatua" (**Libro de versos** 18, "An idyll of smiling life / And of inane happiness"). He thus represents childhood innocence in juxtaposition to Bolívar as the incapacity to apprehend the suffering of others.

Silva repeatedly attempts to use memories of innocent childhood days, recaptured through the mists of time, as a psychological oasis.[3] He depicts images of turning inward, trying to dissociate himself from the disillusionment of adulthood: "Ansiosa el alma torna / A los felices días de la infancia / Que pasaron veloces" (**Intimidades** 181, "Anxiously the soul returns / To the happy days of childhood / That swiftly passed"). He wishes to supersede the suffering of life through memory: "Cómo es de dulce en horas de amarguara / Dirigir al pasado la mirada" (**Libro de versos** 9, "How sweet it is in bitter times / To turn one's gaze to the past"). But sweet childhood memories can also cause pain as a stark reminder of a time forever lost. Adults can only evoke sadly "todo el poema triste de la remota infancia" (**Libro de versos** 12, "the whole sad poem of long-gone childhood"). Silva fully recognizes that "el pasado perfuma los ensueños" (**Libro de versos** 40, "the past perfumes reveries"). Time acts as an idealizing agent on a nebulous past and makes the present all the more unbearable. To Castro, however, memories of youth are distinctly painful because they emphasize the happiness now lacking in her life. Memory forms a source of unending anguish as she realizes that through remembrance human beings recognize their own restlessness (**Follas novas** 301-302). In one poem, for example, Castro uses gold leaves to symbolize an elusive treasure gone—the green of spring and summer and, by extension, youth and hope. Movingly, she indicates the pain she feels whenever she recalls the past: "¿Por qué tan terca, / tan fiel memoria me ha dado el cielo?" (**Sar** 480, "Why such a stubborn, / such a faithful memory has heaven bestowed upon me?"). Ultimately for Castro, memory is one more example of the cruelty and futility of life.

THE AWARENESS AND DISILLUSIONMENT OF ADULTHOOD

Both Castro and Silva portray adulthood as a state of suffering and lost hopes. In the long reflective poem "Orillas del Sar" ("Banks of the River Sar"), Castro describes the increasing disillusionment that maturity brings. The poetic voice looks out the window, surveying a wavy sea of green trees. The trees, observed from a position of height and distance, symbolize gained experience and the greater perspective of age. The passage of time has influenced Castro's life in negative ways as the innocence of youth has given way to pessimism, which she views as a mature acceptance of the possibilities of life. Suggesting withdrawal from the world, the poetic voice speaks in the past tense about the forest once loved. The fluttering leaves reinforce the theme of the vicissitudes of human existence. The green of the leaves may represent the hope of youth, and the birds that dwell among them the lofty aspirations of youth. But the woodland and its symbolism appear utterly foreign now. Somber but resigned, the poetic voice calls

attention to feelings of desolation. The ghosts, made more vivid by the adjective *white,* are the hopes and dreams of youth, which only haunt human beings:

> Bajemos, pues, que el camino
> antiguo nos saldrá al paso,
> aunque triste, escabroso y desierto,
> y cual nosotros cambiado,
> lleno aún de las blancas fantasmas
> que en otro tiempo adoramos.
>
> (*Sar* 459)

> *Let's go down, then, for the path*
> *of old will come to meet us,*
> *although sad, rugged and deserted,*
> *changed like ourselves,*
> *it is still filled with the white ghosts*
> *that at another time we adored.*

Silva also considers maturity as necessarily a symbol of disillusionment. He emphasizes the antipodal nature of youth and old age through juxtaposition in **"La abulea y la nieta"** (**Intimidades** 184-185, **"The Grandmother and the Granddaughter"**). Silva contrasts the granddaughter's white forehead with the grandmother's, darkened and withered by heartache. The grandmother no longer experiences the hope that comes with each new day, as hope is the exclusive property of youth. Silva and Castro express that a consequence of suffering is often a hardening of the mental and emotional self toward others. Silva describes in **"Perdida"** (**"Lost"**) how an idealistic young girl, left pregnant and abandoned, becomes diseased and disillusioned as she avenges herself on all men (**Intimidades** 163-164). Likewise, as beggars are cruelly turned away from the home of one who was once a beggar himself, Castro tragically explains, "la miseria seca el alma / y los ojos además" (*Sar* 502, "suffering dries the soul / and the eyes too").

To underscore their view that humans necessarily change as they mature, becoming more disillusioned over time, Castro and Silva contrast human mutability with such external and concrete items as statues, the seemingly fixed nature of the physical world, stories, nursery rhymes, and bells. In "Na catredal" (*Follas novas* 291-294, "In the Cathedral"), Castro's poetic voice expresses anguish at the loss of her previously intact religious beliefs. During a visit to a cathedral of younger days, she experiences feelings of spiritual orphanhood that heighten her sense of disorientation and inner change as she surveys the frozen statues she knew at a more innocent time in her life when her religious faith was strong. Observing the predominance of old people in various corners, Castro now views faith in its capacity to provide support to those who will soon face death. Matching her depressed mood is the organ that emits melancholy tones to which sad bells respond from afar. Castro's poetic voice notices how the statue of the Messiah seems still to be perspiring blood (291). Throughout her poem she utilizes the present tense to emphasize the continuous, unchanged physical environment of the cathedral in contrast to her evolving pessimism. Her frequent use of interrogatives and exclamations also conveys her anguish at change in herself, and repetition serves to highlight her nervousness. The predominance of *s* in the lines below (1, 2, 5, 7, 10) also suggests a privation of sound that reinforces her theme of emptiness in the wake of her loss of faith:

> ¡Como me miran eses calabres
> i aqueles deños!
> ¡Como me miran facendo moecas
> dende as colunas onde os puxeron!
> ¿Será mentira, será verdade?
> Santos do ceo,
> ¿saberán eles que son a mesma
> daqueles tempos? . . .
> Pero xa orfa, pero enloitada,
> pero insensibre cal eles mesmos . . .
> ¡Como me firen! . . . Voume, si, voume,
> ¡que teño medo!
>
> (*Follas novas* 293)

> *How these demons look at me*
> *and those dead!*
> *How they look at me grimacing*
> *from the columns where they are!*
> *Is it true, or is it a lie?*
> *Saints in heaven,*
> *do they know that I am the same one*
> *of that time?*
> *And now an orphan, and in mourning,*
> *and insensible as they are . . .*
> *How they hurt me! . . . . I am going, yes, I am going,*
> *for I am afraid!*

Self-consciously she feels the statues are staring and grimacing at her, and she eloquently projects her fear and guilt at having lost her faith. The verticality of the cathedral columns represents an upward impulse, a deep desire for self-affirmation in the faith of her forebears. Columns also symbolize the stability lost along with faith. Toward the end of the poem, sunlight streaming on a high chandelier sheds reflections on the cathedral floor and produces dreams of religious illumination. Swiftly, however, the shadows of religious doubt appear and, once more, "todo é negrura, todo é misterio" (293, "all is darkness, all is mystery"). The poetic subject flees the cathedral in fear as now everything is a hurtful reminder of her pessimistic outlook about God's existence. Continuously Castro stresses that her problematic religious faith is the source of her prevailing sadness and confusion.

In another poem she contrasts the indifference of nature and eternal renewal to human beings, who inevitably change during the course of their lives. As critic Kathleen Kulp affirms, Castro "is preoccupied with irrevocable change and temporality, and the Heraclitean concept that man cannot step twice into the same stream" (186). In the poem "¡ Adios!" ("Good-bye") her poetic voice describes how she leaves home as "os vaiviéns da fertuna / pra lonxe me arrastran" (*Follas novas* 289, "the ups and downs of

fortune / drag me far away"). Before departing, she pensively surveys the town cathedral and surrounding countryside. She emphasizes, on an uncertain future return, that nature and the cathedral will remain the same, but the people she has left behind will be different. She measures this transformation in terms of the misfortunes they will have endured (289). Castro's depictions of the painful changes and transformations that the human being undergoes caused her husband Manuel Murguía to comment that "los montes que ve desde su ventana son los mismos que veía en otros tiempos; todo es igual: sólo que faltan alrededor suyo algunos seres, y en su corazón muchas esperanzas; sólo ella, siendo la misma, es distinta" (1944: 155, "the mountains she sees from her window are the same she saw in the past; everything is the same: but missing are some persons around her, and many hopes in her heart; only she, while the same, is different").

In other poems Castro compares the human being's changefulness with the changes in nature. She likens the dissolution of clouds to the dissolution of youthful dreams and hopes. Clouds, always in a state of metamorphosis, convey well the mutability of the human being as time passes (*Follas novas* 290). In another poem, seeing some flowers and stars that seem to be the same as ones she had known when she was younger and had strong faith in God, Castro's poetic voice notes that in reality the flowers and stars are different, just as she is different: she is less innocent. The awareness of how she has changed is a source of deep sorrow:

> Alma que vas huyendo de ti misma,
> ¿qué buscas, insensata, en las demás?
> Si secó en ti la fuente del consuelo,
> secas todas las fuentes has de hallar.
> ¡Que hay en el cielo estrellas todavía,
> y hay en la tierra flores perfumadas!
> ¡ Sí! . . . Mas no son ya aquellas
> que tú amaste y te amaron, desdichada.
>
> (*Sar* 479)

> *Soul in flight from yourself,*
> *what do you expect, fool, to find in others?*
> *If the spring of consolation dried up in you,*
> *dried up all other springs you will find.*
> *There are still stars in the sky,*
> *and on earth scented flowers!*
> *Yes! . . . But they are not those*
> *that you loved and that loved you, wretched one.*

She writes the poem in hendecasyllables except for line 7, which is heptasyllabic, thereby reinforcing the brevity of all things, even of those that may appear eternal. Her self-deprecatory tone implies that she should be well aware of negative change in herself. In a thematically similar poem daisies that grow amid the green grass symbolize lost naiveté and youthful resilience. The tone of the first three stanzas of the poem is calm and hopeful. But as seasons pass her poetic voice contrasts the flowers' apparent changelessness with her own variability (*Sar* 508-509).

Like Castro, Silva mourns human mutability. In **"Crepús-culo"** (**"Twilight"**), he contrasts human transformations with the archetypal permanence of children's stories (*Libro de versos* 14-16). The unvarying dodecasyllabic rhythm and consonant rhyme of this poem additionally emphasize the persistence of beloved storybooks through memory in disenchanted adulthood. In **"Los maderos de San Juan"** (**"The Wood of Saint John"**) Silva also contrasts an unchanging nursery rhyme with the tragic changes the human being experiences (*Libro de versos* 11-13). In **"Día de difuntos"** (**"Day of the Dead"**), he pessimistically juxtaposes the solemn bells that ring eternally for the dead with the brittle, crystalline voice of the hour bell that flippantly measures the inconstancy of human sentiment:

> Y hay algo angustioso e incierto
> Que mezcla a ese sonido su sonido,
> E inarmónico vibra en el concierto
> Que alzan los bronces al tocar a muerto,
>   Por todos los que han sido!
>
>   (*Libro de versos* 65)

> *And there is something anguished and uncertain,*
> *That adds to that sound its own,*
> *And inharmoniously rings in the chorus*
> *Of the bells that ring for the dead,*
>   *For all those who have been!*

Silva ruefully affirms that loved ones who have passed away remain but a day in the memory of the living. He reinforces the fugacity of memory through metrical variation. Yet he also employs repetition of lines, words, and even rhythms at various points to contrast the persistent tolling of bells with the painful recognition of human change, implicitly including his own, from innocence to disillusionment.

Bells that evoke awareness of a more innocent conception of life also peal in Castro's poetry and often inspire acute feelings of *saudade* (*Cantares gallegos* 529-532, 541-543, [*Galician Songs*]; *Follas novas* 289, 291, 314; *Sar* 458, 514). In "O toque da alba" ("The Ringing of the Bells at Dawn") her poetic voice describes the sad, grave tone of a cathedral bell and recalls how, when young, she had awakened to the ringing with hopeful anticipation. But now this constant sound is a distressing gauge of psychological change. Through apostrophe she pathetically wonders to what end the bell brings painful awareness of personal maturation. She concludes her poem by ascribing to the bell a continuity that will transcend her own final transformation: "Mais ben pronto . . . ben pronto, os meus oídos / nin te oirán na tarde nin na aurora" (*Follas novas* 302, "But very soon . . . very soon, my ears / will not hear you at dusk or at dawn"). Through repetition of verses, as well as the steady rhythm of heptasyllables and hendecasyllables, Castro stylistically reinforces regularity and continuity, as represented by the bell vis-à-vis recognition of her present pessimism.

Clearly Poe's "The Bells" (20-23) influenced Castro's "O toque da alba" (*Follas novas* 301-302), "Las campanas"

(*Sar* 537), and Silva's **"Día de difuntos"** (*Libro de versos* 64-68). Each of these writers symbolically contrasts the permanence of sounding bells with the mutable, changing human being who lives and suffers in an unpredictable world. In the case of all three authors their poems were written toward the end of their careers and are thus enriched by life experience. In his poem Poe describes four kinds of bells that swing at different periods of human life; there are sleigh bells that represent youthful innocence, wedding bells that supposedly foretell future happiness, alarm bells that relate directly to the uncertainty of existence, and funeral bells, which signify death with all of its philosophical and fearful implications. From a technical standpoint Castro's and Silva's poems also resemble "The Bells." Poe varies his meter to fit his sequence of themes and employs repetition, consonant rhyme, and onomatopoeia to build a crescendo of sound that imitates the bells that terrifyingly symbolize, as in Castro and Silva, the irrevocable flow of time. Another similarity of these poems is that the authors project human voices or attitudes on the bells. Such identification signals their impossible desire to reconcile the durability of the bells with the instability of humans, as well as their need to discover the very purpose of existence in their consciousness of the passage of time.

LIMITATIONS ON THE HUMAN BEING'S ABILITY FOR SELF-CREATION

Castro and Silva suggest that the uncertain struggle for self-creation is part of what leads to the disillusionment of adulthood. They recognize with sadness that although human beings have the potential to become and do many things, they do not have infinite potential. Specifically the authors depict the limitations that society and personal circumstances impose on human beings as they try to choose and fulfill their life projects. Castro feels restricted by social attitudes toward women authors and uses her writings to expose such injustice. She also reveals the tragic results in human terms of forced Galician emigration. Silva, for his part, depicts not only the horrors of poverty (though much less insistently than Castro) but also the artistic, cultural, and intellectual constraints of Colombian bourgeois society.

CASTRO: LIMITATIONS BECAUSE OF GENDER

As critic Marina Mayoral accurately affirms, "Rosalía, en el prólogo a *La hija del mar,* se refiere muy claramente a las limitaciones que el ser mujer impone a una escritora" (*Actas,* 1986: 342, "Rosalía, in the prologue to *Daughter of the Sea,* refers very clearly to the limitations that being a woman imposes upon a female writer").[4] In this prologue Castro excuses and justifies her "pecado inmenso e indigno de perdón" (47, "immense sin unworthy of forgiveness") of having produced a book. She cites men such as Feijóo, who have supported the intellectual pursuits of women, and then names successful women who have gained fame for their political, religious, and artistic endeavors, such as Joan of Arc, Saint Teresa de Jesus, and George Sand. Castro ends her prologue with a powerful indictment of a society that tragically limits women in expressing themselves affectively and intellectually (48). In the prologue to *Follas novas* she adopts a pose of humility to soften negative public and critical response to a supposedly unfeminine inquiry into metaphysics. In an attempt to undermine censorship she belittles her capacity as a woman to formulate profound thought: "O pensamento da muller é lixeiro, góstanos como ás borboletas, voar de rosa en rosa, sobre as cousas tamén lixeiras; non é feito para nós o duro traballo da meditación" (*Follas novas* 270, "The thoughts of women are light, thus like butterflies, we like to fly from rose to rose, over the lightest of things; not for us the arduous task of thinking"). After this subtle opening, however, she proceeds to challenge furtively patriarchal society and its preconceived notions about female writing in the brief opening poem. Her challenge is in the form of an unanswered question. She affirms that she does not sing of doves and flowers, yet she is a woman:

> Daquelas que cantan as pombas i as frores
> todos din que teñen alma de muller,
> pois eu que n'as canto, Virxe da Paloma,
> ¡ai!, ¿de que a terei?
>
> (*Follas novas* 277)

> *Of those who sing of doves and flowers*
> *it is said that they have the soul of woman,*
> *I do not sing of them, most sainted Virgin,*
> *oh!, what is mine [soul] like?*

Doves and flowers represent acceptable female discourse in Castro's time, discourse consisting of the sentimental, the beautiful, and, of course, the insubstantial. Though a woman, Castro affirms that she prefers quite naturally to explore more meaningful topics. Castro herself was more fortunate than most women as she wrote with the approval and encouragement of her husband.[5] Critic Janet Pérez notes that Castro "probably experienced diminished literary discrimination thanks to Murguía's support" (33).

In *Lieders* (*Songs*) and *Las literatas* (*Literary Women*) Castro assumes a more forceful pose and passionately censures social constraints on women. She exclaims in *Lieders* that "el patrimonio de la mujer son los grillos de la esclavitud" (41, "the patrimony of woman are the shackles of slavery").[6] Under the guise of reading a letter (the *Carta a Eduarda* [*Letter to Eduarda*]) that she finds while walking on the outskirts of the city, Castro is able to reveal more directly the unfair treatment of women writers by society.[7] She divulges how the female author is the object not only of masculine but also of feminine derision: "Las mujeres ponen en [*sic!*] relieve hasta el más escondido de tus defectos y los hombres no cesan de decirte . . . que una mujer de talento es una verdadera calamidad, que vale más casarse con la burra de Balaam" (*Las literatas* 657-658, "Women bring to the fore the most hidden of your defects and men do not stop telling you . . . that a talented woman is a real misfortune, that it is better to wed the ass of Balaam"). She describes how male writers think that women should attend to more feminine pursuits, such as mending their husband's socks if they have a husband

and if not "aunque sean los del criado" (658, "even those of the manservant"), in this way reinforcing their lowly status and inconsequential purpose in life. Castro's testimony, undeniably referring to herself, exposes how the existing patriarchal system convinces women that writing is incompatible with the true measure of their worth, which lies in the conscientious execution of domestic duties:

> Cosa fácil era para algunas abrir el armario y plantarle delante de las narices los zurcidos pacientemente trabajados, para probarle que el escribir algunas páginas no le hace a todas olvidarse de sus quehaceres domésticos, pudiendo añadir que los que tal murmuran saben olvidarse, en cambio, de que no han nacido más que para tragar el pan de cada día y vivir como los parásitos.
>
> (658)

> *It was easy for some to open the closet and thrust under their noses the patiently worked darnings, to prove that writing some pages does not make all women forgo their domestic chores, and could even add that those who so gossip know how to forget, on the other hand, that they were not born only to consume their daily bread and live like parasites.*

Injustice in any form angered Castro and is evident above in her disparaging tone. She creates an alter ego in her character Mara (*Flavio*), a young woman who feels social pressure and struggles pathetically to justify her literary vocation to herself. Poignantly Castro describes how Mara, out of shame, needs to hide her verses, "cuyos renglones ella hubiera preferido borrar quizá con su propia sangre antes de que un ojo profano detuviese en ellos su imprudente mirada" (299, "whose lines she would have preferred to erase perhaps with her own blood rather than have a profane eye scan them with its imprudent glance"). Mara reflects the attitudes of society concerning "correct" female behavior, which precludes expressing thoughts and true emotions in written form.

In *El caballero de las botas azules* (*The Gentleman of the Blue Boots*) Castro points out an important reason why women's potential is limited from the start. In the character of Dorotea she reveals that the prevailing mindset of educators is that it is actually their duty to provide an inferior education to young women.[8] Satirically, Castro depicts the proud Dorotea's conversation with Melchor, the young sexton engaged to Dorotea's niece and charge, Mariquita. Dorotea prides herself in preserving Mariquita's intellectual and worldly ignorance, presenting it as an asset to her future spouse: "Eso sí; no sabe nada de nada y no como otras, que en todo quieren meterse y aprender lo que no les conviene. . . . Cieguita la tengo, como un gatito recien nacido" (59, "Rather she knows nothing about anything not like others, who would have a hand in everything and learn what is not good for them to know. . . . Blind I keep her, like a newborn kitten"). With typical fairmindedness Castro represents Dorotea as an obscurantist who fervently opposes a man, fellow schoolteacher Ricardito Majón, arguing for a liberal education for young women (184). Castro thus shows that women share some of the blame for their lack of intellectual freedom, as they sometimes condemn their own gender to ignorance.

LIMITATIONS BECAUSE OF POVERTY

Silva, like Castro, portrays how circumstances may impede self-realization. He describes, for instance, the limits that poverty imposes on the human being's potential by showing the inevitable fate of poor women of the time.[9] He depicts an impoverished young woman who, left pregnant and abandoned, bitterly descends into a life of prostitution (*Intimidades* 163-164). His wealthy protagonist walks through poor London neighborhoods, observing the "caras marchitas de chicuelas desvergonzadas, corroídas ya por el vicio, y que tienen todavía aire de inocencia no destruida por la incesante venta de sus pobres caricias inhábiles" (*De sobremesa* 279, "worn faces of shameless young girls, corrupted already by vice, who still keep an air of innocence not destroyed by the incessant selling of their poor, clumsy caresses" [*After-Dinner Chat*]). In **"El Recluta" ("The Recruit")** Silva also represents how a poor man is drafted into the army and dies tragically. His mother leads, as he did before, a meaningless life in her poverty (*Poesías varias* 104-105 [*Miscellaneous Poems*]). It is important to remember, however, that although Silva sympathizes with the poor, he does not identify with the poor in his writings as Castro does. He describes their plight from an aristocratic distance. Castro, on the other hand, most closely associated with the humble folk and was always very conscious of the social aspect of her work.

In relating to the poor Castro particularly praises the nobleness of those who suffer in silence (*Follas novas* 407).[10] Through her poetic adaptation of a Galician story about an orphan who reaches adulthood in abject poverty and must beg for a living, Castro illustrates how poverty dehumanizes and limits possibilities for self-affirmation because "donde houbera / pobreza, e soledade e desventura, / groira, dicha e querer correndo pasan" (*Cantares gallegos* 582, "where there is poverty, loneliness and misfortune, / glory, happiness and love flee" [*Galician Songs*]).[11] The slaughter of a pig, in which Vidal does not participate, represents the good living, which lies beyond the poor (*Cantares gallegos* 584).

In particular, Castro describes how her impoverished, unemployed Galician countrymen often had to seek work in other areas of Spain or Portugal, as well as in Latin America.[12] Poverty robs Galicians of the possibility of staying in their beloved homeland:

> ¡Van a deixa-la patria! . . .
> Forzoso, mais supremo sacrificio.
> A miseria está negra en torno deles,
> ¡ai!, i adiante está o abismo! . . .
>
> (*Follas novas* 406)

> *They are going to leave the homeland! . . .*
> *Necessary, supreme sacrifice.*
> *The most abject misery surrounds them,*
> *oh!, before them is the abyss! . . .*

Exclamations convey the intensity of Castro's empathy. The unjust and arbitrary aspects of forced emigration un-

questionably influenced her view of existence. In answer to poet Ventura Ruiz Aguilera's query as to whether the Galician bagpipe sings or cries, Castro unhesitantly responds, as she thinks of the Galician emigres, "eu podo decirche: / Non canta, que chora" (*Cantares gallegos* 605, "I can say to you: It does not sing, rather it cries"). In this poem Castro describes not only how the poverty-stricken Galicians must leave a land that cannot sustain them but also how the rest of Spain has tragically forgotten Galicia. Castro continually depicts Galicia as the abandoned child of Spain, battling the perception "que Galicia é o rincón máis despreciable da terra" (*Cantares gallegos* 490, "that Galicia is the most despicable corner of the earth"). Metaphorically she links Galicia to her prevailing theme of orphanhood because of the mass exodus of its men: "Galicia, sin homes quedas / que te poidan traballar. / Tés, en cambio, orfos e orfas" (*Follas novas* 407, "Galicia, you are left without men / to work the land. / You are left with orphans"). She particularly comments on the distressing results of emigration on women and children (*El primer loco* 684 [*The First Madman*]). Castro also expresses anguish at the fact that even when poor Galicians attempt to better their lot by emigrating to places where work is available, they do not always succeed. She emphasizes the anxiety caused by this uncertainty as she compares the Galician emigrants to doves driven away from their native nest by the fox and kite: Galicians leave their homeland to aid their families, perhaps only to find withered fruit in other plains (*Sar* 491). In addition to describing these physical hardships, Castro also conveys the psychological impact of emigration and the acute loneliness it engenders as spouses, fathers, brothers, and sons depart. She describes with sadness how physical subsistence becomes the primary objective of life and denies personal fulfillment. Perhaps, as critic Rof Carballo maintains, Castro's own lack of a father image when she was growing up allows her to express with greater artistic depth the pain of the widows of the living and the dead: "La ausencia del padre, emigrado muchas veces, es un factor nada menospreciable en la constitución del alma galaica. La niña no tiene 'imago paternal,' núcleo viril sobre el que cristalizar lo más profundo de su ser" (121, "The absence of the father, often an emigrant, is a factor not to be discounted in the formation of the Galician soul. The little girl lacks a father image, manly nucleus on which to crystallize the deepest part of her being").[13]

LIMITATIONS BECAUSE OF SOCIETY

As with Castro, Silva reveals constraints to self-actualization. Particularly he points out the circumscription he experiences in Colombian bourgeois society. Through his characters, especially José Fernández, his alter ego (Orjuela, 1976: 19), he expresses the intellectual and cultural void that exists among the general public and seriously limits motivation and personal achievement. Fernández categorically renounces "la vida burguesa sin emociones y sin curiosidades" (*De sobremesa* 233, "middle-class life without emotions and interests"), which he perceives as mediocre and vulgar. Cynically he explains to friends, who insist he not squander his literary talents, that readers lack apperception and sensitivity to appreciate his poems.[14] In a voice that becomes increasingly vehement Fernández asks his friend Saenz, "¿Ya no recuerdas el artículo de Andrés Ramírez en que me llamó asqueroso pornógrafo y dijo que mis versos eran una mezcla de agua bendita y de cantáridas? Pues esa suerte correría el poema que escribiera" (236, "Don't you remember anymore the article of Andrés Ramírez in which he called me a disgusting pornographer and said that my verses were a mixture of holy water and blisters? The same fate would await any I poem I were to write"). While thinking about the essence of life, Fernández poignantly expresses his sense of isolation (233). He stands apart from other characters because he cannot accept, as they do, the incoherence and mystery of life. Yet ultimately, he gives up his search for impossible answers to existence, as well as his art, which so few understand. According to Dr. Charvet, he must live simply and without questions if he is to lead a normal life (314).

Similarly, in his poem **"El mal del siglo"** (*Gotas amargas* 74, **"Mal du siécle"** [*Bitter Drops*]), Silva describes how a patient's statements of alienation fall on the deaf ears of a doctor who, like the doctors in *De sobremesa* (285, 314), attends mainly to the body without penetrating the deeper sources of human malaise, such as the clash between the sensitive, intelligent human being with the mediocrity and harshness of society. The patient's reflections about life, his feelings of hopeless maladjustment, and his obvious learning contrast with the superficial remedy of the doctor for his depression. The dialogic format of the poem further opposes patient and doctor. Through the doctor Silva exposes the intellectual deficiency of a society filled with easy solutions, which concentrates wholly on the physical rather than on the philosophical aspects of life. Melancholy, boredom, and disillusionment characterize the patient's malady, which parallels the world-weariness of the early French romantics, who suffered the *mal de siécle*. The patient resembles the young philosopher of **"Psicopatía"** (*Libro de versos* 58-60, **"Mental Disorder"**), as both characters' fruitless reflections on life ultimately lead them to despair and prevent their social integration. Through the ignorant doctor Silva criticizes a society that feels threatened in its mediocrity by the philosopher's intellectualization of life. Indeed, society treats the introspective philosopher as if diseased and punishes him with ostracism.[15]

The Human Being's Inability to Escape Limitations

Acknowledging the insufficiency of human life, Castro and Silva thematically represent a desire to escape the limitations of existence. The contemplative tendency to embellish everyday life through dreams, the aspiration to elevate reality to a higher plane, to transform the real into the ideal, is consistent throughout Castro's and Silva's works. Through the image of soaring, Castro represents a human being's dream of transcending the baseness of existence:

Mas aun sin alas cree o sueña que cruza el aire, los espacios,
y aun entre el lodo se ve limpio, cual de la nieve el copo blanco.

(Sar 500)

Even without wings she believes or dreams that she flies through the air, through space,
and even in the mud she imagines herself clean, as the snowflake is white.

Because of the inadequacies of life, Castro shows how the frightened human being may choose to live in a partial dream world as a means of psychological survival: "Astros y fuentes y flores, no murmuréis de mis sueños; / sin ellos, ¿cómo admiraros, ni cómo vivir sin ellos?" (*Sar* 519, "Stars and fountains and flowers, do not whisper about my dreams; / without them, how to admire you or how to live without them?"). However, she also represents an awareness of dreaming at a very conscious level; she is no longer a child who confuses the realms of dreams and reality (*Sar* 488). She sees her graying hair and the frost in the fields yet continues to envision the eternal spring of life (*Sar* 519). Dreams allow Castro to preserve some of the fresh hopefulness of youth. However, despite this tendency to drift into make-believe worlds (*Follas novas* 361-362; *Sar* 466, 487-488, 489-490, 499-500, 501, 519), the rational prevails in her works because she wishes to expose the radical insufficiency of being human. Most urgently, she wishes to portray the harshness of daily life for women and children living in an impoverished land (*Cantares gallegos* 555-556, 557-561, 598-601; *Follas novas* 272, 299, 306, 368-369, 374-376, 399, 407, 414-415, 428-429, 437-438; *Sar* 493, 502-503). Her conceptual imagery often supports stylistically a poetic vision directed firmly to this world. In fact, she shows how angst can arise from the violent juxtaposition of the human being's dream with the strictures of reality: "siempre a soñar condenado, / nunca puede sosegar" (*Sar* 501, "always condemned to dream, / never at rest").

By contrast, Silva typically employs the realistic only for shock effect, as in the closing lines of **"Psicopatía"** (*Libro de versos* 60). He generally expresses the wish to avoid a reality he consistently depicts as cruel and which he cannot change (*Libro de versos* 8-9, 27, 50, 76-77; *Intimidades* 129, 131, 134, 137, 142, 148-150, 154-155, 161-162, 165, 167, 181, 201-202, 203, 207). Although both he and Castro at times portray dreaming as a technique for adapting to existence, the boundary between dreams and life is more clearly defined in Castro than in Silva. Indeed, Silva's **"Futura"** (**"Future"**) is a criticism of a society that rejects the dreamy idealism of Don Quixote (*Gotas amargas* 82-83, [*Bitter Drops*]). Although Silva's authorship of **"Nidos"** (**"Nests"**) is still unconfirmed, the imagery and conclusion certainly are characteristic of Silva: "¡Descansad en el mundo de los sueños / Y en la calma infinita de las cosas!" (Orjuela, 1990: 221, "Rest in the world of dreams / And the infinite calm of things!"). In **"Las noches del hogar"** (**"Nights at Home"**) Silva reinforces his theme of desiring refuge from the "movible océano" (*Intimidades* 162, "moving ocean"), that is, the unstable world. There is the sense in these verses that Silva's poetic voice wishes to hide from the pain of life and shield his identity from society at large. Silva's simile likening the conch to a home, symbolic of the womb, and pearls to humans inside the womb expresses another more subtle view of his psyche and, by extension, of his writing. When a foreign substance, like a grain of sand or a parasite, enters the body of a mollusk, the nacre-forming cells cover the invading substance until the foreign body is enclosed, and the pearl comes into being. The pearl is therefore the product of something completely isolated, independent, and removed. Silva's writings, like exquisite pearls, are a tangible attempt to insulate himself from a world that was a constant irritant. Silva usually represents life in his poetry in more impressionistic terms than Castro. Whenever reality pierces too deeply, he attempts to reach above it, creating worlds of softer contours. He fills his writing with insulated interiors and muted lights that implicitly reveal a longing for the softness lacking in his own frenetic life (*De sobremesa* 229).

In many of Silva's works the beauty of life is relegated to dreams. Through dreams, for instance, he represents a desire to achieve idealized romantic intimacy with women in faraway, fictionalized settings. While listening to his beloved play the piano, Silva's poetic voice imagines a scene in which both are suddenly transported to a Gothic castle, he as a blond page and she as a noblewoman (*Libro de versos* 27). Silva's alter ego, his novelistic protagonist José Fernández, also engages in dreamy reverie. He fantasizes about the deceased Russian writer and artist María Bashkirtseff, romantically delineating a feminine counterpart of himself (*De sobremesa* 241). When he first sees Helena Scilly Dancourt, the fifteen-year-old who becomes his amorous obsession, he also slips away to a realm of illusion as he visualizes the two of them together (*De sobremesa* 272). When Helena and her father leave with no forwarding address, Fernández embarks on a relentless but futile search as he pursues her image around the world. His physician Dr. Rivington insists that Fernández look for the real Helena, not the vision he has created (*De sobremesa* 287). Rivington warns Fernández that "el sueño es un veneno para usted" (*De sobremesa* 298, "dreaming is poisonous for you"). Silva is clearly aware that persistent dreaming in which life and people are idealized (to relieve psychological pressure in contact with bitter reality) can lead to permanent maladjustment. He shows that the contrast between the real and the imagined ends inevitably in painful disillusionment. In the case of his novelistic protagonist fantasy and reality become inextricably fused, and Fernández is therefore incapable of enjoying a fulfilling existence.

Silva also portrays the dangers of becoming too immersed in dreams in his poem **"Lentes ajenos"** (*Gotas amargas* 76-77, **"Borrowed Spectacles"**). Here he presents the schizophrenic Juan de Dios, who utilizes books to avoid engaging fully in life. From a young age Juan de Dios imitates various literary characters with his own lovers. Such excessive imagining prevents him from ever experiencing meaningful love with another human being or establishing a happy, integrated family life. Although acknowledging the temporary regenerative power of dreaming that sustains Juan de Dios, in the poetic sequel, **"Cápsulas"** (*Gotas amargas* 78, **"Capsules"**), Silva graphically underscores the danger of living in a dream world; when real suffering penetrates the fragile shield, the human being remains defenseless. When love and life become painful to Juan de Dios and he has no recourse to honest and open communication with other human beings, because of inability to communicate, he commits suicide in his extreme isolation (*Gotas amargas* 78).

More often than Castro, Silva contrasts the beauty and tenderness of dreams with reality in order to express more vividly the tragedy of human life:

> Mas cuando el alma en sus ensueños flota,
> La realidad asoma de improviso
> No más resuena la encantada nota. . . .
> Brotan espinas do la rosa brota,
> Y en crüel se torna el paraíso.
>
> (*Intimidades* 149)

> *When the soul floats on dreams,*
> *Reality suddenly intrudes*
> *No more can the enchanted note be heard. . . .*
> *Thorns spring where the rose blossoms,*
> *And there is cruelty in paradise.*

The rose symbolizes a fragile dream, the thorns the harshness of life. Acknowledging the perils of dreaming, however, Silva recognizes in his **"Prólogo al poema intitulado 'Bienaventurados los que lloran' de Rivas Frade"** (**"Prologue to the Poem Entitled 'Blessed Are Those Who Cry' by Rivas Frade"**) that certain people are more prone to dreaming and introspection than others. In explaining the spiritual affinity between writers Rivas Frade, Heine, Bécquer, José Angel Porras, and Antonio Escobar, he could easily have been writing about himself:

> Todos esos poetas son espíritus delicadísimos y complicados a quienes su misma delicadeza enfermiza ahuyenta de las realidades brutales de la vida e imposibilita para encontrar en los amores fáciles y en las felicidades sencillas la satisfacción de sus deseos; a quienes lastiman a cada paso las piedras del camino y las durezas de los hombres, y que se refugian en sus sueños.
>
> (366)

> *All these poets are very delicate and complicated spirits whose same sickly sensitivity keeps them from the brutal realities of life and makes it impossible for them to find in easy love and simple happiness the satisfaction of their desires; they are constantly hurt by the pebbles on their path and the roughness of men, and take refuge in their dreams.*

Many critics claim that Silva also took refuge from reality by creating his character José Fernández, whom Silva consistently portrays as eluding prosaic reality.[16] Fernández is high-born, handsome, and wealthy, and he possesses superior literary talent. As critic Rafael Maya affirms:

> El gran sueño frustrado del poeta iba a cobrar vida espléndida por medio de la creación artística. *De sobremesa* es la novela de la evasión y de la compensación. De la evasión, porque le permitió a Silva sustraerse metódicamente a las vulgares necesidades que lo acuciaban, en días verdaderamente amargos, y de la compensación, porque vivió sus mejores sueños en la figura de su protagonista, que estaba modelado con los mas amplios toques de la imaginación creadora.
>
> (101-102)

> *The great frustrated dream of the poet was going to take splendid life through artistic creation.* **After-Dinner Chat** *is a novel of evasion and compensation. Evasion because it allowed Silva methodically to separate himself from the crass and vulgar needs that haunted him, in truly bitter days, and compensation, because he lived his best dreams in the person of his protagonist, construed with the most ample strokes of creative imagination.*

Castro and Silva also recognize elements of dreaming in the composition of human society itself, such as in the affirmation of an Afterlife. Reflecting on human longing for immortality, Castro wistfully writes, "Mas ¿quién sabe si en tanto hacia su fin caminan, / como el hombre, los astros con ser eternos sueñan?" (*Sar* 497, "But who knows if as they move toward their end, / like man, the stars dream of being eternal?"). Gazing at stars once adored by the Magi, Silva expresses a similar yearning without possibility of a cosmic response from the stars: "¿Por qué os calláis si estáis vivas / Y por qué alumbráis si estáis muertas? . . ." (**Libro de versos** 44, "Why are you silent if you are alive / And why do you give off light if you are dead? . . ."). The ellipsis, a privation, speaks eloquently as the words themselves. Castro's desire for immortality anthropomorphizes the cosmos, whereas Silva's longing clashes with his skepticism produced by science. Castro's experience has also taught her that her view of truth as something divine and pure is nothing but a dream, another deception, in the emptiness of existence. She describes how clouds, constantly changing, symbolize the inexistence of an immutable higher truth (*Sar* 481). At times she indicates the hollowness of dreams (*Sar* 501). Silva similarly refers to daydreams as empty (**Libro de versos** 27). Nevertheless, both authors realize that dreams are poignant testimonies to the brutal, uncertain struggle of life, provoking the need for such mental and emotional separation. Whereas Castro suggests that dreams help prevent succumbing to despair, the disparity between dreams and life ultimately leads Silva to despair.

The Lack of Guiding Principles in Human Life

Castro and Silva express deep feelings of emptiness and a longing for guiding principles to explain human existence and to help them live their lives. They especially reveal a desire for religious guidance that resembles a thirst in its intensity. Castro herself repeatedly uses the image of thirst (*Follas novas* 283, 294, 314-315, 415; *Sar* 461, 471-472, 479, 499-500, 500-501). In one poem she compares the blistering sands on the beach, untouched by the cool waves, to her soul, which thirsts for immortality among the seraphims (*Sar* 471-472). Silva also views human worship of an untenable God as a quenchless thirst, though in a more characteristically sarcastic vein:

> Tiene instantes de intensas amarguras
> la sed de idolatrar que al hombre agita,
> del Supremo Señor la faz bendita
> ya no ríe del cielo en las alturas.
>
> (*Poesías varias* 115)

> *There are moments of intense bitterness*
> *the thirst of adoration that incites man,*
> *of the Supreme Lord the blessed face*
> *does not laugh from the height of heaven.*

Nevertheless, although Castro and Silva deeply wish to believe in God, their uncertainty yields anxiety. Religious doubt prevents them from accepting Catholic doctrine unconditionally as they would like and is a further testimony to the sincerity of their religious struggle. Silva describes the human being's journey in faith as uncertain, but he ultimately considers the likelihood of an afterlife in pessimistic terms:

> Sin columna de luz, que en el desierto
> guíe su paso a punto conocido,
> continua el crüel peregrinaje,
>
> para encontrar en el futuro incierto
> las soledades hondas del olvido
> tras las fatigas del penoso viaje.
>
> (*Poesías varias* 115)

> *Without a ray of light in the desert*
> *to guide his steps to a known destination,*
> *the cruel pilgrimage continues,*
>
> *to find in the uncertain future*
> *the deep solitude of oblivion*
> *after the weariness of the hard journey.*

The column of light is very like a reference to the pillar of fire with which God led the Israelites by night toward the Promised Land (Exod. 13:22). The privation of light Silva describes indicates, therefore, the lack of a tangible spiritual presence in the emptiness of life. The sonnet format may also relate to an underlying human need for structure. In a thematically similar poem, ". . . ? . . ." (**Libro de versos** 44), Silva also refers to the agonizing limitations of human knowledge. The poetic voice tenderly probes the immensity and mystery of the universe while gazing at stars that shine in the night. The stars may symbolize Silva's spiritual struggle, that is, his unsuccessful search for religious illumination in the darkness of human existence.

Silva emphasizes how the stars shed no light on the meaning of life. There is not even the promise of daylight, which would indicate possible enlightenment in the future. The ellipses before and after the interrogative may signify the lack of understanding about the beginning and end of existence. The question Silva delicately poses at the conclusion of the poem expresses a deep desire for intercommunication between the human being and the cosmos. Yet life is in essence an unanswered and unanswerable question.

For Silva religious faith belongs to the past. He represents a society utterly lacking in Christian ethics, in which prostitution, adultery, and violence are rampant, signaling a lack of fear of divine retribution (***Intimidades*** 163-164; ***De sobremesa*** 255, 279, 334, 342). His own loss of religious faith is a source of deep personal sorrow. He contrasts how in the past the ancient Romans sought relief and solace from the emptiness of life through their belief in Christ but how today science has destroyed that faith among people:

> La fe ciega que en su regazo de sombra les ofrecía una almohada donde descansar las cabezas a los cansados de la vida, ha desaparecido del universo. El ojo humano al aplicarlo al lente del microscopio que investiga lo infinitesimal y al lente del enorme telescopio que, vuelto hacia la altura, le revela el cielo, ha encontrado, arriba y abajo, en el átomo y en la inconmensurable nebulosa, una sola materia, sujeta a las mismas leyes que nada tienen que ver con la suerte de los humanos.

> (***De sobremesa*** 335-336)

> *Blind faith which on its shadowy lap offered a pillow rest for the heads of those tired with life, has disappeared from the universe. When the human eye looks through the lens of the microscope which investigates the infinitesimal and through the lens of the enormous telescope, which pointed to the heights, reveals the heavens, it has found, above and below, in the atom and in the incommensurable nebula, only one matter, subject to the same laws which have nothing to do with the fate of humans.*

Yet Silva affirms that science, after destroying faith, is itself in no better position to provide guidelines for human life. This negative view of science is evident in **"Zoospermos"** (***Gotas amargas*** 84-86, **"Sperm"**). Through the image of renowned German scientist Cornelius van Kerinken, peering through a microscope at spermatazoids, Silva conveys not only the narrow focus of science but also the inherent limitations of humans studying themselves. He reduces science to mere speculation as van Kerinken wildly predicts what the spermatazoids would have become had they been allowed to live. Silva's sarcastic sense of humor emerges when van Kerinken calls the most minute spermatazoid a lyrical poet and the largest a scientist. But underlying such self-deprecation Silva indicates the unfortunate minimization of the professional poet and the aggrandizement of the scientist, which prevails in society to this day:

> el otro, el pequeñísimo,
> algún poeta lírico;
> y el otro, aquél enorme,
> un profesor científico
> que hubiera escrito un libro
> sobre espermatozoides.

> (85)

> *the other one, the smallest,*
> *a lyrical poet;*
> *and the other, that huge one,*
> *a professor of science*
> *who would have written a book*
> *about spermatozoa.*

Van Kerinken goes insane on realizing that science cannot answer eternal questions or truly understand human nature.

Silva reveals his stance that neither faith nor science can explain the meaning and purpose of life in his portrayal of human beings who search hopelessly, without direction, for another truth, faith, or reality to serve as support in the void of existence. **"Filosofías"** (**"Philosophy"**) is Silva's own hopeless negation of everything in life that could possibly give the human being a sense of purpose (***Gotas amargas*** 89-91). Through his poetic caricature, "Don Juan de Covadonga, un calavera, / Sin Dios, ni rey, ni ley" (***Libro de versos*** 61, "Don Juan de Covadonga, a rake, / Without God, without king, without law"), he represents the human being's unsuccessful search for religious consolation within the corruption of earthly existence. After leading a life of debauchery Don Juan de Covadonga decides to join his brother Hernando in the convent where he is a prior. However, Hernando quickly disabuses Don Juan of the notion that he will find tranquility, affirming that "todo reviste / Un aspecto satánico, mis horas / Tienen angustias indecibles" (***Libro de versos*** 62, "everything is sheathed / In a satanic aura, my hours / Have unspeakable anguish"). Enjambement supports the intentionally prosaic monotony of Hernando's long description of true convent life. Ascetic confines guarantee nothing, not even a measure of psychic peace.

In his novel Silva further portrays the difficulties and angst that human beings experience in attempting to give meaning to existence. Deeply dissatisfied with his life, his protagonist searches for an external source of guidance only to realize that none exists in a world comprising chance happenings and human fabrications. Fernández declares, "La vida. ¿Quién sabe lo que es? Las religiones no, puesto que la consideran como un paso para otras regiones; la ciencia no, porque apenas investiga las leyes que la rigen sin descubrir su causa ni su objeto" (***De sobremesa*** 234, "Life. Who knows what it is? Religions do not know, as they consider it a step to other regions; science does not know, because it barely investigates the laws that govern it without discovering its cause nor its object"). Fernández reveals his desperate desire for a plan to which he can devote his life. Silva's own depressed sense of worthlessness is audible in Fernández's searing condemnation of what he perceives as his desultory existence:

Ese obrero que pasa por la calle con su blusa azul lavada por la mujercita cariñosa y que tiene las manos ásperas por el trabajo duro, vale más que tú porque quiere a alguien, y el anarquista que guillotinaron antier porque lanzó una bomba que reventó un edificio, vale más que tú porque realizó una idea que se había encarnado en él! Eres un miserable que gasta diez minutos en pulirse las uñas como una cortesana y un inútil hinchado de orgullo monstruoso! . . .

(**De sobremesa** 250)

That worker who walks down the street with his blue shirt washed by his loving wife and whose hands are roughened by hard work, is worthier than you because he loves someone, and the anarchist who was guillotined the day before yesterday because he threw a bomb which blew up a building is worthier than you because he turned into action an idea that had taken hold of him! You are a miserable being who spends ten minutes polishing your nails like a courtesan and a good-for-nothing swollen by a monstrous pride! . . .

Tragically, none of Fernández's quests to find a guiding norm are wholly successful. He does not find consolation or anything to direct him "por entre las negruras de la vida" (**De sobremesa** 282, "through the darkness of life"), despite the power and opportunities his wealth gives him to obtain the best medical advice available, to travel as he pleases, to purchase what he wishes, and to associate at leisure with high society. He is ultimately left with an incorrigible sense of emptiness, and consumes his life in worthless dissipation (**De sobremesa** 231).

Like Silva, Castro reveals that neither faith nor science provides a successful means for guiding human beings. Throughout her works she repeats images of the desert and the abyss that convey feelings of emptiness without the support of faith: "¡Que no fondo ben fondo das entrañas / hai un deserto páramo" (*Follas novas* 281, "Down deep inside of one's being / lies a bleak desert"). Castro affirms that in the innermost core of the human being lies an abyss that neither laughter nor happiness can fill. Only suffering fills the emptiness. Yet suffering too is baseless for the skeptical human being and leads to self-destruction as only religious faith grants meaning to human pain. When Castro desperately searches for God, all she finds is "la soledad inmensa del vacío" (*Sar* 465, "the immense loneliness of nothingness"). The loss of faith results in feelings of insecurity: "¿Por que, en fin, Dios meu, / a un tempo me faltan / a terra i o ceu?" (*Follas novas* 300, "Why, then, my God, / I lack at the same time / both the earth and the heavens?"). As her religious faith dwindles, Castro recognizes, as does Silva, that science also fails to provide a satisfactory solution for human beings seeking direction. Castro compares the light of a firefly with that generated by a star, concluding that science is unable to answer even basic questions such as the endurance of things in the world:

Una luciérnaga entre el musgo brilla
y un astro en las alturas centellea;
abismo arriba, y en el fondo abismo;

¿qué es al fin lo que acaba y lo que queda?
En vano el pensamiento
indaga y busca en lo insondable, ¡oh ciencia!
Siempre, al llegar al término, ignoramos
qué es al fin lo que acaba y lo que queda.

(*Sar* 464)

*A firefly shines amid the moss
and a star blinks in the heights;
an abyss above, and an abyss below;
at the last what ends and what remains?
In vain the mind
searches and looks for answers in the unfathomable,
    oh science!
Always, when we arrive at the finish, we are ignorant
of what ends and what remains.*

The imagery in line three can be related to Genesis (1:1) and the darkness of earth and sky before God brought forth light. Castro equates light with a search for spiritual illumination. The light from the firefly and the star contrasts feebly with the darkness of night and relates symbolically to the impotence of human attempts to understand existence. In these lines Castro makes comparisons involving opposites in terms of size, space, depth, and also employs words that imply opposition (*arriba* [above] and *el fondo* [below]; *acaba* [ends] and *queda* [remains]; *indaga* [searches] and *insondable* [unfathomable]) to show the complex, contradictory nature of life. Science, that is, human reason, cannot penetrate beneath or beyond the perplexities of existence to ascertain with certainty if God exists. Addressing doctors, Castro declares that science is incapable of curing or comprehending deeply rooted human suffering:

O meu mal i o meu sofrir
é o meu propio corazón:
¡quitaimo sin compasión!
Despois: ¡faceme vivir!

(*Follas novas* 366)

*My sickness and my suffering
is my own heart:
wrench it from me without compassion!
Then: make me live!*

The alliterating *m* in lines one and two skillfully imitates the sound of human moaning, reinforced by the rhyming of *sofrir* (suffering) and *vivir* (live). For Castro, as for Silva, living and suffering are hopelessly and inexplicably interconnected.

In another poem Castro affirms that in the past, faith guided the hermit to the desert. The hermit symbolizes all humanity who once believed utterly in God. "Desert" for the hermit implicitly signifies the domain of the sun, that is, of heavenly radiance and divine revelation. For Castro it represents a negative landscape in its emptiness as she writes from the perspective of one who has shed blind faith. Like the faithful of former times, she describes how scientists of her day also arrive at the threshold of nothingness. Yet neither the hermit nor the scientist perceives the illusory nature of the reality they have themselves created. Castro concludes that she does not await Ulysses; that is, she does not await a savior in any form but instead affirms that, like Penelope, "tejo y destejo sin cesar mi tela, / pensando que ésta es del destino humano / la incansable tarea" (*Sar* 544, "I ravel and unravel my cloth incessantly, / thinking that this is in human life / the unending task"). Through this image she emphasizes the radical insufficiency of being human as there is no predetermined design or purpose to life that human beings can discover by faith or science.

Castro writes that, like herself, the new generation is adrift "sin paz, sin rumbo e sin fe" (*Follas novas* 298, "without peace, without direction and without faith"). She shows how society no longer turns to religion for direction, as faith, particularly among the young, is fading (*Flavio* 317). Churches are empty (*Sar* 465, 516), and the sacred alter is covered with dust (*Sar* 465). Like Silva, Castro maintains that Christian values are no longer socially operative; there is a collective disregard for the emotional and physical well-being of others, including children (*Follas novas* 368-369). Even as she knows society's search will ultimately be fruitless, she reveals the directionless behavior of those seeking a system of beliefs for guidance:

> ¡Aturde la confusa gritería
> que se levanta entre la turba inmensa!
> Ya no saben qué quieren ni qué piden;
> mas embriagados de soberbia, buscan
> un ídolo o una víctima a quien hieran.
>
> (*Sar* 502)

> *Bewildering is the noisy confusion*
> *that arises from the immense crowd!*
> *They no longer know what they want or what they*
>   *seek;*
> *but inebriated with pride, they search*
> *for an idol or a victim to injure.*

The expression "ya no" ("no longer") indicates that the masses have lost the orientation they once enjoyed. Not sure where to find meaning, a confused society destroys and inflicts pain arbitrarily. In these images Castro thus portrays the lack of transcending purpose in this life, in which suffering, injustice, and confusion prevail. Similarly, Silva believes that lawlessness results from the decline of Catholicism in society. In one poem nihilists "en una súbita explosión / . . . / Vuelan estatua y orador" (*Gotas amargas* 83, "in a sudden explosion / . . . / burst both the statue and the orator").[17]

In their agonizing conception of human life as radical insufficiency Castro and Silva show how people live without support of any kind. Castro often employs imagery of sickness, depicting pathetically human beings who are infirm and in need of religious sustenance. Adjectives and nouns indicating an absence of health are also frequent in Silva's works reflecting the uncertainty of life and his view of human beings as imperfect, needy, and fragile.

Biological orphanhood, symbolic of spiritual orphanhood, is also a thematic constant in Castro's works (*Cantares gallegos* 500, 581; *Follas novas* 272, 282, 293, 309, 316, 354, 369, 407, 425, 432, 438; *Sar* 465, 467, 512, 516). Plaintively she identifies with the moon, "Astro das almas orfas" (*Follas novas* 309, "Star of orphaned souls"). In *La hija del mar* (*Daughter of the Sea*) Castro presents a succession of women (Teresa, Esperanza, Candora) who are illegitimate, orphaned, and abandoned. Movingly, Teresa declares that "las caricias maternales son el rocío que da vida a esas pobres plantas que salen al mundo en un día de dolor" (82, "maternal caresses are the life-giving dew to those poor plants that come to the world in a day of suffering"), thus emphasizing the human need for security. Flavio, Rosa (*Flavio*), and Luis (*El primer loco*) are also orphans who desperately seek meaning in life, which, significantly, they do not find. Likewise, Silva's disoriented novelistic protagonist is an orphan. During his psychoanalysis of José Fernández, Rivington implies that Fernández's desperate groping for spiritual guidance, which has crystallized in an impossible search for the perfect, virginal woman, results from his initial orphanhood (*De sobremesa* 292). He lost his mother and other family members at a tender age. On the death of his grandmother he feels completely forsaken (*De sobremesa* 251).

CONCLUSION

Unlike Silva, Castro associates herself throughout her writings with humble things and persons. In one poem her speaker is a "diminuto insecto de alas de oro" (*Sar* 533, "tiny insect with golden wings") and in another a peasant who has neither food nor firewood in her bare home (*Follas novas* 374-376). As Castro embraces the concerns of humankind, she especially highlights the deprivation that women and children endure through no fault of their own. She is aware that society perceives her as inherently inferior because she is a woman and imposes strict guidelines on her conduct. It was relatively easy for her, therefore, to identify psychologically with the deprived and the lowly, especially considering the circumstances of her birth. Anything she achieved apart from her husband was greeted by surprise and, in the case of her writing, as an outright affront. Silva, on the other hand, affiliates himself mostly with the grandiose, disdaining the mediocrity of society. He imagines living in castles (*Libro de versos* 27) and exalts Bolívar, who possesses "majestad de semidiós" (*Libro de versos* 17, "majesty of a demi-god"). His constant references to items of luxury also contrast sharply with Castro's imagery, usually taken from nature.

Although Silva's and Castro's response to the limitations of society sometimes differs, both felt restricted by nineteenth-century attitudes. Society expected nothing of Castro because she was a woman and consistently downplayed her literary achievements. Silva, conversely, absorbed his family's and society's high expectations of him as a man, especially with regard to financial security. Silva believed that he had fallen short of these expectations. He was a poet and philosopher at heart, not a businessman.

Through his alter ego in *De sobremesa,* a novel filled with wish fulfillment, Silva tragically denounces literary pursuits in favor of materialistic ones. He often uses writing as an unsuccessful attempt to overcome limitations, whereas Castro views writing as a means of exposing injustice wherever she has found it.

Both authors vividly portray experience as negative, with the past denying future endeavors and influencing their general outlook on life. As traditional preconceptions about the meaning and purpose of existence disappear, people remain with nothing but to create a reality based on this experience. Yet Castro and Silva wonder how human beings can create a reality they can tolerate when their experience is only pain and suffering. The two writers convey the deep feelings of emptiness that result from their realization that humans must attempt alone to create their lives in a world permeated by uncertainty. Castro often captures the terrifying force and ubiquity of unforeseen misfortune: "Teño medo á desgracia traidora / que vén, e que nunca se sabe onde vén" (*Follas novas* 279, "I am afraid of treacherous misfortune / that comes, and can never be foreseen"). Silva similarly writes of the dismaying uncertainty inherent in existence: "Se mezclan a nuestras vidas, / De la ausencia o de la muerte, / Las penas desconocidas" (**Libro de versos** 57, "They blend into our lives, / From absence or from death, / unfamiliar suffering"). Both often use interrogatives to reveal their metaphysical angst as they question traditional notions about life. Their frequent questioning, irregular rhythms, and use of ellipses display a similar sense of inner chaos, confusion, and fear in the absence of established values. Both are well aware of the anguish resulting from their conception of existence.[18] Their attitude toward life is genuinely and frighteningly speculative. In a church Castro questions in despair, "¿Qué somos? ¿Qué es la muerte?" (*Sar* 464, "What are we? What is death?"). Similarly, Silva kneels and asks Mother Earth in desperate tones, "¿Qué somos? ¿A do vamos?" (*Gotas amargas* 75, "What are we? Where are we going?") He further implores, "Mi angustia sacia y a mi ansiedad contesta" (*Gotas amargas* 75, "Sate my anguish and answer my anxiety"). For Castro and Silva, suffering has not only very specific outer causes, such as death or poverty, but is also the result of their futile search for enlightenment about human existence. In simple language and sincere voices they transform their suffering into works of art.

Notes

1. Childhood seems to have formed but a brief period of happiness in Castro's and Silva's own lives. Murguía probably refers to Castro's early awareness of social reproach and curiosity as the illegitimate daughter of a priest and a woman of noble descent when he writes, "¡Y cuán amargos y tristes para los que, tocando apenas en los límites de la juventud, tienen ya que luchar con la tristísima realidad!" (1944: 137, "How bitter and sad for those who, barely into their youth, have to fight already sad reality!"). Silva, for his part, had trouble mixing with schoolmates. He was always conspicuous for his intellectual precocity and arrestingly elegant attire. His aloof demeanor and scrupulous manners earned him the nickname "José Presunción." Silva poignantly wished, however, to behave like other children his age:

   > An introvert by nature, he compensated for his lack of communication with others by displaying his superior ability as a student. However, the intensity of his desire to be like the very children whom he exasperated is revealed in an anecdote portraying his excessive behavior when advised by a friend of the family to stop acting like an adult and to indulge in more childish pastimes, like throwing stones at the pigeons. A short time later, José Asunción was observed on the roof getting ready to throw an eleven-or-twelve-pound rock at the pigeons in the courtyard.

   > (Osiek, 1978: 23)

   Castro's and Silva's sensitivity and precociousness made them painfully aware of personal incongruency. In Silva's case, as he grew older he consciously cultivated idiosyncrasies in passive aggression against a world that disdained him and that he in turn disdained.

2. Related to the Spanish *soledad,* the word *saudade* derives from the Latin *solitatem* (Kulp-Hill 49). *Saudade* connotes sorrowful loneliness, nostalgia, and sad recollections. Kulp defines *saudade* as "one of the most Galician (and Portuguese) of sentiments. It is a complicated emotion, a longing for someone or something absent—for a parted loved one, for the dead, for the homeland or for happier former days" (144). See Ramón Piñeiro's article "A saudade en Rosalía" for a thorough treatment of this theme.

3. Unamuno discerningly wrote, "Tal vez se cortó Silva por propia mano el hilo de la vida por no poder seguir siendo niño en ella, porque el mundo le rompía con brutalidades el sueño poético de la infancia" (1979: 421, "Perhaps Silva himself cut the thread of his own life because he could no longer continue to be a child as the world broke the poetic dream of childhood with its harshness"). Unamuno has captured the essential tragedy of Silva's life. In his youth Silva was an idealist who truly believed in the fulfillment of hopes and dreams. As he continued to live, he grew undeceived. His experience with creditors, including his own grandmother, affected him deeply. Continually the victim of adverse circumstances, Silva became a pessimist who could only look back longingly to simpler days. His tragic financial situation and constant retrospection defeated him.

4. For articles treating feminist perspectives see Matilde Albert Robatto, *Rosalía de Castro y la condición feminina* (1981, *Rosalía de Castro and the Feminine Position*) and Andrés Pociña, "La crítica feminista ante la obra de Rosalía de Castro" ("Feminist Criti-

cism and the Work of Rosalía de Castro") in *Crítica y ficción literaria: mujeres españolas contemporáneas* (1989, *Criticism and Literary Fiction: Contemporary Spanish Women*).

5. Murguía wrote the first critical article on Castro's work, titled "La flor, poesías de la señorita Rosalía de Castro" ("The Flower, Poems of Miss Rosalía de Castro"), published on May 12, 1857, in *La Iberia,* a Madrid newspaper. Murguía clairvoyantly wonders in his article whether Castro "ha nacido para ser algo más que una mujer, tal vez para legar un nombre honoroso a su patria" (Kulp-Hill 35, "has been born to be more than a woman, perhaps to bequeathe an honorable name to her homeland"). Critics dispute Murguía's claim that he was personally unacquainted with his future wife when he wrote his article (Mayoral, *Rosalía de Castro* 21-22). Although Murguía probably did know her when he evaluated *La flor,* this does not diminish his unusual perspicacity, especially when comparing the relative value of this first volume of poetry with Castro's later literary accomplishments.

6. In a letter to her husband we can clearly hear Castro's frustration with nineteenth-century parameters regarding female behavior: "Si yo fuera hombre, saldría en este momento y me dirigiría a un monte, pues el día está soberbio; tengo, sin embargo, que resignarme a permanecer encerrada en mi gran salón. *Sea.*" (*Cartas* 602, "If I were a man, I would leave this minute and go to a mountain, as it is a beautiful day; I must, however, resign myself and remain cooped up in my grand parlor. So be it." *Correspondence.*)

7. Machado da Rosa affirms that Castro may have published *Las literatas* as a reaction to rumors that Murguía was helping her with her writing (74). Birute Ciplijauskaite puts Castro's literary woes in historical context: "Hay que recordar que en comparación con el resto de Europa, en la España de mediados del siglo XIX la mujer como creadora aún apenas estaba admitida" (323, "It should be remembered that compared to the rest of Europe, in mid-nineteenth century Spain, women as creators were hardly accepted").

8. Castro herself as an adolescent attended a school sponsored by the 'Sociedad Económica de Amigos del País' (Economic Society of Friends of the Region). Pérez affirms that the name of the school "implies low-cost schooling with emphasis on Galicia and things Galician" (31). It seems that Castro's education was actually rather scanty. Her preserved manuscripts are filled with spelling errors (Mayoral, 1974: 574). Murguía also confirms that Castro possessed "un temperamento por entero musical. De haber tenido una educación a propósito, hubiera sido una tan gran compositora como fue gran poeta" (1993, 449, "a wholly musical temperament. Had she been educated differently, she would have become as

great a composer as she was a poet"). Through references and quotations in her first novel it is evident, though, that Castro read widely on her own.

Castro believed in promoting education for women. She encouraged young aspiring women authors (Carballo Calero 311), and in 1872 she went to live in Santiago so that her daughter Alejandra could perfect her drawing skills (Costa Clavell 80-81).

9. Certainly Silva's precarious financial situation limited his literary output. According to Miramón, Silva's mother blamed the family's continuing financial plight on Silva's penchant for writing: "El claro sentido mercantil de doña Vicenta sabía medir toda la gravedad de la situación, y desesperada en su escasez, achacaba los desastres al afán de Silva por los versos y a su afición a la lectura" (120, "With her clear business sense doña Vicenta was able to gauge the seriousness of the situation, and desperate in her financial straits, blamed the disasters on Silva's love of verses and desire to read"). However, doña Vicenta's grandson, Camilo de Brigard Silva, countered Miramón's assertion, affirming that his grandmother was supportive of her son in every way (Osiek, 1978: 34).

Silva's life truly became a financial nightmare following the death of his father on June 1, 1887. Silva wrote a one-hundred-page letter to Guillermo Uribe, his main creditor, explaining why he was unable to repay his debts. Uribe insisted, however, that Silva immediately repay both the business debts owed to him by his father and the money Silva had borrowed for such necessities as Elvira's funeral. Silva became involved in a long series of bankruptcy proceedings involving not only Uribe but other creditors. Ironically, Silva was not allowed to accept employment of any kind until all of the proceedings were terminated. According to Osiek,

> Uribe did not want to help Silva, and although he had been a longtime friend and business associate of his father he developed a violent antipathy toward the son of his old friend, and actually tried to harm him as much as he could. Not only did he use his influence to keep the debtors from agreement among themselves, but he was one of the first to notify the banks in Bogotá of Silva's likelihood of going broke, causing them to deny him the possibility of borrowing funds from them.
>
> (1978: 40-41)

10. As a sixteen-year-old witness to the horrific "Año del Hambre" (Year of the Famine) in Santiago in 1853, Castro reveals her empathy for the poor and hungry, which would become a distinguishing feature of her work. For moving testimony of this tragedy in Castro's own words, see Alonso Montero (1972: 19-20).

11. "La Choina," a childhood nurse of Castro's, taught her the songs and lore of Galicia (Kulp 2). Castro's

dialect is from the shores of the Sar River, of Santiago de Compostela and the Amabia and Ulla River areas (Kulp 42). Courteau advances the interesting theory that Castro wrote her Spanish poetic texts with the intention of codifying Galician culture through Castilian by incorporating Celtic symbols and beliefs (1991: 87).

12. *Follas novas* first appeared in 1880 in Havana, where it was financed by Galician emigrés.

13. Born February 24, 1837, María Rosalita Rita was the illegitimate daughter of thirty-three-year-old María Teresa da Cruz y Abadía, who belonged to a family of minor Galician nobility, and of thirty-nine-year-old José Martínez Viojo, "variously termed seminarian, presbiter or priest" (Pérez 31). He later served as priest in Padrón. María Francisca Martínez, a faithful servant of her mother's, first cared for Castro until she went to live with her paternal aunts in Ortuño (Albert Robatto, 1995: 126). Although illegitimate children were relatively common in Galicia because of emigration (March 104), Castro felt the rejection of society as the product of a sacrilegious union. Castro lived under her mother's care when she was between the ages of ten and thirteen. The extent of her relationship with her father is unknown. According to José Filgueira Valverde, director of the museum of Pontevedra, there were those who told Castro's descendents how she would run at night to her father's door throughout her difficult life to ask him for help (189-190).

García Sabell and Rof Carballo emphasize, as do many critics, Castro's initial orphanhood when interpreting her works. According to García Sabell, Castro is "víctima de una ausencia irreparable—la del padre" (46, "victim of an irreparable absence—that of the father"). Rof Carballo adds that "la impresión más justa con la que puede resumirse la totalidad, el conjunto, de sus poesías es ésta: Son un gran vagabundaje, un merodeo en busca del rostro maternal, en busca de esa insaciada imagen arquetípica de la Madre, que es decisiva en la vida de todo hombre" (115-116, "the most appropriate impression with which to summarize all her poetry is this: It is a broad wandering, a roaming in search of the maternal face, looking for that archetypical unsated image of the mother, which is decisive in the life of every man").

14. Silva's own genius was not recognized during his life or for years afterward. Lorenzo Marroquín, with the collaboration of José María Rivas Groot, atrociously satirized him in *Pax: Novela de Costumbres Latinoamericanas* (*Pax: Novel of Latin American Customs*). The 'Imprenta de la Luz' published the novel in Bogotá in 1907. One of the characters, S. C. Mata, was a clear caricature of Silva, whose name even mercilessly refers to the manner of Silva's death (Osiek, 1978: 45). The novel also contains an insensitive, vulgar parody of Silva's famous "Nocturno" ("Nocturne"), in which a monk commits suicide be-

cause he is afraid that he will succumb to the spell of a beautiful woman (McGrady 685-686).

15. Like Silva, Castro also shows feelings of being singled out and mocked. She compares malicious society to a pack of heartless dogs that pursue her incessantly: "Ladraban contra min, que camiñaba / casi que sin alento" (*Follas novas* 299, "They were barking against me, who was walking / already almost out of breath," *New Leaves*). As with Silva she experiences alienation because of her propensity for introspection.

16. From the works lost in *L'Amérique* Silva reconstructed only *De sobremesa* at the fortunate insistence of his friend Hernando Villa (Orjuela, 1990: 441). Villa feared that Silva might be contemplating suicide (Miramón 161).

17. In addition to portraying religion and science as incapable of guiding humans, Silva and Castro also denounce positivism as a guiding philosophy. Silva criticizes the positivist Max Nordau and his scientific oversimplifications with regard to the judgment of art and the artist: "(Oh! grotesco doctor Max Nordau, si tu fe en la ciencia miope ha suprimido en ti el sentido del misterio" (*De sobremesa* 247, "Oh! grotesque Doctor Max Nordau, your belief in myopic science has suppressed in you the sense of mystery"). Castro also speaks against positivism as she comments on her century from a historical and literary standpoint, maintaining that "el positivismo mata el genio" (*La hija del mar* 78, "positivism kills genius" [*Daughter of the Sea*]).

18. Although Castro does refer to materialistic-minded priests (*Follas novas* 348), neither she nor Silva embrace anticlericalism as a theme. They continued to admire Christian ethics and respected always the faith of others.

Works Cited

Albert Robatto, Matilde. *Rosalía de Castro y Emilia Pardo Bazán: Afinidades y contrastes*. A Coruña: Ediciós de Castro, 1995.

———. *Rosalía de Castro y la condición femenina*. Madrid: Partenón, 1981.

Alonso Montero, Xesús. *Rosalía de Castro*. Madrid: Júcar, 1972.

Carballo Calero, Ricardo. "Referencias a Rosalía en cartas de sus contemporáneos." *CEG* [*Cuadernos de Estudios Gallegos*] 54 (1958): 303-313.

Castro, Rosalía de. *Obras completas*. 2 vols. Madrid: Biblioteca Castro, 1993.

Ciplijauskaite, Birute. "La 'cárcel estrecha' y sus modulaciones." *Actas do congreso internacional de estudios sobre Rosalía de Castro e o seu tempo*. Vol. 2. Santiago de Compostela: Universidad de Santiago de Compostela, 1986. 321-329.

Costa Clavell, Javier. *Rosalía de Castro.* Barcelona: Plaza y Janes, 1967.

Courteau, Joannna. "Language and Ethnicity: The Case of Rosalía de Castro." *Language and Ethnicity, Focusschrift in Honor of Joshua A. Fishman on the Occasion of his 65th Birthday.* Amsterdam/Philadelphia: Benjamins, 1991. 83-94.

Filgueira Valverde, José. "Cinco visiones contemporáneas sobre Rosalía de Castro." *Rosalía de Castro, la luz de la negra sombra.* Madrid: Silex, 1985. 189-190.

García Sabell, Domingo. "Rosalía y su sombra." *7 (Siete) ensayos sobre Rosalía.* Vigo: Galaxia, 1952. 41-56.

Kulp, Kathleen. *Manner and Mood in Rosalía de Castro.* Madrid: Porrua Turanzas, 1968.

Kulp-Hill, Kathleen. *Rosalía de Castro.* Boston: Twayne, 1977.

McGrady, Donald. "Una caricatura literaria de José Asunción Silva." *Poesía y prosa de José Asunción Silva.* Bogotá: Biblioteca Básica Colombiana, 1979. 680-689.

Machado da Rosa, Alberto. "Heine in Spain (1856-67)—Relations with Rosalía de Castro." *Monatshefte* 49 (1957): 65-82.

March, Kathleen, N. "Rosalía de Castro." *Spanish Women Writers: A Bio-Bibliographical Source Book.* Westport, CT: Greenwood P, 1993. 104-112.

Mayoral, Marina. *La poesía de Rosalía de Castro.* Madrid: Gredos, 1974.

———. *Rosalía de Castro.* Madrid: Cátedra, 1986.

Miramón, Alberto. *José Asunción Silva.* Colombia: Nacional, 1937.

Murguía, Manuel. "Prólogo." *En las orillas del Sar.* Madrid: Biblioteca Castro, 1993. 445-456.

———. "Rosalía de Castro." *Los precursores.* Buenos Aires: Emecé, 1944. 132-155.

Orjuela, Héctor H., ed. *José Asunción Silva, obra completa.* Nanterre: Université Paris X, 1990.

Osiek, Betty Tyree. *José Asunción Silva.* Boston: Twayne, 1978.

Pérez, Janet. "Rosalía de Castro." *Modern and Contemporary Spanish Women Poets.* New York: Twayne, 1996. 30-37.

Piñeiro, Ramón. "A Saudade en Rosalía." *7 (Siete) ensayos sobre Rosalía.* Vigo: Galaxia, 1952. 95-109.

Pociña, Andrés. "La crítica feminista ante la persona y la obra de Rosalía de Castro." *Crítica y ficción literaria: Mujeres españolas contemporáneas.* Granada: Universidad de Granada, 1989. 61-83.

Rof Carballo, J. "Rosalía, Anima galaica." *7 (Siete) ensayos sobre Rosalía.* Vigo: Galaxia, 1952. 111-149.

Unamuno, Miguel de. "José Asunción Silva." *Poesía y prosa, José Asunción Silva.* Bogotá: Biblioteca Básica Colombiana, 1979. 419-424.

FURTHER READING

Criticism

González, Aníbal. "Modernist Prose." In *The Cambridge History of Latin American Literature,* Vol. 2, edited by Roberto González Echevarría and Enrique Pupo-Walker, pp. 69-113. Cambridge: Cambridge University Press, 1996.

>   Examines the prose works of the major writers of Spanish American modernism, including Silva's novel *De sobremesa.*

Hazera, Lydia D. "The Spanish American Modernist Novel and the Psychology of the Artistic Personality." *Hispanic Journal* 8, no. 1 (fall 1986): 69-83.

>   A discussion of three novels associated with Spanish American modernism: Silva's *De sobremesa* and Diaz Rodriguez's *Ídolos rotos* and *Sangre patricia.*

Jrade, Cathy L. "Modernist Poetry." In *The Cambridge History of Latin American Literature,* Vol. 2, edited by Roberto González Echevarría and Enrique Pupo-Walker, pp. 7-68. Cambridge: Cambridge University Press, 1996.

>   Discusses the leading figures of Latin American modernist poetry, including a brief section on Silva's "Nocturno" and other poems.

———. Modernismo, *Modernity, and the Development of Spanish American Literature.* Austin: University of Texas Press, 1998, 193 p.

>   A study of the *modernista* movement, including a brief discussion of Silva's writings.

LoDato, Rosemary C. *Beyond the Glitter: The Language of Gems in Modernista Writers Rubén Darío, Ramón del Valle-Inclán, and José Asunción Silva.* Lewisburg, PA: Bucknell University Press, 1999.

>   Examines the significance of precious stones in the aesthetics of three writers of the Modernismo movement, among them Silva and his relationship to art nouveau jewelry.

Molloy, Sylvia. "Voice Snatching: *De Sobremesa,* Hysteria, and the Impersonation of Marie Bashkirtseff." *Latin American Literary Review* 25, no. 50 (July-December 1997): 11-29.

>   Discusses Silva's references to the Russian diarist and cult figure Marie Bashkirtseff, claiming that in his novel Silva appropriates the voice of the famous sensualist.

Villanueva-Collado, Alfredo. "Gender Ideology and Spanish American Critical Practice: José Asunción Silva's Case." In *From Romanticism to* Modernismo *in Latin America,* edited by David William Foster and Daniel Altamiranda, pp. 269-81. New York: Garland, 1997.

>   Discusses conventional notions of masculinity in the Spanish-American critical tradition, suggesting that speculation on Silva's possible homosexuality may have distorted assessments of his life and work.

How to Use This Index

The main references

> **Calvino, Italo**
> 1923-1985 .... **CLC 5, 8, 11, 22, 33, 39,**
> **73; SSC 3**

list all author entries in the following Gale Literary Criticism series:

BLC = *Black Literature Criticism*
CLC = *Contemporary Literary Criticism*
CLR = *Children's Literature Review*
CMLC = *Classical and Medieval Literature Criticism*
DA = *DISCovering Authors*
DAB = *DISCovering Authors: British*
DAC = *DISCovering Authors: Canadian*
DAM = *DISCovering Authors: Modules*
    DRAM: *Dramatists Module;* *MST:* *Most-Studied Authors Module;*
    MULT: *Multicultural Authors Module;* *NOV:* *Novelists Module;*
    POET: *Poets Module;* *POP:* *Popular Fiction and Genre Authors Module*
DC = *Drama Criticism*
HLC = *Hispanic Literature Criticism*
LC = *Literature Criticism from 1400 to 1800*
NCLC = *Nineteenth-Century Literature Criticism*
NNAL = *Native North American Literature*
PC = *Poetry Criticism*
SSC = *Short Story Criticism*
TCLC = *Twentieth-Century Literary Criticism*
WLC = *World Literature Criticism, 1500 to the Present*

The cross-references

> See also CANR 23; CA 85-88;
> obituary CA116

list all author entries in the following Gale biographical and literary sources:

AAYA = *Authors & Artists for Young Adults*
AITN = *Authors in the News*
BEST = *Bestsellers*
BW = *Black Writers*
CA = *Contemporary Authors*
CAAS = *Contemporary Authors Autobiography Series*
CABS = *Contemporary Authors Bibliographical Series*
CANR = *Contemporary Authors New Revision Series*
CAP = *Contemporary Authors Permanent Series*
CDALB = *Concise Dictionary of American Literary Biography*
CDBLB = *Concise Dictionary of British Literary Biography*
DLB = *Dictionary of Literary Biography*
DLBD = *Dictionary of Literary Biography Documentary Series*
DLBY = *Dictionary of Literary Biography Yearbook*
HW = *Hispanic Writers*
JRDA = *Junior DISCovering Authors*
MAICYA = *Major Authors and Illustrators for Children and Young Adults*
MTCW = *Major 20th-Century Writers*
SAAS = *Something about the Author Autobiography Series*
SATA = *Something about the Author*
YABC = *Yesterday's Authors of Books for Children*

Literary Criticism Series
Cumulative Author Index

Agustini, Delmira 1886-1914
See also CA 166; HLCS 1; HW 1, 2; LAW
Aherne, Owen
See Cassill, R(onald) V(erlin)
Ai 1947- .... **CLC 4, 14, 69**
See also CA 85-88; CAAS 13; CANR 70;
DLB 120
Aickman, Robert (Fordyce)
1914-1981 .... **CLC 57**
See also CA 5-8R; CANR 3, 72, 100; DLB
261; HGG; SUFW
Aiken, Conrad (Potter) 1889-1973 .... **CLC 1,
3, 5, 10, 52; PC 26; SSC 9**
See also AMW; CA 5-8R; 45-48; CANR 4,
60; CDALB 1929-1941; DAM NOV,
POET; DLB 9, 45, 102; EXPS; HGG;
MTCW 1, 2; RGAL 4; RGSF 2; SATA 3,
30; SSFS 8
Aiken, Joan (Delano) 1924- .... **CLC 35**
See also AAYA 1, 25; CA 9-12R, 182;
CAAE 182; CANR 4, 23, 34, 64; CLR 1,
19; DLB 161; FANT; HGG; JRDA; MAI-
CYA 1, 2; MTCW 1; RHW; SAAS 1;
SATA 2, 30, 73; SATA-Essay 109; WYA;
YAW
Ainsworth, William Harrison
1805-1882 .... **NCLC 13**
See also DLB 21; HGG; RGEL 2; SATA
24; SUFW
Aitmatov, Chingiz (Torekulovich)
1928- .... **CLC 71**
See also CA 103; CANR 38; MTCW 1;
RGSF 2; SATA 56
Akers, Floyd
See Baum, L(yman) Frank
Akhmadulina, Bella Akhatovna
1937- .... **CLC 53**
See also CA 65-68; CWP; CWW 2; DAM
POET
Akhmatova, Anna 1888-1966 ..... **CLC 11, 25,
64, 126; PC 2**
See also CA 19-20; 25-28R; CANR 35;
CAP 1; DA3; DAM POET; EW 10;
MTCW 1, 2; RGWL 2
Aksakov, Sergei Timofeyvich
1791-1859 .... **NCLC 2**
See also DLB 198
Aksenov, Vassily
See Aksyonov, Vassily (Pavlovich)
Akst, Daniel 1956- .... **CLC 109**
See also CA 161
Aksyonov, Vassily (Pavlovich)
1932- .... **CLC 22, 37, 101**
See also CA 53-56; CANR 12, 48, 77;
CWW 2
Akutagawa Ryunosuke
1892-1927 .... **TCLC 16; SSC 44**
See also CA 117; 154; DLB 180; MJW;
RGSF 2; RGWL 2
Alain 1868-1951 .... **TCLC 41**
See also CA 163; GFL 1789 to the Present
Alain de Lille c. 1116-c. 1203 .... **CMLC 53**
See also DLB 208
Alain-Fournier .... **TCLC 6**
See also Fournier, Henri Alban
See also DLB 65; GFL 1789 to the Present;
RGWL 2
Alanus de Insluis
See Alain de Lille
Alarcon, Pedro Antonio de
1833-1891 .... **NCLC 1**
Alas (y Urena), Leopoldo (Enrique Garcia)
1852-1901 .... **TCLC 29**
See also CA 113; 131; HW 1; RGSF 2
Albee, Edward (Franklin III) 1928- . **CLC 1,
2, 3, 5, 9, 11, 13, 25, 53, 86, 113; DC
11; WLC**
See also AITN 1; AMW; CA 5-8R; CABS
3; CAD; CANR 8, 54, 74; CD 5; CDALB

1941-1968; DA; DA3; DAB; DAC; DAM
DRAM, MST; DFS 2, 3, 8, 10, 13, 14;
DLB 7; INT CANR-8; LAIT 4; MTCW
1, 2; RGAL 4; TUS
Alberti, Rafael 1902-1999 .... **CLC 7**
See also CA 85-88; 185; CANR 81; DLB
108; HW 2; RGWL 2
Albert the Great 1193(?)-1280 ...... **CMLC 16**
See also DLB 115
Alcala-Galiano, Juan Valera y
See Valera y Alcala-Galiano, Juan
Alcayaga, Lucila Godoy
See Godoy Alcayaga, Lucila
Alcott, Amos Bronson 1799-1888 .... **NCLC 1**
See also DLB 1, 223
Alcott, Louisa May 1832-1888 . **NCLC 6, 58,
83; SSC 27; WLC**
See also AAYA 20; AMWS 1; BPFB 1;
BYA 2; CDALB 1865-1917; CLR 1, 38;
DA; DA3; DAB; DAC; DAM MST, NOV;
DLB 1, 42, 79, 223, 239, 242; DLBD 14;
FW; JRDA; LAIT 2; MAICYA 1, 2; NFS
12; RGAL 4; SATA 100; WCH; WYA;
YABC 1; YAW
Aldanov, M. A.
See Aldanov, Mark (Alexandrovich)
Aldanov, Mark (Alexandrovich)
1886(?)-1957 .... **TCLC 23**
See also CA 118; 181
Aldington, Richard 1892-1962 .... **CLC 49**
See also CA 85-88; CANR 45; DLB 20, 36,
100, 149; RGEL 2
Aldiss, Brian W(ilson) 1925- . **CLC 5, 14, 40;
SSC 36**
See also AAYA 42; CA 5-8R; CAAE 190;
CAAS 2; CANR 5, 28, 64; CN 7; DAM
NOV; DLB 14, 261; MTCW 1, 2; SATA
34; SFW 4
Alegria, Claribel 1924- .... **CLC 75; HLCS 1;
PC 26**
See also CA 131; CAAS 15; CANR 66, 94;
CWW 2; DAM MULT; DLB 145; HW 1;
MTCW 1
Alegria, Fernando 1918- .... **CLC 57**
See also CA 9-12R; CANR 5, 32, 72; HW
1, 2
Aleichem, Sholom .... **TCLC 1, 35; SSC 33**
See also Rabinovitch, Sholem
Aleixandre, Vicente 1898-1984 ... **TCLC 113;
HLCS 1**
See also CANR 81; DLB 108; HW 2;
RGWL 2
Alencon, Marguerite d'
See de Navarre, Marguerite
Alepoudelis, Odysseus
See Elytis, Odysseus
See also CWW 2
Aleshkovsky, Joseph 1929-
See Aleshkovsky, Yuz
See also CA 121; 128
Aleshkovsky, Yuz .... **CLC 44**
See also Aleshkovsky, Joseph
Alexander, Lloyd (Chudley) 1924- ... **CLC 35**
See also AAYA 1, 27; BPFB 1; BYA 5, 6,
7, 9, 10, 11; CA 1-4R; CANR 1, 24, 38,
55; CLR 1, 5, 48; CWRI 5; DLB 52;
FANT; JRDA; MAICYA 1, 2; MAICYAS
1; MTCW 1; SAAS 19; SATA 3, 49, 81,
129; SUFW; WYA; YAW
Alexander, Meena 1951- .... **CLC 121**
See also CA 115; CANR 38, 70; CP 7;
CWP; FW
Alexander, Samuel 1859-1938 .... **TCLC 77**
Alexie, Sherman (Joseph, Jr.)
1966- .... **CLC 96, 154**
See also AAYA 28; CA 138; CANR 95;
DA3; DAM MULT; DLB 175, 206;
MTCW 1; NNAL

Alfau, Felipe 1902-1999 .... **CLC 66**
See also CA 137
Alfieri, Vittorio 1749-1803 .... **NCLC 101**
See also EW 4; RGWL 2
Alfred, Jean Gaston
See Ponge, Francis
Alger, Horatio, Jr. 1832-1899 .... **NCLC 8, 83**
See also DLB 42; LAIT 2; RGAL 4; SATA
16; TUS
Al-Ghazali, Muhammad ibn Muhammad
1058-1111 .... **CMLC 50**
See also DLB 115
Algren, Nelson 1909-1981 ..... **CLC 4, 10, 33;
SSC 33**
See also AMWS 9; BPFB 1; CA 13-16R;
103; CANR 20, 61; CDALB 1941-1968;
DLB 9; DLBY 1981, 1982, 2000; MTCW
1, 2; RGAL 4; RGSF 2
Ali, Ahmed 1908-1998 .... **CLC 69**
See also CA 25-28R; CANR 15, 34
Alighieri, Dante
See Dante
Allan, John B.
See Westlake, Donald E(dwin)
Allan, Sidney
See Hartmann, Sadakichi
Allan, Sydney
See Hartmann, Sadakichi
Allard, Janet .... **CLC 59**
Allen, Edward 1948- .... **CLC 59**
Allen, Fred 1894-1956 .... **TCLC 87**
Allen, Paula Gunn 1939- .... **CLC 84**
See also AMWS 4; CA 112; 143; CANR
63; CWP; DA3; DAM MULT; DLB 175;
FW; MTCW 1; NNAL; RGAL 4
Allen, Roland
See Ayckbourn, Alan
Allen, Sarah A.
See Hopkins, Pauline Elizabeth
Allen, Sidney H.
See Hartmann, Sadakichi
Allen, Woody 1935- .... **CLC 16, 52**
See also AAYA 10; CA 33-36R; CANR 27,
38, 63; DAM POP; DLB 44; MTCW 1
Allende, Isabel 1942- . **CLC 39, 57, 97; HLC
1; WLCS**
See also AAYA 18; CA 125; 130; CANR
51, 74; CDWLB 3; CWW 2; DA3; DAM
MULT, NOV; DLB 145; DNFS 1; FW;
HW 1, 2; INT CA-130; LAIT 5; LAWS
1; MTCW 1, 2; NCFS 1; NFS 6; RGSF
2; SSFS 11; WLIT 1
Alleyn, Ellen
See Rossetti, Christina (Georgina)
Alleyne, Carla D. .... **CLC 65**
Allingham, Margery (Louise)
1904-1966 .... **CLC 19**
See also CA 5-8R; 25-28R; CANR 4, 58;
CMW 4; DLB 77; MSW; MTCW 1, 2
Allingham, William 1824-1889 ...... **NCLC 25**
See also DLB 35; RGEL 2
Allison, Dorothy E. 1949- .... **CLC 78, 153**
See also CA 140; CANR 66, 107; CSW;
DA3; FW; MTCW 1; NFS 11; RGAL 4
Alloula, Malek .... **CLC 65**
Allston, Washington 1779-1843 .... **NCLC 2**
See also DLB 1, 235
Almedingen, E. M. .... **CLC 12**
See also Almedingen, Martha Edith von
See also SATA 3
Almedingen, Martha Edith von 1898-1971
See Almedingen, E. M.
See also CA 1-4R; CANR 1
Almodovar, Pedro 1949(?)- .... **CLC 114;
HLCS 1**
See also CA 133; CANR 72; HW 2
Almqvist, Carl Jonas Love
1793-1866 .... **NCLC 42**

Atheling, William, Jr.
See Blish, James (Benjamin)

Atherton, Gertrude (Franklin Horn)
1857-1948 .... **TCLC 2**
See also CA 104; 155; DLB 9, 78, 186;
HGG; RGAL 4; SUFW; TCWW 2

Atherton, Lucius
See Masters, Edgar Lee

Atkins, Jack
See Harris, Mark

Atkinson, Kate .... **CLC 99**
See also CA 166; CANR 101

Attaway, William (Alexander)
1911-1986 .... **CLC 92; BLC 1**
See also BW 2, 3; CA 143; CANR 82;
DAM MULT; DLB 76

Atticus
See Fleming, Ian (Lancaster); Wilson,
(Thomas) Woodrow

Atwood, Margaret (Eleanor) 1939- ... **CLC 2,
3, 4, 8, 13, 15, 25, 44, 84, 135; PC 8;
SSC 2, 46; WLC**
See also AAYA 12; BEST 89:2; BPFB 1;
CA 49-52; CANR 3, 24, 33, 59, 95; CN
7; CP 7; CPW; CWP; DA; DA3; DAB;
DAC; DAM MST, NOV, POET; DLB 53,
251; EXPN; FW; INT CANR-24; LAIT
5; MTCW 1, 2; NFS 4, 12, 13, 14; PFS 7;
RGSF 2; SATA 50; SSFS 3, 13; YAW

Aubigny, Pierre d'
See Mencken, H(enry) L(ouis)

Aubin, Penelope 1685-1731(?) .... **LC 9**
See also DLB 39

Auchincloss, Louis (Stanton) 1917- .. **CLC 4,
6, 9, 18, 45; SSC 22**
See also AMWS 4; CA 1-4R; CANR 6, 29,
55, 87; CN 7; DAM NOV; DLB 2, 244;
DLBY 1980; INT CANR-29; MTCW 1;
RGAL 4

Auden, W(ystan) H(ugh) 1907-1973 . **CLC 1,
2, 3, 4, 6, 9, 11, 14, 43, 123; PC 1;
WLC**
See also AAYA 18; AMWS 2; BRW 7;
BRWR 1; CA 9-12R; 45-48; CANR 5, 61,
105; CDBLB 1914-1945; DA; DA3;
DAB; DAC; DAM DRAM, MST, POET;
DLB 10, 20; EXPP; MTCW 1, 2; PAB;
PFS 1, 3, 4, 10; WP

Audiberti, Jacques 1900-1965 .... **CLC 38**
See also CA 25-28R; DAM DRAM

Audubon, John James 1785-1851 . **NCLC 47**
See also ANW; DLB 248

Auel, Jean M(arie) 1936- .... **CLC 31, 107**
See also AAYA 7; BEST 90:4; BPFB 1; CA
103; CANR 21, 64; CPW; DA3; DAM
POP; INT CANR-21; NFS 11; RHW;
SATA 91

Auerbach, Erich 1892-1957 .... **TCLC 43**
See also CA 118; 155

Augier, Emile 1820-1889 .... **NCLC 31**
See also DLB 192; GFL 1789 to the Present

August, John
See De Voto, Bernard (Augustine)

Augustine, St. 354-430 .... **CMLC 6; WLCS**
See also DA; DA3; DAB; DAC; DAM
MST; DLB 115; EW 1; RGWL 2

Aunt Belinda
See Braddon, Mary Elizabeth

Aunt Weedy
See Alcott, Louisa May

Aurelius
See Bourne, Randolph S(illiman)

Aurelius, Marcus 121-180 .... **CMLC 45**
See also Marcus Aurelius
See also RGWL 2

Aurobindo, Sri
See Ghose, Aurabinda

Austen, Jane 1775-1817 ...... **NCLC 1, 13, 19,
33, 51, 81, 95; WLC**
See also AAYA 19; BRW 4; BRWR 2; BYA
3; CDBLB 1789-1832; DA; DA3; DAB;
DAC; DAM MST, NOV; DLB 116;
EXPN; LAIT 2; NFS 1, 14; WLIT 3;
WYAS 1

Auster, Paul 1947- .... **CLC 47, 131**
See also CA 69-72; CANR 23, 52, 75;
CMW 4; CN 7; DA3; DLB 227; MTCW
1

Austin, Frank
See Faust, Frederick (Schiller)
See also TCWW 2

Austin, Mary (Hunter) 1868-1934 . **TCLC 25**
See also Stairs, Gordon
See also ANW; CA 109; 178; DLB 9, 78,
206, 221; FW; TCWW 2

Averroes 1126-1198 .... **CMLC 7**
See also DLB 115

Avicenna 980-1037 .... **CMLC 16**
See also DLB 115

Avison, Margaret 1918- .... **CLC 2, 4, 97**
See also CA 17-20R; CP 7; DAC; DAM
POET; DLB 53; MTCW 1

Axton, David
See Koontz, Dean R(ay)

Ayckbourn, Alan 1939- ...... **CLC 5, 8, 18, 33,
74; DC 13**
See also BRWS 5; CA 21-24R; CANR 31,
59; CBD; CD 5; DAB; DAM DRAM;
DFS 7; DLB 13, 245; MTCW 1, 2

Aydy, Catherine
See Tennant, Emma (Christina)

Ayme, Marcel (Andre) 1902-1967 ... **CLC 11;
SSC 41**
See also CA 89-92; CANR 67; CLR 25;
DLB 72; EW 12; GFL 1789 to the Present;
RGSF 2; RGWL 2; SATA 91

Ayrton, Michael 1921-1975 .... **CLC 7**
See also CA 5-8R; 61-64; CANR 9, 21

Azorin .... **CLC 11**
See also Martinez Ruiz, Jose
See also EW 9

Azuela, Mariano 1873-1952 .. **TCLC 3; HLC
1**
See also CA 104; 131; CANR 81; DAM
MULT; HW 1, 2; LAW; MTCW 1, 2

Baastad, Babbis Friis
See Friis-Baastad, Babbis Ellinor

Bab
See Gilbert, W(illiam) S(chwenck)

Babbis, Eleanor
See Friis-Baastad, Babbis Ellinor

Babel, Isaac
See Babel, Isaak (Emmanuilovich)
See also EW 11; SSFS 10

Babel, Isaak (Emmanuilovich)
1894-1941(?) .... **TCLC 2, 13; SSC 16**
See also Babel, Isaac
See also CA 104; 155; MTCW 1; RGSF 2;
RGWL 2

Babits, Mihaly 1883-1941 .... **TCLC 14**
See also CA 114; CDWLB 4; DLB 215

Babur 1483-1530 .... **LC 18**

Babylas 1898-1962
See Ghelderode, Michel de

Baca, Jimmy Santiago 1952- .... **PC 41**
See also CA 131; CANR 81, 90; CP 7;
DAM MULT; DLB 122; HLC 1; HW 1, 2

Baca, Jose Santiago
See Baca, Jimmy Santiago

Bacchelli, Riccardo 1891-1985 .... **CLC 19**
See also CA 29-32R; 117

Bach, Richard (David) 1936- .... **CLC 14**
See also AITN 1; BEST 89:2; BPFB 1; BYA
5; CA 9-12R; CANR 18, 93; CPW; DAM
NOV, POP; FANT; MTCW 1; SATA 13

Bache, Benjamin Franklin
1769-1798 .... **LC 74**
See also DLB 43

Bachman, Richard
See King, Stephen (Edwin)

Bachmann, Ingeborg 1926-1973 .... **CLC 69**
See also CA 93-96; 45-48; CANR 69; DLB
85; RGWL 2

Bacon, Francis 1561-1626 .... **LC 18, 32**
See also BRW 1; CDBLB Before 1660;
DLB 151, 236, 252; RGEL 2

Bacon, Roger 1214(?)-1294 .... **CMLC 14**
See also DLB 115

Bacovia, George 1881-1957 .... **TCLC 24**
See also Vasiliu, Gheorghe
See also CDWLB 4; DLB 220

Badanes, Jerome 1937- .... **CLC 59**

Bagehot, Walter 1826-1877 .... **NCLC 10**
See also DLB 55

Bagnold, Enid 1889-1981 .... **CLC 25**
See also BYA 2; CA 5-8R; 103; CANR 5,
40; CBD; CWD; CWRI 5; DAM DRAM;
DLB 13, 160, 191, 245; FW; MAICYA 1,
2; RGEL 2; SATA 1, 25

Bagritsky, Eduard 1895-1934 .... **TCLC 60**

Bagrjana, Elisaveta
See Belcheva, Elisaveta Lyubomirova

Bagryana, Elisaveta -1991 .... **CLC 10**
See also Belcheva, Elisaveta Lyubomirova
See also CA 178; CDWLB 4; DLB 147

Bailey, Paul 1937- .... **CLC 45**
See also CA 21-24R; CANR 16, 62; CN 7;
DLB 14; GLL 2

Baillie, Joanna 1762-1851 .... **NCLC 71**
See also DLB 93; RGEL 2

Bainbridge, Beryl (Margaret) 1934- . **CLC 4,
5, 8, 10, 14, 18, 22, 62, 130**
See also BRWS 6; CA 21-24R; CANR 24,
55, 75, 88; CN 7; DAM NOV; DLB 14,
231; MTCW 1, 2

Baker, Carlos (Heard)
1909-1987 .... **TCLC 119**
See also CA 5-8R; 122; CANR 3, 63; DLB
103

Baker, Elliott 1922- .... **CLC 8**
See also CA 45-48; CANR 2, 63; CN 7

Baker, Jean H. .... **TCLC 3, 10**
See also Russell, George William

Baker, Nicholson 1957- .... **CLC 61**
See also CA 135; CANR 63; CN 7; CPW;
DA3; DAM POP; DLB 227

Baker, Ray Stannard 1870-1946 .... **TCLC 47**
See also CA 118

Baker, Russell (Wayne) 1925- .... **CLC 31**
See also BEST 89:4; CA 57-60; CANR 11,
41, 59; MTCW 1, 2

Bakhtin, M.
See Bakhtin, Mikhail Mikhailovich

Bakhtin, M. M.
See Bakhtin, Mikhail Mikhailovich

Bakhtin, Mikhail
See Bakhtin, Mikhail Mikhailovich

Bakhtin, Mikhail Mikhailovich
1895-1975 .... **CLC 83**
See also CA 128; 113; DLB 242

Bakshi, Ralph 1938(?)- .... **CLC 26**
See also CA 112; 138; IDFW 3

Bakunin, Mikhail (Alexandrovich)
1814-1876 .... **NCLC 25, 58**

Baldwin, James (Arthur) 1924-1987 . **CLC 1,
2, 3, 4, 5, 8, 13, 15, 17, 42, 50, 67, 90,
127; BLC 1; DC 1; SSC 10, 33; WLC**
See also AAYA 4, 34; AFAW 1, 2; AMWS
1; BW 1; CA 1-4R; 124; CABS 1; CAD;
CANR 3, 24; CDALB 1941-1968; CPW;
DA; DA3; DAB; DAC; DAM MST,
MULT, NOV, POP; DFS 15; DLB 2, 7,

Bassani, Giorgio 1916-2000 .... **CLC 9**
See also CA 65-68; 190; CANR 33; CWW
2; DLB 128, 177; MTCW 1; RGWL 2

Bastian, Ann .... **CLC 70**

Bastos, Augusto (Antonio) Roa
See Roa Bastos, Augusto (Antonio)

Bataille, Georges 1897-1962 .... **CLC 29**
See also CA 101; 89-92

Bates, H(erbert) E(rnest)
1905-1974 .... **CLC 46; SSC 10**
See also CA 93-96; 45-48; CANR 34; DA3;
DAB; DAM POP; DLB 162, 191; EXPS;
MTCW 1, 2; RGSF 2; SSFS 7

Bauchart
See Camus, Albert

Baudelaire, Charles 1821-1867 . **NCLC 6, 29, 55; PC 1; SSC 18; WLC**
See also DA; DA3; DAB; DAC; DAM
MST, POET; DLB 217; EW 7; GFL 1789
to the Present; RGWL 2

Baudouin, Marcel
See Peguy, Charles (Pierre)

Baudouin, Pierre
See Peguy, Charles (Pierre)

Baudrillard, Jean 1929- .... **CLC 60**

Baum, L(yman) Frank 1856-1919 ... **TCLC 7**
See also CA 108; 133; CLR 15; CWRI 5;
DLB 22; FANT; JRDA; MAICYA 1, 2;
MTCW 1, 2; NFS 13; RGAL 4; SATA 18,
100; WCH

Baum, Louis F.
See Baum, L(yman) Frank

Baumbach, Jonathan 1933- .... **CLC 6, 23**
See also CA 13-16R; CAAS 5; CANR 12,
66; CN 7; DLBY 1980; INT CANR-12;
MTCW 1

Bausch, Richard (Carl) 1945- .... **CLC 51**
See also AMWS 7; CA 101; CAAS 14;
CANR 43, 61, 87; CSW; DLB 130

Baxter, Charles (Morley) 1947- . **CLC 45, 78**
See also CA 57-60; CANR 40, 64, 104;
CPW; DAM POP; DLB 130; MTCW 2

Baxter, George Owen
See Faust, Frederick (Schiller)

Baxter, James K(eir) 1926-1972 .... **CLC 14**
See also CA 77-80

Baxter, John
See Hunt, E(verette) Howard, (Jr.)

Bayer, Sylvia
See Glassco, John

Baynton, Barbara 1857-1929 .... **TCLC 57**
See also DLB 230; RGSF 2

Beagle, Peter S(oyer) 1939- .... **CLC 7, 104**
See also BPFB 1; BYA 9, 10; CA 9-12R;
CANR 4, 51, 73; DA3; DLBY 1980;
FANT; INT CANR-4; MTCW 1; SATA
60, 130; SUFW; YAW

Bean, Normal
See Burroughs, Edgar Rice

Beard, Charles A(ustin)
1874-1948 .... **TCLC 15**
See also CA 115; 189; DLB 17; SATA 18

Beardsley, Aubrey 1872-1898 .... **NCLC 6**

Beattie, Ann 1947- ..... **CLC 8, 13, 18, 40, 63, 146; SSC 11**
See also AMWS 5; BEST 90:2; BPFB 1;
CA 81-84; CANR 53, 73; CN 7; CPW;
DA3; DAM NOV, POP; DLB 218; DLBY
1982; MTCW 1, 2; RGAL 4; RGSF 2;
SSFS 9

Beattie, James 1735-1803 .... **NCLC 25**
See also DLB 109

Beauchamp, Kathleen Mansfield 1888-1923
See Mansfield, Katherine
See also CA 104; 134; DA; DA3; DAC;
DAM MST; MTCW 2; TEA

Beaumarchais, Pierre-Augustin Caron de
1732-1799 .... **LC 61; DC 4**
See also DAM DRAM; DFS 14; EW 4;
GFL Beginnings to 1789; RGWL 2

Beaumont, Francis 1584(?)-1616 .... **LC 33; DC 6**
See also BRW 2; CDBLB Before 1660;
DLB 58

Beauvoir, Simone (Lucie Ernestine Marie Bertrand) de 1908-1986 .... **CLC 1, 2, 4, 8, 14, 31, 44, 50, 71, 124; SSC 35; WLC**
See also BPFB 1; CA 9-12R; 118; CANR
28, 61; DA; DA3; DAB; DAC; DAM
MST, NOV; DLB 72; DLBY 1986; EW
12; FW; GFL 1789 to the Present; MTCW
1, 2; RGSF 2; RGWL 2

Becker, Carl (Lotus) 1873-1945 ..... **TCLC 63**
See also CA 157; DLB 17

Becker, Jurek 1937-1997 .... **CLC 7, 19**
See also CA 85-88; 157; CANR 60; CWW
2; DLB 75

Becker, Walter 1950- .... **CLC 26**

Beckett, Samuel (Barclay)
1906-1989 .. **CLC 1, 2, 3, 4, 6, 9, 10, 11, 14, 18, 29, 57, 59, 83; SSC 16; WLC**
See also BRWR 1; BRWS 1; CA 5-8R; 130;
CANR 33, 61; CBD; CDBLB 1945-1960;
DA; DA3; DAB; DAC; DAM DRAM,
MST, NOV; DFS 2, 7; DLB 13, 15, 233;
DLBY 1990; GFL 1789 to the Present;
MTCW 1, 2; RGSF 2; RGWL 2; SSFS
15; WLIT 4

Beckford, William 1760-1844 .... **NCLC 16**
See also BRW 3; DLB 39, 213; HGG;
SUFW

Beckman, Gunnel 1910- .... **CLC 26**
See also CA 33-36R; CANR 15; CLR 25;
MAICYA 1, 2; SAAS 9; SATA 6

Becque, Henri 1837-1899 .... **NCLC 3**
See also DLB 192; GFL 1789 to the Present

Becquer, Gustavo Adolfo
1836-1870 .... **NCLC 106; HLCS 1**
See also DAM MULT

Beddoes, Thomas Lovell
1803-1849 .... **NCLC 3; DC 15**
See also DLB 96

Bede c. 673-735 .... **CMLC 20**
See also DLB 146

Bedford, Donald F.
See Fearing, Kenneth (Flexner)

Beecher, Catharine Esther
1800-1878 .... **NCLC 30**
See also DLB 1, 243

Beecher, John 1904-1980 .... **CLC 6**
See also AITN 1; CA 5-8R; 105; CANR 8

Beer, Johann 1655-1700 .... **LC 5**
See also DLB 168

Beer, Patricia 1924- .... **CLC 58**
See also CA 61-64; 183; CANR 13, 46; CP
7; CWP; DLB 40; FW

Beerbohm, Max
See Beerbohm, (Henry) Max(imilian)

Beerbohm, (Henry) Max(imilian)
1872-1956 .... **TCLC 1, 24**
See also BRWS 2; CA 104; 154; CANR 79;
DLB 34, 100; FANT

Beer-Hofmann, Richard
1866-1945 .... **TCLC 60**
See also CA 160; DLB 81

Beg, Shemus
See Stephens, James

Begiebing, Robert J(ohn) 1946- .... **CLC 70**
See also CA 122; CANR 40, 88

Behan, Brendan 1923-1964 ...... **CLC 1, 8, 11, 15, 79**
See also BRWS 2; CA 73-76; CANR 33;
CBD; CDBLB 1945-1960; DAM DRAM;
DFS 7; DLB 13, 233; MTCW 1, 2

Behn, Aphra 1640(?)-1689 .... **LC 1, 30, 42; DC 4; PC 13; WLC**
See also BRWS 3; DA; DA3; DAB; DAC;
DAM DRAM, MST, NOV, POET; DLB
39, 80, 131; FW; WLIT 3

Behrman, S(amuel) N(athaniel)
1893-1973 .... **CLC 40**
See also CA 13-16; 45-48; CAD; CAP 1;
DLB 7, 44; IDFW 3; RGAL 4

Belasco, David 1853-1931 .... **TCLC 3**
See also CA 104; 168; DLB 7; RGAL 4

Belcheva, Elisaveta Lyubomirova
1893-1991 .... **CLC 10**
See also Bagryana, Elisaveta

Beldone, Phil "Cheech"
See Ellison, Harlan (Jay)

Beleno
See Azuela, Mariano

Belinski, Vissarion Grigoryevich
1811-1848 .... **NCLC 5**
See also DLB 198

Belitt, Ben 1911- .... **CLC 22**
See also CA 13-16R; CAAS 4; CANR 7,
77; CP 7; DLB 5

Bell, Gertrude (Margaret Lowthian)
1868-1926 .... **TCLC 67**
See also CA 167; DLB 174

Bell, J. Freeman
See Zangwill, Israel

Bell, James Madison 1826-1902 ... **TCLC 43; BLC 1**
See also BW 1; CA 122; 124; DAM MULT;
DLB 50

Bell, Madison Smartt 1957- ...... **CLC 41, 102**
See also AMWS 10; BPFB 1; CA 111, 183;
CAAE 183; CANR 28, 54, 73; CN 7;
CSW; DLB 218; MTCW 1

Bell, Marvin (Hartley) 1937- .... **CLC 8, 31**
See also CA 21-24R; CAAS 14; CANR 59,
102; CP 7; DAM POET; DLB 5; MTCW
1

Bell, W. L. D.
See Mencken, H(enry) L(ouis)

Bellamy, Atwood C.
See Mencken, H(enry) L(ouis)

Bellamy, Edward 1850-1898 ...... **NCLC 4, 86**
See also DLB 12; NFS 15; RGAL 4; SFW
4

Belli, Gioconda 1949-
See also CA 152; CWW 2; HLCS 1

Bellin, Edward J.
See Kuttner, Henry

Belloc, (Joseph) Hilaire (Pierre Sebastien Rene Swanton) 1870-1953 ...... **TCLC 7, 18; PC 24**
See also CA 106; 152; CWRI 5; DAM
POET; DLB 19, 100, 141, 174; MTCW 1;
SATA 112; WCH; YABC 1

Belloc, Joseph Peter Rene Hilaire
See Belloc, (Joseph) Hilaire (Pierre Sebastien Rene Swanton)

Belloc, Joseph Pierre Hilaire
See Belloc, (Joseph) Hilaire (Pierre Sebastien Rene Swanton)

Belloc, M. A.
See Lowndes, Marie Adelaide (Belloc)

Bellow, Saul 1915- . **CLC 1, 2, 3, 6, 8, 10, 13, 15, 25, 33, 34, 63, 79; SSC 14; WLC**
See also AITN 2; AMW; BEST 89:3; BPFB
1; CA 5-8R; CABS 1; CANR 29, 53, 95;
CDALB 1941-1968; CN 7; DA; DA3;
DAB; DAC; DAM MST, NOV, POP;
DLB 2, 28; DLBD 3; DLBY 1982;
MTCW 1, 2; NFS 4, 14; RGAL 4; RGSF
2; SSFS 12

Belser, Reimond Karel Maria de 1929-
See Ruyslinck, Ward
See also CA 152

Bely, Andrey .... TCLC 7; PC 11
See also Bugayev, Boris Nikolayevich
See also EW 9; MTCW 1

Belyi, Andrei
See Bugayev, Boris Nikolayevich
See also RGWL 2

Bembo, Pietro 1470-1547 .... LC 79
See also RGWL 2

Benary, Margot
See Benary-Isbert, Margot

Benary-Isbert, Margot 1889-1979 .... CLC 12
See also CA 5-8R; 89-92; CANR 4, 72;
CLR 12; MAICYA 1, 2; SATA 2; SATA-
Obit 21

Benavente (y Martinez), Jacinto
1866-1954 .... TCLC 3; HLCS 1
See also CA 106; 131; CANR 81; DAM
DRAM, MULT; GLL 2; HW 1, 2; MTCW
1, 2

Benchley, Peter (Bradford) 1940- .. CLC 4, 8
See also AAYA 14; AITN 2; BPFB 1; CA
17-20R; CANR 12, 35, 66; CPW; DAM
NOV, POP; HGG; MTCW 1, 2; SATA 3,
89

Benchley, Robert (Charles)
1889-1945 .... TCLC 1, 55
See also CA 105; 153; DLB 11; RGAL 4

Benda, Julien 1867-1956 .... TCLC 60
See also CA 120; 154; GFL 1789 to the
Present

Benedict, Ruth (Fulton)
1887-1948 .... TCLC 60
See also CA 158; DLB 246

Benedikt, Michael 1935- .... CLC 4, 14
See also CA 13-16R; CANR 7; CP 7; DLB
5

Benet, Juan 1927-1993 .... CLC 28
See also CA 143

Benet, Stephen Vincent 1898-1943 . TCLC 7;
SSC 10
See also CA 104; 152; DA3; DAM POET;
DLB 4, 48, 102, 249; DLBY 1997; HGG;
MTCW 1; RGAL 4; RGSF 2; SUFW;
WP; YABC 1

Benet, William Rose 1886-1950 ..... TCLC 28
See also CA 118; 152; DAM POET; DLB
45; RGAL 4

Benford, Gregory (Albert) 1941- ..... CLC 52
See also BPFB 1; CA 69-72, 175; CAAE
175; CAAS 27; CANR 12, 24, 49, 95;
CSW; DLBY 1982; SCFW 2; SFW 4

Bengtsson, Frans (Gunnar)
1894-1954 .... TCLC 48
See also CA 170

Benjamin, David
See Slavitt, David R(ytman)

Benjamin, Lois
See Gould, Lois

Benjamin, Walter 1892-1940 .... TCLC 39
See also CA 164; DLB 242; EW 11

Benn, Gottfried 1886-1956 .. TCLC 3; PC 35
See also CA 106; 153; DLB 56; RGWL 2

Bennett, Alan 1934- .... CLC 45, 77
See also CA 103; CANR 35, 55, 106; CBD;
CD 5; DAB; DAM MST; MTCW 1, 2

Bennett, (Enoch) Arnold
1867-1931 .... TCLC 5, 20
See also BRW 6; CA 106; 155; CDBLB
1890-1914; DLB 10, 34, 98, 135; MTCW
2

Bennett, Elizabeth
See Mitchell, Margaret (Munnerlyn)

Bennett, George Harold 1930-
See Bennett, Hal
See also BW 1; CA 97-100; CANR 87

Bennett, Hal .... CLC 5
See also Bennett, George Harold
See also DLB 33

Bennett, Jay 1912- .... CLC 35
See also AAYA 10; CA 69-72; CANR 11,
42, 79; JRDA; SAAS 4; SATA 41, 87;
SATA-Brief 27; WYA; YAW

Bennett, Louise (Simone) 1919- ...... CLC 28;
BLC 1
See also BW 2, 3; CA 151; CDWLB 3; CP
7; DAM MULT; DLB 117

Benson, E(dward) F(rederic)
1867-1940 .... TCLC 27
See also CA 114; 157; DLB 135, 153;
HGG; SUFW

Benson, Jackson J. 1930- .... CLC 34
See also CA 25-28R; DLB 111

Benson, Sally 1900-1972 .... CLC 17
See also CA 19-20; 37-40R; CAP 1; SATA
1, 35; SATA-Obit 27

Benson, Stella 1892-1933 .... TCLC 17
See also CA 117; 155; DLB 36, 162; FANT

Bentham, Jeremy 1748-1832 .... NCLC 38
See also DLB 107, 158, 252

Bentley, E(dmund) C(lerihew)
1875-1956 .... TCLC 12
See also CA 108; DLB 70; MSW

Bentley, Eric (Russell) 1916- .... CLC 24
See also CA 5-8R; CAD; CANR 6, 67;
CBD; CD 5; INT CANR-6

Beranger, Pierre Jean de
1780-1857 .... NCLC 34

Berdyaev, Nicolas
See Berdyaev, Nikolai (Aleksandrovich)

Berdyaev, Nikolai (Aleksandrovich)
1874-1948 .... TCLC 67
See also CA 120; 157

Berdyayev, Nikolai (Aleksandrovich)
See Berdyaev, Nikolai (Aleksandrovich)

Berendt, John (Lawrence) 1939- ...... CLC 86
See also CA 146; CANR 75, 93; DA3;
MTCW 1

Beresford, J(ohn) D(avys)
1873-1947 .... TCLC 81
See also CA 112; 155; DLB 162, 178, 197;
SFW 4; SUFW

Bergelson, David 1884-1952 .... TCLC 81

Berger, Colonel
See Malraux, (Georges-)Andre

Berger, John (Peter) 1926- .... CLC 2, 19
See also BRWS 4; CA 81-84; CANR 51,
78; CN 7; DLB 14, 207

Berger, Melvin H. 1927- .... CLC 12
See also CA 5-8R; CANR 4; CLR 32;
SAAS 2; SATA 5, 88; SATA-Essay 124

Berger, Thomas (Louis) 1924- .. CLC 3, 5, 8,
11, 18, 38
See also BPFB 1; CA 1-4R; CANR 5, 28,
51; CN 7; DAM NOV; DLB 2; DLBY
1980; FANT; INT CANR-28; MTCW 1,
2; RHW; TCWW 2

Bergman, (Ernst) Ingmar 1918- ...... CLC 16,
72
See also CA 81-84; CANR 33, 70; DLB
257; MTCW 2

Bergson, Henri(-Louis) 1859-1941 . TCLC 32
See also CA 164; EW 8; GFL 1789 to the
Present

Bergstein, Eleanor 1938- .... CLC 4
See also CA 53-56; CANR 5

Berkeley, George 1685-1753 .... LC 65
See also DLB 101, 252

Berkoff, Steven 1937- .... CLC 56
See also CA 104; CANR 72; CBD; CD 5

Berlin, Isaiah 1909-1997 .... TCLC 105
See also CA 85-88; 162

Bermant, Chaim (Icyk) 1929-1998 ... CLC 40
See also CA 57-60; CANR 6, 31, 57, 105;
CN 7

Bern, Victoria
See Fisher, M(ary) F(rances) K(ennedy)

Bernanos, (Paul Louis) Georges
1888-1948 .... TCLC 3
See also CA 104; 130; CANR 94; DLB 72;
GFL 1789 to the Present; RGWL 2

Bernard, April 1956- .... CLC 59
See also CA 131

Berne, Victoria
See Fisher, M(ary) F(rances) K(ennedy)

Bernhard, Thomas 1931-1989 ..... CLC 3, 32,
61; DC 14
See also CA 85-88; 127; CANR 32, 57; CD-
WLB 2; DLB 85, 124; MTCW 1; RGWL
2

Bernhardt, Sarah (Henriette Rosine)
1844-1923 .... TCLC 75
See also CA 157

Bernstein, Charles 1950- .... CLC 142,
See also CA 129; CAAS 24; CANR 90; CP
7; DLB 169

Berriault, Gina 1926-1999 .... CLC 54, 109;
SSC 30
See also CA 116; 129; 185; CANR 66; DLB
130; SSFS 7,11

Berrigan, Daniel 1921- .... CLC 4
See also CA 33-36R; CAAE 187; CAAS 1;
CANR 11, 43, 78; CP 7; DLB 5

Berrigan, Edmund Joseph Michael, Jr.
1934-1983
See Berrigan, Ted
See also CA 61-64; 110; CANR 14, 102

Berrigan, Ted .... CLC 37
See also Berrigan, Edmund Joseph Michael,
Jr.
See also DLB 5, 169; WP

Berry, Charles Edward Anderson 1931-
See Berry, Chuck
See also CA 115

Berry, Chuck .... CLC 17
See also Berry, Charles Edward Anderson

Berry, Jonas
See Ashbery, John (Lawrence)
See also GLL 1

Berry, Wendell (Erdman) 1934- ... CLC 4, 6,
8, 27, 46; PC 28
See also AITN 1; AMWS 10; ANW; CA
73-76; CANR 50, 73, 101; CP 7; CSW;
DAM POET; DLB 5, 6, 234; MTCW 1

Berryman, John 1914-1972 ... CLC 1, 2, 3, 4,
6, 8, 10, 13, 25, 62
See also AMW; CA 13-16; 33-36R; CABS
2; CANR 35; CAP 1; CDALB 1941-1968;
DAM POET; DLB 48; MTCW 1, 2; PAB;
RGAL 4; WP

Bertolucci, Bernardo 1940- ...... CLC 16, 157
See also CA 106

Berton, Pierre (Francis Demarigny)
1920- .... CLC 104
See also CA 1-4R; CANR 2, 56; CPW;
DLB 68; SATA 99

Bertrand, Aloysius 1807-1841 .... NCLC 31
See also Bertrand, Louis oAloysiusc

Bertrand, Louis oAloysiusc
See Bertrand, Aloysius
See also DLB 217

Bertran de Born c. 1140-1215 .... CMLC 5

Besant, Annie (Wood) 1847-1933 ..... TCLC 9
See also CA 105; 185

Bessie, Alvah 1904-1985 .... CLC 23
See also CA 5-8R; 116; CANR 2, 80; DLB
26

Bethlen, T. D.
See Silverberg, Robert

Beti, Mongo .... CLC 27; BLC 1
See also Biyidi, Alexandre
See also AFW; CANR 79; DAM MULT;
WLIT 2

Bradbury, Malcolm (Stanley)
1932-2000 .... **CLC 32, 61**
See also CA 1-4R; CANR 1, 33, 91, 98;
CN 7; DA3; DAM NOV; DLB 14, 207;
MTCW 1, 2

Bradbury, Ray (Douglas) 1920- .... **CLC 1, 3,**
10, 15, 42, 98; SSC 29, 53; WLC
See also AAYA 15; AITN 1, 2; AMWS 4;
BPFB 1; BYA 4, 5, 11; CA 1-4R; CANR
2, 30, 75; CDALB 1968-1988; CN 7;
CPW; DA; DA3; DAB; DAC; DAM MST,
NOV, POP; DLB 2, 8; EXPN; EXPS;
HGG; LAIT 3, 5; MTCW 1, 2; NFS 1;
RGAL 4; RGSF 2; SATA 11, 64, 123;
SCFW 2; SFW 4; SSFS 1; SUFW; YAW

Braddon, Mary Elizabeth
1837-1915 .... **TCLC 111**
See also Aunt Belinda
See also CA 108; 179; CMW 4; DLB 18,
70, 156; HGG

Bradford, Gamaliel 1863-1932 .... **TCLC 36**
See also CA 160; DLB 17

Bradford, William 1590-1657 .... **LC 64**
See also DLB 24, 30; RGAL 4

Bradley, David (Henry), Jr. 1950- ... **CLC 23,**
118; BLC 1
See also BW 1, 3; CA 104; CANR 26, 81;
CN 7; DAM MULT; DLB 33

Bradley, John Ed(mund, Jr.) 1958- . **CLC 55**
See also CA 139; CANR 99; CN 7; CSW

Bradley, Marion Zimmer
1930-1999 .... **CLC 30**
See also Chapman, Lee; Dexter, John; Gard-
ner, Miriam; Ives, Morgan; Rivers, Elfrida
See also AAYA 40; BPFB 1; CA 57-60; 185;
CAAS 10; CANR 7, 31, 51, 75, 107;
CPW; DA3; DAM POP; DLB 8; FANT;
FW; MTCW 1, 2; SATA 90; SATA-Obit
116; SFW 4; YAW

Bradshaw, John 1933- .... **CLC 70**
See also CA 138; CANR 61

Bradstreet, Anne 1612(?)-1672 ...... **LC 4, 30;**
PC 10
See also AMWS 1; CDALB 1640-1865;
DA; DA3; DAC; DAM MST, POET; DLB
24; EXPP; FW; PFS 6; RGAL 4; WP

Brady, Joan 1939- .... **CLC 86**
See also CA 141

Bragg, Melvyn 1939- .... **CLC 10**
See also BEST 89:3; CA 57-60; CANR 10,
48, 89; CN 7; DLB 14; RHW

Brahe, Tycho 1546-1601 .... **LC 45**

Braine, John (Gerard) 1922-1986 . **CLC 1, 3,**
41
See also CA 1-4R; 120; CANR 1, 33; CD-
BLB 1945-1960; DLB 15; DLBY 1986;
MTCW 1

Bramah, Ernest 1868-1942 .... **TCLC 72**
See also CA 156; CMW 4; DLB 70; FANT

Brammer, William 1930(?)-1978 ...... **CLC 31**
See also CA 77-80

Brancati, Vitaliano 1907-1954 .... **TCLC 12**
See also CA 109

Brancato, Robin F(idler) 1936- .... **CLC 35**
See also AAYA 9; BYA 6; CA 69-72; CANR
11, 45; CLR 32; JRDA; MAICYA 2;
MAICYAS 1; SAAS 9; SATA 97; WYA;
YAW

Brand, Max
See Faust, Frederick (Schiller)
See also BPFB 1; TCWW 2

Brand, Millen 1906-1980 .... **CLC 7**
See also CA 21-24R; 97-100; CANR 72

Branden, Barbara .... **CLC 44**
See also CA 148

Brandes, Georg (Morris Cohen)
1842-1927 .... **TCLC 10**
See also CA 105; 189

Brandys, Kazimierz 1916-2000 .... **CLC 62**

Branley, Franklyn M(ansfield)
1915- .... **CLC 21**
See also CA 33-36R; CANR 14, 39; CLR
13; MAICYA 1, 2; SAAS 16; SATA 4, 68

Brathwaite, Edward Kamau 1930- . **CLC 11;**
BLCS
See also BW 2, 3; CA 25-28R; CANR 11,
26, 47, 107; CDWLB 3; CP 7; DAM
POET; DLB 125

Brathwaite, Kamau
See Brathwaite, Edward Kamau

Brautigan, Richard (Gary)
1935-1984 ..... **CLC 1, 3, 5, 9, 12, 34, 42**
See also BPFB 1; CA 53-56; 113; CANR
34; DA3; DAM NOV; DLB 2, 5, 206;
DLBY 1980, 1984; FANT; MTCW 1;
RGAL 4; SATA 56

Brave Bird, Mary
See Crow Dog, Mary (Ellen)
See also NNAL

Braverman, Kate 1950- .... **CLC 67**
See also CA 89-92

Brecht, (Eugen) Bertolt (Friedrich)
1898-1956 ..... **TCLC 1, 6, 13, 35; DC 3;**
WLC
See also CA 104; 133; CANR 62; CDWLB
2; DA; DA3; DAB; DAC; DAM DRAM,
MST; DFS 4, 5, 9; DLB 56, 124; EW 11;
IDTP; MTCW 1, 2; RGWL 2

Brecht, Eugen Berthold Friedrich
See Brecht, (Eugen) Bertolt (Friedrich)

Bremer, Fredrika 1801-1865 .... **NCLC 11**
See also DLB 254

Brennan, Christopher John
1870-1932 .... **TCLC 17**
See also CA 117; 188; DLB 230

Brennan, Maeve 1917-1993 ... **CLC 5; TCLC**
124
See also CA 81-84; CANR 72, 100

Brent, Linda
See Jacobs, Harriet A(nn)

Brentano, Clemens (Maria)
1778-1842 .... **NCLC 1**
See also DLB 90; RGWL 2

Brent of Bin Bin
See Franklin, (Stella Maria Sarah) Miles
(Lampe)

Brenton, Howard 1942- .... **CLC 31**
See also CA 69-72; CANR 33, 67; CBD;
CD 5; DLB 13; MTCW 1

Breslin, James 1930-
See Breslin, Jimmy
See also CA 73-76; CANR 31, 75; DAM
NOV; MTCW 1, 2

Breslin, Jimmy .... **CLC 4, 43**
See also Breslin, James
See also AITN 1; DLB 185; MTCW 2

Bresson, Robert 1901(?)-1999 .... **CLC 16**
See also CA 110; 187; CANR 49

Breton, Andre 1896-1966 .. **CLC 2, 9, 15, 54;**
PC 15
See also CA 19-20; 25-28R; CANR 40, 60;
CAP 2; DLB 65, 258; EW 11; GFL 1789
to the Present; MTCW 1, 2; RGWL 2; WP

Breytenbach, Breyten 1939(?)- .. **CLC 23, 37,**
126
See also CA 113; 129; CANR 61; CWW 2;
DAM POET; DLB 225

Bridgers, Sue Ellen 1942- .... **CLC 26**
See also AAYA 8; BYA 7, 8; CA 65-68;
CANR 11, 36; CLR 18; DLB 52; JRDA;
MAICYA 1, 2; SAAS 1; SATA 22, 90;
SATA-Essay 109; WYA; YAW

Bridges, Robert (Seymour)
1844-1930 .... **TCLC 1; PC 28**
See also BRW 6; CA 104; 152; CDBLB
1890-1914; DAM POET; DLB 19, 98

Bridie, James .... **TCLC 3**
See also Mavor, Osborne Henry
See also DLB 10

Brin, David 1950- .... **CLC 34**
See also AAYA 21; CA 102; CANR 24, 70;
INT CANR-24; SATA 65; SCFW 2; SFW
4

Brink, Andre (Philippus) 1935- . **CLC 18, 36,**
106
See also AFW; BRWS 6; CA 104; CANR
39, 62, 109; CN 7; DLB 225; INT CA-
103; MTCW 1, 2; WLIT 2

Brinsmead, H. F(ay)
See Brinsmead, H(esba) F(ay)

Brinsmead, H. F.
See Brinsmead, H(esba) F(ay)

Brinsmead, H(esba) F(ay) 1922- ...... **CLC 21**
See also CA 21-24R; CANR 10; CLR 47;
CWRI 5; MAICYA 1, 2; SAAS 5; SATA
18, 78

Brittain, Vera (Mary) 1893(?)-1970 . **CLC 23**
See also CA 13-16; 25-28R; CANR 58;
CAP 1; DLB 191; FW; MTCW 1, 2

Broch, Hermann 1886-1951 .... **TCLC 20**
See also CA 117; CDWLB 2; DLB 85, 124;
EW 10; RGWL 2

Brock, Rose
See Hansen, Joseph
See also GLL 1

Brod, Max 1884-1968 .... **TCLC 115**
See also CA 5-8R; 25-28R; CANR 7; DLB
81

Brodkey, Harold (Roy) 1930-1996 .. **CLC 56;**
TCLC 123
See also CA 111; 151; CANR 71; CN 7;
DLB 130

Brodskii, Iosif
See Brodsky, Joseph
See also RGWL 2

Brodsky, Iosif Alexandrovich 1940-1996
See Brodsky, Joseph
See also AITN 1; CA 41-44R; 151; CANR
37, 106; DA3; DAM POET; MTCW 1, 2

Brodsky, Joseph . **CLC 4, 6, 13, 36, 100; PC**
9
See also Brodsky, Iosif Alexandrovich
See also AMWS 8; CWW 2; MTCW 1

Brodsky, Michael (Mark) 1948- .... **CLC 19**
See also CA 102; CANR 18, 41, 58; DLB
244

Brodzki, Bella ed. .... **CLC 65**

Brome, Richard 1590(?)-1652 .... **LC 61**
See also DLB 58

Bromell, Henry 1947- .... **CLC 5**
See also CA 53-56; CANR 9

Bromfield, Louis (Brucker)
1896-1956 .... **TCLC 11**
See also CA 107; 155; DLB 4, 9, 86; RGAL
4; RHW

Broner, E(sther) M(asserman)
1930- .... **CLC 19**
See also CA 17-20R; CANR 8, 25, 72; CN
7; DLB 28

Bronk, William (M.) 1918-1999 .... **CLC 10**
See also CA 89-92; 177; CANR 23; CP 7;
DLB 165

Bronstein, Lev Davidovich
See Trotsky, Leon

Bronte, Anne 1820-1849 ..... **NCLC 4, 71, 102**
See also BRW 5; BRWR 1; DA3; DLB 21,
199

Bronte, (Patrick) Branwell
1817-1848 .... **NCLC 109**

Bronte, Charlotte 1816-1855 ...... **NCLC 3, 8,**
33, 58, 105; WLC
See also AAYA 17; BRW 5; BRWR 1; BYA
2; CDBLB 1832-1890; DA; DA3; DAB;
DAC; DAM MST, NOV; DLB 21, 159,
199; EXPN; LAIT 2; NFS 4; WLIT 4

Buell, John (Edward) 1927- .... **CLC 10**
See also CA 1-4R; CANR 71; DLB 53

Buero Vallejo, Antonio 1916-2000 ... **CLC 15, 46, 139; DC 18**
See also CA 106; 189; CANR 24, 49, 75; DFS 11; HW 1; MTCW 1, 2

Bufalino, Gesualdo 1920(?)-1990 ...... **CLC 74**
See also CWW 2; DLB 196

Bugayev, Boris Nikolayevich
1880-1934 .... **TCLC 7; PC 11**
See also Bely, Andrey; Belyi, Andrei
See also CA 104; 165; MTCW 1

Bukowski, Charles 1920-1994 ... **CLC 2, 5, 9, 41, 82, 108; PC 18; SSC 45**
See also CA 17-20R; 144; CANR 40, 62, 105; CPW; DA3; DAM NOV, POET; DLB 5, 130, 169; MTCW 1, 2

Bulgakov, Mikhail (Afanas'evich)
1891-1940 .... **TCLC 2, 16; SSC 18**
See also BPFB 1; CA 105; 152; DAM DRAM, NOV; NFS 8; RGSF 2; RGWL 2; SFW 4

Bulgya, Alexander Alexandrovich
1901-1956 .... **TCLC 53**
See also Fadeyev, Alexander
See also CA 117; 181

Bullins, Ed 1935- ... **CLC 1, 5, 7; BLC 1; DC 6**
See also BW 2, 3; CA 49-52; CAAS 16; CAD; CANR 24, 46, 73; CD 5; DAM DRAM, MULT; DLB 7, 38, 249; MTCW 1, 2; RGAL 4

Bulwer-Lytton, Edward (George Earle
Lytton) 1803-1873 .... **NCLC 1, 45**
See also DLB 21; RGEL 2; SFW 4; SUFW

Bunin, Ivan Alexeyevich
1870-1953 .... **TCLC 6; SSC 5**
See also CA 104; RGSF 2; RGWL 2

Bunting, Basil 1900-1985 ...... **CLC 10, 39, 47**
See also BRWS 7; CA 53-56; 115; CANR 7; DAM POET; DLB 20; RGEL 2

Bunuel, Luis 1900-1983 ... **CLC 16, 80; HLC 1**
See also CA 101; 110; CANR 32, 77; DAM MULT; HW 1

Bunyan, John 1628-1688 ..... **LC 4, 69; WLC**
See also BRW 2; BYA 5; CDBLB 1660-1789; DA; DAB; DAC; DAM MST; DLB 39; RGEL 2; WCH; WLIT 3

Buravsky, Alexandr .... **CLC 59**

Burckhardt, Jacob (Christoph)
1818-1897 .... **NCLC 49**
See also EW 6

Burford, Eleanor
See Hibbert, Eleanor Alice Burford

Burgess, Anthony . **CLC 1, 2, 4, 5, 8, 10, 13, 15, 22, 40, 62, 81, 94**
See also Wilson, John (Anthony) Burgess
See also AAYA 25; AITN 1; BRWS 1; CD-BLB 1960 to Present; DAB; DLB 14, 194, 261; DLBY 1998; MTCW 1; RGEL 2; RHW; SFW 4; YAW

Burke, Edmund 1729(?)-1797 .... **LC 7, 36; WLC**
See also BRW 3; DA; DA3; DAB; DAC; DAM MST; DLB 104, 252; RGEL 2

Burke, Kenneth (Duva) 1897-1993 ... **CLC 2, 24**
See also AMW; CA 5-8R; 143; CANR 39, 74; DLB 45, 63; MTCW 1, 2; RGAL 4

Burke, Leda
See Garnett, David

Burke, Ralph
See Silverberg, Robert

Burke, Thomas 1886-1945 .... **TCLC 63**
See also CA 113; 155; CMW 4; DLB 197

Burney, Fanny 1752-1840 .... **NCLC 12, 54, 107**
See also BRWS 3; DLB 39; RGEL 2

Burney, Frances
See Burney, Fanny

Burns, Robert 1759-1796 ... **LC 3, 29, 40; PC 6; WLC**
See also BRW 3; CDBLB 1789-1832; DA; DA3; DAB; DAC; DAM MST, POET; DLB 109; EXPP; PAB; RGEL 2; WP

Burns, Tex
See L'Amour, Louis (Dearborn)
See also TCWW 2

Burnshaw, Stanley 1906- .... **CLC 3, 13, 44**
See also CA 9-12R; CP 7; DLB 48; DLBY 1997

Burr, Anne 1937- .... **CLC 6**
See also CA 25-28R

Burroughs, Edgar Rice 1875-1950 . **TCLC 2, 32**
See also AAYA 11; BPFB 1; BYA 4, 9; CA 104; 132; DA3; DAM NOV; DLB 8; FANT; MTCW 1, 2; RGAL 4; SATA 41; SCFW 2; SFW 4; YAW

Burroughs, William S(eward)
1914-1997 .. **CLC 1, 2, 5, 15, 22, 42, 75, 109; TCLC 121; WLC**
See also Lee, William; Lee, Willy
See also AITN 2; AMWS 3; BPFB 1; CA 9-12R; 160; CANR 20, 52, 104; CN 7; CPW; DA; DA3; DAB; DAC; DAM MST, NOV, POP; DLB 2, 8, 16, 152, 237; DLBY 1981, 1997; HGG; MTCW 1, 2; RGAL 4; SFW 4

Burton, Sir Richard F(rancis)
1821-1890 .... **NCLC 42**
See also DLB 55, 166, 184

Burton, Robert 1577-1640 .... **LC 74**
See also DLB 151; RGEL 2

Busch, Frederick 1941- ... **CLC 7, 10, 18, 47**
See also CA 33-36R; CAAS 1; CANR 45, 73, 92; CN 7; DLB 6, 218

Bush, Ronald 1946- .... **CLC 34**
See also CA 136

Bustos, F(rancisco)
See Borges, Jorge Luis

Bustos Domecq, H(onorio)
See Bioy Casares, Adolfo; Borges, Jorge Luis

Butler, Octavia E(stelle) 1947- .... **CLC 38, 121; BLCS**
See also AAYA 18; AFAW 2; BPFB 1; BW 2, 3; CA 73-76; CANR 12, 24, 38, 73; CLR 65; CPW; DA3; DAM MULT, POP; DLB 33; MTCW 1, 2; NFS 8; SATA 84; SCFW 2; SFW 4; SSFS 6; YAW

Butler, Robert Olen, (Jr.) 1945- .... **CLC 81**
See also BPFB 1; CA 112; CANR 66; CSW; DAM POP; DLB 173; INT CA-112; MTCW 1; SSFS 11

Butler, Samuel 1612-1680 .... **LC 16, 43**
See also DLB 101, 126; RGEL 2

Butler, Samuel 1835-1902 .... **TCLC 1, 33; WLC**
See also BRWS 2; CA 143; CDBLB 1890-1914; DA; DA3; DAB; DAC; DAM MST, NOV; DLB 18, 57, 174; RGEL 2; SFW 4; TEA

Butler, Walter C.
See Faust, Frederick (Schiller)

Butor, Michel (Marie Francois)
1926- .... **CLC 1, 3, 8, 11, 15, 161**
See also CA 9-12R; CANR 33, 66; DLB 83; EW 13; GFL 1789 to the Present; MTCW 1, 2

Butts, Mary 1890(?)-1937 .... **TCLC 77**
See also CA 148; DLB 240

Buxton, Ralph
See Silverstein, Alvin; Silverstein, Virginia B(arbara Opshelor)

Buzo, Alexander (John) 1944- .... **CLC 61**
See also CA 97-100; CANR 17, 39, 69; CD 5

Buzzati, Dino 1906-1972 .... **CLC 36**
See also CA 160; 33-36R; DLB 177; RGWL 2; SFW 4

Byars, Betsy (Cromer) 1928- .... **CLC 35**
See also AAYA 19; BYA 3; CA 33-36R, 183; CAAE 183; CANR 18, 36, 57, 102; CLR 1, 16, 72; DLB 52; INT CANR-18; JRDA; MAICYA 1, 2; MAICYAS 1; MTCW 1; SAAS 1; SATA 4, 46, 80; SATA-Essay 108; WYA; YAW

Byatt, A(ntonia) S(usan Drabble)
1936- .... **CLC 19, 65, 136**
See also BPFB 1; BRWS 4; CA 13-16R; CANR 13, 33, 50, 75, 96; DA3; DAM NOV, POP; DLB 14, 194; MTCW 1, 2; RGSF 2; RHW

Byrne, David 1952- .... **CLC 26**
See also CA 127

Byrne, John Keyes 1926-
See Leonard, Hugh
See also CA 102; CANR 78; INT CA-102

Byron, George Gordon (Noel)
1788-1824 ..... **NCLC 2, 12, 109; PC 16; WLC**
See also BRW 4; CDBLB 1789-1832; DA; DA3; DAB; DAC; DAM MST, POET; DLB 96, 110; EXPP; PAB; PFS 1, 14; RGEL 2; WLIT 3; WP

Byron, Robert 1905-1941 .... **TCLC 67**
See also CA 160; DLB 195

C. 3. 3.
See Wilde, Oscar (Fingal O'Flahertie Wills)

Caballero, Fernan 1796-1877 .... **NCLC 10**

Cabell, Branch
See Cabell, James Branch

Cabell, James Branch 1879-1958 .... **TCLC 6**
See also CA 105; 152; DLB 9, 78; FANT; MTCW 1; RGAL 4; SUFW

Cabeza de Vaca, Alvar Nunez
1490-1557(?) .... **LC 61**

Cable, George Washington
1844-1925 .... **TCLC 4; SSC 4**
See also CA 104; 155; DLB 12, 74; DLBD 13; RGAL 4

Cabral de Melo Neto, Joao
1920-1999 .... **CLC 76**
See also CA 151; DAM MULT; LAW; LAWS 1

Cabrera Infante, G(uillermo) 1929- . **CLC 5, 25, 45, 120; HLC 1; SSC 39**
See also CA 85-88; CANR 29, 65; CDWLB 3; DA3; DAM MULT; DLB 113; HW 1, 2; LAW; LAWS 1; MTCW 1, 2; RGSF 2; WLIT 1

Cade, Toni
See Bambara, Toni Cade

Cadmus and Harmonia
See Buchan, John

Caedmon fl. 658-680 .... **CMLC 7**
See also DLB 146

Caeiro, Alberto
See Pessoa, Fernando (Antonio Nogueira)

Caesar, Julius .... **CMLC 47**
See also Julius Caesar
See also AW 1; RGWL 2

Cage, John (Milton, Jr.) 1912-1992 . **CLC 41**
See also CA 13-16R; 169; CANR 9, 78; DLB 193; INT CANR-9

Cahan, Abraham 1860-1951 .... **TCLC 71**
See also CA 108; 154; DLB 9, 25, 28; RGAL 4

Cain, G.
See Cabrera Infante, G(uillermo)

Cain, Guillermo
See Cabrera Infante, G(uillermo)

Cain, James M(allahan) 1892-1977 .. **CLC 3, 11, 28**
See also AITN 1; BPFB 1; CA 17-20R; 73-76; CANR 8, 34, 61; CMW 4; DLB 226; MSW; MTCW 1; RGAL 4

Caine, Hall 1853-1931 .... **TCLC 97**
See also RHW

Caine, Mark
See Raphael, Frederic (Michael)

Calasso, Roberto 1941- .... **CLC 81**
See also CA 143; CANR 89

Calderon de la Barca, Pedro
1600-1681 .... **LC 23; DC 3; HLCS 1**
See also EW 2; RGWL 2

Caldwell, Erskine (Preston)
1903-1987 .... **CLC 1, 8, 14, 50, 60; SSC 19; TCLC 117**
See also AITN 1; AMW; BPFB 1; CA 1-4R; 121; CAAS 1; CANR 2, 33; DA3; DAM NOV; DLB 9, 86; MTCW 1, 2; RGAL 4; RGSF 2

Caldwell, (Janet Miriam) Taylor (Holland)
1900-1985 .... **CLC 2, 28, 39**
See also BPFB 1; CA 5-8R; 116; CANR 5; DA3; DAM NOV, POP; DLBD 17; RHW

Calhoun, John Caldwell
1782-1850 .... **NCLC 15**
See also DLB 3, 248

Calisher, Hortense 1911- ..... **CLC 2, 4, 8, 38, 134; SSC 15**
See also CA 1-4R; CANR 1, 22, 67; CN 7; DA3; DAM NOV; DLB 2, 218; INT CANR-22; MTCW 1, 2; RGAL 4; RGSF 2

Callaghan, Morley Edward
1903-1990 .... **CLC 3, 14, 41, 65**
See also CA 9-12R; 132; CANR 33, 73; DAC; DAM MST; DLB 68; MTCW 1; RGEL 2; RGSF 2

Callimachus c. 305B.C.-c.
240B.C. .... **CMLC 18**
See also AW 1; DLB 176; RGWL 2

Calvin, Jean
See Calvin, John
See also GFL Beginnings to 1789

Calvin, John 1509-1564 .... **LC 37**
See also Calvin, Jean

Calvino, Italo 1923-1985 .... **CLC 5, 8, 11, 22, 33, 39, 73; SSC 3, 48**
See also CA 85-88; 116; CANR 23, 61; DAM NOV; DLB 196; EW 13; MTCW 1, 2; RGSF 2; RGWL 2; SFW 4; SSFS 12

Camden, William 1551-1623 .... **LC 77**
See also DLB 172

Cameron, Carey 1952- .... **CLC 59**
See also CA 135

Cameron, Peter 1959- .... **CLC 44**
See also CA 125; CANR 50; DLB 234; GLL 2

Camoens, Luis Vaz de 1524(?)-1580
See also EW 2; HLCS 1

Camoes, Luis de 1524(?)-1580 .... **LC 62; HLCS 1; PC 31**
See also RGWL 2

Campana, Dino 1885-1932 .... **TCLC 20**
See also CA 117; DLB 114

Campanella, Tommaso 1568-1639 .... **LC 32**
See also RGWL 2

Campbell, John W(ood, Jr.)
1910-1971 .... **CLC 32**
See also CA 21-22; 29-32R; CANR 34; CAP 2; DLB 8; MTCW 1; SCFW; SFW 4

Campbell, Joseph 1904-1987 .... **CLC 69**
See also AAYA 3; BEST 89:2; CA 1-4R; 124; CANR 3, 28, 61, 107; DA3; MTCW 1, 2

Campbell, Maria 1940- .... **CLC 85**
See also CA 102; CANR 54; CCA 1; DAC; NNAL

Campbell, Paul N. 1923-
See hooks, bell
See also CA 21-24R

Campbell, (John) Ramsey 1946- ..... **CLC 42; SSC 19**
See also CA 57-60; CANR 7, 102; HGG; INT CANR-7; SUFW

Campbell, (Ignatius) Roy (Dunnachie)
1901-1957 .... **TCLC 5**
See also AFW; CA 104; 155; DLB 20, 225; MTCW 2; RGEL 2

Campbell, Thomas 1777-1844 .... **NCLC 19**
See also DLB 93, 144; RGEL 2

Campbell, Wilfred .... **TCLC 9**
See also Campbell, William

Campbell, William 1858(?)-1918
See Campbell, Wilfred
See also CA 106; DLB 92

Campion, Jane .... **CLC 95**
See also AAYA 33; CA 138; CANR 87

Campion, Thomas 1567-1620 .... **LC 78**
See also CDBLB Before 1660; DAM POET; DLB 58, 172; RGEL 2

Camus, Albert 1913-1960 ...... **CLC 1, 2, 4, 9, 11, 14, 32, 63, 69, 124; DC 2; SSC 9; WLC**
See also AAYA 36; AFW; BPFB 1; CA 89-92; DA; DA3; DAB; DAC; DAM DRAM, MST, NOV; DLB 72; EW 13; EXPN; EXPS; GFL 1789 to the Present; MTCW 1, 2; NFS 6; RGSF 2; RGWL 2; SSFS 4

Canby, Vincent 1924-2000 .... **CLC 13**
See also CA 81-84; 191

Cancale
See Desnos, Robert

Canetti, Elias 1905-1994 .. **CLC 3, 14, 25, 75, 86**
See also CA 21-24R; 146; CANR 23, 61; 79; CDWLB 2; CWW 2; DA3; DLB 85, 124; EW 12; MTCW 1, 2; RGWL 2

Canfield, Dorothea F.
See Fisher, Dorothy (Frances) Canfield

Canfield, Dorothea Frances
See Fisher, Dorothy (Frances) Canfield

Canfield, Dorothy
See Fisher, Dorothy (Frances) Canfield

Canin, Ethan 1960- .... **CLC 55**
See also CA 131; 135

Cankar, Ivan 1876-1918 .... **TCLC 105**
See also CDWLB 4; DLB 147

Cannon, Curt
See Hunter, Evan

Cao, Lan 1961- .... **CLC 109**
See also CA 165

Cape, Judith
See Page, P(atricia) K(athleen)
See also CCA 1

Capek, Karel 1890-1938 .... **TCLC 6, 37; DC 1; SSC 36; WLC**
See also CA 104; 140; CDWLB 4; DA; DA3; DAB; DAC; DAM DRAM, NOV; DFS 7, 11 !**; DLB 215; EW 10; MTCW 1; RGSF 2; RGWL 2; SCFW 2; SFW 4

Capote, Truman 1924-1984 . **CLC 1, 3, 8, 13, 19, 34, 38, 58; SSC 2, 47; WLC**
See also AMWS 3; BPFB 1; CA 5-8R; 113; CANR 18, 62; CDALB 1941-1968; CPW; DA; DA3; DAB; DAC; DAM MST, NOV, POP; DLB 2, 185, 227; DLBY 1980, 1984; EXPS; GLL 1; LAIT 3; MTCW 1, 2; NCFS 2; RGAL 4; RGSF 2; SATA 91; SSFS 2

Capra, Frank 1897-1991 .... **CLC 16**
See also CA 61-64; 135

Caputo, Philip 1941- .... **CLC 32**
See also CA 73-76; CANR 40; YAW

Caragiale, Ion Luca 1852-1912 ...... **TCLC 76**
See also CA 157

Card, Orson Scott 1951- .... **CLC 44, 47, 50**
See also AAYA 11, 42; BPFB 1; BYA 5, 8; CA 102; CANR 27, 47, 73, 102, 106; CPW; DA3; DAM POP; FANT; INT CANR-27; MTCW 1, 2; NFS 5; SATA 83, 127; SCFW 2; SFW 4; YAW

Cardenal, Ernesto 1925- .... **CLC 31, 161; HLC 1; PC 22**
See also CA 49-52; CANR 2, 32, 66; CWW 2; DAM MULT, POET; HW 1, 2; LAWS 1; MTCW 1, 2; RGWL 2

Cardozo, Benjamin N(athan)
1870-1938 .... **TCLC 65**
See also CA 117; 164

Carducci, Giosue (Alessandro Giuseppe)
1835-1907 .... **TCLC 32**
See also CA 163; EW 7; RGWL 2

Carew, Thomas 1595(?)-1640 . **LC 13; PC 29**
See also BRW 2; DLB 126; PAB; RGEL 2

Carey, Ernestine Gilbreth 1908- ...... **CLC 17**
See also CA 5-8R; CANR 71; SATA 2

Carey, Peter 1943- .... **CLC 40, 55, 96**
See also CA 123; 127; CANR 53, 76; CN 7; INT CA-127; MTCW 1, 2; RGSF 2; SATA 94

Carleton, William 1794-1869 .... **NCLC 3**
See also DLB 159; RGEL 2; RGSF 2

Carlisle, Henry (Coffin) 1926- .... **CLC 33**
See also CA 13-16R; CANR 15, 85

Carlsen, Chris
See Holdstock, Robert P.

Carlson, Ron(ald F.) 1947- .... **CLC 54**
See also CA 105; CAAE 189; CANR 27; DLB 244

Carlyle, Thomas 1795-1881 ..... **NCLC 22, 70**
See also BRW 4; CDBLB 1789-1832; DA; DAB; DAC; DAM MST; DLB 55, 144, 254; RGEL 2

Carman, (William) Bliss
1861-1929 .... **TCLC 7; PC 34**
See also CA 104; 152; DAC; DLB 92; RGEL 2

Carnegie, Dale 1888-1955 .... **TCLC 53**

Carossa, Hans 1878-1956 .... **TCLC 48**
See also CA 170; DLB 66

Carpenter, Don(ald Richard)
1931-1995 .... **CLC 41**
See also CA 45-48; 149; CANR 1, 71

Carpenter, Edward 1844-1929 .... **TCLC 88**
See also CA 163; GLL 1

Carpenter, John (Howard) 1948- ... **CLC 161**
See also AAYA 2; CA 134; SATA 58

Carpentier (y Valmont), Alejo
1904-1980 . **CLC 8, 11, 38, 110; HLC 1; SSC 35**
See also CA 65-68; 97-100; CANR 11, 70; CDWLB 3; DAM MULT; DLB 113; HW 1, 2; LAW; RGSF 2; RGWL 2; WLIT 1

Carr, Caleb 1955(?)- .... **CLC 86**
See also CA 147; CANR 73; DA3

Carr, Emily 1871-1945 .... **TCLC 32**
See also CA 159; DLB 68; FW; GLL 2

Carr, John Dickson 1906-1977 .... **CLC 3**
See also Fairbairn, Roger
See also CA 49-52; 69-72; CANR 3, 33, 60; CMW 4; MSW; MTCW 1, 2

Carr, Philippa
See Hibbert, Eleanor Alice Burford

Carr, Virginia Spencer 1929- .... **CLC 34**
See also CA 61-64; DLB 111

Carrere, Emmanuel 1957- .... **CLC 89**
See also CA 200

Carrier, Roch 1937- .... **CLC 13, 78**
See also CA 130; CANR 61; CCA 1; DAC; DAM MST; DLB 53; SATA 105

Carroll, James P. 1943(?)- .... **CLC 38**
See also CA 81-84; CANR 73; MTCW 1

Carroll, Jim 1951- .... **CLC 35, 143**
See also AAYA 17; CA 45-48; CANR 42

Carroll, Lewis ... NCLC 2, 53; PC 18; WLC
  See also Dodgson, Charles L(utwidge)
  See also AAYA 39; BRW 5; BYA 5, 13; CD-
    BLB 1832-1890; CLR 2, 18; DLB 18,
    163, 178; DLBY 1998; EXPN; EXPP;
    FANT; JRDA; LAIT 1; NFS 7; PFS 11;
    RGEL 2; SUFW; WCH
Carroll, Paul Vincent 1900-1968 ...... CLC 10
  See also CA 9-12R; 25-28R; DLB 10;
    RGEL 2
Carruth, Hayden 1921- ..... CLC 4, 7, 10, 18,
    84; PC 10
  See also CA 9-12R; CANR 4, 38, 59; CP 7;
    DLB 5, 165; INT CANR-4; MTCW 1, 2;
    SATA 47
Carson, Rachel Louise 1907-1964 .... CLC 71
  See also AMWS 9; ANW; CA 77-80; CANR
    35; DA3; DAM POP; FW; LAIT 4;
    MTCW 1, 2; NCFS 1; SATA 23
Carter, Angela (Olive) 1940-1992 ...... CLC 5,
    41, 76; SSC 13
  See also BRWS 3; CA 53-56; 136; CANR
    12, 36, 61, 106; DA3; DLB 14, 207, 261;
    EXPS; FANT; FW; MTCW 1, 2; RGSF 2;
    SATA 66; SATA-Obit 70; SFW 4; SSFS
    4, 12; WLIT 4
Carter, Nick
  See Smith, Martin Cruz
Carver, Raymond 1938-1988 ..... CLC 22, 36,
    53, 55, 126; SSC 8, 51
  See also AMWS 3; BPFB 1; CA 33-36R;
    126; CANR 17, 34, 61, 103; CPW; DA3;
    DAM NOV; DLB 130; DLBY 1984,
    1988; MTCW 1, 2; RGAL 4; RGSF 2;
    SSFS 3, 6, 12, 13; TCWW 2
Cary, Elizabeth, Lady Falkland
    1585-1639 .... LC 30
Cary, (Arthur) Joyce (Lunel)
    1888-1957 .... TCLC 1, 29
  See also BRW 7; CA 104; 164; CDBLB
    1914-1945; DLB 15, 100; MTCW 2;
    RGEL 2
Casanova de Seingalt, Giovanni Jacopo
    1725-1798 .... LC 13
Casares, Adolfo Bioy
  See Bioy Casares, Adolfo
  See also RGSF 2
Casas, Bartolome de las 1474-1566
  See Las Casas, Bartolome de
  See also WLIT 1
Casely-Hayford, J(oseph) E(phraim)
    1866-1903 .... TCLC 24; BLC 1
  See also BW 2; CA 123; 152; DAM MULT
Casey, John (Dudley) 1939- .... CLC 59
  See also BEST 90:2; CA 69-72; CANR 23,
    100
Casey, Michael 1947- .... CLC 2
  See also CA 65-68; CANR 109; DLB 5
Casey, Patrick
  See Thurman, Wallace (Henry)
Casey, Warren (Peter) 1935-1988 .... CLC 12
  See also CA 101; 127; INT 101
Casona, Alejandro .... CLC 49
  See also Alvarez, Alejandro Rodriguez
Cassavetes, John 1929-1989 .... CLC 20
  See also CA 85-88; 127; CANR 82
Cassian, Nina 1924- .... PC 17
  See also CWP; CWW 2
Cassill, R(onald) V(erlin) 1919- ... CLC 4, 23
  See also CA 9-12R; CAAS 1; CANR 7, 45;
    CN 7; DLB 6, 218
Cassiodorus, Flavius Magnus c. 490(?)-c.
    583(?) .... CMLC 43
Cassirer, Ernst 1874-1945 .... TCLC 61
  See also CA 157
Cassity, (Allen) Turner 1929- .... CLC 6, 42
  See also CA 17-20R; CAAS 8; CANR 11;
    CSW; DLB 105

Castaneda, Carlos (Cesar Aranha)
    1931(?)-1998 .... CLC 12, 119
  See also CA 25-28R; CANR 32, 66, 105;
    DNFS 1; HW 1; MTCW 1
Castedo, Elena 1937- .... CLC 65
  See also CA 132
Castedo-Ellerman, Elena
  See Castedo, Elena
Castellanos, Rosario 1925-1974 .... CLC 66;
    HLC 1; SSC 39
  See also CA 131; 53-56; CANR 58; CD-
    WLB 3; DAM MULT; DLB 113; FW;
    HW 1; LAW; MTCW 1; RGSF 2; RGWL
    2
Castelvetro, Lodovico 1505-1571 .... LC 12
Castiglione, Baldassare 1478-1529 ...... LC 12
  See also Castiglione, Baldesar
  See also RGWL 2
Castiglione, Baldesar
  See Castiglione, Baldassare
  See also EW 2
Castillo, Ana (Hernandez Del)
    1953- .... CLC 151
  See also AAYA 42; CA 131; CANR 51, 86;
    CWP; DLB 122, 227; DNFS 2; FW; HW
    1
Castle, Robert
  See Hamilton, Edmond
Castro (Ruz), Fidel 1926(?)-
  See also CA 110; 129; CANR 81; DAM
    MULT; HLC 1; HW 2
Castro, Guillen de 1569-1631 .... LC 19
Castro, Rosalia de 1837-1885 ... NCLC 3, 78;
    PC 41
  See also DAM MULT
Cather, Willa (Sibert) 1873-1947 .... TCLC 1,
    11, 31, 99; SSC 2, 50; WLC
  See also AAYA 24; AMW; AMWR 1; BPFB
    1; CA 104; 128; CDALB 1865-1917; DA;
    DA3; DAB; DAC; DAM MST, NOV;
    DLB 9, 54, 78, 256; DLBD 1; EXPN;
    EXPS; LAIT 3; MAWW; MTCW 1, 2;
    NFS 2; RGAL 4; RGSF 2; RHW; SATA
    30; SSFS 2, 7; TCWW 2
Catherine II
  See Catherine the Great
  See also DLB 150
Catherine the Great 1729-1796 .... LC 69
  See also Catherine II
Cato, Marcus Porcius
    234B.C.-149B.C. .... CMLC 21
  See also Cato the Elder
Cato the Elder
  See Cato, Marcus Porcius
  See also DLB 211
Catton, (Charles) Bruce 1899-1978 . CLC 35
  See also AITN 1; CA 5-8R; 81-84; CANR
    7, 74; DLB 17; SATA 2; SATA-Obit 24
Catullus c. 84B.C.-54B.C. .... CMLC 18
  See also AW 2; CDWLB 1; DLB 211;
    RGWL 2
Cauldwell, Frank
  See King, Francis (Henry)
Caunitz, William J. 1933-1996 .... CLC 34
  See also BEST 89:3; CA 125; 130; 152;
    CANR 73; INT 130
Causley, Charles (Stanley) 1917- .... CLC 7
  See also CA 9-12R; CANR 5, 35, 94; CLR
    30; CWRI 5; DLB 27; MTCW 1; SATA
    3, 66
Caute, (John) David 1936- .... CLC 29
  See also CA 1-4R; CAAS 4; CANR 1, 33,
    64; CBD; CD 5; CN 7; DAM NOV; DLB
    14, 231
Cavafy, C(onstantine) P(eter) ... TCLC 2, 7;
    PC 36
  See also Kavafis, Konstantinos Petrou
  See also CA 148; DA3; DAM POET; EW
    8; MTCW 1; RGWL 2; WP

Cavallo, Evelyn
  See Spark, Muriel (Sarah)
Cavanna, Betty .... CLC 12
  See also Harrison, Elizabeth (Allen) Ca-
    vanna
  See also JRDA; MAICYA 1; SAAS 4;
    SATA 1, 30
Cavendish, Margaret Lucas
    1623-1673 .... LC 30
  See also DLB 131, 252; RGEL 2
Caxton, William 1421(?)-1491(?) .... LC 17
  See also DLB 170
Cayer, D. M.
  See Duffy, Maureen
Cayrol, Jean 1911- .... CLC 11
  See also CA 89-92; DLB 83
Cela, Camilo Jose 1916-2002 .... CLC 4, 13,
    59, 122; HLC 1
  See also BEST 90:2; CA 21-24R; CAAS
    10; CANR 21, 32, 76; DAM MULT;
    DLBY 1989; EW 13; HW 1; MTCW 1, 2;
    RGSF 2; RGWL 2
Celan, Paul -1970 .... CLC 10, 19, 53, 82; PC
    10
  See also Antschel, Paul
  See also CDWLB 2; DLB 69; RGWL 2
Celine, Louis-Ferdinand .. CLC 1, 3, 4, 7, 9,
    15, 47, 124
  See also Destouches, Louis-Ferdinand
  See also DLB 72; EW 11; GFL 1789 to the
    Present; RGWL 2
Cellini, Benvenuto 1500-1571 .... LC 7
Cendrars, Blaise .... CLC 18, 106
  See also Sauser-Hall, Frederic
  See also DLB 258; GFL 1789 to the Present;
    RGWL 2; WP
Centlivre, Susanna 1669(?)-1723 .... LC 65
  See also DLB 84; RGEL 2
Cernuda (y Bidon), Luis 1902-1963 . CLC 54
  See also CA 131; 89-92; DAM POET; DLB
    134; GLL 1; HW 1; RGWL 2
Cervantes, Lorna Dee 1954- .... PC 35
  See also CA 131; CANR 80; CWP; DLB
    82; EXPP; HLCS 1; HW 1
Cervantes (Saavedra), Miguel de
    1547-1616 .... LC 6, 23; HLCS; SSC 12;
    WLC
  See also BYA 1, 14; DA; DAB; DAC; DAM
    MST, NOV; EW 2; LAIT 1; NFS 8; RGSF
    2; RGWL 2
Cesaire, Aime (Fernand) 1913- . CLC 19, 32,
    112; BLC 1; PC 25
  See also BW 2, 3; CA 65-68; CANR 24,
    43, 81; DA3; DAM MULT, POET; GFL
    1789 to the Present; MTCW 1, 2; WP
Chabon, Michael 1963- .... CLC 55, 149
  See also CA 139; CANR 57, 96
Chabrol, Claude 1930- .... CLC 16
  See also CA 110
Challans, Mary 1905-1983
  See Renault, Mary
  See also CA 81-84; 111; CANR 74; DA3;
    MTCW 2; SATA 23; SATA-Obit 36
Challis, George
  See Faust, Frederick (Schiller)
  See also TCWW 2
Chambers, Aidan 1934- .... CLC 35
  See also AAYA 27; CA 25-28R; CANR 12,
    31, 58; JRDA; MAICYA 1; SAAS 12;
    SATA 1, 69, 108; WYA; YAW
Chambers, James 1948-
  See Cliff, Jimmy
  See also CA 124
Chambers, Jessie
  See Lawrence, D(avid) H(erbert Richards)
  See also GLL 1

Cooper, Henry St. John
See Creasey, John
Cooper, J(oan) California (?)- .... **CLC 56**
See also AAYA 12; BW 1; CA 125; CANR
55; DAM MULT; DLB 212
Cooper, James Fenimore
1789-1851 .... **NCLC 1, 27, 54**
See also AAYA 22; AMW; BPFB 1;
CDALB 1640-1865; DA3; DLB 3, 183,
250, 254; LAIT 1; NFS 9; RGAL 4; SATA
19; WCH
Coover, Robert (Lowell) 1932- ...... **CLC 3, 7, 15, 32, 46, 87, 161; SSC 15**
See also AMWS 5; BPFB 1; CA 45-48;
CANR 3, 37, 58; CN 7; DAM NOV; DLB
2, 227; DLBY 1981; MTCW 1, 2; RGAL
4; RGSF 2
Copeland, Stewart (Armstrong)
1952- .... **CLC 26**
Copernicus, Nicolaus 1473-1543 .... **LC 45**
Coppard, A(lfred) E(dgar)
1878-1957 .... **TCLC 5; SSC 21**
See also CA 114; 167; DLB 162; HGG;
RGEL 2; RGSF 2; SUFW; YABC 1
Coppee, Francois 1842-1908 .... **TCLC 25**
See also CA 170; DLB 217
Coppola, Francis Ford 1939- ... **CLC 16, 126**
See also AAYA 39; CA 77-80; CANR 40,
78; DLB 44
Corbiere, Tristan 1845-1875 .... **NCLC 43**
See also DLB 217; GFL 1789 to the Present
Corcoran, Barbara (Asenath)
1911- .... **CLC 17**
See also AAYA 14; CA 21-24R; CAAE 191;
CAAS 2; CANR 11, 28, 48; CLR 50;
DLB 52; JRDA; MAICYA 2; MAICYAS
1; RHW; SAAS 20; SATA 3, 77, 125
Cordelier, Maurice
See Giraudoux, Jean(-Hippolyte)
Corelli, Marie .... **TCLC 51**
See also Mackay, Mary
See also DLB 34, 156; RGEL 2; SUFW
Corman, Cid .... **CLC 9**
See also Corman, Sidney
See also CAAS 2; DLB 5, 193
Corman, Sidney 1924-
See Corman, Cid
See also CA 85-88; CANR 44; CP 7; DAM
POET
Cormier, Robert (Edmund)
1925-2000 .... **CLC 12, 30**
See also AAYA 3, 19; BYA 1, 2, 6, 8, 9;
CA 1-4R; CANR 5, 23, 76, 93; CDALB
1968-1988; CLR 12, 55; DA; DAB; DAC;
DAM MST, NOV; DLB 52; EXPN; INT
CANR-23; JRDA; LAIT 5; MAICYA 1,
2; MTCW 1, 2; NFS 2; SATA 10, 45, 83;
SATA-Obit 122; WYA; YAW
Corn, Alfred (DeWitt III) 1943- .... **CLC 33**
See also CA 179; CAAE 179; CAAS 25;
CANR 44; CP 7; CSW; DLB 120; DLBY
1980
Corneille, Pierre 1606-1684 .... **LC 28**
See also DAB; DAM MST; EW 3; GFL Be-
ginnings to 1789; RGWL 2
Cornwell, David (John Moore)
1931- .... **CLC 9, 15**
See also le Carre, John
See also CA 5-8R; CANR 13, 33, 59, 107;
DA3; DAM POP; MTCW 1, 2
Cornwell, Patricia (Daniels) 1956- . **CLC 155**
See also AAYA 16; BPFB 1; CA 134;
CANR 53; CMW; CPW; CSW; DAM
POP; MSW; MTCW 1
Corso, (Nunzio) Gregory 1930-2001 . **CLC 1, 11; PC 33**
See also CA 5-8R; 193; CANR 41, 76; CP
7; DA3; DLB 5, 16, 237; MTCW 1, 2;
WP

Cortazar, Julio 1914-1984 ... **CLC 2, 3, 5, 10, 13, 15, 33, 34, 92; HLC 1; SSC 7**
See also BPFB 1; CA 21-24R; CANR 12,
32, 81; CDWLB 3; DA3; DAM MULT,
NOV; DLB 113; EXPS; HW 1, 2; LAW;
MTCW 1, 2; RGSF 2; RGWL 2; SSFS 3;
WLIT 1
Cortes, Hernan 1485-1547 .... **LC 31**
Corvinus, Jakob
See Raabe, Wilhelm (Karl)
Corvo, Baron
See Rolfe, Frederick (William Serafino Aus-
tin Lewis Mary)
See also GLL 1; RGEL 2
Corwin, Cecil
See Kornbluth, C(yril) M.
Cosic, Dobrica 1921- .... **CLC 14**
See also CA 122; 138; CDWLB 4; CWW
2; DLB 181
Costain, Thomas B(ertram)
1885-1965 .... **CLC 30**
See also BYA 3; CA 5-8R; 25-28R; DLB 9;
RHW
Costantini, Humberto 1924(?)-1987 . **CLC 49**
See also CA 131; 122; HW 1
Costello, Elvis 1955- .... **CLC 21**
Costenoble, Philostene 1898-1962
See Ghelderode, Michel de
Costenoble, Philostene 1898-1962
See Ghelderode, Michel de
Cotes, Cecil V.
See Duncan, Sara Jeannette
Cotter, Joseph Seamon Sr.
1861-1949 .... **TCLC 28; BLC 1**
See also BW 1; CA 124; DAM MULT; DLB
50
Couch, Arthur Thomas Quiller
See Quiller-Couch, Sir Arthur (Thomas)
Coulton, James
See Hansen, Joseph
Couperus, Louis (Marie Anne)
1863-1923 .... **TCLC 15**
See also CA 115; RGWL 2
Coupland, Douglas 1961- .... **CLC 85, 133**
See also AAYA 34; CA 142; CANR 57, 90;
CCA 1; CPW; DAC; DAM POP
Court, Wesli
See Turco, Lewis (Putnam)
Courtenay, Bryce 1933- .... **CLC 59**
See also CA 138; CPW
Courtney, Robert
See Ellison, Harlan (Jay)
Cousteau, Jacques-Yves 1910-1997 .. **CLC 30**
See also CA 65-68; 159; CANR 15, 67;
MTCW 1; SATA 38, 98
Coventry, Francis 1725-1754 .... **LC 46**
Coverdale, Miles c. 1487-1569 .... **LC 77**
See also DLB 167
Cowan, Peter (Walkinshaw) 1914- .... **SSC 28**
See also CA 21-24R; CANR 9, 25, 50, 83;
CN 7; DLB 260; RGSF 2
Coward, Noel (Peirce) 1899-1973 . **CLC 1, 9, 29, 51**
See also AITN 1; BRWS 2; CA 17-18; 41-
44R; CANR 35; CAP 2; CDBLB 1914-
1945; DA3; DAM DRAM; DFS 3, 6;
DLB 10, 245; IDFW 3, 4; MTCW 1, 2;
RGEL 2
Cowley, Abraham 1618-1667 .... **LC 43**
See also BRW 2; DLB 131, 151; PAB;
RGEL 2
Cowley, Malcolm 1898-1989 .... **CLC 39**
See also AMWS 2; CA 5-8R; 128; CANR
3, 55; DLB 4, 48; DLBY 1981, 1989;
MTCW 1, 2
Cowper, William 1731-1800 ..... **NCLC 8, 94; PC 40**
See also BRW 3; DA3; DAM POET; DLB
104, 109; RGEL 2

Cox, William Trevor 1928-
See Trevor, William
See also CA 9-12R; CANR 4, 37, 55, 76,
102; DAM NOV; INT CANR-37; MTCW
1, 2
Coyne, P. J.
See Masters, Hilary
Cozzens, James Gould 1903-1978 . **CLC 1, 4, 11, 92**
See also AMW; BPFB 1; CA 9-12R; 81-84;
CANR 19; CDALB 1941-1968; DLB 9;
DLBD 2; DLBY 1984, 1997; MTCW 1,
2; RGAL 4
Crabbe, George 1754-1832 .... **NCLC 26**
See also BRW 3; DLB 93; RGEL 2
Crace, Jim 1946- .... **CLC 157**
See also CA 128; 135; CANR 55, 70; CN
7; DLB 231; INT CA-135
Craddock, Charles Egbert
See Murfree, Mary Noailles
Craig, A. A.
See Anderson, Poul (William)
Craik, Mrs.
See Craik, Dinah Maria (Mulock)
See also RGEL 2
Craik, Dinah Maria (Mulock)
1826-1887 .... **NCLC 38**
See also Craik, Mrs.; Mulock, Dinah Maria
See also DLB 35, 163; MAICYA 1, 2;
SATA 34
Cram, Ralph Adams 1863-1942 ..... **TCLC 45**
See also CA 160
Cranch, Christopher Pearse
1813-1892 .... **NCLC 115**
See also DLB 1, 42, 243
Crane, (Harold) Hart 1899-1932 .... **TCLC 2, 5, 80; PC 3; WLC**
See also AMW; CA 104; 127; CDALB
1917-1929; DA; DA3; DAB; DAC; DAM
MST, POET; DLB 4, 48; MTCW 1, 2;
RGAL 4
Crane, R(onald) S(almon)
1886-1967 .... **CLC 27**
See also CA 85-88; DLB 63
Crane, Stephen (Townley)
1871-1900 ...... **TCLC 11, 17, 32; SSC 7; WLC**
See also AAYA 21; AMW; BPFB 1; BYA 3;
CA 109; 140; CANR 84; CDALB 1865-
1917; DA; DA3; DAB; DAC; DAM MST,
NOV, POET; DLB 12, 54, 78; EXPN;
EXPS; LAIT 2; NFS 4; PFS 9; RGAL 4;
RGSF 2; SSFS 4; WYA; YABC 2
Cranshaw, Stanley
See Fisher, Dorothy (Frances) Canfield
Crase, Douglas 1944- .... **CLC 58**
See also CA 106
Crashaw, Richard 1612(?)-1649 .... **LC 24**
See also BRW 2; DLB 126; PAB; RGEL 2
Craven, Margaret 1901-1980 .... **CLC 17**
See also BYA 2; CA 103; CCA 1; DAC;
LAIT 5
Crawford, F(rancis) Marion
1854-1909 .... **TCLC 10**
See also CA 107; 168; DLB 71; HGG;
RGAL 4; SUFW
Crawford, Isabella Valancy
1850-1887 .... **NCLC 12**
See also DLB 92; RGEL 2
Crayon, Geoffrey
See Irving, Washington
Creasey, John 1908-1973 .... **CLC 11**
See also Marric, J. J.
See also CA 5-8R; 41-44R; CANR 8, 59;
CMW 4; DLB 77; MTCW 1
Crebillon, Claude Prosper Jolyot de (fils)
1707-1777 .... **LC 1, 28**
See also GFL Beginnings to 1789

Danvers, Dennis 1947- .... **CLC 70**

Danziger, Paula 1944- .... **CLC 21**
See also AAYA 4, 36; BYA 6, 7, 14; CA 112; 115; CANR 37; CLR 20; JRDA; MAICYA 1, 2; SATA 36, 63, 102; SATA-Brief 30; WYA; YAW

Da Ponte, Lorenzo 1749-1838 .... **NCLC 50**

Dario, Ruben 1867-1916 ... **TCLC 4; HLC 1; PC 15**
See also CA 131; CANR 81; DAM MULT; HW 1, 2; LAW; MTCW 1, 2; RGWL 2

Darley, George 1795-1846 .... **NCLC 2**
See also DLB 96; RGEL 2

Darrow, Clarence (Seward)
1857-1938 .... **TCLC 81**
See also CA 164

Darwin, Charles 1809-1882 .... **NCLC 57**
See also BRWS 7; DLB 57, 166; RGEL 2; WLIT 4

Darwin, Erasmus 1731-1802 .... **NCLC 106**
See also DLB 93; RGEL 2

Daryush, Elizabeth 1887-1977 ...... **CLC 6, 19**
See also CA 49-52; CANR 3, 81; DLB 20

Dasgupta, Surendranath
1887-1952 .... **TCLC 81**
See also CA 157

Dashwood, Edmee Elizabeth Monica de la Pasture 1890-1943
See Delafield, E. M.
See also CA 119; 154

da Silva, Antonio Jose
1705-1739 .... **NCLC 114**
See also Silva, Jose Asuncion

Daudet, (Louis Marie) Alphonse
1840-1897 .... **NCLC 1**
See also DLB 123; GFL 1789 to the Present; RGSF 2

Daumal, Rene 1908-1944 .... **TCLC 14**
See also CA 114

Davenant, William 1606-1668 .... **LC 13**
See also DLB 58, 126; RGEL 2

Davenport, Guy (Mattison, Jr.)
1927- .... **CLC 6, 14, 38; SSC 16**
See also CA 33-36R; CANR 23, 73; CN 7; CSW; DLB 130

David, Robert
See Nezval, Vitezslav

Davidson, Avram (James) 1923-1993
See Queen, Ellery
See also CA 101; 171; CANR 26; DLB 8; FANT; SFW 4; SUFW

Davidson, Donald (Grady)
1893-1968 .... **CLC 2, 13, 19**
See also CA 5-8R; 25-28R; CANR 4, 84; DLB 45

Davidson, Hugh
See Hamilton, Edmond

Davidson, John 1857-1909 .... **TCLC 24**
See also CA 118; DLB 19; RGEL 2

Davidson, Sara 1943- .... **CLC 9**
See also CA 81-84; CANR 44, 68; DLB 185

Davie, Donald (Alfred) 1922-1995 .... **CLC 5, 8, 10, 31; PC 29**
See also BRWS 6; CA 1-4R; 149; CAAS 3; CANR 1, 44; CP 7; DLB 27; MTCW 1; RGEL 2

Davie, Elspeth 1919-1995 .... **SSC 52**
See also CA 120; 126; 150; DLB 139

Davies, Ray(mond Douglas) 1944- ... **CLC 21**
See also CA 116; 146; CANR 92

Davies, Rhys 1901-1978 .... **CLC 23**
See also CA 9-12R; 81-84; CANR 4; DLB 139, 191

Davies, (William) Robertson
1913-1995 .... **CLC 2, 7, 13, 25, 42, 75, 91; WLC**
See also Marchbanks, Samuel
See also BEST 89:2; BPFB 1; CA 33-36R; 150; CANR 17, 42, 103; CN 7; CPW; DA; DA3; DAB; DAC; DAM MST, NOV, POP; DLB 68; HGG; INT CANR-17; MTCW 1, 2; RGEL 2

Davies, Walter C.
See Kornbluth, C(yril) M.

Davies, William Henry 1871-1940 ... **TCLC 5**
See also CA 104; 179; DLB 19, 174; RGEL 2

Da Vinci, Leonardo 1452-1519 ..... **LC 12, 57, 60**
See also AAYA 40

Davis, Angela (Yvonne) 1944- .... **CLC 77**
See also BW 2, 3; CA 57-60; CANR 10, 81; CSW; DA3; DAM MULT; FW

Davis, B. Lynch
See Bioy Casares, Adolfo; Borges, Jorge Luis

Davis, Gordon
See Hunt, E(verette) Howard, (Jr.)

Davis, H(arold) L(enoir) 1896-1960 . **CLC 49**
See also ANW; CA 178; 89-92; DLB 9, 206; SATA 114

Davis, Rebecca (Blaine) Harding
1831-1910 .... **TCLC 6; SSC 38**
See also CA 104; 179; DLB 74, 239; FW; NFS 14; RGAL 4

Davis, Richard Harding
1864-1916 .... **TCLC 24**
See also CA 114; 179; DLB 12, 23, 78, 79, 189; DLBD 13; RGAL 4

Davison, Frank Dalby 1893-1970 ..... **CLC 15**
See also CA 116; DLB 260

Davison, Lawrence H.
See Lawrence, D(avid) H(erbert Richards)

Davison, Peter (Hubert) 1928- .... **CLC 28**
See also CA 9-12R; CAAS 4; CANR 3, 43, 84; CP 7; DLB 5

Davys, Mary 1674-1732 .... **LC 1, 46**
See also DLB 39

Dawson, Fielding 1930-2002 .... **CLC 6**
See also CA 85-88; CANR 108; DLB 130

Dawson, Peter
See Faust, Frederick (Schiller)
See also TCWW 2, 2

Day, Clarence (Shepard, Jr.)
1874-1935 .... **TCLC 25**
See also CA 108; DLB 11

Day, John 1574(?)-1640(?) .... **LC 70**
See also DLB 62, 170; RGEL 2

Day, Thomas 1748-1789 .... **LC 1**
See also DLB 39; YABC 1

Day Lewis, C(ecil) 1904-1972 . **CLC 1, 6, 10; PC 11**
See also Blake, Nicholas
See also BRWS 3; CA 13-16; 33-36R; CANR 34; CAP 1; CWRI 5; DAM POET; DLB 15, 20; MTCW 1, 2; RGEL 2

Dazai Osamu .... **TCLC 11; SSC 41**
See also Tsushima, Shuji
See also CA 164; DLB 182; MJW; RGSF 2; RGWL 2

de Andrade, Carlos Drummond
See Drummond de Andrade, Carlos

de Andrade, Mario 1892-1945
See Andrade, Mario de
See also CA 178; HW 2

Deane, Norman
See Creasey, John

Deane, Seamus (Francis) 1940- ...... **CLC 122**
See also CA 118; CANR 42

de Beauvoir, Simone (Lucie Ernestine Marie Bertrand)
See Beauvoir, Simone (Lucie Ernestine Marie Bertrand) de

de Beer, P.
See Bosman, Herman Charles

de Brissac, Malcolm
See Dickinson, Peter (Malcolm)

de Campos, Alvaro
See Pessoa, Fernando (Antonio Nogueira)

de Chardin, Pierre Teilhard
See Teilhard de Chardin, (Marie Joseph) Pierre

Dee, John 1527-1608 .... **LC 20**
See also DLB 136, 213

Deer, Sandra 1940- .... **CLC 45**
See also CA 186

De Ferrari, Gabriella 1941- .... **CLC 65**
See also CA 146

Defoe, Daniel 1660(?)-1731 .. **LC 1, 42; WLC**
See also AAYA 27; BRW 3; BRWR 1; BYA 4; CDBLB 1660-1789; CLR 61; DA; DA3; DAB; DAC; DAM MST, NOV; DLB 39, 95, 101; JRDA; LAIT 1; MAICYA 1, 2; NFS 9, 13; RGEL 2; SATA 22; WCH; WLIT 3

de Gourmont, Remy(-Marie-Charles)
See Gourmont, Remy(-Marie-Charles) de

de Hartog, Jan 1914- .... **CLC 19**
See also CA 1-4R; CANR 1; DFS 12

de Hostos, E. M.
See Hostos (y Bonilla), Eugenio Maria de

de Hostos, Eugenio M.
See Hostos (y Bonilla), Eugenio Maria de

Deighton, Len .... **CLC 4, 7, 22, 46**
See also Deighton, Leonard Cyril
See also AAYA 6; BEST 89:2; BPFB 1; CDBLB 1960 to Present; CMW 4; CN 7; CPW; DLB 87

Deighton, Leonard Cyril 1929-
See Deighton, Len
See also CA 9-12R; CANR 19, 33, 68; DA3; DAM NOV, POP; MTCW 1, 2

Dekker, Thomas 1572(?)-1632 ..... **LC 22; DC 12**
See also CDBLB Before 1660; DAM DRAM; DLB 62, 172; RGEL 2

Delafield, E. M. .... **TCLC 61**
See also Dashwood, Edmee Elizabeth Monica de la Pasture
See also DLB 34; RHW

de la Mare, Walter (John)
1873-1956 . **TCLC 4, 53; SSC 14; WLC**
See also CA 163; CDBLB 1914-1945; CLR 23; CWRI 5; DA3; DAB; DAC; DAM MST, POET; DLB 19, 153, 162, 255; EXPP; HGG; MAICYA 1, 2; MTCW 1; RGEL 2; RGSF 2; SATA 16; SUFW; WCH

Delaney, Franey
See O'Hara, John (Henry)

Delaney, Shelagh 1939- .... **CLC 29**
See also CA 17-20R; CANR 30, 67; CBD; CD 5; CDBLB 1960 to Present; CWD; DAM DRAM; DFS 7; DLB 13; MTCW 1

Delany, Martin Robison
1812-1885 .... **NCLC 93**
See also DLB 50; RGAL 4

Delany, Mary (Granville Pendarves)
1700-1788 .... **LC 12**

Delany, Samuel R(ay), Jr. 1942- . **CLC 8, 14, 38, 141; BLC 1**
See also AAYA 24; AFAW 2; BPFB 1; BW 2, 3; CA 81-84; CANR 27, 43; DAM MULT; DLB 8, 33; MTCW 1, 2; RGAL 4; SCFW

De La Ramee, (Marie) Louise 1839-1908
See Ouida
See also SATA 20

de la Roche, Mazo 1879-1961 .... **CLC 14**
  See also CA 85-88; CANR 30; DLB 68;
  RGEL 2; RHW; SATA 64
De La Salle, Innocent
  See Hartmann, Sadakichi
Delbanco, Nicholas (Franklin)
  1942- .... **CLC 6, 13**
  See also CA 17-20R; CAAE 189; CAAS 2;
  CANR 29, 55; DLB 6, 234
del Castillo, Michel 1933- .... **CLC 38**
  See also CA 109; CANR 77
Deledda, Grazia (Cosima)
  1875(?)-1936 .... **TCLC 23**
  See also CA 123; RGWL 2
Deleuze, Gilles 1925-1995 .... **TCLC 116**
Delgado, Abelardo (Lalo) B(arrientos) 1930-
  See also CA 131; CAAS 15; CANR 90;
  DAM MST, MULT; DLB 82; HLC 1; HW
  1, 2
Delibes, Miguel .... **CLC 8, 18**
  See also Delibes Setien, Miguel
Delibes Setien, Miguel 1920-
  See Delibes, Miguel
  See also CA 45-48; CANR 1, 32; HW 1;
  MTCW 1
DeLillo, Don 1936- ..... **CLC 8, 10, 13, 27, 39,
  54, 76, 143**
  See also AMWS 6; BEST 89:1; BPFB 1;
  CA 81-84; CANR 21, 76, 92; CN 7; CPW;
  DA3; DAM NOV, POP; DLB 6, 173;
  MTCW 1, 2; RGAL 4
de Lisser, H. G.
  See De Lisser, H(erbert) G(eorge)
  See also DLB 117
De Lisser, H(erbert) G(eorge)
  1878-1944 .... **TCLC 12**
  See also de Lisser, H. G.
  See also BW 2; CA 109; 152
Deloire, Pierre
  See Peguy, Charles (Pierre)
Deloney, Thomas 1543(?)-1600 .... **LC 41**
  See also DLB 167; RGEL 2
Deloria, Vine (Victor), Jr. 1933- ...... **CLC 21,
  122**
  See also CA 53-56; CANR 5, 20, 48, 98;
  DAM MULT; DLB 175; MTCW 1;
  NNAL; SATA 21
Del Vecchio, John M(ichael) 1947- .. **CLC 29**
  See also CA 110; DLBD 9
de Man, Paul (Adolph Michel)
  1919-1983 .... **CLC 55**
  See also CA 128; 111; CANR 61; DLB 67;
  MTCW 1, 2
DeMarinis, Rick 1934- .... **CLC 54**
  See also CA 57-60, 184; CAAE 184; CAAS
  24; CANR 9, 25, 50; DLB 218
Dembry, R. Emmet
  See Murfree, Mary Noailles
Demby, William 1922- .... **CLC 53; BLC 1**
  See also BW 1, 3; CA 81-84; CANR 81;
  DAM MULT; DLB 33
de Menton, Francisco
  See Chin, Frank (Chew, Jr.)
Demetrius of Phalerum c.
  307B.C.- .... **CMLC 34**
Demijohn, Thom
  See Disch, Thomas M(ichael)
Deming, Richard 1915-1983
  See Queen, Ellery
  See also CA 9-12R; CANR 3, 94; SATA 24
Democritus c. 460B.C.-c. 370B.C. . **CMLC 47**
de Montherlant, Henry (Milon)
  See Montherlant, Henry (Milon) de
Demosthenes 384B.C.-322B.C. ...... **CMLC 13**
  See also AW 1; DLB 176; RGWL 2
de Natale, Francine
  See Malzberg, Barry N(athaniel)

de Navarre, Marguerite 1492-1549 ..... **LC 61**
  See also Marguerite d'Angouleme; Mar-
  guerite de Navarre
Denby, Edwin (Orr) 1903-1983 .... **CLC 48**
  See also CA 138; 110
Denham, John 1615-1669 .... **LC 73**
  See also DLB 58, 126; RGEL 2
Denis, Julio
  See Cortazar, Julio
Denmark, Harrison
  See Zelazny, Roger (Joseph)
Dennis, John 1658-1734 .... **LC 11**
  See also DLB 101; RGEL 2
Dennis, Nigel (Forbes) 1912-1989 ...... **CLC 8**
  See also CA 25-28R; 129; DLB 13, 15, 233;
  MTCW 1
Dent, Lester 1904(?)-1959 .... **TCLC 72**
  See also CA 112; 161; CMW 4; SFW 4
De Palma, Brian (Russell) 1940- ...... **CLC 20**
  See also CA 109
De Quincey, Thomas 1785-1859 ..... **NCLC 4,
  87**
  See also BRW 4; CDBLB 1789-1832; DLB
  110, 144; RGEL 2
Deren, Eleanora 1908(?)-1961
  See Deren, Maya
  See also CA 192; 111
Deren, Maya .... **CLC 16, 102**
  See also Deren, Eleanora
Derleth, August (William)
  1909-1971 .... **CLC 31**
  See also BPFB 1; BYA 9, 10; CA 1-4R; 29-
  32R; CANR 4; CMW 4; DLB 9; DLBD
  17; HGG; SATA 5; SUFW
Der Nister 1884-1950 .... **TCLC 56**
de Routisie, Albert
  See Aragon, Louis
Derrida, Jacques 1930- .... **CLC 24, 87**
  See also CA 124; 127; CANR 76, 98; DLB
  242; MTCW 1
Derry Down Derry
  See Lear, Edward
Dersonnes, Jacques
  See Simenon, Georges (Jacques Christian)
Desai, Anita 1937- .... **CLC 19, 37, 97**
  See also BRWS 5; CA 81-84; CANR 33,
  53, 95; CN 7; CWRI 5; DA3; DAB; DAM
  NOV; DNFS 2; FW; MTCW 1, 2; SATA
  63, 126
Desai, Kiran 1971- .... **CLC 119**
  See also CA 171
de Saint-Luc, Jean
  See Glassco, John
de Saint Roman, Arnaud
  See Aragon, Louis
Desbordes-Valmore, Marceline
  1786-1859 .... **NCLC 97**
  See also DLB 217
Descartes, Rene 1596-1650 .... **LC 20, 35**
  See also EW 3; GFL Beginnings to 1789
De Sica, Vittorio 1901(?)-1974 .... **CLC 20**
  See also CA 117
Desnos, Robert 1900-1945 .... **TCLC 22**
  See also CA 121; 151; CANR 107; DLB
  258
Destouches, Louis-Ferdinand
  1894-1961 .... **CLC 9, 15**
  See also Celine, Louis-Ferdinand
  See also CA 85-88; CANR 28; MTCW 1
de Tolignac, Gaston
  See Griffith, D(avid Lewelyn) W(ark)
Deutsch, Babette 1895-1982 .... **CLC 18**
  See also BYA 3; CA 1-4R; 108; CANR 4,
  79; DLB 45; SATA 1; SATA-Obit 33
Devenant, William 1606-1649 .... **LC 13**
Devkota, Laxmiprasad 1909-1959 . **TCLC 23**
  See also CA 123

De Voto, Bernard (Augustine)
  1897-1955 .... **TCLC 29**
  See also CA 113; 160; DLB 9, 256
De Vries, Peter 1910-1993 ..... **CLC 1, 2, 3, 7,
  10, 28, 46**
  See also CA 17-20R; 142; CANR 41; DAM
  NOV; DLB 6; DLBY 1982; MTCW 1, 2
Dewey, John 1859-1952 .... **TCLC 95**
  See also CA 114; 170; DLB 246; RGAL 4
Dexter, John
  See Bradley, Marion Zimmer
  See also GLL 1
Dexter, Martin
  See Faust, Frederick (Schiller)
  See also TCWW 2
Dexter, Pete 1943- .... **CLC 34, 55**
  See also BEST 89:2; CA 127; 131; CPW;
  DAM POP; INT 131; MTCW 1
Diamano, Silmang
  See Senghor, Leopold Sedar
Diamond, Neil 1941- .... **CLC 30**
  See also CA 108
Diaz del Castillo, Bernal 1496-1584 .. **LC 31;
  HLCS 1**
  See also LAW
di Bassetto, Corno
  See Shaw, George Bernard
Dick, Philip K(indred) 1928-1982 ... **CLC 10,
  30, 72**
  See also AAYA 24; BPFB 1; BYA 11; CA
  49-52; 106; CANR 2, 16; CPW; DA3;
  DAM NOV, POP; DLB 8; MTCW 1, 2;
  NFS 5; SCFW; SFW 4
Dickens, Charles (John Huffam)
  1812-1870 .... **NCLC 3, 8, 18, 26, 37, 50,
  86, 105, 113; SSC 17, 49; WLC**
  See also AAYA 23; BRW 5; BYA 1, 2, 3,
  13, 14; CDBLB 1832-1890; CMW 4; DA;
  DA3; DAB; DAC; DAM MST, NOV;
  DLB 21, 55, 70, 159, 166; EXPN; HGG;
  JRDA; LAIT 1, 2; MAICYA 1, 2; NFS 4,
  5, 10, 14; RGEL 2; RGSF 2; SATA 15;
  SUFW; TEA; WCH; WLIT 4; WYA
Dickey, James (Lafayette)
  1923-1997 .... **CLC 1, 2, 4, 7, 10, 15, 47,
  109; PC 40**
  See also AITN 1, 2; AMWS 4; BPFB 1;
  CA 9-12R; 156; CABS 2; CANR 10, 48,
  61, 105; CDALB 1968-1988; CP 7; CPW;
  CSW; DA3; DAM NOV, POET, POP;
  DLB 5, 193; DLBD 7; DLBY 1982, 1993,
  1996, 1997, 1998; INT CANR-10; MTCW
  1, 2; NFS 9; PFS 6, 11; RGAL 4
Dickey, William 1928-1994 .... **CLC 3, 28**
  See also CA 9-12R; 145; CANR 24, 79;
  DLB 5
Dickinson, Charles 1951- .... **CLC 49**
  See also CA 128
Dickinson, Emily (Elizabeth)
  1830-1886 ... **NCLC 21, 77; PC 1; WLC**
  See also AAYA 22; AMW; AMWR 1;
  CDALB 1865-1917; DA; DA3; DAB;
  DAC; DAM MST, POET; DLB 1, 243;
  EXPP; MAWW; PAB; PFS 1, 2, 3, 4, 5,
  6, 8, 10, 11, 13; RGAL 4; SATA 29; WP;
  WYA
Dickinson, Mrs. Herbert Ward
  See Phelps, Elizabeth Stuart
Dickinson, Peter (Malcolm) 1927- .. **CLC 12,
  35**
  See also AAYA 9; BYA 5; CA 41-44R;
  CANR 31, 58, 88; CLR 29; CMW 4; DLB
  87, 161; JRDA; MAICYA 1, 2; SATA 5,
  62, 95; SFW 4; WYA; YAW
Dickson, Carr
  See Carr, John Dickson
Dickson, Carter
  See Carr, John Dickson

Dove, Rita (Frances) 1952- .... **CLC 50, 81; BLCS; PC 6**
See also AMWS 4; BW 2; CA 109; CAAS 19; CANR 27, 42, 68, 76, 97; CDALBS; CP 7; CSW; CWP; DA3; DAM MULT, POET; DLB 120; EXPP; MTCW 1; PFS 1, 15; RGAL 4

Doveglion
See Villa, Jose Garcia

Dowell, Coleman 1925-1985 .... **CLC 60**
See also CA 25-28R; 117; CANR 10; DLB 130; GLL 2

Dowson, Ernest (Christopher)
1867-1900 .... **TCLC 4**
See also CA 105; 150; DLB 19, 135; RGEL 2

Doyle, A. Conan
See Doyle, Sir Arthur Conan

Doyle, Sir Arthur Conan
1859-1930 .... **TCLC 7; SSC 12; WLC**
See also Conan Doyle, Arthur
See also AAYA 14; BRWS 2; CA 104; 122; CDBLB 1890-1914; CMW 4; DA; DA3; DAB; DAC; DAM MST, NOV; DLB 18, 70, 156, 178; EXPS; HGG; LAIT 2; MSW; MTCW 1, 2; RGEL 2; RGSF 2; RHW; SATA 24; SCFW 2; SFW 4; SSFS 2; WCH; WLIT 4; WYA; YAW

Doyle, Conan
See Doyle, Sir Arthur Conan

Doyle, John
See Graves, Robert (von Ranke)

Doyle, Roddy 1958(?)- .... **CLC 81**
See also AAYA 14; BRWS 5; CA 143; CANR 73; CN 7; DA3; DLB 194

Doyle, Sir A. Conan
See Doyle, Sir Arthur Conan

Dr. A
See Asimov, Isaac; Silverstein, Alvin; Silverstein, Virginia B(arbara Opshelor)

Drabble, Margaret 1939- ...... **CLC 2, 3, 5, 8, 10, 22, 53, 129**
See also BRWS 4; CA 13-16R; CANR 18, 35, 63; CDBLB 1960 to Present; CN 7; CPW; DA3; DAB; DAC; DAM MST, NOV, POP; DLB 14, 155, 231; FW; MTCW 1, 2; RGEL 2; SATA 48

Drapier, M. B.
See Swift, Jonathan

Drayham, James
See Mencken, H(enry) L(ouis)

Drayton, Michael 1563-1631 .... **LC 8**
See also DAM POET; DLB 121; RGEL 2

Dreadstone, Carl
See Campbell, (John) Ramsey

Dreiser, Theodore (Herman Albert)
1871-1945 .... **TCLC 10, 18, 35, 83; SSC 30; WLC**
See also AMW; CA 106; 132; CDALB 1865-1917; DA; DA3; DAC; DAM MST, NOV; DLB 9, 12, 102, 137; DLBD 1; LAIT 2; MTCW 1, 2; NFS 8; RGAL 4

Drexler, Rosalyn 1926- .... **CLC 2, 6**
See also CA 81-84; CAD; CANR 68; CD 5; CWD

Dreyer, Carl Theodor 1889-1968 ...... **CLC 16**
See also CA 116

Drieu la Rochelle, Pierre(-Eugene)
1893-1945 .... **TCLC 21**
See also CA 117; DLB 72; GFL 1789 to the Present

Drinkwater, John 1882-1937 .... **TCLC 57**
See also CA 109; 149; DLB 10, 19, 149; RGEL 2

Drop Shot
See Cable, George Washington

Droste-Hulshoff, Annette Freiin von
1797-1848 .... **NCLC 3**
See also CDWLB 2; DLB 133; RGSF 2; RGWL 2

Drummond, Walter
See Silverberg, Robert

Drummond, William Henry
1854-1907 .... **TCLC 25**
See also CA 160; DLB 92

Drummond de Andrade, Carlos
1902-1987 .... **CLC 18**
See also Andrade, Carlos Drummond de
See also CA 132; 123; LAW

Drury, Allen (Stuart) 1918-1998 .... **CLC 37**
See also CA 57-60; 170; CANR 18, 52; CN 7; INT CANR-18

Dryden, John 1631-1700 ..... **LC 3, 21; DC 3; PC 25; WLC**
See also BRW 2; CDBLB 1660-1789; DA; DAB; DAC; DAM DRAM, MST, POET; DLB 80, 101, 131; EXPP; IDTP; RGEL 2; TEA; WLIT 3

Duberman, Martin (Bauml) 1930- ..... **CLC 8**
See also CA 1-4R; CAD; CANR 2, 63; CD 5

Dubie, Norman (Evans) 1945- .... **CLC 36**
See also CA 69-72; CANR 12; CP 7; DLB 120; PFS 12

Du Bois, W(illiam) E(dward) B(urghardt)
1868-1963 ... **CLC 1, 2, 13, 64, 96; BLC 1; WLC**
See also AAYA 40; AFAW 1, 2; AMWS 2; BW 1, 3; CA 85-88; CANR 34, 82; CDALB 1865-1917; DA; DA3; DAC; DAM MST, MULT, NOV; DLB 47, 50, 91, 246; EXPP; LAIT 2; MTCW 1, 2; NCFS 1; PFS 13; RGAL 4; SATA 42

Dubus, Andre 1936-1999 ..... **CLC 13, 36, 97; SSC 15**
See also AMWS 7; CA 21-24R; 177; CANR 17; CN 7; CSW; DLB 130; INT CANR-17; RGAL 4; SSFS 10

Duca Minimo
See D'Annunzio, Gabriele

Ducharme, Rejean 1941- .... **CLC 74**
See also CA 165; DLB 60

Duchen, Claire .... **CLC 65**

Duclos, Charles Pinot- 1704-1772 .... **LC 1**
See also GFL Beginnings to 1789

Dudek, Louis 1918- .... **CLC 11, 19**
See also CA 45-48; CAAS 14; CANR 1; CP 7; DLB 88

Duerrenmatt, Friedrich 1921-1990 ... **CLC 1, 4, 8, 11, 15, 43, 102**
See also Durrenmatt, Friedrich
See also CA 17-20R; CANR 33; CMW 4; DAM DRAM; DLB 69, 124; MTCW 1, 2

Duffy, Bruce 1953(?)- .... **CLC 50**
See also CA 172

Duffy, Maureen 1933- .... **CLC 37**
See also CA 25-28R; CANR 33, 68; CBD; CN 7; CP 7; CWD; CWP; DFS 15; DLB 14; FW; MTCW 1

Du Fu
See Tu Fu
See also RGWL 2

Dugan, Alan 1923- .... **CLC 2, 6**
See also CA 81-84; CP 7; DLB 5; PFS 10

du Gard, Roger Martin
See Martin du Gard, Roger

Duhamel, Georges 1884-1966 .... **CLC 8**
See also CA 81-84; 25-28R; CANR 35; DLB 65; GFL 1789 to the Present; MTCW 1

Dujardin, Edouard (Emile Louis)
1861-1949 .... **TCLC 13**
See also CA 109; DLB 123

Dulles, John Foster 1888-1959 .... **TCLC 72**
See also CA 115; 149

Dumas, Alexandre (pere)
1802-1870 .... **NCLC 11, 71; WLC**
See also AAYA 22; BYA 3; DA; DA3; DAB; DAC; DAM MST, NOV; DLB 119, 192; EW 6; GFL 1789 to the Present; LAIT 1, 2; NFS 14; RGWL 2; SATA 18; WCH

Dumas, Alexandre (fils)
1824-1895 .... **NCLC 9; DC 1**
See also DLB 192; GFL 1789 to the Present; RGWL 2

Dumas, Claudine
See Malzberg, Barry N(athaniel)

Dumas, Henry L. 1934-1968 .... **CLC 6, 62**
See also BW 1; CA 85-88; DLB 41; RGAL 4

du Maurier, Daphne 1907-1989 .. **CLC 6, 11, 59; SSC 18**
See also AAYA 37; BPFB 1; BRWS 3; CA 5-8R; 128; CANR 6, 55; CMW 4; CPW; DA3; DAB; DAC; DAM MST, POP; DLB 191; HGG; LAIT 3; MSW; MTCW 1, 2; NFS 12; RGEL 2; RGSF 2; RHW; SATA 27; SATA-Obit 60; SSFS 14

Du Maurier, George 1834-1896 ..... **NCLC 86**
See also DLB 153, 178; RGEL 2

Dunbar, Paul Laurence 1872-1906 . **TCLC 2, 12; BLC 1; PC 5; SSC 8; WLC**
See also AFAW 1, 2; AMWS 2; BW 1, 3; CA 104; 124; CANR 79; CDALB 1865-1917; DA; DA3; DAC; DAM MST, MULT, POET; DLB 50, 54, 78; EXPP; RGAL 4; SATA 34

Dunbar, William 1460(?)-1520(?) .... **LC 20**
See also DLB 132, 146; RGEL 2

Duncan, Dora Angela
See Duncan, Isadora

Duncan, Isadora 1877(?)-1927 .... **TCLC 68**
See also CA 118; 149

Duncan, Lois 1934- .... **CLC 26**
See also AAYA 4, 34; BYA 6, 8; CA 1-4R; CANR 2, 23, 36; CLR 29; JRDA; MAICYA 1, 2; MAICYAS 1; SAAS 2; SATA 1, 36, 75, 133; WYA; YAW

Duncan, Robert (Edward)
1919-1988 .... **CLC 1, 2, 4, 7, 15, 41, 55; PC 2**
See also CA 9-12R; 124; CANR 28, 62; DAM POET; DLB 5, 16, 193; MTCW 1, 2; PFS 13; RGAL 4; WP

Duncan, Sara Jeannette
1861-1922 .... **TCLC 60**
See also CA 157; DLB 92

Dunlap, William 1766-1839 .... **NCLC 2**
See also DLB 30, 37, 59; RGAL 4

Dunn, Douglas (Eaglesham) 1942- .... **CLC 6, 40**
See also CA 45-48; CANR 2, 33; CP 7; DLB 40; MTCW 1

Dunn, Katherine (Karen) 1945- .... **CLC 71**
See also CA 33-36R; CANR 72; HGG; MTCW 1

Dunn, Stephen (Elliott) 1939- .... **CLC 36**
See also CA 33-36R; CANR 12, 48, 53, 105; CP 7; DLB 105

Dunne, Finley Peter 1867-1936 ...... **TCLC 28**
See also CA 108; 178; DLB 11, 23; RGAL 4

Dunne, John Gregory 1932- .... **CLC 28**
See also CA 25-28R; CANR 14, 50; CN 7; DLBY 1980

Dunsany, Lord .... **TCLC 2, 59**
See also Dunsany, Edward John Moreton Drax Plunkett
See also DLB 77, 153, 156, 255; FANT; IDTP; RGEL 2; SFW 4; SUFW

Dunsany, Edward John Moreton Drax Plunkett 1878-1957
See Dunsany, Lord
See also CA 104; 148; DLB 10; MTCW 1

Estleman, Loren D. 1952- .... **CLC 48**
  See also AAYA 27; CA 85-88; CANR 27,
  74; CMW 4; CPW; DA3; DAM NOV,
  POP; DLB 226; INT CANR-27; MTCW
  1, 2

Etherege, Sir George 1636-1692 .... **LC 78**
  See also BRW 2; DAM DRAM; DLB 80;
  PAB; RGEL 2

Euclid 306B.C.-283B.C. .... **CMLC 25**

Eugenides, Jeffrey 1960(?)- .... **CLC 81**
  See also CA 144

Euripides c. 484B.C.-406B.C. .... **CMLC 23,
  51; DC 4; WLCS**
  See also AW 1; CDWLB 1; DA; DA3;
  DAB; DAC; DAM DRAM, MST; DFS 1,
  4, 6; DLB 176; LAIT 1; RGWL 2

Evan, Evin
  See Faust, Frederick (Schiller)

Evans, Caradoc 1878-1945 ... **TCLC 85; SSC
  43**
  See also DLB 162

Evans, Evan
  See Faust, Frederick (Schiller)
  See also TCWW 2

Evans, Marian
  See Eliot, George

Evans, Mary Ann
  See Eliot, George

Evarts, Esther
  See Benson, Sally

Everett, Percival
  See Everett, Percival L.
  See also CSW

Everett, Percival L. 1956- .... **CLC 57**
  See also Everett, Percival
  See also BW 2; CA 129; CANR 94

Everson, R(onald) G(ilmour)
  1903-1992 .... **CLC 27**
  See also CA 17-20R; DLB 88

Everson, William (Oliver)
  1912-1994 .... **CLC 1, 5, 14**
  See also CA 9-12R; 145; CANR 20; DLB
  5, 16, 212; MTCW 1

Evtushenko, Evgenii Aleksandrovich
  See Yevtushenko, Yevgeny (Alexandrovich)
  See also RGWL 2

Ewart, Gavin (Buchanan)
  1916-1995 .... **CLC 13, 46**
  See also BRWS 7; CA 89-92; 150; CANR
  17, 46; CP 7; DLB 40; MTCW 1

Ewers, Hanns Heinz 1871-1943 ..... **TCLC 12**
  See also CA 109; 149

Ewing, Frederick R.
  See Sturgeon, Theodore (Hamilton)

Exley, Frederick (Earl) 1929-1992 .... **CLC 6,
  11**
  See also AITN 2; BPFB 1; CA 81-84; 138;
  DLB 143; DLBY 1981

Eynhardt, Guillermo
  See Quiroga, Horacio (Sylvestre)

Ezekiel, Nissim 1924- .... **CLC 61**
  See also CA 61-64; CP 7

Ezekiel, Tish O'Dowd 1943- .... **CLC 34**
  See also CA 129

Fadeyev, A.
  See Bulgya, Alexander Alexandrovich

Fadeyev, Alexander .... **TCLC 53**
  See also Bulgya, Alexander Alexandrovich

Fagen, Donald 1948- .... **CLC 26**

Fainzilberg, Ilya Arnoldovich 1897-1937
  See Ilf, Ilya
  See also CA 120; 165

Fair, Ronald L. 1932- .... **CLC 18**
  See also BW 1; CA 69-72; CANR 25; DLB
  33

Fairbairn, Roger
  See Carr, John Dickson

Fairbairns, Zoe (Ann) 1948- .... **CLC 32**
  See also CA 103; CANR 21, 85; CN 7

Fairfield, Flora
  See Alcott, Louisa May

Fairman, Paul W. 1916-1977
  See Queen, Ellery
  See also CA 114; SFW 4

Falco, Gian
  See Papini, Giovanni

Falconer, James
  See Kirkup, James

Falconer, Kenneth
  See Kornbluth, C(yril) M.

Falkland, Samuel
  See Heijermans, Herman

Fallaci, Oriana 1930- .... **CLC 11, 110**
  See also CA 77-80; CANR 15, 58; FW;
  MTCW 1

Faludi, Susan 1959- .... **CLC 140**
  See also CA 138; FW; MTCW 1; NCFS 3

Faludy, George 1913- .... **CLC 42**
  See also CA 21-24R

Faludy, Gyoergy
  See Faludy, George

Fanon, Frantz 1925-1961 .... **CLC 74; BLC 2**
  See also BW 1; CA 116; 89-92; DAM
  MULT; WLIT 2

Fanshawe, Ann 1625-1680 .... **LC 11**

Fante, John (Thomas) 1911-1983 ..... **CLC 60**
  See also CA 69-72; 109; CANR 23, 104;
  DLB 130; DLBY 1983

Farah, Nuruddin 1945- .. **CLC 53, 137; BLC
  2**
  See also AFW; BW 2, 3; CA 106; CANR
  81; CDWLB 3; CN 7; DAM MULT; DLB
  125; WLIT 2

Fargue, Leon-Paul 1876(?)-1947 .... **TCLC 11**
  See also CA 109; CANR 107; DLB 258

Farigoule, Louis
  See Romains, Jules

Farina, Richard 1936(?)-1966 .... **CLC 9**
  See also CA 81-84; 25-28R

Farley, Walter (Lorimer)
  1915-1989 .... **CLC 17**
  See also BYA 14; CA 17-20R; CANR 8,
  29, 84; DLB 22; JRDA; MAICYA 1, 2;
  SATA 2, 43, 132; YAW

Farmer, Philip Jose 1918- .... **CLC 1, 19**
  See also AAYA 28; BPFB 1; CA 1-4R;
  CANR 4, 35; DLB 8; MTCW 1; SATA
  93; SCFW 2; SFW 4

Farquhar, George 1677-1707 .... **LC 21**
  See also BRW 2; DAM DRAM; DLB 84;
  RGEL 2

Farrell, J(ames) G(ordon)
  1935-1979 .... **CLC 6**
  See also CA 73-76; 89-92; CANR 36; DLB
  14; MTCW 1; RGEL 2; RHW; WLIT 4

Farrell, James T(homas) 1904-1979 . **CLC 1,
  4, 8, 11, 66; SSC 28**
  See also AMW; BPFB 1; CA 5-8R; 89-92;
  CANR 9, 61; DLB 4, 9, 86; DLBD 2;
  MTCW 1, 2; RGAL 4

Farrell, Warren (Thomas) 1943- ...... **CLC 70**
  See also CA 146

Farren, Richard J.
  See Betjeman, John

Farren, Richard M.
  See Betjeman, John

Fassbinder, Rainer Werner
  1946-1982 .... **CLC 20**
  See also CA 93-96; 106; CANR 31

Fast, Howard (Melvin) 1914- ... **CLC 23, 131**
  See also AAYA 16; BPFB 1; CA 1-4R; 181;
  CAAE 181; CAAS 18; CANR 1, 33, 54,
  75, 98; CMW 4; CN 7; CPW; DAM NOV;
  DLB 9; INT CANR-33; MTCW 1; RHW;
  SATA 7; SATA-Essay 107; TCWW 2;
  YAW

Faulcon, Robert
  See Holdstock, Robert P.

Faulkner, William (Cuthbert)
  1897-1962 .... **CLC 1, 3, 6, 8, 9, 11, 14,
  18, 28, 52, 68; SSC 1, 35, 42; WLC**
  See also AAYA 7; AMW; AMWR 1; BPFB
  1; BYA 5; CA 81-84; CANR 33; CDALB
  1929-1941; DA; DA3; DAB; DAC; DAM
  MST, NOV; DLB 9, 11, 44, 102; DLBD
  2; DLBY 1986, 1997; EXPN; EXPS;
  LAIT 2; MTCW 1, 2; NFS 4, 8, 13;
  RGAL 4; RGSF 2; SSFS 2, 5, 6, 12

Fauset, Jessie Redmon
  1882(?)-1961 .... **CLC 19, 54; BLC 2**
  See also AFAW 2; BW 1; CA 109; CANR
  83; DAM MULT; DLB 51; FW; MAWW

Faust, Frederick (Schiller)
  1892-1944(?) .... **TCLC 49**
  See also Austin, Frank; Brand, Max; Challis, George; Dawson, Peter; Dexter, Martin; Evans, Evan; Frederick, John; Frost,
  Frederick; Manning, David; Silver, Nicholas
  See also CA 108; 152; DAM POP; DLB
  256

Fawkes, Guy
  See Benchley, Robert (Charles)

Fearing, Kenneth (Flexner)
  1902-1961 .... **CLC 51**
  See also CA 93-96; CANR 59; CMW 4;
  DLB 9; RGAL 4

Fecamps, Elise
  See Creasey, John

Federman, Raymond 1928- .... **CLC 6, 47**
  See also CA 17-20R; CAAS 8; CANR 10,
  43, 83, 108; CN 7; DLBY 1980

Federspiel, J(uerg) F. 1931- .... **CLC 42**
  See also CA 146

Feiffer, Jules (Ralph) 1929- ...... **CLC 2, 8, 64**
  See also AAYA 3; CA 17-20R; CAD; CANR
  30, 59; CD 5; DAM DRAM; DLB 7, 44;
  INT CANR-30; MTCW 1; SATA 8, 61,
  111

Feige, Hermann Albert Otto Maximilian
  See Traven, B.

Feinberg, David B. 1956-1994 .... **CLC 59**
  See also CA 135; 147

Feinstein, Elaine 1930- .... **CLC 36**
  See also CA 69-72; CAAS 1; CANR 31,
  68; CN 7; CP 7; CWP; DLB 14, 40;
  MTCW 1

Feke, Gilbert David .... **CLC 65**

Feldman, Irving (Mordecai) 1928- ..... **CLC 7**
  See also CA 1-4R; CANR 1; CP 7; DLB
  169

Felix-Tchicaya, Gerald
  See Tchicaya, Gerald Felix

Fellini, Federico 1920-1993 .... **CLC 16, 85**
  See also CA 65-68; 143; CANR 33

Felsen, Henry Gregor 1916-1995 ..... **CLC 17**
  See also CA 1-4R; 180; CANR 1; SAAS 2;
  SATA 1

Felski, Rita .... **CLC 65**

Fenno, Jack
  See Calisher, Hortense

Fenollosa, Ernest (Francisco)
  1853-1908 .... **TCLC 91**

Fenton, James Martin 1949- .... **CLC 32**
  See also CA 102; CANR 108; CP 7; DLB
  40; PFS 11

Ferber, Edna 1887-1968 .... **CLC 18, 93**
  See also AITN 1; CA 5-8R; 25-28R; CANR
  68, 105; DLB 9, 28, 86; MTCW 1, 2;
  RGAL 4; RHW; SATA 7; TCWW 2

Ferdowsi, Abu'l Qasem 940-1020 . **CMLC 43**
  See also RGWL 2

Ferguson, Helen
  See Kavan, Anna

Gardam, Jane (Mary) 1928- .... **CLC 43**
    See also CA 49-52; CANR 2, 18, 33, 54,
        106; CLR 12; DLB 14, 161, 231; MAI-
        CYA 1, 2; MTCW 1; SAAS 9; SATA 39,
        76, 130; SATA-Brief 28; YAW
Gardner, Herb(ert) 1934- .... **CLC 44**
    See also CA 149; CAD; CD 5
Gardner, John (Champlin), Jr.
        1933-1982 ...... **CLC 2, 3, 5, 7, 8, 10, 18,
        28, 34; SSC 7**
    See also AITN 1; AMWS 6; BPFB 2; CA
        65-68; 107; CANR 33, 73; CDALBS;
        CPW; DA3; DAM NOV, POP; DLB 2;
        DLBY 1982; FANT; MTCW 1; NFS 3;
        RGAL 4; RGSF 2; SATA 40; SATA-Obit
        31; SSFS 8
Gardner, John (Edmund) 1926- .... **CLC 30**
    See also CA 103; CANR 15, 69; CMW 4;
        CPW; DAM POP; MTCW 1
Gardner, Miriam
    See Bradley, Marion Zimmer
    See also GLL 1
Gardner, Noel
    See Kuttner, Henry
Gardons, S. S.
    See Snodgrass, W(illiam) D(e Witt)
Garfield, Leon 1921-1996 .... **CLC 12**
    See also AAYA 8; BYA 1, 3; CA 17-20R;
        152; CANR 38, 41, 78; CLR 21; DLB
        161; JRDA; MAICYA 1, 2; MAICYAS 1;
        SATA 1, 32, 76; SATA-Obit 90; WYA;
        YAW
Garland, (Hannibal) Hamlin
        1860-1940 .... **TCLC 3; SSC 18**
    See also CA 104; DLB 12, 71, 78, 186;
        RGAL 4; RGSF 2; TCWW 2
Garneau, (Hector de) Saint-Denys
        1912-1943 .... **TCLC 13**
    See also CA 111; DLB 88
Garner, Alan 1934- .... **CLC 17**
    See also AAYA 18; BYA 3, 5; CA 73-76;
        178; CAAE 178; CANR 15, 64; CLR 20;
        CPW; DAB; DAM POP; DLB 161, 261;
        FANT; MAICYA 1, 2; MTCW 1, 2; SATA
        18, 69; SATA-Essay 108; SUFW; YAW
Garner, Hugh 1913-1979 .... **CLC 13**
    See also Warwick, Jarvis
    See also CA 69-72; CANR 31; CCA 1; DLB
        68
Garnett, David 1892-1981 .... **CLC 3**
    See also CA 5-8R; 103; CANR 17, 79; DLB
        34; FANT; MTCW 2; RGEL 2; SFW 4;
        SUFW
Garos, Stephanie
    See Katz, Steve
Garrett, George (Palmer) 1929- .. **CLC 3, 11,
        51; SSC 30**
    See also AMWS 7; BPFB 2; CA 1-4R;
        CAAE 202; CAAS 5; CANR 1, 42, 67,
        109; CN 7; CP 7; CSW; DLB 2, 5, 130,
        152; DLBY 1983
Garrick, David 1717-1779 .... **LC 15**
    See also DAM DRAM; DLB 84, 213;
        RGEL 2
Garrigue, Jean 1914-1972 .... **CLC 2, 8**
    See also CA 5-8R; 37-40R; CANR 20
Garrison, Frederick
    See Sinclair, Upton (Beall)
Garro, Elena 1920(?)-1998
    See also CA 131; 169; CWW 2; DLB 145;
        HLCS 1; HW 1; LAWS 1; WLIT 1
Garth, Will
    See Hamilton, Edmond; Kuttner, Henry
Garvey, Marcus (Moziah, Jr.)
        1887-1940 .... **TCLC 41; BLC 2**
    See also BW 1; CA 120; 124; CANR 79;
        DAM MULT

Gary, Romain .... **CLC 25**
    See also Kacew, Romain
    See also DLB 83
Gascar, Pierre .... **CLC 11**
    See also Fournier, Pierre
Gascoyne, David (Emery)
        1916-2001 .... **CLC 45**
    See also CA 65-68; 200; CANR 10, 28, 54;
        CP 7; DLB 20; MTCW 1; RGEL 2
Gaskell, Elizabeth Cleghorn
        1810-1865 .... **NCLC 5, 70, 97; SSC 25**
    See also BRW 5; CDBLB 1832-1890; DAB;
        DAM MST; DLB 21, 144, 159; RGEL 2;
        RGSF 2
Gass, William H(oward) 1924- . **CLC 1, 2, 8,
        11, 15, 39, 132; SSC 12**
    See also AMWS 6; CA 17-20R; CANR 30,
        71, 100; CN 7; DLB 2, 227; MTCW 1, 2;
        RGAL 4
Gassendi, Pierre 1592-1655 .... **LC 54**
    See also GFL Beginnings to 1789
Gasset, Jose Ortega y
    See Ortega y Gasset, Jose
Gates, Henry Louis, Jr. 1950- .... **CLC 65;
        BLCS**
    See also BW 2, 3; CA 109; CANR 25, 53,
        75; CSW; DA3; DAM MULT; DLB 67;
        MTCW 1; RGAL 4
Gautier, Theophile 1811-1872 .. **NCLC 1, 59;
        PC 18; SSC 20**
    See also DAM POET; DLB 119; EW 6;
        GFL 1789 to the Present; RGWL 2;
        SUFW
Gawsworth, John
    See Bates, H(erbert) E(rnest)
Gay, John 1685-1732 .... **LC 49**
    See also BRW 3; DAM DRAM; DLB 84,
        95; RGEL 2; WLIT 3
Gay, Oliver
    See Gogarty, Oliver St. John
Gay, Peter (Jack) 1923- .... **CLC 158**
    See also CA 13-16R; CANR 18, 41, 77;
        INT CANR-18
Gaye, Marvin (Pentz, Jr.)
        1939-1984 .... **CLC 26**
    See also CA 195; 112
Gebler, Carlo (Ernest) 1954- .... **CLC 39**
    See also CA 119; 133; CANR 96
Gee, Maggie (Mary) 1948- .... **CLC 57**
    See also CA 130; CN 7; DLB 207
Gee, Maurice (Gough) 1931- .... **CLC 29**
    See also AAYA 42; CA 97-100; CANR 67;
        CLR 56; CN 7; CWRI 5; MAICYA 2;
        RGSF 2; SATA 46, 101
Gelbart, Larry (Simon) 1928- .... **CLC 21, 61**
    See also Gelbart, Larry
    See also CA 73-76; CANR 45, 94
Gelbart, Larry 1928-
    See Gelbart, Larry (Simon)
    See also CAD; CD 5
Gelber, Jack 1932- .... **CLC 1, 6, 14, 79**
    See also CA 1-4R; CAD; CANR 2; DLB 7,
        228
Gellhorn, Martha (Ellis)
        1908-1998 .... **CLC 14, 60**
    See also CA 77-80; 164; CANR 44; CN 7;
        DLBY 1982, 1998
Genet, Jean 1910-1986 .. **CLC 1, 2, 5, 10, 14,
        44, 46**
    See also CA 13-16R; CANR 18; DA3;
        DAM DRAM; DFS 10; DLB 72; DLBY
        1986; EW 13; GFL 1789 to the Present;
        GLL 1; MTCW 1, 2; RGWL 2
Gent, Peter 1942- .... **CLC 29**
    See also AITN 1; CA 89-92; DLBY 1982
Gentile, Giovanni 1875-1944 .... **TCLC 96**
    See also CA 119
Gentlewoman in New England, A
    See Bradstreet, Anne

Gentlewoman in Those Parts, A
    See Bradstreet, Anne
Geoffrey of Monmouth c.
        1100-1155 .... **CMLC 44**
    See also DLB 146
George, Jean
    See George, Jean Craighead
George, Jean Craighead 1919- .... **CLC 35**
    See also AAYA 8; BYA 2, 4; CA 5-8R;
        CANR 25; CLR 1; 80; DLB 52; JRDA;
        MAICYA 1, 2; SATA 2, 68, 124; WYA;
        YAW
George, Stefan (Anton) 1868-1933 . **TCLC 2,
        14**
    See also CA 104; 193; EW 8
Georges, Georges Martin
    See Simenon, Georges (Jacques Christian)
Gerhardi, William Alexander
    See Gerhardie, William Alexander
Gerhardie, William Alexander
        1895-1977 .... **CLC 5**
    See also CA 25-28R; 73-76; CANR 18;
        DLB 36; RGEL 2
Gerson, Jean 1363-1429 .... **LC 77**
    See also DLB 208
Gersonides 1288-1344 .... **CMLC 49**
    See also DLB 115
Gerstler, Amy 1956- .... **CLC 70**
    See also CA 146; CANR 99
Gertler, T. .... **CLC 134**
    See also CA 116; 121
Ghalib .... **NCLC 39, 78**
    See also Ghalib, Asadullah Khan
Ghalib, Asadullah Khan 1797-1869
    See Ghalib
    See also DAM POET; RGWL 2
Ghelderode, Michel de 1898-1962 ..... **CLC 6,
        11; DC 15**
    See also CA 85-88; CANR 40, 77; DAM
        DRAM; EW 11
Ghiselin, Brewster 1903-2001 .... **CLC 23**
    See also CA 13-16R; CAAS 10; CANR 13;
        CP 7
Ghose, Aurabinda 1872-1950 .... **TCLC 63**
    See also CA 163
Ghose, Zulfikar 1935- .... **CLC 42**
    See also CA 65-68; CANR 67; CN 7; CP 7
Ghosh, Amitav 1956- .... **CLC 44, 153**
    See also CA 147; CANR 80; CN 7
Giacosa, Giuseppe 1847-1906 .... **TCLC 7**
    See also CA 104
Gibb, Lee
    See Waterhouse, Keith (Spencer)
Gibbon, Lewis Grassic .... **TCLC 4**
    See also Mitchell, James Leslie
    See also RGEL 2
Gibbons, Kaye 1960- .... **CLC 50, 88, 145**
    See also AAYA 34; AMWS 10; CA 151;
        CANR 75; CSW; DA3; DAM POP;
        MTCW 1; NFS 3; RGAL 4; SATA 117
Gibran, Kahlil 1883-1931 . **TCLC 1, 9; PC 9**
    See also CA 104; 150; DA3; DAM POET,
        POP; MTCW 2
Gibran, Khalil
    See Gibran, Kahlil
Gibson, William 1914- .... **CLC 23**
    See also CA 9-12R; CAD 2; CANR 9, 42,
        75; CD 5; DA; DAB; DAC; DAM
        DRAM, MST; DFS 2; DLB 7; LAIT 2;
        MTCW 2; SATA 66; YAW
Gibson, William (Ford) 1948- ... **CLC 39, 63;
        SSC 52**
    See also AAYA 12; BPFB 2; CA 126; 133;
        CANR 52, 90, 106; CN 7; CPW; DA3;
        DAM POP; DLB 251; MTCW 2; SCFW
        2; SFW 4

Gide, Andre (Paul Guillaume)
1869-1951 ..... TCLC 5, 12, 36; SSC 13; WLC
See also CA 104; 124; DA; DA3; DAB; DAC; DAM MST, NOV; DLB 65; EW 8; GFL 1789 to the Present; MTCW 1, 2; RGSF 2; RGWL 2

Gifford, Barry (Colby) 1946- .... CLC 34
See also CA 65-68; CANR 9, 30, 40, 90

Gilbert, Frank
See De Voto, Bernard (Augustine)

Gilbert, W(illiam) S(chwenck)
1836-1911 .... TCLC 3
See also CA 104; 173; DAM DRAM, POET; RGEL 2; SATA 36

Gilbreth, Frank B(unker), Jr.
1911-2001 .... CLC 17
See also CA 9-12R; SATA 2

Gilchrist, Ellen (Louise) 1935- .. CLC 34, 48, 143; SSC 14
See also BPFB 2; CA 113; 116; CANR 41, 61, 104; CN 7; CPW; CSW; DAM POP; DLB 130; EXPS; MTCW 1, 2; RGAL 4; RGSF 2; SSFS 9

Giles, Molly 1942- .... CLC 39
See also CA 126; CANR 98

Gill, Eric 1882-1940 .... TCLC 85

Gill, Patrick
See Creasey, John

Gillette, Douglas .... CLC 70

Gilliam, Terry (Vance) 1940- .... CLC 21, 141
See also Monty Python
See also AAYA 19; CA 108; 113; CANR 35; INT 113

Gillian, Jerry
See Gilliam, Terry (Vance)

Gilliatt, Penelope (Ann Douglass)
1932-1993 .... CLC 2, 10, 13, 53
See also AITN 2; CA 13-16R; 141; CANR 49; DLB 14

Gilman, Charlotte (Anna) Perkins (Stetson)
1860-1935 ..... TCLC 9, 37, 117; SSC 13
See also BYA 11; CA 106; 150; DLB 221; EXPS; FW; HGG; LAIT 2; MAWW; MTCW 1; RGAL 4; RGSF 2; SFW 4; SSFS 1

Gilmour, David 1946- .... CLC 35

Gilpin, William 1724-1804 .... NCLC 30

Gilray, J. D.
See Mencken, H(enry) L(ouis)

Gilroy, Frank D(aniel) 1925- .... CLC 2
See also CA 81-84; CAD; CANR 32, 64, 86; CD 5; DLB 7

Gilstrap, John 1957(?)- .... CLC 99
See also CA 160; CANR 101

Ginsberg, Allen 1926-1997 .... CLC 1, 2, 3, 4, 6, 13, 36, 69, 109; PC 4; TCLC 120; WLC
See also AAYA 33; AITN 1; AMWS 2; CA 1-4R; 157; CANR 2, 41, 63, 95; CDALB 1941-1968; CP 7; DA; DA3; DAB; DAC; DAM MST, POET; DLB 5, 16, 169, 237; GLL 1; MTCW 1, 2; PAB; PFS 5; RGAL 4; WP

Ginzburg, Eugenia .... CLC 59

Ginzburg, Natalia 1916-1991 .... CLC 5, 11, 54, 70
See also CA 85-88; 135; CANR 33; DFS 14; DLB 177; EW 13; MTCW 1, 2; RGWL 2

Giono, Jean 1895-1970 .... CLC 4, 11; TCLC 124
See also CA 45-48; 29-32R; CANR 2, 35; DLB 72; GFL 1789 to the Present; MTCW 1; RGWL 2

Giovanni, Nikki 1943- .... CLC 2, 4, 19, 64, 117; BLC 2; PC 19; WLCS
See also AAYA 22; AITN 1; BW 2, 3; CA 29-32R; CAAS 6; CANR 18, 41, 60, 91; CDALBS; CLR 6, 73; CP 7; CSW; CWP; CWRI 5; DA; DA3; DAB; DAC; DAM MST, MULT, POET; DLB 5, 41; EXPP; INT CANR-18; MAICYA 1, 2; MTCW 1, 2; RGAL 4; SATA 24, 107; YAW

Giovene, Andrea 1904-1998 .... CLC 7
See also CA 85-88

Gippius, Zinaida (Nikolayevna) 1869-1945
See Hippius, Zinaida
See also CA 106

Giraudoux, Jean(-Hippolyte)
1882-1944 .... TCLC 2, 7
See also CA 104; 196; DAM DRAM; DLB 65; EW 9; GFL 1789 to the Present; RGWL 2

Gironella, Jose Maria 1917-1991 ..... CLC 11
See also CA 101; RGWL 2

Gissing, George (Robert)
1857-1903 .... TCLC 3, 24, 47; SSC 37
See also BRW 5; CA 105; 167; DLB 18, 135, 184; RGEL 2

Giurlani, Aldo
See Palazzeschi, Aldo

Gladkov, Fyodor (Vasilyevich)
1883-1958 .... TCLC 27
See also CA 170

Glanville, Brian (Lester) 1931- .... CLC 6
See also CA 5-8R; CAAS 9; CANR 3, 70; CN 7; DLB 15, 139; SATA 42

Glasgow, Ellen (Anderson Gholson)
1873-1945 .... TCLC 2, 7; SSC 34
See also AMW; CA 104; 164; DLB 9, 12; MAWW; MTCW 2; RGAL 4; RHW; SSFS 9

Glaspell, Susan 1882(?)-1948 . TCLC 55; DC 10; SSC 41
See also AMWS 3; CA 110; 154; DFS 8; DLB 7, 9, 78, 228; MAWW; RGAL 4; SSFS 3; TCWW 2; YABC 2

Glassco, John 1909-1981 .... CLC 9
See also CA 13-16R; 102; CANR 15; DLB 68

Glasscock, Amnesia
See Steinbeck, John (Ernst)

Glasser, Ronald J. 1940(?)- .... CLC 37

Glassman, Joyce
See Johnson, Joyce

Gleick, James (W.) 1954- .... CLC 147
See also CA 131; 137; CANR 97; INT CA-137

Glendinning, Victoria 1937- .... CLC 50
See also CA 120; 127; CANR 59, 89; DLB 155

Glissant, Edouard 1928- .... CLC 10, 68
See also CA 153; CWW 2; DAM MULT

Gloag, Julian 1930- .... CLC 40
See also AITN 1; CA 65-68; CANR 10, 70; CN 7

Glowacki, Aleksander
See Prus, Boleslaw

Gluck, Louise (Elisabeth) 1943- .. CLC 7, 22, 44, 81, 160; PC 16
See also AMWS 5; CA 33-36R; CANR 40, 69, 108; CP 7; CWP; DA3; DAM POET; DLB 5; MTCW 2; PFS 5, 15; RGAL 4

Glyn, Elinor 1864-1943 .... TCLC 72
See also DLB 153; RHW

Gobineau, Joseph-Arthur
1816-1882 .... NCLC 17
See also DLB 123; GFL 1789 to the Present

Godard, Jean-Luc 1930- .... CLC 20
See also CA 93-96

Godden, (Margaret) Rumer
1907-1998 .... CLC 53
See also AAYA 6; BPFB 2; BYA 2, 5; CA 5-8R; 172; CANR 4, 27, 36, 55, 80; CLR 20; CN 7; CWRI 5; DLB 161; MAICYA 1, 2; RHW; SAAS 12; SATA 3, 36; SATA-Obit 109

Godoy Alcayaga, Lucila
1899-1957 .... TCLC 2; HLC 2; PC 32
See also Mistral, Gabriela
See also BW 2; CA 104; 131; CANR 81; DAM MULT; DNFS; HW 1, 2; MTCW 1, 2

Godwin, Gail (Kathleen) 1937- ..... CLC 5, 8, 22, 31, 69, 125
See also BPFB 2; CA 29-32R; CANR 15, 43, 69; CN 7; CPW; CSW; DA3; DAM POP; DLB 6, 234; INT CANR-15; MTCW 1, 2

Godwin, William 1756-1836 .... NCLC 14
See also CDBLB 1789-1832; CMW 4; DLB 39, 104, 142, 158, 163, 262; HGG; RGEL 2

Goebbels, Josef
See Goebbels, (Paul) Joseph

Goebbels, (Paul) Joseph
1897-1945 .... TCLC 68
See also CA 115; 148

Goebbels, Joseph Paul
See Goebbels, (Paul) Joseph

Goethe, Johann Wolfgang von
1749-1832 ... NCLC 4, 22, 34, 90; PC 5; SSC 38; WLC
See also CDWLB 2; DA; DA3; DAB; DAC; DAM DRAM, MST, POET; DLB 94; EW 5; RGWL 2

Gogarty, Oliver St. John
1878-1957 .... TCLC 15
See also CA 109; 150; DLB 15, 19; RGEL 2

Gogol, Nikolai (Vasilyevich)
1809-1852 .... NCLC 5, 15, 31; DC 1; SSC 4, 29, 52; WLC
See also DA; DAB; DAC; DAM DRAM, MST; DFS 12; DLB 198; EW 6; EXPS; RGSF 2; RGWL 2; SSFS 7

Goines, Donald 1937(?)-1974 . CLC 80; BLC 2
See also AITN 1; BW 1, 3; CA 124; 114; CANR 82; CMW 4; DA3; DAM MULT, POP; DLB 33

Gold, Herbert 1924- ... CLC 4, 7, 14, 42, 152
See also CA 9-12R; CANR 17, 45; CN 7; DLB 2; DLBY 1981

Goldbarth, Albert 1948- .... CLC 5, 38
See also CA 53-56; CANR 6, 40; CP 7; DLB 120

Goldberg, Anatol 1910-1982 .... CLC 34
See also CA 131; 117

Goldemberg, Isaac 1945- .... CLC 52
See also CA 69-72; CAAS 12; CANR 11, 32; HW 1; WLIT 1

Golding, William (Gerald)
1911-1993 ..... CLC 1, 2, 3, 8, 10, 17, 27, 58, 81; WLC
See also AAYA 5; BPFB 2; BRWR 1; BRWS 1; BYA 2; CA 5-8R; 141; CANR 13, 33, 54; CDBLB 1945-1960; DA; DA3; DAB; DAC; DAM MST, NOV; DLB 15, 100, 255; EXPN; HGG; LAIT 4; MTCW 1, 2; NFS 2; RGEL 2; RHW; SFW 4; WLIT 4; YAW

Goldman, Emma 1869-1940 .... TCLC 13
See also CA 110; 150; DLB 221; FW; RGAL 4

Goldman, Francisco 1954- .... CLC 76
See also CA 162

Goldman, William (W.) 1931- ...... **CLC 1, 48**
See also BPFB 2; CA 9-12R; CANR 29, 69, 106; CN 7; DLB 44; FANT; IDFW 3, 4

Goldmann, Lucien 1913-1970 .... **CLC 24**
See also CA 25-28; CAP 2

Goldoni, Carlo 1707-1793 .... **LC 4**
See also DAM DRAM; EW 4; RGWL 2

Goldsberry, Steven 1949- .... **CLC 34**
See also CA 131

Goldsmith, Oliver 1730-1774 .. **LC 2, 48; DC 8; WLC**
See also BRW 3; CDBLB 1660-1789; DA; DAB; DAC; DAM DRAM, MST, NOV, POET; DFS 1; DLB 39, 89, 104, 109, 142; IDTP; RGEL 2; SATA 26; TEA; WLIT 3

Goldsmith, Peter
See Priestley, J(ohn) B(oynton)

Gombrowicz, Witold 1904-1969 .... **CLC 4, 7, 11, 49**
See also CA 19-20; 25-28R; CANR 105; CAP 2; CDWLB 4; DAM DRAM; DLB 215; EW 12; RGWL 2

Gomez de Avellaneda, Gertrudis 1814-1873 .... **NCLC 111**
See also LAW

Gomez de la Serna, Ramon 1888-1963 .... **CLC 9**
See also CA 153; 116; CANR 79; HW 1, 2

Goncharov, Ivan Alexandrovich 1812-1891 .... **NCLC 1, 63**
See also DLB 238; EW 6; RGWL 2

Goncourt, Edmond (Louis Antoine Huot) de 1822-1896 .... **NCLC 7**
See also DLB 123; EW 7; GFL 1789 to the Present; RGWL 2

Goncourt, Jules (Alfred Huot) de 1830-1870 .... **NCLC 7**
See also DLB 123; EW 7; GFL 1789 to the Present; RGWL 2

Gongora (y Argote), Luis de 1561-1627 .... **LC 72**
See also RGWL 2

Gontier, Fernande 19(?)- .... **CLC 50**

Gonzalez Martinez, Enrique 1871-1952 .... **TCLC 72**
See also CA 166; CANR 81; HW 1, 2

Goodison, Lorna 1947- .... **PC 36**
See also CA 142; CANR 88; CP 7; CWP; DLB 157

Goodman, Paul 1911-1972 ..... **CLC 1, 2, 4, 7**
See also CA 19-20; 37-40R; CAD; CANR 34; CAP 2; DLB 130, 246; MTCW 1; RGAL 4

Gordimer, Nadine 1923- ...... **CLC 3, 5, 7, 10, 18, 33, 51, 70, 123, 160, 161; SSC 17; WLCS**
See also AAYA 39; AFW; BRWS 2; CA 5-8R; CANR 3, 28, 56, 88; CN 7; DA; DA3; DAB; DAC; DAM MST, NOV; DLB 225; EXPS; INT CANR-28; MTCW 1, 2; NFS 4; RGEL 2; RGSF 2; SSFS 2, 14; WLIT 2; YAW

Gordon, Adam Lindsay 1833-1870 .... **NCLC 21**
See also DLB 230

Gordon, Caroline 1895-1981 . **CLC 6, 13, 29, 83; SSC 15**
See also AMW; CA 11-12; 103; CANR 36; CAP 1; DLB 4, 9, 102; DLBD 17; DLBY 1981; MTCW 1, 2; RGAL 4; RGSF 2

Gordon, Charles William 1860-1937
See Connor, Ralph
See also CA 109

Gordon, Mary (Catherine) 1949- .... **CLC 13, 22, 128**
See also AMWS 4; BPFB 2; CA 102; CANR 44, 92; CN 7; DLB 6; DLBY 1981; FW; INT CA-102; MTCW 1

Gordon, N. J.
See Bosman, Herman Charles

Gordon, Sol 1923- .... **CLC 26**
See also CA 53-56; CANR 4; SATA 11

Gordone, Charles 1925-1995 .. **CLC 1, 4; DC 8**
See also BW 1, 3; CA 93-96; 180; 150; CAAE 180; CAD; CANR 55; DAM DRAM; DLB 7; INT 93-96; MTCW 1

Gore, Catherine 1800-1861 .... **NCLC 65**
See also DLB 116; RGEL 2

Gorenko, Anna Andreevna
See Akhmatova, Anna

Gorky, Maxim .... **TCLC 8; SSC 28; WLC**
See also Peshkov, Alexei Maximovich
See also DAB; DFS 9; EW 8; MTCW 2

Goryan, Sirak
See Saroyan, William

Gosse, Edmund (William) 1849-1928 .... **TCLC 28**
See also CA 117; DLB 57, 144, 184; RGEL 2

Gotlieb, Phyllis Fay (Bloom) 1926- .. **CLC 18**
See also CA 13-16R; CANR 7; DLB 88, 251; SFW 4

Gottesman, S. D.
See Kornbluth, C(yril) M.; Pohl, Frederik

Gottfried von Strassburg fl. c. 1170-1215 .... **CMLC 10**
See also CDWLB 2; DLB 138; EW 1; RGWL 2

Gotthelf, Jeremias 1797-1854 .... **NCLC 115**
See also DLB 133; RGWL 2

Gould, Lois 1932(?)-2002 .... **CLC 4, 10**
See also CA 77-80; CANR 29; MTCW 1

Gourmont, Remy(-Marie-Charles) de 1858-1915 .... **TCLC 17**
See also CA 109; 150; GFL 1789 to the Present; MTCW 2

Govier, Katherine 1948- .... **CLC 51**
See also CA 101; CANR 18, 40; CCA 1

Gower, John c. 1330-1408 .... **LC 76**
See also BRW 1; DLB 146; RGEL 2

Goyen, (Charles) William 1915-1983 .... **CLC 5, 8, 14, 40**
See also AITN 2; CA 5-8R; 110; CANR 6, 71; DLB 2, 218; DLBY 1983; INT CANR-6

Goytisolo, Juan 1931- .... **CLC 5, 10, 23, 133; HLC 1**
See also CA 85-88; CANR 32, 61; CWW 2; DAM MULT; GLL 2; HW 1, 2; MTCW 1, 2

Gozzano, Guido 1883-1916 .... **PC 10**
See also CA 154; DLB 114

Gozzi, (Conte) Carlo 1720-1806 .... **NCLC 23**

Grabbe, Christian Dietrich 1801-1836 .... **NCLC 2**
See also DLB 133; RGWL 2

Grace, Patricia Frances 1937- .... **CLC 56**
See also CA 176; CN 7; RGSF 2

Gracian y Morales, Baltasar 1601-1658 .... **LC 15**

Gracq, Julien .... **CLC 11, 48**
See also Poirier, Louis
See also CWW 2; DLB 83; GFL 1789 to the Present

Grade, Chaim 1910-1982 .... **CLC 10**
See also CA 93-96; 107

Graduate of Oxford, A
See Ruskin, John

Grafton, Garth
See Duncan, Sara Jeannette

Graham, John
See Phillips, David Graham

Graham, Jorie 1951- .... **CLC 48, 118**
See also CA 111; CANR 63; CP 7; CWP; DLB 120; PFS 10

Graham, R(obert) B(ontine) Cunninghame
See Cunninghame Graham, Robert (Gallnigad) Bontine
See also DLB 98, 135, 174; RGEL 2; RGSF 2

Graham, Robert
See Haldeman, Joe (William)

Graham, Tom
See Lewis, (Harry) Sinclair

Graham, W(illiam) S(idney) 1918-1986 .... **CLC 29**
See also BRWS 7; CA 73-76; 118; DLB 20; RGEL 2

Graham, Winston (Mawdsley) 1910- .... **CLC 23**
See also CA 49-52; CANR 2, 22, 45, 66; CMW 4; CN 7; DLB 77; RHW

Grahame, Kenneth 1859-1932 .... **TCLC 64**
See also BYA 5; CA 108; 136; CANR 80; CLR 5; CWRI 5; DA3; DAB; DLB 34, 141, 178; FANT; MAICYA 1, 2; MTCW 2; RGEL 2; SATA 100; WCH; YABC 1

Granger, Darius John
See Marlowe, Stephen

Granin, Daniil .... **CLC 59**

Granovsky, Timofei Nikolaevich 1813-1855 .... **NCLC 75**
See also DLB 198

Grant, Skeeter
See Spiegelman, Art

Granville-Barker, Harley 1877-1946 .... **TCLC 2**
See also Barker, Harley Granville
See also CA 104; DAM DRAM; RGEL 2

Granzotto, Gianni
See Granzotto, Giovanni Battista

Granzotto, Giovanni Battista 1914-1985 .... **CLC 70**
See also CA 166

Grass, Guenter (Wilhelm) 1927- ... **CLC 1, 2, 4, 6, 11, 15, 22, 32, 49, 88; WLC**
See also BPFB 2; CA 13-16R; CANR 20, 75, 93; CDWLB 2; DA; DA3; DAB; DAC; DAM MST, NOV; DLB 75, 124; EW 13; MTCW 1, 2; RGWL 2

Gratton, Thomas
See Hulme, T(homas) E(rnest)

Grau, Shirley Ann 1929- .... **CLC 4, 9, 146; SSC 15**
See also CA 89-92; CANR 22, 69; CN 7; CSW; DLB 2, 218; INT CA-89-92, CANR-22; MTCW 1

Gravel, Fern
See Hall, James Norman

Graver, Elizabeth 1964- .... **CLC 70**
See also CA 135; CANR 71

Graves, Richard Perceval 1895-1985 .... **CLC 44**
See also CA 65-68; CANR 9, 26, 51

Graves, Robert (von Ranke) 1895-1985 .. **CLC 1, 2, 6, 11, 39, 44, 45; PC 6**
See also BPFB 2; BRW 7; BYA 4; CA 5-8R; 117; CANR 5, 36; CDBLB 1914-1945; DA3; DAB; DAC; DAM MST, POET; DLB 20, 100, 191; DLBD 18; DLBY 1985; MTCW 1, 2; NCFS 2; RGEL 2; RHW; SATA 45

Graves, Valerie
See Bradley, Marion Zimmer

Gray, Alasdair (James) 1934- .... **CLC 41**
See also CA 126; CANR 47, 69, 106; CN 7; DLB 194, 261; HGG; INT CA-126; MTCW 1, 2; RGSF 2

Gray, Amlin 1946- .... **CLC 29**
See also CA 138

Gray, Francine du Plessix 1930- ..... **CLC 22, 153**
See also BEST 90:3; CA 61-64; CAAS 2; CANR 11, 33, 75, 81; DAM NOV; INT CANR-11; MTCW 1, 2

Gray, John (Henry) 1866-1934 ...... **TCLC 19**
See also CA 119; 162; RGEL 2

Gray, Simon (James Holliday)
1936- .... **CLC 9, 14, 36**
See also AITN 1; CA 21-24R; CAAS 3; CANR 32, 69; CD 5; DLB 13; MTCW 1; RGEL 2

Gray, Spalding 1941- ..... **CLC 49, 112; DC 7**
See also CA 128; CAD; CANR 74; CD 5; CPW; DAM POP; MTCW 2

Gray, Thomas 1716-1771 .... **LC 4, 40; PC 2; WLC**
See also BRW 3; CDBLB 1660-1789; DA; DA3; DAB; DAC; DAM MST; DLB 109; EXPP; PAB; PFS 9; RGEL 2; WP

Grayson, David
See Baker, Ray Stannard

Grayson, Richard (A.) 1951- .... **CLC 38**
See also CA 85-88; CANR 14, 31, 57; DLB 234

Greeley, Andrew M(oran) 1928- ...... **CLC 28**
See also BPFB 2; CA 5-8R; CAAS 7; CANR 7, 43, 69, 104; CMW 4; CPW; DA3; DAM POP; MTCW 1, 2

Green, Anna Katharine
1846-1935 .... **TCLC 63**
See also CA 112; 159; CMW 4; DLB 202, 221; MSW

Green, Brian
See Card, Orson Scott

Green, Hannah
See Greenberg, Joanne (Goldenberg)

Green, Hannah 1927(?)-1996 .... **CLC 3**
See also CA 73-76; CANR 59, 93; NFS 10

Green, Henry .... **CLC 2, 13, 97**
See also Yorke, Henry Vincent
See also BRWS 2; CA 175; DLB 15; RGEL 2

Green, Julian (Hartridge) 1900-1998
See Green, Julien
See also CA 21-24R; 169; CANR 33, 87; DLB 4, 72; MTCW 1

Green, Julien .... **CLC 3, 11, 77**
See also Green, Julian (Hartridge)
See also GFL 1789 to the Present; MTCW 2

Green, Paul (Eliot) 1894-1981 .... **CLC 25**
See also AITN 1; CA 5-8R; 103; CANR 3; DAM DRAM; DLB 7, 9, 249; DLBY 1981; RGAL 4

Greenaway, Peter 1942- .... **CLC 159**
See also CA 127

Greenberg, Ivan 1908-1973
See Rahv, Philip
See also CA 85-88

Greenberg, Joanne (Goldenberg)
1932- .... **CLC 7, 30**
See also AAYA 12; CA 5-8R; CANR 14, 32, 69; CN 7; SATA 25; YAW

Greenberg, Richard 1959(?)- .... **CLC 57**
See also CA 138; CAD; CD 5

Greenblatt, Stephen J(ay) 1943- ...... **CLC 70**
See also CA 49-52

Greene, Bette 1934- .... **CLC 30**
See also AAYA 7; BYA 3; CA 53-56; CANR 4; CLR 2; CWRI 5; JRDA; LAIT 4; MAICYA 1, 2; NFS 10; SAAS 16; SATA 8, 102; WYA; YAW

Greene, Gael .... **CLC 8**
See also CA 13-16R; CANR 10

Greene, Graham (Henry)
1904-1991 .... **CLC 1, 3, 6, 9, 14, 18, 27, 37, 70, 72, 125; SSC 29; WLC**
See also AITN 2; BPFB 2; BRWR 2; BRWS 1; BYA 3; CA 13-16R; 133; CANR 35, 61; CBD; CDBLB 1945-1960; CMW 4; DA; DA3; DAB; DAC; DAM MST, NOV; DLB 13, 15, 77, 100, 162, 201, 204; DLBY 1991; MSW; MTCW 1, 2; RGEL 2; SATA 20; SSFS 14; WLIT 4

Greene, Robert 1558-1592 .... **LC 41**
See also DLB 62, 167; IDTP; RGEL 2; TEA

Greer, Germaine 1939- .... **CLC 131**
See also AITN 1; CA 81-84; CANR 33, 70; FW; MTCW 1, 2

Greer, Richard
See Silverberg, Robert

Gregor, Arthur 1923- .... **CLC 9**
See also CA 25-28R; CAAS 10; CANR 11; CP 7; SATA 36

Gregor, Lee
See Pohl, Frederik

Gregory, Lady Isabella Augusta (Persse)
1852-1932 .... **TCLC 1**
See also BRW 6; CA 104; 184; DLB 10; IDTP; RGEL 2

Gregory, J. Dennis
See Williams, John A(lfred)

Grekova, I. .... **CLC 59**

Grendon, Stephen
See Derleth, August (William)

Grenville, Kate 1950- .... **CLC 61**
See also CA 118; CANR 53, 93

Grenville, Pelham
See Wodehouse, P(elham) G(renville)

Greve, Felix Paul (Berthold Friedrich)
1879-1948
See Grove, Frederick Philip
See also CA 104; 141, 175; CANR 79; DAC; DAM MST

Greville, Fulke 1554-1628 .... **LC 79**
See also DLB 62, 172; RGEL 2

Grey, Zane 1872-1939 .... **TCLC 6**
See also BPFB 2; CA 104; 132; DA3; DAM POP; DLB 9, 212; MTCW 1, 2; RGAL 4; TCWW 2

Grieg, (Johan) Nordahl (Brun)
1902-1943 .... **TCLC 10**
See also CA 107; 189

Grieve, C(hristopher) M(urray)
1892-1978 .... **CLC 11, 19**
See also MacDiarmid, Hugh; Pteleon
See also CA 5-8R; 85-88; CANR 33, 107; DAM POET; MTCW 1; RGEL 2

Griffin, Gerald 1803-1840 .... **NCLC 7**
See also DLB 159; RGEL 2

Griffin, John Howard 1920-1980 ..... **CLC 68**
See also AITN 1; CA 1-4R; 101; CANR 2

Griffin, Peter 1942- .... **CLC 39**
See also CA 136

Griffith, D(avid Lewelyn) W(ark)
1875(?)-1948 .... **TCLC 68**
See also CA 119; 150; CANR 80

Griffith, Lawrence
See Griffith, D(avid Lewelyn) W(ark)

Griffiths, Trevor 1935- .... **CLC 13, 52**
See also CA 97-100; CANR 45; CBD; CD 5; DLB 13, 245

Griggs, Sutton (Elbert)
1872-1930 .... **TCLC 77**
See also CA 123; 186; DLB 50

Grigson, Geoffrey (Edward Harvey)
1905-1985 .... **CLC 7, 39**
See also CA 25-28R; 118; CANR 20, 33; DLB 27; MTCW 1, 2

Grillparzer, Franz 1791-1872 . **NCLC 1, 102; DC 14; SSC 37**
See also CDWLB 2; DLB 133; EW 5; RGWL 2

Grimble, Reverend Charles James
See Eliot, T(homas) S(tearns)

Grimke, Charlotte L(ottie) Forten
1837(?)-1914
See Forten, Charlotte L.
See also BW 1; CA 117; 124; DAM MULT, POET

Grimm, Jacob Ludwig Karl
1785-1863 .... **NCLC 3, 77; SSC 36**
See also DLB 90; MAICYA 1, 2; RGSF 2; RGWL 2; SATA 22; WCH

Grimm, Wilhelm Karl 1786-1859 .. **NCLC 3, 77; SSC 36**
See also CDWLB 2; DLB 90; MAICYA 1, 2; RGSF 2; RGWL 2; SATA 22; WCH

Grimmelshausen, Hans Jakob Christoffel von
See Grimmelshausen, Johann Jakob Christoffel von
See also RGWL 2

Grimmelshausen, Johann Jakob Christoffel von 1621-1676 .... **LC 6**
See also Grimmelshausen, Hans Jakob Christoffel von
See also CDWLB 2; DLB 168

Grindel, Eugene 1895-1952
See Eluard, Paul
See also CA 104; 193

Grisham, John 1955- .... **CLC 84**
See also AAYA 14; BPFB 2; CA 138; CANR 47, 69; CMW 4; CN 7; CPW; CSW; DA3; DAM POP; MSW; MTCW 2

Grossman, David 1954- .... **CLC 67**
See also CA 138; CWW 2

Grossman, Vasily (Semenovich)
1905-1964 .... **CLC 41**
See also CA 124; 130; MTCW 1

Grove, Frederick Philip .... **TCLC 4**
See also Greve, Felix Paul (Berthold Friedrich)
See also DLB 92; RGEL 2

Grubb
See Crumb, R(obert)

Grumbach, Doris (Isaac) 1918- . **CLC 13, 22, 64**
See also CA 5-8R; CAAS 2; CANR 9, 42, 70; CN 7; INT CANR-9; MTCW 2

Grundtvig, Nicolai Frederik Severin
1783-1872 .... **NCLC 1**

Grunge
See Crumb, R(obert)

Grunwald, Lisa 1959- .... **CLC 44**
See also CA 120

Guare, John 1938- .... **CLC 8, 14, 29, 67**
See also CA 73-76; CAD; CANR 21, 69; CD 5; DAM DRAM; DFS 8, 13; DLB 7, 249; MTCW 1, 2; RGAL 4

Gubar, Susan (David) 1944- .... **CLC 145**
See also CA 108; CANR 45, 70; FW; MTCW 1; RGAL 4

Gudjonsson, Halldor Kiljan 1902-1998
See Laxness, Halldor
See also CA 103; 164; CWW 2

Guenter, Erich
See Eich, Guenter

Guest, Barbara 1920- .... **CLC 34**
See also CA 25-28R; CANR 11, 44, 84; CP 7; CWP; DLB 5, 193

Guest, Edgar A(lbert) 1881-1959 ... **TCLC 95**
See also CA 112; 168

Guest, Judith (Ann) 1936- .... **CLC 8, 30**
See also AAYA 7; CA 77-80; CANR 15, 75; DA3; DAM NOV, POP; EXPN; INT CANR-15; LAIT 5; MTCW 1, 2; NFS 1

Guevara, Che .... **CLC 87; HLC 1**
See also Guevara (Serna), Ernesto

Guevara (Serna), Ernesto
1928-1967 .... **CLC 87; HLC 1**
See also Guevara, Che
See also CA 127; 111; CANR 56; DAM MULT; HW 1

Guicciardini, Francesco 1483-1540 ..... **LC 49**

Guild, Nicholas M. 1944- .... **CLC 33**
See also CA 93-96

Guillemin, Jacques
See Sartre, Jean-Paul

Guillen, Jorge 1893-1984 . **CLC 11; HLCS 1; PC 35**
See also CA 89-92; 112; DAM MULT, POET; DLB 108; HW 1; RGWL 2

Guillen, Nicolas (Cristobal)
1902-1989 .... **CLC 48, 79; BLC 2; HLC 1; PC 23**
See also BW 2; CA 116; 125; 129; CANR 84; DAM MST, MULT, POET; HW 1; LAW; RGWL 2; WP

Guillen y Alavarez, Jorge
See Guillen, Jorge

Guillevic, (Eugene) 1907-1997 .... **CLC 33**
See also CA 93-96; CWW 2

Guillois
See Desnos, Robert

Guillois, Valentin
See Desnos, Robert

Guimaraes Rosa, Joao
See Rosa, Joao Guimaraes
See also LAW

Guimaraes Rosa, Joao 1908-1967
See also CA 175; HLCS 2; LAW; RGSF 2; RGWL 2

Guiney, Louise Imogen
1861-1920 .... **TCLC 41**
See also CA 160; DLB 54; RGAL 4

Guinizelli, Guido c. 1230-1276 ...... **CMLC 49**

Guiraldes, Ricardo (Guillermo)
1886-1927 .... **TCLC 39**
See also CA 131; HW 1; LAW; MTCW 1

Gumilev, Nikolai (Stepanovich)
1886-1921 .... **TCLC 60**
See also CA 165

Gunesekera, Romesh 1954- .... **CLC 91**
See also CA 159; CN 7

Gunn, Bill .... **CLC 5**
See also Gunn, William Harrison
See also DLB 38

Gunn, Thom(son William) 1929- .. **CLC 3, 6, 18, 32, 81; PC 26**
See also BRWS 4; CA 17-20R; CANR 9, 33; CDBLB 1960 to Present; CP 7; DAM POET; DLB 27; INT CANR-33; MTCW 1; PFS 9; RGEL 2

Gunn, William Harrison 1934(?)-1989
See Gunn, Bill
See also AITN 1; BW 1, 3; CA 13-16R; 128; CANR 12, 25, 76

Gunn Allen, Paula
See Allen, Paula Gunn

Gunnars, Kristjana 1948- .... **CLC 69**
See also CA 113; CCA 1; CP 7; CWP; DLB 60

Gurdjieff, G(eorgei) I(vanovich)
1877(?)-1949 .... **TCLC 71**
See also CA 157

Gurganus, Allan 1947- .... **CLC 70**
See also BEST 90:1; CA 135; CN 7; CPW; CSW; DAM POP; GLL 1

Gurney, A(lbert) R(amsdell), Jr.
1930- .... **CLC 32, 50, 54**
See also AMWS 5; CA 77-80; CAD; CANR 32, 64; CD 5; DAM DRAM

Gurney, Ivor (Bertie) 1890-1937 ... **TCLC 33**
See also BRW 6; CA 167; PAB; RGEL 2

Gurney, Peter
See Gurney, A(lbert) R(amsdell), Jr.

Guro, Elena 1877-1913 .... **TCLC 56**

Gustafson, James M(oody) 1925- ... **CLC 100**
See also CA 25-28R; CANR 37

Gustafson, Ralph (Barker)
1909-1995 .... **CLC 36**
See also CA 21-24R; CANR 8, 45, 84; CP 7; DLB 88; RGEL 2

Gut, Gom
See Simenon, Georges (Jacques Christian)

Guterson, David 1956- .... **CLC 91**
See also CA 132; CANR 73; MTCW 2; NFS 13

Guthrie, A(lfred) B(ertram), Jr.
1901-1991 .... **CLC 23**
See also CA 57-60; 134; CANR 24; DLB 6, 212; SATA 62; SATA-Obit 67

Guthrie, Isobel
See Grieve, C(hristopher) M(urray)

Guthrie, Woodrow Wilson 1912-1967
See Guthrie, Woody
See also CA 113; 93-96

Guthrie, Woody .... **CLC 35**
See also Guthrie, Woodrow Wilson
See also LAIT 3

Gutierrez Najera, Manuel 1859-1895
See also HLCS 2; LAW

Guy, Rosa (Cuthbert) 1925- .... **CLC 26**
See also AAYA 4, 37; BW 2; CA 17-20R; CANR 14, 34, 83; CLR 13; DLB 33; DNFS 1; JRDA; MAICYA 1, 2; SATA 14, 62, 122; YAW

Gwendolyn
See Bennett, (Enoch) Arnold

H. D. .... **CLC 3, 8, 14, 31, 34, 73; PC 5**
See also Doolittle, Hilda

H. de V.
See Buchan, John

Haavikko, Paavo Juhani 1931- .. **CLC 18, 34**
See also CA 106

Habbema, Koos
See Heijermans, Herman

Habermas, Juergen 1929- .... **CLC 104**
See also CA 109; CANR 85; DLB 242

Habermas, Jurgen
See Habermas, Juergen

Hacker, Marilyn 1942- .. **CLC 5, 9, 23, 72, 91**
See also CA 77-80; CANR 68; CP 7; CWP; DAM POET; DLB 120; FW; GLL 2

Hadrian 76-138 .... **CMLC 52**

Haeckel, Ernst Heinrich (Philipp August)
1834-1919 .... **TCLC 83**
See also CA 157

Hafiz c. 1326-1389(?) .... **CMLC 34**
See also RGWL 2

Haggard, H(enry) Rider
1856-1925 .... **TCLC 11**
See also BRWS 3; BYA 4, 5; CA 108; 148; DLB 70, 156, 174, 178; FANT; MTCW 2; RGEL 2; RHW; SATA 16; SCFW; SFW 4; SUFW; WLIT 4

Hagiosy, L.
See Larbaud, Valery (Nicolas)

Hagiwara, Sakutaro 1886-1942 .... **TCLC 60; PC 18**
See also CA 154

Haig, Fenil
See Ford, Ford Madox

Haig-Brown, Roderick (Langmere)
1908-1976 .... **CLC 21**
See also CA 5-8R; 69-72; CANR 4, 38, 83; CLR 31; CWRI 5; DLB 88; MAICYA 1, 2; SATA 12

Hailey, Arthur 1920- .... **CLC 5**
See also AITN 2; BEST 90:3; BPFB 2; CA 1-4R; CANR 2, 36, 75; CCA 1; CN 7; CPW; DAM NOV, POP; DLB 88; DLBY 1982; MTCW 1, 2

Hailey, Elizabeth Forsythe 1938- ..... **CLC 40**
See also CA 93-96; CAAE 188; CAAS 1; CANR 15, 48; INT CANR-15

Haines, John (Meade) 1924- .... **CLC 58**
See also CA 17-20R; CANR 13, 34; CSW; DLB 5, 212

Hakluyt, Richard 1552-1616 .... **LC 31**
See also DLB 136; RGEL 2

Haldeman, Joe (William) 1943- .... **CLC 61**
See also Graham, Robert
See also AAYA 38; CA 53-56, 179; CAAE 179; CAAS 25; CANR 6, 70, 72; DLB 8; INT CANR-6; SCFW 2; SFW 4

Hale, Sarah Josepha (Buell)
1788-1879 .... **NCLC 75**
See also DLB 1, 42, 73, 243

Halevy, Elie 1870-1937 .... **TCLC 104**

Haley, Alex(ander Murray Palmer)
1921-1992 .... **CLC 8, 12, 76; BLC 2**
See also AAYA 26; BPFB 2; BW 2, 3; CA 77-80; 136; CANR 61; CDALBS; CPW; CSW; DA; DA3; DAB; DAC; DAM MST, MULT, POP; DLB 38; LAIT 5; MTCW 1, 2; NFS 9

Haliburton, Thomas Chandler
1796-1865 .... **NCLC 15**
See also DLB 11, 99; RGEL 2; RGSF 2

Hall, Donald (Andrew, Jr.) 1928- ...... **CLC 1, 13, 37, 59, 151**
See also CA 5-8R; CAAS 7; CANR 2, 44, 64, 106; CP 7; DAM POET; DLB 5; MTCW 1; RGAL 4; SATA 23, 97

Hall, Frederic Sauser
See Sauser-Hall, Frederic

Hall, James
See Kuttner, Henry

Hall, James Norman 1887-1951 ..... **TCLC 23**
See also CA 123; 173; LAIT 1; RHW 1; SATA 21

Hall, (Marguerite) Radclyffe
1880-1943 .... **TCLC 12**
See also BRWS 6; CA 110; 150; CANR 83; DLB 191; MTCW 2; RGEL 2; RHW

Hall, Rodney 1935- .... **CLC 51**
See also CA 109; CANR 69; CN 7; CP 7

Hallam, Arthur Henry
1811-1833 .... **NCLC 110**
See also DLB 32

Halleck, Fitz-Greene 1790-1867 .... **NCLC 47**
See also DLB 3, 250; RGAL 4

Halliday, Michael
See Creasey, John

Halpern, Daniel 1945- .... **CLC 14**
See also CA 33-36R; CANR 93; CP 7

Hamburger, Michael (Peter Leopold)
1924- .... **CLC 5, 14**
See also CA 5-8R; CAAE 196; CAAS 4; CANR 2, 47; CP 7; DLB 27

Hamill, Pete 1935- .... **CLC 10**
See also CA 25-28R; CANR 18, 71

Hamilton, Alexander
1755(?)-1804 .... **NCLC 49**
See also DLB 37

Hamilton, Clive
See Lewis, C(live) S(taples)

Hamilton, Edmond 1904-1977 .... **CLC 1**
See also CA 1-4R; CANR 3, 84; DLB 8; SATA 118; SFW 4

Hamilton, Eugene (Jacob) Lee
See Lee-Hamilton, Eugene (Jacob)

Hamilton, Franklin
See Silverberg, Robert

Hamilton, Gail
See Corcoran, Barbara (Asenath)

Hamilton, Mollie
See Kaye, M(ary) M(argaret)

Hamilton, (Anthony Walter) Patrick
1904-1962 .... **CLC 51**
See also CA 176; 113; DLB 10, 191

Hatteras, Owen .... **TCLC 18**
  See also Mencken, H(enry) L(ouis); Nathan,
  George Jean
Hauptmann, Gerhart (Johann Robert)
  1862-1946 .... **TCLC 4; SSC 37**
  See also CA 104; 153; CDWLB 2; DAM
  DRAM; DLB 66, 118; EW 8; RGSF 2;
  RGWL 2
Havel, Vaclav 1936- ..... **CLC 25, 58, 65, 123;**
  DC 6
  See also CA 104; CANR 36, 63; CDWLB
  4; CWW 2; DA3; DAM DRAM; DFS 10;
  DLB 232; MTCW 1, 2
Haviaras, Stratis .... **CLC 33**
  See also Chaviaras, Strates
Hawes, Stephen 1475(?)-1529(?) .... **LC 17**
  See also DLB 132; RGEL 2
Hawkes, John (Clendennin Burne, Jr.)
  1925-1998 .. **CLC 1, 2, 3, 4, 7, 9, 14, 15,**
  27, 49
  See also BPFB 2; CA 1-4R; 167; CANR 2,
  47, 64; CN 7; DLB 2, 7, 227; DLBY
  1980, 1998; MTCW 1, 2; RGAL 4
Hawking, S. W.
  See Hawking, Stephen W(illiam)
Hawking, Stephen W(illiam) 1942- . **CLC 63,**
  105
  See also AAYA 13; BEST 89:1; CA 126;
  129; CANR 48; CPW; DA3; MTCW 2
Hawkins, Anthony Hope
  See Hope, Anthony
Hawthorne, Julian 1846-1934 .... **TCLC 25**
  See also CA 165; HGG
Hawthorne, Nathaniel 1804-1864 ... **NCLC 2,**
  10, 17, 23, 39, 79, 95; SSC 3, 29, 39;
  WLC
  See also AAYA 18; AMW; AMWR 1; BPFB
  2; BYA 3; CDALB 1640-1865; DA; DA3;
  DAB; DAC; DAM MST, NOV; DLB 1,
  74, 183, 223; EXPN; EXPS; HGG; LAIT
  1; NFS 1; RGAL 4; RGSF 2; SSFS 1, 7,
  11, 15; SUFW; WCH; YABC 2
Haxton, Josephine Ayres 1921-
  See Douglas, Ellen
  See also CA 115; CANR 41, 83
Hayaseca y Eizaguirre, Jorge
  See Echegaray (y Eizaguirre), Jose (Maria
  Waldo)
Hayashi, Fumiko 1904-1951 .... **TCLC 27**
  See also Hayashi Fumiko
  See also CA 161
Hayashi Fumiko
  See Hayashi, Fumiko
  See also DLB 180
Haycraft, Anna (Margaret) 1932-
  See Ellis, Alice Thomas
  See also CA 122; CANR 85, 90; MTCW 2
Hayden, Robert E(arl) 1913-1980 . **CLC 5, 9,**
  14, 37; BLC 2; PC 6
  See also AFAW 1, 2; AMWS 2; BW 1, 3;
  CA 69-72; 97-100; CABS 2; CANR 24,
  75, 82; CDALB 1941-1968; DA; DAC;
  DAM MST, MULT, POET; DLB 5, 76;
  EXPP; MTCW 1, 2; PFS 1; RGAL 4;
  SATA 19; SATA-Obit 26; WP
Hayek, F(riedrich) A(ugust von)
  1899-1992 .... **TCLC 109**
  See also CA 93-96; 137; CANR 20; MTCW
  1, 2
Hayford, J(oseph) E(phraim) Casely
  See Casely-Hayford, J(oseph) E(phraim)
Hayman, Ronald 1932- .... **CLC 44**
  See also CA 25-28R; CANR 18, 50, 88; CD
  5; DLB 155
Hayne, Paul Hamilton 1830-1886 . **NCLC 94**
  See also DLB 3, 64, 79, 248; RGAL 4
Hays, Mary 1760-1843 .... **NCLC 114**
  See also DLB 142, 158; RGEL 2

Haywood, Eliza (Fowler)
  1693(?)-1756 .... **LC 1, 44**
  See also DLB 39; RGEL 2
Hazlitt, William 1778-1830 ...... **NCLC 29, 82**
  See also BRW 4; DLB 110, 158; RGEL 2
Hazzard, Shirley 1931- .... **CLC 18**
  See also CA 9-12R; CANR 4, 70; CN 7;
  DLBY 1982; MTCW 1
Head, Bessie 1937-1986 .... **CLC 25, 67; BLC**
  2; SSC 52
  See also AFW; BW 2, 3; CA 29-32R; 119;
  CANR 25, 82; CDWLB 3; DA3; DAM
  MULT; DLB 117, 225; EXPS; FW;
  MTCW 1, 2; RGSF 2; SSFS 5, 13; WLIT
  2
Headon, (Nicky) Topper 1956(?)- ..... **CLC 30**
Heaney, Seamus (Justin) 1939- ..... **CLC 5, 7,**
  14, 25, 37, 74, 91; PC 18; WLCS
  See also BRWR 1; BRWS 2; CA 85-88;
  CANR 25, 48, 75, 91; CDBLB 1960 to
  Present; CP 7; DA3; DAB; DAM POET;
  DLB 40; DLBY 1995; EXPP; MTCW 1,
  2; PAB; PFS 2, 5, 8; RGEL 2; WLIT 4
Hearn, (Patricio) Lafcadio (Tessima Carlos)
  1850-1904 .... **TCLC 9**
  See also CA 105; 166; DLB 12, 78, 189;
  HGG; RGAL 4
Hearne, Vicki 1946-2001 .... **CLC 56**
  See also CA 139; 201
Hearon, Shelby 1931- .... **CLC 63**
  See also AITN 2; AMWS 8; CA 25-28R;
  CANR 18, 48, 103; CSW
Heat-Moon, William Least .... **CLC 29**
  See also Trogdon, William (Lewis)
  See also AAYA 9
Hebbel, Friedrich 1813-1863 .... **NCLC 43**
  See also CDWLB 2; DAM DRAM; DLB
  129; EW 6; RGWL 2
Hebert, Anne 1916-2000 .... **CLC 4, 13, 29**
  See also CA 85-88; 187; CANR 69; CCA
  1; CWP; CWW 2; DA3; DAC; DAM
  MST, POET; DLB 68; GFL 1789 to the
  Present; MTCW 1, 2
Hecht, Anthony (Evan) 1923- ...... **CLC 8, 13,**
  19
  See also AMWS 10; CA 9-12R; CANR 6,
  108; CP 7; DAM POET; DLB 5, 169; PFS
  6; WP
Hecht, Ben 1894-1964 ..... **CLC 8; TCLC 101**
  See also CA 85-88; DFS 9; DLB 7, 9, 25,
  26, 28, 86; FANT; IDFW 3, 4; RGAL 4
Hedayat, Sadeq 1903-1951 .... **TCLC 21**
  See also CA 120; RGSF 2
Hegel, Georg Wilhelm Friedrich
  1770-1831 .... **NCLC 46**
  See also DLB 90
Heidegger, Martin 1889-1976 .... **CLC 24**
  See also CA 81-84; 65-68; CANR 34;
  MTCW 1, 2
Heidenstam, (Carl Gustaf) Verner von
  1859-1940 .... **TCLC 5**
  See also CA 104
Heifner, Jack 1946- .... **CLC 11**
  See also CA 105; CANR 47
Heijermans, Herman 1864-1924 .... **TCLC 24**
  See also CA 123
Heilbrun, Carolyn G(old) 1926- .... **CLC 25**
  See also Cross, Amanda
  See also CA 45-48; CANR 1, 28, 58, 94;
  FW
Hein, Christoph 1944- .... **CLC 154**
  See also CA 158; CANR 108; CDWLB 2;
  CWW 2; DLB 124
Heine, Heinrich 1797-1856 .... **NCLC 4, 54;**
  PC 25
  See also CDWLB 2; DLB 90; EW 5;
  RGWL 2

Heinemann, Larry (Curtiss) 1944- .. **CLC 50**
  See also CA 110; CAAS 21; CANR 31, 81;
  DLBD 9; INT CANR-31
Heiney, Donald (William) 1921-1993
  See Harris, MacDonald
  See also CA 1-4R; 142; CANR 3, 58; FANT
Heinlein, Robert A(nson) 1907-1988 . **CLC 1,**
  3, 8, 14, 26, 55
  See also AAYA 17; BPFB 2; BYA 4, 13;
  CA 1-4R; 125; CANR 1, 20, 53; CLR 75;
  CPW; DA3; DAM POP; DLB 8; EXPS;
  JRDA; LAIT 5; MAICYA 1, 2; MTCW 1,
  2; RGAL 4; SATA 9, 69; SATA-Obit 56;
  SCFW; SFW 4; SSFS 7; YAW
Helforth, John
  See Doolittle, Hilda
Heliodorus fl. 3rd cent. - .... **CMLC 52**
Hellenhofferu, Vojtech Kapristian z
  See Hasek, Jaroslav (Matej Frantisek)
Heller, Joseph 1923-1999 . **CLC 1, 3, 5, 8, 11,**
  36, 63; WLC
  See also AAYA 24; AITN 1; AMWS 4;
  BPFB 2; BYA 1; CA 5-8R; 187; CABS 1;
  CANR 8, 42, 66; CN 7; CPW; DA; DA3;
  DAB; DAC; DAM MST, NOV, POP;
  DLB 2, 28, 227; DLBY 1980; EXPN; INT
  CANR-8; LAIT 4; MTCW 1, 2; NFS 1;
  RGAL 4; YAW
Hellman, Lillian (Florence)
  1906-1984 .. **CLC 2, 4, 8, 14, 18, 34, 44,**
  52; DC 1; TCLC 119
  See also AITN 1, 2; AMWS 1; CA 13-16R;
  112; CAD; CANR 33; CWD; DA3; DAM
  DRAM; DFS 1, 3, 14; DLB 7, 228;
  DLBY 1984; FW; LAIT 3; MAWW;
  MTCW 1, 2; RGAL 4
Helprin, Mark 1947- .... **CLC 7, 10, 22, 32**
  See also CA 81-84; CANR 47, 64;
  CDALBS; CPW; DA3; DAM NOV, POP;
  DLBY 1985; FANT; MTCW 1, 2
Helvetius, Claude-Adrien 1715-1771 .. **LC 26**
Helyar, Jane Penelope Josephine 1933-
  See Poole, Josephine
  See also CA 21-24R; CANR 10, 26; CWRI
  5; SATA 82
Hemans, Felicia 1793-1835 ...... **NCLC 29, 71**
  See also DLB 96; RGEL 2
Hemingway, Ernest (Miller)
  1899-1961 .... **CLC 1, 3, 6, 8, 10, 13, 19,**
  30, 34, 39, 41, 44, 50, 61, 80; SSC 1, 25,
  36, 40; TCLC 115; WLC
  See also AAYA 19; AMW; AMWR 1; BPFB
  2; BYA 2, 3, 13; CA 77-80; CANR 34;
  CDALB 1917-1929; DA; DA3; DAB;
  DAC; DAM MST, NOV; DLB 4, 9, 102,
  210; DLBD 1, 15, 16; DLBY 1981, 1987,
  1996, 1998; EXPN; EXPS; LAIT 3, 4;
  MTCW 1, 2; NFS 1, 5, 6, 14; RGAL 4;
  RGSF 2; SSFS 1, 6, 8, 9, 11; WYA
Hempel, Amy 1951- .... **CLC 39**
  See also CA 118; 137; CANR 70; DA3;
  DLB 218; EXPS; MTCW 2; SSFS 2
Henderson, F. C.
  See Mencken, H(enry) L(ouis)
Henderson, Sylvia
  See Ashton-Warner, Sylvia (Constance)
Henderson, Zenna (Chlarson)
  1917-1983 .... **SSC 29**
  See also CA 1-4R; 133; CANR 1, 84; DLB
  8; SATA 5; SFW 4
Henkin, Joshua .... **CLC 119**
  See also CA 161
Henley, Beth .... **CLC 23; DC 6, 14**
  See also Henley, Elizabeth Becker
  See also CABS 3; CAD; CD 5; CSW;
  CWD; DFS 2; DLBY 1986; FW
Henley, Elizabeth Becker 1952-
  See Henley, Beth
  See also CA 107; CANR 32, 73; DA3;
  DAM DRAM, MST; MTCW 1, 2

Hiraoka, Kimitake 1925-1970
See Mishima, Yukio
See also CA 97-100; 29-32R; DA3; DAM DRAM; MTCW 1, 2

Hirsch, E(ric) D(onald), Jr. 1928- .... **CLC 79**
See also CA 25-28R; CANR 27, 51; DLB 67; INT CANR-27; MTCW 1

Hirsch, Edward 1950- .... **CLC 31, 50**
See also CA 104; CANR 20, 42, 102; CP 7; DLB 120

Hitchcock, Alfred (Joseph)
1899-1980 .... **CLC 16**
See also AAYA 22; CA 159; 97-100; SATA 27; SATA-Obit 24

Hitchens, Christopher (Eric)
1949- .... **CLC 157**
See also CA 149; CANR 89

Hitler, Adolf 1889-1945 .... **TCLC 53**
See also CA 117; 147

Hoagland, Edward 1932- .... **CLC 28**
See also ANW; CA 1-4R; CANR 2, 31, 57, 107; CN 7; DLB 6; SATA 51; TCWW 2

Hoban, Russell (Conwell) 1925- ... **CLC 7, 25**
See also BPFB 2; CA 5-8R; CANR 23, 37, 66; CLR 3, 69; CN 7; CWRI 5; DAM NOV; DLB 52; FANT; MAICYA 1, 2; MTCW 1, 2; SATA 1, 40, 78; SFW 4

Hobbes, Thomas 1588-1679 .... **LC 36**
See also DLB 151, 252; RGEL 2

Hobbs, Perry
See Blackmur, R(ichard) P(almer)

Hobson, Laura Z(ametkin)
1900-1986 .... **CLC 7, 25**
See also Field, Peter
See also BPFB 2; CA 17-20R; 118; CANR 55; DLB 28; SATA 52

Hoccleve, Thomas c. 1368-c. 1437 ...... **LC 75**
See also DLB 146; RGEL 2

Hoch, Edward D(entinger) 1930-
See Queen, Ellery
See also CA 29-32R; CANR 11, 27, 51, 97; CMW 4; SFW 4

Hochhuth, Rolf 1931- .... **CLC 4, 11, 18**
See also CA 5-8R; CANR 33, 75; CWW 2; DAM DRAM; DLB 124; MTCW 1, 2

Hochman, Sandra 1936- .... **CLC 3, 8**
See also CA 5-8R; DLB 5

Hochwaelder, Fritz 1911-1986 .... **CLC 36**
See also Hochwalder, Fritz
See also CA 29-32R; 120; CANR 42; DAM DRAM; MTCW 1

Hochwalder, Fritz
See Hochwaelder, Fritz
See also RGWL 2

Hocking, Mary (Eunice) 1921- .... **CLC 13**
See also CA 101; CANR 18, 40

Hodgins, Jack 1938- .... **CLC 23**
See also CA 93-96; CN 7; DLB 60

Hodgson, William Hope
1877(?)-1918 .... **TCLC 13**
See also CA 111; 164; CMW 4; DLB 70, 153, 156, 178; HGG; MTCW 2; SFW 4; SUFW

Hoeg, Peter 1957- .... **CLC 95, 156**
See also CA 151; CANR 75; CMW 4; DA3; DLB 214; MTCW 2

Hoffman, Alice 1952- .... **CLC 51**
See also AAYA 37; AMWS 10; CA 77-80; CANR 34, 66, 100; CN 7; CPW; DAM NOV; MTCW 1, 2

Hoffman, Daniel (Gerard) 1923- . **CLC 6, 13, 23**
See also CA 1-4R; CANR 4; CP 7; DLB 5

Hoffman, Stanley 1944- .... **CLC 5**
See also CA 77-80

Hoffman, William 1925- .... **CLC 141**
See also CA 21-24R; CANR 9, 103; CSW; DLB 234

Hoffman, William M(oses) 1939- ..... **CLC 40**
See also CA 57-60; CANR 11, 71

Hoffmann, E(rnst) T(heodor) A(madeus)
1776-1822 .... **NCLC 2; SSC 13**
See also CDWLB 2; DLB 90; EW 5; RGSF 2; RGWL 2; SATA 27; SUFW; WCH

Hofmann, Gert 1931- .... **CLC 54**
See also CA 128

Hofmannsthal, Hugo von
1874-1929 .... **TCLC 11; DC 4**
See also CA 106; 153; CDWLB 2; DAM DRAM; DFS 12; DLB 81, 118; EW 9; RGWL 2

Hogan, Linda 1947- .... **CLC 73; PC 35**
See also AMWS 4; ANW; BYA 12; CA 120; CANR 45, 73; CWP; DAM MULT; DLB 175; NNAL; SATA 132; TCWW 2

Hogarth, Charles
See Creasey, John

Hogarth, Emmett
See Polonsky, Abraham (Lincoln)

Hogg, James 1770-1835 .... **NCLC 4, 109**
See also DLB 93, 116, 159; HGG; RGEL 2; SUFW

Holbach, Paul Henri Thiry Baron
1723-1789 .... **LC 14**

Holberg, Ludvig 1684-1754 .... **LC 6**
See also RGWL 2

Holcroft, Thomas 1745-1809 .... **NCLC 85**
See also DLB 39, 89, 158; RGEL 2

Holden, Ursula 1921- .... **CLC 18**
See also CA 101; CAAS 8; CANR 22

Holderlin, (Johann Christian) Friedrich
1770-1843 .... **NCLC 16; PC 4**
See also CDWLB 2; DLB 90; EW 5; RGWL 2

Holdstock, Robert
See Holdstock, Robert P.

Holdstock, Robert P. 1948- .... **CLC 39**
See also CA 131; CANR 81; DLB 261; FANT; HGG; SFW 4

Holinshed, Raphael fl. 1580- .... **LC 69**
See also DLB 167; RGEL 2

Holland, Isabelle (Christian)
1920-2002 .... **CLC 21**
See also AAYA 11; CA 21-24R; 181; CAAE 181; CANR 10, 25, 47; CLR 57; CWRI 5; JRDA; LAIT 4; MAICYA 1, 2; SATA 8, 70; SATA-Essay 103; SATA-Obit 132; WYA

Holland, Marcus
See Caldwell, (Janet Miriam) Taylor (Holland)

Hollander, John 1929- .... **CLC 2, 5, 8, 14**
See also CA 1-4R; CANR 1, 52; CP 7; DLB 5; SATA 13

Hollander, Paul
See Silverberg, Robert

Holleran, Andrew 1943(?)- .... **CLC 38**
See also Garber, Eric
See also CA 144; GLL 1

Holley, Marietta 1836(?)-1926 .... **TCLC 99**
See also CA 118; DLB 11

Hollinghurst, Alan 1954- .... **CLC 55, 91**
See also CA 114; CN 7; DLB 207; GLL 1

Hollis, Jim
See Summers, Hollis (Spurgeon, Jr.)

Holly, Buddy 1936-1959 .... **TCLC 65**

Holmes, Gordon
See Shiel, M(atthew) P(hipps)

Holmes, John
See Souster, (Holmes) Raymond

Holmes, John Clellon 1926-1988 ...... **CLC 56**
See also CA 9-12R; 125; CANR 4; DLB 16, 237

Holmes, Oliver Wendell, Jr.
1841-1935 .... **TCLC 77**
See also CA 114; 186

Holmes, Oliver Wendell
1809-1894 .... **NCLC 14, 81**
See also AMWS 1; CDALB 1640-1865; DLB 1, 189, 235; EXPP; RGAL 4; SATA 34

Holmes, Raymond
See Souster, (Holmes) Raymond

Holt, Victoria
See Hibbert, Eleanor Alice Burford
See also BPFB 2

Holub, Miroslav 1923-1998 .... **CLC 4**
See also CA 21-24R; 169; CANR 10; CD-WLB 4; CWW 2; DLB 232

Homer c. 8th cent. B.C.- .... **CMLC 1, 16; PC 23; WLCS**
See also AW 1; CDWLB 1; DA; DA3; DAB; DAC; DAM MST, POET; DLB 176; EFS 1; LAIT 1; RGWL 2; TWA; WP

Hongo, Garrett Kaoru 1951- .... **PC 23**
See also CA 133; CAAS 22; CP 7; DLB 120; EXPP; RGAL 4

Honig, Edwin 1919- .... **CLC 33**
See also CA 5-8R; CAAS 8; CANR 4, 45; CP 7; DLB 5

Hood, Hugh (John Blagdon) 1928- . **CLC 15, 28; SSC 42**
See also CA 49-52; CAAS 17; CANR 1, 33, 87; CN 7; DLB 53; RGSF 2

Hood, Thomas 1799-1845 .... **NCLC 16**
See also BRW 4; DLB 96; RGEL 2

Hooker, (Peter) Jeremy 1941- .... **CLC 43**
See also CA 77-80; CANR 22; CP 7; DLB 40

hooks, bell .... **CLC 94**
See also Watkins, Gloria Jean
See also DLB 246

Hope, A(lec) D(erwent) 1907-2000 .... **CLC 3, 51**
See also BRWS 7; CA 21-24R; 188; CANR 33, 74; MTCW 1, 2; PFS 8; RGEL 2

Hope, Anthony 1863-1933 .... **TCLC 83**
See also CA 157; DLB 153, 156; RGEL 2; RHW

Hope, Brian
See Creasey, John

Hope, Christopher (David Tully)
1944- .... **CLC 52**
See also AFW; CA 106; CANR 47, 101; CN 7; DLB 225; SATA 62

Hopkins, Gerard Manley
1844-1889 .... **NCLC 17; PC 15; WLC**
See also BRW 5; BRWR 2; CDBLB 1890-1914; DA; DA3; DAB; DAC; DAM MST, POET; DLB 35, 57; EXPP; PAB; RGEL 2; WP

Hopkins, John (Richard) 1931-1998 .. **CLC 4**
See also CA 85-88; 169; CBD; CD 5

Hopkins, Pauline Elizabeth
1859-1930 .... **TCLC 28; BLC 2**
See also AFAW 2; BW 2, 3; CA 141; CANR 82; DAM MULT; DLB 50

Hopkinson, Francis 1737-1791 .... **LC 25**
See also DLB 31; RGAL 4

Hopley-Woolrich, Cornell George 1903-1968
See Woolrich, Cornell
See also CA 13-14; CANR 58; CAP 1; CMW 4; DLB 226; MTCW 2

Horace 65B.C.-8B.C. .... **CMLC 39**
See also AW 2; CDWLB 1; DLB 211; RGWL 2

Horatio
See Proust, (Valentin-Louis-George-Eugene-)Marcel

Horgan, Paul (George Vincent
O'Shaughnessy) 1903-1995 .. **CLC 9, 53**
See also BPFB 2; CA 13-16R; 147; CANR 9, 35; DAM NOV; DLB 102, 212; DLBY 1985; INT CANR-9; MTCW 1, 2; SATA 13; SATA-Obit 84; TCWW 2

Jackson, Shirley 1919-1965 . **CLC 11, 60, 87; SSC 9, 39; WLC**
See also AAYA 9; AMWS 9; BPFB 2; CA 1-4R; 25-28R; CANR 4, 52; CDALB 1941-1968; DA; DA3; DAC; DAM MST; DLB 6, 234; EXPS; HGG; LAIT 4; MTCW 2; RGAL 4; RGSF 2; SATA 2; SSFS 1; SUFW

Jacob, (Cyprien-)Max 1876-1944 .... **TCLC 6**
See also CA 104; 193; DLB 258; GFL 1789 to the Present; GLL 2; RGWL 2

Jacobs, Harriet A(nn)
1813(?)-1897 .... **NCLC 67**
See also AFAW 1, 2; DLB 239; FW; LAIT 2; RGAL 4

Jacobs, Jim 1942- .... **CLC 12**
See also CA 97-100; INT 97-100

Jacobs, W(illiam) W(ymark)
1863-1943 .... **TCLC 22**
See also CA 121; 167; DLB 135; EXPS; HGG; RGEL 2; RGSF 2; SSFS 2; SUFW

Jacobsen, Jens Peter 1847-1885 .... **NCLC 34**

Jacobsen, Josephine 1908- .... **CLC 48, 102**
See also CA 33-36R; CAAS 18; CANR 23, 48; CCA 1; CP 7; DLB 244

Jacobson, Dan 1929- .... **CLC 4, 14**
See also AFW; CA 1-4R; CANR 2, 25, 66; CN 7; DLB 14, 207, 225; MTCW 1; RGSF 2

Jacqueline
See Carpentier (y Valmont), Alejo

Jagger, Mick 1944- .... **CLC 17**

Jahiz, al- c. 780-c. 869 .... **CMLC 25**

Jakes, John (William) 1932- .... **CLC 29**
See also AAYA 32; BEST 89:4; BPFB 2; CA 57-60; CANR 10, 43, 66; CPW; CSW; DA3; DAM NOV, POP; DLBY 1983; FANT; INT CANR-10; MTCW 1, 2; RHW; SATA 62; SFW 4; TCWW 2

James I 1394-1437 .... **LC 20**
See also RGEL 2

James, Andrew
See Kirkup, James

James, C(yril) L(ionel) R(obert)
1901-1989 .... **CLC 33; BLCS**
See also BW 2; CA 117; 125; 128; CANR 62; DLB 125; MTCW 1

James, Daniel (Lewis) 1911-1988
See Santiago, Danny
See also CA 174; 125

James, Dynely
See Mayne, William (James Carter)

James, Henry Sr. 1811-1882 .... **NCLC 53**

James, Henry 1843-1916 ..... **TCLC 2, 11, 24, 40, 47, 64; SSC 8, 32, 47; WLC**
See also AMW; AMWR 1; BPFB 2; BRW 6; CA 104; 132; CDALB 1865-1917; DA; DA3; DAB; DAC; DAM MST, NOV; DLB 12, 71, 74, 189; DLBD 13; EXPS; HGG; LAIT 2; MTCW 1, 2; NFS 12; RGAL 4; RGEL 2; RGSF 2; SSFS 9; SUFW

James, M. R.
See James, Montague (Rhodes)
See also DLB 156, 201

James, Montague (Rhodes)
1862-1936 .... **TCLC 6; SSC 16**
See also James, M. R.
See also CA 104; HGG; RGEL 2; RGSF 2; SUFW

James, P. D. .... **CLC 18, 46, 122**
See also White, Phyllis Dorothy James
See also BEST 90:2; BPFB 2; BRWS 4; CDBLB 1960 to Present; DLB 87; DLBD 17; MSW

James, Philip
See Moorcock, Michael (John)

James, Samuel
See Stephens, James

James, Seumas
See Stephens, James

James, Stephen
See Stephens, James

James, William 1842-1910 .... **TCLC 15, 32**
See also AMW; CA 109; 193; RGAL 4

Jameson, Anna 1794-1860 .... **NCLC 43**
See also DLB 99, 166

Jameson, Fredric (R.) 1934- .... **CLC 142**
See also CA 196; DLB 67

Jami, Nur al-Din 'Abd al-Rahman
1414-1492 .... **LC 9**

Jammes, Francis 1868-1938 .... **TCLC 75**
See also CA 198; GFL 1789 to the Present

Jandl, Ernst 1925-2000 .... **CLC 34**
See also CA 200

Janowitz, Tama 1957- .... **CLC 43, 145**
See also CA 106; CANR 52, 89; CN 7; CPW; DAM POP

Japrisot, Sebastien 1931- .... **CLC 90**
See also Rossi, Jean Baptiste
See also CMW 4

Jarrell, Randall 1914-1965 .... **CLC 1, 2, 6, 9, 13, 49; PC 41**
See also AMW; BYA 5; CA 5-8R; 25-28R; CABS 2; CANR 6, 34; CDALB 1941-1968; CLR 6; CWRI 5; DAM POET; DLB 48, 52; EXPP; MAICYA 1, 2; MTCW 1, 2; PAB; PFS 2; RGAL 4; SATA 7

Jarry, Alfred 1873-1907 .... **TCLC 2, 14; SSC 20**
See also CA 104; 153; DA3; DAM DRAM; DFS 8; DLB 192, 258; EW 9; GFL 1789 to the Present; RGWL 2

Jarvis, E. K.
See Silverberg, Robert

Jawien, Andrzej
See John Paul II, Pope

Jaynes, Roderick
See Coen, Ethan

Jeake, Samuel, Jr.
See Aiken, Conrad (Potter)

Jean Paul 1763-1825 .... **NCLC 7**

Jefferies, (John) Richard
1848-1887 .... **NCLC 47**
See also DLB 98, 141; RGEL 2; SATA 16; SFW 4

Jeffers, (John) Robinson 1887-1962 .. **CLC 2, 3, 11, 15, 54; PC 17; WLC**
See also AMWS 2; CA 85-88; CANR 35; CDALB 1917-1929; DA; DAC; DAM MST, POET; DLB 45, 212; MTCW 1, 2; PAB; PFS 3, 4; RGAL 4

Jefferson, Janet
See Mencken, H(enry) L(ouis)

Jefferson, Thomas 1743-1826 . **NCLC 11, 103**
See also ANW; CDALB 1640-1865; DA3; DLB 31, 183; LAIT 1; RGAL 4

Jeffrey, Francis 1773-1850 .... **NCLC 33**
See also Francis, Lord Jeffrey

Jelakowitch, Ivan
See Heijermans, Herman

Jellicoe, (Patricia) Ann 1927- .... **CLC 27**
See also CA 85-88; CBD; CD 5; CWD; CWRI 5; DLB 13, 233; FW

Jemyma
See Holley, Marietta

Jen, Gish .... **CLC 70**
See also Jen, Lillian

Jen, Lillian 1956(?)-
See Jen, Gish
See also CA 135; CANR 89

Jenkins, (John) Robin 1912- .... **CLC 52**
See also CA 1-4R; CANR 1; CN 7; DLB 14

Jennings, Elizabeth (Joan)
1926-2001 .... **CLC 5, 14, 131**
See also BRWS 5; CA 61-64; 200; CAAS 5; CANR 8, 39, 66; CP 7; CWP; DLB 27; MTCW 1; SATA 66

Jennings, Waylon 1937- .... **CLC 21**

Jensen, Johannes V. 1873-1950 ...... **TCLC 41**
See also CA 170; DLB 214

Jensen, Laura (Linnea) 1948- .... **CLC 37**
See also CA 103

Jerome, Jerome K(lapka)
1859-1927 .... **TCLC 23**
See also CA 119; 177; DLB 10, 34, 135; RGEL 2

Jerrold, Douglas William
1803-1857 .... **NCLC 2**
See also DLB 158, 159; RGEL 2

Jewett, (Theodora) Sarah Orne
1849-1909 .... **TCLC 1, 22; SSC 6, 44**
See also AMW; CA 108; 127; CANR 71; DLB 12, 74, 221; EXPS; FW; MAWW; NFS 15; RGAL 4; RGSF 2; SATA 15; SSFS 4

Jewsbury, Geraldine (Endsor)
1812-1880 .... **NCLC 22**
See also DLB 21

Jhabvala, Ruth Prawer 1927- . **CLC 4, 8, 29, 94, 138**
See also BRWS 5; CA 1-4R; CANR 2, 29, 51, 74, 91; CN 7; DAB; DAM NOV; DLB 139, 194; IDFW 3, 4; INT CANR-29; MTCW 1, 2; RGSF 2; RGWL 2; RHW

Jibran, Kahlil
See Gibran, Kahlil

Jibran, Khalil
See Gibran, Kahlil

Jiles, Paulette 1943- .... **CLC 13, 58**
See also CA 101; CANR 70; CWP

Jimenez (Mantecon), Juan Ramon
1881-1958 .... **TCLC 4; HLC 1; PC 7**
See also CA 104; 131; CANR 74; DAM MULT, POET; DLB 134; EW 9; HW 1; MTCW 1, 2; RGWL 2

Jimenez, Ramon
See Jimenez (Mantecon), Juan Ramon

Jimenez Mantecon, Juan
See Jimenez (Mantecon), Juan Ramon

Jin, Ha .... **CLC 109**
See also Jin, Xuefei
See also CA 152; DLB 244

Jin, Xuefei 1956-
See Jin, Ha
See also CANR 91

Joel, Billy .... **CLC 26**
See also Joel, William Martin

Joel, William Martin 1949-
See Joel, Billy
See also CA 108

John, Saint 107th cent. -100 .... **CMLC 27**

John of the Cross, St. 1542-1591 .... **LC 18**
See also RGWL 2

John Paul II, Pope 1920- .... **CLC 128**
See also CA 106; 133

Johnson, B(ryan) S(tanley William)
1933-1973 .... **CLC 6, 9**
See also CA 9-12R; 53-56; CANR 9; DLB 14, 40; RGEL 2

Johnson, Benjamin F., of Boone
See Riley, James Whitcomb

Johnson, Charles (Richard) 1948- .... **CLC 7, 51, 65; BLC 2**
See also AFAW 2; AMWS 6; BW 2, 3; CA 116; CAAS 18; CANR 42, 66, 82; CN 7; DAM MULT; DLB 33; MTCW 2; RGAL 4

Johnson, Denis 1949- .... **CLC 52, 160**
See also CA 117; 121; CANR 71, 99; CN 7; DLB 120

Johnson, Diane 1934- .... **CLC 5, 13, 48**
See also BPFB 2; CA 41-44R; CANR 17, 40, 62, 95; CN 7; DLBY 1980; INT CANR-17; MTCW 1

Johnson, Eyvind (Olof Verner)
1900-1976 .... **CLC 14**
See also CA 73-76; 69-72; CANR 34, 101; DLB 259; EW 12

Johnson, J. R.
See James, C(yril) L(ionel) R(obert)

Johnson, James Weldon
1871-1938 . **TCLC 3, 19; BLC 2; PC 24**
See also AFAW 1, 2; BW 1, 3; CA 104; 125; CANR 82; CDALB 1917-1929; CLR 32; DA3; DAM MULT, POET; DLB 51; EXPP; MTCW 1, 2; PFS 1; RGAL 4; SATA 31

Johnson, Joyce 1935- .... **CLC 58**
See also CA 125; 129; CANR 102

Johnson, Judith (Emlyn) 1936- .... **CLC 7, 15**
See also Sherwin, Judith Johnson
See also CA 25-28R; 153; CANR 34

Johnson, Lionel (Pigot)
1867-1902 .... **TCLC 19**
See also CA 117; DLB 19; RGEL 2

Johnson, Marguerite (Annie)
See Angelou, Maya

Johnson, Mel
See Malzberg, Barry N(athaniel)

Johnson, Pamela Hansford
1912-1981 .... **CLC 1, 7, 27**
See also CA 1-4R; 104; CANR 2, 28; DLB 15; MTCW 1, 2; RGEL 2

Johnson, Paul (Bede) 1928- .... **CLC 147**
See also BEST 89:4; CA 17-20R; CANR 34, 62, 100

Johnson, Robert .... **CLC 70**

Johnson, Robert 1911(?)-1938 .... **TCLC 69**
See also BW 3; CA 174

Johnson, Samuel 1709-1784 .... **LC 15, 52; WLC**
See also BRW 3; BRWR 1; CDBLB 1660-1789; DA; DAB; DAC; DAM MST; DLB 39, 95, 104, 142, 213; RGEL 2; TEA

Johnson, Uwe 1934-1984 .. **CLC 5, 10, 15, 40**
See also CA 1-4R; 112; CANR 1, 39; CD-WLB 2; DLB 75; MTCW 1; RGWL 2

Johnston, George (Benson) 1913- ... **CLC 51**
See also CA 1-4R; CANR 5, 20; CP 7; DLB 88

Johnston, Jennifer (Prudence)
1930- .... **CLC 7, 150**
See also CA 85-88; CANR 92; CN 7; DLB 14

Joinville, Jean de 1224(?)-1317 ..... **CMLC 38**

Jolley, (Monica) Elizabeth 1923- ..... **CLC 46; SSC 19**
See also CA 127; CAAS 13; CANR 59; CN 7; RGSF 2

Jones, Arthur Llewellyn 1863-1947
See Machen, Arthur
See also CA 104; 179; HGG

Jones, D(ouglas) G(ordon) 1929- ..... **CLC 10**
See also CA 29-32R; CANR 13, 90; CP 7; DLB 53

Jones, David (Michael) 1895-1974 .... **CLC 2, 4, 7, 13, 42**
See also BRW 6; BRWS 7; CA 9-12R; 53-56; CANR 28; CDBLB 1945-1960; DLB 20, 100; MTCW 1; PAB; RGEL 2

Jones, David Robert 1947-
See Bowie, David
See also CA 103; CANR 104

Jones, Diana Wynne 1934- .... **CLC 26**
See also AAYA 12; BYA 6, 7, 9, 11, 13; CA 49-52; CANR 4, 26, 56; CLR 23; DLB 161; FANT; JRDA; MAICYA 1, 2; SAAS 7; SATA 9, 70, 108; SFW 4; YAW

Jones, Edward P. 1950- .... **CLC 76**
See also BW 2, 3; CA 142; CANR 79; CSW

Jones, Gayl 1949- ...... **CLC 6, 9, 131; BLC 2**
See also AFAW 1, 2; BW 2, 3; CA 77-80; CANR 27, 66; CN 7; CSW; DA3; DAM MULT; DLB 33; MTCW 1, 2; RGAL 4

Jones, James 1931-1978 ...... **CLC 1, 3, 10, 39**
See also AITN 1, 2; BPFB 2; CA 1-4R; 69-72; CANR 6; DLB 2, 143; DLBD 17; DLBY 1998; MTCW 1; RGAL 4

Jones, John J.
See Lovecraft, H(oward) P(hillips)

Jones, LeRoi .... **CLC 1, 2, 3, 5, 10, 14**
See Baraka, Amiri
See also MTCW 2

Jones, Louis B. 1953- .... **CLC 65**
See also CA 141; CANR 73

Jones, Madison (Percy, Jr.) 1925- ...... **CLC 4**
See also CA 13-16R; CAAS 11; CANR 7, 54, 83; CN 7; CSW; DLB 152

Jones, Mervyn 1922- .... **CLC 10, 52**
See also CA 45-48; CAAS 5; CANR 1, 91; CN 7; MTCW 1

Jones, Mick 1956(?)- .... **CLC 30**

Jones, Nettie (Pearl) 1941- .... **CLC 34**
See also BW 2; CA 137; CAAS 20; CANR 88

Jones, Preston 1936-1979 .... **CLC 10**
See also CA 73-76; 89-92; DLB 7

Jones, Robert F(rancis) 1934- .... **CLC 7**
See also CA 49-52; CANR 2, 61

Jones, Rod 1953- .... **CLC 50**
See also CA 128

Jones, Terence Graham Parry
1942- .... **CLC 21**
See also Jones, Terry; Monty Python
See also CA 112; 116; CANR 35, 93; INT 116; SATA 127

Jones, Terry
See Jones, Terence Graham Parry
See also SATA 67; SATA-Brief 51

Jones, Thom (Douglas) 1945(?)- .... **CLC 81**
See also CA 157; CANR 88; DLB 244

Jong, Erica 1942- .... **CLC 4, 6, 8, 18, 83**
See also AITN 1; AMWS 5; BEST 90:2; BPFB 2; CA 73-76; CANR 26, 52, 75; CN 7; CP 7; CPW; DA3; DAM NOV, POP; DLB 2, 5, 28, 152; FW; INT CANR-26; MTCW 1, 2

Jonson, Ben(jamin) 1572(?)-1637 .. **LC 6, 33; DC 4; PC 17; WLC**
See also BRW 1; BRWR 1; CDBLB Before 1660; DA; DAB; DAC; DAM DRAM, MST, POET; DFS 4, 10; DLB 62, 121; RGEL 2; WLIT 3

Jordan, June 1936- .... **CLC 5, 11, 23, 114; BLCS; PC 38**
See also Meyer, June
See also AAYA 2; AFAW 1, 2; BW 2, 3; CA 33-36R; CANR 25, 70; CLR 10; CP 7; CWP; DAM MULT, POET; DLB 38; GLL 2; LAIT 5; MAICYA 1, 2; MTCW 1; SATA 4; YAW

Jordan, Neil (Patrick) 1950- .... **CLC 110**
See also CA 124; 130; CANR 54; CN 7; GLL 2; INT 130

Jordan, Pat(rick M.) 1941- .... **CLC 37**
See also CA 33-36R

Jorgensen, Ivar
See Ellison, Harlan (Jay)

Jorgenson, Ivar
See Silverberg, Robert

Joseph, George Ghevarughese .... **CLC 70**

Josephson, Mary
See O'Doherty, Brian

Josephus, Flavius c. 37-100 .... **CMLC 13**
See also AW 2; DLB 176

Josiah Allen's Wife
See Holley, Marietta

Josipovici, Gabriel (David) 1940- ...... **CLC 6, 43, 153**
See also CA 37-40R; CAAS 8; CANR 47, 84; CN 7; DLB 14

Joubert, Joseph 1754-1824 .... **NCLC 9**

Jouve, Pierre Jean 1887-1976 .... **CLC 47**
See also CA 65-68; DLB 258

Jovine, Francesco 1902-1950 .... **TCLC 79**

Joyce, James (Augustine Aloysius)
1882-1941 ... **TCLC 3, 8, 16, 35, 52; DC 16; PC 22; SSC 3, 26, 44; WLC**
See also AAYA 42; BRW 7; BRWR 1; BYA 11, 13; CA 104; 126; CDBLB 1914-1945; DA; DA3; DAB; DAC; DAM MST, NOV, POET; DLB 10, 19, 36, 162, 247; EXPN; EXPS; LAIT 3; MTCW 1, 2; NFS 7; RGSF 2; SSFS 1; WLIT 4

Jozsef, Attila 1905-1937 .... **TCLC 22**
See also CA 116; CDWLB 4; DLB 215

Juana Ines de la Cruz, Sor
1651(?)-1695 ...... **LC 5; HLCS 1; PC 24**
See also FW; LAW; RGWL 2; WLIT 1

Juana Inez de La Cruz, Sor
See Juana Ines de la Cruz, Sor

Judd, Cyril
See Kornbluth, C(yril) M.; Pohl, Frederik

Juenger, Ernst 1895-1998 .... **CLC 125**
See also Junger, Ernst
See also CA 101; 167; CANR 21, 47, 106; DLB 56

Julian of Norwich 1342(?)-1416(?) . **LC 6, 52**
See also DLB 146

Julius Caesar 100B.C.-44B.C.
See Caesar, Julius
See also CDWLB 1; DLB 211

Junger, Ernst
See Juenger, Ernst
See also CDWLB 2; RGWL 2

Junger, Sebastian 1962- .... **CLC 109**
See also AAYA 28; CA 165

Juniper, Alex
See Hospital, Janette Turner

Junius
See Luxemburg, Rosa

Just, Ward (Swift) 1935- .... **CLC 4, 27**
See also CA 25-28R; CANR 32, 87; CN 7; INT CANR-32

Justice, Donald (Rodney) 1925- .. **CLC 6, 19, 102**
See also AMWS 7; CA 5-8R; CANR 26, 54, 74; CP 7; CSW; DAM POET; DLBY 1983; INT CANR-26; MTCW 2; PFS 14

Juvenal c. 60-c. 130 .... **CMLC 8**
See also AW 2; CDWLB 1; DLB 211; RGWL 2

Juvenis
See Bourne, Randolph S(illiman)

Kabakov, Sasha .... **CLC 59**

Kacew, Romain 1914-1980
See Gary, Romain
See also CA 108; 102

Kadare, Ismail 1936- .... **CLC 52**
See also CA 161

Kadohata, Cynthia .... **CLC 59, 122**
See also CA 140

Kafka, Franz 1883-1924 . **TCLC 2, 6, 13, 29, 47, 53, 112; SSC 5, 29, 35; WLC**
See also AAYA 31; BPFB 2; CA 105; 126; CDWLB 2; DA; DA3; DAB; DAC; DAM MST, NOV; DLB 81; EW 9; EXPS; MTCW 1, 2; NFS 7; RGSF 2; RGWL 2; SFW 4; SSFS 3, 7, 12

Kahanovitsch, Pinkhes
See Der Nister

Kahn, Roger 1927- .... **CLC 30**
See also CA 25-28R; CANR 44, 69; DLB 171; SATA 37

Kain, Saul
See Sassoon, Siegfried (Lorraine)

Kunikida Doppo 1869(?)-1908
See Doppo, Kunikida
See also DLB 180

Kunitz, Stanley (Jasspon) 1905- .. **CLC 6, 11, 14, 148; PC 19**
See also AMWS 3; CA 41-44R; CANR 26, 57, 98; CP 7; DA3; DLB 48; INT CANR-26; MTCW 1, 2; PFS 11; RGAL 4

Kunze, Reiner 1933- .... **CLC 10**
See also CA 93-96; CWW 2; DLB 75

Kuprin, Aleksander Ivanovich
1870-1938 .... **TCLC 5**
See also CA 104; 182

Kureishi, Hanif 1954(?)- .... **CLC 64, 135**
See also CA 139; CBD; CD 5; CN 7; DLB 194, 245; GLL 2; IDFW 4; WLIT 4

Kurosawa, Akira 1910-1998 ..... **CLC 16, 119**
See also AAYA 11; CA 101; 170; CANR 46; DAM MULT

Kushner, Tony 1957(?)- .... **CLC 81; DC 10**
See also AMWS 9; CA 144; CAD; CANR 74; CD 5; DA3; DAM DRAM; DFS 5; DLB 228; GLL 1; LAIT 5; MTCW 2; RGAL 4

Kuttner, Henry 1915-1958 .... **TCLC 10**
See also CA 107; 157; DLB 8; FANT; SCFW 2; SFW 4

Kuzma, Greg 1944- .... **CLC 7**
See also CA 33-36R; CANR 70

Kuzmin, Mikhail 1872(?)-1936 ...... **TCLC 40**
See also CA 170

Kyd, Thomas 1558-1594 .... **LC 22; DC 3**
See also BRW 1; DAM DRAM; DLB 62; IDTP; RGEL 2; TEA; WLIT 3

Kyprianos, Iossif
See Samarakis, Antonis

Labrunie, Gerard
See Nerval, Gerard de

La Bruyere, Jean de 1645-1696 .... **LC 17**
See also EW 3; GFL Beginnings to 1789

Lacan, Jacques (Marie Emile)
1901-1981 .... **CLC 75**
See also CA 121; 104

Laclos, Pierre Ambroise Francois
1741-1803 .... **NCLC 4, 87**
See also EW 4; GFL Beginnings to 1789; RGWL 2

Lacolere, Francois
See Aragon, Louis

La Colere, Francois
See Aragon, Louis

La Deshabilleuse
See Simenon, Georges (Jacques Christian)

Lady Gregory
See Gregory, Lady Isabella Augusta (Persse)

Lady of Quality, A
See Bagnold, Enid

La Fayette, Marie-(Madelaine Pioche de la Vergne) 1634-1693 .... **LC 2**
See also GFL Beginnings to 1789; RGWL 2

Lafayette, Rene
See Hubbard, L(afayette) Ron(ald)

La Fontaine, Jean de 1621-1695 .... **LC 50**
See also EW 3; GFL Beginnings to 1789; MAICYA 1, 2; RGWL 2; SATA 18

Laforgue, Jules 1860-1887 . **NCLC 5, 53; PC 14; SSC 20**
See also DLB 217; EW 7; GFL 1789 to the Present; RGWL 2

Layamon
See Layamon
See also DLB 146

Lagerkvist, Paer (Fabian)
1891-1974 .... **CLC 7, 10, 13, 54**
See also Lagerkvist, Par
See also CA 85-88; 49-52; DA3; DAM DRAM, NOV; MTCW 1, 2

Lagerkvist, Par .... **SSC 12**

See also Lagerkvist, Paer (Fabian)
See also DLB 259; EW 10; MTCW 2; RGSF 2; RGWL 2

Lagerloef, Selma (Ottiliana Lovisa)
1858-1940 .... **TCLC 4, 36**
See also Lagerlof, Selma (Ottiliana Lovisa)
See also CA 108; MTCW 2; SATA 15

Lagerlof, Selma (Ottiliana Lovisa)
See Lagerloef, Selma (Ottiliana Lovisa)
See also CLR 7; SATA 15

La Guma, (Justin) Alex(ander)
1925-1985 .... **CLC 19; BLCS**
See also AFW; BW 1, 3; CA 49-52; 118; CANR 25, 81; CDWLB 3; DAM NOV; DLB 117, 225; MTCW 1, 2; WLIT 2

Laidlaw, A. K.
See Grieve, C(hristopher) M(urray)

Lainez, Manuel Mujica
See Mujica Lainez, Manuel
See also HW 1

Laing, R(onald) D(avid) 1927-1989 . **CLC 95**
See also CA 107; 129; CANR 34; MTCW 1

Lamartine, Alphonse (Marie Louis Prat) de
1790-1869 .... **NCLC 11; PC 16**
See also DAM POET; DLB 217; GFL 1789 to the Present; RGWL 2

Lamb, Charles 1775-1834 ..... **NCLC 10, 113; WLC**
See also BRW 4; CDBLB 1789-1832; DA; DAB; DAC; DAM MST; DLB 93, 107, 163; RGEL 2; SATA 17

Lamb, Lady Caroline 1785-1828 ... **NCLC 38**
See also DLB 116

Lamming, George (William) 1927- ... **CLC 2, 4, 66, 144; BLC 2**
See also BW 2, 3; CA 85-88; CANR 26, 76; CDWLB 3; CN 7; DAM MULT; DLB 125; MTCW 1, 2; NFS 15; RGEL 2

L'Amour, Louis (Dearborn)
1908-1988 .... **CLC 25, 55**
See also Burns, Tex; Mayo, Jim
See also AAYA 16; AITN 2; BEST 89:2; BPFB 2; CA 1-4R; 125; CANR 3, 25, 40; CPW; DA3; DAM NOV, POP; DLB 206; DLBY 1980; MTCW 1, 2; RGAL 4

Lampedusa, Giuseppe (Tomasi) di
.... **TCLC 13**
See also Tomasi di Lampedusa, Giuseppe
See also CA 164; EW 11; MTCW 2; RGWL 2

Lampman, Archibald 1861-1899 ... **NCLC 25**
See also DLB 92; RGEL 2

Lancaster, Bruce 1896-1963 .... **CLC 36**
See also CA 9-10; CANR 70; CAP 1; SATA 9

Lanchester, John .... **CLC 99**
See also CA 194

Landau, Mark Alexandrovich
See Aldanov, Mark (Alexandrovich)

Landau-Aldanov, Mark Alexandrovich
See Aldanov, Mark (Alexandrovich)

Landis, Jerry
See Simon, Paul (Frederick)

Landis, John 1950- .... **CLC 26**
See also CA 112; 122

Landolfi, Tommaso 1908-1979 .... **CLC 11, 49**
See also CA 127; 117; DLB 177

Landon, Letitia Elizabeth
1802-1838 .... **NCLC 15**
See also DLB 96

Landor, Walter Savage
1775-1864 .... **NCLC 14**
See also BRW 4; DLB 93, 107; RGEL 2

Landwirth, Heinz 1927-
See Lind, Jakov
See also CA 9-12R; CANR 7

Lane, Patrick 1939- .... **CLC 25**
See also CA 97-100; CANR 54; CP 7; DAM POET; DLB 53; INT 97-100

Lang, Andrew 1844-1912 .... **TCLC 16**
See also CA 114; 137; CANR 85; DLB 98, 141, 184; FANT; MAICYA 1, 2; RGEL 2; SATA 16; WCH

Lang, Fritz 1890-1976 .... **CLC 20, 103**
See also CA 77-80; 69-72; CANR 30

Lange, John
See Crichton, (John) Michael

Langer, Elinor 1939- .... **CLC 34**
See also CA 121

Langland, William 1332(?)-1400(?) ..... **LC 19**
See also BRW 1; DA; DAB; DAC; DAM MST, POET; DLB 146; RGEL 2; WLIT 3

Langstaff, Launcelot
See Irving, Washington

Lanier, Sidney 1842-1881 .... **NCLC 6**
See also AMWS 1; DAM POET; DLB 64; DLBD 13; EXPP; MAICYA 1; PFS 14; RGAL 4; SATA 18

Lanyer, Aemilia 1569-1645 .... **LC 10, 30**
See also DLB 121

Lao Tzu c. 6th cent. B.C.-3rd cent. B.C. .... **CMLC 7**

Lao-Tzu
See Lao Tzu

Lapine, James (Elliot) 1949- .... **CLC 39**
See also CA 123; 130; CANR 54; INT 130

Larbaud, Valery (Nicolas)
1881-1957 .... **TCLC 9**
See also CA 106; 152; GFL 1789 to the Present

Lardner, Ring
See Lardner, Ring(gold) W(ilmer)
See also BPFB 2; CDALB 1917-1929; DLB 11, 25, 86, 171; DLBD 16; RGAL 4; RGSF 2

Lardner, Ring W., Jr.
See Lardner, Ring(gold) W(ilmer)

Lardner, Ring(gold) W(ilmer)
1885-1933 .... **TCLC 2, 14; SSC 32**
See also Lardner, Ring
See also AMW; CA 104; 131; MTCW 1, 2; TUS

Laredo, Betty
See Codrescu, Andrei

Larkin, Maia
See Wojciechowska, Maia (Teresa)

Larkin, Philip (Arthur) 1922-1985 ... **CLC 3, 5, 8, 9, 13, 18, 33, 39, 64; PC 21**
See also BRWS 1; CA 5-8R; 117; CANR 24, 62; CDBLB 1960 to Present; DA3; DAB; DAM MST, POET; DLB 27; MTCW 1, 2; PFS 3, 4, 12; RGEL 2

Larra (y Sanchez de Castro), Mariano Jose de 1809-1837 .... **NCLC 17**

Larsen, Eric 1941- .... **CLC 55**
See also CA 132

Larsen, Nella 1893-1963 ...... **CLC 37; BLC 2**
See also AFAW 1, 2; BW 1; CA 125; CANR 83; DAM MULT; DLB 51; FW

Larson, Charles R(aymond) 1938- ... **CLC 31**
See also CA 53-56; CANR 4

Larson, Jonathan 1961-1996 .... **CLC 99**
See also AAYA 28; CA 156

Las Casas, Bartolome de 1474-1566 . **LC 31; HLCS**
See also Casas, Bartolome de las
See also LAW

Lasch, Christopher 1932-1994 .... **CLC 102**
See also CA 73-76; 144; CANR 25; DLB 246; MTCW 1, 2

Lasker-Schueler, Else 1869-1945 ... **TCLC 57**
See also CA 183; DLB 66, 124

Laski, Harold J(oseph) 1893-1950 . **TCLC 79**
See also CA 188

Latham, Jean Lee 1902-1995 .... **CLC 12**
See also AITN 1; BYA 1; CA 5-8R; CANR 7, 84; CLR 50; MAICYA 1, 2; SATA 2, 68; YAW

Leger, (Marie-Rene Auguste) Alexis Saint-Leger 1887-1975 .. **CLC 4, 11, 46; PC 23**
See also Perse, Saint-John; Saint-John Perse
See also CA 13-16R; 61-64; CANR 43; DAM POET; MTCW 1

Leger, Saintleger
See Leger, (Marie-Rene Auguste) Alexis Saint-Leger

Le Guin, Ursula K(roeber) 1929- ..... **CLC 8, 13, 22, 45, 71, 136; SSC 12**
See also AAYA 9, 27; AITN 1; BPFB 2; BYA 5, 8, 11, 14; CA 21-24R; CANR 9, 32, 52, 74; CDALB 1968-1988; CLR 3, 28; CN 7; CPW; DA3; DAB; DAC; DAM MST, POP; DLB 8, 52, 256; EXPS; FANT; FW; INT CANR-32; JRDA; LAIT 5; MAICYA 1, 2; MTCW 1, 2; NFS 6, 9; SATA 4, 52, 99; SCFW; SFW 4; SSFS 2; SUFW; WYA; YAW

Lehmann, Rosamond (Nina) 1901-1990 .... **CLC 5**
See also CA 77-80; 131; CANR 8, 73; DLB 15; MTCW 2; RGEL 2; RHW

Leiber, Fritz (Reuter, Jr.) 1910-1992 .... **CLC 25**
See also BPFB 2; CA 45-48; 139; CANR 2, 40, 86; DLB 8; FANT; HGG; MTCW 1, 2; SATA 45; SATA-Obit 73; SCFW 2; SFW 4; SUFW

Leibniz, Gottfried Wilhelm von 1646-1716 .... **LC 35**
See also DLB 168

Leimbach, Martha 1963-
See Leimbach, Marti
See also CA 130

Leimbach, Marti .... **CLC 65**
See also Leimbach, Martha

Leino, Eino .... **TCLC 24**
See also Loennbohm, Armas Eino Leopold

Leiris, Michel (Julien) 1901-1990 ..... **CLC 61**
See also CA 119; 128; 132; GFL 1789 to the Present

Leithauser, Brad 1953- .... **CLC 27**
See also CA 107; CANR 27, 81; CP 7; DLB 120

Lelchuk, Alan 1938- .... **CLC 5**
See also CA 45-48; CAAS 20; CANR 1, 70; CN 7

Lem, Stanislaw 1921- ...... **CLC 8, 15, 40, 149**
See also CA 105; CAAS 1; CANR 32; CWW 2; MTCW 1; SCFW 2; SFW 4

Lemann, Nancy 1956- .... **CLC 39**
See also CA 118; 136

Lemonnier, (Antoine Louis) Camille 1844-1913 .... **TCLC 22**
See also CA 121

Lenau, Nikolaus 1802-1850 .... **NCLC 16**

L'Engle, Madeleine (Camp Franklin) 1918- .... **CLC 12**
See also AAYA 28; AITN 2; BPFB 2; BYA 2, 4, 5, 7; CA 1-4R; CANR 3, 21, 39, 66, 107; CLR 1, 14, 57; CPW; CWRI 5; DA3; DAM POP; DLB 52; JRDA; MAICYA 1, 2; MTCW 1, 2; SAAS 15; SATA 1, 27, 75, 128; SFW 4; WYA; YAW

Lengyel, Jozsef 1896-1975 .... **CLC 7**
See also CA 85-88; 57-60; CANR 71; RGSF 2

Lenin 1870-1924
See Lenin, V. I.
See also CA 121; 168

Lenin, V. I. .... **TCLC 67**
See also Lenin

Lennon, John (Ono) 1940-1980 .. **CLC 12, 35**
See also CA 102; SATA 114

Lennox, Charlotte Ramsay 1729(?)-1804 .... **NCLC 23**
See also DLB 39; RGEL 2

Lentricchia, Frank, (Jr.) 1940- .... **CLC 34**
See also CA 25-28R; CANR 19, 106; DLB 246

Lenz, Gunter .... **CLC 65**

Lenz, Siegfried 1926- .... **CLC 27; SSC 33**
See also CA 89-92; CANR 80; CWW 2; DLB 75; RGSF 2; RGWL 2

Leon, David
See Jacob, (Cyprien-)Max

Leonard, Elmore (John, Jr.) 1925- . **CLC 28, 34, 71, 120**
See also AAYA 22; AITN 1; BEST 89:1, 90:4; BPFB 2; CA 81-84; CANR 12, 28, 53, 76, 96; CMW 4; CN 7; CPW; DA3; DAM POP; DLB 173, 226; INT CANR-28; MSW; MTCW 1, 2; RGAL 4; TCWW 2

Leonard, Hugh .... **CLC 19**
See also Byrne, John Keyes
See also CBD; CD 5; DFS 13; DLB 13

Leonov, Leonid (Maximovich) 1899-1994 .... **CLC 92**
See also CA 129; CANR 74, 76; DAM NOV; MTCW 1, 2

Leopardi, (Conte) Giacomo 1798-1837 .... **NCLC 22; PC 37**
See also EW 5; RGWL 2; WP

Le Reveler
See Artaud, Antonin (Marie Joseph)

Lerman, Eleanor 1952- .... **CLC 9**
See also CA 85-88; CANR 69

Lerman, Rhoda 1936- .... **CLC 56**
See also CA 49-52; CANR 70

Lermontov, Mikhail Iur'evich
See Lermontov, Mikhail Yuryevich
See also DLB 205

Lermontov, Mikhail Yuryevich 1814-1841 .... **NCLC 5, 47; PC 18**
See also Lermontov, Mikhail Iur'evich
See also EW 6; RGWL 2

Leroux, Gaston 1868-1927 .... **TCLC 25**
See also CA 108; 136; CANR 69; CMW 4; SATA 65

Lesage, Alain-Rene 1668-1747 .... **LC 2, 28**
See also EW 3; GFL Beginnings to 1789; RGWL 2

Leskov, N(ikolai) S(emenovich) 1831-1895
See Leskov, Nikolai (Semyonovich)

Leskov, Nikolai (Semyonovich) 1831-1895 .... **NCLC 25; SSC 34**
See also Leskov, Nikolai Semenovich

Leskov, Nikolai Semenovich
See Leskov, Nikolai (Semyonovich)
See also DLB 238

Lesser, Milton
See Marlowe, Stephen

Lessing, Doris (May) 1919- ... **CLC 1, 2, 3, 6, 10, 15, 22, 40, 94; SSC 6; WLCS**
See also AFW; BRWS 1; CA 9-12R; CAAS 14; CANR 33, 54, 76; CD 5; CDBLB 1960 to Present; CN 7; DA; DA3; DAB; DAC; DAM MST, NOV; DLB 15, 139; DLBY 1985; EXPS; FW; LAIT 4; MTCW 1, 2; RGEL 2; RGSF 2; SFW 4; SSFS 1, 12; WLIT 2, 4

Lessing, Gotthold Ephraim 1729-1781 . **LC 8**
See also CDWLB 2; DLB 97; EW 4; RGWL 2

Lester, Richard 1932- .... **CLC 20**

Levenson, Jay .... **CLC 70**

Lever, Charles (James) 1806-1872 .... **NCLC 23**
See also DLB 21; RGEL 2

Leverson, Ada 1865(?)-1936(?) .... **TCLC 18**
See also Elaine
See also CA 117; DLB 153; RGEL 2

Levertov, Denise 1923-1997 .. **CLC 1, 2, 3, 5, 8, 15, 28, 66; PC 11**
See also AMWS 3; CA 1-4R, 178; 163; CAAE 178; CAAS 19; CANR 3, 29, 50, 108; CDALBS; CP 7; CWP; DAM POET; DLB 5, 165; EXPP; FW; INT CANR-29; MTCW 1, 2; PAB; PFS 7; RGAL 4; WP

Levi, Jonathan .... **CLC 76**
See also CA 197

Levi, Peter (Chad Tigar) 1931-2000 .... **CLC 41**
See also CA 5-8R; 187; CANR 34, 80; CP 7; DLB 40

Levi, Primo 1919-1987 ...... **CLC 37, 50; SSC 12; TCLC 109**
See also CA 13-16R; 122; CANR 12, 33, 61, 70; DLB 177; MTCW 1, 2; RGWL 2

Levin, Ira 1929- .... **CLC 3, 6**
See also CA 21-24R; CANR 17, 44, 74; CMW 4; CN 7; CPW; DA3; DAM POP; HGG; MTCW 1, 2; SATA 66; SFW 4

Levin, Meyer 1905-1981 .... **CLC 7**
See also AITN 1; CA 9-12R; 104; CANR 15; DAM POP; DLB 9, 28; DLBY 1981; SATA 21; SATA-Obit 27

Levine, Norman 1924- .... **CLC 54**
See also CA 73-76; CAAS 23; CANR 14, 70; DLB 88

Levine, Philip 1928- .. **CLC 2, 4, 5, 9, 14, 33, 118; PC 22**
See also AMWS 5; CA 9-12R; CANR 9, 37, 52; CP 7; DAM POET; DLB 5; PFS 8

Levinson, Deirdre 1931- .... **CLC 49**
See also CA 73-76; CANR 70

Levi-Strauss, Claude 1908- .... **CLC 38**
See also CA 1-4R; CANR 6, 32, 57; DLB 242; GFL 1789 to the Present; MTCW 1, 2

Levitin, Sonia (Wolff) 1934- .... **CLC 17**
See also AAYA 13; CA 29-32R; CANR 14, 32, 79; CLR 53; JRDA; MAICYA 1, 2; SAAS 2; SATA 4, 68, 119; SATA-Essay 131; YAW

Levon, O. U.
See Kesey, Ken (Elton)

Levy, Amy 1861-1889 .... **NCLC 59**
See also DLB 156, 240

Lewes, George Henry 1817-1878 ... **NCLC 25**
See also DLB 55, 144

Lewis, Alun 1915-1944 .... **TCLC 3; SSC 40**
See also BRW 7; CA 104; 188; DLB 20, 162; PAB; RGEL 2

Lewis, C. Day
See Day Lewis, C(ecil)

Lewis, C(live) S(taples) 1898-1963 .... **CLC 1, 3, 6, 14, 27, 124; WLC**
See also AAYA 3, 39; BPFB 2; BRWS 3; CA 81-84; CANR 33, 71; CDBLB 1945-1960; CLR 3, 27; CWRI 5; DA; DA3; DAB; DAC; DAM MST, NOV, POP; DLB 15, 100, 160, 255; FANT; JRDA; MAICYA 1, 2; MTCW 1, 2; RGEL 2; SATA 13, 100; SCFW; SFW 4; SUFW; WCH; WYA; YAW

Lewis, Cecil Day
See Day Lewis, C(ecil)

Lewis, Janet 1899-1998 .... **CLC 41**
See also Winters, Janet Lewis
See also CA 9-12R; 172; CANR 29, 63; CAP 1; CN 7; DLBY 1987; RHW; TCWW 2

Lewis, Matthew Gregory 1775-1818 .... **NCLC 11, 62**
See also DLB 39, 158, 178; HGG; RGEL 2; SUFW

Lewis, (Harry) Sinclair 1885-1951 . **TCLC 4, 13, 23, 39; WLC**
See also AMW; BPFB 2; CA 104; 133; CDALB 1917-1929; DA; DA3; DAB;

Lopate, Phillip 1943- .... **CLC 29**
    See also CA 97-100; CANR 88; DLBY
    1980; INT 97-100

Lopez, Barry (Holstun) 1945- .... **CLC 70**
    See also AAYA 9; ANW; CA 65-68; CANR
    7, 23, 47, 68, 92; DLB 256; INT CANR-7,
    -23; MTCW 1; RGAL 4; SATA 67

Lopez Portillo (y Pacheco), Jose
    1920- .... **CLC 46**
    See also CA 129; HW 1

Lopez y Fuentes, Gregorio
    1897(?)-1966 .... **CLC 32**
    See also CA 131; HW 1

Lorca, Federico Garcia
    See Garcia Lorca, Federico
    See also DFS 4; EW 11; RGWL 2; WP

Lord, Bette Bao 1938- .... **CLC 23; AAL**
    See also BEST 90:3; BPFB 2; CA 107;
    CANR 41, 79; INT CA-107; SATA 58

Lord Auch
    See Bataille, Georges

Lord Brooke
    See Greville, Fulke

Lord Byron
    See Byron, George Gordon (Noel)

Lorde, Audre (Geraldine)
    1934-1992 .. **CLC 18, 71; BLC 2; PC 12**
    See also Domini, Rey
    See also AFAW 1, 2; BW 1, 3; CA 25-28R;
    142; CANR 16, 26, 46, 82; DA3; DAM
    MULT, POET; DLB 41; FW; MTCW 1,
    2; RGAL 4

Lord Houghton
    See Milnes, Richard Monckton

Lord Jeffrey
    See Jeffrey, Francis

Loreaux, Nichol .... **CLC 65**

Lorenzini, Carlo 1826-1890
    See Collodi, Carlo
    See also MAICYA 1, 2; SATA 29, 100

Lorenzo, Heberto Padilla
    See Padilla (Lorenzo), Heberto

Loris
    See Hofmannsthal, Hugo von

Loti, Pierre .... **TCLC 11**
    See also Viaud, (Louis Marie) Julien
    See also DLB 123; GFL 1789 to the Present

Lou, Henri
    See Andreas-Salome, Lou

Louie, David Wong 1954- .... **CLC 70**
    See also CA 139

Louis, Father M.
    See Merton, Thomas

Lovecraft, H(oward) P(hillips)
    1890-1937 .... **TCLC 4, 22; SSC 3, 52**
    See also AAYA 14; BPFB 2; CA 104; 133;
    CANR 106; DA3; DAM POP; HGG;
    MTCW 1, 2; RGAL 4; SCFW; SFW 4;
    SUFW

Lovelace, Earl 1935- .... **CLC 51**
    See also BW 2; CA 77-80; CANR 41, 72;
    CD 5; CDWLB 3; CN 7; DLB 125;
    MTCW 1

Lovelace, Richard 1618-1657 .... **LC 24**
    See also BRW 2; DLB 131; EXPP; PAB;
    RGEL 2

Lowell, Amy 1874-1925 ... **TCLC 1, 8; PC 13**
    See also AMW; CA 104; 151; DAM POET;
    DLB 54, 140; EXPP; MAWW; MTCW 2;
    RGAL 4

Lowell, James Russell 1819-1891 ... **NCLC 2,**
    90
    See also AMWS 1; CDALB 1640-1865;
    DLB 1, 11, 64, 79, 189, 235; RGAL 4

Lowell, Robert (Traill Spence, Jr.)
    1917-1977 .... **CLC 1, 2, 3, 4, 5, 8, 9, 11,**
    15, 37, 124; PC 3; WLC
    See also AMW; CA 9-12R; 73-76; CABS
    2; CANR 26, 60; CDALBS; DA; DA3;
    DAB; DAC; DAM MST, NOV; DLB 5,
    169; MTCW 1, 2; PAB; PFS 6, 7; RGAL
    4; WP

Lowenthal, Michael (Francis)
    1969- .... **CLC 119**
    See also CA 150

Lowndes, Marie Adelaide (Belloc)
    1868-1947 .... **TCLC 12**
    See also CA 107; CMW 4; DLB 70; RHW

Lowry, (Clarence) Malcolm
    1909-1957 .... **TCLC 6, 40; SSC 31**
    See also BPFB 2; BRWS 3; CA 105; 131;
    CANR 62, 105; CDBLB 1945-1960; DLB
    15; MTCW 1, 2; RGEL 2

Lowry, Mina Gertrude 1882-1966
    See Loy, Mina
    See also CA 113

Loxsmith, John
    See Brunner, John (Kilian Houston)

Loy, Mina .... **CLC 28; PC 16**
    See also Lowry, Mina Gertrude
    See also DAM POET; DLB 4, 54

Loyson-Bridet
    See Schwob, Marcel (Mayer Andre)

Lucan 39-65 .... **CMLC 33**
    See also AW 2; DLB 211; EFS 2; RGWL 2

Lucas, Craig 1951- .... **CLC 64**
    See also CA 137; CAD; CANR 71, 109;
    CD 5; GLL 2

Lucas, E(dward) V(errall)
    1868-1938 .... **TCLC 73**
    See also CA 176; DLB 98, 149, 153; SATA
    20

Lucas, George 1944- .... **CLC 16**
    See also AAYA 1, 23; CA 77-80; CANR
    30; SATA 56

Lucas, Hans
    See Godard, Jean-Luc

Lucas, Victoria
    See Plath, Sylvia

Lucian c. 125-c. 180 .... **CMLC 32**
    See also AW 2; DLB 176; RGWL 2

Lucretius c. 94B.C.-c. 49B.C. .... **CMLC 48**
    See also AW 2; CDWLB 1; DLB 211; EFS
    2; RGWL 2

Ludlam, Charles 1943-1987 .... **CLC 46, 50**
    See also CA 85-88; 122; CAD; CANR 72,
    86

Ludlum, Robert 1927-2001 .... **CLC 22, 43**
    See also AAYA 10; BEST 89:1, 90:3; BPFB
    2; CA 33-36R; 195; CANR 25, 41, 68,
    105; CMW 4; CPW; DA3; DAM NOV,
    POP; DLBY 1982; MSW; MTCW 1, 2

Ludwig, Ken .... **CLC 60**
    See also CA 195; CAD

Ludwig, Otto 1813-1865 .... **NCLC 4**
    See also DLB 129

Lugones, Leopoldo 1874-1938 ...... **TCLC 15;**
    HLCS 2
    See also CA 116; 131; CANR 104; HW 1;
    LAW

Lu Hsun .... **TCLC 3; SSC 20**
    See also Shu-Jen, Chou

Lukacs, George .... **CLC 24**
    See also Lukacs, Gyorgy (Szegeny von)

Lukacs, Gyorgy (Szegeny von) 1885-1971
    See Lukacs, George
    See also CA 101; 29-32R; CANR 62; CD-
    WLB 4; DLB 215, 242; EW 10; MTCW
    2

Luke, Peter (Ambrose Cyprian)
    1919-1995 .... **CLC 38**
    See also CA 81-84; 147; CANR 72; CBD;
    CD 5; DLB 13

Lunar, Dennis
    See Mungo, Raymond

Lurie, Alison 1926- .... **CLC 4, 5, 18, 39**
    See also BPFB 2; CA 1-4R; CANR 2, 17,
    50, 88; CN 7; DLB 2; MTCW 1; SATA
    46, 112

Lustig, Arnost 1926- .... **CLC 56**
    See also AAYA 3; CA 69-72; CANR 47,
    102; CWW 2; DLB 232; SATA 56

Luther, Martin 1483-1546 .... **LC 9, 37**
    See also CDWLB 2; DLB 179; EW 2;
    RGWL 2

Luxemburg, Rosa 1870(?)-1919 ..... **TCLC 63**
    See also CA 118

Luzi, Mario 1914- .... **CLC 13**
    See also CA 61-64; CANR 9, 70; CWW 2;
    DLB 128

L'vov, Arkady .... **CLC 59**

Lyly, John 1554(?)-1606 .... **LC 41; DC 7**
    See also BRW 1; DAM DRAM; DLB 62,
    167; RGEL 2

L'Ymagier
    See Gourmont, Remy(-Marie-Charles) de

Lynch, B. Suarez
    See Borges, Jorge Luis

Lynch, David (K.) 1946- .... **CLC 66**
    See also CA 124; 129

Lynch, James
    See Andreyev, Leonid (Nikolaevich)

Lyndsay, Sir David 1485-1555 .... **LC 20**
    See also RGEL 2

Lynn, Kenneth S(chuyler)
    1923-2001 .... **CLC 50**
    See also CA 1-4R; 196; CANR 3, 27, 65

Lynx
    See West, Rebecca

Lyons, Marcus
    See Blish, James (Benjamin)

Lyotard, Jean-Francois
    1924-1998 .... **TCLC 103**
    See also DLB 242

Lyre, Pinchbeck
    See Sassoon, Siegfried (Lorraine)

Lytle, Andrew (Nelson) 1902-1995 ... **CLC 22**
    See also CA 9-12R; 150; CANR 70; CN 7;
    CSW; DLB 6; DLBY 1995; RGAL 4;
    RHW

Lyttelton, George 1709-1773 .... **LC 10**
    See also RGEL 2

Lytton of Knebworth, Baron
    See Bulwer-Lytton, Edward (George Earle
    Lytton)

Maas, Peter 1929-2001 .... **CLC 29**
    See also CA 93-96; 201; INT CA-93-96;
    MTCW 2

Macaulay, Catherine 1731-1791 .... **LC 64**
    See also DLB 104

Macaulay, (Emilie) Rose
    1881(?)-1958 .... **TCLC 7, 44**
    See also CA 104; DLB 36; RGEL 2; RHW

Macaulay, Thomas Babington
    1800-1859 .... **NCLC 42**
    See also BRW 4; CDBLB 1832-1890; DLB
    32, 55; RGEL 2

MacBeth, George (Mann)
    1932-1992 .... **CLC 2, 5, 9**
    See also CA 25-28R; 136; CANR 61, 66;
    DLB 40; MTCW 1; PFS 8; SATA 4;
    SATA-Obit 70

MacCaig, Norman (Alexander)
    1910-1996 .... **CLC 36**
    See also BRWS 6; CA 9-12R; CANR 3, 34;
    CP 7; DAB; DAM POET; DLB 27; RGEL
    2

MacCarthy, Sir (Charles Otto) Desmond
    1877-1952 .... **TCLC 36**
    See also CA 167

Author Index

Mayo, Jim
  See L'Amour, Louis (Dearborn)
  See also TCWW 2
Maysles, Albert 1926- .... **CLC 16**
  See also CA 29-32R
Maysles, David 1932-1987 .... **CLC 16**
  See also CA 191
Mazer, Norma Fox 1931- .... **CLC 26**
  See also AAYA 5, 36; BYA 1, 8; CA 69-72;
    CANR 12, 32, 66; CLR 23; JRDA; MAI-
    CYA 1, 2; SAAS 1; SATA 24, 67, 105;
    WYA; YAW
Mazzini, Guiseppe 1805-1872 .... **NCLC 34**
McAlmon, Robert (Menzies)
    1895-1956 .... **TCLC 97**
  See also CA 107; 168; DLB 4, 45; DLBD
    15; GLL 1
McAuley, James Phillip 1917-1976 .. **CLC 45**
  See also CA 97-100; DLB 260; RGEL 2
McBain, Ed
  See Hunter, Evan
  See also MSW
McBrien, William (Augustine)
    1930- .... **CLC 44**
  See also CA 107; CANR 90
McCabe, Patrick 1955- .... **CLC 133**
  See also CA 130; CANR 50, 90; CN 7;
    DLB 194
McCaffrey, Anne (Inez) 1926- .... **CLC 17**
  See also AAYA 6, 34; AITN 2; BEST 89:2;
    BPFB 2; BYA 5; CA 25-28R; CANR 15,
    35, 55, 96; CLR 49; CPW; DA3; DAM
    NOV, POP; DLB 8; JRDA; MAICYA 1,
    2; MTCW 1, 2; SAAS 11; SATA 8, 70,
    116; SFW 4; WYA; YAW
McCall, Nathan 1955(?)- .... **CLC 86**
  See also BW 3; CA 146; CANR 88
McCann, Arthur
  See Campbell, John W(ood, Jr.)
McCann, Edson
  See Pohl, Frederik
McCarthy, Charles, Jr. 1933-
  See McCarthy, Cormac
  See also CANR 42, 69, 101; CN 7; CPW;
    CSW; DA3; DAM POP; MTCW 2
McCarthy, Cormac .... **CLC 4, 57, 59, 101**
  See also McCarthy, Charles, Jr.
  See also AAYA 41; AMWS 8; BPFB 2; CA
    13-16R; CANR 10; DLB 6, 143, 256;
    TCWW 2
McCarthy, Mary (Therese)
    1912-1989 .. **CLC 1, 3, 5, 14, 24, 39, 59;
      SSC 24**
  See also AMW; BPFB 2; CA 5-8R; 129;
    CANR 16, 50, 64; DA3; DLB 2; DLBY
    1981; FW; INT CANR-16; MAWW;
    MTCW 1, 2; RGAL 4
McCartney, (James) Paul 1942- . **CLC 12, 35**
  See also CA 146
McCauley, Stephen (D.) 1955- .... **CLC 50**
  See also CA 141
McClaren, Peter .... **CLC 70**
McClure, Michael (Thomas) 1932- ... **CLC 6,
    10**
  See also CA 21-24R; CAD; CANR 17, 46,
    77; CD 5; CP 7; DLB 16; WP
McCorkle, Jill (Collins) 1958- .... **CLC 51**
  See also CA 121; CSW; DLB 234; DLBY
    1987
McCourt, Frank 1930- .... **CLC 109**
  See also CA 157; CANR 97; NCFS 1
McCourt, James 1941- .... **CLC 5**
  See also CA 57-60; CANR 98
McCourt, Malachy 1932- .... **CLC 119**
  See also SATA 126
McCoy, Horace (Stanley)
    1897-1955 .... **TCLC 28**
  See also CA 108; 155; CMW 4; DLB 9

McCrae, John 1872-1918 .... **TCLC 12**
  See also CA 109; DLB 92; PFS 5
McCreigh, James
  See Pohl, Frederik
McCullers, (Lula) Carson (Smith)
    1917-1967 .... **CLC 1, 4, 10, 12, 48, 100;
      SSC 9, 24; WLC**
  See also AAYA 21; AMW; BPFB 2; CA
    5-8R; 25-28R; CABS 1, 3; CANR 18;
    CDALB 1941-1968; DA; DA3; DAB;
    DAC; DAM MST, NOV; DFS 5; DLB 2,
    7, 173, 228; EXPS; FW; GLL 1; LAIT 3,
    4; MAWW; MTCW 1, 2; NFS 6, 13;
    RGAL 4; RGSF 2; SATA 27; SSFS 5;
    YAW
McCulloch, John Tyler
  See Burroughs, Edgar Rice
McCullough, Colleen 1938(?)- .. **CLC 27, 107**
  See also AAYA 36; BPFB 2; CA 81-84;
    CANR 17, 46, 67, 98; CPW; DA3; DAM
    NOV, POP; MTCW 1, 2; RHW
McDermott, Alice 1953- .... **CLC 90**
  See also CA 109; CANR 40, 90
McElroy, Joseph 1930- .... **CLC 5, 47**
  See also CA 17-20R; CN 7
McEwan, Ian (Russell) 1948- ..... **CLC 13, 66**
  See also BEST 90:4; BRWS 4; CA 61-64;
    CANR 14, 41, 69, 87; CN 7; DAM NOV;
    DLB 14, 194; HGG; MTCW 1, 2; RGSF
    2
McFadden, David 1940- .... **CLC 48**
  See also CA 104; CP 7; DLB 60; INT 104
McFarland, Dennis 1950- .... **CLC 65**
  See also CA 165
McGahern, John 1934- ... **CLC 5, 9, 48, 156;
      SSC 17**
  See also CA 17-20R; CANR 29, 68; CN 7;
    DLB 14, 231; MTCW 1
McGinley, Patrick (Anthony) 1937- . **CLC 41**
  See also CA 120; 127; CANR 56; INT 127
McGinley, Phyllis 1905-1978 .... **CLC 14**
  See also CA 9-12R; 77-80; CANR 19;
    CWRI 5; DLB 11, 48; PFS 9, 13; SATA
    2, 44; SATA-Obit 24
McGinniss, Joe 1942- .... **CLC 32**
  See also AITN 2; BEST 89:2; CA 25-28R;
    CANR 26, 70; CPW; DLB 185; INT
    CANR-26
McGivern, Maureen Daly
  See Daly, Maureen
McGrath, Patrick 1950- .... **CLC 55**
  See also CA 136; CANR 65; CN 7; DLB
    231; HGG
McGrath, Thomas (Matthew)
    1916-1990 .... **CLC 28, 59**
  See also AMWS 10; CA 9-12R; 132; CANR
    6, 33, 95; DAM POET; MTCW 1; SATA
    41; SATA-Obit 66
McGuane, Thomas (Francis III)
    1939- .... **CLC 3, 7, 18, 45, 127**
  See also AITN 2; BPFB 2; CA 49-52;
    CANR 5, 24, 49, 94; CN 7; DLB 2, 212;
    DLBY 1980; INT CANR-24; MTCW 1;
    TCWW 2
McGuckian, Medbh 1950- ... **CLC 48; PC 27**
  See also BRWS 5; CA 143; CP 7; CWP;
    DAM POET; DLB 40
McHale, Tom 1942(?)-1982 .... **CLC 3, 5**
  See also AITN 1; CA 77-80; 106
McIlvanney, William 1936- .... **CLC 42**
  See also CA 25-28R; CANR 61; CMW 4;
    DLB 14, 207
McIlwraith, Maureen Mollie Hunter
  See Hunter, Mollie
  See also SATA 2
McInerney, Jay 1955- .... **CLC 34, 112**
  See also AAYA 18; BPFB 2; CA 116; 123;
    CANR 45, 68; CN 7; CPW; DA3; DAM
    POP; INT 123; MTCW 2

McIntyre, Vonda N(eel) 1948- .... **CLC 18**
  See also CA 81-84; CANR 17, 34, 69;
    MTCW 1; SFW 4; YAW
McKay, Claude .... **TCLC 7, 41; BLC 3; PC
    2; WLC**
  See also McKay, Festus Claudius
  See also AFAW 1, 2; AMWS 10; DAB;
    DLB 4, 45, 51, 117; EXPP; GLL 2; LAIT
    3; PAB; PFS 4; RGAL 4; WP
McKay, Festus Claudius 1889-1948
  See McKay, Claude
  See also BW 1, 3; CA 104; 124; CANR 73;
    DA; DAC; DAM MST, MULT, NOV,
    POET; MTCW 1, 2
McKuen, Rod 1933- .... **CLC 1, 3**
  See also AITN 1; CA 41-44R; CANR 40
McLoughlin, R. B.
  See Mencken, H(enry) L(ouis)
McLuhan, (Herbert) Marshall
    1911-1980 .... **CLC 37, 83**
  See also CA 9-12R; 102; CANR 12, 34, 61;
    DLB 88; INT CANR-12; MTCW 1, 2
McMillan, Terry (L.) 1951- .... **CLC 50, 61,
    112; BLCS**
  See also AAYA 21; BPFB 2; BW 2, 3; CA
    140; CANR 60, 104; CPW; DA3; DAM
    MULT, NOV, POP; MTCW 2; RGAL 4;
    YAW
McMurtry, Larry (Jeff) 1936- .. **CLC 2, 3, 7,
    11, 27, 44, 127**
  See also AAYA 15; AITN 2; AMWS 5;
    BEST 89:2; BPFB 2; CA 5-8R; CANR
    19, 43, 64, 103; CDALB 1968-1988; CN
    7; CPW; CSW; DA3; DAM NOV, POP;
    DLB 2, 143, 256; DLBY 1980, 1987;
    MTCW 1, 2; RGAL 4; TCWW 2
McNally, T. M. 1961- .... **CLC 82**
McNally, Terrence 1939- .... **CLC 4, 7, 41, 91**
  See also CA 45-48; CAD; CANR 2, 56; CD
    5; DA3; DAM DRAM; DLB 7, 249; GLL
    1; MTCW 2
McNamer, Deirdre 1950- .... **CLC 70**
McNeal, Tom .... **CLC 119**
McNeile, Herman Cyril 1888-1937
  See Sapper
  See also CA 184; CMW 4; DLB 77
McNickle, (William) D'Arcy
    1904-1977 .... **CLC 89**
  See also CA 9-12R; 85-88; CANR 5, 45;
    DAM MULT; DLB 175, 212; NNAL;
    RGAL 4; SATA-Obit 22
McPhee, John (Angus) 1931- .... **CLC 36**
  See also AMWS 3; ANW; BEST 90:1; CA
    65-68; CANR 20, 46, 64, 69; CPW; DLB
    185; MTCW 1, 2
McPherson, James Alan 1943- .. **CLC 19, 77;
    BLCS**
  See also BW 1, 3; CA 25-28R; CAAS 17;
    CANR 24, 74; CN 7; CSW; DLB 38, 244;
    MTCW 1, 2; RGAL 4; RGSF 2
McPherson, William (Alexander)
    1933- .... **CLC 34**
  See also CA 69-72; CANR 28; INT
    CANR-28
McTaggart, J. McT. Ellis
  See McTaggart, John McTaggart Ellis
McTaggart, John McTaggart Ellis
    1866-1925 .... **TCLC 105**
  See also CA 120; DLB 262
Mead, George Herbert 1873-1958 . **TCLC 89**
Mead, Margaret 1901-1978 .... **CLC 37**
  See also AITN 1; CA 1-4R; 81-84; CANR
    4; DA3; FW; MTCW 1, 2; SATA-Obit 20
Meaker, Marijane (Agnes) 1927-
  See Kerr, M. E.
  See also CA 107; CANR 37, 63; INT 107;
    JRDA; MAICYA 1, 2; MAICYAS 1;
    MTCW 1; SATA 20, 61, 99; SATA-Essay
    111; YAW

Medoff, Mark (Howard) 1940- .... **CLC 6, 23**
  See also AITN 1; CA 53-56; CAD; CANR
  5; CD 5; DAM DRAM; DFS 4; DLB 7;
  INT CANR-5
Medvedev, P. N.
  See Bakhtin, Mikhail Mikhailovich
Meged, Aharon
  See Megged, Aharon
Meged, Aron
  See Megged, Aharon
Megged, Aharon 1920- .... **CLC 9**
  See also CA 49-52; CAAS 13; CANR 1
Mehta, Ved (Parkash) 1934- .... **CLC 37**
  See also CA 1-4R; CANR 2, 23, 69; MTCW
  1
Melanter
  See Blackmore, R(ichard) D(oddridge)
Meleager c. 140B.C.-c. 70B.C. ...... **CMLC 53**
Melies, Georges 1861-1938 .... **TCLC 81**
Melikow, Loris
  See Hofmannsthal, Hugo von
Melmoth, Sebastian
  See Wilde, Oscar (Fingal O'Flahertie Wills)
Meltzer, Milton 1915- .... **CLC 26**
  See also AAYA 8; BYA 2, 6; CA 13-16R;
  CANR 38, 92, 107; CLR 13; DLB 61;
  JRDA; MAICYA 1, 2; SAAS 1; SATA 1,
  50, 80, 128; SATA-Essay 124; WYA;
  YAW
Melville, Herman 1819-1891 ..... **NCLC 3, 12,**
  29, 45, 49, 91, 93; SSC 1, 17, 46; WLC
  See also AAYA 25; AMW; AMWR 1;
  CDALB 1640-1865; DA; DA3; DAB;
  DAC; DAM MST, NOV; DLB 3, 74, 250,
  254; EXPN; EXPS; LAIT 1, 2; NFS 7, 9;
  RGAL 4; RGSF 2; SATA 59; SSFS 3
Members, Mark
  See Powell, Anthony (Dymoke)
Membreno, Alejandro .... **CLC 59**
Menander c. 342B.C.-c. 293B.C. .... **CMLC 9,**
  51; DC 3
  See also AW 1; CDWLB 1; DAM DRAM;
  DLB 176; RGWL 2
Menchu, Rigoberta 1959- .. **CLC 160; HLCS**
  2
  See also CA 175; DNFS 1; WLIT 1
Mencken, H(enry) L(ouis)
  1880-1956 .... **TCLC 13**
  See also AMW; CA 105; 125; CDALB
  1917-1929; DLB 11, 29, 63, 137, 222;
  MTCW 1, 2; RGAL 4
Mendelsohn, Jane 1965- .... **CLC 99**
  See also CA 154; CANR 94
Mercer, David 1928-1980 .... **CLC 5**
  See also CA 9-12R; 102; CANR 23; CBD;
  DAM DRAM; DLB 13; MTCW 1; RGEL
  2
Merchant, Paul
  See Ellison, Harlan (Jay)
Meredith, George 1828-1909 ... **TCLC 17, 43**
  See also CA 117; 153; CANR 80; CDBLB
  1832-1890; DAM POET; DLB 18, 35, 57,
  159; RGEL 2
Meredith, William (Morris) 1919- .... **CLC 4,**
  13, 22, 55; PC 28
  See also CA 9-12R; CAAS 14; CANR 6,
  40; CP 7; DAM POET; DLB 5
Merezhkovsky, Dmitry Sergeyevich
  1865-1941 .... **TCLC 29**
  See also CA 169
Merimee, Prosper 1803-1870 ... **NCLC 6, 65;**
  SSC 7
  See also DLB 119, 192; EW 6; EXPS; GFL
  1789 to the Present; RGSF 2; RGWL 2;
  SSFS 8; SUFW
Merkin, Daphne 1954- .... **CLC 44**
  See also CA 123
Merlin, Arthur
  See Blish, James (Benjamin)

Merrill, James (Ingram) 1926-1995 .. **CLC 2,**
  3, 6, 8, 13, 18, 34, 91; PC 28
  See also AMWS 3; CA 13-16R; 147; CANR
  10, 49, 63, 108; DA3; DAM POET; DLB
  5, 165; DLBY 1985; INT CANR-10;
  MTCW 1, 2; PAB; RGAL 4
Merriman, Alex
  See Silverberg, Robert
Merriman, Brian 1747-1805 .... **NCLC 70**
Merritt, E. B.
  See Waddington, Miriam
Merton, Thomas 1915-1968 ..... **CLC 1, 3, 11,**
  34, 83; PC 10
  See also AMWS 8; CA 5-8R; 25-28R;
  CANR 22, 53; DA3; DLB 48; DLBY
  1981; MTCW 1, 2
Merwin, W(illiam) S(tanley) 1927- ... **CLC 1,**
  2, 3, 5, 8, 13, 18, 45, 88
  See also AMWS 3; CA 13-16R; CANR 15,
  51; CP 7; DA3; DAM POET; DLB 5, 169;
  INT CANR-15; MTCW 1, 2; PAB; PFS
  5, 15; RGAL 4
Metcalf, John 1938- .... **CLC 37; SSC 43**
  See also CA 113; CN 7; DLB 60; RGSF 2
Metcalf, Suzanne
  See Baum, L(yman) Frank
Mew, Charlotte (Mary) 1870-1928 .. **TCLC 8**
  See also CA 105; 189; DLB 19, 135; RGEL
  2
Mewshaw, Michael 1943- .... **CLC 9**
  See also CA 53-56; CANR 7, 47; DLBY
  1980
Meyer, Conrad Ferdinand
  1825-1905 .... **NCLC 81**
  See also DLB 129; EW; RGWL 2
Meyer, Gustav 1868-1932
  See Meyrink, Gustav
  See also CA 117; 190
Meyer, June
  See Jordan, June
  See also GLL 2
Meyer, Lynn
  See Slavitt, David R(ytman)
Meyers, Jeffrey 1939- .... **CLC 39**
  See also CA 73-76; CAAE 186; CANR 54,
  102; DLB 111
Meynell, Alice (Christina Gertrude
  Thompson) 1847-1922 .... **TCLC 6**
  See also CA 104; 177; DLB 19, 98; RGEL
  2
Meyrink, Gustav .... **TCLC 21**
  See also Meyer, Gustav
  See also DLB 81
Michaels, Leonard 1933- .... **CLC 6, 25; SSC**
  16
  See also CA 61-64; CANR 21, 62; CN 7;
  DLB 130; MTCW 1
Michaux, Henri 1899-1984 .... **CLC 8, 19**
  See also CA 85-88; 114; DLB 258; GFL
  1789 to the Present; RGWL 2
Micheaux, Oscar (Devereaux)
  1884-1951 .... **TCLC 76**
  See also BW 3; CA 174; DLB 50; TCWW
  2
Michelangelo 1475-1564 .... **LC 12**
  See also AAYA 43
Michelet, Jules 1798-1874 .... **NCLC 31**
  See also EW 5; GFL 1789 to the Present
Michels, Robert 1876-1936 .... **TCLC 88**
Michener, James A(lbert)
  1907(?)-1997 .. **CLC 1, 5, 11, 29, 60, 109**
  See also AAYA 27; AITN 1; BEST 90:1;
  BPFB 2; CA 5-8R; 161; CANR 21, 45,
  68; CN 7; CPW; DA3; DAM NOV, POP;
  DLB 6; MTCW 1, 2; RHW
Mickiewicz, Adam 1798-1855 . **NCLC 3, 101;**
  PC 38
  See also EW 5; RGWL 2

Middleton, Christopher 1926- .... **CLC 13**
  See also CA 13-16R; CANR 29, 54; CP 7;
  DLB 40
Middleton, Richard (Barham)
  1882-1911 .... **TCLC 56**
  See also CA 187; DLB 156; HGG
Middleton, Stanley 1919- .... **CLC 7, 38**
  See also CA 25-28R; CAAS 23; CANR 21,
  46, 81; CN 7; DLB 14
Middleton, Thomas 1580-1627 .... **LC 33; DC**
  5
  See also BRW 2; DAM DRAM, MST; DLB
  58; RGEL 2
Migueis, Jose Rodrigues 1901- .... **CLC 10**
Mikszath, Kalman 1847-1910 .... **TCLC 31**
  See also CA 170
Miles, Jack .... **CLC 100**
  See also CA 200
Miles, John Russiano
  See Miles, Jack
Miles, Josephine (Louise)
  1911-1985 .... **CLC 1, 2, 14, 34, 39**
  See also CA 1-4R; 116; CANR 2, 55; DAM
  POET; DLB 48
Militant
  See Sandburg, Carl (August)
Mill, Harriet (Hardy) Taylor
  1807-1858 .... **NCLC 102**
  See also FW
Mill, John Stuart 1806-1873 .... **NCLC 11, 58**
  See also CDBLB 1832-1890; DLB 55, 190,
  262; FW 1; RGEL 2
Millar, Kenneth 1915-1983 .... **CLC 14**
  See also Macdonald, Ross
  See also CA 9-12R; 110; CANR 16, 63,
  107; CMW 4; CPW; DA3; DAM POP;
  DLB 2, 226; DLBD 6; DLBY 1983;
  MTCW 1, 2
Millay, E. Vincent
  See Millay, Edna St. Vincent
Millay, Edna St. Vincent
  1892-1950 ... **TCLC 4, 49; PC 6; WLCS**
  See Boyd, Nancy
  See also AMW; CA 104; 130; CDALB
  1917-1929; DA; DA3; DAB; DAC; DAM
  MST, POET; DLB 45, 249; EXPP;
  MAWW; MTCW 1, 2; PAB; PFS 3;
  RGAL 4; WP
Miller, Arthur 1915- ...... **CLC 1, 2, 6, 10, 15,**
  26, 47, 78; DC 1; WLC
  See also AAYA 15; AITN 1; AMW; CA
  1-4R; CABS 3; CAD; CANR 2, 30, 54,
  76; CD 5; CDALB 1941-1968; DA; DA3;
  DAB; DAC; DAM DRAM, MST; DFS 1,
  3; DLB 7; LAIT 1, 4; MTCW 1, 2; RGAL
  4; TUS; WYAS 1
Miller, Henry (Valentine)
  1891-1980 .... **CLC 1, 2, 4, 9, 14, 43, 84;**
  WLC
  See also AMW; BPFB 2; CA 9-12R; 97-
  100; CANR 33, 64; CDALB 1929-1941;
  DA; DA3; DAB; DAC; DAM MST, NOV;
  DLB 4, 9; DLBY 1980; MTCW 1, 2;
  RGAL 4
Miller, Jason 1939(?)-2001 .... **CLC 2**
  See also AITN 1; CA 73-76; 197; CAD;
  DFS 12; DLB 7
Miller, Sue 1943- .... **CLC 44**
  See also BEST 90:3; CA 139; CANR 59,
  91; DA3; DAM POP; DLB 143
Miller, Walter M(ichael, Jr.)
  1923-1996 .... **CLC 4, 30**
  See also BPFB 2; CA 85-88; CANR 108;
  DLB 8; SCFW; SFW 4
Millett, Kate 1934- .... **CLC 67**
  See also AITN 1; CA 73-76; CANR 32, 53,
  76; DA3; DLB 246; FW; GLL 1; MTCW
  1, 2

Millhauser, Steven (Lewis) 1943- .... **CLC 21, 54, 109**
See also CA 110; 111; CANR 63; CN 7; DA3; DLB 2; FANT; INT CA-111; MTCW 2

Millin, Sarah Gertrude 1889-1968 ... **CLC 49**
See also CA 102; 93-96; DLB 225

Milne, A(lan) A(lexander)
1882-1956 .... **TCLC 6, 88**
See also BRWS 5; CA 104; 133; CLR 1, 26; CMW 4; CWRI 5; DA3; DAB; DAC; DAM MST; DLB 10, 77, 100, 160; FANT; MAICYA 1, 2; MTCW 1, 2; RGEL 2; SATA 100; WCH; YABC 1

Milner, Ron(ald) 1938- .... **CLC 56; BLC 3**
See also AITN 1; BW 1; CA 73-76; CAD; CANR 24, 81; CD 5; DAM MULT; DLB 38; MTCW 1

Milnes, Richard Monckton
1809-1885 .... **NCLC 61**
See also DLB 32, 184

Milosz, Czeslaw 1911- ...... **CLC 5, 11, 22, 31, 56, 82; PC 8; WLCS**
See also CA 81-84; CANR 23, 51, 91; CDWLB 4; CWW 2; DA3; DAM MST, POET; DLB 215; EW 13; MTCW 1, 2; RGWL 2

Milton, John 1608-1674 ..... **LC 9, 43; PC 19, 29; WLC**
See also BRW 2; BRWR 2; CDBLB 1660-1789; DA; DA3; DAB; DAC; DAM MST, POET; DLB 131, 151; EFS 1; EXPP; LAIT 1; PAB; PFS 3; RGEL 2; TEA; WLIT 3; WP

Min, Anchee 1957- .... **CLC 86**
See also CA 146; CANR 94

Minehaha, Cornelius
See Wedekind, (Benjamin) Frank(lin)

Miner, Valerie 1947- .... **CLC 40**
See also CA 97-100; CANR 59; FW; GLL 2

Minimo, Duca
See D'Annunzio, Gabriele

Minot, Susan 1956- .... **CLC 44, 159**
See also AMWS 6; CA 134; CN 7

Minus, Ed 1938- .... **CLC 39**
See also CA 185

Miranda, Javier
See Bioy Casares, Adolfo
See also CWW 2

Mirbeau, Octave 1848-1917 .... **TCLC 55**
See also DLB 123, 192; GFL 1789 to the Present

Miro (Ferrer), Gabriel (Francisco Victor)
1879-1930 .... **TCLC 5**
See also CA 104; 185

Misharin, Alexandr .... **CLC 59**

Mishima, Yukio ... **CLC 2, 4, 6, 9, 27; DC 1; SSC 4**
See also Hiraoka, Kimitake
See also BPFB 2; DLB 182; GLL 1; MJW; MTCW 2; RGSF 2; RGWL 2; SSFS 5, 12

Mistral, Frederic 1830-1914 .... **TCLC 51**
See also CA 122; GFL 1789 to the Present

Mistral, Gabriela
See Godoy Alcayaga, Lucila
See also DNFS 1; LAW; RGWL 2; WP

Mistry, Rohinton 1952- .... **CLC 71**
See also CA 141; CANR 86; CCA 1; CN 7; DAC; SSFS 6

Mitchell, Clyde
See Ellison, Harlan (Jay); Silverberg, Robert

Mitchell, James Leslie 1901-1935
See Gibbon, Lewis Grassic
See also CA 104; 188; DLB 15

Mitchell, Joni 1943- .... **CLC 12**
See also CA 112; CCA 1

Mitchell, Joseph (Quincy)
1908-1996 .... **CLC 98**
See also CA 77-80; 152; CANR 69; CN 7; CSW; DLB 185; DLBY 1996

Mitchell, Margaret (Munnerlyn)
1900-1949 .... **TCLC 11**
See also AAYA 23; BPFB 2; BYA 1; CA 109; 125; CANR 55, 94; CDALBS; DA3; DAM NOV, POP; DLB 9; LAIT 2; MTCW 1, 2; NFS 9; RGAL 4; RHW; WYAS 1; YAW

Mitchell, Peggy
See Mitchell, Margaret (Munnerlyn)

Mitchell, S(ilas) Weir 1829-1914 .... **TCLC 36**
See also CA 165; DLB 202; RGAL 4

Mitchell, W(illiam) O(rmond)
1914-1998 .... **CLC 25**
See also CA 77-80; 165; CANR 15, 43; CN 7; DAC; DAM MST; DLB 88

Mitchell, William 1879-1936 .... **TCLC 81**

Mitford, Mary Russell 1787-1855 ... **NCLC 4**
See also DLB 110, 116; RGEL 2

Mitford, Nancy 1904-1973 .... **CLC 44**
See also CA 9-12R; DLB 191; RGEL 2

Miyamoto, (Chujo) Yuriko
1899-1951 .... **TCLC 37**
See also Miyamoto Yuriko
See also CA 170, 174

Miyamoto Yuriko
See Miyamoto, (Chujo) Yuriko
See also DLB 180

Miyazawa, Kenji 1896-1933 .... **TCLC 76**
See also CA 157

Mizoguchi, Kenji 1898-1956 .... **TCLC 72**
See also CA 167

Mo, Timothy (Peter) 1950(?)- ... **CLC 46, 134**
See also CA 117; CN 7; DLB 194; MTCW 1; WLIT 4

Modarressi, Taghi (M.) 1931-1997 ... **CLC 44**
See also CA 121; 134; INT 134

Modiano, Patrick (Jean) 1945- .... **CLC 18**
See also CA 85-88; CANR 17, 40; CWW 2; DLB 83

Mofolo, Thomas (Mokopu)
1875(?)-1948 .... **TCLC 22; BLC 3**
See also AFW; CA 121; 153; CANR 83; DAM MULT; DLB 225; MTCW 2; WLIT 2

Mohr, Nicholasa 1938- .... **CLC 12; HLC 2**
See also AAYA 8; CA 49-52; CANR 1, 32, 64; CLR 22; DAM MULT; DLB 145; HW 1, 2; JRDA; LAIT 5; MAICYA 2; MAICYAS 1; RGAL 4; SAAS 8; SATA 8, 97; SATA-Essay 113; WYA; YAW

Mojtabai, A(nn) G(race) 1938- ..... **CLC 5, 9, 15, 29**
See also CA 85-88; CANR 88

Moliere 1622-1673 ..... **LC 10, 28, 64; DC 13; WLC**
See also DA; DA3; DAB; DAC; DAM DRAM, MST; DFS 13; EW 3; GFL Beginnings to 1789; RGWL 2

Molin, Charles
See Mayne, William (James Carter)

Molnar, Ferenc 1878-1952 .... **TCLC 20**
See also CA 109; 153; CANR 83; CDWLB 4; DAM DRAM; DLB 215; RGWL 2

Momaday, N(avarre) Scott 1934- ...... **CLC 2, 19, 85, 95, 160; PC 25; WLCS**
See also AAYA 11; AMWS 4; ANW; BPFB 2; CA 25-28R; CANR 14, 34, 68; CDALBS; CN 7; CPW; DA; DA3; DAB; DAC; DAM MST, MULT, NOV, POP; DLB 143, 175, 256; EXPP; INT CANR-14; LAIT 4; MTCW 1, 2; NFS 10; NNAL; PFS 2, 11; RGAL 4; SATA 48; SATA-Brief 30; WP; YAW

Monette, Paul 1945-1995 .... **CLC 82**
See also AMWS 10; CA 139; 147; CN 7; GLL 1

Monroe, Harriet 1860-1936 .... **TCLC 12**
See also CA 109; DLB 54, 91

Monroe, Lyle
See Heinlein, Robert A(nson)

Montagu, Elizabeth 1720-1800 .... **NCLC 7**
See also FW

Montagu, Mary (Pierrepont) Wortley
1689-1762 .... **LC 9, 57; PC 16**
See also DLB 95, 101; RGEL 2

Montagu, W. H.
See Coleridge, Samuel Taylor

Montague, John (Patrick) 1929- ..... **CLC 13, 46**
See also CA 9-12R; CANR 9, 69; CP 7; DLB 40; MTCW 1; PFS 12; RGEL 2

Montaigne, Michel (Eyquem) de
1533-1592 .... **LC 8; WLC**
See also DA; DAB; DAC; DAM MST; EW 2; GFL Beginnings to 1789; RGWL 2

Montale, Eugenio 1896-1981 ... **CLC 7, 9, 18; PC 13**
See also CA 17-20R; 104; CANR 30; DLB 114; EW 11; MTCW 1; RGWL 2

Montesquieu, Charles-Louis de Secondat
1689-1755 .... **LC 7, 69**
See also EW 3; GFL Beginnings to 1789

Montessori, Maria 1870-1952 ...... **TCLC 103**
See also CA 115; 147

Montgomery, (Robert) Bruce 1921(?)-1978
See Crispin, Edmund
See also CA 179; 104; CMW 4

Montgomery, L(ucy) M(aud)
1874-1942 .... **TCLC 51**
See also AAYA 12; BYA 1; CA 108; 137; CLR 8; DA3; DAC; DAM MST; DLB 92; DLBD 14; JRDA; MAICYA 1, 2; MTCW 2; RGEL 2; SATA 100; WCH; WYA; YABC 1

Montgomery, Marion H., Jr. 1925- .... **CLC 7**
See also AITN 1; CA 1-4R; CANR 3, 48; CSW; DLB 6

Montgomery, Max
See Davenport, Guy (Mattison, Jr.)

Montherlant, Henry (Milon) de
1896-1972 .... **CLC 8, 19**
See also CA 85-88; 37-40R; DAM DRAM; DLB 72; EW 11; GFL 1789 to the Present; MTCW 1

Monty Python
See Chapman, Graham; Cleese, John (Marwood); Gilliam, Terry (Vance); Idle, Eric; Jones, Terence Graham Parry; Palin, Michael (Edward)
See also AAYA 7

Moodie, Susanna (Strickland)
1803-1885 .... **NCLC 14, 113**
See also DLB 99

Moody, Hiram F. III 1961-
See Moody, Rick
See also CA 138; CANR 64

Moody, Minerva
See Alcott, Louisa May

Moody, Rick .... **CLC 147**
See also Moody, Hiram F. III

Moody, William Vaughan
1869-1910 .... **TCLC 105**
See also CA 110; 178; DLB 7, 54; RGAL 4

Mooney, Edward 1951-
See Mooney, Ted
See also CA 130

Mooney, Ted .... **CLC 25**
See also Mooney, Edward

Moorcock, Michael (John) 1939- ...... **CLC 5, 27, 58**
See also Bradbury, Edward P.
See also AAYA 26; CA 45-48; CAAS 5; CANR 2, 17, 38, 64; CN 7; DLB 14, 231, 261; FANT; MTCW 1, 2; SATA 93; SFW 4; SUFW

Moore, Brian 1921-1999 ... **CLC 1, 3, 5, 7, 8, 19, 32, 90**
See also Bryan, Michael
See also CA 1-4R; 174; CANR 1, 25, 42, 63; CCA 1; CN 7; DAB; DAC; DAM MST; DLB 251; FANT; MTCW 1, 2; RGEL 2

Moore, Edward
See Muir, Edwin
See also RGEL 2

Moore, G. E. 1873-1958 .... **TCLC 89**
See also DLB 262

Moore, George Augustus
1852-1933 .... **TCLC 7; SSC 19**
See also BRW 6; CA 104; 177; DLB 10, 18, 57, 135; RGEL 2; RGSF 2

Moore, Lorrie .... **CLC 39, 45, 68**
See also Moore, Marie Lorena
See also AMWS 10; DLB 234

Moore, Marianne (Craig)
1887-1972 .... **CLC 1, 2, 4, 8, 10, 13, 19, 47; PC 4; WLCS**
See also AMW; CA 1-4R; 33-36R; CANR 3, 61; CDALB 1929-1941; DA; DA3; DAB; DAC; DAM MST; POET; DLB 45; DLBD 7; EXPP; MAWW; MTCW 1, 2; PAB; PFS 14; RGAL 4; SATA 20; WP

Moore, Marie Lorena 1957-
See Moore, Lorrie
See also CA 116; CANR 39, 83; CN 7; DLB 234

Moore, Thomas 1779-1852 .... **NCLC 6, 110**
See also DLB 96, 144; RGEL 2

Moorhouse, Frank 1938- .... **SSC 40**
See also CA 118; CANR 92; CN 7; RGSF 2

Mora, Pat(ricia) 1942-
See also CA 129; CANR 57, 81; CLR 58; DAM MULT; DLB 209; HLC 2; HW 1, 2; MAICYA 2; SATA 92

Moraga, Cherríe 1952- .... **CLC 126**
See also CA 131; CANR 66; DAM MULT; DLB 82, 249; FW; GLL 1; HW 1, 2

Morand, Paul 1888-1976 .... **CLC 41; SSC 22**
See also CA 184; 69-72; DLB 65

Morante, Elsa 1918-1985 .... **CLC 8, 47**
See also CA 85-88; 117; CANR 35; DLB 177; MTCW 1, 2; RGWL 2

Moravia, Alberto .... **CLC 2, 7, 11, 27, 46; SSC 26**
See also Pincherle, Alberto
See also DLB 177; EW 12; MTCW 2; RGSF 2; RGWL 2

More, Hannah 1745-1833 .... **NCLC 27**
See also DLB 107, 109, 116, 158; RGEL 2

More, Henry 1614-1687 .... **LC 9**
See also DLB 126, 252

More, Sir Thomas 1478(?)-1535 .... **LC 10, 32**
See also BRWS 7; DLB 136; RGEL 2; TEA

Moreas, Jean .... **TCLC 18**
See also Papadiamantopoulos, Johannes
See also GFL 1789 to the Present

Moreton, Andrew Esq.
See Defoe, Daniel

Morgan, Berry 1919- .... **CLC 6**
See also CA 49-52; DLB 6

Morgan, Claire
See Highsmith, (Mary) Patricia
See also GLL 1

Morgan, Edwin (George) 1920- .... **CLC 31**
See also CA 5-8R; CANR 3, 43, 90; CP 7; DLB 27

Morgan, (George) Frederick 1922- .. **CLC 23**
See also CA 17-20R; CANR 21; CP 7

Morgan, Harriet
See Mencken, H(enry) L(ouis)

Morgan, Jane
See Cooper, James Fenimore

Morgan, Janet 1945- .... **CLC 39**
See also CA 65-68

Morgan, Lady 1776(?)-1859 .... **NCLC 29**
See also DLB 116, 158; RGEL 2

Morgan, Robin (Evonne) 1941- .... **CLC 2**
See also CA 69-72; CANR 29, 68; FW; GLL 2; MTCW 1; SATA 80

Morgan, Scott
See Kuttner, Henry

Morgan, Seth 1949(?)-1990 .... **CLC 65**
See also CA 185; 132

Morgenstern, Christian (Otto Josef Wolfgang) 1871-1914 .... **TCLC 8**
See also CA 105; 191

Morgenstern, S.
See Goldman, William (W.)

Mori, Rintaro
See Mori Ogai
See also CA 110

Moricz, Zsigmond 1879-1942 .... **TCLC 33**
See also CA 165; DLB 215

Morike, Eduard (Friedrich)
1804-1875 .... **NCLC 10**
See also DLB 133; RGWL 2

Mori Ogai
See Mori Ogai
See also DLB 180

Mori Ogai 1862-1922 .... **TCLC 14**
See also Mori Ogai; Ogai
See also CA 164; TWA

Moritz, Karl Philipp 1756-1793 .... **LC 2**
See also DLB 94

Morland, Peter Henry
See Faust, Frederick (Schiller)

Morley, Christopher (Darlington)
1890-1957 .... **TCLC 87**
See also CA 112; DLB 9; RGAL 4

Morren, Theophil
See Hofmannsthal, Hugo von

Morris, Bill 1952- .... **CLC 76**

Morris, Julian
See West, Morris L(anglo)

Morris, Steveland Judkins 1950(?)-
See Wonder, Stevie
See also CA 111

Morris, William 1834-1896 .... **NCLC 4**
See also BRW 5; CDBLB 1832-1890; DLB 18, 35, 57, 156, 178, 184; FANT; RGEL 2; SFW 4; SUFW

Morris, Wright 1910-1998 .. **CLC 1, 3, 7, 18, 37; TCLC 107**
See also AMW; CA 9-12R; 167; CANR 21, 81; CN 7; DLB 2, 206, 218; DLBY 1981; MTCW 1, 2; RGAL 4; TCWW 2

Morrison, Arthur 1863-1945 .... **TCLC 72; SSC 40**
See also CA 120; 157; CMW 4; DLB 70, 135, 197; RGEL 2

Morrison, Chloe Anthony Wofford
See Morrison, Toni

Morrison, James Douglas 1943-1971
See Morrison, Jim
See also CA 73-76; CANR 40

Morrison, Jim .... **CLC 17**
See also Morrison, James Douglas

Morrison, Toni 1931- . **CLC 4, 10, 22, 55, 81, 87; BLC 3**
See also AAYA 1, 22; AFAW 1, 2; AMWS 3; BPFB 2; BW 2, 3; CA 29-32R; CANR 27, 42, 67; CDALB 1968-1988; CN 7; CPW; DA; DA3; DAB; DAC; DAM MST, MULT, NOV, POP; DLB 6, 33, 143;

DLBY 1981; EXPN; FW; LAIT 2, 4; MAWW; MTCW 1, 2; NFS 1, 6, 8, 14; RGAL 4; RHW; SATA 57; SSFS 5; YAW

Morrison, Van 1945- .... **CLC 21**
See also CA 116; 168

Morrissy, Mary 1958- .... **CLC 99**

Mortimer, John (Clifford) 1923- ..... **CLC 28, 43**
See also CA 13-16R; CANR 21, 69, 109; CD 5; CDBLB 1960 to Present; CMW 4; CN 7; CPW; DA3; DAM DRAM, POP; DLB 13, 245; INT CANR-21; MSW; MTCW 1, 2; RGEL 2

Mortimer, Penelope (Ruth)
1918-1999 .... **CLC 5**
See also CA 57-60; 187; CANR 45, 88; CN 7

Mortimer, Sir John
See Mortimer, John (Clifford)

Morton, Anthony
See Creasey, John

Morton, Thomas 1579(?)-1647(?) .... **LC 72**
See also DLB 24; RGEL 2

Mosca, Gaetano 1858-1941 .... **TCLC 75**

Mosher, Howard Frank 1943- .... **CLC 62**
See also CA 139; CANR 65

Mosley, Nicholas 1923- .... **CLC 43, 70**
See also CA 69-72; CANR 41, 60, 108; CN 7; DLB 14, 207

Mosley, Walter 1952- .... **CLC 97; BLCS**
See also AAYA 17; BPFB 2; BW 2; CA 142; CANR 57, 92; CMW 4; CPW; DA3; DAM MULT, POP; MSW; MTCW 2

Moss, Howard 1922-1987 . **CLC 7, 14, 45, 50**
See also CA 1-4R; 123; CANR 1, 44; DAM POET; DLB 5

Mossgiel, Rab
See Burns, Robert

Motion, Andrew (Peter) 1952- .... **CLC 47**
See also BRWS 7; CA 146; CANR 90; CP 7; DLB 40

Motley, Willard (Francis)
1912-1965 .... **CLC 18**
See also BW 1; CA 117; 106; CANR 88; DLB 76, 143

Motoori, Norinaga 1730-1801 .... **NCLC 45**

Mott, Michael (Charles Alston)
1930- .... **CLC 15, 34**
See also CA 5-8R; CAAS 7; CANR 7, 29

Mountain Wolf Woman 1884-1960 .. **CLC 92**
See also CA 144; CANR 90; NNAL

Moure, Erin 1955- .... **CLC 88**
See also CA 113; CP 7; CWP; DLB 60

Mowat, Farley (McGill) 1921- .... **CLC 26**
See also AAYA 1; BYA 2; CA 1-4R; CANR 4, 24, 42, 68, 108; CLR 20; CPW; DAC; DAM MST; DLB 68; INT CANR-24; JRDA; MAICYA 1, 2; MTCW 1, 2; SATA 3, 55; YAW

Mowatt, Anna Cora 1819-1870 ..... **NCLC 74**
See also RGAL 4

Moyers, Bill 1934- .... **CLC 74**
See also AITN 2; CA 61-64; CANR 31, 52

Mphahlele, Es'kia
See Mphahlele, Ezekiel
See also AFW; CDWLB 3; DLB 125, 225; RGSF 2; SSFS 11

Mphahlele, Ezekiel 1919- .... **CLC 25, 133; BLC 3**
See also Mphahlele, Es'kia
See also BW 2, 3; CA 81-84; CANR 26, 76; CN 7; DA3; DAM MULT; MTCW 2; SATA 119

Mqhayi, S(amuel) E(dward) K(rune Loliwe)
1875-1945 .... **TCLC 25; BLC 3**
See also CA 153; CANR 87; DAM MULT

Mrozek, Slawomir 1930- .... **CLC 3, 13**
See also CA 13-16R; CAAS 10; CANR 29; CDWLB 4; CWW 2; DLB 232; MTCW 1

Neruda, Pablo 1904-1973 .. **CLC 1, 2, 5, 7, 9, 28, 62; HLC 2; PC 4; WLC**
See also CA 19-20; 45-48; CAP 2; DA; DA3; DAB; DAC; DAM MST, MULT, POET; DNFS 2; HW 1; LAW; MTCW 1, 2; PFS 11; RGWL 2; WLIT 1; WP

Nerval, Gerard de 1808-1855 ... **NCLC 1, 67; PC 13; SSC 18**
See also DLB 217; EW 6; GFL 1789 to the Present; RGSF 2; RGWL 2

Nervo, (Jose) Amado (Ruiz de) 1870-1919 .... **TCLC 11; HLCS 2**
See also CA 109; 131; HW 1; LAW

Nesbit, Malcolm
See Chester, Alfred

Nessi, Pio Baroja y
See Baroja (y Nessi), Pio

Nestroy, Johann 1801-1862 .... **NCLC 42**
See also DLB 133; RGWL 2

Netterville, Luke
See O'Grady, Standish (James)

Neufeld, John (Arthur) 1938- .... **CLC 17**
See also AAYA 11; CA 25-28R; CANR 11, 37, 56; CLR 52; MAICYA 1, 2; SAAS 3; SATA 6, 81; SATA-Essay 131; YAW

Neumann, Alfred 1895-1952 .... **TCLC 100**
See also CA 183; DLB 56

Neumann, Ferenc
See Molnar, Ferenc

Neville, Emily Cheney 1919- .... **CLC 12**
See also BYA 2; CA 5-8R; CANR 3, 37, 85; JRDA; MAICYA 1, 2; SAAS 2; SATA 1; YAW

Newbound, Bernard Slade 1930-
See Slade, Bernard
See also CA 81-84; CANR 49; CD 5; DAM DRAM

Newby, P(ercy) H(oward) 1918-1997 .... **CLC 2, 13**
See also CA 5-8R; 161; CANR 32, 67; CN 7; DAM NOV; DLB 15; MTCW 1; RGEL 2

Newcastle
See Cavendish, Margaret Lucas

Newlove, Donald 1928- .... **CLC 6**
See also CA 29-32R; CANR 25

Newlove, John (Herbert) 1938- .... **CLC 14**
See also CA 21-24R; CANR 9, 25; CP 7

Newman, Charles 1938- .... **CLC 2, 8**
See also CA 21-24R; CANR 84; CN 7

Newman, Edwin (Harold) 1919- .... **CLC 14**
See also AITN 1; CA 69-72; CANR 5

Newman, John Henry 1801-1890 . **NCLC 38, 99**
See also BRWS 7; DLB 18, 32, 55; RGEL 2

Newton, (Sir) Isaac 1642-1727 ...... **LC 35, 53**
See also DLB 252

Newton, Suzanne 1936- .... **CLC 35**
See also BYA 7; CA 41-44R; CANR 14; JRDA; SATA 5, 77

New York Dept. of Ed. .... **CLC 70**

Nexo, Martin Andersen 1869-1954 .... **TCLC 43**
See also DLB 214

Nezval, Vitezslav 1900-1958 .... **TCLC 44**
See also CA 123; CDWLB 4; DLB 215

Ng, Fae Myenne 1957(?)- .... **CLC 81**
See also CA 146

Ngema, Mbongeni 1955- .... **CLC 57**
See also BW 2; CA 143; CANR 84; CD 5

Ngugi, James T(hiong'o) .... **CLC 3, 7, 13**
See also Ngugi wa Thiong'o

Ngugi wa Thiong'o
See Ngugi wa Thiong'o
See also DLB 125

Ngugi wa Thiong'o 1938- .... **CLC 36; BLC 3**
See also Ngugi, James T(hiong'o); Ngugi wa Thiong'o
See also AFW; BW 2; CA 81-84; CANR 27, 58; CDWLB 3; DAM MULT, NOV; DNFS 2; MTCW 1, 2; RGEL 2

Nichol, B(arrie) P(hillip) 1944-1988 . **CLC 18**
See also CA 53-56; DLB 53; SATA 66

Nichols, John (Treadwell) 1940- .... **CLC 38**
See also CA 9-12R; CAAE 190; CAAS 2; CANR 6, 70; DLBY 1982; TCWW 2

Nichols, Leigh
See Koontz, Dean R(ay)

Nichols, Peter (Richard) 1927- .... **CLC 5, 36, 65**
See also CA 104; CANR 33, 86; CBD; CD 5; DLB 13, 245; MTCW 1

Nicholson, Linda ed. .... **CLC 65**

Ni Chuilleanain, Eilean 1942- .... **PC 34**
See also CA 126; CANR 53, 83; CP 7; CWP; DLB 40

Nicolas, F. R. E.
See Freeling, Nicolas

Niedecker, Lorine 1903-1970 ...... **CLC 10, 42**
See also CA 25-28; CAP 2; DAM POET; DLB 48

Nietzsche, Friedrich (Wilhelm) 1844-1900 .... **TCLC 10, 18, 55**
See also CA 107; 121; CDWLB 2; DLB 129; EW 7; RGWL 2

Nievo, Ippolito 1831-1861 .... **NCLC 22**

Nightingale, Anne Redmon 1943-
See Redmon, Anne
See also CA 103

Nightingale, Florence 1820-1910 ... **TCLC 85**
See also CA 188; DLB 166

Nijo Yoshimoto 1320-1388 .... **CMLC 49**
See also DLB 203

Nik. T. O.
See Annensky, Innokenty (Fyodorovich)

Nin, Anais 1903-1977 ..... **CLC 1, 4, 8, 11, 14, 60, 127; SSC 10**
See also AITN 2; AMWS 10; BPFB 2; CA 13-16R; 69-72; CANR 22, 53; DAM NOV, POP; DLB 2, 4, 152; GLL 2; MAWW; MTCW 1, 2; RGAL 4; RGSF 2

Nisbet, Robert A(lexander) 1913-1996 .... **TCLC 117**
See also CA 25-28R; 153; CANR 17; INT CANR-17

Nishida, Kitaro 1870-1945 .... **TCLC 83**

Nishiwaki, Junzaburo 1894-1982 .... **PC 15**
See also Nishiwaki, Junzaburo
See also CA 194; 107; MJW

Nishiwaki, Junzaburo 1894-1982
See Nishiwaki, Junzaburo
See also CA 194

Nissenson, Hugh 1933- .... **CLC 4, 9**
See also CA 17-20R; CANR 27, 108; CN 7; DLB 28

Niven, Larry .... **CLC 8**
See also Niven, Laurence Van Cott
See also AAYA 27; BPFB 2; BYA 10; DLB 8; SCFW 2

Niven, Laurence Van Cott 1938-
See Niven, Larry
See also CA 21-24R; CAAS 12; CANR 14, 44, 66; CPW; DAM POP; MTCW 1, 2; SATA 95; SFW 4

Nixon, Agnes Eckhardt 1927- .... **CLC 21**
See also CA 110

Nizan, Paul 1905-1940 .... **TCLC 40**
See also CA 161; DLB 72; GFL 1789 to the Present

Nkosi, Lewis 1936- .... **CLC 45; BLC 3**
See also BW 1, 3; CA 65-68; CANR 27, 81; CBD; CD 5; DAM MULT; DLB 157, 225

Nodier, (Jean) Charles (Emmanuel) 1780-1844 .... **NCLC 19**
See also DLB 119; GFL 1789 to the Present

Noguchi, Yone 1875-1947 .... **TCLC 80**

Nolan, Christopher 1965- .... **CLC 58**
See also CA 111; CANR 88

Noon, Jeff 1957- .... **CLC 91**
See also CA 148; CANR 83; SFW 4

Norden, Charles
See Durrell, Lawrence (George)

Nordhoff, Charles (Bernard) 1887-1947 .... **TCLC 23**
See also CA 108; DLB 9; LAIT 1; RHW 1; SATA 23

Norfolk, Lawrence 1963- .... **CLC 76**
See also CA 144; CANR 85; CN 7

Norman, Marsha 1947- .... **CLC 28; DC 8**
See also CA 105; CABS 3; CAD; CANR 41; CD 5; CSW; CWD; DAM DRAM; DFS 2; DLBY 1984; FW

Normyx
See Douglas, (George) Norman

Norris, (Benjamin) Frank(lin, Jr.) 1870-1902 .... **TCLC 24; SSC 28**
See also AMW; BPFB 2; CA 110; 160; CDALB 1865-1917; DLB 12, 71, 186; NFS 12; RGAL 4; TCWW 2; TUS

Norris, Leslie 1921- .... **CLC 14**
See also CA 11-12; CANR 14; CAP 1; CP 7; DLB 27, 256

North, Andrew
See Norton, Andre

North, Anthony
See Koontz, Dean R(ay)

North, Captain George
See Stevenson, Robert Louis (Balfour)

North, Captain George
See Stevenson, Robert Louis (Balfour)

North, Milou
See Erdrich, Louise

Northrup, B. A.
See Hubbard, L(afayette) Ron(ald)

North Staffs
See Hulme, T(homas) E(rnest)

Northup, Solomon 1808-1863 ...... **NCLC 105**

Norton, Alice Mary
See Norton, Andre
See also MAICYA 1; SATA 1, 43

Norton, Andre 1912- .... **CLC 12**
See also Norton, Alice Mary
See also AAYA 14; BPFB 2; BYA 4, 10, 12; CA 1-4R; CANR 68; CLR 50; DLB 8, 52; JRDA; MAICYA 2; MTCW 1; SATA 91; SUFW; YAW

Norton, Caroline 1808-1877 .... **NCLC 47**
See also DLB 21, 159, 199

Norway, Nevil Shute 1899-1960
See Shute, Nevil
See also CA 102; 93-96; CANR 85; MTCW 2

Norwid, Cyprian Kamil 1821-1883 .... **NCLC 17**

Nosille, Nabrah
See Ellison, Harlan (Jay)

Nossack, Hans Erich 1901-1978 .... **CLC 6**
See also CA 93-96; 85-88; DLB 69

Nostradamus 1503-1566 .... **LC 27**

Nosu, Chuji
See Ozu, Yasujiro

Notenburg, Eleanora (Genrikhovna) von
See Guro, Elena

Nova, Craig 1945- .... **CLC 7, 31**
See also CA 45-48; CANR 2, 53

Novak, Joseph
See Kosinski, Jerzy (Nikodem)

Novalis 1772-1801 .... **NCLC 13**
See also CDWLB 2; DLB 90; EW 5; RGWL 2

Novis, Emile
See Weil, Simone (Adolphine)

Nowlan, Alden (Albert) 1933-1983 ... **CLC 15**
See also CA 9-12R; CANR 5; DAC; DAM MST; DLB 53; PFS 12

Noyes, Alfred 1880-1958 ...... **TCLC 7; PC 27**
See also CA 104; 188; DLB 20; EXPP; FANT; PFS 4; RGEL 2

Nunn, Kem .... **CLC 34**
See also CA 159

Nwapa, Flora 1931-1993 .... **CLC 133; BLCS**
See also BW 2; CA 143; CANR 83; CD-WLB 3; CWRI 5; DLB 125; WLIT 2

Nye, Robert 1939- .... **CLC 13, 42**
See also CA 33-36R; CANR 29, 67, 107; CN 7; CP 7; CWRI 5; DAM NOV; DLB 14; FANT; HGG; MTCW 1; RHW; SATA 6

Nyro, Laura 1947-1997 .... **CLC 17**
See also CA 194

Oates, Joyce Carol 1938- .. **CLC 1, 2, 3, 6, 9, 11, 15, 19, 33, 52, 108, 134; SSC 6; WLC**
See also AAYA 15; AITN 1; AMWS 2; BEST 89:2; BPFB 2; BYA 11; CA 5-8R; CANR 25, 45, 74; CDALB 1968-1988; CN 7; CP 7; CPW; CWP; DA; DA3; DAB; DAC; DAM MST, NOV, POP; DLB 2, 5, 130; DLBY 1981; EXPS; FW; HGG; INT CANR-25; LAIT 4; MAWW; MTCW 1, 2; NFS 8; RGAL 4; RGSF 2; SSFS 1, 8

O'Brian, Patrick 1914-2000 .... **CLC 152**
See also CA 144; 187; CANR 74; CPW; MTCW 2; RHW

O'Brien, Darcy 1939-1998 .... **CLC 11**
See also CA 21-24R; 167; CANR 8, 59

O'Brien, E. G.
See Clarke, Arthur C(harles)

O'Brien, Edna 1936- ..... **CLC 3, 5, 8, 13, 36, 65, 116; SSC 10**
See also BRWS 5; CA 1-4R; CANR 6, 41, 65, 102; CDBLB 1960 to Present; CN 7; DA3; DAM NOV; DLB 14, 231; FW; MTCW 1, 2; RGSF 2; WLIT 4

O'Brien, Fitz-James 1828-1862 ..... **NCLC 21**
See also DLB 74; RGAL 4; SUFW

O'Brien, Flann .... **CLC 1, 4, 5, 7, 10, 47**
See also O Nuallain, Brian
See also BRWS 2; DLB 231; RGEL 2

O'Brien, Richard 1942- .... **CLC 17**
See also CA 124

O'Brien, (William) Tim(othy) 1946- . **CLC 7, 19, 40, 103**
See also AAYA 16; AMWS 5; CA 85-88; CANR 40, 58; CDALBS; CN 7; CPW; DA3; DAM POP; DLB 152; DLBD 9; DLBY 1980; MTCW 2; RGAL 4; SSFS 5, 15

Obstfelder, Sigbjoern 1866-1900 .... **TCLC 23**
See also CA 123

O'Casey, Sean 1880-1964 .... **CLC 1, 5, 9, 11, 15, 88; DC 12; WLCS**
See also BRW 7; CA 89-92; CANR 62; CBD; CDBLB 1914-1945; DA3; DAB; DAC; DAM DRAM, MST; DLB 10; MTCW 1, 2; RGEL 2; TEA; WLIT 4

O'Cathasaigh, Sean
See O'Casey, Sean

Occom, Samson 1723-1792 .... **LC 60**
See also DLB 175; NNAL

Ochs, Phil(ip David) 1940-1976 .... **CLC 17**
See also CA 185; 65-68

O'Connor, Edwin (Greene)
1918-1968 .... **CLC 14**
See also CA 93-96; 25-28R

O'Connor, (Mary) Flannery
1925-1964 .... **CLC 1, 2, 3, 6, 10, 13, 15, 21, 66, 104; SSC 1, 23; WLC**
See also AAYA 7; AMW; BPFB 3; CA 1-4R; CANR 3, 41; CDALB 1941-1968; DA; DA3; DAB; DAC; DAM MST, NOV; DLB 2, 152; DLBD 12; DLBY 1980; EXPS; LAIT 5; MAWW; MTCW 1, 2; NFS 3; RGAL 4; RGSF 2; SSFS 2, 7, 10

O'Connor, Frank .... **CLC 23; SSC 5**
See also O'Donovan, Michael John
See also DLB 162; RGSF 2; SSFS 5

O'Dell, Scott 1898-1989 .... **CLC 30**
See also AAYA 3; BPFB 3; BYA 1, 2, 3, 5; CA 61-64; 129; CANR 12, 30; CLR 1, 16; DLB 52; JRDA; MAICYA 1, 2; SATA 12, 60; WYA; YAW

Odets, Clifford 1906-1963 ..... **CLC 2, 28, 98; DC 6**
See also AMWS 2; CA 85-88; CAD; CANR 62; DAM DRAM; DFS 3; DLB 7, 26; MTCW 1, 2; RGAL 4

O'Doherty, Brian 1928- .... **CLC 76**
See also CA 105; CANR 108

O'Donnell, K. M.
See Malzberg, Barry N(athaniel)

O'Donnell, Lawrence
See Kuttner, Henry

O'Donovan, Michael John
1903-1966 .... **CLC 14**
See also O'Connor, Frank
See also CA 93-96; CANR 84

Oe, Kenzaburo 1935- .. **CLC 10, 36, 86; SSC 20**
See also Oe Kenzaburo
See also CA 97-100; CANR 36, 50, 74; DA3; DAM NOV; DLBY 1994; MTCW 1, 2

Oe Kenzaburo
See Oe, Kenzaburo
See also CWW 2; DLB 182; EWL 3; MJW; RGSF 2; RGWL 2

O'Faolain, Julia 1932- .... **CLC 6, 19, 47, 108**
See also CA 81-84; CAAS 2; CANR 12, 61; CN 7; DLB 14, 231; FW; MTCW 1; RHW

O'Faolain, Sean 1900-1991 ...... **CLC 1, 7, 14, 32, 70; SSC 13**
See also CA 61-64; 134; CANR 12, 66; DLB 15, 162; MTCW 1, 2; RGEL 2; RGSF 2

O'Flaherty, Liam 1896-1984 .... **CLC 5, 34; SSC 6**
See also CA 101; 113; CANR 35; DLB 36, 162; DLBY 1984; MTCW 1, 2; RGEL 2; RGSF 2; SSFS 5

Ogai
See Mori Ogai
See also MJW

Ogilvy, Gavin
See Barrie, J(ames) M(atthew)

O'Grady, Standish (James)
1846-1928 .... **TCLC 5**
See also CA 104; 157

O'Grady, Timothy 1951- .... **CLC 59**
See also CA 138

O'Hara, Frank 1926-1966 .. **CLC 2, 5, 13, 78**
See also CA 9-12R; 25-28R; CANR 33; DA3; DAM POET; DLB 5, 16, 193; MTCW 1, 2; PFS 8; 12; RGAL 4; WP

O'Hara, John (Henry) 1905-1970 . **CLC 1, 2, 3, 6, 11, 42; SSC 15**
See also AMW; BPFB 3; CA 5-8R; 25-28R; CANR 31, 60; CDALB 1929-1941; DAM NOV; DLB 9, 86; DLBD 2; MTCW 1, 2; NFS 11; RGAL 4; RGSF 2

O Hehir, Diana 1922- .... **CLC 41**
See also CA 93-96

Ohiyesa 1858-1939
See Eastman, Charles A(lexander)

Okigbo, Christopher (Ifenayichukwu)
1932-1967 .... **CLC 25, 84; BLC 3; PC 7**
See also AFW; BW 1, 3; CA 77-80; CANR 74; CDWLB 3; DAM MULT, POET; DLB 125; MTCW 1, 2; RGEL 2

Okri, Ben 1959- .... **CLC 87**
See also AFW; BRWS 5; BW 2, 3; CA 130; 138; CANR 65; CN 7; DLB 157, 231; INT CA-138; MTCW 2; RGSF 2; WLIT 2

Olds, Sharon 1942- .. **CLC 32, 39, 85; PC 22**
See also AMWS 10; CA 101; CANR 18, 41, 66, 98; CP 7; CPW; CWP; DAM POET; DLB 120; MTCW 2

Oldstyle, Jonathan
See Irving, Washington

Olesha, Iurii
See Olesha, Yuri (Karlovich)
See also RGWL 2

Olesha, Yuri (Karlovich) 1899-1960 .. **CLC 8**
See also Olesha, Iurii
See also CA 85-88; EW 11

Oliphant, Mrs.
See Oliphant, Margaret (Oliphant Wilson)
See also SUFW

Oliphant, Laurence 1829(?)-1888 .. **NCLC 47**
See also DLB 18, 166

Oliphant, Margaret (Oliphant Wilson)
1828-1897 .... **NCLC 11, 61; SSC 25**
See also Oliphant, Mrs.
See also DLB 18, 159, 190; HGG; RGEL 2; RGSF 2

Oliver, Mary 1935- .... **CLC 19, 34, 98**
See also AMWS 7; CA 21-24R; CANR 9, 43, 84, 92; CP 7; CWP; DLB 5, 193; PFS 15

Olivier, Laurence (Kerr) 1907-1989 . **CLC 20**
See also CA 111; 150; 129

Olsen, Tillie 1912- ... **CLC 4, 13, 114; SSC 11**
See also BYA 11; CA 1-4R; CANR 1, 43, 74; CDALBS; CN 7; DA; DA3; DAB; DAC; DAM MST; DLB 28, 206; DLBY 1980; EXPS; FW; MTCW 1, 2; RGAL 4; RGSF 2; SSFS 1

Olson, Charles (John) 1910-1970 .. **CLC 1, 2, 5, 6, 9, 11, 29; PC 19**
See also AMWS 2; CA 13-16; 25-28R; CABS 2; CANR 35, 61; CAP 1; DAM POET; DLB 5, 16, 193; MTCW 1, 2; RGAL 4; WP

Olson, Toby 1937- .... **CLC 28**
See also CA 65-68; CANR 9, 31, 84; CP 7

Olyesha, Yuri
See Olesha, Yuri (Karlovich)

Omar Khayyam
See Khayyam, Omar
See also RGWL 2

Ondaatje, (Philip) Michael 1943- .... **CLC 14, 29, 51, 76; PC 28**
See also CA 77-80; CANR 42, 74, 109; CN 7; CP 7; DA3; DAB; DAC; DAM MST; DLB 60; MTCW 2; PFS 8; TWA

Oneal, Elizabeth 1934-
See Oneal, Zibby
See also CA 106; CANR 28, 84; MAICYA 1, 2; SATA 30, 82; YAW

Oneal, Zibby .... **CLC 30**
See also Oneal, Elizabeth
See also AAYA 5, 41; BYA 13; CLR 13; JRDA; WYA

O'Neill, Eugene (Gladstone)
1888-1953 ...... **TCLC 1, 6, 27, 49; WLC**
See also AITN 1; AMW; CA 110; 132; CAD; CDALB 1929-1941; DA; DA3; DAB; DAC; DAM DRAM, MST; DFS 9, 11, 12; DLB 7; LAIT 3; MTCW 1, 2; RGAL 4; TUS

Onetti, Juan Carlos 1909-1994 ... **CLC 7, 10; HLCS 2; SSC 23**
   See also CA 85-88; 145; CANR 32, 63; CD-WLB 3; DAM MULT, NOV; DLB 113; HW 1, 2; LAW; MTCW 1, 2; RGSF 2

O Nuallain, Brian 1911-1966
   See O'Brien, Flann
   See also CA 21-22; 25-28R; CAP 2; DLB 231; FANT

Ophuls, Max 1902-1957 .... **TCLC 79**
   See also CA 113

Opie, Amelia 1769-1853 .... **NCLC 65**
   See also DLB 116, 159; RGEL 2

Oppen, George 1908-1984 ..... **CLC 7, 13, 34; PC 35; TCLC 107**
   See also CA 13-16R; 113; CANR 8, 82; DLB 5, 165

Oppenheim, E(dward) Phillips
   1866-1946 .... **TCLC 45**
   See also CA 111; 202; CMW 4; DLB 70

Opuls, Max
   See Ophuls, Max

Origen c. 185-c. 254 .... **CMLC 19**

Orlovitz, Gil 1918-1973 .... **CLC 22**
   See also CA 77-80; 45-48; DLB 2, 5

Orris
   See Ingelow, Jean

Ortega y Gasset, Jose 1883-1955 ... **TCLC 9; HLC 2**
   See also CA 106; 130; DAM MULT; EW 9; HW 1, 2; MTCW 1, 2

Ortese, Anna Maria 1914- .... **CLC 89**
   See also DLB 177

Ortiz, Simon J(oseph) 1941- ..... **CLC 45; PC 17**
   See also AMWS 4; CA 134; CANR 69; CP 7; DAM MULT, POET; DLB 120, 175, 256; EXPP; NNAL; PFS 4; RGAL 4

Orton, Joe .... **CLC 4, 13, 43; DC 3**
   See also Orton, John Kingsley
   See also BRWS 5; CBD; CDBLB 1960 to Present; DFS 3, 6; DLB 13; GLL 1; MTCW 2; RGEL 2; WLIT 4

Orton, John Kingsley 1933-1967
   See Orton, Joe
   See also CA 85-88; CANR 35, 66; DAM DRAM; MTCW 1, 2

Orwell, George .... **TCLC 2, 6, 15, 31, 51; WLC**
   See also Blair, Eric (Arthur)
   See also BPFB 3; BRW 7; BYA 5; CDBLB 1945-1960; CLR 68; DAB; DLB 15, 98, 195, 255; EXPN; LAIT 4, 5; NFS 3, 7; RGEL 2; SCFW 2; SFW 4; SSFS 4; WLIT 4; YAW

Osborne, David
   See Silverberg, Robert

Osborne, George
   See Silverberg, Robert

Osborne, John (James) 1929-1994 .... **CLC 1, 2, 5, 11, 45; WLC**
   See also BRWS 1; CA 13-16R; 147; CANR 21, 56; CDBLB 1945-1960; DA; DAB; DAC; DAM DRAM, MST; DFS 4; DLB 13; MTCW 1, 2; RGEL 2

Osborne, Lawrence 1958- .... **CLC 50**
   See also CA 189

Osbourne, Lloyd 1868-1947 .... **TCLC 93**

Oshima, Nagisa 1932- .... **CLC 20**
   See also CA 116; 121; CANR 78

Oskison, John Milton 1874-1947 ... **TCLC 35**
   See also CA 144; CANR 84; DAM MULT; DLB 175; NNAL

Ossian c. 3rd cent. - .... **CMLC 28**
   See also Macpherson, James

Ossoli, Sarah Margaret (Fuller)
   1810-1850 .... **NCLC 5, 50**
   See also Fuller, Margaret; Fuller, Sarah Margaret

See also CDALB 1640-1865; FW; SATA 25

Ostriker, Alicia (Suskin) 1937- .... **CLC 132**
   See also CA 25-28R; CAAS 24; CANR 10, 30, 62, 99; CWP; DLB 120; EXPP

Ostrovsky, Alexander 1823-1886 .. **NCLC 30, 57**

Otero, Blas de 1916-1979 .... **CLC 11**
   See also CA 89-92; DLB 134

Otto, Rudolf 1869-1937 .... **TCLC 85**

Otto, Whitney 1955- .... **CLC 70**
   See also CA 140

Ouida .... **TCLC 43**
   See also De La Ramee, (Marie) Louise
   See also DLB 18, 156; RGEL 2

Ouologuem, Yambo 1940- .... **CLC 146**
   See also CA 111; 176

Ousmane, Sembene 1923- ... **CLC 66; BLC 3**
   See also Sembene, Ousmane
   See also BW 1, 3; CA 117; 125; CANR 81; CWW 2; MTCW 1

Ovid 43B.C.-17 .... **CMLC 7; PC 2**
   See also AW 2; CDWLB 1; DA3; DAM POET; DLB 211; RGWL 2; WP

Owen, Hugh
   See Faust, Frederick (Schiller)

Owen, Wilfred (Edward Salter)
   1893-1918 ... **TCLC 5, 27; PC 19; WLC**
   See also BRW 6; CA 104; 141; CDBLB 1914-1945; DA; DAB; DAC; DAM MST, POET; DLB 20; EXPP; MTCW 2; PFS 10; RGEL 2; WLIT 4

Owens, Rochelle 1936- .... **CLC 8**
   See also CA 17-20R; CAAS 2; CAD; CANR 39; CD 5; CP 7; CWD; CWP

Oz, Amos 1939- .... **CLC 5, 8, 11, 27, 33, 54**
   See also CA 53-56; CANR 27, 47, 65; CWW 2; DAM NOV; MTCW 1, 2; RGSF 2

Ozick, Cynthia 1928- .... **CLC 3, 7, 28, 62, 155; SSC 15**
   See also AMWS 5; BEST 90:1; CA 17-20R; CANR 23, 58; CN 7; CPW; DA3; DAM NOV, POP; DLB 28, 152; DLBY 1982; EXPS; INT CANR-23; MTCW 1, 2; RGAL 4; RGSF 2; SSFS 3, 12

Ozu, Yasujiro 1903-1963 .... **CLC 16**
   See also CA 112

Pacheco, C.
   See Pessoa, Fernando (Antonio Nogueira)

Pacheco, Jose Emilio 1939-
   See also CA 111; 131; CANR 65; DAM MULT; HLC 2; HW 1, 2; RGSF 2

Pa Chin .... **CLC 18**
   See also Li Fei-kan

Pack, Robert 1929- .... **CLC 13**
   See also CA 1-4R; CANR 3, 44, 82; CP 7; DLB 5; SATA 118

Padgett, Lewis
   See Kuttner, Henry

Padilla (Lorenzo), Heberto
   1932-2000 .... **CLC 38**
   See also AITN 1; CA 123; 131; 189; HW 1

Page, Jimmy 1944- .... **CLC 12**

Page, Louise 1955- .... **CLC 40**
   See also CA 140; CANR 76; CBD; CD 5; CWD; DLB 233

Page, P(atricia) K(athleen) 1916- ...... **CLC 7, 18; PC 12**
   See also Cape, Judith
   See also CA 53-56; CANR 4, 22, 65; CP 7; DAC; DAM MST; DLB 68; MTCW 1; RGEL 2

Page, Stanton
   See Fuller, Henry Blake

Page, Stanton
   See Fuller, Henry Blake

Page, Thomas Nelson 1853-1922 .... **SSC 23**
   See also CA 118; 177; DLB 12, 78; DLBD 13; RGAL 4

Pagels, Elaine Hiesey 1943- .... **CLC 104**
   See also CA 45-48; CANR 2, 24, 51; FW

Paget, Violet 1856-1935
   See Lee, Vernon
   See also CA 104; 166; GLL 1; HGG

Paget-Lowe, Henry
   See Lovecraft, H(oward) P(hillips)

Paglia, Camille (Anna) 1947- .... **CLC 68**
   See also CA 140; CANR 72; CPW; FW; GLL 2; MTCW 2

Paige, Richard
   See Koontz, Dean R(ay)

Paine, Thomas 1737-1809 .... **NCLC 62**
   See also AMWS 1; CDALB 1640-1865; DLB 31, 43, 73, 158; LAIT 1; RGAL 4; RGEL 2

Palamas, Kostes 1859-1943 .... **TCLC 5**
   See also CA 105; 190; RGWL 2

Palazzeschi, Aldo 1885-1974 .... **CLC 11**
   See also CA 89-92; 53-56; DLB 114

Pales Matos, Luis 1898-1959
   See Pales Matos, Luis
   See also HLCS 2; HW 1; LAW

Paley, Grace 1922- .. **CLC 4, 6, 37, 140; SSC 8**
   See also AMWS 6; CA 25-28R; CANR 13, 46, 74; CN 7; CPW; DA3; DAM POP; DLB 28, 218; EXPS; FW; INT CANR-13; MAWW; MTCW 1, 2; RGAL 4; RGSF 2; SSFS 3

Palin, Michael (Edward) 1943- .... **CLC 21**
   See also Monty Python
   See also CA 107; CANR 35, 109; SATA 67

Palliser, Charles 1947- .... **CLC 65**
   See also CA 136; CANR 76; CN 7

Palma, Ricardo 1833-1919 .... **TCLC 29**
   See also CA 168; LAW

Pancake, Breece Dexter 1952-1979
   See Pancake, Breece D'J
   See also CA 123; 109

Pancake, Breece D'J .... **CLC 29**
   See also Pancake, Breece Dexter
   See also DLB 130

Panchenko, Nikolai .... **CLC 59**

Pankhurst, Emmeline (Goulden)
   1858-1928 .... **TCLC 100**
   See also CA 116; FW

Panko, Rudy
   See Gogol, Nikolai (Vasilyevich)

Papadiamantis, Alexandros
   1851-1911 .... **TCLC 29**
   See also CA 168

Papadiamantopoulos, Johannes 1856-1910
   See Moreas, Jean
   See also CA 117

Papini, Giovanni 1881-1956 .... **TCLC 22**
   See also CA 121; 180

Paracelsus 1493-1541 .... **LC 14**
   See also DLB 179

Parasol, Peter
   See Stevens, Wallace

Pardo Bazan, Emilia 1851-1921 .... **SSC 30**
   See also FW; RGSF 2; RGWL 2

Pareto, Vilfredo 1848-1923 .... **TCLC 69**
   See also CA 175

Paretsky, Sara 1947- .... **CLC 135**
   See also AAYA 30; BEST 90:3; CA 125; 129; CANR 59, 95; CMW 4; CPW; DA3; DAM POP; INT CA-129; MSW; RGAL 4

Parfenie, Maria
   See Codrescu, Andrei

Parini, Jay (Lee) 1948- .... **CLC 54, 133**
   See also CA 97-100; CAAS 16; CANR 32, 87

Park, Jordan
   See Kornbluth, C(yril) M.; Pohl, Frederik

Park, Robert E(zra) 1864-1944 ..... **TCLC 73**
   See also CA 122; 165

Parker, Bert
See Ellison, Harlan (Jay)
Parker, Dorothy (Rothschild)
1893-1967 .. **CLC 15, 68; PC 28; SSC 2**
See also AMWS 9; CA 19-20; 25-28R; CAP 2; DA3; DAM POET; DLB 11, 45, 86; EXPP; FW; MAWW; MTCW 1, 2; RGAL 4; RGSF 2
Parker, Robert B(rown) 1932- .... **CLC 27**
See also AAYA 28; BEST 89:4; BPFB 3; CA 49-52; CANR 1, 26, 52, 89; CMW 4; CPW; DAM NOV, POP; INT CANR-26; MSW; MTCW 1
Parkin, Frank 1940- .... **CLC 43**
See also CA 147
Parkman, Francis, Jr. 1823-1893 .. **NCLC 12**
See also AMWS 2; DLB 1, 30, 183, 186, 235; RGAL 4
Parks, Gordon (Alexander Buchanan)
1912- .... **CLC 1, 16; BLC 3**
See also AAYA 36; AITN 2; BW 2, 3; CA 41-44R; CANR 26, 66; DA3; DAM MULT; DLB 33; MTCW 2; SATA 8, 108
Parks, Tim(othy Harold) 1954- ...... **CLC 147**
See also CA 126; 131; CANR 77; DLB 231; INT CA-131
Parmenides c. 515B.C.-c.
450B.C. .... **CMLC 22**
See also DLB 176
Parnell, Thomas 1679-1718 .... **LC 3**
See also DLB 95; RGEL 2
Parra, Nicanor 1914- ... **CLC 2, 102; HLC 2; PC 39**
See also CA 85-88; CANR 32; CWW 2; DAM MULT; HW 1; LAW; MTCW 1
Parra Sanojo, Ana Teresa de la 1890-1936
See de la Parra, (Ana) Teresa (Sonojo)
See also HLCS 2; LAW
Parrish, Mary Frances
See Fisher, M(ary) F(rances) K(ennedy)
Parshchikov, Aleksei .... **CLC 59**
Parson, Professor
See Coleridge, Samuel Taylor
Parson Lot
See Kingsley, Charles
Parton, Sara Payson Willis
1811-1872 .... **NCLC 86**
See also DLB 43, 74, 239
Partridge, Anthony
See Oppenheim, E(dward) Phillips
Pascal, Blaise 1623-1662 .... **LC 35**
See also EW 3; GFL Beginnings to 1789; RGWL 2
Pascoli, Giovanni 1855-1912 .... **TCLC 45**
See also CA 170; EW 7
Pasolini, Pier Paolo 1922-1975 .. **CLC 20, 37, 106; PC 17**
See also CA 93-96; 61-64; CANR 63; DLB 128, 177; MTCW 1; RGWL 2
Pasquini
See Silone, Ignazio
Pastan, Linda (Olenik) 1932- .... **CLC 27**
See also CA 61-64; CANR 18, 40, 61; CP 7; CSW; CWP; DAM POET; DLB 5; PFS 8
Pasternak, Boris (Leonidovich)
1890-1960 ...... **CLC 7, 10, 18, 63; PC 6; SSC 31; WLC**
See also BPFB 3; CA 127; 116; DA; DA3; DAB; DAC; DAM MST, NOV, POET; EW 10; MTCW 1, 2; RGSF 2; RGWL 2; TWA; WP
Patchen, Kenneth 1911-1972 .... **CLC 1, 2, 18**
See also CA 1-4R; 33-36R; CANR 3, 35; DAM POET; DLB 16, 48; MTCW 1; RGAL 4

Pater, Walter (Horatio) 1839-1894 . **NCLC 7, 90**
See also BRW 5; CDBLB 1832-1890; DLB 57, 156; RGEL 2; TEA
Paterson, A(ndrew) B(arton)
1864-1941 .... **TCLC 32**
See also CA 155; DLB 230; RGEL 2; SATA 97
Paterson, Katherine (Womeldorf)
1932- .... **CLC 12, 30**
See also AAYA 1, 31; BYA 1, 2, 7; CA 21-24R; CANR 28, 59; CLR 7, 50; CWRI 5; DLB 52; JRDA; LAIT 4; MAICYA 1, 2; MAICYAS 1; MTCW 1; SATA 13, 53, 92, 133; WYA; YAW
Patmore, Coventry Kersey Dighton
1823-1896 .... **NCLC 9**
See also DLB 35, 98; RGEL 2; TEA
Paton, Alan (Stewart) 1903-1988 ...... **CLC 4, 10, 25, 55, 106; WLC**
See also AAYA 26; AFW; BPFB 3; BRWS 2; BYA 1; CA 13-16; 125; CANR 22; CAP 1; DA; DA3; DAB; DAC; DAM MST, NOV; DLB 225; DLBD 17; EXPN; LAIT 4; MTCW 1, 2; NFS 3, 12; RGEL 2; SATA 11; SATA-Obit 56; WLIT 2
Paton Walsh, Gillian 1937- .... **CLC 35**
See also Paton Walsh, Jill; Walsh, Jill Paton
See also CA 262; CANR 38; CLR 2, 65; DLB 161; JRDA; MAICYA 1, 2; SAAS 3; SATA 4, 72, 109; YAW
Paton Walsh, Jill
See Paton Walsh, Gillian
See also BYA 1, 8
Patton, George S(mith), Jr.
1885-1945 .... **TCLC 79**
See also CA 189
Paulding, James Kirke 1778-1860 ... **NCLC 2**
See also DLB 3, 59, 74, 250; RGAL 4
Paulin, Thomas Neilson 1949-
See Paulin, Tom
See also CA 123; 128; CANR 98; CP 7
Paulin, Tom .... **CLC 37**
See also Paulin, Thomas Neilson
See also DLB 40
Pausanias c. 1st cent. - .... **CMLC 36**
Paustovsky, Konstantin (Georgievich)
1892-1968 .... **CLC 40**
See also CA 93-96; 25-28R
Pavese, Cesare 1908-1950 .. **TCLC 3; PC 13; SSC 19**
See also CA 104; 169; DLB 128, 177; EW 12; RGSF 2; RGWL 2
Pavic, Milorad 1929- .... **CLC 60**
See also CA 136; CDWLB 4; CWW 2; DLB 181
Pavlov, Ivan Petrovich 1849-1936 . **TCLC 91**
See also CA 118; 180
Payne, Alan
See Jakes, John (William)
Paz, Gil
See Lugones, Leopoldo
Paz, Octavio 1914-1998 . **CLC 3, 4, 6, 10, 19, 51, 65, 119; HLC 2; PC 1; WLC**
See also CA 73-76; 165; CANR 32, 65, 104; CWW 2; DA; DA3; DAB; DAC; DAM MST, MULT, POET; DLBY 1990, 1998; DNFS 1; HW 1, 2; LAW; LAWS 1; MTCW 1, 2; RGWL 2; SSFS 13; WLIT 1
p'Bitek, Okot 1931-1982 ..... **CLC 96; BLC 3**
See also AFW; BW 2, 3; CA 124; 107; CANR 82; DAM MULT; DLB 125; MTCW 1, 2; RGEL 2; WLIT 2
Peacock, Molly 1947- .... **CLC 60**
See also CA 103; CAAS 21; CANR 52, 84; CP 7; CWP; DLB 120

Peacock, Thomas Love
1785-1866 .... **NCLC 22**
See also BRW 4; DLB 96, 116; RGEL 2; RGSF 2
Peake, Mervyn 1911-1968 .... **CLC 7, 54**
See also CA 5-8R; 25-28R; CANR 3; DLB 15, 160, 255; FANT; MTCW 1; RGEL 2; SATA 23; SFW 4
Pearce, Philippa
See Christie, Philippa
See also CA 5-8R; CANR 4, 109; CWRI 5; FANT; MAICYA 2
Pearl, Eric
See Elman, Richard (Martin)
Pearson, T(homas) R(eid) 1956- .... **CLC 39**
See also CA 120; 130; CANR 97; CSW; INT 130
Peck, Dale 1967- .... **CLC 81**
See also CA 146; CANR 72; GLL 2
Peck, John (Frederick) 1941- .... **CLC 3**
See also CA 49-52; CANR 3, 100; CP 7
Peck, Richard (Wayne) 1934- .... **CLC 21**
See also AAYA 1, 24; BYA 1, 6, 8, 11; CA 85-88; CANR 19, 38; CLR 15; INT CANR-19; JRDA; MAICYA 1, 2; SAAS 2; SATA 18, 55, 97; SATA-Essay 110; WYA; YAW
Peck, Robert Newton 1928- .... **CLC 17**
See also AAYA 3, 43; BYA 1, 6; CA 81-84, 182; CAAE 182; CANR 31, 63; CLR 45; DA; DAC; DAM MST; JRDA; LAIT 3; MAICYA 1, 2; SAAS 1; SATA 21, 62, 111; SATA-Essay 108; WYA; YAW
Peckinpah, (David) Sam(uel)
1925-1984 .... **CLC 20**
See also CA 109; 114; CANR 82
Pedersen, Knut 1859-1952
See Hamsun, Knut
See also CA 104; 119; CANR 63; MTCW 1, 2
Peeslake, Gaffer
See Durrell, Lawrence (George)
Peguy, Charles (Pierre)
1873-1914 .... **TCLC 10**
See also CA 107; 193; DLB 258; GFL 1789 to the Present
Peirce, Charles Sanders
1839-1914 .... **TCLC 81**
See also CA 194
Pellicer, Carlos 1900(?)-1977
See also CA 153; 69-72; HLCS 2; HW 1
Pena, Ramon del Valle y
See Valle-Inclan, Ramon (Maria) del
Pendennis, Arthur Esquir
See Thackeray, William Makepeace
Penn, William 1644-1718 .... **LC 25**
See also DLB 24
PEPECE
See Prado (Calvo), Pedro
Pepys, Samuel 1633-1703 ... **LC 11, 58; WLC**
See also BRW 2; CDBLB 1660-1789; DA; DA3; DAB; DAC; DAM MST; DLB 101, 213; RGEL 2; WLIT 3
Percy, Thomas 1729-1811 .... **NCLC 95**
See also DLB 104
Percy, Walker 1916-1990 .... **CLC 2, 3, 6, 8, 14, 18, 47, 65**
See also AMWS 3; BPFB 3; CA 1-4R; 131; CANR 1, 23, 64; CPW; CSW; DA3; DAM NOV, POP; DLB 2; DLBY 1980, 1990; MTCW 1, 2; RGAL 4
Percy, William Alexander
1885-1942 .... **TCLC 84**
See also CA 163; MTCW 2
Perec, Georges 1936-1982 .... **CLC 56, 116**
See also CA 141; DLB 83; GFL 1789 to the Present

Rabelais, Francois 1494-1553 .... **LC 5, 60;
WLC**
See also DA; DAB; DAC; DAM MST; EW
2; GFL Beginnings to 1789; RGWL 2

Rabinovitch, Sholem 1859-1916
See Aleichem, Sholom
See also CA 104

Rabinyan, Dorit 1972- .... **CLC 119**
See also CA 170

Rachilde
See Vallette, Marguerite Eymery

Racine, Jean 1639-1699 .... **LC 28**
See also DA3; DAB; DAM MST; EW 3;
GFL Beginnings to 1789; RGWL 2

Radcliffe, Ann (Ward) 1764-1823 ... **NCLC 6,
55, 106**
See also DLB 39, 178; HGG; RGEL 2;
SUFW; WLIT 3

Radclyffe-Hall, Marguerite
See Hall, (Marguerite) Radclyffe

Radiguet, Raymond 1903-1923 ...... **TCLC 29**
See also CA 162; DLB 65; GFL 1789 to the
Present; RGWL 2

Radnoti, Miklos 1909-1944 .... **TCLC 16**
See also CA 118; CDWLB 4; DLB 215;
RGWL 2

Rado, James 1939- .... **CLC 17**
See also CA 105

Radvanyi, Netty 1900-1983
See Seghers, Anna
See also CA 85-88; 110; CANR 82

Rae, Ben
See Griffiths, Trevor

Raeburn, John (Hay) 1941- .... **CLC 34**
See also CA 57-60

Ragni, Gerome 1942-1991 .... **CLC 17**
See also CA 105; 134

Rahv, Philip .... **CLC 24**
See also Greenberg, Ivan
See also DLB 137

Raimund, Ferdinand Jakob
1790-1836 .... **NCLC 69**
See also DLB 90

Raine, Craig (Anthony) 1944- .. **CLC 32, 103**
See also CA 108; CANR 29, 51, 103; CP 7;
DLB 40; PFS 7

Raine, Kathleen (Jessie) 1908- ..... **CLC 7, 45**
See also CA 85-88; CANR 46, 109; CP 7;
DLB 20; MTCW 1; RGEL 2

Rainis, Janis 1865-1929 .... **TCLC 29**
See also CA 170; CDWLB 4; DLB 220

Rakosi, Carl .... **CLC 47**
See also Rawley, Callman
See also CAAS 5; CP 7; DLB 193

Ralegh, Sir Walter
See Raleigh, Sir Walter
See also BRW 1; RGEL 2; WP

Raleigh, Richard
See Lovecraft, H(oward) P(hillips)

Raleigh, Sir Walter 1554(?)-1618 .... **LC 31,
39; PC 31**
See also Ralegh, Sir Walter
See also CDBLB Before 1660; DLB 172;
EXPP; PFS 14; TEA

Rallentando, H. P.
See Sayers, Dorothy L(eigh)

Ramal, Walter
See de la Mare, Walter (John)

Ramana Maharshi 1879-1950 .... **TCLC 84**

Ramoacn y Cajal, Santiago
1852-1934 .... **TCLC 93**

Ramon, Juan
See Jimenez (Mantecon), Juan Ramon

Ramos, Graciliano 1892-1953 .... **TCLC 32**
See also CA 167; HW 2; LAW; WLIT 1

Rampersad, Arnold 1941- .... **CLC 44**
See also BW 2, 3; CA 127; 133; CANR 81;
DLB 111; INT 133

Rampling, Anne
See Rice, Anne
See also GLL 2

Ramsay, Allan 1686(?)-1758 .... **LC 29**
See also DLB 95; RGEL 2

Ramsay, Jay
See Campbell, (John) Ramsey

Ramuz, Charles-Ferdinand
1878-1947 .... **TCLC 33**
See also CA 165

Rand, Ayn 1905-1982 ...... **CLC 3, 30, 44, 79;
WLC**
See also AAYA 10; AMWS 4; BPFB 3;
BYA 12; CA 13-16R; 105; CANR 27, 73;
CDALBS; CPW; DA; DA3; DAC; DAM
MST, NOV, POP; DLB 227; MTCW 1, 2;
NFS 10; RGAL 4; SFW 4; YAW

Randall, Dudley (Felker) 1914-2000 . **CLC 1,
135; BLC 3**
See also BW 1, 3; CA 25-28R; 189; CANR
23, 82; DAM MULT; DLB 41; PFS 5

Randall, Robert
See Silverberg, Robert

Ranger, Ken
See Creasey, John

Rank, Otto 1884-1939 .... **TCLC 115**

Ransom, John Crowe 1888-1974 .. **CLC 2, 4,
5, 11, 24**
See also AMW; CA 5-8R; 49-52; CANR 6,
34; CDALBS; DA3; DAM POET; DLB
45, 63; EXPP; MTCW 1, 2; RGAL 4

Rao, Raja 1909- .... **CLC 25, 56**
See also CA 73-76; CANR 51; CN 7; DAM
NOV; MTCW 1, 2; RGEL 2; RGSF 2

Raphael, Frederic (Michael) 1931- ... **CLC 2,
14**
See also CA 1-4R; CANR 1, 86; CN 7;
DLB 14

Ratcliffe, James P.
See Mencken, H(enry) L(ouis)

Rathbone, Julian 1935- .... **CLC 41**
See also CA 101; CANR 34, 73

Rattigan, Terence (Mervyn)
1911-1977 .... **CLC 7; DC 18**
See also BRWS 7; CA 85-88; 73-76; CBD;
CDBLB 1945-1960; DAM DRAM; DFS
8; DLB 13; IDFW 3, 4; MTCW 1, 2;
RGEL 2

Ratushinskaya, Irina 1954- .... **CLC 54**
See also CA 129; CANR 68; CWW 2

Raven, Simon (Arthur Noel)
1927-2001 .... **CLC 14**
See also CA 81-84; 197; CANR 86; CN 7

Ravenna, Michael
See Welty, Eudora (Alice)

Rawley, Callman 1903-
See Rakosi, Carl
See also CA 21-24R; CANR 12, 32, 91

Rawlings, Marjorie Kinnan
1896-1953 .... **TCLC 4**
See also AAYA 20; AMWS 10; ANW;
BPFB 3; BYA 3; CA 104; 137; CANR 74;
CLR 63; DLB 9, 22, 102; DLBD 17;
JRDA; MAICYA 1, 2; MTCW 2; RGAL
4; SATA 100; WCH; YABC 1; YAW

Ray, Satyajit 1921-1992 .... **CLC 16, 76**
See also CA 114; 137; DAM MULT

Read, Herbert Edward 1893-1968 ..... **CLC 4**
See also BRW 6; CA 85-88; 25-28R; DLB
20, 149; PAB; RGEL 2

Read, Piers Paul 1941- .... **CLC 4, 10, 25**
See also CA 21-24R; CANR 38, 86; CN 7;
DLB 14; SATA 21

Reade, Charles 1814-1884 .... **NCLC 2, 74**
See also DLB 21; RGEL 2

Reade, Hamish
See Gray, Simon (James Holliday)

Reading, Peter 1946- .... **CLC 47**
See also CA 103; CANR 46, 96; CP 7; DLB
40

Reaney, James 1926- .... **CLC 13**
See also CA 41-44R; CAAS 15; CANR 42;
CD 5; CP 7; DAC; DAM MST; DLB 68;
RGEL 2; SATA 43

Rebreanu, Liviu 1885-1944 .... **TCLC 28**
See also CA 165; DLB 220

Rechy, John (Francisco) 1934- ...... **CLC 1, 7,
14, 18, 107; HLC 2**
See also CA 5-8R; CAAE 195; CAAS 4;
CANR 6, 32, 64; CN 7; DAM MULT;
DLB 122; DLBY 1982; HW 1, 2; INT
CANR-6; RGAL 4

Redcam, Tom 1870-1933 .... **TCLC 25**

Reddin, Keith .... **CLC 67**
See also CAD

Redgrove, Peter (William) 1932- . **CLC 6, 41**
See also BRWS 6; CA 1-4R; CANR 3, 39,
77; CP 7; DLB 40

Redmon, Anne .... **CLC 22**
See also Nightingale, Anne Redmon
See also DLBY 1986

Reed, Eliot
See Ambler, Eric

Reed, Ishmael 1938- .. **CLC 2, 3, 5, 6, 13, 32,
60; BLC 3**
See also AFAW 1, 2; AMWS 10; BPFB 3;
BW 2, 3; CA 21-24R; CANR 25, 48, 74;
CN 7; CP 7; CSW; DA3; DAM MULT;
DLB 2, 5, 33, 169, 227; DLBD 8; MSW;
MTCW 1, 2; PFS 6; RGAL 4; TCWW 2

Reed, John (Silas) 1887-1920 .... **TCLC 9**
See also CA 106; 195

Reed, Lou .... **CLC 21**
See also Firbank, Louis

Reese, Lizette Woodworth 1856-1935 . **PC 29**
See also CA 180; DLB 54

Reeve, Clara 1729-1807 .... **NCLC 19**
See also DLB 39; RGEL 2

Reich, Wilhelm 1897-1957 .... **TCLC 57**
See also CA 199

Reid, Christopher (John) 1949- .... **CLC 33**
See also CA 140; CANR 89; CP 7; DLB 40

Reid, Desmond
See Moorcock, Michael (John)

Reid Banks, Lynne 1929-
See Banks, Lynne Reid
See also CA 1-4R; CANR 6, 22, 38, 87;
CLR 24; CN 7; JRDA; MAICYA 1, 2;
SATA 22, 75, 111; YAW

Reilly, William K.
See Creasey, John

Reiner, Max
See Caldwell, (Janet Miriam) Taylor
(Holland)

Reis, Ricardo
See Pessoa, Fernando (Antonio Nogueira)

Remarque, Erich Maria 1898-1970 . **CLC 21**
See also AAYA 27; BPFB 3; CA 77-80; 29-
32R; CDWLB 2; DA; DA3; DAB; DAC;
DAM MST, NOV; DLB 56; EXPN; LAIT
3; MTCW 1, 2; NFS 4; RGWL 2

Remington, Frederic 1861-1909 ..... **TCLC 89**
See also CA 108; 169; DLB 12, 186, 188;
SATA 41

Remizov, A.
See Remizov, Aleksei (Mikhailovich)

Remizov, A. M.
See Remizov, Aleksei (Mikhailovich)

Remizov, Aleksei (Mikhailovich)
1877-1957 .... **TCLC 27**
See also CA 125; 133

Renan, Joseph Ernest 1823-1892 .. **NCLC 26**
See also GFL 1789 to the Present

Renard, Jules 1864-1910 .... **TCLC 17**
See also CA 117; GFL 1789 to the Present

Robbins, Tom .... **CLC 9, 32, 64**
   See also Robbins, Thomas Eugene
   See also AAYA 32; AMWS 10; BEST 90:3;
     BPFB 3; DLBY 1980; MTCW 2
Robbins, Trina 1938- .... **CLC 21**
   See also CA 128
Roberts, Charles G(eorge) D(ouglas)
   1860-1943 .... **TCLC 8**
   See also CA 105; 188; CLR 33; CWRI 5;
     DLB 92; RGEL 2; RGSF 2; SATA 88;
     SATA-Brief 29
Roberts, Elizabeth Madox
   1886-1941 .... **TCLC 68**
   See also CA 111; 166; CWRI 5; DLB 9, 54,
     102; RGAL 4; RHW; SATA 33; SATA-
     Brief 27; WCH
Roberts, Kate 1891-1985 .... **CLC 15**
   See also CA 107; 116
Roberts, Keith (John Kingston)
   1935-2000 .... **CLC 14**
   See also CA 25-28R; CANR 46; DLB 261;
     SFW 4
Roberts, Kenneth (Lewis)
   1885-1957 .... **TCLC 23**
   See also CA 109; 199; DLB 9; RGAL 4;
     RHW
Roberts, Michele (Brigitte) 1949- ..... **CLC 48**
   See also CA 115; CANR 58; CN 7; DLB
     231; FW
Robertson, Ellis
   See Ellison, Harlan (Jay); Silverberg, Rob-
     ert
Robertson, Thomas William
   1829-1871 .... **NCLC 35**
   See also Robertson, Tom
   See also DAM DRAM
Robertson, Tom
   See Robertson, Thomas William
   See also RGEL 2
Robeson, Kenneth
   See Dent, Lester
Robinson, Edwin Arlington
   1869-1935 .... **TCLC 5, 101; PC 1, 35**
   See also AMW; CA 104; 133; CDALB
     1865-1917; DA; DAC; DAM MST,
     POET; DLB 54; EXPP; MTCW 1, 2;
     PAB; PFS 4; RGAL 4; WP
Robinson, Henry Crabb
   1775-1867 .... **NCLC 15**
   See also DLB 107
Robinson, Jill 1936- .... **CLC 10**
   See also CA 102; INT 102
Robinson, Kim Stanley 1952- .... **CLC 34**
   See also AAYA 26; CA 126; CN 7; SATA
     109; SCFW 2; SFW 4
Robinson, Lloyd
   See Silverberg, Robert
Robinson, Marilynne 1944- .... **CLC 25**
   See also CA 116; CANR 80; CN 7; DLB
     206
Robinson, Smokey .... **CLC 21**
   See also Robinson, William, Jr.
Robinson, William, Jr. 1940-
   See Robinson, Smokey
   See also CA 116
Robison, Mary 1949- .... **CLC 42, 98**
   See also CA 113; 116; CANR 87; CN 7;
     DLB 130; INT 116; RGSF 2
Rochester
   See Wilmot, John
   See also RGEL 2
Rod, Edouard 1857-1910 .... **TCLC 52**
Roddenberry, Eugene Wesley 1921-1991
   See Roddenberry, Gene
   See also CA 110; 135; CANR 37; SATA 45;
     SATA-Obit 69
Roddenberry, Gene .... **CLC 17**
   See also Roddenberry, Eugene Wesley
   See also AAYA 5; SATA-Obit 69

Rodgers, Mary 1931- .... **CLC 12**
   See also BYA 5; CA 49-52; CANR 8, 55,
     90; CLR 20; CWRI 5; INT CANR-8;
     JRDA; MAICYA 1, 2; SATA 8, 130
Rodgers, W(illiam) R(obert)
   1909-1969 .... **CLC 7**
   See also CA 85-88; DLB 20; RGEL 2
Rodman, Eric
   See Silverberg, Robert
Rodman, Howard 1920(?)-1985 .... **CLC 65**
   See also CA 118
Rodman, Maia
   See Wojciechowska, Maia (Teresa)
Rodo, Jose Enrique 1871(?)-1917
   See also CA 178; HLCS 2; HW 2; LAW
Rodolph, Utto
   See Ouologuem, Yambo
Rodriguez, Claudio 1934-1999 .... **CLC 10**
   See also CA 188; DLB 134
Rodriguez, Richard 1944- .... **CLC 155; HLC 2**
   See also CA 110; CANR 66; DAM MULT;
     DLB 82, 256; HW 1, 2; LAIT 5; NCFS 3;
     WLIT 1
Roelvaag, O(le) E(dvart) 1876-1931
   See Rolvaag, O(le) E(dvart)
   See also CA 117; 171
Roethke, Theodore (Huebner)
   1908-1963 .... **CLC 1, 3, 8, 11, 19, 46,**
     101; PC 15
   See also AMW; CA 81-84; CABS 2;
     CDALB 1941-1968; DA3; DAM POET;
     DLB 5, 206; EXPP; MTCW 1, 2; PAB;
     PFS 3; RGAL 4; WP
Rogers, Samuel 1763-1855 .... **NCLC 69**
   See also DLB 93; RGEL 2
Rogers, Thomas Hunton 1927- .... **CLC 57**
   See also CA 89-92; INT 89-92
Rogers, Will(iam Penn Adair)
   1879-1935 .... **TCLC 8, 71**
   See also CA 105; 144; DA3; DAM MULT;
     DLB 11; MTCW 2; NNAL
Rogin, Gilbert 1929- .... **CLC 18**
   See also CA 65-68; CANR 15
Rohan, Koda
   See Koda Shigeyuki
Rohlfs, Anna Katharine Green
   See Green, Anna Katharine
Rohmer, Eric .... **CLC 16**
   See also Scherer, Jean-Marie Maurice
Rohmer, Sax .... **TCLC 28**
   See also Ward, Arthur Henry Sarsfield
   See also DLB 70; MSW; SUFW
Roiphe, Anne (Richardson) 1935- .. **CLC 3, 9**
   See also CA 89-92; CANR 45, 73; DLBY
     1980; INT 89-92
Rojas, Fernando de 1475-1541 .... **LC 23;**
   HLCS 1
   See also RGWL 2
Rojas, Gonzalo 1917-
   See also CA 178; HLCS 2; HW 2; LAWS 1
Rolfe, Frederick (William Serafino Austin
   Lewis Mary) 1860-1913 .... **TCLC 12**
   See also Corvo, Baron
   See also CA 107; DLB 34, 156; RGEL 2
Rolland, Romain 1866-1944 .... **TCLC 23**
   See also CA 118; 197; DLB 65; GFL 1789
     to the Present; RGWL 2
Rolle, Richard c. 1300-c. 1349 ...... **CMLC 21**
   See also DLB 146; RGEL 2
Rolvaag, O(le) E(dvart) .... **TCLC 17**
   See also Roelvaag, O(le) E(dvart)
   See also DLB 9, 212; NFS 5; RGAL 4
Romain Arnaud, Saint
   See Aragon, Louis
Romains, Jules 1885-1972 .... **CLC 7**
   See also CA 85-88; CANR 34; DLB 65;
     GFL 1789 to the Present; MTCW 1

Romero, Jose Ruben 1890-1952 .... **TCLC 14**
   See also CA 114; 131; HW 1; LAW
Ronsard, Pierre de 1524-1585 . **LC 6, 54; PC 11**
   See also EW 2; GFL Beginnings to 1789;
     RGWL 2
Rooke, Leon 1934- .... **CLC 25, 34**
   See also CA 25-28R; CANR 23, 53; CCA
     1; CPW; DAM POP
Roosevelt, Franklin Delano
   1882-1945 .... **TCLC 93**
   See also CA 116; 173; LAIT 3
Roosevelt, Theodore 1858-1919 ..... **TCLC 69**
   See also CA 115; 170; DLB 47, 186
Roper, William 1498-1578 .... **LC 10**
Roquelaure, A. N.
   See Rice, Anne
Rosa, Joao Guimaraes 1908-1967 ... **CLC 23;**
   HLCS 1
   See also Guimaraes Rosa, Joao
   See also CA 89-92; DLB 113; WLIT 1
Rose, Wendy 1948- .... **CLC 85; PC 13**
   See also CA 53-56; CANR 5, 51; CWP;
     DAM MULT; DLB 175; NNAL; PFS 13;
     RGAL 4; SATA 12
Rosen, R. D.
   See Rosen, Richard (Dean)
Rosen, Richard (Dean) 1949- .... **CLC 39**
   See also CA 77-80; CANR 62; CMW 4;
     INT CANR-30
Rosenberg, Isaac 1890-1918 .... **TCLC 12**
   See also BRW 6; CA 107; 188; DLB 20,
     216; PAB; RGEL 2
Rosenblatt, Joe .... **CLC 15**
   See also Rosenblatt, Joseph
Rosenblatt, Joseph 1933-
   See Rosenblatt, Joe
   See also CA 89-92; CP 7; INT 89-92
Rosenfeld, Samuel
   See Tzara, Tristan
Rosenstock, Sami
   See Tzara, Tristan
Rosenstock, Samuel
   See Tzara, Tristan
Rosenthal, M(acha) L(ouis)
   1917-1996 .... **CLC 28**
   See also CA 1-4R; 152; CAAS 6; CANR 4,
     51; CP 7; DLB 5; SATA 59
Ross, Barnaby
   See Dannay, Frederic
Ross, Bernard L.
   See Follett, Ken(neth Martin)
Ross, J. H.
   See Lawrence, T(homas) E(dward)
Ross, John Hume
   See Lawrence, T(homas) E(dward)
Ross, Martin 1862-1915
   See Martin, Violet Florence
   See also DLB 135; GLL 2; RGEL 2; RGSF
     2
Ross, (James) Sinclair 1908-1996 ... **CLC 13;**
   SSC 24
   See also CA 73-76; CANR 81; CN 7; DAC;
     DAM MST; DLB 88; RGEL 2; RGSF 2;
     TCWW 2
Rossetti, Christina (Georgina)
   1830-1894 .... **NCLC 2, 50, 66; PC 7;**
   WLC
   See also BRW 5; BYA 4; DA; DA3; DAB;
     DAC; DAM MST, POET; DLB 35, 163,
     240; EXPP; MAICYA 1, 2; PFS 10, 14;
     RGEL 2; SATA 20; TEA; WCH
Rossetti, Dante Gabriel 1828-1882 . **NCLC 4, 77; WLC**
   See also BRW 5; CDBLB 1832-1890; DA;
     DAB; DAC; DAM MST, POET; DLB 35;
     EXPP; RGEL 2
Rossi, Cristina Peri
   See Peri Rossi, Cristina

Saint, H(arry) F. 1941- .... **CLC 50**
    See also CA 127
St. Aubin de Teran, Lisa 1953-
    See Teran, Lisa St. Aubin de
    See also CA 118; 126; CN 7; INT 126
Saint Birgitta of Sweden c.
    1303-1373 .... **CMLC 24**
Sainte-Beuve, Charles Augustin
    1804-1869 .... **NCLC 5**
    See also DLB 217; EW 6; GFL 1789 to the
    Present
Saint-Exupery, Antoine (Jean Baptiste
    Marie Roger) de 1900-1944 .... **TCLC 2,**
    56; WLC
    See also BPFB 3; BYA 3; CA 108; 132;
    CLR 10; DA3; DAM NOV; DLB 72; EW
    12; GFL 1789 to the Present; LAIT 3;
    MAICYA 1, 2; MTCW 1, 2; RGWL 2;
    SATA 20
St. John, David
    See Hunt, E(verette) Howard, (Jr.)
St. John, J. Hector
    See Crevecoeur, Michel Guillaume Jean de
Saint-John Perse
    See Leger, (Marie-Rene Auguste) Alexis
    Saint-Leger
    See also EW 10; GFL 1789 to the Present;
    RGWL 2
Saintsbury, George (Edward Bateman)
    1845-1933 .... **TCLC 31**
    See also CA 160; DLB 57, 149
Sait Faik .... **TCLC 23**
    See also Abasiyanik, Sait Faik
Saki .... **TCLC 3; SSC 12**
    See also Munro, H(ector) H(ugh)
    See also BRWS 6; LAIT 2; MTCW 2;
    RGEL 2; SSFS 1; SUFW
Sakutaro, Hagiwara
    See Hagiwara, Sakutaro
Sala, George Augustus 1828-1895 . **NCLC 46**
Saladin 1138-1193 .... **CMLC 38**
Salama, Hannu 1936- .... **CLC 18**
Salamanca, J(ack) R(ichard) 1922- .. **CLC 4,**
    15
    See also CA 25-28R; CAAE 193
Salas, Floyd Francis 1931-
    See also CA 119; CAAS 27; CANR 44, 75,
    93; DAM MULT; DLB 82; HLC 2; HW
    1, 2; MTCW 2
Sale, J. Kirkpatrick
    See Sale, Kirkpatrick
Sale, Kirkpatrick 1937- .... **CLC 68**
    See also CA 13-16R; CANR 10
Salinas, Luis Omar 1937- ... **CLC 90; HLC 2**
    See also CA 131; CANR 81; DAM MULT;
    DLB 82; HW 1, 2
Salinas (y Serrano), Pedro
    1891(?)-1951 .... **TCLC 17**
    See also CA 117; DLB 134
Salinger, J(erome) D(avid) 1919- .. **CLC 1, 3,**
    8, 12, 55, 56, 138; SSC 2, 28; WLC
    See also AAYA 2, 36; AMW; BPFB 3; CA
    5-8R; CANR 39; CDALB 1941-1968;
    CLR 18; CN 7; CPW 1; DA; DA3; DAB;
    DAC; DAM MST, NOV, POP; DLB 2,
    102, 173; EXPN; LAIT 4; MAICYA 1, 2;
    MTCW 1, 2; NFS 1; RGAL 4; RGSF 2;
    SATA 67; WYA; YAW
Salisbury, John
    See Caute, (John) David
Salter, James 1925- .... **CLC 7, 52, 59**
    See also AMWS 9; CA 73-76; CANR 107;
    DLB 130
Saltus, Edgar (Everton) 1855-1921 . **TCLC 8**
    See also CA 105; DLB 202; RGAL 4
Saltykov, Mikhail Evgrafovich
    1826-1889 .... **NCLC 16**
    See also DLB 238:

Saltykov-Shchedrin, N.
    See Saltykov, Mikhail Evgrafovich
Samarakis, Antonis 1919- .... **CLC 5**
    See also CA 25-28R; CAAS 16; CANR 36
Sanchez, Florencio 1875-1910 .... **TCLC 37**
    See also CA 153; HW 1; LAW
Sanchez, Luis Rafael 1936- .... **CLC 23**
    See also CA 128; DLB 145; HW 1; WLIT
    1
Sanchez, Sonia 1934- .... **CLC 5, 116; BLC 3;**
    PC 9
    See also BW 2, 3; CA 33-36R; CANR 24,
    49, 74; CLR 18; CP 7; CSW; CWP; DA3;
    DAM MULT; DLB 41; DLBD 8; MAI-
    CYA 1, 2; MTCW 1, 2; SATA 22; WP
Sand, George 1804-1876 ..... **NCLC 2, 42, 57;**
    WLC
    See also DA; DA3; DAB; DAC; DAM
    MST, NOV; DLB 119, 192; EW 6; FW;
    GFL 1789 to the Present; RGWL 2
Sandburg, Carl (August) 1878-1967 . **CLC 1,**
    4, 10, 15, 35; PC 2, 41; WLC
    See also AAYA 24; AMW; BYA 1, 3; CA
    5-28R; 25-28R; CANR 35; CDALB 1865-
    1917; CLR 67; DA; DA3; DAB; DAC;
    DAM MST, POET; DLB 17, 54; EXPP;
    LAIT 2; MAICYA 1, 2; MTCW 1, 2;
    PAB; PFS 3, 6, 12; RGAL 4; SATA 8;
    WCH; WP; WYA
Sandburg, Charles
    See Sandburg, Carl (August)
Sandburg, Charles A.
    See Sandburg, Carl (August)
Sanders, (James) Ed(ward) 1939- .... **CLC 53**
    See also Sanders, Edward
    See also CA 13-16R; CAAS 21; CANR 13,
    44, 78; CP 7; DAM POET; DLB 16, 244
Sanders, Edward
    See Sanders, (James) Ed(ward)
    See also DLB 244
Sanders, Lawrence 1920-1998 .... **CLC 41**
    See also BEST 89:4; BPFB 3; CA 81-84;
    165; CANR 33, 62; CMW 4; CPW; DA3;
    DAM POP; MTCW 1
Sanders, Noah
    See Blount, Roy (Alton), Jr.
Sanders, Winston P.
    See Anderson, Poul (William)
Sandoz, Mari(e Susette) 1900-1966 .. **CLC 28**
    See also CA 1-4R; 25-28R; CANR 17, 64;
    DLB 9, 212; LAIT 2; MTCW 1, 2; SATA
    5; TCWW 2
Saner, Reg(inald Anthony) 1931- .... **CLC 9**
    See also CA 65-68; CP 7
Sankara 788-820 .... **CMLC 32**
Sannazaro, Jacopo 1456(?)-1530 .... **LC 8**
    See also RGWL 2
Sansom, William 1912-1976 . **CLC 2, 6; SSC**
    21
    See also CA 5-8R; 65-68; CANR 42; DAM
    NOV; DLB 139; MTCW 1; RGEL 2;
    RGSF 2
Santayana, George 1863-1952 .... **TCLC 40**
    See also AMW; CA 115; 194; DLB 54, 71,
    246; DLBD 13; RGAL 4
Santiago, Danny .... **CLC 33**
    See also James, Daniel (Lewis)
    See also DLB 122
Santmyer, Helen Hooven
    1895-1986 .... **CLC 33**
    See also CA 1-4R; 118; CANR 15, 33;
    DLBY 1984; MTCW 1; RHW
Santoka, Taneda 1882-1940 .... **TCLC 72**
Santos, Bienvenido N(uqui)
    1911-1996 .... **CLC 22**
    See also CA 101; 151; CANR 19, 46; DAM
    MULT; RGAL 4
Sapir, Edward 1884-1939 .... **TCLC 108**
    See also DLB 92

Sapper .... **TCLC 44**
    See also McNeile, Herman Cyril
Sapphire
    See Sapphire, Brenda
Sapphire, Brenda 1950- .... **CLC 99**
Sappho fl. 6256th cent. B.C.- ... **CMLC 3; PC**
    5
    See also CDWLB 1; DA3; DAM POET;
    DLB 176; RGWL 2; WP
Saramago, Jose 1922- ..... **CLC 119; HLCS 1**
    See also CA 153; CANR 96
Sarduy, Severo 1937-1993 .... **CLC 6, 97;**
    HLCS 2
    See also CA 89-92; 142; CANR 58, 81;
    CWW 2; DLB 113; HW 1, 2; LAW
Sargeson, Frank 1903-1982 .... **CLC 31**
    See also CA 25-28R; 106; CANR 38, 79;
    GLL 2; RGEL 2; RGSF 2
Sarmiento, Domingo Faustino 1811-1888
    See also HLCS 2; LAW; WLIT 1
Sarmiento, Felix Ruben Garcia
    See Dario, Ruben
Saro-Wiwa, Ken(ule Beeson)
    1941-1995 .... **CLC 114**
    See also BW 2; CA 142; 150; CANR 60;
    DLB 157
Saroyan, William 1908-1981 ... **CLC 1, 8, 10,**
    29, 34, 56; SSC 21; WLC
    See also CA 5-8R; 103; CAD; CANR 30;
    CDALBS; DA; DA3; DAB; DAC; DAM
    DRAM, MST, NOV; DLB 7, 9, 86; DLBY
    1981; LAIT 4; MTCW 1, 2; RGAL 4;
    RGSF 2; SATA 23; SATA-Obit 24; SSFS
    14
Sarraute, Nathalie 1900-1999 .... **CLC 1, 2, 4,**
    8, 10, 31, 80
    See also BPFB 3; CA 9-12R; 187; CANR
    23, 66; CWW 2; DLB 83; EW 12; GFL
    1789 to the Present; MTCW 1, 2; RGWL
    2
Sarton, (Eleanor) May 1912-1995 ..... **CLC 4,**
    14, 49, 91; PC 39; TCLC 120
    See also AMWS 8; CA 1-4R; 149; CANR
    1, 34, 55; CN 7; CP 7; DAM POET; DLB
    48; DLBY 1981; FW; INT CANR-34;
    MTCW 1, 2; RGAL 4; SATA 36; SATA-
    Obit 86; TUS
Sartre, Jean-Paul 1905-1980 . **CLC 1, 4, 7, 9,**
    13, 18, 24, 44, 50, 52; DC 3; SSC 32;
    WLC
    See also CA 9-12R; 97-100; CANR 21; DA;
    DA3; DAB; DAC; DAM DRAM, MST,
    NOV; DFS 5; DLB 72; EW 12; GFL 1789
    to the Present; MTCW 1, 2; RGSF 2;
    RGWL 2; SSFS 9
Sassoon, Siegfried (Lorraine)
    1886-1967 .... **CLC 36, 130; PC 12**
    See also BRW 6; CA 104; 25-28R; CANR
    36; DAB; DAM MST, NOV, POET; DLB
    20, 191; DLBD 18; MTCW 1, 2; PAB;
    RGEL 2; TEA
Satterfield, Charles
    See Pohl, Frederik
Satyremont
    See Peret, Benjamin
Saul, John (W. III) 1942- .... **CLC 46**
    See also AAYA 10; BEST 90:4; CA 81-84;
    CANR 16, 40, 81; CPW; DAM NOV,
    POP; HGG; SATA 98
Saunders, Caleb
    See Heinlein, Robert A(nson)
Saura (Atares), Carlos 1932-1998 .... **CLC 20**
    See also CA 114; 131; CANR 79; HW 1
Sauser-Hall, Frederic 1887-1961 ...... **CLC 18**
    See also Cendrars, Blaise
    See also CA 102; 93-96; CANR 36, 62;
    MTCW 1

Stael, Germaine de
See Stael-Holstein, Anne Louise Germaine
Necker
See also DLB 119, 192; FW; GFL 1789 to
the Present; TWA

**Stael-Holstein, Anne Louise Germaine
Necker** 1766-1817 .... **NCLC 3, 91**
See also Stael; Stael, Germaine de

Stafford, Jean 1915-1979 .. **CLC 4, 7, 19, 68;
SSC 26**
See also CA 1-4R; 85-88; CANR 3, 65;
DLB 2, 173; MTCW 1, 2; RGAL 4; RGSF
2; SATA-Obit 22; TCWW 2

Stafford, William (Edgar)
1914-1993 .... **CLC 4, 7, 29**
See also CA 5-8R; 142; CAAS 3; CANR 5,
22; DAM POET; DLB 5, 206; EXPP; INT
CANR-22; PFS 2, 8; RGAL 4; WP

Stagnelius, Eric Johan 1793-1823 . **NCLC 61**

Staines, Trevor
See Brunner, John (Kilian Houston)

Stairs, Gordon
See Austin, Mary (Hunter)
See also TCWW 2

Stairs, Gordon 1868-1934
See Austin, Mary (Hunter)

Stalin, Joseph 1879-1953 .... **TCLC 92**

Stancykowna
See Szymborska, Wislawa

Stannard, Martin 1947- .... **CLC 44**
See also CA 142; DLB 155

Stanton, Elizabeth Cady
1815-1902 .... **TCLC 73**
See also CA 171; DLB 79; FW

Stanton, Maura 1946- .... **CLC 9**
See also CA 89-92; CANR 15; DLB 120

Stanton, Schuyler
See Baum, L(yman) Frank

Stapledon, (William) Olaf
1886-1950 .... **TCLC 22**
See also CA 111; 162; DLB 15, 255; SFW
4

Starbuck, George (Edwin)
1931-1996 .... **CLC 53**
See also CA 21-24R; 153; CANR 23; DAM
POET

Stark, Richard
See Westlake, Donald E(dwin)

Staunton, Schuyler
See Baum, L(yman) Frank

Stead, Christina (Ellen) 1902-1983 ... **CLC 2,
5, 8, 32, 80**
See also BRWS 4; CA 13-16R; 109; CANR
33, 40; DLB 260; FW; MTCW 1, 2;
RGEL 2; RGSF 2

Stead, William Thomas
1849-1912 .... **TCLC 48**
See also CA 167

Stebnitsky, M.
See Leskov, Nikolai (Semyonovich)

Steele, Sir Richard 1672-1729 .... **LC 18**
See also BRW 3; CDBLB 1660-1789; DLB
84, 101; RGEL 2; WLIT 3

Steele, Timothy (Reid) 1948- .... **CLC 45**
See also CA 93-96; CANR 16, 50, 92; CP
7; DLB 120

Steffens, (Joseph) Lincoln
1866-1936 .... **TCLC 20**
See also CA 117

Stegner, Wallace (Earle) 1909-1993 .. **CLC 9,
49, 81; SSC 27**
See also AITN 1; AMWS 4; ANW; BEST
90:3; BPFB 3; CA 1-4R; CAAS 9;
CANR 1, 21, 46; DAM NOV; DLB 9,
206; DLBY 1993; MTCW 1, 2; RGAL 4;
TCWW 2

Stein, Gertrude 1874-1946 .... **TCLC 1, 6, 28,
48; PC 18; SSC 42; WLC**
See also AMW; CA 104; 132; CANR 108;
CDALB 1917-1929; DA; DA3; DAB;
DAC; DAM MST, NOV, POET; DLB 4,
54, 86, 228; DLBD 15; EXPS; GLL 1;
MAWW; MTCW 1, 2; RGAL 4; RGSF 2;
SSFS 5; WP

Steinbeck, John (Ernst) 1902-1968 ... **CLC 1,
5, 9, 13, 21, 34, 45, 75, 124; SSC 11,
37; WLC**
See also AAYA 12; AMW; BPFB 3; BYA 2,
3, 13; CA 1-4R; 25-28R; CANR 1, 35;
CDALB 1929-1941; DA; DA3; DAB;
DAC; DAM DRAM, MST, NOV; DLB 7,
9, 212; DLBD 2; EXPS; LAIT 3; MTCW
1, 2; NFS 1, 5, 7; RGAL 4; RGSF 2;
RHW; SATA 9; SSFS 3, 6; TCWW 2;
WYA; YAW

Steinem, Gloria 1934- .... **CLC 63**
See also CA 53-56; CANR 28, 51; DLB
246; FW; MTCW 1, 2

Steiner, George 1929- .... **CLC 24**
See also CA 73-76; CANR 31, 67, 108;
DAM NOV; DLB 67; MTCW 1, 2; SATA
62

Steiner, K. Leslie
See Delany, Samuel R(ay), Jr.

Steiner, Rudolf 1861-1925 .... **TCLC 13**
See also CA 107

Stendhal 1783-1842 .. **NCLC 23, 46; SSC 27;
WLC**
See also DA; DA3; DAB; DAC; DAM
MST, NOV; DLB 119; EW 5; GFL 1789
to the Present; RGWL 2; TWA

Stephen, Adeline Virginia
See Woolf, (Adeline) Virginia

Stephen, Sir Leslie 1832-1904 .... **TCLC 23**
See also BRW 5; CA 123; DLB 57, 144,
190

Stephen, Sir Leslie
See Stephen, Sir Leslie

Stephen, Virginia
See Woolf, (Adeline) Virginia

Stephens, James 1882(?)-1950 .... **TCLC 4;
SSC 50**
See also CA 104; 192; DLB 19, 153, 162;
FANT; RGEL 2; SUFW

Stephens, Reed
See Donaldson, Stephen R(eeder)

Steptoe, Lydia
See Barnes, Djuna
See also GLL 1

Sterchi, Beat 1949- .... **CLC 65**

Sterling, Brett
See Bradbury, Ray (Douglas); Hamilton,
Edmond

Sterling, Bruce 1954- .... **CLC 72**
See also CA 119; CANR 44; SCFW 2; SFW
4

Sterling, George 1869-1926 .... **TCLC 20**
See also CA 117; 165; DLB 54

Stern, Gerald 1925- .... **CLC 40, 100**
See also AMWS 9; CA 81-84; CANR 28,
94; CP 7; DLB 105; RGAL 4

Stern, Richard (Gustave) 1928- ... **CLC 4, 39**
See also CA 1-4R; CANR 1, 25, 52; CN 7;
DLB 218; DLBY 1987; INT CANR-25

Sternberg, Josef von 1894-1969 .... **CLC 20**
See also CA 81-84

Sterne, Laurence 1713-1768 .... **LC 2, 48;
WLC**
See also BRW 3; CDBLB 1660-1789; DA;
DAB; DAC; DAM MST, NOV; DLB 39;
RGEL 2

Sternheim, (William Adolf) Carl
1878-1942 .... **TCLC 8**
See also CA 105; 193; DLB 56, 118;
RGWL 2

Stevens, Mark 1951- .... **CLC 34**
See also CA 122

Stevens, Wallace 1879-1955 ...... **TCLC 3, 12,
45; PC 6; WLC**
See also AMW; AMWR 1; CA 104; 124;
CDALB 1929-1941; DA; DA3; DAB;
DAC; DAM MST, POET; DLB 54; EXPP;
MTCW 1, 2; PAB; PFS 13; RGAL 4; WP

Stevenson, Anne (Katharine) 1933- .. **CLC 7,
33**
See also BRWS 6; CA 17-20R; CAAS 9;
CANR 9, 33; CP 7; CWP; DLB 40;
MTCW 1; RHW

Stevenson, Robert Louis (Balfour)
1850-1894 ...... **NCLC 5, 14, 63; SSC 11,
51; WLC**
See also AAYA 24; BPFB 3; BRW 5;
BRWR 1; BYA 1, 2, 4, 13; CDBLB 1890-
1914; CLR 10, 11; DA; DA3; DAB;
DAC; DAM MST, NOV; DLB 18, 57,
141, 156, 174; DLBD 13; HGG; JRDA;
LAIT 1, 3; MAICYA 1, 2; NFS 11; RGEL
2; RGSF 2; SATA 100; SUFW; TEA;
WCH; WLIT 4; WYA; YABC 2; YAW

Stewart, J(ohn) I(nnes) M(ackintosh)
1906-1994 .... **CLC 7, 14, 32**
See also CA 85-88; 147; CAAS 3; CANR
47; CMW 4; MTCW 1, 2

Stewart, Mary (Florence Elinor)
1916- .... **CLC 7, 35, 117**
See also AAYA 29; BPFB 3; CA 1-4R;
CANR 1, 59; CMW 4; CPW; DAB;
FANT; RHW; SATA 12; YAW

Stewart, Mary Rainbow
See Stewart, Mary (Florence Elinor)

Stifle, June
See Campbell, Maria

Stifter, Adalbert 1805-1868 .. **NCLC 41; SSC
28**
See also CDWLB 2; DLB 133; RGSF 2;
RGWL 2

Still, James 1906-2001 .... **CLC 49**
See also CA 65-68; 195; CAAS 17; CANR
10, 26; CSW; DLB 9; DLBY 01; SATA
29; SATA-Obit 127

Sting 1951-
See Sumner, Gordon Matthew
See also CA 167

Stirling, Arthur
See Sinclair, Upton (Beall)

Stitt, Milan 1941- .... **CLC 29**
See also CA 69-72

Stockton, Francis Richard 1834-1902
See Stockton, Frank R.
See also CA 108; 137; MAICYA 1, 2; SATA
44; SFW 4

Stockton, Frank R. .... **TCLC 47**
See also Stockton, Francis Richard
See also BYA 4, 13; DLB 42, 74; DLBD
13; EXPS; SATA-Brief 32; SSFS 3;
SUFW; WCH

Stoddard, Charles
See Kuttner, Henry

Stoker, Abraham 1847-1912
See Stoker, Bram
See also CA 105; 150; DA; DA3; DAC;
DAM MST, NOV; HGG; SATA 29; TEA

Stoker, Bram .... **TCLC 8; WLC**
See also Stoker, Abraham
See also AAYA 23; BPFB 3; BRWS 3; BYA
5; CDBLB 1890-1914; DAB; DLB 36, 70,
178; RGEL 2; SUFW; WLIT 4

Stolz, Mary (Slattery) 1920- .... **CLC 12**
See also AAYA 8; AITN 1; CA 5-8R;
CANR 13, 41; JRDA; MAICYA 1, 2;
SAAS 3; SATA 10, 71, 133; YAW

Teternikov, Fyodor Kuzmich 1863-1927
See Sologub, Fyodor
See also CA 104

Tevis, Walter 1928-1984 .... **CLC 42**
See also CA 113; SFW 4

Tey, Josephine .... **TCLC 14**
See Mackintosh, Elizabeth
See also DLB 77; MSW

Thackeray, William Makepeace
1811-1863 .... **NCLC 5, 14, 22, 43; WLC**
See also BRW 5; CDBLB 1832-1890; DA;
DA3; DAB; DAC; DAM MST, NOV;
DLB 21, 55, 159, 163; NFS 13; RGEL 2;
SATA 23; TEA; WLIT 3

Thakura, Ravindranatha
See Tagore, Rabindranath

Thames, C. H.
See Marlowe, Stephen

Tharoor, Shashi 1956- .... **CLC 70**
See also CA 141; CANR 91; CN 7

Thelwell, Michael Miles 1939- .... **CLC 22**
See also BW 2; CA 101

Theobald, Lewis, Jr.
See Lovecraft, H(oward) P(hillips)

Theocritus c. 310B.C.- .... **CMLC 45**
See also AW 1; DLB 176; RGWL 2

Theodorescu, Ion N. 1880-1967
See Arghezi, Tudor
See also CA 116

Theriault, Yves 1915-1983 .... **CLC 79**
See also CA 102; CCA 1; DAC; DAM
MST; DLB 88

Theroux, Alexander (Louis) 1939- .... **CLC 2,
25**
See also CA 85-88; CANR 20, 63; CN 7

Theroux, Paul (Edward) 1941- ..... **CLC 5, 8,
11, 15, 28, 46**
See also AAYA 28; AMWS 8; BEST 89:4;
BPFB 3; CA 33-36R; CANR 20, 45, 74;
CDALBS; CN 7; CPW 1; DA3; DAM
POP; DLB 2, 218; HGG; MTCW 1, 2;
RGAL 4; SATA 44, 109

Thesen, Sharon 1946- .... **CLC 56**
See also CA 163; CP 7; CWP

Thespis fl. 6th cent. B.C.- .... **CMLC 51**

Thevenin, Denis
See Duhamel, Georges

Thibault, Jacques Anatole Francois
1844-1924
See France, Anatole
See also CA 106; 127; DA3; DAM NOV;
MTCW 1, 2

Thiele, Colin (Milton) 1920- .... **CLC 17**
See also CA 29-32R; CANR 12, 28, 53,
105; CLR 27; MAICYA 1, 2; SAAS 2;
SATA 14, 72, 125; YAW

Thomas, Audrey (Callahan) 1935- .... **CLC 7,
13, 37, 107; SSC 20**
See also AITN 2; CA 21-24R; CAAS 19;
CANR 36, 58; CN 7; DLB 60; MTCW 1;
RGSF 2

Thomas, Augustus 1857-1934 .... **TCLC 97**

Thomas, D(onald) M(ichael) 1935- . **CLC 13,
22, 31, 132**
See also BPFB 3; BRWS 4; CA 61-64;
CAAS 11; CANR 17, 45, 75; CDBLB
1960 to Present; CN 7; CP 7; DA3; DLB
40, 207; HGG; INT CANR-17; MTCW 1,
2; SFW 4

Thomas, Dylan (Marlais)
1914-1953 ... **TCLC 1, 8, 45, 105; PC 2;
SSC 3, 44; WLC**
See also BRWS 1; CA 104; 120; CANR 65;
CDBLB 1945-1960; DA; DA3; DAB;
DAC; DAM DRAM, MST, POET; DLB
13, 20, 139; EXPP; LAIT 3; MTCW 1, 2;
PAB; PFS 1, 3, 8; RGEL 2; RGSF 2;
SATA 60; WLIT 4; WP

Thomas, (Philip) Edward
1878-1917 .... **TCLC 10**
See also BRW 6; BRWS 3; CA 106; 153;
DAM POET; DLB 19, 98, 156, 216; PAB;
RGEL 2

Thomas, Joyce Carol 1938- .... **CLC 35**
See also AAYA 12; BW 2, 3; CA 113; 116;
CANR 48; CLR 19; DLB 33; INT CA-
116; JRDA; MAICYA 1, 2; MTCW 1, 2;
SAAS 7; SATA 40, 78, 123; WYA; YAW

Thomas, Lewis 1913-1993 .... **CLC 35**
See also ANW; CA 85-88; 143; CANR 38,
60; MTCW 1, 2

Thomas, M. Carey 1857-1935 .... **TCLC 89**
See also FW

Thomas, Paul
See Mann, (Paul) Thomas

Thomas, Piri 1928- .... **CLC 17; HLCS 2**
See also CA 73-76; HW 1

Thomas, R(onald) S(tuart)
1913-2000 .... **CLC 6, 13, 48**
See also CA 89-92; 189; CAAS 4; CANR
30; CDBLB 1960 to Present; CP 7; DAB;
DAM POET; DLB 27; MTCW 1; RGEL
2

Thomas, Ross (Elmore) 1926-1995 .. **CLC 39**
See also CA 33-36R; 150; CANR 22, 63;
CMW 4

Thompson, Francis (Joseph)
1859-1907 .... **TCLC 4**
See also BRW 5; CA 104; 189; CDBLB
1890-1914; DLB 19; RGEL 2; TEA

Thompson, Francis Clegg
See Mencken, H(enry) L(ouis)

Thompson, Hunter S(tockton)
1937(?)- .... **CLC 9, 17, 40, 104**
See also BEST 89:1; BPFB 3; CA 17-20R;
CANR 23, 46, 74, 77; CPW; CSW; DA3;
DAM POP; DLB 185; MTCW 1, 2

Thompson, James Myers
See Thompson, Jim (Myers)

Thompson, Jim (Myers)
1906-1977(?) .... **CLC 69**
See also BPFB 3; CA 140; CMW 4; CPW;
DLB 226; MSW

Thompson, Judith .... **CLC 39**
See also CWD

Thomson, James 1700-1748 .... **LC 16, 29, 40**
See also BRWS 3; DAM POET; DLB 95;
RGEL 2

Thomson, James 1834-1882 .... **NCLC 18**
See also DAM POET; DLB 35; RGEL 2

Thoreau, Henry David 1817-1862 .. **NCLC 7,
21, 61; PC 30; WLC**
See also AAYA 42; AMW; ANW; BYA 3;
CDALB 1640-1865; DA; DA3; DAB;
DAC; DAM MST; DLB 1, 183, 223;
LAIT 2; NCFS 3; RGAL 4; TUS

Thorndike, E. L.
See Thorndike, Edward L(ee)

Thorndike, Edward L(ee)
1874-1949 .... **TCLC 107**
See also CA 121

Thornton, Hall
See Silverberg, Robert

Thucydides c. 455B.C.-c. 395B.C. . **CMLC 17**
See also AW 1; DLB 176; RGWL 2

Thumboo, Edwin Nadason 1933- .... **PC 30**
See also CA 194

Thurber, James (Grover)
1894-1961 .. **CLC 5, 11, 25, 125; SSC 1,
47**
See also AMWS 1; BPFB 3; BYA 5; CA
73-76; CANR 17, 39; CDALB 1929-1941;
CWRI 5; DA; DA3; DAB; DAC; DAM
DRAM, MST, NOV; DLB 4, 11, 22, 102;
EXPS; FANT; LAIT 3; MAICYA 1, 2;
MTCW 1, 2; RGAL 4; RGSF 2; SATA
13; SSFS 1, 10; SUFW

Thurman, Wallace (Henry)
1902-1934 .... **TCLC 6; BLC 3**
See also BW 1, 3; CA 104; 124; CANR 81;
DAM MULT; DLB 51

Tibullus c. 54B.C.-c. 18B.C. .... **CMLC 36**
See also AW 2; DLB 211; RGWL 2

Ticheburn, Cheviot
See Ainsworth, William Harrison

Tieck, (Johann) Ludwig
1773-1853 .... **NCLC 5, 46; SSC 31**
See also CDWLB 2; DLB 90; EW 5; IDTP;
RGSF 2; RGWL 2; SUFW

Tiger, Derry
See Ellison, Harlan (Jay)

Tilghman, Christopher 1948(?)- .... **CLC 65**
See also CA 159; CSW; DLB 244

Tillich, Paul (Johannes)
1886-1965 .... **CLC 131**
See also CA 5-8R; 25-28R; CANR 33;
MTCW 1, 2

Tillinghast, Richard (Williford)
1940- .... **CLC 29**
See also CA 29-32R; CAAS 23; CANR 26,
51, 96; CP 7; CSW

Timrod, Henry 1828-1867 .... **NCLC 25**
See also DLB 3, 248; RGAL 4

Tindall, Gillian (Elizabeth) 1938- ...... **CLC 7**
See also CA 21-24R; CANR 11, 65, 107;
CN 7

Tiptree, James, Jr. .... **CLC 48, 50**
See also Sheldon, Alice Hastings Bradley
See also DLB 8; SCFW 2; SFW 4

Tirso de Molina
See Tirso de Molina
See also RGWL 2

Tirso de Molina 1580(?)-1648 ..... **LC 73; DC
13; HLCS 2**
See also Tirso de Molina

Titmarsh, Michael Angelo
See Thackeray, William Makepeace

**Tocqueville, Alexis (Charles Henri Maurice
Clerel Comte) de** 1805-1859 .. **NCLC 7,
63**
See also EW 6; GFL 1789 to the Present

Tolkien, J(ohn) R(onald) R(euel)
1892-1973 .... **CLC 1, 2, 3, 8, 12, 38;
WLC**
See also AAYA 10; AITN 1; BPFB 3;
BRWS 2; CA 17-18; 45-48; CANR 36;
CAP 2; CDBLB 1914-1945; CLR 56;
CPW 1; CWRI 5; DA; DA3; DAB; DAC;
DAM MST, NOV, POP; DLB 15, 160,
255; EFS 2; FANT; JRDA; LAIT 1; MAI-
CYA 1, 2; MTCW 1, 2; NFS 8; RGEL 2;
SATA 2, 32, 100; SATA-Obit 24; SFW 4;
SUFW; TEA; WCH; WYA; YAW

Toller, Ernst 1893-1939 .... **TCLC 10**
See also CA 107; 186; DLB 124; RGWL 2

Tolson, M. B.
See Tolson, Melvin B(eaunorus)

Tolson, Melvin B(eaunorus)
1898(?)-1966 .... **CLC 36, 105; BLC 3**
See also AFAW 1, 2; BW 1, 3; CA 124; 89-
92; CANR 80; DAM MULT, POET; DLB
48, 76; RGAL 4

Tolstoi, Aleksei Nikolaevich
See Tolstoy, Alexey Nikolaevich

Tolstoi, Lev
See Tolstoy, Leo (Nikolaevich)
See also RGSF 2; RGWL 2

Tolstoy, Alexey Nikolaevich
1882-1945 .... **TCLC 18**
See also CA 107; 158; SFW 4

Tolstoy, Leo (Nikolaevich)
1828-1910 .. **TCLC 4, 11, 17, 28, 44, 79;
SSC 9, 30, 45, 54; WLC**
See also Tolstoi, Lev
See also CA 104; 123; DA; DA3; DAB;
DAC; DAM MST, NOV; DLB 238; EFS
2; EW 7; EXPS; IDTP; LAIT 2; NFS 10;
SATA 26; SSFS 5

Literary Criticism Series
Cumulative Topic Index

This index lists all topic entries in Gale's *Classical and Medieval Literature Criticism, Contemporary Literary Criticism, Drama Criticism, Literature Criticism from 1400 to 1800, Nineteenth-Century Literature Criticism,* and *Twentieth-Century Literary Criticism.*

Topic Index

NCLC Cumulative Nationality Index

AMERICAN

Adams, John **106**
Alcott, Amos Bronson **1**
Alcott, Louisa May **6, 58, 83**
Alger, Horatio Jr. **8, 83**
Allston, Washington **2**
Apess, William **73**
Audubon, John James **47**
Barlow, Joel **23**
Beecher, Catharine Esther **30**
Bellamy, Edward **4, 86**
Bird, Robert Montgomery **1**
Brackenridge, Hugh Henry **7**
Brentano, Clemens (Maria) **1**
Brown, Charles Brockden **22, 74**
Brown, William Wells **2, 89**
Brownson, Orestes Augustus **50**
Bryant, William Cullen **6, 46**
Calhoun, John Caldwell **15**
Channing, William Ellery **17**
Child, Lydia Maria **6, 73**
Chivers, Thomas Holley **49**
Cooke, John Esten **5**
Cooke, Rose Terry **110**
Cooper, James Fenimore **1, 27, 54**
Crèvecoeur, Michel Guillaume Jean de **105**
Crockett, David **8**
Dana, Richard Henry Sr. **53**
Delany, Martin Robinson **93**
Dickinson, Emily (Elizabeth) **21, 77**
Douglass, Frederick **7, 55**
Dunlap, William **2**
Dwight, Timothy **13**
Emerson, Mary Moody **66**
Emerson, Ralph Waldo **1, 38, 98**
Field, Eugene **3**
Foster, Hannah Webster **99**
Foster, Stephen Collins **26**
Frederic, Harold **10**
Freneau, Philip Morin **1, 111**
Hale, Sarah Josepha (Buell) **75**
Halleck, Fitz-Greene **47**
Hamilton, Alexander **49**
Hammon, Jupiter **5**
Harris, George Washington **23**
Hawthorne, Nathaniel **2, 10, 17, 23, 39, 79, 95**
Hayne, Paul Hamilton **94**
Holmes, Oliver Wendell **14, 81**
Horton, George Moses **87**
Irving, Washington **2, 19, 95**
Jackson, Helen Hunt **90**
Jacobs, Harriet A(nn) **67**
James, Henry Sr. **53**
Jefferson, Thomas **11, 103**
Kennedy, John Pendleton **2**
Kirkland, Caroline M. **85**
Lanier, Sidney **6**
Lazarus, Emma **8, 109**
Lincoln, Abraham **18**
Longfellow, Henry Wadsworth **2, 45, 101, 103**

Lowell, James Russell **2, 90**
Melville, Herman **3, 12, 29, 45, 49, 91, 93**
Mowatt, Anna Cora **74**
Murray, Judith Sargent **63**
Parkman, Francis Jr. **12**
Parton, Sara Payson Willis **86**
Paulding, James Kirke **2**
Pinkney, Edward **31**
Poe, Edgar Allan **1, 16, 55, 78, 94, 97**
Rowson, Susanna Haswell **5, 69**
Sedgwick, Catharine Maria **19, 98**
Shaw, Henry Wheeler **15**
Sheridan, Richard Brinsley **5, 91**
Sigourney, Lydia Howard (Huntley) **21, 87**
Simms, William Gilmore **3**
Smith, Joseph Jr. **53**
Solomon, Northup **105**
Southworth, Emma Dorothy Eliza Nevitte **26**
Stowe, Harriet (Elizabeth) Beecher **3, 50**
Taylor, Bayard **89**
Thoreau, Henry David **7, 21, 61**
Timrod, Henry **25**
Trumbull, John **30**
Truth, Sojourner **94**
Tyler, Royall **3**
Very, Jones **9**
Warner, Susan (Bogert) **31**
Warren, Mercy Otis **13**
Webster, Noah **30**
Whitman, Sarah Helen (Power) **19**
Whitman, Walt(er) **4, 31, 81**
Whittier, John Greenleaf **8, 59**
Wilson, Harriet E. Adams **78**
Winnemucca, Sarah **79**

ARGENTINIAN

Echeverria, (Jose) Esteban (Antonino) **18**
Hernández, José **17**

AUSTRALIAN

Adams, Francis **33**
Clarke, Marcus (Andrew Hislop) **19**
Gordon, Adam Lindsay **21**
Harpur, Charles **114**
Kendall, Henry **12**

AUSTRIAN

Grillparzer, Franz **1, 102**
Lenau, Nikolaus **16**
Nestroy, Johann **42**
Raimund, Ferdinand Jakob **69**
Sacher-Masoch, Leopold von **31**
Stifter, Adalbert **41**

CANADIAN

Crawford, Isabella Valancy **12**
Haliburton, Thomas Chandler **15**
Lampman, Archibald **25**
Moodie, Susanna (Strickland) **14, 113**
Richardson, John **55**
Traill, Catharine Parr **31**

COLOMBIAN

Isaacs, Jorge Ricardo **70**
Silva, José Asunción **114**

CUBAN

Avellaneda, Gertrudis Gómez de **111**
Martí (y Pérez), José (Julian) **63**

CZECH

Macha, Karel Hynek **46**

DANISH

Andersen, Hans Christian **7, 79**
Grundtvig, Nicolai Frederik Severin **1**
Jacobsen, Jens Peter **34**
Kierkegaard, Søren **34, 78**

ENGLISH

Ainsworth, William Harrison **13**
Arnold, Matthew **6, 29, 89**
Arnold, Thomas **18**
Austen, Jane **1, 13, 19, 33, 51, 81, 95**
Bagehot, Walter **10**
Barbauld, Anna Laetitia **50**
Barham, Richard Harris **77**
Barnes, William **75**
Beardsley, Aubrey **6**
Beckford, William **16**
Beddoes, Thomas Lovell **3**
Bentham, Jeremy **38**
Blake, William **13, 37, 57**
Borrow, George (Henry) **9**
Bowles, William Lisle **103**
Brontë, Anne **4, 71, 102**
Brontë, Charlotte **3, 8, 33, 58, 105**
Brontë, Emily (Jane) **16, 35**
Brontë, (Patrick) Branwell **109**
Browning, Elizabeth Barrett **1, 16, 61, 66**
Browning, Robert **19, 79**
Bulwer-Lytton, Edward (George Earle Lytton) **1, 45**
Burney, Fanny **12, 54, 107**
Burton, Richard F(rancis) **42**
Byron, George Gordon (Noel) **2, 12, 109**
Carlyle, Thomas **22, 70**
Clare, John **9, 86**
Clough, Arthur Hugh **27**
Cobbett, William **49**
Coleridge, Hartley **90**
Coleridge, Samuel Taylor **9, 54, 99, 111**
Coleridge, Sara **31**
Collins, (William) Wilkie **1, 18, 93**
Cowper, William **8, 94**
Crabbe, George **26**
Craik, Dinah Maria (Mulock) **38**
Darwin, Charles **57**
Darwin, Erasmus **106**
De Quincey, Thomas **4, 87**
Dickens, Charles (John Huffam) **3, 8, 18, 26, 37, 50, 86, 105, 113**
Disraeli, Benjamin **2, 39, 79**

NCLC-114 Title Index

ISBN 0-7876-5978-9

90000

9 780787 659783